FIGURE 5.11. A remarkable example of teamwork in weaver ants of the genus *Oecophylla* (Hölldobler & Wilson 1990). Rows of workers pull from the edge of a leaf until a second team binds the two edges with a silk produced by larvae.

FIGURE 6.9. The coelacanth *Latimeria,* a living … Ocean. (Photograph courtesy of Traute Kleinschmidt.

COMPARATIVE PSYCHOLOGY
Evolution and Development of Behavior

MAURICIO R. PAPINI
Texas Christian University

Upper Saddle River, New Jersey 07458

Library of Congress Cataloging-in-Publication Data

Papini, Mauricio R.
Comparative psychology: evolution and development of behavior/by Mauricio R. Papini.
p. cm.
Includes bibliographical references and index.
ISBN 0-13-080429-0
1. Psychology, Comparative. I. Title
BF671 .P37 2002
156—dc21

2001021516

VP/Editorial Director: Laura Pearson
Acquisitions Editor: Jayme Heffler
Editorial Assistant: April Dawn Klemm
Senior Managing Editor: Mary Rottino
Production Liaison: Fran Russello
Editorial/Production Supervision: Marianne Hutchinson (Pine Tree Composition, Inc.)
Prepress and Manufacturing Buyer: Tricia Kenny
Art Director: Jayne Conte
Cover Designer: Bruce Kenselaar
Cover Art: Arte Romana: Bordur decorativa con scene nilotiche. Napoli. Roman decorative border with marine scene. Museo Archeologico Nazionale, Naples, Italy
Director, Image Resource Center: Melinda Lee Reo
Manager, Rights & Permissions: Key Dellosa
Image Specialist: Beth Boyd
Photo Researcher: Karen Pugliano
Marketing Manager: Sharon Cosgrove

For permission to use copyrighted material, grateful acknowledgment is made to the copyright holders on pages 615–616, which are hereby made part of this copyright page.

This book was set in 10/12 New Aster by Pine Tree Composition, Inc., and was printed and bound by R.R. Donnelley & Sons Company.
The cover was printed by Phoenix Color Corp.

Printed in the United States of America
10 9 8 7 6 5 4 3 2 1

ISBN 0-13-080429-0

Pearson Education LTD., *London*
Pearson Education Australia PTY. Limited, *Sydney*
Pearson Education Singapore, Pte. Ltd
Pearson Education North Asia Ltd., *Hong Kong*
Pearson Education Canada, Ltd., *Toronto*
Pearson Educatión de Mexico, S.A. de C.V.
Pearson Education—Japan, *Tokyo*
Pearson Education Malaysia, Pte. Ltd
Pearson Education, Upper Saddle River, New Jersey

A mis queridos padres, Elena y Victorio

Brief Contents

Contents

Preface

Any scientific discipline has two major goals: to promote original research leading to new knowledge in its area of interest and to become a source of education for itself and for the larger science within which it is inserted. As a teacher, my graduate and undergraduate courses on comparative psychology and animal behavior have always been organized with both goals in mind. I have tried to convey to the students the excitement I feel about comparative research—the same excitement that drove me into this profession during my undergraduate years at the University of Buenos Aires. I have also striven to provide psychology students with a firm grasp of evolutionary science as it is applied to the understanding of the behavior and psychological processes of human and nonhuman animals. My problem has always been the lack of textbooks that I considered appropriate for this task. Most current textbooks on animal behavior do not cover evolutionary principles in detail because they are written with the biology student in mind. Unlike psychology majors, biology students have plenty of opportunities to be exposed to evolutionary principles. The main incentive to write this book was, in fact, to try to fill this gap.

For these reasons, this is not a typical book on animal behavior. First, this book was written for undergraduate psychology majors who take a course on comparative psychology or animal behavior. As a result, it includes more general information about evolutionary theory, human evolution, and brain evolution than is typical of most animal behavior textbooks. Second, this book provides extensive coverage of areas that continue to be at the core of comparative psychology, including behavioral development, learning, and cognition. I expect students to develop and deepen their understanding of evolutionary principles in general, and of the application of such principles to the study of behavior in particular. In my opinion, one of the main contributions of comparative psychology to the science of psychology is to provide students with a firm grasp of evolutionary thinking from within psychology.

I also hope that this book will contribute to strengthening the identity of comparative psychology as a research discipline. I have struggled to provide comparative psychologists with a tool to expose students in psychology and the social sciences to the intricacies of evolutionary science. Psychology is increasingly influenced by the development of biological disciplines including neuroscience, molecular biology, and genetics. Many of the newest scientific developments have a tremendous potential to increase our understanding of behavior and psychological processes. However, this task demands a new generation of psychologists equipped with the conceptual machinery capable of absorbing biological principles without losing the behavioral perspective. I believe comparative psychologists are in an ideal position to carry out this task for the benefit of their own discipline, as well as of psychology as a whole.

The organization of this book reflects years of teaching experience during which I changed and adjusted the sequence of topics to be covered in class according to the experience I was gaining in the process. Its relatively unorthodox structure made it particularly necessary for me to receive feedback from my colleagues and students. I have made important changes in the content and structure of this book as a result of their reviews and comments, for which I am very grateful. They have undoubtedly improved the final product.

I appreciate and acknowledge the contributions made by those who read one or more chapters of the manuscript, including Marifran Arias, Jeff Bitterman, Aaron Blaisdell, Daniela Brunner, Mike Domjan, Francisco Fernández Serra, Gary Greenberg, Douglas Grimsley, Jerry Hirsch, Geoffrey Hall, Anita Hartmann, Jennifer Higa, John Horner, Masato Ishida, H. Wayne Ludvigson, Euan M. Macphail, Roger Mellgren, Rubén N. Muzio, Jesse E. Purdy, Duane Rumbaugh, Pablo Tubaro, and Jeannette P. Ward. Francisco Fernández Serra introduced me to the work of Gómez Pereira, described in Chapter 1, whereas Jim Chambers and several contributors of the Romarch discussion list guided me through the story of human sacrifices in Ancient Carthage included in Chapter 5. Several graduate and undergraduate students also made significant contributions to the manuscript, including especially Ixchel Alvarez, Bambi Bonilla, Dawn Hansen, Dawn McVicar, Des Robinson, Steven Stout, and Cindy Weldon. Many students made indirect contributions by commenting on the organization of my courses; their views are now reflected in this book. I also appreciate the diligence with which many colleagues responded to my request for photographs and drawings of their research, including Michael Domjan, Irit Gazit, Francisco González-Lima, Karen Hissmann, Tetsuro Matsuzawa, Rubén Muzio, Katharine Rankin, Duane Rumbaugh, William Smotherman, Josef Terkel, Keiichiro Tsuji, Pablo Tubaro, Jeannette Ward, Masakata Watanabe, Emily Weiss, and Shuhai Xiao. I am fortunate for the support I received from my colleagues and staff in the Psychology Department and in the Mary Couts Burnett Library at TCU. I am especially thankful to David Cross, Jennifer Higa, Tim Hubbard, Tamy Joyce, and Dawn McVicar for their valuable help. I am also thankful to the staff at Prentice Hall who worked around my schedule and provided support during the three years it took me to complete the manuscript.

My deepest appreciation to Jeff Bitterman and Bruce Overmier, who, over the past twenty years, have provided me with the best advice and greatest challenges a student of animal learning and behavior could hope to receive from a mentor; and to Enrique Gandolfi, who brought to my attention the intricacies and rewards of a scientific view of psychology during my undergraduate years. Whatever value readers may find in this book is surely a reflection of their influence. Writing a book is such a complicated task that it would be impossible to accomplish without affecting the lives of those around us. I will be forever grateful to my sons, Santiago and Angel, to Mirta, and to my parents, Elena and Victorio, for their unqualified support, without which I would have never been able to complete this book.

Mauricio R. Papini
Texas Christian University

CHAPTER 1

Introduction

MAIN GENERALIZATIONS OF CHAPTER 1

- *Comparative psychology originated during the second half of the 19th century as a result of the confluence of evolutionary biology and experimental psychology.*
- *Darwin's concepts of evolution by natural selection and mental continuity across species provided an evolutionary framework for comparative studies of the behavioral capacities of animals.*
- *Mechanistic views of behavior such as those of Pereira and Descartes and the emergence of physiology as a laboratory science provided an experimental model that could be applied to the study of behavior.*
- *The distinction between instinct and intelligence, expressed as the nature-nurture dichotomy, shaped much of the initial progress of comparative psychology.*
- *Behavior can be explained according to four levels of causal analysis: adaptive significance, phylogenetic history, mechanism, and development.*

Thus the sum of things is ever being renewed,
and mortal creatures live dependent one upon another.
Some species increase, other diminish,
and in a short space the generations of living creatures are changed
and, like runners, pass the torch of life.
Lucretius, *De Rerum Natura* (book 2, lines 75–79).

Standing on top of a hill and overlooking the surrounding valleys and streams, a small group of Cro-Magnon humans are planning tomorrow's hunt. Their concern is to determine when and where to attack the herd, and the solution to this problem will require some behavioral knowledge. Where would these animals be tomorrow? Could they be better approached at night? Which ones are the most vulnerable? Although imaginary, scenarios such as this one must have been common throughout much of the evolutionary history of humans, unprotected and unequipped by means other than their intelligence and social organization to face all types of environmental challenge.

It could be easily hypothesized that, for early humans, knowledge about the behavior of animals must have had important practical implications. Of course, this is true even today, although the actual applications may be considerably different. In our time, research on animal behavior has widespread practical implications: The testing of drugs before they are released for medical treatment; the development of animal models for a wide variety of pathological conditions; animal production; the treatment of maladaptive behavior in domestic animals; the implementation of conservation efforts to preserve endangered species; and many other applications. Most contemporary researchers would agree, however, that to meet many of these practical goals it is first necessary to answer many basic "why" and "how" questions about animal behavior. In scientific research, the raising of these questions usually leads not just to improved understanding of natural phenomena but to new ideas of great practical importance. It is this set of basic questions about the origin and causal control of behavior that constitutes the core of this book.

Psychology is one of the disciplines concerned with the study of behavior in a broad sense, from social behavior and the properties of social groups to the physiological basis of simple motor movements. Psychologists ask many different kinds of questions about behavior and, consequently, are forced to use a wide variety of research procedures to find the answers. Psychology is indeed a broad discipline, and it is sometimes difficult to see connections between the many areas of inquiry. The connecting theme is behavior: What can organisms do? Why do they do it? How can they do it? This book concentrates on what might be called the "biological extreme" of psychology, an area that is traditionally known as comparative psychology.

Comparative psychology is almost an interdisciplinary area by definition. As will be shown later in this chapter, it originated from the intersection of experimental psychology and evolutionary biology in the last portion of the 19th century, and it is presently concerned with the study of the evolution and development of behavior, using experimental and field methods of observation and covering a wide range of species. The main goal of comparative psychology is to uncover common and divergent behavioral processes among species, including our own. In this context, the "comparative" aspect addresses the assumption that this discipline will ultimately provide a better understanding of the evolutionary origins of human behavior and a clear view of the unique and common behavioral properties of our own species, relative to the rest of the animal kingdom.

One feature that characterizes behavioral phenomena is their *complexity* (see ***Chapter 14, section 4,*** pp. 580–583). Even a simple monosynaptic reflex involving essentially a sensory and motor neuron in a feed-forward circuitry, in which information flows in only one direction, poses serious empirical and theoretical obstacles. The question of just how much integration there is among similarly simple reflexes becomes almost intractable, and the addition of systems that can influence or modulate the reflex pathway, without being strictly speaking a part of it, adds even more complexity to this picture. Behaviors that are relatively discrete and well organized, such as a chick pecking at grain on the floor or a frog calling during the mating season, are influenced by many internal and external factors, and it is probably correct to say that all behavior is caused by a multitude of independent and interacting factors. Such *multicausality* invites interdisciplinary interaction, and that, as it has already been said, is an ubiquitous feature of research in comparative psychology. ***Figure 1.1*** provides a general overview of some of the interactions among the areas within comparative psychology and other fields of knowledge that have developed independently. Fruitful interaction is often accompanied by the emergence of new theories or even the crystallization of a new area. Many examples will be discussed in this book, including the application of adaptive functional analysis to human social behavior, the correlations between brain size (or the size of specific brain nuclei) and behavioral capacities such as spatial memory or foraging strategies, and the combination of a wide range of genetic techniques to understand behavioral development.

1. Classic Roots

The view that the evolution and development of behavior should be studied within a special scientific discipline is relatively new, although there is a long history of interest in the origin of behavioral capacities and the place of the human species in nature. Greek philosophers left an early record of their attempts to explain physical reality within the constraints of natural principles. Anaximandros of Miletos [ca. 610–545 B.C.], for example, seems to have suggested that all life originated in the seas and that, therefore, human beings had evolved from fish. Empedocles [ca. 493–433 B.C.], Leucipus [ca. 450–370 B.C.], Democritus [ca. 460–370 B.C.], and Epicurus [ca. 341–270 B.C.] emphasized the role of random combination of basic primordial elements in the formation of physical bodies. Greek philosophers called these primordial elements "atomoi,"—"uncutables,"—and thus their view of the universe is known as atomic theory. (Notice that these "atomoi" are equivalent to the subatomic particles of modern physics.) Atomic theory led to an interest in the origin of life, although, unfortunately, only fragments were preserved of the writings of these philosophers. The problem of the origin of life was treated by a later Epicurean,

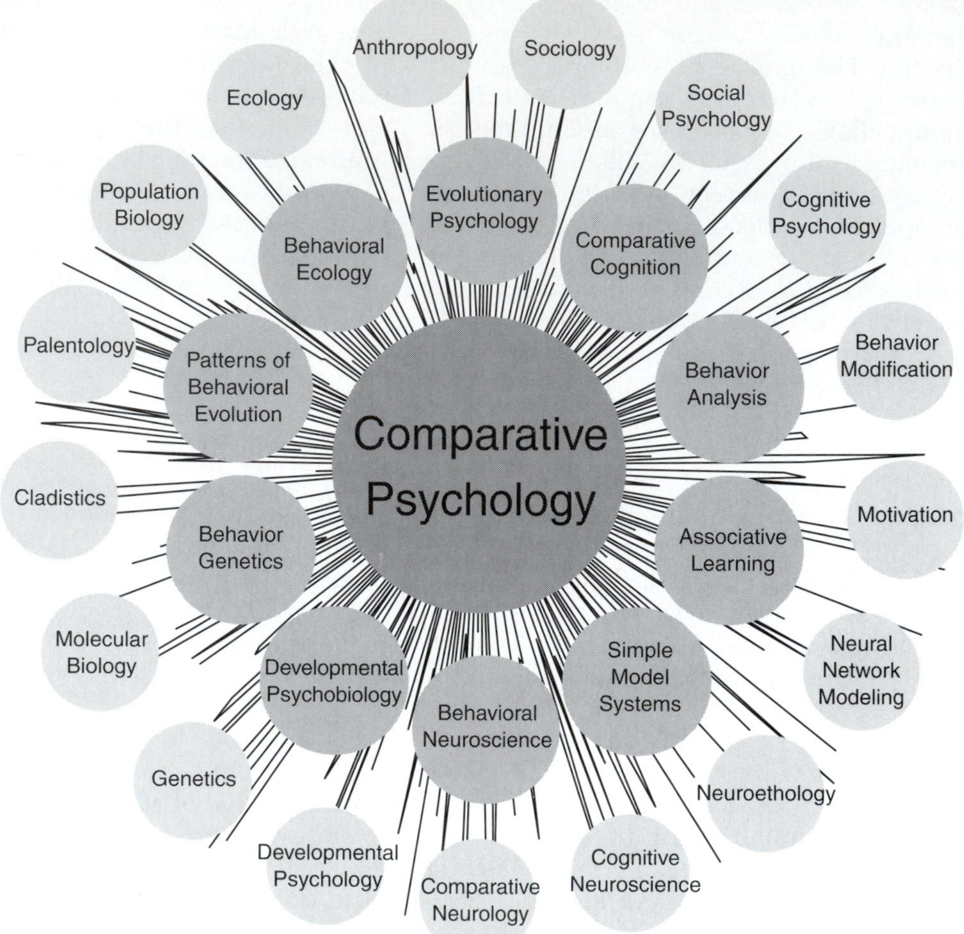

FIGURE 1.1. Relationship between the main research areas of comparative psychology and a variety of disciplines in the social and biological sciences. The scientific scene is constantly changing as new areas of research are redefined and created. The scheme is intended to show the interdisciplinary nature of comparative psychology and its relevance to both the social and biological sciences. (Drawing by D. Robinson)

the Roman philosopher Titus Lucretius Caro [95–55 B.C.].

Lucretius's poem *De Rerum Natura* (*On the Nature of the Universe*) is intriguing to a reader acquainted with the modern notions of evolution and natural selection. Particles of all kinds, dispersed randomly throughout the universe, gave rise to all bodies, including the earth, moon, sun, and stars. A believer in *spontaneous generation,* Lucretius suggested that living organisms originated in the "mother earth":

> *And even now many creatures arise from the earth, formed by the rain and the warm heat of the sun* (book V, verses 793–794).

Since *"all things move, all are changed by nature and compelled to alter"* (book V, verses 830–831), many of these organisms were aberrant, simply resulting from trial and error in the random combination of particles. It followed that many of these organisms (*"monsters"* in Lucretius's terms) were not fit to survive and reproduce, and thus became extinct. Lucretius wrote (book V, verses 849–854) in the first century B.C.:

> *For we see that living beings need many things in conjunction, so that they may be able by procreation to forge out the chain of the generations: First there must be food, next there must be a way for the life-giving seeds to ooze through the frame and be discharged from the body, and that male and female be joined they must both have the means to exchange mutual pleasures.*

Aristotle [384–322 B.C.], who vigorously opposed atomic theory, has often been considered the father of both biology and psychology. Aristotle must have been greatly impressed with the fauna and flora specimens that officials in Alexander the Great's army were collecting specially for him. Taxonomic principles originated in his efforts to organize this vast information. He recognized and classified 540 animal species, segregating them into the enaima (or vertebrates) and the anaima (or invertebrates), depending on the presence or absence of blood, respectively. In his *Historia Animalium,* Aristotle proposed the concept of *scala naturae* to explain what he viewed as a gradual transition from the inanimate to plants, animals, and humans. He wrote:

> *Nature proceeds from the inanimate to the animals by such small steps that, because of the continuity, we fail to see to which side the boundary and the middle between them belongs* (book VII, 588b).

From plants to animals, the ladder (an appropriate metaphor for Aristotle's scala naturae notion) suggested that *"one after another shows more possession of life and movement"* (book VII, 588b). Whereas reproduction is common to all living forms, reproductive behavior distinguishes simple from complex species (book VII, 589a):

> *Now some* [animals] *simply like plants accomplish their own reproduction according to the seasons; others take trouble as well to complete the nourishing of their young, but once that is accomplished they separate from them and have no further association; but those that have more understanding and possess some memory continue the association, and have a more social relationship with their offspring.*

Aristotle suggested (book I, 488b) that:

> *Many animals have the power of memory and can be trained; but the only one which can recall past events at will is man.*

Aristotle also left extensive behavioral descriptions, ranging from quite accurate to completely wrong. Errors can often be justified by the conditions under which Aristotle made his observations—that is, the lack of instruments and reference sources (Sarton 1952). Aristotle's descriptions of the foraging and social behavior of bees, migratory behavior of cranes and pelicans, electric discharge of the torpedo fish, brood parasitism by European cuckoos, and parental care behavior of the catfish, among many other behavioral descriptions, reflect his systematic and objective approach.

The centuries that followed, from the Hellenistic period to the European Renaissance, were marked by a decline in the support for the study of the basic sciences and by a progressive concentration on theological issues. Roman and Arab philosophers and scientists were predominantly occupied with applied problems: Physics and geometry were displaced by architecture and engineering, while biology gave way to medicine and hygiene (Sthal 1962). Aristotle's notion of scala naturae was seen as logically ending with God as the ultimate expression of perfection (Sarton 1952). And although the ladder illustrated a progression, such a progression was perfectly compatible with a view according to which species were immutable and fixed. For centuries, such a view of life's diversity and of the place of humans in this picture, known as *creationism,* was taken literally from the Bible. The essential postulate was that all species had been created simultaneously and independently by a superior being.

2. PRE-DARWINIAN ROOTS

Western philosophy has been dominated by the Aristotelian view that humans enjoy a special status in the hierarchy of life as the most advanced species. This idea, which is still a matter of philosophical and scientific debate, led to a curious development in the work of several philosophers during the Renaissance in Europe. Any serious attempt at establishing the psychological superiority of humans was bound to provide a convincing account of animal behavior on the basis of totally material and mechanistic processes. Many philosophers found it unconvincing that the immortal soul, assigned to humans on a religious basis and seen as the foundation of conscious experience, could be something shared by all life forms.

Among the first to develop a mechanistic theory of animal behavior was the Spanish philosopher Gómez Pereira [1500–1558] in a book entitled *Antoniana Margarita,* first published in 1554. Pereira was influenced by recent advances in the physics of motion, and he attempted to apply these notions to the movement (behavior) of animals without assuming that animals possess any capacity for conscious perception and mental life (Bandrés & Llavona 1992). Thus, Pereira distinguished between voluntary movements, assigned only to humans, and vital movements, assigned to animals. Animals were capable of three kinds of vital movements. First, those directly produced by sensory experience, involving approach and withdrawal, such as the movements observed in a predator-prey interaction. These movements, called *instincts,* were thought to depend on the way the animal was built by the Creator. Pereira's example of instinct is the ability of chicks to peck at appropriate grains soon after hatching and without the apparent benefit of experience (see ***Chapter 11, section 2.g.,*** pp. 430–434). Second, movements produced in the absence of external stimuli were caused by a residue or trace left by the stimulus (which Pereira called "phantom") in the occipital part of the brain (called the "triclinio"). Internal factors determined whether the phantom was transferred to the frontal part of the brain (called the "synciput"), where it was translated into motor movements. These two classes of movements already contained all the elements of a *reflex*—that is, a sensory input that gives rise to a response after processing in the central nervous system. The third type of movement involved *learning,* and it was achieved by the association of phantoms in the brain by mere repetition. As examples, Pereira mentioned the training of parrots to talk, and the rapid approach of chickens and dogs when they are offered food. According to Pereira, the phantoms of the master's calls and the food provided by him become associated in the occipital part of the brain. Eventually, when the animal hears again the call, the food memory is activated and the animal is compelled to approach in a mechanical manner.

Pereira thus managed to explain behaviors ranging in complexity from a simple reaction to a stimulus to the effects of domestication and training, without resorting to mental or conscious processes, but attributing them entirely to mechanical influences among different parts of the animal's body. Pereira's views were highly controversial and provoked a number of rebuttals over the following centuries. However, the notion that a mechanistic view of animal behavior was possible became firmly established. Among those who articulated this view most influentially was the French philosopher René Descartes [1596–1650], particularly in his *Treatise on Man,* first published in 1664 (Descartes 1664/1985).

Two aspects of Descartes' contribution are relevant for comparative psychology. One was the notion that humans are unique and different from all other animals because of their ability for mental experience (i.e., the rational mind). In Descartes' view, such mental processes could not be reduced to the operation of some mechanism—*mind-body dualism.* Cartesian dualism has had a deep influence in the historical development of comparative psychology. The idea that our species is unique continues to be pervasive, although researchers and philosophers favor a variety of reasons for this uniqueness, including technology, language, and higher cognitive processes (e.g., Macphail 1982; Popper & Eccles 1977).

The second, and perhaps more productive, aspect of Descartes' contributions was his mechanical theory of animal behavior, inspired in the moving statues located in the gardens of the Saint Germane palace. Like Pereira's, Descartes' view embodied the notion of reflex, which was eventually to become central to the analysis of behavior (see ***Chapter 7, section 2.b.,*** pp. 233–236). These statues were actually operated by the visitors themselves, as they inadvertently stepped on tiles that activated valves allowing water to flow through an intricate circuitry of tubes. Descartes conceived animals as essentially complex moving statues, equipped with far finer tubings and much faster and lighter fluids he called animal spirits. These spirits were pulled from cavities of the brain much as air is moved into the "wind-chests" of a church organ, and they were released by sensory events just as air is released in an organ by the pressing of the keys that open appropriate valves. Sensory events moved nerve fluids that, in turn, pulled valves in the interior surface of the brain. Descartes said (p. 101),

> *Through these pores the animal spirits in the cavities of the brain immediately begin to make their way into the nerves and so to the muscles which serve to cause movements in the machine quite similar to those we are naturally prompted to make when our senses are affected in the same way.*

This is why, according to Descartes, a person is able not only to withdraw his leg from a burning fire but also to turn his head toward the fire. According to Descartes, this mechanism operated in both animals and humans, but the difference was that humans also have subjective experience. Whereas both animals and humans withdrew from the fire, only humans felt the heat of the flame as an internal experience. This was accomplished because *"God unites a rational soul to this machine,"* argued Descartes (p. 102).

Descartes did not speculate about the origin of this machinery that allowed for animal movement, but soon others entertained the possibility that experience could provide the means to build on the basis of these reflexes (Boakes 1984). David Hartley [1705–1757], for example, suggested that reflexes could be acquired through experience. In his *Observations on Man, His Frame, His Duty, and His Expectations,* Hartley (1749/1966) suggested that learned behavior could be explained in terms of brain processes and that differences in intellectual capacity of humans and animals were related to brain size, the quality of the nerves, the possession of language, and a greater dependence of humans on education rather than instinct. Hartley suggested that animals with smaller brains had less brain mass available for the formation of associations than animals with large brains. At about the same time, Julien de La Mettrie [1709–1751] also proposed that education was largely responsible for intellectual differences between humans and animals. In a book entitled *Man a Machine,* La Mettrie (1748/1953) actually suggested that properly educated apes should be able to acquire human speech, given the similarities in brain structure between humans and apes (see ***Chapter 14, section 3.d.,*** pp. 572–576).

Hartley and La Mettrie were reacting to Descartes' view that humans were essentially different from animals by arguing that the difference, although obvious and clear, was only a matter of degree. By this time, philosophers like John Locke [1632–1704], David Hume [1711–1776], and Thomas Brown [1778–1820] in Britain and Etienne Condillac [1714–1780] and Destutt de Tracy [1754–1836] in France were speculating about the origin of knowledge. They were all stressing one critical idea—namely, that the human mind is originally like a blank tablet (i.e., mind as *tabula rasa*), on which ideas derived from sensory experience are imprinted by the operation of associative processes. It was a theoretical framework that tended to interpret psychological differences between species as mainly related to external factors, given the predominant role attributed to sensory experience in the acquisition of knowledge. This view also stimulated thinking in terms of neural processes because sensory experience could be clearly linked to receptor organs and nerves. However, physiological information in the 17th and 18th centuries did not permit much progress. Basic anatomical and electrophysiological principles were being developed, but it was only during the 19th century that such basic notions as the spinal control of involuntary movements [Robert Whytt, 1714–1766], the sensory-motor theory [François Magendi, 1783–1855], the reflex arc [Marshall Hall, 1790–1857], physiological inhibition [Eduard F. W. Weber, 1806–1871], and the modulation of spinal reflexes by the brain [Ivan M. Sechenov, 1829–1905] were postulated. Moreover, new techniques were developed that allowed for accurate measurements of electrical potentials [Luigi Galvani, 1737–1798; Alessandro Volta, 1745–1827] and the speed of nerve conduction [Hermann von Helmholtz, 1821–1894]. These advances made possible the emergence of neurophysiology.

These contributions were also important because they set the stage for an experimental approach to biological research that would eventually develop intensely during the 19th and 20th centuries. The experimental study of biological systems was in part a reaction to *vitalism* and an attempt to demonstrate that the analysis of isolated organs could lead to orderly results. According to the vitalist view, a mysterious force, called the "élan vital," was necessary to explain properties of life that seemed to appear nowhere in the realm of the nonliving, such as the ability to vary, adapt, and reproduce (Jacob 1973). But this vital force implicated the animal as a whole, and thus, breaking the animal apart for analysis would seem to lead nowhere as that isolated part would lack the essential force that kept it alive. *Mechanicism* of the kind that was first developed in great detail by Pereira and Descartes to explain animal behavior—and subsequently expanded by those who dared to look into the nervous system to uncover its basic anatomical organization and physiology—eventually became the dominant approach in the biological sciences.

Meanwhile, the European view of the world was changing very fast during these centuries. Just as Alexander's military campaigns expanded the known world for the Greeks, the worldwide exploration that started in the Renaissance revolutionized the natural sciences. For the first time naturalists were exposed to a range of diversity in life forms that was far greater than anyone had anticipated. A feature that soon became obvious to European naturalists working on specimens collected in all the continents was the presence of regional faunas. For example, there was a South American fauna involving camelids (llamas, alpacas), edentates (armadillos), and marsupials (opossums), among other groups. This territorial uniqueness was even more obvious in islands all over the world. How could these assemblages have been formed if all the species had been created in a single place?

The Spanish naturalist Félix de Azara [1746–1821] was among the first to propose alternatives to creationism. Azara (1934) suggested that local faunas implied that species had been created in different continents and argued that creation could have occurred at different times, based on the observation that certain species are locked together in terms of predator-prey interactions. Prey species must have been created first, or else predators would have perished. Azara accepted the possibility of transgenerational change within a species and viewed variability in morphological characters as part of the natural endowment of animal populations. He based these conclusions on the study of *domestication,* the conscious pairing of animals with the purpose of improving their form or organs. Azara pointed out that domestication increased morphological variability and also suggested that stronger species could cause the extinction of weaker ones. The notion that character variability is not just noise distorting a prototypical form would become, a few decades later, one of the critical assumptions underlying the theory of natural selection proposed by Darwin and Wallace.

At about the time Azara was describing the South American fauna and the nervous system was becoming an object of intense scrutiny, European zoologists were rediscovering the classic idea that change is an ubiquitous property of nature. Jean B. Lamarck [1744–1829], a French zoologist and botanist, developed a theory that accounted for the gradual modification of one species into another. Lamarck proposed in 1801 the theory of the *inheritance of acquired traits,* which, simply put, suggested that the use and disuse of parts determined the degree to which they were passed across generations. This specific theory is now widely regarded as wrong (Avers 1989), but the emphasis on function over structure—the basic postulate that evolutionary change starts with a change in behavior (i.e., the use of a part) and that morphological changes follow—continues to be of paramount importance in contemporary evolutionary theory (Gottlieb 1992; Wyles et al. 1983).

Lamarck (1809/1984) also developed a theory of the evolutionary stages of neural organization and speculated on the functional correlates of brain structure (see ***Figure 1.2***). Lamarck's theory is based on a primary dichotomy between living organisms that do not possess a nervous system—such as plants, infusorians (unicellular protists such as *Volvox* and *Amoeba*), and polyps (e.g., sponges)—and those with some degree of neural development. Organisms without nervous systems also lack muscles and can move only by *irritability;* they are unable to initiate movements from within, acting only in reaction to external conditions. Therefore, these organisms lack both instincts and intelligence, both of which require sensory-motor integration.

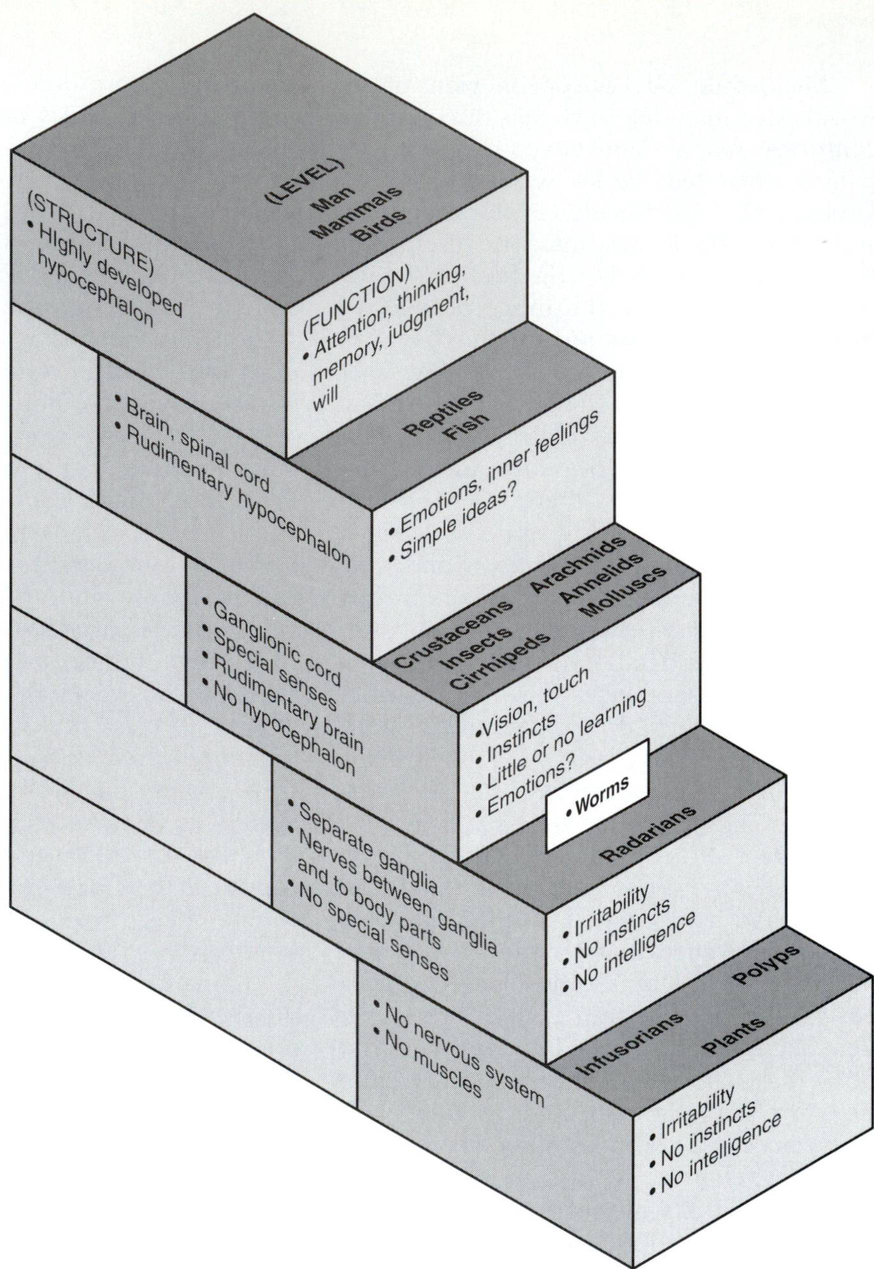

FIGURE 1.2. A representation of Lamarck's progressive theory of the evolution of the nervous system and behavioral capacities (adapted from Lamarck's *Zoological Philosophy*). The ladder represents the idea that lower levels are more general, both structurally and functionally, and that as one moves toward the top, forms become increasingly more "perfect." Each step in the ladder contains unique properties as well as all the properties of lower levels and rudiments of properties that will appear in full development in the upper steps. (Drawing by D. Robinson)

The four levels that follow represent a progression from the most "imperfect" to the most "perfect" nervous systems, a progression that is accompanied by functional improvements and the emergence of new psychological capacities. At the level of radiarians (e.g., jellyfish), cords of ganglia connected by nerves with one another and with the various bodily parts control and organize simple movements as well as the functioning of internal organs. These animals, however, lack special senses such as vision and audition, and thus the nervous system is solely responsible for movement. Nematodes and flatworms represent, according to Lamarck, an intermediate group in which there is certainly the sense of touch, and perhaps some rudiments of vision. The next level is characterized by a ganglionic longitudinal cord, usually ending in a ganglion that could be called a rudimentary brain. A variety of invertebrate groups are characterized by this level of organization, in which special senses are already fully developed and a sensory-motor distinction is already present in the nerves connecting the cord with muscles and organs. These animals show clear evidence of instinctive behaviors, which, according to Lamarck, originated in habits repeated during many ancestral generations until they became fixed. Such animals, however, have no power to vary their actions and thus possess no intelligence. It is at the level of fish and reptiles (which in Lamarck's classification includes the amphibians) that the nervous cord ends in a rudimentary accessory organ, also called hypocephalon: the hemispheres. Lamarck distinguishes between the brain (the seat of sensory processing) and the hypocephalon (the hemispheres, responsible for higher psychological functions). It is the hypocephalon that allows for the emergence of inner emotions, a sense of the internal state of the organism. Lamarck's most perfect level of organization is that of birds and mammals, in which a highly developed hypocephalon is evident. It is in our own species that the hemispheres have reached the highest degree of complexity, and, according to Lamarck, it is this complexity that allows for the highest psychological functions, including attention, thinking (formation of ideas), memory (association of ideas), and judgment (comparison of ideas). Whereas Lamarck's notion of the evolution of brain and intelligence continues to attract research interest (see chapters in ***Parts II*** and ***IV***), his Aristotelian view of evolutionary progress as the inevitable transformation of species toward a more "perfect" organization has been abandoned by contemporary comparative psychologists.

By the mid 19th century the natural sciences were ready to accept the possibility of "transformation"—that is, the generational change that leads to the origin of new species that is now called *evolution*. Working in parallel, physiologists were discovering the mechanisms of neural functioning, and neurobiologists were for the first time able to look at the building blocks of the nervous system, the neuron cells. In the face of diversity, both zoologists and physiologists were struggling to reduce the apparent complexity of the natural order to the operation of a few basic principles.

3. Natural Selection and Mental Continuity

One general principle was discovered independently by Charles Darwin [1809–1882] and Alfred Wallace [1823–1913], two British naturalists with extensive field experience. The idea was very simple and already evident in the process of domestication. Just as humans consciously paired animals to develop breeds with advantageous characteristics, so too nature operated on existing variations, promoting those that favored the animal's ability to survive and reproduce, and eliminating those that led to less success or premature death. In his influential book *On the Origin of Species,* Darwin (1859/1993, p. 88) wrote

> *Owing to this struggle* [for life], *variations, however slight and from whatever cause proceeding, if they be in any degree profitable to the individuals of a species, in their infinitely complex relations to other organic beings and to their physical conditions of life, will tend to the preservation of such individuals, and will generally be inherited by the offspring. The offspring, also, will thus have a better chance of surviving, for, of the many individuals of any species which are periodically born, but a small number can survive. I have called this principle, by which each slight variation, if useful, is preserved, by the term Natural Selection, in order to mark its relation to man's power of selection.*

As a process, *natural selection* was assumed to be gradual and to work in a cumulative fashion across many generations, thus requiring a long period of time to explain the diversity of life known to 19th-century naturalists. Natural selection also needed a theory of heredity because only those variations that could actually be inherited would have an impact in the process of speciation. Neither of these assumptions could be sustained with scientific observations by the mid 1800s; the earth was thought to be quite young, and the problem of heredity had not been resolved yet. So natural selection was taken as another possible factor in evolution; many naturalists (including Darwin and Wallace) continued to advocate alternative evolutionary mechanisms, including Lamarck's inheritance of acquired traits. But whereas the dominance of natural selection as the main factor in evolution had to await the modern synthesis of the 1930s, the notion of evolution as a fact had become firmly rooted in scientific circles of that time.

Evolutionary ideas revitalized the problem of man's place in nature. If known species were all tied up by deep genealogical links, then human origins must be found in nonhuman animals. The same should apply to every human attribute, from bodily organs to physiology, behavior, and higher psychological functions. Even such seemingly unique attributes as imagination, language, and moral judgment should be found in "lower" animals, although perhaps in rudimentary form. *Mental continuity* was required by a theory that placed such an emphasis on gradualism. But whereas other notions of mental continuity, including Aristotle's and Lamarck's, implied progress in a teleological sense (i.e., evolution proceeding toward the goal of producing increasingly "perfect" beings), Darwin's mental continuity simply implied that no trait would be absolutely new in evolution. Whereas a ladder is an appropriate metaphor for Aristotle's view of nature, a tree branching in all possible directions is the adequate metaphor for a view of evolution based on natural selection.

With evolution firmly established in scientific circles, it is not surprising that the idea of comparing animals in terms of their psychological capacities became increasingly popular. Herbert Spencer [1820–1903] developed an evolutionary perspective of mental processes in his *Principles of Psychology,* published in 1855, and the German zoologist David F. Weinland [1829–1915] defined, in 1858 and perhaps for the first time, comparative animal psychology as the study of the psychological life and the movements of animals (Cadwallader 1984). Under the influence of Darwin's hypothesis of mental continuity, the first attempts at collecting relevant evidence appeared during the second half of the 19th century. Darwin himself can be said to have made the initial efforts to explain human intelligence, emotions, and moral faculties from an evolutionary perspective (Darwin 1871, 1872), and his disciple George Romanes [1848–1894] provided the first comprehensive account of mental continuity in his book *Animal Intelligence,* published in 1882.

The predominant methodology used in these works was based on direct observation from which inferences about the animal's mental states were made by analogy to human subjective experiences known by introspection. Behavior was considered only as the "ambassador" of the mind (Romanes 1882, p. 1), an unavoidable obstacle given the impossibility of direct observation of mental events. But these initial books on comparative psychology were also rich in "anecdotal evidence" published or volunteered by people of various levels of expertise. As an example, Romanes transcribes an account given by an eyewitness of an episode in which rats were supposedly observed to rob eggs: The rats *"form a line from the egg baskets to their hole, and handed the eggs from one to another in their fore-paws"* (Romanes 1882, p. 40). Uncritical acceptance of these anecdotes as evidence for mental continuity soon aroused severe criticisms. C. Lloyd Morgan [1852–1936], author of *An Introduction to Comparative Psychology* (1894, p. 53), in a sentence that became known as *Morgan's canon* of parsimony, warned that

> *In no case may we interpret an action as the outcome of the exercise of a higher psychical faculty, if it can be interpreted as the outcome of the exercise of one which stands lower in the psychological scale.*

An extraordinary example of the kind of experimenter bias that justified Morgan's canon is the case of the horse Clever Hans, which became notorious in the early 1900s. According to its trainer, Herr von Osten, Hans had learned to perform mathematical calculations and to spell words. Standing before a board that read "2 × 2 =" the horse would answer correctly by tapping four times on the floor with one of its hoofs, for doing which it would usually receive some reward. Clever Hans became so famous in Germany that a commission was appointed to study the horse's mental capacities from a scientific point of view. After many carefully designed tests, the psychologist Oskar Pfungst concluded that the horse had no mathematical skills whatsoever, but only the ability, learned by trial and error, to respond to subtle and unintentional facial movements of its trainer that signaled when to start and stop tapping on the floor (Pfungst 1965).

Not always were accounts of animal behavior so biased and anecdotal. A case in point is provided by Darwin's (1881) observations on the intelligence of worms. Darwin was intrigued by the habit of worms to plug the opening of their burrows, and he carefully recorded the types of objects used (usually leaves or petioles) and how the worms drew them into the burrow. In addition, he provided the worms with paper triangles varying in shape and size. Darwin found that these objects were not drawn by just any part, but most frequently by the object's apex. ***Figure 1.3*** shows the results in quantitative format. Darwin (1881, p. 97) concluded that

> *If worms are able to judge, either before drawing or after having drawn an object close to the mouths of their burrows, how best to drag it in, they must acquire some notion of its general shape. This they probably acquire by touching it in many places with the anterior extremity of their bodies, which serves as a tactile organ. . . . If worms have the power of acquiring some notion, however crude, of the shape of an object and of their burrows, as seems to be the case, they deserve to be called intelligent; for they then act in nearly the same manner as would a man under similar circumstances.*

By the end of the 19th century it was clear that little was gained from unreliable information and biased interpretation of

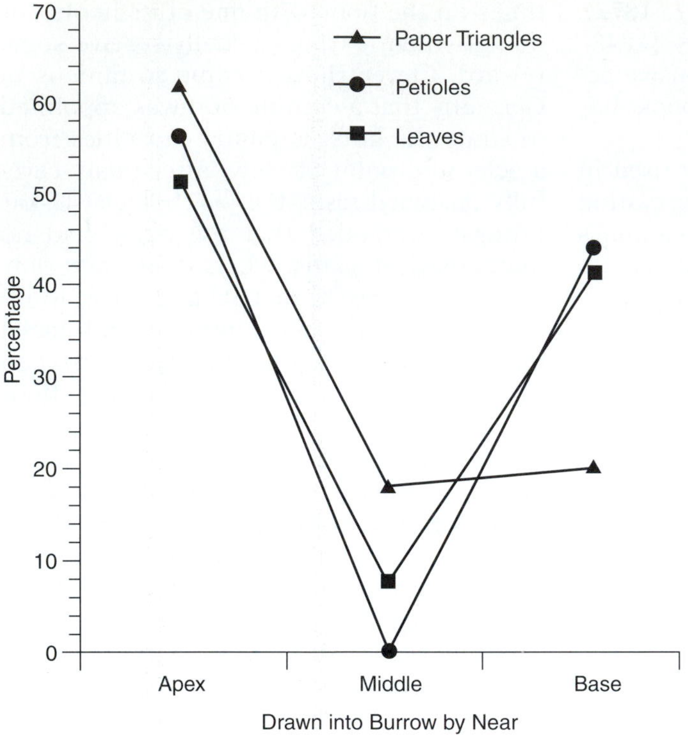

FIGURE 1.3. Results reported by Darwin (1881) on the manner in which worms draw various kinds of objects into their burrows. Worms tended to draw objects from the apex or base, a result that suggested to Darwin that they had formed a rudimentary representation of the object. The actual results were reported in a table; the means for leaves, petioles, and paper triangles are plotted as percentages of total observations.

the evidence. Quantitative methods and experimental procedures of the kind being developed by physiologists were required. Experimental attempts were made in several areas: Pierre Flourens [1794–1867] assessed the effects of brain lesions on the behavior of birds; Douglas Spalding [1840–1877] studied the effects of visual deprivation in embryos and very young chicks on the development of behavior; Edward L. Thorndike [1874–1949] published the first doctoral dissertation based on the experimental study of trial-and-error learning in animals; Ivan P. Pavlov [1849–1936] developed an experimental procedure to study basic associative processes and a theory that explained learned behavior in terms of brain processes; Herbert S. Jennings [1868– 1947] studied the behavior of single-celled organisms and primitive animals; and Jacques Loeb [1859–1924] studied how gravity and light affected the behavior of simple animals, developing his mechanistic theory of tropisms. Robert Yerkes [1876–1956] was especially important in the early history of comparative psychology as coeditor, with C. L. Herrick, of the *Journal of Comparative Neurology and Psychology* between 1904 and 1910 (after 1910 this journal resumed its original and present title, *Journal of Comparative Neurology*) and editor of the *Journal of Animal Behavior* and the *Comparative Psychology Monographs,* both founded in 1911 and the first entirely devoted to comparative psychology. Yerkes is also known for his research on motivation, discrimination learning, and problem solving in species ranging from frogs and turtles to monkeys and apes (Boakes 1984).

As behavioral phenomena were increasingly brought under the control of experimental techniques in the laboratory, researchers began to shift their attention away from inferring the animal's mental states and toward behavior itself. The "ambassador" became the "king." It was John B. Watson [1878–1958] who expressed this shift most vehemently in a manifesto put forth as an attempt to shift psychology's object of study from the mind to behavior (Watson 1913). Watson's view became known as *behaviorism*. Although behaviorism arose from the unquestionable problems generated by attempts to interpret the minds of animals, it spread to all areas of psychology. Behaviorism was a reaction to anecdotalism and introspectionism, an attempt to build a science of psychology based on purely objective facts and on the Darwinian hypothesis of species continuity. Watson's (1913, p. 158) opening paragraph reveals the core of his insight:

> *Psychology as the behaviorist views it is a purely objective experimental branch of natural science. Its theoretical goal is the prediction and control of behavior. Introspection forms no essential part of its methods, nor is the scientific value of its data dependent upon the readiness with which they lend themselves to interpretation in terms of consciousness. The behaviorist, in his efforts to get a unitary scheme of animal response, recognizes no dividing line between man and brute. The behavior of man, with all of its refinement and complexity, forms only a part of the behaviorist's total scheme of investigation.*

4. Evolution of Instincts

The distinction between intelligence and instinct has been a ubiquitous feature in the history of comparative psychology. In traditional schemes, such as those of Aristotle, Descartes, and Lamarck, intelligence occupied the highest level in the hierarchy, whereas instinctive reactions were thought to be simpler forms of psychological functioning. Intelligent acts were typically described as fundamentally variable and involving some degree of adjustment, whereas instincts were typically stereotypic forms of behavior. Their relationship could be complex, however, as in the case of Lamarck's theory of habits: these, he claimed, after repetitive use across many generations, could become inheritable and turn into fixed instincts.

Darwin (1859/1993) approached the problem of instincts by trying to fit them into his own principle of natural selection; thereby, he clearly perceived several fundamental problems. He defined an *instinct* as an action performed *"without experience,"* and *"by many individuals in the same way, without their knowing for what purpose it is performed"* (p. 317). He wrote: *"instincts are as important as corporeal structures for the welfare of each species"* (p. 321), and thus equally subject to natural selection. But how could natural selection have shaped instincts if they are so fixed? How could instincts have evolved in cases where the organisms are reproductively sterile, such as in the worker castes of bees and ants? Moreover, how could such complex instinctive behavior as that observed in social insects have evolved gradually by natural selection?

Part of Darwin's effort went into proving that most instincts do show variability and that their performance is far from completely fixed. Ultimately, however, he did not see a way out of these problems, and so he developed an eclectic view of the evolutionary origins of instincts, according to which they could evolve via different mechanisms. For example, a Lamarckian mechanism was said to be responsible for the tameness of domestic rabbits, attributed to a *"long-continued close confinement"* (p. 326), and for the chicken's inability to fly, said to have been *"lost by disuse"* (p. 327). Natural selection accounted for the evolution of egg-parasitism in cuckoos. Darwin suggested that this *"aberrant habit"* might have helped females to profit by being able *"to migrate earlier"*; having inherited this tendency, the chicks would then tend to follow the same instinct as their mothers, laying eggs occasionally in other birds' nests (p. 328). A third mechanism was correlation of characters, which Darwin applied to the habit of titmouse birds to hold a seed with their feet while they hammer it with the beak. Darwin argued that while *"the beak is supposed to be slowly modified by natural selection,"* the feet could have become larger through correlation with the beak. Darwin suggested that

> *It is not improbable that such larger feet would lead the bird to climb more and more until it acquired the remarkable climbing instinct and power of the nuthatch* (p. 351).

Finally, the insuperable difficulty of the evolution of sterile castes in insects was approached from a point of view that suggests a *group selection* principle (see ***Chapter 2, section 5.f.,*** pp. 54–56). Darwin thought that *"selection may be applied to the family, as well as to the individual"* (p. 354). According to Darwin (p. 352), if

> *. . . it had been profitable to the community that a number* [of insects] *should have been annually born capable of work, but incapable of procreation, I can see no especial difficulty in this having been effected through natural selection.*

Despite the fall of Lamarckian and group selection ideas, current views of evolution retain the eclectic flavor that characterizes Darwin's account of instincts. While natural selection continues to be central, other mechanisms, including correlation of characters (allometry) and genetic drift, contribute to the evolutionary process, as reviewed in ***Chapter 2.*** But perhaps the most interesting idea stemming from Darwin's chapter on instincts is the hypothesis that instincts can be used to reconstruct the history of a lineage. Darwin suggested that graded forms of instincts, just as in the case of morphological traits such as the shape of a bird's beak, should be found in *"collateral lines of descent"* (p. 320). This hypothesis suggested that the study of a particular instinct in a group of related species (i.e., species with a relatively recent common ancestor) should permit a reconstruction of the evolutionary history of that instinct. Following Darwin's principles, instances of that instinct that appeared complex, in the sense of involving many behavioral elements, could be interpreted as derived, whereas simpler forms of the same behavior could correspond more closely to the primitive state of that instinct. Among the first to develop this idea into a research program were Charles Whitman [1842–1910], who described the behavior of related species of pigeons (Columbidae), and Oskar Heinroth [1871–1945], who published a similar account for duck species (Anatinae). They both concluded that the constancy of these behavioral displays was so remarkable that they could be used as traits for taxonomic purpose.

It was this basic idea that eventually led to the emergence of *ethology* during the first half of the 20th century, mainly through the work of Konrad Lorenz [1901–1989]. Lorenz (1941) published a detailed description of the reproductive displays of the Anatinae, assuming simply that the motor patterns were innate (i.e., inherited and fixed) and that similarity of behavior could be used to infer common evolutionary origin (i.e., homology). According to Lorenz (1941, p. 16),

> *Correspondence* [of behavioral characters] *with the related morphological characters would permit solid defense of the application of the phylogenetic homology concept to species-specific behaviour patterns, such that the pre-conditions for comparative psychology in the narrowest sense would be provided.*

> *Only such fine systematic studies of an exactly investigated group of animals is able to provide us with information about the manner in which phylogenetic alterations of instinctive motor patterns, taxes, innate schemata, and—later on—of all psychological mechanisms, occur.*

Lorenz's account of the phylogenetic history of these displays and similar studies that followed led to the introduction of a family of new concepts that greatly stimulated research on behavioral evolution. The word "instinct" was replaced by a variety of more specific words. For example, *fixed action patterns* (FAPs) referred to innate responses that, once initiated, would continue to completion without interference from external stimuli. Such patterns were thought to be neural programs directly under genetic control that, once activated, would unload a stream of outputs leading to an observable FAP. One example was the so-called egg-retrieval response of the graylag goose. These ground-nesting birds would retrieve an egg displaced away from the nest with characteristic movements of the beak. Lorenz observed that once the movements were initiated, they would continue even if the egg was removed in the process. It was as if the goose was rolling an imaginary egg. By contrast, *taxes* were movements that depended on continuous sensory feedback. These motor responses were thus referred to as orienting reactions. In the egg-retrieval example, when the bird is rolling an egg, slight sideways movements of the egg cause compensatory movements of the bird's beak that completely disappear when the egg is removed. Such movements were classified as taxes. But motor patterns occur, in most cases, in the presence of some particular stimulus. In courtship displays, the stimulus is provided by the behavior or appearance of a conspecific, and it was referred to as *sign stimulus*. A puzzling property of sign stimuli was their apparent simplicity. For example, male European robins compete aggressively for the possession of reproductive territories. Whereas casual observation would appear to indicate that a resident male responds to the presence of an intruder, in fact only a patch of red feathers controls the resident's aggressive behavior and not the perception of the entire intruder as a complex stimulus. It was as if these simple stimuli were keys that selectively unlocked a FAP. A second perplexing observation was that in some cases animals exhibited preferences for extreme versions of the stimulus. For example, given a choice between its own egg and a giant egg several times larger, oystercatchers preferred the giant egg and spent substantial amounts of time attempting to sit on top of it. These were called *supernormal stimuli.*

Lorenz emphasized fieldwork over the laboratory, qualitative description over quantitative research, and natural behavior over what he considered to be artificial responses of rats pressing levers in the simplified environment of a conditioning chamber. He also stressed the point that instincts were rigid and invariant, and although they were considered to be the product of natural selection, he rarely studied how animal behavior related to the general fitness of the animal. With its emphasis on fixity, Lorenz's view of instincts is dramatically different from that of Darwin. Darwin's gradualist view had permeated almost everything, and the dichotomy between instinct and intelligence was no exception. William James [1842–1910] wrote, on the basis of work by Darwin, Romanes, and others, the following passage:

> *In the instincts of mammals, and even of lower creatures, the uniformity and infallibility which, a generation ago, were considered as essential characters do not exist.*

According to James (1890, vol. 2, p. 391),

> *What is called an instinct is usually only a tendency to act in a way of which the average is pretty constant, but which need not be mathematically 'true.'*

A similar view was advanced by Wallace Craig [1876–1954], who distinguished between *appetitive* and *consummatory* behaviors as constituents of instincts. Craig (1918) argued that whereas consummatory responses (e.g., eating food or drinking water) tend to be relatively fixed and stereotyped, appetitive responses (e.g., searching for or orienting toward food or water sources) are flexible and complex.

Lorenz did not provide adequate quantitative information to support his claims of behavioral fixity. Nonetheless, it was obvious that the study of behavior under natural conditions was leading to a different set of problems from those that originally had shaped comparative psychology. It was Niko Tinbergen's [1907–1988] main contribution to show empirical ways to illuminate the connection between natural selection and behavior through the use of simple experimental techniques under field conditions (see ***Chapters 4*** and ***5*** for a discussion of the adaptive significance of behavior). The emphasis placed by ethologists like Lorenz and Tinbergen on the distinction between innate and acquired behaviors, and on the idea that innate behavior is fixed and stereotyped, contrasted dramatically with the emphasis on behavioral plasticity that had developed as a result of some key assumptions behind the behavioristic approach. Eventually, these two views of animal behavior collided.

5. Nature Versus Nurture

The 20th century began with major progress in the two areas that had troubled Darwin the most. Geologists demonstrated that the earth originated much earlier than anybody had previously thought, thus providing the time needed for natural selection to create the immense diversity in life forms. But most relevant to the present discussion, biologists finally started to understand heredity. The work of Gregor Mendel [1822–1884], rediscovered in 1900, suggested that germ cells contain enough information to generate an entire organism through development. Knowledge about heredity led to a series of principles (discussed in ***Chapters 2*** and ***3***) and, among them, to the idea that information flows from the genome to the organism but not vice versa. This principle, proposed by August Weismann [1834–1914], was contrary to Lamarckian notions of use and disuse and suggested that parents could not genetically transmit to their progeny those behavioral and physical traits developed during their own life.

In a different vein, Thorndike's (1898, 1911) comparative work on learning, and the subsequent research it inspired, seemed to provide support for the Darwinian idea of mental continuity. This research suggested that the basic underlying mechanisms of learning were the same across a wide range of animals, although perhaps there were differences in the amount of learning that different types of animals could accomplish. Species differences in learning abilities, a key to understanding complex behavior, were progressively seen as merely quantitative. Thorndike's general view of learning, as well as Weismann's principle, contributed to a gradual transformation of comparative research toward an increasing emphasis on underlying mechanisms at the expense of true comparative work. Just as geneticists were uncovering the laws of heredity by studying a few plant and animal models, so comparative psychologists progressively concentrated on the study of behavioral processes related to issues of perception, learning, motivation, and development by concentrating on a few animal models, mainly the albino rat and, later, the pigeon and rhesus monkey.

There were two other sources for this shift in research emphasis. One was provided by developmental research begun by Spalding (1873/1954), who had described the phenomenon of *imprinting* (the development through learning of a mother-infant bond in ducks and other precocial birds; see ***Chapter 12, section 1,*** pp. 442–458) as an imperfect instinct. Spalding found that the duckling had to be exposed to its mother for some time before an attachment would develop, and he interpreted this as evidence that the instinct was incomplete at birth and hence "imperfect." This view was changed even more drastically by Zing Yang Kuo [1898–1970], who found that male pigeons reared in social interaction with ring doves, a different species, would display courtship behavior toward ring dove females but not toward females of their own species. This phenomenon, known as sexual imprinting, suggested to Kuo (1921, p. 657) that

> *All our sexual appetites are the result of social stimulations. The organism possesses no ready-made reaction to the other sex, any more than it possesses innate ideas.*

A second factor driving comparative psychologists away from the study of instinctive behavior was the influence of behaviorism. For example, Watson's (1924) research on the perceptual, motor, and learning abilities of human infants convinced him that instincts played a minor role in the development of behavior, compared to environmental influences. Watson's (1924, p. 104) environmentalist claims became famous because of his extreme formulation:

> *Give me a dozen healthy infants, well-formed, and my own specified world to bring them up in and I'll guarantee to take any one at random and train him to become any type of specialist I might select—doctor, lawyer, artist, merchant-chief and, yes, even beggar-man and thief, regardless of his talents, penchants, tendencies, abilities, vocations, and race of his ancestors.*

Although he conceded to be *"going beyond my facts"* (p. 104), he insisted that the empirical evidence for the existence of human and animal instincts was weak, at best.

Such an extreme emphasis on *nurture* provoked a reaction from the ethologists, who saw inherited and fixed patterns of behavior dominating the scene when the observer concentrated on animals living in their natural environment. According to the ethological emphasis on *nature,* genes inherited from the parents set up circuits in the central nervous system via unknown mechanisms, and once these circuits become functional, the resulting behavior can emerge even in the absence of practice and learning. Since behavior contributed to the process of biological adaptation, genetic information had to somehow predict the problems the animal would face in its environment and equip it with the adequate behavioral repertoire. For example, Tinbergen (1951) suggested a hierarchical system of neural centers controlling the complex reproductive behavior of the stickleback fish. A major instinct, such as reproduction, involved a variety of coordinated actions, such as male-male aggression, nesting, and courtship, and each in turn involved even more specific actions, down to the level of activation of motor units and muscles. Lorenz (1965) suggested that innate mechanisms were so prevalent that even learning abilities were preestablished. One of the prime examples was, in fact, imprinting, which Lorenz viewed as a form of preprogrammed learning whereby a young animal is innately predisposed to acquire information during a specific interval of time called the *critical period.* So ethologists emphasized "nature" over "nurture" and set up the stage for one of the most vivid controversies in comparative psychology.

The nature-nurture debate led to a view of behavioral development known as *epigenesis,* according to which structures and functions of the organism arise during development, as opposed to being preformed in the egg, as believed by 19th-century biologists (Gottlieb 1992). At the behavioral level, this notion was most forcefully advanced by T. C. Schneirla [1902–1968] and Daniel S. Lehrman [1919–1972], whose main argument was that the notion of "innate" and "acquired" as exclusive categories in the classification of behaviors was oversimplistic, as was the notion, implied by ethologists, that the road from genes to behavior was relatively direct. These arguments were forcefully developed by Lehrman (1953), who carefully analyzed some of the classic examples of FAPs and taxes, such as the egg-retrieval behavior of the graylag goose.

Lehrman pointed out a serious limitation of isolation experiments that have been taken by Lorenz and Tinbergen as the primary evidence for the argument that particular instances of behavior are innate. In isolation experiments of the kind first carried out by Spalding in the 19th century, a developing animal is prevented from a particular kind of experience, and so, if the behavior develops normally, it is appropriate to conclude that the particular type of experience eliminated in the experiment is not required for the normal development of the behavior. What is inappropriate is to conclude that all kinds of experience are excluded, as is implied in the conclusion that the behavior is innate. According to Lehrman, such a conclusion drives attention away from developmental processes and from an understanding of factors that may contribute at every stage of development to the normal behavioral pattern. He pointed out that even developing embryos provide themselves with experience, as had been shown in Kuo's (1932) research on the pecking behavior of chicks. Moreover, the emergence of a behavior may depend on the prior development of other types of behavior subserving different functions. For example, prior experience with carrying food in the mouth affected the development of pup-carrying behavior in female rats. Lehrman also pointed out that even the fact that a behavior is species-specific and stable enough to have taxonomic usefulness does not necessarily imply that it is innate in Lorenz's sense; most members of a particular species tend to develop in similar environments.

Perhaps the most important message left by the nature-nurture controversy is that behavior develops as a result of complex interactions between a nested set of contexts, from the genetic information encoded in the DNA within the cells, to the internal physiological processes, and hence to organism-environment interactions. It has proven more profitable for comparative psychologists to concentrate on these developmental processes to explain behavioral patterns than to stop at the attribution that a particular behavior is "innate" or "acquired," as if these words had some explanatory power. These issues are developed in greater detail in the chapters on behavioral development, ***Part III.***

6. Levels of Analysis

It has become customary in the natural sciences to refer to levels of organization of natural phenomena from elementary particles to atoms, molecules, cells, tissues, organs, systems, behaviors, and social groups. The idea of levels is also evident in Aristotle's scala naturae, as well as in more modern views of nature, such as Lamarck's view of the evolution of the nervous system discussed earlier. In evolutionary theory, the concept of levels of organization is related to the notion of evolutionary *grade:* the sharing of derived features in taxonomic groups that have evolved them independently (e.g., mammals and birds share the ability to maintain a constant internal temperature, endothermy, that has evolved in parallel from different ancestral groups of reptiles). In behavioral theory, the concept of levels has been used to organize behavioral capacities in order of complexity, as Schneirla (1949) did with individual behavior and Evans (1966) did with the social behavior of insects.

There is yet another use for the concept of levels. The nature-nurture controversy showed that behavioral theories can be based upon alternative views of causality. As an example, consider the singing behavior of passerine birds such as the sparrow or the canary. A full account of such singing behavior would require answers to four basic questions.

Singing, like most behaviors, has consequences for the animal. It can affect the male's ability to attract females or to repel competing males from a territory during the reproductive season. Such consequences may determine the male's degree of reproductive success—that is, how capable the male will be in passing copies of its own genes into the next generation by producing offspring. This capability is referred to as the *adaptive significance* of singing behavior.

The song of a particular male will likely be common to all males of that species, at least in some fundamental sense, and it will likely be different from the song exhibited by males of other species. Songs of a group of related species tend to be similar. An analysis of the songs' components and main features may lead to an understanding of their *phylogenetic history.*

Singing behavior can be explained in terms of the underlying neurological and peripheral *mechanisms* that allow a bird to produce sound and to modulate it appropriately. Additional aspects of such a mechanistic theory involve brain processes responsible for the production of the song and the general environmental (e.g., annual cycles) and physiological (e.g., hormonal) influences that modulate song production.

Singing can also be viewed as the outcome of a *developmental* process. As such, singing might depend on the maturation of particular brain areas, on the animal's exposure to specific types of experience, including social exposure to singing adults and the auditory feedback from the animal's own singing, and other similar variables. Perhaps the song develops in stages, and perhaps the organism is particularly sensitive to acquiring song-related information at a particular stage of development.

When researchers are interested in the adaptive significance or phylogenetic history of a particular behavior, behavioral phenomena are said to be explained in terms of the *ultimate causes* of their origin. By contrast, mechanistic and developmental accounts refer to factors operating in the animal under observation. Consequently, these two levels of analysis are referred to as *proximate causes.* Ultimate causes are responsible for the evolution of mechanisms and developmental programs, which in turn are directly responsible for the production of behavior. This idea is represented in ***Figure 1.4.***

These subtle distinctions between causal levels was first proposed by Tinbergen (1963), on the basis of a similar classification suggested by the biologist Julian S. Huxley [1887–1975], who saw this as a major problem in biology. Such distinction is presently widely accepted in the study of animal behavior, although it is risky to think of these levels of causal analysis as completely independent. Rather, as suggested in ***Figure 1.4,*** there is substantial overlap in the reach of these levels. Obviously, knowledge of one type of determinant may affect how behavior is understood at another level. Nonetheless, theories should be evaluated with this distinction of causal levels in mind.

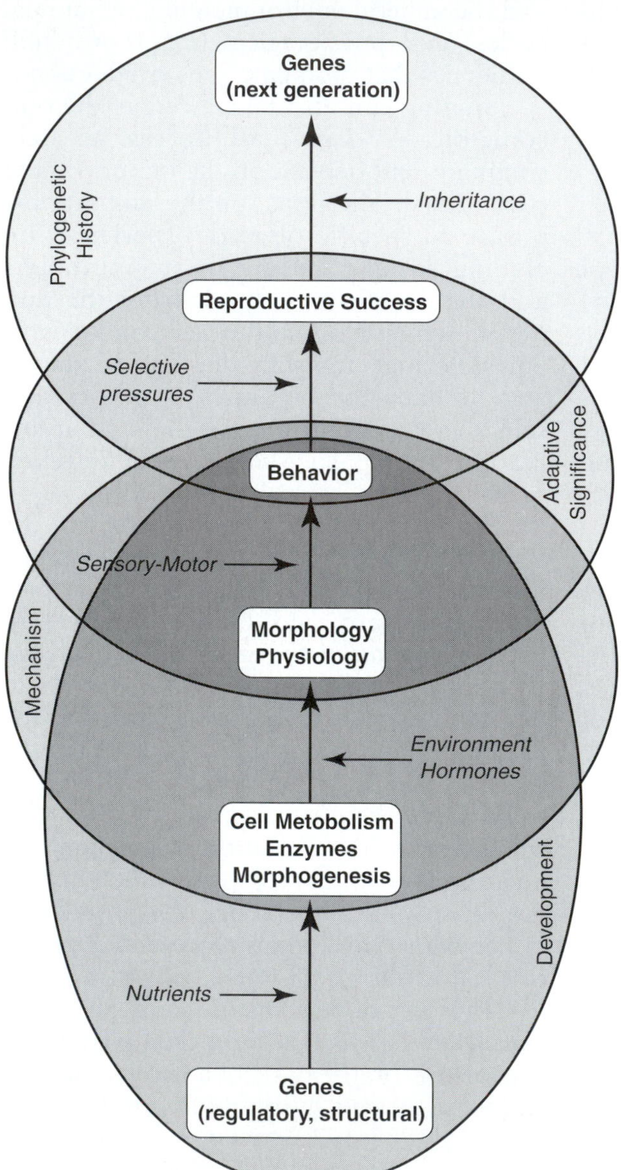

Figure 1.4. Levels of causality in the study of behavior are represented here in a dynamic fashion. From the unfolding of developmental programs (bottom) to the transmission of genetic material to the next generation (top), the various causal levels can be viewed as fitting some period within the scheme, but with substantial overlapping. Examples of factors that modulate the developmental process are provided on the sides. (Drawing by D. Robinson)

7. ORGANIZATION OF THIS BOOK

The organization of this book reflects Tinbergen's four-level notion of causality. The chapters in ***Part I*** describe evolutionary processes and deal with the adaptive significance of behavior, especially in terms of feeding and social behavior. The main principle underlying all of these chapters is that behavioral traits vary, are selected, and are inherited according to the same rules that apply to morphological traits. An understanding of the adaptive significance of behavior also requires the acquisition of a terminology that is essential for any evolutionary approach to the study of behavior.

The chapters in ***Part II*** are concerned with the phylogenetic history of animals in general, and vertebrates and primates in particular. For a comparative psychologist trying to understand the evolution of behavior, what is especially important is to be able to relate behavior to its underlying neural structure and function. Accordingly, these chapters provide a comprehensive view of the evolution of neural systems and behavior. It is also important that students of animal behavior recognize major trends in animal evolution and the general phylogenetic relationships among species used as models in the analysis of behavior. Taxonomic classifications provide us with a wealth of biological knowledge and a general picture that serves to organize information obtained through research with specific species.

The chapters in ***Part III*** deal with the development of behavior. At this point, the reader is equipped with a sophisticated view of evolutionary theory and its application to behavior that provides a background for an evolutionary approach to development. This is both a traditional area in comparative psychology and also the cutting edge of evolutionary science. Much remains to be done to integrate evolutionary principles with the study of behavioral development, and these chapters provide a minimum set of concepts that will guide such integration.

Finally, ***Part IV*** refers to a mechanistic study of learning and cognitive processes, also a traditional area of comparative psychology, perhaps the one that most clearly relates to the origins of the discipline and also the one that continues to dominate the field. Most of the research on animal behavior carried out in psychology departments is concerned with learning and cognitive processes, their environmental determinants and their brain correlates. These chapters provide a view of comparative learning and cognition that is consistent with the evolutionary principles developed during the initial portions of the book.

8. KEY TERMS

adaptive significance 21
appetitive-consummatory behavior 18
behaviorism 15
comparative psychology 2
complexity 3
creationism 6
critical period 19
developmental causes 21
domestication 9
ethology 16
epigenesis 20
evolution 11
fixed action pattern (FAP) 17
grade 21
group selection 16
imprinting 19

inheritance of acquired traits 9
instincts 6
irritability 9
learning 6
mechanicism 8
mechanism 21
mental continuity 12
mind-body dualism 7
multicausality 3
Morgan's canon 13
nature-nurture 19
natural selection 12
phylogenetic history 21
proximate causes 21
psychology 2
reflex 6
scala naturae 5
sign stimulus 17
spontaneous generation 4
supernormal stimulus 17
tabula rasa 8
taxes 17
ultimate causes 21
vitalism 8

9. HISTORICAL CONTRIBUTIONS TO COMPARATIVE PSYCHOLOGY

Author	*Date*	*Contribution (Chapter)*
Aesop	620–560 B.C.	Animal fables (4)
Anaximandros	610–545 B.C.	Life originated in the sea (1)
Empedocles	493–433 B.C.	Atomic theory of nature (1)
Leucipus	540–370 B.C.	Atomic theory of nature (1)
Democritus	460–370 B.C.	Atomic theory of nature (1)
Aristotle	384–322 B.C.	Taxonomy, scala naturae, behavior observations (1, 6)
Epicurus	341–270 B.C.	Atomic theory of nature (1)
Lucretius	95–55 B.C.	Atomic theory, rudiments of natural selection (1)
Gómez Pereira	1500–1558	Mechanistic theory of movements (1)
René Descartes	1596–1650	Mind-body dualism, mechanistic theory (1)
John Locke	1632–1704	Associationism (1)
David Hartley	1705–1757	Learned reflexes (1)
Carolus Linaeus	1707–1778	Taxonomy (2, 6)
G. L. L. Buffon	1707–1788	Taxonomy (2)
Julien de La Mettrie	1709–1751	Mechanistic theory of human behavior (1, 9, 14)
David Hume	1711–1776	Associationism (1)
Etienne Condillac	1714–1780	Associationism (1)
Robert Whytt	1714–1766	Spinal function (1)
Lazzaro Spallanzani	1729–1799	Acoustic perception in bats (4)
Luigi Galvani	1737–1798	Techniques for measuring electric potentials (1)
Jean B. Lamarck	1744–1829	Inheritance of acquired traits, neural evolution (1)
Alessandro Volta	1745–1827	Techniques for measuring electric potentials (1)
Félix de Azara	1746–1821	Local creationism, evolution and domestication (1)
Destutt de Tracy	1754–1836	Associationism (1)

Author	*Date*	*Contribution (Chapter)*
Georges Cuvier	1769–1832	Taxonomy (1)
Thomas Brown	1778–1820	Associationism (1)
François Magendi	1783–1855	Sensory-motor theory (1)
Marshall Hall	1790–1857	Reflex arc (1)
Karl von Baer	1792–1876	Comparative embryology (2, 8, 10)
Pierre Flourens	1794–1867	Brain lesions and behavior (1, 8)
Antoine Desmoulins	1796–1828	Brain lesions and behavior (8)
Eduard F. W. Weber	1806–1871	Physiological inhibition (1)
Charles Darwin	1809–1882	Natural selection, mental continuity (1-6)
Herbert Spencer	1820–1903	Evolution of mental processes (1)
H. von Helmholtz	1821–1894	Speed of nerve conduction (1)
Gregor Mendel	1822–1884	Genetics (1, 2)
Francis Galton	1822–1911	Nature-nurture dichotomy (10)
Alfred Wallace	1823–1913	Evolution by natural selection (1)
Ivan M. Sechenov	1829–1905	Modulation of spinal reflexes by the brain (1)
David F. Weinland	1829–1915	Comparative psychology (1)
Ernest Haeckel	1834–1919	Ontogeny and phylogeny (2, 6, 10)
August Weismann	1834–1914	Inheritance (2)
Douglas Spalding	1840–1877	Early experience (1)
William Preyer	1841–1897	Behavioral embryology (11)
William James	1842–1910	Instinct versus intelligence (1)
Charles Whitman	1842–1910	Taxonomy and behavior (1)
George Romanes	1848–1894	Anecdotal evidence for mental continuity (1)
Ivan P. Pavlov	1849–1936	Classical conditioning (1, 13)
S. Ramón y Cajal	1852–1934	Histology of the nervous system (8, 10)
C. Lloyd Morgan	1852–1936	First textbook, canon of parsimony (1)
Vladimir Bechterev	1857–1927	Escape-avoidance learning (13)
Charles Sherrington	1857–1952	Spinal reflexes (8)
Jacques Loeb	1859–1924	Theory of animal tropisms (1)
James Baldwin	1861–1934	Genetic assimilation (10)
Korbinian Brodman	1868–1918	Cortical cytoarchitecture (8)
Herbert S. Jennings	1868–1947	Behavior of simple organisms (1)
Walter Garstang	1868–1949	Development and evolution (10)
Oskar Heinroth	1871–1945	Taxonomy and behavior (1)
Edward L. Thorndike	1874–1949	Trial-and-error learning (1, 13, 14)
Robert Yerkes	1876–1956	Animal learning, language in apes (1, 14)
Wallace Craig	1876–1954	Appetitive versus consummatory behavior (1)
John B. Watson	1878–1958	Behaviorism (1)
Clark L. Hull	1884–1952	S-R theory of learning (14)
Edward C. Tolman	1886–1959	Cognitive view of learning (14)
Karl von Frisch	1886–1982	Sensory-perceptual processes in bees (13)
Julian S. Huxley	1887–1975	Levels of causation (1)

Author	Date	Contribution (Chapter)
Karl S. Lashley	1890–1958	Mass action principle of brain function (8)
Jean Piaget	1896–1980	Stages of psychological development (11)
Wolfgang Köhler	1897–1967	Tool use and insight learning in chimpanzees (4, 14)
Zing Yang Kuo	1898–1970	Early experience (1, 10)
Konrad Lorenz	1901–1989	Theory of instincts (1, 12)
T. C. Schneirla	1902–1968	Behavioral development, levels of organization (1, 10)
William H. Thorpe	1902–1988	Bird song (12)
B. F. Skinner	1904–1990	Schedules of reinforcement (13)
Donald O. Hebb	1904–1985	Early experience (10)
Harry F. Harlow	1905–1981	Attachment in primates (12)
John P. Scott	1906–2000	Development of socialization in dogs (12)
Niko Tinbergen	1907–1988	Ecology and behavior, levels of causation (1)
Frank A. Beach	1911–1988	Hormones and behavior (10)
Daniel S. Lehrman	1919–1972	Critique of the theory of instinct (1, 10)
W. D. Hamilton	1936–2000	Evolution of social behavior (4, 5)

10. REFERENCES

Aristotle (1965). *Historia animalium.* Books I–III. Translated by A. L. Peck. Cambridge, MA: Harvard University Press.

Aristotle (1991). *Historia animalium.* Books VII–X. Translated by D. M. Balme. Cambridge, MA: Harvard University Press.

Avers, C. J. (1989). *Process and pattern in evolution.* New York: Oxford University Press.

Azara, F. de (1934). Antología. In E. Alvarez López (Ed.), *Félix de Azara.* Madrid: Aguilar.

Bandres, J., & Llavona, R. (1992). Minds and machines in renaissance Spain: Gomez Pereira's theory of animal behavior. *Journal of the History of the Behavioral Sciences,* **28,** 158–168.

Boakes, R. (1984). *From Darwin to behaviourism. Psychology and the minds of animals.* Cambridge, UK: Cambridge University Press.

Cadwallader, T. C. (1984). Neglected aspects of the evolution of American comparative and animal psychology. In G. Greenberg & E. Tobach (Eds.), *Behavioral evolution and integrative levels* (pp. 15–48). Hillsdale, NJ: Erlbaum.

Craig, W. (1918). Appetites and aversions as constituents of instincts. *Biological Review,* **34,** 91–107.

Darwin, C. (1859/1993). *The origin of species.* New York: Random House.

Darwin, C. (1871/1981). *The descent of man and selection in relation to sex.* Princeton, NJ: Princeton University Press.

Darwin, C. (1872/1965). *The expression of the emotions in man and animals.* Chicago: University of Chicago Press.

Darwin, C. (1881/1982). *The formation of vegetable mould, through the action of worms, with observations of their habits.* Chicago: University of Chicago Press.

Descartes, R. (1664/1985). *Treatise on man.* In *The philosophical writings of Descartes.* Translated by J. Cottingham, R. Stoothoff, & D. Murdoch (Vol. 1, pp. 99–108). Cambridge, UK: Cambridge University Press.

Evans, H. E. (1962). The evolution of prey-carrying mechanisms in wasps. *Evolution,* **16,** 468–483.

Gottlieb, G. (1992). *Individual development and evolution. The genesis of novel behavior.* New York: Oxford University Press.

Hartley, D. (1664/1966). *Observations on man, his frame, his duty, and his expectations.* Gainsville, FL: Scholars' Facsimiles & Reprints.

Jacob, F. (1973). *The logic of life. A history of heredity.* Translated by B. E. Spillmann. Princeton, NJ: Princeton University Press.

James, W. (1890). *The principles of psychology.* New York: Holt.

Kuo, Z. Y. (1921). Giving up instincts in psychology. *Journal of Philosophy,* **18,** 645–664.

Kuo, Z. Y. (1932). Ontogeny of embryonic behavior in Aves. IV. The influence of embryonic movements upon the behavior after hatching. *Journal of Comparative Psychology,* **14,** 109–122.

Lamarck, J. B. (1809/1984). *Zoological philosophy.* Translated by H. Elliot. Chicago, IL: University of Chicago Press.

Lehrman, D. S. (1953). A critique of Konrad Lorenz's theory of instinctive behavior. *Quarterly Review of Biology,* **28,** 337–363.

Lorenz, K. (1941). Comparative studies of the motor patterns of Anatinae. In R. Martin (Ed. and translator), *Studies in animal and human behavior* (Vol. 2, 1971). Cambridge, MA: Harvard University Press.

Lorenz, K. (1965). *Evolution and modification of behavior.* Chicago, IL: University of Chicago Press.

Lorenz, K., & Tinbergen, N. (1938). Taxis und instinkthandlung in der Eirollbewegung der Graugans. I. *Zeitschrift fur Tierpsychologie,* **2,** 1–29.

Lucretius Caro, T. (1943). *De rerum natura.* Translated by W. H. D. Rouse. Cambridge, MA: Harvard University Press.

Macphail, E. M. (1982). *Brain and intelligence in vertebrates.* Oxford, UK: Clarendon Press.

Mettrie, J. O. de la (1748/1953). *Man a machine.* La Salle, IL: Open Court.

Morgan, C. L. (1894). *An introduction to comparative psychology.* London: Scott.

Pfungst, O. (1908/1965). *Clever Hans: The horse of Mr. von Osten.* New York: Holt.

Popper, K. S., & Eccles, J. C. (1977). *The self and its brain.* Berlin: Springer.

Romanes, G. C. (1882). *Animal intelligence.* London: Kegan, Paul, Trench.

Sarton, G. (1952). *A history of science. Ancient science through the golden age of Greece.* Cambridge, MA: Harvard University Press.

Spalding, D. A. (1873/1954). Instinct; with original observations on young animals. In J. B. S. Haldane (Ed.), Introducing Douglas Spalding. *British Journal of Animal Behaviour,* **2,** 1–11.

Stahl, W. H. (1962). *Roman science. Origins, development, and influence to later Middle Ages.* Madison, WI: University of Wisconsin Press.

Thorndike, E. L. (1898). Animal intelligence: an experimental study of the associative processes in animals. *Psychological Review,* **2,** 1–109.

Thorndike, E. L. (1911). *Animal intelligence.* New York: Macmillan.

Tinbergen, N. (1950). The hierarchical organization of nervous mechanisms underlying instinctive behaviour. *Symposium of the Society for Experimental Biology,* **4,** 305–312.

Tinbergen, N. (1960). The Herring gull's world. A study of the social behavior of birds. New York: Basic Books.

Tinbergen, N. (1963). On aims and methods of ethology. *Zeitschrift für Tierpsychologie,* **20,** 410–433.

Watson, J. B. (1913). Psychology as the behaviorist views it. *Psychological Review,* **20,** 158–177.

Watson, J. B. (1924). *Behaviorism.* New York: Norton.

Wyles, J. S., Kunkel, J. G., Wilson, A. C. (1983). Birds, behavior, and anatomical evolution. *Proceedings of the National Academy of Sciences* (USA), **80,** 4394–4397.

PART I
Behavior and the Evolutionary Process

The organization of this book reflects to a large extent Tinbergen's classification of levels of analysis. The chapters in ***Part I*** focus predominantly on evolutionary processes and on the functional analysis of behavior or, in other words, the study of how behavior contributes to fitness. This part begins with an introduction to evolution in ***Chapter 2.*** What is evolution, and what is the evidence for it? A deep understanding of evolution will require considering evidence from a wide variety of sources, from studies of the molecular structure of proteins and DNA to paleontology and biogeography. This evidence opens the way for a description of evolution as a process—genetic variability, the laws of inheritance, and natural selection—to be covered in ***Chapter 3.*** The emphasis will be on processes as they are studied in a wide range of species and without strict reference to their phylogenetic history (issues of evolutionary patterns will be covered in ***Part II***). The last two chapters in this part deal with functional units of behavior, including feeding behavior from the predator's and prey's points of view (***Chapter 4***), and reproductive and social behavior (***Chapter 5***). The emphasis, again, will be on the processes that are hypothetically responsible for the evolutionary origin of such behaviors.

The goal of ***Part I*** is, therefore, to develop an understanding of the ways in which behavior contributes to individual fitness in evolving animal populations.

CHAPTER 2

Biological Evolution

MAIN GENERALIZATIONS OF CHAPTER 2

- *Evolution is the product of the interplay of processes (e.g., natural selection, genetic drift) and patterns (e.g., phylogenetic history).*
- *Natural selection, a main force driving evolutionary processes, is the result of phenotypic variation, differential reproductive success, and inheritance.*
- *Lifetime reproductive success is assessed in terms of inclusive fitness (i.e., the sum of direct and indirect fitness).*

Evolution can be defined as a phenomenon that results from the interplay of *evolutionary processes,* such as natural selection and genetic drift, and *evolutionary patterns,* such as the constraints imposed by phylogenetic history. Processes can be viewed as "innovative forces" that give rise to novelty and change, whereas phylogenetic patterns can be viewed as "conservative forces" that provide the raw material for change. For example, in the evolution of terrestrial vertebrates, including amphibians, reptiles, birds, and mammals, an impressive variety of forms has evolved, adapted to live under a wide range of environmental conditions. But no matter how diverse these animals might be, they are all constrained to a body plan involving four limbs, whether they are used for locomotion, swimming, climbing, jumping, or flying. In fact, the entire taxon is known as tetrapods, literally four-footed animals.

Organisms, therefore, contain a mixture of unique and common characters. Unique characters permit a clear-cut appreciation of the fit of the organism's form and function to its environment. Uniqueness is illustrated by bipedal locomotion and language, two distinctive human characters that suggest adaptation to open grassland and social environments, respectively. Commonality of characters allows for the tracing of *phylogenies,* that is, lineages of ancestors and descendants. The pentadactyl (five-digit) hand is an instance of a character shared by humans and other tetrapods, one widely considered to be primitive among extant tetrapods.

1. Evidence for Evolution

1.a. Molecular Genetics. Evolution is generally considered a fact, although it is not a directly observable fact because of its slow pace. Many other facts are equally difficult to observe, from such familiar events as the growth of a plant to the essential constituents of matter—molecules, atoms, and subatomic particles. In the former case, it is possible to use fast-speed video to actually watch the growth of the leaves and branches of a plant, compressing a few days into a few seconds. But other events have to be detected indirectly by the effects they have upon measurable variables. The fast-video example could be analogous to artificial selection experiments. By greatly accelerating the process of evolutionary divergence under laboratory conditions, artificial selection experiments show that it is possible to evolve lines of reproductively isolated organisms whose ancestors were capable of interbreeding. Artificial selection will be reviewed in ***Chapter 3.*** But there is, in addition, a large body of indirect evidence for evolution.

Above all, evolution implies genealogical links, so the best evidence is provided by the existence of common biological traits among living forms. Perhaps the most important of these common traits is the *genetic code,* shared by nearly all known living organisms (unicellular and multicellular; see ***Table 2.1***) Let's review a few basic terms in molecular genetics. Genetic information is encoded in the sequence of nucleotides that constitute the *deoxyribonucleic acid* (*DNA*) molecule located inside the cell, either floating in the cytoplasm, as in *prokaryote* bacteria, or surrounded by a nuclear membrane, as in *eukaryote* organisms. DNA contains four nucleotides: adenine, thymine, guanine, and cytosine (A, T, G, and C). Cell division involves the replication of the DNA molecule. The expression of genetic information involves the transcription of DNA into *RNA* (*ribonucleic acid*), its splicing into messenger RNA (mRNA), and the translation of mRNA into protein molecules in the cytoplasm. The RNA molecule copies the nucleotides, with the exception that it replaces thymine by uracil. Triplets of nucleotide molecules, arranged in a specific order and called codons, are translated into the 20 known amino acids, the blocks with which all proteins are built. Translation occurs according to the code described in ***Table 2.1***.

In each codon, the first base is that closest to the 5′ end of the mRNA molecule. Particular amino acids may be coded by more than one codon. Synonymous codons tend to differ in the third base. There are also triplets coding for a STOP command. This genetic code is common to all animals and, with few exceptions (e.g., mitochondrial DNA), common to all living organisms. The universality of such a specific genetic code strongly suggests that all life forms currently present in our planet have evolved from a common ancestor.

Molecular techniques can be used to determine the exact sequence of amino acids in a particular protein. This sequential information, in turn, allows for a comparison of a variety of molecules that are presumed to be *homologous* (i.e., to have evolved from a common ancestor) across many species. Such comparisons provide information about the molecular similarity of a particular protein across species. The assumption is that the more similar protein structure is among two different species, the less time there has been since their evolutionary divergence. With this information it is possible to

TABLE 2.1 Genetic Code

Amino Acid	*Abbreviation*	*mRNA Codons*
Alanine	ala	GCA, GCC, GCG, GCU
Arginine	arg	AGA, AGG, CGA, CGC, CGG, CGU
Asparagine	asn	AAC, AAU
Aspartic acid	asp	GAC, GAU
Cysteine	cys	UGC, UGU
Glutamine	gln	CAA, CAG
Glutamic acid	glu	GAA, GAG
Glycine	gly	GGA, GGC, GGG, GGU
Histidine	his	CAC, CAU
Isoleucine	ile	AUA, AUC, AUU
Leucine	leu	CUA, CUC, CUG, CUU, UUA, UUG,
Lysine	lys	AAA, AAG
Methionine	met	AUG
Phenylalanine	phe	UUC, UUU
Proline	pro	CCA, CCC, CCG, CCU
Serine	ser	AGC, AGU, UCA, UCC, UCG, UCU
Threonine	thr	ACA, ACC, ACG, ACU
Tryptophan	trp	UGG
Tyrosine	tyr	UAC, UAU
Valine	val	GUA, GUC, GUG, GUU
Stop		UAA, UGA, UAG

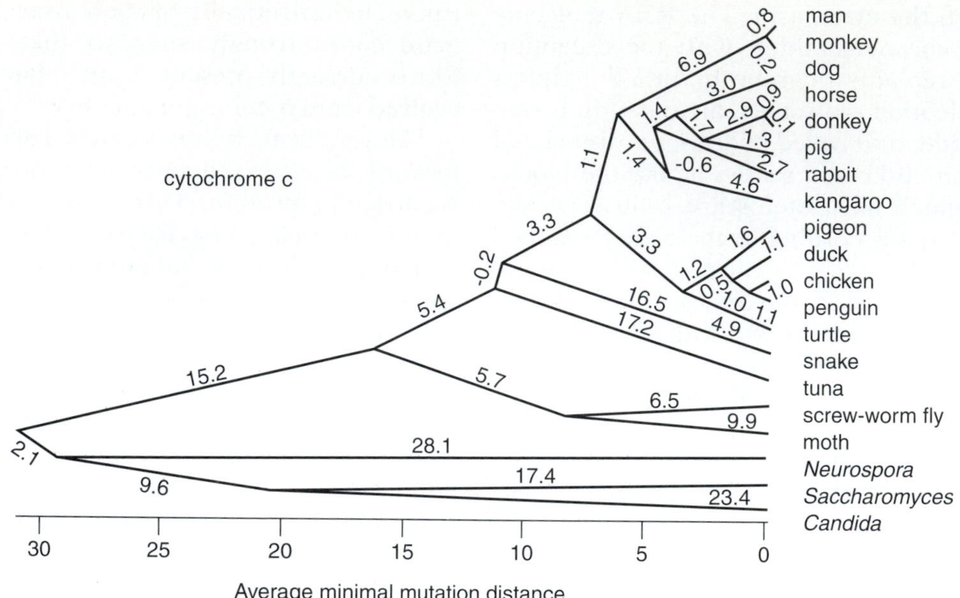

FIGURE 2.1. A phylogenetic tree based on sequential analysis of amino acids in the cytochrome c molecule (Fitch & Margoliash 1967). Because this molecule is present in a wide range of organisms, its sequencing allows comparisons not only across species but also across kingdoms (e.g., animals, plants, and fungi). Such genotypic comparisons are crucial given that most morphological aspects of the phenotype are completely different across kingdoms and therefore do not allow for phylogenetic relationships to be established on their basis.

plot the relative position of each species in a *phylogenetic tree* that captures their genealogical relationships. ***Figure 2.1*** shows a phylogenetic tree developed on the basis of the analysis of the protein cytochrome c (Fitch & Margoliash 1967). Cytochrome c participates in the respiratory cycle as part of the electron transport chain.

Molecular evidence may also be used to obtain information about the time elapsed since the divergence of different lineages. If changes in the genetic code occur at a constant rate, then the accumulation of molecular differences could provide a time scale for evolutionary events. This is referred to as the *molecular clock*. A comparison of divergence times obtained from a variety of different proteins and with information from independent sources, such as the fossil record, should then provide a database for the generation of phylogenetic hypotheses. Although the notion of molecular clock is not without problems (see ***section 4.h.*** below), it has contributed significantly to the study of broad phylogenetic patterns. More recently, it has become possible to analyze DNA sequences directly, rather than having to infer genetic differences from the analysis of protein structure. This topic will be considered in further detail in ***Chapter 6,*** in the context of a discussion of evolutionary patterns.

1.b. Embryology. The unfolding of genetic information in constant interaction with internal and external factors gives rise to the development of the organism. Development proceeds from stages of relative undifferentiation to the adult organism, and thus commonalities would be expected to be particularly noticeable in early stages of development. It was Karl E. von Baer [1792–1876] who first called attention to the fact that the younger a vertebrate embryo, the more difficult it is to identify the species. Specific features tend to develop as the embryo matures into its later stages of development, as shown in a classic drawing from Ernst Haeckel [1834–1919], perhaps the first to establish links between evolution and development in the late 19th century (***Figure 2.2***). Basic vertebrate characters such as the notochord, pharynx, and dorsal

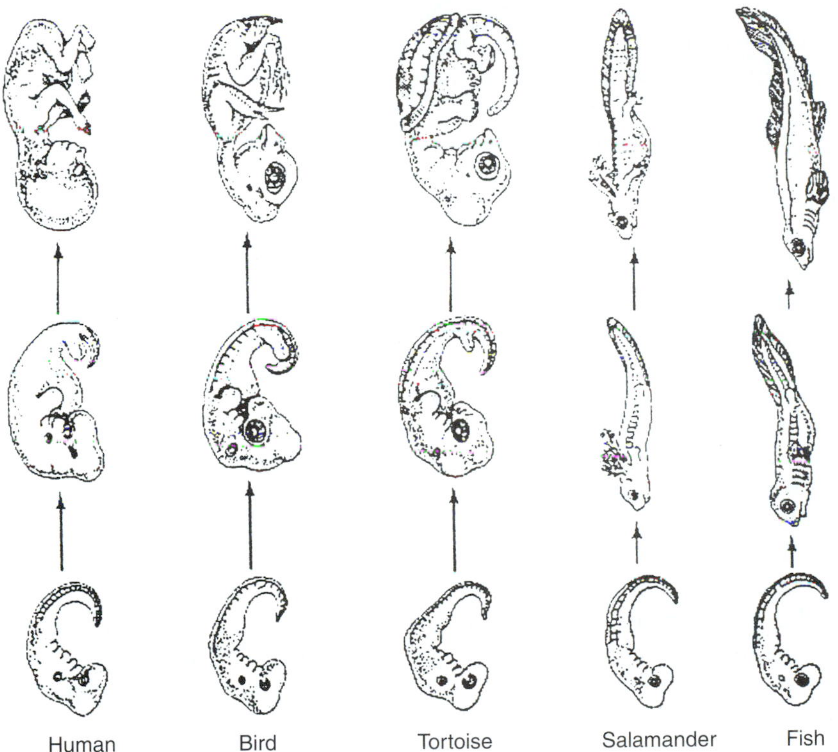

Figure 2.2. Stages of vertebrate development as visualized by Haeckel (1879). The earliest stage in this figure, called the phylotypic stage (bottom row), is really quite advanced relative to fertilization. Phylotypic stages vary across phyla but are highly conserved within a particular phylum. This observation was first made in 1828 by Ernest von Baer, who suggested that generalized traits develop earlier than traits unique to the embryo's own species. Substantial species variation in development may occur before and after the phylotypic stage.

neural tube appear earlier than derived characters typical of specific groups, such as gill pouches (a fish trait) and the five-digit limb (a tetrapod trait). The stage in which the characters typical of a particular phylum (such as the chordates) appear is referred to as the *phylotypic stage,* that is, a highly conserved stage that remains stable across species that can vary enormously in their adult morphology (see ***Chapter 10, section 1.c.,*** pp. 365–367). The presence of a phylotypic stage also suggests common ancestry.

Embryological research also shows the genetic ties among species in terms of developmental trajectories. For example, in some species, evolution appears to have acted as if new stages of development had been added in descendant species, relative to their ancestors. Development in descendant species goes through stages that resemble the adult forms of ancestral species. This is one among several possible developmental strategies (classically referred to as recapitulation; see ***Chapter 10, section 2,*** pp. 372–385) and is clearly observed in crustaceans. Higher crustaceans, including crabs and lobsters, develop through stages, passing from one to the other through a series of molting episodes. Larvae of lower crustacean species stop development at early molting stages, whereas larvae of higher crustaceans continue their development into additional phases. Common developmental stages add evidence supporting the hypothesis of genetic relatedness among different lineages.

1.c. Anatomy. Anatomical similarity has been the major criterion for classification since Aristotle. As late as the 18th century, taxonomists such as Carolus Linaeus [1707–1778], G. L. L. Buffon [1707–1788], and Georges Cuvier [1769–1832] based their influential taxonomic views almost exclusively on *character similarity.* After Darwin, morphological similarity is interpreted as evidence of evolutionary homology, particularly when similarity can be tracked down to details of design. Traits are homologous when their similarity can be attributed to inheritance from a common ancestor.

A clear example of morphological homology can be found in the comparative anatomy of limb structure in tetrapod vertebrates (amphibians, reptiles, birds, and mammals). As seen in ***Figure 2.3,*** limb bones differ somewhat in shape and size because they have evolved to fit different demands. Nonetheless, these bones are clearly recognizable as homologous in terms of their relative position. Such commonality points to shared ancestry. Variation and constancy show the combined effect of process (adaptation) and pattern (phylogenetic constraint) in the evolution of limb structure.

1.d. Biogeography. The observation that plant and animal species tend to be geographically restricted played a key role in the evolutionary thinking of both Darwin and Wallace. There are many examples of faunas that are limited to particular continents (South American monkeys), large islands (marsupials in Australia and lemurs in Madagascar), lakes (cichlid fish of African lakes), and archipelagos (finches in the Galapagos and fruitflies in the Hawaiian Islands). Darwin was impressed by the resemblance of South American fossil glyptodonts to living armadillos in their armors, and by the continental character of the birds he found in the Galapagos Islands.

A group of these Galapagos birds, known as Darwin's finches, are notable for the variation in beak size and shape that occurs in species that have entered the various islands in the archipelago. Changes in the

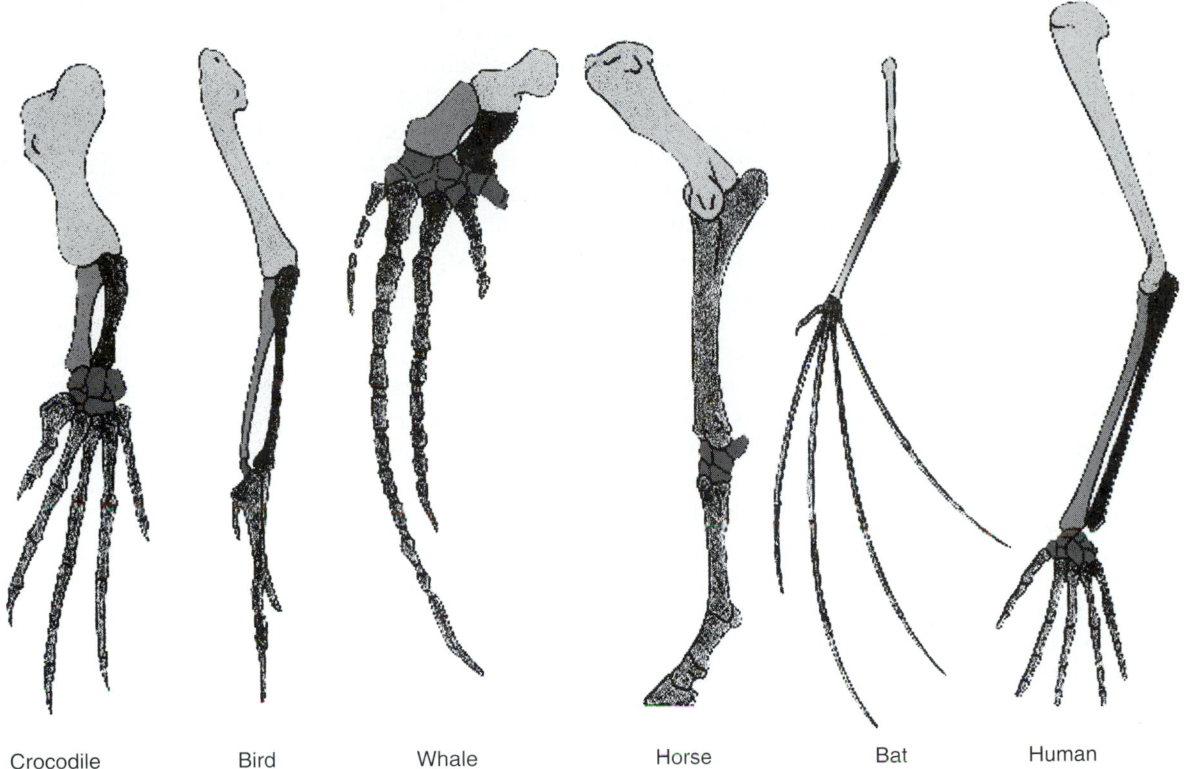

FIGURE 2.3. Homology in limb structure across several species of tetrapod vertebrates. The size and shape of the particular bones differ dramatically across species. Some of the bones are missing or drastically reduced in some of the species. However, the relative position of the bones has been conserved. Notice that whereas these limbs are structurally homologous, they have diverged widely in terms of function (wings for flying, flippers for swimming, legs for running, and hands for grasping). (From Curtis & Barnes 1989)

beak are correlated with island differences in food resources. The beaks of species that evolved as seed eaters are short and strong, whereas the beak of cactus eaters is significantly longer. Species that feed on insects also exhibit beaks appropriate for the type of insect prey they typically exploit as food. These species differences are easily interpreted as variations on a basic pattern inherited from the common ancestor, probably a species that originally migrated from the mainland of South America.

Studies by Grant (1986) show, in fact, how natural selection works in a population of Galapagos finches, *Geospiza fortis*. Between 1975 and 1985, considerable variation in rainfall produced marked changes in vegetation. After several annual droughts during 1977, 1980, and 1982, a sharp reduction in seed availability was recorded; large and hard seeds were more abundant than small seeds in these years. The finch population declined during these years, but the surviving population involved predominantly birds of large body and beak size. Small birds presumably had trouble opening large seeds and thus tended to die differentially. After years of normal or abundant rainfall, small birds were more likely to survive, thus reversing the tendency. If similar environmental changes were to influence a population across a sufficient number of generations, some traits would most likely be lost, giving rise to speciation events.

1.e. Paleontology. Fossils come to mind when one thinks of evolution, although the mere evidence of extinct species does not force evolutionary views. In ancient Greece and Rome, the fossilized remains of large mammals that are common in the Mediterranean region (e.g., bears, rhinos, mammoths, etc.) may have fueled mythological stories such as that of the battle of the giants, or gigantomachy (Mayor 2000). Cuvier is considered by most the father of vertebrate paleontology and among the first to extensively describe extinct species. Yet Cuvier believed in separate creationism and interpreted the evidence as arising from a series of catastrophic events that had resulted in the extinction of some species. Striking evidence of evolution in the fossil record is found in the sequential appearance of the various animal groups.

Among the vertebrates, for example, the most primitive fish appear in rocks of the Cambrian period, some 500 Mya, which in turn yield no evidence of land vertebrates. Terrestrial vertebrates appear clearly some hundred million years later, during the Devonian period, which in turn provides no evidence of birds or mammals. It is only during the Jurassic period, some 200 Mya, that higher vertebrates (birds and mammals) appear as fossils, and only during the last 60 million years that the mammals have diverged into the multiplicity of species that characterize the extant mammalian fauna. This sequential order is also replicated within more restricted taxonomic groups. In the case of horses, for example, small body size and multiple digits are primitive characters; derived characters, such as large body size and reduced digit number, appear in more recent fossils. In the case of primates there is also a similar increase in body size, with the largest species (apes and hominids) evolving relatively more recently than the smallest species (prosimians). It should not be inferred from this, however, that evolution proceeds in a linear fashion (i.e., scala naturae); both horses and primates evolved species with relatively large body size in several lineages.

Despite its many problems (see ***Chapter 6***), the fossil record provides compelling evidence of the genealogical links among broad groups of animals. Perhaps the most famous case is that of *Archaeopteryx lithographica,* a fossil bird from the Jurassic discovered in Germany in 1862. The importance of *Archaeopteryx* derives from the mixture of reptilian and avian characters that makes it a transitional form of the type predicted by Darwin's notion of continuity. A bony tail and teeth are typical reptilian characters, whereas the body appears to have been covered by feathers similar to those of modern birds.

2. Genotype and Phenotype

The evidence reviewed thus far supports the evolutionary assumption that life forms are tied by links of relatedness. These links are ultimately to be found in the genetic makeup of species. It is therefore not surprising that evolution is often characterized and defined in genetic terms.

Evolution involves a change in the biological traits characterizing a population of animals over a number of generations. These *traits* may be morphological, such as the length of the giraffe's neck or the shape of a finch's beak, or functional, such as the capacity of the panda bear's digestive system to process sugar cane leaves or the ability of bats to use echoes from their own high-frequency calls to locate moving prey. Organisms can be thought of as collections of traits, although this concept is complicated by the difficulties in defining a priori whether a particular feature is, in fact, a trait. Such a collection is referred to as the *phenotype*—that is, the outcome of a complex set of developmental interactions between genetic information and the environment. This genetic information is, in turn, known as the *genotype*.

The relationship between genotype and phenotype is not simple, however. For example, only a relatively small set of traits are known to bear a 1:1 relationship to the genotype. The genetics of these traits is referred to as *Mendelian* because this 1:1 relationship held for the traits first studied by Mendel in garden peas (see ***section 4.a.***, pp. 38–40). In most cases, many genes contribute to the development of a particular trait—a phenomenon known as *polygeny;* and any particular gene may affect the development of many traits—a phenomenon known as *pleiotropy*. Examples of polygeny are the rule; any complex morphological or functional character (e.g., organs, metabolic processes, reproductive behavior) is likely to be the result of the interplay of many genes with nongenetic factors. Pleiotropic effects are easily seen if one thinks of the cascade of effects that a change in the normal composition of a particular protein can have. For example, sickle-cell hemoglobin in humans leads to abnormal red blood cells, which in turn cause any number of symptoms from impaired cognitive function (due to anemia), to paralysis (due to brain damage), and kidney failure.

The relationship between genotype and phenotype is further complicated by the fact that the same set of genes can lead to significant differences in development, depending on the organism's environment. For example, the age at which humans reach sexual maturity depends on a complex set of physiological processes involving hormones that are ultimately regulated by specific genes. However, the process is modulated by early nutrition, among other factors. In women, for example, nutritional differences are responsible for a range of variation in age of sexual maturity from 10 years to as much as 20 years of age. This is referred to as the *norm of reaction* for age, in this example. Similarly, many aspects of behavioral and neural development of adult animals depend on early experience. Norms of reaction highlight the basic principle that behavior and other aspects of an animal's phenotype are the result of complex interactions between genetic and nongenetic factors.

Evolution occurs when changes in the phenotype of individual organisms lead to their reproductive isolation. One general assumption of this definition is that often such phenotypic change involves also a change at the genotypic level. It is possible, however, that phenotypes change because of the expression of genetic information that was previously silent or, as shown above, because of genetic-environment interactions (e.g., the concept of reaction norm). So phenotypic change does not necessarily imply genotypic change.

3. LOGIC OF NATURAL SELECTION

Darwin pointed out that species have an impressive reproductive potential. If a pair of sexually mature elephants were to procreate freely, and their offspring were to procreate freely, and so on, the earth would be covered with elephants in a relatively small number of generations. Despite the possibility of exponential growth, animal populations remain relatively constant over moderately long periods of time. Darwin suggested that the force keeping population numbers steady was natural selection, the differential survival and reproduction of individual animals.

Natural selection is the result of three basic properties of animal populations, illustrated in ***Figure 2.4.*** First, individuals within a population exhibit phenotypic variation (e.g., individual male deer vary in their ability to defend a group of reproductive females from other males). Secondly, some phenotypic traits are related to the individual's ability to produce offspring; these traits can be said to confer differential reproductive success to their bearers (e.g., large male deer can defend female groups more successfully than small males, thus increasing their reproductive output). Thirdly, there is a consistent relationship between the phenotypes of parents and offspring due to inheritance (e.g., large male deer tend to produce relatively large male offspring).

Phenotypic variation, differential reproductive success, and inheritance are necessary and sufficient for the process of natural selection to occur. Since natural selection acts only on traits having some genetic basis, the raw material for evolution is the genetic variability available in the population, or gene pool.

4. Origin and Preservation of Genetic Variability

4.a. Mendelian Genetics. As already mentioned, the simplest genotype-phenotype relationships are those first described by Gregor Mendel [1822–1884] in his research with garden peas. Mendel published his findings in 1866, but they remained unnoticed until 1900. Before Mendel, the prevail-

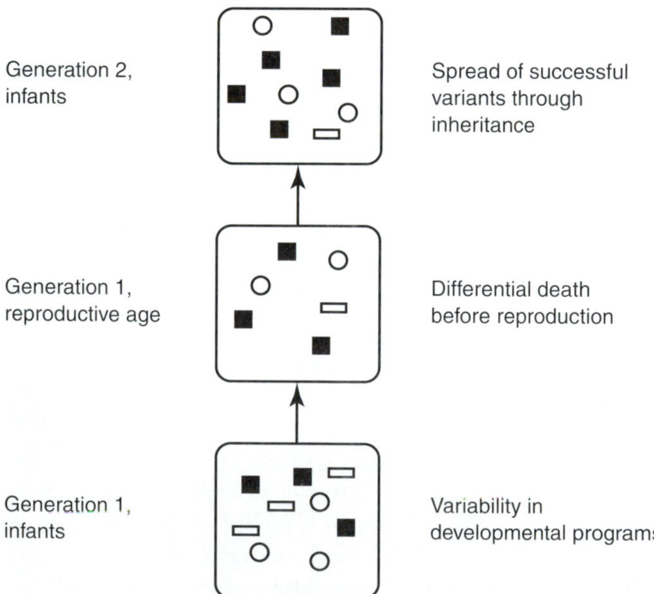

Figure 2.4. This drawing represents the logic of natural selection in a simplified fashion. At the bottom, a group of infant animals varies in terms of developmental programs. Three different programs are represented by different geometric forms. Whereas the initial frequency of each program is the same, when animals reach sexual maturity the frequency of some phenotypes has decreased due to differential death. This represents the action of natural selection on developing animals. In the top drawing, the second generation of infants is represented. The frequency distribution of developmental programs has changed because of the combined effects of differential death and inheritance of developmental programs.

ing view of inheritance was that the qualities provided by the parents were blended in the offspring. Darwin realized that such blending would tend to attenuate the effects of natural selection on a specific trait, which would tend to be diluted by sexual reproduction. By contrast, Mendel found that traits that were apparently lost in one generation could, in some cases, reappear in a following generation. Such reappearance of the original character clearly indicated that no blending was taking place and that the determinants of these traits preserved their identity across one or more generations. These units are referred to as *genes* and are nothing more than sections within the DNA molecule contained in the chromosomes. The fact that genes maintain their identity across generations is one major mechanism for the preservation of genetic variation.

Let's review a few key concepts in genetics. Although germ cells (sperm and egg cells) contain a single copy of each chromosome and, therefore, a single copy of each gene, fertilization leads to a duplication of chromosomes. Germ cells are *haploid,* whereas a fertilized egg, as well as all other cells in the organism (somatic cells), are *diploid* because they contain two copies of each chromosome and, therefore, of each gene within the chromosomes. Different versions of homologous genes (genes located in the same locus in homologous chromosomes) are called *alleles.* Alleles are produced by mutations that alter the sequence of bases in the DNA molecule. In any given organism, there might be up to two alleles for each gene, but in a population it is possible to find cases in which more than two alleles occur for a particular gene.

Mendelian genetics can be illustrated with a simple example, such as one from Mendel's own research with garden peas. Mendel had seeds from pea plants that were known to consistently yield either round *(R)* or wrinkled *(r)* peas. *R* and *r* represent alternative phenotypes that, because of the consistency with which they are produced, can be assumed to be each under the control of a pair of identical genes. This condition, described as *homozygous,* is usually represented as *RR* or *rr,* and these plants constitute the parental population, P_1. Two homozygous plants can be crossed by taking the pollen of the plant producing *R* peas and mixing it with that of one producing *r* peas. Mendel showed that such a cross yields plants that produce only *R* peas. This first filial generation is labeled F_1. However, if now F_1 plants are crossed with each other, the peas produced by plants from the F_2 generation will be a mixture of *R* and *r,* with a precise distribution: *3R:1r.* Schematically:

P_1: round × wrinkled
F_1: all round, round × round
F_2: 3 round for every 1 wrinkled

Mendel deduced his first law, usually referred to as the *law of segregation,* from this finding. The idea is that alleles controlling biological characteristics segregate from each other and are restored after fertilization. That is, there is no blending of genes.

Mendel also reasoned that although the *r* character was not observed in F_1, the fact that it reappeared in F_2 meant that it was always present but somehow its expression was repressed. When an organism has both alleles present (i.e., *Rr*), the condition is described as *heterozygous.* In this particular example, Mendel also reasoned that in the heterozygous condition the allele that was expressed *(R* in F_1*)* was dominant, whereas the allele that was suppressed *(r* in F_1*)* was recessive (hence the lowercase letter). The particular *3:1* ratio obtained in F_2 follows from the crossing of heterozygous plants, as shown in ***Table 2.2.***

In other words, each of the four possible genotypes in F_2 represents 25% of the plants produced by F_1 crossings. Because *r* is recessive, 75% of the plants will express the *R* phenotype, whereas only 25% will express the *r* phenotype (i.e., the *3:1* ratio). Mendel discovered that the *3:1* ratio held for a variety of traits, including the color of the seed and flower and the height of the stem. Each of these phenotypes are, therefore, under the control of a single gene. Mendel also extended his analysis to the case of two characters, each one controlled independently by its own gene, again by producing hybrids and recording the frequency of appearance of the various combinations of the two traits.

4.b. Hardy-Weinberg Equilibrium. Since recessive alleles are an important source of genetic variability, one may ask why do recessive alleles persist and are not eliminated by dominant ones? This question was answered independently by G. H. Hardy and G. Weinberg in 1908, and their solution is known as the *Hardy-Weinberg equilibrium.* To understand this rule, consider again a very simple situation involving two alleles of a single gene: *A* the dominant and *a* the recessive. Assume, further, that the following five conditions apply to this hypothetical population: (1) there are no mutations, (2) there is no gene migration (no gene inflow from outside populations), (3) the population is very large, (4) mating is random, and (5) the alleles are equally viable.

TABLE 2.2. Genotypic and Phenotypic Outcomes of a Cross of Heterozygous Genotypes

Generation	*Genotype*	*Phenotype*
F_1	***Rr* × *Rr***	***R* × *R***
F_2	***RR, Rr, rR, rr***	***R, R, R, r***

Note. *R*, round phenotype. *r*, wrinkled phenotype.

If the frequency of *A* is represented by *p* and the frequency of *a* is represented by *q*, then $p + q = 1$. It is possible to assume that the distribution of these alleles is unequal. For example, $p = 0.8$ and $q = 0.2$. In algebraic terms, because $p + q = 1$, then

$$(p+q)(p+q)=1(1)=1$$

that is,

$$(0.8+0.2)(0.8+0.2)=1$$

or, as derived from an expansion of the binomial $(p + q)^2$,

$$p^2+2pq+q^2=1$$

that is,

$$0.8^2+2(0.8)(0.2)+0.2^2=1$$

This expression describes the distribution of *A* and *a* in a population exhibiting the five features listed above. For example:

p^2 represents the frequency of *AA*, which is 0.64;

$2pq$ represents the frequency of *Aa*, which is 0.32; and

q^2 represents the frequency of *aa*, which is 0.04.

From these frequencies it is possible to determine the frequencies of the individual alleles in the following manner:

A: 0.64 plus one half of 0.32, or 0.64 + 0.16 = 0.80

a: 0.04 plus one half of 0.32, or 0.04 + 0.16 = 0.20

The conclusion is, therefore, that in an ideal population that meets the five former conditions, the frequencies of individual alleles do not change from generation to generation. Thus genetic variability tends to be constant.

The Hardy-Weinberg equation is useful for determining the presence and direction of a generational change. Suppose, for example, that the frequency of a condition assumed to be homozygous recessive, *aa*, is determined by screening infants in a population to be 1 out of 10,000 infants. Then, $q^2 = 0.0001$, $p^2 = 0.9801$, and hence,

$q = 0.01$ (square root of 0.0001),

$p = 0.99$ (square root of 0.9801), and

$2qp = 0.0198$ (i.e., approximately 2% of the infants are heterozygous).

Now suppose that the frequency of the same condition is measured again 5 and 10 years later. The values for q are found to be 0.009 and 0.008, instead of the 0.01 initial value. The meaning of these numbers is that evolution is occurring: One allele, *a*, is decreasing in frequency while the other, *A*, is increasing. Notice that the Hardy-Weinberg equilibrium shows that the genetic variability within a population is not related to the allele's being dominant or recessive.

Obviously, the five features of the hypothetical population described above would rarely be met in natural populations, and some of the violations can have important consequences for the preservation of genetic diversity. For example, mutations will increase the number of alleles to the extent that they are neutral or beneficial to the organism. Reproductive interactions between members of different populations (gene flow) will also tend to maintain variability, which natural selection could eliminate if the population remained isolated. As is shown in ***Chapter 3,*** geographical isolation, which reduces or eliminates gene flow, is a major mechanism of speciation. Mating is also rarely random. Many cases have been described in which two distinct phenotypes are maintained in a population because individuals tend to mate according to those phenotypes. White snow geese, for example, mate preferentially with white individuals, whereas blue snow geese tend to mate with blue individuals. Such assortative mating can have important consequences for the preservation of these so-called *polymorphisms,* another way of preserving genetic variability in the population.

4.c. Genetic Drift. One of the conditions assumed for the hypothetical population was its large size. Many factors can reduce the number of individuals in a population. Genetic variation is more likely to diminish across generations in small populations for reasons unrelated to natural selection. The simple combination of genotypes during reproduction can lead to the loss of alleles.

Consider the following extreme example. This population has only two heterozygous individuals (*Aa, Aa*), so the proportion of each allele is the same: $p = q = 0.5$. If these two individuals mate, they have a chance of 0.5 of producing a heterozygous offspring. But if by chance they produce two homozygous dominant offspring, then the population would change in an irreversible manner because the recessive allele would be lost forever. The proportion of alleles would then be $p = 1$ and $q = 0$. Natural selection played no role in this change, which is referred to as *genetic drift.*

Genetic drift can result in relatively rapid, nonselective genetic change. The potential importance of genetic drift in the process of speciation is currently debated, but there is reasonable agreement that it plays a major role in two cases in which populations are drastically reduced in numbers. One case is that of a small population that branches off the main, larger population and becomes reproductively isolated. This situation is referred to as the *founder effect* because it could be a common scenario preceding the origin of new species. For example, a small group of animals may reach an island (this is supposed to have occurred with the ancestors of the Galapagos finches; Grant 1986) and become reproductively isolated because of geographical barriers. Since the founding group is small, it is unlikely to represent the larger population, so that otherwise infrequent alleles may become more common through inbreeding.

A second situation involves a drastic reduction in population size, referred to as a *population bottleneck*. For example, the northern elephant seal was hunted so intensely during the 19th century that as few as 20 animals were left in some breeding sites in 1884, when protection laws were passed in the United States and Mexico. This population has increased since then to approximately 100,000 animals in the 1990s, along the coasts of California and Baja California. Despite this repopulation, analyses of genetic diversity show that individuals tend to be homozygous for a greater proportion of gene loci than is usual for mammals. Population bottlenecks may result in the elimination of some alleles, as well as the spread of otherwise uncommon alleles through the population.

In some cases, although the number of animals in a population can be relatively large, only a small proportion participates in reproduction. Species displaying a mating system based on intense competition between males for access to receptive females (i.e., polygyny; see ***Chapter 5, section 2.a.,*** pp. 131–134) can result in the exclusion of a large proportion of males from the reproductive process. In such cases, a census of the number of animals may overestimate the size of the population and hide a bottleneck. Counting only those animals that participate in reproduction would more accurately represent the size of the population; this is known as the effective population number.

4.d. Exons and Introns. The problem of genetic variability has been approached thus far considering the gene as a black box. Mendelian genetics illustrates how a gene's integrity is protected from blending and how recessive alleles can continue to exist despite their expression being prevented by dominant alleles. Genes have also been described superficially as chunks of DNA. It is now possible to open this particular black box and describe with greater precision the structure of genes.

Figure 2.5 presents a schematic view of an eukaryote gene, arbitrarily arranged with the 5′ end at the bottom and the 3′ end at the top. The DNA molecule is organized in two major components, exons and introns. *Exons* are coding segments of DNA. Ultimately, exons are responsible for the building of proteins. *Introns,* by contrast, are noncoding sequences that intervene between exons. A particular gene may be structured with one or several exons mixed in tandem with introns. The entire chunk of DNA is transcribed into RNA, and introns will eventually be excised to give rise to messenger RNA, or mRNA, which is used to build a protein. This RNA editing process is known as splicing. Toward the 5′ end there is a promoter region, so called because the bases found there (GC, CAAT, and TATA boxes) control the initial binding of the RNA polymerase and the start point of tran-

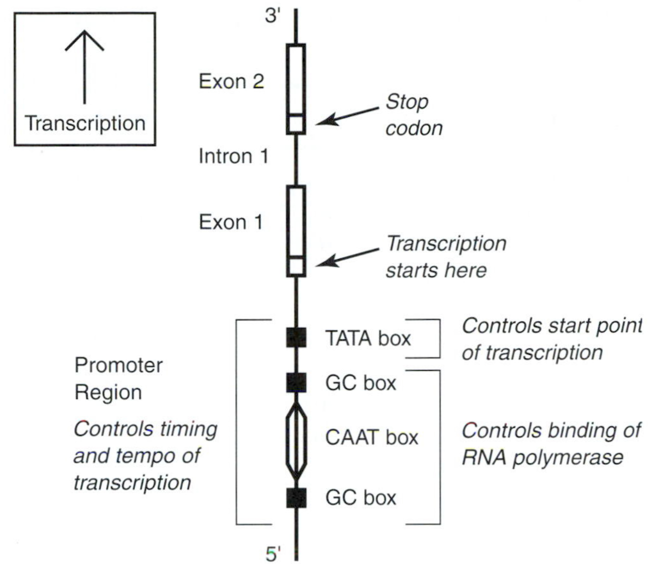

Figure 2.5. Schematic representation of the various regions of a gene. The particular elements represented in the promoter region vary across genes. Some genes lack GC and CAAT elements, some lack the TATA element. Exons contain information useful for translation purposes, whereas introns include nontranslatable information. Both exons and introns are transcribed into pre-messenger RNA. Intron regions are excised, and the remaining RNA is spliced to form mature mRNA, subsequently used as a template to build a protein.

scription. The specific components of the promoter region (e.g., GC box, CAAT box, etc.) vary across genes. Finally, the 3′ end contains a stop codon signaling the termination of transcription.

It has been suggested that the crossing over of introns could lead to exon duplication and exchange between genes. The best evidence for the existence of this so-called *exon shuffling* lies in the fact that most genes appear to be mosaics of other genes, rather than entirely novel nucleotide sequences. For example, the genes coding for the low density lipoprotein and the epidermal growth factor have a homologous region consisting of eight contiguous exons (105 to 228 base pairs). Five of the nine introns interrupt the sequence at precisely the same amino acid in these two genes. Such a degree of coincidence suggests that these two genes derive from a common ancestral gene; it seems unlikely that these two sequences of nucleotides resemble each other that much out of chance convergence.

Roughly speaking, the number of introns appears to increase directly with the complexity of the organism. Exon shuffling would lead to genetic variability at a much faster rate than that of mutations (see below). In addition, the exon-intron arrangement can allow for greater phenotypic plasticity, as has been shown to be the case for the immune system (Langman 1989). For example, genes coding for antigen-specific binding regions in higher vertebrates are typically formed by a constant exon attached to several variable exons. These exons are separated by introns that, during RNA splicing, allow for the formation of a variety of mRNA combinations between the constant exon and any of the variable exons. Antibodies formed in this manner, called rearranging immunoglobulins, can deal with an enormous variety of pathogens.

4.e. Structural and Regulatory Genes. Genes involving a DNA sequence that encodes the information necessary to build proteins are referred to as *structural genes.* Proteins are ultimately involved in cell differentiation, tissue development, and the organization of the entire body of the organism. Since copies of these structural genes are present in all cells within a multicellular animal, something else must be responsible for their differentiation. Cell differentiation, as well as a variety of other processes dependent on DNA transcription, are based on the regulation of the process by the selective activation of genes. Such *regulatory genes* encode information to build proteins that, in turn, regulate the transcription of other genes.

Regulatory genes thus determine when transcription of some gene should start and stop, and so these genes play a critical role in developmental processes and perhaps in the evolution of new species. For example, analyses of homologous proteins of humans and chimpanzees have shown an impressive degree of similarity that contrasts with their obviously dissimilar phenotypes. Since the proteins compared in this study reflect the level of similarity in structural genes, King and Wilson (1975) suggested that, in this particular case, evolution has acted predominantly at the level of regulatory genes.

4.f. Mutation. As mentioned earlier, *mutations* are random alterations in the sequence of nucleotides within the DNA molecule that result in seemingly minor changes in the code. Mutations can be thought of as copying errors that occur at the time of DNA replication, although radiation and chemical substances can also induce changes in the sequence of nucleotides. Mutations result in a sudden change of genotype, and, consequently, an animal may inherit a mutated gene that would code for an "abnormal" sequence of amino acids in a particular protein.

Although the substitution of one amino acid for another in a protein containing many such building blocks may seem a small change, the consequences can escalate in a series of effects depending on the number of cellular processes in which that protein participates (i.e., the degree of pleiotropy). As one might anticipate, such random changes should more often than not lead to maladaptive consequences and very rarely to some functional or structural improvement. Mutations are, therefore, usually deleterious for the organism. In the case of sickle-cell anemia (mentioned previously to illustrate pleiotropic effects), a blood pathology involving abnormal hemoglobin that leads to the clogging of blood vessels and premature death, the abnormal phenotype is caused by a change in a single amino acid (from the normal glutamic acid to the sickle valine). Another point mutation for the same locus involves a change from the normal glutamic to lysine. The latter mutation is not as severe, although it still causes anemia.

Mutations can be induced experimentally and thus used as a research tool. In the fruitfly *Drosophila melanogaster,* an animal model in genetic research, mutations are routinely induced by exposure to X rays, extreme temperatures, and chemical substances. Mutants thus created are then bred selectively giving rise to mutated strains. Several mutations are known to affect *Drosophila*'s behavior, including effects on activity levels, phototactic behavior, courtship, and learning processes (see ***Chapter 3, section 3,*** pp. 73–78. The molecular effects of some mutations have been determined, thus allowing for an understanding of the causal links between genes and behavior. In most of these cases, mutations affect structural genes. When mutations occur in regulatory genes, the transcription of structural genes could be affected in terms of its timing or frequency.

4.g. C-value Paradox. Because genes are ultimately responsible for bodily structures, it would appear perfectly reasonable that more complex organisms would require a greater number of genes. The amount of DNA can be estimated in terms of its molecular weight or in terms of the number of base pairs, and this is called the C-value. Broadly speaking, there is a direct relationship between complexity and the C-value. For example, a prokaryote bacterium such as *Escherichia coli* contains a single chromosome with some 4.7 million base pairs within the DNA molecule. However, algae and fungi require a minimum of 20 million base pairs, and the minimum number increases to 100 million base pairs in multicellular plants and animals. For *Homo sapiens* an estimated 2.6 billion base pairs are distributed in 23 chromosomes.

The *C-value paradox* becomes evident only when the amount of DNA among animals is considered, and it arises from the lack of a clear correlation between morphological complexity and the C-value across a wide range of animal groups. ***Figure 2.6*** illustrates this point, using the approximate number of cell types and of descriptive morphological terms as indices of morphological complexity. It is not clear, for example, why some amphibian species would require 100 times more DNA than any mammal or bird, or why birds and worms would require about the same DNA amount. Sometimes, closely related species have widely different amounts of DNA, as is the case of some flowering plants and salamanders.

The C-value paradox seems to be related to the amount of *repetitive DNA*—that is, portions of the DNA molecule that represent multiple copies of the same genes. As much as 80% of all DNA may be repetitive in some amphibians and flowering plants, whereas in unicellular protists and simple multicellular organisms only 10% to 20% is repetitive. What could be the function of repetitive DNA? Repetitive DNA may be vital to chromosome structure. For example, long segments with the same sequence of bases repeated over and over again are found around the chromosome's centromere and in the tips of chromosomes. In animals, repetitive DNA may play a role in the movements of chromosomes toward the poles during the division of the cell nucleus. Another functional account relates to the large amount of DNA in salamanders, which is often considered puzzling. Salamanders may have evolved simplified brains from ancestors possessing somewhat more differentiated brains (i.e., simplification as a derived, not primitive, condition), and it has been argued that this process is related to the accumulation of multiple gene replications (Roth et al. 1997).

4.h. Neutral Theory of Molecular Evolution. The C-value paradox raises another intriguing possibility. Perhaps some, or even most, of the genetic variation accumulated in the form of noncoding, repetitive DNA reflects the operation of a random evolutionary process. The notion that most molecular variation in DNA structure is basically neutral was suggested by Kimura (1983), and it has been labeled the *neutral theory* of molecular evolution. Kimura's theory was initially postulated to deal with an observation that was considered puzzling earlier in this chapter. When the notion of a molecular clock was introduced (see ***section 1.a.,*** p. 32, above), it was mentioned that the clock seems to run at a constant speed, at least when the structure of many homologous proteins is considered (individual proteins may vary substantially in their rate of change). Since it has now become possible to compare the similarity of nucleotide sequences in essentially the entire genome of different species, it is possible to estimate their rate of change, and in many cases it seems to be relatively constant. This

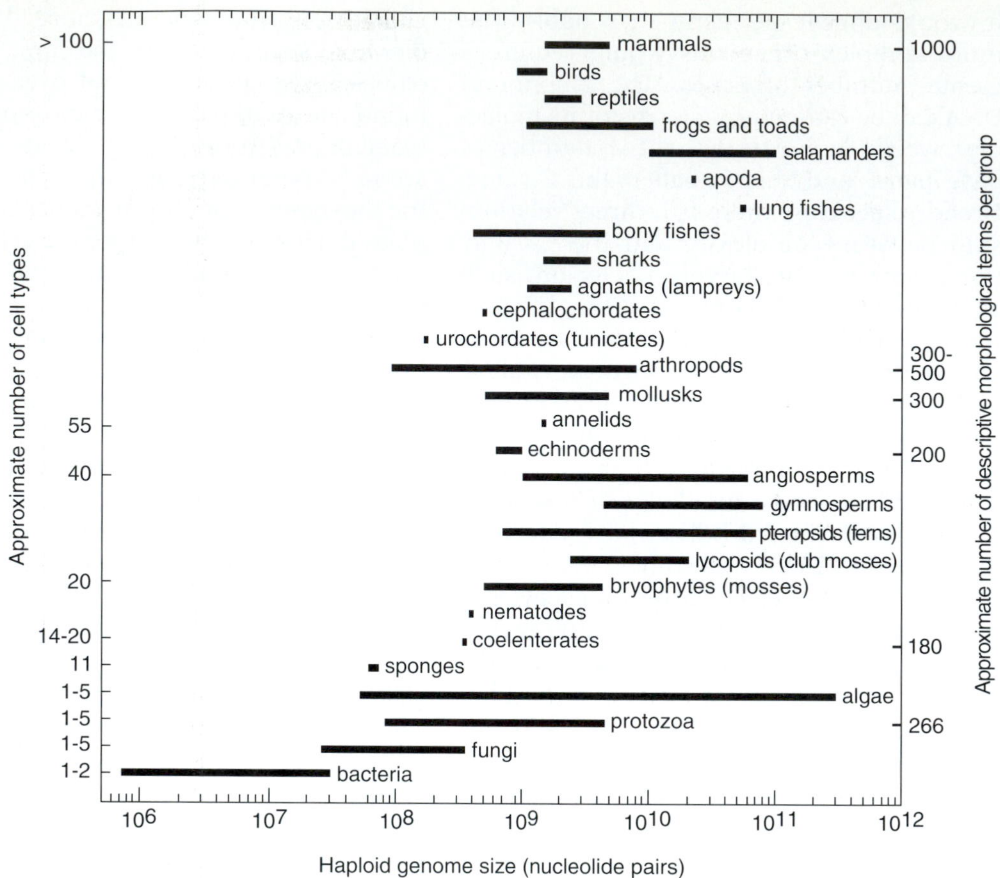

FIGURE 2.6. The C-value paradox is the apparent lack of correlation between the size of the genotype (indexed here by the number of nucleotide pairs) and phenotypic complexity (indexed here in terms of number of cell types and descriptive terms used by experts). The paradox becomes particularly obvious if one compares groups of animals. (From Raff & Kaufman 1983)

seems to make little sense given the irregular speed of morphological change observed in the fossil record. However, as Kimura argued, this is precisely what one might expect if neutral or nearly neutral mutations were to spread in a population by a purely random process. DNA variations can be said to be selectively neutral if the DNA information is not expressed in the phenotype and cannot, therefore, be subjected to natural selection. Neutral evolution collides with the Darwinian view that genotypic variation is the result of natural selection; this has led to a so-called selectionist-neutralist controversy. The two theories are not necessarily incompatible, however.

It has more recently been shown that molecular change in DNA sequence across species is related to generation time and to other demographic variables, after all—at least in some cases. For example, a comparison of the rate of evolution of homologous genes from DNA material sampled from rodents and primates shows a greater rate of change in the former group. Apparently, and in terms of molecular changes, rodents are evolving faster than primates (Wu & Li 1985). Such differences in the rate of DNA change can be reduced if generation time is taken into account. However, as Wu and Li noticed, this need not argue against the neutral theory of molecular evolution. Since rodents reproduce at a higher rate than most other mammals, the accumulation of neutral mutations should be accelerated.

The C-value paradox and neutral molecular evolution suggest that there might be vast amounts of unexpressed genetic information in the gene pool of most animal populations. This information has the potential to produce important phenotypic changes if its expression could somehow be activated, as it might when the environment changes as a result of geologic, climatic, or biotic factors. In fact, it has been argued that natural selection could be responsible for the evolution, early in the history of life, of mechanisms that allow for the accumulation of neutral mutations (Sibly & Ahlquist 1990). According to this argument, such mechanisms would build up a reserve of *preadaptations*—that is, momentarily silent genes that could eventually express themselves phenotypically and thus come under the shaping influence of natural selection. Lineages involving a relatively large amount of silent genetic polymorphisms would tend to include individuals that might be able to cope with a changing environment and leave descent, whereas lineages poor in such genetic variability might become extinct in the face of changing environmental challenges.

4.i. Sexual Reproduction. There are, therefore, processes that increase genetic variability (e.g., mutation) and processes that decrease it (e.g., genetic drift). Because such variability is critical for natural selection to produce adaptations, it is theoretically important to understand how, once generated, genetic variability is preserved in a population. What processes, other than the random drift of neutral mutations, maintain genetic variability? It was shown earlier that recessive alleles can be preserved and passed on from one generation to the next via sexual reproduction. Diploidy, the presence of two sets of alleles in any given cell within the organism, ensures the preservation of such recessive genes. But sexual reproduction contributes to the preservation of genetic variability in additional ways.

A major source of genetic variation occurs during meiosis in the germ cells of sexually reproducing species. Unlike mitosis (the fractionation of a cell into two sister diploid cells), in meiosis the end cell is haploid (egg or sperm cell). Diploidy is restored during fertilization of the egg by a sperm cell. During meiosis, pairs of alleles located in different chromosomes are segregated without regard to other alleles located in different chromosomes. This process, called *independent assortment,* occurs only in germ cells and implies that the chromosomes in the fertilized egg are really a mosaic of intermixed alleles from both parents. Such shuffling of alleles is partly responsible for the high levels of genetic variability that characterize sexually reproducing species.

Independent assortment was Mendel's second law, and it simply states that alleles coding for different traits segregate independently from each other, thus leading to a potentially large amount of phenotypic variability. Consider the following example. At the time of meiosis, a genotype with a haploid number n (with an n number of unique chromosomes) will produce 2^n possible gametes. In the case of humans, with 23 chromosomes in germ cells, these produce 2^{23} different combinations of gametes, or 8,388,608 genetically different combinations of germ cells!

Novel genotypic combinations can also be produced by a variety of additional processes during meiosis, some involving the interchange of chromosome parts during duplication, and some involving the failure of chromosomes to separate completely. Crossing-over, inversion, deletion, and insertion, as illustrated in ***Figure 2.7,*** involve changes in sections of chromosomes, whereas monosomy and trisomy are conditions in which chromosomes fail to fully separate during meiosis. Changes in chromosome number usually lead to infertility and in some cases to anatomical defects. For example, men with three copies of the X chromosome are feminized, whereas trisomy of chromosome 21 leads to the Down syndrome, which includes mental retardation among other consequences.

The relationship between sexual reproduction and genetic diversity can be best appreciated in the life cycles of species that exhibit both sexual and asexual reproduction. Conditions that make the environment less predictable in terms of food availability, competition with other species, or parasite infestation tend to encourage a switch toward sexual reproduction. Many invertebrate species reproduce asexually when food supply is plentiful, thus producing an explosive population growth, but turn to a sexual mode when food becomes scanty. Presumably, sexual reproduction enhances the organism's ability to produce offspring that would be able to adjust to changing environmental conditions. In some species of snails, for example, sexual reproduction predominates in the environment of lakes,

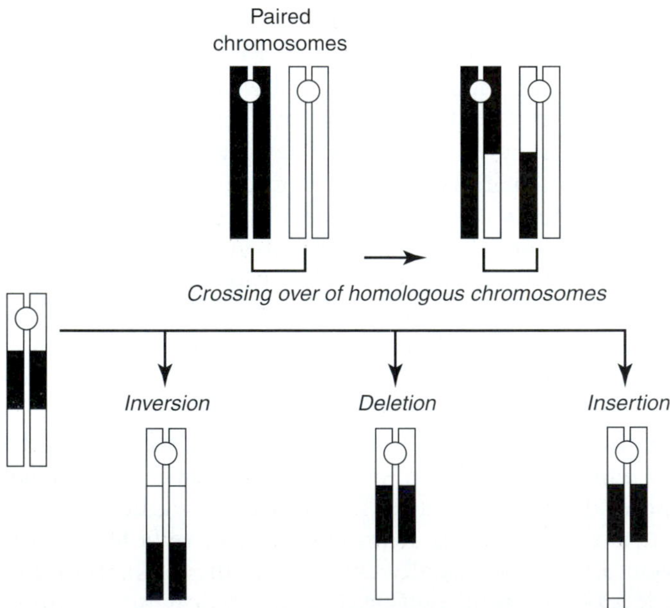

FIGURE 2.7. Changes in chromosome structure can lead to rearrangements that produce novel combinations of the same genes. Breaks in parts of a chromosome may lead to the interchange of those parts across homologous chromosomes, as in crossing over, or to the deletion, inversion, or insertion of the part. The figure represents paired chromosomes in terms of rectangles and the centromere as a circle.

but not streams. Snails living in lakes show a greater level of infestation by parasites than those living in streams, which tend to reproduce asexually (Lively 1987).

There are some known cases in which the heterozygous individuals exhibit a higher fitness or reproductive success than homozygous counterparts, a condition known as *heterosis*. In the case of human sickle-cell anemia mentioned earlier, although the homozygous recessive condition is deleterious (the blood disorder leads to general debilitating effects and death), heterozygous individuals are resistant to malaria and females are known to be more fertile—two unrelated pleiotropic effects.

5. NATURAL SELECTION

It was argued earlier that the theory of natural selection has three main components: variability, selection, and inheritance. Genetic variability was considered in the previous section, in which some of the laws of inheritance have also been described (more on inheritance in ***Chapter 3***). Consider now some rules governing natural selection.

Natural selection was identified previously with reproductive success—that is, the ability of organisms to reproduce and thus pass their genes onto the next generation. This is usually referred to as *Darwinian,* or *direct fitness,* because it involves maximization of direct descent (i.e., offspring). Notice that natural selection is not defined here in terms of survival value, as in the famous, but misleading, phrase "survival of the fittest," first coined by Spencer (1855). Survival is now generally regarded as secondary in importance to reproductive success. Other things being equal, and within a given species, animals that live longer tend to bear more offspring than animals that live shorter lives. This assumption is supported by the fact that longevity and fecundity are positively correlated in a variety of species (Stearns 1992).

After the work of William D. Hamilton [1926–2000], it has become clear that there are ways of "passing on" genes from one generation to the other that do not involve direct descent (Hamilton 1964). For example, helping behavior resulting in an increase in the reproductive success of a genetically related organism (i.e., a relative) can lead to the spread of the helper's genes, even if the helper's own direct fitness is reduced. Relatively well-studied examples of helping behavior directed at relatives involve some cases of breeding behavior in birds and antipredator strategies in mammals. Because *indirect fitness* implies some type of interaction among conspecifics, it might be of critical importance to understand the evolution of antipredator and social behavior, and therefore it will be described in detail in ***Chapters 4*** and ***5.***

An organism's fitness may thus be considered to be equal to the sum of its direct (number of offspring) plus its indirect (offspring of relatives surviving because of the organism's helping behavior) fitness components. This is referred to as *inclusive fitness.* For the moment, however, let's concentrate on the direct component of fitness.

5.a. Types of Direct Fitness.

According to Darwin's theory of natural selection, the reproductive success of any given organism is measured in terms of the number of offspring it can contribute to the next generation, compared to the numbers produced by other conspecifics. Because individual organisms cannot reproduce ad libitum but, rather, are constrained by limited resources, fitness is always understood as a relative measure. Alternative characters (presumably based on alternative alleles of the same gene), expressed in different organisms within a population, may convey differential fitness. It is such relative differential fitness that determines the evolutionary fate of the alternative characters—the one correlated with a greater fitness may spread in the population over many generations, while the one correlated with relatively lower fitness may entirely disappear. Because most organisms reproduce either continuously or during several breeding seasons, their direct fitness must be measured not just in terms of a single episode but in relation to their entire reproductive life. Direct fitness is, thus, the relative reproductive success achieved by an individual organism during its reproductively active lifetime, or *lifetime reproductive success (LRS).*

Three different types of direct fitness can be recognized. The first and perhaps most obvious case is that of traits that contribute to LRS by improving the chances of survival. The second is the less obvious case of characters that themselves may not contribute directly to LRS but that are correlated with characters that do enhance LRS (i.e., pleiotropic traits). These two cases will be discussed in this chapter after a brief consideration of some features of natural selection (see ***sections 5.d.*** and ***5.e.*** below). The third type of direct fitness is that of characters that evolved through sexual selection. Sexual selection refers to the evolution of traits that contribute to LRS either by improving intrasexual competition (e.g., male-male competition for access to females) or by affecting the choice of sexual partner. Sexual selection will be discussed in greater detail in ***Chapter 5*** (***section 2,*** pp. 130–141) in connection with mating systems.

5.b. Measuring LRS. Since fitness is a relative concept, the assessment of a trait's direct fitness requires an estimation of the contribution of that trait to LRS, relative to the contribution to LRS of an alternative form, or allele, of that trait. It is easy to realize how difficult it is to find good evidence of LRS, particularly for species characterized by a long reproductively active life, such as is the case for most mammals. One good example involves the study of grouping behavior of lions, *Panthera leo* (Bygott et al. 1979).

Lions are the only cats that live in stable social groups. Males form stable coalitions that take over female prides. Typically, a taking over implies the killing of the cubs when they are 6 months old or younger. It has been estimated that about 27% of all cubs die because of infanticide. This male behavior (which in a superficial sense appears deleterious for the species; see ***section 7*** below) is advantageous for males because they are able to speed up the females' return to sexual receptivity by an average of 8 months. This group dynamic suggests that reproductive advantages for males and females are likely to differ. Thus the question of how social grouping contributes to LRS has to be answered separately for males and females.

With LRS defined as the number of offspring reaching 12 months of age, the case of males is relatively clear. In males, LRS increases steadily with the size of the coalition. Most solitary males never reproduce, whereas males forming coalitions of up to 6 animals have increasingly larger LRS, as shown in ***Figure 2.8-a.*** In females the relationship between grouping and LRS is more complex. As shown in ***Figure 2.8-b,*** very small (1 or 2 individuals) or very large (more than 10 individuals) groups of females are correlated with very low LRS. However, an intermediate group size (3 to 10 females) has the largest LRS. Rather than being stable as in males, female groups tend to show

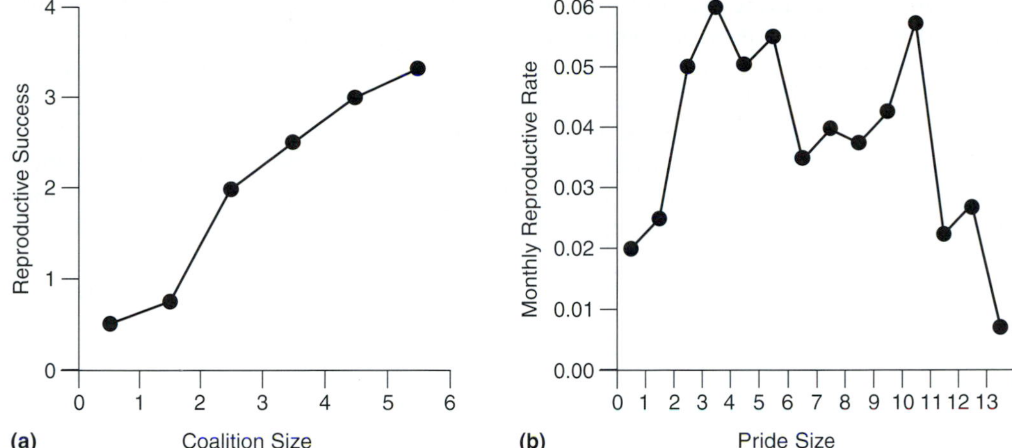

FIGURE 2.8. Lifetime reproductive success in the lion (*Pantera leo*). The data were obtained in the Serengeti and Ngorongoro areas of Tanzania (Packer et al. 1988). (***a***) Reproductive success in males increases as a direct function of coalition size. (***b***) Monthly reproductive rates of females increase as a function of pride size up to a point, and then decrease for groups of more than 10 animals. The frequency of takeovers by males is very high in large groups; takeovers lower the female's reproductive success because the new males usually kill unweaned cubs.

fluctuations in time. The function relating the probability of a successful takeover by a coalition as a function of size of the female group is a mirror image of the previous function. This suggests that intermediate groups with the largest LRS are also the ones experiencing less takeovers by males. Since takeover episodes are almost always followed by infanticide, females living in intermediate size groups can prevent losses more effectively. Notice that the relative nature of the concept of LRS always requires a comparison of alternative characters, such as the tendency of male lions to be solitary rather than to associate with other males.

5.c Natural Selection and Diversity. In the case of the evolution of social behavior in lions, the selective pressures exerted on the population of males and females are different. For males, fitness seems to increase toward a relatively unconstrained upper value (larger groups are more successful than smaller groups). When fitness increases towards one end of the scale, and assuming there is genetic variability available in the population, one possible outcome is that the population mean for that character will gradually increase over many generations. Within certain limits, it is possible that the optimal size of male coalitions has been increasing in the recent evolution of lions. This is called *directional selection* (***Figure 2.9-a***). Of course, there is always a "certain limit" that tends to prevent a runaway trend; in this case, for example, it would be unreasonable to expect the evolution of group size to continue indefinitely because, eventually, increasing numbers would give rise to negative selective pressures for group size.

Such a limit on selective change is clearly measured in the case of grouping in females, for which relatively small or large groups are correlated with lower fitness than an intermediate size group. This is called *stabilizing selection* because variability in the character tends to be reduced over a sufficient number of generations (***Figure 2.9-b***). Thus natural selection will favor the evolution of any mechanism that allows female lions to remain in groups that are close to the optimal size and to move away from groups that are either smaller or larger than the optimal size. Stabilizing selection illustrates the interplay of opposing selective forces since the optimal group size presumably reflects a compromise.

Polymorphisms were mentioned previously (see ***section 4.b.,*** p. 41, above) as an example of sustained genetic variability. Polymorphisms, or the coexistence of discretely different phenotypes in an interbreeding population, also illustrate the action of *disruptive selection,* a third variety of selection that, unlike stabilizing selection, results in increased diversity (***Figure 2.9-c***). In disruptive selection extreme phenotypes have greater fitness than intermediate ones. For example, North Pacific salmon males returning from the ocean into freshwater rivers for reproduction can be either 2 or 3 years old. The younger males can be up to about a third of the body size of the older males. Gross (1985) has shown that these two types of males exhibit different reproductive behavior. Among the 3-year-old males, competition for access to spawning females is the rule, and thus larger males have an advantage over smaller ones. The 2-year-old males remain still, nearby rocks

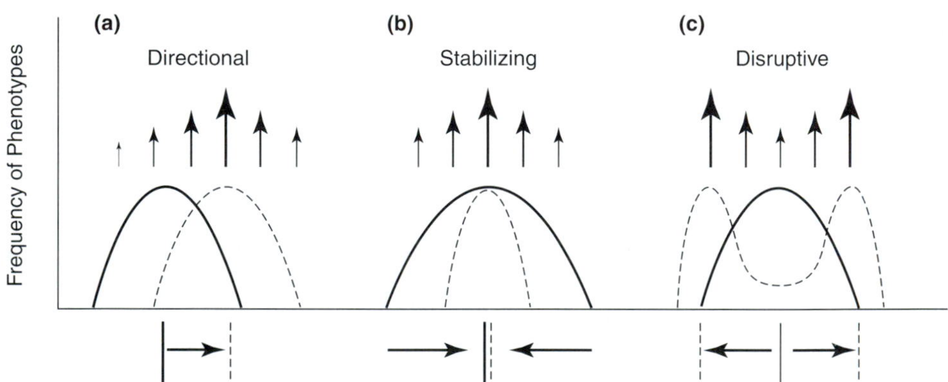

FIGURE 2.9. Three examples of natural selection that can result in changes in the distribution of a particular character: **(a)** directional, **(b)** stabilizing, and **(c)** disruptive selection. The strength of the selective pressure is represented by the length of the vertical arrows above each pair of distributions. In each case, evolution is represented as a change from the distribution drawn with a continuous line to the one drawn in dotted line. The dotted line distribution conforms better to the selective pressures. The vertical lines below each pair of distributions represent the position of the mode and the direction of the evolutionary change. Natural selection can lead to either a decrease in diversity (e.g., stabilizing selection) or an increase in diversity (e.g., disruptive selection).

and plants, until an opportunity to fertilize eggs arises (fertilization is external in salmon). These two strategies, which are in apparent equilibrium, are the result of disruptive selection.

5.d. Traits Contributing to Survival. Many events have to occur at the appropriate time and in the appropriate order for a normal and healthy organism to develop and survive until reproductive age. No multicellular organism is capable of reproduction immediately after fertilization or, if it applies, immediately after birth. Natural selection might be relatively "blind" to traits that develop after the organism has completed its reproductive stage, but it will work intensely upon the evolution of traits that are expressed before this reproductive stage. Mutations and other genetic changes that affect genes expressing relatively early in the development of the organism can be easily eliminated if they result in nonviable organisms. It is this differential survival and death of prereproductive organisms that has resulted in the evolution of complex developmental programs involving the coordinated action of thousands of genes and intricate gene-environment interactions that result in the development of a reproductively viable individual. As emphasized throughout this chapter, however, from the point of view of natural selection, survival is important only to the extent that it implies increased reproductive chances for the organism; survival is not worth in its own right.

A classic example illustrating the evolution of characters that contribute to survival involved changes in protective coloration of peppered moths, *Biston betularia,* in England (Bishop & Cook 1980). Light-colored individuals predominated until industrial pollution darkened the tree trunks in some regions. As light-colored individuals settled on the trunks, they were easily detected by birds that normally fed on these moths. Predatory pressures then led to a shift in the relative frequencies of these two characters, and presumably also of their underlying alleles, such that in heavily industrial areas the dark-colored variety eventually predominated over the light-colored one, but in less industrialized areas the light-colored individuals continued to predominate. When air pollution came under the control of more severe legislation, trees recovered their original coloration and light-colored individuals again spread in the population. It is important to notice that this example illustrates only changes in allele frequencies, and not the evolution of a new species. The process was driven by predatory pressures, and it was probably not long enough (in terms of the number of generations) to lead to the evolution of different species.

5.e. Correlated Traits. As mentioned previously (see ***section 2*** above), a particular gene (or set of genes) may exert its effects on a variety of characters as the organism develops. Imagine a situation in which characters dependent on this gene contribute differentially to LRS. If one of the characters contributes significantly to fitness and is, thus, under strong positive selection, this could cause *correlated traits* also to evolve even if they do not have themselves adaptive significance. It has been suggested, for example, that the miniaturization of the forelimbs of certain dinosaurs, as in *Tyrannosaurus rex,* could be a correlated consequence of selection for an increase in head size (Gould & Lewontin 1979). Whether or not this was the case is something that perhaps will never be firmly established, but the example makes a good point: It would be fruitless to search for the adaptive function of forelimb reduction.

An additional point made by the example just given is that evolution can occur by altering entire sets of characters, rather than one character at a time. In some cases, characters that spread because of correlation may eventually provide some benefit for the animal when environmental conditions change. The accumulation of a pigment, such as melanin, could result from strong selection of an enzyme that regulates some metabolic process. If external coloration becomes a factor in terms of fitness, as it did in the example of the peppered moth cited previously, then coloration itself might come under the control of selective pressures. Characters that are available for selection in this manner are referred to as preadaptations and show the opportunistic nature of evolution.

Changes in entire patterns of characters can have important behavioral implications. Consider a simple example. If natural selection were to favor the evolution of increased body size, say in a particular lineage of mammals, perhaps because of reduced predatory pressure, this might bring about a variety of developmental changes. Since it would almost certainly take longer to achieve a larger body size, the patterns of parental care, social interactions, and the relative importance of environmental experience might consequently all change. The entire adaptive pattern is called a *life-history strategy;* the word "strategy" simply suggests that traits evolve in a coordinated fashion. A number of life-history correlations have been demonstrated in mammals, although they can be taken only as broad trends (Eisenberg 1981). For example, as body size increases across species of mammals, longevity increases too, but the number of offspring per birth decreases. The size of the brain, like that of other organs, also increases directly with body size, and, interestingly, larger-brained mammals tend to produce infants that remain for relatively longer periods in attachment with their parents and siblings.

5.f. Darwinian Fitness and Adaptation. Not only is LRS difficult to measure, but it is also impossible to even estimate in many cases, most notably when fossil evidence is under analysis. Entire functional theories of behavior are based on unsubstantiated assumptions about the relationship between LRS and whatever variable happens to be actually measured. This will become obvious in ***Chapter 4*** (***section 2***, pp. 85–93), where I review optimal foraging theory; such models often assume a positive relationship between some type of feeding behavior and LRS, which, although likely to be correct, is usually not empirically tested. Biologists have traditionally approached this problem by assuming that complexity of design and degree of fit to the environment imply the operation of natural selection. Such traits are referred to as *adaptations,* and the view that organisms are collections of adaptive traits that evolved by natural selection is labeled *adaptationism.* Thus the complex wings of pterosaurs (a morphological trait) and the sophisticated foraging behavior of Hawaiian honeycreepers (a functional trait) are viewed as adaptations because it is presently not possible to understand their evolution without reference to natural selection.

According to the adaptationist viewpoint, the environment poses a problem and an adaptation represents the solution to that problem. Solving the problem ultimately translates into inclusive fitness. There are several problems with this view of evolution. As Williams (1966) pointed out, the principle of natural selection goes beyond the physics and chemistry of the natural order and thus should be invoked only when more basic processes cannot explain the facts. As an example, Williams points to the behavior of flying fish of returning to the water after an aerial flight. Because flying fish cannot survive outside the water, it might be postulated that returning to the water is an adaptation selected through natural selection. Such an explanation would require alternative traits, given that natural selection is always a relative concept, but it is hard to imagine, for example, flying fish that never return to water and thus die of oxygen deprivation. This hypothesis is clearly unnecessary (i.e., nonparsimonious), for the return to water is caused simply by gravity.

Williams also noted that adaptations should not be recognized solely on the basis of the benefit a particular trait confers to the organism, because that benefit may be secondary to the function of that trait. For example, a fox may take the same way to a foraging site after a heavy snowfall because, once the path is opened, it is easier to travel through the snow. However, it would be a mistake to conclude that the shape of the fox's paws is adapted for constructing paths in the snow, even if this involves a significant saving in energy and time ultimately crucial for reproductive success. The paws are clearly adapted for walking and running, and the fact that they open a path through the snow is simply an accidental by-product.

It would be a mistake also to assume that a trait constitutes the best possible solution to a particular environmental problem. Solutions evolved out of sets of genes that are grouped together for historical reasons—because they have been successful in the ancestors from which they have been inherited. Thus, solutions have to be worked out from the available genetic information and within the constraints imposed by the evolutionary history of the species. This is nicely illustrated by the example of the panda's "thumb" (Gould & Lewontin 1979). Pandas are herbivorous mammals that evolved from carnivorous ancestors. As it is the case with most carnivores, the panda's ancestors used the first digit for running, and it is therefore not mobile. But pandas have evolved a bone in the wrist that plays the role of a thumb, allowing the animal to strip the leaves from bamboo shoots. It is likely that developmental constraints restrict the possibility of change in the structure of digits because the arm evolved toward a running function; however, the wrist bones may have been less resistant to change. Consequently, evolution favored a modification of the wrist bones, generating an original solution to a feeding problem.

Historical factors can also restrict the particular evolutionary pathway taken by a population of animals. Lewontin (1978) illustrated this point with the example of the one-horn Indian rhinoceros and two-horn African rhinoceros. It appears unlikely that the one-horn phenotype is more adaptive in India than in Africa, but the opposite is true for the two-horn phenotype. It is simpler to assume that the founder populations of these two species differed in the type of genetic material upon which natural selection operated.

Whereas the importance of natural selection in the evolution of adaptations should not be underestimated, it would be erroneous to assume that all behaviors (and all traits, in general) are adaptations that evolved as solutions to environmental problems, just as an engineer solves a design problem on a drawing board. As was eloquently put by Jacob (1977), evolution is an opportunistic process: It draws from available information to come up with the best solution, which need not be the best in absolute terms, but just the one that is possible given the limits of inherited information. Unlike the engineer, evolution cannot start the design of a new species with a blank piece of paper; rather, it has to take the old design and transform it. When this is not possible, the lineage may simply become extinct.

5.g. Units of Natural Selection. The popularity of the phrase "survival of the fittest" is matched by an equally popular and misleading phrase suggesting that natural selection acts at the group level. People would often say, in colloquial conversations, that behaviors and morphological features evolved "for the benefit of the species." Animals are thought to do the things they do "to perpetuate the species." However, Darwin's view of natural selection works best if the individual organism, rather than some supra-individual entity such as the group, population, or species, is seen as the level at which natural selection operates. So whereas evolutionary change occurs in populations, natural selection acts at the individual level. Indeed, it has become popular after the influential work of Dawkins (1976) to conceptualize natural selection as acting at the level of individual alleles, rather than the entire individual, a view usually labeled the *selfish gene view*. Dawkins (1982) recognized that the levels of analysis exemplified by the organism and the gene often lead to the same conclusions, although they might in some cases lead to conflicting predictions.

The *group-selection view* was developed in great detail by Wynne-Edwards (1962). His basic hypothesis was that almost all social behavior is directed at avoiding the overexploitation of resources important for the survival of the group (population or species). The implication is that species that possessed mechanisms for the regulation of populations survived up to the present, whereas those that did not have become extinct. Wynne-Edwards (1963) argued that "the individual member has to be governed by the homeostatic system even when, as commonly happens, this means his exclusion from food in the midst of apparent plenty, or detention from reproduction when others are breeding." Notice that instead of selection acting on alternative traits, intergroup selection involves the relative success of entire groups of animals. According to this view, it is the groups, not the individual's traits, that vary and are positively (or negatively) selected.

Wynne-Edwards suggested that animal groups compete for a limited amount of resources, and under some conditions, the individual animals within the groups may have to sacrifice their own reproductive potential as a contribution to the welfare of the group. Groups in which such altruistic individuals are common would, presumably, manage to survive relative to groups of selfish individuals. In support of intergroup selection, Wynne-Edwards cites the fact that animal groups tend to perpetuate themselves by individuals returning to the breeding grounds, thus constituting real biological units. In the face of resource depletion, groups exercise self-regulation through the individual behavior of their members, including territoriality, social hierarchies, and intraspecific aggression. Such patterns result in the spacing of individuals that permits a more balanced exploitation of environmental resources.

Although this view may seem similar to Darwin's theory of natural selection, closer analysis reveals that intergroup selection is an entirely different mechanism. According to Darwin, only traits that promote individual fitness spread in a population. If a trait prompts an animal to sacrifice its own reproductive success, how could this trait be passed on to the next generation? Moreover, in a population of self-sacrificing individuals, a selfish mutant would enjoy such a selective advantage that in a few generations the underlying selfish genes would replace the self-sacrificing genes.

Fitness at the individual (or gene) level has far stronger consequences than fitness at the group level. A case in point is that of infanticide in lions mentioned previously, a behavior that has been observed in other species as well. Such infanticidal behavior is clearly deleterious for the species as a whole as it implies the loss of young animals before they have a chance to contribute to the "survival of the species." However, because infanticide prompts the females into sexual receptivity, it provides for an increase in the fitness of males and it is, therefore, favored by natural selection.

6. KEY TERMS

adaptation 54
adaptationism 54
allele 39
character similarity 34
correlated traits 53
C-value paradox 45
Darwinian (or direct) fitness 49
diploid 39
directional selection 51
disruptive selection 52
DNA (deoxyribonucleic acid) 30
eukaryote 30
evolutionary pattern 30
evolutionary process 30
exon 42
exon shuffling 43
founder effect 42
gene 39
genetic code 30
genetic drift 41
genotype 37
group selection view 56
haploid 39
Hardy-Weinberg equilibrium 40
heterosis 49
heterozygous 39
homology 31
homozygous 39
inclusive fitness 49
independent assortment 47
indirect fitness 49
intron 42
law of segregation 39
life-history strategy 54
lifetime reproductive success (LRS) 50
Mendelian genetics 37
molecular clock 32
mutation 44
natural selection 38
neutral theory 45
norm of reaction 37
phenotype 37
phylogeny 30
phylogenetic tree 32
phylotypic stage 34
pleiotropy 37
polygeny 37
polymorphisms 41
population bottleneck 42
preadaptation 47
prokaryote 30
regulatory genes 44
repetitive DNA 45
RNA (ribonucleic acid) 30
selfish gene view 56
stabilizing selection 52
structural genes 43
trait 36

7. REFERENCES

Bishop, J. A., & Cook, L. M. (1980). Industrial melanism and the urban environment. *Advances in Ecological Research,* **11,** 373–404.

Bygott, J. D., Bertram, B. C. R., & Hanby, C. R. (1979). Male lions in large coalitions gain reproductive advantages. *Nature,* **282,** 839–841.

Curtis, H., & Barnes, N. S. (1989). *Biology* (5th ed.). New York: Worth.

Dawkins, R. (1976). *The selfish gene.* Oxford, UK: Oxford University Press.

Dawkins, R. (1982). *The extended phenotype.* Oxford, UK: Oxford University Press.

Eisenberg, J. F. (1981). *The mammalian radiations. An analysis of trends in evolution, adaptation, and behaviour.* London: Athlone Press.

Fitch, W. M., & Margoliash, E. (1967). Construction of phylogenetic trees. *Science,* **155,** 279–284.

Gould, S. J., & Lewontin, R. C. (1979). The spandrels of San Marco and the Panglossian paradigm: A critique of the adaptationist programme. *Proceedings of the Royal Society,* London B, **205,** 581–598.

Grant, P. R. (1986). *Ecology and evolution of Darwin's finches.* Princeton, NJ: Princeton University Press.

Gross, M. R. (1985). Disruptive selection for alternative life histories in salmon. *Nature,* **313,** 47–48.

Haeckel, E. (1879). *The evolution of man: A popular exposition of the principal points of human ontogeny and phylogeny.* New York: Appleton & Century.

Hamilton, W. D. (1964). The genetical evolution of social behavior, I and II. *Journal of Theoretical Biology,* **7,** 1–52.

Hrdy, S. B. (1977). Infanticide as a primate reproductive strategy. *American Scientist,* **65,** 40–49.

Jacob, F. (1977). Evolution and tinkering. *Science,* **196,** 1161.

Kimura, M. (1983). *The neutral theory of molecular evolution.* Cambridge, UK: Cambridge University Press.

King, M. C., & Wilson, A. C. (1975). Evolution at two levels: molecular similarities and biological differences between humans and chimpanzees. *Science,* **188,** 107–116.

Langman, R. E. (1989). *The immune system.* San Diego, CA: Academic Press.

Lewontin, R. C. (1978). Adaptation. *Scientific American,* **239,** 156–169.

Lively, C. M. (1987). Evidence from a New Zealand snail for the maintenance of sex by parasitism. *Nature,* **328,** 519–521.

Mayor, A. (2000). *The first fossil hunters. Paleontology in Greek and Roman times.* Princeton, NJ: Princeton University Press.

Mock, D. W., & Ploger, B. J. (1987). Parental manipulation of optimal hatch asynchrony in cattle egrets: An experimental study. *Animal Behaviour,* **35,** 150–160.

Packer, C., Herbst, L., Pusey, A. E., Bygott, J. D., Hanby, J. P., Cairns, S. J., & Mulder, M. B. (1988). Reproductive success of lions. In T. H. Clutton-Brock (Ed.), *Reproductive success* (pp. 363–383). Chicago, IL: University of Chicago Press.

Raff, R. A., & Kaufman, T. C. (1983). *Embryos, genes, and evolution.* Bloomington, IN: Indiana University Press.

Roth, G., Nishikawa, K. C., & Wake, D. B. (1997). Genome size, secondary simplification, and the evolution of the brain in salamanders. *Brain, Behavior, & Evolution,* **50,** 50–59.

Sibley, C. G., & Ahlquist, J. E. (1990). *Phylogeny and classification of birds. A study in molecular evolution.* New Haven, CT: Yale University Press.

Spencer, H. (1855). *Principles of psychology.* London: Longman.

Stearns, S. C. (1992). *The evolution of life histories.* Oxford, UK: Oxford University Press.

Williams, G. C. (1966). *Adaptation and natural selection.* Princeton, NJ: Princeton University Press.

Wu, C.-I., & Li, W.-H. (1985). Evidence for higher rates of nucleotide substitution in rodents than in man. *Proceedings of the National Academy of Sciences* (USA), **82,** 1741–1745.

Wynne-Edwards, V. C. (1962). *Animal dispersion in relation to social behaviour.* Edinburgh: Oliver & Boyd.

Wynne-Edwards, V. C. (1963). Intergroup selection in the evolution of social systems. *Nature,* **200,** 623–626.

CHAPTER 3

Genes and Behavior

MAIN GENERALIZATIONS OF CHAPTER 3

- *Behavior develops as a result of complex interactions between genetic and nongenetic information.*
- *Some complex behaviors appear to have a simple Mendelian basis, whereas others are the result of the action of many genes.*
- *While the rates of evolution observed in laboratory experiments, field experiments, and fossil lineages are very different, the same evolutionary process appears to operate in all these cases.*

An understanding of the mechanisms by which behavior arises during development is critical for comparative psychology. Behavior and other aspects of the phenotype of an animal are the result of a complex set of interactions involving genetic and nongenetic information. To avoid simplistic reductionisms, it might be appropriate to remember exactly why this interaction is described as "complex." On the one hand, the number of genetic and, particularly, nongenetic factors is considerably large. Some behaviors bearing a one-to-one relationship with genes are amenable to the type of genetic analysis introduced by Mendel during the 19th century. By far, however, behaviors are the result of the action of large numbers of genes (i.e., polygeny). The pathway from genes to behavior is also quite indirect; after all, genes produce only proteins, not cells, organs, networks, or behavioral traits (see ***Figure 3.1***). Moreover, nongenetic information involves such factors as direct environmental influences (e.g., temperature, nutrition, social context, etc.), as well as the various nested environments internal to the organism: systems, organs, physiological processes, and cellular and nuclear environments. Even nongenetic maternal factors that are transmitted in the egg's cytoplasm can influence development.

On the other hand, even if such interaction is reduced to its simplest expression—one in which a particular phenotype results from the interplay of genotype and the external environment—the number of potential outcomes of such a process would still be considerably large. Identical twins are genetically identical, but, otherwise, organisms are genetically unique because of the independent assortment of alleles in meiosis. Something similar also holds for environments: To the extent that it is the organism that defines its environment, environments are also unique. Additionally, the interaction of genotypes and environments implies that even when one of them is held constant, variation in the other term can lead to different phenotypes.

Interest in the genetic basis of behavior is based on two different but complementary goals. First, from the point of view of proximate causes, genes contribute important information for the development of individual behavior. Second, from the point of view of ultimate causes, a genetic basis for behavior implies that behavior can be the result of an evolutionary process, as Darwin (1859) envisioned in his discussion of instincts. More recently it has become clear that behavior can, at least in some cases, start the evolutionary process; it is behavioral "decisions" that drive animals into geographical isolation and into the exploitation of new resources.

Let's then begin by looking at a relatively complex set of behaviors that appear to have a relatively simple genetics.

1. Mendelian Behavior Genetics

1.a. Hygienic Behavior of Honeybees. With tens of thousands of individuals, honeybee colonies are spectacularly complex. Individual bees carry out a variety of duties, from reproduction (a privilege reserved only for the colony's queen and drones) to building and cleaning the hive, nurturing the pupae, defending the colony, and foraging for food. Together with other social insects (ants, wasps, and termites), the honeybees represent a pinnacle in the evolution of social behavior (see ***Chapter 5, section 5.a.,*** pp. 157–159). The behaviors of interest here are carried out by sterile females, called workers, and are observed only in some honeybee colonies. In certain

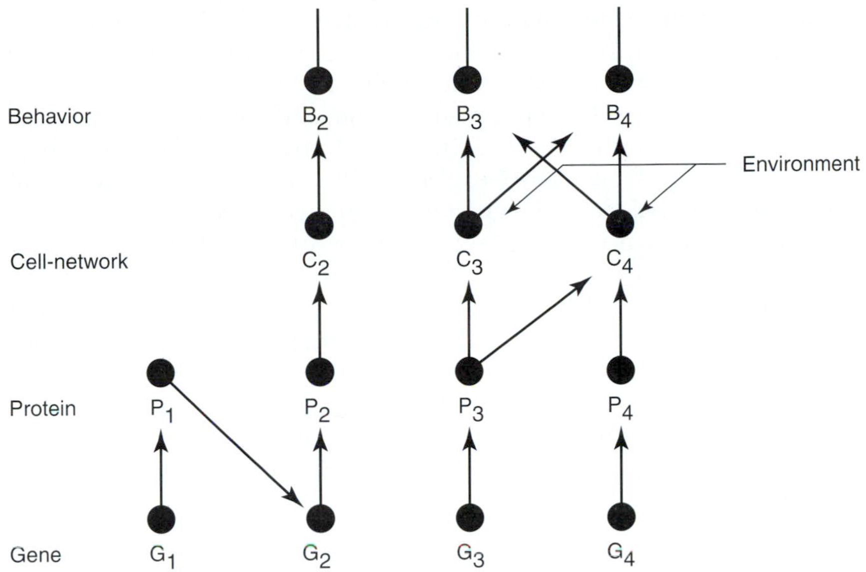

FIGURE 3.1. Schematic representation of the relationship between genes and behavior. All genes represented here can ultimately affect behavior, but only in indirect ways. G_1 represents a regulatory gene whose main action is to regulate another gene's transcription. G_2 represents a lineal relationship that could be described as a 1:1 relationship between gene and behavior. Mendelian traits probably work in a similar fashion. G_3 and G_4 represent both pleiotropic (1:many) or polygenic (many:1) relationships between gene:behavior connections. Nongenetic factors are symbolized here by the environment, although it should be remembered that this is a gross oversimplification.

colonies, workers periodically check developing eggs and larvae stored inside combs and remove those that have died. Checking a comb involves opening, or uncapping, the closure. Two behaviors are thus observed in these colonies: the uncapping of combs and the removal of dead eggs and larvae. Death usually results from bacterial infection and, therefore, these behaviors prevent the spread of infection in the colony. In other colonies, workers neither check combs nor remove dead eggs and larvae, thus allowing infections to spread to neighboring combs.

Rothenbuhler (1964) reported the results of cross-breeding experiments of these lines of hygienic and nonhygienic honeybees. The five colonies resulting from the cross (the F_1 generation) displayed clear evidence of nonhygienic behavior, from which it was concluded that the genes controlling these hygienic behaviors were recessive. If the behaviors are based on *Mendelian inheritance,* then a backcross between F_1 males and hygienic queens should produce an F_2 progeny with a very specific distribution of phenotypes, depending on the number of genes involved. Sperm cells from F_1 drones were used to artificially inseminate inbreed hygienic queens. Control crosses were run involving inbreeding of hygienic and nonhygienic animals, as well as a backcross of F_1 drones with nonhygienic queens.

As expected, control crosses yielded the appropriate behavior in the colonies produced. The backcross against nonhygienic queens yielded seven colonies, none of which displayed hygienic behavior. The main results, involving the backcross against the hygienic queens, were very clear. Six of 29 F_2 colonies (21%) displayed hygienic behavior, uncapping and removing dead individuals in a normal fashion, whereas the other 23 colonies displayed nonhygienic behavior. However, there were interesting differences among these nonhygienic colonies. In 9 of these colonies (31%), combs with dead larvae inside were uncapped but the larvae were not removed, suggesting that only one of the hygienic behaviors (uncapping) was present. The remaining 14 colonies did not uncap combs, but again a surprising result was obtained when combs were uncapped by the experimenter, thus allowing expression for the other hygienic behavior. In 6 of these colonies (21%), exposed dead larvae were promptly removed from their comb, although in the final 8 colonies (27%), exposed dead larvae were not removed. The obtained distribution of frequencies, 21:31:21:27, approximates a 1:1:1:1 distribution typical of diallelic cases. As in Mendel's experiments, "uncapping" and "removing" can be considered each to be under the independent control of a single gene.

1.b. Further Mendelian Analysis. It is surprising to find relatively complex behaviors, such as those expressed in hygienic honeybee workers, that depend upon single genes. Although, as already said, most behaviors do involve polygenic control, there are some further examples that illustrate Mendelian behavior genetic rules. An interesting one is the control of avoidance behavior in mice (*Mus musculus*), which is also useful to illustrate an elaboration of the cross-breeding technique.

As is true for other behavioral phenotypes, the acquisition of avoidance behavior in randomly bred mice shows substantial variability. Training in *active avoidance learning* is typically administered in a two-compartment shuttle-box apparatus. The experimenter arranges the situation such that the presentation of some stimulus (e.g., a tone) in one of the compartments is followed a few seconds later by a painful electric shock delivered to the animal's feet, unless the animal shuttles to the other compartment during the presentation of the stimulus and before the shock begins. Such shuttling responses allow the animal to avoid the shock. Some individuals acquire avoidance behaviors at a relatively high level, shuttling in more than 50% of the trials, whereas others are poor learners, avoiding only in approximately 10% of the trials. Mouse strains of individuals that are either high or low in their avoidance learning capacities can be assumed to be homozygous for many alleles as a result of intense inbreeding. Such inbred strains can be used to determine whether avoidance behavior is under Mendelian control.

A crossing of individuals from the inbred lines produces a heterozygous F_1, and a further crossing produces a variety of F_2 combinations. Brother-sister pairing of individuals from F_2 leads, over many generations, to highly inbred strains called *recombinant inbred strains*. Oliverio et al. (1973) used such a method on a parental population of mice known to be high (so-called BALB/c strain) and low (so-called C57BL strain) in avoidance learning, from which seven inbred strains were developed. In the F39, avoidance performance was segregated in an almost dichotomous manner, with three of the strains scoring very high in avoidance (as the parental BALB/c mice), and four scoring very low (as the parental C57BL mice). It is the absence of mice showing intermediate levels of avoidance behavior that suggests that a single gene is responsible for the behavioral differences. If a single gene is responsible for the behavioral difference between high and low parental strains, then each inbred line has a probability equal to 0.5 of fixating one of the two alleles, or, in other words, about half of the inbred strains should resemble each of the parental populations. Typically, this recombinant inbred strain method yields intermediate phenotypes, which suggests that more than one gene is involved in the control of the phenotype under study.

2. Quantitative Genetics

2.a. Artificial Selection. Darwin's insight on natural selection embodies an analogy. Just as humans have domesticated animals and plants through a process of selective breeding called *artificial selection,* so it must happen under natural conditions with all living organisms. *Natural selection* must work according to a set of criteria based on survival and reproductive success. Much of what is known today about the genetic basis of behavior comes from experiments using the technique of artificial selection. This technique is simple and surprisingly powerful.

Some character is first measured in a parental population of randomly bred animals. In most cases, the frequency of scores for the characters approaches a normal distribution (i.e., intermediate scores are the most common). Then, individuals scoring high are bred with one another, as are individuals scoring low, thus giving rise to a first filial generation. Typically, the F_1 generation shows some overlap in phenotype distributions, and such an overlap may persist across several generations. In each generation, extreme phenotypes are paired selectively. Experiments of this type also involve a control line in which individuals chosen randomly from each generation are paired and bred; this procedure eliminates the contribution of factors other than selective breeding to the evolution of high (H) and low (L) strains. Control breeding lines usually retain the average phenotypic value of the parental population. Selective breeding thus involves directional selection (see ***Figure 2.9,*** p. 52).

There are many examples of rapid response of behavioral phenotypes to selective breeding. Roubertoux (1992) found rapid changes in lines of male guppy fish (*Poecilia reticulata*) selected for presence-versus-absence of the sigmoid response, a behavior that is part of the male's courtship display. High and low lines evolved within three generations, whereas a control, unselected line exhibited little change. In this particular case, however, most of the change in behavior was obtained in the low line. As will be discussed later, behavior that responds little to artificial selection and occurs relatively frequently may indicate that the phenotype has undergone intense natural selection in the ancestors of those animals used in the experiment.

A second example of artificial selection is also useful to illustrate the criteria that must be adopted to define the phenotype for the purpose of selection. Zawistowski and Hirsch (1984) reported an experiment in which blowflies (*Phormia regina*) were selected for high and low discriminative performance in a classical conditioning situation (see ***Chapter 13, section 1.b.,*** pp.

491–493). Such a phenotype is complex in that discrimination implies differential responding to stimuli paired with reward (or S+) and with nonreward (or S–). Such differential behavior may arise because of high responding to the S+, low responding to the S–, or both, and the criterion for selection must therefore specify these possibilities. Some flies in this experiment were exposed to trials in which a sodium chloride (N) solution was followed by exposure to sucrose, which induces proboscis extension, whereas a potassium chloride (K) solution was not paired with sucrose (i.e., N+/K– procedure). For other flies, the conditions of pairing were reversed: K+/N–. This procedure of counterbalancing stimulus validity across flies is necessary to ensure that selective breeding will affect the flies' learning ability, rather than their ability to sense a particular stimulus. Conditioning was assessed by the occurrence of proboscis extension responses to the S+, before the sucrose solution is presented in each trial. Flies were given 15 S+ trials and 15 S– trials, and their performance in the last 8 trials was selected for analysis. The high line was derived from flies scoring 6 to 8 responses to the S+, 0 to 3 responses to the S–, and a difference between S+ and S– equal or greater than 4. By contrast, the low line was derived from flies scoring 1 to 3 responses to S+ or S–, and a difference score between –2 and +2. These criteria clearly illustrate the complexity of the phenotype under selection.

The results with the F_{11} generation are presented in ***Figure 3.2,*** which also includes the performance of the parental (P) population and that of a random breeding control (C).

Bidirectional selection had a particularly strong effect on the response of flies to the S+: Notice that responding to the S+ was particularly high in the H line and low in the L line, relative to both the parental and control lines. The same could be said of the difference scores, that is, the subtraction of responses to the S+ minus responses to the S–: Again, the H line exhibited a strong difference score relative to both controls, P and C, whereas the L line showed a difference that was less than that of the controls. Since the response to the stimuli was practically nil during the first trial of the training session (not shown in the figure), it can be concluded that selection did not affect the unconditioned reactions to the sodium and potassium chloride solutions per se.

Examples of successful selective breeding responses are abundant in the literature. ***Table 3.1*** provides a sense of the power of this technique to produce behavioral changes in strains of organisms.

2.b. Heritability. The success of artificial selection techniques implies the existence of considerable amounts of genetic variability for behavioral traits. The rate and extent to which filial generations respond to artificial selection allows for an estimation of the degree to which a character is heritable. Notice, however, that heritability applies to the distribution of phenotypic values in a population, and not to the proportion of a particular trait that can be explained by genetic factors in an individual animal. In the extreme cases, a character that depends on a single gene and is highly heritable will respond fast and strongly to artificial selection. By contrast, a phenotype that has zero heritability should not exhibit any change across generations of selective breeding. Between these two extremes lies a continuum of intermediate values of heritability that produce intermediate rates of generational change. Intermediate rates imply that the behavioral phenotype is under polygenic control.

A change in phenotype between two successive generations is a function of two factors. The first factor is the difference between the mean phenotype for the entire

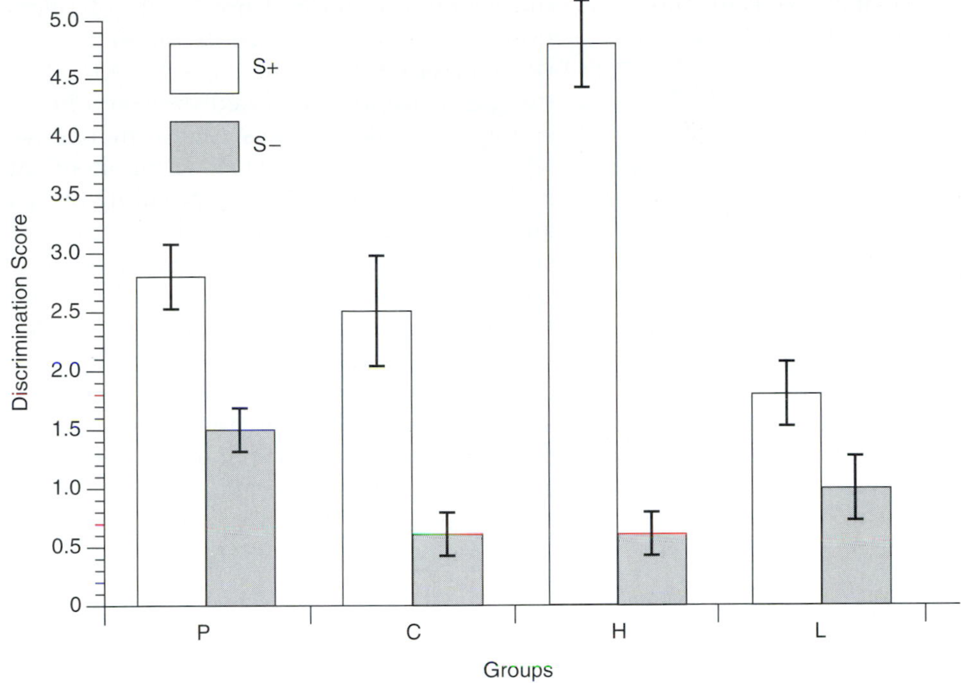

FIGURE 3.2. Discrimination learning in individual fruitflies, *Drosophila melanogaster,* was measured in terms of proboscis extension in an experiment reported by Zawistowski and Hirsch (1984). Responses were recorded in the presence of both the stimulus paired with sucrose, or *S+*, and the stimulus paired with nothing, or *S−*. Four groups of fruitflies received training: a group sampled from the parental population, *P;* a group of randomly mated control flies, *C;* and groups obtained from the *H* and *L* lines of artificially selected animals.

parental population and the mean phenotype of the subpopulation selected for inbreeding. This variable is called *selection differential,* or *S,* and it reflects the degree to which the selected phenotypic value is extreme, relative to the parental population. The second factor is the difference between the mean of the filial generation and the mean of the parental generation. This variable is referred to as the *gain,* or *G,* and it reflects the response of the phenotype to selective breeding. When $G = 0$, heritability also equals zero, and the implication is, of course, that the trait has little or no genetic basis. When $G = S$, then heritability is equal to 1, and the implication is that the phenotype has a strong genetic component. Therefore, *heritability* (labeled h^2) is a direct function of *G* and an inverse function of *S:*

$$h^2 = \frac{G}{S}$$

Heritability is frequently estimated after several generations of selective breeding, in

TABLE 3.1 Variety of Traits That Respond to Artificial Selection

Phenotype	*Species*
Relative brain size	Mice
Audiogenic seizures	Mice
Geotaxis, phototaxis	Fruitflies
Tonic immobility	Quail
Exploratory behavior, activity levels	Fruitflies, mice
Mating behavior	Fruitflies, quail, chickens
Nest building	Mice
Aggressive behavior	Stickleback fish, mice
Sensitivity to alcohol consumption	Mice
Frustration in consummatory contrast	Rats
Appetitive conditioning	Fruitflies, honeybees
Avoidance learning	Mice, rats
Maze learning performance	Rats

which case it is labeled *realized* h^2. Realized h^2 does not reflect necessarily the absolute degree to which a trait is heritable in the parental population, but rather how well the trait responded to selective breeding, given the initial values. The same trait can, thus, result in different values of h^2 depending on the original distribution. Realized h^2 values equal or greater than 0.40 are common for characters that respond well to artificial selection, such as those listed above.

2.c. Limits of Artificial Selection. A relatively rapid response to selection is typical of selective breeding experiments, as already pointed out. There are, however, important limitations to this technique. In some cases, well-defined behaviors do not seem to respond to selective breeding. In the example described previously of selection for components of courtship in guppies (Roubertoux 1992), whereas selection effectively and rapidly modified the sigmoid response of males, it was totally ineffective when applied to another component of male courtship involving a spreading of fins and curving of the body while the male is snout-to-snout with the female (so-called gonopodial swinging). Such a differential response to selective breeding of these behaviors implies a different genetic basis and development. However, negative outcomes of this sort are hard to interpret; perhaps the behavior would respond to selection if more generations were added (i.e., perhaps the behavior involves many different genes and thus responds slowly to artificial selection).

A second limitation of artificial selection may actually be quite informative regarding the natural history of the behavioral pattern under selective breeding. Whereas high and low lines are usually easily evolved, in some cases the response to selective breeding is observable in only one of the lines. For example, fruitflies (*Drosophila melanogaster*) selected for H and L ability to develop aversive olfactory conditioning exhibit a significant selective response in the L line but no response in the H line, a result that can be appreciated in ***Figure 3.3*** (Hewitt et al. 1983). This *directional dominance* for selection can be interpreted as resulting from lack of genetic variation to increase the efficiency of olfactory conditioning. Since one factor leading to reduced genetic variability is natural selection, this failure to develop a H line indicates that this behavioral trait is already under strong selective pressure. Therefore, artificial selection may help identify behaviors that have been under strong positive natural selection in the ancestors of animals exposed to experimental conditions.

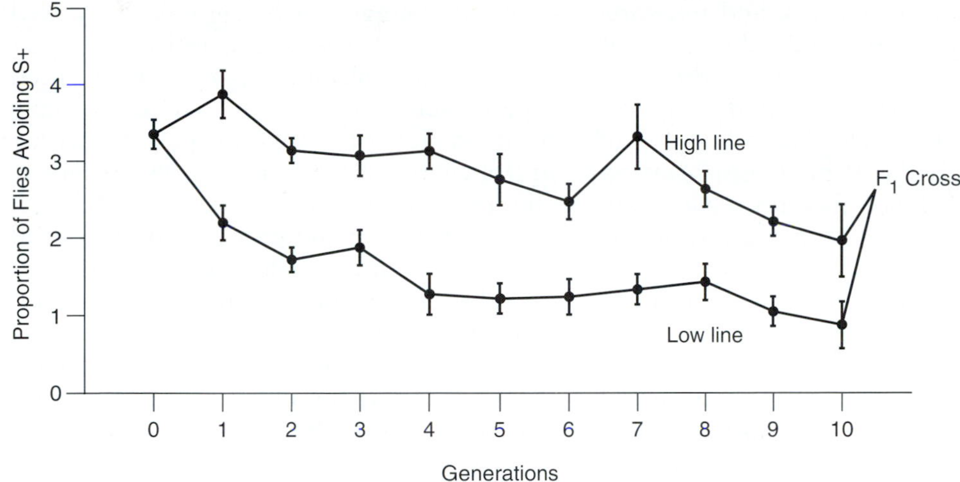

FIGURE 3.3. Bidirectional selection for avoidance of an odor paired with electric shock during 10 generations in the fruitfly *Drosophila melanogaster* (Hewitt et al. 1983). Notice that whereas there was a good response to selection in the L line, there was no response in the H line, which actually exhibited inbreeding depression (i.e., scores decreased across generations). This differential responding of H and L lines to artificial selection is referred to as *directional dominance.* The last point shows the scores obtained in the progeny of a H × L cross. The recovery observed in this progeny suggests that inbreeding depression was caused by the accumulation of deleterious recessive alleles.

In the selective breeding experiment reported by Hewitt et al. (1983), there was a further outcome of interest. The H line not only did not respond to selection, but it actually showed *inbreeding depression:* The conditioning scores steadily decreased over the 10 generations. Furthermore, a hybrid generation produced as a result of interbreeding individuals from the H and L lines exhibited a greater conditioning score than that of the H line. Such a regression toward the values of the P generation is referred to as *hybrid vigor* or *heterosis.* Inbreeding depression and heterosis are the two sides of the same coin. They imply that the genetic architecture of the trait under selection involves dominant alleles. Inbreeding (crossing among closely related individuals, such as brothers and sisters or cousins) causes deleterious recessive alleles to cluster in homozygous pairs across generations, thus leading to the depression of phenotypic values. Heterozygosis is reestablished in hybrids, allowing the dominant alleles to mask the effects of recessive alleles. Such a masking invigorates phenotypic scores.

A third problem with artificial selection is one of validity. In some cases, selection for a particular trait results in a significant response in H and L lines, but upon further analysis, the trait may not be what it was assumed to be in the first place. A classic experiment illustrates this problem. Tryon (1934) exposed a population of rats to a complex maze-learning task and measured the number of errors individual animals made before solving the task. An error was counted every time an animal entered a blind alley in the maze. The average number of errors in the P population was approximately 14. Tryon then proceeded to inbreed animals with low scores, which he termed the "bright line," and animals with high scores, called the "dull line." In just a few generations, Tryon observed the emergence of bright and dull rats, and by the F_{20} there was no overlap between these strains. Brights were making approximately 9 errors on average to solve the maze, whereas dulls were making twice as many errors. If, in fact, Tryon was selecting for H and L intelligence, then it should be possible to obtain good and poor performance in other learning tasks because such an ability should generalize beyond the confinements of the original training situation. Subsequent experiments with bright and dull rats showed that in other tasks (e.g., aversive conditioning) the dulls were actually better than the brights (Searle 1949). Although the criterion for selection was considered a priori a measure of learning ability, the lines diverged because they differed in terms of what might be called *emotionality*. Dull rats were not necessarily poorer in learning ability, but just more emotional and easily disturbed. An increased emotionality impaired performance in a food-reinforced maze task, but it enhanced acquisition of an aversively motivated task. This problem will be expanded below in ***section 2.e.***

A fourth problem of artificial selection experiments concerns the consequences of relaxing selective pressures after some number of generations. Although artificial breeding typically leads to the rapid evolution of H and L lines, when selective breeding is discontinued and animals are allowed free mating, scores typically regress to the parental average. Such regression is called *genetic homeostasis,* and it reflects the fact that although strains might have diverged rapidly, selective breeding does not usually result in stable new phenotypes. According to Dobzhansky (1970), the alleles present in any population are *coadapted* with each other because of the past action of natural selection; artificial selection disrupts that equilibrium, but only partially. As a result, when the selective pressure is relaxed the phenotypes regress to their usual values. Lines produced through artificial selection may be said to evolve in the sense that phenotypic changes occur across generations, but not in the sense that new species are produced. However, some artificial selection experiments demonstrate the evolution of stable lines that do not regress to parental phenotypic values when selective pressures are relaxed. This suggests that artificial selection may induce a novel coadaptation of genes.

2.d. Speciation in the Laboratory? The artificial selection procedure operates like a magnifier glass in the sense that in the laboratory it is possible to minimize competing selective pressures and to concentrate the power of selective breeding by carefully planning mating episodes. In nature, net fitness depends on many factors, some enhancing and others interfering with reproductive success. Nevertheless, it takes extensive selective breeding under the favorable conditions of the laboratory to observe substantial and stable genetic changes. Several such experiments have been reported, but, for comparative psychologists, it is particularly interesting when selection is based on a behavioral character. Hirsch and collaborators have accomplished such an outcome by selecting H and L lines for *geotaxis* in *D. melanogaster.* Fruitflies are placed in a maze allowing upward and downward turns. Flies that end in high tubes made upward turns and thus display negative geotaxis, whereas those that end in low tubes display positive geotaxis because they tend to move toward the floor. The tube in which flies are collected at the exit of the maze provides a score of geotaxis which, in the actual experiment, could vary between zero (i.e., all turns were toward the floor) and 16 (i.e., 15 turns against gravity). Hundreds of flies can be left in such a maze for periods of up to 24 hr until they are collected in the goal tubes (Ricker & Hirsch 1985).

The experiment was begun in 1957 with two stocks of wild flies and one stock from the laboratory. The P population had average scores of about 6 to 7 on the geotaxis scale. A rapid but gradual change in geotaxis was observed over the initial 100 generations, and, thereafter, scores exhibited considerable fluctuation, particularly during short periods in which selective pressures were relaxed (for many years these populations of flies were kept only for educational purposes). By 1983 there had been 550 generations of flies, and the scores for the H and L lines had diverged extensively to approximate values of 14 and 1, respectively. Starting in F_{415} and for the next 26 generations, selective pressures were relaxed, but, surprisingly, no regression was observed in either line. A stable level of geotaxis suggests that genes controlling positive and negative geotaxis had become associated in clusters. Such coadaptation of gene clusters implies the accumulation of genes associated with high fitness, which, in turn, might be the result of extensive artificial selection. In fact, a similar process is likely to be responsible for *speciation,*—that is, the evolution of new species through directional selection in natural populations (see ***Chapter 6, section 4.b.,*** 209–210).

One test of the hypothesis that the H and L lines have achieved new stable phenotypic levels is based on counterselection and relaxation. If H and L lines were now selected for intermediate scores and the filial populations obtained were relaxed, would the resulting animals regress toward middle geotactic scores or toward their new H and L levels? Ricker and Hirsch (1988) reported such an experiment of reversed selection and relaxation over several filial generations, and the results are presented in ***Figure 3.4.*** Relaxation produced mixed results for the H line, which regressed toward high scores in some cases but toward middle scores in other cases. However, regression toward the new phenotypic level was very clear in the L line, after artificial counterselection toward middle scores. This result indicates that the L phenotype has achieved a new homeostatic level.

Is this evidence sufficient to conclude that speciation was observed in the laboratory? Whereas the evidence clearly indicates that selective breeding has caused a type of phenotypic change across generations that appears to be stable, the most important feature in the evolution of a new species (as different from the evolution of a variety or strain within a single species) is the *reproductive isolation* of the new populations. Genetic changes would be stable and set into divergent paths if gene migration between the newly formed populations could be drastically reduced or completely eliminated. Local selective pressures would then take over and the isolation would deepen across generations.

Lofdahl et al. (1992) reported an initial analysis of reproductive isolation in the H and L geotaxis lines and compared that to mating among control lines of fruitflies. In these mating tests, males and females of the H and L lines are mixed in a bottle and allowed some period of time for mating. Animals are marked, and mating preferences are determined by direct observation. ***Fig-***

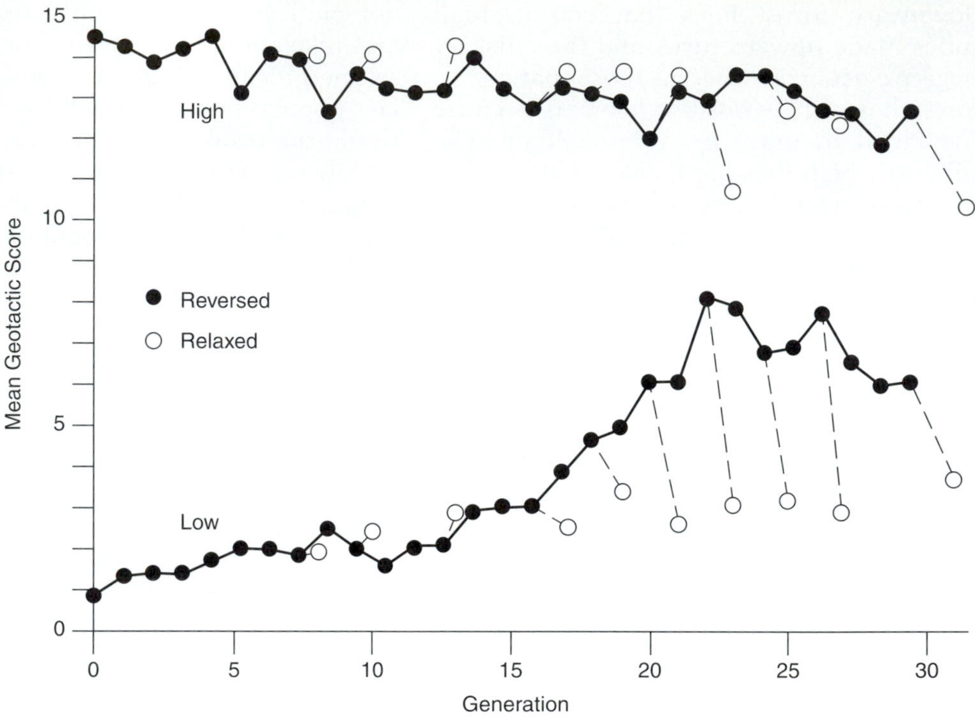

FIGURE 3.4. H and L lines of fruitfly *Drosophila melanogaster* extensively selected for negative and positive geotaxis, respectively, were now exposed to reverse selective pressures (Ricker & Hirsch 1988). Periodically, the pressure was relaxed allowing for free mating. The scores in these relaxed experiments regressed to the new level in the L line (rather than to intermediate geotactic levels as was the case for the parental population). The results for the H line were more ambiguous. Regression toward the new behavioral level suggest that prior artificial selection has resulted in the evolution of new gene coadaptations.

ure 3.5 shows the results summarized from a large number of experiments performed with a variety of testing procedures. There was a partial, but significant, degree of assortative mating—that is, a preference for male and female flies to copulate within the H and L lines rather than across lines. For comparison purposes, similar mating preferences between wild-type controls and Adh lines were determined, and they indicate that the testing procedure is not biased toward one type of crossing. Thus, artificial selection of H and L lines of fruitflies has led to stable phenotypes and partial reproductive isolation. The results can be interpreted as providing evidence for incipient speciation.

2.e. Genetics of Aversively Motivated Behavior. Aversively motivated behaviors are among the easiest to influence through artificial selection procedures, and they

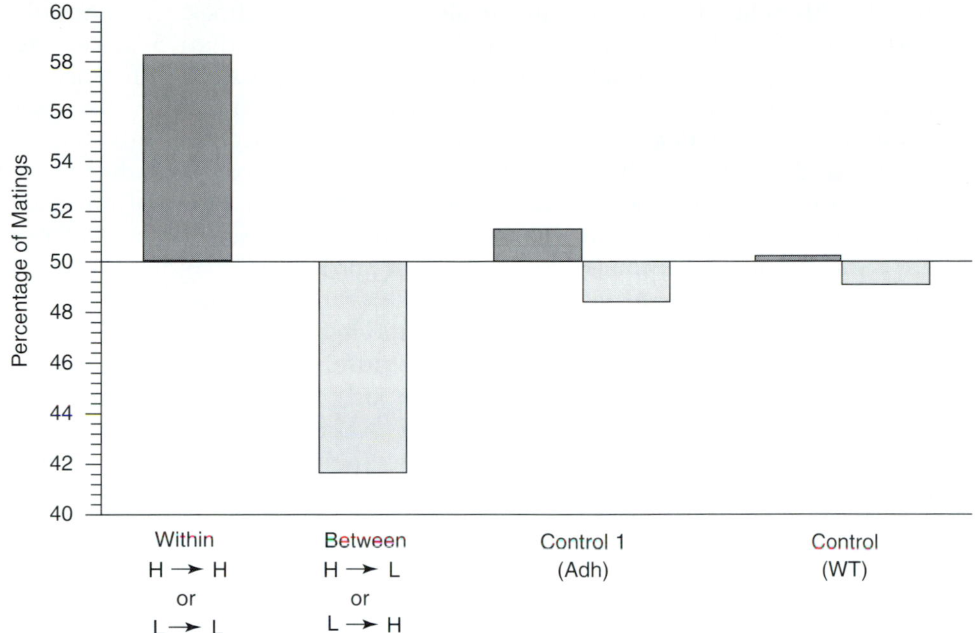

FIGURE 3.5. Partial reproductive isolation among lines of *Drosophila melanogaster* extensively selected for negative and positive geotaxis (Lofdahl et al. 1992). The 50% preference line represents random mating. Male-female crosses between fast and slow *Adh* strains (selected for reaction to alcohol dehydrogenase) and Champaign and Oregon-R strains (*WT,* or wild-type flies) yielded random mating. Male-female crosses between the H or L line for geotaxis exhibited a partial, but significant, tendency to mate preferentially with individuals from the same strain, as shown by the two bars on the left.

provide data interesting both in their own right, as well as a way of understanding the widespread consequences of artificial selection procedures. The effects of selection for H and L active avoidance performance in mice *(Mus musculus)* were previously considered in the context of recombinant inbred strains. In the active avoidance task, animals have to engage an explicit response (such as shuttle from one side of a box to the other) during the presentation of a warning stimulus (such as a light or a tone) to avoid a painful footshock. In the context of this task, H and L refer to strains of animals that can engage the response in a large or small proportion of the trials, respectively. Avoidance learning thus involves two separable processes: the acquisition of fear in response to the warning signal that predicts shock and the acquisition of a response that eliminates the fear state (see ***Chapter 13, section 3.d.,*** pp. 518–522).

Although artificial selection is nominally based on response acquisition, the correlation between the acquisition of fear and the acquisition of the response is such that the selective process could have effects different from those intended. Moreover, efficient active avoidance performance may depend on a number of additional processes that are not directly related to learning mechanisms and are referred to as *contextual variables* (e.g., sensory-perceptual, motivational, and motor variables). Examples of contextual variables in this case include pain threshold and general activity levels. Efficient active avoiders might be either animals that are particularly sensitive to shock-induced pain or simply animals that move around a lot. Which part of the avoidance learning process is actually being affected by artificial selection?

There is evidence that suggests that poor active avoidance acquisition does not necessarily imply poor aversive learning ability in general. For example, a mouse strain that performs well in active avoidance tasks, the so-called DBA strain, actually exhibits very poor passive avoidance learning (Iso & Shimai 1991). *Passive avoidance* tasks require that the animal does not enter a compartment where it has previously received shock. In fact, DBA mice left undisturbed in an open-field apparatus show relatively high levels of locomotor activity (Kvist 1984). It appears, therefore, that a selective regime that enhances active avoidance learning achieves its effects by affecting general levels of activity. Mice are efficient at learning active tasks because these situations require more behavior; for the same reason, however, the same animals are poor at acquiring passive avoidance responses that are largely dependent on the animal's ability to inhibit behavior.

In another long-term study, H and L strains of rats (*Rattus norvegicus*) were selected on the basis of their performance in an active avoidance task (Brush et al. 1979). The obtained strains are known as Syracuse high-avoidance line (SHA) and Syracuse low-avoidance line (SLA). The criteria for selection involved two different features. First, all rats had to exhibit a short-latency response to the warning signal (a tone+light compound stimulus) in a series of pretraining trials in which no shock was administered. Latencies of less than 5 s were required to control for possible differences in activity across strains, as those discussed previously for mice. Second, rats had to perform highly or poorly in the active avoidance task during a series of 60 trials. Out of 60 active avoidance trials, SHA rats (whether male or female) avoided the shock in about 70% of those trials, whereas SLA rats avoided in less than 5% of the trials. As usual, strain differences emerged fast: Clear behavioral effects were observed starting in F_{12}. Several subsequent studies were designed to further understand the consequences of the selective protocol.

For example, Brush et al. (1985) found that SHA and SLA rats were not different in terms of a number of contextual variables. No strain differences were found in the frequency of intertrial responses (which suggests similar background activity levels) in the latency to escape to the shock (which indicates similar thresholds for electric shock) and in the latency to respond to the warning signal (which simply reflects the first selection criterion). Sensitivity to shock was tested independently by applying current to the rat's tail immediately before presenting a loud noise that triggered a startle response. Tail shock inhibited the startle reflex but, of course, only when the shock was perceived by the animal. Using this procedure, absolute perceptual thresholds for shock were found to be 57.5 μA for the SHA animals, and 65.0 μA for the SLA animals; the difference was not significant. Animals from both lines did not differ either in terms of general locomotor activity, as measured in an open field apparatus. However, two interesting results were found in this series of experiments. The first result was a significant difference in an index of emotionality in the open field: SLA rats defecated more than SHA rats. The second result was a negative one: No differences were found in the acquisition of a series of food-reinforced visual discriminations. Together, these two results suggest that artificial selection for H and L active avoidance may have produced its result by affecting the animals' general emotionality (a contextual variable) and not the animals' general learning ability.

The higher emotionality levels of SLA rats suggests that they may actually be better than the SHA in aversive learning tasks other than active avoidance. Subsequent research found a series of interesting reversals of efficiency in learning. SLA rats are better than SHA rats in the following tasks: (1) shock-induced *conditioned suppression,* a situation analogous to passive avoidance training; (2) *flavor aversion,* in which a saccharin+almond compound solution is paired with lithium chloride, a toxin that produces strong gastrointestinal disease; and (3) *successive negative contrast,* in which a 4% sucrose solution is rejected after experience with a much sweeter, 32% solution (Brush et al. 1988; Flaherty & Rowan 1991; von Kluge & Brush 1992). In all three situations, learning leads to some sort of behavioral inhibition, either in terms of locomotion or bar pressing (as in conditioned suppression) or in terms of fluid intake (as in flavor aversions and negative contrast). Whether the aversiveness of the task comes from the presentation of some event such as shock or gastrointestinal disease or comes from the removal of an otherwise expected appetitive event, such as a sweet solution, does not seem to matter.

The research reviewed in this section, and other similar lines of research, provide evidence that performance in some learning tasks can be influenced by genes through a variety of mechanisms. Even when selective criteria are explicitly set to direct indices of learning, resulting transgenerational changes in behavior can be accounted for in terms of changes in contextual variables, such as general activity levels or emotionality, rather than through a direct influence of genetic information on learning processes.

3. Behavioral Mutants

The fact that some behaviors have a Mendelian basis suggests that it should be possible to find single-point mutations that affect behavior in a relatively specific way. Mutations can be "spontaneous," or they can be induced by applying chemicals, X rays, and other mutagens on germ cells. Mutant lines have been extensively studied in *Drosophila* fruitflies, mice, and other animal models for genetic research. Behavioral screening is then used to determine the presence of some behavioral abnormality that might be attributable to a mutation. Hundreds of animals have to be tested behaviorally before a putative mutant is detected. Then, these animals are bred according to a protocol designed to obtain a substantial number of animals that are homozygous for the mutation.

Crossing a putative mutant with a wild-type animal should provide heterozygous offspring for the mutation in F_1 according to a 1:4 ratio. Crossing these heterozygous mutants should produce homozygous animals in F_2 according, again, to a 1:4 ratio. Further inbreeding of the homozygous mutants leads to a population of behavioral mutants that can be studied intensely. Such a procedure has been used to uncover the genetics of circadian rhythms and learning.

3.a. Genetics of Circadian Rhythms. Many organisms, from bacteria to plants and animals, display temporal regularities in phase with annual, lunar, or daily cycles. *Circadian rhythms* are cycles with a period of about 24 hr that tune organisms to the obvious changes in the physical and biotic aspects of the environment that occur as the Earth rotates on its axis. The study of circadian rhythms has recently entered a phase of molecular analysis that has allowed the uncovering of fundamental mechanisms of behavior. In fact, some molecular aspects of rhythmicity are so general that they seem to be shared by organisms as distantly related as cyanobacteria, fungi, fruitflies, and mice (Hall 1995). So there are ultimate and proximate implications of this research.

Circadian mutants have been isolated in the fruitfly *Drosophila melanogaster,* in which at least two genes are involved in the regulation of rhythmic activity cycles (Dunlap 1996). These genes are known as *period* (*per*) and *timeless* (*tim*); up to seven alleles are known for *tim,* which provides an estimate of the amount of genetic variability underlying this trait. These genes regulate themselves according to a negative feedback loop of processes occurring within neurons in the fruitfly's central nervous system. The protein products of these genes are labeled PER and TIM. PER also affects processes outside the cells in which it is synthesized, eventually leading to regulation of behavioral levels of activity. An overview of this circadian mechanism is graphically represented in ***Figure 3.6.*** Transcription of genes *per* and *tim* peak in the early evening, but it is only in early night hours that enough accumulation of TIM is possible to boost levels of PER in the cytoplasm. Light is perceived by photoreceptors in the ommatidia (elements of the insect's compound eye), and through a series of influences it results in the rapid turnover of TIM. Under constant light, for example, TIM does not accumulate, and, as a result, PER cannot be translated to high levels; flies show no cyclic behavior under these conditions.

Similar mechanisms control circadian rhythms in mammals. The gene *clock,* for example, has been isolated in research with mice treated with the mutagen substance N-ethyl-N-nitrosourea (Vitaterna et al. 1994). Mice that are heterozygous for the *clock* mutation display a cycle with a period slightly above 24 hr, which results in a gradual shift in activity cycles when they are housed in complete darkness. Interestingly, homozygous clock mutants typically show nearly normal cycles until they are shifted to complete darkness. Under these conditions, mutant mice show an initial period of about 28 hr followed by a breakdown of circadian rhythms and a random distribution of activity bouts.

3.b. Learning Mutants. Similar behavioral screening of mutant animals has been used to uncover *learning mutants.* Such an approach, however, is complicated by the very nature of learning phenomena. First, the learning process involves several distinguishable phases, including acquisition, storage, retrieval, and behavioral expression of information acquired as a result of experience. While it might seem plausible to expect mutations to affect one of these phases while leaving the others relatively normal, such a result would be extremely surprising. At the molecular level, some of the subprocesses may be shared across phases of learning. For example, the same metabolic pathway may participate in both acquisition and retrieval processes; a mutation affecting a critical enzyme for such a pathway may disrupt both phases of learning.

Second, learning phenomena can be extremely varied. Fruitflies, for example, can be aversively conditioned to avoid an odor after odor-shock pairings, to extend their proboscis to a stimulus paired with a sucrose solution, or to change posture to avoid a source of heat, among other possibilities (Dudai 1988). Ideally, a learning mutation that affects acquisition, for in-

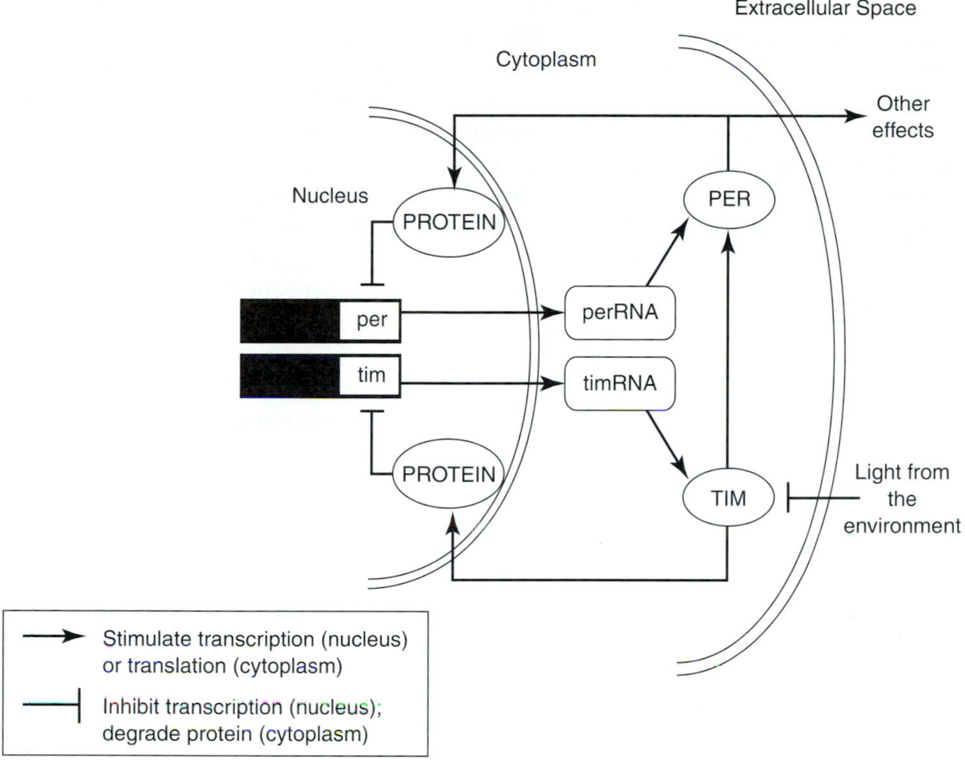

FIGURE 3.6. A representation of the cellular circadian clock proposed by Dunlap (1996). Two genes, *per* and *tim,* and their associated proteins, *PER* and *TIM,* are involved in this pacemaker. *TIM* regulates *PER* and is regulated by external light; they also turn off gene transcription. *PER* has other effects leading, eventually, to circadian behavioral rhythms. This system is considerably more complex in mammals. Several genes are expressed, including three different *per* genes, whose proteins give rise to several interacting feedback loops in neurons of the hypothalamic region known as the suprachiasmatic nucleus (Shearman et al. 2000).

stance, should disrupt acquisition in all of these tasks; such a pattern of results is not commonly observed.

Third, behavioral performance in a learning task can be affected by a variety of contextual factors in addition to those strictly related to learning. It is possible that a mutation affects the fruitfly's ability to sense the stimulus (sensory deficit) or to control its behavior (motor deficit), thus giving the impression that the mutation disrupts some aspect of the learning process. A similar problem was encountered previously in the genetic analysis of learning in mice and rats. This problem can be resolved by incorporating appropriate behavioral control conditions in which animals receive exposure to the critical components of the task but in a different order (Mihalek et al. 1997). Presumably, associative learning occurs as a result of experiencing a pairing of two events, not by experiencing each isolated event on its own (see ***Chapter 13, section 2.a.,*** pp. 495–497).

Research with *Drosophila* has yielded several lines, including *ruttabaga* (*rut*), *dunce* (*dnc*), and *amnesiac* (*amn*), that have been proposed to carry gene mutations affecting some, but not all, processes involved in learning (Dudai 1988). However, detailed behavioral analyses showed some of the problems outlined above. For example, *dnc* mutants exhibit normal appetitive and aversive conditioning, but forgetting is faster than normal. Although this might suggest the *dnc* mutation is involved in storage processes, *dnc* mutants also show acquisition deficits in a different olfactory conditioning task (Tully & Quinn 1985). To complicate matters further, *dnc* mutants exhibit normal forgetting in the heat-avoidance task (Mariath 1985).

Perhaps there is still something useful to be learned from these learning mutants. Some of the mutations observed in the fruitfly affect genes encoding for proteins involved in the *cyclic adenosine monophosphate* (*cAMP*) pathway. cAMP is referred to as a second messenger, because of its effects within the cell (neurotransmitters are the first messengers, and their influence is exerted between neurons). The cAMP pathway is activated in neurons undergoing rapid stimulation, such as occurs during behavioral training. One consequence of increased cytoplasmatic levels of cAMP is to induce cAMP-dependent enzymes to enter the cell nucleus, where they bind to proteins that induce the transcription of specific genes, as represented in ***Figure 3.7.*** It is thought that the resulting proteins may change synaptic efficacy on a long-term basis, perhaps by altering the density of neurotransmitter receptors in the postsynaptic membrane (Nestler & Greengard 1994). Interestingly enough, cAMP is also a critical component of learning in distantly related species, from the marine slug *Aplysia californica* to vertebrates (Cedar et al. 1972; Huang & Kandel 1994), which suggests that at least some cell-molecular components underlying learning processes are common across widely divergent species (see ***Chapter 13, section 4.c.,*** pp. 522–534).

Learning mutants have also been produced in the nematode *Caenorhabditis elegans,* another popular animal model in genetic research. Nematodes exposed to the mutagen substance ethylmethanesulfonate are behaviorally screened, and those showing learning deficits are selectively bred. The evolution of learning mutant lines is facilitated by the fact that *C. elegans* is predominantly a hermaphrodite animal. Wen et al. (1997) have identified two different mutations, *lrn-1* and *lrn-2,* that affect associative learning in a variety of tasks but that seem to leave sensory and motor functions intact. In a typical conditioning task, food-deprived nematodes are placed in a plate in which a salt-based solution (the signal) and a layer of bacteria (the reinforcer) have been evenly spread (an S+ trial). In other trials, the same nematodes are placed in a plate containing a chloride solution but no food (S– trials). Nematodes feed on the bacteria in the presence of the salty stimulus but not in the presence of the chloride solution. In the critical test session, the animals are transferred to the center of a new plate containing a gradient with a high concentration of the salt on one end and of the chloride on the other end. Learning is demonstrated if the animals move toward the S+ and away from the S– in the test trial. Wild-type nematodes show a significant 75% preference for the S+ end of the test tube, whether after individual or after group training; by contrast, *lrn-1* and *lrn-2* mutants show 48% and 47% preference, respectively (i.e., essentially a random distrib-

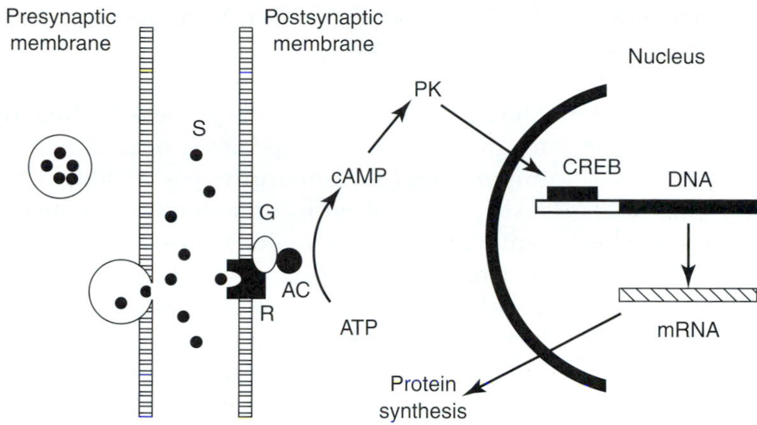

FIGURE 3.7. Transcriptional function of cAMP. The neurotransmitter serotonin (*S*), released by the presynaptic neuron, activates a receptor (*R*) complex involving a *G* protein and adenyl cyclase (*AC*). AC is responsible for converting ATP into cAMP, which activates levels of protein kinase (*PK*) enzymes. These enzymes can enter the cell nucleus where they attach themselves to a so-called cAMP-response-element-binding protein (or *CREB*). CREB binds to the promoter of specific genes, affecting (i.e., increasing or decreasing) gene transcription. The proteins produced can then change structural and, therefore, functional properties of the postsynaptic neuron, which, as a result, could become more responsive to serotonin. (Modified from Nestler & Greengard 1994.)

ution in the test plate). Backcrosses of these learning mutant animals with wild-type nematodes produced F_2 nonlearners with a proportion of 1:4, suggesting that the learning deficit results from a single gene that behaves as a recessive Mendelian trait.

3.c. Selective Gene Knockout. It is possible to alter the genome of an animal by manipulating individual genes using a complex sequence of treatments. *Embryonic stem cells* (*ES*) are taken from the blastocyst of a developing mouse, during the morula stage in early development (see ***Chapter 10, section 1.a.,*** pp. 362–365). These cells would normally develop into an adult animal, but they can be cultured in a medium that prevents their differentiation but not their growth and multiplication. Arrested ES cells can then be subjected to one of a variety of procedures for inserting segments of DNA in specific locations. The resulting ES cells can be tested to determine whether they carry the modified DNA sequence. For example, if the inserted gene confers resistance to a specific antibiotic, cells with this new gene will grow in a medium containing the antibiotic. Once it has been determined that the cells carry the appropriate gene, the cells are injected into a recipient blastocyst, and this blastocyst is implanted into a recipient female. The resulting mouse is referred to as a *chimeric* animal because it is created with DNA fragments from more than two different organisms. This procedure generally results in the disruption of a particular gene in the chimeric animal. In some cases, these chimeric animals can be detected visually by their coat pattern. *Gene knockout* mice lines can then be produced according to standard breeding protocols.

Knockout techniques have been used to produce strains of mice that lack particular neurotransmitter receptor proteins. The resulting animals are therefore deficient in their ability to respond to a very specific neurotransmitter. For example, disrupting the gene that codes for one of *serotonin*'s receptor types, called 5-HT_{1B}, produces serotonin-receptor–deficient mice that exhibit a variety of behavioral effects. These mice are generally more aggressive, develop addiction for cocaine faster, and respond faster in learning tasks than wild-type mice (Brunner & Hen 1997). These results are consistent with more conventional studies suggesting that serotonin is implicated in regulating general levels of activation or impulsivity. A similar case could be made for another neurotransmitter, *dopamine,* which also has several receptor types in the nervous system of mammals. A knockout strain deficient in one of these receptors, called D_3, is notorious for a tendency to enter open spaces (Steiner et al. 1998). Normal mice's avoidance of open spaces is part of their antipredator behavior repertoire. Serotonin-receptor– and dopamine-receptor–deficient mice are thus more impulsive than their wild-type conspecifics.

Notice, however, that in these cases the genetic change is introduced very early in development, thus allowing for compensatory reactions to take place. When the goal is to understand gene-behavior relationships, it would be desirable to be able to switch genes on and off in specific tissues (e.g., in a specific brain area, at a specific moment). Inducible knockouts would minimize compensatory processes.

4. Another Look at Natural Selection

The role of behavior in the process leading to the evolution of new species is of paramount importance for comparative psychology. The research reviewed in this chapter is consistent with Darwin's analogy between artificial and natural selection, and suggests that it should be possible to detect the action of selective pressures on behavioral and morphological changes in natural populations. Ample evidence now exists of relatively rapid changes (in the order of years) in phenotype that appear to result from natural selection. The speed of these changes is actually surprisingly high; it had been thought until recently that a large number of generations were necessary to change a character such as body size, but a variety of field observations and experiments suggest otherwise.

I have already mentioned a long-term study of the Galapagos finches in ***Chapter 2, section 1.d.*** (pp. 34–36). That study showed that a population of *Geospiza fortis* living in the small island of Daphne experienced rapid change in the average depth of the beak and in body size as a result of unusually dry weather during 1977 and 1978 (Grant 1983). Such changes were correlated with differential survival of relatively larger animals, which was most likely the result of limited availability of small seeds. Considerable strength must be exercised to peel the hard coats from large seeds, for which task larger beaks might be functionally advantageous. It was not clear, however, which character (i.e., body size or beak width) was being selected or whether one of them was simply changing by correlation. Interestingly, when rainfall—and thus the availability of small seeds—returned to normal levels, there was a regression toward the original population values in both characters that was equally fast (Gibbs & Grant 1987).

Similar changes have been documented in two other vertebrates using a rather different strategy: transfer of individual animals to a new area. In one study carried out at Trinidad Island in the Caribbean, populations of guppies (*Poecilia reticulata*) were transferred to river sections above waterfalls where these fish did not occur and where they encountered relatively more relaxed predatory pressures (Reznick et al. 1997). Guppies living downstream in the same currents were naturally exposed to a variety of predatory species, including several cichlid fish that prey preferentially on large guppies. By contrast, the guppies introduced into upstream currents were exposed to a single predator, the killifish *Rivulus hartii*, an omnivore that may occasionally attack guppies. Leaving the guppies undisturbed for several years, researchers then returned periodically to measure body size and age of the descendant guppies. These measurements were compared with populations left undisturbed in the downstream, high-predation areas. Even after 4 years (approximately 7 generations), male guppies exposed to the upstream, low-predation environment were exhibiting significant increases in size and age. Female size and age had increased significantly by the second measurement, after 7.5 years and approximately 13 generations. After 11 years (or about 18 generations), measures of body size and age were significantly larger in the low-predation areas than in the control areas. There were additional changes in these transplanted guppies. The onset of reproduction was delayed and the number of fries per litter decreased relative to downstream populations. These phenotypic changes are interesting because they involve a life-history pattern, not just an isolated trait.

A similar study involved colonization of small islands of the Bahamas by the lizard *Anolis sagrei* (Losos et al. 1997). The animals were originally introduced in 1977, and a variety of morphological measurements of their descendants were taken in 1991. There were consistent differences in vegetation between the island where these lizards are naturally found (in this study, all lizards were originally from Staniel Cay Island) and the 14 small islands in which they were introduced. After 14 years, a comparison of hindlimb length of lizards from several islands with the average diameter of perching branches in each of the islands yielded a positive correlation. The various lizard populations had then responded to variation in vegetation by adjusting body dimensions.

Two cautionary notes are in order when interpreting the results of studies such as those described in this section. The first is that the observed changes in morphology in finches, guppies, and lizards cannot be unambiguously interpreted as resulting from natural selection. Not only did seed size, predatory pressures, or vegetation differ across years or locations, but probably many other correlated factors might have accounted for the observed changes in phenotype. In the case of the guppies, for example, the upstream environment might have differed in terms of food availability, in addition to predatory pressures. It may be that the changes observed really involved purely phenotypic changes. The notion of *phenotypic plasticity* has been invoked to explain changes in characters that result from the influence of environmental factors on the development of the animals. A change in the type of food items or in the amount of food available may modify body size without any changes in allele frequency in the population. A second critical point is that whereas phenotypic changes were observed in all of these instances, it is important to remember that there was no evidence of speciation. That is, the transplanted guppies and lizards did not evolve into new species. Obviously, this might simply depend on the relatively short number of generations involved in these studies.

5. Rates of Evolution

Although speciation is an elusive phenomenon for direct observation, morphological and behavioral change can be produced relatively easily, whether in natural populations or in the laboratory. Speciation events can be measured in the fossil record in cases in which it is particularly well preserved. These observations permit an assessment of the rate of phenotypic change. Haldane (1949) suggested a measure of evolutionary rate for cases in which a particular character can be estimated in ancestor-descendant populations over a known period of time. *Evolutionary rate, r,* is then defined according to a simple formula:

$$r = \frac{[ln(X_2) - ln(X_1)]}{t_2 - t_1},$$

in which X_1 is the character in its initial state at t_1 and X_2 the same character in its final state at t_2. The natural log is used because it is proportional change, rather than absolute change, that matters. Haldane named the unit of change the darwin (d).

The rates of change in body size in the guppy populations described previously varied between 8,000 and 16,400 d after 11 years of reproductive isolation in the low-predatory environments. Similarly, the rate of evolution for hindlimb length in the *Anolis* lizards varied between 89 and 1,195 d. A comparison of rates obtained in analogous colonization studies shows a geometric mean of 370 d, far lower than the mean obtained in laboratory experiments based on artificial selection procedures. At average rates of 58,700 d, artificial selection is, in fact, extremely powerful in comparison. Interestingly, the rates are extremely low for fossil characters: Geometric means vary between 0.07 and 0.73 d (Gingerich 1983). These vast differences in evolutionary rate may imply that real evolutionary changes (as recorded in fossils) depend on processes other than those engaged in laboratory experiments or colonization studies. Alternatively, it might be that short-term studies yield higher rate values because they are less likely to be sensitive to bidirectional variations in traits produced by unstable environments. A good example of this is provided by the finches. As mentioned previously, body size increased during a year of drought, but it decreased again after a year of normal rainfall. A measure of change over the entire period would be insensitive to local changes because increases and decreases would tend to cancel each other.

Perhaps the important message of laboratory and colonization studies is that populations can respond to sustained selective pressures in a relatively short number of generations. The implication is that rapid change in the fossil record need not reflect the operation of processes different from those invoked to understand within-species phenotypic change.

6. Key Terms

active avoidance learning 62
artificial selection 63
cAMP (cyclic adenosine monophosphate) 76

chimeric animal 77
circadian rhythms 73
coadaptation 68
conditioned suppression 73
contextual variables 72
directional dominance 66
dopamine 78
embryonic stem cells (ES) 77
emotionality 68
evolutionary rate 80
flavor aversion 73
gain (G) 65
gene knockout 78
genetic homeostasis 68
geotaxis 68
heritability (h^2) 65
heterosis (or hybrid vigor) 67
inbreeding depression 67
learning mutants 74
Mendelian inheritance 61
natural selection 63
passive avoidance learning 72
phenotypic plasticity 79
realized heritability 66
recombinant inbred strains 62
reproductive isolation 69
selection differential (S) 65
serotonin 78
speciation 69
successive negative contrast 73

7. REFERENCES

Brunner, D., & Hen, R. (1997). Insights into the neurobiology of impulsive behavior from serotonin receptor knockout mice. *Annals of the New York Academy of Sciences,* **836,** 81–105.

Brush, F. R., Baron, S., Froehlich, J. C., Ison, J. R., Pellegrino, L. J., Phillips, D. S., Sakellaris, P. C., & Williams, V. N. (1985). Genetic differences in avoidance learning by *Rattus norvegicus:* Escape/avoidance responding, sensitivity to electric shock, discrimination learning, and open-field behavior. *Journal of Comparative Psychology,* **99,** 60–73.

Brush, F. R., Del Paine, S. N., Pellegrino, L. J., Rykaszewski, I. M., Dess, N. K., & Collins, P. Y. (1988). CER suppression, passive avoidance learning, and stress-induced suppression of drinking in the Syracuse high- and low-avoidance strains of rats (*Rattus norvegicus*). *Journal of Comparative Psychology,* **102,** 337–349.

Brush, F. R., Froehlich, J. C., & Sakellaris, P. C. (1979). Genetic selection for avoidance behavior in the rat. *Behavior Genetics,* **9,** 309–316.

Cedar, H., Kandel, E. R., & Schwartz, J. H. (1972). Cyclic adenosine monophosphate in the nervous system of *Aplysia californica.* I. Increased synthesis in response to synaptic stimulation. *Journal of General Physiology,* **60,** 558–569.

Darwin, C. (1859/1993). *The origin of species.* New York: Random House.

Dobzhansky, T. (1970). *Genetics of the evolutionary process.* New York: Columbia University Press.

Dudai, Y. (1988). Neurogenetic dissection of learning and short-term memory in *Drosophila. Annual Review of Neuroscience,* **11,** 537–563.

Dunlap, J. C. (1996). Genetic and molecular analysis of circadian rhythms. *Annual Review of Genetics,* **30,** 579–601.

Flaherty, C. F., & Rowan, G. A. (1989). Rats selected to differ in avoidance performance also differ in response to novelty stress, in glycemic conditioning, and in reward contrast. *Behavioral & Neural Biology,* **51,** 145–164.

Gibbs, H. L., & Grant, P. R. (1987). Oscillating selection on Darwin's finches. *Nature,* **327,** 511–513.

Gingerich, P. D. (1983). Rates of evolution: Effects of time and temporal scaling. *Science,* **222,** 159–161.

Haldane, J. B. S. (1949). Suggestions as to quantitative measurements of rates of evolution. *Evolution,* **3,** 51–56.

Hall, J. C. (1995). Tripping along the trail to the molecular mechanisms of biological clocks. *Trends in Neuroscience,* **18,** 230–240.

Hewitt, J. K., Fulker, D. W., & Hewitt, C. A. (1983). Genetic architecture of olfactory discriminative avoidance conditioning in *Drosophila melanogaster. Journal of Comparative Psychology,* **97,** 52–58.

Huang, Y.-Y., & Kandel, E. R. (1994). Recruitment of long-lasting and protein kinase A-dependent long-term potentiation in the CA1 region of hippocampus requires repeated tetanization. *Learning & Memory,* **1,** 74–82.

Iso, H., & Shimai, S. (1991). Running-wheel avoidance learning in mice (*Mus musculus*): Evidence of contingency learning and differences among inbred strains. *Journal of Comparative Psychology,* **105,** 190–202.

Kvist, B. (1984). Strain differences in open field activity after learning in mice. *Scandinavian Journal of Psychology,* **25,** 370–380.

Lofdahl, K. L., Hu, D., Ehrman, L., Hirsch, J., & Skoog, L. (1992). Incipient reproductive isolation and evolution in laboratory *Drosophila melanogaster* selected for geotaxis. *Animal Behaviour,* **44,** 783–786.

Losos, J. B., Warheit, K. I., & Schoener, T. W. (1997). Adaptive differentiation following experimental island colonization in *Anolis* lizards. *Nature,* **387,** 70–73.

Mariath, H. A. (1985). Operant conditioning in *Drosophila melanogaster* wild-type and learning mutants with defects in the cyclic AMP metabolism. *Journal of Insect Physiology,* **31,** 779–787.

Mihalek, R. M., Jones, C. J., & Tully, T. (1997). The *Drosophila* mutation *turnip* has pleiotropic behavioral effects and does not specifically affect learning. *Learning & Memory,* **3,** 425–444.

Nestler, E. J., & Greengard, P. (1994). Protein phosphorylation and the regulation of neuronal function. In G. J. Siegel, B. W. Agranoff, R. W. Albers, & P. B. Molinoff (Eds.), *Basic neurochemistry* 5th ed., pp. 449–474). New York: Raven Press.

Oliverio, A., Eleftheriou, B. E., & Bailey, D. W. (1973). A gene influencing active avoidance performance in mice. *Physiology & Behavior,* **11,** 497–501.

Reznick, D. N., Shaw, F. H., Rodd, F. H., & Shaw, R. G. (1997). Evaluation of the rate of evolution in natural populations of guppies (*Poecilia reticulata*). *Science,* **275,** 1934–1937.

Ricker, J. P., & Hirsch, J. (1985). Evolution of an instinct under long-term divergent selection for geotaxis in domesticated populations of *Drosophila melanogaster. Journal of Comparative Psychology,* **99,** 380–390.

Ricker, J. P., & Hirsch, J. (1988). Reversal of genetic homeostasis in laboratory populations of *Drosophila melanogaster* under long-term selection for geotaxis and estimates of gene correlates: Evolution of behavior-genetic systems. *Journal of Comparative Psychology,* **102,** 203–214.

Rothenbuhler, W. C. (1964). Behavior genetics of nest cleaning in honeybees. IV. Responses of F_1 and backcross generations to disease-killed brood. *American Zoologist,* **4,** 111–123.

Roubertoux, P. L. (1992). Courtship behavior in the male guppy (*Poecilia reticulata*): A genetic analysis. *International Journal of Comparative Psychology,* **5,** 145–163.

Searle, L. V. (1949). The organization of hereditary maze-brightness and maze-dullness. *Genetic Psychology Monographs,* **39,** 279–325.

Shearman, L. P., Sriram, S., Weaver, D. R., Maywood, E. S., Chaves, I., Zheng, B., Kume, K., Lee, C. C., van der Horst, G. T. J., Hastings, M. H., & Reppert, S. M. (2000). Interacting molecular loops in the mammalian circadian clock. *Science,* **288,** 1013–1019.

Steiner, H., Fuchs, S., & Accili, D. (1997). D3 dopamine receptor-deficient mouse: Evidence for reduced anxiety. *Physiology & Behavior,* **63,** 137–141.

Tryon, R. C. (1934). Individual differences. In F. A. Moss (Ed.), *Comparative psychology* (pp. 409–445). Englewood Cliffs, NJ: Prentice-Hall.

Tully, T., & Quinn, W. G. (1985). Classical conditioning and retention in normal and mutant *Drosophila melanogaster. Journal of Comparative Physiology,* **157,** 263–277.

Vitaterna, M. H., King, D. P., Chang, A.-M., Kornhauser, J. M., Lowrey, P. L., McDonald, J. D., Dover, W. F., Pinto, L. H., Turek, F. W., & Takahashi, J. S. (1994). Mutagenesis and mapping of a mouse gene, *Clock,* essential for circadian behavior. *Science,* **264,** 719–725.

von Kluge, S., & Brush, F. R. (1992). Conditioned taste and taste-potentiated odor aversions in the Syracuse high- and low-avoidance (SHA/Bru and SLA/Bru) strains of rats (*Rattus norvegicus*). *Journal of Comparative Psychology,* **106,** 248–253.

Wen, J. Y. M., Kumar, N., Morrison, G., Rambaldini, G., Runciman, S., Rousseau, J., & van der Kooy, D. (1997). Mutations that prevent associative learning in *C. elegans. Behavioral Neuroscience,* **111,** 354–268.

Zawistowski, S., & Hirsch, J. (1984). Conditioned discrimination in the blowfly, *Phormia regina*: Controls and bidirectional selection. *Animal Learning & Behavior,* **12,** 402–408.

CHAPTER 4

Predators and Preys

MAJOR GENERALIZATIONS OF CHAPTER 4

- *All animals obtain the resources they need to support all vital functions by feeding on other living organisms.*
- *Six basic types of interactions describe the feeding behavior of animals: competitive exclusion, cooperation, mutualism, parasitism, predator-prey interaction, and altruism.*
- *Natural selection, coevolution, kin selection, and reciprocity are the major principles that account for the evolution of feeding behavior.*

Living organisms perform a variety of functions that must be sustained by an influx of substances. In addition, multicellularity imposes further requirements of growth to achieve cell differentiation and normal adult size. Development, growth, and maintenance are based on the availability of nutrients that must be collected, pursued, manipulated, and processed so that the components can be used. Because animals must obtain the vast majority of nutrients from other living organisms, the study of feeding behavior will be approached from the perspective of both the predator and the prey.

Evolution has shaped many aspects of the phenotype according to selective pressures related to the efficient use of feeding resources and avoidance of predators. This chapter reviews the area of feeding behavior predominantly from the point of view of adaptive significance (see ***Chapter 1, section 6,*** pp. 20–22), emphasizing aspects of the natural foraging behavior of animals. There will be, however, some opportunities to highlight underlying mechanisms of behavior as the dynamics of predatory and antipredatory behaviors are considered. Comparative psychologists have also made extensive use of feeding behavior in their research on such topics as learning, motivation, and cognition, but these issues will be discussed in ***Parts III*** and ***IV*** in greater detail.

1. COMPETITION

Divergent evolution is driven to a large extent by specialization in the exploitation of resources. For example, if two animals compete over a limited amount of one type of food that can sustain only one of them, there are two possible outcomes. Either one of them dies, or else it finds another type of food that can replace the first one. This is known as the principle of *competitive exclusion.* Darwin (1859) pointed out that competition should be particularly intense within a species because the "conflict" remains unresolved. However, if one looks at how food resources are exploited by a set of highly related species coexisting in a particular habitat (i.e., a *sympatric distribution*), it may be possible to detect evidence of a successful resolution of such an evolutionary conflict. A few examples will suffice to illustrate this point.

Diamond (1973) studied sympatric pigeons of the genera *Ducula* and *Ptilinopus,* all living in the rain forest of New Guinea and feeding on various types of fruit. The body size of these species varies between 50 g for the smallest to up to 800 g for the largest, and the size of the fruits they prey upon also varies concomitantly. Up to four species within a size category may feed on a given type of fruit. However, trees producing large fruits attract large pigeons preferentially, and, within a single tree, smaller pigeons tend to forage in the periphery of the tree where the fruits are smaller. Therefore, even if different species of pigeons are collecting food from the same tree, they can successfully reduce competition by specializing in a particular fruit size.

One way to refer to such degree of specialization in resource exploitation is to think of each species as finding its own *ecological niche.* Although the word "niche" suggests a spatial dimension, there are more subtle ways of partitioning resources, as illustrated by the pigeons foraging on different parts of the same tree. An ecological niche is in fact defined by all the factors necessary to sustain the life of a particular population of animals. These include physical factors (e.g., temperature, pH, etc.), biological factors (e.g., food sources), and behavioral factors (e.g., patterns of daily activity, predatory behavior, etc.). Different species can coexist by feeding on different food sources: Some African ungulates, such as antelopes, feed on lower tree branches, while giraffes feed on higher ones. Obviously, antelopes and giraffes may not be currently in competition, but rather represent the end points of a divergent event driven by competitive exclusion. Presumably, natural selection favored the evolution of anatomical specializations, including the giraffe's long neck, that would optimize resource exploitation. Such *character displacement* is therefore a consequence of prior competition.

An interesting example of character displacement is observed in the Galapagos finch *Geospiza fortis* (Schluter et al. 1985). The average beak depth of birds living in small islands with relatively little competition from other finches (e.g., Daphne Island) is approximately 10 mm. However, in islands such as Charles and Chatham, the average beak depth reaches 13 mm. This increase in beak depth can be accounted for by the presence in these islands of a second species, *G. fuliginosa,* of smaller body size and average beak depth of about 9 mm. Thus, substantial competition for seeds with a smaller species may have favored the displacement of beak depth in *G. fortis* away from values that are typical of habitats where competition is reduced.

It is possible that present-day competition at Charles and Chatham Islands is keeping average beak depth in check, but the appropriate experiment (i.e., removal of *G. fuliginosa* from the island) can obviously not be done. In other cases, however, precisely such a field experiment can be carried out to determine whether interspecies competition is occurring in the present. For example, Connell (1961) reported relevant data from two species of barnacles, small crustaceans that attach themselves to rocks at the sea edge. One of the species (*Chthamalus stellatus*) lives normally in the upper rocks where sea water reaches only at high tide, whereas the other (*Semibalanus balanoides*) lives in lower parts where moisture and food are more constant. Although it might appear that these barnacles have partitioned the environment to avoid competition, removal of the species living in the lower rocks results in the rapid spread of the species normally present only in the upper parts. Spatial segregation of these species is therefore actively maintained by interspecies competition.

2. Optimal Foraging Theory

2.a. Foraging and Reproductive Success. In addition to interspecies competition and predatory pressures, animals looking for food face a variety of other problems. They need to sample information about prey distribution in the environment, develop appropriate search patterns, select the right food items, and procure and handle the prey. Decisions have to be made about where in the environment to search and when to leave a patch that is no longer yielding as much food as before. All these problems arise in part because resources vary and are generally limited, as is the time available to perform these activities. Feeding for too long may not leave enough time for other important behaviors, such as caring for the body, building a nest, guarding a territory, or resting. Ultimately, feeding behavior is constrained by reproductive success. Even the most efficient predator will not make a mark, in evolutionary terms, if it is sterile. To be reproductively successful, animals must be capable of maintaining good health and storing sufficient energy to perform reproductive activities, which, in some species, are extremely physically demanding. Foraging decision rules must, therefore, be under the influence of natural selection, which should positively select traits that allow individuals to achieve (by whichever mechanisms) the most efficient of the available solutions. Such a solution need not be precisely the optimal one, as determined by some mathematical rule, but just the most efficient among the alternative solutions against which it is in competition.

An important assumption made by all *optimal foraging models* is that these alternative foraging solutions correlate with variation in reproductive success such that the most efficient solution will be positively selected. As in the case of any other functional problem, foraging behavior can be interpreted in economic terms as a trade-off between cost and benefit. Animals engaged in feeding must invest energy and time in all the activities that are necessary to procure food; this is the cost term of the equation. In turn, they gain the energy and nutrients they need to continue foraging and to perform other activities. Notice that this *cost-benefit analysis* ultimately relates to reproductive success: Costs and benefits are eventually translated into offspring lost or gained (the so-called currency of natural selection) as a result of foraging decisions.

Foraging models assume that some aspect of the foraging strategy is being optimized (under certain constraints), and the task is to identify that factor (as well as the constraints). Optimization may involve maximizing energy intake, maximizing some critical nutrient, minimizing energy expenditure, or some complex interaction of these. Although the assumption that foraging strategies are positively correlated with reproductive success is rarely tested empirically, research can help identify which aspect of a particular strategy is actually being optimized.

Field observations suggest that indeed not all types of diets are equally correlated with reproductive success. In one study involving herring gulls (*Larus argentatus*) on Great Island, Newfoundland, Pierotti and Annett (1987) found that whereas feeding preferences were variable in the population as a whole, about 80% of individual gulls exhibited a specialized diet. The three major items consumed by these specialists were mussels, petrels, and human garbage consisting of remains of chicken, beef, pork, and fish. These food items were analyzed for content of calories, fat, and proteins, and in all cases mussels turned out to be the poorest source. However, most of the specialized gulls (60%) actually fed on mussels, in contrast to those that fed on garbage (25%) and on petrels (14%). Measurement of various indices of reproductive success indicated, surprisingly, that mussel specialists were ahead of the rest. For example, mussel-specialist gulls laid eggs earlier in the spring, had a larger clutch size (three eggs, as opposed to two eggs for petrel- and garbage-specialists), laid heavier eggs, had greater hatching success (i.e., they laid fewer infertile eggs), produced heavier chicks at hatching, and had a greater proportion of their offspring survive to become independent from their parents. The fact that the majority of the gulls specialized in a diet based on mussels could be explained, in an ultimate sense, by the greater relative reproductive success of these animals in the population.

An interesting aspect of the data reported by Pierotti and Annett (1987) is the dependence of the diet on the reproductive condition of the breeding pair. All specialist birds incubating eggs exhibited a drastic switch in diet to capelin fish during the first week after hatching, and then a second drastic switch to squid during the third post-hatching week when the chicks are usually fledging. Such a change in diet was not caused by a shift in prey availability, but rather by demands of parental care. A diet rich in fish after hatching is correlated with greater survival rates, whereas the switch to squid appears to be related mainly to the ability of chicks to handle larger food pieces after 3 weeks of age. A capelin fish weighs 10 to 20 g, whereas a typical squid weighs 100 to 200 g. Small chicks given large pieces of food that cannot be swallowed rapidly are at high risk both because they are not receiving sufficient nourishment and because they can be injured by adult gulls attracted to the nest by the leftovers.

One difference between foraging for mussels or garbage, as gulls do before they need to provide for their offspring, and foraging for small fish and squid, as they do after their offspring hatch, lies in the predictability of these items. Mussels and garbage are both highly predictable items since they can be obtained in relatively stable locations, whereas fish and squid are less predictable sources of food. The presence of chicks causes the parents to switch from a risk-averse mode (i.e., preference for predictable food) to a risk-prone mode (Caraco 1981).

The foraging behavior of herring gulls is then affected by a variety of factors, not all necessarily obvious a priori. The complexity of foraging is reduced in optimal foraging models by making simplistic assumptions about the foraging behavior of animals. Important factors can thus be identified and subsequently manipulated in field or laboratory experiments to test specific models (Shettleworth 1989).

2.b. The Marginal Value Theorem. A highly influential model of foraging proposed by Charnov (1976) is based on a set of simple assumptions and is referred to as the *marginal value theorem* (*MVT*). Recall that these models are not concerned with "how" the animal achieves the solution (a proximate, mechanistic issue) but rather with dictating how the animal "should" behave so that the outcome is optimal (an ultimate, functional issue). Nonetheless, it will become apparent that it is impossible to ignore proximate processes as assumptions about how animals make decisions are specified. MVT assumes that animals have a perfect knowledge of the distribution of food in their environment that allows them to estimate the average food rate. The model further assumes that food is patchily distributed so that animals collect items in discrete areas but need to travel from one area to another as their predatory behavior depletes the patch. Two main problems are suggested by MVT for analysis. First, when should animals leave the current patch and search for another one? Second, how should travel time between patches affect the decision to leave the patch? For each case, and given certain properties of the environment, there is a solution that will maximize the rate of food intake for a given foraging period.

2.c. Time Allocation. The optimal solution to the problem of deciding when to leave the current patch seems obvious: The animal should leave when the rate of food intake in the patch decreases below the rate in the environment as a whole. For the purpose of testing this hypothesis, however, it is necessary to find an index of the animal's assessment of food rate while feeding in a particular patch. One possibility is that animals use the time since the last capture to estimate the quality of the patch. When this time exceeds a particular value, called the giving-up time (GUT), the patch should be deemed poor and the animal should leave and search for food elsewhere. MVT predicts that for any given habitat, the value of GUT should be constant across patches, although the GUT value should shorten when

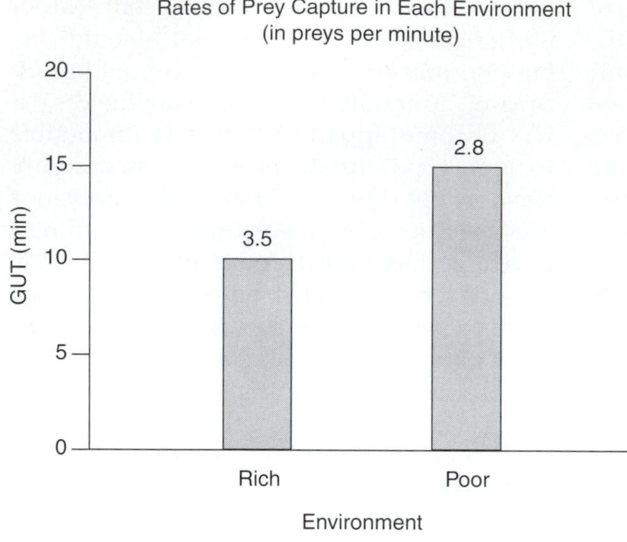

FIGURE 4.1. Chickadees abandon a rich patch (measured as giving-up time, GUT) significantly sooner than a poor patch. Rich and poor patches are defined in terms of the average rate of prey capture (Krebs et al. 1974).

the habitat becomes richer and lengthen when it becomes poorer. This hypothesis was tested in black-capped chickadees (*Parus atricapillus*) foraging for meal worms in a test aviary (Krebs et al. 1974). Chickadees encountered artificial trees in which patches of four artificial cones were filled each with either one mealworm (poor patch) or three mealworms (rich patch). As shown in ***Figure 4.1,*** birds gave up faster in the rich patch than in the poor patch. The MVT also predicts that when poor and rich patches are equally distributed in the environment, the GUT should be constant for all patches, as was also shown to be the case.

Despite the apparent success of this particular model, it seems clear that not all food resources deplete in the same fashion and that not any type of foraging strategy would result in the same rate of depletion. There are conditions of foraging (both because of the distribution of prey and because of the predator's behavior) in which other rules will be more efficient than one based on the GUT. For example, predators could search using a random rule according to which any location has an equal probability of being visited, whether or not the animal has already been there; or they could search systematically by avoiding previously visited locations within a patch. Rules alternative to the GUT could involve assessing the average time between successive rewards or the total time allocated to a particular patch. Although the mathematical computations to arrive at an optimal solution may be complex, animals are not required to be performing exactly the same computation. For example, as noted previously, the richness of a patch can be determined by the GUT, a rather simple variable to measure, compared to the amount of information that would be required for an exact assessment of patch quality. Evolution is expected to favor such so-called *rules of thumb* as shortcuts to optimal solutions.

2.d. Travel Time. The second problem derived from the MVT is that of travel time between patches. Decisions about leaving a patch should depend not only on its yield but also on how difficult it is to get there, either in terms of time or energy. If patches within a habitat are far apart from each other, animals should be expected to stay longer in any given patch than if patches are close together. This prediction, like many others derived from optimal foraging models, has been tested using the operant learning techniques developed by comparative psychologists interested in the study of learning (see ***Chapter 13, section 3,*** pp. 510–522). In one experiment (Redhead & Tyler 1988), rats (*Rattus norvegicus*) were trained to obtain food by pressing two levers. Each lever was considered a patch yielding either a high or a low reward rate (rich and poor patches, respectively). Patch depletion was simulated by using a progressive time schedule, according to which the animal waits a longer period of time from one reward to the next. In the rich patch, the animal waited 0, 1, 2, 4, 8, 12, 22, 40, and 64 seconds to collect successive rewards, whereas in the poor patch the progressive times were 2, 6, 10, 18, 40, 64, and 122 seconds. When the patch was exhausted, the rat had to wait for the other patch to become available. This waiting time (simulating traveling between patches) could be either 5 or 25 seconds long. Whether the environment consisted purely of rich patches or poor patches, rats remained significantly more time pressing the lever for food when the travel time was longer than when it was shorter. Rats were also found to use the interreinforcement interval rather than the GUT to decide when to shift patches. Rats switched patches when the time between successive rewards approximately equated travel time plus time to the first reward in the alternative patch.

Rats could adjust rapidly when the transition was from a rich to a poor environment, or vice versa. However, adjustment was far more gradual when animals had been exposed to variable environments—that is, sessions containing a mixture of rich and poor patches. Perhaps under variable circumstances it takes longer to collect relevant information about the distribution of food in the environment.

2.e. Sampling. Environments are typically unstable in terms of food availability. Appropriate foraging decisions must require some amount of information, particularly when conditions change (e.g., at the beginning of the spring or after a flood) or when the predator enters a new habitat. Under such conditions, the behavior of an animal may be suboptimal in the short term, although the information gathered through *sampling* may be critical for the development of an optimal strategy. The critical problem is thus to determine how to balance sampling and exploitation optimally.

An animal facing two alternative patches of different quality should collect information about each patch and then allocate all its behavior to the richer patch. The amount of sampling needed would therefore depend on the discrepancy in prey rate across patches. The greater the difference, the easier it would be for the animal to determine which patch is the richer, and the faster should the animal switch from sampling to exploiting. Krebs et al. (1978) tested this idea in an experiment with great tits (*Parus major*) by exposing the birds to two patches yielding mealworms with varying probabilities across sessions. The percentage probabilities varied in the following manner: 50:0, 40:10, 35:15, and 30:20. The finding of interest was that the amount of sampling of the alternatives (i.e., before animals devoted their time almost exclusively to the richer of the two patches) decreased as a function of the difference in reward probability across patches.

2.f. Diet Selection. Animals foraging for food in the wild are usually exposed to a variety of food items, facing moment-to-moment decisions about what to consume. This is the problem of *diet selection*. For example, carnivorous savanna monitor lizards (*Varanus albigularis*) prey on snails. Snails vary in size and in the amount of work necessary to grab them and to swallow them. If the currency the lizard is maximizing is, for example, net energy gain, then the amount gained from consuming the prey must be weighed against the energy lost in searching and handling the prey. When encountering a prey item, therefore, the lizards must decide if it would pay more to stop and catch this particular snail than to continue the search for a more profitable prey. In this particular example, small snails are consumed readily when food is scanty but are ignored in favor of large ones when food is abundant (Kaufman et al. 1994). Optimality concepts can help make sense of this type of choice.

The simplest possible problem is that of a predator feeding on two types of prey that differ, say, in size, as in the lizard example (Charnov 1976). The *profitability* of each prey is directly related to the amount of the currency being maximized (i.e., energy, nutrients) and inversely related to the time and energy invested in handling the prey. This could be represented as a ratio of energy to handling time, or *E/h*. For two preys, specialization on prey number 1, for example, would occur if

$$\frac{E_1}{h_1} > \frac{E_2}{h_2} \tag{1}$$

When the predator encounters prey 1, it should immediately eat it because it is the most profitable prey. To the extent that preys differ in profitability, predators should never specialize in the less profitable prey, no matter how abundant (i.e., predators should always consume the larger prey as it is encountered). Upon encountering prey 2, however, the predator should eat it only when net energy gain is greater than the net energy gained from prey 1 weighted by the amount of search time needed to find one such item. That is, the predator should consume prey 2 only if

$$\frac{E_2}{h_2} > \frac{E_1}{h_1 + S_1} \tag{2}$$

where S_1 represents the cost of searching for prey 1. Clearly, then, whether the predator chooses to consume prey 2 depends not on the prey's own abundance but on the abundance of the more profitable prey 1. This is a straightforward prediction that can be put to test.

Krebs et al. (1977) exposed predators (great tits, *Parus major*) to relatively large and small worms presented over a short period of about half a second through a window (the worms were actually placed on a conveyor belt). Seizing one of the worms would imply missing the few ones that followed because of the handling time. The main manipulation was to vary the relative frequency of the large prey while leaving the frequency of the small prey constant. This manipulation could be interpreted as resulting in variations in S_1 [see (2) above]. The results provided qualitative agreement with the optimal diet model in two respects: First, large preys were always consumed when encountered, and second, small prey were consumed more as the large prey became less abundant. Notice, however, that the model predicts a sharp change in the degree of specialization: Animals should display exclusive preference for prey 1 until the value for S_1 in (2) increases enough to shift the inequation in the opposite direction. In other words, the degree of specialization should follow a step function, with indifference for both prey types occurring when search for prey 1 is long enough to compensate exactly for the net gain obtained from prey 1 itself. In contrast to the predicted sharp transition in specialization, great tits actually showed a more graded shift in preference for small prey.

2.g. Constraints. Foraging decisions are limited by a number of factors generally referred to as *constraints*. For example, foraging must be based not on reliable information but on rules of thumb that allow only for a rough approximation to the critical parameters. Time and effort are also limited by activities other than foraging that are important. Consider, as an example, that predators might become prey if they are not careful and vigilant. Time allocated to searching for food must be shared with time allocated to detecting the presence of potential danger. Also, an animal must carry out a number of additional activities, from resting to reproductively related activities (e.g., nest building, patrolling a territory, courting females, responding to displaying males, caring for the young, etc.). There are also limits imposed by the very resource a predator is exploiting. Prey may be available during a restricted period within the day or year, or the environmental conditions may limit the predator's ability to search for prey. Such limits can have important implications for foraging decisions, as is illustrated in the following two examples.

In the first example, we look at how diet selection changes as a function of time allocated to foraging. Suppose a predator can determine whether the time for foraging is approaching an end on the basis of some signal (e.g., changes in natural light at dawn or dusk). Assume, in addition, that this predator has been foraging for two types of prey and has shown preference for the larger of the two. Should preference for the small prey change near the end of a foraging episode? Preference may actually change if the probability of having sufficient time to search for a more profitable prey is decreasing sharply. Again, this is a simple problem that can be tested under rigorous conditions in the laboratory.

In one such test, Yoerg and Kamil (1988) trained blue jays (*Cyanocitta cristata*) to peck at a response key to obtain mealworms as a reward. The preys were made differentially profitable by changing the temporal delay between a response to a positive stimulus and access to the mealworm. Moreover, the total time allowed for foraging could be either 20 min or 10 min in different phases of the experiment. The question of interest was whether the probability of attacking the less profitable prey at the end of the 10-min session was greater than the attack probability in the middle of a 20-min session. As ***Figure 4.2*** shows, preference for the least profitable prey actually increased at the end of the 10-min foraging session, suggesting that diet selection is dependent on such constraints as the total time allowed for searching and feeding.

The second example illustrates the interaction between feeding and predatory risk. An animal searching for food is also likely to be an easy target for a predator unless the forager can adjust its feeding strategy to minimize predatory risks. One way to do this is to carry some of the food items to a safe location (e.g., a burrow, a nest) rather than consuming the food where it is found. Such a behavior is referred to as *central place foraging*. Other features besides predatory risk may induce central place foraging, including caring for offspring at a nest or protecting food from conspecifics. Notice that it will take time and energy to carry the item to a

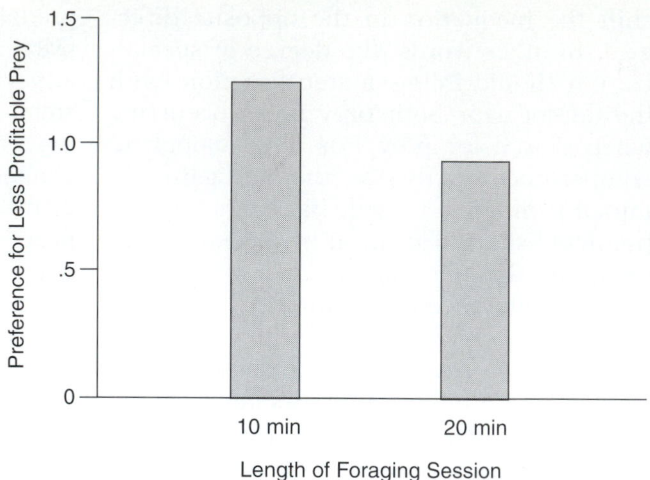

FIGURE 4.2. The results of Yoerg and Kamil's (1988) experiment demonstrate that the preference for the less profitable prey is higher at the end of a 10-min-long session than it is at the 10th min of a 20-min-long session. So the comparison is done at the same time within the session, but the time horizon involved is different: The session is ending in the 10-min group, but it is halfway to the end in the 20-min group. Because animals had been given many training sessions with these lengths, it is assumed that they had learned to estimate the time horizon involve in each case. Blue jays tended to accept a less profitable prey when the foraging session was close to its end and thus the expectation of having enough time to find a more profitable prey was low.

central location; this expenditure will thus detract from the item's profitability. An optimal decision should involve both information about the food item, such as its size, and about the central place location, such as its distance from the source of food. Specifically, animals are expected to practice central place foraging as the size of the food item increases and the distance of the central location to the food source decreases.

The common rat, *Rattus norvegicus,* is an animal known to practice central place foraging in the wild (Barnett 1975) and one that can be induced to do the same under special laboratory conditions. The architecture of the typical underground burrows built by rodents can be simulated in the lab by a maze with a central platform from which a series of arms radiate in all directions. This so-called radial-arm maze contains, therefore, a safe location in the center and a series of patches at the end of each arm. Using a four-arm maze, Phelps and Roberts (1989) found that the tendency to carry pieces of cheddar cheese from one of the arms to the central platform increased directly with the weight of the piece. Pieces of cheese weighing 0.05 g were always eaten on the spot, whereas pieces weighing more than 3 g were invariably consumed at the central platform. When the time and energy required to travel from the arm to the central location and back was increased by adding wooden barriers to the arm, the foraging pattern changed. Intermediate pieces of cheese that would normally be carried to the central location were instead consumed on the arms. Interestingly, enclosing the arms with walls changed again the foraging behavior of rats. Whereas in an open radial maze 98% of 0.90-g cheese pieces were transported to the central platform, with the covered arms only 13% were transported. Apparently, then, the safety provided by adding walls to the maze discouraged central place foraging.

Constraints are a very important component of foraging models. If, for example, foraging decisions were analyzed exclusively in relation to such factors as the energy provided by the food item and the time required to handle the item, the behavior of animals such as the gulls' foraging for capelin fish (***section 2.a.***) or of the rats practicing central place foraging would have to be considered far from optimal. In reality, however, animals cope with changes in the environment by adjusting their foraging behavior. When these constraints are included in the analysis, the animal's behavior appears to be functionally fit.

3. Search

3.a. Sit-and-Wait. Animals differ in their foraging styles. Some animals, such as most mammals and birds, actively search for prey. Others, such as many species of fish and reptiles, passively wait until a prey becomes available nearby to attack. To a large extent, whether an animal favors one or the other foraging strategy correlates with the characteristics of the prey. Herbivore animals feeding on plants, fruits, seeds, and other vegetal items are forced to search actively because their food does not move around. Insectivore and carnivore predators prey on other animals, and since animals move around substantially, it pays in certain cases to sit and wait for the prey to approach the predator.

Sit-and-wait predators have evolved specializations to remain cryptic to their prey and even lure their prey to approach until they are within attack distance. Many lizards, for example, have evolved cryptic coloration and are capable of remaining motionless for long periods. These features allow them to stay relatively unnoticed by flying insects, birds, or small rodents. The chameleon, for example, can change its external appearance to match the background. When an insect is within attack distance, the chameleon flips its tongue, captures the insect on the tip, and retrieves it for consumption in a fraction of a second. Some of the specializations include an anterior insertion of the tongue in the mouth that allows for its fast unfolding and a substance in the tongue that acts as a glue for the prey. In addition, chameleons have a keen sensitivity for motion detection and the ability to coordinate visuomotor information so that they strike the exact location where their prey is flying.

Some fish have evolved ingenious devices to attract prey into their proximity. For example, an anglerfish of the genus *Antennarius* remains motionless on the sea floor, looking like a sponge, while wagging a specialized spine (a modified portion of the dorsal fin) inserted at the tip of the snout, which has a fishlike structure in its tip. The appearance of a small fish swimming in that location attracts other fish, which are then attacked by the anglerfish as they approach (Pietsch & Grobecker 1978). The anglerfish just described belongs to the teleost order Lophiiformes which contains approximately 200 species, most of which use similar methods for attracting prey. In some deep-sea species, such as the anglerfish *Thaumatichthys axeli,* organs filled with light-emitting bacteria lure small prey right into the fish's mouth (Gartner et al. 1997).

3.b. Exploratory Behavior. For active predators, a considerable amount of time in their lives is devoted to searching for food. Many animals have evolved complex ways of collecting information from the environment that might eventually be relevant for feeding or for avoiding predators. Comparative psychologists have been fascinated over the years by such *exploratory behavior* because it shows how complex the interaction between organism and environment can be (see ***Chapter 11, section 2.b.,*** pp. 414–415). The laboratory rat has been a traditional subject to study exploratory behavior. As an omnivorous animal, the rat seems to be constantly looking for food and is motivated to sniff, manipulate, and taste almost any object in its environment.

A classic experiment on exploratory behavior in the rat shows that these animals not only move around in their environment but actually learn about structural aspects of that environment. Such aspects may be currently irrelevant, but as the environment changes they may become important in feeding. Tolman and Honzik (1930) exposed two groups of rats to a complex maze containing many blind alleys and a central location. This location, called the goal box, was baited with food for one group but not for the other. All rats had an opportunity to run through the maze during ten daily sessions, while the experimenters recorded the number of times they entered into the blind alleys. The results are shown in ***Figure 4.3.*** Whereas rats reinforced with food learned slowly to locate the goal box, nonrewarded animals also actively explored the maze. Interestingly, when previously nonrewarded rats were given access to food after ten days

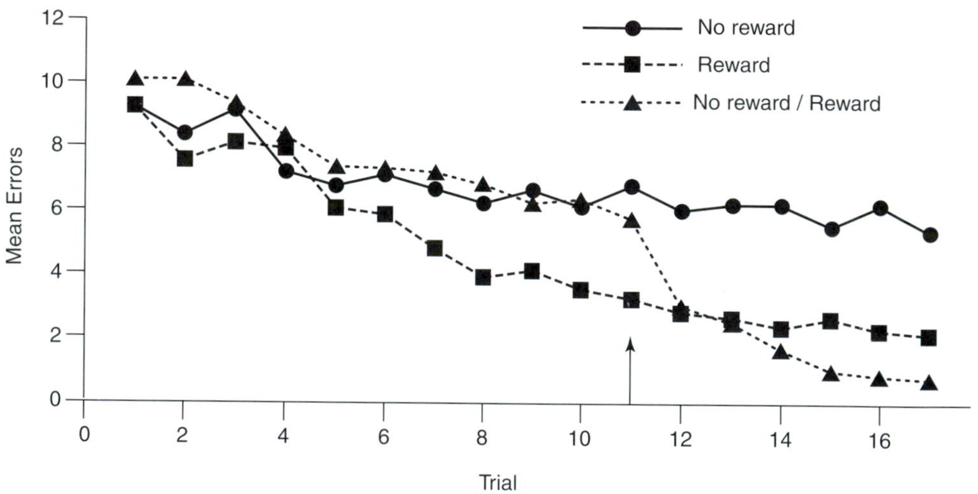

FIGURE 4.3. Rats exploring a complex maze with no food as an incentive show immediate changes in accuracy of their behavior when a reward is introduced after session 11. Such a rapid change in behavior suggests that the exploratory behavior of prior trials resulted in the acquisition of information about the environment. Because such information remained available but was used only when food was introduced, this phenomenon is referred to as latent learning (Tolman & Honzik 1930).

of exposure to the maze, they immediately developed a performance level equal to that of the reinforced animals. This experiment shows that exploring rats not only move around but they actually learn about aspects of the environment. Such learning is called *latent learning* because it involves information that is not used immediately after being acquired. In an analogous experiment, Renner (1988) found that familiarity with an environment allowed rats later to escape through a hidden route when a simulated predator was introduced (a toy car controlled remotely by the experimenter so that it would chase the rats for 180 s without touching them!).

3.c. Specialized Search. Many foraging specializations have evolved by natural selection as a way of reducing competition for limited food resources. Among the primates, for example, most species are diurnal and thus base their food-searching behavior primarily on visual cues. However, owl monkeys (*Aotus nancymai*), a species of New World monkey inhabiting the rain forests of South America, have evolved nocturnal habits. Bolen and Green (1997) found that owl monkeys exhibit a stronger tendency to use olfactory cues to locate hidden food than do diurnal capuchin monkeys (*Cebus apella*). Interestingly, the correlation between a nocturnal lifestyle and reliance on olfactory cues can be extended to the brain. Brain areas in charge of processing olfactory information are enlarged in owl monkeys, compared to other New World primates, in relation to body size (Stephan et al. 1981).

Among the rodents, for instance, there are interesting variations in the types of cues used by animals in their foraging, depending on the type of prey (Langley 1987). Rodents that are specialized for a carnivorous diet, such as the grasshopper mouse (*Onychomys leucogaster*), which feeds on beetles, crickets, and other nocturnally active insects, rely extensively upon auditory information. In contrast, omnivorous rodents such as the golden hamster (*Mesocricetus auratus*), which feeds on insects but also on a variety of plant items, rely on visual information to attack animal prey. The African water rat (*Colomys goslingi*) is unusual in its preference for aquatic invertebrates and its reliance on tactile information provided by its vibrissae for locating them.

The bifurcated tongues of certain snakes and lizards have evolved to detect edges of pheromonal trails left by predators and conspecifics (Schwenk 1994). These animals possess a specialized organ, called the vomeronasal organ, located in the nasal cavity and communicating with the oral cavity through a pair of fenestrae. After touching the ground, the forked tongue is rapidly retracted into the mouth and inserted in the fenestrae to deliver odor molecules into the vomeronasal organ. The tips of the forked tongue, which can be separated by a distance as large as the width of the animal's head, act as a delivery device, picking up chemosensory information that allows the animal to establish the presence of a trail. Forked tongues have evolved in reptiles that track prey over large distances, but not in sit-and-wait predators.

3.d. Search Image. Active foragers may in some cases develop preference for a particular prey based on recent experience rather than on the real density of available items. This resembles the so-called recency effect seen in research on memory, according to which recently experienced material is easily remembered. The predator behaves as if it had a "mental image" of the prey it is after (i.e., a *search image*).

The search image hypothesis easily lends itself to experimental testing using standard operant training procedures. ***Figure 4.4*** describes a procedure used by Pietriewicz and Kamil (1979) with blue jays (*Cyanocitta cristata*). Birds rapidly learn to peck a key for a piece of mealworm as reward. Response keys could be illuminated from behind using colors or projecting slides showing natural images. In this experiment, slides were of two kinds: Some were pictures of a moth on a tree trunk (a cryptic prey that tends to stay on surfaces that match its own coloration and pattern), whereas others were pictures of the same trunk without the moth. In this procedure, a peck on the red key gave way to two possible trials. In one type of trial, the blue jays had a choice between the red key and a slide containing a moth (marked Slide+ in ***Figure 4.4***). Responding to the pos-

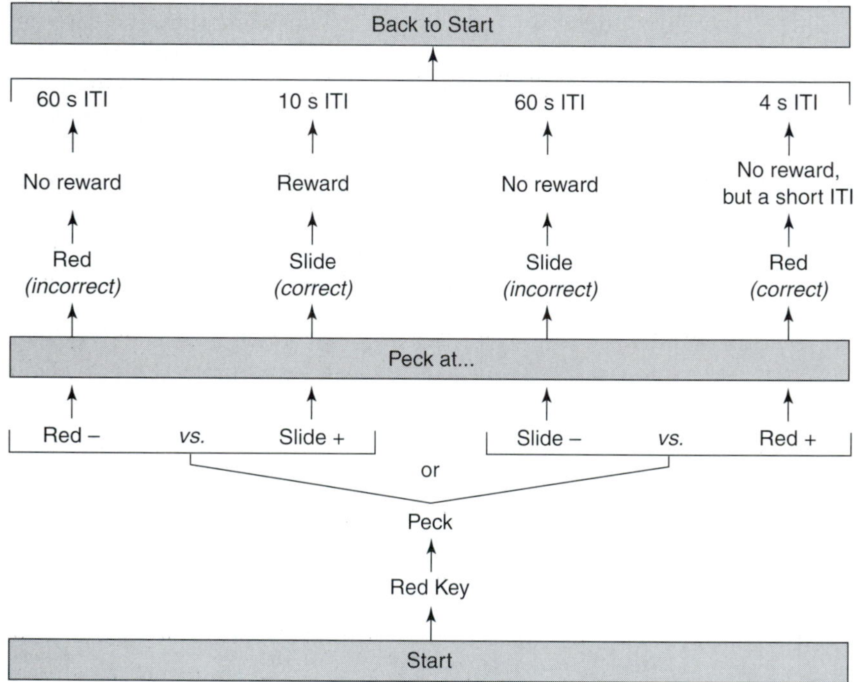

FIGURE 4.4. A visual representation of the design used by Pietriewicz and Kamil (1979) to provide empirical support for the search image hypothesis. Blue jays pecked at a red key to initiate a trial sequence. One of two pairs of slides are presented on the side. In one pair (left), the positive stimulus is a slide showing an image containing a cryptic prey, whereas the negative stimulus is a red slide. In the other pair (right), the positive slide is the red stimulus, whereas the negative slide shows a picture of the background without the cryptic moth. Thus, when the cryptic prey is there, choice of the slide is rewarded (by food); but when only the background is there, choice of the red stimulus is rewarded (by a short intertrial interval, ITI, and a rapid opportunity for a new trial). The question of interest is whether discrimination of the cryptic prey is enhanced when the blue jay has to detect a single moth species versus two moth species (see Figure 4.5 for the results).

itive slide resulted in reinforcement and a short intertrial interval, whereas responding to the red key resulted in no reinforcement and a long interval. In the other type of trial, the slide without the moth (labeled Slide– in ***Figure 4.4***) was presented together with the red key. In this case, responding to the red key was correct, although no food was provided (just a short intertrial interval).

The question of interest is whether detection of the positive slide would increase in a run of eight successive trials as a function of whether the blue jay is exposed to one versus two species of moth. According to the search image hypothesis, exposure to one type of prey should increase detection accuracy because the animal should be able to develop a precise expectation of the prey it should be looking for in the slide. As ***Figure 4.5*** shows, the percentage of correct responses (preference for the Slide+ key) increased when the birds were exposed to positive slides of a single moth but not to positive slides containing moths of different species. Interestingly, accuracy also improved (preference for the red key, in this case) in the trials in which blue jays had a choice between the negative slide and the red key. Recent experience with a particular prey, and its visual appearance in this particular example, may bias the predator toward selecting that type of item over others that may be available in the habitat.

3.e. Social Interactions. Many important aspects of the feeding behavior of animals are related to their ability to interact with other members of the species. Given the principle of competitive exclusion discussed at the outset of this chapter, it should not be surprising to find many examples of within-species competition for food resources. Rats, for example, actively steal food from a conspecific (Galef et al. 2001), and in fact very specific behavioral patterns have evolved to prevent theft of food (Whishaw & Tomie 1987). Rats would pick up food that was previously left on the floor as they see an approaching competitor, and they would turn away from the conspecific at an angle of approximately 175 degrees. Such *dodging behavior* is ex-

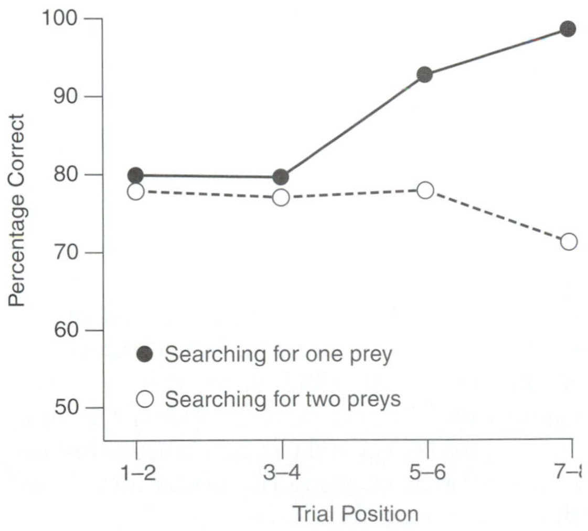

FIGURE 4.5. Blue jays were exposed to series of trials in which either one type of prey was presented or two different preys were intermixed randomly across the trials (see Figure 4.4 for a view of the training procedure). Exposure to a single prey led to improved accuracy in the discrimination across the series, suggesting the development of a search image (Pietriewicz & Kamil 1979).

tremely efficient; in a sample of 277 interactions between pairs of rats, dodging failed to occur in only 17 occasions and in all of them the robber could grab the piece of food. However, in all of the remaining 260 interactions, food defense was successful. But, apparently, theft of food can be prevented in some cases not by evasive maneuvers but by providing incorrect information to the potential robber. Some cases of learned *deception* have been claimed to occur in chimpanzees (*Pan troglodytes*). For example, a subdominant animal that had repeatedly lost food to a dominant one was observed to develop a variety of behaviors that prevented loss of food, such as avoiding the baited location while the dominant animal was nearby or waiting to collect the food until the dominant animal was searching in a different location (Menzel 1973).

Perhaps more surprising are examples of *cooperation* to obtain and share food among conspecifics. Young ravens (*Corvus corax*) search for food over large distances in the woods of Maine until they find, for example, the carcass of a large animal. Typically, adult ravens can defend successfully such a resource, so a flying-by juvenile may not stop and bother to try to get some food. Instead, the juvenile would return to a roost of other juveniles and communicate the finding through special calls. As a group, the juveniles can easily overthrow adult animals that might be defending the catch and obtain access to the food. Heinrich and Marzluff (1995) have used DNA fingerprinting techniques to show that these juveniles are not relatives (i.e., closely genetically related), which discards selection based on kinship as the plausible evolutionary mechanism (see ***section 4.f.*** below). It is cooperation of this sort that allows naive ravens released at the site of the roost to be able to be at a feeding site the next morning. The ability to share information regarding potential sources of food may be an important selective pressure underlying the evolution of social behavior. Ward and Zahavi (1973) suggested that animal groups (e.g., bird roosts, breeding colonies) may function as *information centers*. Clearly, animals that share information in this manner can benefit only if they are unable to access the food source by themselves.

Group foraging may have multiple effects in highly social species, depending on the conditions of the environment. Just as there are signals of food in physical features of the environment, the behavior of conspecifics may also indicate that food is available. The feeding behavior of one animal may induce another one to look for food in the same location and to direct the search to the same features of the environment, a phenomenon called *social enhancement*. For example, Burmese fowl (*Gallus gallus*) observing conspecifics obtaining food from one of four available patches would, 48 hr later, search for food preferentially in the same patches where their conspecifics had found seeds earlier (McQuoid & Galef 1992). A process of social enhancement may be responsible for the spread of new behavioral traits in a population of animals. In some cases, such a spread has been interpreted in terms of imitation, a process that is not required by social enhancement. In a famous case, an urban population of English tits (*Parus* spp.) showed the rapid development and adoption of an unusual behavior: They learned to open milk bottles placed on the thresholds of houses early in the morning and drink the cream from the top. Fisher and Hinde (1949) interpreted the spread of this behavior in terms of imitation. However, as Sherry and Galef (1984) showed in an experiment involving chickadees (*Parus atricapillus*), animals exposed to open bottles, but not to other birds opening the bottle, developed the behavior on their own.

Under experimental conditions, it is possible to pair or dissociate the presence of a conspecific and the food so as to show the power of social enhancement upon the foraging decisions of animals. In an experiment designed along these lines (Coleman & Mellgren 1997), zebra finches (*Taeniopygia guttata*) foraged for seeds in pairs in two adjacent enclosures containing four patches, each marked with colored paper. Birds could observe each other during the foraging sessions. When one of the finches found food in the green patch, the other tended to search first in the green patch. As a result, foraging was enhanced when food for the second bird happened to be in the same location, the green patch; but foraging could be greatly interfered with when food was located in a different patch. When birds were searching for food individually, their ability to find the baited patch was intermediate; thus social enhancement facilitated or interfered with the feeding, depending on the distribution of food. As one might suspect, however, finches showed a great deal of plasticity in their behavior, eventually disregarding social cues and approaching the paper color that had been most reliably paired with the seeds.

3.f. Social Learning. Social interactions can also have a powerful effect on the development of food preferences and aversions through *social learning.* In rats (*Rattus norvegicus*), interactions between a naive rat (called the *observer*) and one that has eaten a piece of food distinctively flavored (called the *demonstrator*) result in the development of a strong and specific preference for the flavor (Galef 1990). ***Figure 4.6*** describes the basic procedure used in these experiments. Detailed analysis of this type of interaction has uncovered the nature of the information and the context in which such information is used. For example, the preference does not develop simply because of exposure to the flavor. Moreover, observer rats exposed to demonstrators that have eaten a cinnamon-flavored food do not prefer to build nests using cinnamon-marked shredded paper, a material favored by rats for building nests (Galef et al. 1994); so the flavor preference seems to be specific for feeding.

An interesting aspect of these social interactions is that they seem to be quite effective in changing an animal's own experience with a given type of food. In an example reported by Galef (1986), rats that received training in which a flavored food was paired

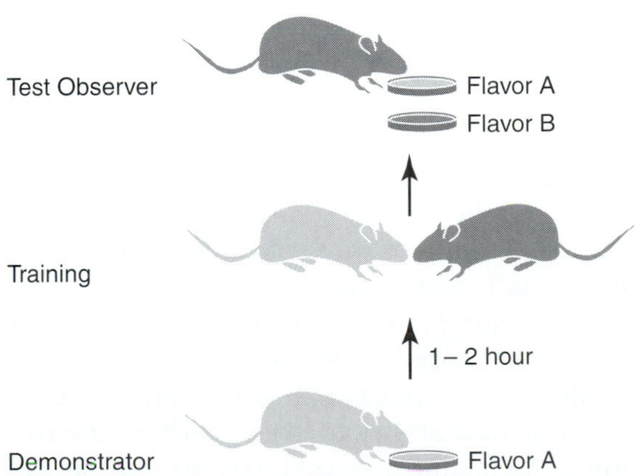

FIGURE 4.6. A representation of the basic design used by Galef and his associates to demonstrate social transmission of food preferences. In the bottom figure, the demonstrator rat is exposed to the target flavor. Subsequently, the demonstrator and a naive rat are allowed to interact. In a final test, the naive rat is given a choice between the flavor previously given to the demonstrator and a novel flavor. Social learning is manifested by the observer's preference for the flavor given originally to the demonstrator.

with a drug that produces gastrointestinal disease (in this case, lithium chloride) rapidly developed a strong aversion to that type of food. Yet this *food aversion learning* was reversed by exposure to a conspecific that had eaten the same type of food earlier; the reversal was even stronger if the poisoned rat was exposed to two, rather than one, demonstrators. Female spotted hyenas (*Crocuta crocuta*), which kill and consume their prey in groups, also show socially induced reversal of food aversions. If the dominant hyena is given meat poisoned with lithium chloride and tested individually, it shows a strong, and usually total, rejection of the same type of meat, even days after the conditioning episode. However, the same dominant hyena would readily consume that type of meat in a social group. Moreover, a group feeding experience totally reverses the aversion (Yoerg 1991).

Social interaction may not only occur, as it did in the examples reviewed so far, but actually be promoted when the individual animals involved in the interaction bear a special degree of kinship. In primates, for example, the strong mother-infant bond is important, among other things, because it provides information about the types of food that are appropriate for the infant. Hikami et al. (1990) reported that infant Japanese macaques (*Macaca fuscata*) can reverse a food aversion (produced by the now-familiar procedure of pairing the food item with a toxin) when their mother accepts and consumes that type of food in their presence. The social learning of foraging skills by young primates can have significant consequences on their survival. Primates are generally herbivores and are thus exposed to a variety of naturally poisonous plants that they must learn to avoid. To a large extent, infants get this natural training while foraging with their mothers during the initial months of their lives. In a study of free-ranging vervet monkeys (*Cercopithecus aethiops*) in Kenya, Hauser (1993) found that the infant's age at death (a measure of its survival success) correlated positively with the proportion of foraging time in which the infant had been observed to be eating the same type of food as its mother. An infant that either ate separately from its mother or ate by its mother's side but consumed different types of food tended to die prematurely. Interestingly, the infant's age at death did not correlate with such variables as the quality of the feeding territory or the social rank of its mother. A great deal of learning and teaching is involved in food selection and foraging efficiency in primates.

3.g. Retrieving Previously Stored Food. Central place foraging implies a time delay between finding and consuming food (see ***section 2.g.***, p. 91). Some species, including many mammals, birds, and arthropods, have evolved a striking ability not only to displace food from one location to another but also to store it for later consumption during periods ranging between hours and months. Given its taxonomic distribution, it seems clear that *food-hoarding behavior* has evolved independently in many lineages and must therefore be related to similar ecological pressures (Vander Wall 1990). Among these pressures is the seasonality of food resources. Scarcity of food during the winter months can be compensated for by storing nutrients somewhere in the environment; items can be retrieved later, at an appropriate time. Many of these species inhabit temperate to subartic habitats and would probably not survive through the winter without access to stored food. Such behavior also confers reproductive advantages in terms of an increased ability to breed early in the following season. In some birds, food is stored near the nest during the egg-incubation period, to be used later for the nestlings. Many morphological features are specialized for the purpose of transporting large amounts of food. Rodents possess cheek pouches, jays have distensible esophagi, and bees store pollen in special sacs in their hind legs called corbiculae.

Food hoarding may also require the evolution of specialized behavioral capacities. For example, one species of the family Corvidae, Clark's nutcrackers (*Nucifraga columbina*), stored pine seeds and nuts at distances of up to 20 km from the site in which they were found (Kamil & Balda 1985). A single animal may store as much as 20,000 to 100,000 seeds per year and recover the cache up to several months after hoarding. Nutcrackers depend on this food supply to survive during the cold winters in the mountainous region of western North America, and they rely on *spatial learning* to access this food supply. A similar storing ability is observed in some species of the family Paridae, small songbirds distributed over the northern hemisphere. Laboratory experiments show that black-capped chickadees (*Parus atricapillus*) exhibit a bias toward the acquisition of spatial information. To demonstrate such a bias, chickadees are first trained to find food on the basis of both spatial and color information (so-called spatial-color compound stimuli). Later, only one of these components is presented in a test trial, either the spatial (e.g., right vs. left) or the color (e.g., green vs. red). Under such conditions, chickadees show efficient performance when they can use spatial cues, but random efficacy when food can be found only on the basis of color cues, whereas nonstoring species tend to show no bias for either spatial or color cues (Brodbeck 1994; Brodbeck & Shettleworth 1995).

I mentioned previously that monkeys that actively forage during the night use olfactory cues and have relatively larger olfactory areas in their brains (see ***section 3.c.***, p. 95). A similar behavior-brain relationship has been established between the spatial abilities of food-storing birds and the size of their *hippocampal formation*. The hippocampal formation is located in the medial and dorsal portions of the telencephalon (i.e., the cerebral hemispheres of the brain), and it has been found to be implicated, among other things, in the spatial learning abilities shown by birds and mammals (Sherry et al. 1992). In a study of the hippocampal size of species from 13 families of song birds, Sherry et al. (1989) found that those species that exhibit food-hoarding behavior have a larger hippocampus relative to both body size and telencephalon size than nonstoring species (see ***Chapter 14, section 2.c.***, pp. 547–549). A relative increase in the size of a particular brain nucleus is one way in which natural selection shapes the evolution of specialized behavioral abilities.

3.h. Tool Using and Tool Manufacturing. The aye-aye (*Daubentonia madagascariensis*) is a primate endemic to Madagascar that has evolved a peculiarly long middle finger, which it uses to extract insect larvae from their burrowing places in trees and fruit pulp. Perhaps the absence of other species exploiting these resources (e.g., there are no woodpeckers in Madagascar), combined with appropriate genetic variability, has permitted natural selection to give rise to an elongated middle finger in the aye-aye's ancestors. But such morphological specializations are not the only way to solve the problem of food procurement. In some species, evolution has favored an alternative solution, and rather than lengthening a finger (as in the aye-aye) or shaping a beak (as in the woodpecker), it has led to the development of an ability to use a tool to compensate for the lack of an appropriate bodily structure to exploit a food resource. Using tools requires that an animal engages in interaction with some physical object that will serve its function (e.g., aid in procuring food) later in time. Tool use has traditionally been thought of as a higher behavioral capacity, but it is now known to be present in a variety of animals (Beck 1980).

For example, some solitary digger wasps of the genus *Ammophila* store eggs and paralyzed prey (to be used as food by emerging larvae) in a burrow; the wasp then selects a stone of the appropriate size and transports it to the burrow's entrance, where it is used to seal the hole. Several analogous examples of tool use have been described in birds and mammals. In the Galapagos Islands, where there are also no native woodpeckers, the woodpecker finch *Cactospiza pallida* is famous for using cactus spines to poke into insect burrows in trees, much as the aye-aye does with its finger in Madagascar (Grant 1986). New Zealand crows (*Corvus moneduloides*) actually manufacture hook-shaped tools by cutting twigs from the base and using them repeatedly to obtain insect larvae from tree holes (Hunt 1996). Egyptian vultures (*Neophron percnopterus*) have been observed to throw stones at eggs, while the African banded mongoose (*Mungos mungo*) throws the egg onto a hard stone to break it. The sea otter (*Enhydra lutris*) forages for mussels and bivalves on the sea floor and surfaces with its prey and a flat stone. Floating on its back, the otter strikes the mussel against the stone, which is held against its chest and functions as an anvil, until it can crush the shell with its teeth (Hall & Schaller 1964).

The most familiar examples of *tool use and manufacture* are found, not surprisingly, among primates. It is somewhat obvious that tool-related behavior is particularly facilitated by manual dexterity, visual acuity, and a propensity and motivation to manipulate objects. These characteristics are typical of primates (see also ***Chapter 11, section 3.b.,*** pp. 436–438). Many early reports on the "intelligent behavior" of monkeys and apes involved their seemingly spontaneous use of stones and sticks to reach otherwise inaccessible food. The classic work of the German comparative psychologist Wolfgand Kohler [1897–1967] with a group of chimpanzees (*Pan troglodytes*) at Tenerife Island showed that experienced individuals rapidly figure out ways of reaching food, even when the solution requires assembling a series of short sticks to create a long one, or piling up two boxes to reach a piece of food hanging from the ceiling (Kohler 1927). Field observations show that chimpanzees use a wide variety of tools to obtain food (***Figure 4.7, see front inside cover***). For example, they use leaves as sponges to absorb water from tree holes, stones and wood pieces as hammers and anvils to crack hard nuts, and carefully manufactured twigs and sticks to collect termites from their nests (Goodall 1986; Inoue-Nakamura & Matsuzawa 1997; Suzuki et al. 1995).

A similar *toolkit* has been described in capuchin monkeys (*Cebus apella*), New World primates thought to be phylogenetically more conservative than apes. Laboratory observations show that capuchin monkeys can manufacture sticks from tree branches to dip into corn syrup through holes in a specially designed apparatus. Monkeys also rapidly learn to use a variety of objects as sponges (paper towels, leaves, etc.) to absorb fruit juice from a source that was actually directly accessible to the animals (Westergaard & Fragaszy 1987). Whereas it is obvious that tool users from wasps to vultures, otters, monkeys, and chimpanzees display similar behavioral capacities and achieve analogous outcomes (the functional aspect of feeding behavior emphasized in this chapter), the development of such behavior may show important species differences. In one experiment, capuchin monkeys (*Cebus apella*), chimpanzees (*Pan troglodytes*), bonobos (*Pan paniscus*), and an orangutan (*Pongo pygmaeus*) rapidly learned to insert a stick into a clear tube in order to remove a piece of food placed inside the tube (Visalberghi et al. 1995). However, differences between the capuchin monkeys and the apes emerged when the task was made more complex by bundling three sticks together so that they would not fit inside the tube. The capuchin monkeys solved this problem by trial and error, attempting first, unsuccessfully, to insert the bundle into the tube. Thus prior training with the stick interfered with the resolution of the new problem, a phenomenon called *negative transfer*. By contrast, all the apes solved this problem without ever attempting to insert the bundle into the tube. This can be interpreted as an instance of *positive transfer* in that prior training with a single stick facilitated the resolution of the new problem with the bundled sticks. Although these species exhibited a readiness to use a tool in the appropriate way and adjusted to a new situation by finding the correct solution, the results suggest that prior experience in the task transfers negatively in the case of monkeys but positively in the case of apes (see ***Chapter 8, section 4.e.,*** pp. 309–314, and ***Chapter 14, section 2.g.,*** pp. 556–559, for further comparative studies of transfer in primates). A general principle worth emphasizing here is that a given adaptive function (e.g., food procurement through the use of tools) can be achieved via different mechanisms.

3.i. Symbiosis: Mutualism and Parasitism. Just as individuals of the same species compete and cooperate in searching and procuring their food, there are numerous examples in which the animals involved in the interaction belong to different species. Such an association is referred to as *symbiosis*. Symbiotic relationships in which both parts benefit (called *mutualism*) or in which one part benefits while the other incurs a cost (called *parasitism*) result in evolutionary changes that affect both species involved. Such a process is referred to as *coevolution*, and it is thought to be responsible for some notable species associations, such as that between flowering plants and their pollinators (insects, birds, etc.) and that between active predators and their preys (see ***section 4*** below).

The consequences of coevolution can be clearly appreciated in the association between ants of the genus *Pseudomyrmex* and *Acacia* trees (Janzen 1966). Ants establish their colonies in the tree's thorns and repel insects and other animals, including mammals, that approach and make contact with the tree. In addition, they will chew and destroy twigs and sprouts of plants growing around the acacia tree, thus helping it to grow rapidly. If the ants are removed, the acacia trees grow slowly and are vulnerable to herbivorous insects that prey on the leaves. In turn, acacia trees evolved the Bentian bodies, specialized structures located at the tip of young leaflets that contain nutrients and nectar used as food by the ants.

An equally fascinating example of mutualism involves a small bird, the greater honeyguide (*Indicator indicator*), and the Boran people, a nomadic culture from Kenya (Isack & Reyer 1989). Boran men have been collecting honey from beehives for perhaps thousands of years, following a procedure that was considered by many a myth until recently. Men call the honeyguides by blowing a whistle when they are ready to search for honey. Honeyguides appear flying and perch in a nearby tree, moving rapidly from branch to branch while displaying their white tail feathers and emitting a special call. When the men approach, the honeyguides take off to another nearby tree and repeat the behavioral display. As the men follow the honeyguides, they keep blowing the whistle and talk loudly because they claim this maintains the birds' interest in the guiding process. Eventually, they will discover a honeybee hive, usually in a tree, in between rock cracks, or in an abandoned termite mound. Once at the hive, the Boran men use smoke to drive the bees away and tools to open the hive and take the honey. The honeyguides will then feed on the exposed larvae and remaining pieces of honeycomb.

Boran men have learned to interpret aspects of the behavior of honeyguides and extract information about the distance to the hive. For example, the shorter the distance to the honeybee colony, the shorter the disappearance of the honeyguide between the first and second encounters, the shorter the distance between successive perches, and the lower the height of the perch. It is not necessary to assume that the bird provides the information "intentionally" but only that the information is available in its behavior. A still unproved claim by Boran men could provide such decisive evidence: They claim that a honeyguide may sometimes "deceive" them into believing that a hive is near, when in fact the hive may be located 2 km away; presumably, this behavior keeps the men focused on the task.

Field experiments indicate that a honeyguide is capable of guiding men to a hive (which is not destroyed in this case) repeatedly through a relatively direct pathway, but not necessarily using the same route. Interestingly, if men call from different locations, the honeyguide will invariably guide them more or less directly to the same hive. Obviously, these birds have learned a detailed representation of the features of a particular location, much like the exploring rats of Tolman and Honzik had learned the complex maze (see ***section 3.b.,*** pp. 94–95). Such a representation, referred to as a *cognitive map,* allows the animal to chose the most direct path to the goal from whichever point in the map it happens to be located. The man-honeyguide relationship is clearly mutualistic. On their own, Boran men may look for hives unsuccessfully in some occasions or spend an average of 8.9 hr in a successful search. In contrast, the time drops to 3.2 hr if a honeyguide is helping. And from the point of view of the honeyguides, only 4% of the hives are accessible without human help.

Symbiotic interactions cannot be always described as win-win situations. In many cases, an animal's effort in procuring food is wasted when the food is stolen by competitors—a win-lose situation. The "robber" is referred to as a parasite, whereas the "robbed" is the host. The most obvious case is that of the many species of conventional parasites that live in the internal organs of their hosts and cause a variety of illnesses. From the evolutionary point of view, parasites benefit if they can complete some crucial part of their life cycle before they kill their host. Hosts, by contrast, are benefited by an early rejection of the parasite. These two selective pressures work to cancel each other across generations, and thus they result in the evolution of adaptations and counteradaptations from both sides.

The parasitic mode of life appears to be appealing, judging from the number of specialized taxa. Two of the three classes of flatworms, Trematoda and Cestoda, and many of the species in the phyla Nematoda, Nematomorpha, and Acanthocephala are parasites either continuously or during some part of their life cycle (Curtis &

Barnes 1989). For example, the three species of the genus *Schistosoma* (trematodes responsible for the symptoms of schistosomiasis in humans) begin their life cycle in freshwater currents, in the digestive system of snails. A single snail can release approximately 100,000 larvae during a 6-month period. Larvae can easily penetrate the bloodstream of a person through the skin, and, once inside, they reproduce in the intestines, bladder, liver, and other organs, where they feed on nutrients taken from the host's bloodstream. Egg proliferation causes blockage of vessels and hemorrhages. Some similar flatworms, such as *Taenia pisiformis* (a cestodan worm that parasitizes dogs), have specialized to the extreme of losing their own digestive systems and so are dependent entirely on their hosts for nutrients.

There are also less conventional parasites, including many that act as such only occasionally. In the case of species that store food, there are many documented cases in which the caches are systematically exploited by occasional parasites (Vander Wall & Smith 1987). For example, grizzly bears (*Ursus arctos*) regularly raid locations where red squirrels (*Tamiasciurus hudsonicus*) have hoarded nuts, and wood pigeons (*Columba palumbus*) consume seeds stored by Jays (*Garrulus glandarius*). The paralyzed prey that digger wasps provide for their own larvae, as mentioned previously, are a major target for several other arthropods that steal the cache either by directly consuming the prey or by using it as provision for their own larvae.

4. PREDATOR-PREY INTERACTIONS

Symbiosis provided examples of feeding behavior in which animals of different species interact in either cooperative or competitive ways. When the interaction is competitive, as it is in parasitism, it approaches the more common scenario of the predator and the prey. In the latter case, however, the predator uses the prey itself as a source of nutrients and energy, and not the food that the host has eaten or stored, as in the case of parasitism. But just as in the case of symbiosis, *predator-prey systems* also coevolve. Natural selection would favor, other things being equal, predator species that evolve more efficient means of detecting, capturing, and consuming prey. But such an increase in efficiency would generate, in turn, a selective pressure for the prey species to evolve traits that counteract the predator's new features. Since this reminds us of the political situation during the decades of the Cold War, many refer to this situation as an arms race. Among the clearest examples of arms races are those between herbivore insects and their plant preys. The *Passiflora* vine, for example, has evolved the ability to produce toxins as a defense against the butterfly *Heliconius,* which, in turn, has evolved resistance to those toxins as a counterdefense. Some vine species possess specialized structures aimed at controlling predation by butterflies, including hooklike filaments that immobilize larvae until they starve (Gilbert 1971).

The coevolution of predators and preys implies the evolution of adaptations and counteradaptations that can be best described as a system, just as in the case of symbiosis. The coevolution of behavior in predator-prey systems is particularly obvious when predators are specialized for the consumption of one (or a few related) species and preys are predominantly hunted by one (or a few related) species. This is so because the selective pressures and counterpressures involved in such a case tend to be homogeneous and consistent across generations, allowing for the directional selection of traits. Let's consider the bat-moth system, which has been studied in detail.

4.a. Bats and Moths: From Function to Mechanism. Bats of the suborder Microchiroptera are generally adapted for feeding on flying insects and have evolved a highly specialized system of *echolocation* for this purpose. Large populations of the little brown bat (*Myotis lucifugus*), a species extensively used in echolocation experiments, hibernate in caves during the winter. Clouds of flying bats can be seen coming out of these caves during the spring and moving into feeding locations. These bats forage for moths during the night in the warm period of the year, while females are raising their offspring in large communal colonies. It has been known since the time of Lazzaro Spallanzani [1729–1799], that bats use their ears to fly during the night, but it was only since the 1930s that the actual mechanism began to be understood. The development of sonar, an instrument used during World War I to detect submarines, provided a nice technological analogy, and the invention of ultrasonic recorders conclusively showed that bats were emitting sounds, although at a frequency range above the auditory threshold for humans (Griffin 1958).

Echolocation is based on the animal's ability to extract information from the echo of its own high-frequency calls (above 45 kHz). Bats are amazingly effective in obtaining information from these echoes about various properties of flying moths, including their distance, their size, whether they are beating their wings, how fast they are moving, and how high is their elevation. The little brown bat emits calls that rapidly fall in frequency about one octave. Such calls are referred to as frequency modulated (FM) calls, and the bat uses them efficiently to infer the prey's distance from the time elapsed between the emission of the call to the reception of the echo. As the prey gets closer to the bat, the rate at which these calls are emitted can increase up to 200 calls per second, as the bat processes information about small changes in the position of its flying prey. Such FM calls appear to be appropriate for foraging in open air. However, bats that forage in relatively dense vegetation, such as the mustached bat (*Pteronotus parnellii*), emit calls characterized by a constant frequency (CF calls) and use a unique mechanism to decode information about the movement of objects by analyzing the Doppler shift of echoes. Echoes from motionless objects, such as a tree or a wall, are compressed in frequency when reflected as the bat flies toward the object (much as the pitch of a truck's honk gets higher as it overtakes you on a freeway). Echoes from moving objects (such as flying insects) contain oscillating frequency components that signal the presence of beating wings. Mustached bats can use this information to follow a moth even through dense vegetation (Suga 1990). There is, therefore, a correlation between the typical foraging environment (open air vs. dense vegetation) and the echolocation system used by the bat (FM vs. CF).

This efficient system for capturing moths poses an intense predatory pressure upon moth species to evolve counteradaptations. It is illuminating, at this point, to consider an important difference in the selective forces acting upon the moth and the bat: Whereas the moth is flying for its life, the bat is flying only for its dinner. Following a famous fable involving a fox and a rabbit, written by the Greek author Aesop [620–560 B.C.], Dawkins and Krebs (1979) referred to this asymmetry as the *life-dinner principle.* Perhaps as a reflection of this principle, some species of moth have evolved a simple, but surprisingly effective, auditory system that appears to exist for the exclusive purpose of detecting bats (Roeder 1967).

Moth species of the family Noctuidae possess a pair of ears located in the abdomen, underneath the wings. Attached to a tympanic membrane are two neurons, labeled A1 and A2, that fire action potentials to the central nervous system in the presence of different, but specific, types of sounds. A1 responds more or less proportionally to the intensity of the sound, and it is thus capable of signaling the approach of a sound-emitting bat. However, A1 would keep responding only when sound is emitted in pulses of high-frequency calls, like those typical of bats. Sensory adaptation rapidly develops in A1 receptors responding to steady sounds. By comparing A1 pulses from each side of the abdomen, or the difference between the frequencies when the wings are up or down, the moths can obtain information about the location of an approaching bat. Low-intensity sound induces directional escape—that is, the moth flies away from the source. A2 cells, on the other hand, respond only when the intensity of the stimulus is relatively high, as would happen when the bat is close by. Apparently, the activation of A2 receptors triggers a rapid change in the moth's flying trajectory, which would typically shift directions randomly. In fact, any high-frequency sound can trigger this behavior at night. Typically, moths stop flapping the wings and take a dive toward the ground, although occasional flapping may change its direction in a more or less random fashion. The random trajectory makes the bat's task more difficult and increases the moth's chances of survival. ***Figure 4.8*** shows two examples of bat-moth interaction, one in which the moth takes a dive and escapes the bat (***a***), and another in which the bat and moth trajectories meet, indicating that the bat caught the moth in the air (***b***). Field observations demonstrate that the chance of surviving is 40% greater for moths that exhibit such random shifts in flying trajectory than for moths that do not show evasive behavior (Roeder & Treat 1961).

4.b. Frequency-Dependent Selection. Predator-prey systems also illustrate the fact that the strength of the predatory pressure may depend in some cases upon the frequency with which a particular species of prey is found in the habitat. Of course, what makes this situation interesting is that, in turn, the frequency of the prey depends on the strength of the predatory pressure. A preview of this issue was found in the discussion of the search image (see ***section 3.d.,*** p. 95); the point was then made that the frequent encounter with a particular type of prey may result in an almost exclusive search for that particular prey at the expense of other, available preys. *Frequency-dependent selection* may be responsible for many instances of polymorphisms found in nature. Recall that reference has already been made already to disruptive selection, a situation in which selection may favor extreme versions of a particular phenotype, thus resulting in the preservation of genetic diversity (see ***Figure 2.9-c,*** p. 52). When the fitness of a particular variation increases if it is rare in the population but decreases if it becomes abundant, frequency-dependent selection would tend to preserve that variation.

The example I have chosen to illustrate this point is interesting, moreover, because it shows the combined effects of predation and parasitism in a multiple-species system (Losey et al. 1997). Pea aphids (*Acyrthosiphon pisum*) occur in two different color variations, red and green. The abundance of each variation is regulated by different but balancing selective pressures, as shown in

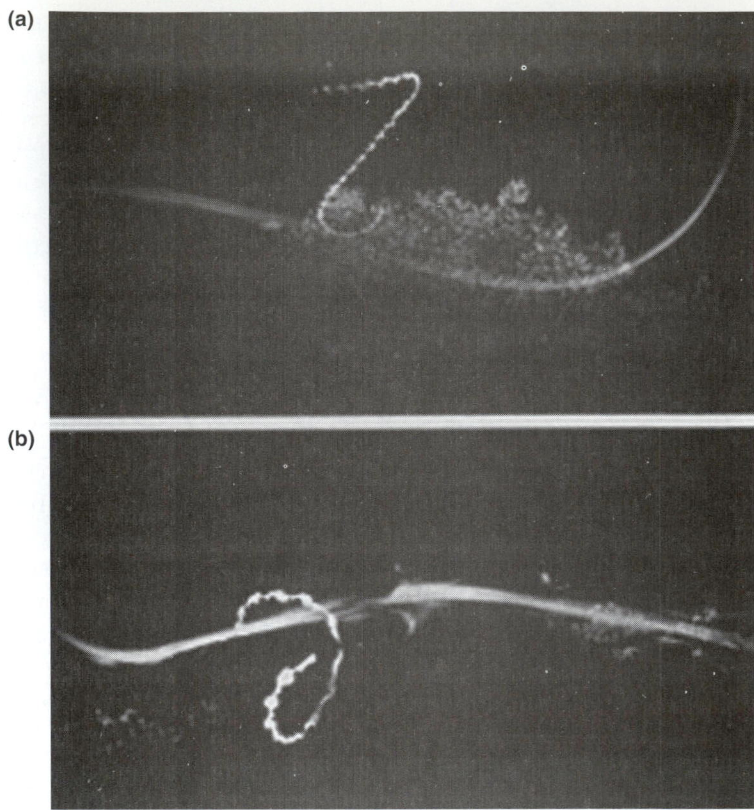

FIGURE 4.8. Tracks of bats and moths during the night (Roeder 1967). Moths are tossed into the air by the experimenter while a camera captures the flying of both animals. ***(a)*** A bat enters the picture from the left while the moth dives and turns upward. The moth is able to escape, as demonstrated by the fact that the moth's trajectory continues above that of the bat. ***(b)*** A bat enters from the right while the moth is turning in an upward loop. The moth's trajectory ends on the bat's, indicating a successful capture for the bat.

Figure 4.9. Aphid populations are affected by the parasitoid wasp *Aphidius ervi*. This wasp inserts eggs into the aphid's body, and the developing larvae feed on the aphid, eventually killing it. Field observations show that although wasps parasitize both variants, they exhibit a significant tendency to parasitize the green variants. Aphids are also vulnerable to predation by ladybird beetles of several species (e.g., *Coccinella septempunctata*). Observations in a greenhouse environment show that ladybird beetles prey significantly more on the red variants than on the green variants. The density of these three species measured in several fields in Wisconsin shows an orderly trend: Fields where parasitoid wasps predominate over ladybird beetles are characterized by a relatively greater abundance of the red variants (their fitness is higher, given the low preda-

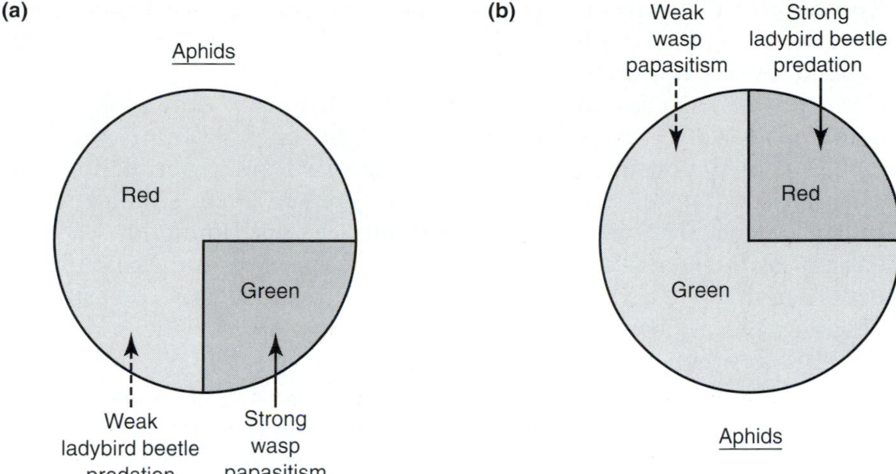

FIGURE 4.9. A polymorphism (red and green aphids, *Acyrthosiphon pisum*) maintained by frequency-dependent and balanced selective pressures (Losey et al. 1997). Ladybird beetles (*Coccinella septempunctata*) prey more selectively on the red morphs, whereas parasitoid wasps (*Aphidius ervi*) attack more frequently the green morphs. (***a***) The red morphs predominate in areas where predatory pressure by beetles is weak. (***b***) In contrast, the green morphs predominate in areas where parasitism by wasps is weak.

tory pressure), whereas fields with a larger proportion of ladybird beetles than wasps are notable for the relative abundance of the green variant (their fitness is higher, given the low parasitic pressure).

Only some aspects of how this interaction is achieved are understood. It is possible, for example, that the differential density of aphids across fields is caused by factors unrelated to balanced parasitism and predation. Two such factors were measured and proved to be nonsignificant. One is the relative reproductive rate, which was similar in green and red aphids. The other factor in which variants are similar is the frequency of a species-typical defensive behavior displayed by aphids in the presence of a predator—they tend to drop from the plant. So green (or red) aphid variants are not abundant in a particular field because they reproduce at a higher rate or are more efficient in antipredator defenses than red (or green) variants. It is thought that ladybird beetles detect the aphids on the basis of visual cues. For example, experiments show that ladybird beetles prey significantly on red aphids when they are released in green containers (simulating the background provided by a leaf); but predation is heavier on the green variants when the test is conducted in a red container. So the ladybird beetles do not seem to have a tendency to prey upon the red variant per se, but rather seem to base their preference on visual discriminability (i.e., a matter of figure-background contrast). However, similar experiments show that parasitism by wasps is not dependent on the color of the container where the tests are performed. Exactly how wasps choose their hosts has not yet been determined.

4.c. Cryptic and Aposematic Coloration. The ability of green aphids to blend with the background provided by vegetation is referred to as *crypticity*. Many species of both preys and predators have evolved cryptic coloration as a solution to the problem of detection. Sit-and-wait predators (see ***section 3.a.,*** p. 93) display *aggressive mimicry* by matching features of their environment or some innocuous animal (e.g., the angler fish mimics a sponge) as a means of minimizing detection by a prey. Chameleons not only can mimic the background of the place they have chosen to sit and wait for prey, but they have the ability to adjust their bodily appearance as they move from one location to another. Skin color is achieved by changes in pigment molecules, such as black melanin, located in skin cells called chromatophores. Some cephalopods, such as octopi and cuttlefish, display astonishingly fast and diverse changes in coloration, which are achieved by chromatophores that contain a variety of pigments. The difference in coloration of polar and grizzly bears provides an example of closely related species that evolved a coloration appropriate to the visual characteristics of their habitats as camouflage. Many species of insects have evolved extraordinary adaptations for crypticity, either to remain unnoticed by predators, such as insects that mimic leaves and sticks, or to repel them. For example, several species of moth and butterflies display dark spots resembling the eyes of a rapacious bird when they open their wings, and some caterpillars change their heads to the shape of snakes when touched by a predator. Eyespots are also displayed by the South American frog *Physalaemus nattereri* on its back. When threatened by a predator, this frog turns around, raises its hind limbs, inflates its trunk, and displays the dark spots; in addition, the latter contain a gland that secretes a toxic substance (see Owen 1980, and similar books for impressive photographic records).

Crypticity obviously draws from the problem of *figure-background discrimination,* a familiar issue in experimental psychology. The greater their similarity, the more difficult the discrimination. By the same token, a simple way of making the figure-background discrimination easier on the predator is to enhance the prey's coloration. But what type of prey would be favored by such a strategy? Many of the species that advertise their presence by displaying bright colors and clear patterns are distasteful animals. Such so-called *aposematic coloration* has apparently evolved by exploiting the learning abilities of predators. Consider the example of the monarch butterfly *Danaus plexippus.* The caterpillar is adapted for processing toxic plant substances, and, as a byproduct, it becomes distasteful to its typical predators (mostly birds) even as an adult butterfly. Birds search for their food almost entirely on the basis of visual cues, and so they are prone to associating the color of the butterfly with the taste that follows. Blue jays, for example, have been observed to vomit recently eaten monarch butterflies. Although that particular butterfly dies in the interaction, the blue jay is likely to develop an aversion to the coloration preceding the bitter taste and therefore is likely also to avoid similar color patterns in future foraging trips. Since learning is facilitated by the salience of the stimulus, it is thus not entirely surprising that natural selection has favored the evolution of aposematic coloration. (A careful reader might have noticed the potential for a group-selection argument in this example, as the monarch butterfly would seem to sacrifice itself for the benefit of the species; more about this in ***section 4.f.*** below.)

Predatory pressures upon insect populations are so intense that aposematic coloration tends to be convergent among unrelated species. Many unpalatable insects signal their poisonous nature by displaying a characteristic yellow-and-black striping pattern, or some similarly salient combination of colors. This example of convergent evolution, referred to as *Müllerian mimicry,* underscores the importance of conveying a unified message to facilitate learning by the predator. Müllerian mimicry also suggests that evolution is exploiting a property of learning known as *stimulus generalization*—that is, the tendency to respond in a like manner to similar stimuli. Such a use of generalization is evident in another twist of this predator-prey story: Some species display aposematic coloration and yet are not distasteful, but perfectly edible. The convergence in coloration of mimic, edible species with their toxic models is referred to as *Batesian mimicry.*

The coexistence of mimic and toxic species poses further constraints on evolution that are also related to the learning abilities of predators. One problem is that of inexperienced predators that will tend to kill both mimic and toxic animals. If predators were to kill many mimics, then mimicry would not work very well; by attacking and killing both types, the predators would tend to learn that the coloration is appetitive, rather than toxic. An occasional experience with a bitter prey may not support enough learning to produce consistent avoidance behavior in the avian predators. Thus, for Batesian mimicry to evolve, the proportion of mimic to toxic preys needs to remain in favor of the latter. Moreover, if birds were to encounter first the palatable mimic, they would tend to learn the "wrong" message. For example, if you learn that red = sweet, this learning will interfere with your ability to subsequently learn that red = bitter. As a way of avoiding this negative transfer problem, mimic species tend to emerge after toxic species, thus increasing the chances that the predator's initial experience will be with toxic animals.

4.d. Active and Passive Defense. Just as there is active and passive (e.g., sit-and-wait) foraging behavior, there is also active and passive antipredator behavior. The *fight-flight reaction* typical of many animals cornered by a predator is an example of an active antipredator strategy. Active escape is perhaps most familiar in the large herbivores of the African grasslands, such as wildebeests, antelopes, and zebras, that can run at high speed when attacked by large carnivores. An arms-race scenario is immediately obvious when one considers the extraordinary speed (close to 70 mph) achieved by cheetahs in pursuit of their active prey. Both active escape and pursuit imply a large amount of energy expenditure. It is thus not surprising that in some cases some sort of communication has evolved between the prey and its predator. This appears to be the case with the *stotting display* of gazelles (*Gazella thomsoni*) when confronted with carnivore predators such as cheetahs (*Acinonyx jubatus*) or wild dogs (*Lycaon pictus*). Stotting gazelles jump with all four legs extended and detached from the ground. It has been observed that cheetahs tend to abandon the pursuit of gazelles that stott and concentrate their hunting on those that do not stott (Caro 1986). Stotting appears to be advantageous perhaps because it "informs" the cheetah that the gazelle will be hard to catch as it is in excellent physical shape. The gazelle is also "saying" that it has seen the predator and is ready to escape. Cheetahs can sustain their pursuit speed for only a short time, and thus it would be advantageous for them to try to catch a gazelle that is not in good physical shape or that shows no sign of having detected their presence.

If stotting gazelles represent one end of the antipredator behavior continuum, then the opossum's (*Didelphis virginiana*) *tonic immobility* reaction would be clearly at the other end. When confronted with a predator, an opossum will curl its body and lie on its side as if it were dead ("playing possum," as the saying goes). Active predators would typically leave dead animals untouched. Tonic immobility is observed in a variety of species, including many snakes, birds, and mammals. A similarly passive antipredator behavior is that of rolling into a ball. The South American armadillo *Tolypeutes mataco* rolls into a locking position in which head and tail complement each other in shape, exposing its hard armor while protecting the soft ventral parts inside the ball. Eisenberg (1981) suggested that mammals that have evolved passive antipredator strategies tend to have smaller brains than close relatives that exhibit active antipredator behaviors. ***Table 4.1*** shows average *encephalization quotients* (a measure of relative brain size; see ***Chapter 8, section 4,*** pp. 302–315) in selected species from various mammalian orders of similar body size but contrasting antipredator behavior. Such differences suggest that the demands of neural processing for active escape (both perceptual and motor) are larger than those implied by passive defensive responses and probably require additional neural tissue, resulting in the evolution of a relatively larger brain.

TABLE 4.1 Degree of Encephalization in Mammals That Exhibit Active vs. Passive Antipredator Behavior

	Antipredator Behavior	
Taxon	***Active***	***Passive***
Marsupials	0.94	0.72
Insectivores	0.74	0.45
Edentates	1.45	0.79
Rodents	1.09	0.72

Note. Numbers are average encephalization quotients (EQs). The EQ measure is an index of the brain size of a particular species relative to the brain size of its class (in this case, mammals). An EQ = 1 means that the brain size of the species is equal to that expected for a mammal of its body size. EQs greater and smaller than 1 imply a brain size or greater or smaller, respectively, than that expected for a mammal of the same body size. The original data (EQ values for individual species) were reported by Eisenberg (1991).

Tonic immobility has been studied in some detail in birds, which have been used in popular demonstrations of the power of magicians for centuries. In one such demonstration of "animal magnetism," as it was called during the 19th century, the magician would rapidly turn a chicken upside down, while holding the animal in his palm, thus inducing a state of complete muscular inhibition that presumably demonstrated the magician's ability to hypnotize the animal. In reality, the sudden movement had triggered tonic immobility as an antipredator response. Fear seems to be a major component in this reaction, which is accompanied, for example, by increases in the plasma concentration of stress hormones (e.g., corticosterone). Japanese quail (*Coturnix japonica*), artificially selected for long tonic immobility reactions triggered by restraint, not only freeze for longer periods but also vocalize, defecate, and locomote less than animals selected for short tonic immobility. Statistical analyses show that these behavioral measurements represent variations in a single underlying factor, thus suggesting that artificial selection for long and short tonic immobility affects a general tendency, referred to as *fearfulness*, rather than a stimulus-specific response (Jones et al. 1991).

4.e. Social Aspects of Defensive Behavior. Animals from many species have the ability to use social cues provided by conspecifics to protect themselves against predators. In fact, it is likely that predatory pressures have contributed significantly to the evolution of social behavior, from fish schools (large aggregates of fish swimming coordinately) to herds of herbivore mammals in the African plains. Grouping may be advantageous to individual animals because it would increase the efficiency of vigilance and detection and thus facilitate antipredator defense. Fish schools may, in addition, have the ability to foster learning of predator recognition, even in the absence of direct contact with the predator, which is clearly advantageous. A case in point is provided by the zebra danio fish, *Brachydanio rerio* (Suboski et al. 1990).

Zebra danio fish form schools even in the relatively restricted confinement of an aquarium tank, in the laboratory. If fluids obtained from a fish that has undergone skin damage are pumped into the tank, the school shows an alarm reaction consisting of swimming and staying at the very bottom of the tank for a period of several minutes. This is a defensive reaction observed in other fish exposed to extracts of damaged skin from a conspecific, and it has been assumed that the extract contains a heretofore undetected pheromone, referred to as an *alarm substance*. Obviously, such a substance would tend to be released when a predator has caught a zebra danio fish, and thus the defensive reaction of the surviving members of the school would protect them against a close predator.

An interesting extension of this basic effect suggests how predator recognition might be learned and transmitted socially (see ***Figure 4.10***). Some experiments have assessed the effects of adding an otherwise neutral odor compound (such as morpholine) or a distinct visual cue (such as a bright light) to the alarm substance. The result of such manipulation is that the added odor or light acquires warning properties similar to those of the alarm substance. This provides the fish with a mechanism to acquire an evasive response when a predator is approaching before making contact with a conspecific. But even more surprising is the fact that when zebra danio fish that have never encountered the alarm substance are placed with experienced fish and together experience the odor or visual cue, they develop the antipredator behavior just as well. These fish must be acquiring this defensive behavior by observing other fish in the group.

In some notable cases, preys adopt a strategy best described by the saying "the best defense is a good offense." Rats, for example, may freeze when a predator is at some distance, but they vocalize, jump, and attack a predator at closer distance (Blanchard et al. 1986). In some cases, the presence of a predator acts as a grouping factor for the intended prey, which may end up disturbing and even attacking the predator. Such behavior is referred to as *mobbing*, and it has been observed in many species of fish, birds, and mammals. The adaptive significance of mobbing seems to depend on the ability of the mob to drive the predator away. But mobbing also facilitates a kind of predator recognition similar to that described previously for zebra danio fish. For example, a blackbird (*Turdus merula*) displaying active defense in the presence of a typical predator (e.g., an owl) may attract other blackbirds to the site and induce mobbing. Experiments show that a blackbird can learn to mob a nonpredator model if it sees this neutral model together with another blackbird displaying defensive behaviors. Using an ingenious technique, Curio et al. (1978) were able to induce mob-

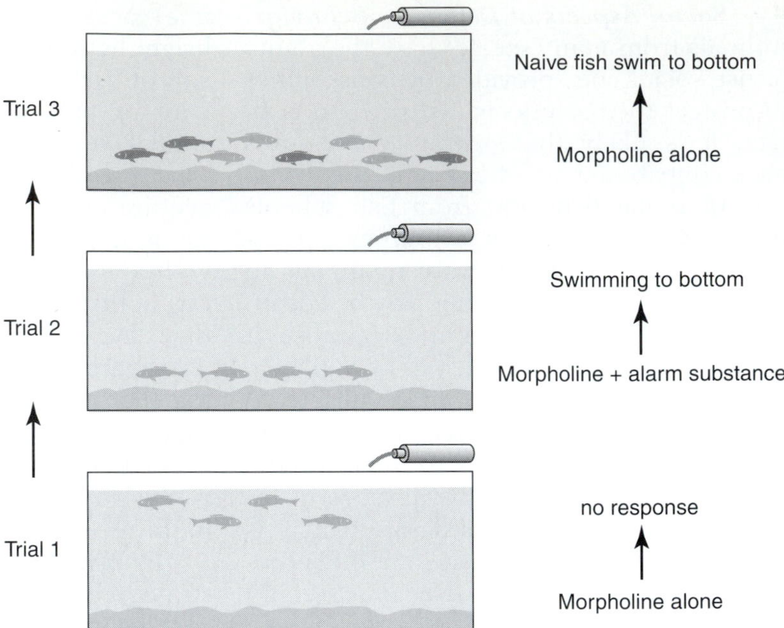

FIGURE 4.10. A representation of social learning in zebra danio fish, *Brachydanio rerio,* based on a procedure used by Suboski et al. (1990). In ***trial 1,*** an undisturbed group shows no specific response to a neutral odor, morpholine. In ***trial 2,*** the same group is exposed to a compound of morpholine and the alarm substance. Fish dive to the bottom of the tank and remain in the substratum. In ***trial 3,*** the same animals trained in the previous trial, plus a group of naive fish, are exposed only to the morpholine. Notice that trained animals respond to the morpholine by diving to the bottom, unlike the case in trial 1. Also notice that naive animals, never exposed to the alarm substance or to morpholine, acquire a recognition of the morpholine as an alarm substance by social learning.

bing in one blackbird by exposing it to an owl; the owl was not visible to a second blackbird (the observer), which could, however, see the other blackbird mobbing (the demonstrator) and a neutral model of a nonpredator animal (an Australian honeyeater dummy) or even a plastic bottle. In subsequent tests, the observer blackbird displayed mobbing behavior toward the previously neutral object (the honeyeater dummy or the bottle). A conditioning process is thus responsible for the social transmission of predator recognition in some species (see ***Chapter 13***).

A remarkable ability to inform conspecifics about the presence of a predator has evolved in several species of primates, including ringtailed lemurs (*Lemur catta*) and vervet monkeys (*Cercopithecus aethiops*). These animals are capable of emitting calls with different acoustic properties depending on the type of predator, a phenomenon that approaches linguistic properties. For example, vervets have distinctive calls for leopards, snakes, and eagles, common predators in the Amboseli National Park of Kenya, where this behavior has been carefully observed and studied using call playbacks (Seyfarth et al. 1980). Interestingly, monkeys walking on the ground tended to move up the trees when hearing a playback of a "leopard call," whereas they would rapidly move down a tree when they heard an "eagle call." A "snake call" tended to induce a looking-down behavior, and if vervets were on the ground, they would adopt a bipedal posture while looking around them. These behaviors are notable because they are appropriate to the typical location of the predator (ground or air).

4.f. Alarm Reactions and Indirect Fitness. The apparent paradox of aposematic coloration was briefly mentioned in ***section 4.c.*** What would be the benefit of aposematic coloration for the individual animal that gets eaten by the inexperienced predator? Following the concept of group selection (see ***Chapter 2, section 5.g,*** pp. 56–57), one could argue that whereas the individual animal dies, its conspecifics are more likely to survive. A trait that confers some advantage to a conspecific at a cost to the bearer is defined as *altruistic.* Obviously, "advantage" and "cost" are here, once again, defined in terms of reproductive output, although the most direct implication of aposematic coloration is related to survival. Altruistic traits seem hard to explain because they lead to the bearer's death, which therefore prevents the transmission of the underlying genes to the next generation. How could the genes coding for aposematic coloration spread in a population if the individuals first showing such a trait would tend to die?

One possible answer to this question is provided by *kinship theory,* a set of principles first proposed by the British biologist William D. Hamilton [1936–2000] and widely believed to provide an explanation for the evolution of many traits that are altruistic (Hamilton 1964). The basic idea of kinship theory, briefly pointed out in ***Chapter 2,*** is that an individual's fitness involves the classic Darwinian component called direct fitness (i.e., producing direct descent through offspring) and also an indirect component; the addition of these two is referred to as inclusive fitness. It is indirect fitness that can help us understand the evolution of traits that reduce the bearer's direct fitness (for example, by causing its death) but that might increase its indirect fitness sufficiently to compensate for the loss and allow for the underlying genes to spread. For example, if a moth lays several hundred eggs in a plant and the emerging caterpillars develop aposematic coloration, the death of one of them in attracting an inexperienced predator may provide protection for the others, which are all relatives. If the eggs have been fertilized by a single male, then the caterpillars in this particular bush will all be siblings and thus will share, on average, 50% of their genes. The shared genes that are critical in this example are those that determine individual variability within a particular species (obviously, many shared genes are species specific, but kinship theory is not concerned with these genes). The altruist trait is thus contributing to the spread of its underlying genes by increasing the fitness of those likely to bear copies of such genes because of kinship. Notice that the word "altruistic" applies to the character in a superficial sense; since the character promotes the inclusive fitness of kin, it is as genetically "selfish" as any regular character that promotes the inclusive fitness of direct descendants.

Two corollaries must be obvious from this brief description of kinship theory. First, any theory emphasizing a role for genes shared among conspecifics must have important implications for the evolution of social behavior. The bulk of examples will be discussed in ***Chapter 5*** because they bear predominantly on patterns of reproductive behavior. Below, however, the case of alarm calls in mammals will be discussed in detail. Second, any serious attempt to test kinship theory should involve individual identification of animals in natural populations, as well as a measurement of their degree of genetic relatedness. It is easy to imagine the practical difficulties incurred by such demands!

These requirements were met by a long-term research project that concentrated on the functional significance of *alarm calls* in the Belding's ground squirrel, *Spermophilus beldingi* (Sherman 1985). Two basic pieces of empirical evidence are necessary to test kinship theory. First, the theory demands for alarm calls to be costly if they are to be classified as altruistic traits. Second, the theory predicts that individuals with relatives living nearby and thus benefiting from the calls should be more likely to exhibit altruistic alarm calls than individuals with few or no nearby relatives. Sherman studied ground squirrels in a population of marked individuals located in the Sierra Nevada Mountains of California since 1969. A pedigree was developed for the animals in this particular colony that allowed the observers to identify each of the animals in any particular episode involving a predator, as well as their degree of relatedness. Ground squirrels live in burrows and forage actively on the ground during the day. They periodically rear on their hind legs to gather information about the immediate surroundings. Alarm calls are emitted in this posture when predators are detected.

Ground squirrels emit different types of calls, depending on whether the predator is approaching on the ground (e.g., a coyote) or from the air (e.g., a hawk). A comparison of callers and noncallers in predatory encounters involving terrestrial and aerial predators shows that callers pay with their lives proportionately more often in the case of ground predators. Kinship theory therefore suggests that alarm calls about terrestrial (but not aerial) predators are altruistic. One possibility is that the additional cost of these calls is compensated by a relatively high degree of genetic relatedness between the caller and the conspecifics being warned by the call. Whereas the caller stands a chance of being captured that is twice the size of that of a noncaller, its relatives benefit by escaping into the safety of the burrow. By contrast, callers appear to benefit directly when the alarm refers to an aerial predator; that is, their own chances of being caught are substantially reduced by that behavior. Observations suggest that calls induced by aerial predators incite a generalized reaction in those squirrels that are nearby; the scene may be one of visual confusion for the predator, since rapacious birds hunt predominantly by vision.

Ground squirrels, like other social mammals, have a dispersal pattern that varies as a function of the animal's sex. Males usually leave their original group after the first year of life and enter into new groups as juveniles. By contrast, females tend to remain in the area where they were born. This peculiar dispersal pattern implies that genetic relatedness among individuals living in spatial proximity would tend to be higher for females than for males. This feature allows for a test of kinship theory within the same species, as the theory clearly predicts that altruistic alarm calls (terrestrial predators)

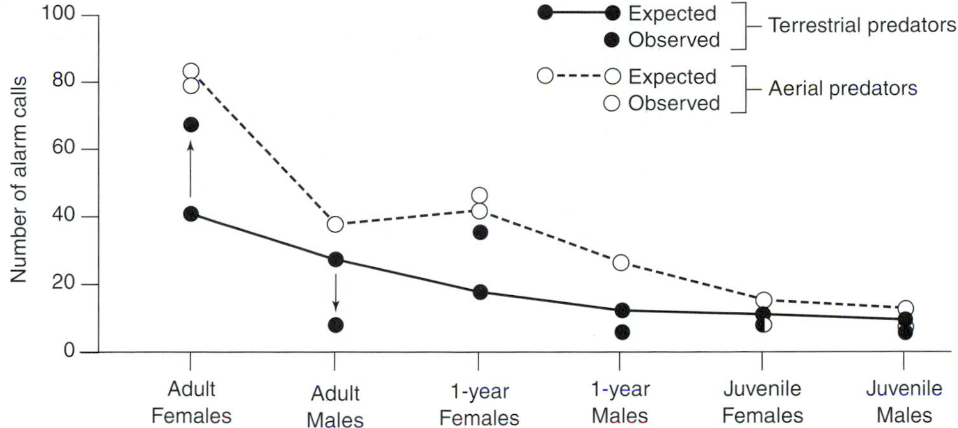

FIGURE 4.11. Adult female Belding ground squirrels (*Spermophilus beldingi*) emit a greater-than-chance number of alarm calls and males emit a less-than-chance number of calls after detecting a terrestrial predator (dark circles; see arrows). Because females, but not males, are likely to benefit relatives living in the same area, and because calls for terrestrial predators are costly, this behavior is defined as altruistic. Such cases of altruistic behavior can be explained in terms of kinship theory. The number of expected and observed calls for aerial predators (open circles) is very similar, suggesting that this type of call is not altruistic (Sherman 1985).

should be performed predominantly by females, but there should be no sexual differences in the frequency of nonaltruistic calls (aerial predators). The main results are presented in ***Figure 4.11,*** in which the continuous and broken lines represent the distribution of alarm calls expected by chance alone for terrestrial and aerial predators, respectively. Although females emit both types of alarm calls more frequently than males, the distribution of observed and expected calls differs (particularly in adult animals) more for the terrestrial predators than for the aerial predators. When a coyote or some similar ground predator is approaching, it is the females that predominantly alarm the community, at a measurable cost of paying with their own lives for doing so. Males, on the other hand, only rarely engage in this antipredator behavior. These data support the conclusion that, at least in some instances, altruistic behaviors evolve because of the reproductive benefits conferred by the altruist animal to its genetic relatives.

5. TYPES OF INTERACTION: A SUMMARY

Several types of interactions between individual animals were covered in this chapter and it may be clarifying to try to summarize their main features (see ***Table 4.2***). Although these interactions turned around feeding behavior, they can also be observed in the context of other types of function, notably reproductive behavior. These will be covered in ***Chapter 5.***

TABLE 4.2 Types of Interactions

Interaction	*Type*	*Benefits*	*Example (section)*
Competition	Interspecific	Only one animal	Galapagos finches *(1)*
Cooperation	Intraspecific	All individuals	Juvenile ravens *(3.e.)*
Mutualism	Interspecific	All individuals	Honeyguides–Boran men *(3.i.)*
Parasitism	Interspecific	Parasite (at host's cost)	Bears robbing hoarded food *(3.i.)*
Predator-Prey	Interspecific	Predator (at prey's cost)	Bat-moth *(4.a.)*
Altruism	Intraspecific	Recipient (at altruist's cost)	Ground squirrel alarm calls *(4.f.)*

6. KEY TERMS

aggressive mimicry 110
alarm calls 116
alarm substance 113
altruism 115
aposematic coloration 110
Batesian mimicry 111
central place foraging 91
character displacement 85
coevolution 103
cognitive map 104
competitive exclusion 84
constraints 91
cooperation 98
cost-benefit analysis 86
crypticity 110
deception 98
demonstrator 99
diet selection 90
dodging behavior 97
echolocation 106
ecological niche 84
encephalization quotient (EQ) 112
exploratory behavior 94
fearfulness 112
fight-flight reaction 111
figure-background discrimination 110
food aversion learning 100
food-hoarding behavior 100
frequency-dependent selection 107
hippocampal formation 101
information center 98
kinship theory 115
latent learning 95
life-dinner principle 106
marginal value theorem 87
mobbing 113
Müllerian mimicry 111
mutualism 103
negative transfer 103
observer 99
optimal foraging models 86
parasitism 103
positive transfer 103
predator-prey system 105
profitability 90
rules of thumb 88
sampling 89
search image 95
sit-and-wait predators 93
social enhancement 98
social learning 99
spatial learning 101
stimulus generalization 111
stotting display 111

7. REFERENCES

Barnett, S. A. (1975). *The rat.* Chicago: Chicago University Press.

Beck, B. B. (1980). *Animal tool behavior: The use and manufacture of tools by animals.* New York: Garland Press.

Blanchard, R. J., Flannelly, K. J., & Blanchard, D. C. (1986). Defensive behaviors of laboratory and wild *Rattus norvegicus*. *Journal of Comparative Psychology,* **100,** 101–107.

Bolen, R. H., & Green, S. M. (1997). Use of olfactory cues in foraging by owl monkeys (*Aotus nancymai*) and capuchin monkeys (*Cebus apella*). *Journal of Comparative Psychology,* **111,** 152–158.

Brodbeck, D. R. (1994). Memory for spatial and local cues: A comparison of a storing and a nonstoring species. *Animal Learning & Behavior,* **22,** 119–133.

Brodbeck, D. R., & Shettleworth, S. J. (1995). Matching location and color of a compound stimulus: Comparison of a food-storing and a nonstoring bird species. *Journal of Experimental Psychology: Animal Behavior Processes,* **21,** 64–77.

Caraco, T. (1981). Risk sensitivity and foraging groups. *Ecology,* **62,** 527–531.

Caro, T. M. (1986). The functions of stotting in Thomson's gazelles: Some tests of the predictions. *Animal Behaviour,* **34,** 663–684.

Charnov, E. L. (1976). Optimal foraging: The marginal value theorem. *Theoretical Population Biology,* **9,** 129–136.

Coleman, S. L., & Mellgren, R. L. (1997). Social enhancement and interference of food finding in zebra finches (*Taeniopygia guttata*). *Journal of Comparative Psychology,* **111,** 242–250.

Connell, J. H. (1961). The influence of interspecific competition and other factors on the distribution of the barnacle *Chthamalus stellatus*. *Ecology,* **42,** 710–723.

Curio, E., Ernest, U., & Vieth, W. (1978). Cultural transmission of enemy recognition: One function of mobbing. *Science,* **202,** 899–901.

Curtis, H., & Barnes, N. S. (1989). *Biology* (5th ed.). New York: Worth.

Darwin, C. (1859/1993). *The origin of species.* New York: Random House.

Dawkins, R., & Krebs, J. R. (1979). Arms race between and within species. *Proceedings of the Royal Society of London,* **B205,** 489–511.

Diamond, J. M. (1973). Distributional ecology of New Guinea birds. *Science,* **179,** 759–769.

Eisenberg, J. F. (1981). *The mammalian radiations.* Chicago: Chicago University Press.

Fisher, J., & Hinde, R. A. (1949). The opening of milk bottles by birds. *British Birds,* **42,** 347–357.

Galef, B. G. Jr. (1986). Social interaction modifies learned aversions, sodium appetite, and both palatability and handling-time induced dietary preferences in rats (*R. norvegicus*). *Journal of Comparative Psychology,* **100,** 432–439.

Galef, B. G. Jr. (1990). An adaptationist perspective on social learning, social feeding, and social foraging in Norway rats. In D. A. Dewsbury (Ed.), *Contemporary issues in comparative psychology* (pp. 55–79). Sunderland: Sinauer.

Galef, B. G. Jr., Iliffe, C. P., & Whiskin, E. E. (1994). Social influences on rats' (*Rattus norvegicus*) preferences for flavored foods, scented nest materials, and odors associated with harborage sites: Are flavored foods special? *Journal of Comparative Psychology,* **108,** 266–273.

Galef, B. G. Jr., Marczinski, C. A., Murray, K. A., & Whiskin, E. E. (2001). Food stealing by young Norway rats (*Rattus norvegicus*). *Journal of Comparative Psychology,* **115,** 16–21.

Gartner, J. V. Jr., Crabtree, R. E., & Sulak, K. J. (1997). Feeding at depth. In D. J. Randall & A. P. Farrell (Eds.), *Deep-sea fishes* (pp. 115–193). New York: Academic Press.

Gilbert, L. E. (1971). Butterfly-plant coevolution: Has *Passiflora adenopoda* won the selectional race with heliconiine butterflies? *Science,* **172,** 585–586.

Goodall, J. (1986). *The chimpanzees of Gombe.* Cambridge: Harvard University Press.

Grant, P. R. (1986). *Ecology and evolution of Darwin's finches.* Princeton: Princeton University Press.

Griffin, D. R. (1958). *Listening in the dark. The acoustic orientation of bats and men.* New Haven: Yale University Press.

Hall, K., & Schaller, G. (1964). Tool-using behavior of the California sea otter. *Journal of Mammalogy,* **45,** 287–298.

Hamilton, W. D. (1964). The genetical evolution of social behavior, I and II. *Journal of Theoretical Biology,* **7,** 1–52.

Hauser, M. D. (1993). Ontogeny of foraging behavior in wild vervet monkeys (*Cercopithecus aethiops*): Social interactions and survival. *Journal of Comparative Psychology,* **107,** 276–282.

Heinrich, B., & Marzluff, J. (1995). Why ravens share. *American Scientist,* **83,** 342–355.

Hikami, K., Hasegawa, Y., & Matsuzawa, T. (1990). Social transmission of food preferences in Japanese monkeys (*Macaca fuscata*) after mere exposure or aversion training. *Journal of Comparative Psychology,* **104,** 233–237.

Hunt, G. R. (1996). Manufacture and use of hook-tools by New Caledonian crows. *Nature,* **379,** 249–251.

Inoue-Nakamura, N., & Matsuzawa, T. (1997). Development of stone tool use by wild chimpanzees (*Pan troglodytes*). *Journal of Comparative Psychology,* **111,** 159–173.

Isack, H. A., & Reyer, H.-U. (1989). Honeyguides and honey gatherers: Interspecific communication in a symbiotic relationship. *Science,* **243,** 1343–1346.

Janzen, D. H. (1966). Coevolution of mutualism between ants and acacias in Central America. *Evolution,* **20,** 249–275.

Jones, R. B., Mills, A. D., & Faure, J.-M. (1991). Genetic and experiential manipulations of fear-related behavior in Japanese quail chicks (*Coturnix coturnix japonica*). *Journal of Comparative Psychology,* **105,** 15–24.

Kamil, A. C., & Balda, R. P. (1985). Cache recovery and spatial memory in Clark's nutcrackers (*Nucifraga columbiana*). *Journal of Experimental Psychology: Animal Behavior Processes,* **11,** 95–111.

Kaufman, J. D., Burghardt, G. M., & Phillips, J. A. (1994). Density-dependent foraging strategy of a large carnivorous lizard, the savanna monitor (*Varanus albigularis*). *Journal of Comparative Psychology,* **108,** 381–384.

Kohler, W. (1927). *The mentality of apes.* London: Routledge & Kegan Paul.

Krebs, J. R., Erichsen, J. T., Webber, M. I., & Charnov, E. L. (1977). Optimal prey selection in the great tit, *Parus major. Animal Behaviour,* **25,** 30–38.

Krebs, J. R., Kacelnik, A., & Taylor, P. (1978). Test of optimal sampling by foraging great tits. *Nature,* **275,** 27–31.

Krebs, J. R., Ryan, J., & Charnov, E. L. (1974). Hunting by expectation or optimal foraging? A study of patch use by chickadees. *Animal Behaviour,* **22,** 953–964.

Langley, W. M. (1987). Specializations in the predatory behavior of grasshopper mice (*Onychomys leucogaster* and *O. torridus*): A comparison with the golden hamster (*Mesocricetus auratus*). *Journal of Comparative Psychology,* **101,** 322–327.

Losey, J. E., Ives, A. R., Harmon, J., Ballantyne, F., & Brown, C. (1997). A polymorphism maintained by opposite patterns of parasitism and predation. *Nature,* **388,** 269–272.

McQuoid, L. M., & Galef, B. G. Jr. (1992). Social influences on feeding site selection by Burmese fowl (*Gallus gallus*). *Journal of Comparative Psychology,* **106,** 137–141.

Menzel, E. W. Jr. (1973). Leadership and communication in young chimpanzees. In E. W. Menzel, Jr. (Ed.), *Precultural primate behavior* (pp. 192–225). Basel: Karger.

Owen, D. (1980). *Camouflage and mimicry.* Chicago, IL: Chicago University Press.

Phelps, M. R., & Roberts, W. A. (1989). Central-place foraging by *Rattus norvegicus* on the radial maze. *Journal of Comparative Psychology,* **103,** 326–338.

Pierotti, R., & Annett, C. (1987). Reproductive consequences of dietary specialization and switching in an ecological generalist. In A. C. Kamil, J. R. Krebs, & H. R. Pulliam (Eds.), *Foraging behavior* (pp. 417–442). New York: Plenum.

Pietriewicz, A. T., & Kamil, A. C. (1979). Search image formation in the blue jay (*Cyanocitta cristata*). *Science,* **204,** 1332–1333.

Pietsch, T. W., & Grobecker, D. B. (1978). The compleat angler: Aggressive mimicry in an antennariid anglerfish. *Science,* **201,** 369–370.

Redhead, E., & Tyler, P. A. (1988). An experimental analysis of optimal foraging behaviour in patchy environments. *Quarterly Journal of Experimental Psychology,* **40B,** 83–102.

Renner, M. J. (1988). Learning during exploration: The role of behavioral topography during exploration in determining subsequent adaptive behavior. *International Journal of Comparative Psychology,* **2,** 43–56.

Roeder, K. D. (1967). *Nerve cells and insect behavior.* Cambridge, MA: Harvard University Press.

Roeder, K. D., & Treat, A. E. (1961). The detection and evasion of bats by moths. *American Scientist,* **49,** 135–148.

Schluter, D., Price, T. D., & Grant, P. R. (1985). Ecological character displacement in Darwin's finches. *Science,* **227,** 1056–1059.

Schwenk, K. (1994). Why snakes have forked tongues. *Science,* **263,** 1573–1577.

Seyfarth, R. M., Cheney, D. L., & Marler, P. (1980). Monkey responses to three different alarm calls: Evidence for predator classification and semantic communication. *Science,* **210,** 801–803.

Sherman, P. W. (1985). Alarm calls of Belding's ground squirrels to aerial predators: Nepotism or self-preservation? *Behavioral Ecology & Sociobiology,* **17,** 313–323.

Sherry, D. F., & Galef, B. G. Jr. (1984). Cultural transmission without imitation: Milk bottle opening by birds. *Animal Behaviour,* **32,** 937–938.

Sherry, D. F., Jacobs, L. F., & Gaulin, S. J. C. (1992). Spatial memory and adaptive specialization of the hippocampus. *Trends in Neuroscience,* **15,** 298–303.

Sherry, D. F., Vaccarino, A. L., Buckenham, K., & Herz, R. S. (1989). The hippocampal complex of food-storing birds. *Brain, Behavior, and Evolution,* **34,** 308–317.

Shettleworth, S. J. (1989). Animals foraging in the lab: Problems and promises. *Journal of Experimental Psychology: Animal Behavior Processes,* **15,** 81–87.

Stephan, H., Frahm, H., & Baron, G. (1981). New and revised data on volumes of brain structures in insectivores and primates. *Folia Primatologica,* **35,** 1–29.

Suboski, M. D., Bain, S., Carty, A. E., McQuoid, L. M., Seelen, M. I., & Seifert, M. (1990). Alarm reaction in acquisition and social transmission of simulated-predator recognition by zebra danio fish (*Brachydanio rerio*). *Journal of Comparative Psychology,* **104,** 101–112.

Suga, N. (1990). Biosonar and neural computation in bats. *Scientific American,* **262** (June), 60–68.

Suzuki, S., Kuroda, S., & Nishihara, T. (1995). Tool-set for termite-fishing by chimpanzees in the Ndoki forest, Congo. *Behaviour,* **132,** 219–235.

Tolman, E. C., & Honzik, C. H. (1930). Introduction and removal of reward and maze performance in rats. *University of California Publications in Psychology,* **4,** 257–275.

Vander Wall, S. B. (1990). *Food hoarding in animals.* Chicago: Chicago University Press.

Vander Wall, S. B., & Smith, K. G. (1987). Cache-protecting behavior of food-hoarding animals. In A. C. Kamil, J. R. Krebs, & H. R. Pullian (Eds.), *Foraging behavior* (pp. 611–644). New York: Plenum.

Visalberghi, E., Fragaszy, D. M., & Savage-Rumbaugh, S. (1995). Performance in a tool-using task by common chimpanzees (*Pan troglodytes*), bonobos (*Pan paniscus*), an orangutan (*Pongo pygmaeus*), and capuchin monkeys (*Cebus apella*). *Journal of Comparative Psychology,* **109,** 52–60.

Ward, P., & Zahavi, A. (1973). The importance of certain assemblages of birds as "information-centers" for food-finding. *Ibis,* **115,** 517–534.

Westergaard, G. C., & Fragaszy, D. M. (1987). The manufacture and use of tools by capuchin monkeys (*Cebus apella*). *Journal of Comparative Psychology,* **101,** 159–168.

Whishaw, I. Q., & Tomie, J.-A. (1987). Food wresting and dodging: Strategies used by rats (*Rattus norvegicus*) for obtaining and protecting food from conspecifics. *Journal of Comparative Psychology,* **101,** 202–209.

Yoerg, S. I. (1991). Social feeding reverses learned flavor aversions in spotted hyenas (*Crocuta crocuta*). *Journal of Comparative Psychology,* **105,** 185–189.

Yoerg, S. I., & Kamil, A. C. (1988). Diet choices of blue jays (*Cyanocitta cristata*) as a function of time spent foraging. *Journal of Comparative Psychology,* **102,** 230–235.

CHAPTER 5

Reproductive and Social Behavior

MAIN GENERALIZATIONS OF CHAPTER 5

- *The association of males and females in sexually reproducing species and of mother and offspring in species displaying parental care are the building blocks of sociality.*
- *Properties of social groups, such as the mating system, emerge out of individual traits, both behavioral and neurobiological.*
- *Natural selection, sexual selection, kinship, cooperation, and reciprocity are key concepts for an understanding of social evolution.*

Reproductive and social behaviors are a direct consequence of *sexual reproduction*—that is, the production of new individuals by the joint contribution of germ cells from a male and a female. Sexual reproduction is based on two major processes: meiosis and fertilization. In meiosis, germ cells are formed that contain a single set of chromosomes (haploid), as opposed to the double number of chromosomes (diploid) typical of all other types of cells, referred to as somatic cells. Fertilization is the process whereby the female's egg (defined as the larger of the two germ cells, usually nonmotile) is penetrated by a male's sperm cell (defined as the smaller and more motile of the germ cells) to form a fertilized egg, called a zygote. The diploid number is thus restored in the zygote, from which a new organism will grow through a series of complex developmental processes. Fertilization requires the coming together of individual organisms, thus creating a variety of problems with important behavioral implications. Sexual partners must find each other, they must agree to engage in sexual interaction, and they must ensure that the resulting young will develop to achieve maturity so that the process will repeat itself in the next generation. These basic problems generate such behavioral categories as courtship, territoriality, aggression and competition, mate choice, reciprocity, parental care, and many others that will be reviewed in this chapter.

But not all animals reproduce sexually. For example, the cnidarian *Hydra,* an animal that lives as a solitary polyp and possesses a diffuse nerve net, can reproduce by the outgrowth of a bodily part that fragments itself and forms a new individual. This process, called budding, occurs in other cnidarians, such as sea anemones, as well as in some sponges and worms. In other animals, including some species of insects, fish, frogs, and lizards, females are capable of producing viable offspring out of unfertilized eggs, a process labeled parthenogenesis. These examples of *asexual reproduction* do not involve meiosis or fertilization and can lead to a fast reproductive rate. Cell division, or mitosis, is the basis for the proliferation of cells leading to a complete adult. The resulting offspring, however, will all be clones, possessing the same genotype and therefore constituting a highly uniform population. Some species are known to be exclusively parthenogenetic, such as the whiptail lizard, *Cnemidophorus uniparens,* a species consisting only of females (Crews & Moore 1986). In fact, one-third of the 45 lizard species of this genus are known to be parthenogenetic! Usually, however, sexual and asexual modes of reproduction coexist in the same animals, which can be said to switch from one modality to the other depending on some environmental factors, such as the abundance of food resources (see ***Chapter 2, section 4.i.,*** pp. 47–49). This situation exemplifies a trade-off between genetic diversity (a key consequence of sexual reproduction) and speed of reproduction (the hallmark of asexual reproduction), each conferring greater fitness depending on prevailing ecological conditions.

Sexual reproduction forces animals to engage in a minimum amount of interaction in the context of courtship and copulation. This may be seen as the building block for other forms of interaction, which may include the mother-offspring form, the male-male form, and eventually, the grouping of animals into societies with various degrees of structure and stratification. Such grouping could have, in turn, important consequences for the evolution of lineages in which social behavior is a prominent feature. Wyles et al. (1983) argued, for example, that social interactions may cause the spread of new behaviors, perhaps introduced into the group by some particularly "creative" animal, such that the group is driven to novel ecological pressures. For example, an animal may develop a way of exploiting a new source of food, perhaps through the use of a tool, that may subsequently spread throughout the group by social enhancement or by imitation. As a result of this behavioral innovation and its social transmission, the animals' fitness may be affected by the capacity of their digestive system to process the new type of food and by their ingenuity for designing the required tools to access the resource. Interestingly enough, the rate of morphological evolution (as estimated from the fossil record) is positively correlated with the relative size of the brain in a selected set of vertebrate species, including salamanders, frogs, lizards, birds, and mammals. Because the size of the brain is related to the animal's capacity for behavioral plasticity (see ***Chapter 8***), this finding supports the view that behavioral complexity is associated with high rates of evolutionary change. It follows then that behavior not only evolves, but it can also affect the evolutionary process, at least in certain species.

1. Mechanisms Underlying Social Behavior

Comparative psychologists have traditionally emphasized the idea that living organisms are organized according to layers or levels, like a Mayan pyramid. Physicochemical processes lie at the bottom of the pyramid, and cellular, tissue, organ, system, and behavioral levels are placed in order on top. In such a view it has been typically assumed that social interactions occupy the uppermost level of organization. But social behavior, whatever its type, must be sustained upon a variety of capacities exhibited by individual organisms. It is, for example, hard to imagine how natural selection could directly affect whether a group of animals displays a monogamic or polygynic mating system (discussed in ***section 2***, below), because these properties are not really part of the organism's phenotype but are properties that emerge from the way animals organize themselves. Natural selection must, therefore, be influencing some behavioral capacities that, in interaction with prevailing ecological conditions, result in specific group properties, such as the formation of monogamous pairs or polygynous harems. Generally speaking, the social behavior of animals is based upon processes that are expressed in individuals. Examples of such processes are the ability to discriminate faces, the sensitivity to social reinforcement, and the capacity to discriminate between kin and non-kin, among others.

1.a. Perceptual Basis of Social Behavior. The social dynamics of a group may demand the capacity for *individual recognition* of group members. Garter snakes (*Thamnophis radix*) within the same litter vary in their dietary preferences, but when two snakes show preference for the same type of food, they might engage in costly combat. This snake attacks a prey, such as a worm, preferentially when it is in the mouth of another snake, and it may end up eating the other snake in the process of catching the worm. Experiments show that garter snakes tend to stay in close contact with other snakes that have proved to be noncompetitors in prior encounters involving competition for food (that is, snakes that do not fight over the same type of food). Snakes separated for a period of 5 months still had the ability to recognize a previous noncompetitor with which they had established an association (Yeager & Burghardt 1991).

While it seems clear that garter snakes have the ability to recognize a specific individual on the basis of prior experience, exactly how such recognition is achieved has not yet been determined.

It is interesting that an ability so intimately related to social behavior of the most sophisticated kind, such as individual recognition, is present in snakes, which are not characterized by their social culture. Such abilities may evolve in highly restricted contexts, and once they are available, they may come to play a part in a larger or different context. Relative to this ulterior function, such traits are said to be preadaptations: prerequisites for one function (as individual recognition is to complex social behavior) that evolved for a somewhat different function (perhaps, as in the snake example, as a way of aggregating with noncompetitor foragers). This is a dangerous concept to use because it is potentially tainted with teleological meaning; an adaptation cannot evolve for some future function, no matter how appropriate it might seem. Current adaptive function provides the selective context within which biological traits evolve. However, once a beneficial by-product of an adaptation is available, it provides raw material from which natural selection can work further.

The ability to discriminate individuals within a group would seem a prerequisite for social situations involving the establishment of bonds among specific animals, as is the case in monogamic species. In Australian budgerigars (*Melopsittacus undulatus*), a small parrot that nests in colonies, monogamic pairs are established for life. Budgerigars recognize individuals by their faces, in terms of the colors and patterns of markings in the feathers of the head, and the size and color of the eye's iris (Brown & Dooling 1992, 1993). Extensive experiments with real and computer-generated images of conspecifics show that the most perceptually salient markings are those that provide information about the animal's sex, age, and group. For example, face color is more easily discriminated by these birds than body color, which may be how budgerigars recognize members of their breeding colony. Furthermore, female budgerigars (but not males) find it easy to discriminate faces in which the size of the iris is varied, a cue used by males during courtship (males rapidly contract the pupil, thus showing a large iris, as part of the courtship display).

Another social situation that may require individual recognition is that of highly structured groups in which access to resources (e.g., receptive females, food, etc.) depends on the position occupied by an animal within the social hierarchy. Primates, for example, live in groups that are characterized by a *leadership* structure. Social interactions can have, as a result, definite consequences for these animals. Displaying "inappropriate" behavior toward a dominant animal may result in aggressive interactions in which there is a risk of bodily injury and even death. Chimpanzees (*Pan troglodytes*) exposed to pictures of individuals from their own group with whom they tend to have aggressive interactions exhibit an increase in heart rate. By contrast, their heart rate does not change much when they are exposed to pictures of companions, and it decreases in frequency for images of strangers (Boysen & Berntson 1989).

Such changes in heart rate indicate the chimpanzee's ability to discriminate a specific individual according to prior social interactions. Indeed, it has been claimed that chimpanzees can actually discriminate a self-image from that of a another chimpanzee (Gallup 1970). In the original observations, a mark was placed in the chimpanzee's ear and eyebrow ridge (i.e., outside their direct view) while the animal was under anesthesia. Subsequently, the number of times the animal touched the marks was recorded before the introduction of a mirror and during access to the mirror. Many of the chimpanzees subjected to this or similar testing procedures exhibited a tendency to touch the marked places when confronted with the mirror. This evidence suggests the possibility that chimpanzees possess the ability of *self-recognition*. Studies with other primates, including New World monkeys, Old World monkeys, and other apes further suggested that self-recognition may be restricted to a few species. However, these results should be taken with caution given the small sample size of most of the studies. Chimpanzees are the exception since more than 150 chimpanzees have been tested systematically; the evidence indicates extensive individual differences, with some studies finding evidence of mirror self-recognition in only a small fraction of the sample (only 1 out of 11 chimpanzees passed the mirror test in a study reported by Swartz & Evans 1991). While there is little doubt that some chimpanzees use the mirror image to explore their own body rather than the image in the mirror, the extent to which this reflects a self-recognition capacity is still unclear (de Veer & van den Bos 1999).

1.b. Social Reinforcement. The emotional effect afforded by the image of a conspecific in the example of the chimpanzee described previously suggests that social interactions have the potential to be reinforcing. Just as the behavior of a hungry animal is affected by food reinforcement, that of a social animal may be affected by social reinforcement. *Social reinforcement* refers to the ability of certain animals to learn about situations in which the motivationally important event is the presence of a conspecific or the opportunity to interact with it. Examples of social reinforcement may be found in the context of mother-offspring, sibling, male-female, or male-male interactions, among others.

The reproductive behavior of marmoset monkeys (*Callithrix jacchus*) is characterized by a substantial amount of helping in rearing the young. Female marmosets give birth to twins; whereas the mother provides care and nurture for the infants, other members of the family and even unrelated adults also contribute to caring for the twins. It is not surprising, therefore, that the maternal behavior of female marmosets is highly dependent on prior experience in infant care. Using an ingenious apparatus, Pryce et al. (1993) demonstrated that these females are motivated to learn a seemingly arbitrary response for a social consequence. In a typical session, a female is housed in a chamber in which there is a bar that can be pressed downwards while, at the same time, a tape recorder is playing back an infant's distress call. By pressing the bar, the female can stop the distress call and turn on the lights on an adjacent compartment to see a replica of an infant sitting there; this lasts for 15 s, and then the trial starts all over again. It is in fact somewhat surprising that such a reinforcement was effective at all, since no direct contact with an infant was involved in this procedure.

Direct approach to a group of siblings is a powerful social reinforcer for domestic chicks (*Gallus gallus*), as shown in experiments in which these animals learn to walk through a straight alley toward a goal chamber (Vallortigara et al. 1990). Four-day-old chicks rapidly learn to approach a goal where they find five other chicks with which they spent the initial days of their lives. Interestingly, although all chicks learn to run this alley for social reinforcement, females appear to be more sensitive than males to social reinforcement because they learn significantly faster. By contrast, males are better than females when the behavior is reinforced with food. This indicates that this difference does not reflect a general gender effect on learning, but rather gender-specific sensitivity to the kind of reinforcement involved in the situation.

An obvious and perhaps nearly universal source of social reinforcement should be found in the context of *copulatory behavior,* which involves male-female interactions. Clearly, motivation for seeking copulatory interactions could be seen as a proxy (or "rule of thumb") for reproductive success. But copulatory behavior is subject to somewhat peculiar conditions when compared to, say, feeding behavior. In many species, breeding is restrained in time to a season, or females may become receptive according to some cycle (e.g., the estrous cycle of many female mammals). In addition, male sexual behavior may undergo a postejaculatory refractory period immediately after copulation, during which the motivational power of sexual reinforcement decreases drastically. These peculiarities have forced comparative psychologists to develop special procedures to study sexual reinforcement. One way to reduce the impact of refractory periods is to train males to work not for access to a female but for the presentation of a stimulus that has reliably signaled access to a receptive female in the past. This procedure is based on the ability of *primary reinforcers* (such as copulation) to transfer part of their motivational properties to signaling cues, which can subsequently be used as *secondary reinforcers.* For example, Everitt et al. (1987) presented male rats (*Rattus norvegicus*) with a light for 30 s and subsequently introduced a receptive female into the male's chamber. After a few such light-copulation temporal pairings, the males were able to acquire a bar-pressing response whose only consequence was to turn on that same light. As a secondary reinforcer, the light supported motivated behavior, but it did not support actual copulation and ejaculation; therefore, the males were not exposed to postejaculatory refractory periods.

Learning in a male-male context can be easily illustrated in species exhibiting strong territorial behavior, such as is the case with several species of fish (sticklebacks, blue gouramies, and Siamese fighting fish are popular experimental models). Male Siamese fighting fish (*Betta splendens*), for example, exhibit a variety of behaviors toward intruding males, including a frontal approach display involving the erection of all fins and gill covers. Interestingly, *Betta* males treat their own image reflected by a mirror as if they were dealing with an intruder, a feature that has practical value for designing experimental situations. For example, Thompson and Sturn (1965) presented a light followed 10 s later by a mirror reflection lasting for 15 s. After a few such trials, those same responses begun to be controlled by the light. Such a transfer of reinforcing value indicates that males are willing to respond to visual cues that reliably predict an approaching male. Does the resident male benefit from predicting the impending presence of a competitor?

1.c. From Social Reinforcement to Reproductive Success. This question shifts our attention from proximate to ultimate causes of behavior because by "benefit" I, in fact, mean "reproductive benefit" (see ***Chapter 2, section 5,*** pp. 49–59). Perhaps the functional advantage of predicting biologically important events is that the organism can prepare for their imminent arrival (Hollis 1982). One way to approach this issue is to look at the reproductive success of animals for which important events are either predictable or unpredictable. For example, would territorial males be more efficient in defending their territory if intruders were reliably signaled? Would these males increase their chances of copulating with a receptive female if they were already expecting her arrival? Since defending territories and copulating with females can be safely assumed to be positively correlated with reproductive success, a positive answer to these questions would provide support for the idea that sensitivity to social reinforcement has adaptive significance.

Experiments with blue gourami fish (*Trichogaster trichopterus*) and Japanese quail (*Coturnix japonica*) show that males gain a reproductive advantage when the environment provides signals for the impending presence of another male or of a female. In both species, males typically set up small territories early in the reproductive season and defend them against intruders; females rarely pair with males lacking a territory. For these males, a major problem consists in discriminating whether the approaching conspecific is another male or a receptive female. If the residential male fails to discriminate, it may end up courting an intruder male or attacking a receptive female, both of which would be maladaptive. But if males can predict the sex of the arriving animal, they might be at an advantage.

In one experiment (Hollis et al. 1995), blue gourami males received training in which either a light was paired with the presentation of another male (L+ males), or followed by nothing (L– males; these males were in fact given access to a rival 6 hr later serving as unpaired controls). In a subsequent contest, 10 of the 11 L+ males won the encounter, whereas only 1 of the 11 L– males actually managed to chase away the other male. But this winning experience seems to have also a long-lasting effect on future encounters. When a few days later these animals were confronted with new intruders—and even without the benefit of a signal—6 of the 11 L+ males proved able to win this second contest, whereas none of the 11 L– males managed to win the second contest. Notice that it is not a characteristic of the male that allows it to win or lose the contest, but rather a feature of the environment (presence vs. absence of a signal). Once a male wins a contest, its chances of staying a winner are very high; losers, however, tend to stay losers.

Gutiérrez and Domjan (1996) trained quail males in an auditory discrimination test in which a tone signaled the presence of a female, whereas another tone signaled its absence. In a crucial test, the males were placed in the same arena and given exposure to a tone. The trick was, however, that this tone predicted the female for one of the males (the T+ male), but not for the other (the T– male). As ***Figure 5.1-a*** shows, T+ males copulated faster with the female than T– males. When the tone was presented, T+ males rapidly approached the area where the female usually appeared in the arena, whereas T– males remained unaltered. It is this anticipatory approach response that provides a copulatory advantage for the T+ males. In fact, male quail given paired training release a significantly larger number of sperm cells than unpaired controls (Domjan et al. 1998). Experiments with male blue gouramis show that paired training can have striking reproductive benefits (Hollis et al. 1997). In this case it was possible to compare the number of offspring produced by males exposed to pairings of a light with the presentation of a female (L+ males) with those produced by males given unpaired presentations of the light and the female (L– males). The results, shown in ***Figure 5.1-b,*** clearly indicate that L+ males were able to foster a significantly larger number of offspring than L– males. The reason for this difference is related to the discrimination problem mentioned above. L– males engage in substantially more aggressive behavior than L+ males, which more readily court the incoming female. L– males lose many courtship opportunities because they discourage females with their aggressive displays.

1.d. Kin Recognition. There are at least two reasons to expect the evolution of kin-recognition mechanisms. On the one hand, kinship effects, such as the alarm calls reviewed in ***Chapter 4*** (pp. 115–117), require kin-recognition abilities. Kinship theory suggests that the evolution of seemingly *altruistic behavior* could be driven by *indirect fitness,* that is, the transfer of benefits (at a cost to the altruist animal) to genetically related individuals. This functional idea implies the evolution of proximate mechanisms that would allow animals to recognize relatives so as to properly allocate their costly altruistic behavior. For example, although female ground squirrels are generally prone to emit alarm calls, they are more so if there are relatives living in the same area than if they are surrounded by nonrelatives (Sherman 1977).

On the other hand, the avoidance of inbreeding, which, as mentioned in ***Chapter 3*** (p. 67), may lead to inbreeding depression because of the accumulation of deleterious genes in a homozygous condition, may also require kin-recognition abilities. Obviously, kin recognition can be seen as a special case of *species recognition,* typically occurring at the time of courtship. Imagine that there is a continuum from, say, a sibling (maximum genetic relatedness) to a member of another species (minimum genetic relatedness). Op-

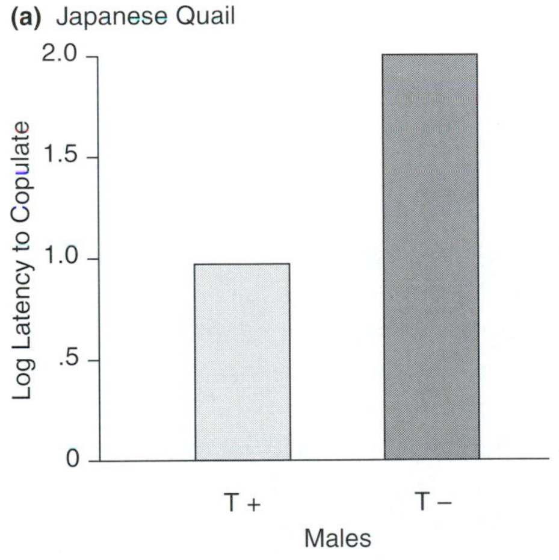

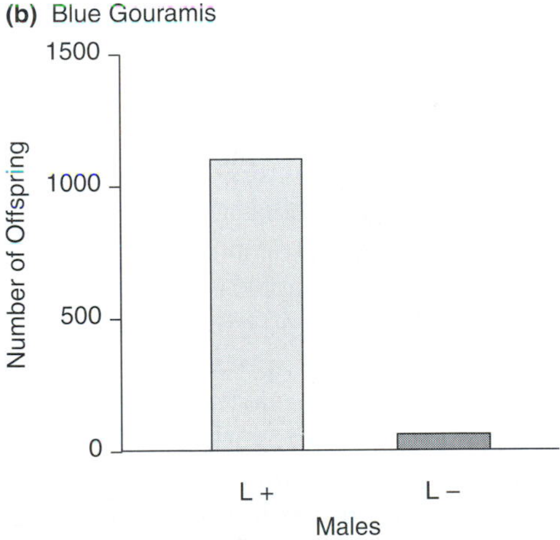

FIGURE 5.1. (*a*) Male Japanese quail (*Coturnix japonica*) copulate faster (i.e., shorter latencies) when the arrival of the female is preceded by a tone that had signaled incoming females in the past (T+) than when the tone had not been paired with a female (T–; Gutiérrez & Domjan 1996). (*b*) Male blue gouramis (*Trichogaster trichopterus*) sired more offspring when the female was preceded by a light that in the past had signaled incoming females (L+), than when the light had not been paired with females in the past (L–; Hollis et al. 1997).

timal reproductive behavior requires animals not only to avoid interspecific copulation (extreme outbreeding), which translates into wasted, nonviable hybrids, but also to avoid mating with closely related individuals (extreme inbreeding), which translates into inbreeding depression (Bateson 1983).

How does kin recognition work? Given the difficulties that we have to establish the genealogical tree of our own families, one might expect animals to follow relatively simple rules of thumb to distinguish their kin. Perhaps the simplest one is to recognize between familiar and stranger animals; if two animals have grown together, the chance is good that they are genetically related. On the other hand, strangers are likely to come from outside of the animal's circle of relatives. Experiments can easily dissociate "familiarity" from "relatedness" by a manipulation of litter or group composition. Such dissociations suggest that in some cases the rule based on familiarity is at work, whereas in other cases, kin recognition appears to involve something other than simple familiarity.

For example, some primates aggregate in terms of familiarity, ignoring relatives with whom they have had little previous interaction (Frederickson & Sackett 1984). In the Galapagos mockingbird (*Nesomimus parvulus*), kin recognition appears to be based on simple associative learning: Birds recognize those that provided them with food when they were nestlings (Curry & Grant 1990). Birds are more likely to provide help to a nest if they had been fed by both of the adults currently breeding in that nest than when they had been fed by only one or none of them. Usually, nestlings are fed by their parents, and so this associative rule of thumb would normally lead to the allocation of altruistic behavior (by the helper bird) to kin (the breeding pair). In contrast, female ground squirrels (*Spermophilus beldingi*) are able to discriminate relatives even when they have been reared apart by different mothers (Holmes & Sherman 1982). In the laboratory, newborns were interchanged among different mothers to create various combinations. As adults, females reared apart engaged in less aggressive behavior when they were siblings than when they were unrelated. In female ground squirrels, therefore, kin recognition appears to be based on more than simple familiarity, although it is not yet clear exactly how females can discriminate their relatives (could it be through family-specific odors?). One intriguing possibility is that the information essential for kin recognition in ground squirrels, and perhaps other mammals, is acquired during the period of intrauterine development (Robinson & Smotherman 1991). Rat fetuses are capable of responding to a variety of sensory stimuli and of acquiring preferences and responses through associative learning that affect their postnatal behavior (fetal learning is discussed in detail in ***Chapter 11, section 1.c.,*** pp. 408–410).

2. MATING SYSTEMS

Sexually reproducing species depend on the ability of individual male and female animals to come together to reproduce. Fertilization, whether internal (as in mammals) or external (as in many fish and amphibians), requires some amount of time shared by the male and female. If this male-female relationship is viewed in a sufficiently short time interval, then it could be argued that all species are monogamous. However, when the time interval is stretched to encompass many such fertilization events, species are found to display a variety of mating systems. Indeed, in some species, a specific pair of individuals maintains an exclusive bond for the entire reproductive season and, even more astonishing, for their entire lives in some notable cases. This is referred to as *monogamy.* In other cases, however, only a relatively small proportion of the reproductively able males in a population inseminates most of the females. This arrangement, called *polygyny,* implies the displacement of some males by others from the reproductive scene, a goal achieved through a variety of strategies. In other, relatively rarer cases, the opposite is observed; that is, females compete with each other for access to males, a system that implies that only a relatively small proportion of the females accesses the reproductively active male population. The name for this is *polyandry.* There are many variations of these basic themes, including in some species a combination of the last two in a system that came to be known as *polygynandry,* in which several males and females shared their reproductive potential. What drives mating systems to become so diverse?

2.a. Polygyny. In polygynous systems, the reproductive sex ratio in a population is biased toward females: More females than males reproduce in any given season. Two general issues permeate the study of polygynous systems, namely, *male-male competition* and *female choice* (Darwin 1871). These will be considered in the context of the three major categories of polygyny: resource-defense polygyny, mate-defense polygyny, and lek polygyny.

In *resource-defense polygyny,* males actively compete for and defend some resource from other males. This resource, which is the basis for their reproductive success, could be a nesting area, a feeding territory, or some other similar feature. In many species, the male sets up a nesting territory that he defends from intruding males and where he waits for approaching females. Such is the case for the blue gourami and similar fish species mentioned in the previous section. In the fish *Pseudolabrus celidotus,* for example, the deeper the male's territory, the greater the female's preference for the territory. It is possible that deeper nesting areas experience less predation on the eggs than more superficial territories (Jones 1981). In other species, it is the quality of the territory that counts. Areas with more suitable vegetation for nesting or with more food tend to attract more females. In a field experiment with red-winged blackbirds (*Agelaius phoeniceus*), Wimberger (1988) demonstrated that males provided with extra food in their territories by the experimenter were able to attract more females. Obviously, the food itself may attract the females, and once they are available, the resident male's chances for copulation might increase.

In *mate-defense polygyny* the defended resource is a group of receptive females. This variety of polygyny is particularly ubiquitous in mammals, and it has been argued that it is the common system in our own species, *Homo sapiens.* In the *Ethnographic Atlas* published by Murdock (1967), 850 of a total of 1,170 human societies, roughly 73%, were described as polygynous. As shown by Hartung (1982), the prevalence of polygyny remains even if the *Atlas*'s sample is selected such that major geographic areas or language families are equally represented. On the basis of studies of the sexual lives of leaders in Ancient Rome, Betzig (1992) concluded that power correlates with access to reproductive resources. In classic Rome, marriage was monogamic, but adultery was widely tolerated and even promoted in some cases. Whereas emperors were notorious for their consistently adulterous behavior, similar reproductive benefits may have been accrued by members of the upper class who had access to slaves, sometimes in the thousands. In this regard, imperial Rome appears to be no different from other ancient civilizations, including Egyptian, Aztec, Inca, Indian, and Chinese societies, for which records confirm that leaders could access hundreds and even thousands of women for sexual purposes. Roman data from urban residences show that masters often freed their slaves, an act called manumission, and endowed them with material benefits and good social opportunities. Betzig interpreted such behavior as resulting from father's trying to find a place within mainstream society for their natural children.

While these data are thought-provoking, one must keep in mind the difficulties associated with the measurement of reproductive success. Historical reviews lack the quantitative rigor and precision required for an assessment of human mating systems. For example, different indices of reproductive success may not always co-vary as one might expect. Indirect indices, such as broad patterns of sexual behavior, are easier to observe and record, whereas more direct and valid measures of reproductive success, such as number of surviving offspring, are difficult to determine. Reliable knowledge about paternity would require the use of DNA fingerprinting, which not always is a viable alternative. Whereas the human data are consistent with a polygynous view of our species, precise determination of paternity would be required for a better understanding of human mating systems.

The potential dissociation between different indices of reproductive success, some less direct than others (such as copulations or ejaculations relative to number of offspring, for example) makes an excellent methodological point. However, the fact remains that dominance and reproductive success have been found to be related in research with a variety of species, under both laboratory and field conditions. Detailed observations of the number of intromissions or ejaculations (comparable to sexual life data) and of a more direct measure of reproductive success, such as the actual number of pups sired by dominant and submissive males, were reported by Dewsbury (1981) for male deer mice (*Peromyscus maniculatus*). In these studies, males classified as dominant in aggressive encounters ejaculated more than submissive males, but their production of offspring depended on the test conditions. When the two males were kept in a small enclosure together with a female, the dominant male showed a higher frequency of ejaculation, but it produced a similar number of offspring compared to the submissive male. However, in a seminatural enclosure the dominant males were able to produce a significantly larger number of offspring. One corollary of these observations is that direct (e.g., offspring) and indirect (e.g., copulations) indices of reproductive success need not always tell the same story, despite our intuitions.

What determines dominance in a polygynous species? One important factor is simply the male's body size. A long-term study of an elephant seal (*Mirounga angustirostris*) population in the Año Nuevo rookery, in California, supports the conclusion that dominance and reproductive success (as measured indirectly in terms of copulatory success) are positively correlated. Moreover, it is the larger males that tend to become more dominant by successfully defending a group of females (Haley et al. 1994). A similar field study on red deer (*Cervus elaphus*) shows that the male's reproductive success (as measured in terms of number of offspring per year) depends on its ability to dominate other competing males. Such fighting ability is in turn correlated with body size and age (Clutton-Brock et al. 1982). Interestingly, the effects of male-male competition for dominance can have far-reaching consequences for submissive animals. In one study involving mice (*Mus musculus*), for example, the prior establishment of dominance impaired the reproductive success of submissive males even when the dominant male was not present during the test (D'Amato 1988). A similar effect was described previously for the blue gourami fish (see ***section 1.c.***). Prior winning-losing experience and body size are important factors in the shaping of dominant male behavior.

In *lek polygyny* males defend a specific piece of courtship ground or area, called the lek, itself having no resources. Females usually visit several leks before settling for a specific male. Although most leking species are sexually dimorphic in size or in ornamentation, females may be in some cases more attracted to the location of the lek than to the male itself. In the black grouse (*Tetreo tetrix*), cocks compete intensely for leks located in a central position, in open ground arenas, and these are the males generally favored by females in terms of copulation opportunities (Kruijt & de Vos 1988). Perhaps the most famous of all leking species is the peacock (*Pavo cristatus*). Male peacocks grow their tail feathers very slowly, so that the older ones tend to be those displaying the largest tails. These tail feathers have eye-like structures in the tips, called ocelli, which apparently attract the attention of females. Petrie et al. (1991) found a very strong positive correlation between the number of females attracted by males and the number of ocelli in their tails (varying between 140 and 170 ocelli). Females may thus be manifesting a preference to mate with males that show evidence of longevity in terms of tail size and ornamentation.

In other leking species, notably in the bowerbirds, females are attracted to the conspicuous bowers prepared and guarded by males, themselves not particularly conspicuous (***Figure 5.2***). Most males of the 18 species of bowerbirds collect bright and colorful objects, such as flowers, fruits, shells, butterfly wings, feathers, and even artificial objects (e.g., pieces of paper or plastic) to decorate their bowers. Borgia (1985) observed males of the satin bowerbird (*Ptilonorhynchus violaceus*) destroying other males' bowers and "stealing" decorative objects; blue feathers appeared to be particularly attractive. The number of decorative

FIGURE 5.2. Bowerbird males build these sophisticated structures, called bowers, and adorn them with all sorts of colorful and shining objects (*Encyclopedia of Birds* (1998).

objects apparently signals the male's degree of dominance over other males, a factor that attracts females and allows these males to obtain most of the matings.

2.b. Polygyny and Sexual Selection. Polygynous mating systems are accompanied by a cluster of biological characteristics. *Male-male competition* for access to females involves the establishment and defense of territories (as in the blue gourami fish) or leks (peacocks), the evolution of large male body size (elephant seals), body ornamentation (birds of paradise), and the construction of sophisticated bowers (bowerbirds), among other biological features. These are usually associated with strong sexual dimorphism in *secondary sexual characters* (e.g., body size, feather ornamentation, fur coloration, etc.), behavior, or both. Many of these features puzzled Darwin since they would appear to make the males more vulnerable to predators (e.g., the peacock's bright coloration) or simply involve a costly burden in terms of development and maintenance (e.g., the deer's antlers). Male-male aggression is very vicious in some species; contests often result in physical inferiority, sickness, and even death for the defeated animal. It is in these characters that the importance of reproductive success is appreciated to the fullest degree, since they evolve even though they seem to compromise the animal's own survival. Males engage in such costly behaviors, or in the development of costly morphological traits, because these features contribute to their reproductive success. Such a success is based on their ability to supersede other males and/or in the preference exhibited by females for such features. In some species, females may actively select their mates, and they may even promote competition among the males, a process referred to as *female choice.* This combination of male-male competition and female choice are the two central aspects of what Darwin (1871) called *sexual selection,* a special case of natural selection that clearly illustrates the coevolution of reproductive behavior and morphology among male and female animals.

Sexual selection highlights the fact that males and females within a single species may be exposed to very different selective pressures and thus exhibit different patterns of reproductive success. ***Figure 5.3*** shows one representative example from the research with red deer already mentioned (Clutton-Brock et al. 1982). It is clear that the reproductive success of males is far more dependent on age than that of females. For any given season, therefore, there would tend to be more variability in reproductive success in males than in females. Over the entire lifetime of the animals, reproductive success may balance out, but only for males capable of surviving long enough. The fact that polygynous males and females are subject to very different selective pressures may help explain their sexual dimorphism. For example, males and females often differ in the degree to which they provide care for their young. *Parental investment* has been defined as anything a parent does for an offspring at the expense of the parent's ability to invest in other offspring (Trivers 1972). Bateman (1948) pointed out that the degree of parental investment in the offspring and the degree of variability in reproductive success are inversely related. The sex displaying the greatest amount of parental investment is usually the one with the least variability in reproductive success. This inverse relationship between parental investment and variation in reproductive success of males vs. females is known as *Bateman's principle.* Generally speaking, females need just a few copulations to fertilize most of their eggs,

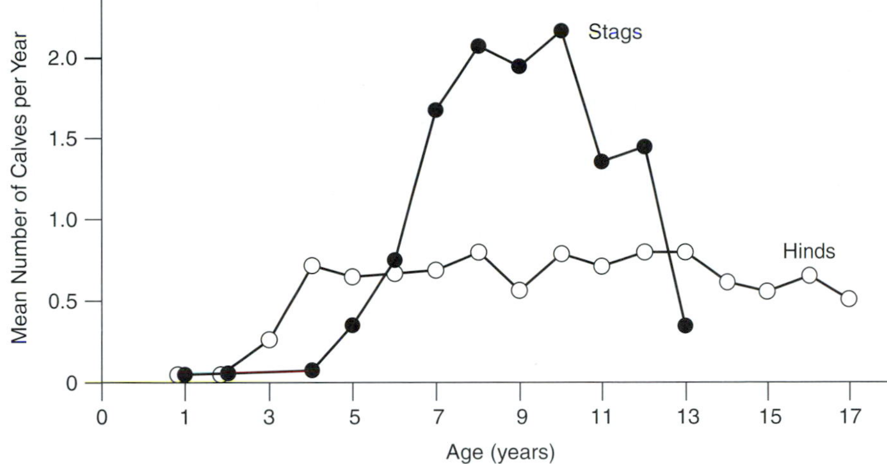

FIGURE 5.3. Reproductive success of male (stags) and female (hinds) red deer (*Cervus elaphus*) as a function of age (Clutton-Brock et al. 1982). Notice that reproductive success peaks at a particular age for males, whereas it is relatively constant for females.

but they are limited by the number of eggs they can produce over their entire life. In contrast, males are primarily limited by the number of copulations with different females, given that sperm cells are relatively more economical to produce (compared to the female's massive egg cell, sperm cells are little more than mere DNA). In addition, females usually invest more in the offspring than males in terms of parental care (consider milk production by female mammals as an example). Bateman (1948) showed this to be the case in experiments with the fruitfly *Drosophila melanogaster*. Males and females were placed in equal numbers in bottles, and their reproductive output was measured as a function of the number of mates. Whereas the reproductive success of males increased as a function of the number of females with which they copulated, the success of females was constant and independent of the number of mates.

2.c. Polyandry and Monogamy. An interesting way to obtain support for a scientific theory is to look at cases that depart from the usual. In polyandrous species, in which several females mate with a single male, sexual selection theory would lead one to expect some interesting departures from the picture described in the previous two sections. For example, females (rather than males) should compete for mates, show more conspicuous secondary sexual characteristics, and exhibit greater variation in success. These predictions seem to apply at least to some species. A well-studied case is that of the spotted sandpiper (*Actitis macularia*). Field studies at Leech Lake, Minnesota, show that males are in charge of providing parental care, including incubation of the eggs (Oring 1985). Females can lay up to five clutches (a clutch size of four eggs is usual) by copulating with different males, but each male can raise only a single clutch in the entire breeding season. As predicted from sexual selection theory, females compete among themselves for territories and mates in intensive aggressive contests. The reproductive success of females is correlated with their age and the size of the territory that they are able to defend (a patch of beach on the lake), and, critically from the theoretical point of view, the female's success increases with the number of mates (Oring et al. 1991).

Species displaying a monogamous system also provide an interesting exception to polygyny. When mates bond for long periods of time, intrasexual competition (male-male or female-female) may be drastically reduced. As a result, variation in reproductive success should be approximately equal across sexes, and the species should show little or no sexual dimorphism. Among the primates, for example, polygyny is the rule, and sexual dimorphism in body size and coloration is particularly salient. Gorillas and baboons provide very good examples; males can be almost double the size of females. The few primates that exhibit a monogamous reproductive behavior, such as gibbons, tamarins, and marmosets, are notorious for their lack of sexual differentiation. Tamarin and marmoset monkeys belong to the family Callitrichidae, endemic to South America and notable because monogamy is the norm among its species. Snowdon (1990) suggested that monogamy in these monkeys is related to infant care. Polygyny is correlated with the female's ability to successfully raise the young on her own. This allows the males to leave the pair after copulation and invest little in the progeny without incurring large reproductive costs. But if the survival of the offspring were dependent on the contribution of both parents, it would pay for males to stay with the female and invest in the offspring. The evolutionary conflict from the male's perspective lies in the relative degree of *paternal uncertainty*. In mammals, for example, the long period of pregnancy and lactation imposes a close mother-offspring association, assuring mothers that they are directing their efforts to their own offspring. Fathers, however, are generally less certain about their paternity. Paternal behaviors directed toward nonrelated infants, at a cost of generating offspring (Triver's definition of parental care), would tend to be eliminated by natural selection. One way in which males could increase their chances of directing costly paternal behavior toward their own offspring is through the development of a bond with the female that excludes other males.

Marmoset and tamarin females of almost all species give birth to identical twins. They live in groups characterized by communal care of the infants. In cotton-top tamarins (*Saguinus oedipus*), there is usually a single reproductive mother who is also in charge of marking the group's territory by depositing a scent in the trees. Such *scent marking* has an additional function: It prevents other mature females from becoming pregnant. Savage et al. (1988) demonstrated that the transfer of wood pieces containing scent into a group cage can significantly delay ovulation in the females of this group. Older siblings, as well as males and females other than the parents, contribute by carrying the babies (these monkeys live almost exclusively in trees) and by providing protection from predators. Young animals stay in the group apparently because direct experience in infant care is required for successful parenting as adults. In a series of experiments with captive marmosets, Epple (1978) found that the most successful monogamic pairs are those in which both parents have cared for infants in the past, and the least successful are those in which both parents lack caregiving experience.

It would probably be a mistake to assume that sexual selection is not present in monogamous systems. If, for example, the males or females of a given population were to differ in some important respect, this could lead to intense competition for mates even if monogamic pairs are formed as a result of such competition. Individuals of either sex may differ in such traits as fecundity, experience, ability to provide parental care, territory quality, and similar features. In some monogamous species there is a small degree of sexual dimorphism that may relate to female preferences. In the swallow (*Hirundo rustica*), females prefer to copulate with males that have long and symmetrical tails, as Møller (1992) was able to demonstrate by artificially modifying the tails of males. There is no obvious male-male competition in these animals, which suggests that the evolution of the male swallow's tail is probably based mainly on female choice. Female choice may also be responsible for the widespread occurrence of extra-pair copulations. In many species presumed to be monogamous and, therefore, sexually exclusive, DNA fingerprinting techniques demonstrate that females may copulate with males other than the apparent father in the nest (Westneat et al. 1990).

2.d. Manipulating Mating Systems. The idea that mating systems are emergent properties of groups of animals interacting for reproductive purposes was suggested at the beginning of this chapter. Intuitively, one would expect such emergent group properties to be very sensitive to prevailing ecological conditions and show a great deal of flexibility as the conditions change. This intuition has been at the basis of some theoretical developments. For example, Orians (1969) suggested that the female's choice of a mate may depend on the quality of the environment that the male is defending. From the female's point of view, it may be preferable to mate with a male that already has a mate if the availability of food in the environment compensates for the reduced contribution in rearing the offspring that she is likely to receive from a polygynous male. That is, given a choice between a single male in a poor habitat and a polygynous male in a rich habitat, it may pay for the female to choose the latter. According to Orians, differences in habitat quality determine whether the female chooses a monogamous or a polygynous system. He refers to such a difference as the *polygyny threshold*.

Emlen and Oring (1977) took this argument a step further and suggested that the temporal and spatial distribution of resources in the environment (such as food) determine the number of females that an individual male can monopolize. Environments have a potential to support polygynous arrangements (i.e., a polygyny threshold) to the extent that their quality makes it possible for a male to defend a group of females. Mate defense is costly in terms of time and energy, and this cost increases with the number of females defended. If the females are scattered in large territories because, for example, food is relatively scarce, it may be impossible for a single male to prevent other males from copulating with the female. Emlen and Oring pointed out that polygyny requires not only appropriate environmental factors but also an appropriate set of biological features that would allow an animal to capitalize on such environmental potential. For example, when care of the young can be assumed entirely by one sex (e.g., female mammals providing milk), or care is highly reduced (e.g., precocial young born with highly developed sensory-motor abilities), the potential for polygyny increases. Because resources fluctuate spatially (in different habitats within the region of distribution of a species) and temporally (during the year, and across years), individuals should be able to adjust their mating behavior so as to maximize reproductive success.

The hypothesis that the nature of the mating system depends on environmental resources can actually be put to test through field experiments, since some of the critical factors can be manipulated in the animal's natural environment. This allows us to shift our attention from pure observation to actual experimentation, a step required to be able to demonstrate a causal connection between ecological factors and mating behavior. A very peculiar bird, the dunnock (*Prunella modularis*), has provided valuable data about the role of environmental variables on mating systems (Davis 1992). Dunnocks are small, sparrow-like passerines found in the open grasslands and woodlands of England that can be easily marked for individual recognition and studied on a long-term basis. The dunnock is peculiar in that practically all the mating systems described previously can be observed within the same population. Monogamy, polygyny (e.g., a male defending 2 females), polyandry (e.g., 2 or 3 males sharing a single female), and even polygynandry (e.g., 2 or 3 males sharing 2, 3, or 4 females) can be found in a population distributed over an area of about 16 hectares, within the botanical gardens of Cambridge University.

Observations had suggested a correlation between the size of the female's territory and the mating system: The smaller the territory, the more likely for the system to be monogamy. If the size of the female's territory was related, on the one hand, to food density and, on the other hand, to the ability of the male to monopolize the female, then it should be possible to induce a shift in mating system by changing food availability in the environment. Additional food was supplied in a set of randomly selected territories. Large cylinders containing oats, bread crumbs, maggots, and mealworms were distributed in these territories, and food was replaced daily during a period of several months. This sudden increase in food availability led to marked changes in the behavior of dunnocks, but some of the critical changes were a function of the animal's sex. For example, food supplements did not affect the size of a male's territory, but they led to a significant decrease in territory size for females. Not only were female territories smaller when food was added, but the territory of specific females shifted in size, suggesting a degree of flexibility to adjust to changing environmental conditions. Most critically, such a shift in territory size for females resulted in a significant change in the prevailing mating systems, as shown in ***Figure 5.4.*** A high incidence of polyandrous groups gave way to an increase in the frequency of monogamous and polygynandrous groups, thus showing that the decrease in the female's territory size made it possible for males either to successfully monopolize (monogamy) a single female or to share (polygynandry) up to four females and defend them from intruding males. Added food also changed the behavior of males, decreasing significantly the amount of time spent foraging and increasing the amount of time spent perching and interacting with conspecifics. However, these changes occurred in all males, independently of the particular mating system they were displaying. It appears, therefore, that food density determines the size of a female's territory, which, in turn, determines the male's ability to defend that female and, in consequence, the type of mating system present in a particular group of dunnocks.

2.e. Alternative Mating Strategies. The intriguing possibility that more than one

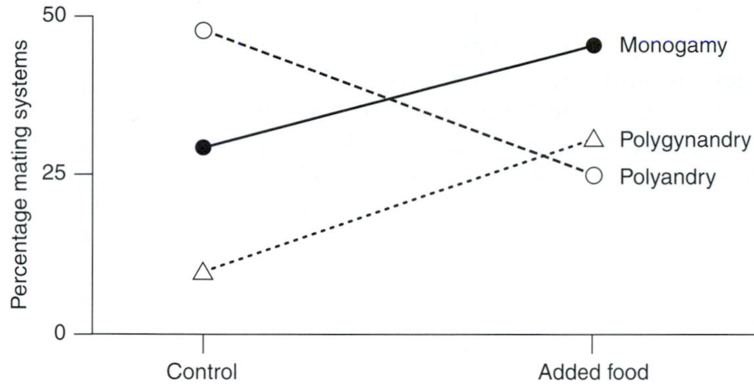

FIGURE 5.4. As a result of the addition of food and the shrinking of female territories, the incidence of monogamy and polygynandry increased, but the frequency of polyandry decreased, in a population of dunnocks, *Prunella modularis* (Davies 1992).

morph would be present in a particular population was discussed in ***Chapter 2, section 5.b.*** (pp. 50–51) in the context of the preservation of genetic diversity. Some of the most interesting examples of morphological and behavioral polymorphisms to be found in nature actually occur in connection with reproductive biology. In many species, sexual selection has driven the male population toward distinctly different but stable phenotypes, usually correlated with a unique mating strategy. As a result, these reproductive tactics are viewed as alternative expressions of a polymorphic trait. A typical case involves males that differ in body size, as described in ***Chapter 2*** for the Pacific salmon (*Oncorhynchus kisutch*). Reproductive success is directly related to male body size, but some males are very small and still manage to obtain access to spawning females by sneaking into the nest (Gross 1985). These differences in body size are, in fact, an expression of different life histories in these male populations. Large males (as well as females, which are also large in size) spend up to 20 months in the open sea before returning to freshwater streams to reproduce. By contrast, small males return from the sea after periods ranging between 5 and 8 months and are, therefore, smaller in size and lacking in secondary sexual characteristics. Because these two mating tactics require different phenotypes, selection is probably disruptive in this particular case (i.e., extreme phenotypes having greater reproductive success than intermediate phenotypes; see ***Figure 2.9-c,*** p. 52).

Alternative mating strategies suggest that what is fit for one male may depend on what other males are doing in the population. If the two strategies have equal reproductive success, then they will establish themselves in a population and will remain stable, with no single strategy being able to displace the other. These are referred to as *evolutionarily stable strategies* (Maynard Smith 1982). In the example of the salmon, alternative males play their chances of reproductive success by following one of two mutually exclusive tactics. Once they commit themselves to one tactic, they are excluded from the other. More commonly, the reproductive tactic exhibited by animals is of a conditional type—that is, it changes depending on some critical factor, such as age and social environment.

Young elephant seal males (*Mirounga angustirostris*), for example, cannot successfully monopolize females, probably because of their still small body size. It pays them to avoid aggressive contests with large resident males, which can be dangerous and costly. Instead, they stay in the periphery of reproductive areas and can occasionally hold a female for a sufficiently long time to copulate (Le Boeuf 1974). As the male ages, its body size will allow for chances to compete for a group of females against a large resident male. Juvenile southern sea lion males (*Otaria byronia*) appear to take a different approach: They gather in peripheral groups of about ten and raid the breeding colony, provoking a great deal of confusion. As a result of this generalized confusion, some resident males lose females and some of the raiders occasionally gain access to a female that they can defend from other males (Campagna et al. 1988). In the green tree frog (*Hyla cinerea*), some males do the calling that attracts females into their vicinity, whereas other males remain silent and simply sneak in when the opportunity for fertilization arises. The latter are called *satellite males*. In a series of field experiments, Perrill et al. (1982) demonstrated that whether a male follows a "caller" or a "satellite" strategy depends on its social context. When calling males were removed, a large proportion of the satellite males begun calling, in some cases as fast as within 5 min of the manipulation. In contrast, when calls were played back through speakers, a significant proportion of the calling males became silent.

A remarkable instance of an alternative mating strategy is illustrated by *sequential hermaphroditism*. In many species of fish in which reproduction is characterized by external fertilization (and thus absence of specialized genitalia and internal embryo growth), females have the capacity to turn into males under certain environmental conditions (Warner 1975). For example, in the blue-head wrasse (*Thalassoma bifasciatum*), animals may develop initially as either male or female. These initial males and females reproduce in groups. As they grow in body size, however, males change in coloration and settle in spawning territories, but so do females, which soon begin to produce sperm. The male-to-male and female-to-male developmental trajectories can be viewed as alternative life histories.

2.f. Mating Systems and Brain Evolution. Let's shift once more, but now from an ultimate to a proximate level of analysis. Just as social behavior is based on perceptual, associative, and motivational mechanisms (see ***section 1*** above), mating systems are similarly based upon the operation of brain mechanisms that are beginning to be understood. The ecological and parental care factors that are known to affect the development of particular mating systems must be evaluated through some proximate mechanism. An understanding of this issue is aided by a comparative study of brain features across closely related species exhibiting different mating systems. The fact that the species are closely related implies that differences in brain morphology and function are less likely the result of an extensive phylogenetic history of independent evolution. Rather, such differences can more safely be attributed to recent divergence driven by contrasting ecological and social selective pressures. This type of information will help us determine how natural selection shapes a mating system.

Rodent species of the genus *Microtus* exhibit differences in mating systems ranging from monogamy, as in pine voles (*M. pinetorum*), to polygyny, as in meadow voles (*M. pennsylvanicus*), and to promiscuous mating, as in montane voles (*M. montanus*). Relative to nonmonogamous vole species, monogamous pine voles show a greater degree of territory overlap between males and females, and a stronger contribution of fathers to infant care. In polygynous meadow voles, males have a territory that is typically between four and seven times larger than that of females. These large male territories appear to be less related to foraging than to polygynous mating, since they occur only during the breeding season. As a result, reproductive success would be far more dependent on complex spatial navigation in polygynous males than in females. Comparative studies demonstrate that polygynous males exhibit both a greater spatial learning ability and a larger hippocampal formation (relative to the size of the brain) than female meadow voles. By contrast, no such gender differences are found in monogamous pine voles that exhibit territory overlap (Sherry et al. 1992).

A similar relationship between spatial abilities and the relative size of the hippocampus has already been pointed out in connection with the food-hoarding behavior of birds (see ***Chapter 4, section 3.g.,*** pp. 100–101). It appears, therefore, that behavioral capacities dependent on complex spatial learning abilities evolve in correlation with changes in the hippocampal formation. An increase in the size of a particular brain region may involve a larger number of neurons, a correspondingly larger number of synapses, and even the development of new neuronal types adapted for specific processing functions. These evolutionary changes in the relative distribution of neural tissue may carry adaptive significance if they permit the expression of behavioral capacities critical for reproductive success.

Natural selection can also affect the evolution of mating systems in more subtle ways. Vole species are also notorious for their diversity in terms of the brain distribution of neurotransmitter receptors involved in social behavior. One such neurotransmitter is arginine vasopressin (AVP), a neuropeptide that plays a role in the regulation of social learning, scent marking, aggression, and partner preference, among other social behaviors. The distribution of AVP receptors in the brain is very different for monogamous and nonmonogamous vole species, although the actual network of connections of AVP neurons appears to be relatively constant. Apparently, then, the social behavior of voles evolved, at least in part, through the differential activation in various brain regions of the gene coding for the AVP receptor protein, rather than through a process of network rewiring (Young et al. 1997). Notice that in both cases, whether via changes in the relative size of a brain area or in the density of neurotransmitter receptors across brain areas, the evolution of behavioral capacities implicated in the various mating systems requires modifications in regulatory genes. Growth processes, whether in terms of cell numbers or in terms of protein density, must be turned on and off, and it is the task of regulatory genes to coordinate the timing of gene transcription. More about this in ***Chapter 10.***

3. Patterns of Reproductive Behavior

3.a. Territorial, Aggressive, and Agonistic Behaviors. It should be clear from the discussion on mating systems that territoriality is a prominent feature of polygynous species. Less clear, perhaps, is the fact that territories are established and actively defended in species exhibiting other types of mating arrangements. Many monogamous species (e.g., marmoset monkeys) defend an area against conspecific intruders, and in some species (e.g., wolves) an entire group may actively defend a territory. Territorial behavior is, in fact, a relatively common aspect of the behavior of animals and not necessarily restricted to reproductive behavior (animals may defend feeding, basking, or resting places from conspecifics). Perhaps the most characteristic feature of territorial behavior is the fact that the resident animal exhibits defensive behavior. Whereas the term *home range* is typically used to imply a nondefended area where an animal may look for needed resources, the term *territory* is reserved for that portion of the environment actively defended by a resident animal. Active defense of a territory may include scent marking, singing, patrolling the area, and aggressive behavior directed at intruders.

Scent marking (prominent in mammals) and singing (prominent in birds) are ways of deterring potential intruders from entering the limits of the territory. These behaviors can be viewed as attempts to provide information to a conspecific, thus constituting examples of animal *communication*. This effort by the resident animal to advertise its presence in a location may pay off if aggressive encounters are avoided. In order to be effective, *territorial aggression* must be immediate and intense, or the intruder may familiarize itself with the territory and take over some of its resources. Aggressive contests may also be costly in terms of physical injuries, which may reduce the resident's ability to further defend its territory and perform costly reproductive behaviors, such as nest building, incubation, or caring of the offspring. Therefore, these costs provide a selective pressure for the evolution of behaviors that may discourage intruders from entering an already occupied location. The term *agonistic behavior* was introduced to refer to the entire spectrum of behaviors that may be activated in an aggressive-defensive context, from overt physical contact to threatening or submissive displays (Scott 1958).

Communication involves a variety of specialized glands for scent marking in mammals. For example, hamsters (*Mesocricetus auratus*) have a pair of sebaceous glands called flank glands, which they rub against hard surfaces to mark a territory. In other mammals, marking is performed by deposition of urine, as in the familiar example of dogs. Mammals mark and countermark—that is, an animal would tend to deposit its own scent on top of the scent of another animal. Laboratory experiments with hamsters show that the top scent can completely mask the bottom scent (Wilcox & Johnston 1995). In birds, on the other hand, communication involves predominantly visual and acoustic signals. Singing often can be shown to deter potential intruders, and in some species it is performed while the bird is in flight, thus increasing the salience of the stimulus. The visual components of aggressive displays are frequently very salient and stereotyped behaviors; Huxley (1923) called them *ritualizations* to emphasize their lack of ambiguity as communication signals. Ritualization is also suggested whenever the aggressive contest is not as intense as it could be, given the strength and weapons exhibited by the animals engaged in the interaction. Snakes use venom to paralyze and kill prey, and large carnivores use a powerful bite to kill their prey; yet these weapons are not necessarily used in aggressive encounters with conspecifics. In birds, ritualization involves the adoption of very specific postures signifying threat and submission. Adelie penguins (*Pygoscelis adeliae*) threat conspecifics by moving their bills underneath one of the flippers (a so-called "bill-to-axilla" response) or by erecting the occipital crest of feathers. Threats may be accompanied by submissive postures which have the effect of appeasing the opponent. Penguins usually exhibit a so-called "slender walk" when they move through the colony, which seems to communicate a nonaggressive disposition to neighboring birds. Actual combat may ensue when intruders are not deterred from approaching a nesting area. Fighting may involve hitting the opponent with the flippers or pecking the other bird, which sometimes leads to an interlock of the opponents (Williams 1995).

Aggressive behavior is also an instrumental part of the development of *dominance*. In many animals, access to resources that are scarce or actively defended depends on a relatively strict order (e.g., the pecking order). For example, aggressive behavior among males may result in a winner and a loser, as seen previously in the case of territorial fish (***section 1.c.***). The development of a dominance hierarchy saves time and energy because it prevents constant aggression among group members. In some cases, dominance also leads to more direct payoffs: It determines access to reproductively fertile females. In deer mice (*Peromyscus maniculatus*), for example, dominant males (i.e., the ones chasing other males) copulate more often than subordinate males, and in some cases they sire more offspring (Dewsbury 1988).

3.b. Courtship Displays. Many of the concepts that are useful in understanding agonistic behavior are applicable to instances of reproductive interactions between males and females. For example, scent marking also allows hamsters to determine the presence of potential mates, and the singing behavior of birds also attracts females. In many different species, courtship involves a type of duet in which two animals maintain a sort of "conversation" based on the emission of very specific and, in some cases, highly ritualized responses. This chain reaction was described in great detail for the threspine stickleback fish (*Gasterosteus aculeatus*) by Tinbergen (1951) and is schematically presented in ***Figure 5.5.*** This is, in fact, a highly idealized representation of the sequence because these behaviors are usually influenced by such factors as motivation and learning. For example, a less motivated female may demand that the male switch from nest-pointing back to the zigzag display for another trial; and recent experience with an intruder may make the male prone to attack, rather than court, an approaching female. The entire display appears to set the stage for fertilization—the most important consequence of courtship and one that might require a great deal of synchrony between the two animals. Obviously, displays of this type also serve the general function of species recognition, a process that becomes particularly important for species with overlapping (i.e., sympatric) distribution that may rely on courtship to avoid hybridization.

It has long been recognized that some of these ritualized responses that act as signals to communicate sexual receptiveness among males and females have their phylogenetic origin in nonreproductive traits (Huxley 1923). This was, in part, the type of insight that led to the emergence of ethology (see ***Chapter 1, sections 4*** and ***5,*** pp. 15–20). For example, avian feathers probably originated as insulation structures useful in thermoregulation and were subsequently used in the context of flight. But feathers also acquired a function related to courtship and display through sexual selection (Morris 1956). Birds display elongated tail feathers, bright coloration of pectoral feathers, crests of feathers that can be erected, and appropriate movements that can make these features even more salient, as shown in ***Figure 5.6.*** The peacock, for example, not only displays his colorful tail but he also shakes these feathers to produce

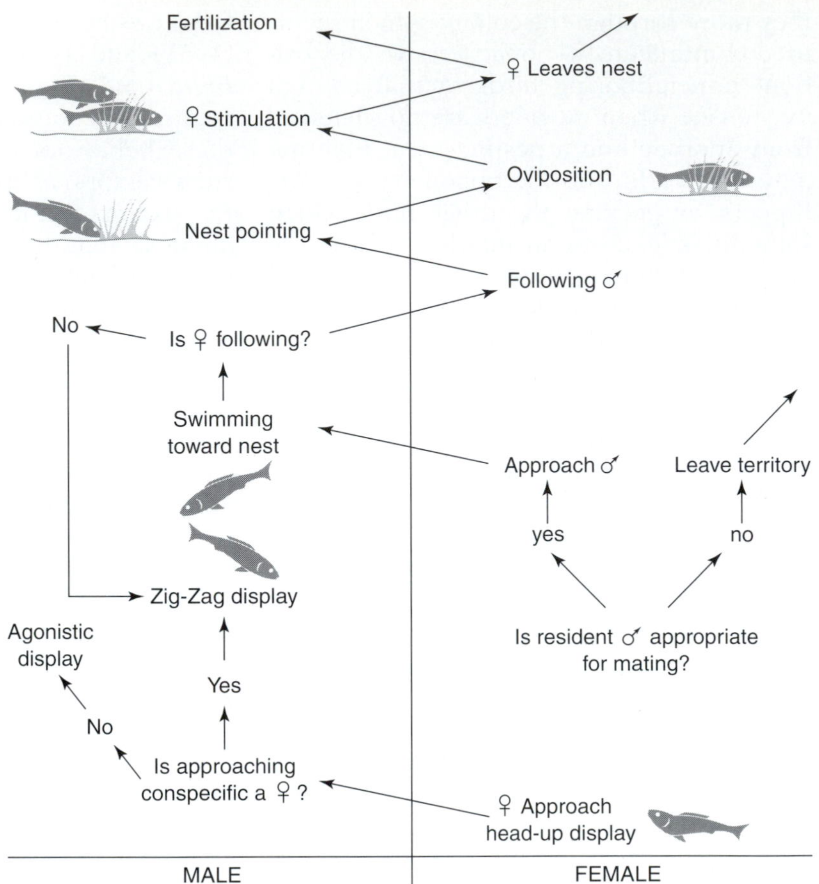

FIGURE 5.5. A classic, idealized description of the interactions of male and female stickleback fish (*Gasterosteus aculeatus*) during courtship (Tinbergen 1951). While the actual form of these behaviors is accurate, in actual courtship episodes the stream of behaviors is more variable, perhaps to some extent because animals vary in their motivation for displaying. Such variability is captured here in terms of decision points.

a sound that adds to the visual dimension of the display. The evolution of motor control over the feathers probably evolved also as a thermoregulatory mechanism. For example, a movement of the feathers from a fully depressed position (lying close to the body) to a partial erection results in varying degrees of insulation; such movements regulate the rate of heat loss and can be used to cool or warm the blood that circulates through peripheral capillaries under the skin. Other examples of behaviors occurring during courtship displays involve movements resembling preening, food-gathering, or nest-building behaviors. Such behavioral mechanisms can be viewed as

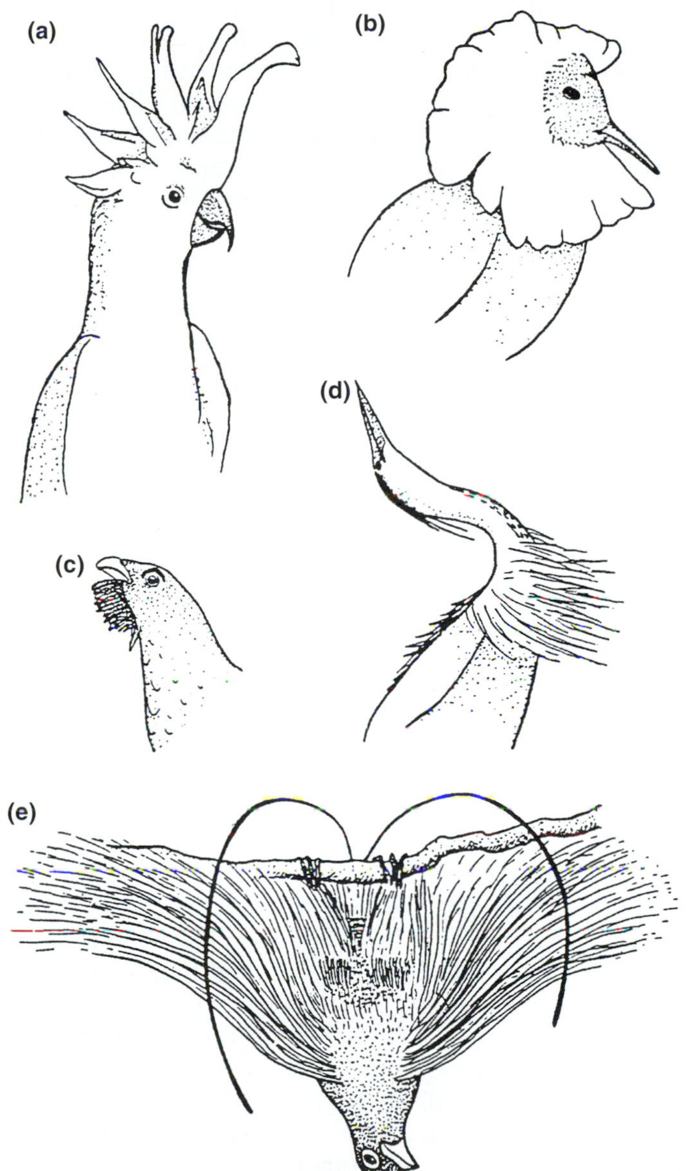

FIGURE 5.6. Courtship displays are accompanied in many species by the presence of colorful and salient plumage. Feathers in the crest ***(a)***, ruff ***(b)***, chin ***(c)***, throat ***(d)***, and flank and tail ***(e)*** have evolved to serve a function in these displays (Morris 1956).

the raw material upon which sexual selection operates. The process that leads to a shift of context for the emission of such behaviors is referred to as *displacement*. Thus, the preening like movements used in courtship by many duck species can be viewed as displaced from their original body-care function. The result seems to be, almost invariably, that the structure becomes more conspicuous or the behavior more ritualized, perhaps in part to reduce signal ambiguity.

Sexual selection can drive these traits to extreme degrees of conspicuousness in more than one way. A puzzling example is provided by the way in which long-tailed manakin males (*Chiroxiphia linearis*) display in courtship (McDonald & Potts 1994). In this species, two males usually cooperate in the display, thus making it apparently more attractive to the female. Manakins exhibit lek polygyny, and so some display areas are highly valued by females. Single-male displays are less successful in attracting females than those involving a pair of males. However, only one of the two displaying males (called the alpha male) actually copulates with the female, while the other (the beta male) contributes almost exclusively to the display. So female choice seems to be responsible for the evolution of this particular method for making the courtship display more conspicuous. Once these associations are established, the roles may remain stable for many years, suggesting that reciprocity is not involved. Alpha and beta males are not genetically related, which discards kin selection as a mechanism. So what keeps the beta male in this altruistic bond? Field observations in Costa Rica indicate that beta males copulate very rarely (only 4 beta copulations were observed out of a total of 263 recorded copulations between 1983 and 1992), that they always succeed the alpha male, that females are highly attached to the lek sites where they copulated before, and that the mating success of beta males in their first alpha season is positively correlated with that of the previous alpha males. Apparently, it is the combination of female choice and the probability to inherit the lek when the alpha male dies (a long-delayed reproductive benefit) that keep the beta male in association with the alpha male.

3.c. Assessing Fitness. Courtship displays also allow females to assess the degree of fitness of courting males. Extreme displays, such as that of the peacock, would seem to be sending a very strange message; it is as if the male were saying, "I am so fit that I can tolerate any handicap from the ornaments, colorfulness, and behavior involved in my display." Obviously, costly ornaments would be even more costly to low-quality males with poor health or deficient means to acquire resources. Zahavi and Zahavi (1997) refer to this as the *handicap principle* and suggest that signals evolve precisely to the extent that they allow the female to assess the male's genetic quality. From the female's point of view, these characters are indices of the male's fitness—a convenient rule of thumb.

An intriguing possibility has received recent attention by evolutionary psychologists: What men and women consider "beautiful" are traits that have evolved by sexual selection as proxies of fitness. In one set of studies, facial beauty has been hypothesized to convey information about the genetic quality of the person. These studies are driven by an intriguing version of sexual selection theory, according to which traits that advertise resistance to parasites are positively selected. Parasite infection lowers the general health of the organism, making it less likely to live a longer life, to compete successfully for mates, and to be able to sustain the hardships of reproduction. Parasite resistance depends on several factors, such as the organism's degree of immunocompetence and its degree of heterozygocity. Immunocompetence refers to the organism's ability to fight parasite infections by activation of the immune system. Many of the hormones that mediate the development of secondary sexual characteristics (androgens and estrogens) also lower immune activity. In men, for example, prominent jaws, chins, and cheekbones are examples of sexual characters controlled by the androgen testosterone. Therefore, hormone-dependent sexual characters may be advertising the genetic quality of the bearer: Only highly fit individuals can tolerate the handicap brought about by such prominent characters. In this context, it is interesting that experiments with human subjects show that extreme versions of features such as "jaw width" are considered particularly attractive by females and a signal of social dominance in a variety of cultures (Grammer & Thornhill 1994; Keating et al. 1981).

Another set of studies involves the so-called *waist-to-hip ratio,* or *WHR,* which appears to be a major determinant of the degree to which men find women attractive. Men from different cultures rate as most attractive and sexy those women who have a WHR of around 0.7 (i.e., the size of the waist is about 70% of the size of the hip, independently of the absolute dimensions). Singh (1993) found this to be true even when male subjects were rating drawings of women varying in "weight" and also in the WHR. For each weight category, the most attractive figures were those of drawings representing a WHR of 0.7, even though underweight and overweight drawings were generally rated as less attractive than normal-weight ones (***Figure 5.7***). This type of evidence is interesting but not particularly compelling from the evolutionary point of view, unless the WHR provides additional information. The WHR approaches the 0.7 value at puberty, it is maintained until menopause, and it obviously increases in pregnant women—all of which provide information about the reproductive status of a woman. A WHR close to 0.7 also signals low risk for several forms of diabetes and cancer, gallbladder disease, hypertension, heart disease, stroke, and mortality, thus providing information about the woman's general health status. Married women with

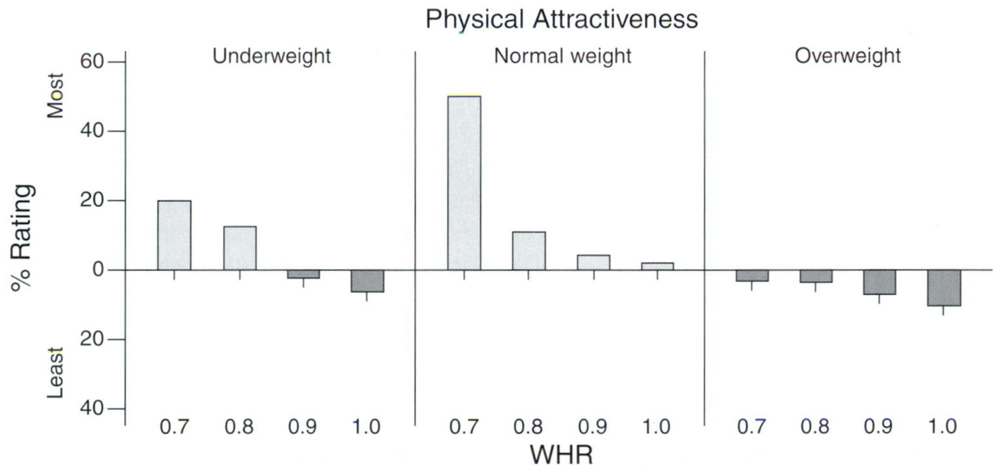

FIGURE 5.7. Men rated a series of drawings representing women that varied in terms of body weight and waist-to-hip ratio (WHR). Attractiveness increased for all drawings as the WHR approached a value of 0.7. The effect of the WHR was evident even when the drawings were considered unattractive on the basis of body weight (Singh 1993).

WHRs approaching 0.7 report less difficulty in becoming pregnant, and they have their first baby at a lower age than women with higher WHRs. Therefore, a WHR close to 0.7 is correlated with higher fertility and lower mortality, two variables known to index lifetime reproductive success from research with many species.

The WHR is shaped by gender-dependent hormones that regulate fat deposition in various regions of the body. The difference between men and women is not so much in the absolute amount of fat tissue as in its distribution. At puberty, estrogen (present in women in larger quantities than in men) favors the deposition of fat tissue in the gluteofemoral region, thus resulting in increased hip length that tends to lower the WHR. By contrast, testosterone (present predominantly in men) favors fat deposition in the abdominal region, keeping the waist length relatively high and thus increasing the WHR value. As a result, the WHR of women and men show a distribution with practically no overlap: 0.67 to 0.80 for healthy women and 0.85 to 0.95 for healthy men.

3.d. Copulatory Behavior. Animal reproduction is achieved by a synchronization of male and female behavior. In some species of fish and amphibians, male and female eject their germ cells in the water, thus reproducing through *external fertilization.* In other species, however, fertilization is achieved by the male's capacity to introduce its sperm cells into the female's body. Such *internal fertilization* requires the evolution of specialized organs (e.g., a male penis and a female cavity to house the fertilized egg) and of specialized copulatory behavior. Internal fertilization also creates other problems, such as paternal uncertainty and maternal investment in pregnancy, which, as seen previously, may have important consequences in terms of mating strategies.

Copulatory behavior is usually highly stereotypic within particular species, although also variable across species. In whiptail lizards, for example, the male usually approaches from behind and bites the neck skin of the female, sometimes riding on top of the female as she walks along sluggishly. The male then bends its tail underneath the female and inserts the penis, which in these species is bifurcated into two symmetrical organs, and then firmly bites her abdomen (Wade & Crews 1997). This male behavior is under testosterone control, and it can also be induced in females by the administration of hormones. As mentioned at the start of this chapter, some species of whiptail lizards are actually parthenogenetic, and while that means that there are no males in the species and that no sperm is required to produce young, it certainly does not imply that there is no courtship. In fact, as the levels of estrogen and progesterone rise during ovulation and the postovulatory period (as it is also generally the case for birds and mammals), females of the parthenogenetic species *Cnemidophorus uniparens* engage in malelike courting and mating, which is known to increase fecundity despite the fact that it is a purely behavioral interaction.

Analogous mating behaviors exhibited by other species also regulate the efficiency of mating. In rats (*Rattus norvegicus*), for example, both male and female emit *ultrasonic vocalizations* during mating. Females exhibit several typical responses, such as *darting behavior,* whereby a female runs and stops in front of a male adopting a posture that permits copulation, or *lordosis,* a curving of the back that exposes the genital area. Males, in turn, show *mounting behavior,* consisting of a rear approach with elevation of the forepaws and grasping of the female by the flanks, which is usually accompanied by intromission of the penis into the female's vagina and ejaculation of sperm. Rats typically perform several intromissions for every time they ejaculate; intromissions followed by ejaculation are distinguished by a slow dismount. Surgical devocalization can severely disturb darting and lordosis responses in females and mounting responses in males. Interestingly, the playback of ultrasonic vocalizations can partially restore mating performance (White & Barfield 1987, 1990).

It would be a mistake, however, to think of this pattern of mating behavior as universal for mammals, or even for rodents. As Dewsbury (1975) has shown, there is an impressive amount of behavioral variability in copulatory behavior across rodent species, a fact suggesting a great deal of evolutionary divergence driven by ecological and social adaptations. Rodents can be classified according to the presence or absence of four basic copulatory behaviors. First, although relatively rare, some species show a vaginal-penile locking after copulation, usually caused by the swelling of the penis. Locking prevents the female from copulating with another male, providing some time for the male's sperm cells to travel through the oviducts. Locking has often been interpreted as a way of ensuring paternity by males. Second, rodents vary in the extent to which they show a single thrust in each insertion. In some species, each mounting by the male is accompanied by repetitive thrusting, as it occurs in the primates. Third, whereas in some species every intromission is followed by an ejaculation, others require multiple intromissions for each ejaculation. Fourth, in most rodent species, a single male-female sexual encounter is characterized by multiple ejaculations. If each of these four behaviors is characterized as present or absent, there are 16 possible combinations of these four features. Dewsbury (1975) described seven of these 16 possibilities, with the popular rat exemplifying one of them (e.g., no lock, no repetitive thrusting, multiple intromissions, and multiple ejaculations). However, since the order Rodentia is particularly prolific in species, new combinations emerge as new rodent species are studied. For example, *Akodon molinae,* a small South American species, has been characterized by a combination of locking, no repetitive thrusting, multiple intromission, and a single ejaculation until satiety (Yunes & Castro Vázquez 1990). The particular combination pattern of these four copulatory responses had never been observed before in a rodent species.

Vaginal-penile locking increases the male's chance that his own sperm will fertilize the female's eggs. If a female were to copulate with two males in succession, then there would be room for *sperm competition,* and the first of the males to copulate would not necessarily be the one fertilizing the eggs. Females of some species can also eject the sperm of one male before copulating with another male, which seems to be related to the evolution in some species of a vaginal plug. Ejaculation by the male may be followed by the delivery of a gelatinous substance that closes the cloaca and prevents further ejaculation during a short period of time. In other species, females can store sperm from several males and use it in a delayed fashion over some period of time. Interestingly, the courtship display sometimes has a component in which the male stimulates the female to eject some of the sperm that has been in storage. For example, the male dunnock pecks at the female's cloaca up to 30 times, which in some cases results in the ejection of a droplet replete with sperm cells from previous matings (Davies 1992). In other species, sperm competition occurs in a concealed fashion. Human females, for example, eject an estimated 35% of the total sperm cells within

30 min of impregnation, in a series of globules containing seminal fluid and other secretions. However, copulatory orgasms occurring in a time window beginning 1 min before ejaculation and extending up to 45 min after ejaculation, can significantly increase sperm retention. Contractions occurring during and after the female's orgasm facilitate the transport of sperm from the vagina into the cervix, therefore increasing chances of fertilization. When a woman shifts from a monogamous to a polyandrous arrangement, the number of copulatory orgasms with the extra-pair male is higher than with the pair male, which favors the extra-pair male in terms of sperm retention. This has been interpreted as a concealed female mechanism (i.e., not obvious to males) for sperm competition (Baker & Bellis, 1993). The cloaca pecking behavior of dunnocks described above, and the concealment of copulatory orgasms in human females (who also conceal ovulation and display continuous sexual receptivity), may be examples of female strategies directed at providing the male with "evidence" of paternity that might ensure his contribution to parental care, whether or not he is responsible for fertilization.

4. Caring for the Young

4.a. Patterns of Parental Care. There is a great deal of diversity in *parental care* patterns among animals. Many species provide absolutely no parental care, leaving the fertilized eggs to their own fate. Marine plankton is populated by developing organisms from thousands of species in which the only parental investment involves the production of germ cells. Similarly, sea turtles typically lay their eggs in a beach and depart before hatching takes place. In many species, one parent may provide food for the offspring but have otherwise no contact with them. Many wasps build a burrow in the sand where they deposit both fertilized eggs and also a paralyzed prey that will serve as food for the larvae. Generations do not overlap in these cases.

In polygynous and polyandrous species, only one of the parents usually takes over the duties of infant care. *Maternal care* is common in many species, but it is the rule in mammals. In placental mammals, the female's ability to nurture the offspring through the placenta during intrauterine development and to provide milk during postnatal development gives her priority in terms of parental care. Marsupial mammals give birth to a highly immature, altricial embryo, which grows to become a large animal by means of extensive maternal care (Eisenberg 1991). A newborn embryo red kangaroo (*Megalia rufa*) weighs about 1 g and may fit in a teaspoon, but it grows to become a 30,000-g adult! A red kangaroo female may have up to three offspring generations living in her body at any one time: a large and relatively independent infant living in the pouch, an embryo attached to a nipple also inside the pouch, and a fertilized egg in *diapause* (a temporary arrest of embryonic development) inside the uterus. But mammalian maternal care not only involves nurturing and protection, but also sensory experience (Ronca et al. 1993). In rats (*Rattus norvegicus*), for example, the mother's behavior during the perinatal period results in tactile, temperature, olfactory, and vestibular stimulation. Behaviors such as activity, rearing, stirring, abdominal grooming, and scratching are prominent during the final stages of pregnancy, when the amount of amniotic fluid has decreased considerably and the fetus is thus more exposed to external influences. Further stimulation is provided by contractions during delivery, as well as by the mother's handling of the newborn in terms of licking, pup retrieval, and body contact (***Figure 5.8***).

Paternal care is relatively common in fish and amphibians, in which fathers do not provide food, but mainly protection from predators. In frogs, the male typically guards the eggs, keeping them moist and providing protection. Experimental removal of guarding male frogs of the species *Eleutherodactylus coqui* has been shown to result in increased egg mortality (Towsand et al. 1984). Surprisingly, a major cause of death is cannibalism by other males. Male crocodiles (*Crocodylus palustris*) transport the young in their mouth, and in large ratite birds, such as the rhea (*Rhea americana*), it is the male that incubates the eggs and raises the young.

In many species, parental care is provided by more than one animal. *Biparental care* is observed in some species of cichlid fish, and it is a prominent feature in birds, for which monogamy is common. Egg incubation, nest guarding, and nurturing are shared by both parents in many species of birds. In mammals, by contrast, biparental care is observed only exceptionally. Among the rodents, for example, the California mouse (*Peromyscus californicus*) exhibits relatively stable patterns of biparental care in both its natural habitat and the laboratory environment (Gubernick & Alberts 1987). Fathers remain at the nest and provide essentially the same care as the mothers, with the exception of nursing. In the dunnock (*Prunella modularis*), the number of fledging chicks is correlated with the amount of parental care provided. A polyandrous trio (one female and two males) in which a predator kills one of the males produces about half the number of fledglings as a trio in which both males provide food for the young (Davies 1992). An analogous type of *group care* of the infants is also observed in some mammals. In a lion pride (*Panthera leo*), reproductively active females cooperate in infant care (Packer et al. 1988). These lionesses tend to be sedentary and thus genetically related within a particular pride, which implies that this pattern of maternal care has evolved in part driven by indirect selection because of the benefits provided to kin. Lionesses do not appear to associate with unrelated females.

At the start of this section it was pointed out that many species do not provide any obvious type of parental care. It is perhaps appropriate to close it by illustrating the case of a species that appears to have lost the ability to provide parental

FIGURE 5.8. Rat mothers engage in a variety of behaviors that stimulate the newborn (Ronca et al. 1993). ***(a)*** Licking and handling the pups. ***(b)*** Pup retrieval. ***(c)*** Vicarious stimulation occurs when the mother gently sits on pups or touches them with the rear paws.

care, at least to some extent, and yet produces offspring that can survive only if provided with the safety of the nest and with abundant food by adults. The European cuckoo (*Cuculus canorus*) is one of a number of species that practice *brood parasitism,* that is, the "infestation" of other species' nests with their own eggs, which are thus incubated by foster parents. Brood parasitism fits the parasite-host system discussed in ***Chapter 4*** in connection with feeding, and therefore one might anticipate the evolution of traits that would make the parasite more successful and of countertraits that would make the host more capable of detecting the parasite.

Female cuckoos search for a suitable host among nests of dunnocks, warblers, robins, and many other species (Davies 1992). However, individual females actually specialize in a particular species, and they may lay eggs that match in external appearance those of some of the host species. There are therefore strains of cuckoos that differ in the type of egg they produce; the female's selectivity for a particular host may depend on early learning of host features while at the nest. In some notable cases, however, the cuckoo's eggs are obviously different from those of the host, and it is hard to understand why they are accepted at all. For example, the dunnock's eggs are small and bluish, yet they are willing to incubate the somewhat larger and greenish-white eggs laid by cuckoos. The most obvious countermeasure by hosts is the abandonment of the nest, although in some cases the host may eject the parasitic egg from the nest. Some host species have evolved an ability to detect eggs that do not match their own in coloration or pattern. For example, experiments with artificial eggs show that red warblers (*Acrocephalus scirpaceus*) reject approximately 62% of egg models not matching their own, but reject 0% of the models matching those of their cuckoo parasite strain, whereas pied wagtails (*Motacila alba*) reject 71% of the nonmatching eggs but only 50% of the models matching their cuckoo strain.

One of the most bizarre consequences of parasitism is the ability of cuckoo chicks to eliminate the competition. As ***Figure 5.9*** (***see inside front cover***) illustrates, a few hours after hatching and while still featherless and with closed eyelids, a cuckoo chick is working hard to eject a warbler's egg out of the nest. Some hosts parents, such as is the case with dunnocks, may remain passive while observing the cuckoo chick ejecting their own eggs from the nest (Davies 1992). The cuckoo chick will subsequently manage to receive all the benefits of parental care for itself, developing at a fast rate. Soon the chick may surpass the foster parent in body size, but this would not stop the host from feeding it. Foster parents may be irresistibly pulled towards this extreme situation by the very large size of the parasite. I mentioned in ***Chapter 1*** (***section 4,*** p. 17) that animals sometimes prefer a stimulus larger than the one typical for their own species; it may well be that the open mouth of cuckoo chicks and their large body size act as supernormal stimuli that make it impossible for the foster parent to refuse parental care. It is easy to see how natural selection could affect the parasite's features to exploit the host's tendency to respond preferentially to supernormal stimuli, although one would expect also that there would be counterselection traits. It is not clear why dunnocks are so vulnerable to parasitism; one possibility is that the dunnock has become a host only recently and countertraits have not yet evolved. Variability in the success of various host species to deal with cuckoo parasites suggests the possibility that cuckoos are forced to shift to new hosts when antiparasite traits evolve in species that have served as hosts for many generations.

4.b. Parent-Offspring Conflict. Parasites and their hosts, and predators and their preys—all are engaged in a sort of evolutionary conflict, as was shown in ***Chapter 4***. A similar evolutionary conflict appears to relate to mating arrangements because the interests of the male and female do not always coincide. Trivers (1974) suggested that parents and offspring are also engaged in an evolutionary conflict.

At the basis of this *parent-offspring conflict* is a set of divergent interests. In sexually reproducing species, parents obviously benefit from providing care for their offspring because they share a proportion of 0.5 of the total genes. As a result, natural selection favors the evolution of responses aimed at protecting the young and providing for their normal growth. Offspring benefit from this parental care because they are not prepared for an independent way of life. As the offspring grow, however, the cost of parental care increases both because the offspring are more demanding (e.g., they need more food) and also because the parent is delaying the production of additional offspring. From the offspring's point of view, by contrast, the longer the period of parental care, the lower the cost of searching for food and exposure to predators. This, of course, would work up to a point because offspring receive an indirect selection benefit from their parents' ability to produce additional kin. Natural selection would thus favor parents that provide enough for their offspring to reach independence but that also reduce the cost of parental care so as to maximize lifetime reproductive success. But natural selection would also favor offspring who can maximize the amount of parental care received, up to some point. Hence the conflict: Offspring should always prefer to receive more care than parents prefer to provide.

Trivers (1974) explored an intriguing implication of his parent-offspring conflict hypothesis—namely, that natural selection could in some cases favor the evolution of offspring behaviors that amount to psychological manipulation of the parent. Trivers reasoned that in a competition between a parent and its offspring, the parent would tend to have the advantage of size and experience, which would eliminate the viability of any strategy based on physical strength on the part of the offspring. Instead, the offspring may come to exploit behaviors that are normal components of early parent-offspring interactions, only out of context and aimed at increasing parental care to a point that makes it no longer adaptive for the parent.

For example, parents tend to be sensitive to signs of distress produced by their infants, such as crying in human babies. These behaviors communicate hunger, discomfort, or similar states that pose a threat to the infant's integrity. It is in the parent's best interest to attend to these situations until the signs of distress disappear. (From a proximate point of view, crying can be intensely aversive to a parent and probably achieves its adaptive function by instigating various forms of escape learning.) An older infant may resort to crying not because of some real threat but rather because the parent refuses some privilege. In an analogous situation, an infant baboon (*Papio anubis*) who is refused access to milk by its mother may display behaviors characteristic of a younger stage, such as a greater degree of attachment to the mother. Trivers pointed out that such a phenomenon is referred to as *regression* in psychology—that is, the display of behavior typical of a younger stage in a situation involving conflict. Indeed, rats (*Rattus norvegi-*

cus) are known to regress to responses acquired earlier in life, when current behaviors are no longer effective in producing the customary rewards (Rashotte & Amsel 1968). By the same token, parents would be favored to evolve the ability to discriminate between infant behaviors that communicate a real threat and those that reflect the infant's attempt at psychological manipulation. It is plausible that the effectiveness of the offspring in such attempts would diminish as parents gained more experience in raising their infants.

4.c. Helpers at the Nest. In some situations the duties of parental care are extended to animals other than the parents. Such animals are called *helpers,* and they provide nesting material, food for the young, and protection against predators. An important aspect of this situation is that although the helpers are usually sexually mature and capable of producing their own young, yet they postpone their reproduction to provide help. Why?

Just as ground squirrels risk their lives to warn relatives of the presence of a terrestrial predator (see ***Chapter 4, section 4.f.,*** pp. 115–117), so helpers put their own reproduction on hold to provide for the raising of relatives. Indeed, helpers appear to be invariably related to the breeding pair that they are assisting at the nest, whether in fish, birds, or mammals. Therefore, indirect selection through kinship may be a main factor in the evolution of this altruistic behavior. In the cichlid fish *Lamprologus brichardi,* helpers remain in the parents' territory cleaning eggs and providing defense against predators. Taborsky (1984) has shown that the clutch size of females assisted by helpers is significantly larger than that of nests in which the parents are on their own. Yet helpers do not appear to be gaining any direct fitness from their behavior. Some of the helper's potential direct benefits include the possibility of taking over the parents' territory, obtaining experience in rearing offspring, or acquiring helpers if the current parents were to reciprocate in the future. All these direct benefits are delayed in time but are nonetheless potentially important, depending on ecological and life-history factors. For example, if there is a shortage of breeding territories, it may pay to wait and take over the parents' territory, while investing in kin in the meantime. Similarly, if the process of rearing offspring is complex, it may pay to delay direct reproduction and acquire relevant experience while helping relatives.

The Florida population of scrub jays (*Aphelocoma coerulescens coerulescens*) has been the subject of a long-term field study (since 1969) that illustrates some of the main features of helping behavior (Woolfender & Fitzpatrick 1997). This population is apparently unique among scrub jays in displaying cooperative breeding; in fact, practically all individuals in the population can be characterized as either breeding animals, dependent young, or helpers (i.e., there are no long-term floaters). Helpers (usually one, sometimes two, and on very rare occasions more than two), are observed in an average of 55% of all nests, to which they contribute by engaging in all the duties of parental care performed by the parents. The main contribution of helpers appears to be their ability to decrease the impact of predators on the nest. Practically all jays die because of predation, so this is a significant selective pressure for the evolution of antipredator behavior. For example, jays display *sentinel behavior* by sitting on an exposed branch and observing the environment; when a predator is detected (e.g., a hawk or snake), distinct alarm calls are emitted that induce other jays to move toward dense vegetation for cover. Predators are sometimes mobbed by groups of jays or directly attacked by individual jays that approach and peck at them. Helpers also provide food for the chicks, and although this does not appear to be a major factor in itself, it frees time for the parents to remain near the nest for longer periods. It has been shown that parents with helper assistance leave a significantly larger number of fledglings than unaided parents, although there seems to be no difference between breeding groups with one or more helpers.

There are two major benefits that might explain why helper scrub jays help. First, individual jays may increase their direct fitness by inheriting the breeding territory of the pair when they die. Because scrub jays exhibit strong dominance—the breeding male being the most dominant and the oldest helper male being dominant over other helpers—and because it is the dominant helper male that tends to inherit the territory, this benefit is particularly important for males. Females, in contrast, tend to disperse away from their nest more than males, and they tend to acquire a nest by pairing with a widower male or with a male that has recently inherited a territory. Second, in an overwhelming majority of the observations, helpers provided assistance to relatives, as shown in ***Figure 5.10.*** By contributing to the raising of siblings, with which they share 50% of the genes, and half siblings, with which they share 25% of the genes through their common parent, helper jays are gaining sufficient fitness to offset the cost of delaying direct reproduction while increasing, at the same time, their chances of acquiring a good breeding territory in the future.

5. COMPLEX ANIMAL SOCIETIES

In the year 310 B.C., Carthage was besieged by Agatocles of Syracuse and many were killed. Carthaginians attributed their misfortune to having lost the favors of the God Cronos-Baal, whom they had traditionally honored by offering the children of the

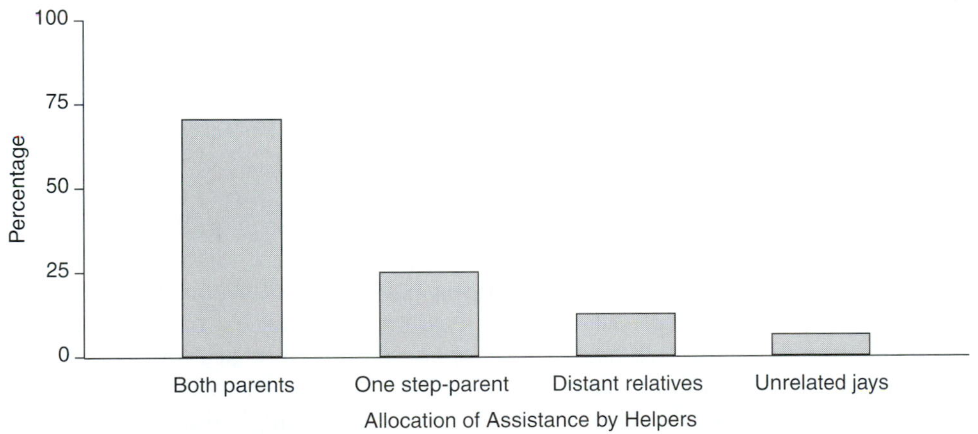

FIGURE 5.10. Scrub jays in the Florida population (*Aphelocoma coerulescens coerulescens*) provide extensive help to young even though this results in the postponement of their own reproduction (Woolfender & Fitzpatrick 1997). These results demonstrate that helpers tend to allocate their helping behavior to nests tended by relatives, thus increasing their own inclusive fitness through the indirect fitness component.

wealthiest families for sacrifice. According to the ancient historians Diodorus Siculus and Plutarch, Carthaginians believed that Cronos-Baal was displeased because many rich families had resorted to buying children from poor families and substituting them for their own in sacrificial ceremonies. This historical episode reveals some of the major elements of human societies, including a family organization, a class structure for the distribution of resources, religious beliefs and rituals, and warfare. Whereas the complexity of human social behavior escapes, for the most part and for the moment, an evolutionary analysis, research with other animals can contribute to our understanding of bits and pieces of this mosaic. Consider kinship as an example. The "cheating" of rich Carthaginians could be seen in the light of the benefits accrued to selfish parents by the workings of natural selection, as it was repeatedly illustrated in this chapter. The decision made by poor parents to sell their babies for the purpose of being sacrificed in these ceremonies is harder to understand from an evolutionary perspective. One might speculate that such parents may have been gambling with the perspective of compensating a current reproductive loss by a future gain; they may have tended to be, for example, relatively young parents with a long reproductive life ahead of them. However, the very existence of this kind of human sacrifice is perplexing from the evolutionary point of view, and it must have required an oppressive culture in order to become dominant among Carthaginians. In this vein, ancient historians describe how parents who cried for their children during a ceremony were socially stigmatized and blamed for the uproar of a God who expected parents to be happy for having a son or a daughter chosen for sacrifice.

The sacrifice of children is an example of a complex social phenomenon that is particularly striking in its violation of a most basic evolutionary rule—namely, the selfish defense of one's own offspring. In fact, when one looks at human social practices from the background provided by animal behavior studies, their complexity becomes astonishing: political structures and procedures, resource administration, leadership systems, legal regulations, science, art, technology, education, and the countless ways in which we entertain ourselves. Nonetheless, the very fact that the sacrifice of young children, as opposed to the sacrifice of defeated leaders or soldiers, has been an uncommon social practice among human societies suggests that although cultures may deviate occasionally from a more fundamental biological order, they are generally limited by evolutionary rules. Social evolution should occur within the limits imposed by biological evolution, just as evolution is constrained by the chemical and physical properties of matter. Thus, one would expect that human cultures would place a great value on preserving their children and ensuring their survival and development so that they could become useful to themselves and to the social group as a whole. As usual, however, specific social realities lie somewhere in between these two extremes.

Why would complex societies ever evolve? What do social individuals gain from grouping? Partial answers to these questions have been attempted in this and previous chapters. For example, lions can increase their lifetime reproductive success by living in groups, as shown in ***Figure 2.8*** (p. 51). Given the ecological and life-history features of lions, individuals with gregarious tendencies are positively selected because they can hunt more successfully and provide better care for their offspring than individualistic lions. ***Chapter 4*** illustrated how social factors aid individuals in their search for food and in their defense against predators. And at the outset of the present chapter, I argued that the basic reproductive interaction between parents and offspring in sexually reproducing species could be considered as the building block of sociality. Complex societies will also be found to be sensitive to factors including foraging efficiency, antipredator defense, and infant care. However, there are additional elements to be considered.

5.a. Eusociality and Haplodiploidy. As was shown in the previous section, many species exhibit patterns of parental care that ensure the survival of the young. Moreover, there are cases in which offspring from a previous generation help the parents at the nest by providing protection against predators and food for the young. Entomologists interested in the evolution of social behavior in insects have traditionally classified species that display these two features (i.e., parental care and overlapping generations) as subsocial. *Subsociality* is, thus, a relatively widespread mode of social organization in many species of birds and mammals, as well as in insects. In some exceptional cases, a third feature is added, —namely a division of reproductive duties according to which one (or a few) individuals produce viable eggs and the rest form *sterile castes* of nonreproductive individuals that provide care for the eggs and defend the nest. Depending on the species, nonreproductive individuals may be entirely sterile or may retain the ability to procreate and express it when the appropriate conditions arise in the colony. Species displaying all three characteristics (i.e., parental care, overlapping generations, and sterile castes) are referred to as *eusocial*. Apart from human societies, perhaps the most complex animal groups are those of eusocial species.

Eusociality is known in species from two distantly related animal phyla, Arthropoda and Chordata. Among arthropods, it is found in insects (ants, wasps, bees, termites, gall thrips, bark beetles, and aphids) and crustaceans (sponge-dwelling shrimp); among chordates, it has been described only in mammals (naked mole-rats). Because of the remote relationship of these taxa and the presence, in each of them, of many closely related groups that do not exhibit eusocial behavior, it is generally agreed that eusociality has evolved independently several times. Therefore, there must be certain features, either in the biology of these organisms or in their ecology, or both, that promote eusociality. One such feature is the genetic system underlying sex determination. In some eusocial species, including termites, bark beetles, shrimp, and naked mole-rats, both male and female individuals are formed out of fertilized eggs and are therefore referred to as *diplodiploid* species (each somatic cell in these organisms has a diploid number of chromosomes, or $2n$). In diplodiploid species, sisters and brothers are not more related to each other than they are to their own offspring. Diplodiploid eusociality is discussed in the following section.

In contrast, in ants, bees, and wasps (classified in the insect order Hymenoptera), and in the less-studied gall thrips (insect order Thysanoptera), sex determination is more complex. Reproductive females (queens) mate with one or more males, usually during a relatively short period. Queens can store sperm for long periods and use it to fertilize their own eggs in order to produce females. However, queens can produce males by laying unfertilized eggs. Therefore, whereas females are diploid (chromosome number equal to $2n$), males are haploid (chromosome number equal to n); the system is referred to as *haplodiploid*. Diplodiploid and haplodiploid systems generate different patterns of genetic relatedness among sisters and brothers. If one assumes monogamous parents, then the *coefficients of relatedness* (r) distribute as shown in ***Table 5.1.***

Notice that haplodiploid daughters display an unusually high degree of genetic relatedness, sharing 3/4 of their genotype, on average. However, mothers and daughters share 1/2 of their genotype, on average, whether the species is diplodiploid or haplodiploid. This implies, of course, that haplodiploid sisters would be genetically more similar to one another (r = 0.75) than they would be to their own offspring (r = 0.5). Hamilton (1964) first noticed this asymmetry and suggested that it would pay for haplodiploid sisters to direct their efforts at caring for other sisters, even if they sacrificed their entire reproductive potential by becoming sterile. In all haplodiploid and eusocial species, sterile castes (e.g., workers in charge of foraging, egg caring, and nest cleaning, and soldiers in charge of nest defense) are exclusively females. Therefore, it is widely believed that haplodiploidy is one of the factors (but not the only one) favoring the evolution of eusociality.

Among the Hymenoptera, all known ants (about 8,800 species, although it is estimated that a total of up to 20,000 species may be extant), an estimated 1,000 species of bees (up to 30,000 species of bees are thought to be extant), and approximately 900 species of wasps (of about 7,000 living species) are eusocial. Hymenopterans account for an estimated 99% of all extant subsocial insects and about 92% of all known eusocial species of insects. Eusociality is thought to have evolved independently several times (up to 11 independent origins have been hypothesized) among the hymenopterans. All together, this information provides a rough estimate of the correlation between haplodiploidy and eusociality in Hymenoptera, a correlation consistent with the hypothesis that haplodiploidy is one factor (among a set of factors) contributing to the repeated evolution of eusociality in this order (Alexander et al. 1991).

A few examples of eusocial organization in hymenopterans will suffice to provide a sense of their complexity. These examples involve ants and were all taken from the impressive account of their biology by Hölldobler and Wilson (1990). Ants provide many intriguing examples of parasitism, some of which are extreme in the dependence of the parasite species on its host. There are several species of slave-making ants, such as the Amazon *Polyergus rufescens,* which steal eggs from a host species and carry them to their own nest. Slave ants will eventually take over all the activities of maintenance in the colony without which *Polyergus* ants would not be able to survive. Some species are also known to have agricultural skills.

TABLE 5.1 Coefficients of Relatedness (r) for Diplodiploid and Haplodiploid Species

	Probability of sharing genes through their			
Relatedness among	***Mother***		***Father***	***r =***
Diplodiploid daughters	$(0.5)^2$	+	$(0.5)^2$	0.5
Haplodiploid daughters	$(0.5)^2$	+	0.5	0.75
Diplodiploid sons	$(0.5)^2$	+	$(0.5)^2$	0.5
Haplodiploid sons	$(0.5)^2$	+	0	0.25

Note. Haploid fathers produce only one set of genes, which are shared by all the haplodiploid daughters produced by the same father, thus producing an unusually high r of 0.75.

Ants of the genera *Atta* and *Acromyrmex* collect plant material and carry it into their nests, where leaves are cut in small pieces, chewed, and mixed with anal secretions. These pieces of pulpy plant material are then deposited in fungus gardens. Each ant species may have a specific association with a particular fungus symbiont. The fungus acts in fact as an ancillary digestive tract, providing nutrients and some enzymes that these ants apparently no longer produce. In return, the fungus symbionts depend on the ants for care and cultivation. Ants protect specific species of fungi by a variety of means: They eliminate unwanted fungus species, fertilize the substrate with nutrients to which their fungus symbionts have become adapted, and produce a hormone that stimulates fungal growth. A final example involves weaver ants of the genus *Oecophylla,* which team in large groups to create cavities with leaves. These ants live in trees and build their nests by pulling together from the edge of a leaf until they can bind the leaf to produce an enclosure (see ***Figure 5.11, front inside cover***). Workers form a living chain to pull one edge close to the other, and then rows of workers keep the two edges together while a second group attempts the binding from the inside of the leaf. Binding is achieved by using a special silk secreted only by the larvae. Workers bring larvae to the building site and stimulate them to produce the silk.

The correlation between haplodiploidy and eusociality is not perfect, as implied previously. First, the existence of eusociality in diplodiploid species (see next section) indicates that haplodiploidy is not necessary for the evolution of eusociality. Second, the presence of many solitary haplodiploids among the Hymenoptera (wasps and bees) and other insect orders demonstrates that haplodiploidy is not sufficient for the evolution of eusociality. For example, only six species of gall thrips, out of an estimated 2,500 species, are eusocial. In fact, Australian gall thrips suggest other sources of selective pressure that might be responsible for the evolution of eusociality (Crespi 1992). For example, these animals live in nests that provide both shelter and food, that are relatively stable, and that are defensible. Many of these features are shared by hymenopterans. Nest defense, for example, is in charge of specialized individuals, the soldiers, possessing bodily parts used as weapons (much like the stingers of wasps and bees) and predisposed to what Alexander et al. (1991) call "heroic acts."

5.b. Eusocial Diplodiploids and Clonals. In the Caribbean sea, off the coast of Belize, colonies of shrimp (*Synalpheus regalis*) dwell inside sponges. These colonies are very stable and contain hundreds of individual shrimp, each about 2 or 3 mm in length, of which only a single female is reproductively active (easily identifiable because of its grown ovaries or brooded eggs). These animals take advantage of the sponge's feeding system and pick up food from the passing current. Because nearly all sponges are occupied in an entire coral-reef area, a main problem for the shrimp must be the defense of the nest by invading organisms, including conspecifics. Sponge-dwelling shrimp are notorious for bearing asymmetric claws, one of which can achieve a relatively large size. The shrimp use these large claws to snap at intruders, kill them, and drag them out of the nest. Species of the genus *Synalpheus* vary in the degree of grouping from eusocial colonies to a single heterosexual pair occupying a sponge. Phylogenetic analysis of a group of 13 *Synalpheus* species shows that eusociality evolved independently in at least three lineages (Duffy et al. 2000). Apparently, social organization confers a competitive advantage in the occupation of sponges; eusocial species tend to exclude other species from the sponges in which they establish their nests more effectively than noneusocial species.

Similar features—extensive parental care, reproductive division of labor with sterile castes, and stable, expandable nests—also characterize the termites (approximately 2,200 extant species, all eusocial; insect order Isoptera) and the naked mole-rats (three known eusocial species; mammalian order Rodentia). In these species, sterility may not be necessarily permanent. For example, removal of a queen from a colony of termites or naked mole-rats is followed by the emergence of a new queen within the colony. Membership in a particular caste (e.g., workers, soldiers) is not determined genetically but by nutritional, hormonal, and pheromonal influences that channel development into one of a series of alternative pathways, not always irreversible. These species are characterized by extensive periods of inbreeding which may be seen as a direct consequence of their habitat and the way in which they exploit resources. For example, termites live in logs and bark from which they also obtain their food. They eat their own residence, and when it is gone, individuals within the colony develop wings (so-called *alates*) and disperse. Many termite species do not go out of their colony to forage for food (Thorne 1997). Similarly, naked mole-rats live almost permanently in underground burrows that the workers keep expanding in search of new sources of food. Under these conditions, extensive inbreeding may lead to unusually high levels of genetic relatedness among colony members (Reeve et al. 1990). Such a pattern of inbreeding may be seen as approaching the situation of haplodiploid species; perhaps, then, a high degree of genetic relatedness may be one factor promoting the evolution of reproductive altruism (sterility) and behavioral altruism ("heroic acts") by workers even in diplodiploid species.

But when it comes to genetic relatedness, an even more extreme case is illustrated by the aphids, insects of the order Hemiptera, in which approximately 50 species, of an estimated 4,400 extant species, exhibit sterile castes (Aoki 1977). Eusocial aphids are particularly interesting because they are strictly *clonal species*—that is, individuals are genetically identical (Stern & Foster 1996). Aphids are small animals (up to 10 mm in length) that live in close association with plant hosts from which they obtain their food and in which they also live in colonies inside galls. During a parthenogenetic phase of reproduction, colonies can grow very fast with a generation turnover of approximately 10 days. These clones move from a primary host (usually a very specific plant species) to a secondary host (there is diversity in the selection of secondary host species). Such a growth is punctuated by a sexual generation in which alate individuals are formed and settle in the primary host. The alate aphid produces male and female offspring, which then mate. The female usually lays a single egg, from which clones are derived by parthenogenesis to repeat the life cycle. There are several known variations in life cycle among aphid species. Aphids produce castes specialized for gall defense. These soldiers develop some body parts into weapons, such as stylets and horns, which are used to defend the colony against intruders. Soldiers also carry out other tasks, such as cleaning and maintenance of the gall.

Because of their clonal reproduction, aphids may be either fully related to the recipients of their altruistic behavior (i.e., $r = 1$) or completely unrelated if the colony is infiltrated by other clones. As Stern and Foster (1996) argued, this seems to have far-reaching implications. Consider the continuum illustrated in ***Figure 5.12.*** At the lower extreme of this continuum are the somatic cells of a multicellular organism. Cells in the skin, heart, hair, etc., are all clones, genetically identical and spatially clumped. Their distribution makes it unlikely for conspecific cells from another organism to invade them, and the division of labor goes on without much genetic conflict. This would be the most extreme case of altruism, in which somatic cells have given up their reproductive potential in favor of germ cells. As one moves upward in this continuum, the components of the colony (whether bacteria, protists, or multicellular organisms) display a greater degree of mobility and individuality. At the upper extreme of the continuum, such species as ants, termites, and naked mole-rats exhibit the lowest degree of genetic relatedness in the continuum and also are more vulnerable to invasion by unrelated organisms. The potential for genetic conflict then increases as one moves upward in the continuum, and to the extent that kinship and reproductive altruism are related, one would expect that altruistic traits would find it increasingly harder to evolve, as is indeed the case. By comparison with the coordinated manner in which differentiated tissues in a multicellular organism cooperate to facilitate the reproductive success of the animal (ultimately achieved by its germ cells), the examples of altruistic eusociality discussed in this section appear far less extreme.

In summary, eusociality in clonal, haplodiploid, and diplodiploid species appears to be linked to various factors. Genetic relatedness, a long lifespan that allows for

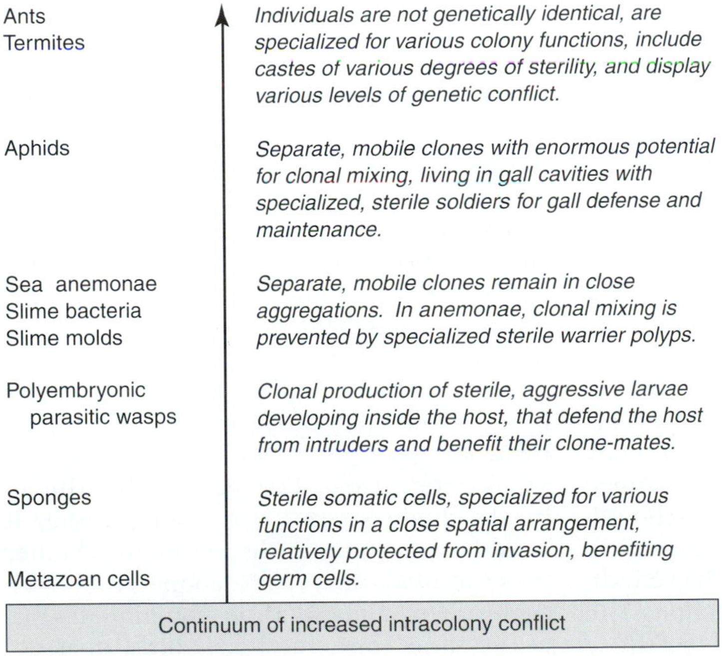

Ants Termites	*Individuals are not genetically identical, are specialized for various colony functions, include castes of various degrees of sterility, and display various levels of genetic conflict.*
Aphids	*Separate, mobile clones with enormous potential for clonal mixing, living in gall cavities with specialized, sterile soldiers for gall defense and maintenance.*
Sea anemonae Slime bacteria Slime molds	*Separate, mobile clones remain in close aggregations. In anemonae, clonal mixing is prevented by specialized sterile warrier polyps.*
Polyembryonic parasitic wasps	*Clonal production of sterile, aggressive larvae developing inside the host, that defend the host from intruders and benefit their clone-mates.*
Sponges Metazoan cells	*Sterile somatic cells, specialized for various functions in a close spatial arrangement, relatively protected from invasion, benefiting germ cells.*

Continuum of increased intracolony conflict

Figure 5.12. The reproductive altruism found in clonal aphids suggests the presence of a continuum of altruism with somatic cells in one extreme and the social insects in the other (Stern & Foster 1996). The continuum presumably extends beyond the social insects into diploid species in which altruistic behavior is extremely rare and a solitary mode of life predominates.

generational overlap, parental care, bodily organs specialized for colony defense (stingers, claws, horns), and a tendency toward monogamy are among the organismic factors that surely play significant roles in the evolution of eusocial behavior and morphology. In addition, such ecological factors as the ability to set up a colony in an enclosed, expandable, and defensible nest site may be essential ingredients in the evolution of eusociality.

5.c. Cooperation and Reciprocity. A careful reader might have noticed the parallels between the lifestyles of eusocial species and humans. In a geologically brief period of time (perhaps within the last 30,000 years), human societies have evolved from relatively small nomadic groups to large aggregates of people, living in expandable habitats (called cities), exhibiting a strong division of labor, and possessing "castes" and tools (rather than bodily parts) specialized for group defense. Family units allow for the expression of a considerable amount of altruism and cooperation among kin, but such behavior also extends beyond immediate relatives. Unlike eusocial insects, however, humans do not display reproductive altruism but preserve selfish reproductive traits common to the vast majority of animals.

Despite this basic genetic selfishness, many species of birds and mammals have evolved relatively sophisticated social behavior. Such behavior is "sophisticated" in the sense that it is based on a considerable degree of cooperation and reciprocity among individuals. *Cooperation* is defined as a type of social interaction in which individuals obtain a benefit that would be difficult or impossible for them to achieve individually. In cooperative interactions, all individuals within the group gain access to some resource more or less simultaneously. In one prototypical example of cooperation, individuals join efforts to kill prey. Examples of cooperative hunting are illuminating because the goal (to obtain food) and the relationship between hunting effectiveness and group size can be easily determined in many cases. Some examples of cooperation among animals were briefly mentioned previously, including the evolution of grouping in lions (see ***Chapter 2, section 5.b.,*** pp. 50–51) and in juvenile ravens (see ***Chapter 4, section 3.e.,*** pp. 97–99).

Bednarz (1988) observed cooperative hunting in Harris' hawks (*Parabuteo unicinctus*) in their natural habitat in New Mexico. Because the hawk groups were very stable, it was possible to follow them and keep records of their hunting strategies and successes. Hawks would converge on a rabbit by flying in from different directions in a surprising manner. When the rabbit found a place to hide, some of the hawks would typically search on the ground while the others would perch above and observe. Rabbits that rushed from cover when disturbed would be caught by one of the perching hawks. The number of kills increased linearly with group size—from no success when hunting was attempted by two or three individuals to the greatest success with groups of up to six hawks. Interestingly, a measure of energy gain and expenditure indicated that a minimum group size of five hawks was necessary to obtain enough energy from the sharing of the kills to maintain balance. Since these groups are really families, there is an important kinship component in this cooperative behavior.

A critical view of cooperative hunting in hawks might suggest, for example, that it would seem hard to discriminate whether these animals are really cooperating with each other or just hunting individually but at the same time. In other words, does cooperation involve more than simply a synchrony among individuals in the same group? Moreover, how can we know whether the perching hawks were waiting for the rabbit, or refusing to participate in the ground search to lower their cost of hunting? While cooperation allows animals the access to resources, it also creates conditions that can be exploited by noncooperative animals. For cooperative behavior to evolve, the animals investing in the interaction must be capable of detecting cheaters—that is, animals that share the benefits but avoid the costs of hunting. If cooperative animals are deprived of the benefits of cooperation by cheaters, then those alleles underlying cooperative behavior would not spread in a population. Or, in other words, cooperation would not become an evolutionarily stable strategy (see ***section 2.e.,*** pp. 138–140).

Boesch (1994) studied the hunting behavior of chimpanzees (*Pan troglodytes*) with these problems in mind: (1) that cooperation should involve more than individuals doing the same thing at the same time; (2) that cooperative hunters should gain more than solitary ones; and (3) that cooperative hunters should be able to control access to the prey by nonhunters (i.e., cheaters), perhaps through some sort of social mechanism. Two populations of wild chimpanzees were studied, one at Taï National Park, in the Ivory Coast, and the other at the Gombe Stream National Park, in Tanzania. These populations differ in the extent and type of group hunting. At Taï, chimpanzees get measurable benefits for cooperating in groups because their prey (*Colobus* monkeys) move in dense vegetation and large trees that allow them to escape fairly easily. In contrast, the chimpanzees at Gombe hunt simultaneously, but each hunter typically follows its own prey. There, *Colobus* monkeys move in smaller trees, and escape routes can easily be blocked by individual chimpanzees. Once a chimpanzee has made a kill, and provided that the prey is a relatively large animal, it would share the meat with other hunters and with animals that did not participate in the hunt and thus might be considered cheaters. In terms of the net energy intake per hunter in each of the two populations, individual hunters paid a cost for cooperating at Gombe; in the Taï population there was some indication that groups of four or more than six chimpanzees did better than solitary hunters.

Taï chimpanzees provide evidence for social regulation of access to the meat. When a chimpanzee kills a relatively large *Colobus,* it typically emits a distinctive "capture call," which creates excitement among group members and attracts other animals to the site. The hunters have generally preferential access to the food, and about 45% of each hunter's portion of meat is actually shared with other animals, particularly with females. For a hunter, therefore, it is not only a matter of obtaining food for himself but also a matter of having food to share with others. In addition to hunters, access to the meat is determined by the age and the dominance rank of the animal. This social mechanism tends to restrict cheaters from access to the meat, but it does not prevent it altogether because of a considerable degree of sharing. It must be noticed that male chimpanzees tend to stay in the group, which suggests that the sharing may benefit genetically related individuals. Sharing meat with females could also have a kinship component if the female is nursing an offspring sired by the hunter. Or, interestingly, the sharing of meat could affect the future interaction of that male with the recipient female; perhaps the female will reciprocate later by allowing the male to copulate with her. Boesch measured the net benefit per hunter and per cheater as a function of group size in both populations. As shown in ***Figure 5.13,*** whereas cooperation and cheating led to differential benefits at Taï, they did not differ at Gombe. The implication is, therefore, that cooperation and cheating are stable strategies at Taï, each yielding some measurable benefit, and none being able to completely displace the other. By contrast, cooperation would not evolve at Gombe because it can be easily invaded by cheating.

The Taï chimpanzees tend to adopt a conditional strategy, sometimes being hunters, and sometimes cheaters. They also provide meat to females, presumably in exchange for sexual access in the future. These are examples of *reciprocity* (also referred to as *reciprocal altruism*; Trivers 1971). Reciprocity occurs when an animal procures some benefit to a recipient (not an immediate relative) at some cost to the animal, and the recipient returns the benefit in the future. In both cooperation and reciprocity all the individuals involved in the social interaction benefit, but whereas the benefits are more or less simultaneous for cooperating animals, they are delayed in time for one of the animals engaged in reciprocity. Reciprocity is even more open to cheating than cooperation, as one might suspect, although it can be an important component of social behavior. In human cultures, for example, reciprocity is a major economic force, but many laws, regulations, and penalties have to be set up for the detection and punishment of cheaters. The system for loaning money is perhaps one of the clearest examples: Creditors benefit their clients but expect the roles to reverse when

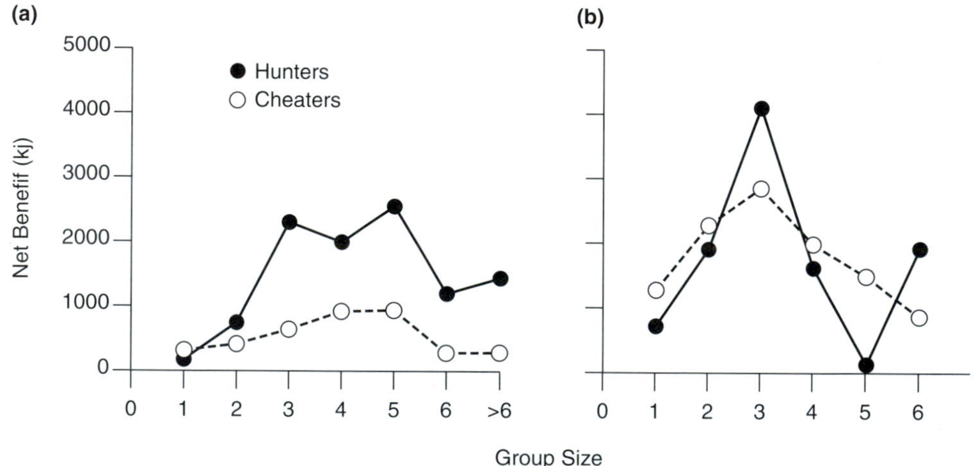

FIGURE 5.13. Total amount of meat obtained by chimpanzee hunters and cheaters (both eaten by them and shared with group members) as a function of group size. ***(a)*** In the Taï population, hunters have a distinct advantage over cheaters, but for both strategies there is an increase in the net benefit as a function of group size, up to a point. ***(b)*** In the Gombe population, hunting and cheating have similar success across various group sizes. Boesch (1994) suggested that these strategies are evolutionarily stable at Taï, but cooperative hunting should not evolve at the Gombe population because it can be easily invaded by a cheating strategy.

clients pay back the loan with interest. Failure to reciprocate is a source of constant social tension among economic agents, ethnic groups, genders, parents, generations, etc., and it illustrates the conflict between selfish and altruistic behavioral tendencies.

Reciprocity can evolve as an evolutionarily stable strategy if several provisions are made. First, the cost incurred by the animal must be sufficiently small to compensate for the delay involved in the return. Obviously, if the altruistic animal were to lose its life during the interaction, there would be no opportunity for reciprocation and the behavior would not evolve. In addition, reciprocity would be particularly likely to evolve in a species with long life span and stable group composition. If the costs are minimal, the benefits are large, and the animal lives long enough for the benefits to have an impact on its reproductive success, then reciprocity may evolve into a stable social behavior. Allogrooming among primates (one individual grooms another) appears to fit this low-cost category while simultaneously providing substantial benefits. The costs associated with grooming another animal may involve changes in the time budget (grooming takes substantial amounts of time) and distraction from potential dangers (predators, unprotected offspring), although attempts to measure these costs have shown the risks to be relatively small. On the other hand, grooming has many potential benefits, the most obvious being that of deparasitation. Less obvious are the social consequences of allogrooming, including the strengthening of bonds among unrelated individuals (i.e., "friends"), which may lead to decreased aggression and to the establishment of *coalitions* that might provide assistance in other contexts.

Another important component of reciprocity is the ability of animals to detect cheaters and exclude them from social interactions, which depends on individual recognition. Only if individuals who reciprocate are discriminated from cheaters, who take the benefit without reciprocating (a cost-efficient strategy which will tend to spread in a population unless it is checked), can reciprocity become stable. Several studies show that helping behavior among unrelated animals is usually directed at individuals that provided help in the past. An example is found in the blood-sharing behavior of female vampire bats (*Desmodus rotundus*) from Costa Rica. These animals roost in specific sites within a hollow tree. In a group of about ten females, the degree of relatedness varies between 0.02 and 0.11 (i.e., distant cousins at best). Vampire bats go on foraging trips every night and look for a mammal from which they can extract blood (cows, horses, and other large animals are typical preys). These bats are likely to starve to death unless they feed at least every other night. Upon returning to the group, individuals that have been unsuccessful beg for food from their neighbors, which, on some occasions, regurgitate some amount of blood into the recipient's mouth. Wilkinson (1984) found that the probability that an individual would regurgitate blood to a specific neighbor can be predicted from the extent of their association, that is, from the degree to which these two particular bats had been observed in close proximity within the group. Furthermore, Wilkinson demonstrated that the cost of giving food for a well-fed bat is small compared to the benefit conferred to the starving bat. The rate of weight loss in starving bats decreases as they approach the point of starvation. As a result, an animal that has recently obtained blood (far from the starvation point) and is providing, say, 5% of its weight to a recipient, will approach the starvation point in a given amount of time, say 10 hr. However, the 5% amount of blood obtained by the recipient will move it away from the starvation point by a comparatively larger amount of time, say 18 hr. This may be enough to allow for another foraging opportunity. Vampire bats that were recently fed by a group member are more likely to become blood donors than bats that did not receive food from a conspecific. These animals have found a way to compensate individual failures in foraging by evolving a stable strategy based on reciprocity.

6. Key Terms

agonistic behavior 142
alternative mating strategy 139
altruistic behavior 129
asexual reproduction 123
Bateman's principle 134
biparental care 151
brood parasitism 152
clonal species 160
coalitions 165
coefficient of relatedness (*r*) 158
communication 142
cooperation 162
copulatory behavior 127
darting behavior 148
diapause 150
diplodiploidy 157
displacement 145
dominance 143
eusociality 157
evolutionarily stable strategy 139
external fertilization 148
female choice 131
group care 151
handicap principle 146
haplodiploidy 157
helpers 154
home range 142
indirect fitness 129
individual recognition 124
internal fertilization 148
leadership 125
lek polygyny 133
lordosis 148
male-male competition 131
mate-defense polygyny 131
maternal care 150
monogamy 131
mounting 148
parent-offspring conflict 153
parental care 150
parental investment 134
paternal care 151
paternal uncertainty 136
polyandry 131
polygynandry 131
polygyny 131
polygyny threshold 137
primary reinforcers 127
reciprocity (or reciprocal altruism) 164
regression 153
resource-defense polygyny 131
ritualizations 142
satellite males 140
scent marking 136
secondary reinforcers 127
secondary sexual characters 134
self-recognition 126
sentinel behavior 154
sequential hermaphroditism 140
sexual reproduction 123

7. REFERENCES

Alexander, R. D., Noonan, K. M., & Crespi, B. J. (1991). The evolution of eusociality. In P. W. Sherman, J. U. M. Jarvis, & R. D. Alexander (Eds.), *The biology of the naked mole-rat* (pp. 3–44). Princeton: Princeton University Press.

Aoki, S. (1977). *Colophina clematis* (Homoptera, Pemphigidae), an aphid species with "soldiers." *Kontyû,* **45,** 276–282.

Baker, R. R., & Bellis, M. A. (1993). Human sperm competition: Ejaculate manipulation by females and a function for the female orgasm. *Animal Behaviour,* **46,** 887–909.

Bateman, A. J. (1948). Intra-sexual selection in *Drosophila. Heredity,* **2,** 349–368.

Bateson, P. (1983). Optimal outbreeding. In P. Bateson (Ed.), *Mate choice* (pp. 257–277). Cambridge, UK: Cambridge University Press.

Bednarz, J. C. (1988). Cooperative hunting in Harris' hawks (*Parabuteo unicinctus*). *Science,* **239,** 1525–1527.

Betzig, L. (1992). Roman polygyny. *Ethology and Sociobiology,* **12,** 309–349.

Boesch, C. (1994). Cooperative hunting in wild chimpanzees. *Animal Behaviour,* **48,** 653–667.

Borgia, G. (1985). Bower quality, number of decorations and mating success of male satin bowerbirds (*Ptilonorhynchus violaceus*): An experimental analysis. *Animal Behaviour,* **33,** 266–271.

Boysen, S. T., & Berntson, G. G. (1989). Conspecific recognition in the chimpanzee (*Pan troglodytes*): Cardiac responses to significant others. *Journal of Comparative Psychology,* **103,** 215–220.

Brown, S. D., & Dooling, R. J. (1992). Perception of conspecific faces by budgerigars (*Melopsittacus undulatus*): I. Natural faces. *Journal of Comparative Psychology,* **106,** 203–216.

Brown, S. D., & Dooling, R. J. (1993). Perception of conspecific faces by budgerigars (*Melopsittacus undulatus*): II. Synthetic models. *Journal of Comparative Psychology,* **107,** 48–60.

Campagna, C., Le Boeuf, B. J., & Cappozzo, H. L. (1988). Group raids: A mating strategy of male southern sea lions. *Behaviour,* **105,** 224–249.

Clutton-Brock, T. H., Guinness, F. E., & Albon, S. D. (1982). *Red deer: Behavior and ecology of two sexes.* Chicago, IL: University of Chicago Press.

Crespi, B. J. (1992). Eusociality in Australian gall thrips. *Nature,* **359,** 724–726.

Crews, D., & Moore, M. C. (1986). Evolution of mechanisms controlling mating behavior. *Science,* **231,** 121–125.

Curry, R. L., & Grant, P. R. (1990). Galapagos mockingbirds: Territorial cooperative breeding in a climatically variable environment. In P. B. Stacey & W. D. Koenig (Eds.), *Cooperative breeding in birds: Long-term studies of ecology and behavior* (pp. 291–331). Cambridge, UK: Cambridge University Press.

D'Amato, F. R. (1988). Effects of male social status on reproductive success and on behavior in mice (*Mus musculus*). *Journal of Comparative Psychology,* **102,** 146–151.

Darwin, C. (1871). *The descent of man, and selection in relation to sex.* London: Murray.

Davies, N. B. (1992). *Dunnock behaviour and social evolution.* Oxford: Oxford University Press.

de Veer, M., & van den Bos, R. (1999). A critical review of methodology and interpretation of mirror self-recognition research in nonhuman primates. *Animal Behaviour,* **58,** 459–468.

Dewsbury, D. A. (1975). Diversity and adaptation in rodent copulatory behavior. *Science,* **190,** 947–954.

Dewsbury, D. A. (1981). Social dominance, copulatory behavior, and differential reproduction in deer mice (*Peromyscus maniculatus*). *Journal of Comparative & Physiological Psychology,* **95,** 880–895.

Dewsbury, D. A. (1988). Kinship, familiarity, aggression, and dominance in deer mice (*Peromyscus maniculatus*) in seminatural enclosures. *Journal of Comparative Psychology,* **102,** 124–128.

Domjan, M., Blesbois, E., & Williams, J. (1998). The adaptive significance of sexual conditioning: Pavlovian control of sperm release. *Psychological Science,* **9,** 411–415.

Dufy, J. E. (1996). Eusociality in a coral-reef shrimp. *Nature,* **381,** 512–514.

Duffy, J. E., Morrison, C. L., & Ríos, R. (2000). Multiple origins of eusociality among sponge-dwelling shrimps *(Synalpheus). Evolution,* **54,** 503–516.

Eisenberg, J. F. (1991). *The mammalian radiations.* Chicago: Chicago University Press.

Emlen, S. T., & Oring, L. W. (1977). Ecology, sexual selection, and the evolution of mating systems. *Science,* **197,** 215–223.

Epple, G. (1978). Reproductive and social behavior of marmosets with special reference to captive breeding. *Primates in Medicine,* **10,** 50–62.

Everitt, B. J., Fray, P., Kostarczyk, E., Taylor, S., & Stacey, P. (1987). Studies of instrumental behavior with sexual reinforcement in male rats (*Rattus norvegicus*): I. Control by brief visual stimuli paired with a receptive female. *Journal of Comparative Psychology,* **101,** 395–406.

Fredrickson, W. T., & Sackett, G. P. (1984). Kin preferences in primates (*Macaca nemestrina*): Relatedness or familiarity? *Journal of Comparative Psychology,* **98,** 29–34.

Gallup, G. G. Jr. (1970). Chimpanzees: Self-recognition. *Science,* **167,** 86–87.

Grammer, K., & Thornhill, R. (1994). Human (*Homo sapiens*) facial attractiveness and sexual selection: The role of symmetry and averageness. *Journal of Comparative Psychology,* **108,** 233–242.

Gubernick, D. J., & Alberts, J. R. (1987). The biparental care system of the California mouse, *Peromyscus californicus. Journal of Comparative Psychology,* **101,** 169–177.

Gutiérrez, G., & Domjan, M. (1996). Learning and male-male sexual competition in Japanese quail (*Coturnix japonica*). *Journal of Comparative Psychology,* **110,** 170–175.

Gross, M. R. (1985). Disruptive selection for alternative life histories in salmon. *Nature,* **313,** 47–48.

Haley, M. P., Deutsch, C. J., & Le Boeuf, B. J. (1994). Size, dominance, and copulatory success in male northern elephant seals, *Mirounga angustirostris. Animal Behaviour,* **48,** 1249–1260.

Hamilton, W. D. (1964). The genetical evolution of social behaviour. I, II. *Journal of Theoretical Biology,* **7,** 1–52.

Hartung, J. (1982). Polygyny and inheritance of wealth. *Current Anthropology,* **23,** 1–12.

Hölldobler, B., & Wilson, E. O. (1990). *The ants.* Cambridge: Harvard University Press.

Hollis, K. L. (1982). Pavlovian conditioning of signal-centered action patterns and autonomic behavior: A biological analysis of function. *Advances in the Study of Behavior,* **12,** 1–64.

Hollis, K. L., Dumas, M. J., Singh, P., & Fackelman, P. (1995). Pavlovian conditioning of aggressive behavior in blue gourami fish (*Trichogaster trichopterus*): Winners become winners and losers stay losers. *Journal of Comparative Psychology,* **109,** 123–133.

Hollis, K. L., Pharr, V. L., Dumas, M. J., Britton, G. B., & Field, J. (1997). Classical conditioning provides paternity advantage for territorial male blue gouramis (*Trichogaster trichopterus*). *Journal of Comparative Psychology,* **111,** 219–225.

Holmes, W. G., & Sherman, P. W. (1982). The ontogeny of kin recognition in two species of ground squirrels. *American Zoologist,* **22,** 491–517.

Huxley, J. S. (1923). Courtship activities in the red-throated diver, *Colymbus stellatus pontopp*; together with a discussion of the evolution of courtship in birds. *Journal of the Linnean Society of London,* **35,** 253–292.

Jones, G. P. (1981). Spawning-site choice by female *Pseudolabrus celidotus* (Pisces: Labridae) and its influence on the mating system. *Behavioral Ecology & Sociobiology,* **8,** 129–142.

Keating, C. F., Mazur, A., & Segall, M. H. (1981). A cross-cultural exploration of physiognomic traits of dominance and happiness. *Ethology & Sociobiology,* **2,** 41–48.

Kruijt, J. P., & de Vos, G. J. (1988). Individual variation in reproductive success in male black grouse, *Tetrao tetrix.* In T. H. Clutton-Brock (Ed.), *Reproductive success* (pp. 279–290). Chicago, IL: Chicago University Press.

Le Boeuf, B. J. (1974). Male-male competition and reproductive success in elephant seals. *American Zoologist,* **14,** 163–176.

Maynard Smith, J. (1982). *Evolution and the theory of games.* Cambridge: Cambridge University Press.

McDonald, D. B., & Potts, W. K. (1994). Cooperative display and relatedness among males in a lek-mating bird. *Science,* **266,** 1030–1032.

Møller, A. P. (1992). Female swallow preference for symmetrical male sexual ornaments. *Nature,* **357,** 238–240.

Morris, D. (1956). The feather postures of birds and the problem of the origin of social signals. *Behaviour,* **9,** 6–113.

Murdock, G. P. (1967). *Ethnographic atlas.* Pittsburg, PA: University of Pittsburg Press.

Orians, G. H. (1969). On the evolution of mating systems in birds and mammals. *American Naturalist,* **103,** 589–603.

Oring, L. W. (1985). Avian polyandry. *Current Ornithology,* **3,** 309–351.

Oring, L. W., Colwell, M. A., & Reed, J. M. (1991). Lifetime reproductive success in the spotted sandpiper (*Actitis macularia*): Sex differences and variance components. *Behavioral Ecology & Sociobiology,* **28,** 425–432.

Packer, C., Herbst, L., Pusey, A. E., Bygott, J. D., Hanby, J. P., Cairns, S. J., & Mulder, M. B. (1988). Reproductive success of lions. In T. H. Clutton-Brock (Ed.), *Reproductive success* (pp. 363–383). Chicago: Chicago University Press.

Perrill, S. A., Gerhardt, H. C., & Daniel, R. (1982). Mating strategy shifts in male green treefrogs (*Hyla cinerea*): An experimental study. *Animal Behaviour,* **30,** 43–48.

Petrie, M., Halliday, T., & Sanders, C. (1991). Peahens prefer peacocks with elaborate trains. *Animal Behaviour,* **41,** 323–331.

Pryce, C. R., Döbeli, M., & Martin, R. D. (1993). Effects of sex steroids on maternal motivation in the common marmoset (*Callithrix jacchus*): Development and application of an operant system with maternal reinforcement. *Journal of Comparative Psychology,* **107,** 99–115.

Rashotte, M. E., & Amsel, A. (1968). Transfer of slow-response rituals to the extinction of a continuously rewarded response. *Journal of Comparative & Physiological Psychology,* **66,** 432–443.

Reeve, H. K., Westneat, D. F., Noon, W. A., Sherman, P. W., & Aquadro, C. F. (1990). DNA "fingerprinting" reveals high levels of inbreeding in colonies of the eusocial naked mole-rat. *Proceedings of the National Academy of Sciences,* (USA), **87,** 2496–2500.

Robinson, S. R., & Smotherman, W. P. (1991). Fetal learning: Implications for the development of kin recognition. In P. G. Hepper (Ed.), *Kin recognition* (pp. 308–334). Cambridge, UK: Cambridge University Press.

Ronca, A. E., Lamkin, C. A., & Alberts, J. R. (1993). Maternal contributions to sensory experience in the fetal and newborn rat (*Rattus norvegicus*). *Journal of Comparative Psychology,* **107,** 61–74.

Savage, A., Ziegler, T. E., & Snowdon, C. T. (1988). Sociosexual development, pairbond formation, and mechanisms of fertility suppression in female cotton-top tamarins (*Saguinus oedipus*). *American Journal of Primatology,* **14,** 345–359.

Scott, J. P. (1958). *Animal behavior.* Chicago: Chicago University Press.

Sherman, P. W. (1977). Nepotism and the evolution of alarm calls. *Science,* **197,** 1246–1253.

Sherry, D. F., Jacobs, L. F., & Gaulin, S. J. C. (1992). Spatial memory and adaptive specialization of the hippocampus. *Trends in Neuroscience,* **15,** 298–303.

Singh, D. (1993). Adaptive significance of female physical attractiveness: Role of the waist-to-hip ratio. *Journal of Personality & Social Psychology,* **65,** 293–307.

Stern, D. L., & Foster, W. A. (1996). The evolution of soldiers in aphids. *Biological Reviews,* **71,** 27–79.

Swartz, K. B., & Evans, S. (1991). Not all chimpanzees (*Pan troglodytes*) show self-recognition. *Primates,* **32,** 583–496.

Taborsky, M. (1984). Broodcare helpers in the cichlid fish *Lamprologus brichardi*: Their costs and benefits. *Animal Behaviour,* **32,** 1236–1252.

Thompson, T., & Sturm, T. (1965). Classical conditioning of aggressive display in Siamese fighting fish. *Journal of the Experimental Analysis of Behavior,* **8,** 397–403.

Thorne, B. L. (1997). Evolution of eusociality in termites. *Annual Review of Ecology & Systematics,* **28,** 27–54.

Towsend, D. S., Stewart, M. M., & Pough, F. H. (1984). Male parental care and its adaptive significance in a neotropical frog. *Animal Behaviour,* **32,** 421–431.

Trivers, R. L. (1971). The evolution of reciprocal altruism. *Quarterly Review of Biology,* **46,** 35–57.

Trivers, R. L. (1972). Parental investment and sexual selection. In B. Campbell (Ed.), *Sexual selection and the descent of man 1871–1971* (pp. 136–179). Chicago, IL: Aldine.

Trivers, R. L. (1974). Parent-offspring conflict. *American Zoologist,* **14,** 249–264.

Vallortiagara, G., Cailotto, M., & Zanforlin, M. (1990). Sex differences in social reinstatement motivation of the domestic chick (*Gallus gallus*) revealed by runway tests with social and nonsocial reinforcement. *Journal of Comparative Psychology,* **104,** 361–367.

Wade, J., & Crews, D. (1997). Biopsychology of lizard reproductive behavior. In G. Greenberg & M. Haraway (Eds.), *Comparative psychology. A handbook* (pp. 348–354). New York: Garland.

Warner, R. R. (1975). The adaptive significance of sequential hermaphroditism in animals. *American Naturalist,* **109,** 61–86.

Westneat, D. F., Sherman, P. W., & Morton, M. L. (1990). The ecology and evolution of extra-pair copulations. *Current Ornithology,* **7,** 331–369.

White, N. R., & Barfield, R. J. (1987). Role of the ultrasonic vocalization of the female rat (*Rattus norvegicus*) in sexual behavior. *Journal of Comparative Psychology,* **101,** 73–81.

White, N. R., & Barfield, R. J. (1990). Effects of male pre-ejaculatory vocalizations on female receptive behavior in the rat (*Rattus norvegicus*). *Journal of Comparative Psychology,* **104,** 140–146.

Wilcox, R. M., & Johnston, J. E. (1995). Scent countermarks: Specialized mechanisms of perception and response to individual odors in golden hamsters (*Mesocricetus auratus*). *Journal of Comparative Psychology,* **109,** 349–356.

Wilkison, G. (1984). Reciprocal food sharing in vampire bats. *Nature,* **308,** 181–184.

Williams, T. D. (1995). *The penguins.* Oxford, UK: Oxford University Press.

Wimberger, P. H. (1988). Food suplement effects on breeding time and harem size in the red-winged blackbird (*Agelaius phoeniceus*). *Auk,* **105,** 799–802.

Woolfenden, G. E., & Fitzpatrick, J. W. (1997). Florida scrub jays: A synopsis after 18 years of study. In P. B. Stacy & W. D. Koenig (Eds.), *Cooperative breeding in birds: Long-term studies of ecology and behavior* (pp. 241–266). Cambridge: Cambridge University Press.

Wyles, J. S., Kunkel, J. G., & Wilson, A. C. (1983). Birds, behavior, and anatomical evolution. *Proceedings of the National Academy of Sciences,* (USA), **80,** 4394–4397.

Yanes, R. M. F., & Castro Vázquez, A. (1990). An unusual pattern of copulatory behavior in a South American cricetid rodent: *Akodon molinae. Journal of Comparative Psychology,* **104,** 263–267.

Yeager, C. P., & Burghardt, G. M. (1991). Effect of food competition on aggregation: Evidence for social recognition in the plains garter snake (*Thamnophis radix*). *Journal of Comparative Psychology,* **105,** 380–386.

Yunes, R. M. F., & Castro-Vázquez, A. (1990). An unusual pattern of copulatory behavior in a South American cricetid rodent: Akodon molinae. *Journal of Comparative Psychology,* **104,** 263–267.

Young, L. J., Winslow, J. T., Nilsen, R., & Insel, T. R. (1997). Species differences in V1a receptor gene expression in monogamous and nonmonogamous voles: Behavioral consequences. *Behavioral Neuroscience,* **111,** 599–605.

Zahavi, A., & Zahavi, A. (1997). *The handicap principle. A missing piece of Darwin's puzzle.* New York: Oxford University Press.

PART II
Patterns of Brain-Behavior Evolution

The chapters in ***Part I*** introduced some basic concepts in evolutionary theory and demonstrated how such concepts can be used to understand behavior. Behavioral evolution was explained mainly from a functional point of view—that is, as a part of the entire phenotype that contributes to the individual's reproductive success. No systematic effort was made to place the examples in a historical context. Such a historical context is given by the specific historical pattern of the evolution of life on our planet. The adaptive significance of biological characters occurs not only in an ecological context but also in the context of inheritance, and inherited information is the result of a particular history of evolution in a specific lineage of organisms. Whereas ecological factors shape the mating system displayed by a particular population of animals, some taxonomic groups have a tendency to display a certain system. As I mentioned, for example, tamarin and marmoset monkeys are characterized by a tendency to form monogamous pairs. It is possible that such a tendency depends on factors inherited from a common ancestor, which would make monogamy the modal system for species within this group.

The chapters in ***Part II*** emphasize evolutionary patterns. First, I look at the evolution of animals and review the concepts that are critical for an understanding of historical information (***Chapter 6***). The chapters that follow look at evolutionary patterns from the point of view of brain-behavior evolution, an issue of central importance in comparative psychology. Simple nervous systems and their behavioral properties are described in ***Chapter 7,*** the evolution of the vertebrate brain and behavior in ***Chapter 8,*** and the evolution of the primate brain and behavior in ***Chapter 9.***

CHAPTER 6

Origin and Evolution of Animals

MAIN GENERALIZATIONS OF CHAPTER 6

- *The phylogenetic history of animals is characterized by mass extinction events, adaptive radiations, migrations, and evolutionary novelties that permitted the colonization of new habitats.*
- *The history of animals can be partially reconstructed on the basis of fossil evidence and taxonomic tools such as those provided by cladistic analyses based on molecular, morphological, and behavioral characters.*

Only one instance of life is known to us—namely, the one that evolved in our own planet. Knowing just a single case of evolution creates problems that are, in many ways, similar to those faced by a historian who is trying to understand a particular episode in ancient history. It is impossible to experiment with particular aspects of history, to vary factors that are thought to be crucial and determine whether the history repeats itself, or whether some crucial difference emerges that would shed light on the underlying causes. The historian can, for example, assess various sources of evidence in trying to understand why Socrates accepted with grace the punishment inflicted upon him by the Athenians, or what drove Julius Caesar to cross the Rubicon River and invade Rome. But these unique episodes in ancient history cannot be treated in the same way scientists treat other phenomena. They cannot be replicated, manipulated, or observed under controlled conditions, all of which are necessary if one is to determine exactly the causes of a particular phenomenon. Similarly, mammalian evolution occurred only once, sometime during the Mesozoic era, and the causes for such an outcome can only be guessed on the basis of fragmentary pieces of information provided by the fossil record. Important episodes, such as the mass extinction event that led to the disappearance of dinosaurs at the end of the Cretaceous period or the drift of a particular continental mass, occurred only once and cannot be reproduced under different circumstances or under controlled conditions.

Scientists interested in evolutionary patterns develop hypotheses about the history of a particular group of animals on the basis of some type of information, such as morphological features of the skeleton, and then test the hypothesis against a new data base derived independently from the original one. Gaps are filled with hypotheses, and these are tested against new information as it arises, perhaps through the discovery of new fossils or through the development of new analytical techniques. This information provides an important frame of reference for an understanding of the evolution of behavior, the main concern of comparative psychology.

1. The Diversity of Life

1.a. Taxonomy. Life forms are practically everywhere. From the Arctic to the Antarctic, from the deep sea to the high mountains, and in the air. In hot springs, around volcanic lava, and in between pieces of ice. Buried in the soil of a garden or underneath sand pebbles. The diversity of life is so astonishing that it is hard to comprehend. More than a million species of animals and plants have been scientifically described, and probably many more remain to be identified. Studies in the remaining rain forests of the world often yield new species of animals and plants. Any person attempting to understand such a reality would probably have to begin by putting together organisms that resemble each other. Aristotle [384–322 B.C.] was among the first scholars to try this exercise (see ***Chapter 1, section 1,*** pp. 5–6), thanks to the services of Alexander the Great, who commissioned assistants to collect biological material and promptly send it to Athens for study. This study gave rise to taxonomy—that is, the branch of biology that deals with the classification of species into groups—and made Aristotle the father of both botany and zoology.

Most of the current rules in taxonomy were developed later by Carolus Linnaeus [1707–1778], a Swedish botanist who, like Aristotle, was exposed to a large number of new species resulting from the worldwide explorations that had started during the Renaissance period. European museums and universities had accumulated a vast amount of biological material that Linnaeus intended to classify according to a standard system. Hierarchical classifications had been used since the time of Aristotle, but Linnaeus developed a set of rules that became universally accepted. For example, each species was scientifically identified by two Latin names, the first corresponding to the genus (usually italicized and capitalized) and the second to the species (usually italicized but not capitalized). Thus, humans are scientifically named *Homo sapiens*, "*Homo*" indicating the genus and "*sapiens*" the species. Words derived from Latin and Greek, and even "Latinized" words, are used to name new species as they are discovered or recognized scientifically. For example, the goldfish is referred to as *auratus*, the Latin word for gold, and the American alligator is named *mississippiensis*, a "Latinized" word which clearly points to the animal's geographic distribution. Whereas common names may be vague (e.g., "sparrow" may refer to several different bird species), scientific names are assigned only after careful description of the biological features of the species.

The hierarchical nature of this system becomes evident at the genus level. Only one species bears the name "*sapiens*," but several different species may be identified by the same genus name based on character similarity (e.g., *Homo sapiens, H. habilis, H. erectus*). Some genera may have a single species, while others may include hundreds (about 300 different species of grasses are grouped in the genus *Panicum*). Similarly, the species within one genus may be restricted to a relatively small location, such as a lake, but those in another genus may be spread over large territories (e.g., opossums, genus *Didelphis*, range from United States to Argentina).

Linnaeus and, later, Ernst Haeckel [1834–1919] further grouped species into higher-order units. Each of these units is called a *taxon* (*taxa* in plural). The most widely used taxonomic categories, from the most general (bottom) to the most specific (top), are shown in ***Figure 6.1***. Intermediate categories can be easily created by adding the prefixes *sub-* and *super-* (e.g., subspecies, superfamily). The criterion for inclusion of a particular taxon in a particular category is always *character similarity*, that is, the sharing of traits. At the time of Linnaeus and Haeckel, the main traits were morphological and embryological, as these were easily open to direct observation. Currently, taxonomists also use behavior, brain neurochemical systems, protein structure, and even the DNA sequential data as sources for taxonomic classification.

A warning note is in order. In the rest of this chapter, I make extensive use of taxonomic scientific names. There are several advantages to this approach. First, phylogenetic descriptions gain in precision. Second, this allows the reader to grasp the complexity of the study of the history of animals. Finally, this terminology provides a taxonomic background useful for any approach to the study of the evolution and development of behavior.

1.b. The Five-Kingdom Classification. How many kingdoms are there? Linnaeus suggested that all living organisms could be classified as either animals (Animalia) or plants (Plantae), a very obvious distinction. Plants tend to remain fixed in a single location and obtain energy and nutrients from sunlight and carbon dioxide, whereas animals are far more active and obtain energy and nutrients by consuming other living organisms. But, of course, there are also inter-

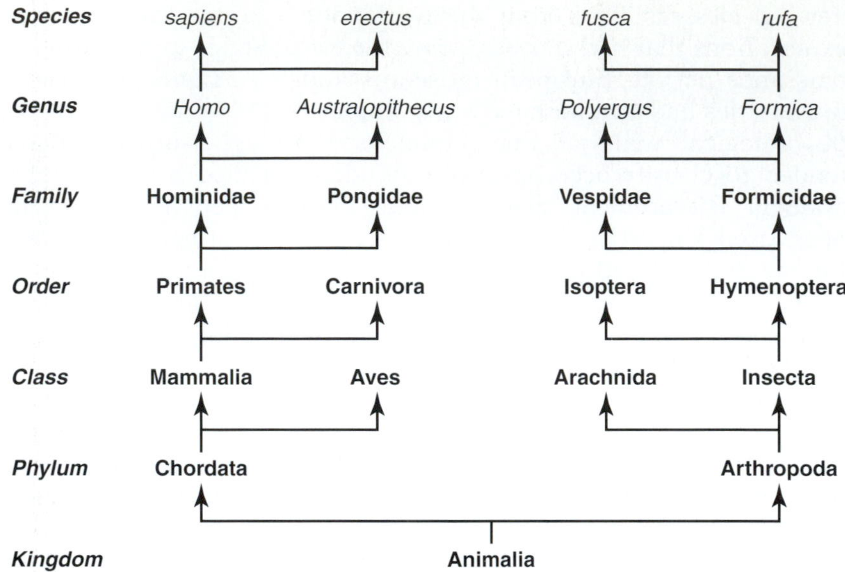

FIGURE 6.1. The most frequently used taxonomic categories arranged hierarchically. The tree represents the hierarchy by means of a branching diagram with specific taxon names for the two examples given above, humans and red ants. Several instances of each particular category (e.g., several orders) are typically included in the immediately higher category (e.g., class). In some rare cases, a single lower category may be assigned to its corresponding category (e.g., some genera include a single species).

---

mediate forms. Carnivorous plants obtain nutrients from insects, whereas some lizards synthesize vitamins in their skin directly from sunlight; there are plants possessing "sensitive" leaves that move when touched (e.g., *Mimosa pudica*), and animals that live attached to a substrate (e.g., coral). Nonetheless, the distinction stands as a useful one.

With the invention of the microscope, the realm of the living was extended to microorganisms. When the microscope was used to observe the various tissues of animals and plants, it was discovered that they are, in fact, made out of unified entities called *cells*. Many different types of cells were discovered in animals and plants, with clearly discriminable morphologies and functions. These are thus referred to as *multicellular organisms*. Microorganisms, on the other hand, seem fundamentally different from animals and plants in that they are made of a single cell; that is, they are *unicellular organisms*.

Although the diversity of unicellulars is also astonishing, broad patterns of similarity are also apparent. A major distinction among unicellulars is that between prokaryotes and eukaryotes. *Prokaryotes* (several types of bacteria) are distinguished by the lack of a membrane-bound nucleus, the absence of mitosis and meiosis, and their relatively small size (ranging between 1 and 10 μm, with 1 μm being equal to a millionth of a meter).

Prokaryotes obtain nutrients from a process of photosynthesis similar to that of plants or through absorption. They typically contain a single chromosome arranged in a double helix structure with few or no associated proteins. The only organelles present in bacteria are the ribosomes, which participate in protein synthesis. During cell division, the chromosome is replicated and the two copies are separated; eventually the bacterium divides itself, giving rise to two daughter cells with equal DNA content. There are no known multicellular prokaryotes.

In contrast, *eukaryotes* are characterized by a clear nucleus-cytoplasm differentiation with a nuclear membrane surrounding the chromosomes. They typically have several distinct chromosomes, many cytoplasmatic organelles (ribosomes, mitochondria, chloroplasts, etc.), and a relatively large size (ranging between 10 and 100 μm). The amoeba, paramecium, and vorticella are among the most famous unicellular eukaryotes. But eukaryotes have given rise to multicellular forms of at least three types: the animals and plants already mentioned, and also the fungi. All these organisms are formed by a mass of eukaryote cells with various degrees of differentiation and coordination, many reproducing sexually and exhibiting true development from a fertilized egg to a sexually mature stage.

The particular taxonomy adopted here is referred to as the five-kingdom system (Whittaker 1969). It is not universally accepted, but it provides a relatively simple way to organize the diversity of life. The following nomenclature is used in this system:

Monera: involves all the prokaryote unicellulars (bacteria).

Protista: (also referred to as *Protozoa*) includes a wide diversity of eukaryote unicellulars.

Plantae: multicellular eukaryotes (algae and plants) that obtain nutrients by photosynthesis.

Fungi: multicellular eukaryotes (mushrooms) that obtain nutrients by absorption.

Animalia: (also referred to as *Metazoa*) multicellular eukaryotes that obtain nutrients by ingestion.

Several points can be made about this classification. First, the way in which organisms obtain their nutrients is the major key to distinguish among the multicellular kingdoms. Second, an evolutionary sequence is implied in this classification, although the specifics are obscure. Monerans are thought to be direct descendants from the most primitive organisms. Protists evolved from monerans and, in turn, gave rise independently to the three multicellular kingdoms: plants, fungi, and animals. Third, viruses are not in this picture, although many biologists would now consider them to be true living organisms, probably related to the monerans. Viruses contain regular DNA and use the familiar genetic code; but, unlike bacteria, viruses lack ribosomes. For this reason, they can only proliferate by "parasiting" a cell and using its cytoplasmatic machinery for the expression of their own DNA.

Comparative psychology is about the evolution and development of animal behavior, and thus this book is restricted to issues involving the kingdom Animalia. Just as our own species needs to be seen in the context of animal evolution, it is important to realize that animals are part of an even larger context of living organisms with which they share many fundamental properties (e.g., the genetic code).

1.c. The Animal Phyla. Most taxonomists agree that animals can be divided into thirty-something phyla, although the exact number is still in dispute. Each animal phylum is thought to represent a more or less unique *body plan* (also referred to as *Bauplan*). A body plan is a basic set of homologous structural features representing a theme that, in many variations, appears in all the members of a particular phylum. Thus the chordates (including fish, toads, humans, etc.) are characterized, among other features, by a ventral digestive system and a dorsal nervous system. Although in bipedal organisms (such as humans and kangaroos), ventral and dorsal can be equated with the animal's front and back, respectively, the relative positions of the digestive and nervous systems remain the same.

Animal phyla can be represented by means of a *phylogenetic tree,* that is, a graphical representation of evolution based on the tree metaphor (see, for example, ***Figure 6.13,*** p. 205). In a phylogenetic tree the branches represent lineages of ancestors and descendants, and the nodes where branches meet represent a common ancestor. Branches stemming from a node symbolize the process of evolutionary *divergence,* that is, the splitting of taxa from a common ancestor. The trunk of the tree can be viewed as the ancestor common to all the lineages represented in the tree. ***Figure 6.2*** represents the phylogenetic relationship among several animal phyla and it illustrates several important points. First, evolutionary links are hypothesis of relatedness based on some set of data (in this case, the phylogeny is based on molecular data obtained from living species of these taxa). These hypotheses can be tested by developing a phylogeny based on an alternative set of traits, such as morphological or behavioral traits.

Second, whereas some aspects of this tree are controversial, others are relatively well established. For example, there is general agreement about the position of the Porifera (sponges) at the basis of the tree as the most primitive phyla (i.e., most conservative in morphology). The Mesozoa (small, tubular animals, made from 20 to 30 cells that live in the kidneys of octopuses and other cephalopods), not shown in this figure, are also generally considered to be a primitive animal phylum. These animals have different cell types, but cells are not organized into different types of tissue, and so the animals lack internal organs. The Cnidaria (sea anemones, jellyfish, coral) and Ctenophora (comb jellies; not shown in the picture) are characterized by *radial symmetry,* that is, their bodies are organized around one (or more than one) central axis. These animals exhibit differentiated tissue and the simplest known nervous systems, organized as diffuse nerve nets. Cnidarians and ctenophorans have a *diploblastic* body plan consisting of two layers of cells: the *ectoderm,* an external layer where skin, muscle, and neuron cells are located; and the *endoderm,* an internal layer that functions as a gut. Nutrients enter and exit the body through a single opening.

All the other animal phyla, many of which are illustrated in ***Figure 6.2,*** are characterized by *bilateral symmetry*—that is, the presence of an anterior-posterior axis and paired bodily parts. Bilaterals possess three cell layers—ectoderm, mesoderm, and endoderm—and are thus called *triploblasts.* The *mesoderm* appears in the simple bilaterals as an intermediate layer that has allowed for the evolution of larger and more complex organs.

Bilateral animals are usually grouped according to two major criteria. One criterion is based on the presence of a coelom. The coelom is a body cavity lined with mesoderm cells where the internal organs are enclosed. This criterion leads to three major groups. (1) The flatworms (Platyhelminthes) are triploblastic but lack a

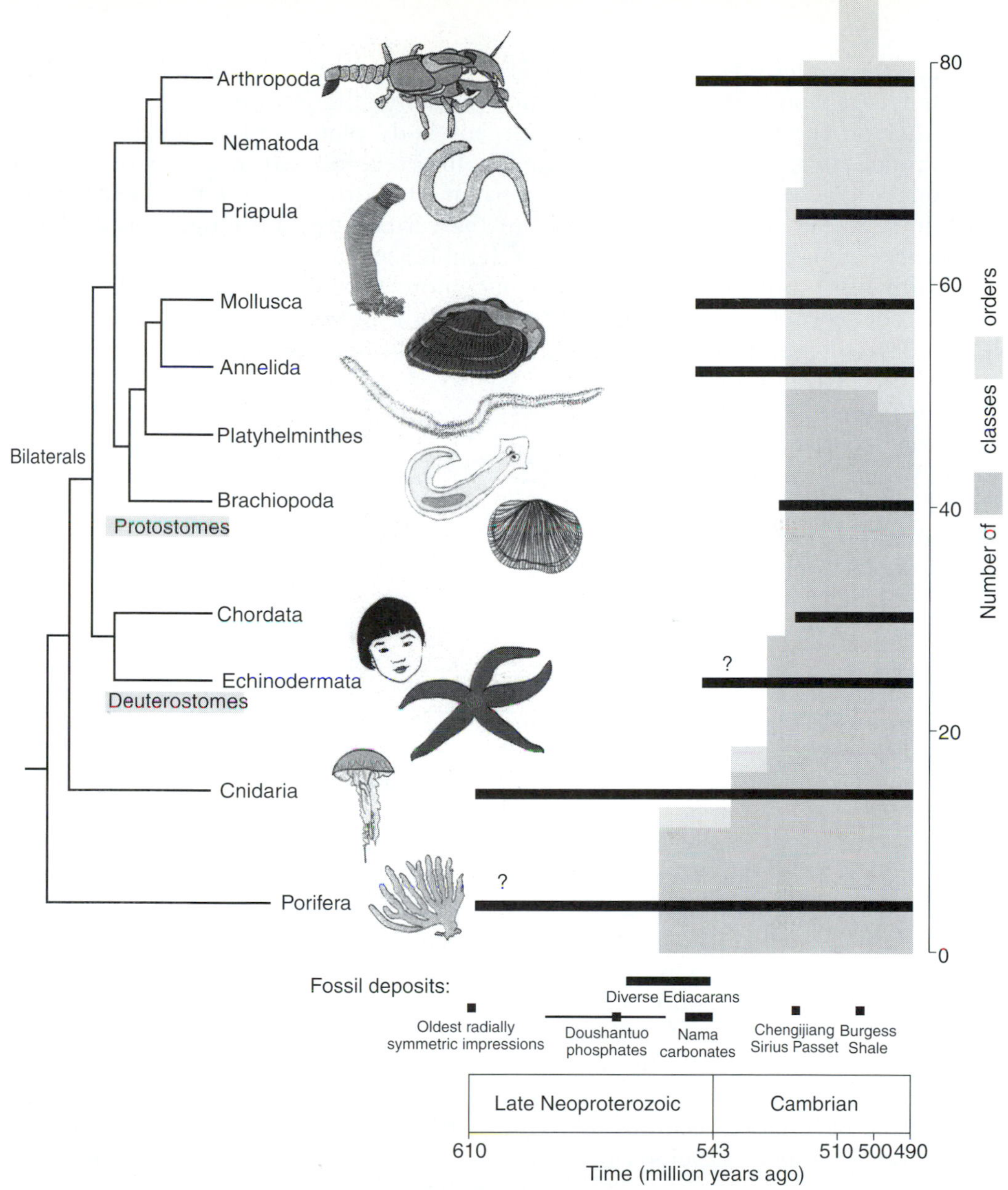

FIGURE 6.2. The phylogenetic relationships among some of the animal phyla (Knoll & Carroll 1999). The phylogenetic tree is based on molecular data obtained from living representatives of these taxa. The black bars on the right denote the presence of these phyla in the fossil faunas listed at the bottom of the figure. For example, cnidarians have been found in all the fossil faunas listed at the bottom. The histograms represent the number of classes (light) and orders (dark) present in each of the fossil faunas. Information from living and extinct specimens serve as independent sources for hypotheses of relatedness. Although there is no universal agreement about the classification of the animal phyla, this tree displays some features that are widely accepted by taxonomists.

coelom and are thus referred to as *acoelomates.* (2) A heterogeneous set of phyla are grouped together on the basis of having a body cavity similar to the coelom but of a clearly different origin because it lacks the mesoderm lining. These are referred to as *pseudocoelomates,* and their phylogenetic relationship with other bilaterals is uncertain. The nematode worm *Caenorhabditis elegans* (Nematoda), is a pseudocoelomate extensively used in research on behavioral genetics (see ***Chapter 3***). (3) *Coelomates* possess a true coelom and have thus evolved larger organs and stronger muscles, allowing for a great diversity of adaptations. The major animal phyla are coelomates, including arthropods, annelids, molluscs, echinoderms, and chordates, among others.

As shown in ***Figure 6.2,*** bilaterals can also be grouped into protostomes and deuterostomes, a distinction based on relatively general embryological features (see ***Chapter 10, section 1,*** pp. 362–365). Soon after fertilization, the embryo develops into a hollow ball of cells referred to as the *blastula stage.* At a point called the blastopore, the cells invaginate to form the precursor of the gut until they eventually produce a second opening. This is called the *gastrula* stage. In *protostomes,* the blastopore (or an adjacent site) gives rise to the mouth of the animal, while the opening distal from the blastopore develops into an anus. In contrast, in *deuterostomes* the opening distal with respect to the blastopore becomes the mouth, while the blastopore develops into an anus.

Figure 6.2 makes an additional point. It is clear that the distinction between *vertebrates* and *invertebrates,* often used in the psychological literature, can be misleading. Vertebrata is considered a subphylum of Chordata (although some give it a phylum status), and thus it possesses a meaningful biological status as a taxon. In contrast, the term "invertebrate" refers to a broad collection of many different phyla with widely divergent body plans and complex phylogenetic interrelations. It may be used as a convenient shortcut to refer to "everything but the vertebrates," although it is perhaps preferable to avoid the term altogether when more specific taxonomic claims are made about the generality of certain behavioral or neurobiological phenomena.

2. Geological Background

2.a. Geological Periods. Now that some of the major characters of the story have been delineated, it is necessary to place them in time. Unlike regular stories, however, the history of life on earth unfolds over periods of time that are hard to grasp unless we make a special effort. Our planet is believed to be at least four and a half billion years old—that is 4,500,000,000 years old! This time span is usually divided into three large time eons: The Archaean eon extends from the formation of the Earth until about 2,500 million years ago (Mya), the Proterozoic eon until about 543 Mya, and the Phanerozoic eon reaches the present time.

Nobody really knows for sure when and how life started, although there is no shortage of theories (Maynard Smith & Szathmary 1995). Evidence of microscopic organisms appears in the oldest rock deposits from the Archaean eon, about 3.5 billion years old. For a very long period of time, the fossil record (that is, the evidence about past life forms derived from the study of rocks) provides no evidence of true multicellular animals. The following exercise may be useful to picture the time spans involved. If your feet represent the point in time when the earth was formed, then the first fossil microorganisms appear at the height of your knees, but the first animal fossils appear only at the level of your neck. All human culture and history would be compressed at the very top of your head.

The history of animal evolution begins approximately 600 Mya, at the end of the Proterozoic, and it extends through the entire Phanerozoic. It is the events in this last period that provide a phylogenetic background for the study of the evolution and development of animal behavior. ***Table 6.1*** summarizes the geological periods.

The appearance of the continents and the climatic conditions of our planet have gone through a great deal of change during the last 600 million years. Continental land masses are part of relatively rigid tectonic plates that float on a layer of melted rock, called the mantle, some 100 km below the surface. Although the plates are rigid, they move around in a very slow fashion, changing places and colliding with one another to generate mountains, a phenomenon referred to as *continental drift*. The number and size of plates have varied in time. Most of today's plates have some continental mass (e.g., African, Antarctic, Australian, Eurasian, North American, and South American plates), but others, such as the Pacific plate, the Nazca plate (located west of South America), and the Cocos plate (located west of Central America) are submerged and carry only islands.

Continental drift made it possible for animals to disperse across land masses. Some patterns of dispersion and isolation would be hard to understand without knowledge of plate tectonics. ***Figure 6.3*** shows the distribution of land masses at various points during the Phanerozoic. For example, there was continuous land communication among continents during the Mesozoic, which explains why specific genera of fresh-water reptiles appear in fossil rocks from South America, Africa, India, and Antarctica. Similarly, the absence of placental mammals from the Australian fauna (with the exception of recently arrived bats and the domestic species introduced by humans) is accounted for by the isolation of Australia from the other land masses during the Cretaceous period, when placental mammals evolved, probably in what is now Asia, North America, or South America. The Australian mammals are, of course, the marsupials (kangaroos, koalas, wombats, etc.), which probably originated in the Americas and reached Australia through Antarctica, before the breakup of these land masses. Australia's combination of isolation and a great variety of ecological niches allowed for the evolution of an impressive diversity of marsupial species.

In addition to continental drift, alterations in the earth's orbit around the sun produced climatic changes during the Phanerozoic. The drift of continental masses resulted in some of them moving in directions that led to progressive cooling or warming. For example, Antarctica was once located closer to the equator and possessed a much warmer climate than today. Moreover, during the cyclic glaciation periods of the Pleistocene, ice caps grew in size, sea levels dropped, and land bridges emerged in places that are covered with water today. For example, the Mediterranean sea separating Europe and Africa was once considerably reduced during these glacial periods, allowing for land bridges that made north-south migrations possible for many species.

2.b. Fossilization. Without fossil evidence it would be impossible to know some of the actual organisms that populated the earth and that are long extinct. Fossil evidence also helps make sense of knowledge of living organisms in many ways. For example, it introduces a temporal order

TABLE 6.1 Ages in the History of Earth

Eon	*Era*	*Period*	*Epoch*	*Brief Description of the Main Events:* • *Geology* • *Biology*
Phanerozoic *(544 to present)*				
	Cenozoic *(65 to present)*			
		Quaternary		
			Pleistocene *(1.8 to present)*	• Four major glaciations; last one ended 10 Kya. • Evolution of *Homo* and worldwide distribution; extinction of large mammals and birds; human civilization.
		Tertiary *(65 to 1.8)*		
			Pliocene *(5 to 1.8)*	• Isthmus of Panama arises. • First Hominidae.
			Miocene *(23 to 5)*	• India and Australia collide with Asia; Africa connected to Europe. • Diversification of grazing mammals and primates.
			Oligocene *(38 to 23)*	• First anthropoid primates.
			Eocene *(54 to 38)*	• Australia separates from Antarctica. North America and Asia connected through the Bering bridge. • Abundant number of placental mammals.
			Paleocene *(65 to 54)*	• Diversification of insects, birds, and mammals.
		Mesozoic *(245 to 65)*		
			Cretaceous *(146 to 65)*	• Greenland, Eurasia, Africa and the Arabian peninsula, India, South America, North America, Antarctica, and Australia are formed. • Mass extinction event at the end of the Cretaceous; extinction of dinosaurs and other large reptiles; first modern birds and mammals.
			Jurassic *(208 to 146)*	• Pangaea breaks into Laurasia (north) and Gondwana (south). • Mass extinction event at the end of the Jurassic; diversification of dinosaurs and other reptiles; first birds and mammals; extinction of therapsids.
			Triassic *(245 to 208)*	• Breakup of Pangaea begins. • Mass extinction event at the end of the Triassic. Insects, bony fish, and reptiles diversify; first dinosaurs.

TABLE 6.1 Ages in the History of Earth (*continued*)

Eon / ***Era*** / ***Period*** / ***Epoch***	***Brief Description of the Main Events:*** • ***Geology*** • ***Biology***
Paleozoic (*544 to 245*)	
Permian (*286 to 245*)	• Most land masses connected in Pangaea supercontinent. • Mass extinction event at the end of the Permian. Extinction of trilobites; insects and reptiles diversify; first therapsids.
Carboniferous (*360 to 286*)	• Parts of Laurentia and Gondwana connected. • Mass extinction event at the end of Carboniferous. Diversification of insects and amphibians; first reptiles.
Devonian (*410 to 360*)	• Northern continents and Gondwana separated by broad sea. • Mass extinction events in middle and late Devonian. Diversification of fishes; sharks and bony fish; trilobites; insects; amphibians.
Silurian (*440 to 410*)	• Invasion of the land by arthropods; extinction of placoderm fish; agnathans diversify.
Ordovician (*505 to 440*)	• Mass extinction event in late Ordovician. Aquatic species diversify; agnathan fish; armored ostracoderms.
Cambrian (*544 to 505*)	• Mass extinction event in early Cambrian. Faunas include most animal phyla, all living in marine environments.
Proterozoic (*2,500 to 544*)	
Neoproterozoic (*900 to 544*)	
Vendian (*650 to 544*)	• Laurentia, Baltica, China, Siberia, Kazakhstania, Gondwana masses were widely separated. • Fossil evidence includes forms resembling cnidarians, trails made by worms, and embryos.
Mesoproterozoic (*1,600 to 900*) Paleoproterozoic (*2,500 to 1,600*)	• Oldest eukaryotes, about 1,250 Mya. Oldest traces made by wormlike bilaterals, about 1,000 Mya. • Increased oxygen in atmosphere, about 2,000 Mya.
Archaean (*4,500 to 2,500*)	• Oldest known rocks, about 3,800 Mya. Formation of oceans and continents. • Oldest known fossils (anaerobic bacteria?), about 3,500 Mya.

Note. All numbers in parentheses are in Mya.

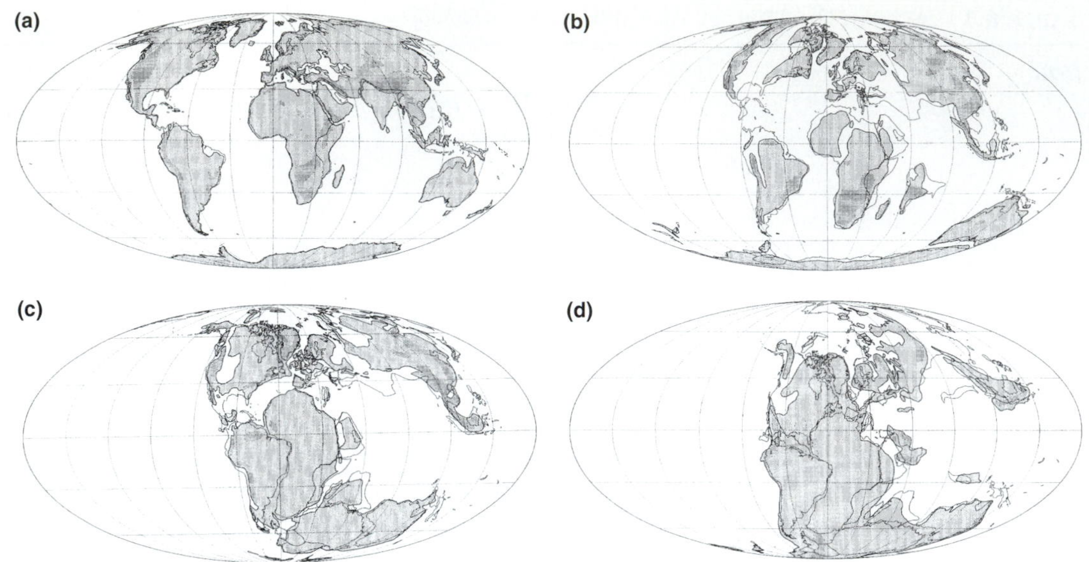

FIGURE 6.3. The relative position of the various land masses (gray areas) during the Phanerozoic eon (Smith et al. 1994). ***(a)*** Pleistocene, 5 Mya. ***(b)*** Late Cretaceous, 70 Mya. ***(c)*** Early Cretaceous, 148 Mya. ***(d)*** Early Triassic, 245 Mya.

among the various taxa, helping to determine which groups are primitive and which are derived; it allows for an identification of lineages that are very conservative (the so-called living fossils, such as sharks, coelacanths, or turtles); and it permits the recognition of relatedness among groups that have diverged extensively, as shown by intermediate forms. Unfortunately, fossil evidence is relatively scanty and biased because of the very way in which fossils are formed.

The process of fossilization begins with the death of an animal whose body remains undetected by large predators. In some extremely rare cases, the animal's soft tissues leave an imprint in the rock. More commonly, however, only the hard parts fossilize, such as the exoskeleton of arthropods (e.g., trilobites) or the bones of vertebrates (e.g., dinosaurs). Fossilization requires that the body of the dead animal is covered by a layer of sediment. Microorganisms in the sediment cause the decay of the soft tissues. Additional layers may cover the terrain over relatively long periods of time, which may result in the dispersion and breakage of the bones, some of which may be lost in the process. Eventually, the various layers of sediment dry and harden, forming a sedimentary rock, by far the most common source of fossils. A process of mineralization slowly transforms what was once living tissue into rock. Amazingly, such a transformation may respect the original form of the animal in great detail. For example, the fine structure of the compound eye (soft tissue!) of some fossil trilobites is so clearly preserved that it can be the subject of scientific research.

A similar process can preserve the trace of an animal that has been walking or moving on a wet terrain. Burial of the specimen can occur as a result of a dust storm, volcanic ash, ice, or amber. An unusual burial medium is found in the tar pits of Rancho La Brea, in southern California. During the Pleistocene, many species of mammals and birds that approached the pools to drink water were trapped by the viscosity of the tar. Many complete skeletons have been preserved in this unusual environment, providing detailed information of the Pleistocene fauna of this region.

Although fossilization must clearly be a rare phenomenon, when the conditions are appropriate it can yield large quantities of material, as anyone who has walked on the plains of Patagonia or central Texas could attest. In these areas, the conditions for fossilization during the Mesozoic produced an abundance of fossils that challenges the notion that fossilization occurs only rarely. Ammonites, shark teeth, sea urchins, bivalves, corals, snails, and many other types of animals turn up in exposed sediments or just on the surface. By the same token, fossilization may lead to biased samples of animals. Entire populations that lived in dry environments or in woodlands may remain unknown forever, given the poor conditions for fossilization that prevail in such environments. As a consequence, the phylogenetic history of some lineages is better documented than that of other lineages.

Fossils acquire major theoretical importance when they can be dated because hypotheses about the history of the lineage can thus be tested. There are two basic methods for dating fossils. The traditional approach is that of stratigraphic dating, a method based on the assumption that deeper deposits, or strata, are older than more superficial ones. Obviously, this alone provides no information on the age of the specimen or even on the relative time separation between different specimens since the rate of sediment accumulation is not constant. Another method, absolute dating, provides information about the actual age of the sample. Absolute dating is based on the fact that radioactive elements decay into nonradioactive elements at a constant rate. It is known, for example, that uranium 238 decays into helium and lead 206, whereas potassium 40 decays into calcium 40 and argon 40. The rate of decay can be estimated independently, and it varies, depending on the radioactive element, from a few thousand years to billions of years. Therefore, if one knows the amount of the radioactive and nonradioactive elements present in a sample, and the rate of decay of one into the other, then the absolute age of the sample can be estimated with a great deal of accuracy.

How good is the history of animal evolution derived from the fossil record? Is our view of animal phylogeny increasingly poorer as older lineages are considered? Since older rocks have a better chance of being destroyed by mere geological activity than younger rocks, it may seem obvious that recent lineages would be better represented in the fossil record than remote lineages. This assertion is generally correct if one considers the evolutionary history of a lineage at the lower taxonomic level of species or genus. Surprisingly, however, the fossil record displays constant quality during the Phanerozoic eon when lineages are studied at the higher taxonomic level of family or order (Benton et al. 2000). Although we will probably never know the history of each animal lineage that evolved during the past 544 million years because of the irreparable loss of fossils, we have a reasonably complete picture of the broad patterns that characterize animal phylogeny.

3. THE ORIGIN AND EVOLUTION OF ANIMALS

3.a. Precambrian Fossils. In addition to geological evidence, ***Table 6.1*** also describes some biological events that provide a general background of animal phylogeny. Fossil evidence from the Archaean and most of the Proterozoic is restricted to microorganisms. Intriguing evidence has been discovered in rocks dated to the last part of the Proterozoic, referred to as the Vendian period, approximately 544 to 650 Mya. These fossils were first discovered in a region called Ediacara Hills, in south Australia, in 1946, but they have subsequently been found in regions as distant from each other as the White Sea in northwestern Russia and the Namibian desert in southern Africa, among others. The oldest of these fossils reaches approximately 555 Mya (Martin et al. 2000).

This so-called *Ediacaran fauna* includes forms that are difficult to categorize because they show few affinities with known phyla (they may not be animals at all) and forms that can be related to known animal phyla. A few are generally agreed to be cnidarians similar to jellyfish or sea pens. *Eoporpita,* for example, may have been a sessile polyp attached to a rock at the floor of precambrian oceans, much like today's sea anemones.

More compelling evidence of precambrian animals is actually found in *fossilized traces,* some of which may be as old as 1,000 Mya. These traces are significant because they must have been made by animals that were bilaterally organized and had a triploblastic body structure (Fedonkin & Runnegar 1992). Traces tend to be superficial, and the animal often seems to have crossed its own path in what appears to be a type of random search behavior. The fact that these precambrian traces were predominantly made at the surface of the sea floor suggests that these animals may have been acoelomate or possess a relatively simple coelom. A coelom may be necessary to exert the type of pushing pressure, through peristaltic motion, needed to burrow substantially below the surface. Perhaps the feeding behavior of these bilateral animals could be characterized as grazing on a layer of bacteria (Seilacher et al. 1998). Unfortunately, no vestiges of the animals making the traces have yet been found.

The discovery of fossil embryos should be rated among the most fascinating ones ever made (see ***Figure 6.4***). On the one hand, they clearly demonstrate the extraordinary degree of detail that can be preserved in mineralized form, and on the other, they help establish the fact that animals were already dwelling in aquatic environments by the end of the Proterozoic. Vendian animal embryos have been found in various formations in China, dating approximately 570–580 Mya (Li et al. 1998; Xiao et al. 1998). Embryos arrested at the two-, four-, and eight-cell stages, as well as later cleavage stages, have been preserved in calcium phosphate, a mineral known to reproduce soft tissue in great detail. Notably, the embryos have a constant size of about half a millimeter in diameter, which is to be expected of animal embryos and not of colonial microorganisms or nonliving mineral formations. It is not clear what type of animals these embryos would have produced; some may be sponges, whereas others may be bilateral animals.

3.b. A Cambrian Explosion? The transition from the Vendian to the Cambrian is marked by the appearance in the fossil record of a wide variety of animals. Such an abrupt transition suggests the idea that a rapid divergence of body plans took place

FIGURE 6.4. Fossilized embryo discovered in Vendian deposits from China. (Photograph courtesy of Shuhai Xiao.)

during this period, in a geologically short time span (about 40 million years) commonly labeled the Cambrian explosion and technically referred to as an *adaptive radiation.* The adaptive radiation of the early Cambrian is special because evidence of animals from many of the major phyla has been recovered, including annelids, arthropods, brachiopods, chordates, echinoderms, hemichordates, and molluscs, among others. These animals possess hard body parts that are likely to mineralize, so it is reasonable to think that animals from other phyla that are less likely to fossilize were already present during the Cambrian.

Perhaps one of the most intriguing pieces of evidence from the viewpoint of comparative psychology is the increase in complexity of the animal traces across the Vendian-Cambrian boundary (see ***Chapter 7*, *section 1.c.***, pp. 229–231). The typically random and superficial Vendian traces give way to traces denoting a more systematic foraging behavior. Cambrian trajectories can take the form of a spiral or a sinusoid, for example, both of which avoid the revisitation of an area and are thus more efficient. Moreover, Cambrian animals seem to have been able to burrow themselves deeper and to build elaborate burrows. This increase in behavioral complexity may be a consequence of the evolution or improvement of a coelom, as noted previously, and it may also imply the evolution of more sophisticated sensory-motor capabilities in centralized nervous systems (Valentine 1995).

Mineralized skeletons of animals from various phyla appear during the early Cambrian period (544 to 520 Mya), including arthropods, molluscs, and equinoderms. However, the fossil record "explodes" in the middle Cambrian thanks to the discovery of thousands of specimens in which the soft parts have been preserved in extraordinary detail. The first locality in yielding such fossils is known as Burgess Shale (in British Columbia, Canada), discovered in 1909. But a number of other localities in North America, China, Greenland, south Australia, Siberia, Spain, and Poland have produced similar fossils, suggesting, as it was the case for the Ediacaran fauna, a worldwide distribution of this fauna (Briggs et al. 1994). A major difference between the Vendian and middle Cambrian faunas is that whereas many specimens of the Ediacaran fauna cannot be clearly identified, the *Burgess Shale fauna* includes specimens that can be clearly linked to extant phyla (see ***Figure 6.5***). The abundance of specimens for particular species has also allowed for the three-dimensional reconstruction of the animals to a great deal of detail, from which life habits can be inferred with some degree of certainty.

The Burgess Shale fauna includes animals that have been assigned to 12 animal phyla, as well as some species whose relationship to known taxa is dubious. ***Figure 6.5,*** numbers 1 to 3, show examples of sponges (Porifera), all presumed to be filter feeders and sessile. The Burgess Shale sponges varied in size from 1 to 30 cm. The sponge *Vauxia* (# 1) is the most common and was built with cylindrical branches that gave it the appearance of a tree. *Nisusia* (# 4) is a bivalve (Brachiopoda) that lived partially buried in the sea floor, pumping water through the mantle cavity as a way of

FIGURE 6.5. A reconstruction of the marine fauna discovered at the Burgess Shale formation, Canada (Briggs et al. 1994). The following species are represented in this drawing: ***1,*** *Vauxia* (Porifera). ***2,*** *Choia* (Porifera). ***3,*** *Pirania* (Porifera). ***4,*** *Nisusia* (Brachiopoda). ***5,*** *Burgessochaeta* (Annelida). ***6,*** *Ottoia* (Priapula). ***7,*** *Louisella* (Priapula). ***8,*** *Olenoides* (Arthropoda). ***9,*** *Sidneyia* (Arthropoda). ***10,*** *Leanchoilia* (Arthropoda). ***11,*** *Marrella* (Arthropoda). ***12,*** *Canadaspis* (Arthropoda). ***13,*** *Molaria* (Arthropoda). ***14,*** *Burgessia* (Arthropoda). ***15,*** *Yohoia* (Arthropoda). ***16,*** *Waptia* (Arthropoda). ***17,*** *Aysheaia* (Arthropoda). ***18,*** *Scenella* (Mollusca). ***19,*** *Echmatocrinus* (Echinodermata). ***20,*** *Pikaia* (Chordata). Undetermined phyla: ***21,*** *Haplophrentis.* ***22,*** *Haplophrentis.* ***23,*** *Dinomischus.* ***24,*** *Wiwaxia.* ***25,*** *Anomalocaris.*

feeding. Some brachiopod species appear to have been gregarious, as they are usually found in large aggregates. Species vary in size from 2 to 22 mm. *Burgessochaeta* (# 5) is a polychaete worm (Annelida) exhibiting a series of body segments, each with a pair of appendages, which are believed to have allowed movement through the sediments by burrowing. Burgess Shale worms varied in size between 1 and 9 cm. Additional burrowing animals are *Ottoia* (# 6) and *Louisella* (# 7) (Priapulida). Some *Ottoia* fossils contain shells in their guts, indicating their carnivorous diet. ***Figure 6.5*** also shows a variety of arthropods, including the trilobite *Olenoides* (# 8). These animals were highly mobile on the sea floor. *Echmatocrinus* (# 19) was a sessile species that fed on particles suspended in sea water (Echinodermata). Several arms radiate from the top of a single foot which, in some specimens, appears attached to a shell. *Pikaia* (# 20) is a 4-cm long animal similar to the lancelet (Chordata). A dorsal notochord and paired muscles are visible in many specimens. It is usually preserved in an undulating posture suggesting swimming habits. *Anomalocaris* (# 25), with its 50-cm length, is the largest animal of this fauna; it appears also in China, Greenland, and Australia, but it has not yet been possible to assign it to a specific taxon. It is clearly a free-swimming predator that used the pair of claws to grab its prey.

It is not clear whether the so-called Cambrian explosion involved the emergence of most animal phyla, or whether it was a more restricted event. It seems possible that a wide variety of soft-bodied animals had existed long before the Cambrian, as indicated by the Ediacaran and trace fossils discussed previously. Perhaps the key innovation achieved by Cambrian animals was the evolution of a skeleton capable of mineralization. Whatever the case, the fossil record clearly demonstrates that by the mid Cambrian, about 520 Mya, chordates, arthropods, and molluscs had already undergone considerable divergence. This is important for comparative psychologists because the species most commonly used in behavioral research belong to these three phyla. When common behavioral processes are identified in comparisons involving these phyla, caution should be exercised in inferring homologous mechanisms because of the extensive opportunity for convergent evolution and the remoteness of the common ancestor.

3.c. Molecular Phylogenies. There is a substantial body on information obtained from living species that actually speaks about the origin of animals. The notion of a *molecular clock,* briefly introduced in ***Chapter 2*** (p. 32), can provide a source of information on the dates of divergence of various lineages that is independent of the fossil record. The fossil record can tell us that arthropods and chordates had already diverged in the mid Cambrian, but it does not tell us how long before that period the divergence took place. A comparison of molecular and fossil information can thus reveal the length of the time period between divergence and first occurrence in the fossil record.

The basic idea of the molecular clock is that changes in protein structure or DNA sequence accumulate linearly in time. If homologous proteins or genes from different species are compared, the more similar they are to each other, the more recent the common ancestor. Two basic values need to be estimated in order to calibrate the molecular clock: the genetic distance of homologous genes from different species and the divergence time of the lineages under study. The degree of genetic similarity is calculated by aligning the sequence of the same protein or gene from the different taxa and determining the number of gaps and substitutions in amino acids (for proteins) or nucleotide bases (for genes) that are necessary to postulate in order to maximize sequence similarity across the genes. There are a variety of methods that yield a quantitative estimate of genetic distance and that can lead to substantial differences in the quantitative estimates. Therefore, most researchers use several statistical programs with the same database to determine if the phylogenetic conclusions depend on the method of analysis. Divergence times are usually estimated from the fossil record of lineages for which fossil information is considered particularly complete. Once a correlation is calculated between genetic distance and divergence time for a target set of lineages, then divergence times for other lineages can be estimated by extrapolation.

The information obtained through such procedures is valuable and interesting, but not always reliable. Studies focusing on different genes or proteins may arrive at very different conclusions. In one study, for example, 57 different enzymes were compared in a variety of taxa (Doolittle et al. 1996). Using that database, the divergence between deuterostomes (e.g., chordates) and protostomes (e.g., arthropods) was estimated to have occurred 670 Mya, a time roughly consistent with the presence of well-differentiated Burgess Shale faunas some 520 Mya. According to this estimate, therefore, it took approximately 150 million years to go from a common ancestor to animals such as *Pikaia* (a deuterostome chordate) and *Olenoides* (a protostome arthropod). However, another study based on sequence information from seven unrelated genes from various phyla yielded an older date of divergence between protostomes and deuterostomes: approximately 1,200 Mya (Wray et al. 1996). This value suggests that the divergence among some of the main animal phyla occurred in the mid Proterozoic and implies that the Cambrian explosion is an artifact of the fossil record.

One problem with this approach is the assumption that molecular change is constant, which is critical if the notion of a molecular clock is to be of any value to establish dates of divergence. Many genes and proteins do not conform to this assumption of constant change in time and, therefore, do not allow a fine tuning of the clock. Using several independent genes or proteins and averaging genetic distances can only be a partial solution because, as it was shown previously, studies can yield very different estimates of divergence times. Still, comparing gene or protein sequences in terms of their similarity can provide information about the degree of relatedness between the various phyla and contribute to developing phylogenetic hypotheses (see ***Figure 2.1,*** p. 32).

Researchers have found a useful application of this "problem" of having differential rates of change of various types of DNA and proteins. There is a graded correspondence between the speed of change of the various types of macromolecules (DNA, RNA, proteins) used in molecular phylogenies, and their sensitivity to comparisons at various taxonomic levels. For example, *ribosomal RNA,* or *rRNA,* has changed at a low rate during phylogeny and is therefore appropriate to compare distantly related organisms (at the level of phyla, for example). However, *DNA-DNA hybridization* is more appropriate to distinguish between species from various families or orders, and within a particular class. This technique has been used by Sibly and Ahlquist (1990) to establish the phylogenetic relationships among birds, for which the fossil record is relatively poor. Some regions of *mitochondrial DNA* change so fast that they have allowed distinctions among subspecies—that is, populations within the same species. This approach has been applied to human evolution (see ***Chapter 9***). Analysis of yet more variable portions of DNA has been used to determine relationships among family members by using *DNA fingerprinting* techniques, such as in studies on kinship and altruistic behavior (see ***Chapter 5***).

Consider animal phylogenies based on the sequencing of specific genes within the rRNA molecule. As already mentioned, rRNA exhibits a relatively slow rate of change, and in addition, homologous portions are present in essentially all animals. These properties allow scientists to use rRNA data to develop theories about animal evolution at the phylum level. Ruiz-Trillo et al. (1999), for example, reported the results of a study based on a section of rRNA known as 18S that included information from 29 phyla. Based on a sequential analysis of 18S data they concluded that the order Acoela (usually classified within the phylum Platyhelminthes, or flatworms) includes living representatives of the earliest bilateral animal. Raff (1996) and Valentine (1995) have also provided a summary from various studies involving rRNA sections 16S and 18S. The phylogeny that emerges is shown in ***Figure 6.6*** Let's "read" this figure carefully.

Figure 6.6 represents a phylogenetic tree of several phyla that are listed on the right. If you start from the bottom left portion you will see that each node (marked by a dark dot) involves two branches. As you move upward in this figure, you are moving toward progressively more recent divergence events. The two branches diverging at any given node are referred to as *sister groups*—that is, taxa with an immediate common ancestor. At each node, the lower branch is referred to as the *outgroup,* whereas the upper branch is the *ingroup.* A major evolutionary innovation is represented before each node, and that innovation applies to all the branches located to its right. The closer a node is to the ending taxa, the more recent the divergent event is, although, in this case, recency can be estimated only in relative terms. For example, the divergence of echinoderms (starfish, sea urchins) and chordates (tunicates, lancelets, vertebrates) is a more recent event than the divergence between Platyhelminthes (flatworms) and all other bilateral animals.

According to these simple rules, rRNA sequence information suggests the following conclusions. Porifera (sponges) is the outgroup of all other animal phyla, which implies that it possesses the most basic attributes of animals, such as, for example, tissue. The ingroup of this first divergence (all animals except the Porifera) is distinguished by the acquisition of some major innovations, such as gastrulation. The next major innovation, the mesoderm, characterizes all bilaterally symmetrical animals, for which Platyhelminthes (flatworms) is the outgroup. The two major divisions in the ingroup, that is, those characterized by a hemocoel (Annelida to Arthropoda) and those characterized by a mesodermic coelom (Echinodermata and Chordata) correspond reasonably well to the distinction between protostomes and deuterostomes. One major implication is, therefore, that the coelom has evolved independently in protostomes and deuterostomes, a controversial hypothesis about which there is yet no universal agreement.

3.d. Early Evolution of Vertebrates. Among the fossils of the Burgess Shale is a small, elongated animal named *Pikaia gracilens.* It averages 4 cm in length and has two features that have convinced many paleontologists that this is an early chordate: a

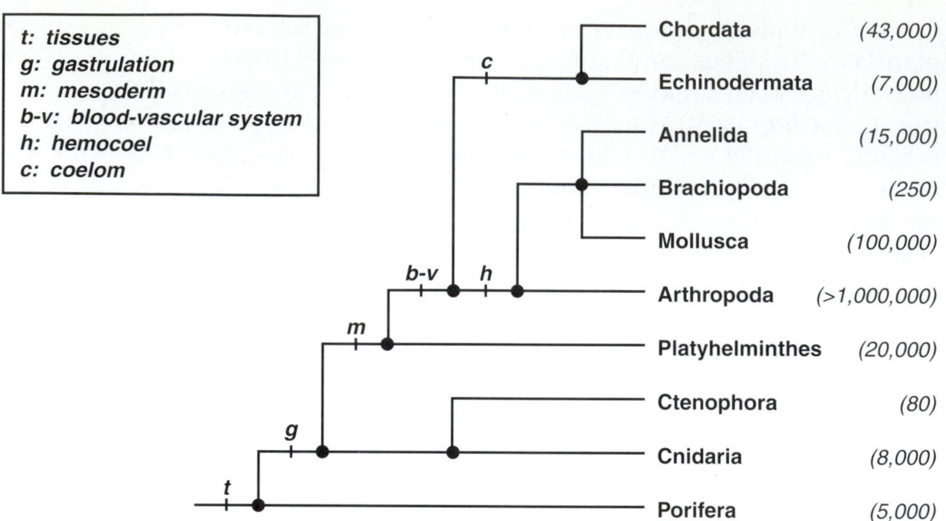

FIGURE 6.6. A cladogram depicting a classification of various animal phyla on the basis of rRNA data (modified from Valentine 1995). Each node (dark circle) represents a divergence event. Major characters included in the cladogram apply to all the lineages located to their right. ***t*** (tissue), cell populations differentiated in structure and function. ***g*** (gastrulation), a stage of embryonic development characterized by the formation of an internal cavity from a hollow ball of cells. ***m*** (mesoderm), a third layer of cells in addition to ectoderm and endoderm. ***b-v*** (blood-vascular system), a circulatory system. ***h*** (hemocoel), a body cavity filled with blood. ***c*** (coelom), a body cavity lined with mesoderm cell. The number in parentheses reflects the approximate number of living species in each phylum.

longitudinal rod thought to be a notochord (the precursor of the spinal cord of vertebrates) and a series of segmented sections along its body that could be myotomes (a series of muscles involved in swimming movements). *Pikaia* is reminiscent of the amphioxus or lancelet, *Brachiostoma,* a primitive living chordate. Similar in morphology and age (530 Mya) are *Yunnanozoon* and *Haikouella,* two lancelet-like chordates discovered in China (Chen et al. 1999).

The phylum Chordata includes three major subphyla: Urochordata, Cephalochordata, and Vertebrata. It is widely accepted that this group is *monophyletic,* that is, derived from a common ancestor. The Urochordata, also called tunicates (about 1,300 species), are all marine animals. The adults of most species live a sedentary life, attaching themselves to a substrate and, in some cases, forming colonies of many individuals. Although most adult urochordates do not resemble the chordate body plan, the free-swimming larvae possess a dorsal chord in their tails called a urochord.

The Cephalochordata, or lancelets (about 28 species), are also all marine species that tend to live partially buried in the sea floor. Lancelets are characterized by a dorsal notochord and V-shaped myotones. Their general appearance is that of a fish, but they have no true bone and the neural tube does not present an anterior brain, but just a vesicle. Nonetheless, it has been widely assumed that the Cephalochordata and the Vertebrata are sister groups derived from a common ancestor that may have looked like *Pikaia*.

The major innovations of the Vertebrata seem to be mostly a function of their active lifestyle. Complex sense organs, motor ganglia, and a well-defined brain are among the most relevant novelties introduced by the first vertebrates that have been retained by their descendants. Eight or nine classes of vertebrates are usually recognized in the literature, depending on the author; Benton's (1990a) classification will be followed here.

Vertebrates are usually segregated into two groups. The *lower vertebrates* include the various classes of fishes, the amphibians and the reptiles, whereas the *higher vertebrates* include the birds and mammals. The words "lower" and "higher" make reference to the fact that the lower vertebrates appear in lower strata of the fossil record, whereas the higher vertebrates are discovered in more recent strata. There are conservative and derived lineages in each of these two groups, as will be shown below, so it would be inappropriate to think of these animals in terms of a lineal order. Moreover, each vertebrate class represents a tree of radiating branches, of which only one may have given rise to another vertebrate class. The ancestral lineage is usually a fossil taxon whose identity is a matter of controversy. Therefore, it would also be inappropriate to take a living species from a group of lower vertebrates and conceptualize it as the ancestor of living species from a different class. For example, mammals are thought to have evolved from a group of fossil reptiles known as the cynodonts; however, it would be erroneous to think of any living reptile (turtles, lizards, crocodiles) as the ancestor of living mammals because these modern reptiles represent other diverging branches of the reptilian tree.

Figure 6.7 summarizes the phylogenetic tree of the vertebrates and includes some of the major evolutionary innovations in their history, whereas ***Figure 6.8*** shows the appearance of the various vertebrate groups in the fossil record. The brief description of each vertebrate class that follows in the next four sections is based on a variety of sources (Benton 1990a, 1990b; Coates & Clack 1991; Cooper & Penny 1997; Cracraft 1986; Estes & Reig 1973; Forey & Janvier 1994; Gauthier et al. 1988; Gorr & Klinschmidt 1993; Horner 1982; Kemp 1988; Lee 1996; Lillegraven et al. 1979; Padian & Chiappe 1998; Romer 1966; Rougier et al. 1995; Sibly & Ahlquist 1990).

3.e. The Fishes and Amphibians. Class **Agnatha,** or jawless fish, is represented today by about 60 species assigned to only two groups: the lampreys and the hagfishes. However, a great diversity of forms has been discovered in fossils from the Ordovician, Silurian, and Devonian periods suggesting that agnathans were once widespread and populated the oceans in great numbers. Many of the Paleozoic fossil species (referred to as ostracoderm fish) show characteristic armors covering the head that have been hypothesized to be antipredator structures, although they could also serve as storage for phosphates or calcium. Extant hagfish are all marine scavengers. Extant lampreys live in fresh water or marine habitats and obtain food by rubbing and wearing away the flesh of other animals. The oldest fossil hagfish and lam-

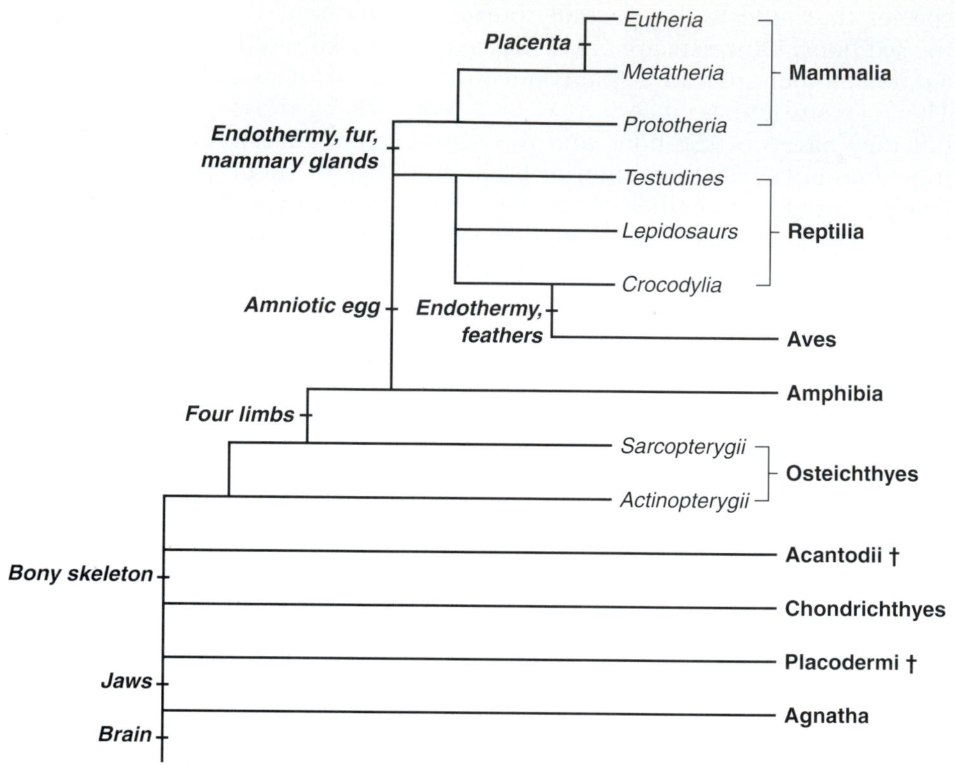

FIGURE 6.7. A tree of the vertebrate classes. Fossil taxa have been excluded, except for the two extinct classes of fish, Placodermi and Acantodii (marked by daggers). Key innovations included in this tree apply to all the lineages above their location in this cladogram. Notice the convergent evolution of endothermy in the mammalian and avian lineages.

preys are from the Carboniferous period, about 300 Mya.

The classes **Placodermi,** or armored fish, and **Acanthodii,** or spiny fish, are both completely extinct. Placoderm fish evolved a variety of bony plates over their heads, and many species are considered to have been bottom feeders. Placoderms are generally thought to be closely related to the sharks (Chondrichthyes). Acanthodians, probably related to bony fish (Osteichthyes), were relatively small, freshwater fish, reaching no more than 20 cm in length and completely covered with small scales. Little is known about their skeleton because they tend to be preserved crushed against the rocks, but they were clearly jawed fish (vertebrates with bony jaws are referred to as Gnathostomata) and, in fact, are the oldest known group of jawed vertebrates (early Silurian, about 400 Mya).

Class **Chondrichthyes,** or cartilaginous fish, appears in fossil rocks from the Carboniferous (360 Mya) and is represented today by about 625 species of chimeras, sharks, and rays. Chimerans are known

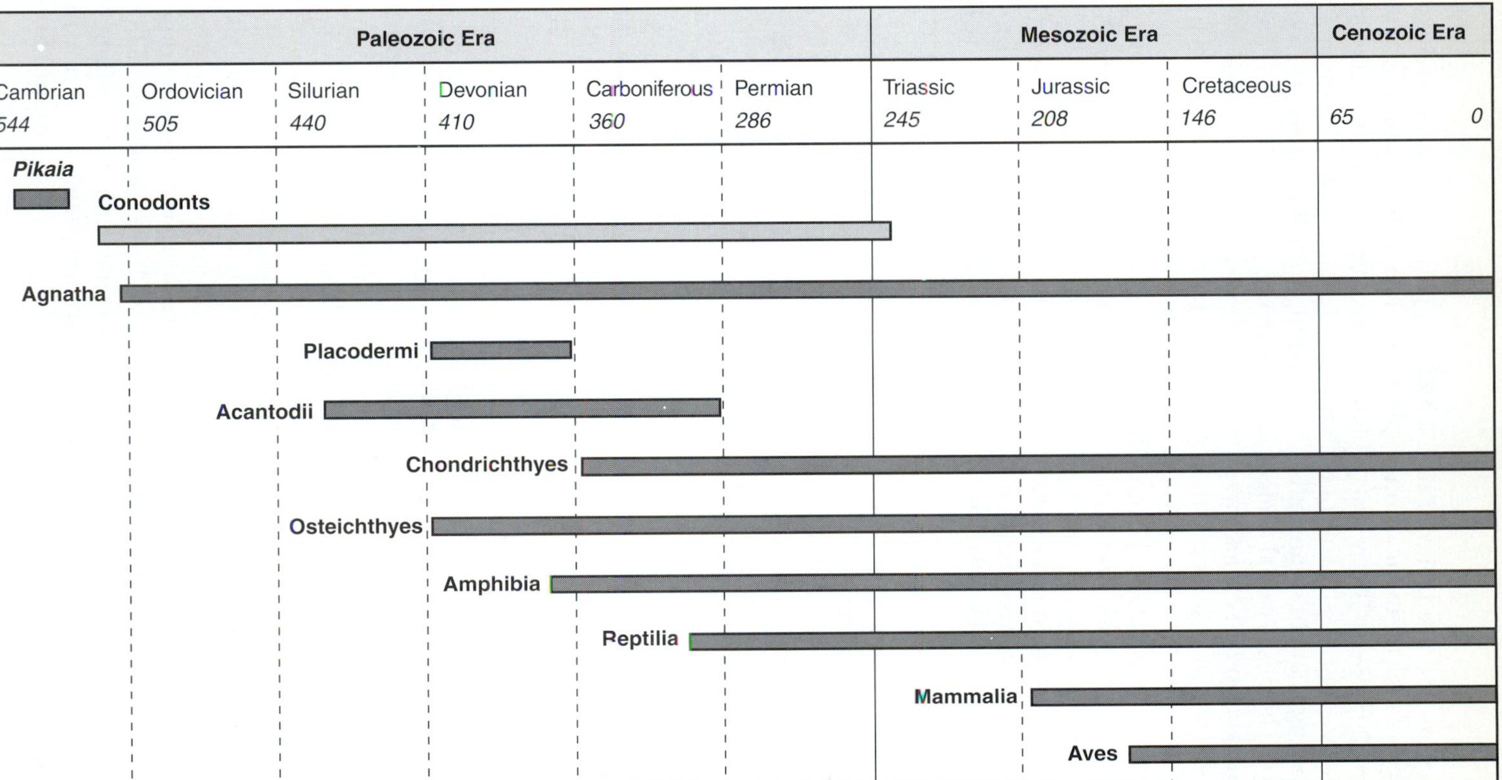

FIGURE 6.8. The fossil record of the various classes of vertebrates. *Pikaia* and the conodonts, both suspected to be chordates, are included for comparison.

from the Carboniferous and are believed to be the most conservative of all living chondrichthyes. Sharks possess a bony jaw, powerful musculature, and a streamlined body design, suggesting that these animals evolved as predators. The post-cranial skeleton is made of cartilage. Some species have reached gigantic sizes. For example, the basking and whale sharks, two living species, can reach a length of 17 m, whereas *Carcharodon,* a species from the Cretaceous known only from its 15-cm-long teeth, might have been 13 m in length. By contrast, the rays are specialized generally as bottom feeders and have evolved flattened bodies.

Class **Osteichthyes,** or bony fish, is the most numerous in today's seas, rivers, and lakes (some 20,000 catalogued species). The skull of osteichthyan fish includes many jointed bony plates, permitting a substantial flexibility that probably supported the evolution of new predatory abilities. Bony fish are classified into two subclasses distinguished by the structure of their fins, the Actinopterygii and the Sarcopterygii, which appear already well differentiated in the early Devonian (400 Mya).

Actinopterygian fish, also called ray-fin fish, are characterized by fins supported by a series of rods radiating from the base. There are three major taxa of actinopterygians, and each has undergone its own adaptive radiation. The chondrosteans flourished during the period extending from the Carboniferous to the Triassic and subsequently declined in numbers. There are relatively few living species of chondrosteans, including the sturgeons and paddlefish. The holosteans radiated in the Jurassic and Triassic periods and subsequently declined. Species of the holostean genus *Lepisosteus* can be tracked as far back as the Cretaceous, at least 65 Mya, which suggests a highly conservative morphology. The third radiation, that of the teleosteans, begun in the Jurassic period, and the degree of species diversity has remained high until the present. With almost 20,000 living species, teleost fish are the most diverse group of aquatic vertebrates. The most common species of fish belong to this group, including the salmon, carps, herring, and the colorful variety of species that inhabit coral reef environments of tropical oceans.

The other subclass of bony fish is the Sarcopterygii, also called lobe-fin fish, with a fossil record that extends to the Devonian. Sarcopterygian fins are characterized by the presence of muscles and a supporting bony skeleton. These lobe fins can acquire a variety of postures and have traditionally been viewed as the evolutionary precursors of the legs of tetrapods (four-limbed vertebrates). Sarcopterygians flourished during the Paleozoic and Mesozoic but lost substantial diversity during the Cenozoic era. Early in their phylogeny, sarcopterygian fish show evidence of a unique tooth structure, characterized by the folding of the enamel (the external layer). Such tooth structure, called *labyrinthine,* is also characteristic of the early tetrapods that invaded the land. Sarcopterygians are presently restricted to the Dipnoi, or lungfish, and the Actinistia, or coelacanths (***Figure 6.9, see front inside cover***). Although a great diversity of lungfish was present during the Devonian, only three genera exist today in freshwater environments of South America, Africa, and Australia. The tooth plates characteristic of lungfish suggest a specialization for crushing the exoskeletons of invertebrates, such as molluscs. The case of Actinistia is particularly revealing of the decline of sarcopterygian fish: Only two extant species are known of a group that showed a great diversity of species during the extensive time period between the Devonian and the Cretaceous. In fact, coelacanths were believed extinct until, unexpectedly, a specimen of *Latimeria chalumnae* was fished out of the Indian Ocean, off the coast of the Comoro Islands, in 1938. The morphology of this animal is so conservative that it has become a paradigmatic case of the living fossil. A second species, *L. menadoensis,* has been discovered off the coast of several Indonesian islands (Fricke et al. 2000). Coelacanths are equipped with sharp teeth that suggest they evolved predominantly as predators.

Class **Amphibia** includes a number of fossil species that are the earliest vertebrates to evolve adaptations for terrestrial life. Major anatomical, physiological, and behavioral changes were involved in the transition from a purely aquatic to an amphibian mode of life. It is generally agreed that the Osteoleptiformes, a group of sarcopterygian fish that flourished between the Devonian and the early Permian, is the sister group of amphibians. There is less agreement about which group of living sarcopterygians, lungfish or coalacanths, is closer to amphibians. A major novelty of amphibians is the evolution of four legs that lifted the body above the ground and moved it by *locomotion.* These legs are supported by bones already evident in the pectoral fins of an early osteoleptiform fish known as *Eusthenopteron* (e.g., humerus, ulna, radius, and wrist bones). Amphibians have some additional bones supporting a series of fingers, which numbered as many as eight in primitive species, but eventually settled at five. The *pentadactyl hand* is thus a primitive trait of tetrapods, including humans.

One of the oldest known tetrapods is *Ichthyostega,* from late Devonian rocks of Greenland and measuring about a meter in length. *Ichthyostega* has many of the typical features of present-day tetrapods, although it would probably be a mistake to picture it as living entirely outside the water because of its tail fin and lateral line system. Another late Devonian amphibian, *Acanthostega,* shows evidence of internal gills and must have been, therefore, predominantly aquatic. This evidence suggests that the legs with digits of early tetrapods may have evolved for walking on the floor of shallow ponds, much as coelacanths do today on the ocean floor, and not exclusively for locomotion in terrestrial environments. By the late Carboniferous, a diverse community of amphibians populated the shallow and open water environments, as well as the marginal areas of lakes and rivers. Living amphibians (about 2,500 species) are thought to have diverged from these groups relatively early in amphibian history. They fall into three distinctive orders, all with a poor fossil record. The Anura (frogs and toads) are specialized for jumping as a mode of locomotion, with extended hind limbs and powerful musculature. The earliest frog has been discovered in Jurassic rocks from Argentina and already presents the typical morphological features of modern anurans. The Urodela (salamanders and newts) have an elongated body with a flattened tail specialized for swimming. The Gymnophiona (apodans) are legless amphibians that look like worms and live buried in the soil in tropical environments. ***Figure 6.10*** summarizes the fishes and amphibians described in this section.

3.f. Reptiles. Early reptiles are thought to have evolved from a group of fossil amphibians known as reptiliomorphs. Class **Reptilia** includes a complex and heterogeneous assemblage of fossils and

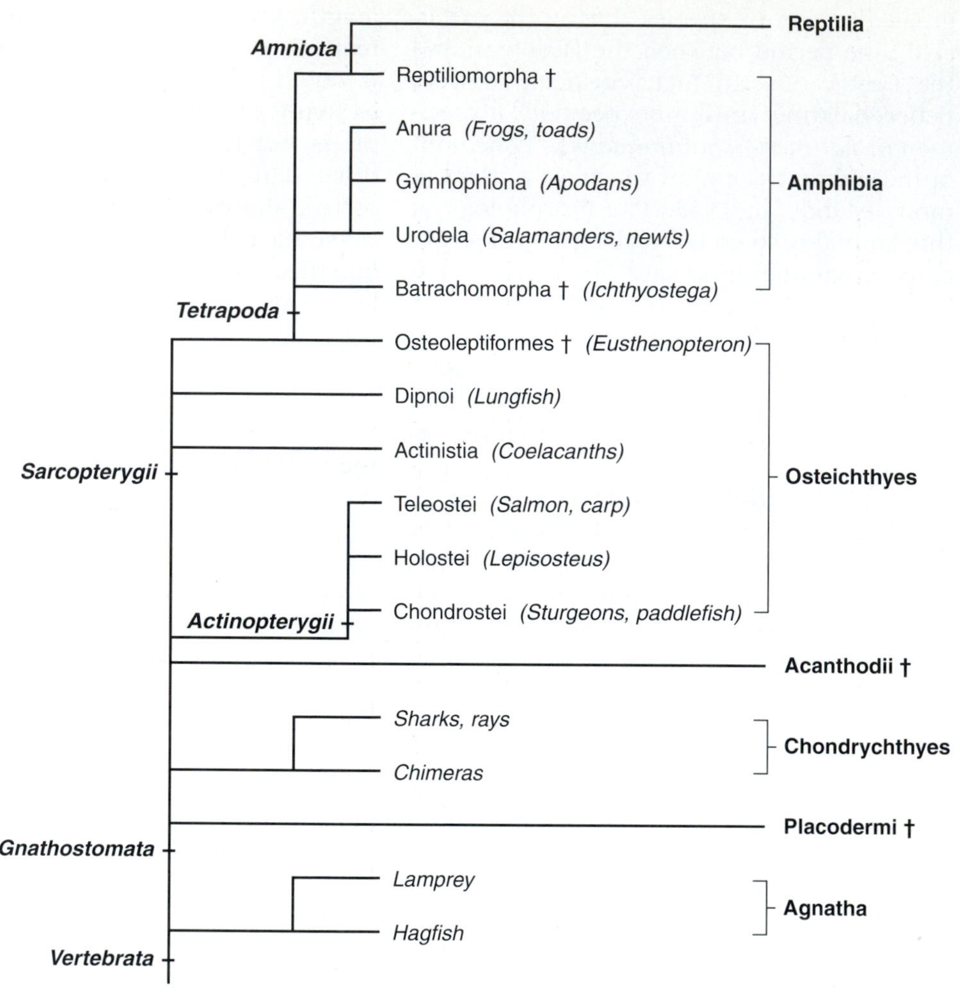

FIGURE 6.10. This tree summarizes the fish classes and the amphibians covered in ***section 3.e.*** The taxonomic labels marked in the cladogram apply to all lineages above their location. Some key extinct groups are included (marked by daggers).

about 6,000 living species. The oldest known reptiles are relatively small, lizard-like animals from the mid Carboniferous (about 300 Mya) of Nova Scotia, in eastern Canada. They were preserved inside of hollow tree trunks together with a rich fauna of millipedes, snails, and small tetrapods that must have constituted their diet. One of the main common characters of reptiles is the evolution of the *amniotic egg,* an innovation that allowed early reptiles to move far from water sources and fully occupy terrestrial environments. Amniotic eggs have a semipermeable shell that reduces dehydration of internal fluids and allows for the embryo to develop in a dry environment. The embryo is surrounded by membranes (chorion, amnion, and allantois), that provide protection and nutrients, participate in respiration, and store digestive waste. It is difficult to know when the amniotic egg evolved because fossil eggs are rare. However, the eggs of all living reptiles, for all their complexity, develop in the same way, suggesting that the amniotic egg evolved only once. The name Amniota is applied to vertebrates possessing this type of egg—that is, reptiles, birds, and mammals. ***Figure 6.11*** summarizes the amniote groups described in the rest of this section.

Amniotes are grouped into four taxa according to the number of *temporal fenestrae,* that is, openings located in the temporal (lateral and posterior) region of the skull. Species of the subclass Anapsida exhibit no temporal openings. Anapsids include a few families of extinct reptiles from the Carboniferous, Permian, and Triassic, and the extant Testudines, or turtles. The fossil record of turtles extends to the late Triassic, about 200 Mya, when they appear in regions as distant as Germany and Argentina. The sister group of turtles is generally agreed to lie within a group of Permian anapsids referred to as "parareptiles." A

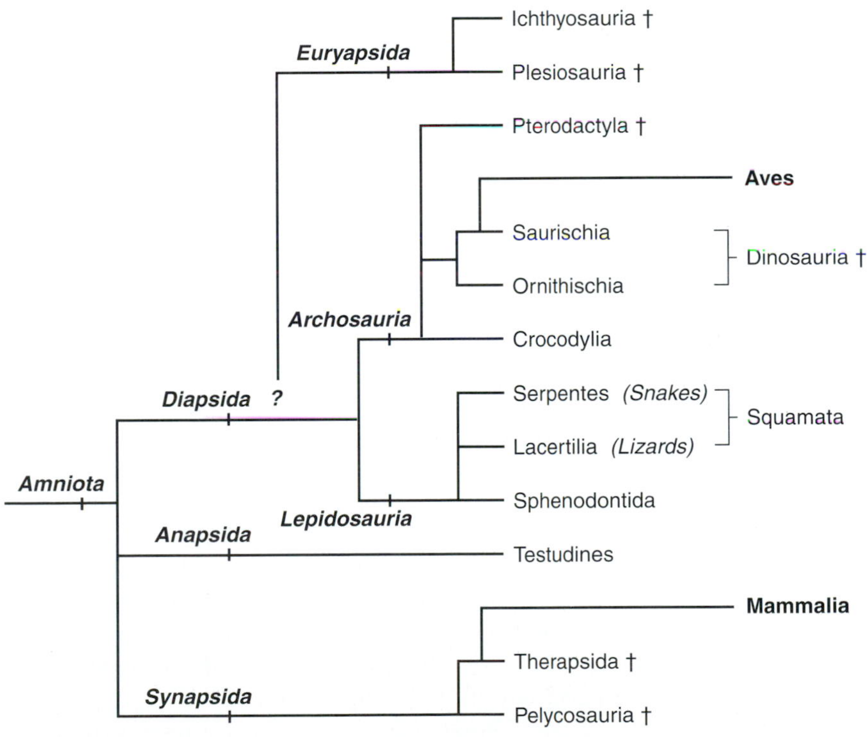

Figure 6.11. A summary of the taxa covered in ***section 3.f.*** Taxonomic labels apply to all lineages to the right of their location. Several extinct groups are included in this tree (marked by daggers).

major characteristic of the turtle body plan is the shell, which serves an obvious protective function and which appears already in the earliest species. Unlike primitive turtles, the modern ones can pull their heads into their carapace.

Species of the subclass Synapsida exhibit a single temporal fenestra located in a lower position. Basal synapsids appear in the late Carboniferous (about 295 Mya), and diversify during the Permian. These are referred to as the pelycosaurs, some of which are characterized by the presence of long spines protruding from the cervical and dorsal vertebrae, as in *Dimetrodon*. These spines were covered with skin and richly vascularized, a fact that has suggested a thermoregulatory function. For example, a predator pelycosaur like *Dimetrodon* could have increased internal temperature much faster by exposing this "sail" to the early morning sun. Pelycosaurs were replaced by the Therapsida, a major synapsid group that appeared during the late Permian, evolved into a variety of forms, and disappeared during the Jurassic period. It is from a group of therapsid reptiles (the cynodonts) that the mammals are thought to have evolved (see ***section 3.h.*** below).

Species of the subclass Diapsida exhibit two temporal openings. Diapsids include extinct groups such as the dinosaurs and pterosaurs (flying reptiles), as well as the extant lizards, snakes, sphenodon, and crocodilians. Birds are also diapsids, but they will be discussed below in ***section 3.g***. The oldest diapsids appear in rocks from the late Carboniferous period (295 Mya) and the group flourished during the Triassic period, after the mass extinction event at the end of the Permian. There are two major groups of living diapsid reptiles, the Lepidosauria and the Archosauria. Lepidosaurs are thought to be relatively more primitive, and they include the Sphenodontida and the Squamata. Sphenodontidans appear in Triassic rocks and include a variety of forms suggesting diverse modes of life and diets. There is only one extant species, the tuatara *Sphenodon punctatum*, which lives in some islands off the coast of New Zealand. *Sphenodon* is lizardlike in external appearance, but the skeleton lacks many of the features that are typical of squamatans and is thus widely considered to be a living fossil. Squamatans include the living species of lizards, snakes, and the legless amphisbaenians. The oldest squamatans are lizards from the late Jurassic period (about 200 Mya); snakes appear much later, in early Cretaceous rocks (140 Mya), whereas amphisbaenians have a poor fossil record.

Archosaurs include the most famous of all fossils, the extinct dinosaurs and pterosaurs, and also crocodilians and birds. The earliest archosaurs appeared at the beginning of the Triassic, approximately 240 Mya, and underwent a series of adaptive radiations of impressive diversity. The crocodilians probably diverged in the early Triassic. Like their modern cousins, Triassic crocodilians lived in rivers and marshes and had a voracious appetite. Some specimens with fossilized stomach contents demonstrate that these animals fed on fish but also hunted small tetrapods that were probably seized outside the water and then carried into the river, where they were consumed. The oldest pterosaurs are found in late Triassic deposits of Italy. These reptiles fed on fish and occupied a variety of niches, diversifying extensively during the Jurassic and Cretaceous, in parallel to the dinosaurs. Pterosaurs exhibit a remarkable variation in body size from the 9-cm length of *Eudimorphodon* to the 1.8-m length of *Pteranodon*, which had a wing span of 5 to 8 m. *Quetzal-*

coatlus, known from fragments of a single wing and dated to the late Cretaceous of Texas, is estimated to have had a wing span between 11 and 15 m—like a small airplane! Some well-preserved fossils demonstrate that pterosaurs had also evolved hair, probably as an insulating material, which implicates endothermy. *Endothermy* is the ability to maintain a constant internal temperature and is characteristic of extant birds and mammals in which the feathers and hair function as insulating material. All living reptiles are *ectothermic;* that is, their internal temperature fluctuates with that of the environment. Endothermy may have allowed pterosaurs the sustained metabolic rate necessary for flight.

A substantial amount of information exists about the evolution of the dinosaurs, partly because their size and unique variations have fascinated scientists and the general public since their discovery. The oldest dinosaurs are from late Triassic rocks (230 Mya) of Argentina, such as *Herrerasaurus,* a 3-m long, bipedal predator with reduced forelimbs. Dinosaurs were rare in the late Triassic, but they achieved worldwide distribution during the Jurassic and Cretaceous, aided by the formation of the supercontinent of Pangaea. Two distinct groups of dinosaurs are generally recognized, possibly diverging at the very beginning of their history on the basis of the shape of the pelvic girdle. Saurischian dinosaurs have a lizard-like hip with the pubis extending forward and the ischium extending backwards. The famous *Tyrannosaurus rex,* a 14-m-long bipedal saurischian, is one of the largest terrestrial carnivores that ever existed. Some of the largest herbivores were also saurischian, such as *Diplodocus.* In ornithischian dinosaurs, by contrast, the pubis extends backwards and becomes parallel with the ischium. Duck-bill dinosaurs, ceratopsians, and stegosaurs are among the most famous ornithischian dinosaurs.

Many recent paleontological discoveries have stirred controversy on the general biology and behavior of dinosaurs. The traditional picture of the dinosaurian mode of life, resembling that of present-day lizards, has been replaced by a view that puts them closer to the birds. There is considerable agreement that birds evolved from a group of saurischian dinosaurs known as Theropoda, which includes the *Tyrannosaurus* and other bipedal carnivores. So there is a phylogenetic connection between dinosaurs and birds. The discovery of richly vascularized bone (suggesting endothermy) and fossilized nests (suggesting parental care and breeding in colonies) has inspired an "avian view" of the dinosaurs. It is possible that traits such as endothermy and parental care of the young, so characteristic of birds, may have evolved originally in the dinosaurs.

The subclass Euryapsida is characterized by a single upper temporal fenestra, and it includes a variety of extinct reptiles that flourished during the Mesozoic. The two main groups, plesiosaurs and ichthyosaurs, include marine reptiles that appeared in the Triassic. Among the adaptations for an aquatic life are the paddles of plesiosaurs and the dolphinlike body shape of ichthyosaurs. The remarkable preservation of a female ichthyosaur that is apparently giving birth to an offspring that developed internally and is emerging tail-first, demonstrates a set of remarkable convergences with modern dolphins and whales.

Reptiles were particularly affected by major *mass extinction* events at the end of the Permian and Cretaceous periods. In the Permian extinction (245 Mya), presently considered the largest of such events (Stanley & Yang 1994), 27 of the 37 families of tetrapods disappeared from the fossil record. Indeed, about 61% of all life forms are thought to have disappeared in the Permian extinction (Benton 1995). The therapsids, for example, were practically exterminated in this event, except for a few lines that continue into the Mesozoic, eventually giving rise to the early mammals. The cause of the Permian extinction event is not known; it could have been a gradual cooling of the Earth or a more catastrophic event such as the fall of an asteroid or a comet. The mass extinction event at the end of the Cretaceous (65 Mya) resulted in the disappearance of dinosaurs, pterosaurs, plesiosaurs, mosasaurs, and of many families of birds and mammals. Among the reptiles, 9 of 44 families became extinct at the end of the Cretaceous. Many of these groups, however, were already in decline before this event, a fact that suggests a gradual process, such as a global change in climate. A sudden extinction is suggested by chemical evidence of an extraterrestrial impact, perhaps a meteorite. A high concentration of iridium and the presence of shock quartz in rocks from the end of the Cretaceous are both consistent with a catastrophic event. Between the Permian and Cretaceous mass extinction events stands the Triassic, a period during which many amniote groups underwent adaptive radiations. Crocodilians, dinosaurs, pterosaurs, turtles, ichthyosaurs, plesiosaurs, cynodonts, and the mammals all arose or flourished during the Triassic.

3.g. Avian Evolution. The estimated 9,000 species of living birds provide a clear illustration of the notion of body plan and its many variations. Some of the derived characters shared by all birds include the feathers, a toothless beak, bipedal posture, and anterior limbs adapted for flight. The many variations in morphology and behavior may alter some of these characters, but the Bauplan is still obvious. For example, some birds have lost the ability to fly, and consequently their wings are reduced (e.g., ostriches and rheas) or they have been reshaped into flippers (e.g., penguins). But ostriches and penguins are still very clearly birds. When did this Bauplan arise?

Fragments of several specimens and fossil traces from the late Triassic and early Jurassic have been suggested to belong to early birds (e.g., *Protoavis,* from the late Triassic of Texas). However, there is yet no universal agreement about the avian nature of these findings because the remains are fragmentary and difficult to date. *Archaeopteryx litographica,* discovered in 1861 in Germany, is still the oldest known fossil that can be unmistakably identified as a bird. Only six skeletons have been recovered from sandstone deposits of what was once a subtropical marine environment, and they have been dated from the late Jurassic (about 140 Mya). *Archaeopteryx* was approximately the size of a modern pigeon and possessed feathers (one of which has been beautifully preserved in a block of sandstone), wings, and a tail. But *Archaeopteryx* also had a number of "reptilian" characters that are not present in extant birds: teeth, a bony tail with more than 20 vertebrae, and three fingers in the wing. Its pubic bone, in the pelvis, was probably intermediate between the forward orientation of basal theropods and the backward orientation of modern birds. The overall shape of the pelvis and the fused wishbones (clavicles) show clear affinities with theropodan dinosaurs.

A question that has ignited substantial debate is the extent to which *Archaeopteryx* could fly. Many of the characters associated with flight in birds, such as hollow bones and the bipedal posture, were already present in theropods. It appears now that even feathers, or a dermal structure resembling the avian feather, are also present in some small dinosaurs from China. One of these, the theropod *Protarchaeopteryx,* shows clusters of feathers that almost certainly play no role in flying. It is possible that *Archaeopteryx* flew only with great difficulty, although it could have been able to glide from a tree. Perhaps feathers evolved as insulating structures connected to temperature regulation, much like hair in mammals. It is also possible that feathers were initially used in the context of courtship displays. Once there for one function (thermoregulation or display), feathers could have been further selected for their contribution to gliding and flapping flight. Fossil birds from the Cretaceous period show a number of characters that indicate an improvement of structures associated to flight, such as a more powerful sternum (the breast bone where muscles involved in flapping attach), a short tail, and perching feet (with the fourth toe curved toward the other three toes to allow for grasping). *Iberomesornis* (from Spain) and *Sinornis* (from China) indicate a clear shift to an arboreal, tree-dwelling mode of life that was probably accompanied by a progressive improvement of flight.

Extant birds are classified into two superorders: Palaeognathae and Neognathae. The distinction was originally based on morphological characters, including the structure of the palate and a variety of skeletal traits associated with the loss of flight. The palaeognathous palate is more similar to that of thecodont dinosaurs and thus thought to be more primitive. More recently, this distinction has been confirmed by molecular analysis of nuclear and mitochondrial DNA sequence. The Palaeognathae include the primitive tinamous birds of Central and South America and the flightless ratites such as the rhea (South America), ostrich (Africa), cassowaries and emus (Australia), and kiwis (New Zealand). Several species of large ratites became extinct only recently, some within historical times, including the 13 or so species of moas from New Zealand. Moas radiated in the islands of New Zealand where there are no native mammals, occupying a variety of niches and reaching enormous sizes; the largest species was about 3 m tall. Moas declined after the arrival of the Polynesians in New Zealand, about a thousand years ago, and became totally extinct in the 18th century. Recent evidence suggests that human settlers, and not natural causes such as climatic changes, may have been responsible for the extinction of some of the giant ratites, such as *Genyornis newtoni,* a flightless bird from Australia that disappeared suddenly about 50,000 years ago (Miller et al. 1999).

The Neognathae are the most abundant of modern species, including such common animals as chicken, ducks, quail, penguins, parrots, pigeons, and the songbirds (sparrows, cardinals, mockingbirds, etc.). The songbirds, or Passeriformes, are the most abundant order of living birds, with almost 6,000 species. Neognathous species of birds are among the most common animal research models in comparative psychology. Unfortunately, however, they have a very poor fossil record, although several orders can be identified already in the late Cretaceous. These animals are generally small, with hollow bones, and living in forested areas, not necessarily in close association with water, all features that would make it unlikely for their remains to fossilize. The lack of information about their phylogeny is a reminder of the biased representation of taxa in the fossil record.

One way to approach the phylogeny of a group like this is to rely on molecular information obtained from living species. Of course, this approach provides no clues as to the actual diversity of neognathous birds during the Cenozoic, but it contributes information about the phylogenetic distance between the various groups, as well as hypotheses of divergent times that could be contrasted against eventual fossil findings. Sibly and Alhquist (1990) undertook the monumental task of assessing living birds, using DNA-DNA hybridization techniques. DNA from two different species is pooled together, and the extent to which the strands hybridize provides an index of their degree of similarity. The closer the divergence between two species, the more similar the DNA sequence and thus the higher the degree of hybridization. ***Figure 6.12*** shows a summarized phylogenetic tree of all avian orders based on molecular evidence.

3.h. Mammalian Evolution. Mammals appear in fossils from the late Triassic period, approximately 200 Mya, but are preceded by the therapsids, a group of reptiles that gradually evolved many of the morphological characters that were to become typical of the class Mammalia, including the jaw joint, the middle ear, and the pattern of tooth replacement. The fossil record of advanced therapsids, known as cynodonts, is so complete that transitional states between basal reptiles and modern mammals have been preserved, thus allowing for a historical reconstruction. *Tooth replacement* is a major character differentiating modern mammals from reptiles. In reptiles, teeth are replaced continuously, whereas in mammals there is a single replacement of the milk teeth by the adult teeth. Advanced cynodonts already had a typically mammalian pattern of tooth replacement. They also possessed a high degree of tooth specialization, with incisors, canines, and massive cheek teeth specialized for crushing. These changes, taken together, suggest major advances in feeding behavior and, in particular, the evolution of a muscle and bone machinery that allowed for chewing.

A small, shrew-like animal called *Morganucodon,* from the late Triassic of Europe and China, and a variety of closely related forms are generally believed to be the oldest known mammals. The body size of these animals is estimated to have varied between 20 and 30 g, which suggests they were at least one order of magnitude smaller than the smallest known cynodonts of the same period. *Morganucodon* shows a brain enlargement that seems concentrated on areas associated with the processing of odors and acoustic signals. Since olfaction and audition are distance senses most useful in nocturnal mammals, it is believed that the first mammals were primarily nocturnal, as are the most conservative marsupial and placental mammals of today (opossums and insectivores, respectively). Some advanced cynodonts have small cavities in the snout, suggesting the presence of a neural and circulatory innervation for whiskers, which, in turn, suggest that cynodonts may have possessed hair and were perhaps endothermic.

An endothermic, small, opportunistic mesozoic animal could have exploited the *nocturnal niche* that the dominant reptiles and the emerging birds, with their visual bias, left open. Jerison (1973) suggested that it was such a move toward a nocturnal mode of life that provided the selective pressures for the evolution of more sophisticated olfactory and auditory neural processing centers and that in turn, led to the increase in relative *brain size* that is so typical of mammals (more about this in ***Chapter 8***).

Jurassic and Cretaceous mammals of a variety of groups have been described, in-

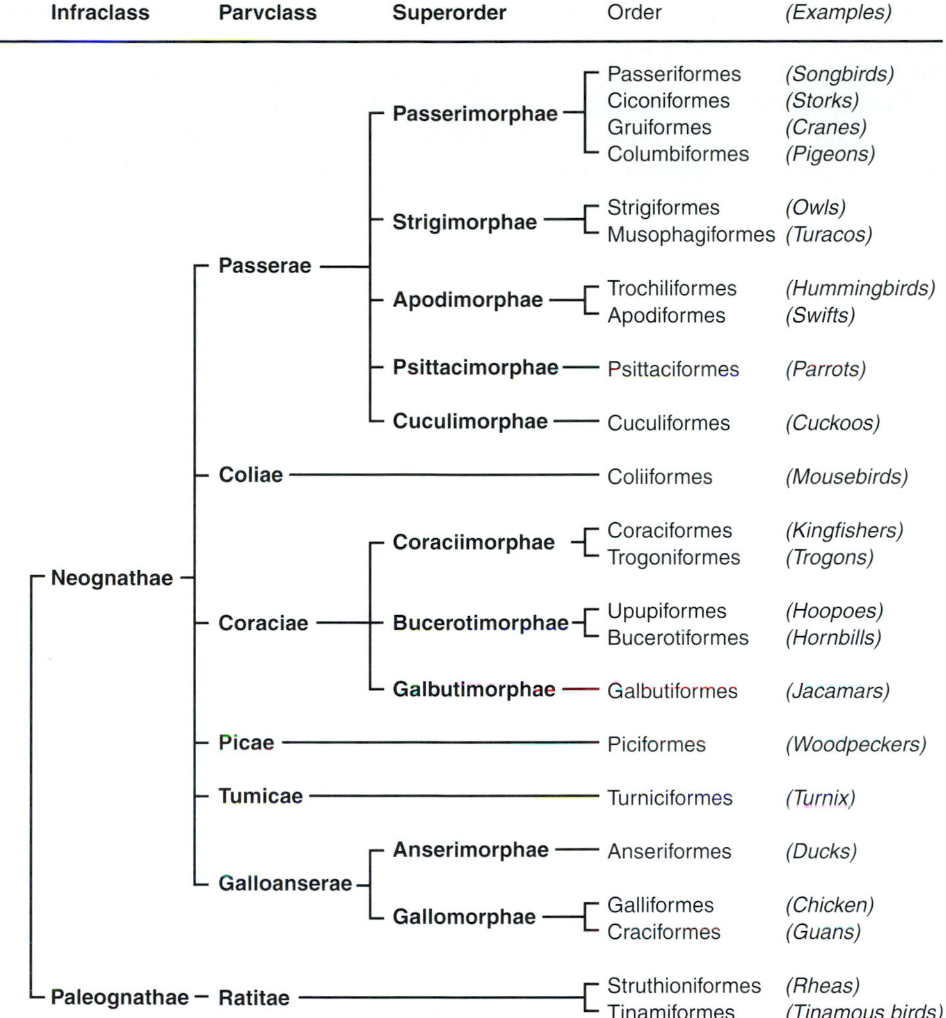

Figure 6.12. A classification of avian orders based on DNA-DNA hybridization data (Sibly & Ahlquist 1990). The phylogenetic history of most of these orders is very poor or completely unknown.

cluding the Multituberculata, Triconodonta, Docodonta, Symmetrodonta, and Pantotheria, among others. Most of these names refer to distinctive features of their dental anatomy. For example, triconodonts possessed molars with three cones, with the central one being longer than the lateral cones; the upper central cone fits the space between two adjacent lower molars, thus yielding a very distinctive occlusal pattern.

Among the living mammals (about 4,500 species), a distinction is often made between the Prototheria (=Monotremata), or egg-lying mammals, and the Theria (marsupials plus placentals). There are only three extant species of prototherians, all living in Australia and New Guinea: the platypus and two species of echidnas. It has been suggested that egg-laying mammals represent what remains of one of these groups that originated in the Jurassic period; the multituberculates have been nominated as possible ancestors of modern prototherians, but the matter is still unresolved. Prototherians are highly specialized and conservative, as demonstrated by their oviparous mode of reproduction. After hatching, monotreme infants move into a pouch and feed on milk secreted by glands widely distributed on the ventral skin of the mother.

Therian mammals include the living Metatheria, or marsupials, and Eutheria, or placentals, and are characterized by a distinctive feature: the *tribosphenic molar.* Three main cusps, a variable number of accessory, small cusps, and the presence of several crests with sharp edges and valleys characterize the tribosphenic molar. This molar represents an improvement in chewing ability and a design that seemed to have reduced the wearing of the enamel, thus prolonging the tooth's functional life.

Mammalian evolution has followed a very peculiar path. While mesozoic mammals remained relatively unchanged during approximately 140 million years of evolution, mammalian diversity increased by the late Cretaceous and literally exploded during the early Paleocene in one of the clearest examples of adaptive radiation (***Figure 6.13***). An intriguing possibility is that the Paleocene adaptive radiation is a direct consequence of the Cretaceous mass extinction event that wiped out a substantial number of both terrestrial and marine reptiles. The "mammalian explosion" of the Paleocene may thus be linked to the relatively sudden opening of a variety of ecological niches that were readily occupied by new orders of mammals, capable of evolving new Bauplans and new behavioral capabilities.

The Metatheria, or marsupials, and Eutheria, or placentals, appeared in the late Cretaceous. They are usually distinguished by the number of premolars (three in marsupials, four in placentals) and molars (four in marsupials, three in placentals). The oldest marsupials were discovered in North and South America, and more recent fossils were found in Europe, north Africa, and Australia. They probably originated somewhere in the Americas, from which they dispersed to Europe and Africa, and to Australia via Antarctica during the Cretaceous, when there were still many land bridges between the continents. There are approximately 260 living species of marsupials, restricted to the Americas, Australia, and some islands north of Australia, as well as New Zealand and Hawaii, where they have been introduced recently by humans. In marsupials, the embryo emerges from the uterus at a very early stage and continues its development in a pouch, where it attaches itself to a teat and extracts milk.

There are approximately 4,250 species of living placentals, distributed in 16 to 18 orders, depending on the classification adopted. The fossil record of some of these groups extends to the Paleocene and even to the late Cretaceous. The earliest Eutheria appeared in the late Cretaceous of Mongolia and the Americas. *Zalambdalestes,* from Mongolia, had long hind legs and feet and must have been specialized for leaping, like rabbits, but most species were relatively small insectivores, wolf-size carnivores, and cow-size herbivores. The adaptive radiation of the Paleocene includes a wide variety of groups that became extinct in the Eocene (about 50 Mya). In a matter of about 10 million years, from the late Cretaceous to the early Eocene, the number of mammalian families increased from 15

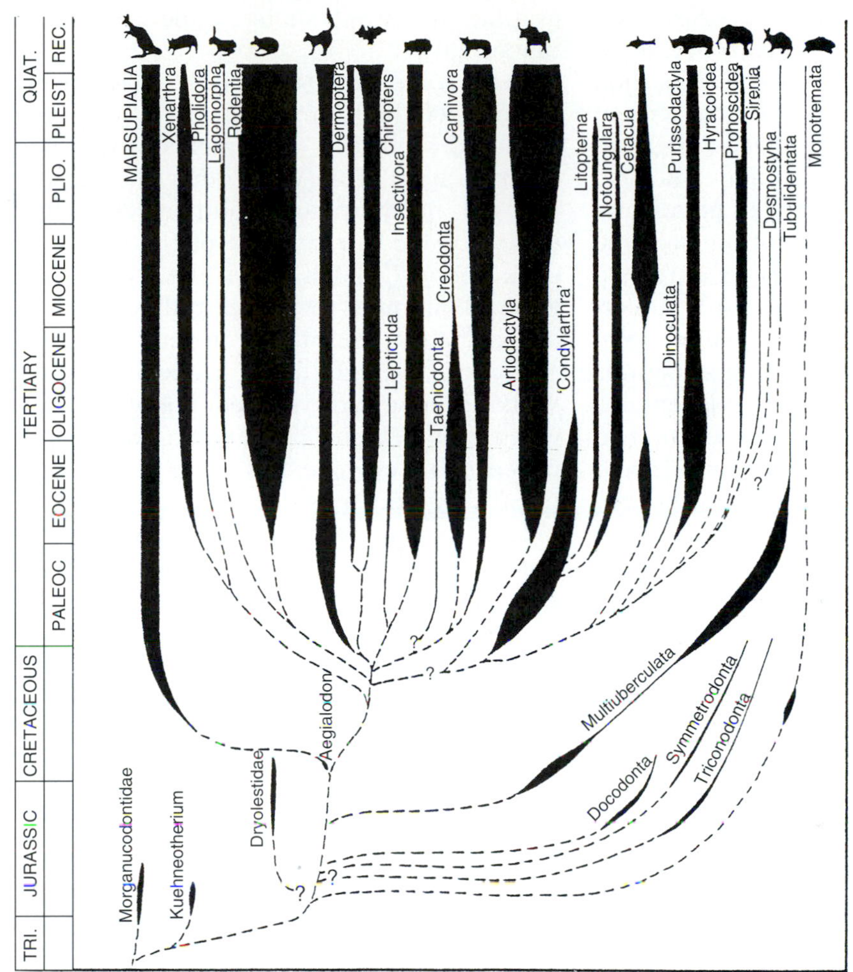

FIGURE 6.13. A phylogenetic tree representing the adaptive radiation of the eutherian mammals during the early Cenozoic (=Tertiary) era (Benton 1990a). Monotremes, marsupials, and several lineages of extinct mammals are also included in this tree.

to 78, and the number of genera from 40 to about 200. What allowed these placental groups to afford such an explosive adaptive radiation? Improved dentition (and hence efficient feeding behavior), extensive parental care, and increased intelligence have traditionally been cited as contributing factors.

If placental mammals originated in the late Cretaceous, and if most of the modern orders were already differentiated in the Paleocene, about 60 Mya, then the subsequent evolution of modern mammals has occurred in parallel. Behavioral capacities and neural structures that underwent substantial change during the Cenozoic, such as social behavior and the neocortex, may have evolved largely in parallel from a set of basic therian features. Parallel evolution can be appreciated among convergent species of marsupials and placentals as illustrated in ***Figure 6.14.*** Similar ecological pressures coupled with similar preadaptations have favored the evolution of some striking similarities among unrelated species, including adaptations for a subterranean mode of life (in marsupial and placental moles) and similar gliding structures (in arboreal marsupials and placentals). There were even analogous saber-toothed species of marsupials (*Thylacosmilus*) and placentals (*Smilodon*) among the carnivorous fauna of South America. Because of this extensive parallel evolution, comparative psychologists must be cautious when comparing mammalian characters that underwent extensive change during the Cenozoic. For example, knowledge about social behavior or neocortical organization and function obtained from the study of a particular order of placental mammals, such as rodents, should be extrapolated cautiously to a different order, such as primates.

4. Patterns of Diversity

4.a. Zoogeographic Regions. The brief survey of the history of animals highlights a number of important features. Some lineages show explosive adaptive radiations, while others exhibit a remarkable evolutionary stasis, leading, in some notorious cases, to the so-called living fossils. Periods of rapid diversification, like the Triassic, alternate with mass extinction events, such as that at the end of the Permian. Continents have moved, allowing some faunas to spread worldwide, such as the dinosaurs in Gondwana, while others have evolved in geographic isolation, such as the Australian marsupials.

On some rare occasions, a relatively rapid geologic change has produced the "sudden" meeting of faunas that had evolved apart from each other. For example, the northern and southern Americas were isolated during most of the Cenozoic until about 7.5 Mya, when their proximity allowed animals to successfully move between the two continents on rafts either directly or through the Caribbean islands. Walking migration started about 3 Mya, when the isthmus of Panama was established. This episode has been dubbed the Great American Interchange (Marshall, 1988). As shown in ***Figure 6.15,*** typical South American mammals, such as the glyptodonts, armadillos, opossums, ground sloths, and porcupines, invaded the northern continent, whereas typical North American mammals, such as wolves, rabbits, horses, and elephants, entered the southern continent. This interchange was followed by similar levels of extinction in both continents, but whereas the southern species did not diversify in North America, the northern species that reached South America underwent extensive diversification. Why were the northern species more successful in South America than vice versa?

It is possible that the relatively higher success of the northern fauna is due to their greater diversity. Not only is North America about 25% larger than South America in territory, but it also had a greater diversity of genera during the time of the interchange. The North American fauna had also been exposed to successive migrations from Europe (connected during the early Cenozoic) and from Asia (connected through the Bering passage at various times during the Cenozoic).

This Great American Interchange illustrates the degree to which animals are seg-

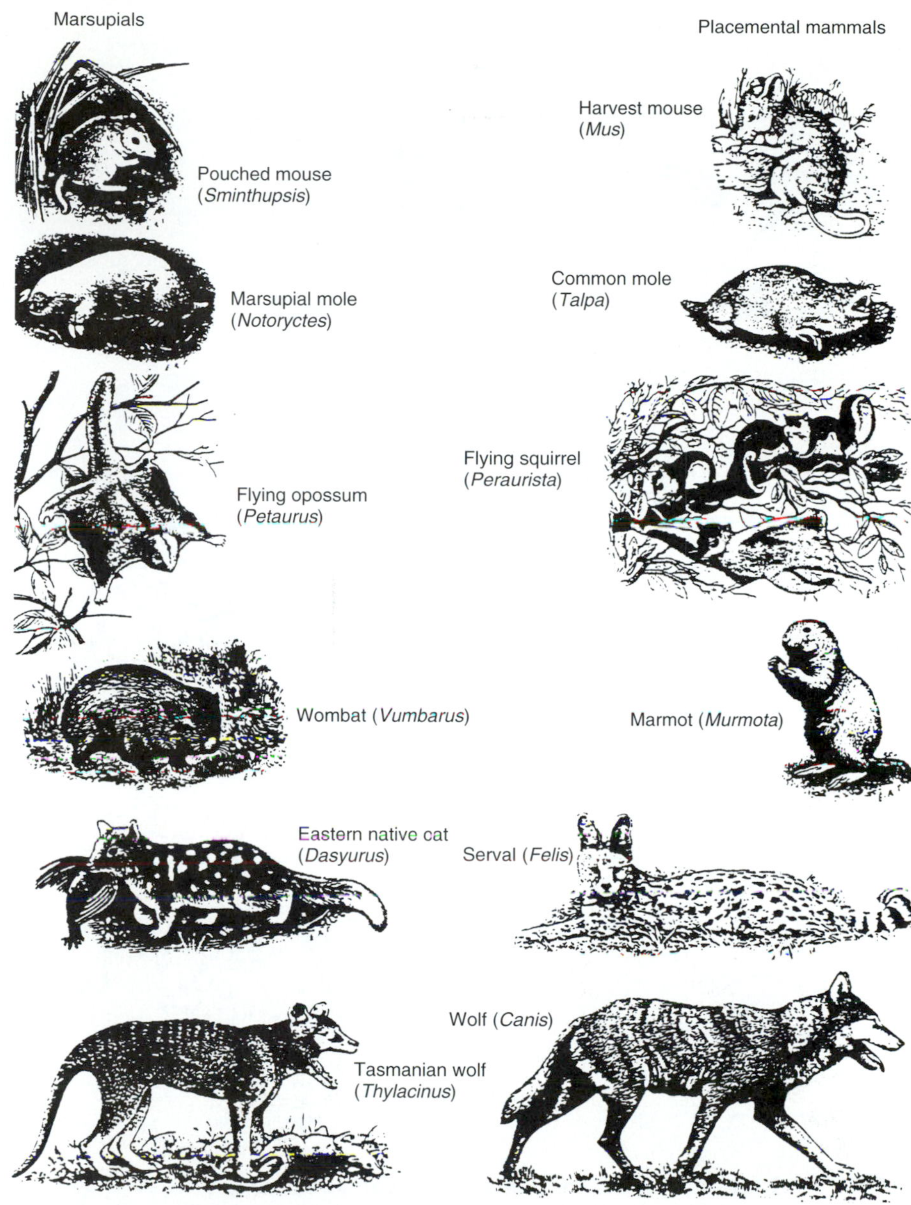

FIGURE 6.14. Evolutionary convergence of independently evolved species of marsupials and placentals that occupy similar ecological niches (Young 1981).

FIGURE 6.15. The Great American Interchange involved the bidirectional migration of a variety of mammals through the isthmus of Panama that started about 3 Mya (Benton 1990a).

regated in space. The land masses of the world are typically divided into zoogeographical regions, such as the Palearctic, Ethiopian, Oriental, Australian, Nearctic, and Neotropical. These regions are characterized by groupings of animals (and plants) that are, to some degree, quite peculiar and unique. For example, the Neotropical fauna, which extends from Patagonia in the south to Central America in the north, is characterized by platyrrhine monkeys (capuchins, marmosets, etc.), a wide variety of edentates (including armadillos, tree sloths, and anteaters) and marsupials, and distinct freshwater fishes, including the electric eels and the lungfish.

Islands and archipelagos are also associated with adaptive radiation events, as well as with the preservation of unique living fossils. For example, the large island of Madagascar, off the east coast of Africa, is a refuge for the lemurs. Once distributed over the African continent, this primitive group of primates has survived and diversified only in Madagascar. The Hawaiian Islands support an estimated 1,000 species of fruitflies of the family Drosophilidae, more than the combined number of species found in the rest of the world. These fruitflies, however, evolved elsewhere, since the oldest Hawaiian Island, Kawai'i, was formed about 5 Mya. The tuatara *Sphenodon* (from New Zealand), and the lungfishes and ratite birds (from South America, Africa, and Australia) are examples of living fossil groups that have been preserved in relative isolation.

4.b. Speciation. A population of animals sharing the same habitat may split into different species by means of so-called *sympatric speciation.* Sympatric speciation may occur when, for example, a mutation affects a critical trait for species recognition. Some species of *Drosophila* seem to have diverged from their sympatric ancestors on the basis of mating preferences that depend on such characters as the shape of the head. Assortative mating may lead to reproductive isolation even when populations overlap in space (Higashi et al. 1999). However, sympatric speciation is generally assumed to be a relatively rare event.

The examples of spatial diversity reviewed in the previous section demonstrate that new species may commonly originate by a process of geographic isolation. This is referred to as *allopatric speciation,* and it assumes that geographical barriers (e.g., mountains, ocean) prevented gene flow among populations that were once capable of interbreeding, leading eventually to the evolution of local varieties and to reproductive isolation (Grant 1998). Allopatric speciation is also the process simulated in laboratory experiments on artificial selection (see ***Chapter 3***). Imagine, for example, an interbreeding population of fish living off the coast of South America, right before the isthmus of Panama was established. When the land bridge emerges, the population is split into a Pacific group and a Caribbean group. Local ecological pressures may not change, but the two populations no longer interbreed. Such gene flow would normally cancel out the effects of local selective pressures and preserve the interbreeding capacity of animals within this particular species. After a sufficient number of generations, a combination of (1) the genetic variation existing in the Pacific and Caribbean founding groups and (2) the cumulative effects of local selective pressures results in the evolution of different species. If the land bridge were to disappear again in, say, 5 million years, then the new species are likely to remain reproductively isolated, even though they might again coexist in the same habitat.

When a species is found in two different habitats and there is considerable phenotypic divergence, it may be the case that some intermediate forms are found in the boundary between the habitats. In cases in which these intermediate forms are actually found, and the hybrid individuals are viable, the two populations are referred to as subspecies. For example, the rat snake (*Elaphe obsoleta*) is distributed over a large area of the eastern and southern United States; several subspecies living in geographically restricted habitats have been identified on the basis of color and the presence of stripes. Such cases of subspecies may be considered to be populations that have undergone some degree of divergence and are on their way to reproductive isolation if the current geographic pattern of distribution were to be maintained for a number of additional generations.

4.c. Macroevolution and Microevolution. In this chapter I have treated the origin of new animal phyla and the origin of new animal species more or less indiscriminately. There are, however, some distinctions that are worth recognizing. Biologists refer to the pattern of evolution above the taxonomic level of species or genus as *macroevolution,* whereas they reserve the term *microevolution* to refer to the origin of new species. Few would argue against the scenarios for speciation described in the previous section; such ideas of speciation are supported by a substantial body of data from field and laboratory studies (see ***Chapter 3***, ***section 4***, pp. 78–80). Reproductive isolation, gene flow, and natural selection are some of the important elements in speciation. Indeed, these are the features that convey the idea that the concept of "species" refers to a real, natural entity—that is, a population of interbreeding organisms distinguishable from other such populations. Obviously, this definition is limited; for example, it is impossible to apply to fossil species, for which no evidence of interbreeding can be obtained, or to asexually reproducing organisms, for which the notion of interbreeding does not apply. In such cases, character similarity is the main basis for discriminating among species.

There is, however, far less agreement about the extent to which a similar set of processes could also account for the emergence of new taxa above the species level. The issue is whether such concepts as "order," "class," or "phylum" are arbitrary units existing only in the taxonomist's mind or whether they are natural units analogous to "species" or "subspecies." The evolution of animals that are built according to novel principles of organization, such as, for example, the evolution of the first bilateral animal or of the first bird, demands an explanation of how an entirely novel suite of characters emerges, given that intermediate forms appear a priori to be impossible or maladaptive. In the extreme case, can a specific set of selective pressures and reproductive isolation be sufficient to understand the evolution of a new body plan, such as that seen when a new order, class, or phylum evolves? Can natural selection accumulate variations gradually until a new body plan emerges? Is macroevolution reducible to the same set of processes that successfully explain microevolution?

Biologists have provided several answers to these critical questions. One common reaction to this problem is to argue that whereas microevolutionary processes can be worked out by direct observations under laboratory or field conditions, macroevolutionary processes are less accessible to direct experimentation. Therefore, researchers should concentrate on the former (Dobzhansky 1937). A critical assumption of this position is that a thorough understanding of microevolution will ultimately lead to an understanding of macroevolutionary patterns.

A second possibility is to argue that macroevolutionary patterns do, in fact, reflect the same processes that operate in populations and lead to speciation, only over much longer periods of time. Perhaps new body plans emerge according to the same process that leads to speciation, but only after a substantially greater accumulation of genetic variation. Proponents of the third possibility, that macroevolution and microevolution are based on different principles, point to the pattern of change in the fossil record as relevant evidence to resolve this issue. Simpson (1944), for example, accepted that the fossil record is incomplete when it comes to documenting the transition between species, but he doubted that the absence of intermediate forms between families, orders, or classes could be easily dismissed as an artifact of an incomplete fossil record. Simpson argued that the reason for the absence of intermediate forms for macroevolutionary transitions was to be found in the speed of the transition. Macroevolutionary events, he thought, must occur very rapidly, perhaps in very small populations and in the absence of intermediate forms. This was referred to as *quantum evolution,* and it was described in terms of a very popular metaphor in evolutionary biology: the adaptive landscape.

The term *adaptive landscape* was first used by Sewall Wright in 1932, who had also suggested the notion of genetic drift—a nonadaptive, random change in allele frequencies that can be particularly fast in small populations (see ***Chapter 2, section 4.c.***, pp. 41–42). An adaptive landscape has peaks and valleys. Populations are supposed to be driven upward by natural selection. Once they are at the top of a peak, it would seem impossible for them to diverge because they would have to move downward—that is, become nonadapted. Simpson suggested that small populations may be able to sustain nonadaptive change through genetic drift and thus jump from the peak to a valley, where natural selection might take over and drive the population with a new set of characters onto another peak.

Simpson's notion of quantum evolution agrees better with a typical feature of the fossil record. As we have seen before, it is fairly common that higher-order taxa appear in relatively short bursts of adaptive radiations and then remain relatively stable during millions of years. For example, modern orders of placental mammals appear in the fossil record more or less abruptly, during the early Paleocene. Typically, macroevolutionary change is restricted to geologically brief periods of time, whereas evolutionary stasis dominates most of the history of particular lineages. This pattern has been named *punctuated equilibria* (Gould & Eldredge 1977) and is distinguished from the gradual and continuous rate of change suggested originally by Darwin and implied in the notion of speciation based on the accumulation of adaptive alleles by natural selection.

According to this notion of quantum evolution or punctuated equilibria, natural selection would play an important role in driving a population toward its adaptive peak (directional selection) and perhaps in keeping it in check (stabilizing selection). However, natural selection would be a minor force in the origin of new taxa, perhaps even in the origin of new species. Some experiments and field observations on the short-term effects of environmental changes on phenotypic characters mentioned previously (see ***Chapter 2, sections 4*** and ***5***, pp. 38–57), suggest that natural selection does keep a population in check with short-term environmental changes. For example, the average size of the beaks of Galapagos finches changed with yearly fluctuations in rainfall. But such rapid phenotypic changes go both ways, canceling each other out in the long term; they would appear in the fossil record as a period of stasis when, in fact, character fluctuations might have been constant.

A more complete understanding of the mechanisms that lead to novel body plans will be achieved when we explore the interconnections between development and evolution in ***Chapter 10.*** For the moment, however, it would seem appropriate to keep in mind the distinction between microevolution and macroevolution, even though no definitive answer can be provided as to whether or not they involve different processes.

4.d. Grades and Clades. Compared to modern reptiles, birds are notoriously more active and display a greater diversity of social behaviors, parental care patterns, and migratory movements, as well as an endothermic physiology and a relatively larger brain. Since all of these avian features are shared with mammals, it is not surprising that some have argued that these two groups are closely related. The name Haemothermia has been used to pool together Aves and Mammalia as sister groups (Gardiner 1982). Notice, however, that such a hypothesis would go against morphological and paleontological evidence suggesting that birds are archosaurs, only distantly related to mammals, which, in turn, are descended from a reptilian group that diverged very early in amniote evolution (see ***Figure 6.11,*** p. 197).

The characters that lead to the Haemothermia hypothesis are predominantly functional. For example, incubation of eggs (in birds and in the egg-laying monotreme mammals), bradycardia during diving, and endothermy. Kemp (1988) has shown that only a minority of these functional characters are, in fact, unique to birds and mammals, and many are shared with other reptiles (e.g., bradycardia during diving is shared with marine snakes). Moreover, Kemp demonstrated that when fossil groups of therapsids and dinosaurs are included in the analysis, the phylogenetic pattern supports a tree similar to that shown in ***Figure 6.11.*** Therefore, these phenotypic similarities must have evolved independently by a process of convergent evolution and not by inheritance from a common ancestor.

As taxonomic devices, both Haemothermia and Archosauria are defined as *clades,* that is, a phylogenetic hypothesis of a set of taxa tied together by a common ancestor. A clade is postulated on the basis of the derived characters that are shared by its members and are not present in any other taxa outside the clade. However, the Haemothermia hypothesis highlights the fact that, in some cases, the grouping of taxa makes sense even if the individual taxa conforming the group have evolved independently. The many common characters of the phenotype of birds and mammals puts them in a similar level, as far as those characters is concerned, and distinguishes them from other vertebrates that possess alternative versions of those characters. Such levels are referred to as *grades,* and they are postulated in connection with the evolution of key innovations. Multicellularity, bilaterality, endothermy, relative brain size, and complex sociality are examples of characters that have been postulated to involve a transition in grade organization. Grades denote the sharing of derived features by taxa that may have evolved these features either from a common ancestor or independently.

5. Elements of Cladistics

The story of the Haemothermia hypothesis versus the Archosauria hypothesis demonstrates that the classification of taxa can follow more than one criterion. In fact, there are three different approaches to developing phylogenetic hypotheses. The first and most traditional procedure, called evolutionary systematics, consists of developing a phylogenetic tree that postulates the genealogical relationship among a group of taxa based on the selection of a particular set of characters. Trees may encode various types of information, including the common ancestor of a particular group, the amount of divergence that occurred in the various lineages, the direction of the evolutionary process, and its time course. ***Figure 6.13,*** p. 205, depicts the evolution of mammals using the tree as a device. In this procedure, the grouping of taxa into higher order categories, such as classes, may depend on the weight given to certain characters by the taxonomist, but not on whether the taxon includes all the descendants. Consider the classes Reptilia, Aves, and Mammalia, derived from a traditional classification and adopted in this text. Whereas these three classes together are monophyletic—that is, they are derived from a common amniote ancestor—the class Reptilia is said to be *paraphyletic* because it does not include some of its descendants, the birds and mammals.

Secondly, taxonomic classifications could be organized on the basis of the degree of character similarity among taxa. This is referred to as phenetics, and the outcome is represented on a *phenogram* in which the proximity of two given taxa is a direct reflection of their degree of character similarity. The Haemothermia hypothesis is an example of a phenetic classification. As was argued above, the main problem with this type of system is that it may lead to the grouping of taxa that may be derived from very different ancestors. Such groups are referred to as *polyphyletic*.

A third approach is provided by cladistics, in which the grouping of taxa is based also on character similarity, but only of those characters that are both derived and unique to the particular group under study. Unlike in the case of evolutionary systematics, it is not the taxonomist that selects the critical characters; rather, the selection is based on the objective criterion that the characters must be shared and derived. Unlike in the case of phenetics, it is not overall similarity that matters, but similarity in terms of shared derived characters. The results are represented in a *cladogram,* which is viewed as a hypothesis of the pattern of divergence within a monophyletic clade. A cladogram looks like a tree, except that the taxa are represented only at the end of each branch; trees may include taxa postulated to be common ancestors and placed at the node from which branches diverge. A cladogram also looks like a phenogram, except that the distance between the branches bears no information; phenograms usually encode information on similarity in terms of the distance between branches and their length.

In cladistic analysis, a critical distinction is made between primitive characters, or *plesiomorphies,* derived characters, or *apomorphies,* and shared derived characters, or *synapomorphies.* By using only synapomorphies to cluster taxa as sister groups, cladistic analysis avoids the formation of paraphyletic and polyphyletic groups. Cladistic analysis aims at determining the structure of clades—that is, the interrelations among all known members of a particular monophiletic group. A clade includes both the ancestral taxon and all the derived lineages. In this context, it would make no sense to have a class Reptilia that excludes some of the derived lineages (i.e., birds and mammals). The correct group would be the Amniota, which would include all reptiles, birds, and mammals, living and fossil, unified in a single clade by the possession of a common synapomorphy: the amniote egg. Further monophyletic subdivisions of the Amniota include the mammals, the mammals plus therapsids, the birds, the birds plus dinosaurs, the turtles, the squamatans, and so forth.

The distinction between these approaches to phylogeny can be illustrated with an example. Suppose you discover a new fossil species of primate and you would like to determine its phylogenetic position. You notice some characters, including "five digits" in hand and foot, a "cranial capacity of 500 ml," and a foot adapted for "bipedal locomotion." In evolutionary systematics, the combination of small cranial capacity and bipedality may lead the scientist to classify this new species as an intermediate form between the hominid line (leading to modern humans) and the pongid line (leading to modern chimpanzees)—a missing link. Phenetic analysis would indicate that this species shares as many characters with pongids (5 digits, 500-ml cranial capacity) as it does with hominids (5 digits, bipedality) and would therefore classify it as equidistant from chimpanzees and humans. Cladistic analysis would proceed in the following fashion: The first character, 5-digit hand/foot, is discarded because it is a plesiomorphy for mammals (i.e., a primitive character not unique to primates). A cranial capacity of 500 ml does not distinguish between hominids and pongids, since it is typical of species that have been assigned to these groups on the basis of other characters. Bipedality, however, is a derived and unique character in the hominid line and is thus treated as a synapomorphy. According to cladistic analysis, the new species is a hominid.

Some basic cladistic elements have already been introduced in the context of ***Figure 6.6,*** p. 190. For example, a cladogram of the Amniota (the ingroup) would include the amphibians as the outgroup. The outgroup is defined as the closest taxon lacking the critical apomorphy defining the ingroup. For example, the amphibians are the closest tetrapod group to the amniota lacking an amniote egg. If the character "amniote egg" is used in a classification such as this one, it can be given two values: 0 = absence and 1 = presence. For this particular character, amphibians score a zero, whereas all the amniotes score a one.

Cladograms are constructed by developing a matrix with a set of character states in one axis and a set of taxa in the other axis. Each character is then scored (either dichotomically, e.g. absence vs. presence, or quantitatively by assigning graded values) for each taxon. An important feature of the matrix is that the characters must be independent from each other—that is, not correlated. Consider the simple matrix shown in ***Figure 6.16*** as an example.

According to this distribution of characters, Taxon X would be the outgroup, whereas Taxa Y and Z would form a derived monophyletic group sharing Characters 1 and 2. This can be represented in a cladogram, such as that shown in ***Figure 6.16-a***. Branches represent lineages, and they diverge from a point of common origin called a node. In this cladogram, the taxa are represented at the end of each line, whereas the characters are inserted between adjacent nodes. Characters 1 and 2 are not present in any lineage below their location (such as in Taxon X), but they are present in all lineages above their location (such as Taxa Y and Z).

Notice, however, that other cladograms based on the same data are possible. In the cladogram shown in ***Figure 6.16-b,*** the order of the taxa is reversed relative to the first cladogram. The distribution of characters is explained by assuming the selective loss of Characters 3 and 4 before the divergence of Taxa X and Y, and the selective loss of Characters 1 and 2 in Taxon X. While this second cladogram is compatible with the data set given above, it postulates a total of eight changes (gain of four characters and loss of four characters); in contrast, the first cladogram requires only four hypotheses of character change (gain of four characters) and is thus considered more parsimonious.

The cladogram depicted in ***Figure 6.16-c*** is also compatible with the original data set, but it has a peculiarity: it hypothesizes that Character 2 evolved independently in Taxa Y and Z. This would be an instance of convergence that adds an additional hypothesis of character change and makes this cladogram less parsimonious than the first one.

The logic used to select the best cladogram is based on the method of *simple parsimony*. The best cladogram to account for a specific character distribution matrix across taxa is the one that makes the smallest number of hypotheses of character change. According to this method, the cladogram shown in ***Figure 6.16-a*** should be selected as the best depiction of the phylogenetic relationship between these taxa, given the character set used in the analysis. Obviously, cladogram ***6.16-c*** may be supported over ***6.16-a*** if there were reliable evidence that Character 2 is actually convergent in Taxa Y and Z. This implies that the best cladogram may not necessarily be the most parsimonious one.

	Character 1	Character 2	Character 3	Character 4
Taxon X	0	0	0	0
Taxon Y	1	1	0	0
Taxon Z	1	1	1	1

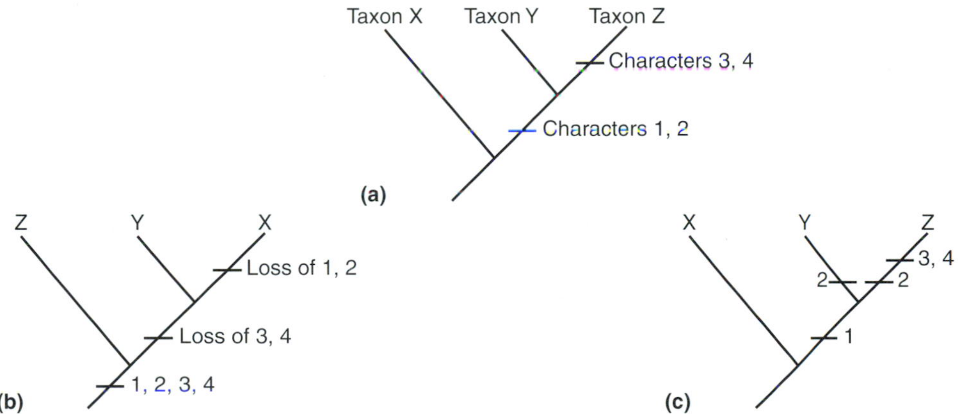

FIGURE 6.16. A hypothetical matrix of four characters distributed over three taxa. The characters assume one of two possible states (e.g., 0 = absence, 1 = presence). The three cladograms are all consistent with the matrix of character distribution, but they differ in terms of parsimony. The cladogram shown in ***(a)*** is the most parsimonious because it postulates four state changes (gain of each of the four characters). Cladogram ***(b)*** hypothesizes eight state changes, whereas cladogram ***(c)*** hypothesizes five state changes, with character 2 evolving independently in two lineages. Simple parsimony is a common criterion for choosing among alternative cladograms.

(a)

Species	123456789	1 0123456789	2 0123456789	3 01234567
Phaethon	000000000	0000000000	0000000000	00000000
Fregata	100000000	0000000000	0000000000	00000300
Pelecanus	110000000	0000000000	0000000000	00001400
M. capensis	111000000	1000000101	0001?10001	01002100
M. serrator	111000000	1000000111	0001110001	01002100
M. bassanus	111000000	1000000111	0000110001	01002100
S. leucogaster	111011030	1000000002	0000100000	10102100
S. dactylatra	111011010	1000000002	0000100000	10102100
S. sula	111011010	1000000002	0000100000	00002100
S. nebouxii	111011020	100000000?	0000?00000	00012100
S. variegata	111011020	100000000?	0000?00000	00012100
Anhinga	111?31011	0???10000	0000001?00	00002500
P. varius	111?31011	0???10000	0000001?00	00002500
P. auritus	101231011	0130110000	0101001200	00002511
P. olivaceus	111231011	0130?10000	1100001?00	00002500
P. carbo	101230111	0110210000	1101001300	00002511
P. penicillatus	111140111	0120110000	0010001000	00002600
P. pelagicus	101140111	0121201000	0001001210	00002710
P. urile	111140111	0121201000	0000001210	00002700
P. aristotelis	111150031	0110300000	0011001100	00002610

(b)

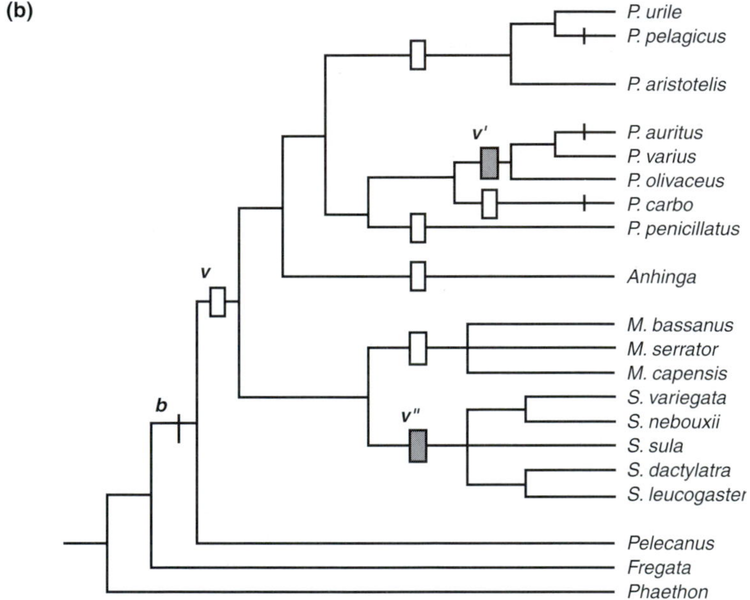

FIGURE 6.17. Cladistic analysis of pelicaniform birds based on their reproductive displays (Kennedy et al. 1996). ***(a)*** Matrix of behavioral character distribution for a group of 20 species of pelicaniform birds. These characters are part of the reproductive display of these species, such as, for example, "presentation of nest material" (character 1), "male advertising" (character 5), and "pre-take-off head raise" (character 22). This information was available in the literature after extensive observations of the reproductive behavior of these species in their natural environment. ***(b)*** A parsimony analysis of this matrix produced 12 shortest cladograms; the cladogram presented here is one derived from these 12 most

Unlike a phylogenetic tree, a cladogram is silent with respect to the ancestral taxon in any particular branch. Cladograms do not tell us which taxon is the ancestral and which is the derived, but rather which states of a particular phenotype are plesiomorphic and which are apomorphic. Cladistic analysis leads to hypotheses about the relative affinity among taxa, and it contributes to identify the ancestral state for a particular character through outgroup analysis, but not necessarily the ancestral taxon. Such an outgroup analysis indicates the *polarity* of evolutionary change by placing the states of a particular character along the primitive-derived dimension (Maddison et al. 1984). For example, placental mammals share the corpus callosum, a brain structure that connects the two cerebral hemispheres. The corpus callosum is a synapomorphy of the placentals because it is present neither in marsupial nor in monotreme mammals, the two immediate outgroups for the placental mammals. Therefore, the ancestors of placental mammals must have lacked a corpus callosum. However, this analysis should not be interpreted as suggesting that either marsupials or monotremes are the ancestors of placental mammals.

The matrix given above is unrealistically simple. Matrices derived from morphological, neurochemical, behavioral, or molecular data can be extremely complex, so they need to be analyzed using computer programs based on a variety of procedures and designed to provide the most parsimonious cladogram. In some cases, two or more cladograms can be equally parsimonious; a decision about which is the most appropriate can be made if additional evidence is available, or else the phylogeny remains undetermined. Kennedy et al. (1996) performed a cladistic analysis of the social displays of pelicaniform birds in order to determine the extent to which such displays reflect phylogenetic relationships among the species, rather than common ecological pressures. Thirty-seven behavioral characters were determined; most of the characters were dichotomous (i.e., presence vs. absence), but some assumed more than two values. Examples of dichotomous characters were the following: "presentation of nest material," "bowing," and "pointing." Examples of characters assuming more than two values were the following: "male advertising" (absent, sky pointing, alternate wings waved, slow rate wing waving, rapid flutter wing waving, darting and throwback) and "post-landing call during display" (absent, males only, males and females identical, males and females differ). The values of these 37 characters were established by field observations of 20 species of pelicaniform birds.

The matrix thus produced (see ***Figure 6.17-a***) was analyzed with PAUP (phylogenetic analysis using parsimony), a computer program that searches for the most parsimonious cladogram that fits a particular matrix.

parsimonious cladograms according to a majority consensus rule. Two characters are examined in these trees. The distribution of "bowing" ("***b***," character 2 in the matrix), represented by a vertical line, among these taxa leads to the following hypothesis: ***b*** originated once and it was lost in *P. pelagicus, P. auritus,* and *P. carbo*. The distribution of "vocalize during male advertising" ("***v***," character 6 in the matrix), is more difficult to understand. One possibility, represented by open rectangles, is that ***v*** evolved only once and was lost in at least five lineages. A second possibility, represented by the gray rectangles, is that ***v*** originated independently in at least two different lineages (independent evolution is represented as ***v***' and ***v***'' in this cladogram)

PAUP identified 12 different cladograms as the most parsimonious, that is, the ones requiring the fewest number of character changes. ***Figure 6.17-b*** shows a majority consensus tree built by retaining those branches that occur in more than half of the 12 shortest trees. These 12 cladograms required 78 character changes, a number referred to as tree length (TL). Given the number of character state changes, the absolute minimum TL is 58. These two numbers can now be used to compute the *consistency index,* a measure of the goodness of fit between the minimum TL and the observed TL, according to a simple ratio: $CI = TL_{min} / TL_{obs}$. For this particular case, CI = 58/78 = 0.74, which is a relatively large CI value. If CI = 1, then the fit would be perfect, whereas a CI approaching zero would imply poor fit.

Kennedy et al. (1996) contrasted these 12 most parsimonious cladograms with two types of alternative cladograms. First, these parsimonious cladograms were compared against a set of 1,000 cladograms generated by randomly assigning characters states to each of the 20 species. Such randomized set of cladograms had an average TL = 135, the shortest being TL = 126, considerably above the TL = 78 obtained for the 12 parsimonious cladograms. This suggests that the obtained parsimonious cladograms contain a significant amount of information. Second, the parsimonious cladograms were compared against cladograms generated on the basis of alternative character sets. Morphological, osteological, and molecular matrices from published information were developed and used to produce parsimonious cladograms that, in turn, were compared against the 12 parsimonious cladograms produced on the basis of the behavioral matrix. There was a significant degree of congruence between the behavioral cladograms and the cladograms generated independently from different databases. The main conclusion is, therefore, that behavioral characters may contain as much phylogenetic information as molecular and morphological characters.

The cladogram can also be used to develop hypotheses about the evolution of particular traits. ***Figure 6.17-b*** shows that a parsimonious explanation of the evolution of "bowing" suggests that it appeared once and it was lost three times. The character "vocalize during male advertising" yields a more complex picture. It either evolved independently twice (a parsimonious possibility), or it evolved once but it was lost independently in at least five lineages.

Cladistic analysis has contributed to the resolution of many important issues in taxonomy, and it has become a very influential and dominant approach in contemporary research. The assumptions of cladistics are rooted in evolutionary theory. Moreover, cladistic analysis is attractive because of its objectivity: Only synapomorphies are used for grouping taxa, and explicit criteria are used for choosing among alternative cladograms (e.g., parsimony).

6. Key Terms

acoelomates 178
adaptive landscape 211
adaptive radiation 185
allopatric speciation 209
amniotic egg 196
Animalia (or Metazoa) 175
apomorphy 213
bilateral symmetry 176
blastula stage 178
body plan (or Bauplan) 176
brain size 202
Burgess Shale fauna 186

7. References

Benton, M. J. (1990a). *Vertebrate paleontology*. London: Unwin Hyman.

Benton, M. J. (1990b). Phylogeny of the major tetrapod groups: Morphological data and divergence dates. *Journal of Molecular Evolution,* **30,** 409–424.

Benton, M. J. (1995). Diversification and extinction in the history of life. *Science,* **268,** 52–58.

Benton, M. J., Wills, M. A., & Hitchin, R. (2000). Quality of the fossil record through time. *Nature,* ***403,*** 534–537.

Briggs, D. E. G., Erwin, D. H., & Collier, F. J. (1994). *The fossils of the Burgess Shale.* Washington: Smithsonian Institution Press.

Chen, J.-Y., Huang, D.-Y., & Li, C.-W. (1999). An early Cambrian craniate-like chordate. *Nature,* **402,** 518–522.

Chiappe, L. M. (1995). The first 85 million years of avian evolution. *Nature,* **378,** 349–355.

Coates, M. I., & Clack, J. A. (1991. Fish-like gills and breathing in the earliest known tetrapod. *Nature,* **352,** 234–236.

Cooper, A., & Penny, D. (1997). Mass survival of birds across the Cretaceous-Tertiary boundary: Molecular evidence. *Science,* **275,** 1109–1113.

Cracraft, J. (1986). The origin and early diversification of birds. *Paleobiology,* **12,** 383–399.

Dobzhansky, T. (1937). *Genetics and the origin of species.* New York: Columbia University Press.

Doolittle, R. F., Feng, D.-F., Tsang, S., Cho, G., & Little, E. (1996). Determining divergence times of the major kingdoms of living organisms with a protein clock. *Science,* **271,** 470–477.

Estes, R., & Reig, O. A. (1973). The early fossil record of frogs: A review of the evidence. In J. Vial (Ed.), *Evolutionary biology of the anurans* (pp. 11–63). Columbia: University of Missouri Press.

Fedonkin, M. A., & Runnegar, B. (1992). Proterozoic metazoan trace fossils. In J. W. Schopf & C. Klein (Eds.), *The proterozoic biosphere* (pp. 389–395). Cambridge, UK: Cambridge University Press.

Forey, P., & Janvier, P. (1994). Evolution of the early vertebrates. *American Scientist,* **82,** 554–565.

Fricke, H., Hissmann, K., Schauer, J., Erdmann, M., Moosa, M. K., & Plante, R. (2000). Biogeography of the Indonesian coelacanths. *Nature,* **403,** 38.

Gauthier, J., Kluge, A. G., & Rowe, T. (1988). Amniote phylogeny and the importance of fossils. *Cladistics,* **4,** 105–209.

Gardiner, B. G. (1982). Tetrapod classification. *Zoological Journal of the Linnean Society,* **74,** 207–232.

Gorr, T., & Klinschmidt, T. (1993). Evolutionary relationships of the coelacanth. *American Scientist,* **81,** 72–82.

Gould, S. J., & Eldredge, N. (1977). Punctuated equilibria: The tempo and mode of evolution reconsidered. *Paleobiology,* **3,** 115–151.

Grant, P. R. (1998). *Evolution on islands.* Oxford: Oxford University Press.

Higashi, M., Takimoto, G., & Yamamura, N. (1999). Sympatric speciation by sexual selection. *Nature,* **402,** 523–526.

Horner, J. R. (1982). Evidence for colonial nesting and "site fidelity" among ornithischian dinosaurs. *Nature,* **297,** 675–676.

Jerison, H. J. (1973). *Evolution of the brain and intelligence.* New York: Academic Press.

Kemp, T. S. (1988). Haemothermia or Archosauria? The interrelations of mammals, birds, and crocodiles. *Zoological Journal of the Linnean Society,* **92,** 67–104.

Kennedy, M., Spencer, H. G., & Gray, R. D. (1996). Hop, step, and gape: Do the social displays of the Pelecaniformes reflect phylogeny? *Animal Behaviour,* **51,** 273–291.

Knoll, A. H., & Carroll, S. B. (1999). Early animal evolution: Emerging views from comparative biology and geology. *Science, 284,* 2129–2137.

Lee, M. S. Y. (1996). Correlated progression and the origin of turtles. *Nature,* **379,** 812–815.

Li, C.-W., Chen, J.-Y., & Hua, T.-E. (1998). Precambrian sponges with cellular structures. *Science,* **279,** 879–882.

Lillegraven, J. A., Kielan-Jaworowska, Z., & Clemens, W. A. (1979). *Mesozoic mammals. The first two-thirds of mammalian history.* Berkeley: University of California Press.

Maddison, W. P., Donoghue, M. J., & Maddison, D. R. (1984). Outgroup analysis and parsimony. *Systematic Zoology,* **33,** 83–103.

Marshall, L. G. (1988). Land mammals and the Great American Interchange. *American Scientist,* **76,** 380–388.

Martin, M. W., Grazhdankin, D. V., Bowring, S. A., Evans, D. A. D., Fedonkin, M. A., & Kirschvink, J. L. (2000). Age of neoproterozoic bilaterian body and trace fossils, White Sea, Russia: Implications for metazoan evolution. *Science,* **288,** 841–845.

Maynard Smith, J., & Szathmary, E. (1995). *The major transitions in evolution.* Oxford: Freeman.

Miller, G. H., Magee, J. W., Johnson, B. J., Fogel, M. L., Spooner, N. A., McCulloch, M. T., & Ayliffe, L. K. (1999). Pleistocene extinction of *Genyornis newtoni*: Human impact on Australian megafauna. *Science,* **283,** 205–208.

Padian, K., & Chiappe, L. M. (1998). The origin of birds and their flight. *Scientific American,* February, 28–37.

Raff, R. A. (1996). *The shape of life.* Chicago: University of Chicago Press.

Romer, A. S. (1966). *Vertebrate paleontology.* (3rd ed.). Chicago: University of Chicago Press.

Rougier, G. W., de la Fuente, M. S., & Arcucci, A. B. (1995). Late Triassic turtles from South America. *Science,* **268,** 855–858.

Ruiz-Trillo, I., Riutort, M., Littlewood, D. T. J., Herniou, E. A., & Baguña, J. (1999). Acoel flatworms: Earliest extant bilaterian metazoans, not members of Platyhelminthes. *Science, 283,* 1919–1923.

Seilacher, A., Bose, P. K., & Pfluger, F. (1998). Triploblastic animals more than 1 billion years ago: Trace fossil evidence from India. *Science,* **282,** 80–83.

Sibly, C. G., & Ahlquist, J. E. (1990). *Phylogeny and classification of birds: A study in molecular evolution.* New Haven: Yale University Press.

Simpson, G. G. (1944). *Tempo and mode in evolution.* New York: Columbia University Press.

Smith, A. G., Smith, D. G., & Funnell, B. M. (1994). *Atlas of Mesozoic and Cenozoic coastlines.* Cambridge: Cambridge University Press.

Stanley, S. M., & Yang, X. (1994). A double mass extinction at the end of the Paleozoic era. *Science,* **266,** 1340–1344.

Valentine, J. W. (1995). Late Precambrian bilaterians: Grades and clades. In W. M. Fitch & F. J. Ayala (Eds.), *Tempo and mode in evolution* (pp. 87–107). Washington: National Academy Press.

Whittaker, R. H. (1969). New concepts of kingdoms of organisms. *Science,* **163,** 150–159.

Wray, G. A., Levinton, J. S., & Shapiro, L. H. (1996). Molecuiar evidence for deep precambrian divergences among metazoan phyla. *Science,* **274,** 568–573.

Xiao, S., Zhang, Y., & Knoll, A. H. (1998). Three-dimensional preservation of algae and animal embryos in a neoproterozoic phosphorite. *Nature,* **391,** 553–558.

Young, J. Z. (1981). *The life of vertebrates* (3rd ed.). Oxford: Oxford University Press.

CHAPTER 7

Simple Nervous Systems and Behavior

MAIN GENERALIZATIONS OF CHAPTER 7

- *The vast majority of animals are characterized by relatively simple behavior and neural organization.*
- *A detailed series of basic properties common to the neurons of cnidarians and bilateral animals suggests that neurons are homologous. Therefore, behaviors dependent on neuronal properties may be based on evolutionarily conserved mechanisms.*
- *The simple systems approach has revealed the neural networks underlying a variety of behaviors.*
- *Basic forms of learning are observed in all animals possessing neurons. Neural plasticity may thus be considered a primitive condition among animals.*

The animal world has traditionally been divided into two major categories, that of the vertebrates, or animals possessing backbones, and that of the invertebrates. As I argued in ***Chapter 6,*** the term "invertebrate" carries little taxonomic meaning; it is just a catchall for a vast diversity of animals with extremely different Bauplans, whose only common feature appears to be, actually, the *lack* of a feature! Nonetheless, it is a convenient shortcut for referring to more than 30 different phyla, largely unknown from the behavioral point of view and characterized by relatively simple neural and behavioral organization.

Scientists have used this relative simplicity in a very positive way. Simple model systems are advantageous because they allow us to understand behavior from a cellular and network point of view. Although the systems are simple, this understanding permits the development of new concepts and methods that invariably influence the way in which more complex systems are studied. This chapter considers the diversity of invertebrates, their nervous systems, and their basic behavioral capacities, including reflexes, modal action patterns, orienting responses, and simple forms of learning, such as habituation and sensitization (more complex learning processes will be described in ***Chapters 13*** and ***14***).

1. THE INVERTEBRATE PHYLA: AN OVERVIEW

The kingdom Animalia includes between 31 and 36 phyla, depending on the taxonomist. This uncertainty reflects a lack of knowledge about the phylogenetic relationships of some of the groups. The term *phylum* must apply to a monophyletic group of animals with a distinctive Bauplan from which derived versions follow. For example, there is a distinctive body plan for the molluscs, even though there are many differences in the appearance of such molluscs as a snail, an oyster, or an octopus. One major problem is that the monophyly of certain groups is far from established (Willmer 1990). For example, it is not universally agreed that arthropods constitute a single phylum; some have argued that Arthropoda is a polyphyletic taxon and have recognized up to three different phyla. Similarly, whereas the monophyly of Animalia is widely supported, some taxonomists argue that sponges, cnidarians, and bilaterals could have evolved from different protist ancestors. ***Table 7.1*** provides a brief description of animal phyla for general reference. This classification follows Nielsen (1995) and differs from others in several respects—for example, what is usually treated as a single phylum, Chordata, is here treated as three separate phyla: Urochordata, Cephalochordata, and Vertebrata. The behavioral and neurobiological information reviewed in the rest of this chapter is restricted to a relatively small set of species from a few phyla.

1.a. Porifera. The simplest living animals are the sponges (Porifera). Their scientific name derives from the many pores that cover their bodies and allow for water and nutrients to penetrate the animal. They are distinguished from the flagellate protists (presumed animal ancestors) by the presence of fibrous proteins in the intercellular space, called collagen, widely considered a metazoan synapomorphy. Sponges also possess spermatozoa of the animal type and exhibit diploidy and meiosis. There are different types of cells but, unlike in other animals, cell differentiation is reversible. Sponges can be dissociated by pushing the animal through a fine filter; cells separate in small clusters and become reunited at the other side of the filter. Differentiated

TABLE 7.1 A Brief Description of the Animal Phyla

Phylum (Species)	***Description***
Porifera (5,000)	See *section 1.a.*
Placozoa (1)	*Trichoplax adhaerens*. A flat animal, 1–2 mm long, lives in association with algae and has a widespread distribution.
Cnidaria (8,000)	See *section 1.b.*
Sipuncula (320)	Unsegmented marine worms.
Mollusca (100,000)	Unsegmented animals with a head and a muscular foot that has been modified in a variety of ways. There are aquatic and terrestrial forms. Common forms include solenogasters, chitons, clams, snails, squids, and octopuses.
Annelida (15,000)	Segmented worms with a clear mouth and anus, head, nervous system, and circulatory system.
Onychophora (80)	Soft-bodied animals with unjointed pairs of legs. Well-defined sensory systems (antennae, eyes) and nervous system.
Arthropoda (>1,000,000)	Largest phylum. Segmented animals with an exoskeleton and paired, jointed appendages. Brain is dorsal, but the nerve cord with paired ganglia are ventral. Digestive tract is dorsal. Common species include horseshoe crab, spiders, crayfish, centipedes, and the insects.
Tardigrada (600)	Very small, segmented, freshwater animals with four pairs of legs.
Entoprocta (150)	Microscopic, sessile animals with a pseudocoelom and a digestive tract.
Ectoprocta (4,000)	Sessile, aquatic animals that form colonies.
Platyhelminthes (20,000)	Bilaterally symmetrical flatworms. Their digestive system has a single opening. No circulatory system.
Nemertini (900)	Mostly aquatic, cylindrical or flat ribbon worms.
Rotifera (1,500)	Pseudocoelomate animals, either elongated like worms or spherical. A circle of cilia in the animal's head appears to rotate like a wheel when in movement.
Acanthocephala (500)	Acoelomate parasitic worms lacking a digestive system and having a head equipped with numerous spines.
Chaetognatha (200)	Marine worms with a cylindrical body and a rounded head. They possess lateral fins and a horizontal tail fin.
Gastrotricha (430)	Small, mostly marine pseudocoelomate animals with an elongated body. Cilia are used to produce movement.
Nematoda (20,000)	Aquatic and terrestrial round worms, pseudocoelomates, and frequently parasites. Each species appears to have a constant number of cells in each organ. Adult *Caenorhabditis elegans*, for example, have 302 neurons and 34 cells in the intestine.
Nematomorpha (325)	Pseudocoelomate worms usually parasitic as larvae but free-living as adults.
Priapula (17)	Predatory, burrowing, cylindrical marine animals.
Kinorhyncha (150)	Small, marine, pseudocoelomate worms with segmented body.
Loricifera (100)	Microscopic animals living in various types of marine sediments.
Ctenophora (80)	Free-swimming, spherical comb jellies. They may be brightly colored and possess bioluminescence. Movement is produced by eight bands of cilia.

Table 7.1 A Brief Description of the Animal Phyla (*Continued*)

Phylum (Species)	***Description***
Phoronida (12)	Marine deuterostome worms that build a chitinous tube where they live. Ciliated tentacles around the mouth are used to obtain food.
Brachiopoda (300)	Marine deuterostome animals, referred to as lamp shells, possessing a pair of shells and resembling the unrelated clams.
Pterobranchia (20)	Marine deuterostome animals, often colonial.
Echinodermata (7,000)	Marine deuterostome animals (sea urchins and starfish), possessing five radial canals, with tubular podia in many species. Adults exhibit pentameral symmetry, but larvae are clearly bilateral.
Urochordata (1,300)	Usually sessile marine animals, called tunicates. The adult exhibits a reduced nervous system and no notochord, but both are clearly present in the free-living larvae.
Cephalochordata (25)	Marine animals resembling fish, called lancelets. They have a permanent notochord, a dorsal nerve cord, but no cartilage or bone.
Vertebrata (41,700)	Active deuterostome animals with complex sensory organs, brain, and cranium (see *Chapter 8*).

Note. Nomenclature and species count from Nielsen (1995). Notice that Chordata is not treated as a phylum in this classification.

cells may become ameboid and cluster with other such ameboids to form a new sponge. Tactile stimuli applied to epithelial cells can induce some responses, such as a closure of the pores, but such irritability is largely due to individual cells acting in isolation. There is no evidence that sponges have true neurons.

1.b. Cnidaria. Cnidarians are generally radially symmetrical, although some degree of bilaterality is observed in a few species. Some cnidarians display a complex life cycle, beginning with fertilization and followed by a sessile stage in which the animal, called a polyp, attaches itself to some substrate. Sessile polyps feed by extending a series of tentacles that surround the mouth and using them to capture prey. As they grow, polyps start producing medusas asexually. The medusa stage involves a pelagic, or free-swimming animal, formed by an umbrella-like structure with tentacles extending downward. This cycle characterizes the jellyfish (class Scyphozoa); however, the hydras (class Hydrozoa) and the coral and sea anemones (class Anthozoa) lack a medusa stage and exist only as polyps. The main synapomorphy of the Cnidaria is the cnidocyte, a type of cell specialized for a prey-catching function. Cnidarians are carnivorous animals. These cnidocytes are located in the animal's tentacles and contain a special device in the inside, the *nematocyst,* which consists of a coiled structure that can be released rapidly to seize a prey. The nematocyst is then discarded and a new one grows inside the cnidocyte.

Cnidarians have true neurons of the three general types: sensory, motor, and interneurons. Based on the appearance of animals very similar to extant cnidarians in the Ediacaran fauna, it could be speculated that the rate of evolutionary change in this phylum has been relatively slow. Evolutionary stasis seems to have been a major feature in the evolution of the Cnidaria. Therefore, it is plausible that an analysis of the neurobiological properties of the cnidarian nervous system might provide clues about the evolutionary origin of neural components and the basic functional properties of neural nets. Cnidarian neurons have many of the functional features that characterize the neurons of more recently evolved animals. The synaptic cleft is about 12 to 20 nm and the neurotransmitter vesicles appear variable in shape. Axons are not myelinated in most invertebrates, and thus the speed of conduction depends heavily on the thickness of the axon. Cnidarians exhibit giant fibers in a net that controls swimming movements in medusas, as described below.

Figure 7.1 shows intracellular recordings from neurons of the medusa *Cyanea capillata* (Anderson 1985). The recording system is relatively simple, as shown in the upper left corner of this figure. A stimulating electrode is inserted into one of the neurons (the presynaptic one) to deliver a depolarizing current. Since the *resting potential* of a neuron is slightly negative (inside negatively charged), a stimulus applied to the cell is said to have a *depolarizing* action, that is, to make the interior of the cell electrically less negative, or even positive, in relation to the intercellular space. Two other recording electrodes, one in each of the two neurons (the presynaptic and postsynaptic neurons), permit a detection of the electrical consequences of the stimulation. ***Figure 7.1-a*** shows that stimuli of various intensities produce graded potentials in the presynaptic neuron, but have no effects on the postsynaptic one. *Graded potentials* bear a proportional correspondence with the intensity of the stimulus, but they do not result in transmission across the synapse (i.e., such depolarizations are local). When the size of the graded potential reaches a threshold value, an *action potential* (*AP*) is generated presynaptically. APs are all-or-none depolarizations of the neuron, capable of traveling through the neuron's axon at constant speed and amplitude. In a *chemical synapse,* the arrival of an AP at the axon terminal causes the release of *neurotransmitter* molecules that were stored in vesicles. Neurotransmitter molecules dissipate in the synaptic cleft and some reach the postsynaptic membrane, where they attach themselves to a receptor protein and change the permeability of various ions through the membrane. Such change in permeability causes a gradual potential in the postsynaptic cell (called an *excitatory postsynaptic potential,* or *EPSP*), which, if sufficiently intense to reach the threshold, will cause the neuron to fire an AP. The last stimulation in ***Figure 7.1-a*** shows that an AP in the presynaptic neuron causes an EPSP followed by an AP in the postsynaptic neuron.

Whereas EPSPs and APs are familiar properties of neurons, ***Figure 7.1-b*** shows a feature that is not so commonly observed in studies with other animals. Usually, chemical transmission through the synapse is directional: from the presynaptic neuron to the postsynaptic neuron. In cnidarians, however, many synapses appear to be bidirectional. These recordings show that when an AP is generated in the postsynaptic neuron (as in ***E*** and ***G***), a small depolarization occurs about 1 msec later in the presynaptic neuron (marked with an arrow). Such an "echo" does not occur if the postsynaptic neuron exhibits only an EPSP, as shown in ***F.***

Cnidarian neurons share several additional properties with those of more advanced animals (Spencer 1989). For example, the synaptic delay in transmission (the time it takes for the neurotransmitter to travel through the cleft and stimulate the postsynaptic neuron) is within the range

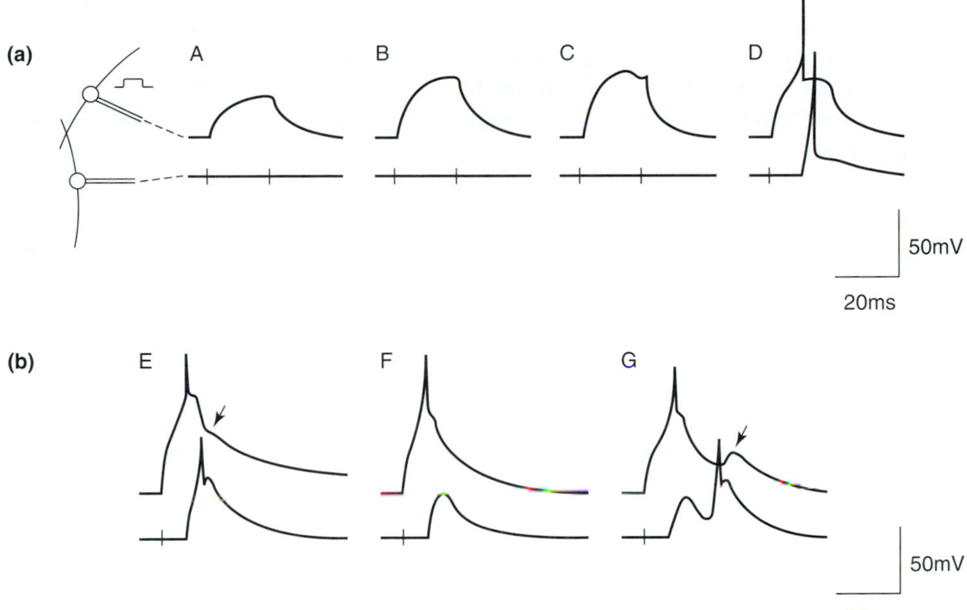

FIGURE 7.1. Intracellular recording from neurons of the scyphomedusa *Cyanea capillata* (Anderson 1985). ***(a)*** Basic experimental setting is sketched in the upper left corner. An intracellular electrode delivers a depolarizing current and also records the membrane potential in a presynaptic neuron. A second electrode records postsynaptic potentials. The electrophysiological responses are seen on the right. Subthreshold stimuli of increasing intensity produce excitatory postsynaptic potentials (EPSPs) of increasing magnitude in the presynaptic cell, but no changes in the postsynaptic cell (***A–C***). In ***D,*** a depolarizing current above threshold produces an action potential (AP) in the presynaptic cell, followed with some delay by an AP in the postsynaptic cell. The delay occurs because of the chemical synapse. ***(b)*** APs inducing another AP in the postsynaptic cell are characterized by a small depolarization in the presynaptic cell (see arrows in ***E*** and ***G***). This notch, or echo, occurs with a small delay, suggesting that it is caused by the release of neurotransmitter by the postsynaptic cell; it does not occur when the postsynaptic cell does not fire an AP (see ***F***).

observed in other species. Moreover, the release of neurotransmitter is dependent on the influx of calcium ions into the axon terminal, as is known to occur in other species. Hydrozoans also exhibit *electrical synapses* in which the APs diffuse with little or no delay between adjacent neurons. The swimming motor network of *Polyorchis penicillatus* displays a rate of spontaneous firing that seems to be caused by the spread of excitation through electrical synapses. An interesting aspect of the neurobiology of Cnidaria is the fact that these familiar properties combine with a relatively simple organization at the system level. Cnidarians do not exhibit the distinction between central and peripheral nervous systems that is so fundamental to more advanced animals. In most species, neurons are distributed in diffuse nets, although the aggregations of neurons observed in some cnidarians could be seen as simple ganglia.

Meech (1989) provided a description of the neural processes underlying a simple type of behavior in the jellyfish *Aglantha digitale:* swimming. There are two types of swimming in these animals; one is related to feeding, while the other is an escape response. During feeding, *Aglantha* moves in a cycle that takes minutes to complete. It passively sinks, with its tentacles extended to pick up food particles, until a slow, rhythmic set of contractions of the bell-shaped mantle drives the animal upward to reinitiate the cycle. The escape reflex is a much faster response to a tactile stimulus (several different potential predators have been shown to elicit this reflex), involving the rapid contraction of the bell-shaped mantle. Such contractions push water and propel the animal in the opposite direction. There are between one and three such contractions, the first one being the most powerful, displacing the animal to a distance of approximately five body lengths. Interestingly, these two types of swimming behaviors are controlled by the same set of neurons. *Aglantha* has eight giant axons originating in the margin and radiating toward the upper part of the mantle. These axons are about 40 μm in diameter. They activate a layer of muscle cells and a series of lateral motoneurons that innervate the muscles lying between the giant axons. Escape responses appear to depend on the differential activation of large populations of lateral motoneurons, resulting in the rapid contraction of muscles.

Substantial behavioral evidence suggests that cnidarians are capable of adjusting to changes in the environment. The ability to change and modify behavior by acquiring, storing, and retrieving information is referred to as *learning.* One of the simplest forms of learning, called *habituation,* consists of a decrease in the frequency or strength of a specific behavior resulting from the repetitive presentation of a relatively innocuous stimulus (more in ***section 3.a.*** below). Animals may initially react even to very mild stimuli, such as noises or moving objects, either by orienting themselves toward the source of stimulation or by exhibiting some form of protective response. However, these responses will tend to diminish in intensity when such stimuli repeat themselves, provided that there has been no other change in the conditions of stimulation.

Experimenters have looked at the habituation of protective responses in several species of Cnidaria (e.g., Haralson & Haralson 1988; Johnson & Wuensch 1994; Logan 1978; Rushforth et al. 1963). For example, bodily contractions induced by mechanical stimuli decrease gradually with repeated stimulation in hydras (*Hydra pirardi*), jellyfish (*Aurelia aurita*), and sea anemones (*Anthopleura elegantissima*). Sea anemones, for example, contract their bodies immediately after being stimulated with a jet of fresh water or a mild shock, and jellyfish in the polyp stage retract their tentacles and shorten their bodies when gently touched at the base of the tentacles. However, such defensive reactions tend to decrease when these stimuli are applied repeatedly.

Suppose that a sea anemone has been habituated to the repeated stimulation of a specific body location. Now, if different points of its body are stimulated in test trials, the sea anemone shows a gradient of *generalization of habituation:* Responding increases as the test location is farther removed from the training location. Moreover, if the animal remains undisturbed for an hour, the reintroduction of the habituating stimulus is accompanied by an almost complete reinstatement of the response, a phenomenon called *spontaneous recovery*. Interestingly, the rehabituation that follows can be faster than the original habituation of the response, suggesting that information of the initial exposure to the stimulus may be stored in the nervous system. Indeed, long-term retention of habituation over several days has been observed in sea anemones (Logan & Beck 1978).

There are at least three alternative explanations for behavioral changes like these. The most interesting possibility is that behavioral habituation reflects a change in synaptic transmission among neurons. However, behavior could decrease because of two other reasons: sensory adaptation and muscular fatigue. *Sensory adaptation* refers to the decrease in activity of the sensory receptor as a result of repeated activation; it is as if the animal were no longer perceiving the stimulus. *Muscular fatigue* refers to the exhaustion of the muscles that are being contracted repeatedly during the experiment; it is as if the animal were tired of responding. A simple manipulation can allow a distinction between the neural hypothesis (habituation reflects synaptic changes) and the peripheral hypothesis (habituation reflects receptor or effector changes). Suppose a novel, relatively intense stimulus is presented while the animal shows habituation to a target stimulus. For example, jellyfish habituated to a tactile stimulus were shaken for 2 s (their home tank was gently moved in a circular fashion) and then reexposed to the tactile stimulus. Such a switch in stimulation resulted in the reinstatement of the defensive response, an outcome that indicates that habituation could not be caused by peripheral factors and must thus reflect a type of neural plasticity. This phenomenon is referred to as *dishabituation* and is used to demonstrate the dependence of habituation on neural processes, rather than on receptor or muscle processes. Because the dishabituating stimulus is not expected to affect peripheral processes, dishabituation of a response should be observed only when habituation is caused by a neural, rather than peripheral, change. I will return to habituation and related learning phenomena in ***section 3***.

1.c. Traces of Early Bilaterals. As mentioned in ***Chapter 6***, ***sections 3.a*** and ***3.b*** (pp. 184–187), the oldest evidence of bilateral animals is found in *fossil traces* from the Vendian and Cambrian periods. An exciting aspect of this fossil evidence is that it provides clues about the behavior of these long-gone animals (Crimes 1992). The transition from the Precambrian (Vendian) to the Cambrian is marked by an increase in the diversity of these traces, which were generally formed in shallow-water environments. A second jump in diversity occurs during the Ordovician period and is probably related to the radiation of animals into deep-water environments. The diversity of fossil traces remains relatively constant until a new increase in deep-water traces is registered in the Cretaceous period.

The increase in the diversity of traces from the Vendian (late Precambrian) to the Tommotian and Atdabanian periods (both early Cambrian in age) is one that can be best described in terms of complexity, as can be appreciated in ***Figure 7.2.*** The earliest traces (Vendian) are straight burrows filled with sediments or, in some cases, superficial, measuring a few millimeters in diameter. Straight traces are recorded up to the Tommotian period, and their most significant change is their increased size. Also from the Vendian are traces characterized by what appears to have been random foraging search behavior, during which the animal seems to have crossed its own path in

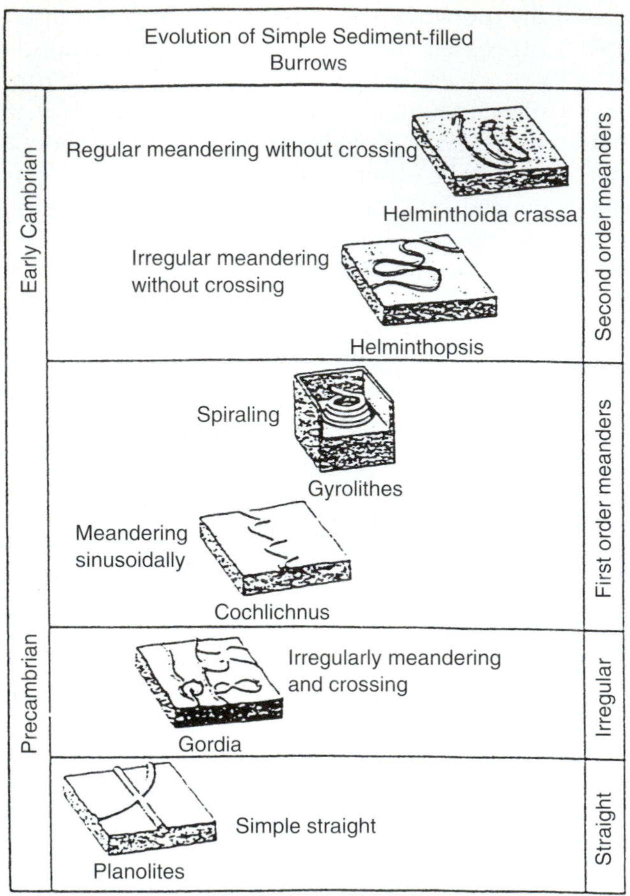

FIGURE 7.2. Evolution of simple sediment-filled burrows across the Precambrian-Cambrian boundary (Crimes 1992). Traces increase in complexity from straight lines to irregular meanders with crossovers, to sinusoidal, spiral, and other types of noncrossing meanders. Traces also increase in size, although this is not shown in the figure.

its wandering through the substrate. These traces are referred to as irregular meanders with crossings and are interpreted as grazing behavior: The animals were moving on a layer of sediment rich in microorganisms that served as food. Irregular meanders from the early Cambrian are also observed in the fossil record, but notably they tend to lack the crossings. These meanders are also interpreted as grazing patterns but are generally considered more efficient since the animal appears to have avoided locations visited previously, where food would have been depleted by its own behavior. Two other interesting types of traces are observed in the Vendian-Tommotian boundary: the sinusoidal and spiral meanderings. These are considered to be advanced feeding traces because of their efficiency in exploiting a feeding location.

Changes in trace complexity can also be appreciated by looking at the structure of the burrows. The straight, Vendian traces seen in ***Figure 7.2*** exhibit no branching. However, subsequent fossil traces show an impressive variety of branching patterns. In late Vendian deposits traces exhibit irregular branching, and in Cambrian rocks a variety of regular branching patterns appear. These are generally interpreted as feeding burrows, although some later specimens described as regular networks are interpreted as possible open tunnel systems.

Fossil traces have been attributed at least five basic functions: feeding, dwelling, resting, crawling, and grazing. A quantitative analysis of the relative frequency of these types of traces during the Vendian-Cambrian boundary suggests some interesting changes. For example, the proportion of simple feeding traces (the most common traces) declined during this period, whereas the proportion of grazing traces increased. It is possible that the decline of simple feeding traces is related to the evolution of more complex and efficient grazing patterns, but the evidence is still ambiguous. It is clear, however, that the transition from simple to complex burrowing patterns occurred relatively rapidly in shallow-water environments of the Vendian-Cambrian boundary.

One implication of the fossil trace evidence is that a remarkable evolution of new sensory-motor capacities occurred during the relatively brief period of the Vendian-Cambrian transition (about 25 million years). Behavioral complexity in burrowing and foraging patterns suggest the emergence of significant innovations in neural organization and function. Once established, some of such innovations may have been conserved for many millions of years. In fact, this could be a quite common pattern for neural evolution: a relatively short period during which some basic neural elements are established, followed by long periods of relative stasis in which minor structural and functional changes are evolved in response to specific ecological pressures.

An example of such neural stasis may be found in the neural circuitry underlying visual perception in arthropods. Such circuitry appears to be homologous even among insects and crustaceans, two classes thought to have diverged as far back as the Silurian and perhaps even earlier (Nielsen 1995). A conclusion of neural homology is based on a number of shared characters, both anatomical and physiological, displayed by the visual neural circuit of these animals (Osorio et al. 1997). The following basic properties have been observed in such animals as fruitflies and grasshoppers (insects), and crayfish (crustaceans). Large monopolar cells (LMCs), located in a structure called the lamina, underneath the compound eye, are anatomically very similar, with axons ranging between 3 and 5 μm. LMCs are the only neurons receiving inputs from the light receptors and are characterized in both insects and crustaceans by an unusual feature: They respond by propagating a graded potential, instead of the usual AP generated by most neurons. LMCs *hyperpolarize* (i.e., the interior of the neuron becomes more negative) when the receptor is directly stimulated, but they depolarize when the stimulus falls outside the receptor's field.

These and other similar shared characters suggest inheritance from a common ancestor, rather than convergence, and are striking in view of the extensive independent evolution of insects and crustaceans and their many behavioral differences. Insects are very active, diurnal, and flying animals, whereas crayfish are sluggish, nocturnal, and aquatic; yet their visual systems are organized according to similar neurobiological properties.

2. BEHAVIOR AND SIMPLE NEURAL NETWORKS

2.a. Basic Neural Properties. Neurons are organized into nervous systems. Despite species variations, these systems exhibit some common features. For example, they extend in an anterior-posterior axis and usually present an anterior enlargement, the *brain,* where neurons are clustered in relatively large numbers. Because bilaterally symmetrical animals generally move forward, the anterior part of the body encounters new stimuli as the animal moves. It is in the head where several key sensory systems (e.g., vision, taste, olfaction) are typically located, so it makes some sense to have the brain nearby as a center for processing sensory information.

In some groups, segmentation of the body is paralleled by a similar segmentation of the nervous system. Such clusters are called *ganglia,* and they typically contain neural circuits that control movement in specific body segments. A useful distinction is also made between the *central nervous system* (*CNS*) and the *peripheral nervous system.* All bilaterals have a true CNS, involving ganglia and the tracts that interconnect them, usually located ventrally with respect to the digestive system and separated from the nerves, sensory receptors, and motor endings located in the periphery. But just as the shape of the body changes drastically across species, so does the macroanatomical structure of the CNS.

Many species exhibit neural features that have played a key role in the development of research on the relationship between behavior and neurophysiological processes. For example, the absolute number of cells in these nervous systems tends to be small and even manageable from the technological point of view, which facilitates the identification of correlates between single cell activity and behavioral outputs. For example, the CNS of the adult nematode *Caenorhabditis elegans* contains only 302 neurons! Obviously, not all invertebrates are like this; for example, a ganglion in an insect may contain a hundred thousand neurons packed into the volume of a cubic millimeter, making it extremely difficult to register the neurons' activity concurrently with the insect's behavior.

Not only are the numbers of neurons reasonably small, but in some species their size is very large, thus facilitating recording and stimulation procedures. Large neurons are adapted for fast conduction. In vertebrates, conduction through the axon is facilitated by the presence of myelin sheets that cover and electrically insulate the axon, except for small points called nodes of Ranvier. APs travel by "jumping" from node to node and thus can achieve substantial speeds. Invertebrates lack myelin cells in their CNSs, but use *giant neurons* to solve the speed of conduction problem. Giant neurons are usually part of neural networks that control behaviors of obvious survival value that must be produced fast, such as antipredator responses. For example, much of the basic physiology of neurons was worked out in the giant axon of the squid *Loligo,* which can reach a diameter of 1 mm. This neuron is part of a circuit that controls the contraction of the mantle and results in the ejection of water through the funnel, used by the animal to propel itself and escape from a predator.

In some species, individual neurons are not only large but also easily identifiable across animals because they tend to develop in the same location within the ganglion. In the mollusc *Aplysia californica,* the cell somas are located in the periphery of a ganglion, which facilitates their direct observation under the microscope, as well as their monitoring in the course of a behavioral experiment. The outer layer contains no axons or dendrites, but only cell bodies. These neurons project a single axon toward the core of the ganglion, called the neuropil, and the dendritic branches emanate from the part of the axon closest to the cell soma.

This type of neuron is referred to as monopolar and is different from the bipolar morphology typical of vertebrate neurons. The position of a neuron in the ganglion and such properties as their spontaneous firing pattern, the pathway of the axon, and its connection to specific neurons can be used as individual markers of that neuron. Several neurons have been individually labeled in the abdominal ganglion of *Aplysia* (Kandel 1976). Experiments can thus be performed on exactly the same neurons (with the same connections and neurochemical properties) in several animals of the same species. In fact, these criteria can be used to identify homologous neurons in different species and compare their properties (see ***section 4*** below).

2.b. Reflexes. A useful strategy to understand the cellular basis of behavior is to start by selecting a simple instance of behavior and a simple nervous system. This approach, often labeled the *simple systems approach,* has led to substantial progress in our understanding of the ways in which neural networks generate behavior.

Reflexes are among the simplest and most pervasive of all behaviors. Several of the examples described previously in this chapter involved reflexes (e.g., the habituation experiments in cnidarians, ***section 1.b.***). A reflex may require as little as two components: a sensory neuron conveying afferent information into the CNS and making synaptic contact with a motoneuron that conveys efferent information into a peripheral structure, such as a muscle or a gland. More complex reflexes may involve interneurons that relay information between the afferent and efferent components. Together, this is referred to as a *reflex arc*. Physicians usually check the integrity of the CNS by inducing the patellar reflex with a gentle tap on the knee, or the pupilary reflex by projecting a light on the eye. As a result, the knee jerks and the pupil contracts. These are familiar examples of reflexes.

The gill-withdrawal reflex in *Aplysia californica* (Mollusca) has been studied extensively, and its underlying circuitry is relatively well understood (Kandel 1979). *Aplysia* is a marine slug which breathes by circulating water through its gill. Tactile stimuli to a variety of bodily parts lead to a retraction of the gill, a reflex that protects a vulnerable and vital structure. In laboratory experiments, the tactile stimulus is typically a jet of water applied to the siphon. As shown in ***Figure 7.3***, this produces a retraction of both the gill and the siphon, and these behaviors are mediated in part by neurons located in the abdominal ganglion. If the abdominal ganglion is removed or if its neurons are chemically inhibited, the gill-withdrawal reflex cannot be induced. This suggests that the abdominal ganglion is the site where this particular siphon-gill reflex arc is integrated.

Some neurons in the abdominal ganglion bring afferent information from the siphon's skin; it is these sensory neurons that detect the water-jet stimulus and relay that information to motor cells also located in the abdominal ganglion. Several of the identifiable neurons in the abdominal ganglion control the retraction of the gill, including neurons L7, LD_{G1}, LD_{G2}, RD_G, $L9_{G1}$, and $L9_{G2}$; some of these cells make direct connections with the gill. A selective lesion of neuron L7 or LD_{G1}, for example, may decrease the magnitude of the gill retraction by 30% to 40% of its full strength. So these two cells account for about 70% of the magnitude of this particular response.

A simplified version of the circuit responsible for the gill-withdrawal reflex is shown in ***Figure 7.4***. Eight sensory neurons are shown, each bringing information from the siphon. A localized stimulus to a point

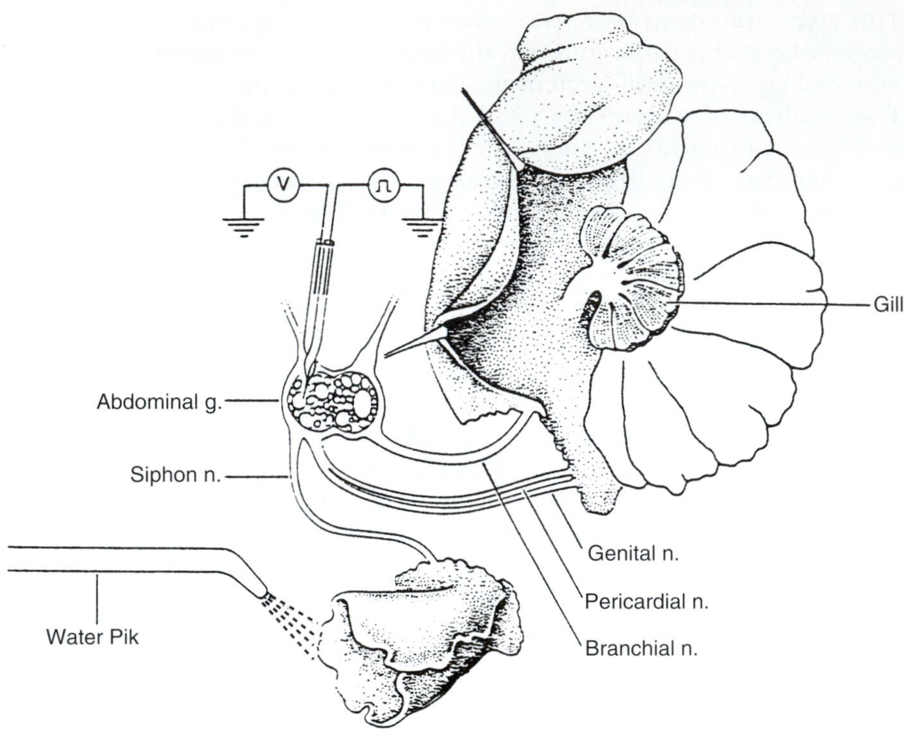

FIGURE 7.3. A scheme showing the main setting to study the gill-withdrawal reflex (GWR) in *Aplysia* (Kandel 1979). A water jet applied to the siphon acts as the stimulus. The siphon is isolated from the rest of the body, except for the siphon nerve which connects it to the abdominal ganglion. Afferent information is carried by sensory neurons into the abdominal ganglion, where it can be recorded by microelectrodes. The abdominal ganglion is also isolated from the body, except for its connections to the gill via several nerves. Motoneurons stimulate the gill and produce its contraction. The GWR is a protective response induced by potentially dangerous tactile stimuli to several parts of the animal's body.

about 0.5 mm in length in the siphon skin activates eight sensory neurons. These sensory neurons make connection both to six motoneurons that innervate the gill and to several interneurons. These connections are all excitatory so that when the sensory neurons are sufficiently activated they will induce APs in both motoneurons and interneurons. Since this reflex can be activated via a single synapse (that between the sensory neurons and the motoneurons), it is referred to as a *monosynaptic reflex.* But the interneurons play a regulatory role. Interneuron L16, for example, has inhibitory connections to other interneurons, whereas interneurons L22 and L23 have excitatory connections to the motoneurons inducing gill retraction. Therefore, this is also a *polysynaptic reflex* if the role of L22 and L23 is taken into account. These neurons potentiate the retraction by providing extra excitation, but such potentiation is regulated by the inhibitory influence of L16. There is also a population of interneurons activated by sensory stimulation of the siphon that inhibit the motoneurons and provide further regulation for this reflex (see Int. II in ***Figure 7.4***).

What about the retraction of the siphon itself? Remember that a stimulus applied to the siphon produces a retraction of both the gill and the siphon. One interesting aspect of this concurrent reflex involving the siphon, which appears to apply also for the gill, is that, at least within a certain range of

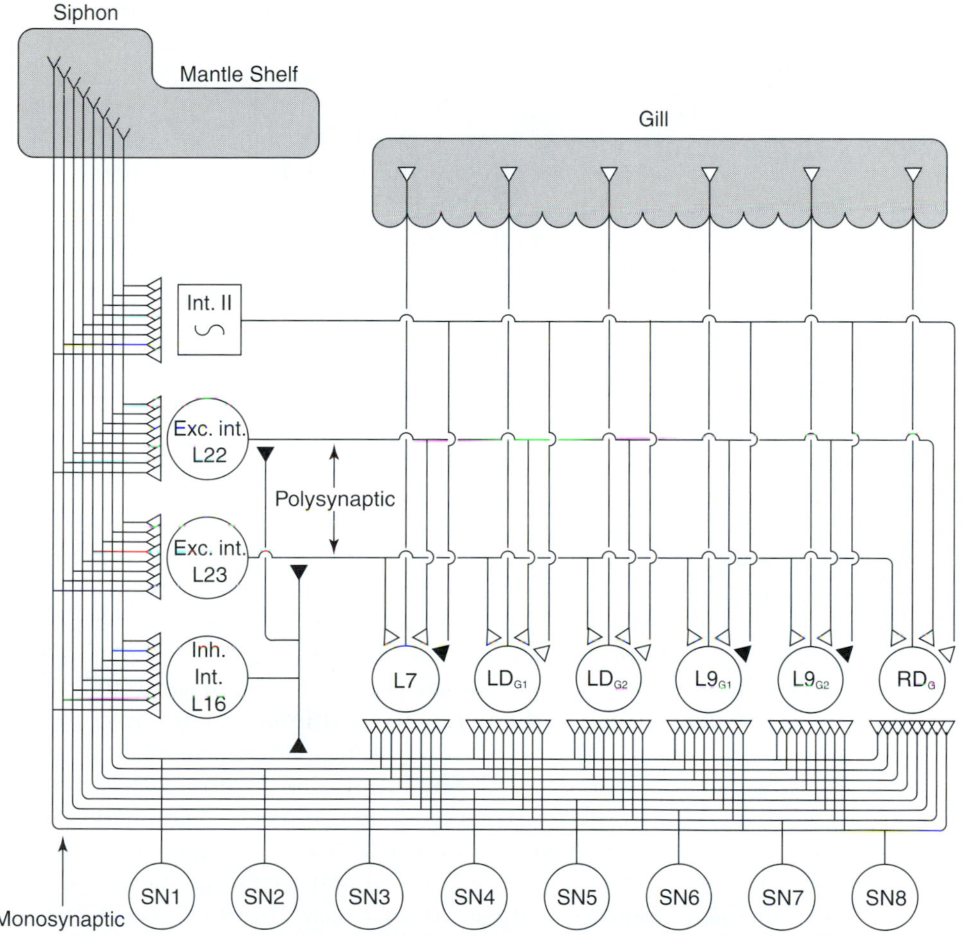

FIGURE 7.4. Circuit of the gill-withdrawal reflex (GWR) of *Aplysia* (Kandel 1979). The monosynaptic circuit involves direct synaptic connections between the mechanosensory neurons of the siphon (a total of about 24 sensory neurons innervate the siphon) and the motoneurons located in the abdominal ganglion. Sensory neurons also connect with excitatory and inhibitory interneurons. This is the polysynaptic component of the GWR circuit. The motoneurons have been individually identified.

stimulation (e.g., with relatively weak stimuli), the retraction of the siphon appears to be mediated entirely by a local, peripheral network. This siphon-withdrawal reflex can be elicited even if the siphon is isolated from the rest of the animal, including the abdominal ganglion. There are about 25 neurons located in the siphon itself that receive input from collateral branches of the sensory neurons and activate muscle fibers in the siphon. This is an example of a *peripheral reflex arc.* Such devices allow for the occurrence of local responses to relatively weak stimuli.

2.c. Modal Action Patterns. A reflexive response bears a relatively simple correspondence with the stimulus that elicits it. The response itself tends to be a relatively unified event. In some instances, however, a stimulus is capable of activating a more extensive pattern of responses, sequentially organized and produced as a unit that involves several discriminable elemental responses. A well-known example is provided by *Tritonia diomedia* (Mollusca), a marine sea slug that exhibits a well-coordinated escape reaction when it contacts a starfish, one of its typical predators (Willows & Hoyle 1969). Chemotactic stimulation induces the flattening of *Tritonia*'s body followed by vigorous dorsal and ventral contractions of the entire body used for swimming. Eventually, these contractions become more relaxed until the animal lands on the sea floor some distance away from the starfish.

This is an example of a *modal action pattern* (*MAP*), a concept that has its origins in the notion of fixed action patterns developed by classic ethologists on the basis of purely qualitative observations (see ***Chapter 1, section 4,*** pp. 15–18). MAPs are instances of sequentially organized behaviors with a clear function (e.g., escape from a predator) that, once activated, develop in a more or less ballistic manner. Although components may be recognized, a MAP is conceptualized as a behavioral unit that is typical of a particular species or of a group of closely related species (Barlow 1977). It is as if the stimulus were activating an entire neural program, and not just an isolated response; once activated, however, such a program unfolds independently of further stimulation. MAPs can be variable and exhibit a degree of adjustment to the environmental conditions in which they occur.

An example of such variability is provided by the sand-digging behavior of the squid *Sepia officinalis* (Mollusca), shown in ***Figure 7.5***. During periods of rest, *Sepia* sinks to the bottom and exhibits a pattern of behaviors that ends when the animal is completely covered by the substrate, usually sand. The entire sequence lasts for about 5 s. Sand digging involves a wiggling motion of the mantle accompanied by the ejection of water jets through the funnel. The funnel can be pointed forward and backward to remove sand from underneath the head and tail. Mather (1986) recorded various properties of this behavior in a group of *Sepia* tested in a tank in which the type of substrate was manipulated by increasing the size of the grains from fine sand (0.5 mm in diameter) to medium sand (0.7 mm), gravel (2.9 mm), and opaque plastic beads (3.7 mm). She found that digging was faster and involved a fewer number of behavioral components in the two sand conditions than in the gravel. When given a choice of substrate, *Sepia* chose fine and medium sand significantly more often than gravel. Interestingly, however, an assessment of variability in the dimensions of digging, such as the latency to start digging, the duration of digging, and the number of individual responses emitted during the entire episode, revealed a substantial amount of variability,

FIGURE 7.5. Schematic representation of the sand-digging modal action pattern (MAP) of the cephalopod mollusc *Sepia officinalis* (Mather 1986). The squid settles on the bottom **(*1–2*)**, blows water to the anterior **(*3*)** and posterior **(*4*)** parts of its body until is partially covered by sand. A lateral wiggling motion **(*5*)** results in the animal being almost completely covered by sand **(*6*)**.

both across individuals and also across trial types for one particular individual.

Behavioral variability can be estimated by computing the *coefficient of variation, CV,* according to the formula

$$CV = (SD/\overline{X}) \times 100.$$

where SD refers to the standard deviation (a measure of variability in a sample of scores) and $\overline{X}$ refers to the mean (a measure of a sample's central tendency). CV thus assesses the proportional relationship that exists between the SD and the X as a percentage. For example, if the duration of a particular behavior is estimated 10 times, $\overline{X} = 8$ s, and SD = 2, then CV = 25%; that is, the size of the variation corresponds to one quarter of the mean size. The smaller the CV, the less variable the behavior (i.e., more

fixed); in the extreme case, a really fixed action pattern should have a CV = 0 when there is no variation across various measurements of the behavior. The CV is preferred over the SD as an index of variability because of a common observation: The size of the SD tends to increase as the $\overline{X}$ becomes larger. If variability were estimated directly by the SD, then behaviors that are longer or involve more components would tend to exhibit larger SD values and therefore appear erroneously to be disproportionately more variable. CV permits a comparison among behavioral measures of different absolute parameters (e.g., short- vs. long-duration MAPs), as well as measured in different units (e.g., duration in s of the entire MAP vs. number of behavioral components in MAP).

Mather (1986) estimated CVs for three different measures of digging: the latency to start digging, the duration of the entire digging sequence, and the number of behaviors in a single episode of digging. All three measurements of digging behavior in this MAP were variable, although the latency to start digging was generally more variable than the duration of digging and the number of response components of the entire MAP. In the fine sand medium, CVs for latency to dig, duration of digging, and number of components were 98, 30, and 23, respectively. Although this particular MAP appears highly stereotyped, as demonstrated by the relatively constant CV for the number of components across various substrates, there is a considerable amount of variation in its various behavioral dimensions.

For comparison purposes, it may be useful to consider the variation reported for other MAPs, such as, for example, the duration of the "waving" display in several species of fiddler crabs (Arthropoda) as described in ***Table 7.2*** (Barlow 1977). Male fiddler crabs have asymmetrical claws; they advertise their presence by waving their large claws laterally. The display occurs whether or not females are present. In *U. rapax* and *U. speciosa,* the presence of a female causes the display to decrease in its total duration because of a shortening of the interval between successive movements of the claw. Interestingly, CVs increase in both species when the male displays in the presence of a female. In *U. rapax* CV goes from 27.4 to 36.1, whereas in *U. speciosa* it goes from 5.1 to 17.4.

TABLE 7.2 Variation in the Duration of Waving Displays in Different Species of Crabs

Species	*CV*
Uca virens	24.8–28.6
U. longisignalis	26.8–27.0
U. pugnax	13.5–24.8
U. rapax	27.4
U. speciosa	5.1

Note. Data from Barlow (1977).

2.d. Sequential Analysis. When MAPs involve several components, as in the digging behavior of the squid described above, or when a more complex set of behaviors is under analysis, the issue of behavioral variability takes a new turn. One can ask whether the components occur in a specific sequential organization. For example, Mather (1986) found that a forward water jet usually starts the digging sequence in *Sepia,* whereas the wiggling of the mantle tends to occur last. An estimation of the complete predictability of the digging sequence in *Sepia* demonstrates that the MAP is highly predictable in medium and fine sand; however, the sequence becomes less fixed when the animal is in a gravel medium.

Sequential analysis can provide interesting clues about the organization of behavior particularly in social interactions. A study of the agonistic behavior of the American lobster, *Homarus americanus* (Arthropoda) provides an appropriate illustration (Huber & Kravitz 1995). Pairs of lobsters were videotaped during 20-min-long test sessions in an aquarium. Each session was divided into discrete, 5-s-long beams of time; during each beam, 17 behavioral categories were scored using a procedure known as *one-zero sampling,* which consists of determining the presence vs. absence of each particular behavior during a particular time interval. Some examples of the behaviors scored were the following: "approach," defined as a lobster advancing towards the opponent and reducing the distance to less than one body length; "retreat," an animal moving or turning away from its opponent; "claw-up," one or both claws lifted and extended laterally; and "antennae whipping," one or both antennae vigorously hitting the opponent in a rapid sequence.

Once a sufficient amount of data have been obtained from observations, statistical treatments may be used to reduce the behavioral categories to clusters of responses that tend to occur together. One such procedure is called principal components analysis (PCA). Behaviors that correlate with each other are grouped into factors. In the case of the agonistic behavior of American lobsters, the list of behaviors was reduced by PCA to six factors, each loaded by a particular combination of behaviors (or by a single behavior in some cases), which exhibit either a positive or a negative correlation with the specific factor. These factors were found in the present study:

"Meral spread": body up, antenna up, claws up, and claw touch.

"Wrestling": antenna up, claw grasp, push/pull.

"Do-si-do": antenna whip, claws down, approach.

"Retreat": approach (negatively correlated), retreat.

"Antenna tap": antenna tap.

"Strike/Rip": strike/rip.

A matrix can then be constructed to show, for each animal, the frequency with which a transition from one of these categories to each of the other five categories occurred during test sessions. A statistical technique called the likelihood-ratio test can be applied to such matrices to determine which transitions occur more (or less) frequently than expected by chance. Moreover, the matrices obtained from different animals can be compared statistically for consistency.

The results can then be summarized in a scheme like that shown in ***Figure 7.6***. The behavioral factors are located in the periphery of the figure. Arrows represent transitions that occur with a probability higher than chance—such as, for instance, the transition between "wrestling" and "strike/rip," which is bidirectional. Dashes, however, represent behavioral transitions that occur rarely, if ever; for example, lobsters do not engage in "wrestling" if they have shown no prior agonistic behavior. Behavioral organization is illustrated by such features as the transition between "antenna tap" and "strike/rip," which is generally mediated by "wrestling."

2.e. Command Neurons. MAPs such as those of *Tritonia* and *Sepia* described above are activated by relatively specific stimuli acting as if they were playing back a tape that contains a complete set of instructions. These behaviors appear to be under the control of a network with a very specific architecture in which individual components influence each other in such a way that, once activated, the output of this small network will produce the MAP. Such networks

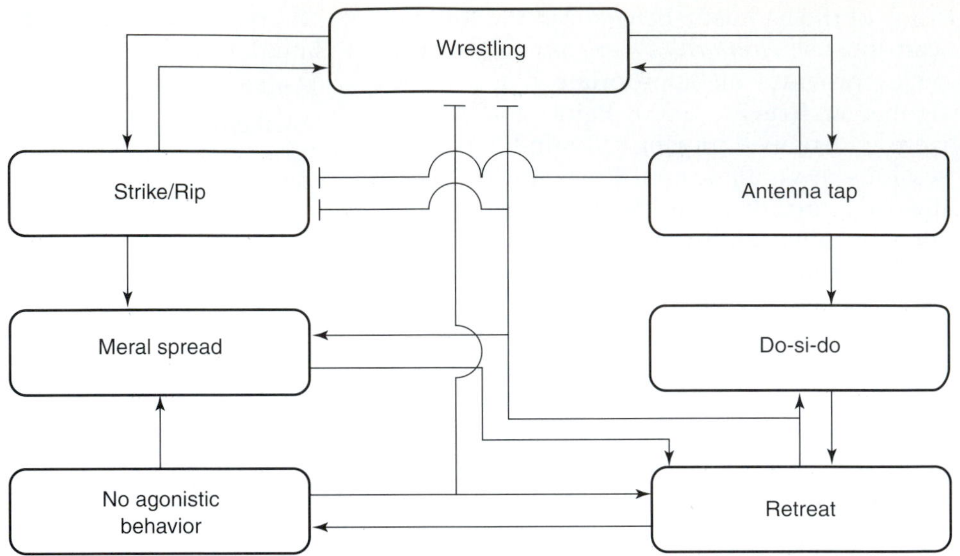

FIGURE 7.6. Sequential analysis of agonistic behavior in the American lobster *Homarus americanus* (Huber & Kravitz 1995). The behavioral components shown in this flowchart were determined by principal component statistical analysis. Transitions that occur with a frequency larger than expected on the basis of chance are shown by arrows. For example, the transition between "antenna tap" and "wrestling" is bidirectional and highly likely. By contrast, transitions that occur with a frequency lower than expected by chance are shown by dashes. For example, animals almost never go from "no agonistic behavior" to "wrestling" during test sessions.

could be generated as a result of a complex set of genetic instructions interacting with some fairly general environmental influences, such that they would develop essentially in the same way in most members of a particular species. What activates a network with these characteristics?

The simplest possibility is that the network responsible for the MAP has a single activating input. This is referred to as a *command neuron,* that is, a neuron capable of producing an input into the network that is both necessary and sufficient to activate the entire output (Kupferman & Weiss 1978). Although research has shown that the command decision is usually distributed among several cells, there are some examples in which a single neuron appears to take control over the occurrence of a MAP. One such example is provided by the crayfish *Procambarus clarkii* (Arthropoda) in which some escape responses are controlled by a command neuron (Wine & Krasne 1982).

Tactile stimulation of the crayfish's abdominal segments results in a vigorous flexion of the tail in an anterior and upward movement. At the same time, other ongoing responses are inhibited during the escape reaction. Tail flexion moves the animal away from the source of stimulation within 20 ms of stimulation. This delay is so small that it suggests the presence of few and fast neurons in the underlying circuitry. In order to understand a simple behavior like this escape reaction, researchers begin by mapping the circuit from the sensory receptors that detect the stimulus, to the interneurons located in specific ganglia in the CNS, and to the motoneurons and muscles that are directly responsible for the pattern.

There are probably thousands of tactile sensory cells (TSCs) located in the crayfish's tail. They project into the CNS, where they make contact with a far more limited number of sensory interneurons (SIs), some of which can be identified. These SIs synapse with lateral giant interneurons (LGIs), easily recognizable because of their large axons, reaching diameters of about 100 μm. There is an LGI in each ganglion and a ganglion in each abdominal segment, and they are interconnected. Each LGI connects to a variety of other cells, but most importantly, to the giant motoneurons (MoG) that innervate the flexor muscle cells of the abdomen and produce the escape response. The connections between SIs and LGIs and between LGIs and MoG involve electrical synapses, which, together with the giant axons of the LGIs and MoG, account for the speed of the escape reaction.

Electrophysiological experiments demonstrate that activity of the LGIs is both necessary and sufficient for the induction of the tail-flexion response. For example, electrical stimulation of an LGI with an intensity capable of producing a single AP results in the activation of the MoG responsible for tail flexion. This satisfies the sufficiency criterion. Moreover, an ingenious procedure may be used to demonstrate that LGI activity is also necessary for the escape response. Sensory cells that synapse with an LGI are stimulated in a manner that produces EPSPs in the LGI. At the same time, an electrode inserted in the LGI can be used to hyperpolarize this neuron, thus preventing it from generating APs. When the LGI is hyperpolarized, the escape response cannot be induced by sensory activation; however, when the LGI is allowed to generate APs, the same sensory stimulation will induce the escape response.

LGIs also affect other neurons that control behaviors that can potentially compete for expression with the escape response. Experiments have shown that LGIs may achieve this influence in a variety of ways. For example, LGI can inhibit neurons that excite muscles responsible for other responses, such as postural adjustments, but they can also excite neurons that normally inhibit such muscle cells. LGIs also inhibit sensory cells and interneurons so that input into the network is temporarily reduced.

2.f. Central Pattern Generators. Most examples of MAPs involve a coordinated sequence of individual responses controlled by a network referred to as a *central pattern generator* (*CPG*). CPGs are good candidates to coordinate any type of action requiring a rhythmic output. Flying, walking, swimming, scratching, heartbeat, breathing, and some ingestive behaviors are typically controlled by neuronal networks that act in a concerted manner. In these cases, however, the major alternative to a CPG is that of a reflex chain. A *reflex chain* also produces a rhythmic output but, unlike in the case of a CPG, the oscillation is maintained by constant sensory input into the circuitry. A CPG generates the pattern independently of sensory input. ***Figure 7.7*** compares these two types of circuits.

It is possible to distinguish between reflex chains and CPGs by surgically eliminating the sensory inputs from the area of the body involved in the behavior. This procedure, called deafferentation, should result in gross behavioral alterations if the cir-

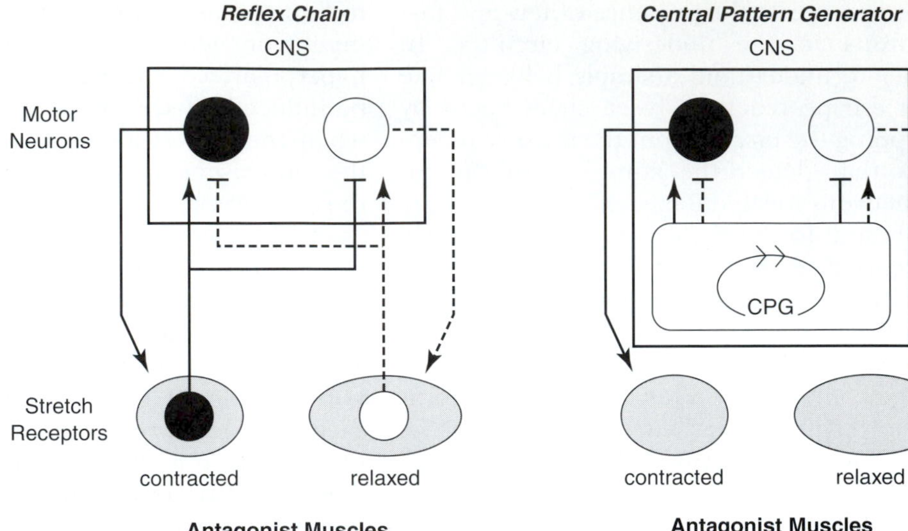

FIGURE 7.7. A comparison of the circuitry underlying a reflex chain and that of a central pattern generator (CPG). The final output is essentially the same. However, the reflex chain coordinates its outputs via afferent sensory inputs, whereas the CPG coordinates its output via its own internal architecture and independently of afferent input. Deafferentation is one of the main experimental procedures to determine if a particular behavior is controlled by a reflex chain or by a CPG.

cuitry is based on a reflex chain, but it should leave the behavior relatively unaffected if the circuitry is a CPG. Such an experimental approach was used to determine if the swimming behavior of the leech *Hirudo medicinalis* (Annelida) is controlled by a CPG (Kristan & Calabrese 1976). Leeches swim by oscillatory dorsoventral movements that require an alternate activation and inhibition of muscles. The leech's body produces a wave that moves toward the posterior end of the animal.

One problem with deafferentation is that the sensory fibers bringing afferent impulses into the CNS usually run side by side with motor fibers bringing efferent impulses into the muscles. Therefore, cutting the nerves results in the isolation of the CNS from peripheral influences. One usual procedure consists of isolating the CNS and recording from various nerves to determine if there are activity patterns analogous to those observed during swimming in the intact animal. Obviously, it may be necessary to stimulate sensory fibers to initiate the output, but the question is whether the pattern will persist for some time in the absence of sensory input. Moreover, such pattern of activity should display a cycle duration that coincides with that of the swimming movements in the intact animal. Experiments with the leech show that several coordinated bursts of activity can be obtained after a short stimulus from different nerves; these bursts closely match the temporal properties of swimming observed in the intact animal. For example, in intact animals the cycle period between bursts of activity varies between 350 and 2,000 ms, whereas in the isolated CNS preparation the cycle is about 385 ms long. Moreover, the undulating wave progresses toward the posterior end at a speed of from 19 to 37 ms per body segment in the intact animal, and at a speed of 20 ms per body segment in the isolated CNS preparation. It appears then that each ganglion in the CNS contains a CPG that controls the local muscles as well as the CPG located downstream. This does not completely rule out the possibility that fine tuning of this network requires sensory input, but it suggests that a large amount of coordination in behavior can be achieved by endogenous oscillators.

Seemingly simple behaviors may demand a complex interaction of CPGs distributed among various ganglia. For example, the mollusc *Aplysia californica* forages for seaweed in intertidal areas where the sea meets the coast in southern and Baja California. Feeding behavior involves the activation of muscles in the buccal and lip areas in a rhythmic fashion. The opening and closing of the lips is coordinated with movements of the mouth. These responses are controlled by a variety of interacting CPGs distributed in the buccal and cerebral ganglia (Perrins & Weiss 1996).

Figure 7.8 shows some of the basic connections between these CPGs and the motoneurons controlling muscles in the lips and buccal area. In the cerebral ganglion, CPGs located in each half of the ganglion control muscles in the same side of the body. This ipsilateral control may allow for asymmetrical lip movement when seaweed activates predominantly one side of the lips. Notice, however, that these cerebral CPGs are regulated by the buccal CPGs as well as by the very motoneurons they control in

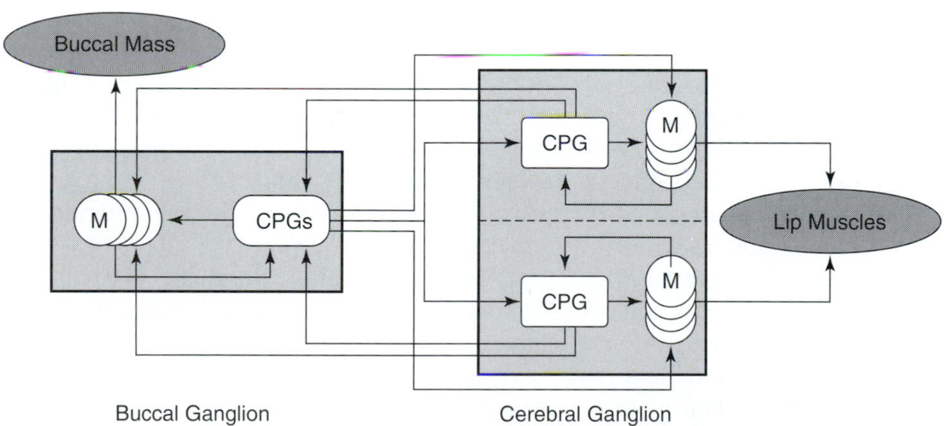

FIGURE 7.8. Interactions among central pattern generators (CPGs) controlling feeding behavior in *Aplysia californica* (Perrins & Weiss 1996). The cerebral ganglion contains one CPG in each side, each controlling ipsilateral lip muscles via ganglion motoneurons. These CPGs are influenced, in turn, by CPGs located in the buccal ganglion, which also bypass the CPG of the cerebral ganglion and influence directly the motoneurons controlling the lip muscles. CPGs do not act in complete isolation.

the cerebral ganglion. Similarly, the buccal CPGs are regulated by input from the cerebral CPGs and also from the buccal motoneurons they control. Although the control of buccal and lip muscles is achieved by their own CPGs, these do not operate in isolation from each other. Rather, there is profuse reciprocal regulation among CPGs, a feature that may allow these animals to use the same network to regulate a variety of feeding behaviors.

3. Behavioral and Neural Plasticity

Are these reflexes and MAPs modifiable? Are animals able to make behavioral adjustments to cope with changes in their environment? Research with cnidarians (see ***section 1.b.,*** pp. 228–229) shows that animals with the simplest nervous systems are able to display some degree of plasticity. Plasticity then appears to be a primitive property of nervous tissue. The term *plasticity* refers to the ability of neurons and synapses to modify their functioning as a result of use and disuse. When this concept of modifiability is applied to behavior, comparative psychologists talk about learning—that is, the ability of organisms to acquire information by individual experience and to use that information to change their own behavior. The simplest types of learning involve behavioral changes that occur as a result of exposure to a single, isolated event, such as in habituation (briefly mentioned previously in this chapter) and sensitization (see ***section 3.f.*** below). These learning phenomena are based on various processes of neural and synaptic plasticity that have been discovered through the development and intensive study of simple systems.

3.a. Properties of Habituation. Let's consider habituation again, now in greater detail. Animals often react to changes in the environment either by orienting toward the source of stimulation or by developing some type of protective response. Other activities that were in progress at the time, such as feeding or courting, may be disrupted or arrested. It is as if the animal were assessing the potential risk afforded by the environmental change. Habituation to a particular event occurs when that event is relatively mild or innocuous, and it translates in the animal's ability to prevent further orienting or protective responses. As a result, the animal can resume normal activities. An organism totally incapable of habituating its reactions to inoffensive events would be constantly disrupted and its fitness seriously compromised. Habituation is, therefore, a way of learning to ignore stimuli that have proven to be unimportant in biological terms. It is not surprising that behavioral habituation is a widespread learning phenomenon. Most, if not all, animals with nervous tissue are capable of detecting a wide range of novel events in their environment and are thus exposed to the problem of distinguishing between potentially harmful and harmless stimuli. Habituation provides a mechanism for this function.

Thompson and Spencer (1966) described nine properties of habituation that have become a useful guideline for research. Some were briefly introduced in a description of habituation in cnidarians (see ***section 1.b.***, pp. 228–229), including spontaneous recovery, generalization of habituation, and dishabituation. ***Figure 7.9*** shows an ideal representation of these nine properties.

(1) The decrease in response frequency or strength that results from the repeated

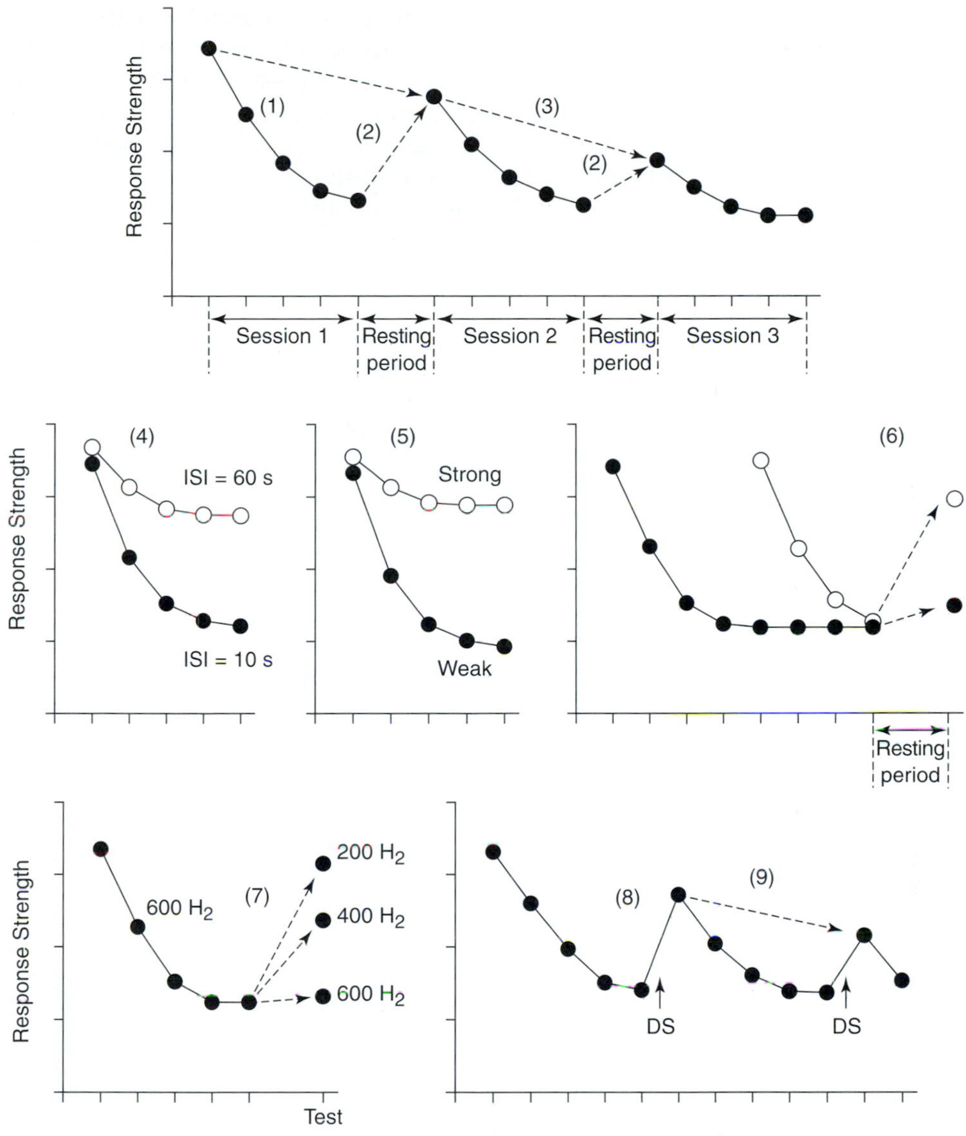

FIGURE 7.9. An idealized representation of Thompson and Spencer's (1966) nine properties of habituation. The numbers in parentheses correspond to each of these properties as described in the text. DS stands for dishabituating stimulus.

presentation of a stimulus is usually a negative exponential function of the number of stimulus presentations. This implies that most of the decrement in response strength occurs early in training and that the amount of change diminishes with the number of stimulus presentations.

(2) If the animal is given a period of rest (i.e., no presentations of the habituating stimulus) after habituation of the response has been achieved, the response will tend to recover over time. The longer the resting period, the greater the recovery of the response. This is called spontaneous recovery.

(3) Suppose that a stimulus is presented in three consecutive sessions, five times per session and once every 30 s; further suppose that there is a resting period of 2 hr between consecutive sessions. The first trial in each of the three sessions will likely yield a higher response level than the last trial of the preceding session because of spontaneous recovery. However, the level of recovery in the first trial will tend to diminish across the three sessions. This is referred to as *habituation of habituation,* and it suggests that there is some amount of retention across the resting interval.

(4) The rate of habituation is faster with shorter interstimulus intervals (ISIs). That is, more frequent presentations lead to faster and deeper response decrements. This is referred to as the *ISI effect.*

(5) Similarly, the rate of habituation is faster with relatively weaker habituating stimuli. That is, *stimulus intensity* and rate of habituation are negatively correlated. In fact, no habituation may occur if a stimulus is very strong. For example, it is hard to habituate to tooth pain.

(6) Suppose now that a response has been habituated but the stimulus continues to be presented for a number of extra trials; what effect this would have on the amount of spontaneous recovery? Although a response cannot occur less than zero times, and so the extra trials would seem to be producing nothing "extra" to this response, the amount of spontaneous recovery can be substantially reduced by overtraining. This is referred to as *below-zero habituation* because it is as if response strength would have dropped below the minimum during overtraining. Below-zero habituation highlights the risk of equating learning and behavior: Although performance does not change during the extra trials, learning appears to continue for some time. This is called the *learning-performance dichotomy* (see ***Chapter 13, section 1.a.***, pp. 490–491).

(7) Habituation is relatively specific to the properties of the stimulus that has been presented repeatedly. This means that similar stimuli would be able to evoke some degree of response suppression, but as the similarity is reduced, the response would show progressively more recovery. This is called generalization of habituation.

(8) The presentation of a novel stimulus, usually also relatively intense, intermixed with the presentation of the habituating stimulus, can lead to substantial recovery of the response. This is referred to as dishabituation, and, as mentioned previously, it is used to distinguish between neural and peripheral causes of response decrement. Only behavioral decrements caused by neural interactions are considered examples of habituation.

(9) But there is also *habituation of dishabituation:* if the dishabituating stimulus is in turn repeatedly presented, its ability to restore the response diminishes.

All together, these properties provide a coherent set of criteria for classifying an instance of behavioral change as habituation. Any response that fulfills these criteria is very likely to be under the control of neural processes within the CNS of the organism. Peripheral processes, such as sensory adaptation and muscular fatigue, cannot fully explain dishabituation and also fail to account for stimulus intensity effects. For example, why should habituation be slower with intense stimuli if they are likely to activate the receptors and muscles more strongly and lead to stronger adaptation and fatigue?

3.b. Habituation of Reflexes and MAPs. The gill-withdrawal reflex of *Aplysia* (***section 2.b.***) and the escape MAP of *Tritonia* (***section 2.c.***) exhibit many of the properties of habituation described above. The escape MAP of *Tritonia* can easily be induced with a jet of sodium chloride applied to the caudal region of the animal (Frost et al. 1996). Experiments show that the application of a relatively strong habituating stimulus at a rate of once every 2 min leads to a negatively exponential function of decay for the swimming response. In this case, habituation is reflected in a reduction in the number of dorsoventral contractions from about eight cycles during the first trial to about three cycles in the tenth trial.

Swimming also shows spontaneous recovery if the habituated *Tritonia* is left undisturbed during various periods of time. Just 5 min after the tenth trial, the number of dorsoventral cycles recovers 24% of its original strength; during the first hr after the tenth trial, recovery reaches 50%. Such a fast rate of spontaneous recovery may explain, at least in part, why habituation proceeds faster with shorter ISIs. In *Tritonia,* for example, habituation was faster when the habituating stimulus was presented once every 2 min rather than every 10 or 30 min.

Results such as these (i.e., negative exponential decrement, spontaneous recovery, and ISI effects) can be accounted for in terms of changes in the CNS, as well as in terms of peripheral changes. Perhaps the decrease in the swimming response is caused by sensory adaptation or muscular fatigue. These alternative explanations are eliminated by the dishabituation experiment in which a different stimulus, presented after habituation has taken place, leads to the recovery of the response. It turns out that dishabituation is hard to obtain in *Tritonia,* particularly if the swimming response has not been completely eliminated by training. But dishabituation is a regular feature in many other preparations. For example, *Aplysia*'s siphon-withdrawal reflex (see ***Figure 7.3***), habituated after repeated administration of a water jet, can be easily dishabituated by the delivery of tactile or electric stimulus to the animal's tail (Marcus et al. 1987).

Notice that the dishabituation experiment requires careful consideration of temporal parameters. The animal is being exposed to a habituating stimulus at a regular rate, say ISI = 1 min. Ideally, the dishabituating stimulus should be presented during the ISI and without disrupting the temporal presentation of the habituating stimulus. If the ISI is lengthened during the presentation of the dishabituating stimulus, it would be unclear whether the recovery of the response was caused by dishabituation or by spontaneous recovery. Moreover, the performance in the trial immediately following the presentation of the dishabituating stimulus should be compared to the performance of a control group that did not receive the dishabituating stimulus.

Figure 7.10 shows a clear example of dishabituation in the crab *Chasmagnathus granulatus* (Arthropoda). The procedure involved passing a shadow over the animal that simulates the presence of a predator. Crabs respond to the shadow by increasing their activity, but activity decreases as the shadow is presented repeatedly. However, if a tactile stimulus is applied to the crab's carapace, then there is a measurable recovery of the response both in comparison with the previous trial and with a control group not exposed to the dishabituating stimulus (Brunner & Maldonado 1988).

3.c. Short-Term and Long-Term Habituation. Several lines of evidence suggest that at least two types of habituation are distinguishable on the basis of the speed at which the habituated response recovers its strength after training. Some training protocols induce a type of habituation that recovers almost completely within hours; this is referred to as *short-term habituation.* Other protocols, however, induce a response depression that may last for days after training; this is called *long-term habituation.* This distinction is important because different mechanisms appear to determine these two types of habituation, as will be shown below.

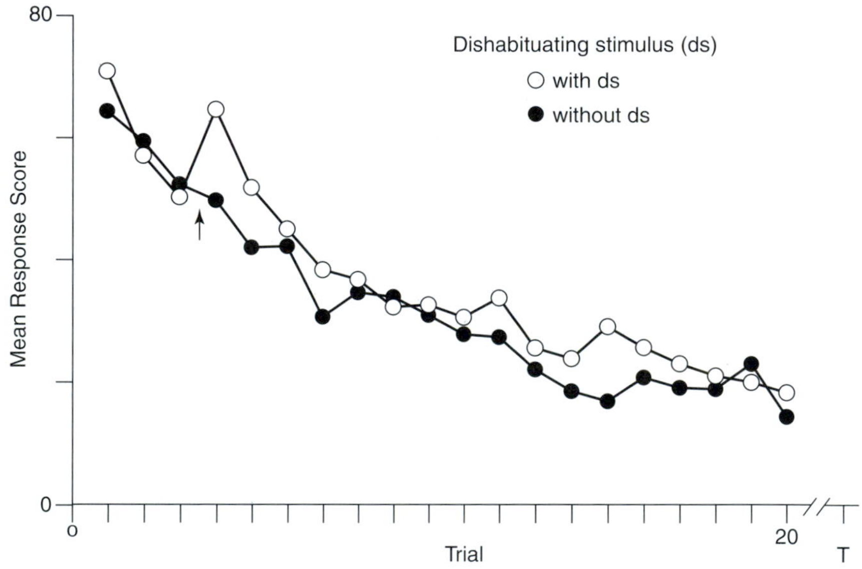

FIGURE 7.10. Dishabituation of shadow-induced activity in the crab *Chasmagnathus granulatus* (Brunner & Maldonado 1988). Crabs are placed in a container and a shadow (simulating a predator, such as a bird) is passed over the animal at regular intervals (ISI = 1 min). The arrow marks the point between the third and fourth trial in which a dishabituating stimulus was introduced: a tactile stimulus on the crab's carapace. This was done without disrupting the timing of the shadow presentations. Trial 4 shows a recovery of activity, but only in the group exposed to the dishabituating stimulus.

Several training variables determine how long it would take for a habituated response to recover. For example, activity induced by a shadow in the crab *C. granulatus* habituates significantly during the session when given 5 or 10 training trials (short-term habituation), but the response is fully recovered 24 hr later. However, simply increasing the amount of training trials to 15 or more leads to substantial response decrements in a retention test administered the following day (Pedreira et al. 1998).

The distribution of trials in time also determines the extent of the response recovery the day after training. In *Aplysia californica,* for example, 40 training trials administered in succession during a single session lead to complete recovery within 24 hr of training. However, if the same 40 trials are now distributed over four daily sessions of 10 trials each, then the response shows signs of depression even a week after training (Carew et al. 1972). Thus, whereas massed training leads to short-term habituation, distributed training induces long-term habituation.

3.d. Neural Basis of Short-Term Habituation. Several features make habituation a good candidate for a cellular analysis of a simple form of learning. The behavioral properties of habituation are well established, and the underlying circuitry of some of the reflexes that undergo habituation is also known. Habituation can actually help us understand one of the most intriguing puzzles of neural functioning: How is it that information is acquired and stored in the CNS of animals?

The nematode *Caenorhabditis elegans* is a good candidate for studies of the cellular basis of habituation because of its simple CNS (recall that the adult hermaphrodite has only 302 neurons in the CNS). Moreover, its neurons are located in the same area and make the same synaptic connections across animals. In fact, there is a database of information about the approximately 5,000 chemical synapses and 2,000 electrical synapses (White et al. 1986). Therefore, the task begins at the behavioral end, with the identification of a model behavior that can be used to study the underlying circuitry, and it proceeds by identifying the location of the site of plasticity. One such preparation involves the tap-withdrawal response (TWR), a reaction induced by mechanosensory stimuli (a tap on the side of the plate where the animal is placed produces a vibration of the substrate; see ***Figure 7.11-a***) consisting of a reverse swimming response (***Figure 7.11-b***). These animals are very small, about 1 cm in length, and thus must be observed under a microscope. Training sessions are videotaped, and the behavior is scored by means of special software. The length or distance of the reverse swimming response can thus be quantified. In addition, individual nematodes can be immobilized and subject to single-cell ablations using a surgical laser. This technique permits the elimination of a specific, individually identified neuron; subsequent behavioral testing determines the extent to which that particular neuron participates in the habituation of the TWR. Reverse swimming also occurs spontaneously; and it can also be induced by thermal stimuli (a heated plate placed close to the nematode but not touching the animal or the medium through which the animal is moving).

Short-term habituation of the TWR shows many of the properties of habituation described previously. For example, it can be dishabituated, and it exhibits ISI effects. Wicks and Rankin (1997) have shown that the reverse swimming that occurs in response to tapping is mediated by the same locomotor CPG that underlies sponta-

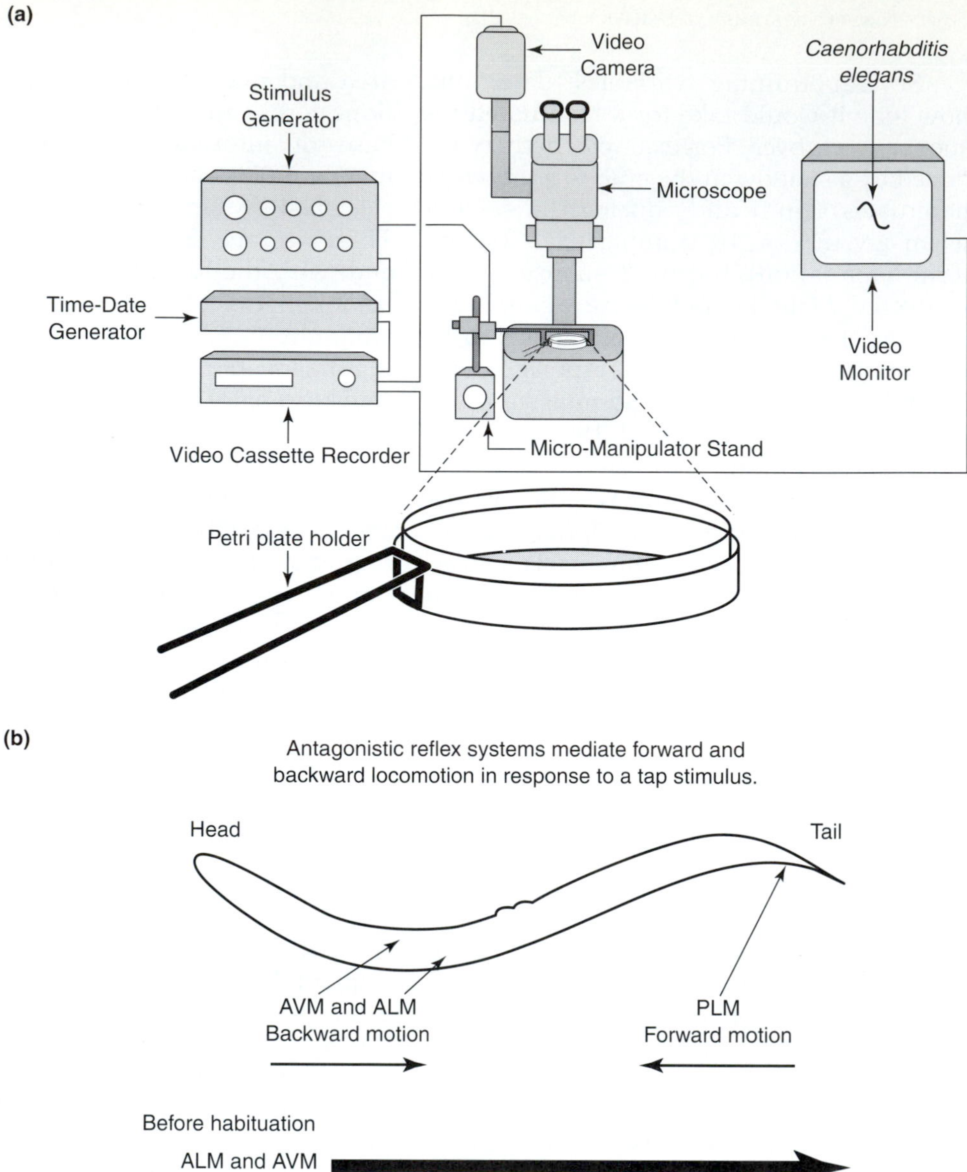

FIGURE 7.11. ***(a)*** Experimental setting to study the tapping withdrawal response (TWR) in *Caenorhabditis elegans.* The animal is placed in a petri plate and a mechanical tapper controlled by a stimulus generator provides the mechanical stimulation of the plate. A camera attached to a microscope tapes the session, and the behavior of the nematode can be quantitatively evaluated from the tape. ***(b)*** AVM, ALM, and PLM refer to mechanosensory neurons that respond to the tap stimulus. Activity in these sensory neurons determines whether the animal moves forward or backward. Before habituation, the backward response to a tap stimulus is very strong. (Drawing courtesy of Catharine Rankin.)

neous reverse swimming. However, when the TWR was subject to habituation, the number and frequency of spontaneous reverse swimming behaviors was not affected. Similarly, reverse swimming elicited by a thermal stimulus was not affected by prior habituation of that response by tapping. This information suggests that habituation of the TWR must occur within the pathway involving mechanoreceptors and not in the locomotor pattern generators or motoneurons controlling reverse swimming. If the latter were the case, then habituation of the TWR should have affected both spontaneous reverse swimming and the reverse swimming elicited by stimuli other than tapping.

The location of the site responsible for short-term habituation has been identified in the case of the gill-withdrawal reflex (GWR) of the mollusc *Aplysia californica*. As shown in ***Figure 7.3,*** the GWR has a monosynaptic pathway that connects sensory neurons detecting information from the siphon and motoneurons innervating the gill muscles. The critical synapse is located in the abdominal ganglion. This ganglion can be isolated from the animal and maintained in a seawater solution long enough to perform habituation experiments (Castellucci & Kandel 1974). The nerve carrying sensory information from the siphon can be electrically stimulated (the habituating stimulus), and activity of one of the critical motoneurons, labeled L7, can be monitored as an output (the response). Repeated activation of the sensory neuron does not affect its own ability to generate an AP, but the EPSP elicited on L7 decreases in magnitude. This decrease in the postsynaptic EPSP is not caused by interneurons, but it results from the repeated activation of the synapse between the sensory neuron and L7. Interestingly, if L7 is repeatedly stimulated, its ability to produce an AP and the magnitude of its own EPSPs are not diminished; this suggests that the source of synaptic plasticity is in the presynaptic sensory neuron.

Because short-term habituation of the GWR is mediated by a single synapse that undergoes a decrease in its excitability, the phenomenon is referred to as *homosynaptic depression*. Homosynaptic depression is caused by a decrease in the amount of neurotransmitter released by the sensory neuron as a result of an AP. Repeated activation reduces the influx of calcium into the sensory neuron's axon terminals. Calcium ions (Ca^{++}) are responsible for mobilizing the vesicles that store neurotransmitter molecules toward the presynaptic membrane, where the vesicles' contents are released into the synaptic cleft. Short-term habituation of the GWR in *Aplysia* is, therefore, a presynaptic phenomenon.

3.e. Long-Term Habituation. Could similar cellular changes, only more prolonged and intense, lead to long-term habituation? While it is true that long-term habituation depends in part on homosynaptic depression, there is more at play. In order to sustain a memory for relatively long periods, the sensory cells undergo structural changes.

Homosynaptic depression was observed after a spaced training protocol in which animals received five daily sessions, each involving 10 presentations of the siphon stimulus (Castellucci et al. 1978). EPSPs obtained from neuron L7 after 1, 7, or 21 days of habituation training were significantly depressed relative to those of control animals that had not been exposed to spaced training. These L7 EPSPs were obtained by inducing a single AP in the sensory neuron. How could such functional changes be sustained over the several days intervening between training and testing of the GWR?

In part, long-term habituation is achieved by the functional deactivation of synaptic connections between sensory and motor neurons. A functional survey showed that only about 30% of the synaptic connections of sensory neurons with L7 are functionally active in habituated animals; by contrast, about 90% of such connections are active in control animals. Although the actual connections remain in place, long-term habituation training reduces the number of sites at which sensory neurons can effectively influence motoneurons. This is called *functional disconnection.*

Interestingly, these changes in synaptic efficiency induced by long-term habituation training can be easily and rapidly reversed by a dishabituating stimulus (Carew et al. 1979). Suppose that habituated *Aplysia* receive an intense electric shock delivered to the head region 2 hr after training and are reexposed to the habituating stimulus after 2 hr. Such dishabituating treatment results in the reinstatement of the GWR to a level of about 70% of the original response strength; habituated animals not exposed to the head shock exhibit a response level of about 10% of the original strength.

3.f. Dishabituation and Short-Term Sensitization. As mentioned before, habituation is impaired when the habituating stimulus is relatively intense and it is reversed by the presentation of a novel, dishabituating stimulus. In fact, responses elicited by relatively intense stimuli can actually exhibit an increase in strength over repeated presentations of the stimulus. This is referred to as *sensitization,* and, in a way, it can be treated as the behavioral opposite to habituation. Unlike habituation, which is specific to the habituating stimulus, sensitization is generally considered a change in the internal state of the organism. A sensitized animal tends to react to almost any stimulus change in the environment. Intense stimuli can put the animal into an alert mode that results in increased responsivity to anything currently happening in the environment. There are short-term and long-term versions of sensitization; let's deal first with the short-term sensitization effect—an increase in response strength that results from the repeated presentation of a relatively intense stimulus and that is fully reversed within hours after training.

In the marine mollusc *Tritonia diomedea,* stimulation with a jet of water leads to an escape response that habituates after repeated trials. However, such a response is elicited under natural conditions by *Tritonia*'s predators, usually starfish. If the water jet is replaced by contact with the starfish *Pycnopodia helianthoides,* one of *Tritonia*'s natural predators, then escape swimming undergoes sensitization (Frost et al. 1998). The escape MAP involves a preparation stage (during which *Tritonia* shortens its body), followed by cycles of dorsoventral contractions. Sensitization is observed in terms of a decrease of the length of this preparation time, a faster onset of swimming, and a larger number of total dorsoventral contractions.

Research with *Aplysia* shows the generalized effects of exposure to intense stimuli. The GWR was habituated in different animals either by stimulation of the siphon or by stimulation of the purple gland, a structure that ejects a dark secretion (called inking behavior) that serves an antipredator function. Then, all animals received a single, strong shock administered to the head area. Siphon-habituated animals exhibited dishabituation of the GWR when stimulated in the siphon, as well as increased responding of the gill when stimulated in the purple gland. On the other hand, purple gland–habituated animals exhibited dishabituation of the GWR when stimulated in the purple gland, and a facilitation of the gill response when stimulated in the siphon

(Pinsker et al. 1970). So a strong shock to the head facilitated both habituated and nonhabituated reflexes. This suggests that the change induced by a strong dishabituating stimulus is not specific to a particular pathway but common to several stimulus-response pathways.

This type of experimental manipulation equates dishabituation and sensitization, although, as will be shown later, these two learning processes appear to be based on different mechanisms. The training protocol involved in a dishabituation experiment includes two sensory inputs, one dealing with the habituating stimulus (siphon tactile stimulation) and the other with the dishabituating stimulus (head shock). This, in turn, suggest that the underlying circuit must involve an architecture slightly more complex than that of habituation. ***Figure 7.12*** illustrates a minimum circuit necessary for dishabituation of the GWR in *Aplysia.* Several electrophysiological findings help us understand the localization of sensitization in this circuit (axo-axonic synapses enclosed in dotted lines in the figure). For example, if a microelectrode is used to stimulate L7 repeatedly, the subsequent elicitation of the GWR is *not* facilitated; since sensitization involves increased activation of L7, this finding suggests that the site of plasticity is presynaptic (Carew et al. 1971).

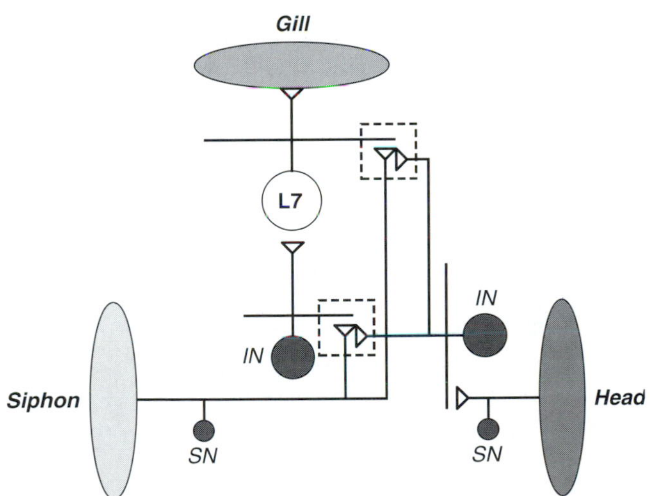

FIGURE 7.12. A schematic representation of the minimum circuit for dishabituation of the gill-withdrawal reflex in *Aplysia californica.* Sensory neurons (SN) from the siphon (carrying the habituating stimulus) and from the head (carrying the dishabituating stimulus) connect interneurons (IN) that, in turn, synapse with the motoneuron L7, partially responsible for contracting the gill. The SN from the siphon also makes direct connection with L7 (the monosynaptic pathway described previously). The IN carrying the dishabituating stimulus makes axo-axonic connection with the SN carrying the habituating stimulus; these are plastic sites (marked with a dotted outline in the figure). In molluscs, dendrites are located in the part of the axon proximal to the neuron's soma

Dishabituation appears to involve an electrophysiological response that is opposite to that seen in short-term habituation (Castellucci & Kandel 1976). Repeated stimulation of the siphon causes a decrease in the amplitude of the EPSPs recorded in L7; this is the homosynaptic depression phenomenon underlying short-term habituation. If, subsequently to habituation training, the sensory neurons innervating the animal's head area (normally carrying the dishabituating stimulus) are stimulated, conduction through the depressed synapse is restored and facilitated. The dishabituating input restores the amplitude of the EPSPs recorded in L7. These sensory neurons establish axo-axonic synapses with the sensory neurons that innervate the siphon, and it is through this synapse that the siphon-L7 synapse is dishabituated. This is referred to as *heterosynaptic facilitation* because the facilitation of the siphon-L7 synapse is achieved by a second synapse, itself not changed during the process. Just as habituation and sensitization involved opposite changes in EPSPs at the L7 neuron, they also appear to involve, respectively, decreases and increases in the amount of neurotransmitter released at the siphon-L7 synapse.

Dishabituation is known to depend on several neurotransmitters, including serotonin (Brunelli et al. 1976). For example, if the isolated abdominal ganglion is bathed in a serotonin-rich solution immediately after habituation training, the amplitude of the EPSPs in L7 is restored much as it is by dishabituating stimulation. However, synaptic facilitation is prevented by application of cinanserin, a drug that prevents serotonin from acting at the synapse (a serotonin antagonist). Finally, depletion of serotonin by the application of a serotonin neurotoxin reduces dishabituation. These pieces of convergent evidence suggest that some facilitatory interneurons use serotonin as neurotransmitter. But the serotonin bath has also a facilitatory effect on nondepressed synapses that is interpreted as short-term sensitization.

Serotonin and other neurotransmitters with similar excitatory effects appear to be responsible for the initiation of a cascade of effects in the siphon sensory neuron that lead to increase synaptic efficacy (Braha et al. 1990). These processes are illustrated in ***Figure 7.13.*** Excitation in these axo-axonic synapses increases cytoplasmatic levels of the protein cyclic adenosine monophosphate, or cAMP, which is directly related to heterosynaptic facilitation. If the abdominal ganglion is exposed to a cAMP analog, the siphon-L7 synapse is facilitated; however, other synapses involving nonsensory cells are not facilitated by such a procedure (Brunelli et al. 1976). Increased cAMP levels at the axon terminals have at least two effects on the permeability of ion channels located in the cell membrane.

First, through its action on cytoplasmatic enzymes, cAMP closes some of the potassium channels present in the cell membrane, thus preventing the flux of this ion from the inside to the outside of the sensory neuron. Normally, an AP depolarizes the cell by allowing a massive influx of positively charged sodium ions (Na^+) into the cell; this induces an outflux current of potassium (K^+), which is also positively charged. This outflux of potassium restabilizes the cell (i.e., it repolarizes it). Because this outflux of potassium is prevented in stimulated sensory neurons, then an arriving AP will last longer than usual. This is called *spike broadening*. This influence of cAMP is mediated by protein kinase A (PKA), a cytoplasmatic enzyme that can modify ion channels.

A second effect of increased levels of cAMP is to lengthen the time during which calcium channels (Ca^{++}) remain open, thus

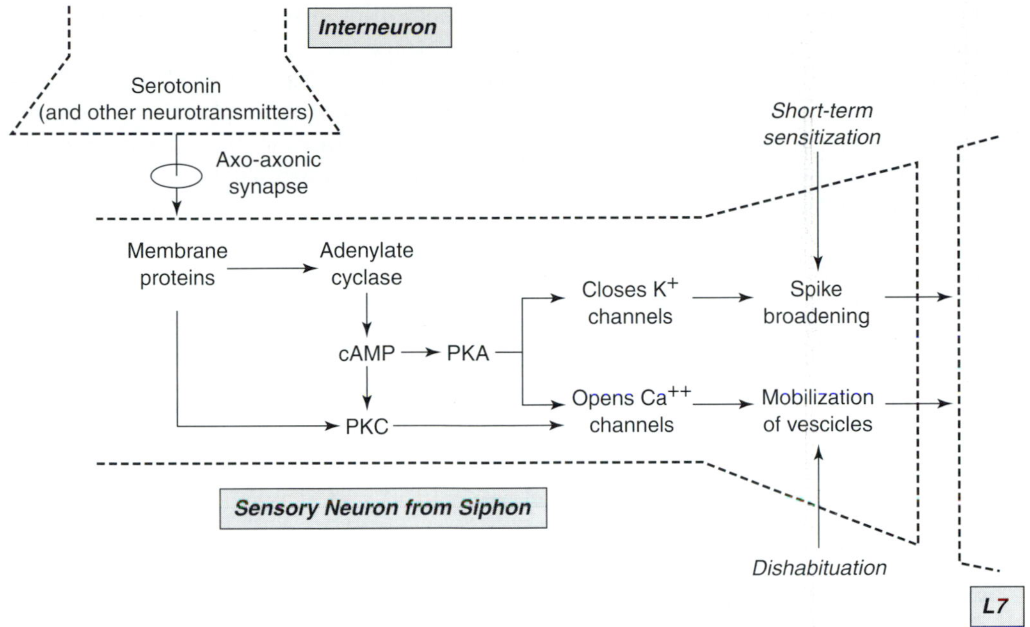

FIGURE 7.13. A schematic representation of the molecular processes underlying dishabituation and short-term sensitization of the gill-withdrawal reflex in *Aplysia californica* (Braha et al. 1990). Neural plasticity occurs in the sensory neuron as a result of activation by excitatory interneurons making axo-axonic contact. Depressed synapses (after habituation treatment) can be dishabituated by a process that results in the opening of calcium channels, the mobilization of vesicles, and the release of large quantities of neurotransmitter into the synapse. Nondepressed synapses can be activated by spike broadening, a mechanism depending on the closing of potassium channels, which keeps the depolarization caused by an AP acting on the axon's terminal for a longer-than-normal period.

increasing calcium influx into the sensory neuron. As mentioned previously, calcium facilitates the release of neurotransmitter into the synapse by mobilizing vesicles toward the cell membrane. This results in *increased excitability* of sensory neurons. This action of cAMP is also mediated in part by PKA, but also by a second enzyme known as protein kinase C (PKC).

Spike broadening and increased excitability are independent from each other and seem to work best under different synaptic conditions (Hochner et al. 1986). For example, if the synapse has been depressed by habituation training, then the increased excitability mechanism may effectively dishabituate that synapse; however, nondepressed synapses are affected by spike broadening. One surprising implication of this is that the molecular mechanisms of dishabituation and sensitization are not the same. Dishabituation results from increased excitability of the sensory neuron produced by the influx of calcium and the mobilization of vesicles, whereas sensitization is based on the spike broadening mechanism.

3.g. Long-Term Sensitization. Just as in the case of habituation, increasing the number of sensitization trials and distributing them over several days results in a type of response facilitation that is sustained for days, rather than hours. This is called long-term sensitization, and there is evidence that it involves mechanisms different from those of its short-term counterpart. In one experiment, the siphon-withdrawal reflex was habituated as usual by stimulating the siphon repeatedly (Pinsker et al. 1973). During the subsequent four days, a group of *Aplysia* received four electric shocks per day delivered to the animal's head, whereas a control group received no sensitization treatment. ***Figure 7.14*** shows the strength of the siphon response 1, 7, and 21 days after sensitization training. The sensitization effect was significant after 1 and 7 days of training but was no longer measurable after 21 days. Heterosynaptic facilitation

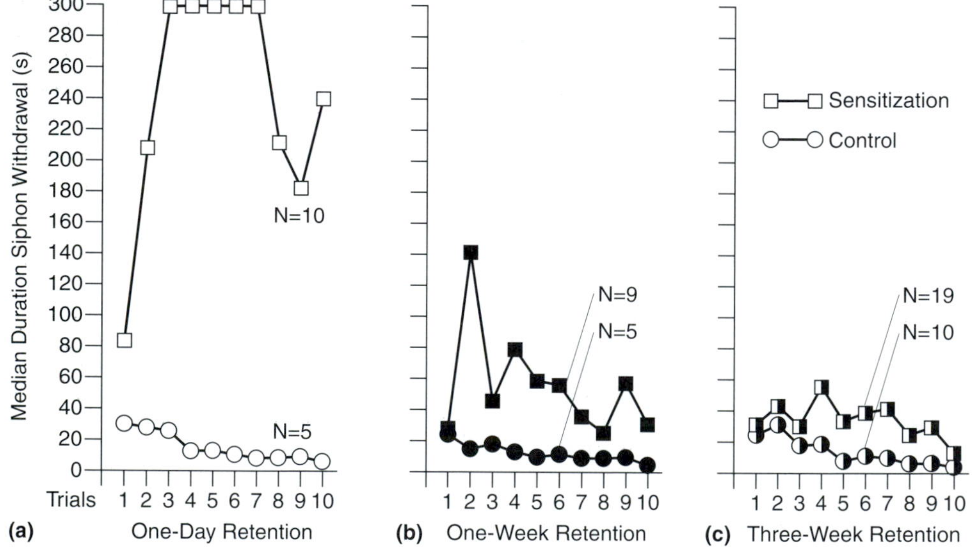

FIGURE 7.14. Long-term sensitization of the siphon-withdrawal reflex in *Aplysia californica* (Pinsker et al. 1973). Each animal in the experimental group received two electric shocks per day over a period of 10 days, delivered to its head, and a single tactile stimulation of the siphon. Control animals received only the siphon stimulus. ***(a)*** Half of the experimental and control animals were tested again 1 day after the last training session. Test trials involved the presentation of the tactile stimulus to the siphon. No electric shocks were delivered. Experimental animals exhibited sensitization in terms of the duration of the siphon withdrawal. ***(b)*** The rest of the animals were given a similar test session 7 days after the last training session. Sensitization of the siphon-withdrawal response is reduced compared to the 1-day test. However, the response is still significantly above the level of the control group. A measurable amount of sensitization could thus be detected a week after training. ***(c)*** All the animals were tested 3 weeks after the last session involving exposure to shock.

can be observed if the isolated abdominal ganglion is bathed five times, each bath lasting 5 min and spaced apart by 15 min, in a serotonin-rich solution. Such facilitation is observed one day after the bathing treatment (Montarolo et al. 1986). One effect of both behavioral training and serotonin treatment of isolated ganglia is to induce an increase in PKC that persists for hours and is thus intermediate between the short-term and the long-term effects (Sossin et al. 1994). PKC may be a molecular mechanism that bridges the gap between the functional changes involved in short-term sensitization and the structural changes underlying long-term sensitization.

Long-term sensitization involves structural changes in the sensory neuron that are mediated by gene expression and protein synthesis. Bailey and Chen (1988), for example, found that sensitized sensory neurons exhibit an increase in the number of axon terminals that synapse with the L7 motoneuron. Such connection sites are called varicosities, and they are, in fact, functional. Increases in varicosities can be obtained by bathing in serotonin and by injections of cAMP, both of which also lead to heterosynaptic facilitation in neurophysiological terms. Many of these experiments have been done with cultured cells, and so it has been possible to determine the cell components that are necessary for varicosities to develop. It is surprising that varicosities develop only in cultures in which the motoneuron was left intact (Glanzman et al. 1990). Thus, although sensitization is a presynaptic phenomenon, the induction of varicosities in the sensory neuron requires the concurrent activation of the motoneuron.

Such morphological changes require the building of new axon terminals. In turn, this must demand the synthesis of proteins. Accordingly, treatments of sensory neurons with protein-synthesis inhibitors (substances that prevent the formation of new proteins) eliminate the long-term sensitizing effects of serotonin injections but do not affect short-term sensitization (Montarolo et al. 1986). In conclusion, although short-term learning effects involve functional adjustments in synaptic transmission, long-term habituation and sensitization require that sensory neurons modify their own anatomy in order to preserve the information for longer periods.

4. EVOLUTION OF LEARNING MECHANISMS IN MOLLUSCS

How general are the electrophysiological and molecular mechanisms of habituation, dishabituation, and sensitization described in *Aplysia*? The ability to identify neurons individually can be used within a comparative framework to determine the evolutionary history of functional properties known to provide a basis for learning.

Suppose that "excitability" and "spike broadening," two of the mechanisms of sensitization described previously, are treated as part of the neuromodulatory phenotype of *Aplysia*'s mechanosensory neurons. Would these mechanisms be present in homologous neurons from other molluscs? If the phylogenetic relationships among these species were determined by independent cladistic analysis, could this tell us something about the evolution of these learning mechanisms? Wright et al. (1996) followed a four-step approach to answer these questions. First, seven species of opistobranch molluscs were selected for analysis (Genera: *Bulla, Akera, Aplysia, Dolabella, Bursatella, Phyllaplysia,* and *Dolabrifera*). Second, their phylogenetic relationships were determined by standard cladistic analysis based on a matrix of morphological characters used in molluscan systematics. Third, they identified sensory neurons in each species that were homologous to the tail-sensory neurons of *Aplysia*. These neurons are stimulated during dishabituation and sensitization experiments. Neuronal homology was based on such features as the neuron's location in the CNS, its size, and its resting physiology, among others. Although none of these features demonstrates that two neurons are homologous, taken together they build up a persuasive argument. Finally, the state of the two neuromodulatory characters (presence or absence of serotonin-induced excitability and spike broadening) was determined for each species and mapped into the cladogram. The resulting distribution is shown in ***Figure 7.15.***

Two main conclusions can be drawn from this phylogenetic analysis. The first conclusion is that increased excitability evolved before spike broadening in this particular population of sensory neurons. This conclusion is based on the presence of excitability and the absence of spike broadening in two outgroups, represented here by *Akera* and *Bulla*. One implication of this finding is that excitability and spike broadening have evolved independently because there are species that show the former but not the latter mechanism. The second conclusion is that both excitability and spike broadening have apparently been lost in the tail-sensory neurons of the ancestors of *Dolabrifera*. Accordingly, training protocols that induce short-term and long-term sensitization in *Aplysia* fail to induce

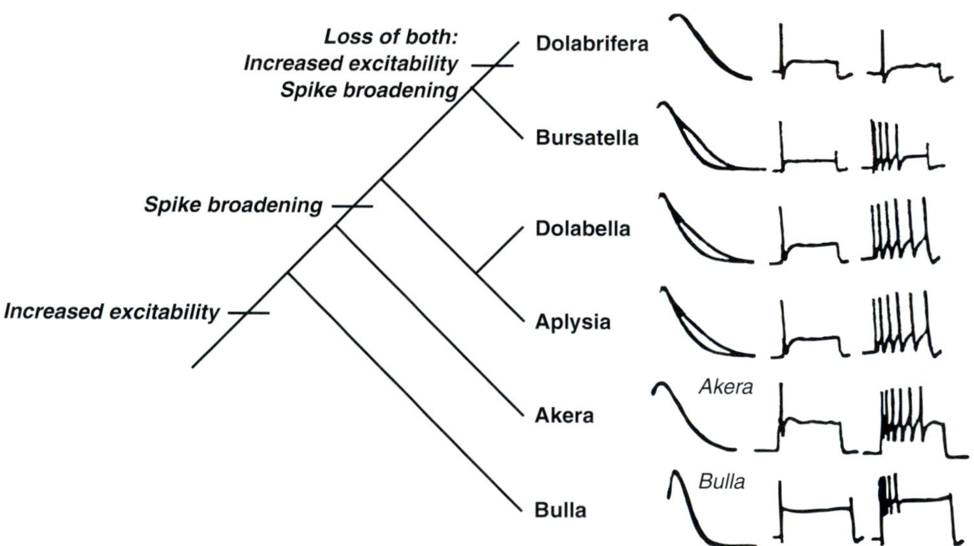

FIGURE 7.15. Cladistic analysis of learning mechanisms in molluscs (Wright et al. 1996). The cladogram was obtained by running the program PAUP on a matrix of 12 morphological characters for the six species. Then, the presence versus absence of two neuromodulatory traits, spike broadening and increased excitability, was established in homologous mechanosensory neurons in these six species and mapped into the cladogram. Two main results are emphasized: Increased excitability evolved before spike broadening, and both mechanisms are lost in *Dolabrifera*.

similar behavioral changes in *Dolabrifera* (Wright 1998). However, these two species exhibit comparable levels of habituation of the mantle-withdrawal response, suggesting that *Dolabrifera* is capable of some forms of learning.

A combination of behavioral, electrophysiological, molecular, and cladistic methods permits the formulation of hypotheses concerning the evolution of learning mechanisms. The uncoupling of learning mechanisms (e.g., spike broadening and excitability) suggests they can evolve independently, and, therefore, the issue of the polarity of change is raised: Which of the two evolved first? Consider the absence of spike broadening in *Bulla* and *Dolabrifera* (see ***Figure 7.15***). The use of cladistic analysis offers different interpretations of what is essentially the same fact: The absence of spike broadening is interpreted as primitive or plesiomorphic in *Bulla,* but as due to evolutionary reversal in *Dolabrifera.*

What is the ultimate origin of the simple examples of behavioral plasticity described in this chapter? A distinction was made previously between habituation, a neuronal phenomenon, and sensory adaptation. Sensory receptors have a pervasive ability to adjust to current stimulus conditions through adaptation. Mechanoreceptors in our skin, for example, stop responding to the light pressure produced by the clothes we wear. Kandel (1976) suggested that such forms of peripheral plasticity may have been the evolutionary precursors of habituation as it occurs in the CNS of animals. The hypothetical evolutionary history is represented in ***Figure 7.16.*** In animals lacking a true CNS, such as cnidarians or their remote ancestors, it is possible that plasticity may have been restricted to a single neuron acting as both receptor and effector. In this stage, changes in behavior would probably be entirely attributable to sensory adaptation. The mechanisms of habituation discovered in molluscs are characterized by the removal of *plastic synapses* from the periphery and into the CNS. Plastic synapses are still found in sensory neurons, but it is their synaptic connections with interneurons and motoneurons inside a ganglion that exhibit plasticity. Kandel also argued that the localization of plasticity in vertebrates is further removed from peripheral detection and found only in interneurons within the CNS. Are there parallels between the central mechanisms of learning and the peripheral effects that initiate the learning process?

Walters (1991) suggested a connection between the learning mechanisms of *Aplysia* and the animal's ability to detect and react to bodily injury. Most experiments with *Aplysia* are based on aversive stimuli that activate mechanoreceptors located in the skin. These cells are in a prime location to detect any type of injury that might threaten the animal's life. As it happens, peripheral damage generates sustained discharges from both the damaged neurons and other sensory neurons located in the vicinity of the damage. During a few seconds after the damage, neurons in the CNS receive high frequency discharges, much as they do during sensitization training. This is followed by synaptic facilitation and cellular repair processes that might involve the growth of axon terminals. Such synaptic facilitation can last for weeks and change the responsiveness of reflexes originated near the injured area. The close parallel between cellular changes following bodily damage and those underlying sensitization suggest a connection between these two processes. Walters (1991) hypothesized that learning mechanisms based on nociceptive signals, such as most of the examples reviewed in this chapter, may have evolved early in the history of animals and thus be common to a wide variety of species.

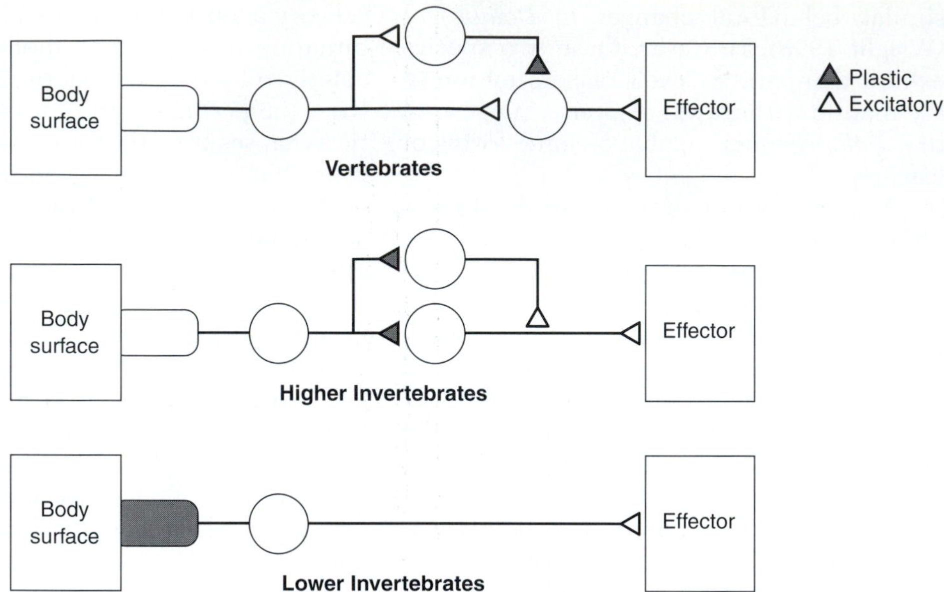

FIGURE 7.16. Kandel's (1979) hypothesis of the evolution of neural plasticity underlying habituation. In lower invertebrates, such as the cnidarians and their ancestors, plasticity was localized at the level of the receptive pole of a sensory-motor unit. In higher invertebrates, such as the molluscs, plasticity is localized in the central nervous system, although it is still present in the afferent sensory neuron. Finally, in vertebrates plasticity is moved farther into the central nervous system and is characteristic of interneurons

5. KEY TERMS

action potential (AP) 226
below-zero habituation 246
brain 232
central nervous system (CNS) 232
chemical synapse 226
central pattern generator (CPG) 241
coefficient of variation (CV) 237
command neuron 240
depolarization 226
dishabituation 229
electrical synapse 227
excitatory postsynaptic potential (EPSP) 226
fossil traces 229
functional disconnection 252
ganglion 232
generalization of habituation 228
giant neurons 232
graded potentials 226
habituation 228
habituation of dishabituation 246
habituation of habituation 246
heterosynaptic facilitation 254
homosynaptic depression 251
hyperpolarization 231

6. REFERENCES

Anderson, P. A. V. (1985). Physiology of a bidirectional, excitatory chemical synapse. *Journal of Neurophysiology,* **53,** 821–835.

Bailey, C. H., & Chen, M. (1988). Long-term memory in *Aplysia* modulates the total number of varicosities of single identified sensory neurons. *Proceedings of the National Academy of Sciences* (USA), **85,** 2373–2377.

Barlow, G. W. (1977). Modal action patterns. In T. A. Sebeok (Ed.), *How animals communicate* (pp. 98–134). Bloomington: Indiana University Press.

Braha, O., Dale, N., Hochner, B., Klein, M., Abrams, T. W., & Kandel, E. R. (1990). Second messengers involved in the two processes of presynaptic facilitation that contribute to sensitization and dishabituation in *Aplysia* sensory neurons. *Proceedings of the National Academy of Sciences* (USA), **87,** 2040–2044.

Brunelli, M., Castellucci, V. F., & Kandel, E. R. (1976). Synaptic facilitation and behavioral sensitization in *Aplysia*: Possible role of serotonin and cyclic AMP. *Science,* **194,** 1178–1181.

Brunner, D., & Maldonado, H. (1988). Habituation in the crab *Chasmagnathus granulatus:* Effect of morphine and naloxone. *Journal of Comparative Physiology A,* **162,** 687–694.

Carew, T. J., Castellucci, V. F., & Kandel, E. R. (1971). An analysis of dishabituation and sensitization of the gill-withdrawal reflex in *Aplysia. International Journal of Neuroscience,* **2,** 79–98.

Carew, T. J., Castellucci, V. F., & Kandel, E. R. (1979). Sensitization in *Aplysia*: Restoration of transmission in synapses inactivated by long-term habituation. *Science,* **205,** 417–419.

Carew, T. J., Pinsker, H. M., & Kandel, E. R. (1972). LTH of a defensive withdrawal response reflex in *Aplysia. Science,* **175,** 451–454.

Castellucci, V. F., Carew, T. J., & Kandel, E. R. (1978). Cellular analysis of long-term habituation of the gill-withdrawal reflex of *Aplysia californica. Science,* **202,** 1306–1308.

Castellucci, V. F., & Kandel, E. R. (1974). A quantal analysis of the synaptic depression underlying habituation of the gill-withdrawal reflex in *Aplysia. Proceedings of the National Academy of Sciences* (USA), **71,** 5004–5008.

Castellucci, V. F., & Kandel, E. R. (1976). Presynaptic facilitation as a mechanism for behavioral sensitization in *Aplysia. Science,* **194,** 1176–1178.

Crimes, T. P. (1992). The record of trace fossils across the Proterozoic-Cambrian boundary. In J. H. Lipps & P. W. Signor (Eds.), *Origin and early evolution of the Metazoa* (pp. 177–202). New York: Plenum.

Frost, W. N., Brandon, C. L., & Mongeluzi, D. L. (1998). Sensitization of the *Tritonia* escape swim. *Neurobiology of Learning & Memory,* **69,** 126–135.

Frost, W. N., Brown, G. D., & Getting, P. A. (1996). Parametric features of habituation of swim cycle number in the marine mollusc *Tritonia diomedia. Neurobiology of Learning & Memory,* **65,** 125–134.

Glanzman, D. L., Kandel, E. R., & Schacher, S. (1990). Target–dependent structural changes accompanying long-term synaptic facilitation in *Aplysia* neurons. *Science,* **249,** 799–802.

Haralson, S. J., & Haralson, J. V. (1988). Habituation in the sea anemone, *Anthopleura elegantissima:*

Spatial discrimination. *International Journal of Comparative Psychology,* **1,** 245–253.

Hochner, B., Klein, M., Schacher, S., & Kandel, E. R. (1986). Additional component in the cellular mechanism of presynaptic facilitation contributes to behavioral dishabituation in *Aplysia. Proceedings of the National Academy of Sciences* (USA), **83,** 8794–8798.

Huber, R., & Kravitz, E. A. (1995). A quantitative analysis of agonistic behavior in juvenile American lobsters (*Homarus americanus* L.). *Brain, Behavior & Evolution,* **46,** 72–83.

Johnson, M. C., & Wuensch, K. L. (1994). An investigation of habituation in the jellyfish *Aurelia aurita. Behavioral & Neural Biology,* **61,** 54–59.

Kandel, E. R. (1976). *Cellular basis of behavior.* San Francisco: Freeman.

Kandel, E. R. (1979). *Behavioral biology of* Aplysia. *A contribution to the comparative study of opistobranch molluscs.* San Francisco: Freeman.

Kristan, W. B. Jr., & Calabrese, R. L. (1976). Rhythmic swimming activity in neurons of the isolated nerve cord of the leech. *Journal of Experimental Biology,* **65,** 643–668.

Kupferman, I., & Weiss, K. R. (1978). The command neuron concept. *Behavioral & Brain Sciences,* **1,** 3–10.

Logan, C. (1975). Topographic changes in responding during habituation to waterstream stimulation in sea anemones (*Anthopleura elegantissima*). *Journal of Comparative & Physiological Psychology,* **89,** 105–117.

Logan, C., & Beck, H. (1978). Long-term retention of habituation in the absence of a central nervous system. *Journal of Comparative & Physiological Psychology,* **92,** 928–934.

Marcus, E. A., Nolen, T. G., Rankin, C. H., & Carew, T. J. (1988). Behavioral dissociation of dishabituation, sensitization, and inhibition in *Aplysia. Science,* **241,** 210–213.

Mather, J. A. (1986). Sand digging in *Sepia officinalis*: Assessment of a cephalopod mollusc's "fixed" behavior pattern. *Journal of Comparative Psychology,* **100,** 315–320.

Meech, R. W. (1989). The electrophysiology of swimming in the jellyfish *Aglantha digitale.* In P. A. V. Anderson (Ed.), *Evolution of the first nervous systems* (pp. 281–298). New York: Plenum Press.

Montarolo, P. G., Goelet, P., Castellucci, V. F., Morgan, J., Kandel, E. R., & Schacher, S. (1986). A critical period for macromolecular synthesis in long-term heterosynaptic facilitation in *Aplysia. Science,* **234,** 1249–1254.

Nielsen, C. (1995). *Animal evolution. Interrelationships of the living phyla.* Oxford: Oxford University Press.

Osorio, D., Bacon, J. P., & Whitington, P. M. (1997). The evolution of arthropod nervous systems. *American Scientist,* **85,** 244–253.

Pedreira, M. E., Romano, A., Tomsic, D., Lozada, M., & Maldonado, H. (1998). Massed and spaced training build up different components of long-term habituation in the crab *Chasmagnathus. Animal Learning & Behavior,* **26,** 34–45.

Perrins, R., & Weiss, K. R. (1996). A cerebral central pattern generator in *Aplysia* and its connections with buccal feeding circuitry. *Journal of Neuroscience,* **16,** 7030–7045.

Pinsker, H. M., Hening, W. A., Carew, T. J., & Kandel, E. R. (1973). Long-term sensitization of a defensive withdrawal reflex in *Aplysia. Science,* **182,** 1039–1042.

Rushforth, N., Burnett, A., & Maynard, R. (1963). Behavior in *Hydra.* Contraction responses of *Hydra pirardi* to mechanical and light stimuli. *Science,* **139,** 760–761.

Sossin, W. S., Sacktor, T. C., & Schwartz, J. H. (1994). Persistent activation of protein kinase C during the development of long-term facilitation in *Aplysia. Learning & Memory,* **1,** 189–202.

Spencer, A. N. (1989). Chemical and electrical synaptic transmission in the Cnidaria. In P. A. V. Anderson (Ed.), *Evolution of the first nervous systems* (pp. 33–53). New York: Plenum Press.

Thompson, R. F., & Spencer, W. A. (1966). Habituation: A model phenomenon for the study of neuronal substrates of behavior. *Psychological Review,* **73,** 16–43.

Walters, E. T. (1991). A functional, cellular, and evolutionary model of nociceptive plasticity in *Aplysia. Biological Bulletin,* **180,** 241–251.

White, J. E., Southgate, E., Thompson, J. N., & Brenner, S. (1986). The structure of the nervous system of the nematode *Caenorhabditis elegans. Philosophical Transactions of the Royal Society of London B314,* 1–340.

Wicks, S. R., & Rankin, C. H. (1997). Effects of tap withdrawal response habituation on other withdrawal behaviors: The localization of habituation in the nematode *Caenorhabditis elegans. Behavioral Neuroscience,* **111,** 342–353.

Willmer, P. (1990). *Invertebrate relationships. Patterns in animal evolution.* Cambridge: Cambridge University Press.

Willows, A. O. D., & Hoyle, G. (1969). Neuronal network triggering a fixed-action pattern. *Science,* **166,** 1549–1551.

Wine, J. J., & Krasne, F. B. (1982). The cellular organization of crayfish escape behavior. In D. E. Bliss, H. Atwood, & D. Sandeman (Eds.), *The biology of* Crustacea. (Vol. IV): *Neural integration.* New York: Academic Press.

Wright, W. G. (1998). Evolution of nonassociative learning: Behavior analysis of a phylogenetic lesion. *Neurobiology of Learning & Memory,* **69,** 326–337.

Wright W. G., Kirschman, D., Rozen, D., & Maynard, D. (1996). Phylogenetic analysis of learning—related neuromodulation in molluscan mechanosensory neurons. *Evolution,* **50,** 2248–2263.

CHAPTER 8

Evolution of the Vertebrate Brain and Behavior

MAIN GENERALIZATIONS OF CHAPTER 8

- *The brain of vertebrates exhibits both a common pattern of organization that reflects phylogeny and a variation in structure that reflects adaptation to particular modes of life.*
- *Cladistic analysis based on neural connections, neurotransmitter systems, and other characters can be used to postulate hypotheses concerning brain evolution.*
- *Brain size increases passively with increments in body size in all vertebrate classes. In addition, encephalization has evolved independently in several lineages, leading to anatomically differentiated brains.*

Vertebrates form a close clade with two other groups of animals: the tunicates (Urochordata) and the lancelets (Cephalochordata). Tunicates are sessile as adults and thus do not resemble chordates at all. However, tunicate larvae show some critical features that put them clearly in the same group with the cephalochordates and vertebrates. All these animals are characterized by four characters; notochord, dorsal nerve cord, gill slits, and tail—the four basic elements of the chordate body plan. The *notochord* is a stiff, dorsal rod that provides support. It is present in the tail of urochordate larvae, but not in the adult tunicate. The notochord is permanent in the cephalochordates and replaced by cartilage or bone in the vertebral column of vertebrates. Chordates also have a *nerve cord* located dorsally with respect to the digestive tract. This is the central nervous system (CNS) which, in all the vertebrates, exhibits an anterior enlargement called the brain. Vertebrate brains are enclosed in a cavity called a cranium, made of cartilage or bone. Two other features common to the chordates are the *gill slits,* critical for breathing, and the *tail,* a postanal structure used in swimming and a main component of the chordates' typically active way of life. Despite their diversity, their sharing of several unique derived characters, or *synapomorphies,* strongly supports the hypothesis that chordates are a monophyletic group (Nielsen 1995).

1. Key Innovations of the Vertebrates

1.a. The Vertebrate Body. It may seem strange to refer to agnathan fish as "vertebrates," given that they do not possess bone and hence lack true vertebrae. However, these primitive fish exhibit the same basic set of specialized characters seen in all vertebrates, including the cranium. For this reason, it would seem more appropriate to refer to agnathan fish as Craniata rather than Vertebrata, although these terms are usually interchangeable. The vertebrate head contains well-defined and -developed sensory organs (e.g., eyes, ears, gustatory papillae), as well as sensory and motor nerves with peripheral ganglia. These are called cranial nerves; some of these nerves can be identified in fossilized crania. The general organization of the vertebrate brain is also quite stable, and although there are many variations, a fundamental theme makes broad sections of the CNS easily identifiable across species. ***Figure 8.1*** shows a prototypical vertebrate brain, as well as the major planes of reference.

The study of brain evolution is particularly facilitated by the skeleton of vertebrates, which fossilizes relatively easily. Whereas the brain decays, as most soft tissues do, after an animal's death, the bones forming the cranial cavity can be preserved, sometimes virtually intact. These bones allow scientists to use the cranium as a mold that yields a cast of the brain that was once located inside. Indeed, on some extraordinary occasions, natural brain casts have been discovered. With this evidence, a substantial amount of information about the shapes and sizes of the brain of extinct animals has been collected over the past century. This information, combined with the relative conservativeness of brains structure and function known from the study of living species, allows for the reconstruction of some general characteristics of the evolution of sensory-motor systems and the brain.

1.b. Agnathan Brains. Forey and Janvier (1993) reported a cladistic analysis of a wide variety of living (hagfish and lampreys) and extinct (ostracoderms) agnathan fish based on 56 morphological characters.

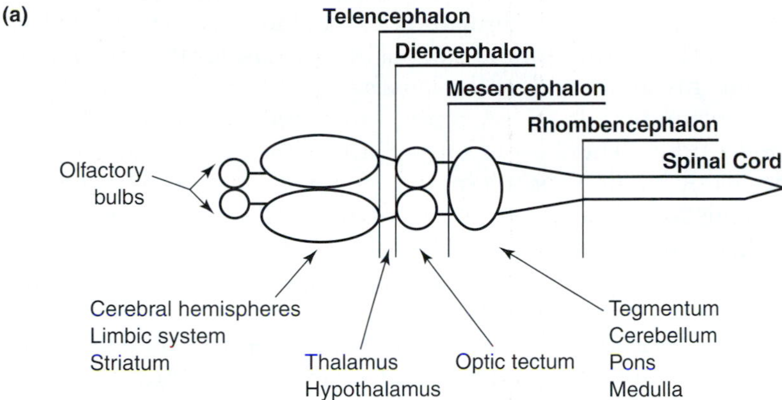

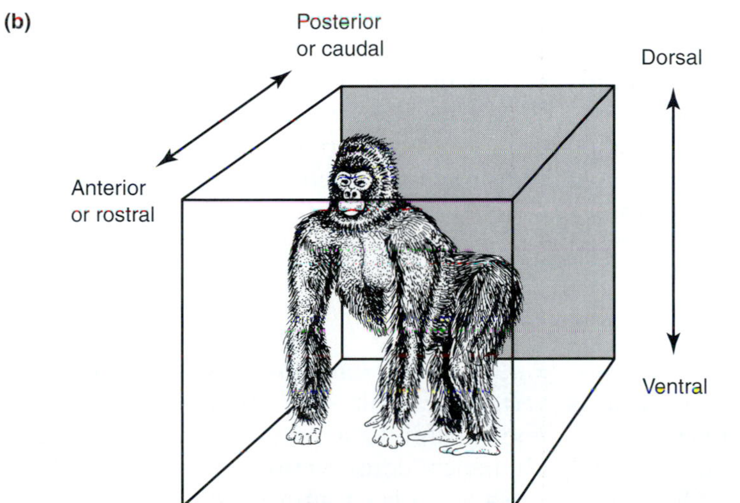

FIGURE 8.1. ***(a)*** Organization of a prototypical vertebrate brain in schematic format. Some of the structures localized in each segment are listed on the bottom. ***(b)*** The planes of reference. Most vertebrates are disposed as shown in the figure. In some species, however, the animal is erected such that dorsal corresponds to the back and ventral to the front (e.g., humans, kangaroos, sea horses).

As mentioned previously, agnathan fish are the most primitive known vertebrates (see ***Chapter 6, section 3.e.,*** pp. 191–195). Two main results were derived from this analysis. First, hagfish are the most primitive of all agnathans, both extant and extinct. The fact that there are living species of hagfish provides comparative psychologists with a great opportunity (not yet realized) to study the behavioral properties of a basal vertebrate. The lampreys are also primitive but are more closely related to living gnathostomes (i.e., jawed vertebrates, including all classes other than Agnatha). Second, all extinct lineages of agnathans, collectively referred to as ostracoderms, fall in between extant agnathans and gnathostomes. In terms of such characters as gross brain morphology, the ostracoderms provide intermediate forms between the lampreys and the gnathostomes.

Figure 8.2 shows a cladogram in which some of the key innovations in neural organization and behavior were overlapped; this is a hypothesis of the historical sequence of those neural characters for which there is some information. The most primitive agnathan fossils, as well as all hagfish species, lived in marine environments; this suggests that vertebrates evolved in the sea and only later entered freshwater habitats. One notorious aspect of the early history of vertebrates is the evolution of new and more complex sensory systems, a process that was accompanied by changes in the brain structures associated with the processing of information from these sensory modalities (Forey & Janvier 1994). For example, hagfish have very simple eyes, without lenses. The lens allows for the focusing of an image in the retina and is present in lampreys and in most other vertebrates. The lensless eyes of hagfish are correlated with the absence of optic tecti, paired structures of the diencephalon that receive direct projections from both retinas, and the presence of a rudimentary cerebellum, an organ involved in the control of the muscles that accommodate the lenses.

A similar progression is observed in the evolution of the inner-ear canals. These semicircular canals are involved in the perception of balance and body orientation in space. Hagfish have very simple internal ears, whereas lampreys have two distinct semicircular canals. These canals contain sensory cells that respond to changes in the up-down and forward-backward directions of bodily motion. Apparently, extinct ostracoderms also possessed two semicircular canals. A third, horizontal canal evolved in the early gnathostomes and has been preserved in most species, including humans. With three semicircular canals, the inner-ear organ can register changes in body movement in each of the spatial dimensions.

2. Comparative Neurology

2.a. Pattern and Process. The CNS of vertebrates, like all other organs of the body, exhibits a certain amount of morphological conservation and variation. Conservation of structures, connections, and neurochemical systems permits the development of hypotheses about the pattern of historical evolution of the brain. Such a pattern is characterized also by specific variations that arise as a result of adaptation to specific modes of life. An example of the interrelationship between pattern and process is provided by the enlarged cerebellum of mormyrid fish. Whereas the large size of the cerebellum is correlated with the importance of electroreception in the natural behavior of these animals, it is still recognizable as a cerebellum and its correspondence with that of other vertebrates is immedi-

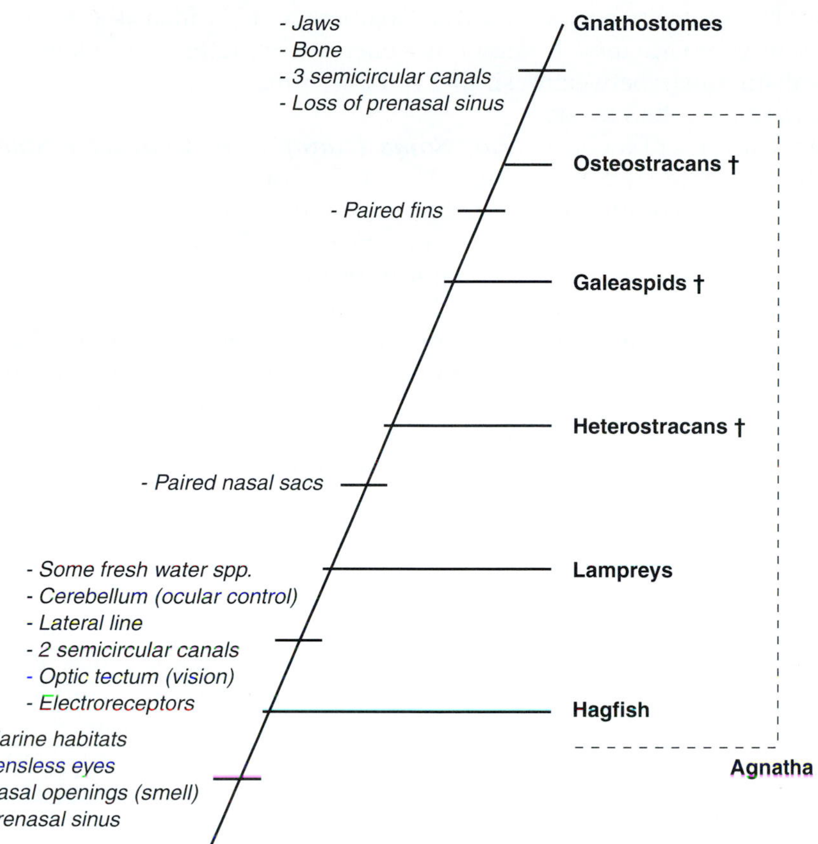

FIGURE 8.2. Key innovations of early vertebrates: the Agnatha or jawless fish. Hagfish and lampreys are extant, but all the other groups (marked with daggers) are extinct.

ately obvious. The same could be said of practically all structures of the CNS of vertebrates.

Brain structures can be subjected to the same evolutionary analyses that apply to other morphological characters and to functional characters, such as behavior (Northcutt 1984). Three main concepts (homology, homoplasy, divergence) have been used previously to understand evolutionary patterns in behavior, and they apply equally well to species comparisons in terms of neural structures, connections among structures, and neurochemical systems. In *homology,* similarity in a character among species is inherited from their immediate common ancestor. *Homoplasy* generally refers to similarity that is not based on common ancestry but evolved independently. There are three different cases of homoplasy: parallelism, convergence, and reversal. In *parallelism,* character similarity evolves from similar primitive characters, whereas in *convergence* the similarity arises from very different primitive characters. It is frequently hard to distinguish between these two possibilities. *Reversal* refers to the evolution in a descendant species of a character that was present in a remote ancestor. Finally, *divergence* refers to the evolution of dissimilarity in characters.

Notice that these concepts are defined by reference to a "common ancestor," although, as already mentioned, this information is not usually available given that the internal structure of the CNS is usually not preserved in fossilized material. How, then can these concepts be applied to the evolution of the brain? Several neurological features are used to develop evolutionary hypotheses. Neural structures are classified as homologous, homoplasic, or divergent across species depending on their topographical position within the CNS, the similarity of their afferent and efferent connections with other brain areas, the details of their cytoarchitecture (i.e., their cellular organization in lamina, layers, etc.), and the degree to which the neurons use similar neurotransmitters. Once homologous structures have been identified, variation in any of the characters mentioned leads to questions of polarity—that is, what variations are primitive and what derived. Polarity can be determined by outgroup analysis (as shown in ***Chapter 6, section 5,*** pp. 212–218), according to which a variation is primitive if it appears in the sister group of the clade under study. In some cases, the polarity of a set of characters can be derived from the study of the developmental sequence leading to the maturation of that character. The embryologist Karl von Baer [1792–1876] noticed that generalized features appear earlier than species-typical features during development (see ***Figure 2.2,*** p. 33). Therefore, neurological features that develop relatively late would tend to be derived characters. This idea is referred to as ontogenetic character precedence, or simply *von Baer's theorem*.

2.b. Some Examples of Character Stability. The CNS of vertebrates is more variable in some sections than in others. Generally speaking, the rostral parts (telencephalon) are more variable across species than the caudal parts. In addition, the interplay of pattern (phylogeny) and process (adaptation) can be appreciated in three general features: the cranial nerves, the neurochemical systems of the brain, and the ventricular system.

Cranial nerves are formed by axons carrying afferent information from sensory receptors in the periphery into the CNS and by axons carrying efferent information from the CNS to peripheral muscles, glands, and sensory receptors cells. Probably all cranial nerves carry some mixture of afferent and efferent fibers, although some of them are predominantly sensory nerves, whereas others are predominantly motor nerves. A list of the cranial nerves of vertebrates is presented in ***Table 8.1*** (Butler & Hodos 1996).

The top 12 cranial nerves, abbreviated in Roman numerals, have been recognized traditionally, whereas the others have been recognized more recently. Not all these nerves appear in all species of vertebrates, and some are restricted to relatively small taxa. For example, humans lack the vomeronasal organ and, consequently, its cranial nerve (VN), but both the organ (located inside the nasal cavity) and the nerve are highly developed in some mammals and also in lizards and snakes. Also stable across species are the relative positions of the nerves as they enter or exit the CNS. Some of these locations are appreciable also in cranial endocasts from extinct species. Once the nerves are identified, an assessment of their relative size provides information about the sensory and/or motor functions that played a critical role in the animal's life.

Also stable across vertebrate species are some of the major *neurochemical systems* of the CNS. These systems involve the internal tracts (bundles of axons) connecting different structures and using a particular neurotransmitter. As mentioned previously (see ***Chapter 7, section 2.a.,*** pp. 231–233), *chemical synapses* act by releasing a *neurotransmitter* that causes electrochemical changes in the postsynaptic cell. Chemical synapses are extremely complex and allow for a variety of modulatory functions. These functions are carried out by the so-called *neuromodulators,* substances that act on various locations (e.g., influencing neurotransmitter receptors in the postsynaptic membrane, or neurotransmitter release and reuptake in the presynaptic membrane). Neurotransmitters and neuromodulators are also surprisingly stable in their functions across species. A partial list of neurotransmitters and neuromodulators is presented in ***Table 8.2*** (Butler & Hodos 1996).

Several of these neurochemical systems are related to the *reticular formation,* a large collection of nuclei located in the brainstem (mesencephalon, pons, and medulla) and projecting fibers both caudally and rostrally to practically all corners of the CNS. The reticular formation carries out a number of critical functions, including particularly those that involve pattern generators, such

TABLE 8.1 Cranial Nerves

Name	*Abbreviation*	*Peripheral Innervation*
Olfactory	I	Olfactory epithelium
Optic	II	Retina
Oculomotor	III	Eye muscles
Trochlear	IV	External eye muscles
Trigeminal	V	Jaw muscles, touch to face, snout, and oral cavity
Abducens	VI	External eye muscles
Dorsal facial	VII_D	Facial muscles, salivary and tear glands
Ventrolateral facial	VII_{VL}	Taste buds
Vestibulocochlear	VIII	Vestibular organs, cochlea, lagena
Dorsal glossopharyngeal	IX_D	Pharynx, salivary glands
Ventrolateral glossopharyngeal	IX_{VL}	Taste buds
Dorsal vagus	X_D	Viscera or thorax and abdomen, larynx, pharynx
Ventrolateral vagus	X_{VL}	Taste buds
Spinal accessory	XI	Neck and shoulder muscles
Hypoglossal	XII	Tongue, syrynx
Terminalis	T	Nasal septum
Vomeronasal	VN	Vomeronasal organ
Epiphyseal	E	Pineal gland, parietal eye
Profundus	P	Skin of the snout
Lateral line (6 nerves)	LL	Lateral line organs

TABLE 8.2 Some of the Neurotransmitters and Neuromodulators of Vertebrates

Substance	***Chemical Group***	***Function***
Neurotransmitters:		
Acetylcholine	Cholinergic	Excitatory or inhibitory, depending on the synapse.
Biogenic amines	Norepinephrine	
	Epinephrine	
	Dopamine	
	Serotonin	
	Histamine	
Amino acids	Glutamate	Excitatory
	Aspartate	
	GABA	Inhibitory
	Glycine	
Neuromodulators:		
Peptides and hormones	VIP	Modulation of synaptic transmission by affecting the release or reuptake of neurotransmitters, or by modifying the sensitivity of the postsynaptic membrane for the neurotransmitter. Some neuromodulators also have neurotransmitterlike activity.
	Substance P	
	Met-enkephalin	
	Leu-enkephalin	
	Cholecystokinin	
	Somatostatin	
	Neurotensin	
	Bombesin	
	Beta-endorphin	
	Angiotensin II	
	Neuropeptide Y	
	Pituitary hormones	
	Insulin	
Second messengers	Cyclic GMP	

as swimming, walking, flying, and chewing. It also regulates muscle tone, integrates sensory information from all modalities, and regulates cycles of sleep and wakefulness, arousal, and attention. Although most of this information comes from research with mammalian species, the morphological stability of the reticular formation across vertebrates suggests that it may have similar functions in a wide range of species. Moreover, such conservativeness is also found in the neurochemical systems that are anatomically closely related to the reticular formation. ***Figures 8.3*** to ***8.5*** describe three of these neurochemical systems based on the neurotransmitters noradrenaline (also called norepinephrine), dopamine, and serotonin. These systems are particularly relevant to an understanding of behavior. It should be kept in mind that not all connections are shown and that species differences do occur in some of the pathways. Other neurochemical systems of behavioral relevance involve such neurotransmitters

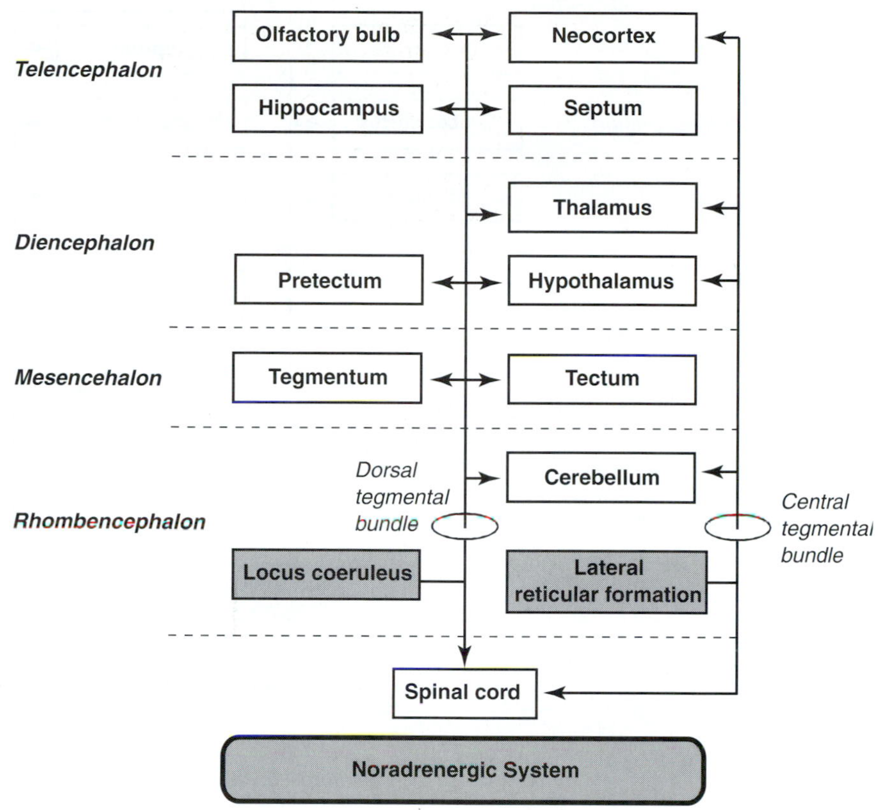

FIGURE 8.3. The noradrenergic system of the brain. Noradrenergic neurons located in the rhombencephalon send axons both rostrally and caudally, influencing the activity of numerous brain areas. Only some areas are represented, and some variations across species may also occur. However, this system is highly conserved.

as acetylcholine and gamma-aminobutyric acid (GABA).

In a vertebrate embryo, the CNS can be described as a hollow cylinder. The walls become the neural structures, and the central cavity develops into the *ventricular system*. Although the specific shape of this system varies with gross macroanatomic variations of the CNS, the main cavities of the systems are highly conserved across species. These cavities are filled with cerebrospinal fluid that provides support and buffers neural tissue against potentially damaging movements of the head. The ventricular system also provides transport for a variety of substances and can, therefore, bridge anatomically distant brain areas. The spinal cord contains a central canal that runs throughout its entire length. There are two central ventricles, one at the level of the rhombencephalon (the fourth ventricle) and one at the level of the diencephalon (third ventricle). Canals communicate these cavities; for example, the cere-

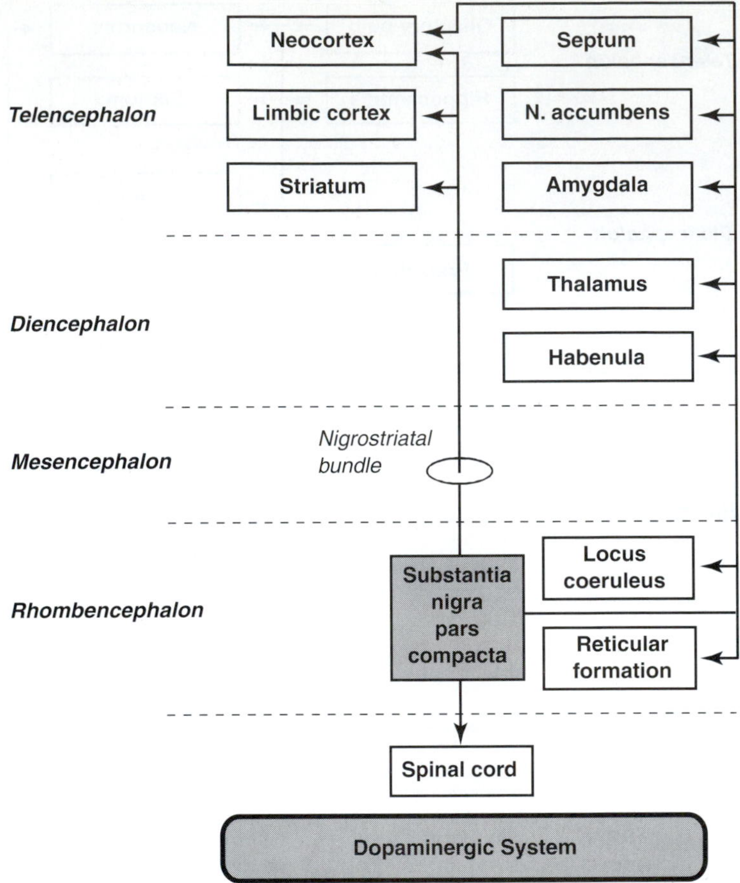

FIGURE 8.4. The dopaminergic system of the brain. The source of this system is neurons located in the substantia nigra of the rhombencephalon. These neurons innervate a variety of rostral areas and also send axons to spinal neurons. Only some areas are represented, and some variations across species may also occur. However, this system is highly conserved.

bral aqueduct links the third and fourth ventricles. Paired ventricles are present in the optic tectum (tectal ventricles) as well as in the telencephalon (lateral ventricles and olfactory ventricles).

Figures 8.3 to ***8.5*** also introduce many brain structures, areas, and nuclei most of which have been experimentally shown to contribute to a wide range of behavioral processes. The anatomical and functional description that follows in the next sections is organized along the lines of major divisions of the CNS of vertebrates, as described in ***Figure 8.1.*** In a caudal-to-rostral direction, such divisions are the spinal cord, rhombencephalon, mesencephalon,

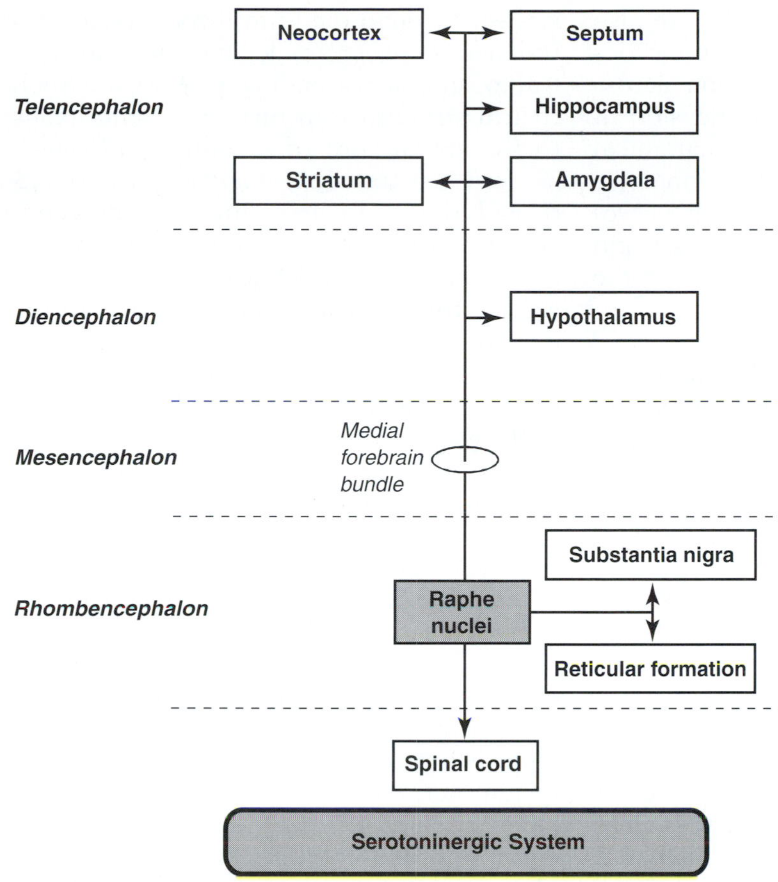

FIGURE 8.5. The serotoninergic system of the brain. Neurons located in the raphe nuclei of the rhombencephalon send axons in a diffuse manner to a wide variety of rostral areas and also send them locally within the rhombencephalon and to the spinal cord. Only some areas are represented, and some variations across species may also occur. However, this system is highly conserved.

diencephalon, and telencephalon. Bear in mind, however, that the CNS is integrated by a large number of pathways (as shown in ***Figures 8.3*** to ***8.5***) and also by nonneural systems, including the circulatory system and the ventricular system, and nonneural components, such as the variety of glial cell types. In addition, although neural communication is emphasized throughout this book, it should be recognized that neurons also transport substances through their axons in both directions. The behavioral relevance of such axonal transport is still obscure. When all these elements are considered, it is easy to see why the CNS of any species is considered to be complex. Of course, comparative psychologists are also interested in the differences and similarities in CNS organization and function across species, which adds another dimension of complexity. The general neuroanatomical information provided in the following sections is based on Hodos & Buttler (1996) and Nieuwenhuys et al. (1998). Let's begin by considering the simplest section: the spinal cord.

2.c. Spinal Cord. The spinal cord may be viewed as a cylinder of nerve tissue enclosed in the core of another cylinder made of cartilage or bone and called the vertebral column. Both the spinal cord and vertebral column display a segmental organization: They are made of an element that repeats itself. In the case of the vertebral column, each segment is referred to as a vertebra. Vertebrae are discrete units. The spinal cord running inside these vertebrae is, however, a continuous mass of tissue; between successive vertebrae, however, the spinal cord presents dorsal and ventral processes called roots. In some agnathan fish, such as the lampreys, segments possess either a dorsal root or a ventral root, each giving rise to a nerve that connects the spinal cord with peripheral structures. In other vertebrates, however, each segment yields both a dorsal and a ventral root that join into a single spinal nerve.

The dorsal root conveys afferent sensory information into the nervous system. The somas of these sensory neurons are located in a chain of ganglia immediately outside the spinal cord, called the dorsal root ganglia. These neurons detect peripheral information from receptors located in the skin, internal organs, muscles, and tendons. Their axons enter at a particular level of the spinal cord and establish synaptic connections with neurons that are, in turn, sending information back either to the periphery through the ventral roots or to central neural structures located in more rostral positions (ascending pathways). Such rostral structures, in turn, also send axons to the spinal cord (descending pathways), as was illustrated in ***Figures 8.3*** to ***8.5*** (I will return to ascending and descending pathways below). Motor neurons located on the ventral horns of gray matter receive this information and relay it to the periphery.

Associated with the ventral roots are a series of sympathetic ganglia that are a part of the *autonomic nervous system* (*ANS*). The ANS includes two branches, the *sympathetic* and *parasympathetic,* usually exhibiting opposing functions on the organs they innervate. For example, sympathetic neurons are responsible for changes associated with escape behaviors, including increase in heart rate and respiratory rate, induction of glucose synthesis and release by the liver, secretion by sweat glands, and a decrease of digestive processes. The parasympathetic system acts to decrease activity in smooth muscles (which results in a decrease of heart rate and respiratory rate, for example), and it controls secretion by certain glands, including the tear and salivary glands. The ANS has been extensively studied in mammals, in which it displays several distinctive features that may not be present in all vertebrates. For example, the chain of sympathetic ganglia mentioned above, aligned by the spinal cord, is present in all tetrapods and in Osteichthyes; sharks and rays also exhibit ganglia, but they are not aligned by the spinal cord, whereas agnathan fish show no sympathetic ganglia. Mammals also possess parasympathetic ganglia located in the vicinity of the organs they innervate. Many of these organs (e.g., stomach, heart, liver, etc.) are innervated by both sympathetic and parasympathetic neurons. Such dual innervation by ANS neurons is less prominent in bony fish and is restricted to the stomach in the case of Chondrichthyes.

An impressive amount of neural information can be processed at the level of the spinal cord, as shown by classic experiments in the so-called *spinal preparation.* The experiments that led to an appreciation of the way in which the spinal cord generates simple reflexes were the product of an age of neurobiological discovery at the end of the 19th century and in the early 20th century. Camillo Golgi [1844–1926] and Santiago Ramón y Cajal [1852–1934] developed and perfected a variety of techniques to stain nerve cells that allowed for the first time a description of the fine structure of the nervous system—that is, its cytoarchitecture. The fact that some of the staining techniques would label specific neurons in a discrete manner led Cajal to suggest the *neuron doctrine* of the nervous system. Essentially, this doctrine is the now universally accepted view that neural networks in the CNS are formed by discrete cells, called neurons, that communicate with each other through tiny gaps. It was Charles S. Sherrington [1857–1952] who coined the term "synapse" in reference to Cajal's idea of cell discontinuity and who developed the spinal preparation. In such a preparation, the spinal cord is severed at some rostral level so as to isolate it from the influence of brain processes. Electrophysiological stimulation and recording, combined with anatomical studies of the structure of the spinal cord, permitted Sherrington and his followers a description of simple reflexes at the cellular level.

Figure 7.12 (p. 253) illustrates the circuitry of monosynaptic and polysynaptic reflexes in *Aplysia.* Similar networks underlie simple behavioral units in vertebrates, and some are fully integrated at the spinal cord level. The flexion reflex (i.e., a flexion of a limb elicited by mechanical or nociceptive stimulation) is an example of a polysynaptic reflex involving the activation of various interneurons at the spinal level. In lower vertebrates, giant neurons located in the rhombencephalon and mesencephalon send projections (giant axons) to the spinal cord, where they coordinate rapid escape responses. In agnathans, for example, Müller cells activate spinal motoneurons, resulting in the contraction of lateral muscles that participate both in regular swimming and in rapid (escape) swimming. Similarly, agnathans, teleost fish, and some species of amphibians possess two giant neurons, located one at each side in the brainstem and called Mauthner cells, that project their giant axon (0.1 mm in diameter) to the spinal cord, where they contact motoneurons responsible for swimming movements (Fetcho 1991). As the giant axon leaves the soma, it crosses to the contralateral side, where it establishes excitatory synaptic connections with motoneurons responsible for muscle activation and with interneurons that also excite the motoneurons. In addition, the Mauthner axon also stimulates (through fast electrical synapses) neurons that project to the contralateral side, at the same segmental level, where they inhibit the neuronal elements responsible for activating muscles from the other side of the body. This results in a C-shaped body posture that rapidly leads to vigorous swimming movements. The Mauthner cells of adult anuran amphibians (tailess toads and frogs) participate in the induction of leaping responses.

Also, evidence of neural plasticity exists at the spinal cord level. For example, in the bullfrog (*Rana catesbeiana*), repeated stimulation of axons in the lateral column of the spinal cord leads to a decreased response output through the ventral root (Farel et al. 1973). This response change is an example of *habituation* that obeys most of the properties described in ***Chapter 7, section 3.a.*** (pp. 244–247). Research has shown that this reflex is monosynaptic and habituation occurs because of changes in the presynaptic neuron. Similar findings were reported by Groves and Thompson (1970) for the flexion reflex in spinal cats.

The mammalian spinal cord seems capable also of associative learning (see ***Chapter 13*** for detailed descriptions of classical and instrumental conditioning). Unlike habituation, in which behavior changes as a result of the repeated presentation of a single stimulus, associative learning involves the joint occurrence of two or more events. Spinal rats, for example, can learn to associate two stimuli presented in temporal succession, such that the presentation of the first stimulus eventually evokes a response similar (or, sometimes, opposite, as will be seen shortly) to the response evoked by the second stimulus. This is called *classical conditioning.* Using a complex design (described in ***Figure 8.6-a***), Grau et al. (1990) demonstrated classical conditioning in spinal rats. Mild shocks were delivered in either the right (R) or left (L) hind limb of restrained animals. One of them was systematically followed by a strong shock, whereas the other was never followed by this strong shock (i.e., R+/L– procedure). Other experiments with intact animals have shown that a stimulus that predicts the imminent presentation of a painful event, such as R in this example, will elicit an analgesic compensatory response. This is called *conditioned analgesia.* After R+/L– training and in order to show whether spinal rats had learned a conditioned analgesic response, the animal's tail was placed on a hot plate and the time before the animal withdrew its tail from the plate was measured. (This tail-flick response provides a measure of how much pain the animal experiences.) Trained spinal rats exposed to the hot plate under the influence of the R stimulus (but without the strong shock), withdrew their tails significantly slower than those exposed under the L stimulus. In other words, the stimulus previously paired with the strong shock induced an analgesic response that allowed the rats to tolerate the heat-induced tail pain for a longer period.

There is also evidence that spinal rats can learn to change their behavior as a function of its consequences, a phenomenon called *instrumental conditioning.* In one experiment (Grau et al. 1998), restrained spinal rats were trained in a situation in which the relaxation of a hind leg led to an electric shock in that leg. To avoid electric shocks, the rat had to learn to keep the leg flexed. An ingenious procedure, known as the *master-yoked procedure,* was used to determine if rats had learned to hold their hind legs flexed simply because of the electric shocks or specifically because of the flexion–no shock contingency (see ***Figure 8.6-b***). Each rat capable of avoiding the shock by flexing its leg (called the "master" rat), also determined when a second rat (the "yoked" rat) received the shock; so whereas master rats had a flexion–no shock contingency enforced in their situation, the yoked rats received the same amount and frequency of shock but independently of their flexion responses. If both groups had increased the frequency of flexion responses, then it would mean that the behavior has been determined purely by the shock. Instead, master rats exhibited a significantly longer flexion duration than yoked animals; in fact, the yoked animals showed as much avoidance behavior as a group of spinal rats that were never shocked in the training situation.

All neural processes resulting in behavioral expression ultimately affect the primary motoneurons of the spinal cord. It

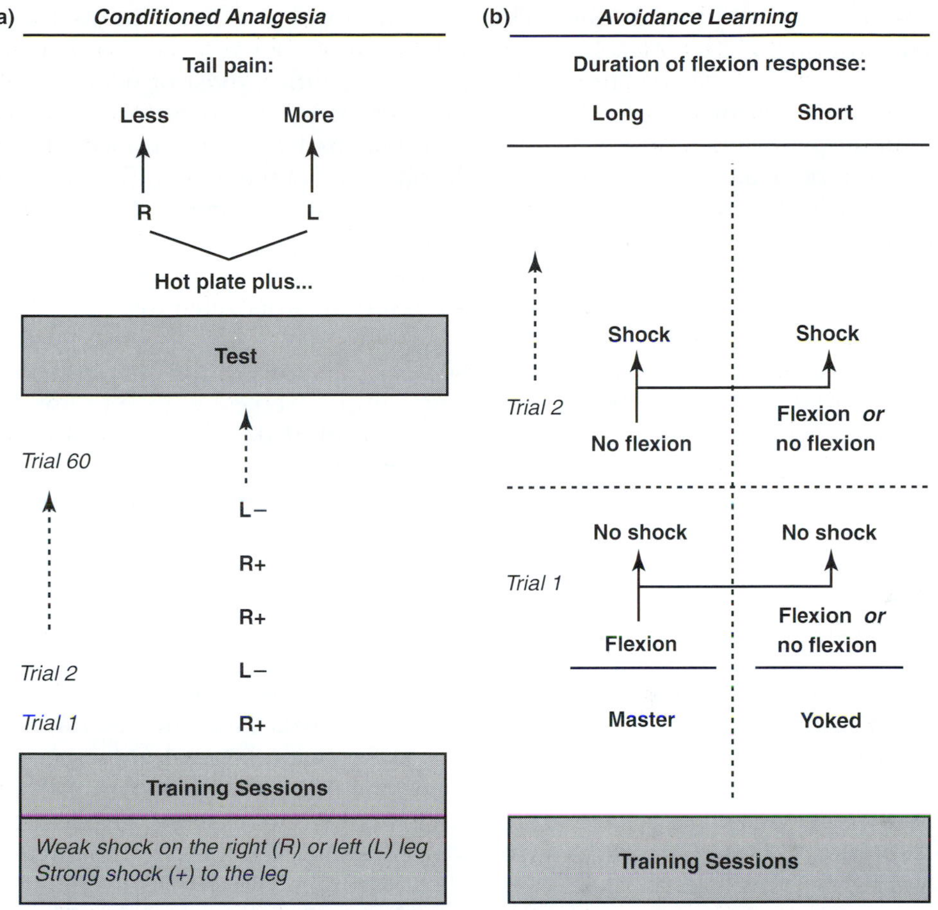

FIGURE 8.6. Learning in spinal animals. ***(a)*** Conditioned analgesia: Training involves the presentation of a weak shock as a signal for a strong shock. A weak shock presented on the right leg is followed by the strong shock (R+), but a weak shock presented on the left is not (L–). During the test, sensitivity to pain is assessed by heating the tail in the presence of either R or L. R induces a compensatory response, making the animals less sensitive to pain—that is, analgesic. Since R has acquired this ability via classical conditioning, it is referred to as conditioned analgesia. ***(b)*** Avoidance learning: During training trials, pairs of animals are exposed to electric shocks except when one of them, called the "master animal," flexes its leg. This leg flexion (the avoidance response) prevents the shock in both the master's situation and the "yoked animal's" situation. Thus both master and yoked animals receive exactly the same amount and frequency of shocks. The longer flexion duration shown by the masters suggests that the flexion–no shock instrumental contingency (and not just exposure to shock) is responsible for the behavioral change. Hence, this is interpreted as an instance of instrumental conditioning.

is these neurons that are responsible for the coordinated contraction of muscles that produces overt behavior. Sherrington noticed that such motoneurons must be shared by descending pathways from a variety of sources and referred to them as the *final common path*. The spinal motoneurons are influenced by sensory inputs directly and through spinal interneurons, by interneurons located in the contralateral side, and by descending brain influences. Motoneurons can also influence themselves through recurrent collateral fibers. Before the axon of a spinal motoneuron leaves the CNS, a collateral branch loops back into the spinal cord and establishes synaptic contact with a Renshaw cell. These cells have an inhibitory influence on the motoneuron that provides negative feedback: The more active a motoneuron, the more it will excite the Renshaw cell, which, in turn, will cause greater inhibition of the motoneuron. Similar recurrent collaterals have been described in Mauthner cells.

2.d. Rhombencephalon and Mesencephalon. Moving in a rostral direction, the spinal cord leads to the medulla, pons, and tegmentum (collectively referred to as *brainstem*). Located dorsal to the medulla and pons is the *cerebellum,* or small cerebrum, and dorsal to the tegmentum is the *optic tectum.* An imaginary line passing between the pons and tegmentum (leaving the cerebellum and optic tectum at each side, respectively), establishes the boundary between rhombencephalon and mesencephalon.

The rhombencephalon contains a wide variety of behaviorally relevant areas. The reticular formation was mentioned above in connection with several neurochemical systems and a variety of behavioral functions. Numerous pathways communicate spinal cord neurons with the reticular formation. The reticular formation is a multisensory processing center that receives input from all sensory modalities, most of which originate in spinal neurons. These are some of the ascending pathways mentioned above. In addition, some of the most influential descending pathways originate in the reticular formation; this is particularly the case in lower vertebrates. These pathways are collectively referred to as reticulospinal pathways.

The nuclei of many of the cranial nerves including cranial nerves V to XII are located at the level of the medulla and pons. As already mentioned, some of these nuclei are particularly enlarged in certain species in accordance with the importance of the sensory information processed by that nucleus. Some teleost fish, such as catfish and carp, exhibit specialized feeding habits that consist of sampling from the bottom of the lakes or rivers where they live. These species have evolved large nuclei for processing gustatory and facial information. The vagal lobe integrates information from cranial nerves IX (glossopharyngeal) and X (vagus). These nerves carry information from the mouth and viscera and relay it in very specific layers within the lobe. The facial lobe receives information from cranial nerve VII (facial), which innervates taste receptors distributed over the animal's skin. The distribution of these afferent fibers is also orderly: Fibers carrying information from the rostral portions of skin make synaptic contact with cells located in the rostral portion of the facial lobe, whereas more caudal afferents enter in caudal portions of the lobe. This organization is, in fact, a general property of neural structures that process some type of sensory information; there is usually a correspondence between the distribution of the receptors in the body or their sensitivity along a particular sensory dimension, and the pattern of connections within the brain center that processes such impulses. This is called *somatotopic organization.*

Several behaviorally important nuclei are also located in the brainstem, including the periaqueductal gray (a nucleus that surrounds the cerebral aqueduct) and several subpopulations of cells distributed in the reticular formation, including the locus coeruleus and the raphe nuclei. These areas are well conserved across vertebrate species. The periaqueductal gray plays a key role in behavior through its massive descending projections. It has been seen as an area that establishes a link between the rostral structures involved in memory, motivation, and perception and their behavioral indices resulting ultimately from the activation of spinal motoneurons. In primates, for example, lesions of the periaqueductal gray disrupt the triggering of vocalizations in social contexts, as well as the initiation of vocal behavior, including language in humans (Jürgens 1990). This area also participates in the control of pain. Many of its neurons respond to neuromodulators such as met-enkephalin and leu-enkephalin. Enkephalins are endogenous molecules capable of activating the same receptors that are also sensitive to morphine, a powerful opiate drug used to produce analgesia (reduced pain perception). Research with mammals suggests that periaqueductal neurons activated by endogenous opioids are responsible for blocking the activity of pathways carrying nociceptive information at the spinal cord level, thus leading to analgesia (Reichling et al. 1988).

The locus coeruleus is a source of noradrenergic neurons projecting to a wide variety of structures, as shown in ***Figure 8.3.*** The raphe nuclei extend from the most caudal regions of the medulla to the pons (see ***Figure 8.5***); its serotoninergic neurons project to various telencephalic and diencephalic structures. Functional research is mostly concentrated in mammalian species, but it seems likely that these nuclei would exhibit similar functions across widely divergent species. In mammals, then, these neurons distribute diffusely through the neocortex. These ascending pathways of the locus coeruleus and raphe nuclei participate in the organization of arousal cycles of sleep and wakefulness.

The optic tectum, in the mesencephalon, receives massive afferent inputs from the retinas of the eyes and is thus particularly enlarged in species that rely on visual information. The processing of visual cues by both retinal and tectal neurons has been studied in detail in common toads (*Bufo bufo*). Although these animals are mostly nocturnal, they use visual information for two main purposes: to procure food and to escape from predators. Toads are mostly sit-and-wait predators, and as prey they deal with their own predators by means of passive strategies, such as freezing and crouching. How does their visual system distinguish between preys and predators?

The retina of visually sophisticated vertebrates can be extremely complex, with several types of light receptors and a variety of neuronal classes organized in layers and with very specific functions. All the visual information processed by these cells ultimately reaches the ganglion neurons, which constitute the only output from the retina (their axons make up cranial nerve II, optic). Each ganglion cell has a receptive field in the retina, which, for simplicity, can be thought of as a circular area. A common field organization involves an excitatory center surrounded by an inhibitory ring, the so-called on-center, off-surround cells. This means that a particular ganglion cell will be most active when the receptors located in the on-center field are active, but less active when the receptors located in the off-surround are active. Other ganglion cells have receptive fields characterized by an off-center, on-surround structure. These conformations of receptive fields are achieved by a combination of excitation and *lateral inhibition*. Light receptors activate two types of cells; bipolar cells have excitatory connection with ganglion cells, whereas horizontal cells have inhibitory connections with several bipolar cells closely distributed in the retina. As a result, activation of a group of bipolars will inhibit other bipolars that surround them (i.e., the off-surround ring). As the axons of ganglion cells leave the retina, they switch over to the contralateral side at the optic chiasm and enter the CNS on their way to the optic tectum. Their distribution is topographic (i.e., retinotopic organization): Each point in the retina is orderly represented in a particular point at the optic tectum level. Therefore, the optic tectum reproduces the receptive fields of ganglion cells in the retina and provides a further level of analysis.

The distinction between "predator" and "prey" cues is achieved in the amphibian optic tectum, where cells of various types have been found to be sensitive to a variety of properties based on the pattern of activation of receptive fields in the retina (Ewert 1997). Cells encode information about the size of the object, its direction of movement, and figure-background contrast. For example, tectal neurons T3 are sensitive to a small object that is approaching the animal, whereas T5.2 respond maximally when the retina is stimulated by an elongated object moving in the direction of its longer axis (like a worm), and T5.4 reacts to a moving large object (like a predator). Obviously, this perceptual information must be integrated with other sources, such as current motivational state and prior experience (both motivation and learning factors affect the tongue-flipping response of toads). Thus, other brain areas, including diencephalic and telencephalic nuclei, influence cells in the optic tectum, which, in turn, send axons to spinal motoneurons controlling the various actual responses involved in prey-catching (orienting toward the source of visual stimulation, approaching the stimulus, and snapping the tongue) or predator-avoidance responses (freezing and crouching).

2.e. Cerebellum. The interplay of pattern and process emerges again clearly when one considers the cerebellum. A comparative overview of the macroanatomy of the cerebellum shows a relatively wide diversity of forms correlated with various modes of life. Natural selection has shaped the gross anatomy of this organ to suit specific functions. When a species emphasizes a particular function for which the cerebellum is a key component, such as motor control (as in birds and mammals) or electroreception (as in mormyrid fish), the species' cerebellum exhibits concomitant morphological features. In mormyrid fish, the corpus cerebelli (the main body of this organ), and the valvula are so enlarged that they extend rostrally on top of the diencephalon and telencephalon, unlike as in most other vertebrates. The mormyrid cerebellum also presents a typical solution to the problem of enlarging the cellular machinery within the constraints of volume imposed by the cranium: folding. The valvula is said to be "hyperfolded" in these animals. In mammals, the corpus cerebelli are "compressed" in the midline and referred to as vermis; lateral to the vermis lie two highly foliated cerebellar hemispheres known as neocerebellum. It is not clear whether the neocerebellum is unique to mammals. A final macrocomponent of the cerebellum is present in all vertebrates except the Agnatha and is called the auricle in fish and the flocculus in tetrapods. The auricle (or flocculus) is usually located in a ventrocaudal position; it receives sensory input from the vestibular system and participates in the control of eye muscles.

Besides these macroanatomic variations, the cerebellum's cell types, cytoarchitecture, and connections with other brain structures clearly show that all vertebrate cerebella originate in a common design that has been greatly conserved. The relative location of the cerebellum in the rhombencephalon is clearly discernible in all vertebrates, even in agnathans, which have the most rudimentary cerebella of all vertebrates. Purkinje cells are distinguishable in all gnathan vertebrates, as are other types of cells, including the stellate cells, granule cells, and Golgi cells. Basket cells are present only in tetrapods. The cortical connections among these cell types is also highly conserved, as is the presence of two sources of cerebellar afferents called the mossy fibers (originating in various brainstem nuclei) and the climbing fibers (originating in the inferior olive, a medullar nucleus). These cellular and fiber elements are organized into three distinct layers: the molecular, Purkinje, and granular layers, from the most superficial to the deepest. Purkinje cells, characterized by a flattened, profuse dendritic arborization, are the only cortical output. In the fishes, the Purkinje cell's axon leaves the cerebellum and establishes connections with various brainstem and spinal cord cell populations. In tetrapods, Purkinje axons are still the only cortical output, but most of them make synaptic connection with the cerebellar subcortical nuclei. Amphibians have only one cerebellar nucleus, but reptiles possess two (the lateral and medial cerebellar nuclei), and birds and mammals have three (the lateral or dentate, interpositus, and medial or fastigial nuclei).

In addition to providing its cellular machinery for the processing of sensory and motor information, the cerebellum plays a role in learning; indeed, according to some researchers, its role is quite critical. Thompson (1986) provided evidence that the cerebellum is the site of storage of one specific case of motor learning. Rabbits (*Oryctolagus cuniculus*) possess both an external eyelid and an internal one called the nictitating membrane. The stimulation of the eye by a puff of air delivered to the cornea (or, in some studies, an electric shock delivered to the cheek), causes three responses that are part of a protective reflex: the external eyelid closes, the eyeball retracts rapidly, and as a result of this retraction, the nictitating membrane closes passively. If that air puff is regularly preceded by a tone, then these responses (eyelid closure, eyeball retraction, and nictitating membrane closure) will occur during the tone and in anticipation of the air puff. This is a well-studied example of classical conditioning (Gormezano et al. 1983), generally referred to as conditioning of the *nictitating membrane response* (*NMR*). The relative facility with which conditioning of the NMR can be induced, the use of fully automated procedures for training and recording relevant behavioral information, and the fact that the animal is immobilized during training (thus permitting concurrent electrophysiological manipulations) have stimulated the use of this preparation for the physiological analysis of conditioning.

Experiments have shown that as the NMR develops to the tone, in anticipation of the air puff, there is a recruitment of activation in neurons located in the dentate and interpositus nuclei of the cerebellum (***Figure 8.7***). What is interesting about this neural correlate of the NMR is that (1) it does not relate to other responses that are being conditioned concurrently, such as

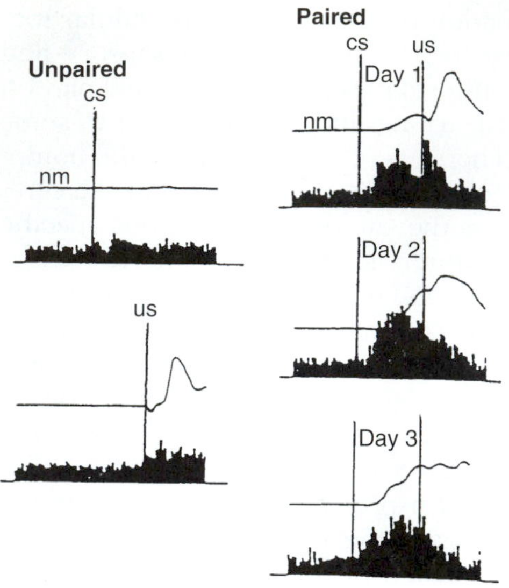

FIGURE 8.7. Neuronal unit activity registered in the dentate and interpositus nuclei during classical conditioning (McCormick & Thompson 1984). This animal received first unpaired presentations of a tone (labeled ***CS***, conditioned stimulus) and an airpuff to the eye (labeled ***US***, unconditioned stimulus), followed by paired presentations in tone-airpuff trials. Neurons responded very little during the unpaired phase of training. During the paired phase, the nictitating membrane response (labeled ***nm***) and the unit activity during the tone increased across three days of paired training, although the unit activity preceded the ***nm*** response by approximately 45 msec. Such changes in unit activity in cerebellar neurons do not occur if the ***CS*** and ***US*** are presented unpaired (i.e., tone and airpuff occurring at different times).

changes in heart rate, and (2) it does not correlate with the response to the air puff itself. Neural activity in these subcortical cerebellar nuclei thus mimics the conditioned NMR (McCormick & Thompson 1984). Moreover, rabbits trained only in one of the eyes and subsequently receiving a lesion of the subcortical nuclei ipsilateral to the trained eye show complete and permanent loss of the conditioned NMR to the tone (McCormick et al. 1982). Interestingly, the response to the air puff itself is not impaired by the lesion, suggesting that the deficit is not motor. A similar result is obtained if a light (instead of a tone) is used to signal the imminent presentation of the air puff, which suggests the deficit is not specific to the auditory modality. In addition, training of the contralateral eye leads to rapid conditioning. The lesion thus results in a selective loss of the conditioned NMR and only in the eye controlled by the lesioned side of the cerebellum. One critical area involved in conditioning of the NMR is, in fact, the anterior portion of the interpositus nucleus.

A second critical cerebellar component of conditioning is the Purkinje cell itself. These are inhibitory cells using GABA as their neurotransmitter. In part, they inhibit the activity of neurons located in the interpositus nucleus. Eyelid conditioning in a strain of mice (*Mus musculus*) that exhibits a selective degeneration of Purkinje cells is impaired but, interestingly, the conditioned response occurs with shorter latencies. These mice respond to the tone and shock just as strongly as wild type mice, suggesting that the deficit is related to associative learning and not to the animal's ability to react to the individual stimuli. Moreover, the residual conditioning that occurs in these mice is completely eliminated by lesions of the anterior interpositus nucleus (Chen et al. 1999).

Thompson (1986) suggested a minimum circuitry (see ***Figure 8.8***) that involves several highly conserved nuclei and

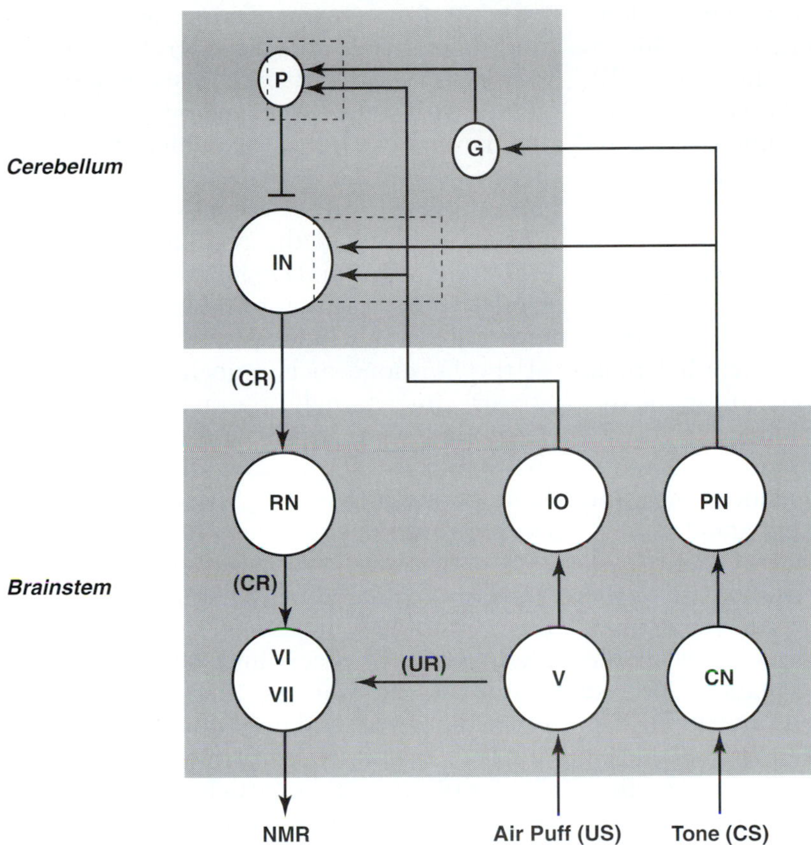

Figure 8.8. Neural network suggested by Thompson (1986) to account for conditioning of the nictitating membrane response in rabbits. The probable sites of neural plasticity are marked with dotted lines. CN, cochlear nucleus; G, granular cell; IN, interpositus nucleus; IO, inferior olive; P, Purkinje cell; PN, pontine nucleus; RN, red nucleus; V, VI, and VII, cranial nerve nuclei.

pathways; if correct, similar types of circuits could be involved in conditioning processes in a wide variety of species. Notice that there are separate pathways for the NMR elicited by the air puff (unconditioned) and by the tone (conditioned); however, these pathways converge on the brainstem nuclei corresponding to cranial nerves VI (abduscens) and VII (facial), both involved in the control of eye-related movements. Most important, however, is the convergence of information about the tone and air puff (or shock) on both the interpositus nucleus and the Purkinje cells. It is such convergence that presumably allows for neural changes to encode the specific information leading to a conditioned NMR. According to this model, the site of neural plasticity is the interpositus nucleus, whereas the Purkinje cells have a modulatory role.

2.f. Diencephalon: Thalamus and Associated Areas. The main parts of the diencephalon, including the pretectum, posterior tuberculum, thalamus, epithalamus, and hypothalamus, are common to all vertebrates. These areas participate in a wide variety of behavioral functions both directly and through their connections with the pineal gland and the pituitary gland.

The pretectal area receives input from the retina of the eyes. As in the case of the optic lobes, the pretectal area also possesses a retinotopic map and participates in the processing of visual information. Teleost fish, such as carp, salmon, and tuna, display highly differentiated pretectal nuclei, compared to all other vertebrates. The posterior tuberculum involves a series of nuclei that process sensory information and that appear only in chondricthyan (e.g., sharks and rays) and osteichthyan (bony) fishes. These nuclei have a function analogous to that served by some thalamic nuclei in other vertebrate groups—that is, they relay sensory information from the periphery to various telencephalic areas. The most dorsal part of the diencephalon is called epithalamus, and it contains the habenula and the pineal gland. The habenula is common to all vertebrates and is widely believed to be a plesiomorphic or primitive character. It is interconnected with various regions of the telencephalon, and in many species it displays an interhemispheric asymmetry, generally being larger on the right side. The pineal gland also appears in most vertebrates and can even be recognized in endocasts of fossil ostracoderm (primitive extinct agnathans) and placoderm (primitive extinct gnathans) fishes. This gland, together with some associated organs, such as the parietal eye of lizards (which includes a pigmented retina) and the frontal organ of amphibians, form the epiphysis. The epiphysis is involved in the regulation of *circadian* (day-night) and *circannual rhythms*, directly by its neural connections with other brain areas and indirectly by the secretion of the hormone melatonin into the bloodstream. Interestingly, the neurotransmitter serotonin (see ***Figure 8.5***) is converted into melatonin in the pineal gland via a metabolic pathway that is highly sensitive to circadian variations in light (Frazer & Hensler 1994). As a result, a variety of cyclic functions are regulated by the epiphysis in various vertebrates, including serotonin-mediated cycles of sleep and wakefulness in mammals, as well as thermorregulation, sexual behavior, and migratory behavior.

The thalamus constitutes a massive cluster of nuclei that participate in a variety of functions, mainly as intermediate relay stations between the rostral telencephalon and many caudal structures. The ventral thalamus, or subthalamus, is implicated in the control of motor functions. The dorsal thalamus, by contrast, is primarily conceptualized as a sensory relay station for a variety of modalities. The dorsal thalamus displays considerable variation in structure across species, and it invites evolutionary analysis. Cladistic analyses of neural structures are based on the comparative study of such characters as sources of afferent fibers, targets of efferent fibers, embryological development, relative concentration of neurotransmitter receptors, and patterns of regulatory gene expression. Consider, for example, the afferent projections to the rostrodorsal portion of the thalamus across various vertebrate taxa. The most rostral part receives input directly from the retina in all vertebrates and from the lemniscal pathways bringing somatosensory (tactile) information in many vertebrates. There is a single rostral nucleus in fish and amphibians, but two in diapsids (lizards, birds), and four in mammals. These are thought to be derived but to constitute a unified field of nuclei labeled *lemnothalamus* (in reference to the lemniscal afferents). By contrast, the most caudal region of the dorsal thalamus is highly conserved across vertebrates. This is labeled the *collothalamus* in reference to the fact that its afferents originate predominantly in the diencephalic nuclei known as superior and inferior colliculi in mammals (torus semicircularis in other vertebrates). These neurons are also sensory, but their connections to peripheral receptors is farther removed than that of lemniscal systems (they are called secondary sensory projections for this reason). The plesiomorphic efferent projections of lemnothalamic nuclei target the pallium, whereas those of the collothalamic nuclei target both the pallium and the striatum, the two basic divisions of the telencephalon as described in ***section 3.*** Based on a characterization of plesiomorphic or primitive characters (in this case, afferent-efferent connections), Butler (1995) suggested the evolutionary history of the dorsal thalamus presented in ***Figure 8.9.***

2.g. Diencephalon: Hypothalamus and Associated Areas. The hypothalamus and its associated preoptic area exhibit an extraordinary degree of complexity both in their internal structure and in the multiplicity of their neural and neuroendocrine functions.

The preoptic area is so labeled because it is rostrally located with respect to the optic chiasm and not because of any involvement in visual processing. Its functions are related to sexual behavior and thermoregulation. In endothermic vertebrates (i.e., birds and mammals), for example, preoptic neurons monitor body temperature and induce corrective responses when needed, such as shivering in response to a drop in body temperature or sweating in response to a rise in body temperature. Interestingly, direct cooling or heating of the preoptic area induces these responses (Nelson & Prosser 1981). The preoptic area is located in the most rostral portion of the hypothalamus, but a large variety of hypothalamic nuclei can be identified in the most caudal portions of this structure, especially in amniotes (i.e., reptiles, birds, and mammals).

The main inputs into the amniote hypothalamus are fibers originating in various regions, both rostral and caudal. For example, serotoninergic axons from the raphe nuclei give rise to the medial forebrain bundle and terminate in the mammillary and suprachiasmatic nuclei, as well as in the preoptic area. This medial forebrain bundle also brings afferent axons from various rostral (telencephalic) regions, including the hippocampus, olfactory bulbs, septum, and amygdala. Neurons located in the hypothalamus send, in turn, their axons to these regions in the same medial forebrain bundle. Another important pathway is the fornix, a tract that brings neural information from the hippocampus into the mammillary bodies and preoptic area.

Although hypothalamic connections have remained relatively conserved across species, they seem to have acquired various functions. This is particularly true of the hormonal products of hypothalamic function. The hypothalamus controls the pituitary gland via both neural and neuroendocrine influences. Hypothalamic neurons release various hormones (e.g., vasopressin, oxy-

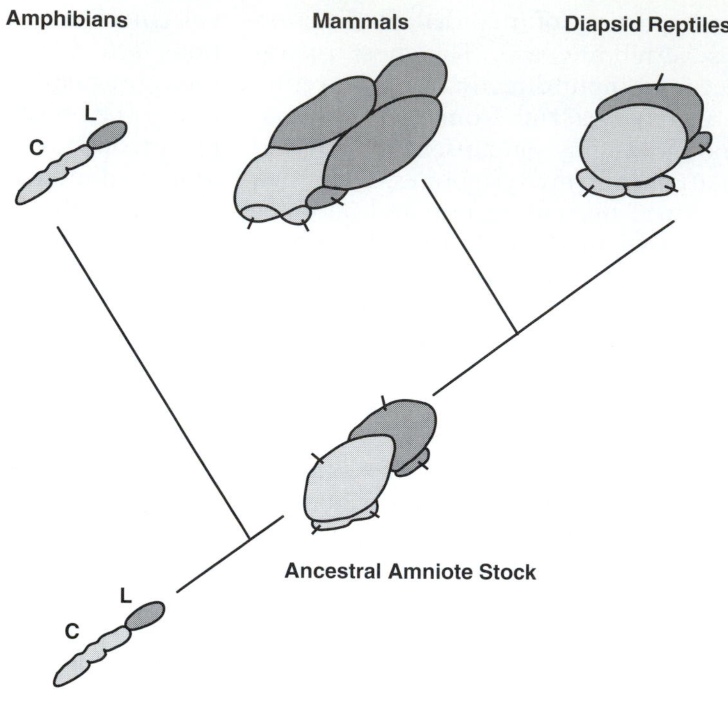

FIGURE 8.9. Hypothesized evolution of the dorsal thalamus of tetrapods (Butler 1995). Two major fields are distinguished according to their main inputs: The collothalamus (C, light gray) receives from the colliculi, whereas the lemnothalamus (L, gray) receives from the lemniscal systems. The collothalamus remains conservative, but the lemnothalamus is expanded from one nucleus in amphibians to several nuclei in mammals and diapsid reptiles. In each case, rostral is toward the right.

tocin) into the bloodstream in the posterior pituitary gland, or the neurohypophysis; these hormones are then transported by the circulatory system to their target organs, such as the kidneys and gonads. A second route involves a connection between hypothalamic neurons and the anterior portion of the pituitary gland, or the adenohypophysis. The adenohypophysis contains an internal circulatory system that receives hypothalamic hormones known as *releasing factors* and activates, in turn, a variety of other pituitary hormones that target other glands and organs of the body. The hypothalamus then allows for another type of regulation of the CNS over various bodily functions, one that is mediated by hormones rather than neural impulses. Although particular hormones may be recognizable as essentially the same molecule in a wide variety of vertebrates, they may display very different functions. For example, prolactin receives its name because it controls the production of milk in mammals; but the same hormone is involved in metamorphosis in amphibians (morphological changes that occur from the tadpole to the adult stage), and it participates in parental care behavior in several species of vertebrates. ***Table 8.3*** summarizes the main hypothalamic releasing factors, pituitary hormones, and their target organs in vertebrates.

3. TELENCEPHALON

3.a. Basic Subdivisions. The telencephalon is probably the most variable part of the CNS of vertebrates and, consequently, has stimulated substantial interest. Not only is it variable in morphology across species but it is also extraordinarily differentiated both in structure and function. One practical consequence of this is the proliferation of different nomenclatures that have historically been applied to the various areas and nuclei of different classes of vertebrates. The most challenging goal of comparative neurologists is, of course, to work their way through these variations in terminology and determine what structures are homologous and what are homoplasic. Similarly, comparative psychologists are interested in the functional side of this picture—that is, the way in which putatively homologous and homoplasic structures

TABLE 8.3 Summary of Hypothalamic-Pituitary Hormonal Influences

Hypothalamic Releasing Hormone	*Pituitary Hormone*	*Target Organ*
Gonadotropic (GnRH)	Follicle stimulating (FSH) Lutenaizing (LH)	Testis, ovary
Corticotropic (CRH)	Adrenocorticotropic (ACTH)	Adrenal cortex
Thyrotropin (TRH)	Thyroid stimulating (TSH)	Thyroid, oviduct
Prolactin (PRH)	Prolactin (PRL)	Ovary, mammary glands (mammals) Skin (reptiles) Crop (birds) Kidney (bony fish)
Growth hormone releasing hormone (GHRH)	Growth hormone (GH)	Skeleton
Hormones produced in the hypothalamus and secreted directly into bloodstream	Arginine vasotocin (AVT)	Kidney, aorta (bony fish, reptiles, birds) Oviduct (bony fish, reptiles, birds)
	Isotocin	Blood vessels and oviduct (bony fish)
	Oxytocin	Uterus, mammary gland (mammals) Kidney (bony fish) Oviduct (reptiles, birds)
	Vasopressin	Kidney

contribute to the control of behavior across species.

The telencephalon of all vertebrates can be subdivided into a pallium and a subpallium. The *pallium* corresponds to all the structures located in the medial, dorsal, and lateral portions of the telencephalon, whereas the *subpallium* corresponds to the most ventral portions of the telencephalon. The subpallial topographical arrangements remain relatively stable across species; by contrast, the relative positions of the various subdivisions of the pallium follow two different patterns of development, called *evagination* and *eversion*. ***Figure 8.10*** shows how these developmental patterns lead to different topographical arrangements. Evagination is considered the plesiomorphic condition because it occurs in agnathans and chondrichthyans, as well as in sarcopterygians (coelacanths, lung fish, and tetrapods); eversion, by contrast, is restricted to actinopterygian fish (see ***Figure 6.7,*** p. 192, for a review of these taxonomic groups).

The numbers in ***Figure 8.10*** identify some of the major components of the telencephalon. If they were labeled according to the terminology used for mammals, then ***1*** corresponds to the hippocampal formation (medial in sarcopterygians, but lateral in actinopterygians), ***2*** corresponds to the neocortex (or isocortex), ***3*** corresponds to the pyriform cortex (or allocortex), ***4*** to the striatum, and ***5*** to the septum. ***Table 8.4*** presents some equivalences in the terminology used to name the main areas of the telencephalon of tetrapods. These equivalences must be taken with caution because many are not considered definitive, as will be discussed in the next sections.

In the simplified view of the vertebrate telencephalon presented in ***Figure 8.10,*** structures ***1 to 3*** are pallial, whereas ***4 to 5*** are subpallial. In the lower vertebrates, these telencephalic areas are not so discrete and well defined as they appear in mammals, for example. Usually, a transversal view of the telencephalon shows a more or less continuous distribution of cell somas with some areas in which the density decreases (called area limitans). These low-density areas mark the boundaries between contiguous areas. ***Figure 8.11*** shows a transversal section of the telencephalon of the toad (*Bufo arenarum*) in which these transitional areas can be clearly appreciated.

3.b. Fish Telencephalon and Behavior. For all its size and complexity, it is somewhat surprising to learn that ablation of the entire telencephalon of fish often produces little or no obvious changes in behavior. Many such observations, particularly in teleost fish, suggest that no critical, life-preserving function is localized in this most anterior part of the brain. Indeed, similar conclusions were achieved during the 19th century by Antoine Desmoulins [1796–1828] and Pierre Flourens [1794–1867]. These French scientists were among the first to cause experimental lesions in the telencephalon and observe their behavioral consequences. In both cases, Demoulins with teleost fish and Flourens with birds, they observed that the postsurgical behavior of their animals (e.g., feeding, swimming, flying) was nearly normal. In order to detect behavioral deficits induced by large ablations of the telencephalon, scientists had to develop refined observational procedures and testing situations.

Flourens noted, for example, that telencephalon-ablated pigeons would tend to react normally to stimuli but would seem to lack some degree of "spontaneity" in their behavior when not stimulated in any particular way. Subsequent research with teleost fish suggests that this conclusion is essen-

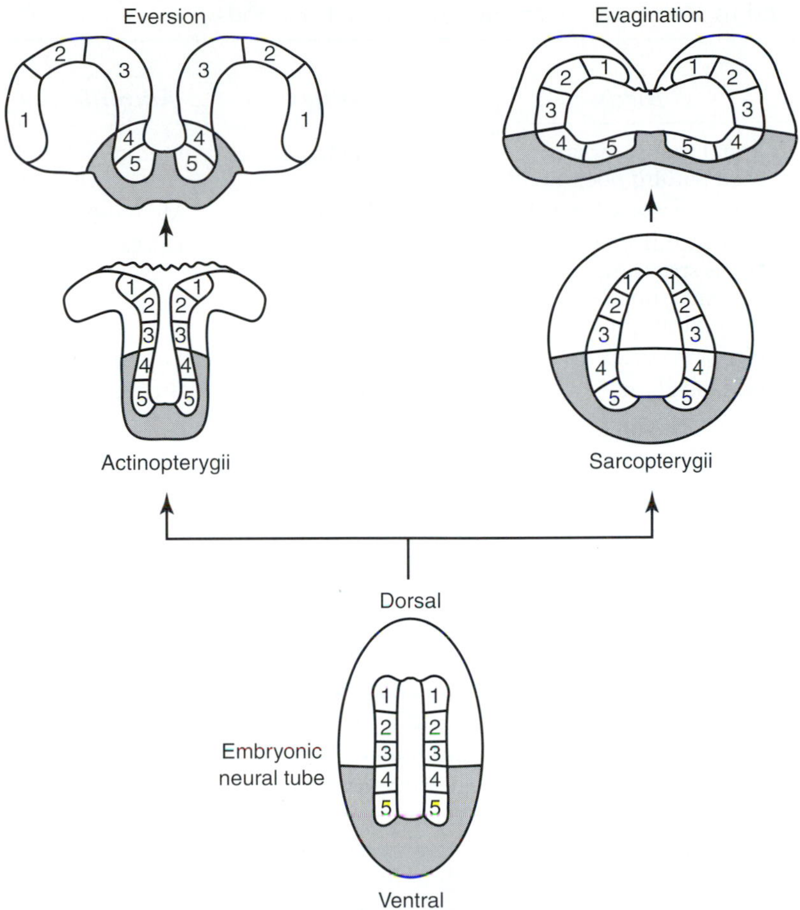

FIGURE 8.10. Patterns of telencephalic development. From an embryonic neural tube, the sarcopterygian telencephalon develop by evagination—that is, by the closure of tissue in the middle line, leading to the formation of lateral ventricles in each hemisphere. In contrast, the actinopterygian telencephalon develops by external eversion of the dorsal tissue. As a result, the topographic disposition of pallial regions is reversed, as shown schematically with the numbers. The pallium (dorsal) is shown in white, whereas the supallium (ventral) is shown in gray.

tially correct (de Bruin 1980). For example, lesioned Siamese fighting fish (*Betta splendens*) exhibit a lower-than-normal frequency in ritualized fighting behavior. However, once initiated, male agonistic behavior is similar to that of nonlesioned animals in its duration and its sequential properties. A three-spine stickleback (*Gasterosteus aculeatus*) with ablation of the telencephalon can initiate the normal zigzag dance in response to an approaching female, but it fails to guide the female toward

TABLE 8.4 Terminology Used to Name Telencephalic Areas in Tetrapods

Figure 8.12	*Mammals*	*Birds*	*Reptiles*	*Amphibians*
1	Amon's horn (CA fields)	Area hippocampalis, Area parahippocampalis?	Dorsomedial cortex	Medial pallium
1	Dentate gyrus	Hippocampus ventral	Medial cortex	Medial pallium
2	Neocortex	Neostriatum, Hyperstriatum, Ectostriatum, Area parahippocampalis?	Dorsal cortex	Dorsal pallium
3	Piriform cortex	Piriform cortex	Lateral cortex	Lateral pallium
4	Caudate, Putamen	Paleostriatum	Striatum	Striatum
4	Nucleus accumbens	N. accumbens	N. accumbens	N. accumbens
5	Septum	Septum	Septum	Septum
5	Amygdala	Archistriatum	Amygdala	Amygdala

Note. The numbers in the first column refer to the telencephalic areas described in *Figure 8.12*.

the nest (see ***Figure 5.5,*** p. 144, for a view of normal courtship).

The behavior of teleost fish in learning situations also shows interesting parallels. Suppose goldfish (*Carassius auratus*) with complete ablation of the telencephalon are trained in a situation in which the presentation of a light is followed a few seconds later by a long electric shock. These animals rapidly develop responses to the light, such as an increase in heart rate and general swimming activity comparable to that of normal animals. They will also respond to the presentation of the shock with an activity burst. If an active response allows the animal to escape the shock as it is being delivered, then ablated fish learn to escape just as well as normal animals. *Escape learning* then appears normal. If, however, the occurrence of this response during the light (and before the shock) allows this animal to completely prevent the shock from ever being delivered, then ablated animals show profound impairments. That is, *avoidance learning* is disturbed by telencephalic lesions (Hainsworth et al. 1967). Interestingly, however, ablated fish would eventually learn to respond to the signal, again suggesting that the telencephalon may be only modulating the process and is not the site where the storage of the critical information occurs. Furthermore, the recovery of avoidance learning impaired by a telencephalic lesion is hastened by increasing the intensity of the electric shock; that is, the behavior of ablated animals recovers to normal levels if they are highly motivated (Overmier & Papini 1986).

3.c. Evolution of the Telencephalon. Variations in the degree of morphological differentiation and topographical arrangement among vertebrates has stimulated an abundant amount of comparative research. An analysis of telencephalic structure using cladistic rules permits the development of hypotheses that characterize the components of a hypothetical ancestral condition. Such a group of characters that must have been present in the common ancestor of a particular taxon is referred to as a *morphotype* (Northcutt 1995). For example, the three pallial divisions—medial, dorsal, and lat-

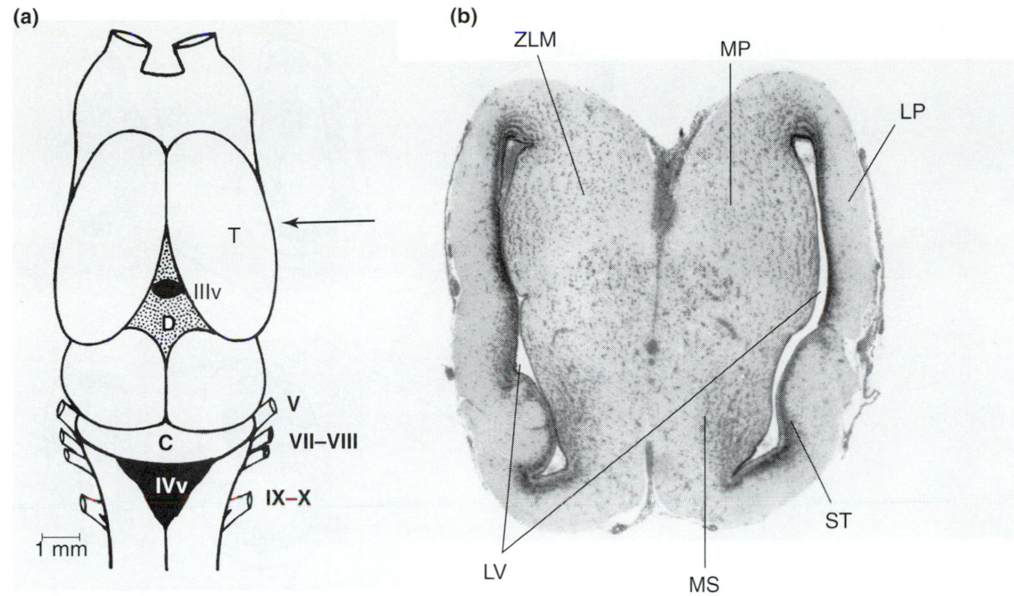

FIGURE 8.11. ***(a)*** Dorsal view of the brain of the toad *Bufo arenarum.* The arrow marks the position of the transversal section shown in ***(b).*** Areas are distinguished by zones where the density of cell somas decreases. C, cerebellum; D, diencephalon; LP, lateral pallium; LV, lateral ventricles; MP, medial pallium; MS, medial septal nucleus; OB, olfactory bulbs; OL, optic lobes; ST, striatum; T, telencephalon; ZLM, zona limitans medialis. (Photograph and drawing courtesy of Rubén Muzio.)

eral—can be found clearly represented in Chondricthyes (sharks and rays) and Osteichthyes (bony fish), and thus these divisions must be plesiomorphic. These three divisions can be recognized even in actinopterygian fish, which, as was shown in ***Figure 8.10,*** have a different folding of telencephalic tissue during development. Chondrichthyans also exhibit a nucleus A, in a lateral position; nucleus A is of dubious homology based on its location. Studies show that it receives inputs from the olfactory tract, which suggests that it might be related to the amygdala of other vertebrates (see ***section 4.e.*** below).

As for the subpallium, chondrichthyans show a clear distinction between a medial cluster of cells, the septal area, and a ventrolateral region known as the striatum. As already mentioned, these regions are extremely conserved in terms of relative position among vertebrates, which suggests they must be part of the ancestral morphotype. ***Figure 8.12*** shows a cladistic analysis of the morphotype that covers the jawed fishes, Chondrichthyes and Osteichthyes. The amphibians represent the tetrapods, and as shown in this figure, their basic organization does not differ substantially from that of sarcopterygian fish (represented by *Protopterus annectens,* an African lungfish).

Although this morphotype represents the basic theme of telencephalic structure, it should be remembered that natural selection has shaped this theme into many varia-

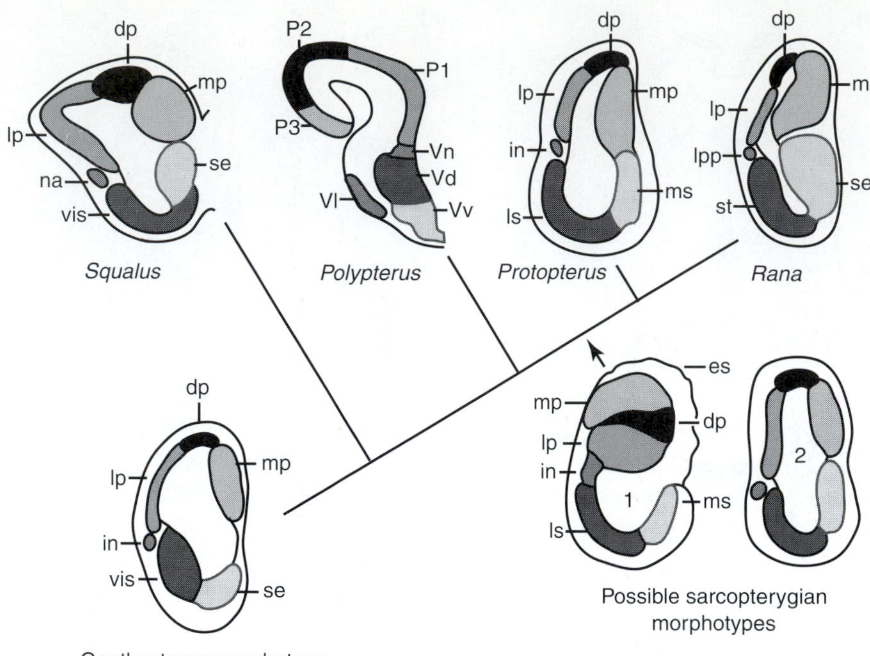

FIGURE 8.12. Hypothesis of the evolution of the vertebrate telencephalon (Northcutt 1995). Gnathostome and sarcopterygian morphotypes are hypothetical. Schematic representations of the brain of a chondrichthyan (*Squalus*), an actinopterygian (*Polypterus*), a lungfish (*Protopterus*), and an amphibian (*Rana*) are shown on the top. Dp, dorsal pallium; es, ependymal septum; in, intercalated nucleus; lp, lateral pallium; lpp, lateral pallial prominence; ls, lateral subpallium; mp, medial pallium; ms, medial subpallium; na, nucleus A; P1–P3, first, second, and third pallial formations; se, septal nuclei; st, striatum; Vd, area ventralis, pars dorsalis; Vl, area ventralis, pars lateralis; Vls, ventrolateral subpallium; Vn, a nucleus dorsal to Vd; Vv, area ventralis, pars ventralis.

tions. The cladogram depicted in ***Figure 8.12*** is based on the most conservative species within each taxon. Other species exhibit derived conditions in which these areas and nuclei appear further subdivided and differentiated. For example, several regions can be distinguished in the dorsal pallium, from which the dorsomedial pallial region is among the most variable in sarcopterygian fish.

A similar analysis for the tetrapods is far more complicated, given the high degree of differentiation displayed by the brains of birds and mammals. Striedter (1997) suggested that a way to understand homologies among the tetrapods is to look at the telencephalon from a developmental perspective. Following von Baer's theorem, according to which structures are more similar in the early developmental stages of different species than in the later stages, it is possible to postulate hypotheses of homology across areas that may appear differently organized in adult brains. ***Figure 8.13*** shows one such

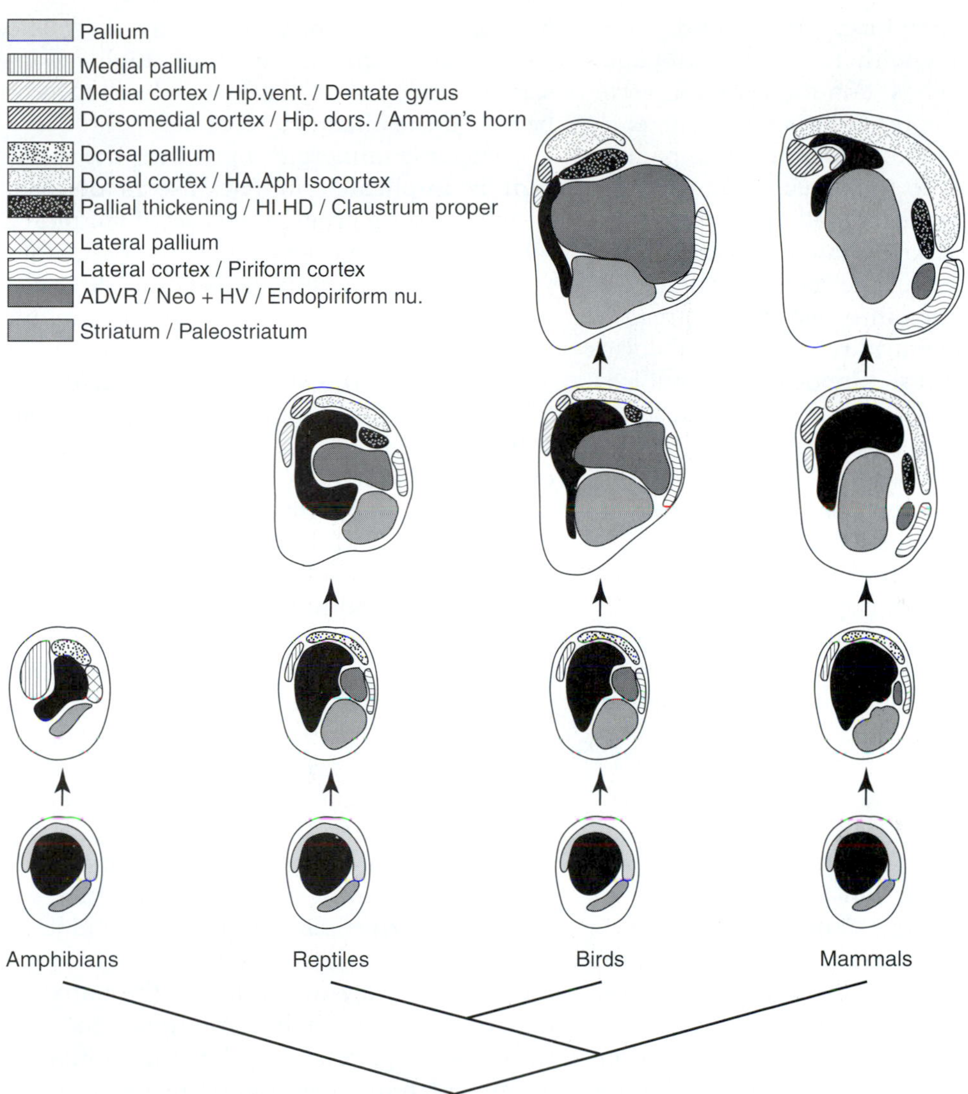

FIGURE 8.13. Hypothesis of the evolution of the telencephalon of tetrapods (Striedter 1997). This hypothesis emphasizes developmental sequences in telencephalic differentiation. The lateral ventricle is represented in black. ADVR, anterior dorsal ventricular ridge; APH, area parahippocampalis; HA, hiperstriatum accessorium; HD, hyperstriatum dorsal; HI, hyperstriatum intercalaris; Hip. dors., hippocampus dorsal; Hip. vent., hippocampus ventral; HV, hyperstriatum ventral; Neo, neostriatum.

analysis, with emphasis on pallial differentiation. It starts with the pallial-subpallial distinction that is common to all vertebrates and thus particularly similar in early development. In amphibians, the pallium differentiates into the three areas that contain the precursors of all the other areas that can be discriminated in other tetrapods. For example, the medial pallium further differentiates into two distinct regions in amniotes, a ventral region (medial cortex in reptiles, ventral hippocampus in birds, and dentate gyrus in mammals) and a dorsal region (dorsomedial cortex in reptiles, dorsal hippocampus in birds, and Amon's horns in mammals). Similarly, the dorsal pallium of amphibians is postulated to be homologous with the dorsal cortex of reptiles, the area parahippocampalis of birds, and the neocortex of mammals. These different regions all receive input from the dorsal thalamus, which suggests that they are homologous.

3.d. Striatum. The striatum of vertebrates has traditionally been conceptualized as an area that participates in the control of motor functions. In this regard, its dopaminergic input from the substantia nigra (the nigro-striatal bundle; see ***Figure 8.4***) and from diencephalic areas is a conserved connection identified in all vertebrates. Dorsal and ventral striatal sections have traditionally been identified within the striatum, and both appear to be plesiomorphic characters for the vertebrates. The dorsal portion is highly differentiated in mammals and, in particular, in primates, where such nuclei as the caudate, putamen, and globus pallidus are clearly discernible (these are also called basal ganglia). The caudate nucleus is a massive structure in the primate telencephalon, involving a rostral head and a tail that loops first dorsally and then ventrorostrally, to end beneath the head and in proximity to the amygdala. The ventral striatum also includes highly conserved nuclei, such as the nucleus accumbens and the olfactory tubercle.

The dopaminergic input into the striatum is implicated in Parkinson's disease, which causes a progressive loss of voluntary motor control in human patients. Behaviors from walking to writing become difficult, and patients lose spontaneity in movement. Similar behavioral effects are observed after lesions of this dopaminergic system in teleost fish and amphibians (Pollard et al. 1992). Lesions can be caused by injections of a toxin known as MPTP, which shows affinity for dopaminergic neurons in the basal ganglia and substantia nigra. Animals lesioned in this manner become lethargic and slow, a condition known as bradykinesia, typical of Parkison's patients.

The striatal system has also been implicated in the acquisition of *stimulus-response habits,* that is, tendencies to respond in a certain way when confronted with a particular stimulus or situation (Mishkin et al. 1984). It has been known for some time, for example, that human patients with brain lesions in the limbic system (see ***section 3.e.*** next) are incapable of remembering event information just acquired (e.g., they would forget the name of a person learned a few minutes ago); yet these same patients display the ability to learn and remember motor tasks, such as simple A+/B– discriminations, for a long time. This latter ability, however, is lost when striatal nuclei (such as the caudate nucleus) are lesioned. Similar results have been reported in monkeys and rats.

3.e. Limbic System and Behavior. The core of the telencephalon includes a series of nuclei and areas collectively referred to as the *limbic system.* Several of the limbic components have been mentioned before, such as the hippocampal formation (or medial pallium), the septum, and the habenula. The limbic system also includes the entorhinal cortex, the cingulate cortex, the mammilary bodies, the olfactory bulbs and tubercles, and the amygdala.

The importance of limbic structures in the control of behavior in all vertebrates studied so far cannot be overemphasized. I mentioned the role of the hippocampal formation in food storing and retrieving behavior in birds (see ***Chapter 4***, ***section 3.g.***, pp. 100–101, and ***Chapter 14***, ***section 2.c.***, pp. 547–549) and in spatial learning related to mating systems in mammals (see ***Chapter 5, section 2.f.***, pp. 140–141). The hippocampus of pigeons (*Columba livia*) has also been implicated in the acquisition of spatial information critical for *homing behavior* (Bingman & Yates 1992). Hippocampal lesions disrupt the ability of young pigeons to learn a homeward path and the ability of adult, experienced pigeons to learn a path when released from a novel location. Similarly, rats (*Rattus norvegicus*) with extensive hippocampal lesions exhibit deficits in *spatial learning* (Morris et al. 1982). For example, normal rats rapidly learn to find a nonvisible platform located always in the same position within a swimming tank. The platform is submerged about 1 cm below the surface, and the water is made opaque by the addition of milk; however, cues outside of the tank (called distal cues), such as a window or a source of noise, can be used to locate the platform even when the animal is released from different starting points.

In many of these experiments with both birds and mammals, hippocampal deficits are specific to spatial tasks, and they disappear when proximal cues are used to signal goal events. For example, hippocampal lesions do not impair the ability of black-capped chickadees (*Parus atricapillus*) to retrieve food when food is cued by a local visual stimulus (Sherry & Vaccarino 1989), and hippocampectomized rats rapidly learn to find the platform if it is made visible by placing it above the water surface (Morris et al. 1982). Interestingly, a similar dissociation between learning with distal cues (spatial learning) and with proximate cues (cue learning) has been reported in goldfish (*Carassius auratus*) with telencephalic ablations (Salas et al. 1996). These animals rapidly learn to exit a tank through an opening that is either directly cued by a proximate visual cue (stripes of black and white vertical lines) or always in the same spatial location (spatial constancy). In this latter case, the fish may have to swim toward the right or toward the visual cue in some trials, but toward the left or away from the visual cues in other trials, but the location is constant relative to distal cues. The results show a selective impairment of the spatial constancy task.

Apparently, such selective deficits are due to damage of the lateral pallium, as experiments with more restricted lesions demonstrate (Broglio 1997). As pointed out previously, actinopterygian fish (such as the goldfish) are characterized by a pattern of eversion in telencephalic development (see ***Figure 8.10***), which implies that what is "lateral" in their adult telencephalon corresponds to what is "medial" in the adult telencephalon of other vertebrates. Hippocampal neurons seem to have evolved a capacity to process spatial information very early in vertebrate evolution, and they have retained that capacity in more recently evolved lineages, such as birds and mammals. That behavioral capacity has been conserved even though the structure itself appears to have undergone significant cytoarchitectural changes. The lateral pallium of actinopterygian fish and the medial pallium of amphibians is characterized by scattered cell somas (see the medial pallium of toads in ***Figure 8.11***). ***Figure 8.14*** shows the organization of this area in amniotes (reptiles, birds, and mammals). A layer of cells is visible in reptiles, and a V-shaped structure appears in birds. In mammals, however, there is an interlocking set of layers, the dentate gyrus and the CA fields (cornu Ammonis, or Ammon's horns), with very specific synaptic connections. The precise homologies among these structures have not been fully established, and, moreover, it is not yet clear whether these architectural differences have functional implications.

Another structure that participates in a wide variety of behavioral functions is the amygdala, clearly visible in all gnathan vertebrates. The mammalian amygdala is a large and heterogeneous area located in the

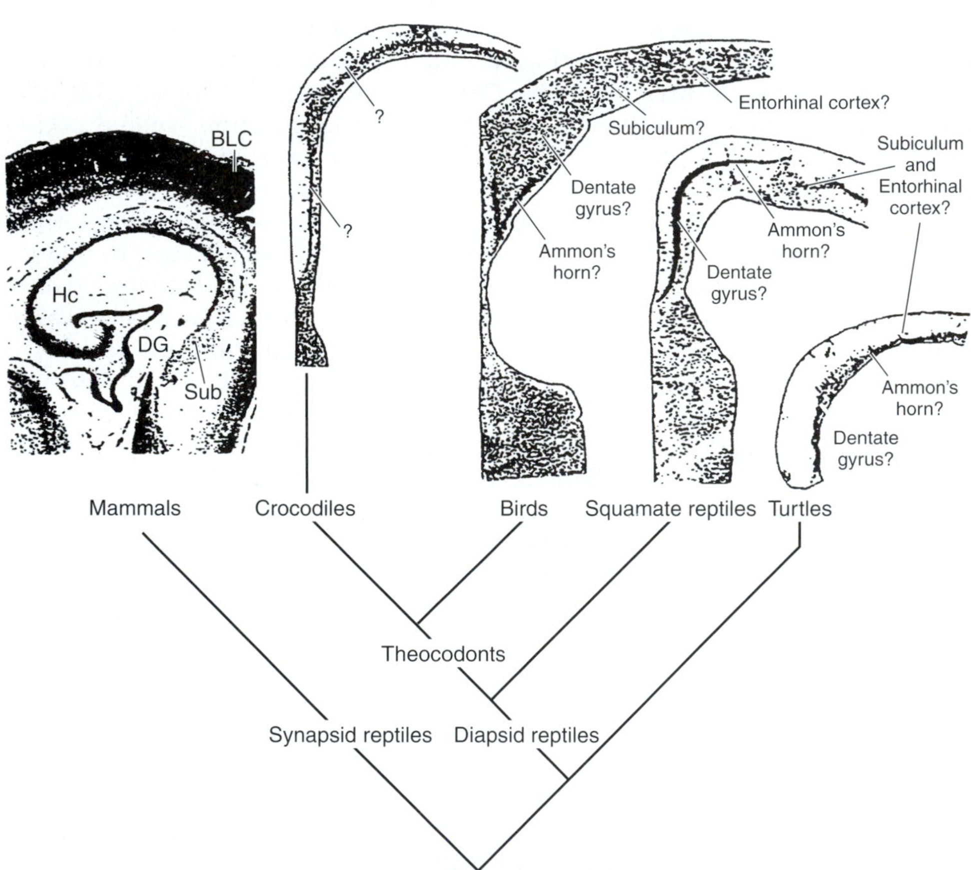

FIGURE 8.14. Comparison of the hippocampal formation in amniotes (reptiles, birds, and mammals). Homologies with respect to the mammalian dentate gyrus (DG), CA fields (Hc), and subiculum (Sub) are not yet fully established. The midline is to the left. (From Butler & Hodos 1996; mammalian hippocampus from Johnson 1977.)

base of the telencephalon and acting as a link between striatal, olfactory, limbic, cortical, and brainstem areas. It has two main regions, the corticomedial and the basolateral, each containing several nuclei. The corticomedial amygdala is linked by reciprocal connections to the hypothalamus and to a variety of brainstem nuclei, including the periaqueductal gray area. It receives direct inputs from the olfactory bulbs and various thalamic nuclei, which implies multisensory processing. The basolateral amygdala has reciprocal connections with the neocortex and various limbic areas, including the hippocampus. Its main efferents target neurons in the hypothalamus and the striatum.

The mammalian amygdala seems to be tied to what could be loosely referred to as aversive behavior. Lesions of the amygdala lead to tameness and reduction or loss of *aggressive behavior.* Consequently, such lesions may modify the interactions among individuals in social species. In rhesus monkeys (*Macaca mulatta*), which normally display very specific hierarchies of social dominance among individuals, lesions of the amygdala lead to significant social changes. In one study, the most dominant male in a group of eight monkeys received an amygdalectomy (Rosvold et al. 1954). After the operation, that monkey quickly became the most submissive animal in the entire group and the target of aggressive behavior from all the other monkeys. Amygdalectomized male monkeys may also display *hypersexuality,* that is, a tendency to engage in copulatory behavior with a variety of sexual partners, including other males and animals of different species.

In a famous experiment, Downer (1961) lesioned the right amygdala of a monkey (leaving the left one intact) and disconnected interhemispheric communication by sectioning the various commissures of the brain (corpus callosum, a bundle that communicates right and left neocortices; the anterior and posterior commissure, dealing with subcortical communication; the hippocampal commissure; the habenular commissure; and the massa intermedia, which communicates thalamic nuclei). In addition, the section of the optic chiasm prevented the eyes from reaching the contralateral hemisphere. As a result, visual stimuli projected on the right eye would be processed by the right hemisphere (where the amygdala was destroyed), but the same stimulus projected on the left eye would be processed by a normal left hemisphere. This animal had been extremely aggressive before the operation, and it continued to be so when both eyes were open and when the left eye was open. The mere sight of a human observer would induce open-mouth display and jumping on the cage. However, when the left eye was sutured and the animal could see only through its right eye (and thus the right, amygdalectomized hemisphere), it became immediately tamed and even willing to take raisins from the hand of the experimenter!

In rats, the role of the amygdala in fear conditioning is also well established. In a typical *fear conditioning* situation (Bouton & Bolles 1980), rats are placed in a novel environment where they are exposed to an arbitrary stimulus (it could be a tone or a light), followed a few seconds later by a painful electric shock delivered to their feet. This is yet another example of classical conditioning. After one or just a few pairings, the rats are brought back to the environment and exposed to the stimulus (which now has become a signal for pain) but not to the electric shock. Of interest is the amount of *freezing response* elicited by the stimulus, that is, how likely the animal is to remain motionless (except for breathing) during the stimulus. The freezing response is part of the rat's antipredatory repertoire. Experiments show that lesions of the lateral nucleus of the amygdala (part of the basolateral amygdala) impair fear conditioning, whether the stimuli are auditory or visual (LeDoux 1995). A model of the circuit involved in fear conditioning is shown in ***Figure 8.15.*** The lateral nucleus receives four main projections. The thalamic projection is crucial in simple conditioning trials (e.g., after tone-shock pairings, or A+ training); the neocortical projections are critical when discrimination training is involved (e.g., tone-shock but light–no shock, or A+/B– training); and the hippocampal projection acquires significance when the shocks are unsignaled and the entire context in which they occur becomes conditioned. Projections from the perirhinal cortex may be involved in integrating signals from various sensory modalities. Information from the lateral nucleus is then sent to the central nucleus (also part of the basolateral amygdala), from which it is relayed to caudal areas, including the periaqueductal gray and hypothalamus, to affect various behavioral and physiological responses, including freezing, autonomic responses, and the release of stress hormones into the blood stream.

3.f. Origin and Evolution of the Cortex. The pallium of amniotes (reptiles, birds, and mammals) is characterized by the migration of cell somas to some portions of the outer surface, where they organize into layers referred to as the *cerebral cortex.* Obviously, these cortical cells have precursors,

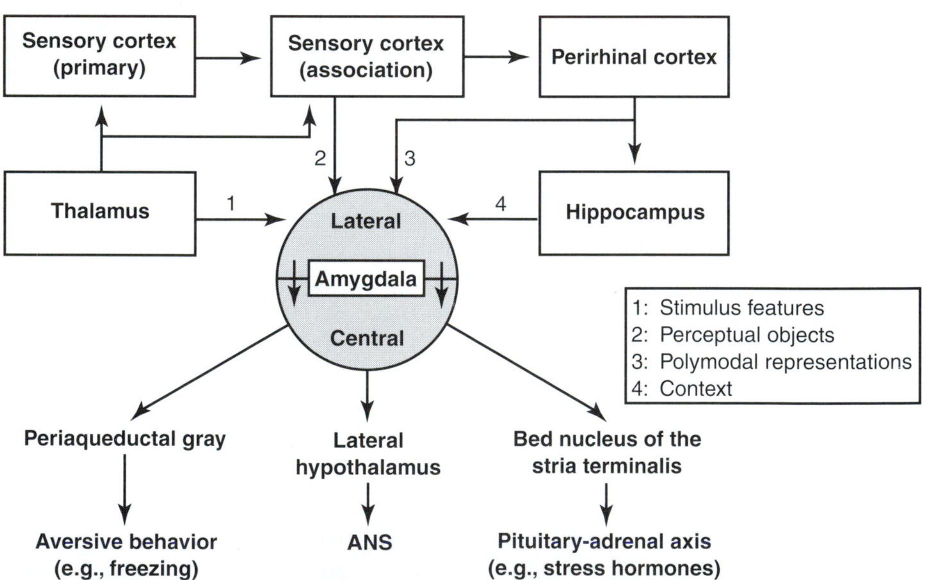

FIGURE 8.15. Neural network hypothesized to underlie fear conditioning in the rat (LeDoux 1995). The amygdala's basolateral field, including the lateral and central nuclei, play an important role in the acquisition of fear and in the expression of various indices of fear, both behavioral and physiological. ANS, autonomic nervous system.

such that homologous neuronal tissue has been found in all vertebrates. However, the cortical type of organization appears to be restricted to amniotes.

Three types of cortical tissue have traditionally been recognized: the archicortex, paleocortex, and neocortex. The prefixes "archi" (extra old), "paleo" (old), and "neo" (new) originally referred to their hypothesized phylogeny, but this is no longer tenable. The term archicortex refers to the hippocampal formation of mammals: dentate gyrus, CA fields, and the subiculum. The interlacing dentate gyrus and CA fields are peculiar to mammals, although, as discussed in the previous section, precursors may be found in all vertebrates (see ***Figure 8.14***).

In mammals, the paleocortex and neocortex are clearly separated by a lateral fissure called the rhinal sulcus; the neocortex lies dorsally and the paleocortex ventrally. These divisions can also be characterized by their cytoarchitecture: the neocortex includes up to six layers, whereas the paleocortex includes up to three layers. The evolution of the paleocortex and neocortex in amniotes has been the subject of intense debate. The immediate precedent of these cortices is the amphibian dorsal pallium. A common feature of the dorsal pallium of tetrapods, in general, is their intimate development with the dorsal thalamus. The two divisions of the dorsal thalamus recognized in ***Figure 8.9,*** the lemnothalamus and the collothalamus, project to the dorsal pallium in all tetrapods; therefore, these projections may be considered plesiomorphic. According to Butler's (1994) cladistic analysis of the dorsal pallium (which included a total of 34 characters), an amniote morphotype can be derived on the basis of the characteristics common to extant species. Among the features of the dorsal pallium common to all amniotes are the following:

(1) Absence of overlap between lemnothalamic and collothalamic projections
(2) Axons from lemnothalamus projecting to the medial part of the dorsal pallium in both hemispheres
(3) Axons from collothalamus projecting to the lateral part of the ipsilateral dorsal pallium
(4) Some reciprocal projections from dorsal pallium to dorsal thalamus

The synapsid line leading to mammals is characterized by several additional features, including the following subset:

(5) Expansion of both divisions of the dorsal pallium
(6) Six-layered cortex in most parts of the dorsal pallium
(7) Direct corticospinal projection
(8) Presence of rhinal sulcus
(9) Presence of corpus callosum (in placental mammals)

Finally, the anapsid-diapsid line leading to turtles, lepidosaur reptiles, crocodiles, and birds is characterized by the following features:

(10) Expansion of the lateral division of the dorsal pallium
(11) Formation of the dorsoventricular ridge
(12) Dorsoventricular ridge with some degree of nuclear organization (in some lizards)
(13) Dorsoventricular ridge with a greater degree of nuclear organization (in crocodiles and birds)

These characters can now be mapped into a cladogram of extant amniotes, as is done in ***Figure 8.16,*** to characterize the

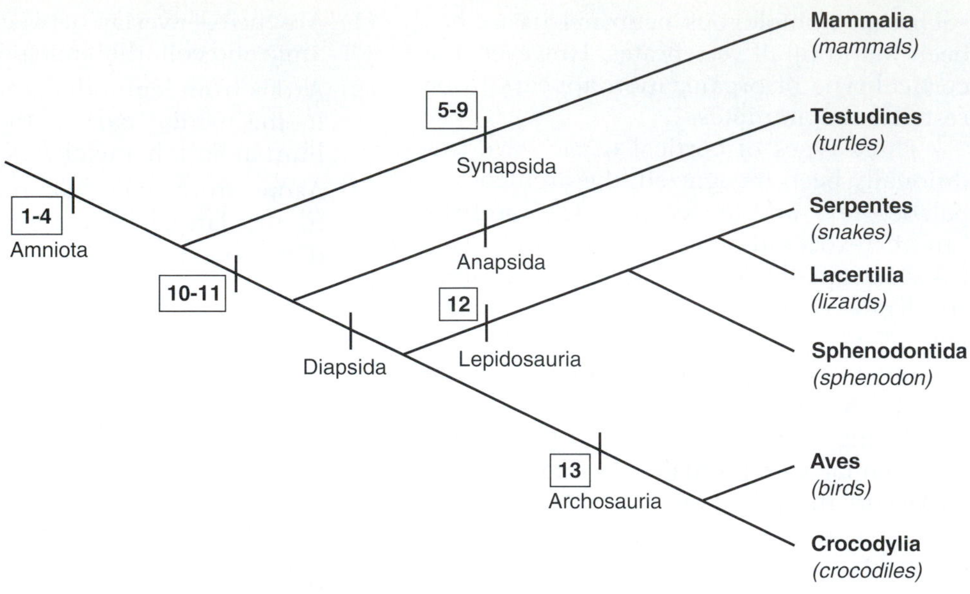

FIGURE 8.16. Cladistic analysis of the evolution of the dorsal pallium of amniotes (Butler 1994). Numbers designate traits as described on p. 299.

major features in the evolution of the cortex. As usual, however, this is considered a hypothesis and, as such, is not universally accepted. Among the controversial issues is that of the relationship between the dorsal ventricular ridge, a prominent reptilian nucleus, and various nuclei present in mammals and birds. According to Striedter (1997; see ***Figure 8.13***), the most anterior portion of the dorsal ventricular ridge (labeled ADVR in that figure), is homologous with the avian neostriatum and ventral hyperstriatum, two relatively large telencephalic structures, but homologous with the endopiriform nucleus in mammals, a rather minor area in relative terms. In Butler's (1994) theory, however, the dorsal ventricular ridge of reptiles and the homologous avian areas are related to the neocortex of mammals.

Probably no other brain structure has captured more attention from researchers and the general public than the mammalian neocortex (also called isocortex). Histological techniques developed at the end of the 19th century made it possible to look at the cytoarchitecture of the neocortex in great detail. The neuroanatomist Korbinian Brodman [1868–1918] found that the neocortex is organized in layers, and he divided the entire surface into areas according to variations in cellular organization. Some of these areas turned out to also have functional coherence. For example, area 4 receives somatosensory projections, whereas area 17 is the primary visual area. The human neocortex appears also complex because of a feature that is by no means general: the folding of the surface to produce convolutions (gyri) and fissures (sulci). Such a condition is referred to as *gyrencephalic*. In contrast, the neocortex of conservative mammals, such as that of opossums, hedgehogs, and armadillos, is smooth, or *lissencephalic*. Human brains, as well as those of other primates, are characterized by the presence of cerebral lobes: Frontal, parietal, occipital, and temporal lobes are visible from an external view; the insula lobe is hidden inside the temporal lobe.

An analysis of endocranial casts of Mesozoic cynodonts (mammalian ancestors) and mammals suggests that they possessed a lissencephalic neocortex (Kielan-Jaworowska 1986). In such endocasts, the rhinal sulcus can be clearly appreciated, and thus the inference of the presence of neocortex is certain. Which is the primitive condition, the lissencephalic or the gyrencephalic? Much has been said about the putative processing power of the highly convoluted cerebral cortex of humans, but apparently this is almost entirely determined by the size of the brain. A study of 48 species of mammals in which the size of the cortical surface (and thus its degree of convolutedness) is correlated against the size of the brain shows an almost perfect correlation (Jerison 1982). One interpretation of such correlation is that the degree of folding is a byproduct of the conservation of the surface-to-volume relationship between the neocortex and brain. The allometric equation has, in fact, an exponent equal to 0.91, which means that the neocortex of species with large brains (such as our own) is actually slightly smaller than expected.

Mesozoic mammals were relatively small and thus likely to have possessed lissencephalic neocortices and relatively high rhinal sulci. Following the mass extinction event at the end of the Cretaceous, there was an adaptive radiation of mammals, and the main extant orders were established (see ***Figure 6.13,*** p. 205). This happened approximately 65 Mya, and since then the mammalian neocortex has evolved in parallel in the various orders. Large brains evolved in many orders independently, including primates (apes and humans), cetaceans (whales), perissodactyles (rhinoceros), carnivores (lions), and proboscideans (elephants). Consequently, whatever properties characterize the neocortex of large species, they may have evolved independently (homoplasy). Some of the primary sensory areas, including the visual, auditory, and somatosensory areas appear to be at least homologous between distantly related rodents and primates. The same applies to the primary motor area of the frontal cortex, although not all mammals may present a clearly distinguishable primary motor area. These areas have topographic representations of the retina (visual), basilar membrane of the internal ear (auditory), body surface (somatosensory), and skeletal muscles (motor), respectively. Monkeys, however, may have somewhere between 20 and 40 supplementary visual areas, depending on the species, at least four times as many as rodents. Thus, many of the secondary visual areas in primates may have no homologous counterpart in rodents. A similar conclusion applies to the auditory, somatosensory, and motor areas of the cortex (Northcutt & Kaas 1995).

In addition to processing sensory and motor information, the neocortex of mammals has integration areas traditionally referred to as *association cortex*. Many psychological processes are based on subtle aspects of the functioning of these areas. For example, simple conditioning processes proceed normally in decorticated animals—that is, animals from which the neocortex was experimentally removed. However, if noninvasive techniques are used to determine what is happening during simple conditioning trials, substantial amounts of neural plasticity are observed, as shown in ***Figure 8.17, see back inside cover*** (Gonzalez-Lima & Scheich 1986). In a typical study, one group of rats receives tone-shock pairings (fear conditioning), while another receives the same number of tone and shock presentations unpaired in time (control). Before a key test session, all the rats are injected with a radioactively labeled substance analogous to glucose (such as 2-fluoro-2-deoxyglucose, FDG). Since glucose (or FDG) is a source of energy, it is taken up by neurons in proportion to their degree of activation. All animals receive exposure to the tone during this test and are sacrificed immediately after the test session. Histological slices of brain tissue are deposited on top of a special type of film sensitive to the radioactive label (usually ^{14}C) carried by FDG. After about 2 weeks, the film is developed, and those areas in which FDG has accumulated appear dark. Such a procedure, called autoradiography, shows high levels of activity in the auditory cortex (and many other brain regions), but only in rats that were exposed to tone-shock pairings. It is not, therefore, a type of activity induced by any tone but only by a tone that has acquired signal value.

The neocortex has taken over additional psychological functions that are particularly well developed and studied in primates. These include planning abilities, expectancy formation (as opposed to stimulus-response habits), memory, and a variety of language-related functions. Some of these topics are covered in ***Chapter 9.***

4. Brain Size

4.a. Principles of Brain Size. The neurological machinery behind a particular behavioral function can be quite localized and restricted. ***Chapter 7,*** for example, provided an appreciation for the extent of such localizationism: Habituation in *Aplysia* could be confined to a monosynaptic pathway. Likewise, vertebrate brains display *functional localization:* Entire regions of the brain may be allocated to the processing of a relatively specific type of information. Are all functions equally localized? And if localization of function is so extreme, what can be gained by looking at the overall size of the brain without distinguishing among its many different regions?

If brain function and brain structure were related in such a simple way as suggested by an extreme localizationist theory, then the way in which brain tissue accomplishes its outcomes (i.e., perception, motivation, learning, memory, consciousness, etc.) would be easy to understand. But such functions appear to require the contribution of many different regions in ways that are not yet fully understood. Isolated vertebrate brains are among the most complex systems known to scientists; if, in addition, brains are seen as active organs, acquiring information and influencing the animal's bodily functions, including behavior, the degree of complexity is almost unimaginable. Brain size provides a useful, initial approach to brain function and a way to illustrate some major generalities (Jerison 1973).

Functional localization, for example, suggests the principle of *proper mass,* according to which there is a positive correlation between the size of a particular neural area and the amount of information involved in the processing of the function allocated to that area. This generalization can be best appreciated by considering the size of the sensory nuclei of various species in relation to the species' natural behavior. Primates, for example, tend to be diurnal and base their foraging and social behavior on visual cues; consequently, it is not surprising to find relatively large brain areas allocated to the processing of visual information. Bottom-feeder fish, such as the bass, detect tactile and gustatory information from the substrate and, consequently, display enlarged hindbrain nuclei that receive afferent input from the vagal and facial nerves.

When functions are extremely localized, the loss of neurons in a particular area may completely and permanently eliminate whatever function these neurons support. However, when the control of a particular function is spread across several brain areas, the extent to which brain damage will affect a specific function may be more related to the magnitude of the damage than to its localization. This is referred to as the principle of *mass action*, and it was first suggested by research on the role of the neocortex of rats in learning. Karl S. Lashley [1890–1958] observed that it was the amount of neocortical tissue ablated, and not its location within the neocortex, that predicted how disrupted rats would be in their ability to learn simple visual discriminations (e.g., learn to approach a sign with vertical white-black lines, instead of one with horizontal lines, to get a food reward). Mass action leads one to expect that sheer brain size would have to be related to the general capacity of an animal to process information.

Such "capacities for processing information" are, in turn, the product of selective pressures that have shaped the evolution of the brain. Brain size can be viewed as a character or trait that responds to such selective pressures. Jerison (1973, p. 15) made this simple assumption explicit in the following general principle: "The brains of all animals have evolved in ways appropriate to life in their niches or adaptive zones, in accordance with principles such as enunciated earlier [proper mass, mass action] that describe the relationship to behavior of the structure of the brain as an organ of the body." Increased brain processing abilities, realized in larger brains, evolved by the same rules that apply to other biological traits.

4.b. Artificial Selection for Brain Size. One way to demonstrate that overall brain size can potentially be affected by natural selection, just as any other morphological trait, is to determine if it responds to artificial selection pressures. *Artificial selection* consists of the breeding of individuals with extreme expressions in a particular phenotype (see ***Chapter 3***). For example, individuals with large (or small) brains are selectively paired for several generations to determine if a strain of animals with large (or small) brains can be developed. But how can such techniques be applied to the size of an internal organ of the body, such as the brain?

One procedure works on the assumption that the brain size of littermates is positively correlated because of their chances of sharing genes that determine this trait. Thus, a subset within a litter is chosen to be sacrificed so that the size of their brains can be measured, whereas the rest are allocated to breeding. A similar procedure was used by Roderick et al. (1973) to develop high (H) and low (L) lines of mice for brain size. The criterion for selective breeding was the absolute weight of the brain. Indeed, H and L strains could be easily developed using this procedure. However, there were correlated changes in body size, even though animals had not been selected for this particular trait. This is already a familiar example from artificial selection experiments: No matter what the criterion for selection is, traits other than the strictly selected one also tend to change. These traits change by correlation because they depend on genes that also determine the trait that is being used as a criterion for selection. Remember that most genes affect the development of many different traits, a property called *pleiotropy*. It is possible, therefore, that increases (and decreases) in brain size are a simple passive consequence of increases (and decreases) in body size.

Would brain size respond to artificial selection when the criterion is based on a measure of brain size relative to body size? Fuller and Geils (1972) provided an affirmative answer to this question. Mice from the Roderick H and L lines were bred according to their scores for relative brain weight, whereas those from the C line were bred randomly. Once litters were obtained from pairs of H and L mice, some were sacrificed and the weights of their brains and bodies were measured. The remainder mice from the same litters were paired according to the brain:body estimates obtained from their litter mates. Mice in which brain weight was higher than expected (or lower than expected) for body weight were paired with each other to yield an H (or an L) generation. These were compared with each other and with randomly mixed mice from the C line at various ages from 5 to 40 days after birth. The results demonstrated that the size of the brain can increase (or decrease) relative to a control line even when the selection criterion is relative, rather than absolute, brain weight. That is, for a given body weight, the H line (or L line) still shows larger (or smaller) brains than the C line. Differences in brain size cannot be fully explained in terms of correlated changes in body size.

Fuller and Geils also measured the brain weight of mouse fetuses from all three lines and found that whereas L and C lines were not different from each other, the H mice had larger relative brain size in late prenatal age. In mammals, the growth of the brain and body occur at about the same rate during embryonic development; but whereas the brain stops growing sometime after birth, the body continues to grow during an additional period. Large brains are achieved by increasing brain growth rate during the same period in which the brain grows in normal animals. By contrast, small brains are achieved by arresting growth earlier than it is the case with normal animals.

4.c. Relative Brain Size. Studies of brain size using artificial selection techniques suggest two conclusions. First, brain size is tied to body size. There must be a common set of genes controlling the growth of these two characters (Lande 1979). There are some growth hormones, for example, which may affect the development of many organs of the body, thus tending to produce a positive correlation between the size of a particular organ (e.g., the brain) and the size of the entire body. This relationship is referred to as *allometric growth* because it fits the generalized allometric equation:

$$E = aS^b$$

where $\boldsymbol{E}$ is brain size or weight (from the French "poids encephalique"), $\boldsymbol{S}$ is body size or weight ("poids somatique"), and $\boldsymbol{a}$ and $\boldsymbol{b}$ are empirical constants for the point of origin and slope, respectively, of the function relating body and brain size. The allometric equation relates changes in the size of one organ or bodily part, to changes in body size according to a power function (Thiessen & Villarreal 1998). Notice that such a function gives a straight line when the variables are transformed to their $\log_{10}$:

$$log(E) = log(a) + b\, log(S)$$

This is why allometric functions are represented either in double log coordinates or in transformed log scores.

The second conclusion is that the size of the brain can increase beyond the size expected on the basis of body size. This active increase in brain size is referred to as *encephalization* and will be discussed in detail in the next section.

It makes sense for the size of the brain and body to be correlated. The brain contains cells that process afferent information from the body (sensory receptors) and control muscles, glands, and organs. For example, an elephant has a larger body surface than a mouse, and so it surely needs more sensory neurons in order to detect tactile information from the skin. The elephant also has a greater number of muscle cells and therefore will need more motoneurons to control its movements than a mouse. The brain of an elephant should be larger than that of a mouse simply because the elephant is a larger animal. But exactly how much larger should one brain be compared to another, even in relative terms?

One way to answer this question is to measure the size of both the brain and the body in a sample of species and plot one against the other. Brain and body can be estimated in terms weight or volume. In cases in which the animal's body is lost (e.g., with fossil species), body size can be extrapolated from the taxon (order or class) to which that animal has been assigned. Jerison (1973) has summarized a variety of methods that are used to measure these variables. When information on brain and body size from a sample of vertebrates is plotted in double logarithmic scales, the resulting functions are linear and fit the allometric equation. ***Figure 8.18*** shows these results in terms of minimum convex polygons for each vertebrate class and for only extant species. Each species provides at least one point for this surface, representing the size (weight, volume) of its brain and body. A sample of mammals, for example, yields a cloud of such points. The polygon for the mammals is the surface that encloses all the points for individual mammalian species. The same is done for the other vertebrate classes.

Jerison (1973) noted that the slopes of these polygons tend to be relatively similar and fall around a value of 0.67. Replacing $\boldsymbol{b}$ in the allometric equation:

$$E = aS^{0.67}$$

If $\boldsymbol{b} = 1$, then for every unit of increase in body size, there would be a unit of increase in brain size; this is called *isometric growth*. But a $\boldsymbol{b} = 0.67$ implies that increases in brain size cannot catch up with increases in body size across species. This is called *negative allometry* (obviously, $\boldsymbol{b} > 1$ implies *positive allometry*). Since the surface of a solid grows with a 2/3 exponent of its volume, Jerison (1973) suggested that the increase in brain volume was dependent on increases in the body surface rather than in body volume.

Jerison's hypothesis was later questioned when it became clear that the value of the exponent can deviate substantially from Jerison's 2/3 value. In mammals, for example, the value of $\boldsymbol{b}$ approximates 0.75—that is, 3/4. The differences in slope values between Jerison's original analyses and subsequent ones are attributable to differences in the size of the samples and to the use in later studies of samples less biased toward small species. Because of negative allometry, any sample in which small species predominate will tend to yield a lower slope value. This 3/4 value for $\boldsymbol{b}$ suggests a connection between brain size and metabolic rate (Armstrong 1990). In mammals, the allometric relationship between metabolic rate and body size has an exponent that approaches 3/4. However, not all classes of vertebrates show the 3/4 slope, suggesting that metabolic rate is not the factor (or at least not the only one) causing evolutionary changes in brain size. More importantly, when basic metabolic rate and brain size are examined in samples of animals with similar body size, the correlation disappears. Other factors, such as the relative timing of brain and body growth (Ritska & Atchley 1985), and ecological factors such as diet in mammals, or life-history factors such as mode of development in birds (Harvey & Krebs 1990), have been postulated to account for the evolution of brain size in vertebrates. ***Table 8.5*** summarizes the slope values for various classes of vertebrates.

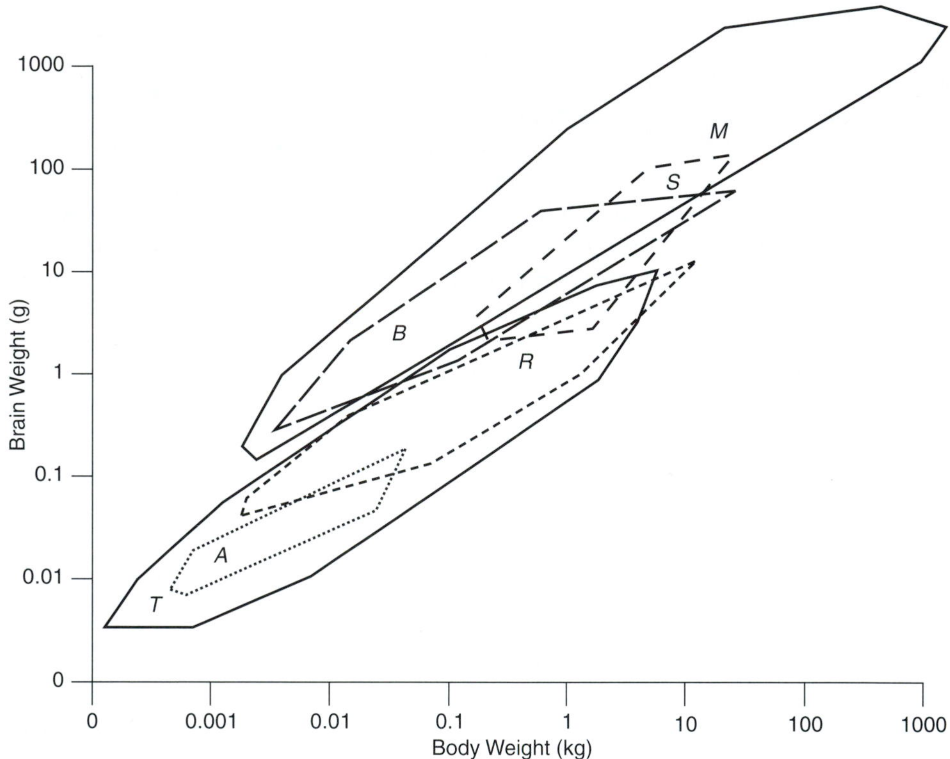

FIGURE 8.18. Relative brain size of various vertebrate classes (Bauchot et al. 1989). A, amphibians; B, birds; M, mammals; R, reptiles; S, sharks and rays; T, teleost fish. Samples include extant species only. Each polygon encloses all the data points for individual species within each class. Extensive overlap exists between birds and mammals and among teleost fish, amphibians, and reptiles, but these two sets are generally segregated. The exceptions are a few species of teleost fish and the sharks and rays that overlap extensively with these two sets. Agnathans (not represented in this figure) have the lowest values of all classes.

TABLE 8.5 Values of the Exponent for the Allometric Equation Obtained in Studies Involving Vertebrates

Class	*b*	*Reference*
Mammalia	0.76	Martin (1981)
	0.74	Eisenberg (1981)
	0.69	Harvey & Krebs (1990)
Aves	0.58	Martin (1981)
Reptilia	0.54	Martin (1981)
	0.60	Platel (1979)
Amphibia (anurans)	0.47	Platel (1979)
Osteichthyes	0.65	Ridet & Bauchot (1990)
Chondrichthyes	0.76	Northcutt (1977)
Agnatha	0.67	Northcutt (1985)

Notice that all exponents are below one, which implies that brain:body relationships obey negative allometry. Moreover, there is some variability in these exponents, particularly if some orders within these classes of vertebrates are analyzed separately. For example, within the Chondrichthyes, skates and rays show very high slopes; Northcutt (1977) reported a ***b*** = 1.04 (isometry) and reanalyzed data from other studies that suggested ***b*** values up to 1.38 (positive allometry). In the other extreme, the slope value for anuran amphibians appears to be the lowest yet reported for any group: ***b*** = 0.47 (Platel 1979). Jerison (1973) had obtained a 0.67 value constant for all of his analyses; such a constant value would suggest that the same factors underlie the evolution of relative brain size in all vertebrate classes. In contrast, diverging slopes suggest that the evolution of relative brain size may be driven by different forces in the various vertebrate groups.

4.d. Encephalization. When the exponents (***b***) of the allometric equation are the same but the point of origin (***a***) is different, then animals of equal weight would have different brain size. For example, Martin (1981) found similar exponents (see above) for samples of extant birds (180 species) and reptiles (59 extant species). However, ***a*** = 2.1 for birds, but ***a*** = 1.2 for reptiles. The difference is not trivial when you realize that these are $\log_{10}$ numbers: the brain of a bird is about 10 times larger than that of a reptile of equal body size! Moreover, there was no overlap between the minimum convex polygon for each class, much as Jerison (1973) had noted earlier. A similar conclusion is true, at least within certain limits of body weight, for the comparison between mammals and reptiles.

Jerison (1973) also calculated brain:body data for a number of extinct species of reptiles, birds and mammals. He found, for example, that the relative brain size of dinosaurs did not deviate significantly from that of living reptiles, although it extended the polygon because of their large body size. Interestingly, some fossil birds (notably *Archaeopteryx,* the oldest known bird) and mammals fell in between the polygons for extant species of these groups and that of reptiles. Apparently, then, the current relative brain size of higher vertebrates evolved during the Mesozoic, with early birds and mammals being already somewhat encephalized relative to reptiles. Why is the brain of a bird or a mammal so much larger than the brain of a reptile?

Jerison (1973) noted that early birds, including *Archaeopteryx,* had larger brains than pterosaurs, their contemporaneous flying reptiles. The implication of this finding is that avian encephalization is probably not related to flying itself, but to some other aspect of the ecological niche of early birds. Like most modern birds, primitive birds probably already lived in a forested environment where perching from branch to branch and avoiding obstacles during flying may have been an important component of their daily behavior. Jerison suggested that it was the perceptual demands of this type of environment that required substantial encephalization in birds. Depth perception accurate enough to make figure-background discriminations while in flight, so that the bird could safely land on a branch, may have required an additional amount of neurons and even substantial rewiring of reptilian brain circuits.

According to Jerison (1973), encephalization in primitive mammals followed an entirely different path. Unlike their reptilian ancestors, Mesozoic mammals may have evolved by exploiting the nocturnal niche—that is, by remaining active at night when most of the then-dominant vertebrates were inactive. The shift from diurnal to nocturnal habits may have demanded a shift from distant perception based primarily on vision (as in reptiles), to one based on olfaction and audition. At night, very little visual information can be acquired (the perception of visual patterns and colors requires substantial illumination). A foraging primitive mammal may have relied extensively on olfactory and auditory cues to detect its prey and avoid danger. Whereas a substantial amount of signal processing can be accomplished in the retina, the internal ear and olfactory epithelium, where sensory receptors are located, are relatively simple peripheral systems. A demand for more complex olfactory and auditory processing was met by enlarging the areas in the CNS allocated to the processing of such signals rather than by making the peripheral organs more complex. In addition, and also unlike in the case of visual stimuli, olfactory and auditory cues must be processed in a serial manner. Such serial processing places a large load on the retention of information over short periods of time in order to interpret incoming signals. Mammalian encephalization may thus be the product of a switch to a nocturnal mode of life that relied on sensory systems requiring a larger proper mass to function adaptively.

While these are plausible and very general scenarios, they rest on several heretofore unstated assumptions about brain size. One of them is that an increase in relative brain size involved predominantly an increase in the number of neurons and their connections rather than an increase in other cells or components of the brain (e.g., glial cells, blood vessels, etc.). The total number of neurons in a particular area could be controlled by modifying the genetic signals that regulate the offset of neuronal reproduction. However, as Jerison (1973) pointed out, neurons are more densely packed in relatively smaller brains, which have a lower density of glial cells relative to neurons than larger brains. Cell numbers are thus confounded with cell density. New types of neurons may also be implicated in the evolution of larger brain size.

Alternatively, it could be that what increases is the size of the cells or their processes (e.g., dendritic arborization, axon terminals). For example, the relatively large hippocampal formation of food-storing birds contains neurons (known as calbindin-like immunoreactive neurons because of the method used to identify them) with somas that are significantly larger than homologous hippocampal neurons from nonstoring species with an average-size hippocampus (Montagnese et al. 1993). In salamanders, for example, brain size is positively correlated with the size of neurons in the optic tectum, an area involved in visual processing (Roth et al. 1994).

In addition, the size of the salamander brain correlates positively with morphological complexity of the optic tectum. Complexity was defined in terms of five categories, depending on the presence of superficial cell somas (cells that migrate away from the ventricular walls) and the number of cell layers. Cellular migration away from the periventricular areas of the telencephalon is also associated with large relative brain size in sharks (Northcutt 1977). Mormyrid teleost fish (Ostheichthyes), such as the elephant-nosed fish, *Gnathonemus petersii,* use weak electric currents to detect food particles in the mud and for intraspecific communication (Kramer 1996). As previously mentioned, the cerebellum of these fish is hypertrophied, folding rostrally on top of the optic tectum and cerebral hemispheres; the valvula, a central structure between the cerebellar hemispheres, is specialized in electroreception and uniquely enlarged in weakly electric fish. As a result, mormyrid fish have among the largest relative brain size scores of all bony fish. Relatively larger brains are also more differentiated morphologically and more complex architecturally than relatively smaller brains.

In summary, relatively encephalized species have evolved in several vertebrate lineages independently from one another. Skates and rays among the Chondrichthyes, mormyrid teleosts among the Ostheichthyes, some salamanders among amphibians, and the birds and mammals among the amniotes all exhibit some degree of independently evolved encephalization.

4.e. Brain Size and Intelligence. Among the most provocative hypotheses advanced by Jerison (1973) was his idea that brain size was related to what he called *biological intelligence,* i.e., "the capacity to construct a perceptual world" (p. 17). Jerison noted that the size of sensory nuclei was roughly equivalent to the importance of that sensory modality in the natural behavior of the animal—the principle of proper mass described previously. However, according to Jerison, the brains of birds and mammals underwent a process of progressive encephalization (related to the unusual ecological demands of their niches) that led to a "surplus" of brain tissue. It is that additional brain mass that allows for more complex representations of the external world and a greater amount of acquired information that can be used to adjust to changing environments.

The term "intelligence" is usually reserved for a variety of psychological capacities, including the ability to learn from experience, to solve problems, and to use information. Is there any information suggesting a connection between brain size and intelligence? There are several ways to answer this question. One approach consists of finding indices for both brain size and intelligence that can be measured in a wide range of species and then determine if they correlate. The obvious assumption behind this approach is that both brain size and intelligence vary gradually and correlate positively. Several indices related to brain size have been suggested in the literature. Jerison (1973) suggested the *encephalization quotient* (*EQ*), defined as the ratio of the obtained brain size of a particular species, E_o, to that expected for the class to which that species has been assigned. Mathemathically, the expected brain size is given by the allometric equation with the constants that correspond to that particular class. The formula then can be expressed thus:

$$EQ = \frac{E_0}{aS^b}$$

According to this equation, if the brain size obtained in a particular species falls on top of the regression line, then the obtained and expected brain sizes are equal, and EQ = 1. Encephalization occurs when EQ > 1. Notice, however, that the solution depends on the particular values assigned to the constants in the allometric equation, which, as was shown previously, differ somewhat across studies. Nonetheless, EQs are extensively used as a life-history trait. ***Table 8.6*** presents a list of EQs for various mammals that provides a general idea of the variation within taxa (from Eisenberg 1981; with $a = 0.05$ and $b = 0.74$).

Jerison (1973) also suggested an index to estimate the amount of cortical neurons in mammals above the number required by the size of the body and called it N_c. This index can be thought of as cortical neurons available for processing information other than that concerned with the body (i.e., sensory and motor). Riddell and Corl (1977) reported that N_c was a good predictor of performance in a variety of learning tasks in mammals, including one known as *learning sets*. In a learning set experiment, animals are trained to choose one of a pair of stimuli and usually given food for correct choices (A+/B–, where "A" and "B" represent a pair of stimuli such as "circle" and "triangle"). Once the first discrimination is learned to a criterion, a new pair of stimuli is introduced (C+/D–) until the new discrimination is mastered, and then, a third pair of stimuli (E+/F–) is introduced, and so on. Eventually, animals may show a typical behavioral pattern when facing a novel discrimination problem: (1) they select one of the stimulus by chance on trial 1, and (2) they respond to the same stimulus if rewarded in trial 1 but respond to the opposite stimulus if nonrewarded in trial 1. This is referred to as the *win-stay/lose-shift strategy*; an animal that achieves this strategy has "learned to learn" new problems (Harlow 1949).

Riddell and Corl (1977) estimated the slopes of learning set performance in published data from a variety of mammalian species, including primates, carnivores, and rodents. They found a very high correlation ($r = 0.98$) between learning set performance and N_c. Does this show that a larger neocortex yields greater intelligence? Perhaps, but one should be cautious when interpreting results like these. For example, the lowest learning set performance was that of rodents and, in particular, rats. Rats are notorious for their relatively clumsy visual abilities, so their taking many trials to master learning set problems based on visual stimuli, such as patterns of stripes or geometric figures, may reflect a sensory-perceptual difficulty rather than poor learning ability. Consistent with this view, faster learning set acquisition (as fast as that exhibited by some primates) has been obtained in rats when tridimensional objects (Kay & Oldfield-Box 1965), spatial cues (Zeldin & Olton 1986), and odors (Slotnick & Katz 1974) were used as discriminative stimuli. So perhaps the correlation between learning set performance and N_c describes a capacity of the mammalian neocortex to process visual information rather than to support a general learning ability.

Rumbaugh and Pate (1984) have used a similar approach in their study of primates'

TABLE 8.6 EQ Values for Selected Species of Mammals

Taxon	*Species*	*Common name*	*EQs*
Monotremata	*Ornithorhynchus anatinus*	Platypus	0.94
	Tachyglossus aculeatus	Echidna	0.72
Marsupialia	*Dasyurus quoll*	Marsupial cat	1.05
	Macropus giganteus	Kangaroo	0.47
	Didelphis marsupialis	Opossum	0.46
Insectivora	*Suncus murinus*	Shrew	0.48
	Setifer setosus	Greater hedgehog	0.45
	Neomys fodiens	Mole	0.75
Edentata	*Choloepus hoffmanni*	Tree sloth	1.09
	Myrmecophaga tridactyla	Ant eater	0.81
	Dasypus novemcinctus	Nine-banded armadillo	0.37
Chiroptera	*Desmodus rotundus*	Vampire bat	1.23
	Pteropus geddeiri	Fruit-eating bat	0.95
	Myotis lucifugus	Little brown bat	0.52
Rodentia	*Atherurus africanus*	Porcupine	1.19
	Rattus norvegicus	Albino rat	0.79
	Hydrochoerus hydrochoeris	Capibara	0.68
Primates	*Homo sapiens*	Human	7.33
	Cebus capuchinus	Cebus monkey	3.40
	Lemur catta	Lemur	1.45
Carnivora	*Vulpes vulpes*	Wild fox	1.89
	Ursus arctos	Bear	0.91
	Panthera leo	Lion	0.70
Cetacea	*Phocaena phocaena*	Porpoise	4.90
	Tursiops tursia	Dolphin	3.23
	Globicephala melaena	Porpoise	1.70
Perissodactyla	*Equus zebra*	Zebra	1.70
	E. caballus	Horse	1.07
	Tapirus bairdi	Tapir	0.87
Artiodactyla	*Bison bison*	Bison	0.35
	Hippopotamus amphibius	Hippopotamus	0.33
	Sus scrofa	Wild pig	0.27

problem-solving abilities. A simple, two-choice situation is presented to the animal in which the choice of one stimulus leads to a piece of food, whereas the choice of a second stimulus leads to nothing (i.e., an A+/B– problem). When animals have achieved some specific acquisition criterion (e.g., accuracy levels of 67% and 84% have been systematically used in this research), the problem is inverted: A–/B+. This is called a *discrimination reversal* task, and it requires that the animal extinguish its response to the previously positive stimulus (A) and develop an approach response to the previously negative stimulus (B). Performance in this reversal discrimination is assessed in terms of a *transfer index* (*TI*) computed as a difference score. Animals receive training in discrimination problems (e.g., A+/B–, C+/D–) until they reach an acquisition criterion of either 67% or 84% correct responses (random performance would yield 50% correct responses). Then, the animal is trained in the reversal of each problem (e.g., A–/B+, C–/D+), and the percentage of correct responses is measured in a block of 11 reversal trials for each reversal problem. TI is computed according to a simple subtraction:

$$TI = [\% \text{ correct responses after } 84\% \text{ criterion}] - [\% \text{ correct responses after } 67\% \text{ criterion}]$$

Negative transfer occurs if learning to a higher criterion of 84% leads to a lower percentage of reversal correct responses than learning to a lower criterion of 67%. Negative transfer indicates that the additional training afforded by the higher acquisition criterion interferes with reversal training. In contrast, *positive transfer* results from better reversal performance after learning to a higher 84% criterion than to a lower 67% criterion. Thus, TI provides a measure of the extent to which prior experience interferes with (negative transfer) or facilitates (positive transfer) reversal performance. As shown in ***Figure 8.19,*** there is a positive correlation between the TI and encephalization in primates. As encephalization rises from prosimians to monkeys and to apes, TI moves from negative to positive values, suggesting that greater behavioral flexibility is correlated with relatively larger brains in primates.

Notice that the underlying hypothesis in studies like those reviewed above is that some relative measure of brain size correlates with a more efficient performance in some learning task, without reference to how the particular degree of encephalization has been achieved. This hypothesis leads one to expect similar performance level in species that reached similar degrees of encephalization, even if brain size similarities had evolved independently. Thus, even though the resulting correlation implies a lineal ordering of species (i.e., a scala naturae), the ordering is not necessarily phylogenetic.

A second approach to the study of the relationship between brain size and intelligence is to study the behavioral capacities of lines artificially selected according to brain size. In the original selection study (see ***section 4.b.*** above), the L line developed retinal degeneration, which rendered many of the mice blind. This did not happen in the H line, and thus these mice were used in several behavioral studies to assess brain size-behavior correlations. Compared to randomly selected controls, C, mice in the H line (after 10 generations of selection for high brain size), were faster to learn brightness discrimination, spatial reversals, and an active avoidance problem. In the spatial reversal problems, mice received training in a T-shaped maze filled with water; they had to swim from the stem of the maze toward one of the arms (always the same for any given animal) that had a small ladder the animals could use to come out of the water. Once the spatial (right vs. left) problem was solved, the reinforced position was reversed until the mice learned the new problem. Two such reversals were administered. H mice learned the original problem just as fast as C mice, but the reversal performance of H mice was significantly superior to that of the controls (Elias 1969, 1970).

Further studies indicated that H mice were superior in tasks that required an active response, but exhibited poorer learning of tasks that required response inhibition. For example, H mice were notoriously inferior in a task in which they were trained to stay in a box to avoid an electric foot shock,

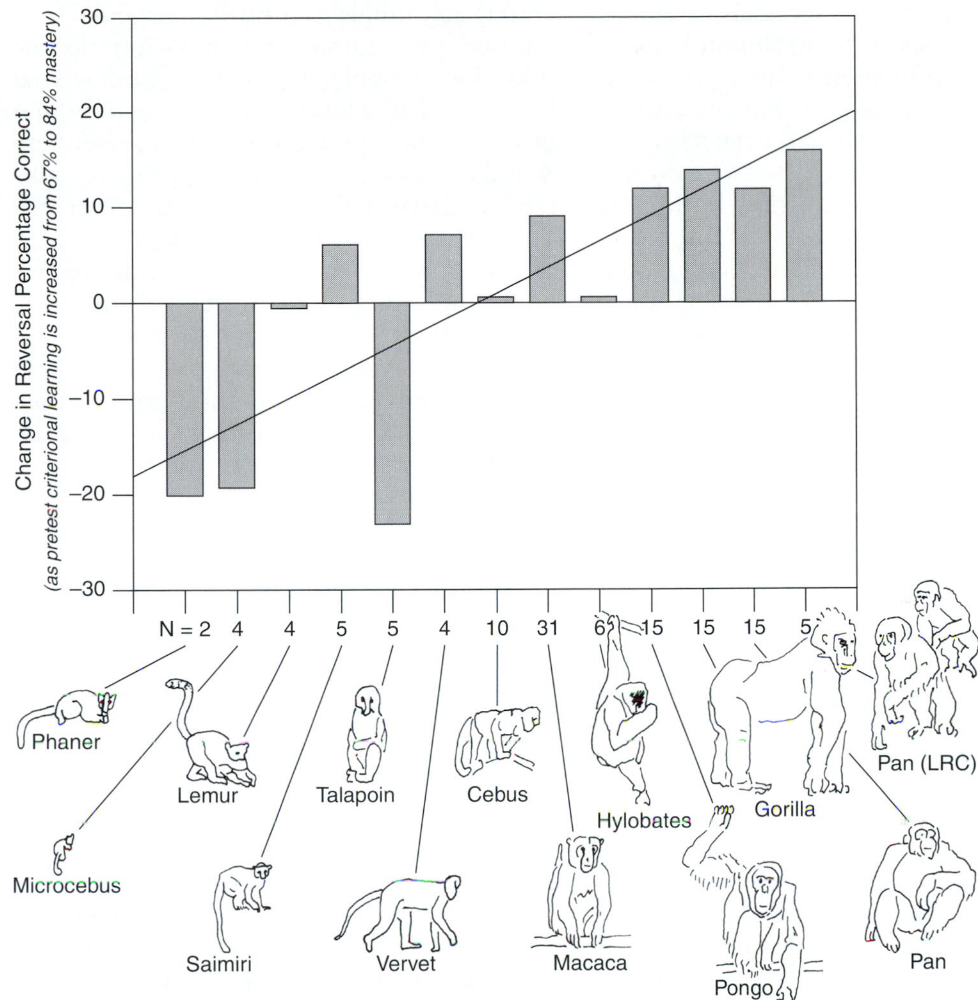

FIGURE 8.19. Performance of several species of primates in the first reversal of a discrimination problem (Rumbaugh & Pate 1984). Learning is measured in terms of a transfer index (see text). Negative numbers mean negative transfer—that is, acquisition of the reversal problem was slower than original acquisition. Positive numbers mean positive transfer—that is, the reversal was acquired faster than the original problem. Prosimians tend to show negative transfer, whereas apes tend to show positive transfer.

---

which was presented only if the animal stepped in another box—so-called *passive avoidance learning*. Furthermore, H mice were significantly more active in an open-field situation than C mice (Wimer et al. 1969). It is thus possible that the relationship between brain size and reversal learning (and perhaps learning set performance too) is caused by a greater tendency of animals with large brains to be generally more active and not by differences in learning mechanisms or abilities per se.

A growing literature implicates a modest but significant positive correlation between brain size and intelligence among humans. These studies also suggest that the correlation holds within a particular species. The most recent studies have relied on noninvasive techniques for measuring brain size, such as magnetic resonance imaging (MRI) techniques. An MRI provides a high-resolution image of the brain and its internal structure that makes it possible to determine brain size with great accuracy. Coefficients of correlation in MRI studies in which normal individuals also take some conventional intelligence test range between 0.30 and 0.60 (e.g., Willerman et al. 1991). Intelligence tests involve various types of problem-solving situations (WAIS), reading ability (NART), and tests designed to minimize cultural biases (CFIT).

4.f. Behavioral Specializations and the Brain. As was shown in this section, there are two main determinants of brain size. The first is the allometric change that occurs primarily as a result of natural selection on body size that passively drives the brain (as well as other organs) toward a larger size. Allometric change is achieved by lengthening the phase of cell proliferation and probably involves minor changes in the internal wiring of the brain. The second change occurs when natural selection favors a particular phenotype that requires additional brain tissue (i.e., proper mass). This type of active change, called encephalization, can involve the entire brain, or some of its substructures and is likely to involve not just lengthened cell proliferation but some degree of rearrangement of connections across brain nuclei and areas (Aboitiz 1996).

Several examples of correlations between behavior and either the whole size of the brain or the size of particular areas within the brain have been discovered among mammals and birds, particularly in relation to feeding strategies. Among the bats, for example, the EQ of species that forage for fruits tends to be higher than that of species that forage for insects (Eisenberg & Wilson 1978). Frugivorous primates also tend to have a larger brain size than primates that have different diets (Mace et al. 1980). Among birds, the nectar-feeding hummingbirds exhibit a relative brain size that is about 2.5 times larger than that of granivorous galliform species such as chickens. Although not yet fully understood, these differences could be related to the demands imposed by these food resources (Rehkamper et al. 1991). Relative brain size can also be linked to other ecological variables. For example, mammalian species that move both on the ground and in trees or water (i.e., three-dimensional lifestyle) tend to have larger brains than species that live predominantly on the ground (i.e., two-dimensional life-style; Eisenberg 1981). These differences in relative brain size evolved as a result of differential ecological demands for information processing afforded by the distribution of food resources and the extent of spatial movement.

Behavioral capacities may demand the evolutionary change of more restricted brain areas. As shown in ***Table 4.1*** (p. 112), the EQs of conservative mammals that display active antipredatory strategies tend to be larger than those of species that escape predators by passive means (e.g., opossums feign death to deter predators). In addition, insectivore mammals that show active (vs. passive) antipredatory strategies have relatively larger limbic areas, known to be involved in emotion, motivation, and aggressive behavior. Moreover, fossorial insectivores that live predominantly in burrows have reduced visual cortical areas and enlarged somatosensory cortical areas, whereas semiaquatic species display enlarged striatal and cerebellar areas, both involved in motor control (Stephan et al. 1991).

Finally, the hippocampal formation varies widely in relative size in correlation with spatial learning abilities. This has been documented in food-hoarding birds (see ***Chapter 4, section 3.g.,*** pp. 100–101, and ***Chapter 14, section 2.c.,*** pp. 547–549) and in polygynous male meadow voles (see ***Chapter 5, section 2.f.,*** pp. 140–141).

5. KEY TERMS

aggressive behavior 297
allometric growth 304
artificial selection 303
association cortex 301
autonomic nervous system (ANS) 274
avoidance learning 290
biological intelligence 310
brainstem 278
cerebellum 278
cerebral cortex 298
chemical synapse 269
circadian rhythms 284
circannual rhythms 284
classical conditioning 276
collothalamus 285
conditioned analgesia 276
convergence 268
diencephalon 284
discrimination reversal 311
divergence 268
encephalization 305
encephalization quotient (EQ) 310
escape learning 290
evagination 288
eversion 288
fear conditioning 297
final common path 278
freezing response 297
functional localization 302
gill slits 264
gyrencephalic 300
habituation 276
homing behavior 295
homology 267
homoplasy 267
hypersexuality 297
instrumental conditioning 276
isometric growth 305
lateral inhibition 280
learning sets 310
lemnothalamus 285
limbic system 294
lissencephalic 301
mass action 303
master-yoked procedure 276
mesencephalon 278
morphotype 290
negative allometry 305
negative transfer 312
nerve cord 264
neurochemical systems 269
neuromodulator 269
neuron doctrine 275
neurotransmitter 269
nictitating membrane response 281
notochord 264
optic tectum 278
pallium 288
parallelism 267
parasympathetic 274
passive avoidance learning 313
pleiotropy 304

positive allometry 305
positive transfer 312
proper mass 302
releasing factors 286
reticular formation 269
reversal 268
rhombencephalon 278
somatotopic organization 279
spatial learning 295
spinal cord 274
spinal preparation 275
stimulus-response habits 294
subpallium 288
sympathetic 274
synapomorphy 264
tail 264
telencephalon 287
transfer index (TI) 312
ventricular system 271
von Baer's theorem 268
win-stay/lose-shift strategy 310

6. References

Aboitiz, F. (1996). Does bigger mean better? Evolutionary determinants of brain size and structure. *Brain, Behavior & Evolution,* **47,** 225–245.

Armstrong, E. (1990). Brain, bodies, and metabolism. *Brain, Behavior & Evolution,* **36,** 166–176.

Bauchot, R., Randall, J., Ridet, J.-M., & Bauchot, M.-L. (1989). Encephalization in tropical teleost fishes and comparison with their mode of life. *Journal für Hirnforschung,* **30,** 645–669.

Bingman, V., & Yates, G. (1992). Hippocampal lesions impair navigational learning in experienced homing pigeons. *Behavioral Neuroscience,* **106,** 229–232.

Bouton, M. E., & Bolles, R. C. (1980). Conditioned fear assessed by freezing and by the suppression of three different baselines. *Animal Learning & Behavior,* **8,** 429–434.

Broglio, C. (1997). Implicacion de diferentes areas telencefalicas en el aprendizaje y la memoria espacial en el carpin dorado (*Carassius auratus*). Unpublished doctoral dissertation, University of Sevilla, Spain.

Butler, A. B. (1994). The evolution of the dorsal pallium in the telencephalon of amniotes: Cladistic analysis and a new hypothesis. *Brain Research Reviews,* **19,** 66–101.

Butler, A. B. (1995). The dorsal thalamus of jawed vertebrates: A comparative viewpoint. *Brain, Behavior & Evolution,* **46,** 209–223.

Butler, A. B., & Hodos, W. (1996). *Comparative vertebrate neuroanatomy. Evolution and adaptation.* New York: Wiley-Liss.

Chen, L., Bao, S., & Thompson, R. F. (1999). Bilateral lesions of the interpositus nucleus completely prevent eyeblink conditioning in Purkinje cell-degeneration mutant mice. *Behavioral Neuroscience,* **113,** 204–210.

de Bruin, J. P. C. (1980). Telencephalon and behavior in teleost fish. A neuroethological approach. In S. O. E. Ebbesson (Ed.), *Comparative neurology of the telencephalon* (pp. 175–201). New York: Plenum.

Downer, J. L. de C. (1961). Changes in visual gnostic functions and emotional behaviour following unilateral temporal pole damage in the "split-brain" monkey. *Nature,* **191,** 50–51.

Eisenberg, J. F. (1981). *The mammalian radiations.* Chicago: Chicago University Press.

Eisenberg, J. F., & Wilson, D. E. (1978). Relative brain size and feeding strategies in the Chiroptera. *Evolution,* **32,** 740–751.

Elias, M. F. (1969). Differences in spatial discrimination reversal learning for mice genetically selected for high brain weight and unselected controls. *Perceptual & Motor Skills,* **28,** 707–712.

Elias, M. F. (1970). Spatial discrimination reversal learning for mice genetically selected for differing brain size: A supplementary report. *Perceptual & Motor Skills,* **30,** 239–245.

Ewert, J.-P. (1997). Neural correlates of key stimulus and releasing mechanism: A case study and two concepts. *Trends in Neuroscience,* **20,** 332–339.

Farel, P. B., Glanzman, D. L., & Thompson, R. F. (1973). Habituation of a monosynaptic resonse in the vertebrate central nervous system: Lateral column–motoneuron pathway in isolated frog spinal cord. *Journal of Neurophysiology,* **36,** 1117–1130.

Fetcho, J. R. (1991). Spinal network of the Mauthner cell. *Brain, Behavior & Evolution,* **37,** 298–316.

Forey, P., & Janvier, P. (1993). Agnathans and the origin of jawed vertebrates. *Nature,* **361,** 129–134.

Forey, P., & Janvier, P. (1994). Evolution of early vertebrates. *American Scientist,* **82,** 554–565.

Frazer, A., & Hensler, J. G. (1994). Serotonin. In G. J. Siegel, B. W. Agranoff, R. W. Albers, & P. B. Molinoff (Eds.), *Basic neurochemistry* (pp. 283–308). New York: Raven.

Fuller, J. L., & Geis, H. D. (1972). Brain growth in mice selected for high and low brain weight. *Developmental Psychobiology,* **5,** 307–318.

Gonzalez-Lima, F., & Scheich, H. (1986). Neural substrates for tone-conditioned bradycardia demonstrated with 2-deoxyglucose. II. Auditory cortex plasticity. *Behavioral Brain Research,* **20,** 281–293.

Gormezano, I., Kehoe, E. J., & Marshall, B. S. (1983). Twenty years of classical conditioning research with the rabbit. *Progress in Psychobiology and Physiological Psychology,* **10,** 197–275.

Grau, J. W., Salinas, J. A., Illich, P. A., & Meagher, M. W. (1990). Associative learning and memory for an antinociceptive response in the spinalized rat. *Behavioral Neuroscience,* **104,** 489–494.

Grau, J. W., Barstrow, D. G., & Joynes, R. L. (1998). Instrumental learning within the spinal cord: I. Behavioral properties. *Behavioral Neuroscience,* **112,** 1366–1386.

Groves, P. M., & Thompson, R. F. (1970). Habituation: A dual-process theory. *Psychological Review,* **77,** 419–450.

Hainsworth, F. R., Overmier, J. B., & Snowden, C. T. (1967). Specific and permanent deficits in instrumental avoidance responding following forebrain ablation in the goldfish. *Journal of Comparative & Physiological Psychology,* **63,** 111–116.

Harlow, H. (1949). The formation of learning sets. *Psychological Review,* **56,** 51–65.

Harvey, P. H., & Krebs, J. R. (1990). Comparing brains. *Science,* **249,** 140–146.

Jerison, H. J. (1973). *Evolution of the brain and intelligence.* New York: Academic Press.

Jerison, H. J. (1982). Allometry, brain size, cortical surface, and convolutedness. In E. Armstrong & D. Falk (Eds.), *Primate brain evolution. Methods and concepts* (pp. 77–84). New York: Plenum.

Johnson, J. I. Jr. (1977). Central nervous system of marsupials. In D. Hunsaker II (Ed.), *The biology of marsupials* (pp. 157–278). New York: Academic Press.

Jürgens, U. (1990). Vocal communication in primates. In R. P. Kesner & D. S. Olton (Eds.), *Neurobiology of comparative cognition* (pp. 51–76). Hillsdale: Erlbaum.

Kay, H., & Oldfield-Box, H. (1965). A study of learning-sets in rats with an apparatus using 3-dimensional shapes. *Animal Behaviour,* **13,** 19–24.

Kielan-Jaworowska, Z. (1986). Brain evolution in Mesozoic mammals. In K. M. Flanagan & J. A. Lilligraven (Eds.), *Vertebrates, phylogeny, and philosophy* (pp. 21–34). Laramie: University of Wyoming Press.

Kramer, B. (1996). *Electroreception and communication in fishes.* Stuttgart: Fisher.

Lande, R. (1979). Quantitative genetic analysis of multivariate evolution, applied to brain:body size allometry. *Evolution,* **33,** 402–416.

Lashley, K. S. (1929). *Brain mechanisms and intelligence.* Chicago: University of Chicago Press.

LeDoux, J. E. (1995). Emotion: Clues from the brain. *Annual Review of Psychology,* **46,** 209–235.

Mace, G. M., Harvey, P. H., & Clutton-Brock, T. H. (1980). Is brain size an ecological variable? *Trends in Neuroscience,* **3,** 193–196.

Martin, R. D. (1981). Relative brain size and basal metabolic rate in terrestrial vertebrates. *Nature,* **293,** 57–60.

McCormick, D. A., Guyer, P. E., & Thompson, R. F. (1982). Superior cerebellar peduncle lesions selectively abolish the ipsilateral classically conditioned nictitating membrane/eyelid response of the rabbit. *Brain Research,* **244,** 347–350.

McCormick, D. A., & Thompson, R. F. (1984). Neuronal responses of the rabbit cerebellum during acquisition and performance of a classically conditioned nictitating membrane-eyelid response. *Journal of Neuroscience,* **4,** 2811–2822.

Mishkin, M., Malamut, B., & Bachevalier, J. (1984). Memories and habits: Two neural systems. In J. L. McGaugh & N. M. Weinberger (Eds.), *Neurobiology of learning and memory* (pp. 68–88). New York: Guilford.

Montagnese, C. M., Krebs, J. R., Székely, A. D., & Csillag, A. (1993). A subpopulation of large calbindin-like immunopositive neurones is present in the hippocampal formation in food-storing but not in non-storing species of bird. *Brain Research,* **614,** 291–300.

Morris, R. G., Garrud, M., Rawlins, J. N. P., & O'Keefe, J. (1982). Place navigation impaired in rats with hippocampal lesions. *Nature,* **297,** 681–683.

Nelson, D. O., & Prosser, C. L. (1981). Intracellular recordings from thermosensitive preoptic neurons. *Science,* **213,** 787–789.

Nielsen, C. (1995). *Animal evolution. Interrelationships of the living phyla.* Oxford: Oxford University Press.

Nieuwenhuys, R., ten Donkelaar, H. J., & Nicholson, C. (1998). *The central nervous system of vertebrates.* (Vols. 1–3). Berlin, Germany: Springer.

Northcutt, R. G. (1977). Elasmobranch central nervous system organization and its possible evolutionary significance. *American Zoologist,* **17,** 411–429.

Northcutt, R. G. (1984). Evolution of the vertebrate central nervous system: Patterns and processes. *American Zoologist,* **24,** 701–716.

Northcutt, R. G. (1985). Brain phylogeny. Speculations on pattern and cause. In M. J. Cohen & F. S. Strumwasser (Eds.), *Comparative neurobiology. Modes of communication in the nervous system* (pp. 351–378). New York: Wiley.

Northcutt, R. G. (1995). The forebrain of gnathostomes: In search of a morphotype. *Brain, Behavior, & Evolution,* **46,** 275–318.

Northcutt, R. G., & Kaas, J. H. (1995). The emergence and evolution of mammalian neocortex. *Trends in Neuroscience,* **18,** 373–379.

Overmier, J. B., & Papini, M. R. (1986). Factors modulating the effects of teleost telencephalon ablation on retention, relearning, and extinction of instrumental avoidance behavior. *Behavioral Neuroscience,* **100,** 190–199.

Platel, R. (1979). Brain weight–body weight relationships. In C. Gans, R. G. Northcutt, & P. Ulinski (Eds.), *Biology of the reptilia* (Vol. 9, pp. 147–171). London: Academic Press.

Pollard, H. B., Dhariwal, K., Adeyemo, O. M., Markey, C. J., Caohuy, H., Levine, M., Markey, S., & Youdim, M. B. H. (1992). A Parkinsonian syndrome induced in the goldfish by the neurotoxin MPTP. *Federation Proceedings of the American Society of Experimental Biology,* **6,** 3108–3116.

Rehkämper, G., Schuchmann, K. L., Schleicher, A., & Zilles, K. (1991). Encephalization in hummingbirds (Trochilidae). *Brain, Behavior, & Evolution,* **37,** 85–91.

Reichling, D. B., Kwiat, G. C., & Basbaum, A. I. (1988). Anatomy, physiology, and pharmacology of the periaqueductal gray contribution to antinociceptive controls. In H. L. Fields & J. M. Besson (Eds.), *Progress in brain research,* (Vol. 77, pp. 31–46). Amsterdam: Elsevier.

Riddell, W. I., & Corl, K. G. (1977). Comparative investigation of the relationship between cerebral indices and learning abilities. *Brain, Behavior, & Evolution,* **14,** 385–398.

Riska, B., & Atchley, W. R. (1985). Genetics of growth predict patterns of brain-size evolution. *Science,* **229,** 668–671.

Roderick, T. H., Wimer, R. E., Wimer, C. C., & Schwartzkroin, P. A. (1973). Genetic and phenotypic variation in weight of brain and spinal cord between inbred strains of mice. *Brain Research,* **64,** 345–353.

Rosvold, H. E., Mirsky, A. F., & Pribram, K. H. (1954). Influence of amygdalectomy on social behavior in monkeys. *Journal of Comparative & Physiological Psychology,* **47,** 173–178.

Roth, G., Blanke, J., & Wake, D. B. (1994). Cell size predicts morphological complexity in the brains of frogs and salamanders. *Proceedings of the National Academy of Sciences,* (USA) **91,** 4796–4800.

Rumbaugh, D. M., & Pate, J. L. (1984). The evolution of cognition in primates: A comparative perspective. In H. L. Roitblat, T. G. Bever, & H. S. Terrace (Eds.), *Animal cognition* (pp. 569–587). Hillsdale: Erlbaum.

Salas, C., Broglio, C., Rodriguez, F., Lopez, J. C., Portavella, M., & Torres, B. (1996). Telencephalic ablation in goldfish impairs performance in a "spatial constancy" problem but not in a cued one. *Behavioural Brain Research,* **79,** 193–200.

Sherry, D. F., & Vaccarino, A. L. (1989). Hippocampus and memory for food caches in black-capped chickadees. *Behavioral Neuroscience,* **103,** 308–318.

Slotnick, B. M., & Katz, H. M. (1974). Olfactory learning-set formation in rats. *Science,* **185,** 796-798.

Stephan, H., Baron, G., & Frahm, H. D. (1991). *Comparative brain research in mammals.* Vol. 1. *Insectivora.* New York: Springer-Verlag.

Striedter, G. F. (1997). The telencephalon of tetrapods in evolution. *Brain, Behavior & Evolution,* **49,** 179–213.

Thiessen, D., & Villarreal, R. (1998). Allometry and comparative psychology. Technique and theory. In G. Greenberg & M. M. Haraway (Eds.), *Comparative psychology. A handbook* (pp. 51–65). New York: Garland.

Thompson, R. F. (1986). The neurobiology of learning and memory. *Science,* **233,** 941–947.

Willerman, L., Schultz, R., Rutledge, J. N., & Bigler, E. D. (1991). *In vivo* brain size and intelligence. *Intelligence,* **15,** 223–228.

Wimer, C., Roderick, T. H., & Wimer, R. E. (1969). Supplementary report: Behavioral differences in mice genetically selected for brain weight. *Psychological Reports,* **25,** 363–368.

Zeldin, R. K., & Olton, D. S. (1986). Rats acquire spatial learning sets. *Journal of Experimental Psychology: Animal Behavior Processes,* **12,** 412–419.

CHAPTER 9

Brain, Behavior, and Evolution of Primates

MAIN GENERALIZATIONS OF CHAPTER 9

- *The evolution of primates in general, and hominids in particular, can be understood in terms of the same set of principles that apply to the evolution of other animal lineages.*
- *Primates are characterized by adaptations for arboreal life, for visual processing of information, and for reproductive strategies biased toward parental care.*
- *Hominids are characterized by a suit of morphological adaptations for bipedal locomotion, encephalization, and complex sociality.*

Mammalian evolution can be divided into two broad periods. The first covers about two-thirds of the entire history of mammals, occurred during the Mesozoic, and is characterized by evolutionary stasis. There is fossil evidence for a variety of lineages, but these species were all relatively small, terrestrial, probably nocturnal, and mainly insectivorous. The second covers the most recent third of this history, occurred during the Cenozoic, and is distinguished by the evolution of a remarkable diversity in body plans and ecological adaptations. This diversity appears in the fossil record during a relatively brief period after the end of the Cretaceous, about 65 Mya. Most mammalian orders were probably established during the last part of the Cretaceous and have been evolving in parallel since then. Among these orders were the Primates.

1. What is a primate?

1.a. Characteristics of Primates. Approximately 200 species of living primates are distributed throughout the world. Three sets of characteristics define a primate (Benton 1990). First, primates possess a suit of adaptations for *arboreal life.* It is plausible that the tree-dwelling mode of life was an essential ecological component in the evolutionary emergence of primates. Among the morphological adaptations appropriate for living in the trees are the *grasping* hands and feet, with opposable thumb and big toe. Walking and moving in trees requires a firm grasp of the branches to avoid dangerous falls to the ground. Grasping is facilitated by the replacement of claws by flat nails and the development of sensitive tactile pads in each digit. The arms of primates are attached to shoulder bones that, compared to other mammals, possess a great deal of mobility. For example, we can stretch our arms and rotate them in a circle because of the mobile shoulder joint. In some primates, such as the gibbon (*Hylobates*), these features are highly developed and critical for *brachiation,* a mode of locomotion that uses the arms to move from branch to branch. In the case of the New World monkeys of South America (e.g., capuchins, marmosets, etc.), which are almost exclusively arboreal, the tail is used as an additional prehensile extremity.

A second set of features involves the visual system. The eyes of primates are located on the front of the face, pointing forward. Consequently, the visual fields overlap extensively. Overlapping visual fields are critical for *depth perception,* that is, for determining the relative distance of different features. When an animal is brachiating, or jumping across branches, the success of locomotion depends on its ability to accurately determine the distance from one branch to the next. The neurological demands of visual processing may also explain the relatively large *brain size* of primates relative to that of other mammals. You may recall that Jerison's (1973) hypothesis about the origin of encephalization in birds was based on the demands of the visual system (see ***Chapter 8, section 4.d.***, pp. 307–309). Similarly, the invasion of the forest by early primates may have strongly selected for accuracy in depth perception, which may require a substantial thalamic and neocortical circuit machinery. A tree-dwelling mode of life may also explain why most extant primates have diurnal habits: If visual depth perception is critical for surviving in the forest, then abundant light is necessary to make accurate perceptual judgments.

A third set of primate features is related to reproductive specializations. In general, it may be said that primates have placed their emphasis on parental investment rather than on reproductive output itself. Unlike most other mammals, primates are characterized by giving birth to a single offspring (twins in some New World species). There is a relatively long period of intrauterine development and a long period of parental care after birth. Infancy can last a few years, which the infant spends in close contact with the mother, peers, and other members of the group. These interactions are crucial if the infant is to learn the social skills that will allow it to fit into the social group and to enhance its reproductive success as an adult. Sexual maturity is delayed, and life span is prolonged relative to other mammals. These features are obviously related to the evolution of complex social groups in many species of primates.

1.b. Taxonomy and Distribution. As usual, taxonomists differ in the details of their classificatory schemes, but some features in primate taxonomy are generally accepted. Discrepancies emerge particularly with respect to fossil species since there is usually very limited material (e.g., isolated teeth, fragmentary cranial and postcranial features). Let's concentrate first on the living groups, following a classification offered by Martin (1992) and reproduced in ***Table 9.1***, and look at their main biological features and biogeographic distribution (Cartmill 1992).

The prosimians are generally considered to retain a greater number of primitive characters. Among these characters are a relatively large pair of olfactory bulbs and the absence of fovea in the retina. Since the fovea is typical of animals that are active during the day, its absence in prosimians implies that the most primitive primates are likely to have been nocturnal. The major prosimian groups are the lemurs (once widely distributed, now found only in Madagascar), galagos or bushbabies (Africa), lorises (rain forests of Africa and southeast Asia), and tarsiers (Borneo, Sumatra, Sulawesi, and the Philippines). Most lemurs are nocturnal, herbivorous, and live almost continuously on trees. The aye-aye (*Daubentonia madagascariensis*) feeds on insects, which it finds in trees by breaking into the wood with its rodent-like incisors and by poking its enlarged middle finger into the openings. Bushbabies and lorises are also all nocturnal and arboreal in habits. Bushbabies tend to have long hind legs that allow them to leap from branch to branch; by contrast, lorises are generally sluggish in their movements.

Tarsiers are in many ways intermediate between lemurs and monkeys. Many anatomical and embryological features resemble more the condition found in anthropoid primates than that of prosimians. For example, they possess a fovea in the retina, and like simians and humans, the fetus develops in close contact with the mother's bloodstream. These and similar traits have convinced many taxonomists that the tarsiers are more related to the anthropoids than they are to the other prosimians. The single living species, *Tarsius bancanus,* is a nocturnal carnivore, feeding on small vertebrates and insects that it catches by leaping. Leaping involves precise visuomotor coordination achieved by highly enlarged eyes and long ankle bones. Tarsiers prefer to rest and move on vertical, rather than horizontal, branches.

The two major taxa grouping the monkeys are distinguished by anatomical features and biogeographic distribution. The platyrrhine monkeys have a broad nose, prehensile tail, and live exclusively in the neotropical forests of South and Central America (this is why they are referred to as New World monkeys). Marmosets and tamarins were mentioned in ***Chapter 5***

TABLE 9.1 Classification of Extant Primates

Suborder	*Infraorder*	*Superfamily*	*Family*	*Subfamily*	*Common Names*
Prosimii (*Prosimians*)	Lemuriformes	Lemuroidea	Cheirogaleidae		*Mouse, dwarf lemurs*
			Lemuridae	Lemurinae	*True lemurs*
				Lepelemurinae	*Sportive lemurs*
			Indridae		*Indri lemurs*
			Daubentoniidae		*Aye-aye*
	Lorisiformes	Lorisoidea	Lorisidae	Lorisinae	*Lorises*
				Galaginae	*Bushbabies*
	Tarsiiformes	Tarsioidea	Tarsiidae		*Tarsiers*
Anthropoidea (*Simians and anthropoids*)	Platyrrhini	Ceboidea (*New World monkeys*)	Cebidae	Aotinae	*Owl monkeys*
				Cebinae	*Capuchin monkeys*
				Atelinae	*Spider monkeys*
				Alouattinae	*Howler monkeys*
				Pitheciinae	*Sakis*
				Callimiconinae	*Goeldi's monkeys*
			Callitrichidae		*Marmosets, tamarins*
	Catarrhini	Cercopithecoidea (*Old World monkeys*)	Cercopithecidae	Cercophithecinae	*Cheek-pouched monkeys*
				Colobinae	*Leaf monkeys*
		Hominioidea (*Apes and humans*)	Hylobatidae	Hylobatinae	*Gibbons*
			Pongidae	Ponginae	*Chimpanzees*
					Gorillas
					Orangutans
			Hominidae	Homininae	*Humans*

(***section 2.c.,*** pp. 135–137) in connection with their monogamic mating system and their regular production of twins. With a few exceptions, platyrrhines are diurnal animals. The owl monkeys (*Aotus*) are the only anthropoids that are predominantly nocturnal (see ***Chapter 4, section 3.c.***, p. 95). Their enlarged eyes are an adaptation to nocturnal habits (as is also true for tarsiers).

Catarrhine monkeys (Family Cercopithecidae) have a narrow nose, teeth specialized for leaf eating, and live in Africa and Asia (hence, they are referred to as Old World monkeys). Most species are arboreal, although some are predominantly terrestrial like the baboons (*Papio*), vervets (*Cercopithecus*), and patas monkeys (*Erythrocebus*). Baboons inhabit the savannas of eastern Africa, characterized by sparse vegetation and long dry seasons. At the other extreme of this distribution are the macaques (*Macaca*), some of which live in islands of the Japanese archipelago, enduring relatively cold winters.

Apes and humans are also catarrhine anthropoids. The apes (Families Hylobatidae and Pongidae) are characterized by elongated arms; they live in the rain forest habitats of Africa and southeast Asia. The two Asian apes, gibbons (*Hylobates*) and orangutans (*Pongo*), are predominantly arboreal and vegetarian in habits. Gibbons were already mentioned because of their brachiating locomotion and agility in trees. Orangutans are far heavier (weighing about 90 kg as adults) and thus move more cautiously when in the trees. The African species are more mixed in their lifestyles. The two species of chimpanzees (*Pan*), the common one and the bonobo or pigmy chimpanzee, live both on the ground and in trees. Common chimpanzees are omnivorous and display a great deal of variation in social behavior. With an average body weight of about 200 kg, the gorilla (*Gorilla*) is the largest primate and cannot afford to live an arboreal life. Gorillas live in small groups, mostly on the ground, where they spent most of their time eating leaves. Humans (*Homo*) are characterized by having lost many anatomical features associated with an arboreal lifestyle (e.g., curved fingers, opposable big toe, elongated arms) and, most distinctively, having evolved a suit of specialization for *bipedal locomotion* (e.g., flat feet). The evolution of language abilities and the development of social communities, culture, and technology to a degree not observed in other animals have allowed humans a cosmopolitan distribution.

1.c. Brain Size. In his extensive account of brain evolution in vertebrates, Jerison (1973) noted that just as mammals, in general, tend to be more highly encephalized than lower vertebrates, the brains of primates tend to be relatively larger than those of other mammals. For example, relative brain size in Jerison's sample of anthropoid species lies entirely above the regression line for Mammalia. In the more complete sample of mammalian *encephalization quotients* (*EQ*s) provided by Eisenberg (1981), the values for every one of the 23 primate species listed are above 1 (remember that an EQ = 1 means that the brain size of a particular species is exactly as expected for a mammal of its body size; ***Chapter 8, section 4.e.,*** pp. 309–310). Jerison (1973) also noted that the brain size of some fossil hominids (extinct australopithecines; see ***section 3.c.*** below), as well as that of humans, lie outside the minimum convex polygon for monkeys and apes. It would appear, therefore, that several episodes of encephalization have characterized the history of primates: the one that led to an increase in relative brain size in early mammals (the primate's ancestors), then in the early primates, and then in the hominids. These episodes are not unique to primates; similar encephalization trends characterize the evolution of other mammalian orders, such as the carnivores and cetaceans.

What is the meaning of primate encephalization? Several factors could contribute to the evolution of relatively large brains. For example, increased motor dexterity and depth perception, both of which are needed for arboreal life, may demand additional neuronal circuits. It is possible that some form of intelligence underlies the evolution of large brains. Primates are generally highly social and respond to cues generated by other animals in the group (e.g., bodily and facial expressions). Perhaps these social skills depend on large integrative neural networks that require additional space. In humans, it is possible that language skills, as will be argued later in this chapter (see ***section 4***), have demanded the contribution of new networks. It is also possible that relatively large brains are obtained not by increasing the rate of growth of neural tissue but by decreasing the rate of growth of the body. This might seem important for species adapted to an arboreal way of life, which places particularly strong demands and risks on a heavy body.

Evidence suggests that several brain structures have changed at different rates among monkeys and apes. This, in turn, implies that different selective pressures have shaped the brains of different primate groups. One example is the cerebellum, which appears to be approximately 45% larger in apes than in monkeys or humans (Rilling & Insel 1998). In this study, brain and cerebellum size were estimated in vivo using magnetic resonance imaging techniques. The sample included humans, all the ape species, 3 species of Old World monkeys, and 2 species of New World monkeys (a total of 11 species, with 2 to 6 individuals per species). The cerebellum correlates allometrically with both brain volume and neocortical volume; however, when brain size is controlled for, gibbons and pongids (chimps, gorillas, and orangutans) have significantly larger cerebellums than monkeys and humans. The functional meaning of this morphological difference is still obscure.

More direct evidence about the possible selective pressures that have shaped the primate brain were provided by Sawaguchi (1988, 1989). Jerison's *index of extra cortical neurons,* N_c, calculated on the basis of body and brain weight (see ***Chapter 8, section 4.e.***, p. 310), was estimated for a sample of 12 prosimian species, 8 New World monkeys, and 27 Old World monkeys. These values were then correlated with three behavioral indices: troop size (average number of animals sharing a common home range), home range (total area used by a troop), and the size of the home range per individual (home range divided by troop size). The results are shown in ***Figure 9.1.*** Although the scatter of data points is considerable, some of the correlations achieved significance. For example, N_c was significantly correlated only to troop size in prosimians, only to home range size in New World monkeys, and to both home range size and home range size per individual in Old World monkeys. To the extent that troop size and home range make different demands upon the behavioral capacities of primates (e.g., social interactions in the case of troop size, but spatial cognition in the case of home range size), these data suggest the possibility that the expansion of the neocortex responded to different selective pressures in prosimians and monkeys. Similarly, New World monkeys that tend to be *polygynous* (groups with a single adult male and two or more adult females) exhibit N_c indices significantly larger

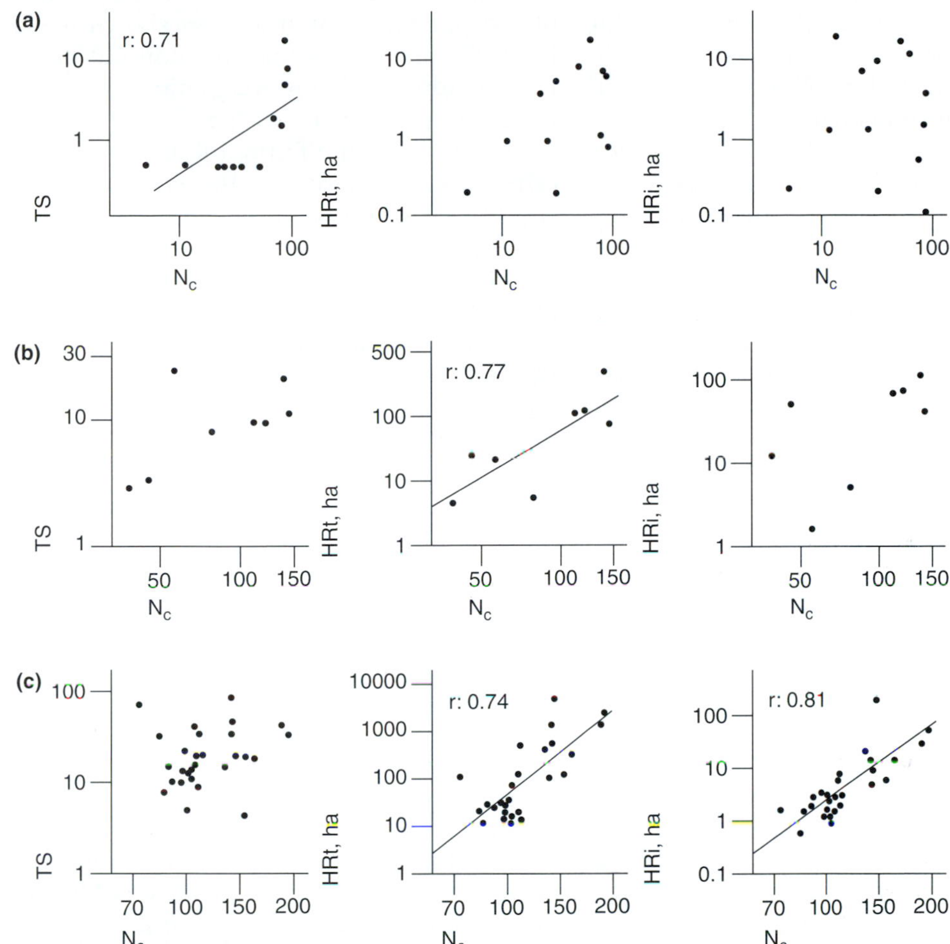

FIGURE 9.1. Correlational analyses of three behavioral indices, troop size (left column), home range (middle column), and home range per individual (right column); and the index of extra cortical neurons in ***(a)*** prosimians, ***(b)*** New World monkeys, and ***(c)*** Old World monkeys (Sawaguchi 1988). Correlation coefficients (*r*) and regression lines are reported only for those analyses that yielded significant results.

than species that tend to be *monogynous* (monogamous or polyandrous groups). This distinction in terms of mating systems did not correlate with N_c in Old World monkeys; in this taxon, however, terrestrial species showed larger N_c values than arboreal species. As in all correlational studies, it is not completely clear whether, for example, "terrestrial" indexes some selective pressure related to the physical environment, to the possibility that terrestrial troops are socially more complex than arboreal troops, or to some other variable. But the general conclusion is that cortical size may be influenced by different factors in different groups of primates.

1.d. The Primate Cortex. The neocortex of primates is morphologically and functionally heterogeneous. The *central sulcus* divides the frontal cortex from the parietal cortex, and the *Sylvian sulcus* separates the more dorsal frontal and parietal lobes from the ventral temporal lobe. The remaining occipital lobe, located on the caudal tip of the brain, does not have a clear boundary with the adjacent parietal and temporal lobes. A substantial amount of research has helped us understand the functional parcellation of the primate neocortex. Some functions are conserved (e.g., primary sensory and motor functions), whereas others could be unique to primates or, at least, particularly developed in primates.

These divisions of the cortex into lobes with clear boundaries is particularly emphasized in primates. The Sylvian sulcus and associated temporal lobe can be said to be unique to primates. The *temporal cortex* is the site of primary auditory processing, and it also includes a variety of secondary auditory areas, as well as areas of sensory integration. In humans, the temporal cortex also contains areas dedicated to the processing of linguistic information, which makes sense given that speech is based on acoustic signals. It also makes sense for the temporal cortex to be associated to musical abilities. An interesting example of brain-behavior correlation has been described in musicians and involves a portion of the temporal cortex known as the *planum temporale.* The planum temporale is thought to be a structure unique to apes and humans, and it is notorious because of its asymmetry: It is usually larger in the left hemisphere. The degree of asymmetry in the size of the planum temporale was shown to be larger for musicians than for nonmusicians in a study involving magnetic resonance imaging (Schlaug et al. 1995).

In addition, the temporal lobe also contains some conservative limbic structures, such as the hippocampus and the amygdala, which actually appear greatly enlarged in primates. The primate *hippocampus,* for example, has migrated from a dorsomedial position in amphibians, reptiles, and insectivore mammals, to a basal location inside the temporal lobe. I also mentioned that hidden behind the temporal lobe is the insular lobe; underneath the insular cortex lies a flat sheet of cell somas known as the *claustrum.* The claustrum has afferent and efferent projections with many cortical areas. However, it is not yet known whether the claustrum is pallial or subpallial, or what its functions are. Its flat shape is, however, unique to primates (it has a more conventional, round shape in other mammals) and it may be related to the particular way in which the Sylvian sulcus folds inwards to create the temporal lobe.

The more caudal portion of the brain is occupied by the *occipital cortex,* which is primarily concerned with visual perception. Given the role that vision plays in primates and the principle of *proper mass* (***Chapter 8, section 4.a.,*** pp. 302–303), it should not be particularly surprising to find a large number of occipital (and also temporal and parietal) areas dedicated to processing the various aspects of visual perception. Brightness, pattern, movement, depth, and color are among the various properties tackled by the visual system to provide a representation of the animal's surround. An interesting feature of anthropoid visual systems is their color vision ability. It is likely that color vision is a plesiomorphic trait in tetrapods, since it is present in many species of amphibians and reptiles. Birds are also prominent in this regard. Primitive placental mammals, such as insectivores, and conservative primates, such as the prosimians, are nocturnal and have reduced color vision abilities or are colorblind. It is thus possible that primate color vision represents an example of evolutionary *reversal,* that is, the recovery of an ancestral trait that was lost with the evolution of the first mammals in a nocturnal niche. However, as it happens in other examples of homoplasy, character resemblance is mostly superficial: Primate color vision involves the evolution of a new color-sensitive pigment and possibly a specialized cortical area.

Color vision depends on several components, including the retina receptors known as cones, the color-sensitive pigments in these cones, and the presence of cortical areas specialized for color perception in the occipital cortex. Pigments are nothing more than proteins, and as such their evolution can be affected by mutation and gene duplication. Primates, for example, have three different types of pigments; two of them are virtually identical (96% identical, to be precise) in terms of the sequence of amino acids constituting the molecule (Nathans et al. 1986). Their peak response corresponds to red and green. They are only about 43% identical to the third, blue-sensitive pigment. Genetic analysis suggests that the divergence of the red and green pigments occurred approximately 40 Mya in some common ancestor of the anthropoids. Interestingly, it is the ancestral anthropoids that shifted from predominantly nocturnal habits (as in most of today's prosimians), to diurnal habits (as in most of today's anthropoids). The evolution of a third pigment may have helped primitive anthropoids discriminate food items in the trees, such as poisonous from edible leaves and fruits.

The *parietal cortex* bordering the central sulcus is the primary area for somatosensory perception—that is, the processing of information arriving from the multitude of receptors located in the skin. At least four separate somatotopic representations of the body were found in the primate somatosensory area. Again in this case, the principle of proper mass helps us understand the relative size of the various parts of the somatotopic representation across species. Raccoons have a relatively large representation of their paws, which are used in handling food, whereas rats have a large area corresponding to their snouts, which corresponds well with the amount of sniffing they display. But the parietal cortex takes over a variety of additional functions. Primates with lesions of the parietal cortex exhibit a variety of deficits related to the processing of spatial information (Friedrich 1990). For example, humans with such lesions have difficulty using maps to find a particular location, or having been exposed to a place, find it difficult to draw a map that shows the relative location of various features. A peculiar perceptual deficit has been described in patients with unilateral lesions of the posterior parietal cortex: They do not recognize parts of their body contralateral to the lesion as being their own. This condition, called unilateral neglect, has been described in other mammals.

The *frontal cortex* extends rostrally with respect to the central sulcus. The band of cortex immediately adjacent to the central sulcus is the primary motor area and, as one might expect, it also contains a topographical representation, in this case, of the muscles of the body. Electrical stimulation of tiny spots in the primary motor area results in movements of discrete parts of the body, such as a finger or the lips. Large, pyramidal neurons located in the primary motor area can influence spinal motoneurons directly via the pyramidal or corticospinal tract. The axons of these neurons descend in between the basal ganglia and cross to the contralateral side at the level of the medulla. This decusation is massive in nonprimates but partial in primates since many axons continue descending on the ipsilateral side. These axons eventually reach the spinal motoneurons. The pyramidal system provides a major source of behavioral control. But, again, several other functions have been taken over by frontal neurons.

Neural networks located in the most anterior part of the frontal cortex play a role in keeping information available during temporal delays. Moreover, some of these neurons encode information about specific objects that are expected in the imminent future. Using a procedure caricatured in ***Figure 9.2***, concurrent with single-cell recordings from the frontal cortex of rhesus monkeys (*Macaca fuscata*), Watanabe (1996) discovered *expectancy-specific neurons*. Monkeys were trained in a situation with three critical steps: First, they saw a

FIGURE 9.2. A cartoon representation of the training procedure first used by Tinklepaugh (1928) to study food expectancies in monkeys. The upper two rows represent two types of training trials, one involving a highly preferred food (banana) and another involving a less preferred but still rewarding food (lettuce). In some test trials, the experimenter replaces the more preferred food by the less preferred food during the delay interval and when the monkey is not able to see what is happening (second frame). During this interval, single-cell recordings demonstrate the presence of expectancy-specific neurons (e.g., neurons active only when the animal expects a banana) in the frontal cortex. (Drawing by Katsuo and Chiharu Tomita.)

particular reward being placed under one of two cups; second, a cover was lowered while they had to wait during a few seconds (a temporal delay); and (3) the cover was raised and they were free to choose one of the two cups. Correct choices were reinforced with access to the reward hidden under the cup. The upper two rows in ***Figure 9.2*** show two types of trials, one involving bananas (a preferred food) and another involving lettuce (a less preferred, but still acceptable, reward). These were the common training trials; however, there were sporadic trials like that depicted in the lowest row. In these test trials, the experimenter changed the banana for the lettuce during the delay period and while the monkey could not see because of the screen. While monkeys accepted a piece of lettuce if they had been expecting it, they rejected it if they had expected a more preferred piece of banana. This result, first reported by Tinklepaugh (1928) using this procedure, suggests that monkeys learn detailed reward expectancies that, when unfulfilled, lead to an emotional behavior. Watanabe (1996) found that specific neurons in the frontal cortex were active only when the animal was expecting banana (or lettuce, or a variety of other types of food) and suggested that the frontal cortex contains neural networks that specify the exact nature of goal events.

This section answered the question "what is a primate?" Let's turn now to the issue of the primate's origin and phylogenetic history. Where do primates come from?

2. EVOLUTION

2.a. Plesiadapiforms: Archaic Primates. The oldest fossils that have been either attributed to primates or considered to be related forms were found in the northern hemisphere. As one might expect, there are considerable doubts about the proper assignment of the oldest specimens since not all the typical characters of primates are present. In addition, many of the oldest fossils are known only in a very fragmentary form (Benton 1990; Simons 1992). A case in point is that of *Purgatorius,* from the late Cretaceous or early Paleocene of Montana (around 65 Mya), known only from a single lower molar. The blades in this molar suggest an insectivorous diet, and its dimensions imply a mouse-size animal. *Purgatorius* could have been a primate (there are some extant small-size insectivorous prosimians), but it may have been an insectivore much like a tree-shrew or a dermopteran (extant dermopterans live in southeast Asia and are represented by a single genus: *Cynocephalus,* or flying lemurs). Both insectivores and dermopterans are candidates for a sister order of the primates. Nonetheless, *Purgatorius* is commonly assigned to a group known as Plesiadapiformes, generally considered to be archaic primates.

The plesiadapiforms include at least five families from the Paleocene and Eocene of North America and Europe, and some of the specimens are more complete than *Purgatorius.* Again, the suit of characters that emerges is ambiguous. For example, they have large eyes but they are positioned sideways, which results in limited binocular vision (binocularity is typical of primates). They have long noses, rodentlike incisors, no opposable thumb or big toe, claws, relatively small brains, a diastema in the lower jaw, and no postorbital bar, none of which is typical of primates (***Figure 9.3***). However, there is evidence in their dentition that their diet had shifted from insects to leaves and fruits. By the end of the Eocene (about 38 Mya), the plesiadapiforms had been completely replaced by ro-

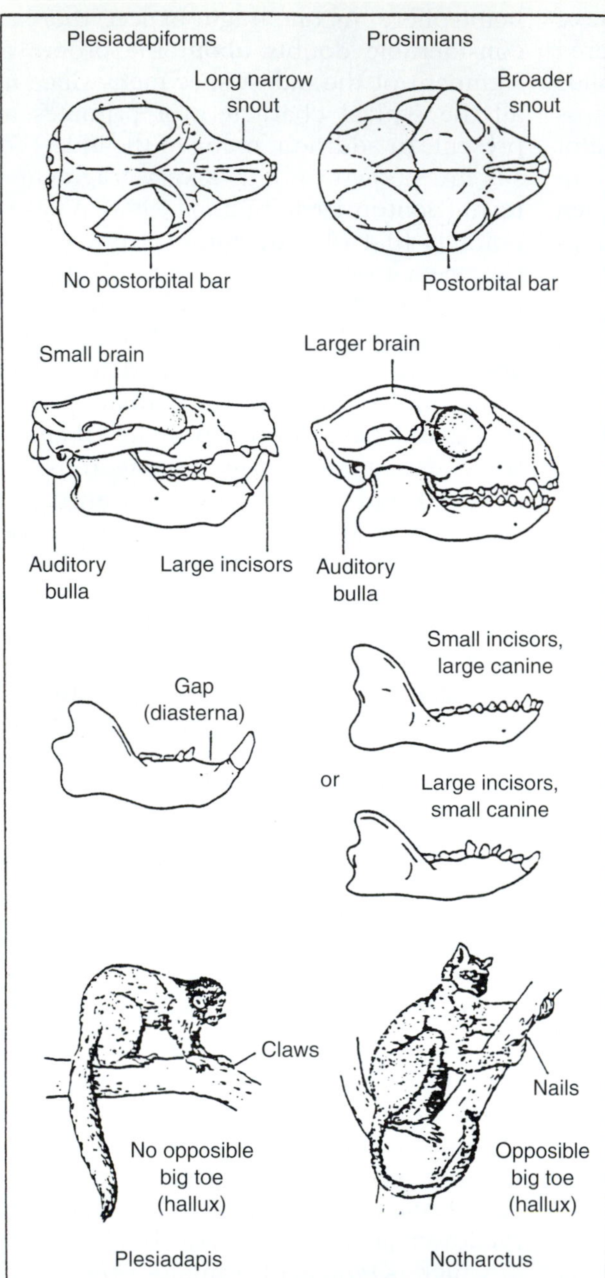

FIGURE 9.3. Some of the anatomical differences between the archaic primates, known as plesiadapiforms, and the prosimians (Simons 1992). Reconstructions of *Plesiadapis* (from the Paleocene of Europe and North America) and *Notharctus* (from the Eocene of North America) are shown at the bottom.

dents and forms more clearly related to modern primates.

Unmistakable primates appear during the Eocene (54–38 Mya) of North America and Europe. These forms exhibit some of the main features of primates, including grasping hands and feet, forward-pointing eyes, presence of postorbital bars (the eyes were thus enclosed by bone), larger brains, and a long tail. They are considered to have been nocturnal on the basis of their large eyes (large eyes are typical of nocturnal living prosimians). Two main families are usually recognized: the Adapidae and the Omomyidae. Adapids could be the ancestors of lemurs and lorises, whereas omomyids are considered to be the ancestors of tarsiers. However, as ***Figure 9.4*** suggests, there are too many gaps in the fossil record to consider these as firm conclusions. The only firm conclusion is that species with characters clearly related to those of primates appeared during the Eocene.

2.b. Anthropoid Primates. There is general agreement that living and fossil tarsiers display many anatomical features (i.e., unique derived characters or synapomorphies) that place them closer to the anthropoids (monkeys, apes, and hominids) than to any other primate group. The Eosimiidae, a group of fossil primates from the middle Eocene of China (approximately 45 Mya), exhibits a combination of prosimianlike and anthropoidlike characters in their dentition and in their foot bones (Gebo et al. 2000). Cladistic analysis of these morphological features suggests that the eosimiids are the sister group of the tarsiers and the basal group of the anthropoids (monkeys, apes, and humans). These findings would suggest that anthropoids originated in Asia during the middle Eocene.

Primate faunas from the late Eocene–early Oligocene (about 38 Mya) of north Africa provide further evidence of fossil anthropoids. They have been assigned to two families: Parapithecidae and Oligopithecidae. One distinct anthropoid synapomorphy is the presence of postorbital plates, a bony structure located behind the eyeballs not present in prosimians but shown by these fossils. The best-known species is the parapithecid *Aegyptopithecus,* a frugivorous, quadruped, and possibly polygynic (given evidence of sexual dimorphism) catarrhine anthropoid found in Egypt.

A number of behavioral characteristics of primitive anthropoids can be inferred from fossil evidence by extrapolating behavioral and morphological correlations known from extant species. Evidence about the diet, daily patterns of activity, and mating behavior can be obtained in this manner (Kay et al. 1997). For example, whether the diet was predominantly based on insects or leaves can be inferred from body size. Insectivorous mammals tend to be relatively small in body size, whereas folivorous mammals tend to be relatively large in body size. A small body size is characterized by a high metabolism, which demands a rich source of energy, such as that provided by insects. Leaves are poor in energy and, to extract enough, an animal needs to consume large quantities and wait for a relatively long digestion. Thus, leaf-eating mammals tend to be large in body size. Since the early fossils of putative anthropoids tend to be small in body size, it is likely that they were predominantly insectivorous. This hypothesis implies that the evolution of anthropoids was probably not driven by a change in diet.

Circadian activity patterns can be inferred from the size of the orbits. As noted previously, living prosimians have large eyes (and, therefore, large orbits), and are predominantly nocturnal. By contrast, living monkeys have smaller eyes and are di-

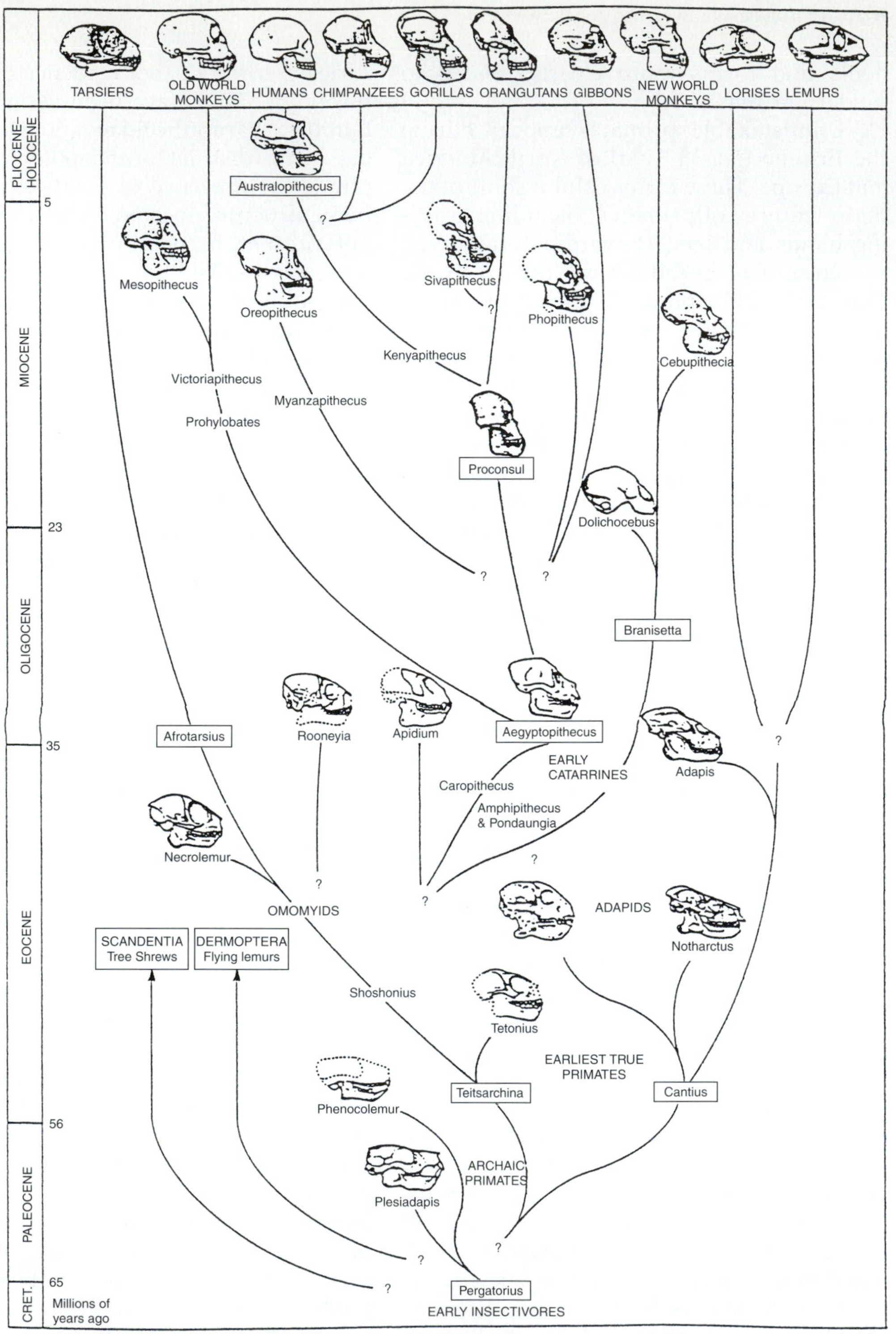
TARSIERS
OLD WORLD MONKEYS
HUMANS
CHIMPANZEES
GORILLAS
ORANGUTANS
GIBBONS
NEW WORLD MONKEYS
LORISES
LEMURS
PLIOCENE–HOLOCENE
MIOCENE
OLIGOCENE
EOCENE
PALEOCENE
CRET.
5
23
35
56
65
Millions of years ago
Australopithecus
Mesopithecus
Oreopithecus
Sivapithecus
Phopithecus
Kenyapithecus
Cebupithecia
Victoriapithecus
Myanzapithecus
Prohylobates
Proconsul
Dolichocebus
Branisetta
Afrotarsius
Rooneyia
Apidium
Aegyptopithecus
EARLY CATARRINES
Adapis
Caropithecus
Amphipithecus & Pondaungia
Necrolemur
OMOMYIDS
ADAPIDS
Notharctus
SCANDENTIA Tree Shrews
DERMOPTERA Flying lemurs
Shoshonius
Tetonius
EARLIEST TRUE PRIMATES
Phenocolemur
Teitsarchina
Cantius
ARCHAIC PRIMATES
Plesiadapis
Pergatorius
EARLY INSECTIVORES

urnal. The correlation between orbit size and nocturnality is particularly strong for small living primates. The small orbit size of some of the putatively anthropoid fossils suggest they were diurnal animals. Additional evidence is provided by the distribution of the *fovea* among the primates. The fovea is the portion of the retina that allows for sharp visual perception (i.e., the image you are sensing right now is projected on your fovea). Among the mammals, foveae are present only in tarsiers and anthropoids, but they are common in fish, reptiles, and birds with diurnal activity and active predatory behavior. Tarsiers have large eyes and nocturnal habits, but they lack the tapetum lucidum (the structure that makes the eyes of cats shine at night and that is typical of nocturnal mammals), which suggests that their ancestors were diurnal. Thus, a shift to diurnal habits may have characterized the first anthropoids.

Sexual dimorphism is associated with polygynous mating systems in a wide variety of mammals, including living primates (see ***Chapter 5*, *section 2.b.***, pp. 134–135). Polygynous males compete for access to females by displaying and engaging in aggressive behavior. In primates, the open-mouth display with exhibition of the canines plays a major role in male-male competition and thus is particularly enlarged in the male. Similar sexual dimorphism in canine size has been found in several species of both parapithecids and oligopithecids, suggesting that these animals lived in relatively complex social groups that included several adult females. Such type of social organization is typical (but not universal) of living monkeys but not of tarsiers, which are rather solitary animals. The picture of the basal anthropoids that emerges is that of small, predominantly insectivorous, diurnal animals with some degree of sociality.

Very little is known about two important episodes in the evolution of primates: the catarrhine-platyrrhine divergence and the pongid-hominid divergence. The origin of the platyrrhine or New World monkeys must have occurred at the latest during the Eocene. Virtually nothing is known about possible ancestors and even the way in which they arrived in South America (there is agreement that New World monkeys originated elsewhere). They could have arrived either from Africa, although not directly because the Atlantic was relatively wide (see ***Figure 6.3-b***, p. 182, for a view of the Atlantic ocean at the end of the Cretaceous), or they could have arrived from North America after the formation of the isthmus of Panama. Despite these uncertainties, the platyrrhines are generally believed to represent the most conservative taxon among extant anthropoids.

The fossil record is relatively rich in Old World monkeys, which have been found in Africa, Europe, and Asia in large quantities and diversity in deposits from the early Miocene (approximately 23 Mya) to the Pleistocene. *Proconsul,* from the early Miocene of eastern Africa, is clearly related to *Aegyptopithecus,* and it is considered to be related to the ancestral group from which apes evolved. However, *Proconsul*'s status as an early ape is in doubt. The greatest diversity and distribution of ape species that ever existed occurred during the late Miocene (Kelley 1992). Thus, Old World monkeys and apes evolved in parallel during this period. Remains of unmistakable apes have been found in Europe, Turkey, Pakistan, and

FIGURE 9.4. A phylogenetic tree of the evolution of Primates (Simons 1992). Uncertainties are marked with question symbols.

China. *Sivapithecus* appears during this period in Turkey, India, and China, and it is thought to be related to modern orangutans. *Gigantopithecus*, a massive animal measuring 2.5 m in height and weighing about 270 kg, was found in Pliocene sediments (5–1 Mya) of southeast Asia. Whereas Old World monkeys expanded and tended to occupy a wide range of habitats, apes diminished in diversity toward the end of the Miocene and remained isolated in rain forests of southeast Asia and eastern Africa. It is unclear whether monkeys displaced apes or whether ape diversity fell because of a reduction in rain forest habitats for which they appear to be highly specialized.

Extant apes (chimpanzees, bonobos, gorillas, orangutans, and gibbons) share a number of biological characters. Relative to monkeys, for example, they exhibit longer gestation periods, more extensive maternal care, longer intervals between successive births, and a longer life span. Apes live in dense vegetation (tropical rain forest habitats), in close dependency with trees, and are generally vegetarian (chimpanzees also hunt monkeys and eat termites). Except the gibbons, which are monogamous, apes show sexual dimorphism and live in polygynous or promiscuous groups. Little is known about the evolution of apes on the African continent, where there is a break in the fossil record for the late Miocene period (10–5 Mya). Such a gap is especially frustrating given the general belief (based on paleontological and molecular genetic analyses) that the ape and hominid lineages diverged during this period.

3. HOMINIDS

3.a. The Pongidae-Hominidae Divergence. The history of primates, since the time of *Purgatorius* to the evolution of the apes during the Miocene, covers a period of about 60 million years (see summary of main events in ***Figure 9.5***). The lineages leading to modern chimpanzees and modern humans diverged sometime between 5 and 10 Mya. It is generally believed that this episode took place on the African continent. As already said, uncertainty about the exact date of this divergence is related to the scarcity of late Miocene fossil evidence in Africa. An alternative way to estimate the date of the pongid-hominid divergence is based on molecular evidence, including the study of protein structure, DNA-DNA hybridization, and mitochondrial DNA. This information can be readily obtained from living species and provides a useful, independent way of approaching evolutionary questions.

The initial evidence came from studies of protein structure published during the 1960s and 1970s. In an influential paper, King and Wilson (1975) reviewed evidence that demonstrated an impressive degree of similarity in the structure of many homologous polypeptides (e.g., cytochrome c, lysozyme, hemoglobin, myoglobin, albumin, etc.) between chimpanzees (*Pan troglodytes*) and humans (*Homo sapiens*). Since protein structure reflects DNA sequence, the implication was that the two species are genetically very close to each other, at least as far as structural genes is concerned. King and Wilson suggested that phenotypic differences between chimps and humans, which are considerable, could not be attributed to structural genes and should, therefore, be caused by regulatory genes (you may recall that the products of regulatory genes control the timing of structural gene transcription).

DNA-DNA hybridization techniques, which look at the similarity of a large amount of DNA material across species, provided an estimate of divergence between chimps and humans ranging between 7 and 4 Mya (Sibley & Ahlquist 1987). This esti-

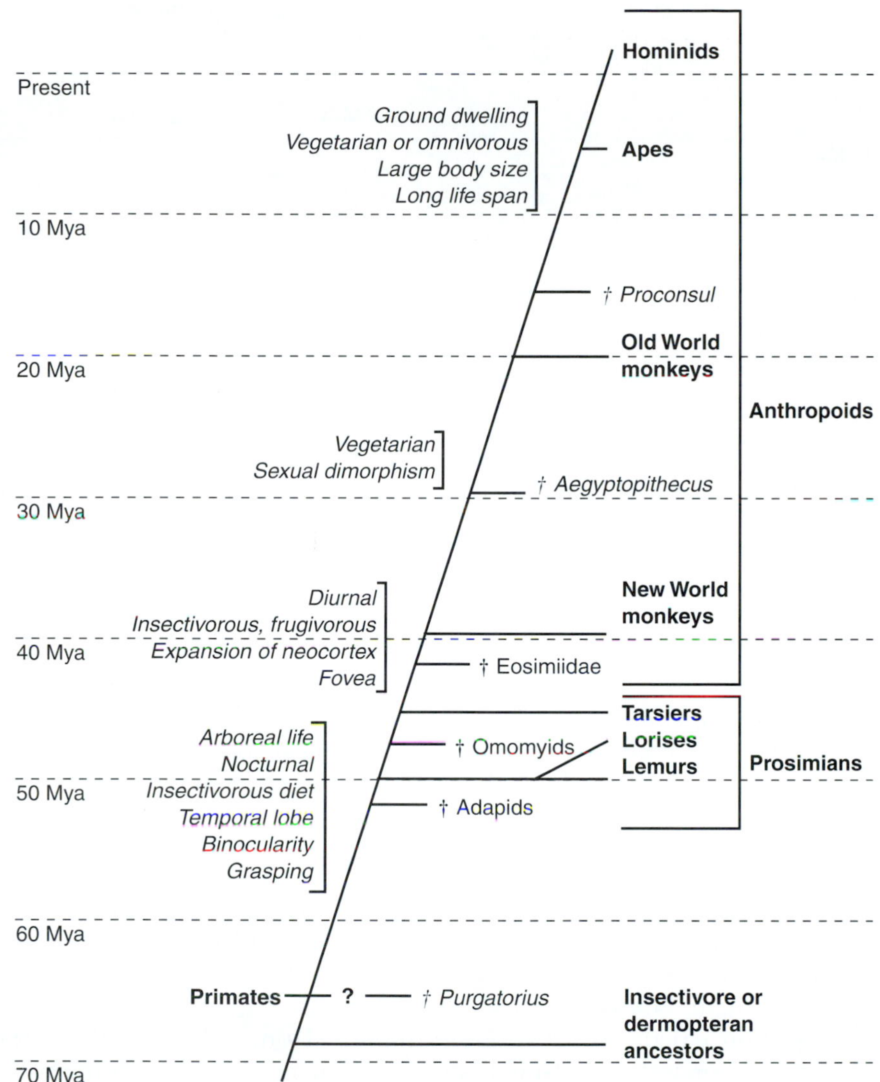

FIGURE 9.5. A phylogenetic tree summarizing the major primate taxa, including some key extinct ones (see daggers), and some of the major evolutionary changes. Approximate times for these events are given on the left.

mate was roughly the same as that provided by comparing the similarity in mitochondrial DNA among primates (Andrews 1985). Mitochondria are cytoplasmatic organelles that carry their own DNA material, which is different from that found in the cell nucleus. A similar outcome was obtained in a study of the similarity of autosomal genes (genes located in chromosomes other than the sexual ones) among

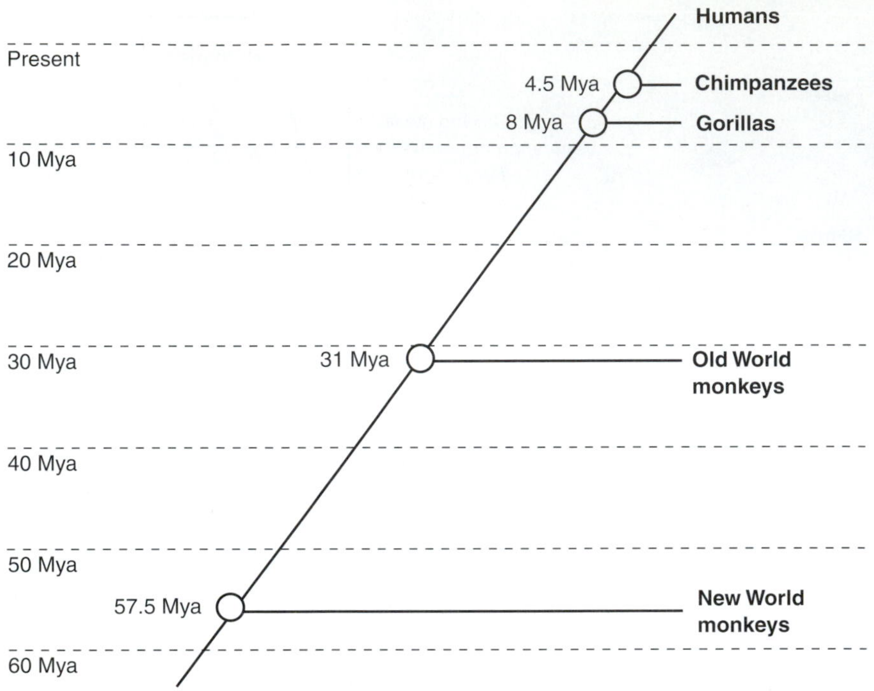

FIGURE 9.6. A phylogenetic tree drawn on the basis of divergence times provided by autosomal gene-sequencing studies (Takahata & Satta 1997). Compare this chronology based on molecular data with that suggested by paleontological evidence presented in ***Figure 9.5***.

anthropoid taxa (Takahata & Satta 1997). ***Figure 9.6*** maps the values reported in this study into a phylogenetic tree that can then be compared to the one shown in ***Figure 9.5,*** which is based primarily on paleontological data. The major discrepancies are related to the relatively older dates of divergence produced by molecular data compared to paleontological data. For example, the Old World monkeys appear in the fossil record in the early Miocene, about 23 Mya, but their divergence from the lineage leading to apes and humans occurred 31 Mya according to molecular data. This is not necessarily puzzling if one assumes that the fossil record does not necessarily preserve the true ancestors of a particular lineage. Again, however, molecular data point to a chimpanzee-hominid divergence close to 5 Mya.

3.b. Hominidae. Hominid evolution is thus restricted to at least the last 5 million years (as usual, dates should be taken with caution). Several species of hominids have been discovered, and continue to be discovered, in southern, eastern, and northern Africa, Eurasia, and the southeast Asian islands. Two broad groups within the Family Hominidae are usually recognized—the more ancient australopithecines and the more recent humans—but the assignment of species and genus names within the Hominidae is highly controversial. Some examples will give you the flavor of this problem.

Most authors recognize two broad groups of australopithecines, one including relatively short and light species (called the gracile australopithecines) and another including relatively larger and massive species (called the robust australopithecines). Despite this general agreement, some authors assign all species to the genus *Australopithecus* (as I will do here), whereas others restrict this name to the gracile group and refer to the robust australopithecines as *Paranthropus*. Such disagreements reflect to some degree not only the lack of fossil information but also the absence of clear-cut criteria for assigning genera names to fossil findings. A similar problem arises with the genus *Homo*. Whereas several species have been assigned to this genus, paleoanthropologists do not yet agree on what synapomorphies define the genus. Controversy also arises because of the paucity of specimens. In some cases, it seems possible that specimens that have been assigned to two different species may in fact be the males and females of a single, sexually dimorphic species. With the discovery of more specimens, paleoanthropologists will be able to estimate the range of population variability in critical traits and assess the degree of overlap in trait distributions among putatively different species. Sometimes, new species are assigned on the basis of what appear to be subtle anatomical details to the nonexpert; in other cases, however, a single species name may be assigned to specimens that exhibit wide variations in morphology over time. For example, some experts designate as *H. erectus* a large set of specimens spanning more than a million years and varying in such characters as cranial capacity from about 800 ml to about 1,200 ml. In other cases, a much smaller increase in cranial capacity appears to be the main basis to assign a particular specimen to a new genus. Despite these problems, the study of hominid evolution remains a fascinating topic about which psychologists will have to become increasingly more familiar in the future.

What are the major synapomorphies of the Hominidae? ***Figure 9.7*** compares various anatomical features of the African pongids (chimpanzees and gorillas) and hominids (australopithecines and humans). The upper four features relate to a major characteristic of hominids, perhaps the one widely considered to be the most important synapomorphy: bipedalism. Among primates, adaptations for bipedalism are present only in hominids; although some species exhibit sporadic bipedal behavior, such as the chimpanzee, none have skeletal adaptations that make the upright posture as energetically efficient as it is in humans. The *foramen magnum* is the opening through which the spinal cord enters the cranial cavity. The portion of the skull that articulates with the first vertebra is called the *occipital condyle*. Bipedalism requires that both the foramen magnum and occipital condyle migrate from a position behind the skull, typical of quadrupeds, to a position underneath the skull more appropriate for a bipedal animal. Similarly, the vertebral column of bipedal hominids adopts an S-like shape that permits the upper body to rest in an upright position while minimizing energy expenditure. Quadruped primates have trouble adopting an upright position in part because the shape of their vertebral column tends to "push" their head forward. Perhaps the most obvious hominid trait related to bipedalism is the shape of the feet, clearly adapted for walking and running on the ground. The loss of grasping ability in the feet is a clear indication of a transition from an arboreal to a ground-dwelling lifestyle. Also, changes in the

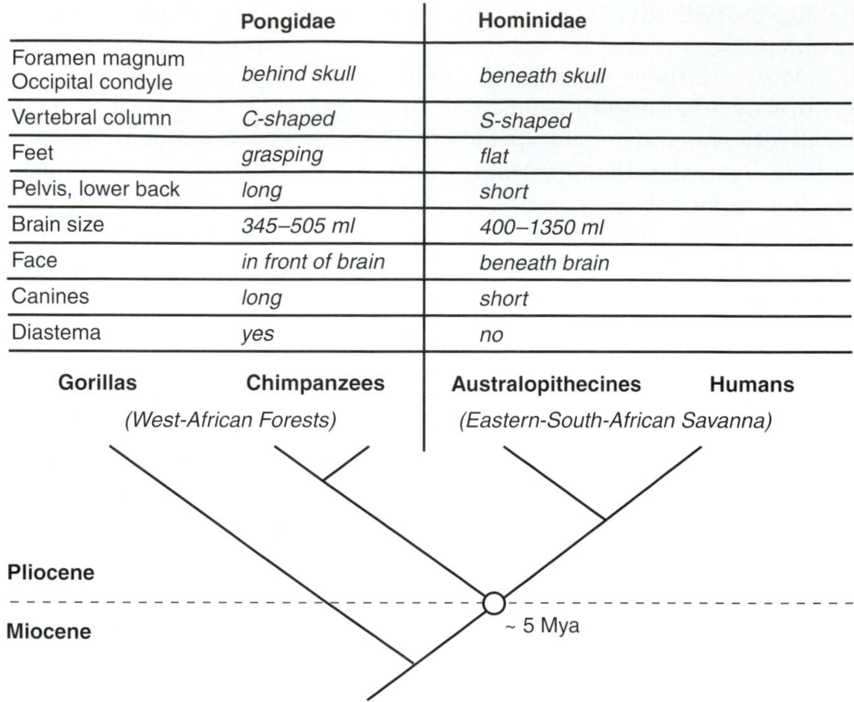

	Pongidae	Hominidae
Foramen magnum Occipital condyle	*behind skull*	*beneath skull*
Vertebral column	*C-shaped*	*S-shaped*
Feet	*grasping*	*flat*
Pelvis, lower back	*long*	*short*
Brain size	*345–505 ml*	*400–1350 ml*
Face	*in front of brain*	*beneath brain*
Canines	*long*	*short*
Diastema	*yes*	*no*

FIGURE 9.7. A comparison of several morphological characters related to bipedalism (upper four rows) and to cranial anatomy (lower four rows) in Pongidae and Hominidae. The divergence of these families is correlated with major environmental changes in eastern Africa over the last 5 million years. During this time, the rain forest in that area receded, giving rise to the gradual development of open grasslands (the savanna habitat).

pelvis, leg bones, and arm bones are related to the adoption of a bipedal posture. Not all these traits appeared at once in the earliest hominids, although a specimen would have to show evidence of adaptations for bipedality in order to be classified as a hominid.

Also evident among the Hominidae is a trend toward an increase in brain size, both in absolute and relative terms. Absolute increase in brain size, as already discussed, may be a passive consequence of the increase in body size that also characterized the hominids. However, EQs computed for a variety of fossil hominid species indicate that the increase in brain size was also relative. Values range between EQ = 2.2 for early australopithecines to EQ = 4.0 for late *Homo erectus* and EQ = 5.8 for *H. sapiens*; these values contrast with an EQ = 2.0 for chimpanzees (*Pan troglodytes*) and EQ = 1.7 for gorillas (*Gorilla gorilla*). Expansion of the brain is thus not a trait that characterizes the earliest hominids, but one that changes during the evolution of the lineage across the 5-million-year period. The position of the face is likely to be a change correlated with brain size, whereas the reduction in canine size is probably related to less intense male-male competition (i.e., less intense polygyny). The *diastema* is a gap in the lower jaw interpolated between the incisors and the canines; the lower jaws of hominids are round and curved, except in the oldest species, which exhibit a diastema similar to that observed in chimpanzees.

Fossils of the earliest hominids have all been found in Africa, and thus there is widespread agreement that our lineage evolved in that continent. It is possible to be even more specific: Those fossils come from the eastern part of Africa. It is known that this region was covered with rain forests before the Pliocene, but it gradually dried out. Patches of forest decreased in size progressively until the habitat became the savanna it is today. A widely held view suggests that the split between pongids and hominids is a case of *allopatric speciation* driven by adaptation to the local features of the rain forest (as in the western African apes) versus those of the increasingly more open grasslands of the savanna (as in the eastern African hominids). Bipedalism seems appropriate for an animal that lives in a savanna environment, but many other mammals (including some Old World monkeys, like the baboons) have adapted to such an environment without evolving bipedality. Perhaps additional selective pressures, including antipredatory vigilance (an upright posture permits animals to scan the landscape, as ground squirrels and other small mammals do) and parental care (transport of infants by releasing the arms from a locomotor function), may have contributed to the evolution of bipedalism in the hominid lineage.

3.c. Australopithecines. ***Figure 9.8*** shows the localities that have yielded evidence of hominids during the period roughly ranging between 5 and 2.5 Mya. Australopithecine species have been discovered in eastern Africa, and they were eventually replaced by species from the genus *Homo* by the end of this period. The record is poor for the initial portion of this period, and, as usual, the evidence is ambiguous (Johanson & Edgar 1996). The oldest tentative hominid, named *Ardipithecus ramidus,* was discovered in Middle Awash, Ethiopia, and dated 5.2 to 5.8 Mya (Haile-Selassie 2001). Foot bones from these remains are consistent with an early form of bipedality.

The oldest australopithecine species is now considered to be *Australopithecus anamensis,* from Kenya, and dated from about 4.2 to 3.9 Mya (Leakey et al. 1995). A preserved tibia indicates that this leg bone articulated in a manner consistent with bipedal locomotion. The lower jaw, however, is apelike in its appearance: It possesses a markedly receding chin. This combination of traits yields an animal that has been described as a "bipedal ape" and provides an intermediate phenotype that helps us understand the polarity of character changes in the hominid line. Of the two broad suits of characters in fossil hominids, those related to bipedality appear first, and those related to cranial changes (including brain size) appear later. Fossils of the better-known species *A. afarensis* also present this intermediate phenotype.

A. afarensis was found in localities at Ethiopia and Tanzania and are dated between 3.9 and 3.0 Mya. The most famous specimen is known as Lucy, and it was discovered in 1974 at Hadar, Ethiopia (Johanson & Edgar 1996). These animals show clear signs of bipedality: The short pelvis, the articulation of the femur and tibia, and a series of humanlike footprints attributed to *afarensis* leave little doubt. However, *afarensis* also had relatively long arms and curved fingers, both features associated with arboreal life. It is possible then that

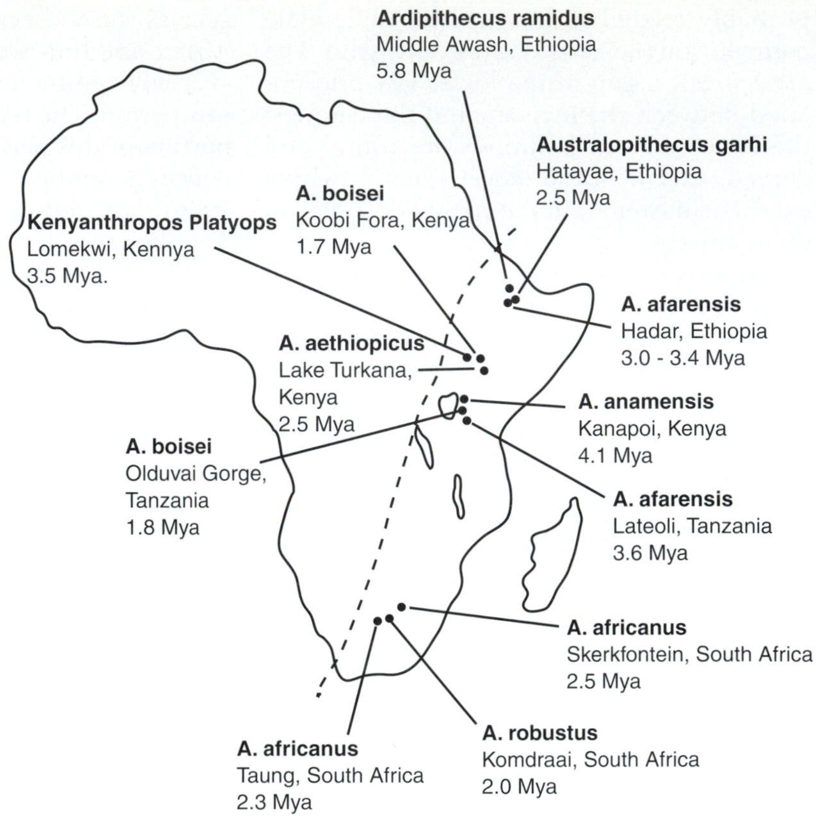

FIGURE 9.8. Major paleontological sites in eastern Africa. All the fossil australopithecines and several species of the genus *Homo* have been discovered in the area east of the dashed line. The northern portion of the line coincides with the East African Rift, a geological formation that may have acted as a geographical barrier to the spread of australopithecines toward the west.

these animals were arboreal to some degree, or, alternatively, that these traits simply reflect *evolutionary inertia* from arboreal ancestors. The skull of *afarensis* is also relatively small, yielding a brain capacity that did not exceed 500 ml in males (Kimbel et al. 1994). The interpretation of cranial capacity (which probably varied between 400 and 500 ml) is complicated by evidence of sexual dimorphism. In any case, for an animal of about 1.0 to 1.2 m in height, this cranial capacity is about the same as that of a chimpanzee. Cranial remains classified as *Kenyanthropus platyops* and dated 3.5 Mya were found near the western shore of Lake Turkana, Kenya (Leakey et al. 2001). A different genus was assigned to these remains because of their age and the combination of a small cranium (estimated to be of a size similar to that of *afarensis*) and relatively flat face (more typical of later *Homo* specimens).

Unfortunately, the absence of postcranial bones prevents an estimation of the degree of bipedality of *K. platyops*. Therefore, on the basis of the biological traits displayed by *anamensis* and *afarensis* it can be argued that early hominids diverged from their ancestors first in terms of adaptations for bipedal locomotion and only later in terms of an increase in brain size.

A third australopithecine species appears in more recent formations: *A. africanus* was discovered in South Africa and dated between 2.8 and 2.4 Mya. Relative to *afarensis, africanus* shows no diastema, smaller canines (less sexual dimorphism?), and larger molars, suggesting a more specialized leaf-eating diet. Its size and cranial capacity were about the same as that of *afarensis*. At about the same time, but in Ethiopia, evidence was found of a fourth species, *A. garhi,* distinguished from *afarensis* by the possession of larger premolars and molars, and from *africanus* by a more primitive, apelike facial morphology (Asfaw et al. 1999). Its age has been estimated to be 2.5 Mya. These four australopithecines, *anamensis, afarensis, africanus,* and *garhi,* were all relatively short and lightly built, clearly bipedal, and with a cranial capacity below 500 ml. They are collectively referred to as gracile; it is widely believed that species of the genus *Homo* first evolved from a gracile australopithecine.

The other branch of the australopithecine tree involves the robust species, of which three have been described so far: *A. aethiopicus* (Kenya, 2.7–1.9 Mya), *A. boisei* (Kenya and Tanzania, 2.3–1.4 Mya), and *A. robustus* (South Africa, 2.0–1.0 Mya). The relationships among the robust species and between them and the graciles is uncertain. Both *afarensis* and *africanus* have been suggested to be potential ancestors of the robust line. It is also possible that robust species evolved in parallel, with a lineage evolving in southern Africa (*africanus* to *robustus*) and another one in eastern Africa (*afarensis* to *aethiopicus* to *boisei*). What is generally agreed upon among experts is that the robust line became extinct without leaving descent.

The robust species possessed massive jaw musculature. They had a sagittal crest on the skull where jaw muscles were implanted and a thick lower jaw. In addition, their massive molars, adapted for crushing and grinding, suggest that they spent most of their time chewing highly fibrous plant material, much like today's gorillas do. Like gorillas, some of these robust australopithecines showed strong sexual dimorphism, with males reaching about twice the size of females. Cranial capacity rises to as much as 550 ml, but part of this increase is passively driven by their generally larger body size (maximum height has been estimated around 1.4 m). It is unclear why they became extinct. Evidence from a cave in South Africa indicates that they might have often been preys of large carnivores. A *robustus* skull was found that exhibits two openings that match the lower canines of a large carnivore found in the same cave. But having been limited to a very specific diet, they might have been vulnerable to climate changes or to competition from other animals, including Old World monkeys.

The evidence described in this section is summarized in ***Figure 9.9***. Relatively well-established conclusions include the following: (1) Bipedality is the main synapomorphy of the Hominidae; (2) changes in cranial capacity were modest in the australopithecines; (3) at least two lines of australopithecines evolved in Africa, the gracile and the robust lines; and (4) *Homo* is generally hypothesized to have evolved from a gracile australopithecine, whereas the robust line is generally believed to have become extinct.

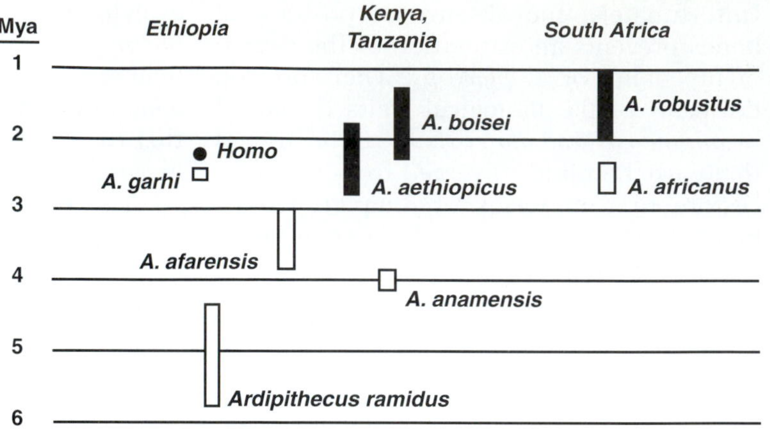

FIGURE 9.9. The location in space and time of the various species of australopithecines found in eastern Africa. *Ardipithecus* and the oldest evidence of *Homo* were included for comparison. Open bars represent the gracile species, whereas black bars represent the robust species.

3.d. Early Homo. The definition of our own genus, *Homo,* is not yet fully worked out by paleoanthropologists. However, the working definitions are surprisingly behavioral: The first humans have traditionally been defined not so much by their own features but by their association with lithic technology—that is, stone tools. Extant apes are known to use tools (see, for example, ***Figure 4.7***, front inside cover), but their tool-making abilities are particularly limited with regard to the use of stone as raw material. Early humans seem to have mastered the ability to take a piece of rock, hold it in one hand, and strike it a few times with another rock to create an edge. This tool could then be used to cut and to crush. This technology is abundantly evident at Olduvai Gorge, in Tanzania, where it was first discovered by Mary Leakey in the early 1960s, who called it the *Oldowan technology* (see ***Figure 9.10-a***). The Oldowan tool kit comprises hammer stones, choppers, scrapers, and similar tools, all relatively rough and simple and traditionally assigned to *Homo habilis* (*habilis* means, in fact, "ingenious" and "skillful" in reference to its presumed tool-making abilities). How far back in time does lithic technology go?

Bones of ungulates and horses bearing cut marks made by stone tools have been found in 2.5 Mya deposits at Hatayae, Ethiopia, in the same formation that yielded evidence of *A. garhi* (de Heinzelin et al. 1999). Some marks imply distal percussion, as in hammering, aimed at breaking the bone, perhaps to access the internal marrow. Other marks imply the cutting of flesh from its associated bone. It is not possible to assign this evidence to any particular hominid species. Moreover, the stone tools that produced the marks have not been found. These uncertainties notwithstanding, a scenario can be suggested for these ancient tool users. This evidence suggest a shift to a more carnivorous diet, although it is not yet possible to determine whether the prey was hunted or scavenged.

(a) Oldowan Technology

(b) Acheulean Technology

(c) Mousterian Technology

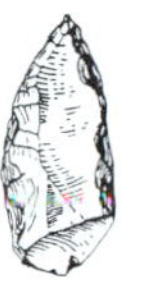
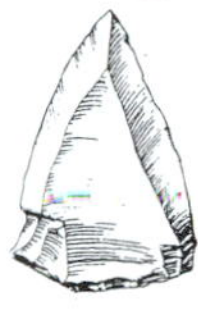

FIGURE 9.10. Some examples of human tools (Gowlett 1992). ***(a)*** Oldowan technology, associated with *Homo habilis* remains, 1.9 to 1.6 Mya (from left to right: trimmed flakes, a flake, a chopper); ***(b)*** Acheulean technology, associated with *H. ergaster,* 1.4 Mya to 150 Kya (handaxe, cleaver, and large flake); and ***(c)*** Mousterian technology, associated with *H. sapiens* and *H. neanderthalensis,* 100 to 40 Kya (point, elongated point, and sidescraper).

Bone marrow is a rich source of fat that may not have been accessible to large carnivores but easily obtainable for a hominid equipped with the appropriate stone tool. It is possible that the scarcity of raw material may have forced the tool makers to carry the tools with them rather than leave them where they had been used. At Olduvai Gorge, for example, tools were made with abundant quartz and basalt, and they were abandoned after use.

The oldest evidence of *Homo* is an upper jaw discovered at Hadar, Ethiopia, and dated about 2.3 Mya (Johanson & Edgar 1996). It is not possible to assign it to a particular species, but it is different from upper jaws assigned to *A. afarensis* found in the same locality. For example, the human maxilla is deeper, rounder, and exhibits less *prognathism* (i.e., the forward projection of the jaws are typical of apes and australopithecines but progressively less typical of humans). The oldest fossil specimens that have been assigned to particular species have been recovered from several localities in eastern Africa and from a time span ranging between 1.9 and 1.6 Mya. These bones have been assigned to *H. rudolfensis* and *H. habilis,* a dichotomy that is not accepted by all experts. If it is correct that these fossils belong to separate species, then one implication is that two distinct human species coexisted in the same period and locality, raising questions about their possible interaction and their possible status as ancestors of later humans. A major problem, as it is usually the case, is to determine whether the morphological differences observed in the fossil specimens are sufficiently important to warrant different species names, or whether they should be seen simply as individual variations within the same species.

H. habilis is also distinguished from australopithecines by the size of its cranium. Australopithecine species for which cranial capacity estimates could be obtained show volumes that do not reach 600 ml. The largest known cranial capacity—approximately 515 ml—is from a specimen of

A. africanus known as "Mrs. Ples," found in South Africa and dated 2.5 Mya: (Conroy et al. 1998). By contrast, a cranial capacity of about 600 ml or greater is now generally considered a synapomorphy of the genus *Homo*. ***Table 9.2*** summarizes the estimates of body and brain size, and provides a more complete list of EQs (McHenry 1995; Tobias 1995). The EQs listed in this table are based on an expected allometric equation for mammals with the following parameters: $E = 0.0589S^{0.76}$ (Martin 1981). Although compared with other similar estimates these values tend to be on the conservative side (i.e., they are smaller than others reported in the literature), the reader is warned that these estimates should be considered with caution. A major problem continues to be the scarcity of crania from which a measure of brain size can be attempted and of postcranial skeletons from which body size can be estimated. A major implication of these numbers is that brain size increased even across hominid species exhibiting similar body size. This implies that there were specific selective pressures for encephalization that are responsible for the peculiar increase in relative brain size that characterizes the hominid lineage. It is plausible that tool making is one of the factors that contributed to the evolution of encephalization in the hominids.

3.e. Homo ergaster and Homo erectus. Until recently, findings from both eastern Africa and Asia, from a 1.8 Mya to 200 Kya time span, and ranging in cranial capacity from 775 ml to 1,225 ml, were pooled together into a single species, *Homo erectus*. The African specimens have been assigned to a new species, *H. ergaster*, which differs from *H. erectus* in lacking several cranial

TABLE 9.2 Estimated Body Size, Brain Size, and EQ for Several Species of Apes and Hominids

Species	***Mya***	***Body Weight (Kg) Males (*)***	***Females (*)***	***Brain Volume (*)***	***(ml) (**)***	***EQ (*)***
Gorilla gorilla	extant	140	70	505	505	1.7
Pan paniscus	extant	38	32	343	344	2.0
Pan troglodytes	extant	49	41	395	383	2.0
Australopithecus afarensis	3.9–3.0	45	29	384	414	2.2
A. africanus	2.8–2.4	41	30	420	440	2.5
A. aethiopicus	2.7–1.9	?	?	399	?	?
A. boisei	2.3–1.4	49	34	488	463	2.6
A. robustus	2.0–1.0	40	32	502	530	2.9
Homo habilis	1.9–1.6	37	32	579	640	3.5
H. rudolfensis	1.9–1.6	60	51	709	?	3.0
H. ergaster	1.8–1.5	58	52	804	?	3.3
H. erectus	0.5–0.3	60	55	980	937	4.0
H. sapiens	0.4–0	58	49	1350	1350	5.8

(*) McHenry (1995)
(**) Tobias (1995)

characters, including thick bones and a depression behind the browridge. An almost complete skeleton of a young *ergaster* boy was found in Kenya and dated 1.6 Mya; the remains correspond to a teenage boy who was 1.8 m tall, weighed nearly 68 kg, and had a cranial capacity of 880 ml. Both *ergaster* and *erectus* were far more similar to modern humans in appearance than any previous species. They were fully bipedal and had lost signs of arboreal adaptations present in previous hominids, such as curved fingers and relatively long arms.

It has been common to assume that *erectus* is derived either from *ergaster* or from some similar, African species. Whatever the case, the biogeographic distribution implies a degree of migratory behavior not observed in any of the preceding hominids, all of which evolved and stayed on the African continent. Evidence of *erectus* was first discovered in Java, in 1891, and later in China, which provides an idea of the extent of this first migratory wave out of Africa. But exactly when does *erectus* (or *ergaster*) first appear on the Asian continent? The Java and China remains are not older than 1 Mya at best. However, human remains (*ergaster? erectus?*) dated 1.8 Mya have been found at Dmanisi, Georgia, between the Caspian and Black Seas (Gabunia & Vekua 1995). This suggests a very ancient migratory wave out of Africa. Consistent with this is the fact that the stone tools recovered in this ancient Georgian site, as well as in the more recent eastern Asian sites, are similar to those characterized as Oldowan technology (appearing in Africa more than 2 Mya). If this early migration occurred somewhere between 2.0 and 1.8 Mya, then this could explain the presence of an Oldowanlike technology in Asia.

Approximately 1.4 Mya, a different tool kit, known as *Acheulean technology,* was developed by *ergaster* populations in Ethiopia (see ***Figure 9.10-b***). These tools were larger and more carefully elaborated (e.g., they were modeled on both sides of the stone) than those typical of the prior Oldowan technology. A wider variety of rocks were used in the making of these tools, including lava rock and flint, and there was an impressive degree of standardization and specialization. Hand axes, picks, and cleavers are commonly found in Acheulean sites ranging from Africa to the Middle East, India, and, starting about 500 Kya, Europe. The degree of standardization in tool making suggests the presence of a manufacturing culture.

During this period and in association with *Homo* remains, there is evidence of the use of fire in several African sites. Starting approximately 500 Kya, sustained used of fire pits occurs in Asian and European locations where climatic conditions may have provided the appropriate incentive to develop control over the production of fire. The importance of fire can hardly be overemphasized. Warmth, light, protection against predators, processing of meat that could be stored before consumption, and an incentive for group members to come into close contact are some of the consequences of controlling fire. Once developed, such traditions may have provided a nurturing environment for the rise of more complex interactions and eventually led to social interchange of information mediated by language.

3.f. Archaic Humans. About 600 Kya, a species with many features intermediate between *ergaster* and modern humans appeared in Africa: *Homo heidelbergensis.* In the past, these fossils were labeled "archaic humans" and attributed to our own species; however, experts now tend to assign these specimens to a different species. Although it is believed that *heildelbergensis* evolved from some African population of *ergaster,* this hypothesis is weakened by a considerable gap in the fossil evidence: The period between the most recent *ergaster,* 1.5 Mya, and the oldest *heidelbergensis,* 600 Kya, is considerable. The original specimen was found in Germany in 1907, and now it seems likely that *heidelbergensis* is the oldest hominid species that entered Europe. Findings in Spain, France, England, and Greece, Europe, and in Zambia, Africa, corresponding to a period ranging between 500 and 250 Kya, are all attributed to *heidelbergensis* (Johanson & Edgar 1996).

Archaic humans are distinguished from *ergaster* and *erectus* by their cranial capacity, among other things (Stringer 1992). Whereas the range for *ergaster-erectus* is between 750 and 1,250 ml, archaic humans exhibit a range between 1,100 and 1,400 ml. These values lie well within those of modern humans, *H. sapiens,* estimated to be between 1,200 and 1,700 ml. Archaic cranial features include a receding frontal bone, prominent brow ridges, and a retracted chin. Generally speaking, these features of the cranium are intermediate between what is observed in *ergaster* or *erectus* and what is typical of modern humans. So, for example, the brow ridges have been gradually reduced and the cranium has become gradually rounder, higher, and shorter.

Archaic humans, like their *ergaster* ancestors, also dispersed from Africa into Europe and Asia. They brought with them the Acheulean technology developed in Africa, which must have been critical in enabling them to adjust to environmental conditions very different from those of the tropical African savanna. Unfortunately, little else is known about the cultural background of these ancient humans.

A second species of archaic humans appeared in Europe about 120 Kya and extended their range to the middle eastern region, only to become extinct, more or less abruptly, approximately 30 Kya. These are the famous Neanderthal humans, or *Homo neanderthalensis.* They have been regarded in the past as a subspecies of *H. sapiens,* but more recently experts have tended to assign them their own species name. Neanderthals display bodily features that seem appropriate for cold climates, including being heavier than modern humans. They inhabited Europe during the glacial periods; traits appropriate to cope with cold weather conditions may have been strongly selected for in Neanderthals. Their range of cranial size, 1,200 to 1,750 ml, is also within the range for modern humans.

There is abundant information about Neanderthals because they tended to live in caves where large amounts of material have been preserved. For example, a cave in Croatia discovered in 1899 has produced thousands of bones from hundreds of individuals and a wide variety of tools. There is evidence of what to us would be familiar cultural practices, including intentional burials, use of clothing, control of fire, caring of the injured, and hunting. Neanderthals shared with contemporary modern humans a tool kit known as *Mousterian technology,* based on the production of flakes that were then turned into a wide variety of tools (see ***Figure 9.10-c***). These tools have refined shapes and were obviously made with great care and patience. It is not clear how Neanderthals and modern humans came to produce very similar tools.

Much has been speculated about the extinction of the Neanderthals and, in particular, the role of modern humans, if any, in their demise. Modern *Homo sapiens* appeared in Europe about 40 Kya, and they start replacing Neanderthals in an orderly fashion, in a western-to-eastern direction. Did Neanderthals evolve into *sapiens?*

The distinct features of *neanderthalensis* and *sapiens* seem to preclude this possibility. Furthermore, analysis of *mitochondrial DNA* recovered from Neanderthal bones supports the hypothesis that the two lineages were highly differentiated (Krings et al. 1997). Comparison of a strain with 328 base pairs among humans shows an average difference in 8 nucleotides; by contrast, Neanderthal mDNA differs from that of contemporary humans by an average of 28 nucleotides. The magnitude of this difference suggests a common ancestor that lived approximately 600 Kya and is consistent with the notion that Neanderthals were a distinct species.

Did *sapiens* exterminate the Neanderthals violently? There is evidence from caves at Mount Carmel, Israel, that Neanderthals and modern humans coexisted during a period of approximately 50,000 years. However, it is not possible to determine the extent to which coexisting populations of Neanderthals and modern humans interacted. In any case, such a long coexistence makes it unlikely that the replacement involved violent means.

Did Neanderthal features (rather than their genes) disappear because they interbred with *sapiens*? This hypothesis is difficult to test. For example, some findings of *sapiens* crania with isolated Neanderthal features (such as an occipital bone that is pointed, rather than rounded as it usually is in *sapiens*) have been interpreted as evidence of interbreeding. Moreover, Neanderthal-like features have been suggested to be present in some modern European populations. The problem arises as a result of the morphological variability that characterizes human populations. There is probably very little in the Neanderthal phenotype that could not be matched by some proportion of the present human population. This fact even questions the extent to which their assignment to a separate species is warranted. If they were a variety of humans, much like a subspecies or a race within a particular species, then spatial proximity would have invariably led to interbreeding.

Were Neanderthals outcompeted by modern humans? It is very likely that the resources exploited by these two populations overlapped extensively. Food, shelter, and raw materials for tools were probably very much the same. Even a small advantage in the ability to exploit these resources of one population over the other, and assuming there was no interbreeding, would eventually cause a replacement. If modern humans were better at selecting their campsites, at planning hunting trips, at obtaining raw materials for tools from distant sources, at interacting with other human groups, and other similar activities, they might have driven Neanderthal populations to extinction.

The evidence suggests that Neanderthals had a restricted distribution, occupying territories in what is now Europe and the Middle East during a period ranging between 120 and 30 Kya. No Neanderthal remains have been found in eastern Asia or even in Africa, a short distance by sea at the Gibraltar point. Unlike their *ergaster* ancestors, Neanderthals seem to have resisted widespread migration. In contrast, modern humans displayed a more dynamic pattern of distribution: During the same period, they entered all the continents, including the Americas, settled in a wide range of ecological conditions, and developed a cultural complexity never before seen in other primates.

3.g. Modern Humans. The oldest fossil evidence attributed to *Homo sapiens* comes from Border Cave and Klasies River Mouth in South Africa, from the Omo Valley in Ethiopia, and from Mount Carmel and

Qafzeh cave in Israel (Vandermeersch 1995). In all these cases, fossils have been dated around 100 Kya in age by various techniques, which implies that the species originated between 200 and 100 Kya, probably in Africa or perhaps in the Middle East. This hypothesis implies, of course, that the earlier *Homo* populations from Asia (*erectus*) and the somewhat contemporary ones from Europe (*neanderthalensis*) cannot be ancestors of *sapiens.*

Sapiens appears in the Asian fossil record as far back as 67 Kya in China, 40 Kya in Borneo, and 24 Kya in the Philippines. Interestingly, Australia has been populated by modern humans (the ancestors of today's aborigines) during the past 60,000 years. In Europe, modern humans, called Cro-Magnons, appear in fossils dated about 40 Kya in age. The American continent was the last one to be invaded by modern humans. Evidence of early settlements during the period between 50 and 30 Kya is somewhat controversial; however, there is agreement that modern human populations were well established by approximately 20 Kya.

Archeological evidence shows that about 40 Kya many of the cultural practices common in today's societies emerged either in *sapiens* or in *neanderthalensis* populations. Tool technology based on bone as raw material allowed for the making of small, delicate tools, such as hooks for fishing. Such delicate tools may have been made earlier in wood or other perishable materials that have left no trace. There is evidence of art, bodily ornaments, huts, intensive exploitation of quarries, a type of commerce with long-distance exchanges of material such as amber and shells (used for ornamental purposes), and the development of means for sea navigation, as demonstrated by the arrival of *sapiens* in Australia. The development of linguistic abilities above some threshold that permitted its application to a wide set of problems may be related to these achievements of the late Paleolithic.

According to one hypothesis, *sapiens* originated in a single population, most likely in sub-Saharan Africa, and from there it spread to northern Africa, Europe, the Middle East, eastern Asia, Australia, and the Americas (Stringer & Gamble 1993). This view, named the *out-of-Africa hypothesis,* is generally considered parsimonious (usually, evolutionary hypotheses claiming a single origin are considered simpler than those claiming more than one origin). At its core, the proposed scenario is the following: Incoming *sapiens* populations progressively enter the regions of the world and replace local populations of archaic humans. In Europe and the middle east, *sapiens* replaced the Neanderthals, whereas in eastern Asia they replaced the last populations of *erectus* that had evolved there. One competing alternative, suggested by Thorne and Wolpoff (1992), is the *multiregional evolution hypothesis,* according to which populations of archaic humans evolved in situ into *Homo sapiens.* This hypothesis is based on the assumption that there has been considerable amount of gene flow between locally evolving populations. These two extreme hypotheses are represented in ***Figure 9.11.***

In evolutionary theory, a pattern of speciation whereby a population gradually evolves from one species into another without any divergence is called *anagenesis.* Speciation by divergence, in which isolated populations evolve into different species by local adaptation, is called *cladogenesis.* Therefore, whereas the out-of-Africa hypothesis implies a cladogenetic pattern in which the initial divergence of *sapiens* is seen as occurring rapidly (perhaps with a strong contribution from genetic drift; see ***Chapter 2, section 4.c.***, pp. 41–42) in relatively small and peripheral populations, the

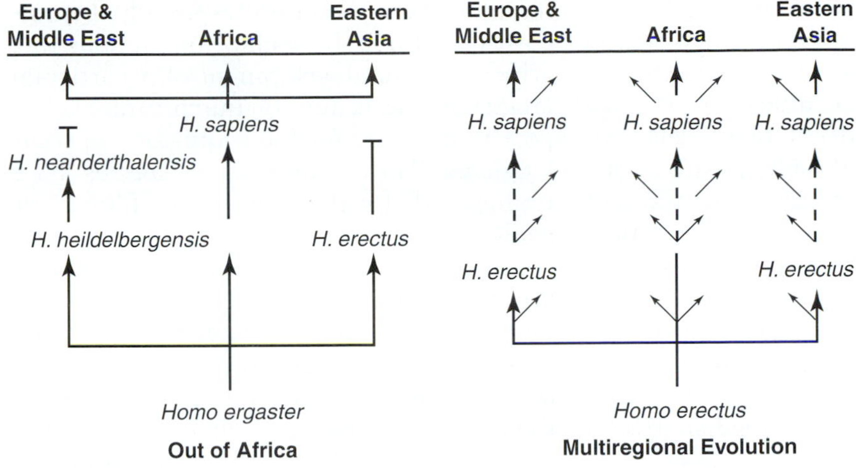

FIGURE 9.11. A graphic representation of the two main hypotheses of the evolution of *Homo sapiens*. The out-of-Africa hypothesis assumes a single origin of *H. sapiens*, perhaps in sub-Saharan Africa, followed by extensive migration, and the replacement of local, archaic populations. The multiregional evolution hypothesis assumes that the evolution of *H. sapiens* occurred in local populations of *H. erectus* that had migrated earlier from Africa. This hypothesis suggests that there was extensive gene flow (see diagonal arrows) among populations.

multiregional evolution hypothesis has a strong anagenetic component according to which all local populations of archaic humans had the potential (i.e., were preadapted) to evolve into *sapiens* independently of the selective pressures originating from the physical environment.

Whereas it is not possible for the moment to select one of these extreme hypotheses, or even one of the more intermediate versions, some of the evidence appears more consistent with the out-of-Africa hypothesis. For example, if the sub-Saharan findings from Ethiopia and South Africa are as old as some have claimed (i.e., older than 100 Kya), this would provide strong evidence for an African origin of *sapiens*. Moreover, the evidence that mDNA from Neanderthals is very different from that of modern humans is also consistent with the out-of-Africa hypothesis.

4. EVOLUTION OF LANGUAGE

4.a. What Is Language? Is it likely that the explosion of cultural developments that characterize the evolution of modern humans follows from the evolutionary emergence of a single trait? I have considered previously that evolution may proceed gradually for long periods, leading to little phenotypic change until, for some reason, an "explosion" of new forms arises in a relative short interval. For example, the transition from the Mesozoic to the Cenozoic witnessed a spectacularly rapid instance of change in the mammalian lineage caused, apparently, by the sudden opening of ecological niches after the mass extinction event of the late Cretaceous. In the case of human evolution, what appears to change drastically with the advent of modern humans is not so much the phenotype of the new species but the cultural environment they provided for themselves. This change is therefore more a "behavioral explosion" rather than a morphological one.

It is likely that the emergence of this novel cultural repertoire is linked to the development of language. Although language itself is unlikely to have emerged suddenly, the application of linguistic skills to a broader context may have occurred relatively rapidly, and once in place it may have prompted behavioral changes that affected most aspects of human social behavior. Language is foremost and most importantly a mode of communication. It is peculiar in that it is based on symbolic units, called *words,* that generally bear no direct resemblance to the objects or actions to which they refer (thus, the word "book" is not related in any obvious way to the object) or that refer to abstract ideas that apply to classes of objects but to no particular object in reality (the word "beautiful" can be applied to many different objects sharing the quality of "beauty"). Words are combined according to specific rules of *syntax* or *grammar* and carry somewhat specific *meanings*—that is, they signify something to the listener. The words, their meaning, and the grammar used by a particular language are all acquired through a process of social learning. Also learned is the ability to use language to communicate via speech (perhaps the original medium in an evolutionary sense), sign language, writing, singing, and reading.

Like any other learning, language depends on the CNS. In particular, various aspects of language appear to map onto different areas of the brain (especially the neocortex). Although social interactions are critical for the development of a particular language, the brains of human infants appear to be ready for the acquisition of some language. How many other species have brains ready for the acquisition of linguistic skills?

As far as it is known, there is no animal other than *sapiens* that uses a mode of communication similar to language. However, many have suggested that the difference is one of education and training. For example, the French philosopher Julien de La Mettrie [1709–1751] suggested that the brains of chimpanzees and humans are so alike that chimpanzees would learn to speak if they were provided with the appropriate education. This suggestion is particularly interesting given that no other living species is more closely related to *sapiens* than the chimpanzee. We now know that chimpanzees raised with human children in a "normal" family environment do not develop full speech abilities (Hayes 1951). Is this inability to speak a reflection of the chimpanzee's poor linguistic capacity? Again the answer appears to be negative. Chimpanzees find it difficult to modulate sounds by adjusting the vocal chords and the larynx as humans do during normal speech. But linguistic abilities are localized in the brain, not in the larynx, so it makes no sense to conclude that chimpanzees do not have linguistic abilities simply because they cannot speak.

Comparative psychologists have been fascinated by the prospect of teaching linguistic abilities to animals in order to determine what aspects of language are shared by humans and nonhumans. This research is reviewed in detail in ***Chapter 14*** (***sections 3.d.*** and ***3.e.***, pp. 572–580), but some conclusions are relevant in the present context.

There is little question that chimpanzees (*Pan troglodytes*) can easily acquire a "vocabulary" of either manual gestures or artificial shapes pressed on a computerlike keyboard (chimpanzees are very skillful in the use of their hands). They can use that vocabulary to request various things, including specific food items (e.g., "apple") and tools (e.g., "wrench") from either an experimenter or another trained chimpanzee. Chimpanzees can also learn to classify words that refer to such things as "apple" and "orange" as "fruit," or "wrench" and "straw" as "tools." A pigmy chimpanzee (*Pan paniscus*) named Kanzi has demonstrated an impressive ability to understand spoken English, which he has acquired "spontaneously" by being present while his surrogate mother was the subject of a language-training program. Naming and classifying objects, and comprehending commands are part of the "linguistic abilities" of several species. To the extent that these are aspects of language, the question of whether nonhuman animals can acquire language may be impossible to answer for one simple reason: Language is not a unitary phenomenon but a complex array of skills. Some of these linguistic skills may be common to several or even many species of higher vertebrates; still others may be unique to humans. Human language may have evolved as an elaboration of intellectual processes that were available to our ancestors and perhaps to a wide range of vertebrates. What are the likely stages of language evolution in early hominids?

4.b. Precursors of Language. One useful property of language is its ability to convey information about many different aspects of the environment. Communication in nonhuman animals tends to involve a narrow correspondence between the signal and the context in which the signal is useful. For example, frog calls have meaning within the context of reproduction, and vervet monkey's alarm signals communicate the presence of specific predators. However, these animals seem to be restricted to using their particular calls in very specific contexts. By contrast, words can be used in a wide variety of contexts: The qualifier "beautiful" can be applied to people, colors, music, actions, and so on. Similarly, language can refer to economic transactions, personal feelings, food, aspects of the environment, and countless other things. Therefore, a wide range of activities can be affected by a single system of communication.

The communicative function of language may have also been, at least in part, an important source of selective pressure during its early evolution. As will be shown in ***section 4.c.*** below, linguistic skills depend heavily on the neocortex. The primate neocortex, in turn, varies extensively in both absolute and relative size among primates, but, interestingly, it shows a positive allometric function when correlated to one index of sociality: group size (Dunbar 1993). Various measurements of neocortical size, including the *neocortex ratio* (volume of the neocortex divided by the volume of the rest of the brain), have been found to correlate with the average size of groups in 36 primate genera, as shown in ***Figure 9.12-a.*** One implication of this correlation is that the neocortex is involved in the processing of social information. Interestingly, group size also correlates positively with the amount of time allocated to grooming in Old World monkeys and apes (***Figure 9.12-b***). Among primates, grooming behavior functions as a way of establishing and strengthening affective bonds among individuals. On the basis of the correlation between group size and neocortex in primates, and knowing the neocortex ratio for humans (which is 4.1), what would be the predicted group size for humans? This value is 147.8

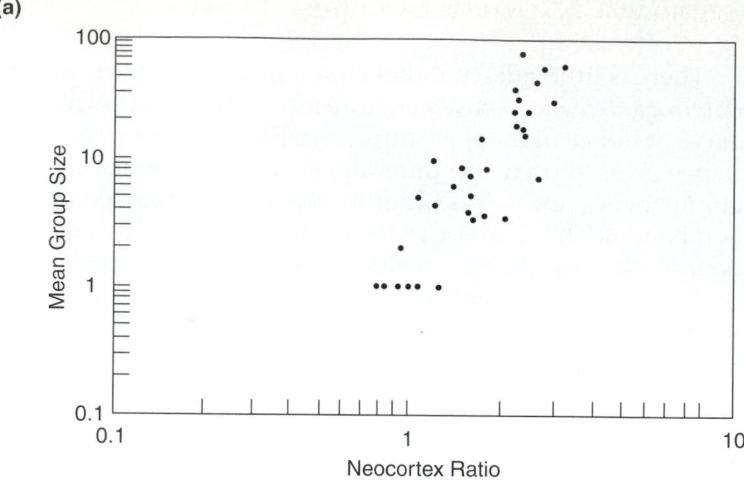

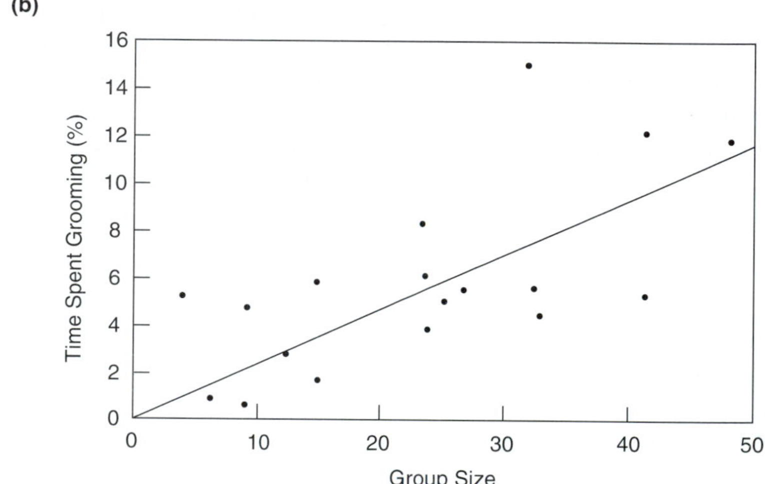

FIGURE 9.12. Correlational evidence used by Dunbar (1993) to suggest possible selective pressures underlying the evolution of language. ***(a)*** Group (or troop) size and the neocortex ratio (volume of neocortex divided by volume of the rest of the brain) correlate positively on double logarithmic coordinates. This study involved 36 genera of primates, including prosimians. ***(b)*** Group size is also positively correlated with the percentage of time spent grooming in Old World monkeys and apes. Based on this evidence, and knowing the neocortex ratio for humans, Dunbar extrapolated to predict that human groups should involve approximately 150 individuals which would require, in turn, an investment in grooming of about 40% of the total time budget. Given the size of this figure, Dunbar suggested that language evolved as a technique that is more efficient than grooming for developing and maintaining social bonds in large groups.

individuals per group. Given this group size, humans would be required to spend about 42% of the total time in grooming, twice the proportion allocated to grooming in other primates. Dunbar (1993) suggested that language may have evolved as a more efficient mechanism to strengthen social bonds in early humans and as an alternative to grooming. Whereas grooming involves pairs of animals engaged in a behavior at the exclusion of other activities, linguistic interactions may involve larger groups and may be engaged even when the group is developing some other activity. However plausible this idea may be, it is unlikely that the evolutionary origin of language could be accounted for in terms of a single selective pressure. Some candidates for selective pressures for the evolution of language include sexual selection, food processing, tool making and teaching, strengthening of social bonds, and planned hunting.

What were the precursors of language? Science may never provide a definitive answer to this question because the key evidence is likely to be irrevocably lost. Plausible answers can be attempted based on available evidence. For example, language research with nonhuman animals suggests that a variety of linguistic properties are relatively widespread. These skills that predated the origin of human language may have formed a basic set of preadaptations from which natural selection shaped more complex linguistic processes. According to Donald (1991), one such preadaptation is the ability of animals for *episodic memory,* that is, the recall of specific events in the person's past (i.e., "I saw Armstrong's first walk on the moon at my aunt Angela's home"). Episodic memory usually involves spatiotemporal information about the event (i.e., "I was a teenager when Armstrong walked on the moon"). Because of the nature of episodic memory, it is hard to find ways to demonstrate that nonverbal organisms possess information about specific events that happened to them. Such information is generally anecdotal and comes from more or less casual observations.

In one experimental attempt to demonstrate episodic memory in animals (Clayton & Dickinson 1998), food-hoarding scrub jays (*Aphelocoma coerulescens*) stored either worms (a type of food that rapidly becomes inedible) or peanuts (a nonperishable food) in different locations. A choice test was scheduled either 4 hr or 120 hr later. Scrub jays showed preference for the worms in the 4-hr test, but their preference rapidly switched to the peanuts in the 120-hr test as jays learned that the worms had decayed. A group of jays for which the worms were replaced before the test showed preference for the worms over the peanuts. This result suggests that the jays remembered where and when the worms had been stored and avoided those locations when chances were good that the worms had become inedible. This report suggests the possibility that episodic memory is within the capacity of nonhuman animals.

The "culture" of an animal capable of representing specific events in memory, including chimpanzees and the australopithecines, can be characterized as an *episodic culture.* Memory for such events may have played a major role in the process of adjustment to the social structure of the group. For example, dominance hierarchies are subject to change after specific events occur within the group (e.g., dominant males may be displaced, females may change status by affiliating with new dominant males, etc.). Remembering the key events that led to such changes could be of prime importance to obtain access to resources, including food and mates.

Donald (1991) further argued that the emergence of *Homo* species brought a transition from an episodic culture to a *mimetic culture.* The systematic tool industry, widespread migration patterns, use of fire, and group hunting that appear to have been typical of *ergaster* and *erectus* introduced this new type of culture. *Mimesis* refers to the ability to reenact an event according to how the actor viewed it. It is similar to the type of imitation that occurs when a child reenacts a tea ceremony with dolls or personifies a super-hero after seeing a movie. Mimesis may have been a preverbal communicative medium that may have allowed early humans to develop greater group cohesiveness, the teaching of tool-making skills, and the planning of group activities, including hunting, ceremonies, and rituals. Speech may have arisen in the context of mimetic acts, as vocalizations that accompanied bodily gestures and facial expressions.

4.c. Biology of Language. Some type of language is present in all human cultures, independently of the culture's degree of complexity (Pinker 1995). It does not seem to be the case that language was "invented" in a particular culture from which it spread to other cultures that had no language, as technological inventions usually do. Language is therefore a biological trait rather than a cultural trait, and it is the product of a vocal tract and brain circuits that may have appeared relatively recently in hominid evolution.

Language may be a synapomorphy of a clade formed by *sapiens, neanderthalensis,* and their common ancestor. Whether or not Neanderthals were capable of speech has been a subject of intense debate. Their peripheral anatomy is ambiguous. On the one hand, their larynx appears to have been too high and the insertion of the pharynx musculature in the basis of the cranium more like that of apes than that of *sapiens.* Moreover, the *basicranial flexure* of Neanderthals was flatter than that of humans and more like that of apes and australopithecines. The basicranial flexure measures the orientation of several points lying at the basis of the cranium and permits an appreciation of the way in which muscles controlling the movements of the vocal apparatus were inserted. These features would have made it difficult for Neanderthals to modulate a large number of sounds. On the other hand, the Neanderthal *hyoid bone* was essentially similar in size and shape to that of *sapiens,* and very different from the chimpanzee hyoid (Arensburg et al. 1989). The hyoid (which is not known from any other extinct hominid), supports larynx muscles that are critical for the modulation of sound and thus for speech. Neanderthals appear to have possessed enough support for some speech abilities, although the degree of development of these abilities is uncertain.

Figure 9.13 shows the vocal tract of chimpanzees and humans from a lateral view (Lieberman 1992). In chimpanzees the larynx is relatively high, as it is also in human infants. In adult humans, however, the larynx acquires a lower position at the neck level, and the soft palate can block the nasal cavity. These changes allow humans to produce a large spectrum of sound frequencies with greater clarity. The rounded tongue of adult humans also permits the production of the sounds defining the vowels [i], [u], and [a] (as in the words "feet," "poor," and "mama") and the consonants [k] and [g], all of which are pervasive phonetic elements of most human languages. The vocal apparatus is part of the production side of language, just as the internal ear is part of the perception part of language. But linguistic abilities go beyond these peripheral components. Humans can, after all, read with their eyes or fingers and express themselves linguistically in writing

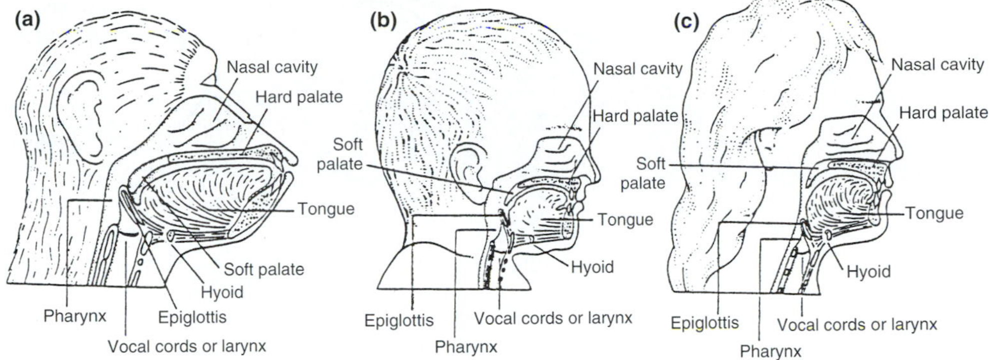

FIGURE 9.13. A lateral view of the head of ***(a)*** a chimpanzee, ***(b)*** an infant, and ***(c)*** an adult (Lieberman 1992). Differences in terms of the shape of the tongue, position of the epiglottis, and height of the larynx between ***(a)*** and ***(c)*** are important in understanding the ability of adult humans to modulate a wide variety of sounds. The shape of the hyoid bone (not appreciable in this drawing) is also associated with speech production. Notice the similarity in these traits between chimpanzees ***(a)*** and infants ***(b)***.

(interestingly, one could write with a computer keyboard, or with a pen attached to the big toe or held between the teeth, so writing is not rigidly tied to the use of one particular medium).

The linguistic skills that allow for such flexibility in peripheral components are localized in the neocortex, particularly in the area surrounding the Sylvian sulcus, but are strongly lateralized. Cortical *lateralization* of function implies that equivalent anatomical areas from each hemisphere may subserve different functions. Lateralization is not unique to language or to humans, but is also expressed in terms of a variety of motor functions and in other primates (see ***Chapter 11***, ***section 3.a.***, pp. 434–436). In humans, the left hemisphere is dominant for language in approximately 90% of the population; the left hemisphere is dominant also in about 70% of the left-handed people and in about 95% of the right-handed people. Some areas implicated in linguistic functions are lateralized morphologically. For example, the planum temporale (implicated in reading, musical talent, and handedness, among other functions) is a portion of temporal cortex located inside of the Sylvian sulcus. It is larger in the left hemisphere than in the right one, although this is also true for chimpanzees (Gannon et al. 1998). Language lateralization may thus have evolved on the basis of preexisting neocortical lateralization for motor skills involving the arms.

Two main areas have traditionally been implicated in linguistic function: Wernicke's area and Broca's area (***Figure 9.14***). Wernicke's area, as well as adjacent areas, plays a role in a variety of linguistic functions related to the semantic properties of language. Patients with lesions in this area may be able to speak fluently, but their speech makes little sense. Moreover, they may fail to understand other people's speech. This is known as *Wernicke's aphasia*. Patients with more restricted le-

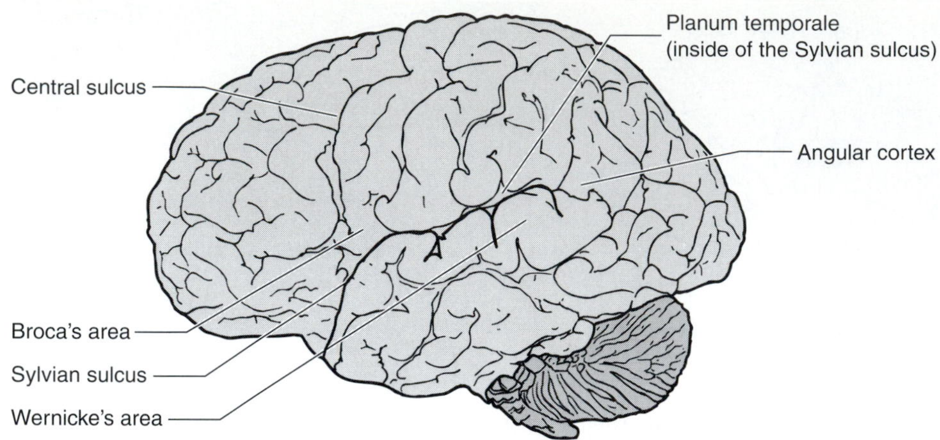

FIGURE 9.14. A lateral view of the human brain. Areas relevant for the processing of linguistic information are marked. Wernicke's area, immediately caudal with respect to the primary auditory area, is involved in language comprehension. Surrounding areas are also responsible for language-related functions, including the planum temporale (hidden in the floor of the Sylvian sulcus) and the angular cortex. Broca's area, at the basis of the central sulcus and in the frontal lobe, controls speech. The arquate fasciculus (not shown) is a tract of axons that connects Wernicke's and Broca's areas. Lesions in this fasciculus lead to comprehension deficits labeled conduction aphasia.

sions may exhibit more specific deficits, such as difficulty in naming objects (nominal aphasia with lesions of the angular cortex), recognizing familiar objects or places (agnosia with lesions of the posterior parietal cortex), or reading (dyslexia with abnormal cell distributions in the planum temporale).

By contrast, patients with lesions in Broca's area display poor and laborious speech articulation. This is called *Broca's aphasia*. Comprehension does not appear to be impaired in this type of aphasia, since words, when produced correctly, have the appropriate meaning for the context. Patients with Broca's aphasia seem to be aware of their problem and struggle to produce the appropriate words.

This view of extreme localization of function should perhaps be taken with caution. Reports have been published of patients having aphasic symptoms and lesions in unexpected cortical areas or, vice versa, having lesions in Broca's or Wernicke's areas but spared linguistic abilities (Caplan et al. 1984). It has been estimated that about 10% of aphasics exhibit lesions in neocortical locations that have not traditionally been related to language, or they show lesions in Broca's area correlated with Wernicke-like symptoms.

Whereas the brain of modern humans has remained virtually unchanged over at least the last 40,000 years, cultural evolution has been impressive. The development of tool technology is particularly notorious.

The Oldowan and Acheulean technologies subsisted practically unchanged for more than a million years. By contrast, the last few thousand years have witnessed the invention of a large variety of tools, manufactured with many different raw materials, some of which have been actually invented (e.g., plastics). The increase in the size of the population, the colonization of virtually the entire planet, the globalization of the economy, the ability to easily relocate, and many other aspects of contemporary culture attest to the success of modern humans. But that very success is creating problems on a similar scale: pollution, poverty, and large-scale environmental changes, among others. The behavioral strategies that have made our cultures so successful may also hinder our own survival.

5. KEY TERMS

Acheulean technology 345
allopatric speciation 339
anagenesis 348
arboreal life 320
basicranial flexure 354
bipedality 323
brachiation 320
brain size 320
Broca's aphasia 356
central sulcus 326
cladogenesis 348
claustrum 326
depth perception 320
diastema 339
encephalization quotient, EQ 323
episodic culture 353
episodic memory 353
evolutionary inertia 340
expectancy-specific neurons 328
foramen magnum 337
fovea 333
frontal cortex 327
grammar 350
grasping 320
index of extra cortical neurons, N_c 324
hippocampus 326
hyoid bone 354
lateralization 355
meaning 350
mimesis 354
mimetic culture 344
mitochondrial DNA 354
monogyny 325
Mousterian technology 346
multiregional evolution hypothesis 348
neocortex ratio 351
occipital condyle 337
occipital cortex 326
Oldowan technology 342
out-of-Africa hypothesis 348
parietal cortex 327
planum temporale 326
polygyny 324
prognathism 343
proper mass 326
reversal 327
sexual dimorphism 333
Sylvian sulcus 326
synapomorphy 354
syntax 350
temporal cortex 326
Wernicke's aphasia 355
words 350

6. References

Andrews, P. (1985). Improved timing of hominoid evolution with a DNA clock. *Nature,* **314,** 498–499.

Arensburg, B., Tillier, A.-M., Vandermeersch, B., Duday, H., Schepartz, L. A., & Rak, Y. (1989). A middle Paleolithic human hyoid bone. *Nature,* **338,** 758–760.

Asfaw, B., White, T., Lovejoy, O., Latimer, B., Simpson, S., & Suwa, G. (1999). *Australopithecus garhi*: A new species of early hominid from Ethiopia. *Science,* **284,** 629–635.

Benton, M. J. (1990). *Vertebrate paleontology.* London: Unwin Hyman.

Caplan, D., Lecours, A. R., & Smith, A. (Eds.) (1984). *Biological perspectives on language.* Cambridge: MIT Press.

Cartmill, M. (1992). Non-human primates. In S. Jones, R. Martin, & D. Pilbeam (Eds.), *Cambridge encyclopedia of human evolution* (pp. 24–32). Cambridge: Cambridge University Press.

Clayton, N. S., & Dickinson, A. (1998). Episodic-like memory during cache recovery by scrub jays. *Nature,* **395,** 272–274.

Conroy, G. C., Weber, G. W., Seidler, H., Tobias, P. V., Kane, A., & Brunsden, B. (1998). Endocranial capacity in an early hominid cranium from Sterkfontein, South Africa. *Science,* **280,** 1730–1731.

de Hainzelin, J., Clark, J. D., White, T., Hart, W., Renne, P., WoldeGabriel, G., Beyene, Y., & Vrba, E. (1999). Environment and behavior of 2.5-million-year-old Bouri hominids. *Science,* **284,** 625–629.

Donald, M. (1991). *Origins of the modern mind.* Cambridge: Harvard University Press.

Dunbar, R. I. M. (1993). Coevolution of neocortical size, group size, and language in humans. *Behavioral and Brain Sciences,* **16,** 681–735.

Eisenberg, J. F. (1981). *The mammalian radiations.* Chicago: University of Chicago Press.

Friedrich, F. J. (1990). Frameworks for the study of human spatial impairments. In R. P. Kesner & D. S. Olton (Eds.), *Neurobiology of comparative cognition* (pp. 317–337). Hillsdale: Erlbaum.

Gabunia, L., & Vekua, A. (1995). A Plio-Pleistocene hominid from Dmanisi, East Georgia, Caucasus. *Nature,* **373,** 509–512.

Gannon, P. J., Holloway, R. L., Broadfield, D. C., & Braun, A. R. (1998). Asymmetry of chimpanzee planum temporale: Humanlike pattern of Wernicke's brain language area homolog. *Science,* **279,** 220–222.

Gebo, D. L., Dagosto, M., Beard, K. C., Qi, T., & Wang, J. (2000). The oldest known anthropoid postcranial fossils and the early evolution of higher primates. *Nature,* **404,** 276–278.

Gowett, J. A. J. (1992). Tools—The Palaeolithic record. In S. Jones, R. Martin, & D. Pilbeam (Eds.), *Cambridge encyclopedia of human evolution* (pp. 350–360). Cambridge: Cambridge University Press.

Haile-Selassie, Y. (2001). Late Miocene Hominids from the Middle Awash, Ethiopia. *Nature,* **412,** 178–181.

Hayes, C. (1951). *The ape in our home.* London: Gollanez.

Jerison, H. J. (1973). *Evolution of the brain and intelligence.* New York: Academic Press.

Johanson, D., & Edgar, B. (1996). *From Lucy to language.* New York: Simon & Shuster.

Kay, R. F., Ross, C., & Williams, B. A. (1997). Anthropoid origins. *Science,* **275,** 797–804.

Kelly, J. (1992). Evolution of apes. In S. Jones, R. Martin, & D. Pilbeam (Eds.), *Cambridge encyclopedia of human evolution* (pp. 223–230). Cambridge: Cambridge University Press.

Kimbel, W. H., Johanson, D. C., & Rak, Y. (1994). The first skull and other new discoveries of *Australopithecus afarensis* at Hadar, Ethiopia. *Nature,* **368,** 449–451.

King, M. C., & Wilson, A. C. (1975). Evolution at two levels: Molecular similarities and biological differences between humans and chimpanzees. *Science,* **188,** 107–116.

Krings, M., Stone, A., Schmitz, R. W., Krainitzki, H., Stoneking, M., & Pääbo, S. (1997). Neanderthal DNA sequences and the origin of modern humans. *Cell,* **90,** 19–30.

Leakey, M. G., Faibel, C. S., McDougall, I., & Walker, A. C. (1995). New four-million-year-old species from Kanapoi and Allia Bay, Kenya. *Nature,* **376,** 565–571.

Leakey, M. G., Spoor, F., Brown, F. H., Gathogo, P. N., Kiarie, C., Leakey, L. N., & McDougall, I. (2001). New hominin genus from eastern Africa shows diverse middle Pliocene lineages. *Nature,* **410,** 433–440.

Lieberman, P. (1992). Human speech and language. In S. Jones, R. Martin, & D. Pilbeam (Eds.), *Cambridge encyclopedia of human evolution* (pp. 134–137). Cambridge: Cambridge University Press.

Martin, R. (1981). Relative brain size and basal metabolic rate in terrestrial vertebrates. *Nature,* **293,** 57–60.

Martin, R. (1992). Classification of primates. In S. Jones, R. Martin, & D. Pilbeam (Eds.), *Cambridge encyclopedia of human evolution* (pp. 20–21). Cambridge: Cambridge University Press.

McHenry, H. M. (1995). Tempo and mode in human evolution. In W. M. Fitch & F. J. Ayala (Eds.), *Tempo and mode in evolution* (pp. 169–186). Washington: National Academy Press.

Nathans, J., Thomas, D., & Hogness, D. S. (1986). Molecular genetics of human color vision: The genes encoding blue, green, and red pigments. *Science,* **232,** 193–202.

Pinker, S. (1995). Facts about human language relevant to its evolution. In J.-P. Changeux & J.

Chavaillon (Eds.), *Origins of the human brain* (pp. 262–283). Oxford: Clarendon Press.

Rilling, J. K., & Insel, T. R. (1998). Evolution of the cerebellum in primates: Differences in relative volume among monkeys, apes and humans. *Brain, Behavior & Evolution,* **52,** 308–314.

Sawaguchi, T. (1988). Correlations of cerebral indices for "extra" cortical parts and ecological variables in primates. *Brain, Behavior & Evolution,* **32,** 129–140.

Sawaguchi, T. (1989). Relationships between cerebral indices for "extra" cortical parts and ecological categories in anthropoids. *Brain, Behavior, & Evolution,* **34,** 281–293.

Schlaug, G., Jänke, L., Huang, Y., & Steinmetz, H. (1995). In vivo evidence of structural brain asymmetry in musicians. *Science,* **267,** 699–701.

Sibly, C. G., & Ahlquist, J. E. (1987). DNA hybridization evidence of hominid phylogeny. *Journal of Molecular Evolution,* **26,** 99–121.

Simons, E. (1992). The fossil history of primates. In S. Jones, R. Martin, & D. Pilbeam (Eds.), *Cambridge encyclopedia of human evolution* (pp. 199–208). Cambridge: Cambridge University Press.

Stringer, C. B. (1992). Evolution of early humans. In S. Jones, R. Martin, & D. Pilbeam (Eds.), *Cambridge encyclopedia of human evolution* (pp. 241–251). Cambridge: Cambridge University Press.

Stringer, C. B., & Gamble, C. (1993). *In search of the Neanderthals. Solving the puzzle of human origins.* New York: Thames and Hudson.

Takahata, N., & Satta, Y. (1997). Evolution of the primate lineage leading to modern humans: Phylogenetic and demographic inferences from DNA sequences. *Proceedings of the National Academy of Sciences* (USA), **94,** 4811–4815.

Thorne, A. G., & Wolpoff, M. H. (1992). The multiregional evolution of humans. *Scientific American,* **266,** 76–83.

Tinklepaugh, O. L. (1928). An experimental study of representative factors in monkeys. *Journal of Comparative Psychology,* **8,** 197–236.

Tobias, P. V. (1995). The brain of the first hominids. In J.-P. Changeux & J. Chavaillon (Eds.), *Origins of the human brain* (pp. 61–81). Oxford: Clarendon Press.

Vandermeersch, B. (1995). The first modern men. In J.-P. Changeux & J. Chavaillon (Eds.), *Origins of the human brain* (pp. 3–10). Oxford: Clarendon Press.

Watanabe, M. (1996). Reward expectancy in primate prefrontal neurons. *Nature,* **382,** 629–632.

PART III
Behavioral Development

The chapters in Part III explore the origin of behavior in a developmental context—that is, across the life span of organisms. Development and evolution are concepts that share an emphasis on change, but differ in the time window over which they apply. Whereas development refers to changes during the life of individual organisms, evolution refers to change across generations. The integration of developmental and evolutionary principles has had an intricate and interesting history, marked by a flourishing period during the 19th century that was followed by a long period of independent progress. Only toward the end of the 20th century did these two sets of principles and fields come together again in an integrated fashion, thanks to progress in molecular biology and its application to the understanding of development in a comparative framework. ***Chapter 10*** deals with the major conceptual innovations and empirical progress in this area. Developmental studies of behavior have been popular since the inception of comparative psychology as a field in the 19th century. As a result, a massive amount of information is available on the developmental basis of many types of behaviors in many different species. Key examples involve fetal behavior and learning, development of associative learning capacities, reproductive and orienting behavior, imprinting, singing behavior, and social behavior, among many others. These topics will be covered in ***Chapters 11*** and ***12.***

CHAPTER 10

Development and Evolution

MAIN GENERALIZATIONS OF CHAPTER 10

- *Developmental processes are the result of complex interactions between genetic and nongenetic factors.*
- *Evolution works by selecting among alternative developmental programs.*
- *New phenotypic characters are often generated by evolutionary changes that affect the timing of developmental processes.*

The concepts of *evolution* and *development* refer to processes that unfold in time and involve a certain amount of change on a stable background. Similar concepts therefore apply to these processes. For example, evolution is referred to as *phylogeny* (the origin of taxa), whereas development is known as *ontogeny* (the origin of individuals); evolution occurs in populations and over the course of generations, whereas development occurs in individual organisms and over the course of an individual's lifetime. Populations evolve, but individuals develop.

Development is defined as the set of processes occurring at all levels of the organism (i.e., genetic, cellular, tissue, organ, system, behavior) in a particular environment and resulting in the formation of a sexually mature animal. Throughout this book I have emphasized the idea that natural selection acts at the level of traits, but, in reality, natural selection usually works by affecting collections of traits. A collection of traits may be nothing other than a life-history strategy (see ***Chapter 2, section 5.e.***, pp. 53–54)—that is, a set of instructions that results in a particular sequence of developmental steps. It follows then that natural selection ultimately selects for specific developmental programs. This is captured in a representation first suggested by the American developmental biologist Walter Garstang [1868–1949] and reproduced in ***Figure 10.1***. This figure portrays a sequence of ancestors and descendants; each fertilized egg, called a *zygote* and symbolized with the letter *Z*, gives rise to an adult form (the letter *A*) via some developmental process (the thick arrows). In the course of development, organisms reproduce (thin arrow) and the cycle repeats itself. However, zygotes might be changed by mutations or other processes, thus leading to evolutionary changes (represented in this figure by the subscript numbers).

Notice that ***Figure 10.1*** represents developmental programs only in metazoans. As a general rule, developmental processes occur only in multicellular organisms, such as animals, plants, and fungi. The reason for this lies in the fact that sexually reproducing organisms must go through a process of zygote formation (a one-cell stage) before more adults can be produced. Thus, adult animals must be formed in each reproductive cycle from the unicellular stage of the zygote, through the production of a variety of specialized cells and organs, during a lengthy process of development. In contrast, when a unicellular bacterium or protist reproduce by division, functional daughter cells are formed in the process. Development begins with a zygote and unfolds through a series of stages leading to a sexually mature organism.

1. Early Development

1.a. Embryogenesis. An *embryo* is an organism in which the structures characteristic of the adult are being formed. In each species and, indeed, in each individual, embryogenesis goes through a series of somewhat unique developmental events. During the course of such a process, features that will be unique to a particular species and to a given individual are produced. Despite such degree of idiosyncrasy, many aspects of development are general and some remarkably constant across a wide range of animals. These constant features will be emphasized here to provide a general background on the biology of development.

Development starts with the *fertilization* of an egg by a sperm cell. Eggs are relatively large haploid cells produced by the female and containing a substantial amount of food material (e.g., proteins, lipids) known as yolk. When meiosis (cell division leading to a

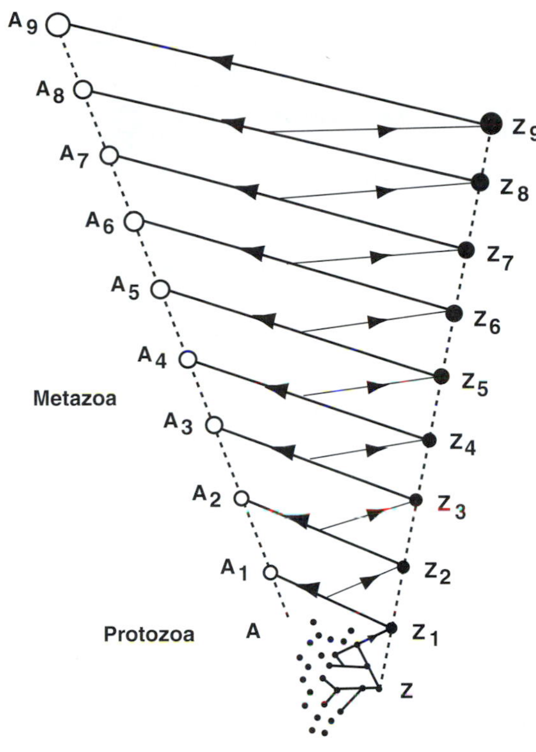

FIGURE 10.1. A representation of the relationship between ontogeny (thick arrows from Zs to As) and phylogeny (divergence illustrated by the subscript numbers) according to Garstand (1928). Adult (A) organisms develop from zygotes (Z) and reproduce at some point. This reproduction initiates a new cycle from the single-cell stage to the adult. Reproduction involves modification in some cases, thus leading to a novel type of zygote slightly divergent from its immediate ancestor. The numbers used as subscripts represent new species that exhibit a novel developmental program.

haploid gamete) is completed before fertilization, the unfertilized egg is called an ovum; but when meiosis is achieved after fertilization, the egg is referred to as an oocyte. Meiosis is completed when the so-called second polar body is released from the egg cell. The point in the zygote at which this second polar body is released is called the animal pole, whereas the point directly opposite is referred to as the vegetal pole.

By contrast, sperm cells are small haploid cells produced by males. In most animal phyla, including the primitive sponges (Porifera) and jellyfish (Cnidaria), sperm cells are formed by an ovoid body containing little more than DNA and a ciliate tail used for locomotion. Sperm cells with two cilia and without cilia have evolved in species from several phyla.

The union of egg and sperm during fertilization restores the diploid number of chromosomes and produces the zygote. The zygote undergoes several cell divisions during a stage called *cleavage.* Cleavage is characterized by the conservation of the overall size of the fertilized egg while it is dividing itself into two, four, eight, etc. cells, called blastomeres. Blastomeres are therefore smaller than the original, fertilized egg. Animals display two broad patterns of cleavage. Deuterostome phyla (including chordates, hemichordates, and equinoderms) display radial cleavage, which is characterized by the overlaying of cells after division. This is shown in ***Figure 10.2*** from a lateral view, with the animal pole on the top. In the eight-cell stage, cells are aligned on top of one another. Species from several proto-

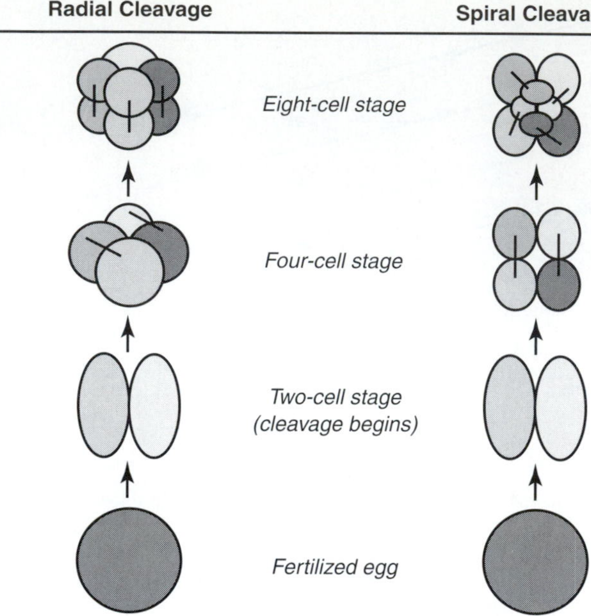

FIGURE 10.2. A simplified representation of the two major forms of cleavage, the radial (characteristic of deuterostome animals, including chordates) and the spiral (characteristic of some protostome phyla, including the molluscs). The lines bridging two cells and their common shading indicate that they are daughter cells. Notice the conservation of volume (i.e., blastomeres become smaller in size) during cleavage.

stome phyla (including molluscs, annelids, and platyhelminths) display spiral cleavage. In this mode of cleavage, the new set of daughter cells lies oriented at an angle relative to the layer below, as shown in ***Figure 10.2*** in a view from the animal pole.

Cleavage is thus a period of cell division without growth that lasts until the blastomeres reach the approximate size they will have in the adult animal. Beyond the eight-cell stage, cells organize in a cluster called the *morula* stage, from which they develop into either a blastula or a discoblastula. A *blastula* stage is characterized by the formation of a hollow ball (or solid in some species) containing a single layer of cells. The fluid-filled cavity in the core is called a blastocoel. The actual shape and density of cells vary greatly across species. Sea urchins (Echinodermata) and frogs (Chordata), two well-studied species, exhibit a blastula stage of development. In birds, the blastula stage involves a flattened disc structure with two distinct layers of cells, called the discoblastula.

In mammals, the morula stage gives rise to the formation of a fluid-filled ball of cells called a blastocyst. Although blastula and blastocyst appear similar (both are hollow spheres), their functions are different. The blastocyst is a device for the implantation of the mammalian embryo in the mother's uterus; it eventually becomes part of the placenta. The blastocyst is thus a mammalian adaptation related to the embryo's dependence on its mother for nutrition. At one end of the blastocyst is an accumulation of cells, known as the inner cell mass, from which the embryo develops. This inner cell mass resembles the avian discoblastula in its organization.

1.b. Gastrulation and Early Organogenesis. To picture the next developmental stage, imagine you are holding a hollow ball in your left hand; the external surface of that blastula is made of a single layer of cells. Now imagine that you push the surface of the ball with the index finger of your right hand. This produces an invagination of the tissue, giving rise to a new stage called *gastrula.* The point at which this invagination starts (i.e., where you pushed with your finger) is called the *blastopore.* As the tissue moves inward, the ball acquires a second layer of cells, connected to the external layer only at the edges of the blastopore. The external layer is called the *ectoderm,* whereas the internal layer is referred to as the *endoderm.*

The process of gastrulation (***Figure 10.3***) occurs in all animals except in sponges (Porifera). In Cnidaria (jellyfish, sea anemones, coral), the adult body involves only two layers of cells, ectoderm and endoderm, and thus those animals are referred to as *diploblastic.* Cnidarians can be viewed as gastrulae in their adult stage, whereas all the bilaterally symmetrical animal phyla have evolved a third cell layer, known as *mesoderm,* which develops by further differentiation. These are called *triploblastic* animals.

Gastrulation is characterized by *cellular differentiation* (cells diverge in morphology and become specialized in their function), *organogenesis* (formation of functionally specialized structures called organs), and *morphogenesis* (the development of the general shape of the organism). In triploblastic animals, each cell layer gives rise to specific organs and structures. For example, the ectoderm layer contains cells that will differentiate into cutaneous glands, hair, sense organs, nasal cavities, mouth, and nerve tissue; the mesoderm gives rise to the notochord, cartilage, bone and bone marrow, muscles, blood, lymphoid tissue, and the epithelium of blood vessels, body cavities, kidneys, and gonads; finally, the endoderm originates such organs as the pharynx, larynx, trachea, lungs, digestive glands and cavities, bladder, vagina, and urethra. In vertebrates, the stage in which the mesoderm is clearly differentiated and the embryo develops a dorsoventral axis is known as the *neurula stage,* a name reflecting the fact that the dorsal neural tissue is among the first to differentiate.

Interestingly, the origin of some of these structures can be tracked down to the position of particular cell groups early in the gastrula stage. In a frog embryo, for instance, the region located around the animal pole of the gastrula develops later as skin, whereas the region immediately below becomes the neural plate, precursor to the central nervous system. This orderly spatial arrangement can be represented in fate maps that indicate what part of the body a particular region of the gastrula will become later in development.

1.c. Phylotypic Stages. The most comprehensive taxonomic category for classifying animals is that of *phylum.* As already mentioned (see ***Table 7.1,*** p. 224), thirty-something phyla have been distinguished, each in-

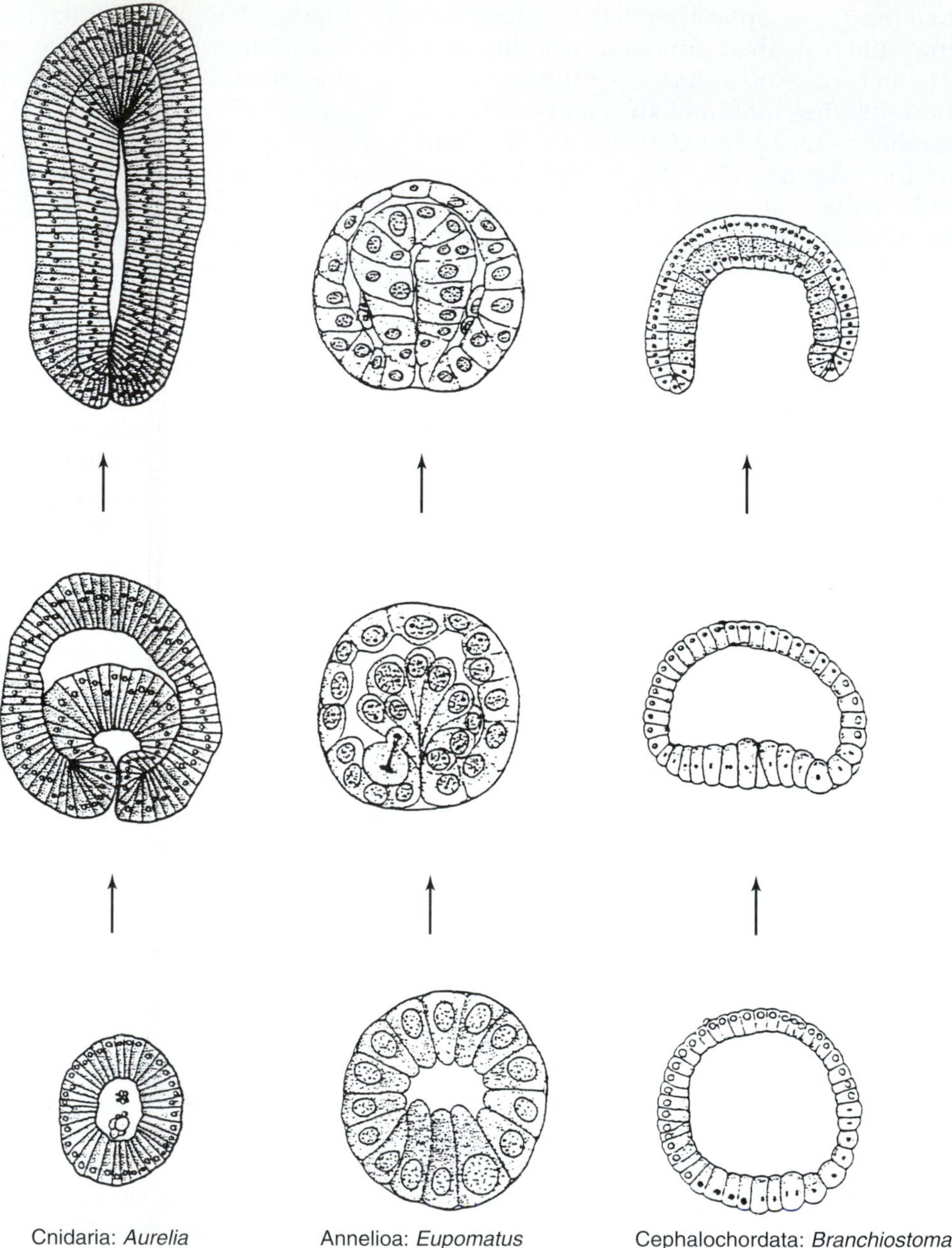

FIGURE 10.3. Variations on gastrulation in several phyla, including the diploblastic cnidarian *Aurelia,* the annelid worm *Eupomatus,* and the cephalochordate *Brachiostoma* (Nielsen 1995).

volving a unique set of characters. For example, all chordates share the presence, at some point during their development, of a dorsal nerve cord, a notochord, gill slits, and a post-anal tail. No phylum other than Chordata possesses these characters, and thus they define the phylum's *body plan*. Each existing phylum therefore represents a unique body plan, whereas the taxonomic divisions below the phylum level (e.g., class, order, family, genus, species) represent variations of this basic organization.

The *phylotypic stage* is the point in development at which the basic features of the phylum's body plan are first distinguished. Karl von Baer [1792–1876] first noted that this stage is extremely stable across species: He had trouble determining whether a particular embryo in his collection was that of a frog, a bird, or a mammal. The bottom row in ***Figure 2.2*** (p. 33) reproduces a classic drawing that shows the phylotypic stage of chordates. Von Baer argued that early in development the morphology of the embryo was generalized and thus indistinguishable from species to species. Structures specific to the class, order, family, genus, and species were developed subsequently, making the organism progressively more recognizable. So development was supposed to involve changes from generalized to specific morphologies. This generalization turned out to be only partially correct. Developmental processes both before and after the phylotypic stage (and not just after, as von Baer argued) are highly variable across species within a single phylum. For example, before reaching their phylotypic stage, vertebrate embryos differ in terms of the size of the egg and the structure developed during the blastula and gastrula stages; after the phylotypic stage, the differences in adult morphology achieved in the various taxa of vertebrates speak for themselves. For some yet unknown reason, development is constrained to pass through a highly conserved stage, common to all species within a given phylum.

Phylotypic stages differ across phyla. In the chordates, for example, it is known as the *pharyngula stage* because the pharyngeal gill slits are first observed. At this point, the vertebrate embryo displays a clear anterior-posterior axis, but exhibits none of the traits that would differentiate the various classes, such as hair, scales, beaks, or teeth, which will begin to appear in later developmental stages. The pharyngula stage occurs at the end of neurulation. In arthropods, however, the phylotypic stage is known as the *segmented germ band stage,* and it occurs during gastrulation. Distinct head, thorax, and abdominal regions are observed at this point in development (Gerhart & Kirschner 1997).

The stability of phylotypic stages suggests that natural selection may be constrained in its ability to modify developmental programs. The extent of such a constraint can be appreciated if one remembers that most of the known animal phyla are represented in Cambrian faunas and were probably established at some point during the pre-Cambrian. It is thus possible that variations in body plan organization were established very early in metazoan evolution and have remained stable since then. The difficulties of tinkering with phylotypic stages may be responsible, at least in part, for the absence of new animal phyla after the Cambrian.

1.d. The Zootype. The formation of the embryo is characterized by the assignment of cell fates to specific cell populations. This results in a very specific spatial patterning of cell differentiation, such that the various populations develop into the regions of the body and differentiate into the various organs that conform the animal. Such spatial patterning of developmental process has been recognized for a long time as a fundamental aspect of ontogeny, but only recently has its underlying genetic basis begun to be understood.

An important feature of phylotypic stages is that they represent a stage during which several gene clusters are maximally active. Moreover, these genes are remarkably stable across many different phyla suggesting very deep links of homology among the metazoans. One example is provided by *homeotic genes,* also known as *Hox genes.* These are regulatory genes; that is, their protein products affect the expression of other genes. They contain a sequence of 180 bases, called the homeobox, which is essentially common across most studied animal phyla. Hox genes are distributed in series in a strain of DNA and expressed in the anterior-posterior axis of the animal in the same order in which they are positioned in the DNA strain, from the 3′ to the 5′ end. Thus those Hox genes closer to the 3′ end affect the development of structures located on the anterior end of the animal (e.g., head), whereas those genes located closer to the 5′ end affect the development of more posterior structures (e.g., tail).

Hox genes were initially discovered in the fruitfly *Drosophila melanogaster* and were called homeotic because their mutation usually leads to the development of similarities in segments of the body normally exhibiting different anatomy (hence their name: "homeo" means "similar"). For example, a mutation of Hox gene number 7, known as ultrabithorax (notice that genes are given very strange names), leads to the development of two pairs of wings in *Drosophila.* In this *bithorax mutant,* the third thoracic segment, which normally has a pair of halters, develops an anatomy similar to that of the second segment, with the halters transformed into a second pair of wings. Interestingly, fruitflies and their relatives belong to the order Diptera (literally two-winged), which implies that this homeotic mutation alters a basic aspect of the dipteran body plan.

The sequence in which Hox genes express their effects is the same in species from many different phyla. ***Figure 10.4*** summarizes the distribution of these genes in a wide range of species, aligning those that have been shown to be homologous on the basis of similarity in base sequence. There are two important features of Hox genes that have implications for an understanding of how evolution works. First, the number of genes in the Hox cluster varies across species, even within the same phylum. Hox genes have evolved by a process of duplication and change. In some taxonomic groups, new genes have been added, whereas in other groups, specific genes have been deleted. Second, the vertebrates present an interesting twist to Hox gene organization. In all known animals except the vertebrates, Hox genes are located in a single strain of DNA, within a single chromosome. In the vertebrates, however, the basic cluster has been extended by at least four additional genes (numbers 10 to 13), and the entire cluster has been quadruplicated, with each strain located in a different chromosome (clusters are known as Hox A, B, C, and D). These variations in the number of Hox genes and in the number of strains may have been necessary prerequisites for the evolution of new traits. For example, the four added Hox genes of vertebrates code for proteins that express in the tail region of the animal. Since the tail is a structure unique to the chordates and highly developed in vertebrates, these genes may be responsible for this evolutionary novelty.

In addition to the Hox cluster, other genes express along the anterior-posterior axis. For example, the genes known as orth-

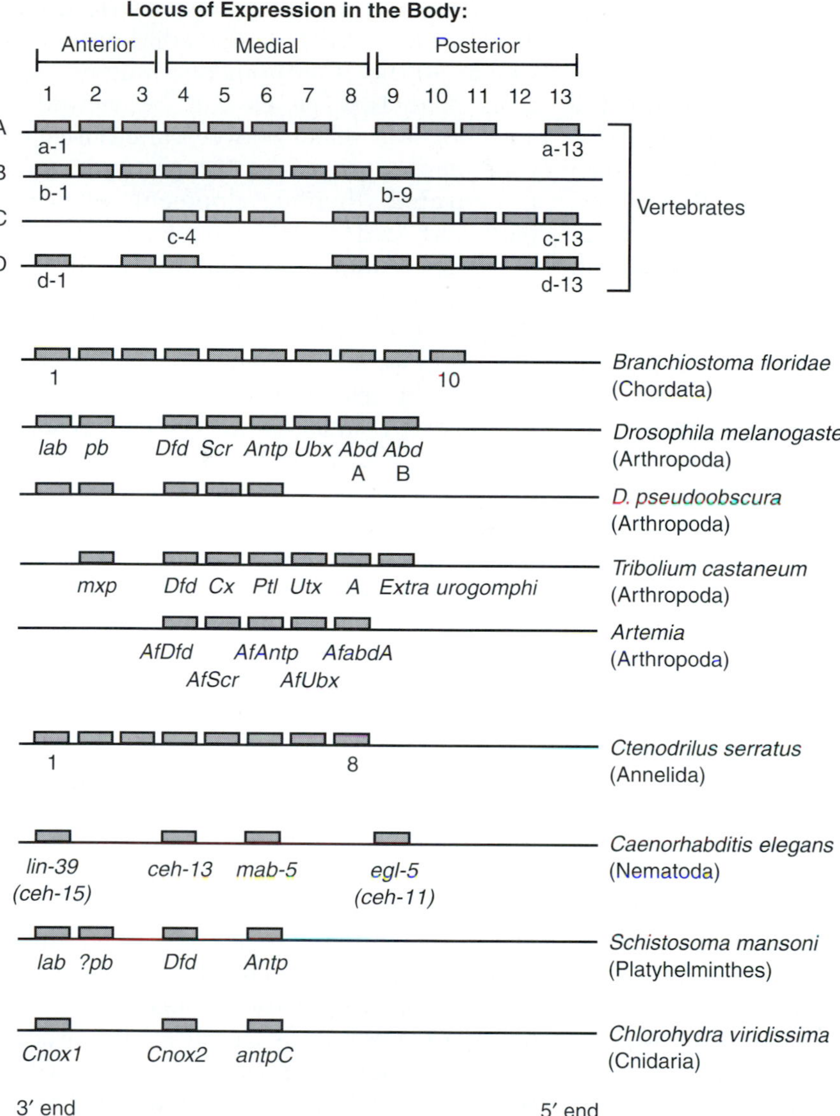

FIGURE 10.4. Hox genes identified in species from widely divergent phyla. Genes considered to be homologous, on the basis of the degree of similarity in the sequence of bases in the DNA molecule, are aligned vertically. Changes include gene additions, deletions, and in vertebrates, quadruplication of the entire linkage group (Hox-A to Hox-D). These linkage groups are called paralogous genes and are located in different chromosomes.

odenticle and empty spiracles express in the anterior end in both mice (a chordate) and fruitflies (an arthropod). These genes, as well as the Hox genes, do not determine the type of structure (i.e., compound eyes, wing, hind leg, etc.) that would develop in any particular region. Rather, they determine the relative position of structures in the anterior-posterior axis of the organism. Hox genes are responsible for determining, for example, that a particular end of the embryo will develop into a head. But additional genes are necessary to determine which type of structures will be present in the head (e.g., compound eyes in insects, but single-lens eyes in a vertebrate).

Because these regulatory genes encode the relative position of bodily parts in practically all studied phyla, Slack et al. (1993) suggested that they actually define the concept of "animal." Their reasoning is as follows: Given that these gene clusters are present in very divergent phyla, that they are homologous, and that they determine the spatial pattern of body organization, their evolution as an organized cluster must have occurred in the ancestor of all the animals. They suggested that these genes should be collectively referred to as the *zootype* (see ***Figure 10.5***). According to this view, an animal is an organism displaying a pattern of gene expression, particularly clearly during its phylotypic stage, known as the zootype.

1.e. Nature-Nurture Interactions. Hox gene number 6, known in arthropods as antennapedia (see Antp in ***Figure 10.4***) is normally expressed in the second thoracic segment and regulates the development of a pair of legs. Antp can be induced to express its regulatory protein in a more anterior segment during an early phase of embryonic development in *Drosophila*. The resulting animal, known as an *antennapedia mutant,* develops a pair of legs where it would normally produce the antennae (Kaufman et al. 1990). The antennapedia mutant, as well as all the other homeotic mutants, suggests that Hox genes can be viewed as switches that select between alternative developmental programs. If a particular gene is activated, then development takes one path and leads to a particular phenotype; however, if that gene remains silent, then development takes a different path. It is likely that many regulatory genes can affect the development of an organism in this manner, by selecting among alternative developmental fates. The critical problem then is that of characterizing those events that determine typical developmental trajectories for a given species.

There is no question that genes are crucial determinants of the process of development. But genes do not act in isolation. Not only do genes regulate each other (i.e., regulatory genes influence structural genes), but they also build systems of nested environments (which we call "organisms"), that give rise to further regulation. When one considers the various levels of interaction (i.e., gene, chromosome, nucleus, cytoplasm, tissue, organism, environment; Weiss 1959), it is easy to see that such reciprocal regulations as those observed during development must achieve an overwhelming level of complexity. Changes and events at any of these levels can affect the process of development, even in subtle ways. Obviously, one such level is related to behavior. As the organism interacts with its environment, it exposes itself to different types of nutrients, to varying degrees of light, to social interactions, and so on, all of which can potentially affect its development.

In psychology, a traditional distinction in conceptualizing developmental processes emphasizes two sources of information, one provided by the genotype and labeled "nature," and another one by the environment

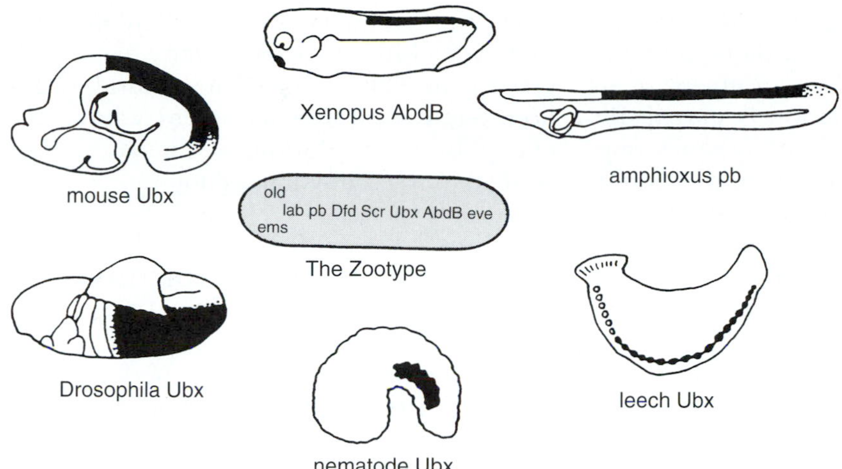

Figure 10.5. The zootype, displayed in the center of this figure, consists of a sequence of regulatory genes ordered in the anterior-posterior axis (anterior to the left). These genes are present in all the animal phyla studied so far and their protein products map in similar parts of the body (Slack et al. 1992). Several species from various phyla are represented also in this figure, including vertebrates (mouse, *Xenopus*), cephalochordates (amphioxus), annelids (leech), nematodes (*Caenorhabditis elegans*), and arthropods (*Drosophila*). The genes in the zootype are labeled according to the nomenclature used for *Drosophila: otd:* orthodenticle; *ems:* empty spiracles; *lab:* labial; *pb:* proboscipedia; *Dfd:* deformed; *scr:* sex combs reduced; *Ubx:* antennapedia-ultrabithorax-abdominal A group; *AbdB:* abdominal B; *eve:* even-skipped. (From NATURE, 361, copyright 1993 by Nature Publishing Group. Reprinted with permission.)

and labeled "nurture." This *nature-nurture dichotomy* has led to extreme views emphasizing either one or the other of them as the most important determinant of development (see ***Chapter 1, sections 4*** and ***5***, pp. 15–20). The dichotomy was first introduced into psychology by Francis Galton [1822–1911], who argued that even the most complex psychological functions of humans are inherited. According to Galton, a major goal of psychology is to measure the relative contribution of nature and nurture to the development of psychological functions. He suggested that monozygous twins could provide such information about the development of psychological abilities. Monozygous twins arise from a single fertilized egg and thus share the same genes.

During the early decades of the 20th century, the nature-nurture dichotomy provided a paradigmatic basis for the study of animal behavior. On one extreme, John B. Watson and other radical behaviorists emphasized the role of experience in the development of adult behavior, even in humans; on the other, Konrad Lorenz and other classic ethologists emphasized the role of genetic information in generating stereotypical, species-specific behavioral patterns, even in humans. The notion that only influences from the external environment interact with genetic information is unrealistic, given the multiple levels of organization. When these levels are taken into account, the dichotomy between nature and nurture becomes less of a dichotomy and more like the end points of a continuum.

Comparative psychologists such as Zing-Yang Kuo [1898–1970], T. C. Schneirla [1902–1968], and Daniel S. Lehrman [1919–1972], among others, suggested that development is essentially an interactive process. According to this view, known as *epigenesis,* interactions (called *coactions*) among existing components of a developing organism give rise to new properties, including new behaviors. According to the epigenetic view (Gottlieb 1992, pp. 159–160):

> Individual development is characterized by an increase of complexity of organization—i.e., the emergence of new structural and functional properties and competencies—at all levels of analysis (molecular, subcellular, cellular, organismic) as a consequence of horizontal and vertical coactions among its parts, including organism-environment interactions.

Horizontal coactions are those that occur within a given level, such as those exemplified by the Hox genes and other regulatory genes. Vertical coactions bridge different levels of organization; for example, behavioral experience may affect the morphological and functional properties of developing neurons within the CNS (see ***section 3.d.*** below).

The epigenetic view suggests that evolutionary processes may be affected by the way in which environmental factors, broadly defined, induce changes in the phenotype. If, for example, animals expose themselves to new influences because of their behavior (e.g., sampling new types of food), these influences may switch on genes that were hitherto silent. Once expressed, these genes are exposed to natural selection. Such vertical coactions may have implications for evolutionary change, as described in the following section.

2. DEVELOPMENT AND EVOLUTION

2.a. Genetic Assimilation. So far, I have treated natural selection as acting upon phenotypic traits that arise from a variety of processes. Such processes as genetic drift, mutations, and recombination in sexual reproduction generate and maintain genetic variability within populations (see ***Chapter 2, section 4***, pp. 38–49). But exactly how are new phenotypes produced? The classic idea, simplistically expressed, is that some process, say mutation, generates variability in structural genes, and natural selection allows those genes that enhance reproductive success to spread at the expense of their alternatives. But molecular genetics provides a picture of the evolutionary process that differs in one important detail from this one: Natural selection probably acts more frequently by selecting among competing regulatory genes rather than structural genes.

The potential importance of regulatory genes was highlighted when it became clear that very different phenotypes may arise from very similar genomes. As mentioned earlier (see ***Chapter 2, section 4.e.***, pp. 43–44), chimpanzees and humans share about 95 to 99% of their genome, and yet adults differ markedly in their phenotypes, enough to be classified within different families. One implication of such findings is that phenotypic differences must be produced not by the activation of different structural genes during development but by their regulation (King & Wilson 1975).

Such regulatory changes probably underlie a very interesting phenomenon known as *genetic assimilation.* The seminal idea was suggested by James Baldwin [1861–1934], a developmental psychologist who sought to apply Darwinian principles to understand the ontogeny of behavior. Baldwin (1902), arguing from a merely theoretical viewpoint, suggested that just as individuals within a population vary in terms of morphological traits, they also vary in terms of their ability to generate certain traits in the presence of appropriate environmental conditions. Some individuals may be more likely to adjust to certain environmental challenges, whereas others may find it too difficult and die in the process. If natural selection were to positively select for "adaptability," then, Baldwin argued, the trait in question could eventually become fixed in the population and able to arise even in the absence of the environmental pressure that originated it in the first place. This genetic assimilation implies no Lamarckian factor, as Baldwin explicitly acknowledged (i.e., no inheritance of acquired traits needs to be assumed).

Evidence for genetic assimilation was first provided by experiments with *Drosophila.* In one experiment (Waddington 1959), flies were raised in bottles containing a concentration of sodium chloride (a salt) sufficient to cause severe mortality. About 60% or more of the individuals produced in any single generation died as a result of this salty environment—a strong selective pressure. The surviving flies could freely mate within the bottles. This process was continued for 20 generations, while the concentration of NaCl was increased to keep the mortality levels constant. A stock of the last generation and an unselected control stock were then exposed to environments with added salt in several concentrations. The results obtained with three different strains of *Drosophila* are shown in ***Figure 10.6.*** In terms of mortality, the three selected lines showed a higher survival rate in most of the salty environments compared to the unselected controls. Most interestingly, the area of a pair of glands called the anal papillae, was enlarged in the selected lines at all salt concentrations. Since this gland participates in osmotic regulation, it was probably the animal's ability to develop large anal papillae that determined its chances of surviving to a reproductive age. Because of differential reproductive success, the 20th generation contained a proportionately large number of individuals that had an enhanced ability to develop relatively large anal papillae, as is also shown in ***Figure 10.6.*** Interestingly, the gland was larger in selected animals even under normal salt concentrations, which implies that the trait (i.e., developing large anal papillae) had been genetically assimilated.

A plausible way in which an outcome such as this one could emerge is via regulation of the genes responsible for determining the size of the anal papillae. Like any organ, an increase in size, relative to that of the organ in the immediate ancestor, could be achieved by delaying the phase in which cells specific to that organ differentiate and reproduce, rather than by producing an entirely new type of cell. In addition, the genetic assimilation experiment suggests that developmental fates that involve certain switches activated by environmental input (i.e., presence of high salinity in the environment) can be changed into programs that unfold relatively independently of those inputs (i.e., natural selection can remove a switch from the program). Waddington referred to such changes as involving different degrees of *canalization.* A trait is highly canalized when the developmental program exhibits few of such switches, but it would be weakly canalized if the final

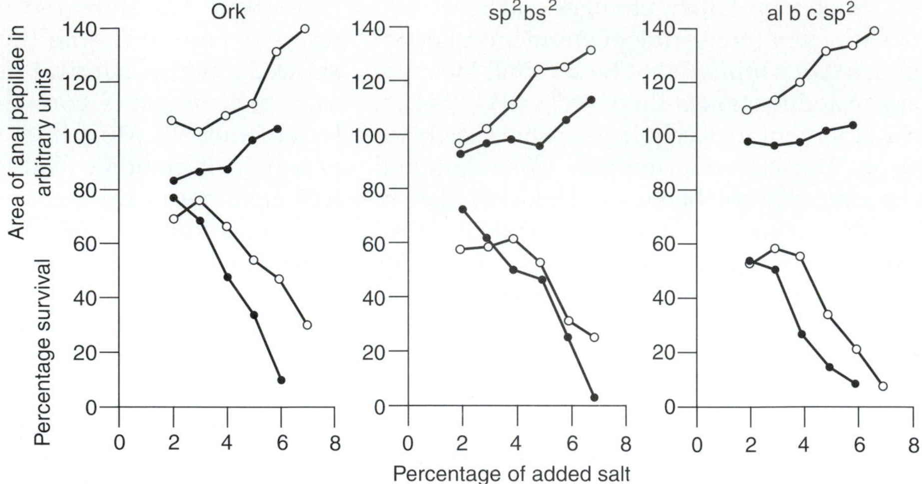

FIGURE 10.6. Results of an experiment relevant to the concept of genetic assimilation (Waddington 1959). *Drosophila* flies from three strains (*OrK, sp2bs2,* and *al b c sp2*) were raised in an environment with a high concentration of salt, which produced 60% mortality in each of 20 generations. Individuals from this 20th generation were then exposed to environments with several different concentrations of salt, and their survival (lower part of the graph) was measured. The selected flies (open circles) survived in greater numbers than the unselected controls (dark circles) as the salinity of the environment increased. They also exhibited larger anal papillae (upper part of the graph), a gland involved in osmotic regulation, even in low-salinity environments. This result suggest that phenotypic plasticity in the development of anal papillae was at least partially assimilated over the course of the experiment. (From NATURE, 183, copyright 1959 by Nature Publishing Group. Reprinted with permission.)

phenotype depends heavily on environmental input. Canalization refers, therefore, to a particular type of vertical coaction.

2.b. Behavioral Neophenotypes. Interestingly, an example of a natural instance of genetic assimilation was provided by Jean Piaget [1896–1980], a developmental psychologist known mainly for his theory of intelligence (Vidal 1994). During the early years of his career, Piaget studied the development of shells in gastropod molluscs from the genus *Limnaea.* Other naturalists had noticed that these gastropods exhibit an elongated shell in most of their distribution, except for species living in some European lakes in which the shells are short. Short-shell *Limnaea* tend to inhabit shallow waters. Experiments showed that species with elongated shells develop short ones when raised in an aquarium with turbulent water. By contrast, species with shorter shells continue to develop shorter shells even when raised in calm waters. Furthermore, short-shell *Limnaea* tend to stay preferentially in shallow waters. Apparently, then, the short-shell morphology and the shallow-water-preference behavior arose initially in response to specific environmental factors. That phenotypic plasticity is still present in species that normally develop elongated shells. However, once the phenotype was in place, further selection resulted in the canalization of the trait so that short-shells are induced even in the absence of the environmental pressure.

A similar study also illustrates how phenotypic variation within a given species may be induced environmentally. Eggs from red-winged blackbirds (*Agelaius phoeniceus*) were transplanted into foster nests between populations living in Tallahassee and the Everglades, in Florida (James 1983). These populations normally differ in the shape of their bills. Everglade eggs transplanted to Tallahassee led to birds exhibiting a bill shape characteristic of the Tallahassee population and significantly different from that of Everglade control birds transplanted within their original habitat. Thus, bill shape exhibited phenotypic plasticity in the Everglade population. By contrast, the Tallahassee eggs transplanted into the Everglades gave rise to birds that were not different from their controls. Matsuda (1987) has argued that cases in which a trait is fit to specific environmental conditions (e.g., short shells induced by turbulent waters) but develops independently of such conditions (e.g., short shells develop even in still waters) probably exemplify traits that have evolved by genetic assimilation.

Gottlieb (1992) suggested that genetic assimilation may provide a general model to conceptualize the evolution of new species (see ***Figure 10.7***). The first step in the speciation process may involve no ge-

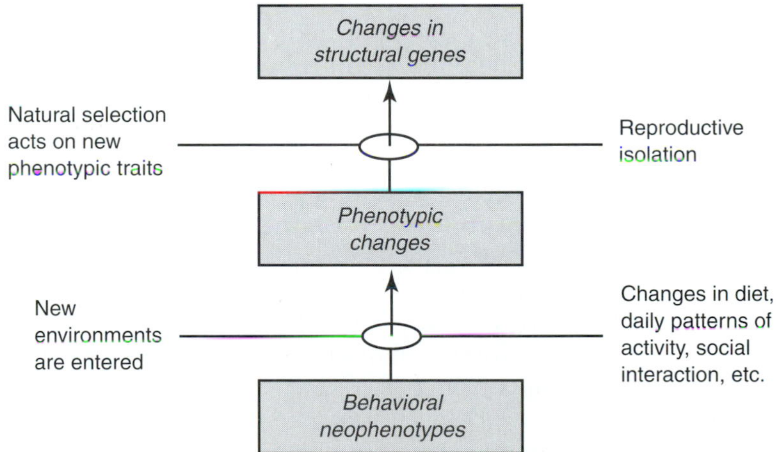

FIGURE 10.7. A representation of Gottlieb's (1992) hypothesis of the behavioral neophenotypes. Neophenotypes arise as a result of animals' entering new environments and becoming exposed to new environmental influences. These factors influence development, leading to new phenotypic traits by changes in gene expression and the activation of previously silent genes. Such phenotypic changes may lead to reproductive isolation even in the absence of substantial genetic changes. Natural selection will subsequently act on the new phenotypes, eventually changing the genetic makeup of the species.

netic change at all but rather a developmental change induced by the adoption of new behaviors. These are called *behavioral neophenotypes*. The second step in the process involves the induction of new morphological and functional traits. New habitat or food preferences, daily cycles of activity, or social interactions may expose animals to environmental conditions capable of inducing novelties in their phenotype. Such novelties arise because developmental programs contain a number of switches activated by nongenetic factors. These changes are produced either by small shifts in regulatory genes or by the expression of hitherto silent genes. At this second stage, a population may become reproductively isolated without having undergone extensive change in terms of structural genes. Such changes may occur in the third stage of this process, when the neophenotypes are exposed to the action of natural selection. And just as in the experiments on genetic assimilation, selection may lead to changes in developmental programs that further refine the new adaptations by either increasing morphological plasticity (as it happened in the case of *Drosophila* exposed to salty environments) or by canalizing the program so that the new phenotypes are induced even if the environmental input that initiated the process fails to occur.

2.c. Heterochrony. One of the most popular statements in evolutionary science says that "ontogeny recapitulates phylogeny." In scientific circles this is known as Ernest Haeckel's [1834–1919] *biogenetic law*. Haeckel suggested it to explain similarities between morphological features of developing embryos and the morphology of the adults from species considered to be ancestral to those embryos. For example, human embryos exhibit gill slits at some point during their development, even though gills never become functional during their lives. Haeckel interpreted this trait as a remnant of humans' ancient fish ancestors. According to the concept of recapitulation, phylogeny (i.e., evolution of new phyla) occurs because novel developmental stages are added during ontogeny. However, each generation must walk through the same sequence of stages as their ancestors before reaching those stages that are unique to their species. Haeckel referred to this as the *principle of terminal addition*.

For decades, the study of the relationship between ontogeny and phylogeny remained in the background of evolutionary science, surrounded by controversy and clouded by the proliferation of a complicated terminology (Haeckel is credited with the invention of many specialized terms, including biology, ontogeny, phylogeny, and heterochrony, among others). However, progress in molecular biology and a standardization of terminology (Gould 1977; McNamara 1986; Raff & Kaufman 1984) have paved the way for an integration of developmental theories in the general framework of evolutionary biology. Such an integration is impacting many disciplines, including molecular genetics and paleontology, and it will eventually influence the study of behavioral development.

Recapitulation turned out to be only one of the possible ways in which ontogeny and phylogeny can be related; thus the biogenetic law is only a partial description of the facts. Recapitulation was subsumed under the more general concept of heterochrony. *Heterochrony* is a term that encompasses a variety of phenomena suggesting evolutionary changes in the rate of development and in the relative time of appearance of phenotypic traits. These timing effects can be seen only when comparing developmental profiles of ancestors and descendants, so heterochronic processes are always relative. For example, developmental rate is said to be accelerated (or retarded) in descendants, relative to the rate observed in their ancestors.

Statements comparing rates of development in different species need common points of reference to make sense. Usually, rate and timing effects are evaluated relative to the point in time when the organisms being compared reach their sexual maturity. *Sexual maturity* refers to the organism's ability to reproduce and typifies the completion of the basic morphology, physiology, and behavior that characterize the adult animal. Another common point of reference across species is provided by an assessment of body size. Changes in the rate of development can result in adult descendants that are either smaller or larger in body size than their ancestors.

Figure 10.8 lists the basic processes of heterochrony. Although there is a tendency to apply labels such as "neotenic" or "hypermorphic" to an entire species (i.e., "humans are neotenic"), it may be more pertinent to think of such processes as applying to a specific trait or to a cluster of traits. Obviously, traits may be regulated independently from each other and exhibit evolutionary change at different rates; this is why evolution is often characterized as a mosaic (i.e., the organism arises from collections of relatively independent traits, just like an entire scene in a Roman mosaic arises from the combination of many independent tesserae). *Mosaic evolution* can be appreciated in your own body. Consider the human hand and foot, the former quite conservatively preserving the ancestral grasping morphology of primates, but the latter displaying recently evolved adaptations for bipedal locomotion.

The simplest cases are those in which the morphology of the descendant and that of the ancestor are very similar, but the descendants have evolved either a smaller (*dwarfism*) or a larger (*giantism*) body size. Such changes in body size with preservation of morphological differentiation can be achieved by the differential action of growth hormones. Mammals, for example, express several of such hormones at different stages of their development. Hormones, of course, are the direct product of genes, and their transcription timing can thus be regulated to change the point in development at which these genes are transcribed. In African pygmies, whose ancestors were larger in body size, the levels of growth hormone are similar to those of larger humans until they reach puberty. During this period of sexual maturation, pygmies lack the burst in growth hormone that is characteristic of other humans, and their adult body size remains proportionally reduced (Merimee et al. 1987). Similar regulatory shifts in genes controlling growth factors may also underlie changes in adult body size among genders within a single species. Sexual dimorphism occurs predominantly in species displaying polygynous mating systems (see ***Chapter 5, section 2.b.***, pp. 134–135), in which males are typically larger than females (e.g., California sea lions and gorillas).

2.d. Paedomorphosis. Some species are characterized by achieving sexual maturity at a stage in their development that corresponds to a juvenile stage in their ancestors. All cases of *paedomorphosis* obviously violate the biogenetic law because the descendant stops its development at a stage that corresponds to an early phase in its ancestor. Paraphrasing Haeckel, this would correspond to a "law of terminal subtraction."

In a classic paper by Garstang (1928), paedomorphosis was postulated to be responsible for the evolution of the vertebrates from tunicate larvae. ***Figure 10.9*** il-

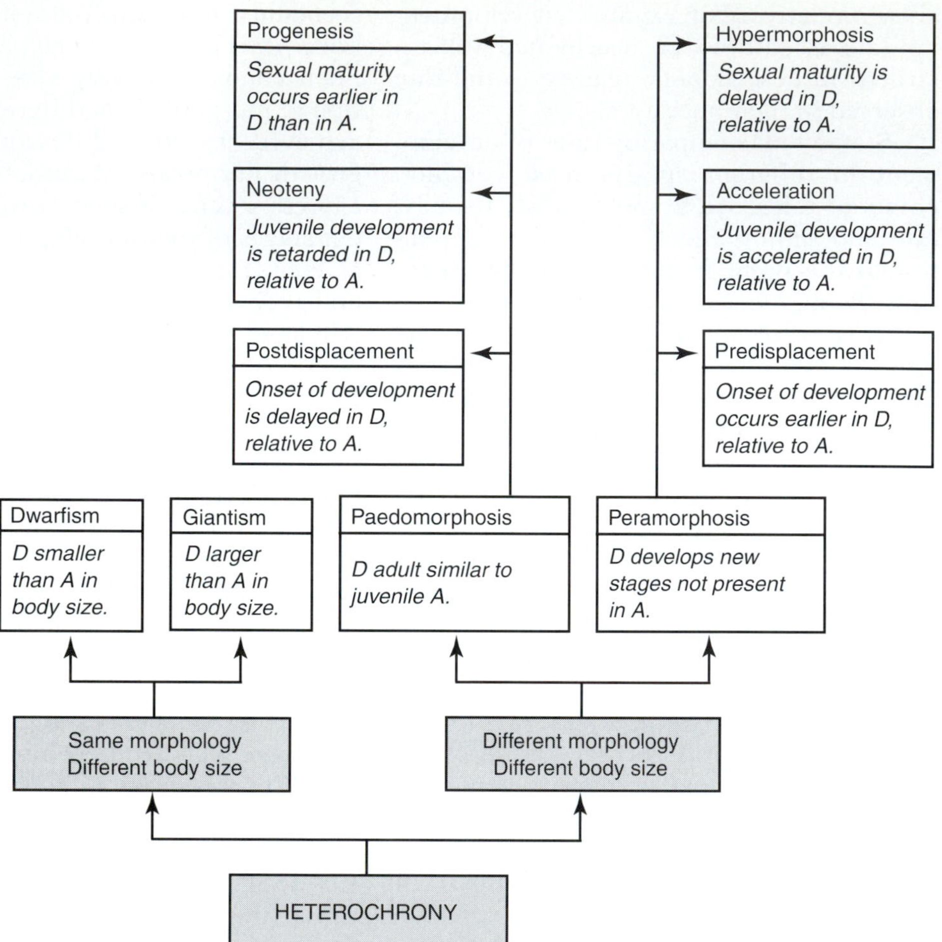

FIGURE 10.8. Summary and characteristics of the main processes of heterochrony. Heterochrony refers to changes in the timing of development of particular traits in descendant species (D) relative to that of their ancestors (A).

lustrates typical larval and adult morphologies of tunicates. Tunicates are usually classified within the phylum Chordata, subphylum Urochordata. What is striking about the adults is how little they resemble a chordate, or even a bilaterally organized animal. Adults live a sessile life, attached to some substrate at the bottom of the sea, in relatively shallow waters. It is the morphology and free-swimming behavior of the larva that establishes a link between tunicates and chordates. Larval tunicates exhibit all four major chordate traits: the notochord, a dorsal nerve cord, gill slits, and a post-anal tail. They are also behaviorally active, as opposed to sessile. According to Garstang's view, vertebrates arose from a tunicate larva that became sexually mature

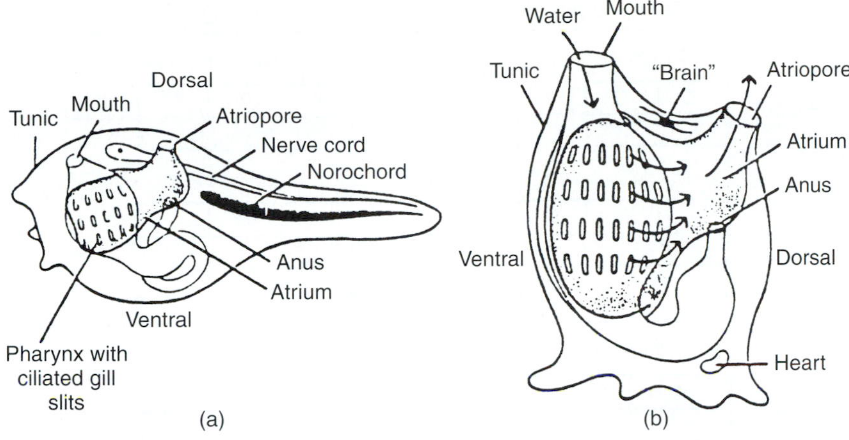

FIGURE 10.9. Garstand (1928) suggested that vertebrates evolved by paedomorphosis from a tunicate larva (tunicates are also called ascidians). Although the adult tunicate ***(b)*** is sessile and quite unlike an actively swimming chordate, the larva ***(a)*** possesses all the attributes of a chordate: dorsal nerve cord, notochord, post-anal tail, and gill slits (Brusca & Brusca 1990).

before the metamorphosis of its body into a sessile adult.

Specific instances of paedomorphosis are represented schematically in ***Figure 10.10-a.*** Each of the three possibilities reflects changes in some of these features:

(1) Onset of development—point in time when a trait begins its differentiation.
(2) Rate of development—the speed at which the trait matures.
(3) Onset of sexual maturity—point in time when sexual reproduction becomes possible.

In *postdisplacement,* the rate of development of a trait and the onset of sexual maturity are similar in descendant and ancestor, but the trait's onset of development is delayed in the descendant. As a result of such delay and because the trait will stop developing at sexual maturity, its adult form will be similar to that of juvenile, rather than adult, ancestors. Postdisplacement may be a developmental mechanism leading to the loss of a character if its development is postponed substantially, as it appears to be the case with the loss of some skull bones in amphibians.

Neoteny involves a similarity in the onset of development, coupled with a decrease in the rate of development and a delay in sexual maturity. Because development is slow, relative to sexual maturity, the animal acquires the capacity to reproduce when its body resembles in many ways the juvenile or larval stage of the ancestor. Species displaying a substantial degree of neoteny are characterized by a relatively large body size. For example, most salamanders pass through an aquatic larval stage and metamorphose into a terrestrial animal before they become sexually mature. In some species, however, sexual maturation is achieved while the animal is still in its aquatic stage, giving rise to "sex-

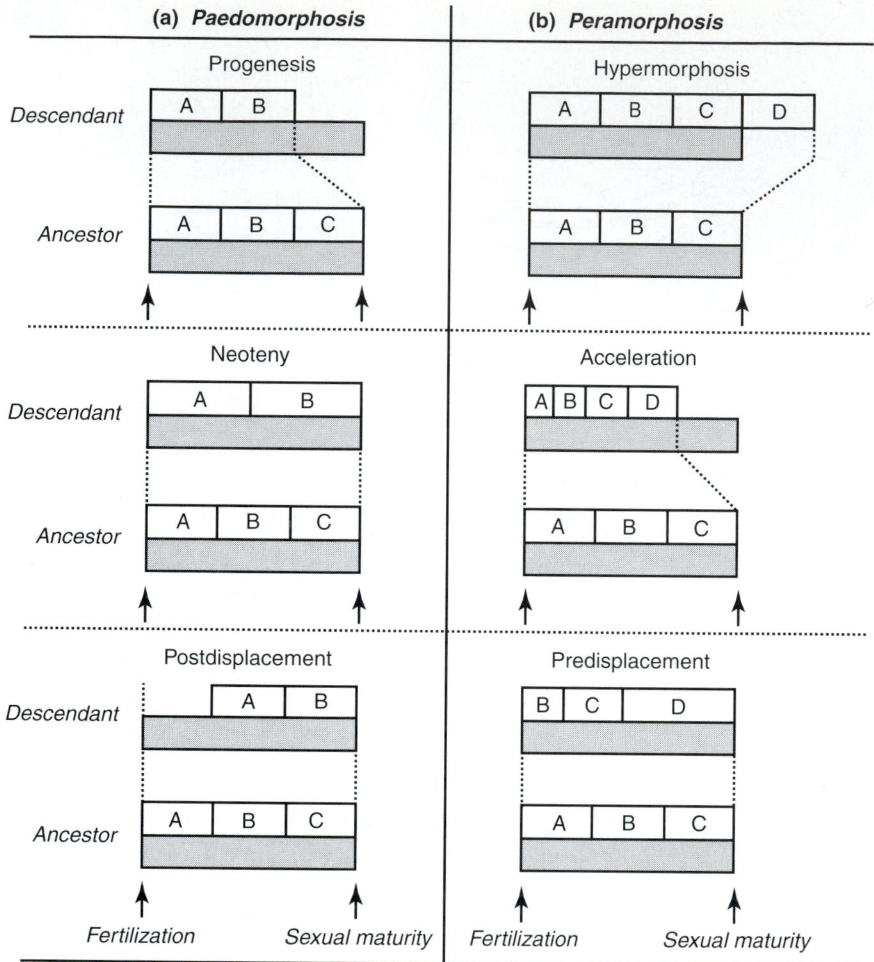

FIGURE 10.10. A representation of ***(a)*** paedomorphosis and ***(b)*** peramorphosis processes. Stages of development of a particular target trait are labeled A, B, C, etc. The shaded bar represents other traits that are concurrently developing in the organism.

ually active larvae" of relatively large body size. The Mexican axolotl (*Ambystoma mexicanum*) provides a classic example of neoteny. The axolotl is a salamander that lives in cave ponds of fresh water. Despite its obvious larval morphology, including external gills and a flattened tail, axolotls achieve sexual maturity and reproduce as typical amphibians, by external fertilization. They do not normally metamorphose into a terrestrial form, as most salamanders do, but metamorphosis can be induced in the laboratory by treatment with the thyroid hormone thyroxin.

Neoteny has been repeatedly postulated as a major mechanism in human evolution.

The idea that "humans are neotenic" has been suggested on the basis of many features of adult humans, both morphological and behavioral, that seem to correspond to those of juvenile primates. Hairlessness, the short face (i.e., reduced prognathism), the relatively large brain size, the extension of curiosity and play behavior into adulthood, and many other characteristics have been suggested at one time or another to imply a neotenic species. As already said, such arguments of general neoteny are hard to support empirically. But some of these features may have evolved by means of neoteny. For example, the human brain continues to grow at a "fetal rate" even after birth, instead of switching to a slower growth rate as is typical of other primates. This produces a relatively (and absolutely) large adult brain size (Deacon 1994). In chimpanzees and other primates, the rate of brain growth decreases sharply after birth, while the body continues to grow for some time.

In the case of *progenesis,* onset and rate of development are similar in descendants and ancestors, but sexual maturity is precocious. As a result, growth and development are stopped in the descendant, when the animal is in a stage similar to that of juvenile ancestors. Progenic descendants are characterized by a relatively small body size. Progenesis could be the mechanism underlying the evolution of species characterized by small body size and high reproductive rate, such as many animals that have adopted a parasitic mode of life. Worms of the phylum Acanthocephala fit such a description. These animals are extremely small (no more than a few millimeters long) and simplified (they lack a digestive system and their brain includes a very small number of neurons). Acanthocephalan worms live in the guts of arthropods and vertebrates, and it seems likely that progenesis has played a key role in their evolution.

2.e. Peramorphosis. Evolution is characterized in some cases by the addition of novel features in the development of specific traits. These are the cases that best fit the classic notion of recapitulation and the biogenetic law. *Peramorphosis,* however, is likely to be just as common as paedomorphosis as an evolutionary mechanism. Three instances of peramorphosis are illustrated in ***Figure 10.10-b,*** each corresponding to an instance of paedomorphosis. Therefore, changes in the same processes are involved in this case, namely, onset of development, rate of development, and onset of sexual maturity.

In these three forms of peramorphosis, the trait in question continues to develop beyond the adult stage of the ancestor, giving rise to phenotypic novelty. *Predisplacement* involves a shift in the onset of development of a particular trait to an earlier stage in the descendant, compared to the ancestor. *Acceleration,* as the word suggests, involves a faster developmental rate in the descendant. And *hypermorphosis* involves a delay in the onset of sexual maturity.

Many examples described before as allometric relationships between a given trait and body size, such as, for example, the increase in relative brain size discussed in ***Chapter 8,*** represent instances of hypermorphosis. Consider the frequent evolutionary trend toward an increase in body size observed in many lineages (so common that, in fact, it is called *Cope's "law"*). When natural selection favors larger body size in the descendant, compared to the ancestors, many bodily organs change by simple allometry. In addition, new structures that may not be present in the ancestors now find ontogenetic room to develop. A classic example are the horns and antlers of certain mammals. In the titanotheres, an extinct family of perissodactyl mammals similar in appearance to modern rhinoceros (a family that also includes the horses and tapirs), such a trend can be observed in the size of the horn. In the oldest fossils from the Eocene (54–38 Mya), which were small in body size, horns are either not observed or appear as a small bump on top of the snout. By contrast, specimens from the Oligocene (38–23 Mya) are larger in body size and exhibit longer horns (***Figure 10.11***). The emergence of horns appears to be in part caused by selection for increased body size.

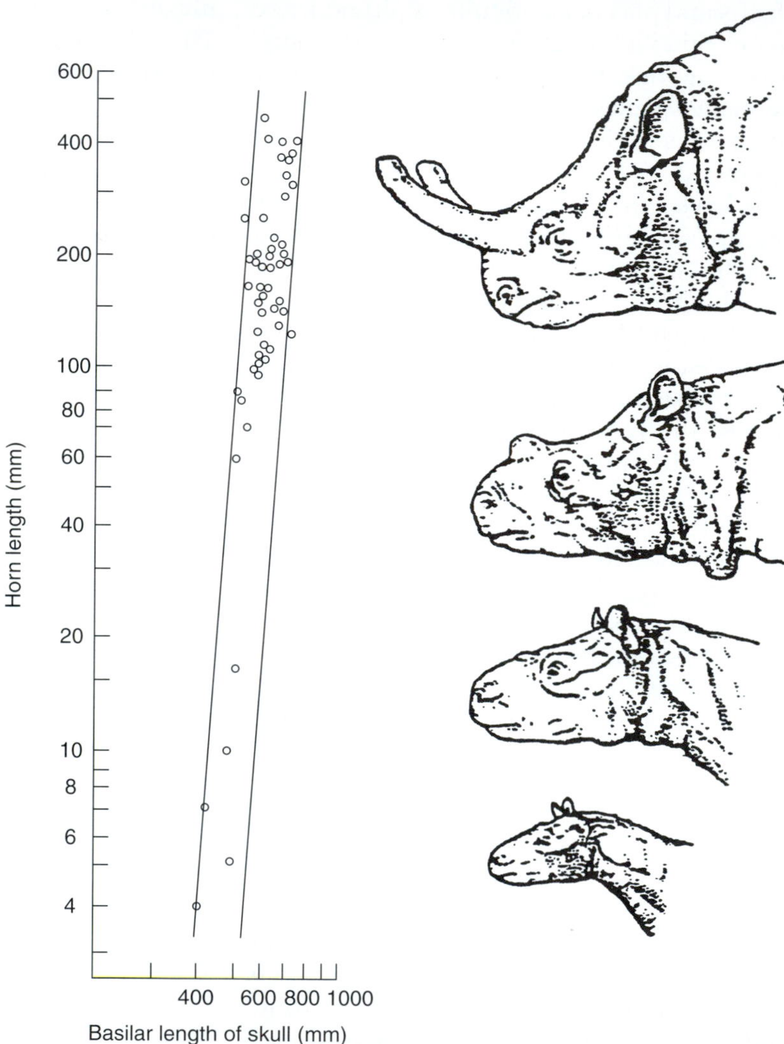

FIGURE 10.11. Horn length as a function of skull length in several species of titanotheres from the Eocene (lower five points) and Oligocene (cloud of upper points). Some examples of species differing in both horn length and body size are shown on the right (McKinney & Schoch 1985).

Interestingly, however, a reanalysis of these data on horn and body size in titanotheres suggests that hypermorphosis may not be enough to account for the evolution of this trait in later specimens (McKinney & Schoch 1985). The slope of the five lower points in ***Figure 10.11,*** which correspond to the Eocene specimens, is similar to that of the upper points, corresponding to the Oligocene specimens; the specific values for these slopes were 5.09 and 4.59, respectively, both indicating positive allometry (i.e., values greater than 1 indicate that horn size growths faster than body size across species). However, the point of origin of these slopes is much higher for the Oligocene forms. This suggests that horns were larger not only because of an increase in body size but also because their development started earlier. This would be a case of predisplacement.

Furthermore, analyses of the slopes of the Oligocene genera show that the relationship between horn and body size varied substantially. In the genus *Allops* the value of the slope was 9.56, whereas in the genus *Brontops* it was 2.95; these values deviate significantly from those of the Eocene species, 5.09, and in opposite directions. The larger value for *Allops* suggests acceleration—that is, an increase in the rate of development relative to the Eocene ancestors. By contrast, the lower value for *Brontops* suggests neoteny—that is, a reduction in the rate of development, again relative to Eocene ancestors. The evolution of relative horn size, a structure probably involved in male-male competition and subject to sexual selection, nicely illustrates how different heterochronic processes may underlie evolutionary changes in the same trait but in different lineages.

2.f. Heterochrony, Ecology, and Behavior. The notion of behavioral neophenotype—that is, that new behaviors can bring about phenotypic changes by modifying gene expression—can also be realized via heterochrony. Behavioral changes may be accompanied by changes in the timing of expression of regulatory genes that, by way of a cascade effect, might result in significant changes in the animal's phenotype. Such effects can be induced under laboratory conditions. In one experiment, groups of the neotropical cichlid fish *Cichlasoma managuense* were fed two different diets during their initial development (Meyer 1987). The diets were based either on juveniles of the crustacean *Artemia salina* or on a mixture of commercial flake food and laboratory-raised nematode worms. These different types of food require different types of feeding behavior, although they are nutritionally equivalent. The group fed with a crustacean diet was significantly longer in body size and in head size, had a longer lower jaw, larger eyes, and longer snout than the fish given a flake-nematode diet. Measurement of developmental rates showed that the fish given the flake-nematode diet displayed a retardation in developmental rate—that is, neoteny. If that diet was changed to a crustacean-based diet at 8 months of age, then the phenotypes converged in approximately 8 more months. However, if those distinct diets were kept constant, the phenotypes remained different.

Cichlid fish are notorious for their species diversity. In the African lakes of Tanganyika, Malawi, and Victoria, there are hundreds of sympatric species (i.e., species with overlapping distribution). Speciation events may be linked, in many cases, to early behavioral shifts which, coupled with developmental plasticity, may give rise to distinct phenotypes (see ***section 2.b*** above). Such phenotypes need not involve drastic genetic changes but only subtle modifications in heterochronic processes. Similar changes appear to be responsible for the evolution of the dog (*Canis familiaris*), during the past 12,000 years, from its wolf ancestors (*Canis lupus*). Morey (1994) analyzed morphological features of the crania of dogs found in archeological sites and compared them to those of wolves of various ages. Early adult dogs were smaller in body size and resembled juvenile, rather than adult, wolves.

Morey (1994) also pointed out that dogs are paedomorphic not only morphologically but also behaviorally. Behavior, as well as body size, might have been a key ingredient in the process that led to the domestication of dogs by humans. The association between humans and the dog's ancestors is likely to have started as a byproduct of similar hunting tactics. Perhaps there were mutual benefits from such an association, such as cooperative hunting of large game or detection of potential predators. Once the link was established, dogs that behaved submissively, following orders and remaining attached to their human companions, may have enjoyed a reproductive advantage over dogs that developed more independent social behavior. Such submissiveness and sensitivity to social reinforcement are behavioral characteristics commonly seen in juvenile wolves but rarely in adults. These behavioral traits may have evolved by way of neoteny. Interestingly, a breeding program based on silver foxes (*Vulpes vulpes*) provides additional evidence on this issue (Trut 1999). Since the 1950s, foxes have been selected on the basis of their degree of tameness—that is, their tendency to respond positively to human contact. About 10% of foxes in the initial population exhibited no fear or withdrawal responses in the presence of humans. After about 30 generations of selective breeding, foxes developed further docility, seeking human company and competing for human attention as dogs do. Such convergence between dogs and foxes suggests that "tamability," a behavioral trait, has been a critical aspect in the process of domestication.

One possible way in which selection may affect levels of tamability is by extending the *sensitive period* for socialization (Scott & Fuller 1965). It is well known that dogs develop social attachment to humans more strongly when they are exposed to human interaction during the initial weeks of life and before they develop fear of the unfamiliar. Such a fear response appears in dogs between 8 and 12 weeks of age. Foxes have a similar sensitive period before fear of the unfamiliar emerges. However, a comparison between domesticated and wild foxes suggests that domestication based on tameness has resulted in the extension of that period; whereas wild foxes exhibit the fear response at about 6 weeks of age, domesticated foxes exhibit it at 9 weeks of age. Domesticated foxes also start responding to external stimuli earlier than wild foxes. In other words, the sensitive period for socialization has widened in the domesticated foxes (descendants), relative to the wild foxes (ancestors).

Foxes also changed in a host of other characters for which they were not explicitly selected, a fact illustrating the pleiotropic effects of genes (i.e., genes usually exert their effects on a variety of traits; see ***Chapter 3***). Domesticated foxes exhibit, for example, soft ears, rolled tails, changes in coat color, shorter legs, and, most interesting, a more frequent receptivity for mating. An entire cluster of traits is actually modified as a result of selection on tameness, as is shown in ***Figure 10.12.*** Many of these characters are actually seen in other domesticated species (e.g., hair color and form, and tail shape are particularly common changes, such as is seen in sheep or pigs). Two implications follow from these observations: First, tame behavior may have been a common selective trait in the domestication of many different

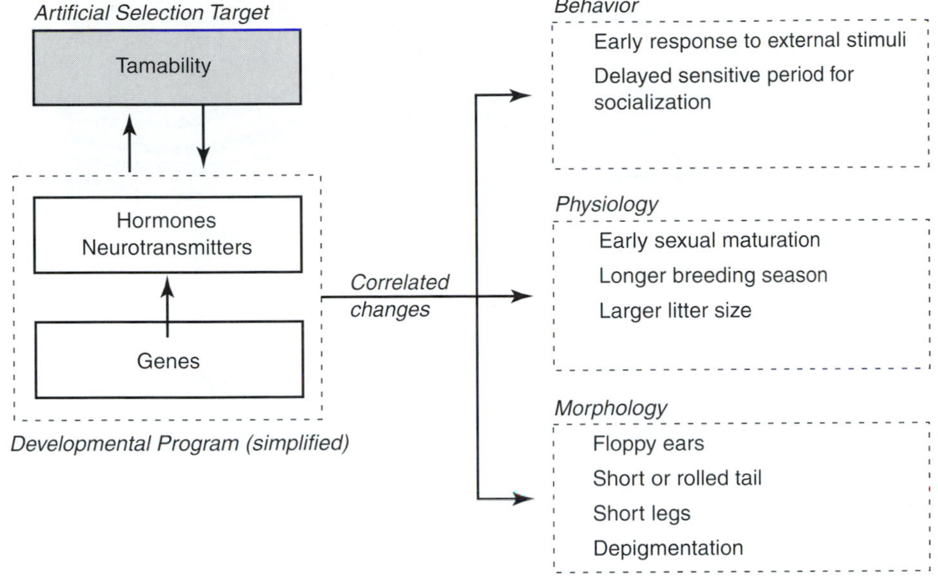

FIGURE 10.12. An extensive program of domestication with wild foxes, *Vulpes vulpes,* carried out in Russia since the late 1950s illustrates the pleiotropic effects of genes. Although the selection was based on tamability—a behavioral trait defined in terms of the fox's response to human contact—other behaviors, physiological responses, and morphological correlates also exhibited changes across generations.

mammals; and second, these species must share homologous developmental programs that link these traits in a correlated fashion, thus leading to changes in similar aspects of the phenotype.

As pointed out at the outset of this chapter, natural selection seems to act most frequently by affecting entire life-history strategies. The behavioral components of these life-history strategies are influenced by affecting the manner in which nervous tissue develops during ontogeny. Behavior is ultimately shaped by evolutionary forces, but it is proximally determined by the functioning of neural networks within the central nervous system of animals. It follows, then, that behavioral evolution is achieved by affecting neurological development.

3. DEVELOPMENT OF THE VERTEBRATE NERVOUS SYSTEM

3.a. Neuroembryology. Nervous tissue is among the first tissues to differentiate during early stages of development in vertebrate embryos. In fact, the neurula stage is thus named precisely because the first nerve cells differentiate from dorsal ectoderm cells. Neurulation is marked by the appearance of a groove in the ectoderm beginning near the blastopore and proceeding toward the caudal region of the embryo. The neural plate is then formed at the sides of the groove, limited by lateral ridges called neural folds. As shown in ***Figure 10.13,*** these folds bend toward the middle line until they become fused

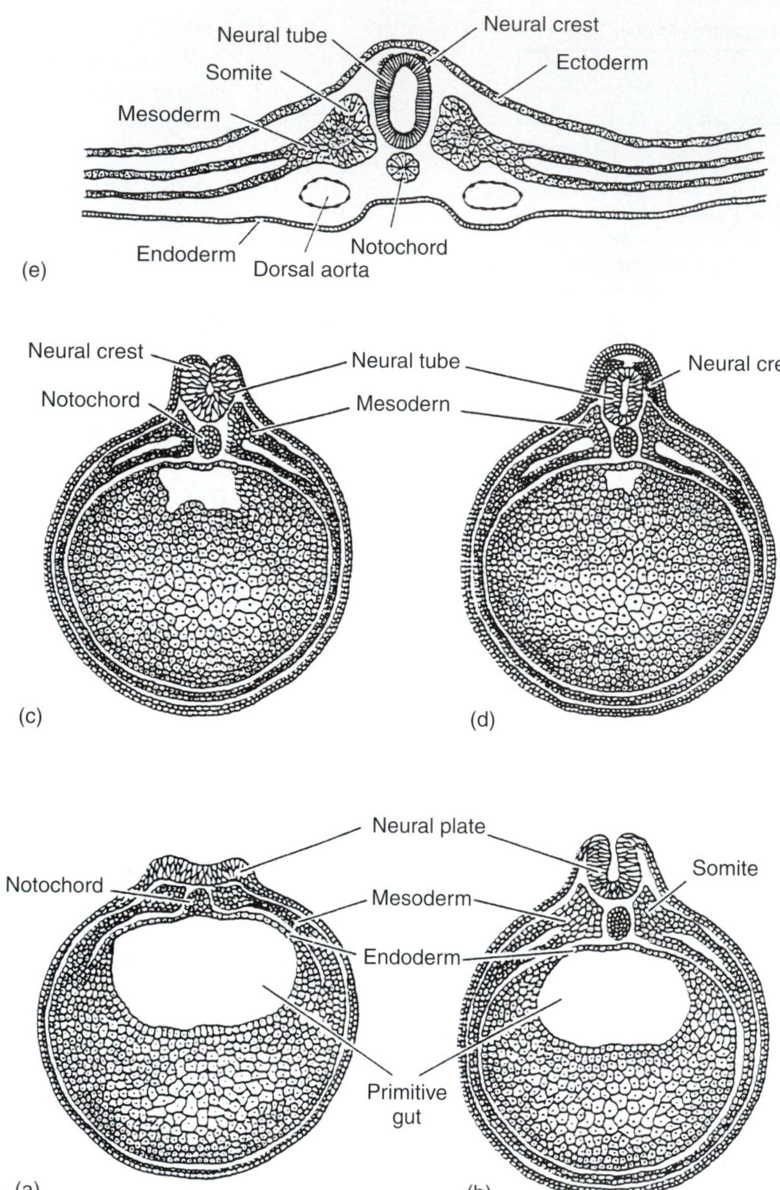

FIGURE 10.13. Development of the neural tube in vertebrates shown here in cross-sections at various stages of development (Saunders 1970). From ***(a)*** to ***(d)*** the neural plate folds and closes, leading to the formation of the neural tube. Such folding and closing usually occurs in progression from the anterior to the posterior end of the embryo. ***(e)*** Neurulation in the chick embryo.

with each other, thus creating the neural tube. Two other key components of the vertebrate body develop also at this stage: the notochord, located below the neural plate and eventually incorporated into the spinal column, and the somites, located laterally and eventually giving rise to the vertebrae, ribs, and skeletal musculature. These structures have a *segmented* organization—that is, a pattern that repeats itself in the anterior-posterior axis of the body. Whereas the central nervous system (CNS) arises from the neural tube, the peripheral nervous system, with its cell types and ganglia, originates from the neural crest, and the tissue that will differentiate into the various sensory organs originates in the ectoderm. Interactions between the cells in the neural crest and ectoderm give rise to the central nuclei serving the cranial nerves.

Neurons proliferate by mitosis in the region bordering the neural tube and then migrate toward the periphery. Mitosis in neurogenic cells is profuse during this stage, but relatively rare beyond embryological development. This is why the effects of brain tissue damage on behavior in adult vertebrates are generally difficult to reverse. As will be discussed later, neuronal reproduction does occur in specific areas of the adult brain of some vertebrate species. Neuronal proliferation also follows anterior-to-posterior and ventral-to-dorsal directions; for example, components of the motor system located in the ventral regions develop before those of the sensory systems located in a dorsal position.

Local cell differentiation and proliferation vary dramatically across the anteroposterior axis. They create a series of swellings that correspond to the telencephalon (brain hemispheres), mesencephalon (optic tectum), and rhombencephalon (cerebellum), as well as the epiphysis, or pineal gland. This feature of CNS development, as well as the development of the vertebral column and somites already cited, emphasize the segmented nature of the vertebrate body. Several gene clusters participate in segmentation, including the Hox genes.

The study of the segmental organization of the CNS is permitting a better understanding of how relatively complex neural networks become organized. During a transient period, vertebrate embryos develop a series of subdivisions along the anterior-posterior axis, called *neuromeres,* which had already been recognized by 19th century neuroanatomists. ***Figure 10.14*** shows these divisions, which are referred to as prosomeres (p1 to p6, in the prosencephalon), a single mesomere (in the mesencephalon), and rhombomeres (r1 to r7, in the rhombencephalon). In the rhombomeres, for example, cell migration across boundaries is severely restricted, so that local circuits are subject to relatively specific influences (Capecchi 1997). Only about 5% of cells have been observed to migrate across rhombomeres. Within each rhombomere there is extensive communication between cells, but such cell-cell communication is practically nonexistent between different rhombomeres. Circuits and cell phenotypes can thus be established locally. These neurons give rise to such central nuclei as those of the cranial nerves.

There is an orderly relationship between the expression of Hox genes and the organization of the rhombomeres in the rhombencephalon of the chick and mouse. Hox genes exhibit a range of expression, and their anterior boundary usually coincides with specific rhombomeres. ***Figure 10.14*** shows the range of expression for several of these genes in the mouse brain. In vertebrates, there are four sets of Hox genes, labeled from A to D and called *paralogous genes* (as shown previously in ***Figure 10.4***). Although only four Hox-A genes are

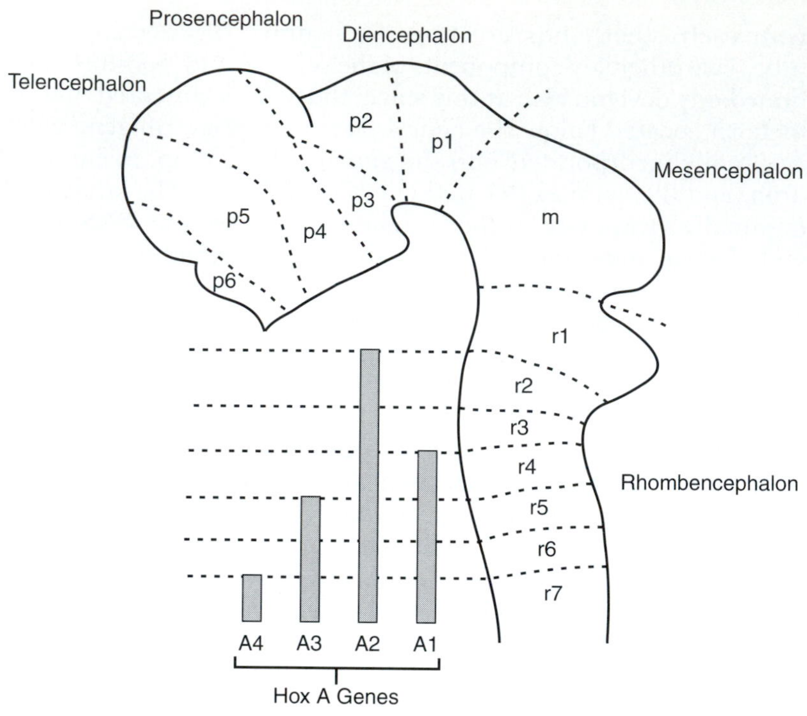

FIGURE 10.14. Formation of neuromeres in the mouse embryo. Six prosomeres have been identified in the prosencephalon, one mesomere in the mesencephalon, and seven rhombomeres in the rhombencephalon. Several regulatory genes, including the four Hox genes illustrated in this figure, have maximum expression profiles that match rhombomere boundaries. Each rhombomere expresses a unique combination of regulatory genes that presumably play a critical role in the development of local circuits.

represented in ***Figure 10.14,*** genes from other Hox linkage groups, as well as other kinds of regulatory genes, are also expressed in these regions, in some cases with a great deal of specificity (e.g., Hox-B1 is expressed maximally in r4). As a result, each rhombomere is marked by a unique combination of Hox gene products. This is thought to lead to rhombomere identity through a cascade of influences.

Tissue transplantation experiments demonstrate that the identity of some rhombomeres is established even before the boundaries are evident. However, some rhombomeres are also influenced by local interactions. For example, transplantation of anterior rhombomeres to posterior regions renders them more influenced by local cells than when the opposite transplantation is performed. Moreover, a rotation in the dorsoventral axis can also modify the identity of some cells. There is also variability in the formation of the same rhombomere at both sides of the rhombencephalon. All these examples suggest that local aspects of the intercellular environment, including cell signals in the posterior portion of the rhombencephalon, in the floor of the neural plate, and in the contralateral side, can influence the development of specific rhombomeres and the neural circuits contained therein.

3.b. Axonal Growth and Synapses. The most proximate cause of behavior is found in the activity of neural networks involving from a few neurons (as in some of the examples reviewed in ***Chapter 7*** on simple systems) to thousands of units. It is such activity that immediately precedes the occurrence of any behavior, from a reflex act to a correct choice in a complex discrimination problem. These networks are established by the growth of axons and the functional activation of the synaptic connections between neurons during early CNS development.

There are millions of neurons in the brain of any vertebrate, each establishing anywhere from a few to thousands of synaptic connections with other neurons and with peripheral tissue. During development, axons grow in bursts toward their target locations, guided by molecular cues for which they possess specific receptors. The tips of axons, named growth cones by the Spanish neurobiologist Santiago Ramón y Cajal [1852–1934] at the end of the 19th century, behave in an ameboid fashion as they develop in a particular direction. The idea that these ameboid movements of growth cones are caused by their response to molecular cues, or the *chemoaffinity hypothesis,* was suggested by Sperry (1963) on the basis of experiments on the amphibian visual system. When the optic nerve is cut, its axons (originating from the ganglion cells of the retina) regenerate and reestablish normal connections with the optic tectum. Such specificity should not be surprising if one considers the stability of anatomical pathways in the CNS of vertebrates.

Axonal guidance mechanisms fall into four categories (Goodman & Tessier-Lavigne 1997). Axons may be attracted or repulsed toward a specific location, and the force may be local (i.e., direct contact) or diffuse (i.e., chemical gradients). Whether the influence is local or diffuse, it is mediated by molecular recognition, and in some cases, such recognition can be quite specific. For example, the limbic system–associated membrane protein (LAMP) stimulates axonal growth of neurons within the limbic system of mammals, including the hippocampus, septum, amygdala, and entorhinal cortex. The particular direction in which a cone grows depends on the local balance of attractor and repulsor molecular influences. Interestingly, similar classes of molecules mediating axonal growth are found in organisms as distantly related as nematodes, arthropods, and vertebrates, suggesting a great deal of conservation of at least some neurodevelopmental processes.

Once axons reach their target field, they establish synaptic connections with a variety of cells in the field (Sanes & Scheller 1997). Synapses are formed between axons and dendrites, cell somas, or other axons, in each case with a great deal of specificity as to the molecular machinery, in both presynaptic and postsynaptic components, that will support synaptic activity. On the presynaptic side, important components involve the mitochondria that provide energy for the metabolic processes involved in synaptic transmission and for the synaptic vesicles that store neurotransmitter. On the postsynaptic side, the main components are the neurotransmitter receptors. But, obviously, the formation of a synapse must involve the reciprocal communication of presynaptic and postsynaptic components via molecular signals. As the axon terminal reaches its target, extensive morphological reorganization of the terminal occurs over a relatively long period. For example, the neuromuscular synapse is formed over a period of 3 weeks in the mouse embryo. Initially, the two cells are in direct physical contact, which permits the interchange of membrane proteins. The synaptic cleft is formed subsequently, as the synaptic vesicles accumulate and active zones appear in the presynaptic membrane. Eventually, the synapse becomes functional, and this activity further determines the preservation of some connections and the elimination of others. At least in vertebrates, experience-dependent rearrangement of synaptic connections occurs throughout the life of the organism.

3.c. Neuronal Aggregations. The CNS of vertebrates shows three basic patterns of neuronal aggregations. The first is the more or less scattered distribution of cell somas with relatively diffuse boundaries, such as is observed in the telencephalon of most fish and some amphibians (see ***Figure 8.11,*** p. 291). In such cases, various brain areas can still be distinguished by their specific connections with other areas and by the presence of very specific neurotransmitter systems. Although random in appearance, these cell aggregates are quite organized and functionally distinct.

A second structural pattern is that of nuclei. A *nucleus* is a cell cluster with relatively clear anatomical boundaries. In some cases, the internal structure of a nucleus includes a laminar pattern established by the alignment of cell somas in layers. For example, the dorsolateral geniculate nucleus of monkeys, a part of the thalamus that receives the projection of the optic nerve originating in the retina, possesses six layers of cells in a disposition resembling an onion. Nerve cells differentiating in the area surrounding the ventricles migrate toward their final location in an orderly fashion. Most nuclei are formed according to a so-called outside-in pattern, that is, the outside layer forms first and the innermost layer last.

A third pattern is illustrated by cortices. A *cortex* is an external (i.e., peripherally located) laminar sheet, usually including several distinct layers of cell somas. The dorsal area of the optic tectum of some salamanders is organized in this manner, although perhaps the most famous example is that of the mammalian, six-layered neocortex. Such cortical structures are usually formed according to a so-called inside-out pattern. The innermost cell layer is usually established first, and more peripheral layers are added by subsequent cell migrations.

Neural development is characterized by the early proliferation of a large number of neurons and neuronal connections. Axons not only grow toward a specific target but also reach transient destinations, often by the development of collateral axonal branches. As the organism matures, there is a selective death of neurons (called *apoptosis*), and many of the neuronal connections previously established are eliminated. A major cause of apoptosis is the failure to establish contact with the appropriate target region. For example, if a normal target (such as an eye or a limb) is surgically removed, then many of the neurons that would normally innervate that target also die. The prevailing view is that more neurons and connections than needed are produced and only those that are functionally successful are preserved. Neural targets in both the central and peripheral nervous system produce a variety of proteins that prevent neuronal death. One such protein is known as the nerve growth factor (Levi-Montalcini 1987). These proteins, collectively known as *neurotrophins,* are absorbed by axon terminals and transported toward the neuron's soma where they facilitate the survival of the neuron. Growing axons compete for access to a limited amount of neurotrophins in a sort of "neuronal Darwinism."

Cell differentiation, migration, and death are all potential determinants of the amount of tissue allocated to a particular aggregate. It is an obvious fact that homologous nuclei and cortical structures vary considerably even among closely related species. For example, the neocortex of primates is quite extensive compared to that of other mammals, such as insectivores or bats. These size differences must be achieved by species differences in developmental processes such as those described in this chapter. Allomeric studies of brain size (see ***Chapter 8, section 4***, pp. 302–315) demonstrate that the vertebrate brain scales to body size. Similarly, neural aggregates also scale in proportion to brain size (Finlay & Darlington 1995).

Among the mammals, for example, such structures as the paleocortex, septum, hippocampus, and cerebellum increase their size in correlation with the size of the entire brain (***Figure 10.15-a***). The increase is, however, steeper for the cerebellum, diencephalon, and striatum (slope value ranging between 0.34 and 0.36) than it is for limbic structures such as the septum and hippocampus (slopes between 0.28 and 0.30), and it is steepest for the neocortex (slope of 0.45). The order in which these structures develop appears to be very stereotyped across mammals, but the point in time at which neurogenic cells differentiate into neurons, and thus no longer reproduce, varies across species. This timing process determines the relative size of the aggregate in the adult. In species in which neurogenic precursors continue to divide for a longer period before yielding true neurons, the terminal size of the structure is relatively larger. It appears that the high-rate growth of the neocortex in primates is achieved by delaying the point in time at which precursor cells differentiate into neurons. ***Figure 10.15-b*** compares the onset and duration of terminal neurogenesis for a wide range of brain structures, on a common scale, for rats and rhesus monkeys. There is substantial overlap in developmental timing, except for some of the layers in the neocortex. In primates, these layers are established relatively late, which allows for the production of a large population of precursor cells that differentiates into neurons.

Notice an apparent paradox in brain evolution. On the one hand, I have described before cases in which a particular structure is relatively enlarged in species that rely heavily on a behavior controlled by that structure (see ***Chapter 8, section 4.f.***, pp. 314–315). For example, the hippocampus of food-storing birds of several families is relatively larger than the hippocampus of nonstoring species. On the other hand, the size of a particular structure, including the hippocampus, appears to depend closely on the size of the brain. Any increase in the size of a particular structure is, therefore, restricted by the size of the brain. These restrictions are referred to as *developmental constraints.* Does this mean that in order for a food-storing species to increase the size of its hippocampus, the entire brain must also increase? An affirmative answer to such a question would imply a very inefficient trade-off since structures that may not be needed would have to increase in size. However, such is not necessarily the case. There is enough variation in the size of specific structures to allow for what would be significant increases in its size in any given species without violating the constraint that relates the structure's size to the size of the

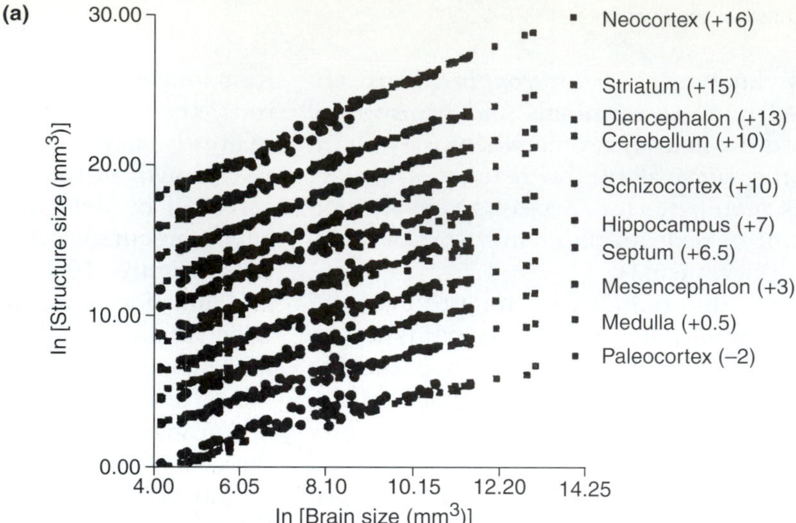

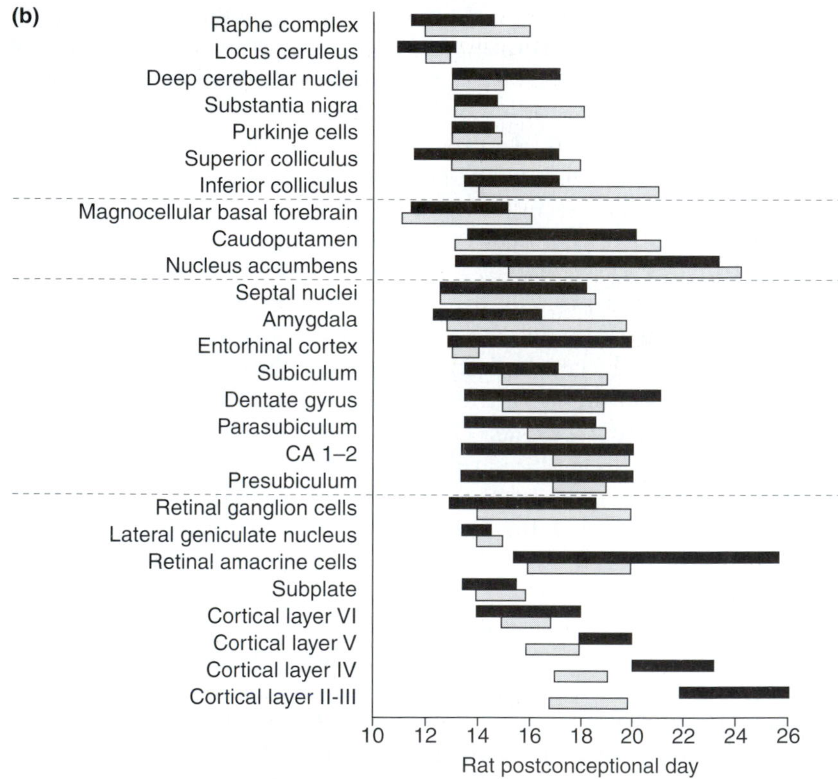

FIGURE 10.15. Comparative aspects of brain development in mammals (Finlay & Darlington 1995). ***(a)*** Size of various brain structures (listed on the right) as a function of brain size, in a sam-

brain. Finlay and Darlington (1995) have estimated that a homologous structure may differ in size among two closely related species by as much as a 2.5 factor (a difference easily detectable as significant) and still be within the size constraint imposed by the species' brain size.

3.d. Brain Development and Experience. The nervous system is in charge of receiving sensory information from the external environment and of coordinating behaviors that allow an organism to effectively interact with its surroundings. It is therefore not entirely surprising that the development of the CNS would be sensitive to what can loosely be referred to as "experience." It was pointed out above that apoptosis depends, to some extent, on the development of appropriate functional connections between neurons: Neurons that fail to connect with the appropriate targets cannot engage in functional interaction and tend to die. Functional neuronal interaction can be viewed as a correlate of experience.

Consider again the case of food-storing behavior in birds. How does the hippocampus of these species become significantly enlarged, relative to that of closely related but nonstoring species? One possibility is that the storing and retrieving experience per se is responsible for the enlargement of the hippocampus. In one experiment, marsh tits (*Parus palustris*) of various ages were allowed the storing of sunflower seeds and their subsequent retrieval. These animals typically store hundreds of seeds on a daily basis during the fall and winter months and then recover them within hours and days. The hippocampus of experienced marsh tits was about 48% larger than that of animals in a control group treated similarly except that storing was not permitted (Clayton & Krebs 1994). Interestingly, this experience affected neither the size of the ectostriatum, a visual area anatomically unrelated to the hippocampus, nor the size of the entire telencephalon, which suggests the effects of experience were rather specific in anatomical terms. Experience caused larger hippocampi by preventing apoptosis: There was a lower number of dead neurons in the hippocampus of experienced animals than in that of controls.

An interesting aspect of the marsh tit data just described is that the effect of expe-

ple of mammalian species from various orders, including primates, insectivores, and bats. The number in parentheses at the right of the figure is a constant value added to the data points to allow for spread and easy visualization of the slopes across brain structures. When represented in logarithmic coordinates, these allometric functions appear linear. Notice small, but consistent, differences in the steepness of the slopes. The steeper the slope, the more the structure changes as a function of brain size. ***(b)*** Duration of terminal neurogenesis in monkeys (solid bars) and rats (open bars) plotted on a common scale. Most structures exhibit overlapping timing, except for neocortical layers II-V, for which terminal neurogenesis occurs relatively late in monkeys, compared to rats. The implication is that a larger mass of neuronal precursors will be available for differentiation since they have been allowed a longer period to reproduce. Such timing effects may cause differences in the relative size of homologous structures across species.

rience on food-storing behavior and hippocampal size was the same across three different ages, covering the transition from juvenile to adult. Apparently, therefore, these effects do not depend on a sensitive period. In other cases, experience affects neural development and behavior only when it occurs within a relatively specific time window during development. I mentioned in ***section 2.f.*** the case of the social behavior of dogs as an example of a developmental process passing through one such sensitive period; further examples will be encountered in subsequent chapters. An important corollary of these findings is that the nervous system seems to have periods during which it is particularly prone to modification by external influences. This neural plasticity may be similar, in many important ways, to the type of plasticity that underlies the acquisition of new memories and the modification of behavior in the adult organism. The approach that has revealed the full strength of neural plasticity in the developing mammalian brain involves the so-called *environmental enrichment* procedure. As in the case of food-storing experience, environmental enrichment brings about changes in the morphology and neurochemistry of the CNS and in the behavior of the animal that do not seem to be greatly restricted by age.

One of the first relevant experiments was done by the Canadian comparative psychologist Donald O. Hebb [1904–1985], who raised a few rats as pets in his home and then compared their adult performance to that of laboratory-reared animals from the same litters. Hebb found the pets to be able to learn several discrimination tasks faster than their cage-reared littermates and concluded that early exposure to a stimulating environment can improve adult problem-solving abilities. Subsequent research showed that early exposure to a complex environment leads to improved performance in a wide variety of learning tasks (Renner & Rosenzweig 1987).

In one of the first reports (Krech et al. 1962), enriched rats were raised in groups of 10 rats placed in a large enclosure containing a small maze and wooden "toys" that were changed daily. Rats in the isolated control group were raised in regular laboratory cages. Rats were placed in these conditions for 30 days immediately after weaning, at about 24 days of age, and then tested in a brightness discrimination reversal problem. In this problem, animals are rewarded with food for choosing one of the alternatives, but nonrewarded if they choose the other (i.e., A+/B– problem). Once a learning criterion is reached (e.g., 19 correct choices out of 20 consecutive trials), the validity of the stimuli is reversed: A–/B+. Rats exposed to enriched environments were about equal to isolated rats in their ability to learn the original A+/B– problem; enriched animals, however, exhibited faster acquisition in all subsequent reversal problems. But how are such behavioral improvements achieved?

It is now well established that many regions of the mammalian brain do not develop rigidly—that is, by the simple unfolding of genetic information. In contrast, brain development exhibits various degrees of phenotypic plasticity, such that neural neophenotypes can be established by manipulating the early environment in which young mammals develop. Infant rats (*Rattus norvegicus*) exposed to complex environments, both socially and physically, develop a heavier and thicker neocortex, hippocampus, superior colliculus, and cerebellar cortex, among other areas (Black & Greenough 1991). The increase in size of these structures may be caused by any of a variety of reasons, including the development of a larger dendritic field and a higher number of dendritic branchings. As a result, there is a significant increase in the number of active synaptic points in enriched animals. Enrichment also affects the number of nonneural cells and structures that provide support for neural networks, including glial cells such as the astrocytes, which regulate levels of ions and neurotransmitters important for neuronal function, and blood vessels, which provide support for tissue function.

3.f. Brain Development and Hormones. The role of hormones in the development of behavior received a considerable impetus from the work of the American comparative psychologist Frank A. Beach [1911–1988]. *Hormones* are proteins synthesized by glands (e.g., pituitary, adrenal, gonads, thyroid, etc.), secreted into the blood stream, and widely distributed in different regions of the body (see ***Table 10.1*** and also ***Table 8.3,*** p. 287). Like neurotransmitters, hormones can affect other cells, but over greater distances than that of the synapse. Two broad effects of hormones can be distinguished—namely, activating and organizing effects—depending on the extent to which the changes are permanent. As usual, however, it may be wise to keep in mind that clear-cut distinctions are usually compromised by a number of exceptions (Arnold & Breedlove 1985).

Activating effects are relatively fast and transient, and are achieved mainly by the hormone's ability to bind to membrane receptors. Receptors for a wide variety of hormones are present in neurons located in various structures of the CNS. Hormones can affect a neuron's firing function by binding to a membrane receptor and modifying the flux of ions through the membrane; hormones can also induce morpho-

TABLE 10.1 Overview of the Mammalian Endocrine System

Gland	***Hormone***	***Some Actions***
Pituitary	Growth hormone (GH)	Regulates growth of all tissues
	Adrenocorticotrophic hormone (ACTH)	Stimulates the adrenal cortex
	Thyroid-stimulating hormone (TSH)	Stimulates the thyroid
	Follicle-stimulating hormone (FSH)	Stimulates the gonads
	Luteinizing hormone (LH)	Regulates growth of the gonads
	Oxytocin	Stimulates release of milk
	Vasopressin	Regulates blood pressure
Pineal	Melatonin	Regulates biological rhythms
Thyroid	Thyroxin	Regulates metabolism
Parathyroid	Parathyroid hormone	Regulates blood calcium levels
Pancreas	Insulin	Regulates metabolism of glucose and fats
Adrenal	Mineralocorticoids	Regulates ion concentration
	Glucocorticoids	Regulate response to stress
	Adrenalin/Noradrenalin	Mimic actions of the sympathetic system
Gonads	Estrogens	Female secondary sexual features
	Progesterone	Prepares uterus for pregnancy
	Testosterone	Male secondary sexual features

Note. Only a sample of hormones and hormonal actions are detailed in this table.

logical changes, including growth and retraction of dendritic fields, neuronal repair following lesions, and neuronal death.

An example of a complex series of activating effects is provided by a family of hormones known as the glucocorticoids. Glucocorticoids are secreted by the adrenal gland, located near the kidneys, and can pass the blood-brain barrier and enter the CNS, where they influence neurons possessing the appropriate membrane receptors. Glucocorticoid receptors are widely distributed in the brain of vertebrates and are particularly concentrated in the hippocampal formation of mammals. Glucocorticoids are released in response to emotionally stressful situations, and their action at the hippocampal level is related to the termination of the stress response. Glucocorticoids also participate in the general response of the organism to stress by reallocating metabolic resources among the various bodily tissues. While under potential danger, peripheral tissues, such as skeletal muscles, receive an abundant blood supply at the expense of internal organs, such as the stomach. This redistribution of resources may contribute to an active escape response by the organism. However, if glucocorticoids are maintained at a high level for long periods of time, they cause cell damage in a variety of organs, including the stomach (where they can be linked to ulcers) and the brain (where they cause neuronal death).

Some types of early experience, such as exposing a rat to an enriched environment or to handling by the experimenter, induce the proliferation of glucocorticoid receptors in many brain regions, including the hippocampus, and lead to lower levels of circulating glucocorticoids in adult animals. Such animals are less prone to stress and less vulnerable to its damaging, long-term effects. For example, stressing rats in their early development by handling procedure leads to abundant glucocorticoid receptors in the brain, a faster turn-off of the stress response, greater survival of hippocampal neurons, and improved memory in a variety of tasks at an old age (Barnes 1991).

The second broad type of effects are referred to as *organizing effects*; these are permanent changes in the morphology of various organs that are usually achieved by the action of hormones during specific sensitive periods. One of the most salient examples of an organizing effect is provided by the role of steroid hormones in the development of mammalian reproductive biology. Steroid hormones (e.g., testosterone, estradiol) can act at the membrane level, but they can also enter the cell, bind to an intracellular receptor, and influence (i.e., turn on or off) gene transcription. This action upon gene activity mediates the development of structural changes, such as the secondary sexual characteristics.

Mammals exhibit gender differences in the size of some brain structures that are established by the action of steroid hormones. For example, a hypothalamic nucleus known as the medial preoptic area (MPO) is larger in male rats than in females (Goy & McEwen 1980). The volume of the MPO is about 0.96 mm^3 for males, but about 0.12 mm^3 for females, a 8:1 size difference! The MPO is a main component of the neural circuit controlling sexual behavior in male mammals largely because of the abundant presence of receptors for the male hormone testosterone. Testosterone injections can induce male sexual behavior and compensate for the effects of castration on male sexual behavior. Male rats castrated at 5 days of age exhibit female sexual behavior as adults. Moreover, female rats injected with testosterone during their first 10 days of life (a sensitive period) develop a masculinized MPO, as well as several other features (e.g., larger clitoris and a steady, rather than cyclic, hormonal production characteristic of males). These females also exhibit male-typical sexual behavior, including mounting other females. Interestingly, infant males injected with estradiol (a female hormone) exhibit no changes in the volume of the MPO. Testosterone, a steroid hormone produced in the testis and, therefore, eliminated when males are castrated, is the source of these organizing brain effects that affect sexual behavior in the adult animal.

Exposure to estrogens (a group of steroid hormones released by the ovaries, such as estradiol) during the early sensitive period also leads to permanent changes in brain structure and behavior. There are estrogen membrane receptors distributed over practically the entire developing telencephalon. These receptors are particularly abundant in another hypothalamic region known as the ventromedial nucleus (VMH). The VMH is larger in females than in males, and it is an important component of the neural circuit controlling female sexual behavior. Female rats respond to estrogen injections in the VMH by increasing their responsivity to males and exhibiting a behavior known as lordosis. *Lordosis* involves the arching of the female's back and the movement of the tail to one side; both of these responses expose the genital area, thus facilitating mounting and penetration by the male. Estrogens appears to be responsible, at least in part, for sexual dimorphism in the VMH of rats. But estrogens have been implicated in a number of additional developmental processes, including the stimulation of neuronal growth and the prevention of neuronal death (Toran-Allerand 1995). Estrogens achieve some of their effects by interacting with receptors of neurotrophins such as the nerve growth factor cited previously. Estrogens and neurotrophins stimulate transcription of an overlapping set of genes during development.

Testosterone and estrogens also have organizing effects in the development of *singing behavior* in birds (see ***Chapter 12, section 3,*** pp. 468–482). In songbirds, only males sing to advertise their presence in a particular territory or to attract females into their territory. Whereas females respond to a male's singing, demonstrating that they can recognize the song, they do not themselves sing. However, zebra finch females (*Poephila guttata*) treated with either testosterone or estrogens shortly after hatching develop the ability to sing as adults. In other words, their brain is masculinized by these hormones. A series of brain sites involved in the circuit controlling song production are significantly enlarged in males, relative to females (Nottebohm & Arnold 1976). These differences arise because of the direct action of estrogens (Gurney & Konishi 1980). In birds, males are characterized by possessing two X chromosomes, or XX, whereas females are XY (notice that this is opposite to mammals, for which males are XY and females XX). The XX conformation permits the production of abundant circulating estrogens, which then facilitate the growth and differentiation of neurons in the song-production circuit. Testosterone, on the other hand, seems to be important in song production in adult males. Interestingly, testosterone facilitates singing in estrogen-treated females but not in normal females, an effect that nicely illustrates the organizing (estrogens) and activating (testosterone) effects of hormones on brain and behavior. The female brain has to be first masculinized by estrogen in order for testosterone to facilitate singing.

4. KEY TERMS

acceleration 381
activating effects 395
antennapedia mutant 370
apoptosis 390
behavioral neophenotypes 376
biogenetic law 376
bithorax mutant 368
blastopore 365
blastula stage 364
body plan (or Bauplan) 367
canalization 373
cellular differentiation 365
chemoaffinity hypothesis 389
cleavage 363
coaction 372
Cope's law 381
cortex 390
development 362
developmental constraints 391
diploblastic animals 365
dwarfism 377
ectoderm 365
embryo 362
endoderm 365
environmental enrichment 394
epigenesis 372
evolution 362
fertilization 362
gastrula stage 365
genetic assimilation 373
giantism 377
heterochrony 376
homeotic (or Hox) genes 368
hormones 395
hypermorphosis 381
lordosis 397
mesoderm 365
morphogenesis 365
morula stage 364
mosaic evolution 377
nature-nurture dichotomy 371
neoteny 379
neuromeres 387
neurotrophins 391
neurula stage 365
nucleus 390
ontogeny 362
organizing effects 396
organogenesis 365
paedomorphosis 377
paralogous genes 387
peramorphosis 381
pharyngula stage 367
phylogeny 362
phylotypic stage 367
phylum 365
postdisplacement 379
predisplacement 381
principle of terminal addition 376
progenesis 381
segmentation 387
segmented germ band stage 367
sensitive period 384
sexual maturity 377
singing behavior 397
triploblastic animals 365
zootype 370
zygote 362

5. REFERENCES

Arnold, A. P., & Breedlove, S. M. (1985). Organizational and activational effects of sex steroids on brain and behavior: A reanalysis. *Hormones & Behavior,* **19,** 469–498.

Baldwin, J. M. (1902). *Development and evolution.* New York: Macmillan.

Barnes, C. A. (1991). Memory changes with age: Neurobiological correlates. In J. L. Martinez, Jr. & R. P. Kesner (Eds.), *Learning and memory. A biological view.* (2nd ed., pp. 259–296). San Diego: Academic Press.

Black, J. E., & Greenough, W. T. (1991). Developmental approaches to the memory process. In J. L. Martinez, Jr. & R. P. Kesner (Eds.), *Learning and memory. A biological view.* (2nd ed., pp. 61–91). San Diego: Academic Press.

Brusca, R. C., & Brusca, G. J. (1990). *Invertebrates.* Sunderland: Sinauer.

Carpecchi, M. R. (1997). The role of Hox genes in hindbrain development. In W. M. Cowan, T. M. Jessell, & S. L. Zipursky (Eds.), *Molecular and cellular approaches to neural development* (pp. 334–355). New York: Oxford University Press.

Clayton, N. S., & Krebs, J. R. (1994). Hippocampal growth and attrition in birds affected by experience. *Proceedings of the National Academy of Sciences* (USA), **91,** 7410–7414.

Deacon, T. W. (1994). The human brain. In S. Jones, R. Martin, & D. Pilbeam (Eds.), *The Cambridge encyclopedia of human evolution* (pp. 115–123). Cambridge: Cambridge University Press.

Finlay, B. L., & Darlington, R. B. (1995). Lined regularities in the development and evolution of mammalian brains. *Science,* **268,** 1578–1584.

Garstand, W. (1922). The theory of recapitulation: A critical re-statement of the biogenetic law. *Journal of the Linnean Society of London, Zoology,* **35,** 81–101.

Garstand, W. (1928). The morphology of the Tunicata, and its bearing on the phylogeny of the Chordata. *Quarterly Journal of Microscopical Science,* **75,** 51–187.

Gerhart, J., & Kirschner, M. (1997). *Cells, embryos, and evolution.* Malden: Blackwell Science.

Goodman, C. S., & Tessier-Lavigne, M. (1997). Molecular mechanisms of axon guidance and target recognition. In W. M. Cowan, T. M. Jessell, & S. L. Zipursky (Eds.), *Molecular and cellular approaches to neural development* (pp. 108–178). New York: Oxford University Press.

Goy, R. W., & McEwen, B. S. (1980). *Sexual differentiation of the brain.* Cambridge: MIT Press.

Gould, S. J. (1977). *Ontogeny and phylogeny.* Cambridge: Harvard University Press.

Gottlieb, G. (1992). *Individual development and evolution. The genesis of novel behavior.* Oxford: Oxford University Press.

Gurney, M., & Konishi, M. (1980). Hormone-induced sexual differentiation of brain and behavior in zebra finches. *Science,* **208,** 1380–1382.

James, F. C. (1983). Environmental component of morphological differentiation in birds. *Science,* **221,** 184–186.

Kaufman, T. C., Seeger, M. A., & Olsen, G. (1990). Molecular and genetic organization of the *Antennapedia* gene complex of *Drosophila melanogaster. Advances in Genetics,* **27,** 309–362.

King, M. C., & Wilson, A. C. (1975). Evolution at two levels: Molecular similarities and biological differences between humans and chimpanzees. *Science,* **188,** 107–116.

Krech, D., Rosenzweig, M. R., & Bennett, E. L. (1962). Relations between brain chemistry and problem-solving among rats raised in enriched and impoverished environments. *Journal of Comparative & Physiological Psychology,* **55,** 801–807.

Levi-Montalcini, R. (1987). The nerve growth factor 35 years later. *Science,* **237,** 1154–1162.

Matsuda, R. (1987). *Animal evolution in changing environments wth special reference to abnormal metamorphosis.* New York: Wiley & Sons.

McKinney, M. L., & Schoch, R. M. (1985). Titanothere allometry, heterochrony, and biomechanics: Revising an evolutionary classic. *Evolution,* **39,** 1352–1363.

McNamara, K. J. (1986). A guide to the nomenclature of heterochrony. *Journal of Paleontology,* **60,** 4–13.

Merimee, T. J., Zapf, J., Hewlet, B., & Cavalli-Sforza, L. L. (1987). Insulin-like growth factors in pygmies: The role of puberty in determining final stature. *New England Journal of Medicine,* **316,** 906–911.

Meyer, A. (1987). Phenotypic plasticity and heterochrony in *Cichlasoma managuense* (Pisces, Cichlidae) and their implications for speciation in cichlid fishes. *Evolution,* **41,** 1357–1369.

Morey, D. F. (1994). The early evolution of the domestic dog. *American Scientist,* **82,** 336–347.

Nielsen, C. (1995). *Animal evolution. Interrelationships of the living phyla.* Oxford: Oxford University Press.

Nottebohm, F., & Arnold, A. P. (1976). Sexual dimorphism in vocal control areas of the songbird brain. *Science,* **194,** 211–213.

Raff, R. A., & Kaufman, T. C. (1983). *Embryos, genes, and evolution.* Bloomington: Indiana University Press.

Renner, M. J., & Rosenzweig, M. R. (1987). *Enriched and impoverished environments: Effects on brain and behavior.* New York: Springer-Verlag.

Sanes, J. R., & Scheller, R. H. (1997). Synapse formation: A molecular perspective. In W. M. Cowan, T.

M. Jessell, & S. L. Zipursky (Eds.), *Molecular and cellular approaches to neural development* (pp. 179–219). New York: Oxford University Press.

Saunders, J. W. (1970). *Patterns and principles of animal development.* New York: Macmillan.

Scott, J. P., & Fuller, J. L. (1965). *Genetics and the social behavior of the dog.* Chicago: University of Chicago Press.

Sperry, R. W. (1963). Chemoaffinity in the orderly growth of nerve fiber patterns and connections. *Proceedings of the National Academy of Sciences USA,* **50,** 703–710.

Slack, J. M. W., Holland, P. W. H., & Graham, C. F. (1993). The zootype and the phylotypic stage. *Nature,* **361,** 490–492.

Toran-Allerand, C. D. (1995). Developmental interactions of estrogens with neurotrophins and their receptors. In P. E. Micevych & R. P. Hammer, Jr. (Eds.), *Neurobiological effects of sex steroid hormones* (pp. 391–411). Cambridge: Cambridge University Press.

Trut, L. N. (1999). Early canid domestication: The farm-fox experiment. *American Scientist,* **87,** 160–169.

Vidal, F. (1994). *Piaget before Piaget.* Cambridge: Harvard University Press.

Waddington, C. H. (1959). Canalization of development and genetic assimilation of acquired characters. *Nature,* **183,** 1654–1655.

Weiss, P. (1959). Cellular dynamics. *Review of Modern Physics,* **31,** 11–20.

CHAPTER 11

Early Learning and Behavior

MAIN GENERALIZATIONS OF CHAPTER 11

- *The sequence of emerging behavioral capacities starts with spontaneous movement unguided by sensory feedback, continues with the sequential activation of various sensory systems, and ends with the emergence of learning and cognitive capacities.*
- *Some species-typical behavior patterns emerge more or less abruptly in development. For the most part, however, behavioral repertoires increase gradually in complexity and degree of integration during development.*
- *Early experience may determine adult behavior in a variety of contexts. However, some early experiences are subject to infantile amnesia.*

Developing animals encounter environmental demands that are different from those that characterize their adult environment. Therefore, they must be appropriately equipped to deal successfully with these developmental transitions. Probably the greatest rates of mortality are observed in populations of young animals (larvae, embryos, infants), which implies that strong selective pressures are at work during early periods of development. Therefore, it would be naive to think of an infant animal merely as an incomplete adult. Rather, the developing animal must be equipped with a set of capacities, including behavioral capacities, that would allow it to survive and develop until sexual maturity is reached. Such traits can be referred to as *ontogenetic adaptations,* and the environment in which a developing animal must survive can be called an *ontogenetic niche.*

Most animals develop through stages that define a succession of ontogenetic niches. For example, tunicates are sessile as adults—that is, they live attached to a substrate in the sea floor; as larvae, however, they are active and free-swimming animals (see ***Figure 10.9,*** p. 379). Similarly, most amphibian species, including frogs and salamanders, live underwater as larvae (the tadpole stage) but develop into terrestrial animals as adults; and fully terrestrial caterpillars develop into free-flying butterflies. Transitions like these involve substantial morphological and functional changes, given the disparate nature of the environments in which these animals live at different stages of their development. Animals are said to go through a process of *metamorphosis*—that is, a morphological and functional reorganization that eliminates adaptations appropriate for the early environment (e.g., the tadpole's gills), while inducing traits that will be needed in the new environment (e.g., the frog's legs).

A substantial amount of information on behavioral development has been collected over the decades by comparative and developmental psychologists. I begin by focusing on the development of individual behavioral capacities in this chapter and continue, in ***Chapter 12,*** with the role of early experience in the development of social behavior. As usual, progress in our understanding of developmental processes depends on the intensive study of a relatively small set of model species. The ready access to the avian embryo in the egg has made birds, and in particular the chicken, a useful model system. But techniques for studying mammalian fetuses have also allowed the stimulation and recording of behaviors during normal development (e.g., in humans), as well as experimental, in-utero techniques that expose the embryo for observation (e.g., in rats). These studies are providing a detailed description of the behavioral, sensory, and learning capacities of highly immature vertebrates.

1. PRENATAL AND PREHATCHING BEHAVIOR

1.a. Mammalian Patterns of Development. Mammals do not metamorphose during development but nonetheless go through drastic transitions in ontogenetic niches. Three major groups of living mammals are segregated mainly on the basis of their reproductive biology: the Prototheria, or egg-laying mammals of Australia and New Guinea; the Metatheria, or marsupials from Australia and the Americas; and the Eutheria, or placentals, with a worldwide distribution. Each represents a unique pattern of development that correlates with often unique behavioral and physiological needs (Eisenberg 1981).

In the Australian platypus and echidnas, the embryo develops inside an egg, from which it hatches much like a reptile. Little is known about these unique egg-laying mammals. Fertilized eggs are retained in the uterus for a few days, and then the female lays them in either a nest (platypus) or a pouch (echidna), where they are incubated. The pouch of echidnas is a transient folding of the ventral skin, present only during the breeding season. During this period of incubation, the developing monotreme feeds on the yolk stored in the egg, as does a reptile. After hatching, there is a relatively extensive period of intensive maternal care, during which the young lick the milk that drops from the loosely scattered mammary glands (monotremes lack nipples). Monotreme young are extremely immature at birth, and they have been observed to open their eyes for the first time about 80 days after hatching.

Marsupial mammals are also born in a highly immature state of development; some of the internal organs are still developing, and so newborns are generally considered to be embryos (Tyndale-Biscoe 1973). However, marsupial embryos exhibit a number of traits that are precociously developed (i.e., acceleration in the language of heterochrony; see ***Chapter 10***). As shown in ***Figure 11.1,*** these embryos exhibit well-developed forelimbs with digits and claws, and a functional olfactory system. The embryo is equipped with an advanced stomach and pancreas, and well-developed musculature in the shoulders and mouth. Spinal reflexes allow the head and forelimbs to move in alternation. These are adaptations for a relatively constant feature of marsupial biology: During birth, embryos move out of the mother's uterus by propelling themselves with their forelimbs until they reach the marsupium, where they typically attach to a nipple. Mothers usually have fewer nipples than embryos, which introduces a strong selective pressure for accelerated development of traits that facilitate locomotion from the uterus to the marsupium. Marsupials complete their development while in the pouch, where they can exhibit a substantial rate of growth; this is particularly obvious in species of large body size, like the kangaroos.

Placental mammals are retained in the mother's uterus for a longer period and thus exhibit a more complete degree of maturation at birth than marsupials. The birth of a placental mammal is more comparable to the exit from the pouch of a marsupial than it is to its birth. Intrauterine development is usually classified into two general periods; an embryonic period, during which the various bodily tissues differentiate and the internal organs are established; and a fetal period, during which the animal grows in size and the internal systems became functional. As will be shown in the following section, fetuses exhibit a variety of behavioral capacities.

The large variation in body size at birth in placental mammals correlates positively with the large variation in body size of adults. At one extreme, the smallest living mammal—the adult white-toothed shrew, *Suncus etruscus* (Insectivora)—weighs about 2 g and produces a young of about 0.2 g at birth; at the other, the largest mammal (and the largest animal, extinct or alive, known to scientists)—the adult blue whale, *Balaenoptera musculus* (Cetacea)—weighs at least 100,000,000 g and gives rise to neonates that weigh as much as 3,000,000 g! Species also vary in the extent to which neonates are immature at birth. In *altricial* species, the young are born with eyes closed, little or no hair, and minimal locomotor abilities; these mammals (like many rodents, for example) complete their development in a nest, usually in close contact

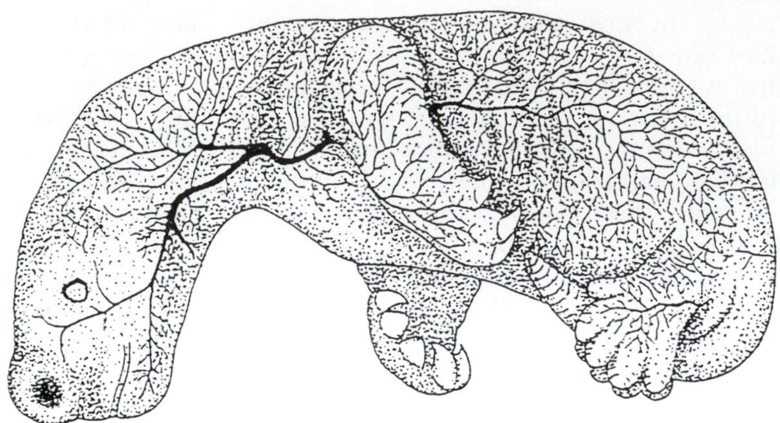

FIGURE 11.1. Newborn embryo of the brush possum, *Trichosurus vulpecula* (Tyndale-Biscoe 1973). Notice the well-developed forelimbs, including the claws. The olfactory system is also functional. These traits contrast with the embryonic state of other parts of the organism. Marsupial embryos free themselves from the amnion and emerge with their heads first. The mother usually licks the amniotic fluid and spreads it throughout the abdominal area, a behavior that probably facilitates the embryo's orientation toward the marsupium. The embryo grasps the mother's fur and advances toward the marsupium with alternating forelimb movements. The entire trip may take as much as 5 min.

with the mother and siblings. In *precocial* species, such as many ungulates (e.g., horses, antelopes, elephants), the young are born in a relatively mature state of development. Motor coordination and active behavior are typically seen within hours of birth.

In all cases, the birth of a mammal involves a sharp transition from a prenatal niche to a postnatal niche that differ in many important elements. A constant element of both niches is the presence of the mother, which may provide incubation, as in monotremes, or the marsupium and intrauterine environments within which marsupial and placental embryos develop. Mothers also provide milk for the newborn, which extends the mother-infant bond considerably and demands a specific behavioral repertoire from the infant, including such abilities as mother recognition, orienting responses (to the mother and to the nipple), and the sucking response.

1.b. Spontaneous Movements. All vertebrate embryos exhibit "spontaneous" activity patterns that occur even in the absence of sensory input and must therefore be considered to be nonreflexive movements. The German biologist William Preyer [1841–1897] noticed that the chick embryo exhibits movements before it responds to sensory stimulation and suggested that such movement occurs in the absence of sensory feedback. This is known as the *motor primacy* *theory* (Gottlieb 1976). Definitive evidence for spontaneous movements was provided much later, also in experiments with chicks.

In one of such studies (Hamburger et al. 1966), 40-hr-old chick embryos received a surgical section of the dorsal spinal roots that carry sensory information from the legs into the spinal cord, as well as a spinal section that isolated the spinal cord from the rest of the CNS. This deafferentation and spinal preparation allowed for the observation of leg movements in the absence of peripheral sensory input and brain modulatory input into the isolated spinal neurons. Leg movements in these animals were about the same as in spinal animals that were not deafferented, thus suggesting that random leg activity occurs in the absence of sensory feedback. The frequency of leg movements in both of these groups decreased after day 15 of embryonic development, suggesting either the spreading of a degenerative neural process initiated by the experimental lesion or the normal onset of reflexes that could not occur in deafferented animals.

The importance of these spontaneous movements is not entirely understood. Movement may stimulate the maturation of a variety of structures and organs in the developing embryo. For example, in birds, leg movements may stimulate the differentiation and growth of specific tissues, prevent muscular atrophy, and facilitate hatching; whereas in mammals, the inflow and outflow of amniotic fluid through the mouth may provide important stimuli for the coordination of perinatal behaviors such as sucking.

1.c. Behavior and Sensory Systems. Gottlieb (1976) noted that sensory systems develop in a fixed sequence, although the timing of development may be different across species. For example, both mammalian and avian embryos respond initially to tactile stimuli and later to vestibular (postural changes), auditory, and visual stimuli. In some species, such as our own, all four of these sensory modalities are functional before birth to some degree, whereas in others, such as the rat, the auditory and visual systems mature largely after birth. The embryo is exposed to a variety of sensory influences, some originating in its own movements and others coming from the environment. Mothers provide a constant source of sensory stimulation. Bird embryos can detect the calls produced by adults, by other embryos in the nest, and by themselves; these sources of auditory experience may have a lasting influence on the developing chicks, aiding in their subsequent ability to respond to species-typical calls (Gottlieb 1991). The human fetus is sensitive to the mother's voice (Fifer & Moon 1988) and, in rats, pregnant mothers provide substantial amounts of experience by engaging in a variety of behaviors that mechanically stimulate the fetus (Ronca et al. 1993; see ***Figure 5.8,*** p. 151, for an example involving newborn rats).

The mammalian fetus responds particularly well to chemical compounds, which is hardly surprising given its immersion in amniotic fluid during intrauterine development. The response of rat fetuses to chemical solutions delivered directly into their mouths demonstrates not only that these substances can be perceived but also that the fetus can discriminate some of them. For example, rat fetuses exposed to small amounts (about 20 μl) of either milk or a lemon solution during the last 3 days of gestation show an increase in general activity; in addition, these substances induce different responses (Smotherman & Robinson 1987). A rat fetus stretches in response to milk in its mouth, whereas it wipes its snout with its forepaws in response to lemon. The *stretching response* involves the dorsal flexion of the body accompanied by extension of the rear limbs. It is similar to that observed in a newborn rat exposed to milk ejection from the mother's nipple, and it facilitates the embryo's contact with the nipple. The *wiping response* involves one or both arms sliding toward the snout, and it can be elicited by other solutions with a strong olfactory component (e.g., mint). Both stretching and wiping responses rarely occur before gestation day 20 and then emerge at this point more or less abruptly. The degree of motor coordination evidenced by these responses differs from the generally unspecific nature of movement in rat fetuses. Such coordination, their sudden emergence, and their functional value suggest that they are *species-typical behavioral patterns*.

Birth and hatching also engage specific behavioral patterns, as well as provide additional sources of experience. Birth is a particularly salient and important event for a mammal, as shown by Molina and Chotro (1991) in an ingenious use of learning techniques. If a relatively innocuous stimulus (called the conditioned stimulus, or CS) occurs right before an important one (called the unconditioned stimulus, or US), the initially innocuous event may acquire control over certain responses. For example, I may salivate when a friend says the word "pizza" (a CS) at lunchtime because this word has been paired many times with the actual taste of pizza (the US) in my past experience. This procedure, known as *classical* (or *Pavlovian*) *conditioning* (see ***Chapter 13***), can be used to determine if a particular event, such as the birth experience, has US properties.

In one experiment, rat fetuses were exposed to both an alcohol and a lemon solution in gestation day 21 (usually, the last day of pregnancy for a rat). In one group—let's call it Group A–L alcohol was administered 40 min before cesarean delivery, whereas lemon was administered 10 min before cesarean delivery. In contrast, in Group L–A the temporal arrangement was the opposite. It is known that the closer in time the CS is to the US, the stronger the conditioning to the CS. Thus, it was expected that, after delivery, the rat pups would respond more to whichever solution, A or L, had been administered closer in time to delivery (i.e., 10 min, rather than 40 min). About 5 hr after delivery, the pups were placed inside an incubator, and their movements were automatically recorded during a 3-min baseline period without stimulation, followed by a 3-min stimulation period with either alcohol or lemon scents. As shown in ***Figure 11.2,*** the change in activity from the baseline to the stimulation period was greater in each group when the test scent was the one administered 10 min before delivery than when the test scent was the one administered 40 min before delivery. This result, and others obtained under similar conditions, suggest that the stimulation associated with birth in a mammal is sufficiently salient and important to act as a US and support learning. Several obvious sources of stimulation during birth may provide the basis for a motivationally significant event, including mechanical stimuli, thermal stimuli, and physiological states derived from respiratory changes (e.g., hypoxia). However, it is not known whether such learning would have any impact on the animal's behavior beyond the effects that could be detected relatively immediately after birth.

The hatching behavior of birds is also interesting because it engages a repertoire of relatively specific responses. For example, embryos exhibit head and leg movements that eventually result in the breaking of the eggshell. These responses may also be ac-

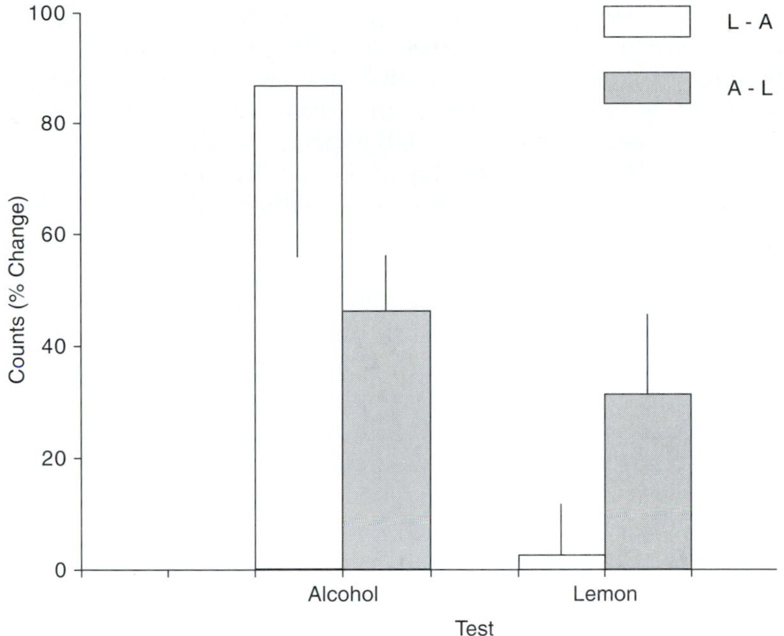

FIGURE 11.2. Motivational impact of birth-related stimulation (Molina & Chotro 1991). Two groups of fetuses (gestation day 21) were exposed to alcohol (A) and lemon (L) solutions, applied in the oral region. The solutions were applied either 40 min or 10 min before cesarean delivery (e.g., L-A means that lemon was applied 40 min before delivery, whereas alcohol was applied 10 min before delivery). In a subsequent test administered 5 hr after delivery, animals exposed to one of the odors exhibited significantly more activation when the test odor was the one administered in closed temporal contiguity to delivery (10 min) than when it was the temporally remote (40 min) odor. This result suggests that the pairing of an odor with delivery cues endows the odor with associative properties, therefore demonstrating that delivery cues are motivationally important.

companied by hatching vocalizations. Head movements bring the beak into contact with the eggshell, plus repetitive extension and flexion of the legs also push against the shell. Interestingly, these responses can be elicited after hatching by adjusting the posture of the chick (Bekoff & Kauer 1982). The key stimuli are provided by the restraint and bending of the chick's neck to one side; this posture, without any changes in other bodily parts, induce synchronized leg movements similar to those observed before hatching. If these stimuli originating in the twisted neck are eliminated (e.g., by local anesthesia), then leg movements are disrupted. Obviously, in the normal chick the movements cease after hatching because the animal is freed from the restraints of the egg.

1.c. Fetal Learning. There is now substantial evidence about the prenatal learning capacity of mammals, particularly in rats and humans. The question is no longer whether fetal learning occurs, but how complex prenatal learning abilities are. As I pointed out above, the ontogenetic niche of a developing fetus is characterized by its immersion in amniotic fluid inside the mother, so it should be able to demonstrate significant learning abilities to associate chemical (gustatory and olfactory) stimuli. This ability can, in fact, be demonstrated in rat fetuses given a relatively restricted amount of practice, which suggests the fetus learns readily.

In a set of experiments, Robinson et al. (1993) exposed rat fetuses in their 20th day of gestation to presentations of an artificial nipple applied to the oral region (the CS) and milk delivered into the mouth (the US). ***Figure 11.3-a*** represents the basic features of the design followed in this experiment. In the experimental group, three such CS-US pairings were administered at 5-min intervals. Notice, however, that the goal of such an experiment is to determine whether the fetus learns to respond to the CS because of its temporal contiguity with the US and not simply because it is exposed three times to these events. Therefore, the behavior of these animals is compared to that of animals that received both the CS and US but in an unpaired fashion—that is, separated in time by at least 2.5 min. Paired and unpaired groups are thus exposed to the same number of individual events, but they differ in terms of the temporal relationship between these events. In addition, groups exposed only to the CS and only to the US were included to assess possible changes in behavior that occur when only one of the two stimuli is presented. (The issue of control conditions in classical conditioning is described in detail in ***Chapter 13, section 2.a.,*** pp. 495–497)

In a single test trial, all the subjects were reexposed to the artificial nipple used as the CS, and their behavior was carefully recorded. For those fetuses exposed to paired CS-US experience, the artificial nipple developed the ability to suppress the wiping response, which occurred in less than 5% of the subjects in this condition. By contrast, 60% or more of the subjects in the unpaired, CS-only, and US-only control conditions exhibited the wiping response. Those fetuses given paired experience seem to have learned to expect a positive outcome (i.e., milk) following the presentation of the CS, such that it suppressed a response designed to rid the animal from a solution applied to the oral cavity. Such positive outcomes are referred to as *appetitive stimuli* because they induce general approach tendencies.

Just as neutral stimuli can acquire a positive value by virtue of being paired with an appetitive US, they can also acquire negative value if they predict the impending presentation of an event that causes some type of discomfort. Contact with an irritating substance, such as the lemon solution mentioned before, induces responses that tend to rid the animal of the stimulus (e.g., wiping responses) and generates a substantial amount of activity. Such outcomes are referred to as *aversive stimuli.* In one experiment (Smotherman & Robinson 1991), a group of rat fetuses (20th gestation day) was exposed to 10 μl oral injections of a sucrose solution (the CS) followed seconds later by a lemon solution (the US). After three such pairings, the activity level in the presence of the CS was measured and compared to that of animals exposed to the same events but in reverse (i.e., first the US and then the CS), to the CS only, to the US only, and to the CS followed by an innocuous saline solution. ***Figure 11.3-b*** represents the basic features of the design followed in this aversive condi-

(a) Appetitive learning

Results Wiping response to nipple significantly suppressed after PAIRED training.

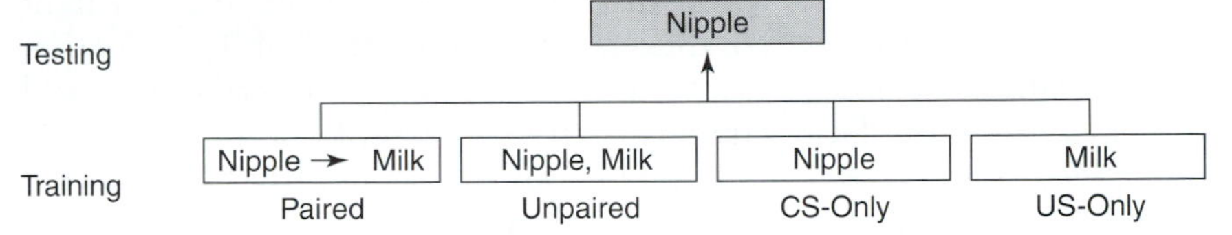

(b) Aversive learning

Results Activity after sucrose presentation significantly increased in PAIRED condition.

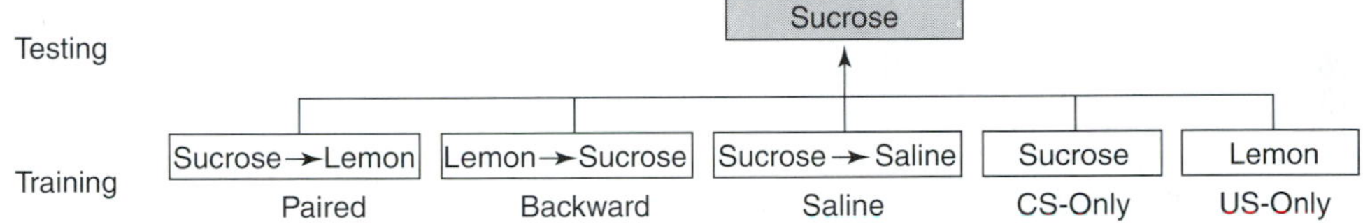

FIGURE 11.3. Schematic representation of the experimental designs used to demonstrate appetitive and aversive learning in the rat fetus. ***(a)*** Appetitive learning is demonstrated by pairing an artificial nipple applied to the mouth (the CS) with milk (the US). This experience leads to a significant degree of suppression of the wiping response in a subsequent test, compared with various control groups (Robinson et al. 1993). ***(b)*** Aversive learning is demonstrated by pairing sucrose (the CS) with lemon (the US), both applied to the oral region of the rat fetus. In a subsequent test, sucrose induces more activity after paired presentations than after various control conditions (Smotherman & Robinson 1991).

tioning experiment. The results indicated that the animals exposed to the CS-US pairings responded significantly more to the sucrose solution CS than any of the control animals. Rat fetuses, therefore, are capable of both appetitive and aversive associative learning at a time in their development when their brain is undergoing a substantial amount of maturation and differentiation. This demonstration of fetal learning abilities relies on the presentation of chemical stimuli for which the mammalian fetus appears to be prepared; both its intrauterine and perinatal niches involve the processing of chemical stimuli (amniotic fluid and milk, respectively) that are critical for the animal's survival.

Human fetuses are notoriously capable of responding to, and learning about, acoustic signals, as I mentioned earlier. Obviously, a salient aspect of their ontogenetic niche is the verbal behavior of their mothers, which can be clearly perceived by the developing fetus in the womb. But acoustic recordings from within the amniotic cavity show that noises from the mother's heartbeat and digestive processes are also salient, as are the voices of other people. Obviously, the fact that the stimuli are present does not necessarily mean that the fetus can perceive them, and this issue of perception is much more difficult to tackle. What is needed is a way of assessing the degree of responsiveness of the fetus when exposed to various stimuli. Several measures have been used in such studies, including changes in heart rate, respiratory frequency, and direct observation of behavior via ultrasound imaging.

A popular procedure for studying learning in the human fetus is based on the phenomenon of *habituation* (see **Chapter 7, section 3.a.,** pp. 244–247). Essentially, the repeated presentation of one stimulus leads to a decrease in the frequency or strength of the initial response to that stimulus; the response recovers after exposure to a novel stimulus (dishabituation) and also after a period of rest (spontaneous recovery). Habituation of the fetus's cardiac rate can be induced with verbal stimuli, such as a sentence or a pair of syllables, repeatedly presented through a speaker located in front of the mother's abdomen (Lecanuet et al. 1992). Typically, the initial cardiac response exhibits a deceleration, although a few cases may actually show an increase in heart rate. With repeated stimulation, however, the response eventually recovers its baseline rate thus providing evidence of habituation in the fetus. Interestingly, if the fetus has habituated to the repeated presentation of a pair of syllables, such as [ba] [bi], reversing the sequence to [bi] [ba] restores the initial response (i.e., dishabituation).

1.e. Long-Term Effects of Early Experience. Many of the topics covered previously clearly demonstrate that highly immature animals can behave in an adaptive fashion. But early influences can also have effects on behavior at subsequent stages of development. In insects, experience during the larval stage may affect various aspects of adult behavior after metamorphosis, including habitat selection and host selection in parasitic species (Caubet et al. 1992). For example, characteristics of the larval environment such as its temperature and light conditions may influence habitat selection in the fly *Drosophila pseudoobscura,* and chemical stimuli present during larval development may subsequently influence the choice of a new nesting site in the ant *Formica polyctena.*

There is also evidence that behavioral preferences induced by conditioning procedures in immature organisms can exert an effect on the choice behavior of adults even after metamorphosis. For example, larvae of the grain beetle (*Tenebrio molitor*) reinforced with food for turning in a particular direction in a T-maze, later show savings in the learning of the same task as adults, compared to untrained larvae (Alloway 1972). Similarly, larvae of the crested newt (*Triturus cristatus*) can be rapidly trained in a visual discrimination task in which approach and contact to one of two small geometrical figures is followed by food, whereas contact with the other figure is nonrewarded (Hershkowitz & Samuel 1973). Newts display a characteristic snapping response to foodlike objects, and the frequency of this response can be increased by food reinforcement. Interestingly, when tested after metamorphosis, newts responded on more than 75% of the trials (which were now nonrewarded) to what had been the correct stimulus during larval training.

Amphibian embryos are also capable of learning by mere exposure to the stimulus during development. For example, injecting orange extract into the eggs of frog embryos (*Rana temporaria*) results in a preference for locations flavored with that odor in both tadpoles and adult frogs (Hepper & Waldman 1992). Since many amphibian species deposit their eggs in ponds and streams, learning the chemical features of the embryonic environment may influence the adults' selection of sites for oviposition. Similarly, chemical stimuli of maternal origin may be responsible in amphibians for the development of *kin recognition,* that is, the ability to discriminate relatives from nonrelatives (Waldman 1981). For example, tadpoles of the toad *Bufo americanus* reared in isolation can discriminate full siblings (same mother and father) from half siblings with the same father, but not from half siblings with the same mother. These results suggest that recognition is mediated by a factor acquired through the mother. Such *maternal factors* include substances from the mother's body that contribute to the formation of the egg and to which the embryo is exposed during development.

In mammals, even the relative *intrauterine position* of the fetus may have important consequences for the adult organism. The intrauterine niche of a pregnant female mouse (*Mus musculus*) is characterized by the presence of several embryos that differ, among other things, in their gender. Since male and female embryos produce different hormones, and these tend to spread in the amniotic fluid forming chemical gradients, fetuses may be exposed to different hormonal influences and to various degrees, depending on the sex of adjacent embryos. Hormones influence neural maturation and, therefore, can affect adult behavior. For example, adult male mice prefer to mate with females that developed as embryos without adjacent males rather than with females that developed in utero with two adjacent males (vom Saal & Bronson 1980). The latter females may present signs of masculinization in the anatomy of their genital organs as a result of exposure to greater levels of circulating androgens during embryonic development.

While it is correct to state that early experience may have long-lasting behavioral consequences, it would be a mistake to conclude that this is always the case. Experience with many early events seem to be substantially forgotten by the adult organism. More about this phenomenon, called infantile amnesia, in ***section 2.f.***, below.

2. INFANT LEARNING AND BEHAVIOR

2.a. Patterns of Behavioral Development. Behavioral development can be profitably described within a naturalistic approach in which the emphasis lies in the description of emergent behavioral patterns and in the order in which such behaviors appear in young animals. Ideally, one would like to have access to the animals in their natural conditions of development, but this is usually difficult or even impossible. Instead, comparative psychologists set up seminatural conditions in a lab, where behavior can be documented in a detailed manner. Such studies are particularly valuable when they focus on species with relatively inaccessible lifestyles. Consider, for example, the blind mole rat, *Spalax ehrenbergi,* studied by Gazit and Terkel (1998).

Blind mole rats are fossorial—that is, they live permanently buried in underground tunnels without exits to the outside world. Fossorial habits have evolved independently in several families of rodents and insectivore mammals, which show extensive convergence in adaptations to that type of environment. The shape of the body, the size of the incisors, the loss or reduction of vision, and even the use of ground vibration as a means of communication are some of the adaptations that characterize blind mole rats. These animals are also solitary as adults, which raises the issue of dispersal from the nest. How do some of these behaviors develop?

Gazit and Terkel (1998) housed several pregnant females each in an enclosure involving five compartments connected by tubes to recreate conditions similar to those found in natural populations (see ***Figure 11.4-a***). Mothers could move in a section of

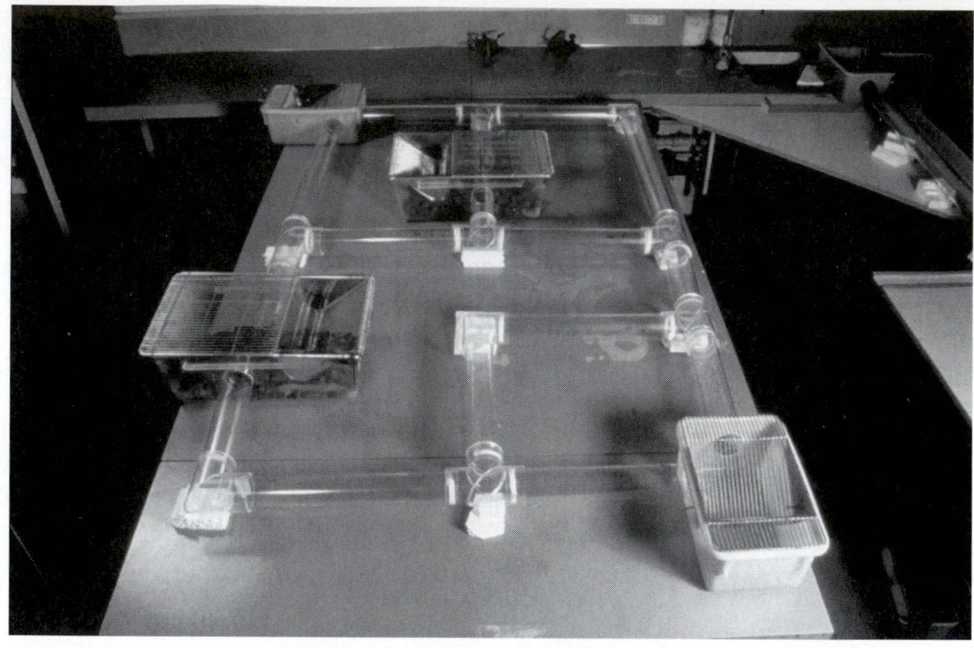

(a)

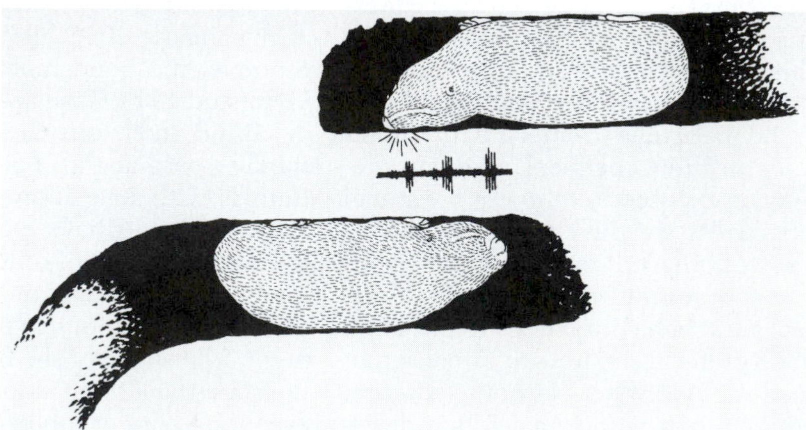

(b)

FIGURE 11.4. *(a)* Seminatural environment set up to study the development of behavior in the blind mole rat. *(b)* Ground vibration used for communication in blind mole rats. (Photographs courtesy of I. Gazit and J. Terkel; drawing by W. Ferguson.)

this environment, but a pair of barriers constrained the tube and prevented the mothers, but not the infants, from entering the other section (mothers were too large to fit through the openings in these barriers). Under these conditions, the date of first appearance of various behavioral patterns was determined as described in ***Table 11.1.*** In general terms, this pattern of development bears many similarities to that of other altricial mammals. For example, the initial weeks after birth are characterized by intensive maternal care, with the pups continuously occupying the nest area. After a month, infants venture out of the nest area and into the tunnels and begin to show more complex interactions. *Play behavior,* for example, appears at this point and is characterized by interactions between siblings involving pushing, pulling, and rolling together. Signs of *aggressive behavior* also appear after a month of life with exposure of the incisors. Aggressive interactions among siblings become more frequent after *weaning* and involve quick movements accompanied by bites and vocalizations. These behaviors are suppressed by the mother's presence and occur at a higher frequency if the pups are removed from the maternal nest. After the second month of life, the pups begin to be the target of aggressive actions by the mother, particularly male pups. Infants retreat to the nest area, but eventually they move to the side of the enclosure where mothers cannot enter, and there

TABLE 11.1 Age (in days) of First Appearance of Various Behaviors in Blind Mole Rats

Behavioral Patterns	*Average Age (days)*
Out of nest into adjacent tube	14.5
Eating solid food in nest	20.7
Gathering food and carrying to mother's nest	31.3
Grooming head with forepaws	31.8
Walking backwards in tunnel	32.5
Use of maternal toilet for excrement	33.0
Scattered digging in maternal cage	34.6
Jaw listening (jaw against tunnel to perceive vibrations)	35.6
Play among siblings	36.7
Exposing incisor teeth without biting	41.0
Weaning	44.0
Forming food storage separate from mother	45.4
Aggression among siblings	52.7
Head drumming (tapping head against tunnel ceiling)	56.5
Aggression between mother and pups	64.5
Sleeping in separate nest during night	66.4
Expulsion from maternal territory	70.3
Forming soil barrier at border of maternal territory	75.0
Duet head drumming between mother and pup	75.0
Urinating against soil barrier	102.0

Note. Weaning and dispersion are underlined as points of reference.

they establish their own territory. ***Figure 11.4-b*** shows the use of ground vibration for communication, a behavior that also emerges during the second month of life.

The transition from living in the mother's territory to living in their own territory is gradual and occurs over a period of 4 to 6 weeks. Interestingly, not only are mothers more aggressive toward their male offspring, but also it is the males that tend to establish themselves on the side of the enclosure where mothers cannot enter. Female infants remain in the mother's side and have to be eventually removed when maternal aggression becomes intense. In the natural environment, it is the males that disperse to more distant areas from the maternal one, whereas females tend to remain closer to the maternal site. It seems plausible that dispersal is mediated by maternal aggression of the type observed in this seminaturalistic study. This pattern of dispersal is quite common among mammals, and it can have important behavioral consequences (see, e.g., ***Chapter 4, section 4.f.***, pp. 115–117).

2.b. Sensorimotor Development. The previous example from the study of blind mole rats illustrates a general, and somewhat obvious, rule of development: Behavioral repertoires tend to become larger and more complex as the animal develops. Although some abrupt transitions do occur (as noted previously for the emergence of the stretching and wiping responses of rat fetuses), behavioral changes are generally gradual. This increase in the complexity of behavioral repertoires during development can be illustrated in terms of the type and degree of interaction of the animal with the objects located in its environment.

Object investigation has been studied in detail in rats (*Rattus norvegicus*), using a modification of the open-field test. The open-field is a simple and widely used apparatus for studying general activity in small animals, such as rodents. Typically, animals are placed in a circular or rectangular arena divided into several sectors, and the session is either taped for later analysis or behaviors are recorded by automatic devices such as photocells or computer software that can track the animals' positions and the types of their movements (e.g., sniffing, rearing, etc.). Since small rodents tend to hesitate to move about in open spaces, a modified open-field procedure consists of installing the home cage underneath the arena and providing a means for the animal to move from the cage to the arena and vice versa. This procedure allows for the emergence of exploratory behaviors that are less contaminated by fear or anxiety responses. Using such a procedure, Renner et al. (1992) found a progressively greater amount of object interaction as a function of age in rats. These animals were exposed to objects classified as either manipulable (e.g., light objects that rats could move about, such as a paper ball) or nonmanipulable (e.g., heavy objects, such as a piece of granite). The total amount of object contact, the number of bouts of object interaction, and length of the bouts all tended to increase with age. Not only was object interaction quantitatively greater in older rats, but the type of responses directed at the objects changed with age. Older, 90-day-old rats not only sniffed more at the objects but made paw contact, placing one or both forelimbs on the object more often than 30-day-old rats; these latter behaviors were seen rarely, if at all, in the younger animals.

Renner et al.'s study represents one of the two typical procedures for studying behavioral development and is referred to as a *cross-sectional design*. In such a design, independent groups of animals differing in age are observed under a certain set of conditions, such as in the open-field situation. One advantage of this design is that the animals are equally naive with respect to the testing situation, and so age differences cannot be attributed to prior experience with the test. An alternative research approach, called a *longitudinal design,* involves observing and describing developmental changes in behavior of a single group of animals. Observations can be scheduled at specific ages or time intervals, or they can be performed in a more or less continuous manner, as in the study with blind mole rats described in the previous section (see ***Table 11.1***).

Longitudinal procedures may be the best option when researchers deal with animals that are observed under natural conditions, that are expensive to keep and maintain, or that are listed as endangered species. For example, Potì and Spinozzi (1994) reported longitudinal observations on the sensorimotor development of chimpanzees (*Pan troglodytes*). *Sensorimotor intelligence* corresponds to the initial stages of intellectual development in the theory proposed by the Swiss developmental psychologist Jean Piaget [1896–1980]. Whereas this theory was aimed at understanding human intelligence, some of the processes postulated by Piaget to characterize a given stage of development have been studied with nonhuman animals. In this particular study, four infants reared by human caretakers were observed for variable periods during their early development, and the age of emergence of various reflexes and behavior was recorded. Sensorimotor development is divided into four stages; presumably, the order in which these stages unfold is relatively fixed and rigid, although the particular age at which behaviors typical of each stage emerge may vary depending on rearing conditions.

The first sensorimotor stage is characterized by reflexes such as sucking and grasping (closing the hand tightly when stimulated on the palm), which appear in full strength during the first week of life, and by the ability to visually follow a moving object evidenced after 4 weeks. The second sensorimotor stage is characterized by a tendency to "explore" objects with the mouth (or *mouthing,* which appears at about 9 weeks of age) and by increased hand-mouth (about 10 weeks) and hand-eye coordination (12 weeks). The third sensorimotor stage involves highly efficient reaching responses—that is, visually guided manual prehension of objects (20 weeks)—and the ability to follow with their eyes the position of objects that are moving rapidly in their visual field. The fourth stage of sensorimotor development is marked by the ability known as *object permanence* (36 weeks)—that is, the ability to look at the appropriate place in which an object that has moved into a hidden location will reappear. The order of development of the behaviors described previously is notoriously similar to that shown by human children, but there are also some differences. In the fourth stage, for example, human babies use so-called *object-object combinations* (e.g., using one object to modify another object, such as using a stick to push a ball) more frequently than do chimpanzees.

2.c. Attention, Habituation, and Latent Inhibition. All environments, no matter how simple and impoverished, include a variety of sensory influences. To the extent that animals have appropriate sensory receptors to detect these environmental influences, one major task consists of determining which stimulus must be actively processed and which can be safely ignored. This ability to orient to and to process particular stimuli is referred to as *attention.* Attention presupposes a certain degree of selectivity, which, in turn, implies that behavior is controlled only by a subset of all the stimuli available in the environment. A basic problem in the study of attention and other similar processes (e.g., learning, memory, motivation, etc.), is that the word "attention" refers to a brain process that is not itself directly observable but that must be inferred from behavioral changes. Psychologists refer to such terms as *intervening variables*—that is, theoretical constructs bearing explicit relationships with definable stimuli and observable responses that are postulated by the theorist to explain empirical observations (Tolman 1938).

Attentional processes are accessible for study when the animal can both perceive stimulus changes in its environment and react to at least some of these changes in some measurable manner. One such behavioral index of attention is the *orienting response,* that is, the ability of an animal to adjust the position of some of its sensory receptors such that contact with a potential source of stimulation is maximized. For example, an adult rat exposed to various types of sound exhibits postural adjustments ranging from a turn of the head in the direction of the source of the sound to a startle response if the stimulus is very intense. As pointed out previously (see ***section 1.c.***), audition develops in rats mostly after birth, so how soon can they orient toward a sound?

Experiments in which cellular recordings from the cochlear nerve (the VIII cranial nerve that conveys auditory information from the internal ear to the CNS) show that cells become responsive to intense noises around days 8 or 9 after birth. However, behavioral experiments demonstrate that postural orientation toward a source of sound emerges only by postnatal day 14 (Kelly et al. 1987). Such orientation depends on the comparison of auditory information detected by both ears; *binaural audition* is a major mechanism for locating the source of a sound in mammals. The accuracy of the orienting response is drastically diminished in monaural 17-day-old rats in which one of the two ear canals has been sutured.

As noted in ***Chapter 7,*** many stimuli that produce orienting and other types of responses after one or a few presentations may lose their eliciting properties after repeated presentations; this is the familiar phenomenon of habituation. Response habituation occurs because of changes in the CNS, and not because of such peripheral factors as sensory adaptation or muscular fatigue. This is demonstrated by the dishabituation effect, in which a habituated response recovers after exposure to a novel, relatively intense stimulus. Thus, habituation may be thought of as involving a decrement in attention—that is, a disruption of the stimulus's ability to evoke a response without affecting the animal's perception of the stimulus and without interfering with the animal's ability to behave if the situation changes.

The ontogeny of habituation has been extensively studied in rats under a variety of conditions. In one experimental preparation, infant rats of various ages are suspended in air and relatively immobilized while a forelimb is stimulated with mild electric shocks and its flexion recorded automatically (Stehouwer & Campbell 1978). Habituation of this leg-flexion reflex meets several of the properties outlined in ***Chapter 7, section 3.a.*** (pp. 244–247), including the following: Leg flexion declines with repeated stimulation in a negative exponential manner (property 1); the rate of habituation is faster with more frequent stimulus presentations (property 4) and with weaker stimuli (property 5); and the presentation of a strong stimulus produces the recovery of the flexion response (property 8). However, the pattern of development is anything but simple.

Figure 11.5 shows the results of varying the interstimulus interval for 3-, 6-, 10-, and 15-day-old rats, all preweanlings (weaning

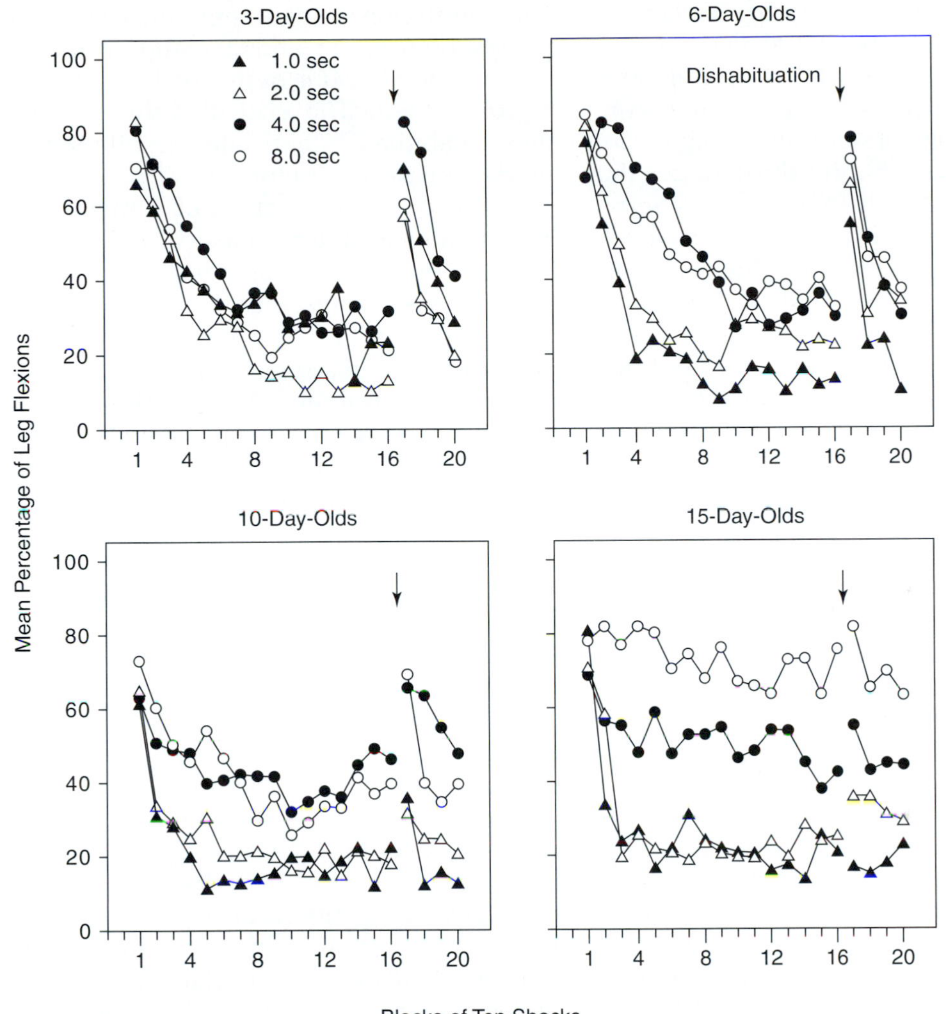

Figure 11.5. Habituation of the leg-flexion response in neonatal rats as a function of age (3-, 6-, 10-, and 15-day-olds) and interstimulus interval (1, 2, 4, or 8 s) (Stehouwer & Campbell 1978). The arrow marks the delivery of a stronger shock used to produce response dishabituation.

in rats occurs at about postnatal day 21). First, notice the exponential decay (property 1) that characterizes most functions. Second, also obvious is the dishabituating effect of a strong stimulus on the leg-flexion response (property 8). But third, notice that habituation is actually more efficient across values of interstimulus intervals (from 1 to 8 s) in younger rats than in older ones: 15-day-old rats barely habituate to a stimulus presented at a rate of once per 8 s, whereas 3-day-olds show impressive behavioral flexibility. As rats mature during these early postnatal days, they are more likely to experience sensitization as a result of repeated stimulation with electric shock. *Sensitization* refers to an increase in the response elicited by a repeatedly presented stimulus. It is often the case that the same stimulus (especially with intermediate intensities) can induce a mixture of habituation and sensitization, such that the actual response levels reflect a sort of algebraic summation of these opposing effects (Groves & Thompson 1970). A hint at sensitization can be appreciated in the performance of 10-day-old rats for interstimulus intervals of 4 and 8 s: Leg flexion increases toward the end of habituation training (see ***Figure 11.5***). More direct tests with a more extensive series of stimulus presentations (500 trials) and intermediate shock intensity (0.18 mA) demonstrate that whereas 3- and 6-day-old rats habituate, 10- and 15-day-olds exhibit both initial habituation followed by sensitization of the leg-flexion response.

Habituation treatments may induce more than a decrement in a particular response. The repeated presentation of a stimulus may develop a tendency to ignore the stimulus—that is, an attentional decrement that could interfere with the processing of such stimulus if the situation were to change. The phenomenon known as *latent inhibition* illustrates such a possibility. A latent inhibition experiment involves two phases of training and a comparison between at least two groups, as illustrated in ***Figure 11.6-a.*** The critical difference between habituation and latent inhibition is in the measurement of the effects of repeated stimulation. Instead of simply measuring changes in a response at the time of stimulus presentation, as it is done in habituation experiments, latent inhibition is measured in terms of a retardation of acquisition in a subsequent phase of classical conditioning training. During this phase, the stimulus repeatedly presented in the first phase is used as a conditioned stimulus in CS-US pairing trials. Such a retardation suggests that animals have learned to ignore the stimulus and have difficulty reversing that tendency when the environment changes and the stimulus becomes a signal for an important event, the US (Lubow 1989).

Experiments with infant rats show that the effects of repeated, nonreinforced exposure to a CS on its conditionability may vary dramatically over the course of the initial 3 weeks of life. In one such experiment (Hoffman & Spear 1989), 10- and 18-day-old preweanling rats received footshocks in the presence of an ambient odor (cotton moistened in methyl salicylate was placed under the grid floor of the conditioning box). In a later test, rats were given the opportunity to choose between two compartments, one marked by the conditioned odor and the other with a neutral odor (see ***Figure 11.6-b***). At both ages, rats exposed to paired odor-shock trials avoided the odor-marked side significantly more than rats exposed to the odor and shock in an unpaired fashion. In the 18-day-old rats, preexposure to the odor for 3, 9, or 27 min before odor-shock conditioning trials led to progressively less avoidance of the odor-marked compartment. This demonstrates a latent

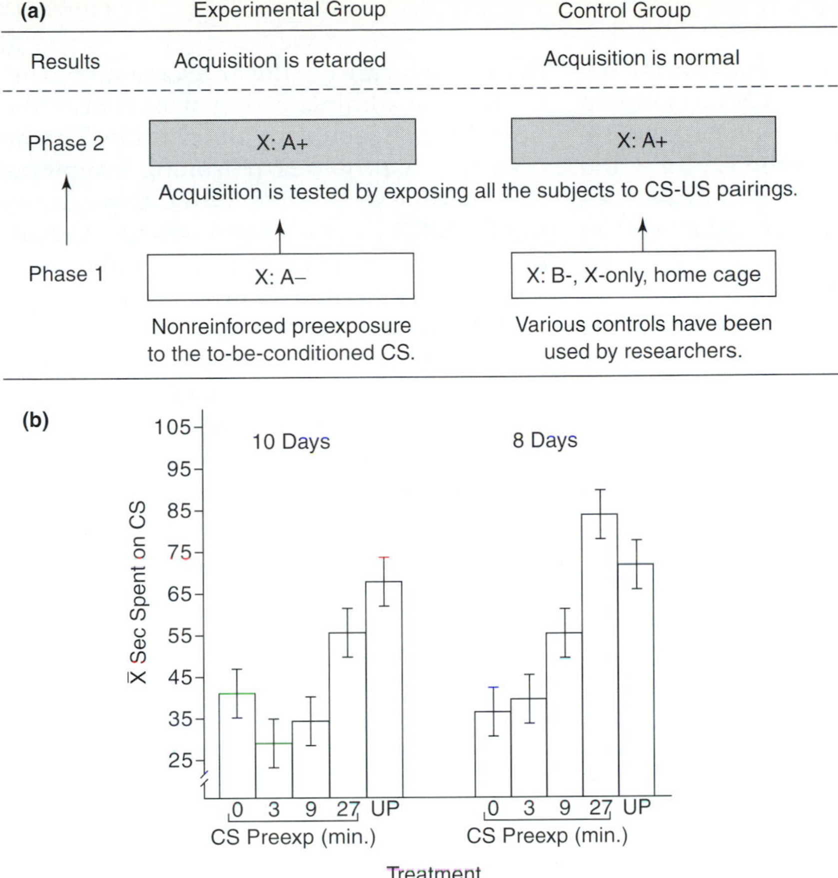

FIGURE 11.6. ***(a)*** Schematic representation of the design used to demonstrate latent inhibition. The experiment involves two phases, but the treatments differ only in the first phase. In phase 1, an experimental group is given nonreinforced preexposure to a to-be-conditioned stimulus (A) in a particular context (X). Various control groups have been used by researchers, including a group that receives a different stimulus (B) in the same context, one exposed to just the context, and one left in its home cage during phase 1. Phase 2 involves pairings of the target CS with the US in the same context as preexposure (represented as X: A+ trials). As a result of nonreinforced preexposure to the CS, experimental animals show retardation of acquisition relative to the control animals. This retardation is referred to as latent inhibition. ***(b)*** Latent inhibition in 10- and 18-day-old rats (Hoffman & Spear 1989). Infants were given various amounts of nonreinforced preexposure to a to-be-conditioned stimulus in phase 1 (0, 3, 9, or 27 min). In phase 2, they received paired presentations of the odor CS and footshock US. A control group received unpaired (UP) presentations of the odor CS and footshock US. In a final test, the results of which are shown in this figure, all the animals were placed in a two-compartment box, and they could choose between a side containing the target odor and another side containing a neutral odor. The less the amount of time spent in the CS side, the stronger the conditioning. Notice, first, that as exposure to the CS increased in phase 1, conditioning decreased in the test (i.e., paired groups are more similar to the UP control); and second, that in 10-day-olds, brief preexposure to the CS (3 or 9 min) actually improved performance relative to the 0-min preexposure control.

inhibition effect that increases with the degree of preexposure to the CS, a standard result in adult animals. However, the 10-day-old rats preexposed to the CS for 3 and 9 min before conditioning actually showed increased avoidance of the odor-marked compartment, that is, a sort of reverse latent inhibition effect. Rather than retarded by preexposure, acquisition was facilitated in 10-day-old rats, at least with a relatively short amount of preexposure.

Infant rats rapidly develop attentional capabilities. They orient toward sources of stimulation, they show habituation rates that may be even greater than those of older rats, and they actually can draw a benefit from being preexposed to an irrelevant stimulus, rather than simply learn to ignore it.

2.d. Neonatal Learning Skills. What is the extent of the learning repertoire of infant mammals? I have already introduced many pieces of evidence in previous sections, and more will be discussed in the following sections and in ***Chapter 12,*** in which social learning is the focus. Let's now concentrate on some of the learning skills exhibited by newborns of two mammalian species that have been studied in detail: rats and humans. Learning in two kinds of procedures will be considered: *classical* (or *Pavlovian*) and *instrumental* (or *operant*) *conditioning.* As was discussed before (see also ***Chapter 13***), classical conditioning involves pairings of two stimuli, called CS and US, that result in changes in the behaviors elicited by the CS, whereas instrumental conditioning involves pairings of a response and an outcome that result in subsequent changes in the frequency or strength of that response.

Since mammalian fetuses demonstrate classical conditioning capabilities, it is not surprising to find similar skills in neonates. For example, 1-day-old rats can be easily trained to acquire a flavor aversion by pairing the oral administration of saccharin (the CS) with an injection of lithium chloride (the US), which provokes poisoning symptoms (Gemberling & Domjan 1982). Exposure to these CS-US pairings decreases the amount of saccharin consumed 5 days later, compared to an unpaired control condition. Similarly, acquired preferences for substances paired with milk can be demonstrated soon after birth. In one experiment (Johanson et al. 1984), pups were exposed to pairings of cedar odor (the CS) and oral infusions of milk (the US) at various ages. After a few pairings, clear signs of conditioning were obtained in 3-day-old pups; for example, during the CS the pups in the CS-US condition exhibited increased frequency of mouthing behavior (defined as movements of the mouth and jaws) and general activity, relative to the levels of these responses scored in neonates exposed to unpaired, CS-only, and US-only control conditions.

Newborn mammals also have the ability to change a particular response as a function of the type of outcome that follows the response during some training trials. Instrumental conditioning of this sort can be demonstrated in 1-day-old rats, using a *master-yoked design* (Johanson & Hall 1979; see also ***Figure 8.6-b,*** p. 277, for another example of the master-yoked procedure). Each occurrence of a manipulative response (e.g., touching a paddle) is reinforced with an oral infusion of milk in the master pups. Within a few hours of continuous exposure to this procedure, the masters develop a relatively high and sustained level of paddle-touching behavior. Yoked controls exposed to the paddle and given milk every time the masters obtain milk for themselves, exhibit a much lower response rate, thus demonstrating that the response-outcome contingency (valid only in master pups) is crucial for this type of learning.

Newborn human babies can also be rapidly conditioned by using sucking as the instrumental response and the mother's voice as the outcome (DeCasper & Fifer 1980). A nonnutritive nipple attached to recording equipment can be used to induce sucking during a period of baseline. After the baseline frequency of sucking bursts is determined, a contingency is introduced aimed at affecting the sucking response. In some babies, sucking above the baseline frequency turned on a tape recorder that presented their mother's voice for a few seconds; in others, sucking below the baseline frequency produced the mother's voice. Under these conditions, 8 of 10 newborn babies modified their sucking frequency (increasing or decreasing it) according to the instrumental contingency enforced during training. Furthermore, babies rapidly learned a simple auditory discrimination. For half of the babies, sucking during the presentation of a tone activated the recording of their mother's voice, whereas sucking during a no-tone period produced no effect (i.e., a T+/noT− discrimination). For the other half, the instrumental contingencies were reversed (i.e., noT+/T− discrimination). As shown in ***Figure 11.7,*** sucking during the S+ component of the discrimination increased in both conditions, which indicates that newborn babies have the ability to adjust their sucking behavior to maximize appetitive consequences not directly linked to food.

The learning abilities of neonatal rats may extend beyond simple forms of associative conditioning. Consider, as an example, our ability to learn in situations involving events that are significant only because of past experience, such as money, praise, or approving comments (e.g., "That was great!" or "Way to go!"). These are referred to as *secondary reinforcers* and are distinguished from *primary reinforcers,* such as milk or illness, which derive motivational power from their direct biological impact upon the organism. The Pavlovian phenom-

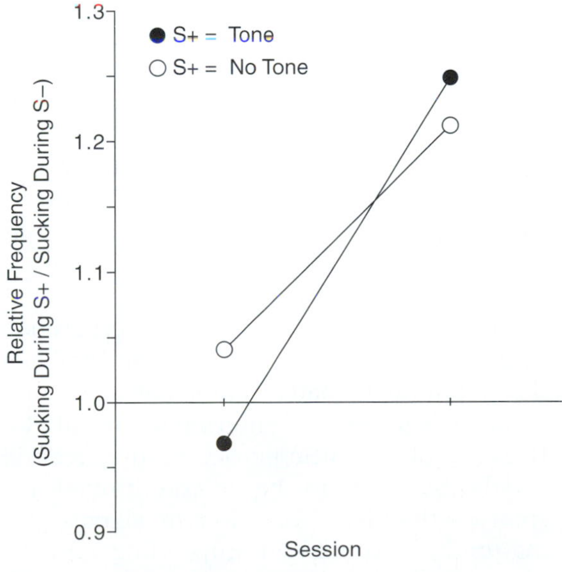

FIGURE 11.7. Auditory discrimination in newborn babies (DeCasper & Fifer 1980). Sucking a nonnutritive nipple turned on a tape recorder that presented the mother's voice for a few seconds, but only when sucking occurred during a particular stimulus (the S+). This S+ was either a tone, or its absence. The results are presented in terms of the relative frequency of sucking, which increased well above 1 under both stimulus conditions. This implies that sucking occurred predominantly during the S+ periods.

enon known as *second-order conditioning* illustrates one way in which secondary reinforcers can affect behavior. ***Figure 11.8-a*** represents the basic design used to demonstrate second-order conditioning, illustrated with the particular stimuli used by Cheatle and Rudy (1979) in a developmental study with rat pups. During phase 1, the experimental group receives typical CS-US pairings (referred to as first-order conditioning), until the stimulus (lemon odor in this study) becomes a good signal for the US (a lithium chloride injection that induces gastrointestinal pain). Phase 1 training was provided in this study when the rats were 1, 3, 5, or 7 days old. In phase 2, the lemon odor was used as a conditioned reinforcer for a second stimulus, orange odor, which was never itself directly paired with the US. The pups were a day older during phase 2 training.

A final test demonstrates the extent to which the orange odor can elicit a conditioned response, in comparison with control groups receiving either backward or unpaired presentations of these events in phase 1 or in phase 2 (i.e., second-order conditioning requires associative experience in both phases). In this test, the pups were placed in a two-compartment box scented in one extreme with the orange odor (the second-order stimulus) and in the other extreme with garlic odor (a neutral stimulus). A second test was subsequently administered to determine the degree of aversiveness developed by the lemon (the first-order stimulus) in comparison with the garlic odor (a neutral stimulus). The time spent in the orange or lemon side, depending on the test, measured the extent of the aversiveness of these odors. As shown in ***Figure 11.8-b,*** first-order conditioning was successful at all ages and in the two groups exposed to the paired procedure, relative to the group receiving backward pairings. In contrast, second-order conditioning was appreciable in 6- and 8-day-old rat pups, but not in 2- or 4-day-olds. Further experiments showed that for second-order conditioning to occur in this situation, phase 2 training must be administered in day 6 after birth or later, although phase 1 training may be administered at any time before day 6.

This brief overview of early learning in rats and humans shows that newborn mammals are equipped with relatively sophisticated learning skills. But this research also shows that just as there are transitions in the emergence of certain behaviors, some learning abilities also emerge during early development. Since the brain is undergoing substantial changes in maturation during early development in most mammals, the gradual emergence of learning effects in ontogeny points to potential brain-behavior parallels, an issue that is further illustrated in the next section.

2.e. Emotion and Learning. These two words allude to the concept of intervening variable discussed previously. Particularly troublesome is the word "emotion" since it has heavy subjective connotations. In order to keep their research within the domain of scientific theorizing, comparative psychologists define concepts such as these carefully and clearly, so that hypotheses can be put to experimental test. Research has concentrated on two emotions familiar to us from personal experience: fear and frustration.

Fear is an emotional state experienced when we anticipate the possible occurrence of an aversive event—that is, one that has the potential to cause pain, harm, or discomfort (e.g., fear of entering a dark alley). Because of its anticipatory nature, fear is widely believed to be a conditioned response—that is, a reaction to signals (no matter how subtle) of impending danger. Thus, training situations involving a US

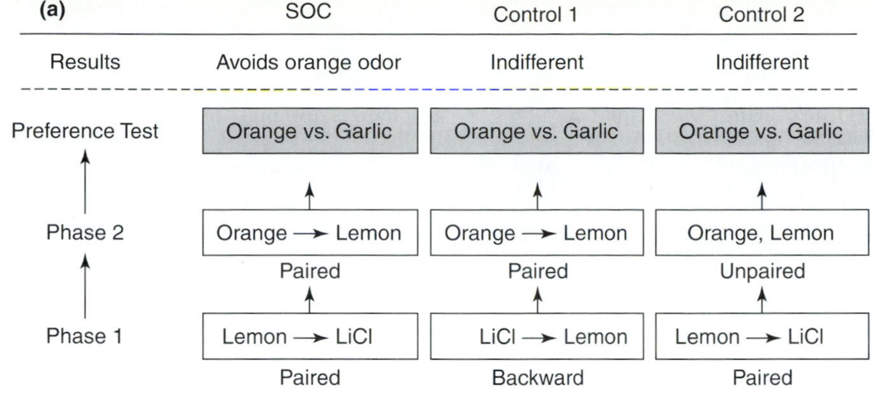

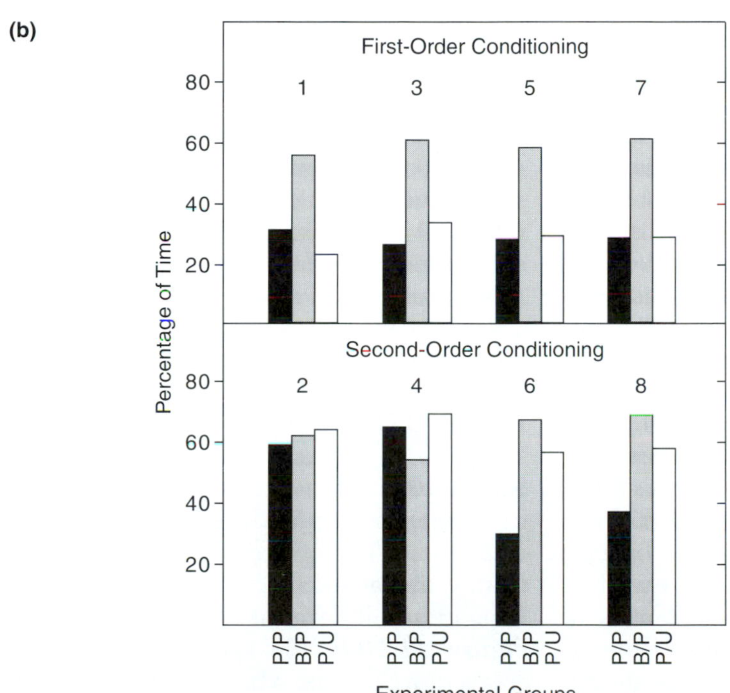

FIGURE 11.8. Second-order conditioning (SOC) in infant rats (Cheatle & Rudy 1979). ***(a)*** A schematic representation of the design used in this experiment. It involves two training phases and a test with three groups. Control 1 received backward pairings during phase 1, whereas Control 2 received unpaired presentations during phase 2. The aim of this design is to demonstrate that paired experience with the stimuli is necessary in both phases for SOC to occur. ***(b)*** Results of the preference tests. The critical test is shown in the bottom. With 6- and 8-day-olds, paired experiences in both phases (P/P) resulted in SOC relative to both controls. However, 2- and 4-day-olds failed to show this effect. The upper graph shows that this deficit in younger rats was not attributable to a failure of first-order conditioning to occur in phase 1.

that causes peripheral pain, such as electric shocks delivered to an animal's feet, are frequently said to lead to *fear conditioning,* or the acquisition of an internal state or response that can influence both the animal's behavior (e.g., induce aggressive responses) and its physiology (e.g., elevate plasma levels of stress hormones). Another index of fear often used in experiments is the ability of signals of painful events to suppress ongoing appetitive behavior. This conditioning preparation is known as *conditioned suppression* and is described in ***Figure 11.9-a.***

In an ontogenetic study involving conditioned suppression, Coulter et al. (1976) administered Pavlovian training to rats that were 11 to 13, 14 to 16, 17 to 19, or 20 to 22 days old, but then waited 32 additional days (a constant period in each age group) to administer instrumental training. Other experiments demonstrate that rats of these ages rapidly learn to suppress their appetitive, food-reinforced behavior when confronted with a signal for shock. However, the question in this study was whether that learning is equally strong after a constant *retention interval.* And as is shown in ***Figure 11.9-b,*** rats failed to exhibit retention of a fear response conditioned at 11 to 16 days of age, although retention improved when conditioning occurred at 17 to 22 days of age. Therefore, the learning skills of immature mammals do not guarantee that the acquired information will be available for use later in its life.

What about frustration? Frustration is induced in situations in which reality turns out to be worse than we expected (e.g., getting a poor grade after studying a lot for an exam). We do not feel frustrated when reward loss can be anticipated (e.g., getting a poor grade after spending no time studying), but only when the loss occurs unexpectedly. Thus this is referred to as *surprising nonreward.* Like fear, frustration is also an aversive internal response with behavioral (e.g., it may also induce aggression) and physiological consequences (e.g., it also increases levels of stress hormones). Frustration can also be a conditioned response (*anticipatory frustration,* as it is technically called). After studying hard and failing in one exam, a student may feel uneasy before a second exam, even after having conscientiously studied the required material. The student is anticipating the possibility of a second failure. Anticipatory frustration can be induced in a situation in which a response reinforced with a more preferred reward is suddenly paired with a less preferred reward. One consequence of this shift in reward condition is that instrumental behavior deteriorates beyond the level of a control group that is exposed only to the less preferred reward. This is called the *successive negative contrast* (*SNC*) effect and is described in ***Figure 11.10-a*** following the procedure used by Chen et al. (1981) with infant rats.

The SNC effect also emerges gradually in developing rats. In one of Chen et al.'s experiments, infants received two sessions of training at postnatal days 16 to 17, 20 to 21, or 25 to 26. They traversed a runway to find a tube at the goal that delivered either a large or small amount of milk. As shown in ***Figure 11.10-b,*** the speed of running increased over trials, which clearly shows that these infants used equivalent learning skills in solving this simple task. However, a downward shift in reward magnitude induced no behavioral change in the 17-day-olds, a hint of a SNC effect in the 21-day-olds, and a significant SNC effect in the 26-day-old rats, which was evident in the undershooting of running speeds during the postshift phase.

A similar SNC effect has also been reported in an experiment involving 3-month-

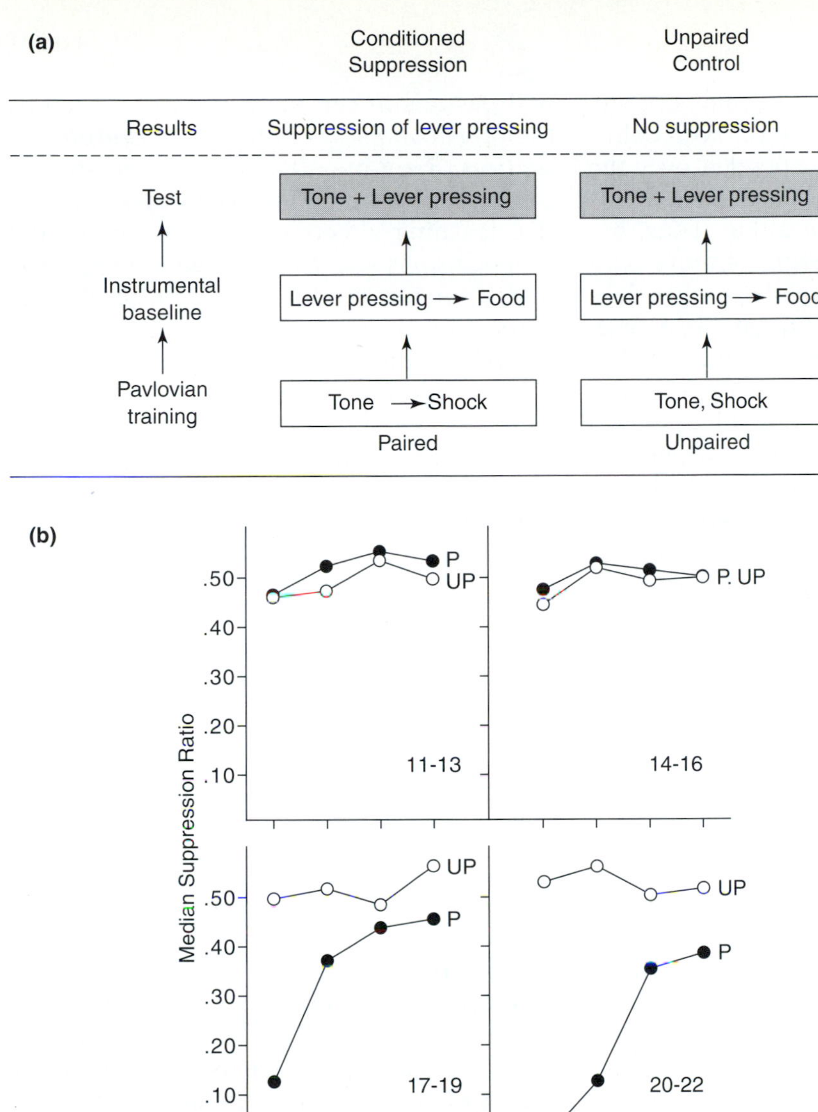

FIGURE 11.9. Fear conditioning in infant rats as measured by the conditioned suppression technique (Coulter et al. 1976). ***(a)*** A schematic representation of the design, involving two training phases and a test with two groups of animals. The groups differ in the treatment administered in phase 1, either paired (P) or unpaired (UP) presentations of the CS and US. In this experiment, the test was administered after a 32-day retention interval. ***(b)*** Rats given phase 1 training when they were 11 to 16 days old *(continued)*

old babies trained with an ingenious procedure (Mast et al. 1980). A mobile with colorful wooden blocks was suspended over the babies' cribs, and a ribbon connected this mobile to the baby's right ankle. Thus, babies could control the amount of movement of this mobile by kicking their right legs (i.e., kicking was the instrumental response, and mobile movement the reinforcer). Babies kicked more frequently when the mobile had 10 colorful wooden blocks than when it had only 2 blocks. Interestingly, an unexpected shift from 10 to 2 blocks led to a significant increase in the frequency of negative vocalizations, including crying and fussing, which clearly indicated the aversiveness of the downward shift. As to kicking behavior per se, after the 10-to-2 shift, kicking frequency increased during the initial 9 min, and then it decreased significantly below the level of the unshifted control group that had been always trained with 2 wooden blocks.

The study describing the emergence of the SNC effect in rats cited previously (Chen et al. 1981) was one of an extensive series of experiments on the development of appetitive learning in infant rats (Amsel 1992). This research shows the gradual emergence, between postnatal day 12 and 26, of several learning phenomena involving behavioral adjustments to the unexpected omission of appetitive reinforcers (see summary in ***Table 11.2***). The behavior of infant rats before the emergence of these learning phenomena resembles that of adult rats with lesions in certain brain areas, such as the *hippocampal formation* (see ***Chapter 8, section 3.e.,*** pp. 294–298). Interestingly, during the same period when these appetitive learning effects emerge, a part of the hippocampus known as the dentate gyrus is undergoing rapid differentiation of its population of granular cells. If this process is disturbed, then the emergence of at least some of these learning phenomena is delayed. For example, exposing rats to X rays between postnatal days 2 and 15, a procedure that disrupts the differentiation of granular cells in the dentate gyrus, eliminates the PREE (see ***Table 11.2***) in 21-day-old rats (Diaz-Granados et al. 1992).

2.f. Infantile Amnesia. As described before in this chapter, there are many cases in which early experience has been shown to have a powerful impact upon adult behavior. Obviously, many of these instances require that some memory of the early experience survives while the animal is developing (anywhere from weeks to years, depending on the species) so that it eventually can affect behavior in the adult animal. But our own experience indicates that it is very difficult to remember events that occurred early in our lives; and the earlier the event, the harder it is for us to remember it (e.g., not many would remember their actual birth). This phenomenon, known as *infantile amnesia,* suggests that some aspects of early experience may never affect adult behavior. This was shown in a descriptive

FIGURE 11.9. (*continued*)
exhibited no evidence of fear conditioning during the test—that is, the presentation of the tone caused no suppression of food-reinforced lever pressing (scores were around 0.5), and there were no differences between the groups. In contrast, the presentation of the tone in rats conditioned at 17 to 22 days of age led to a strong suppression of appetitive lever-pressing performance. The suppression decreases across trials because no shock was administered during the test, thus allowing the extinction of fear.

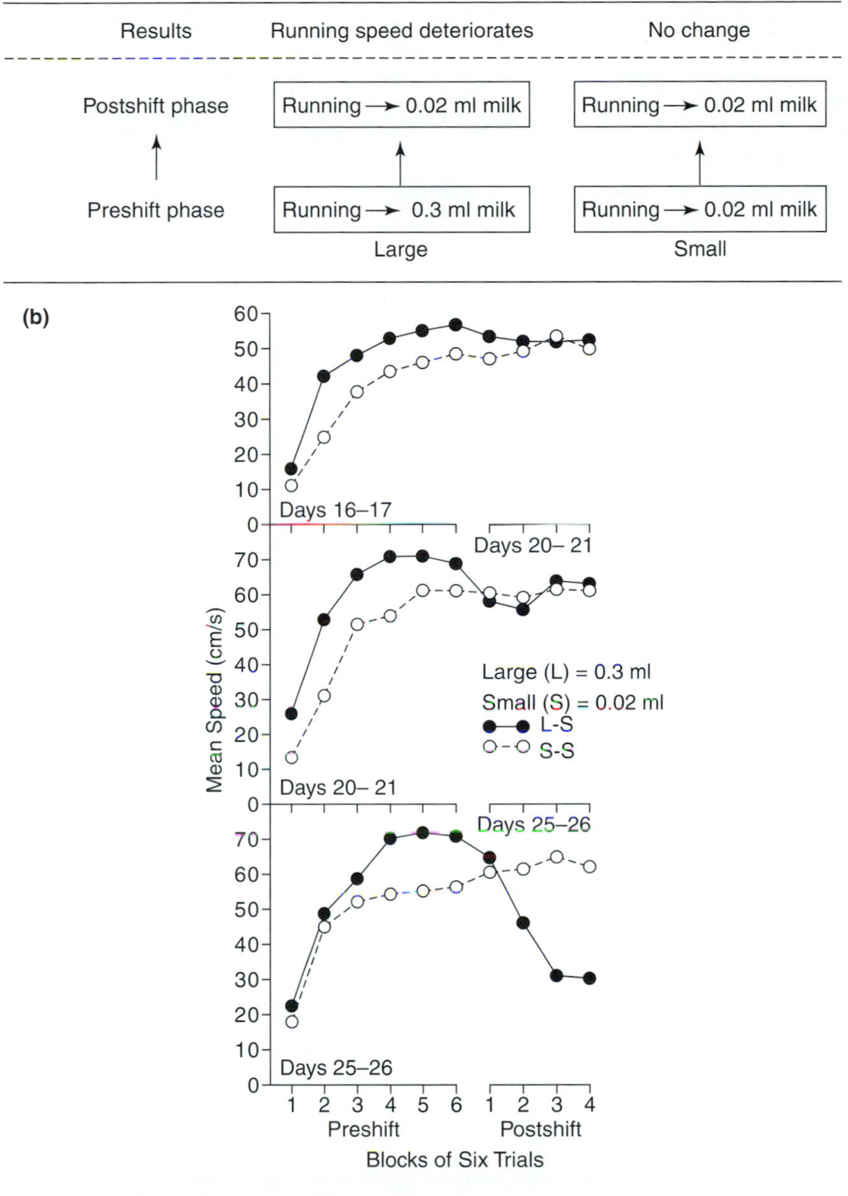

FIGURE 11.10. Emergence of successive negative contrast (SNC) in infant rats (Chen et al. 1981). ***(a)*** A schematic representation of the design, involving two phases of training and two groups. The critical feature is the decrease in the amount of milk reward in the SNC group from phase 1 to phase 2. ***(b)*** Whereas both groups are treated identically in phase 2, the running performance of rats 25 to 26 days old deteriorates significantly below that of the unshifted controls, thus showing the SNC effect. Younger rats show no evidence of a SNC effect. However, rats of all ages learn faster with the large reward than with the small reward, suggesting that the failure of SNC to emerge in younger rats is not caused by an inability to perceive the difference in reward magnitude.

TABLE 11.2 Age of First Appearance of Learning Phenomena Involving Surprising Nonreward

Learning Phenomenon	***Age (days)***
Partial reinforcement extinction effect (PREE) .... -higher behavioral persistence in extinction after acquisition under random 50% reinforcement than after 100%, continuous reinforcement.	12–14
Variable magnitude of reinforcement extinction effect (VMREE) .... -higher behavioral persistence in extinction after acquisition under a random 50% mix of large and small reward magnitudes than after 100%, continuous reinforcement with the large reward.	16–18
Partial delay of reinforcement extinction effect (PDREE) .... -higher behavioral persistence in extinction after acquisition under a random 50% mix of immediate and delayed reinforcement than after 100%, immediate reinforcement.	16–18
Magnitude of reinforcement extinction effect (MREE) .... -higher behavioral persistence in extinction after acquisition with small reward magnitudes than with large reward magnitudes.	20–21
Successive negative contrast (SNC) .... -deterioration of behavior after a downward shift in reward magnitude or quality, compared to an unshifted control.	25–26

study in which a group of college students were asked details about a very significant event in their early lives: the birth of a younger brother or sister (Sheingold & Tenney 1982). Only when such event had occurred when the subjects were 3 years old or older were they able to recall a significant number of details; recall was essentially nil when the subjects were less than 3 years old at the time of the event.

Similar *forgetting* of early experience can be demonstrated in rats trained in a variety of classical and instrumental learning situations. A common outcome of many developmental experiments showing infantile amnesia is that retention of learning is very good immediately after original training. Unlike adult rats, however, infants show a markedly higher rate of forgetting. For example, Campbell and Campbell (1962) delivered foot-shocks in a black compartment to rats of various ages: 18, 23, 38, 54, and 100 days old. During a test session, the rats were placed in the black compartment, but a door allowed them to escape to an adjacent, but previously inaccessible, white compartment. This test did not involve the delivery of shocks, and it was administered either immediately after training or after a retention interval of 7, 21, or 42 days. The results, reproduced in ***Figure 11.11,*** were very clear: Forgetting increased as the retention interval was lengthened, but the forgetting effect was significantly greater for younger rats than for older rats. Similar retention deficits have been found in a variety of tasks, from habituation of responding to auditory stimuli to Pavlovian odor-aversion conditioning, active avoidance maintained by foot shock, and appetitive, food-reinforced instrumental learning. The implication is

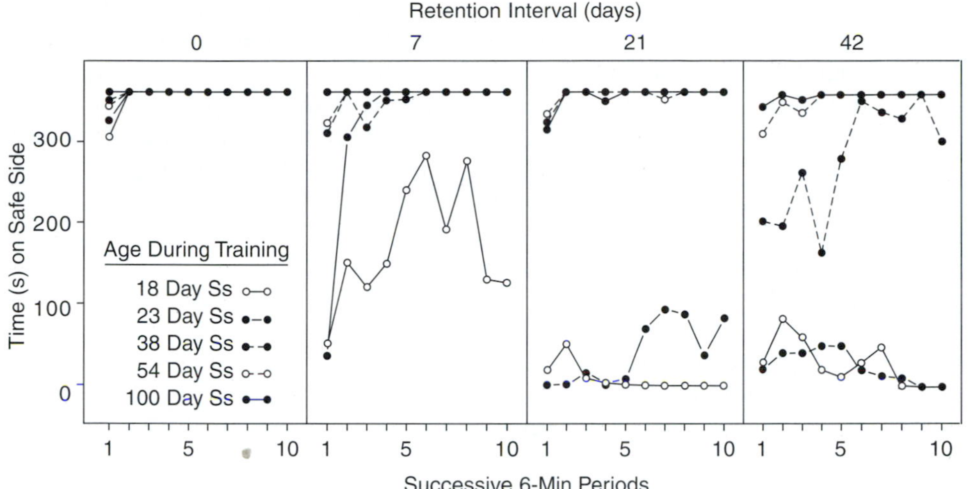

FIGURE 11.11. Infantile amnesia for aversive conditioning in rats (Campbell & Campbell 1962). Rats received footshocks in a black compartment at various ages (18 to 100 days of age) and were tested after various retention intervals (0 to 42 days). Immediate testing (i.e., after a 0 delay) demonstrated that all age groups learn the aversive task equally well. However, as the retention interval increases, groups of younger rats exhibit a progressively greater degree of forgetting.

that infantile amnesia occurs not because the original learning is somewhat weaker in infant rats than it is in adults but because infants are more susceptible to forgetting.

Infantile amnesia may be related to maturational process. For example, the brain of a preweanling rat undergoes extensive maturation, and it continues to grow until at least day 30 after birth. I mentioned previously that hippocampal granular neurons differentiate during the preweanling period; also during this period there is extensive *synaptogenesis* in the cerebral cortex of the rat (i.e., establishment of synaptic connections between neurons). Neurons also increase in size, and their axons become myelinated—that is, covered by sheets of myelin provided by glial cells. *Myelinization* is a critical determinant of the speed with which neurons can conduct action potentials through their axons, and it thus determines the CNS's ability to function normally. These maturational processes may contribute to infantile amnesia if the neural network responsible for storing a particular set of memories is overlaid by networks that develop subsequently. Comparative research provides suggestive evidence for maturation as a source of infantile amnesia.

In ***section 1.a.,*** above, a distinction was drawn between altricial and precocial animals. Altricial species, such as the rat, are born in a relatively immature state and lack many of the locomotor skills that characterize the adult animal. This is a behavioral correlate of their immature CNS. By contrast, precocial species, such as Guinea pigs (*Cavia* spp.), are both behaviorally and neurologically advanced at birth, and they develop rapidly within a few days after birth. Comparisons of altricial and precocial species may thus provide useful information about the extent to which maturational processes relate to infantile amnesia. ***Figure 11.12*** shows the results of one such comparison (Campbell et al. 1974). In the case of rats, retention 1 day after training in an escape-from-shock situation was virtually indistinguishable in animals ranging between 15 and 35 days of age. However, with 7-day and 14-day retention intervals, behavioral scores dropped substantially for the younger animals, again demonstrating that the rate of forgetting in infant rats is higher than it is in postweanling rats. Compare these results with those obtained in Guinea pigs trained in the same situation. Groups of 5-day-old (young) and 100-day-old (adult) Guinea pigs demonstrated equivalent behavioral levels after a 75-day-long retention interval, independently of the amount of original training received.

Does infantile amnesia imply that the forgotten information is irreparably lost? If maturational and other factors induce infantile amnesia by eliminating previously learned information, then no treatment could successfully bring back the behaviors learned in early infancy and subsequently forgotten. However, it is possible, within certain limits, to induce a reactivation of early memories such that behaviors that would otherwise be forgotten can be recovered. An example of the effects of *reactivation treatment* is provided by an experiment involving odor-aversion training in 18-day-old rats (Miller et al. 1991). Infants are placed in a container with lemon odor and then transferred to another compartment with methyl odor. Whereas nothing else happens in the lemon context, methyl is paired with the delivery of several foot-shocks. Subsequent preference tests demonstrate that aversion for the methyl context is present up to 2 hr after the end of original conditioning, but not beyond that time. However, if some aspect of the original training situation is presented before a test administered 24 hr after original training, then aversion for the methyl odor is reinstated. Successful reactivation treatments involve the presentation of the shock, the lemon odor, and exposure to the compartment where infants were originally trained. Such reinstatement of a preference suggests that forgetting in preweanling rats may not necessarily involve the destruction of relevant memories but may involve *retrieval failure*—that is, a deficiency in the recovery of information from memory.

2.g. Early Avian Learning. A substantial amount of research has been done on the effects of early experience on adult behavior in birds. A large part of this research relates to social behavior, including imprinting (e.g., the attachment response of a chick toward its mother) and song learning (e.g., development of vocal communication), and thus is covered in ***Chapter 12.*** This section illustrates some of the basic learning skills of young birds.

Immediately after hatching, chicks of all species face many important problems. For example, they need to stay warm (because temperature regulation takes some time to develop) and procure food (from their parents or directly by themselves). As will be shown below and in the following chapter, birds are also affected by mere exposure to certain features of their environment (e.g., conspecifics, songs, and even the stars in migratory birds). Consider first the temperature-regulation problem.

Young chicks of precocial species rapidly become capable of walking around, but they need some time to develop physiological mechanisms that would allow them to

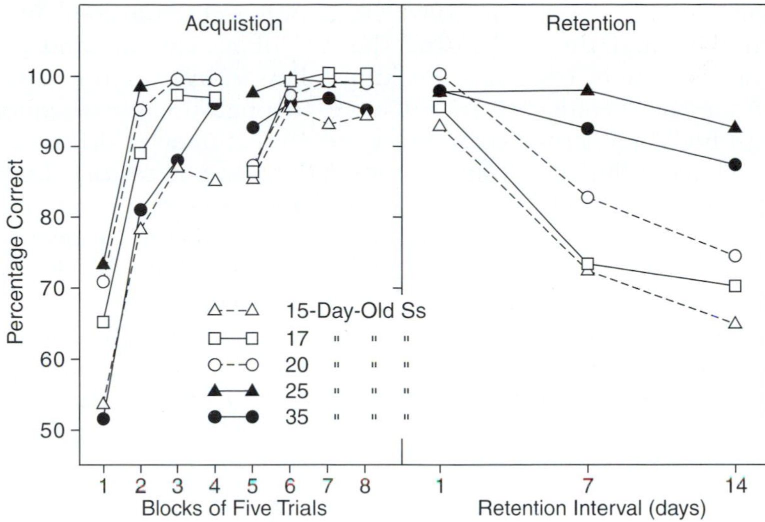

(b) Guinea Pigs

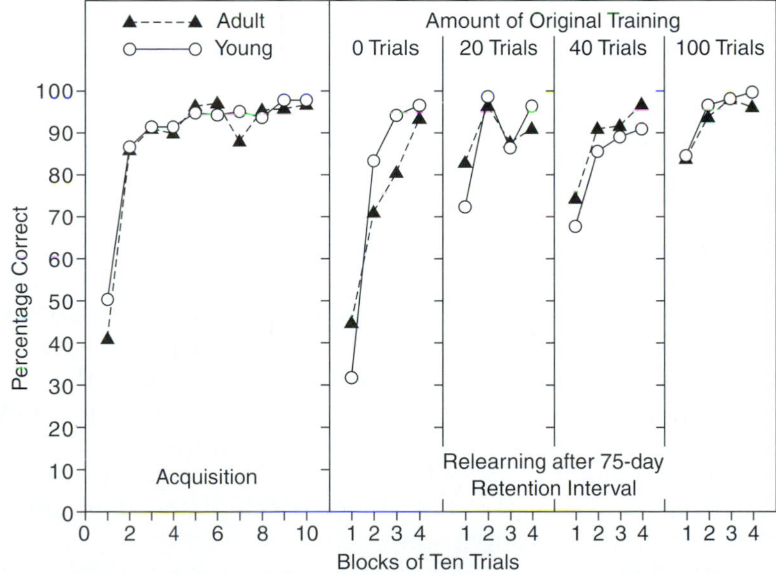

Figure 11.12. Comparative developmental study of infantile amnesia (Campbell et al. 1974). ***(a)*** Rats, an altricial species. ***(b)*** Guinea pigs, a precocial species. Whereas infant rats show forgetting in the retention test, Guinea pigs performed essentially at the same level after a 75-day retention interval and after various amounts of original training. One implication is that maturational processes in altricial species may be responsible to some degree for the phenomenon of infantile amnesia.

maintain a relatively constant internal temperature (i.e., endothermy). The main source of heat is their mother, and their main thermoregulatory mechanism is behavioral: *heat-seeking behavior.* Young chicks respond to a drop in body temperature by approaching and pecking at the hen and then snuggling and rubbing their heads against her feathers; the hen, in turn, may respond by sitting and brooding the chicks. These heat-seeking responses rapidly develop in chicks trained in the laboratory under purely Pavlovian contingencies (Wasserman et al. 1975). For example, 3-day-old chicks (*Gallus gallus*) placed in a chamber kept at a temperature between 4° and 10°C were exposed to temporal pairings of a localized blue light followed 8 s later by the activation of a heat lamp for 4 s. Under these conditions, young chicks learned to peck at the localized light, pecked more often as the percentage of light-heat pairings increased from 33% to 67% and 100%, and learned to discriminate between blue and red lights when only one of them was paired with heat (i.e., B+/R– for some chicks, and R+/B– for others).

Pecking is also a major component of the feeding behavioral system. Many birds forage for seeds scattered on the ground and must, therefore, be able to discriminate between edible and nonedible objects. In precocial birds, such as the domestic chicken, *food recognition* abilities appear so fast after hatching that they would seem to require little learning, whereas, in fact, learning and maturational factors are interacting strongly over a short period of time. Initially, chicks peck at any small object they see on the floor, including food crumbs and sand. Pecking requires the swallowing of some object, but it is not necessary for the chick to be swallowing food in order to peck. However, if chicks have continuous access to both food and sand, they soon demonstrate a preference for food by decreasing the rate of pecking at sand particles. Pecking followed by ingestion and, in turn, by some postingestional consequence (i.e., food in the stomach, decrease in hunger motivation) are necessary for the development of food recognition in chicks. But such experience appears to have little influence before posthatching day 3, which suggests a maturational factor.

The interaction between experience and maturation is nicely illustrated in an experiment with chicks of 1, 2, or 3 days of age (Hogan 1973). Animals were exposed to three phases of training: (1) a 10-min session of exposure to sand; (2) forced feeding, administered either immediately after exposure to sand (paired group) or 2 hr later (unpaired control); and (3) reexposure to the sand test 1.5 hr after forced feeding. If postingestional consequences (food in stomach after forced feeding) influence prior food-selection responses, then these chicks should actually learn to peck at a nonedible substance! The frequency of sand pecking in the retest was not affected by forced feeding in 1- and 2-day-olds, but it was significantly increased in 3-day-old chicks. Sand pecking was also not affected when the postingestional consequence was temporally delayed with respect to the initial sand-pecking training. This suggests that it is not the forced feeding per se that induces learning, but the temporal contiguity between sand pecking and food in the stomach.

The learning skills of precocial species immediately after hatching appear to be quite advanced, reaching well beyond basic phenomena such as those illustrated in the above paragraphs. One way to characterize such skills is to present young animals with a variety of relatively complex tasks and determine the range of solutions that are within their possibilities. Heaton (1978), for example, used such an approach to characterize the learning skills of Peking ducks (*Anas platyrhynchos*) during the first 2 weeks after hatching. Three different tasks were used, and, in all cases, animals were rewarded by accessing a box in which they found food, water, and three colony mates. Consider each of these tasks in turn.

In the *delayed response task,* the animal faced three goal boxes, one of which was illuminated for a brief period so that the animal could see the reinforcers on the other side. The goal boxes were then blocked by an opaque door during a retention interval of variable duration, and afterwards the animal was allowed a choice. If it chose the correct alternative, it could enter the goal box and remain there for 15 s; otherwise, it was detained for 30 s in a compartment. A successful trial implied that the animal remembered which particular location was illuminated in the current trial. Every time an animal made three successive correct choices, the retention interval was increased by 2 s. How long an interval could the animal's memory sustain? Surprisingly, there was no correlation between age and choice accuracy in this task; thus, 1-day-olds and 14-day-olds, and every age in between these values, yielded approximately the same performance level. Accuracy also dropped when the interval was increased from 1 s to 3 s, but this was true for all age groups without exception. Such a decrease in accuracy suggests that performance in this delayed-response task was dependent upon memory.

In the *successive reversal task,* animals were reinforced for turning in one direction, say to the right, in a T-shaped maze, but nonreinforced for turning in the other (i.e., a R+/L– problem). When they reached an acquisition criterion (8 correct choices out of 10), the contingencies were reversed, R–/L+, again until they reached the same criterion, and then reversed again, and so forth. Animals started training at different ages (1, 2, 3, or 4 days posthatching) and received one reversal problem per day for a total of 14 days. The key result was that animals of all ages exhibited the same pattern of problem-solving behavior in this problem: The number of errors increased from the original discrimination problem to the initial reversals, but as reversal training continued, all animals showed a progressive improvement in acquisition, making fewer errors to reach the criterion.

The third and final problem in this series was the *detour task,* in which isolated animals had to learn to move away from a visible but inaccessible reinforcement (a clear Plexiglas barrier blocked direct access), in order to find a tunnel that led to the reinforcement. Six groups of ducklings began their training in posthatching days 1 to 6 and showed equivalent ability to solve this detour problem. These experiments suggest that young precocial birds are equipped with a set of problem-solving abilities that, in many important respects, matches that of adults. The advanced sensorimotor stage of development that characterizes precociality is thus accompanied by adult-like learning skills.

The conclusion that precocial birds are capable learners should not be taken to imply that altricial species have no such abilities. Altriciality is defined by a state of immature sensorimotor development at the time of hatching, which implies an inability to perform the kind of behavioral tasks used by Heaton (1978) with Peking ducks. Nonetheless, altricial chicks have a remarkable ability to acquire information during early development by simple exposure to stimulus conditions. In birds, for example, various sources of information can influence *migratory orientation*, including the earth's magnetic field, polarized light, landmarks, and the stars. In a revealing experiment (Emlen 1970), the structure of the night sky was manipulated in a planetarium by exposing developing indigo buntings (*Passerina cyanea*) to either the normal sky (with stars and constellations rotating around the star Polaris) or a shifted sky (rotating around the star Betelgeuse). A third group was never exposed to the sky during development. Nestlings of this altricial species were removed from their nests 4 to 10 days after hatching and raised in the laboratory. All the birds were completely isolated from viewing the sky until posthatching day 25. Exposure to the normal and altered night skies was given during 3 nights per week for a total of 22 nights. All birds were subsequently tested in the planetarium with the stars in a fixed, nonmoving position.

Buntings develop a restless response when the autumn approaches, jumping in the direction of the migratory flight even when they are in their cages. This behavior allows a detailed record of the direction selected for migration by each bird. Tests indicate that birds raised in isolation from the normal sky do not exhibit a preferred direction in their restless behavior, whereas birds exposed to the normal night sky in the planetarium correctly orient away from the star Polaris, taking a southward direction. Interestingly, birds also exhibit a restless response in the direction opposite to the star Betelgeuse when this particular star was made the center of the rotating pattern of stars in the planetarium. Migratory orientation in indigo buntings depends on the acquisition of information about the structure of the nocturnal sky during development. For this reason, these animals are said to use a star compass.

3. Development of Complex Behavior

3.a. Manual Dexterity and Lateralization. There is extensive interspecies variation among mammals in the degree to which the hands are used for manipulating objects. Rats and raccoons, for example, exhibit extensive manipulation of food with their hands. But manual dexterity has developed to its greatest degree in the primates. The *grasping hand* of primates, although primarily concerned with locomotion on trees, is also a great device to take, hold, and manipulate all kinds of objects. In addition, the great development of vision in primates allows for *eye-hand coordination,* such as is observed in the act of reaching toward an object. In humans, manual dexterity is potentiated by the bipedal posture, which allows them a greater degree of freedom in the use of the hands than it is the case for other primates. Adult humans in all cultures spend a considerable amount of their active time engaged in tasks that require bimanual coordination, such as typing, cooking, or knitting, to mention a few examples.

The arm movements of human neonates appear to be random—that is, independent of objects in their environment and completely unintentional. This is not entirely correct, however, as shown by experiments in which human neonates can adjust their arms in response to the presence of external forces (van der Meer et al. 1995). In one experiment, strings connected to babies' wrists pulled their arms down by virtue of calibrated weights. The babies successfully adjusted the position of their arms if they could see them, either directly or through a TV monitor, and restored the normal movement despite the pulling force. By contrast, an arm that the baby could not see was pulled down by the weight and exhibited little movement. Therefore, seemingly uncoordinated arm movements by human neonates already exhibit some degree of visual coordination and motor control.

Can neonates reach and grab an object? *Prehension* involves a reaching movement of the arm toward an object and a grasping movement of the hand to grab the object. Such movements are regulated by sensory feedback not only from the visual system, which is obvious, but also from propioceptive sensors that provide information about the location and position of the arm, and from touch receptors that coordinate the grasping movements. Prehension thus is finely regulated by sensory feedback, although such regulation appears to become stronger during the first year of life. Neonates are relatively less efficient in achieving contact with static objects, even if they are visually fixated on the object (von Hofsten 1982). Older infants can make appropriate adjustments in prehension even when the goal object is moving in their visual field.

During the second half of their first year of life, human infants develop a progressively greater ability to apply both hands to manipulate an object. Such *bimanual dexterity* implies the differential use of the hands. For example, an 8-month-old baby can use one hand to grab an object while the other hand performs some other movement, such as pushing, pulling, or rotating a part of the object. The emergence of bimanual dexterity is accompanied by *handedness*—that is, the preferential use of one of the hands to reach and grab objects or to perform certain types of movement. Most adult humans prefer to reach and manipulate objects with their right hand, although there is a minority who prefer the left hand and even some who use either hand indistinctively (the so-called ambidextrous condition). Handedness involves *lateralization* of brain function since most of the neural control of each arm depends on the contralateral neocortex. For example, movements of my right hand are controlled by my left neocortex through the descending corticospinal tract that ends in the spinal motoneurons. In the human brain, lateralization involves not only manual movements but also a variety of motor and nonmotor functions. For example, a standing person tends to displace a larger body mass over his or her left side, thus showing postural laterality (Seltzer et al. 1990). Moreover, speech and language comprehension are largely controlled by the left neocortex (see ***Chapter 9, section 4.c.,*** pp. 354–357).

What is the evolutionary origin of brain lateralization? It is now clear that handedness is present even in prosimians, the most primitive group of primates. In a study involving a large sample of five species of the genus *Lemur* (194 individuals were systematically observed), Ward et al. (1990) recorded hand use in reaching for food placed in containers and categorized their observations as involving the mouth, right hand, left hand, or both hands. There was a predominance of ambidexterity (both hands used equally often) during the first year of life, when the use of the mouth to collect food was also predominant. However, most lemurs subsequently developed a strong left-hand preference. Finally, at about 7 years of age, the sample includes as many left-handed as right-handed individuals, so there was no longer a handedness tendency for the sample as a whole. Interestingly, the left-hand preference appeared to be stronger for males than for females. A larger summary of available evidence from African and Malagasy species of prosimians provided further support for this trend: There was a significant tendency toward a left-hand preference in males, but not in females, although samples from individual species showed extensive variability (Ward

1995). It appears then that some degree of brain laterality affecting the animal's posture and the use of the hands may be a primitive feature of primates.

The development of manual dexterity involves the interconnection of several complex processes, including multisensory integration, the assembly of different responses into functionally efficient sequences, and a fine degree of temporal tuning of the responses when grasping is applied to a moving object. Handedness adds to the situation an element of specialization. In turn, the manipulation of objects provides a rich source of experience that shapes the animal's perception of the extent to which it can modify its immediate surroundings; and it also favors the development of detailed representations of those objects that characterize the animal's environment.

3.b. Tool Use and Culture. Primates' use of tools involves extensive manual dexterity. In addition, the study of *tool-using behavior* can contribute to an appreciation of the cognitive abilities of animals (see ***Chapter 4, section 3.h.,*** pp. 101–103). Usually, the context of tool using is well defined functionally—that is, the animal uses a tool in order to achieve a specific end (e.g., procure a piece of food that would otherwise be inaccessible). The components of this behavior are thus constrained by the extent to which they contribute to the goal of the entire act. How does the ability to use a tool develop under natural conditions?

Among the apes, common chimpanzees (*Pan troglodytes*) are notorious for their use of tools to procure various resources. For example, adults insert twigs into termite nests to collect and eat the termites, they select stronger sticks to extract the marrow from the bones of dead animals, and they use leaves as sponges to provide themselves with water. In some cases, male chimpanzees tear up leaves to attract females as part of a courtship display. Some of these behaviors are typical of specific populations of chimpanzees but not of the species as a whole, a fact suggesting the presence of local cultures. A *culture* can be defined as a set of more or less standardized practices, acquired or developed by one or a few individuals, that disseminate to other members of the group and are passed across generations via social learning—that is, learning from observation of conspecifics. This definition of culture, not universally accepted, makes no reference to language and is thus applicable to nonhuman animals. Some suggestive pieces of evidence about the potential for culture in chimpanzee populations are provided by their feeding behavior.

Consider the range of possible relationships between chimpanzees and oil palm nuts (McGrew 1992). In some populations of Senegal (West Africa), chimpanzees live in habitats where there are no oil palm nuts available, suggesting that these are not indispensable for their survival. In other locations, such as in Kasoje, Tanzania (Central Africa), there are oil palm nuts, and they are readily consumed by monkeys and pigs; but chimpanzees seem to completely ignore them. At Gombe, also in Tanzania, chimpanzees have been observed to eat just the outer pulp of the nut, discarding the kernel. But at Bossou, Guinea (West Africa), chimpanzees access the kernel by cracking the nut with a pair of stones, one used as a hammer and the other as an anvil (see ***Figure 4.7,*** front inside cover). Although nonprimates have been observed to use stones as either hammers (to crack an egg, as Egyptian vultures do) or as anvils (to smash mollusc shells, as California sea otters do while floating on their backs), only primates have been observed to use both hammer and anvil in conjunction. The use of stone tools to open oil palm nuts at Bossou sets that population apart from others and raises the question of the ontogenetic origin of such a practice.

At Bossou, for example, chimpanzees younger than 3.5 years of age do not crack nuts with the *hammer-anvil tool*, but they frequently engage in manipulating nuts and stones (Inoue-Nakamura & Matsuzawa 1997). Since the hammer-anvil practice generally develops in a social setting, it is widely believed that social learning plays a major role in its acquisition (***Figure 11.13, see back inside cover.***) Six-month-old chimpanzees do not engage in any type of prerequisite behavior in isolation; they do so only when accompanied by adult members of the group. Mothers are an important source of information for the young, but the skill develops normally even in infants whose mothers do not crack nuts. This suggests that other group members provide just as much information about this practice as the mother. Five basic individual acts have been identified in the hammer-anvil skill, and their integration into a single repertoire occurs gradually during the first 3.5 years of age. The individual acts are "take or pick," "put," "hold," "hit," and "eat." A 2.5-year-old would often put a nut on a stone, hit it with its hand, and then turn toward its mother and eat a kernel from a nut she had cracked before. At this age, then, the behavioral components are present, but they are not organized into a functional sequence. ***Figure 11.14*** depicts the developmental progression of the hammer-anvil practice in terms of the transitions between these five basic behaviors. Not only do certain transitions change in strength, as represented by the thickness of the arrow, but also some emerge with experience. By the age of 3.5 years, all these component acts are interconnected in a reciprocal manner.

The development of tool use has also been studied in human infants. For example, Connolly and Dalgleish (1989) described the emergence of spoon use by 11- and 17-month-old infants. Initially, children exhibit prerequisite acts, such as "put spoon in dish

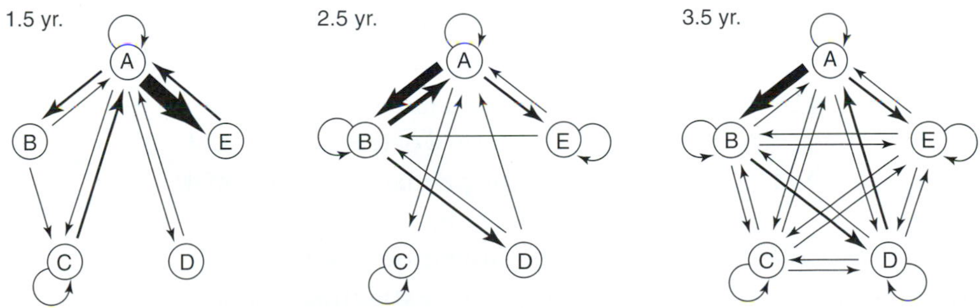

FIGURE 11.13. Development of hammer-anvil tool use in young chimpanzees (Inoue-Nakamura & Matsuzawa 1997). Five basic behaviors are plotted in these diagrams. A: "take or pick"; B: "put"; C: "hold"; D: "hit"; and E: "eat." Arrows represent the tendency for one act to be followed by the other or by itself, whereas the thickness of the arrow represents the statistical strength of that sequential tendency. Notice that at 1.5 years of age all the basic behaviors required for the use of this stone tool are present, but certain transitions do not occur. At 3.5 years of age, all the transitions occur, and the behavior emerges in the animal's repertoire.

and remove it," or "put spoon in mouth and remove it." Such acts are usually functionally inefficient. For example, while one hand may be engaged in these actions, the other may be used to pick up food from the dish. Only later do these two actions become integrated in a larger sequence; additional practice is required before correction loops are incorporated into this sequence (e.g., "check to see if there is enough food in the spoon before putting it into the mouth"). Such a sequence is remarkably similar to that of the hammer-anvil practice in Bossou chimpanzees, but there are some interesting differences. For example, mothers seem to play a more active role as teachers in the case of humans than in the case of chimpanzees, providing verbal instructions, molding the infant's behavior, and reinforcing appropriate responses with social praise. In contrast, infant chimpanzees are pretty much left on their own, and they are not provided with any obvious source of feedback for their actions.

4. Key Terms

aggressive behavior 413
altricial young 403
anticipatory frustration 424
appetitive stimuli 408
attention 415
aversive stimuli 408
bimanual dexterity 435
binaural audition 416
classical (or Pavlovian) conditioning 406
conditioned suppression 424
cross-sectional design 414
culture 436
delayed response task 433
detour task 433
eye-hand coordination 434
fear conditioning 424
food recognition 432
forgetting 428
grasping hand 434
habituation 410
hammer-anvil tool 437
handedness 435
heat-seeking behavior 432
hippocampal formation 426
infantile amnesia 426
instrumental (or operant) conditioning 420
intervening variable 416
intrauterine position 411
kin recognition 411
latent inhibition 418
lateralization 435
longitudinal design 415
master-yoked design 420
maternal factors 411
metamorphosis 402
migratory orientation 434
motor primacy theory 404
mouthing 415
myelinization 429
object investigation 414
object-object combinations 415
object permanence 415
ontogenetic adaptations 402
ontogenetic niche 402
orienting response 416
play behavior 413
precocial young 404
prehension 435

primary reinforcers 421
reactivation treatment 430
retention interval 424
retrieval failure 430
second-order conditioning 422
secondary reinforcers 421
sensitization 418
sensorimotor intelligence 415
species-typical patterns 406
stretching response 406
successive negative contrast (SNC) 424
successive reversal learning 433
surprising nonreward 424
synaptogenesis 429
tool-using behavior 436
weaning 413
wiping response 406

5. REFERENCES

Alloway, T. M. (1972). Retention of learning through metamorphosis in the grain beetle (*Tenebrio molitor*). *American Zoologist,* **12,** 471–477.

Amsel, A. (1992). *Frustration theory. An analysis of dispositional learning and memory.* Cambridge: Cambridge University Press.

Bekoff, A., & Kauer, J. A. (1982). Neural control of hatching: Role of neck position in turning on hatching leg movements in post-hatching chicks. *Journal of Comparative Physiology,* **145,** 497–504.

Campbell, B. A., & Campbell, E. H. (1962). Retention and extinction of learned fear in infant and adult rats. *Journal of Comparative & Physiological Psychology,* **55,** 1–8.

Campbell, B. A., Misanin, J. R., White, B. C., & Lytle, L. D. (1974). Species differences in ontogeny of memory: Indirect support for neural maturation as a determinant of forgetting. *Journal of Comparative & Physiological Psychology,* **87,** 193–202.

Caubet, Y., Jaisson, P., & Lenoir, A. (1992). Preimaginal induction of adult behaviour in insects. *Quarterly Journal of Experimental Psychology,* **44B,** 165–178.

Cheatle, M. D., & Rudy, J. W. (1979). Ontogeny of second-order odor-aversion conditioning in neonatal rats. *Journal of Experimental Psychology: Animal Behavior Processes,* **5,** 142–151.

Chen, J.-S., Gross, K., & Amsel, A. (1981). Ontogeny of successive negative contrast and its dissociation from other paradoxical reward effects in preweanling rats. *Journal of Comparative & Physiological Psychology,* **95,** 146–159.

Connolly, K., & Dalgleish, M. (1989). The emergence of a tool-using skill in infancy. *Developmental Psychology,* **25,** 894–912.

Coulter, X., Collier, A. C., & Campbell, B. A. (1976). Long-term retention of early Pavlovian fear conditioning in infant rats. *Journal of Experimental Psychology: Animal Behavior Processes,* **2,** 48–56.

DeCasper, A. J., & Fifer, W. P. (1980). On human bonding: Newborns prefer their mothers' voices. *Science,* **208,** 1174–1176.

Diaz-Granados, J. L., Greene, P. L., & Amsel, A. (1992). Memory-based learning in preweanling and adult rats after infantile X-irradiation-induced hippocampal granule-cell hypoplasia. *Behavioral Neuroscience,* **106,** 940–946.

Eisenberg, J. F. (1981). *The mammalian radiations.* Chicago: Chicago University Press.

Emlen, S. T. (1970). Celestial rotation: Its importance in the development of migratory orientation. *Science,* **170,** 1198–1201.

Fifer, W. P., & Moon, C. (1988). Auditory experience in the fetus. In W. P. Smotherman & S. R. Robinson (Eds.), *Behavior of the fetus* (pp. 175–188). Caldwell: Telford Press.

Gazit, I., & Terkel, J. (1998). Chronological development of behavior in the blind mole rat (*Spalax ehrenbergi*). *International Journal of Comparative Psychology,* **11,** 1–16.

Gemberling, G. A., & Domjan, M. (1982). Selective associations in one-day-old rats: Taste-toxicosis and texture-shock aversion learning. *Journal of Comparative & Physiological Psychology,* **96,** 105–113.

Gottlieb, G. (1976). Conceptions of prenatal development: Behavioral embryology. *Psychological Review,* **83,** 215–234.

Gottlieb, G. (1991). Experiential canalization of behavioral development: Results. *Developmental Psychology,* **27,** 35–39.

Groves, P. M., & Thompson, R. F. (1970). Habituation: A dual-process theory. *Psychological Review,* **77,** 419–450.

Hamburger, V., Wenger, E., & Oppenheim, R. (1966). Motility in the chick embryo in the absence of sensory input. *Journal of Experimental Zoology,* **162,** 133–160.

Heaton, M. B. (1978). Development of problem-solving abilities in the neonatal Peking duck. *Journal of Comparative & Physiological Psychology,* **92,** 246–254.

Hepper, P. G., & Waldman, B. (1992). Embryonic olfactory learning in frogs. *Quarterly Journal of Experimental Psychology,* **44B,** 179–197.

Hershkowitz, M., & Samuel, D. (1973). The retention of learning during metamorphosis of the crested newt (*Triturus cristatus*). *Animal Behaviour,* **21,** 83–85.

Hoffman, H., & Spear, N. E. (1989). Facilitation and impairment of conditioning in the preweanling rat after prior exposure to the conditioned stimulus. *Animal Learning & Behavior,* **17,** 63–69.

Hogan, J. A. (1973). Development of food recognition in young chicks: I. Maturation and nutrition. *Journal of Comparative & Physiological Psychology,* **83,** 355–366.

Inoue-Nakamura, N., & Matsuzawa, T. (1997). Development of stone tool use by wild chimpanzees (*Pan troglodytes*). *Journal of Comparative Psychology,* **111,** 159–173.

Johanson, I. B., & Hall, W. G. (1979). Appetitive learning in 1-day-old rat pups. *Science,* **205,** 419–421.

Johanson, I. B., Hall, W. G., & Polefrone, J. M. (1984). Appetitive conditioning in neonatal rats: Conditioned ingestive responding to stimuli paired with oral infusions of milk. *Developmental Psychobiology,* **17,** 357–381.

Kelly, J. B., Judge, P. W., & Fraser, I. H. (1987). Development of the auditory orientation response in the albino rat (*Rattus norvegicus*). *Journal of Comparative Psychology,* **101,** 60–66.

Lecanuet, J.-P., Granier-Deferre, C., Jacquet, A.-I., & Busnel, M.-C. (1992). Decelerative cardiac responsiveness to acoustical stimulation in the near term fetus. *Quarterly Journal of Experimental Psychology,* **44B,** 279–303.

Lubow, R. E. (1989). *Latent inhibition and conditioned attention theory.* Cambridge: Cambridge University Press.

Mast, V. K., Fagen, J. W., Rovee-Collier, C. K., & Sullivan, M. W. (1980). Immediate and long-term memory for reinforcement context: The development of learned expectancies in early infancy. *Child Development,* **51,** 700–707.

McGrew, W. C. (1992). *Chimpanzee material culture. Implications for human evolution.* Cambridge: Cambridge University Press.

Miller, J. S., Jagielo, J. A., & Spear, N. E. (1991). Differential effectiveness of various prior-cuing treatments in the reactivation and maintenance of memory. *Journal of Experimental Psychology: Animal Behavior Processes,* **17,** 249–258.

Molina, J. C., & Chotro, M. G. (1991). Association between chemosensory stimuli and cesarean delivery in rat fetuses: Neonatal presentation of similar stimuli increases motor activity. *Behavioral & Neural Biology,* **55,** 42–60.

Potì, P., & Spinozzi, G. (1994). Early sensorimotor development in chimpanzees (*Pan troglodytes*). *Journal of Comparative Psychology,* **108,** 93–103.

Renner, M. J., Bennett, A. J., & White, J. C. (1992). Age and sex as factors influencing spontaneous exploration and object investigation by preadult rats (*Rattus norvegicus*). *Journal of Comparative Psychology,* **106,** 217–227.

Robinson, S. R., Arnold, H. M., Spear, N. E., & Smotherman, W. P. (1993). Experience with milk and an artificial nipple promotes conditioned opioid activity in the rat fetus. *Developmental Psychobiology,* **26,** 375–387.

Ronca, A. E., Lamkin, C. A., & Alberts, J. R. (1993). Maternal contributions to sensory experience in the fetal and newborn rat (*Rattus norvegicus*). *Journal of Comparative Psychology,* **107,** 61–74.

Seltzer, C., Forsythe, C., & Ward, J. P. (1990). Multiple measures of motor lateralization in human primates (*Homo sapiens*). *Journal of Comparative Psychology,* **104,** 159–166.

Sheingold, K., & Tenney, Y. J. (1982). Memory for a salient childhood event. In U. Neisser (Ed.), *Memory observed. Remembering in natural contexts* (pp. 201–212). San Francisco: Freeman.

Smotherman, W. P., & Robinson, S. R. (1987). Prenatal expression of species-typical action patterns in the rat fetus (*Rattus norvegicus*). *Journal of Comparative Psychology,* **101,** 190–196.

Smotherman, W. P., & Robinson, S. R. (1991). Conditioned activation of fetal behavior. *Physiology & Behavior,* **50,** 73–77.

Stehouwer, D. J., & Campbell, B. A. (1978). Habituation of the forelimb-withdrawal response in neonatal rats. *Journal of Experimental Psychology: Animal Behavior Processes,* **4,** 104–119.

Tolman, E. C. (1938). The determiners of behavior at the choice point. *Psychological Review,* **45,** 1–41.

Tyndale-Biscoe, H. (1973). *Life of marsupials.* New York: Elsevier.

van der Meer, A. L. H., van der Weel, F. R., & Lee, D. N. (1995). The functional significance of arm movements in neonates. *Science,* **267,** 693–695.

vom Saal, F., & Bronson, F. (1980). Sexual characteristics of adult female mice are correlated with their blood testosterone levels during prenatal development. *Science,* **208,** 597–599.

von Hofsten, C. (1982). Eye-hand coordination in newborns. *Developmental Psychology,* **18,** 450–461.

Waldman, B. (1981). Sibling recognition in toad tadpoles: The role of experience. *Zeitschrift für Tierpsychologie,* **56,** 341–358.

Ward, J. P. (1995). Laterality in African and Malagasy prosimians. In L. Alterman, G. A. Doyle, & M. K. Izard (Eds.), *Creatures of the dark: The nocturnal prosimians* (pp. 293–309). New York: Plenum Press.

Ward, J. P., Milliken, G. W., Dodson, D. L., Stafford, D. K., & Wallace, M. (1990). Handedness as a function of sex and age in a large population of *Lemur. Journal of Comparative Psychology,* **104,** 167–173.

Wasserman, E. A., Hunter, N. B., Gutowski, K. A., & Bader, S. A. (1975). Autoshaping chicks with heat reinforcement: The role of stimulus-reinforcer and response-reinforcer relations. *Journal of Experimental Psychology: Animal Behavior Processes,* **104,** 158–169.

CHAPTER 12

Early Social Learning and Behavior

MAIN GENERALIZATIONS OF CHAPTER 12

- *The development of adult social behavior is based on a complex set of interactions involving genetic, physiological, and experiential processes.*
- *In higher vertebrates (i.e., birds and mammals), early experience has a pervasive influence upon adult social behavior.*

The adult life of many different kinds of animals is characterized by a substantial amount of social interaction. This is obviously true of most species of higher vertebrates—birds and mammals—for which grouping is relatively common. But sexual reproduction also imposes a certain amount of social interaction in the form of intrasexual competition, territoriality, courtship displays, and parental care. Evolutionary constraints on social interaction can be clearly observed in species that have evolved asexual reproduction from sexually reproducing ancestors. For example, populations of the whiptail lizard *Cnemidophorus uniparens* consists exclusively of parthenogenetic females capable of producing offspring from unfertilized eggs. Interestingly, however, during the breeding season, females come together in large groups and adopt courtship behavioral patterns characteristic of the males of closely related, bisexual species. This would seem to be a waste since no copulation actually takes place; however, such social interactions actually enhance fertility (Crews & Moore 1986). Therefore, even asexually reproducing species may be driven to some degree of social interaction.

Social interactions among conspecifics depend on the development of a variety of basic skills. Some of these skills, such as attention, emotion, learning, and memory, were reviewed in ***Chapter 11*** on the basis of studies involving nonsocial behavioral settings. However, such skills apply equally to situations in which organisms interact. The study of the development of social behavior is complicated by the fact that the experimenter does not have full control over the way in which organisms interact. Often, the behavior of one animal (e.g., a male sparrow is singing) may influence another to respond in a certain way (e.g., a female approaches the male's territory), which, in turn, influences the first to respond, and so on. (Another example of the interactive nature of social behavior is represented in ***Figure 5.5,*** p. 144.) In some lines of research, careful naturalistic observations have given way to experimental research in which a key aspect of the social situation assumes a physical dimension. For example, in their natural environment, ducklings develop an attachment to their mother; however, in the laboratory, attachment is often studied by replacing the real mother with an inanimate object over which the researcher has better control (e.g., a taxidermic model, a moving milk bottle, a geometric figure, an intense light, etc.). Features of such stimuli can thus be manipulated with a great deal of precision, and, moreover, the stimulus "responds" in the same manner in every test. Tapes of vocalizations and substitute mothers have been extensively used in place of the original objects for the same reasons. Obviously, there is another side to this coin: The simplification of social situations by the introduction of artificial stimuli may impoverish the interaction so that some aspect of the process that occurs under natural conditions may be lost in the laboratory situation. Still, the complexity of these behavioral skills is considerable, and their development is often intricate, involving interactions between genetic, physiological, and experiential factors that comparative and developmental psychologists are just beginning to understand.

1. IMPRINTING

1.a. Filial Imprinting. Douglas Spalding [1840–1877] was among the first to make systematic observations on imprinting. As mentioned in ***Chapter 1,*** Spalding (1873/1954) developed the isolation experiment to determine the extent to which the behavior of a newly hatched bird depended on sensory experience. In some of his studies, hoods were placed on the heads of chicks and ducklings immediately after hatching to prevent them from being influenced by visual stimulation. Spalding noticed that chicks would learn to follow him when hoods were removed 1 or 2 days after hatching, much as they would normally learn to follow their mother. Spalding referred to this as the *following reaction* and further noticed that such a reaction would not occur if the hoods were removed 3 or 4 days after hatching. Instead, the chicks exhibited a *fear reaction,* characterized by intense attempts to withdraw from his proximity. These observations were confirmed and elaborated later by the German ethologist Konrad Lorenz [1901–1989], who named this phenomenon filial imprinting (Lorenz 1937).

Filial imprinting, then, refers to a learning process wherein a young bird learns to recognize its mother. As a result of such recognition learning, the young bird follows its mother and exhibits signs of distress when she is not present in its immediate environment. Spalding's and Lorenz's observations suggested that the process was rather fast (hence the word "imprinting," as if the acquired information were stamped in the brain), that it occurred only during a critical period, that it was irreversible, and that it developed in the absence of conventional reinforcement processes. Spalding referred to it as an "imperfect instinct" because chicks could form an attachment with the wrong animal, and Lorenz characterized it as a unique form of learning with both immediate (filial imprinting) and delayed consequences (sexual imprinting; see ***section 2.a.*** below). This characterization stimulated a great amount of research.

Probably the most striking aspect of imprinting is the fact that young birds can develop attachments to all sorts of arbitrary objects. Both Spalding and Lorenz noted that chicks and ducklings easily became attached to them, followed them around, and responded to their presence and absence in much the same way as young birds would respond to their mothers. As noted previously, experimenters have exploited this feature of imprinting to devise testing situations based on a variety of objects. However, not all objects are equally effective, and not all aspects of an effective object control the following response. Objects that can move are particularly effective. For example, a stuffed duck pushed around in a circular motion by a motor, a block of rubber moved back and forth on rails by an electric train motor, and a geometric pattern on a rotating cylinder are particularly effective stimuli. Movement is effective for a variety of species, as shown in ***Figure 12.1*** (Eiserer & Swope 1980). In this experiment, subjects from several precocial species were exposed to either a stationary light or to the same light with a rotating lens (the type of light used in emergency vehicles). Invariably, young birds developed strong approach tendencies to the rotating light, demonstrating that movement is a particularly effective feature of an imprinting stimulus.

Static stimuli can be effective under certain conditions, as shown in an experiment in which ducklings were successfully imprinted to a set of three stationary light bulbs (red, green, and blue lights were used). The strength of the approach response to these lights was as high when they were stationary as when they moved continuously; however, 100-W bulbs were effective, but 7.5-W bulbs were not, demonstrating that effective static cues must be relatively intense for ducklings to learn the following reaction (Eiserer 1980). Therefore, it is not movement per se that facilitates imprinting, but rather the degree of

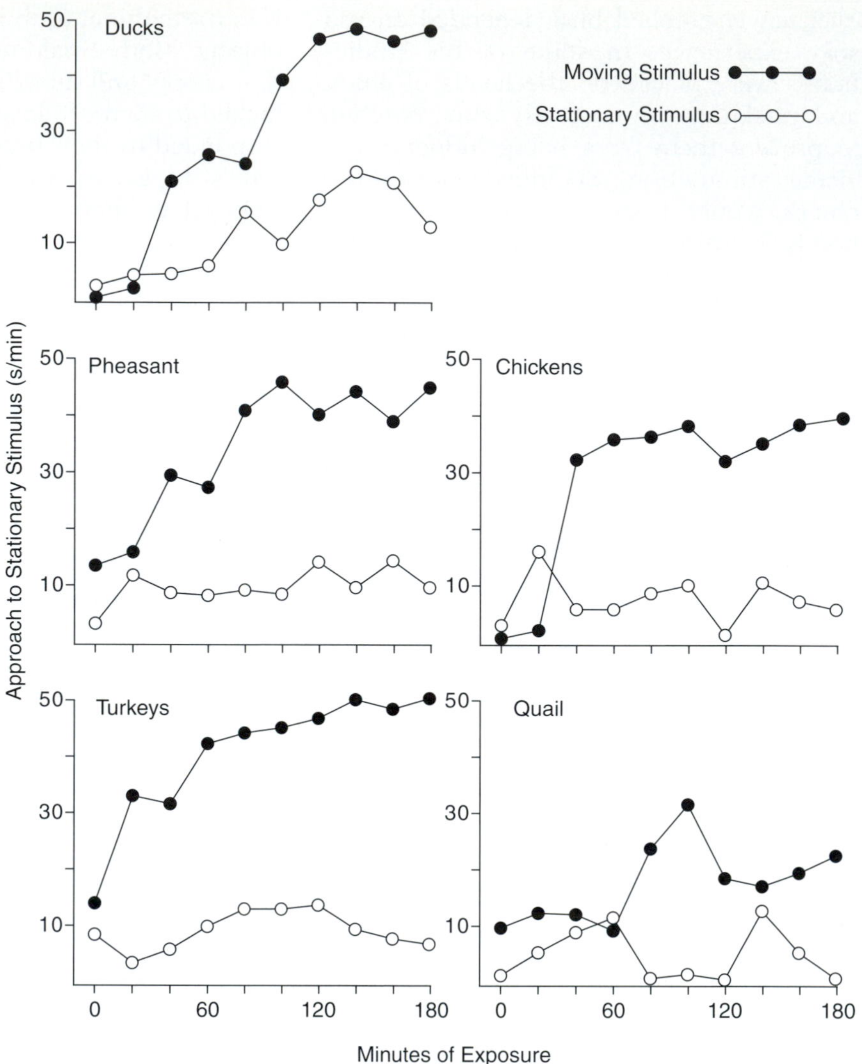

FIGURE 12.1. Effectiveness of a moving imprinting stimulus compared to the same stimulus presented stationary to animals of five different species of precocial birds (Eiserer & Swope 1980).

conspicuousness of the stimulus (i.e., the figure-background contrast).

Arbitrary stimuli have the advantage of being easily amenable to analysis in terms of components. Properties of the object (e.g., intensity, color, shape, speed of movement, etc.) can be manipulated to determine which aspect of the stimulus controls behavior. In the experiment described previously, for example, the intensity of the lights could easily be manipulated by using 100-W instead of 7.5-W lamps. Such manipulations of imprinting stimuli suggest that not all the elements of the configuration control the following response. Naturalistic stimuli, such as a stuffed model, can also be scrambled to produce a variety of patterns, as shown in ***Figure 12.2.*** Dark-reared chicks (*Gallus gallus*) generally prefer the natural model to the scrambled models; they are indifferent, however, when the choice is between the natural model and a stimulus that consists only of the head and neck of the animal (Johnson & Horn 1988). This implies that preference for the natural model is almost entirely based on the head-neck region. Interestingly, they are also indifferent when the choice is between the natural model and another stuffed model displaying a prominent head-neck region, such as that of a bird from a different species, or even that of a polecat, a small carnivorous mammal.

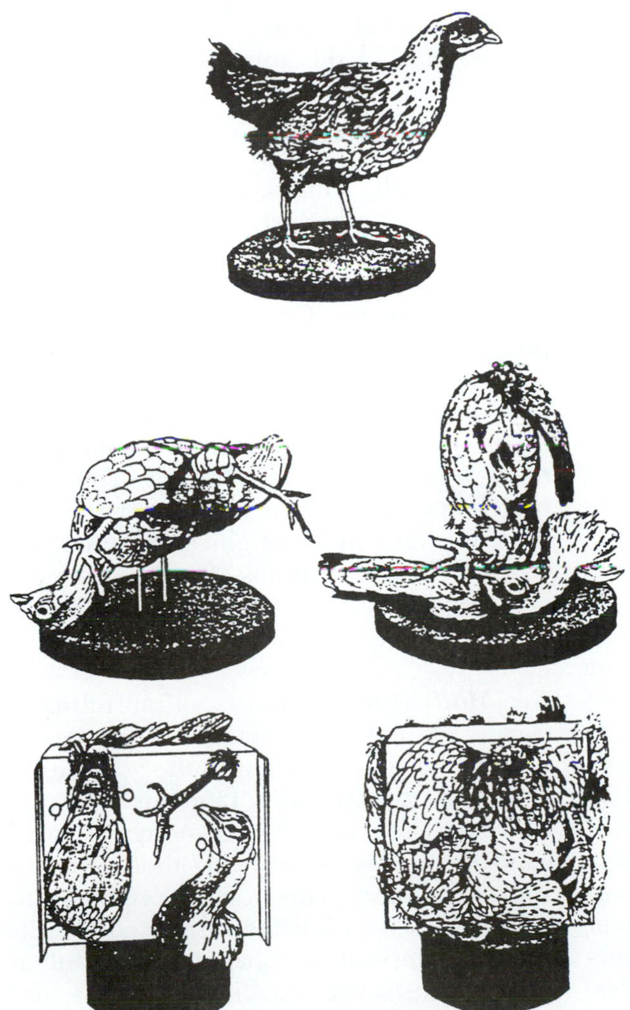

Figure 12.2. Manipulation of a naturalistic stimulus (the stuffed model shown at the top) to determine which element of the configuration controls preference for the imprinting stimulus (Horn 1985). Scrambled configuration containing the head and neck region, such as the one on the bottom left, are as effective as the naturalistic model.

1.b. Sensitive Period and Reversibility. Another aspect of imprinting that attracted substantial attention was the hypothesis that the process could occur only within the limits of a critical period. The notion of *critical period* was borrowed from developmental biology, where it refers to a process that occurs within a precise temporal window of opportunity. Applied to imprinting, it suggested that young birds have a given period of time to become imprinted to an object, and if they fail to do so, they can no longer develop an attachment. Even Spalding's observations suggested a critical period: After 2 days of visual deprivation, seeing a human led to the development of a following response, whereas after 4 days of visual deprivation, the same stimulus induced an intense withdrawal response. Subsequent research demonstrated that the limits of this period are not as rigid as it was originally suggested, so the term was gradually replaced by that of a *sensitive period,* which implies greater susceptibility to learning within graded, rather than abrupt, limits.

The fact that the limits of the sensitive period are malleable suggests that imprinting is not determined by a purely maturational process that unfolds independently of external input. Rather, the process seems to involve vertical coactions between environmental influences and neurophysiological processes. Early sensory experience is one of the factors influencing the upper limit of the sensitive period for imprinting. Birds raised in visual isolation or in environments lacking visual pattern stimulation tend to show an extended upper end for the critical period (Moltz & Stettner 1961). Thus, these visually deprived animals can develop an attachment at older ages than is typical of birds reared in regular environments. However, this tendency may vary across species. In one experiment, 5-month-old ducks (*Anas platyrhynchos*), but not 5-month-old chickens (*Gallus gallus*), developed strong approach tendencies to the set of red-green-blue lights moving horizontally (Eiserer 1980).

The original notion of a critical period for imprinting also led to the expectation that the initial attachment was irreversible. This notion, like that of a rigid limit for learning, has been also questioned by a number of empirical results suggesting that initial preferences are not immutable. In one experiment, domestic chicks were exposed to one of two artificial stimuli (green ball for half of the animals, yellow sponge for the rest) hanging from the cage's ceiling for 3 days (Salzen & Meyer 1968). During a subsequent test session, simultaneous access to both stimuli indicated that the chicks strongly preferred the one to which they had been exposed. Next, each chick was exposed for 3 days to the other object (e.g., the sponge for those previously exposed to the ball, and vice versa) and tested again with both objects. Now, chicks exhibited preference for the more recently exposed stimulus; that is, their original attachment was successfully reversed. This new preference was still present after 3 more days, during which the chicks were not exposed to either stimulus. The development of a second attachment to another stimulus is referred to as *secondary imprinting.*

1.c. Motivational Factors. Imprinting is usually treated as an example of *perceptual learning* because it refers to the acquisition of an object recognition by mere exposure. However, the recognition process works hand in hand with a strong motivation to approach and remain in close proximity to the object. The following response is not itself the imprinting phenomenon, but it clearly illustrates that imprinting is not purely a matter of learning but also involves a motivational component. The young bird seems compelled to follow the imprinting stimulus or to perform any equivalent response that would keep it in the proximity of the imprinting stimulus. It is such a motivational component that has allowed the development of numerous training situations to study imprinting. In an early demonstration, Peterson (1960) placed 1 to 2-day-old ducklings (*Anas rubripes tristis* and *A. platyrhynchos*) in a box with two compartments separated by a translucent wall. The duckling was in one of these compartments and a moving yellow cylinder (the imprinting stimulus) was in the other. Furthermore, a peck on a small key placed in one of the walls of the subject's compartment illuminated the stimulus compartment and set the imprinting stimulus in motion for 40 s. Ducklings rapidly learned to respond to the key (acquisition) and stopped pecking at the key when this behavior no longer resulted in the presentation of the imprinting stimulus (extinction). While these are properties of responses acquired through *instrumental conditioning* with more conventional reinforcers, such as food or water, Peterson noted that the pecking response would persist even after the delivery of hundreds of reinforcements. In other words, there was no sign of satiety effects on a response reinforced by access to an imprinting stimulus, as it usually happens with food- or water-reinforced responses.

A direct comparison of instrumental behavior reinforced by an imprinting stimulus versus one reinforced by water provides further evidence for differences (DePaulo & Hoffman 1981). For example, animals reinforced for responding every 60 s (a so-called fixed-interval schedule) exhibit a characteristic pattern of response distributions called the *scallop*: little responding immediately after a reinforcement, followed by a gradual increase in responding as the time for the next reinforcement approaches. Ducklings trained under a fixed-interval schedule reinforced with water rapidly developed the scallop pattern. In contrast, ducklings of the same age trained under the same conditions except that an imprinting stimulus was used as the reinforcer showed little or no evidence of the fixed-interval scallop. Therefore, whereas imprinting shares several properties with more conventional appetitive reinforcers (e.g., acquisition and extinction), it differs in other respects (e.g., no satiety, little evidence of the scallop).

One of the most interesting demonstrations of the dissociation between recognition learning and the following response in the imprinting situation was provided by an experiment based on *omission training* (see ***Table 13.2,*** p. 512). This procedure is used to determine if a particular response is instrumental—that is, sensitive to its own consequences—by arranging a contingency according to which the occurrence of the response results in the elimination of the reinforcer. If the response is instrumental, then omission contingencies should result in its elimination or drastic reduction (i.e., the animal would be reinforced for emitting any other response).

In an experiment reported by Hoffman et al. (1969a), ducklings were first imprinted to a moving bottle, and once the following response was strongly developed, they were subjected to an omission procedure. During this phase of training, the imprinting stimulus was constantly moving unless the animal approached the section of the box that was closest to the stimulus; in such a case, the stimulus was turned off for 8 s. Ducklings rapidly adjusted to this situation by removing themselves from the closest area. Their behavior was very instructive: They sat on a remote part of the apparatus—thus allowing for the presentation of the imprinting stimulus—and followed the movements of the bottle from the distance. Eventually, the ducklings would again approach the object and the cycle would start again.

The motivational properties of the imprinting situation are also manifested in terms of other behaviors. For example, young birds that are imprinted on a stimulus exhibit *distress calls* when the stimulus is removed from the situation. These vocalizations are brief "peeps" of 3 to 4 kHz, and they occur in aversive situations such as after food deprivation or when the animal is placed in a cold environment. Interestingly, distress calls can also be subjected to the influence of instrumental conditioning, much like the following response. Using a *master-yoked design,* Hoffman et al. (1966) arranged the conditions such that master animals could activate the imprinting stimulus by emitting distress calls. Such calls also activated the imprinting stimulus in the yoked animal's environment, but independently of its behavior. The results indicated that master animals emitted distress calls at a significantly higher frequency than yoked controls, demonstrating that these vocalizations are sensitive to instrumental reinforcement. In the natural environment, distress calls communicate to the mother that something potentially dangerous is occurring. The fact that these vocalizations are sensitive to their consequences in the imprinting situation fits their natural function.

When the imprinting stimulus is presented independently of the chick's behavior and relatively frequently, few distress calls are recorded. Furthermore, if food and water are also available in the situation, eating and drinking tend to occur at the same time the animal is being exposed to the imprinting stimulus (Hoffman et al. 1969b). This pattern of responding is particularly clear when the imprinting stimulus is presented frequently, but it breaks down when presentations are spaced 2 min apart. The presentation of the imprinting stimulus switches the young bird into an appetitive mode, facilitating such behaviors as eating and drinking; these behaviors tend to be suppressed when the imprinting stimulus is off and the animal is in an aversive mode, as suggested by distress calls. Moreover, the administration of electric shocks when the imprinting stimulus is off, presumably making these periods even more aversive, results in a stronger following response (Ratner 1976), whereas injections of morphine, an analgesic drug that would presumably reduce the aversiveness of the situation, lower the frequency of distress calls elicited by the withdrawal of the imprinting stimulus (Panksepp et al. 1978).

1.d. Learning Factors. A few days after hatching, Peking ducklings (*Anas platyrhynchos*) respond to various attributes of their mother hen, including her maternal call (auditory) and her presence in a particular location (visual). Experiments also show that they prefer the species-typical call to that of another species, even when the latter call is accompanied by a stuffed model of an animal of their own species. However, these auditory and visual stimuli go through an interesting developmental trajectory before they become effective stimuli, as demonstrated by careful manipulation of embryonic experience.

Duckling embryos incubated in social isolation, which deprives them from hearing the calls of their mother and siblings, and devocalized, which deprives them from hearing their own calls, no longer exhibit preference for the Peking call over the call of a chicken (Gottlieb 1978). In contrast, socially reared ducklings show an essentially exclusive preference for the species-typical call over a chicken call. The source of *embryonic experience* may thus lie in vocalizations emitted by the mother, by siblings developing in other eggs within the nest, and even by the embryo's own vocalizations, which provide auditory feedback.

Another implication of the results described above is that the duckling responds strongly to some aspect of the imprinting stimulus initially, but after a few days of interaction with the object, stimuli that were previously ineffective develop the ability to control the following response. Several experiments demonstrate that, indeed, different aspects of the configuration acquire control over the duckling's behavior at different rates. For example, ducklings exposed to an inanimate object in motion eventually develop a strong approach response to that object when it is presented stationary in a test session. In contrast, birds always exposed to the stationary object develop a weak approach response (Hoffman et al. 1972). A similar preference develops for a visual stimulus that is accompanied by the species-typical maternal call (Bolhuis & Honey, 1994). One group of ducklings was exposed to a compound stimulus that included a shape projected on a screen (visual feature) accompanied by the maternal call (auditory feature); a second, control group received unpaired exposure to the same features, each one presented in a different session. In a final test, all subjects were given a choice between the familiar shape and a novel shape (the auditory feature was not presented in this test). The ducklings were placed in a running wheel, and these stimuli were presented at either end of the wheel; preference was thus measured in terms of activation of the wheel (in which direction and how much the wheel was turned). Ducklings in the group trained with the audiovisual compound exhibited significantly more preference for the visual feature than ducklings exposed to the same stimuli in an unpaired fashion.

To explain results like these, Hoffman and Ratner (1973) suggested that some feature of the compound imprinting stimulus has a greater initial strength to elicit the following response and to reduce a state of fear responsible for the distress vocalizations. It seems plausible that the particular feature (or features) with high initial strength could vary across species depending on ecological factors. Movement, plumage color, social interaction with siblings, or the species-typical maternal call could be prevalent, depending on the ecological conditions in which the species evolved. For example, auditory features would be relatively more important for sympatric species sharing the same habitats and differing little in terms of plumage, whereas visual features could be more important for species that have evolved a unique plumage pattern. According to Hoffman and Ratner (see ***Figure 12.3-a***), these strong features could act as unconditioned stimuli (USs), endowing accompanying stimuli with strength by virtue of their temporal and spatial contiguity. Thus, for example, static stimulus elements could be thought of as conditioned stimuli (CSs) that are initially neutral but become capable of inducing the following response because of their simultaneous pairing with salient US features. This is known as the classical conditioning theory of imprinting.

The configural nature of the imprinting stimulus is an aspect that differs from more conventional studies of classical conditioning (see ***Chapter 13, section 2.c.,*** pp. 502–505). In typical experiments on classical conditioning, the CS and US are separate events that generally occur at different times (first the CS and then the US) and in different locations. In the imprinting case, however, CS and US are assumed to be features of the same compound stimulus, a characteristic that makes it more difficult

(a) Classical conditioning

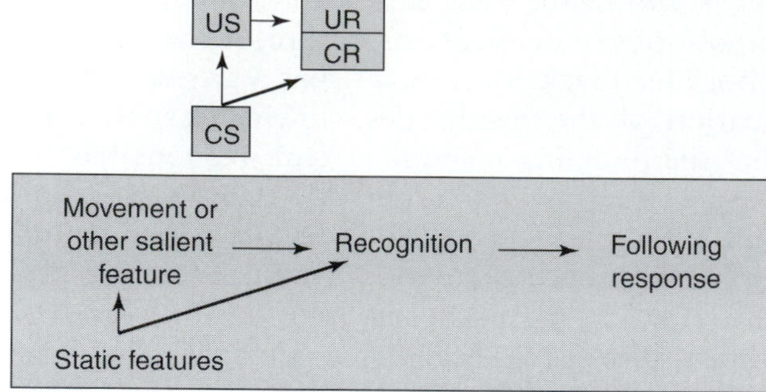

(b) Instrumental conditioning

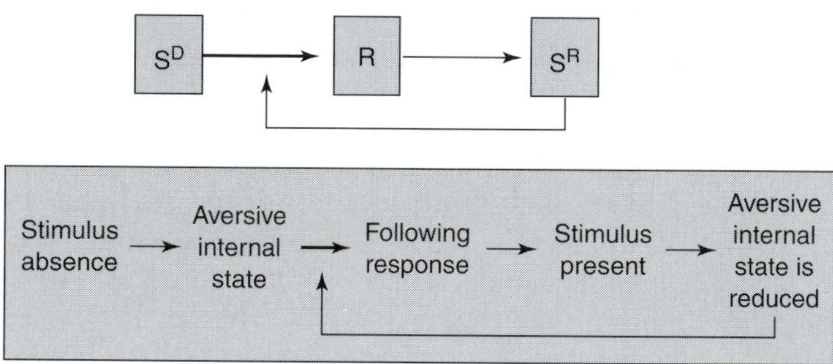

FIGURE 12.3. Role of associative learning in the development of filial imprinting in precocial birds. Acquired associations are shown in bold arrows. ***(a)*** Classical conditioning allows initially ineffective features of the imprinting stimulus (e.g., static stimuli) to become part of the configuration the animal recognizes and follows. In the language of classical conditioning, the effective stimulus (referred to as the unconditioned stimulus, US) has the initial ability to elicit an unconditioned response (UR). An ineffective stimulus (referred to as the conditioned stimulus, CS) acquires the ability to elicit a conditioned response (CR) similar to the UR by virtue of its temporal contiguity with the US. ***(b)*** Instrumental conditioning contributes to the strengthening of the following response by reducing an aversive internal state induced by the withdrawal of the imprinting stimulus. In the terminology of instrumental conditioning, the instrumental response (R) occurs in the presence of a discriminative stimulus (S^D) and is followed by a reinforcement (S^R). According to a classic account of instrumental conditioning, S^R strengthens the associative connection between the S^D and the R.

for experimenters to manipulate these features to generate conditioning phenomena. In turn, this characteristic of the imprinting stimulus (i.e., its configurational nature) invites a view in terms of *within-compound associations*—that is, the ability of the features of a particular compound stimulus to establish associations among themselves by virtue of their joined occurrence. I mentioned above that visual stimuli are preferred significantly more when they are accompanied by the maternal call in an audiovisual compound than when these features are unpaired. Further experiments reported by Bolhuis and Honey (1994) provide additional evidence. After extensive exposure to the audiovisual compound, separate presentations of the auditory feature (the maternal call) reduced the duckling's preference for the visual feature (geometric shapes). Presenting the auditory feature without the visual feature reduced the strength of the within-compound association between these features, thus decreasing the ability of the visual stimulus to elicit a preference.

It is also obvious that the imprinting stimulus introduces a motivational change in the state of the subject, as discussed in the previous section. For instance, if the stimulus is presented in alternating minutes (e.g., present, absent, present, etc.), ducklings would eventually emit most, if not all, of their distress calls during the periods in which the stimulus is absent. This implies that the imprinting stimulus acquires the ability to reduce an aversive state of fear. Interestingly, however, infant birds left in an empty environment do not emit distress calls initially; it is only after they have been exposed to the imprinting stimulus that its absence induces such calls. Therefore, the imprinting stimulus seems to be inducing the need for its very presentation and, consequently, the distress that accompanies its absence. This is consistent with the finding that morphine injections reduce distress calls and naloxone injections increase them (see ***section 1.c.*** above). Morphine is an opioid agonist that reduces pain and fear, whereas naloxone is an opioid antagonist that prevents endogenous opioids from activating their receptors. The following response may thus be instrumentally conditioned by virtue of its pairing with an object that reduces an aversive state of fear (see ***Figure 12.3-b***). Based on these findings, Hoffman (1987) suggested a parallel between filial attachment and drug addiction. According to this hypothesis, salient objects in the duckling's early environment induce the release of endogenous opioids naturally present in the brain, such that the absence of the imprinting stimulus leads to the induction of distress comparable to the withdrawal symptoms experienced by addicts deprived of the drug.

1.e Brain Mechanisms. The previous sections provide a general sense of the amount of behavioral research that has been generated by the phenomenon of filial imprinting. This research permits a comprehensive characterization of the behavioral properties of imprinting and the identification of a number of variables that affect the formation of such attachments. It is thus not surprising that researchers are beginning to take advantage of progress at the behavioral level to uncover the underlying physiological mechanisms of filial imprinting. In this respect, research on imprinting is following a historical pattern similar to that of other areas, as described repeatedly in this book (see, for example, research on mating systems in ***Chapter 5*** or habituation in ***Chapter 7***). Perhaps it would be appropriate to pause and consider this process, as characterized in ***Figure 12.4.***

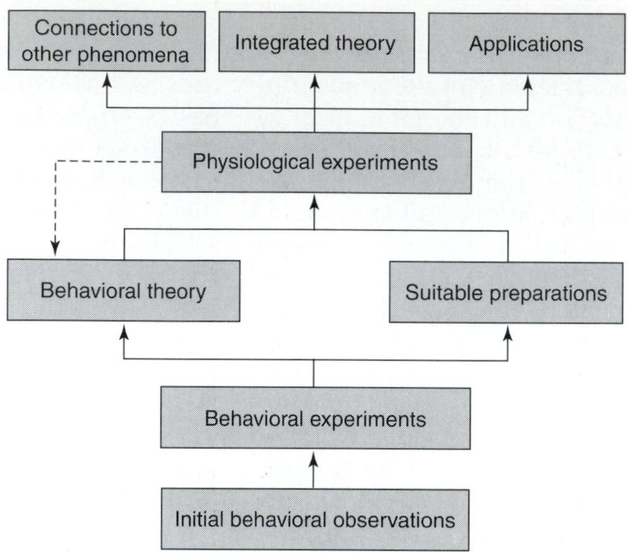

FIGURE 12.4. A general representation of progress in behavioral research. It applies to the case of imprinting research but also to many other areas of comparative psychology as covered in various chapters. There is an initial phase of inductive research wherein the phenomenon is discovered and characterized through observations and behavioral experiments. This information results in the development of testing situations to generate the phenomenon and to construct behavioral theories. These theories usually contain intervening variables—that is, theoretical constructs that provide explanatory power to the theory and guidance for interpreting the results of physiological manipulations. Eventually, a more integrated theory emerges, together with connections to other fields and applications. In the case of imprinting, an example of connections to other fields is provided by Hoffman's characterization of imprinting as a case of addictive behavior **(*section 1.d.*).** Further examples are described in relation to early social experience in primates **(*section 2*)** and vocal learning in birds **(*section 3*).** An example of an application is the notion of chemical imprinting, the development of an attachment to the breeding site, which has been used in the preservation of endangered species **(*section 1.f.*).**

The initial step involves a description of the phenomenon in question at the behavioral level, which usually leads to postulating a series of properties that may stimulate further inquiry. This is followed by a series of behavioral experiments that identify the main properties of the phenomenon and the variables that are important for its production, maintenance, and modulation. These experiments require the development of suitable and standard testing conditions and usually lead to theoretical developments. Behavioral theories often include intervening variables that may act as guides to interpret the effects of physiological variables. Physiological experiments, in turn, often end up enriching the theories that were derived from purely behavioral observations. Finally, these research lines lead to comprehensive theories that provide a deeper understanding of the phenomenon, that link it to various other areas of knowledge, and that are a source of ideas from which applications relevant to human problems often emerge.

What, then, are the physiological processes underlying the development of filial imprinting? There are several ways to approach this problem (Horn 1985). Consider, for example, an approach based on a technique known as autoradiography, which permits an assessment of brain areas that are active at a particular time. Ducklings are first injected with a solution containing radioactively labeled uracil, a base incorporated into RNA. As shown previously (see ***Chapters 2*** and ***3***), transfer RNA assembled in the cell nucleus migrates into the ribosomes of the cell cytoplasm, where it participates in protein synthesis. In any particular neuron, there tends to be a positive correlation between the amount of activation of the neuron, the amount of protein synthesis, and the amount of transfer RNA produced by the neuron. Imprinted animals are then sacrificed immediately after being under the influence of the imprinting stimulus, and their brains are prepared in thin histological slices. These slices are mounted on a special plate and an X ray–sensitive film is placed on top. Active neurons contain a greater amount of transfer RNA labeled with the radioactive uracil base, which leaves a trace on the film.

Autoradiographic studies show that animals exposed to an imprinting stimulus, but not control animals raised in darkness or exposed to a constant light, exhibit a pattern of activation in an area known as the *intermediate and medial part of the hyperstriatum ventrale,* or *IMHV* for short. The position of the HV in an avian brain can be observed in ***Figure 8.13*** (p. 293). The interesting possibility is that information regarding the imprinting stimulus acquired during exposure training is actually stored in the IMHV area. But, of course, this area could be active for a number of other, less interesting reasons. For example, it could be the area responsible for processing visual images or coordinating the motor movements. Interestingly, however, the IMHV area was also found to be active in experiments involving auditory imprinting (suggesting that its activity is not exclusively linked to the visual system) and in the acquisition of passive avoidance behavior—that is, the suppression of a previously punished response (suggesting that its activity is not necessarily linked to motor activation).

A complementary approach consists of lesioning the brain area presumed to be involved in the acquisition of a particular behavior. Brain lesions can be produced in any of a variety of ways: by the aspiration of tissue (ablations), by electric discharges (electrolytic lesions), or by chemicals that induce cell death (chemical lesions). If an area is critical, then its elimination should impair the ability of an animal to acquire the behavior; the lesion should also lead to behavioral deficits in animals that acquired the behavior before the lesion was produced. These are referred to as, respectively, acquisition and retention deficits. In one experiment, the IMHV area was lesioned by inserting an electrode and applying radio waves through its tip (a radiofrequency lesion). This coagulates the tissue surrounding the tip of the electrode, killing all the neurons in the vicinity. Such IMVH lesions performed before a preference for a particular object develops lead to what appears to be a permanent acquisition deficit in imprinting (McCabe et al. 1981). Not only are the animals deficient in terms of the following response, but they are also indifferent when given a choice between the familiar stimulus and a novel one. Furthermore, IMHV lesions produced after establishing a preference for the imprinting stimulus reduce that preference (McCabe et al. 1982). These acquisition and retention deficits in preference are illustrated in ***Figures 12.5-a*** and ***12.5-b,*** respectively.

As in typical lesion studies, results like these do not necessarily demonstrate that the critical information is stored in the lesioned area. Several control conditions and convergent information from other test situations is required to strengthen the hypothesis that the brain region in question is involved in a particular behavior. First of all, lesion treatments are usually contrasted against the effects of a *sham-operated control,* that is, a group of subjects receiving the same surgical treatment as those in the lesion condition (i.e., anesthesia, open scalp and cranium, sutures, etc.), except that the brain tissue itself is not affected. The results described in the previous paragraph come from lesion-sham comparisons. Additionally, lesions of similar size but in different locations are often produced in order to determine if the effect is localized to a particular brain region. For example, similar lesions in the hyperstriatum accessorium (also known as Wulst) and in the lateral telencephalon do not reduce preference for the imprinting stimulus (see ***Figure 12.5-b***),

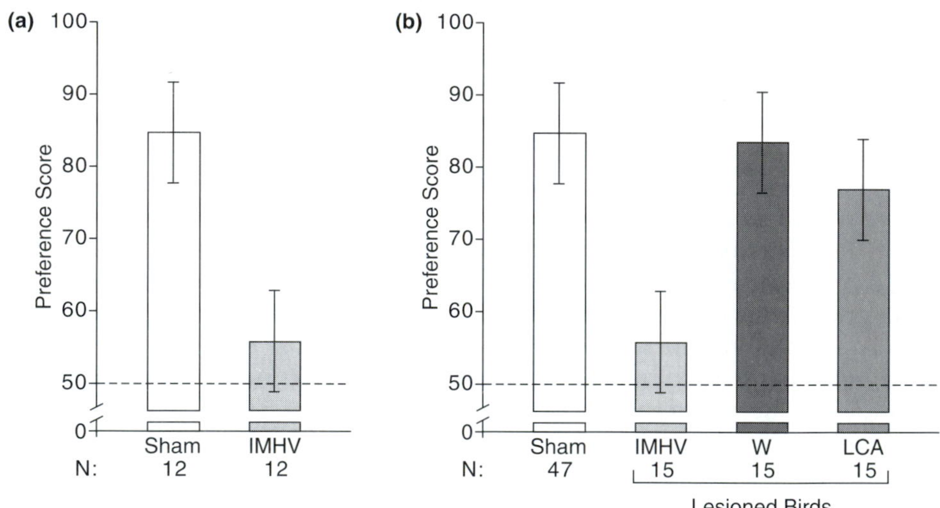

FIGURE 12.5. Effects of lesions in the IMHV on imprinting (McCabe et al. 1982). ***(a)*** Lesions performed before exposure to the imprinting stimulus result in permanent deficits. In this case, lesioned animals exhibit no preference for the imprinting stimulus (chance preference is marked by the dashed line). ***(b)*** Lesions performed after exposure to the imprinting stimulus also cause preference deficits. In both figures, lesioned animals are compared to sham controls receiving the same surgical procedure except that the brain is not damaged. In ***(b)***, further controls involve lesions of similar size but located in the Wulst (W) and the lateral cerebral area (LCA). These controls suggest that size itself is not important, but the location of the lesion in the brain is critical.

suggesting that the effects of IMVH lesions are not caused by the size of the lesion per se but by its location. Finally, important information can be derived from the study of the effects of IMHV lesions on other behaviors. For example, IMHV lesions do not seem to impair feeding behavior or the accuracy of pecking at a moving target. These results suggest that IMHV-lesioned chicks are not impaired in the imprinting situation because they suffer from gross deficits in vision, motivation, or motor coordination. The implication is, therefore, that a piece of information critical to filial imprinting is encoded in neurons located in the IMHV area.

An analysis of several neuroanatomical features of the neurons located in IMHV in chicks exposed to imprinting training for either 20 min (underexposed) or 140 min (overexposed) provides information for the type of change underlying imprinting (Horn et al. 1985). Animals overexposed to the imprinting stimulus exhibit significantly larger synapses between axons of incoming neurons and the dendritic spines of neurons residing in the IMHV area. The synaptic region that is enlarged corresponds to the postsynaptic membrane where neurotransmitter receptors are located. This suggests that one effect of imprinting training is to induce certain cells to produce additional neurotransmitter receptors that presumably facilitate synaptic transmission. One such protein is the receptor for a neurotransmitter known as NMDA (N-methyl-D-aspartate). Substances that bind selectively to the NMDA receptor protein indicate a proliferation of such receptors after training (McCabe & Horn 1988), and NMDA antagonists (substances that bind to the receptor without activating it but without permitting NMDA to act either) injected into the IMHV area decrease the strength of imprinting (Brock et al. 1996). It is possible, therefore, that a critical piece of information concerning imprinting and stored in the IMHV region requires synaptic plasticity based on the proliferation of NMDA receptors in specific neurons.

Figure 12.4 shows a feed-back arrow from "physiological experiments" to "behavioral theory" to signify those cases in which physiological information suggests the existence of processes that were not completely obvious in purely behavioral experiments. Lesion experiments demonstrate that damage to the IMVH region reduces preference for the imprinting stimulus; but this reduction in preference is more drastic when the stimulus is arbitrary (a rotating box) than when it is natural (a rotating stuffed model). Preference for the natural object is reduced by the lesion, relative to a sham control, but it is still significantly greater than chance. Further experiments indicate that the preference for the naturalistic stuffed model is present 24 hr after hatching, but not 2 hr after hatching, and it requires walking experience to emerge. These results suggest that filial imprinting may actually involve two independent processes (Horn 1991). One of these processes is the emergence of a predisposition to recognize naturalistic objects. It is not necessarily the species-typical model that is attractive because, as mentioned previously in ***section 1.a.,*** chicks imprint more readily to a polecat than to an arbitrary geometric shape. The second process is the activation of a learning mechanism that leads to the acquisition of a detailed representation of the imprinting stimulus. It is this learning process that is dependent on the IMHV region.

Whereas the predisposition is perhaps a unique attribute of the phenomenon of filial imprinting, the learning mechanism need not be unique. For example, the development of a detailed representation of the hen may involve classical conditioning (e.g., within-compound associations) or even perceptual learning (e.g., mere exposure learning). All these learning processes are known to occur in a variety of species and situations. In the natural situation, predispositions and learning processes act together and reinforce each other. An emerging predisposition may function to direct attention to a specific set of cues (e.g., head and neck region), while disregarding other cues present in the situation; and the learning process may allow for the development of a detailed representation of other stimulus features that accompany the head-neck configuration. Learning is what permits a precocial chick to eventually recognize the various stimulus attributes of its mother as being part of the same configuration.

1.f. Imprintinglike Phenomena in Other Species. Do other species show evidence of filial imprinting similar to that of precocial birds? What about the development of recognition of objects other than the mother? The two most important criteria used to identify potential cases of imprinting are, first, whether learning by simple exposure is sufficient and, second, whether the learning process displays a sensitive period. Several documented instances of early learning seem to fit these general critera, but it would be a mistake to assume that the underlying processes are necessarily the same as those studied in precocial birds.

Consider, first, the parent-offspring relationship in altricial birds in which the chicks are born in a state of extreme immaturity, lacking any locomotory ability, capable only of waiting in the nest for a parent to come to feed them. Most of the familiar songbirds are altricial, including the sparrows, cardinals, finches, and other similar species grouped in the order Passeriformes. These nestlings may be able to learn to recognize their parents by simple exposure and may even exhibit a sensitive period for such learning. Obviously, one could not test the effects of exposure to an imprinting stimulus in terms of the following response in these nestlings because of their relative immaturity. Recognition can be assessed in terms of the *begging response*: Upon arrival of a parent to the nest, nestlings vigorously open their mouths, a response that induces the parent to deliver the food.

Experiments with blackbird chicks (*Turdus merula*) removed from the nest a few days after hatching and raised in darkness in the laboratory suggest that the development of parent recognition may involve exposure learning. In one experiment, nestlings were exposed to a stuffed model during feeding sessions and later given a preference test between the familiar model and a novel model at ages ranging between 10 and 23 days after hatching (Junco 1988). Preference for the familiar model was measured in terms of the duration of begging responses directed at the familiar model relative to all begging responses during the session. Preference for the familiar model was strongest in 11-day-olds, suggesting the presence of a sensitive period. Obviously, these nestlings are exposed to a natural type of instrumental conditioning training since begging (the response) is reinforced with food in the presence of a parent in the nest (the discriminative stimulus). It is thus possible that conditioning, rather than exposure itself, is responsible for the acquisition of a preference for a familiar visual object. However, further experiments suggest that the preference develops even in the absence of food reinforcement, implying that exposure itself may be sufficient. Junco (1994) suggested that food reinforcement may be necessary for the consolidation of the filial preference.

Suggestive evidence of an imprinting-like process has been collected in experiments with species that exhibit long-range migratory behavior. The idea is that exposure to chemical stimuli characteristic of the early environment leads to the formation of a chemical memory that the adult animal uses to orient toward the hatching site during breeding. Interestingly, this type of *chemical imprinting* has been suggested as a suitable method of repopulating a particular habitat with an endangered species (see "applications" in ***Figure 12.4***). In one such attempt, eggs of the endangered sea turtle *Lepidochelys kempi* collected near Rancho Nuevo, Mexico, were placed in containers with sand from Padre Island, Texas (about 400 km north of Rancho Nuevo, on the Gulf of Mexico), to determine if early exposure could induce the turtles to colonize Padre Island beaches for breeding purposes. In an experimental test of this hypothesis, 4-month-old turtles were exposed to an apparatus that allowed them a choice between four compartments, one with sand and seawater from Padre Island, another with sand and seawater from Galveston, Texas (approximately 300 km northeast of Padre Island), and two untreated control samples (Grassman et al. 1984). Turtles spent a significantly longer time in the compartment labeled with Padre Island sand and seawater than in any of the other compartments. Although many difficulties remain to be resolved in attempts to apply imprinting theory to the management of populations of endangered species of sea turtles (Grassman 1993), the notion of chemical imprinting may prove to be a valuable tool to use in establishing new nesting sites.

Chemical imprinting appears to underlie the migratory behavior of salmon species (Hasler & Sholz 1983). Salmon hatch in freshwater streams in the northern continents and then undergo a developmental process known as smoltification. Smoltification consists of a series of morphological, physiological, and behavioral changes that prepare the juvenile to tolerate seawater in the marine environment to which it soon migrates. However, salmon eventually go back to the continent, entering rivers and swimming upstream to engage in reproductive behavior (i.e., the spawning migration). Adults usually die in these streams after breeding. Salmon are well known for their tendency to return to the very freshwater rivers and streams where they hatched, and it has long been suspected that stream recognition is based on chemical imprinting. Morin et al. (1989) provided evidence that exposure to a particular chemical has a peak effectiveness that suggests the presence of a sensitive period. Fish were exposed to a water current containing the amino acid L-cysteine during one entire day. Independent groups received this exposure at various stages during the smoltification phase. After smoltification was over, fish were placed in a test situation in which the L-cysteine was presented, and changes in heart rate were measured as an index of chemical recognition. The animal's heart rate decreases when exposed to familiar stimuli; such a decrease in heart rate was found to be maximum for fish exposed to the chemical stimulus between day 21 and 28 of the smoltification phase, but not earlier or later.

Imprintinglike phenomena have also been described in some mammalian species. Several attempts at developing attachment to artificial stimuli in precocial mammals, such as the Guinea pig (*Cavia porcellus*), have been generally unsuccessful. In another precocial mammal, the goat (*Capra hircus*), it is the mother, rather than her offspring, that seems to form a bond with the newborn. This *maternal imprinting* develops relatively rapidly and preferentially when the mother is exposed to the newborn shortly after birth—implying a sensitive period for learning in the mother (Gubernick et al. 1979). If a mother is given access to a newborn for 5 min immediately after birth, it would later (in a test carried out several hours afterward) accept this animal as well as all its siblings, allowing them to nurse. Alien infants that spend at least 8 hr with their own mother are vigorously rejected; however, females are more tolerant of alien infants that have been kept in isolation since birth, even hours after giving birth. This last finding suggests that the sensitive period for maternal imprinting is not precisely timed, because an attachment to an alien infant can develop hours after a female has given birth, provided the infant has not been nursed by another female. Maternal imprinting is probably based on a labeling process mediated by licking and nourishing. Chemical stimuli in the mother's saliva and milk allow the mother to recognize her own infants and reject alien ones (Gubernick 1980).

A curious filial attachment (in this case, the "attachment" is literal, as shown in ***Figure 12.6, see back inside cover***) occurs in several shrew species of the family Crocidurinae (order Insectivora). During a relatively short period after birth, the mother stimulates her offspring to grab her fur with their teeth, and this rapidly results in other young holding onto the fur of their siblings. The mother then walks with her offspring holding in line. This entire formation is known as *caravaning behavior,* and it has not been observed outside the Crocidurinae. Observations of caravaning behavior in the musk shrew (*Suncus murinus*) indicate that it tends to occur during a period ranging between 5 and 24 days after birth, peaking at about 12 to 14 days of age, although these values may vary depending on the test situation (Tsuji & Ishikawa 1984, 1986). Musk shrews are altricial mammals that develop from helpless newborns with no vision to sexual maturity in approximately 30 days. Caravaning behavior emerges before the young open their eyes, and it has been assumed to function as a device to retrieve pups into the nest. After vision becomes functional, around day 8 after birth, caravaning behavior exposes the young to a broader set of environmental conditions together with the safety provided by the mother. This curious form of mother-offspring attachment does not seem to pass through a sensitive period in the same sense as in the case of filial imprinting. Rather, the behavior seems to emerge, peak, and disappear as the young age during their first month of life.

2. Reproductive and Social Behavior

2.a. Sexual Imprinting. Early social interactions that contribute to the survival of the developing infant also affect adult social behavior. The importance of early experience in the socialization process was demonstrated in a classic set of studies in dogs by the American comparative psychologist John P. Scott [1909–2000]. Dogs and wolves that are raised in close contact with humans later display few or no fear reactions toward humans and are capable of developing positive social responses. In fact, dogs establish their patterns of social behavior during a sensitive period ranging between 4 and 15 weeks after birth (Scott & Fuller 1965). Experience acquired by the infant may become relevant later in its life, affecting a variety of behaviors, including agonistic and reproductive behaviors. An example of the delayed effect of early experience in adult social behavior is provided by sexual imprinting, which may be viewed as a case of *latent learning* (analogous phenomena include vocal learning, discussed in

section 3 below, and spatial learning, illustrated in ***Figure 4.3,*** p. 94). *Sexual imprinting* refers to early learning that allows the adult to recognize conspecifics in the context of reproductive behavior.

Sexual imprinting has been traditionally tied to filial imprinting on the basis of observations of the sexual behavior of animals that had been imprinted to nonnatural objects as infants. For example, ducklings imprinted to human beings would, as adults, engage in courting humans rather than conspecifics. Thus, the young precocial bird would seem to learn both to recognize a particular object (filial imprinting) and to use that learning to develop a sexual preference for objects similar to the original one later in life (sexual imprinting). In agreement with this hypothesis, chicks receiving IMHV lesions soon after hatching, which, as discussed in ***section 1.e.,*** exhibit deficits in filial imprinting, show no clear sexual preferences as adults (Bolhuis et al. 1989). Filial and sexual imprinting seem to depend on the integrity of the IMHV area to occur normally. Furthermore, studies in which filial and sexual imprinting are induced and tested with arbitrary stimuli suggest that a filial preference correlates well with a sexual preference (Vidal 1980).

However, the nature of the stimulus presented in a test of sexual preference, as well as the social experience of the juvenile bird, can also affect adult sexual preferences. Chicks imprinted to an artificial model and subsequently exposed to conspecifics exhibit a sexual preference for a stuffed natural model later in life, rather than for the artificial imprinting model to which they were attached (Vidal 1980). It appears, therefore, that the establishment of a filial attachment does not rigidly determines adult sexual preferences. Sexual preferences may be significantly influenced by the nature of the stimulus (i.e., natural models may be more effective stimuli than artificial models) and by social interactions that occur after early filial attachments are formed.

There is, in fact, a great deal of diversity among birds in the extent to which social interactions determine adult sexual preferences. In zebra finches (*Taeniopygia guttata*), adult males direct courtship singing either to conspecific females or to female Bengalese finches (*Lonchura striata*), depending on whether they were raised with zebra or Bengalese finches, respectively. If zebra finch males are exposed during development first to conspecifics and later to Bengalese finches, then they exhibit what is known as *dithering behavior,* that is, they direct courtship singing and other social behaviors to females of both species. Sexual preference of ditherer males is stable over time and relatively restricted since they do not engage in sexual courtship with females from other finch species. These two facts have prompted the idea that these males exhibit *double sexual imprinting* (ten Cate 1986). Interestingly, if zebra finch males are raised with conspecifics and Bengalese finches simultaneously, they exhibit adult preference for females of their own species (Immelmann 1972). This preeminence of conspecifics arises from early social interactions between the developing zebra finch and its parents, which tend to direct a greater number of both feeding and aggressive responses to the young zebra finch than do the Bengalese adults.

In other avian species, sexual preferences may be so flexible that social interaction in the adult stage may reverse preferences established earlier in life. In the parasitic cowbird (*Molothrus ater*), sexual preferences toward canaries (*Serinus canaria*) can be established by housing 1-year-old males with both female and male canaries. After several months of such housing, male cowbirds direct most vocalizations to canaries rather than to conspecific females. However, male cowbirds housed with conspecific females sing mostly to them rather than to canaries. The initially strong tendency to respond to canaries can be totally reversed by exposure to conspecific males and females (Freeberg et al. 1995). Social interactions also affect the development of social preferences in lambs (*Capra hircus*). Infants housed with dogs show significant preference for the dogs over sheep in two-choice tests; however, this preference is completely reversed after a period of 4 months of housing with a group of sheep (Cairns & Johnson 1965). Results like these deviate in important ways from what would be expected to be the result of a process of sexual imprinting. Although sexual imprinting may occur in certain species, the adult sexual preferences of other species may be quite malleable and susceptible to social experience.

2.b. Mother-Infant Interactions in Mammals. The *mother-infant bond* is bound to have a great biological importance in mammals because of the central role played by the mother in the survival of the newborn and infant mammal. In all species of mammals, the mother provides nourishment in the form of milk. She is also generally in charge of building and maintaining a nest area, as in many small-size species (e.g., insectivores, rodents), or of providing behavioral guidance and support, as in many aquatic species (e.g., dolphins and whales). By and large, the mother-infant relationship in mammals is more malleable than in precocial birds, so the concept of filial imprinting has generally been avoided. However, much like imprinting, early experience does play a significant role in the adjustment of the animal to both infantile and adult social situations, which suggests the presence of important parallels (i.e., the "connections" referred to in ***Figure 12.4***). Let's consider first the mother-infant bond in rodents.

The order Rodentia is a prolific monophyletic group with hundreds of species adapted to a large variety of habitats and exhibiting substantial variation in terms of life-history strategies (e.g., altricial vs. precocial). These biological features of rodents and their ability to easily breed under laboratory conditions have made them prime research models for comparative developmental studies. A substantial amount of research has been done with the albino rat (*Rattus norvegicus*), an altricial species. Rosenblatt and Siegel (1980) suggested that *maternal behaviors* (e.g., nest building, nursing, retrieving pups into the nest, etc.), are an extension of the reproductive physiology of the female during pregnancy. The pregnant female's physiology is regulated by a complex set of interactions among *hormones,* including progesterone, estradiol, and prolactin among others, that regulate such physiological responses as uterine contractions and milk production. Progesterone levels, for instance, increase steadily during pregnancy and then drop drastically about 4 days before parturition. This decrease in the level of circulating progesterone disinhibits maternal behavior; if progesterone is kept at high levels experimentally, the female rat does not respond to pups placed in her nest. The onset of maternal behavior is also dependent on relatively high circulating levels of estradiol, prolactin, and oxytocin. If these hormones are pharmacologically blocked or their source surgically eliminated (e.g., hypophysectomy, i.e., ablation of the pituitary gland, eliminates prolactin), then the female shows significant deficits in maternal behavior. As discussed before (see, for example, ***Chapter 8, section 2.g.,*** pp. 285–287), hormones are produced inside endocrine cells, released into the bloodstream, and distributed throughout the organism; they act by fitting into a membrane receptor and inducing a variety of changes in their target cells. Some of their targets are peripheral organs; for example, oxytocin released from the hypothalamus and pituitary gland acts, among other sites, in the mammary glands, where it facilitates milk ejection immediately after birth. Other targets are neurons located inside the CNS; these central effects allow hormones to affect behavior directly. For example, injections of oxytocin directly into the ventricles of the rat brain induce maternal behavior; oxytocin administered in this manner probably acts in a variety of brain areas where numerous cells with membrane receptors respond to this hormone, especially in the diencephalon (Insel 1992). Lesions of such diencephalic areas as the preoptic nucleus and the bed nucleus of the stria terminalis abolish maternal behavior in rats.

After parturition, the control of reproductive behavior shifts from hormones to sensory stimulation. The interchange of stimulation between mother and pup is referred to as *trophallaxis* (a term also applied to the interchange of food between individuals in the social insects). This initial maternal behavior is relatively insensitive to manipulations of hormone levels, either by exogenous administration of hormones or by the surgical removal of the ovaries or adrenal glands. Moreover, hormonal manipulations that disrupt maternal behavior in virgin females, such as injections of oxytocin receptor antagonists, fail to affect behavior in experienced females. The maternal behavior of the female rat depends on exposure to the pups during the first hours after partum. Mothers that are deprived of this experience by the experimental removal of their pups shortly after birth exhibit almost no maternal behavior when pups are reintroduced on the 3rd or 5th day after partum. The introduction of pups after 5 days induces no nursing or retrieval behavior in these deprived mothers. In contrast, separation of mother and pup for the same amount of time, but after the bond has been established, does not disrupt maternal behavior when pups are reintroduced. Maternal behavior is maintained by a repertoire of infant reactions and responses that stimulates the mother to engage in a variety of protective and nourishing activities. As the infant develops and matures, these responses disappear and maternal behavior decreases in frequency. Interestingly, a female rat can be induced to persist in her maternal responses by replacing the older pups with younger ones. In a classic study, Wiesner and Sheard (1933) were able to maintain maternal behavior for more than a year by substituting younger pups for older ones every two weeks!

Female rats respond to a variety of stimuli generated by the pups, including odors, body contact (gustatory, tactile, and thermal stimuli), and ultrasonic vocalizations. Female rodents of a variety of altricial species respond to ultrasonic vocalizations emitted by their infants (Smith & Sales 1980). These distress vocalizations communicate hunger, low body temperature, or some other aversive state of the pup. In most of these species, the newborn is *ectothermic*—that is, incapable of maintaining a constant body temperature—and it must regulate behaviorally by seeking the mother's warmth. *Endothermy* develops gradually in altricial species, taking days or weeks to achieve adultlike efficiency. The distress vocalizations of rodents vary in frequency and duration depending on the species and the age of the infant. In general, their frequency tends to increase with age, but the calls become shorter. In rats, for example, the frequency may vary between 30 and 100 kHz and the calls may last up to 200 ms. These calls are sometimes referred to as ultrasonic because their lowest frequencies are rarely below 20 kHz and are usually above 30 kHz; for this reason, they are usually imperceptible to the human ear (for most people, sounds of 20 to 30 kHz lie in the upper limit of audition; hence the adjective "ultrasonic"). The distress vocalizations of rodents are characterized by being extremely stereotyped.

Proximal cues also play an important role in regulating the behavior of the mother and pups. For example, oral stimulation provided by the mother's licking behavior stimulates the pup to nurse; in turn, tactile stimulation of the mother's ventrum by the pups induces quiescence in the mother, which further exposes her ventrum to other pups in the litter. Oral stimulation of the mother's ventrum eventually triggers a response consisting of flexing the ventrum, arching the back, and extending the rear legs to accommodate the pups (Stern & Johnson 1989). When the mother assumes this posture, milk becomes available to the pups. Rat pups direct a variety of behaviors at the mother's ventrum to stimulate nursing. This was studied by Polan and Hofer (1999) using an ingenious device that enclosed a pup in a circular compartment underneath a floor where various types of stimuli, including the pup's mother, could be presented. The anesthetized mother (anesthetized to prevent movement) was very effective in eliciting a variety of orienting responses relative to several other stimuli (e.g., open roof, wire, cotton, or pelt). For example, pups stimulated by the mother's ventrum turned upside down, lying on their back, and pressed their snout against the fur by flexing the neck. Moreover, overnight isolation from the mother intensified these behaviors and the pups' general level of arousal, even if they were housed with their siblings. These maternally oriented behaviors appear to be influenced by internal motivational factors, functioning so that they help the altricial pup to establish closer contact with its mother for nourishment, warmth, and protection.

The maternal behavior of rats is so dependent on sensory stimulation that it can be induced in virgin females and even in males simply by exposing them to rat pups for a few days. This so-called *sensitized maternal behavior* can also be induced immediately after weaning (after postnatal day 21 in the rat), as well as in adult animals (Gray & Chesley 1984). Exposure to toys of similar size and weight does not induce as much behavior, suggesting that social interaction is important to sensitize maternal behavior. After a few days of group housing, both weanling and adult rats tend to exhibit substantially more sniffing and licking of the pups than corresponding controls exposed to the toys. Experimental rats also tend to position themselves on top of the pups, much as mothers normally do. However, weanlings exhibit more maternal behavior than adults that have not been exposed to pups before the experiment, suggesting that early exposure to pups may contribute to the development of maternal behavior in rats.

2.c. Attachment. As shown in the previous section, a rat mother and her pups affect each other by interacting in a complex manner in the context of nursing and maternal care. Does this mean that the mother and pup have established an attachment? I used the word "attachment" before, in the context of filial imprinting, but it is now time to define it more precisely (Ainsworth 1972). *Attachment* refers to the bond that develops between the mother and her infants, and it is usually defined by three characteristics: first, recognition of the attachment object and discrimination from other objects; second, preference for the attachment object over other objects; third, aversive response to the removal of the attachment object. Clearly, filial imprinting in precocial birds fits these criteria and is thus an example of attachment. What about the mother-infant bond in mammals?

In the case of rats, neither the mother nor the pups seem to exhibit *individual recognition.* I mentioned before that maternal behavior can be prolonged by replacing older pups with younger ones. One implication of this observation is that the mother fails to recognize her own offspring. Mothers accept and nurse alien pups so long as they acquire the odors of her litter (Leon 1975). Thus, the mother appears to respond to the pups' odor in a generic sense rather than on an individual basis. Pups, in turn, do not discriminate between their own mother and an alien mother, so long as they are both lactating females and their diets are the same. Pups respond to chemical cues provided by the milk, which, in turn, can be affected by the female's diet. Both mothers and pups also respond to separation, exhibiting aversive reactions, but these reactions do not demonstrate individual recognition. For example, plasma levels of the stress hormone corticosterone are raised when a mother is deprived of her litter, but controls show that these changes are due to handling during the experimental procedure rather than to the specific absence of the pups (Smotherman et al. 1977). Pups separated from their mother emit a higher level of distress vocalizations, but these calls are reduced to normal levels if the pups are placed in a warm environment and provided with tactile stimulation (Hofer 1975). Distress calls can be experimentally affected by exposing the pups to various aversive treatments. For example, placing them in a novel location, handling them, and administering electric shocks induced three progressively more intense levels of distress-call emission. In turn, mothers reunited with pups exposed to these treatments show a progressively higher level of plasma corticosterone (Smotherman et al. 1977). Obviously, therefore, the rat mother can sense the level of distress in her pups and respond adequately without individually recognizing them, while the rat pup has a complex repertoire of responses that induce maternal care without being able to individually recognize its mother. Rats, and perhaps many other species of mammals that exhibit a degree of mother-infant bond, do not meet the criteria for attachment.

In other species, however, there is some evidence that at least the mother recognizes her offspring individually. This could be true of sheep, which can discriminate the odor of their own lambs from that of others (Kendrick et al. 1992), and of the northern elephant seal (*Mirounga angustirostris*), in which individual recognition may be based on the infant's vocalizations (Petrinovich 1974). But the most extensive evidence of attachment comes from the study of the mother-infant bond in primates. For example, vervet (*Cercopithecus aethiops*) and squirrel monkey (*Saimiri sciureus*) mothers recognize their own offspring and prefer them to other infants, including familiar alien infants (Cheney & Seyfarth 1980). Similarly, infant squirrel monkeys can recognize their mother and discriminate her from other females (Kaplan & Russell 1974).

A number of studies also suggest that the aversive response of both a mother and her infant to a relatively short period of separation is specific to the pair and is not spared by the presence of other familiar animals in the immediate environment. Separation-induced stress is conveniently measured in terms of plasma concentrations of corticosteroid hormones (e.g., corticosterone in rodents and cortisol in primates). These hormones reflect the degree of activation of the so-called *hypothalamo-pituitary-adrenal axis,* which is involved in the organism's response to aversive situations. In one experiment (Coe et al. 1978), mother-infant pairs of squirrel monkeys were housed in groups that included a late-term female that could potentially act as an "aunt" for the infant, providing care in the absence of the mother. Nonetheless, removal of either the mother or the infant from a group induced an elevation of cortisol levels in both the mother and the infant. Interestingly, high cortisol levels were observed even in infants that received "aunt" care during the period of separation from its mother, a fact suggesting that the stress state induced by separation is specific to the absence of the mother.

The stress derived from separation has a significant impact on the organism's general health state. In rhesus monkeys (*Macaca mulatta*), for example, maternal separation not only increases cortisol levels but also decreases the amount of bacteria that are a normal component of the intestinal flora, such as *Lactobacillus* (Bailey & Coe 1999). These bacteria buffer the organism against the proliferation of pathogenic microorganisms like *Salmonella.* A decrease of the intestinal flora following maternal separation makes the infant rhesus monkeys prone to infections by pathogens that are kept at a subclinical level in infants housed with their mothers. There is also some indication that social isolation in cebus monkeys (*Cebus apella*) may impair immune system activity, leaving the organism more vulnerable to disease (Kling et al. 1992). Infant primates appear to be under strong selective pressure to develop and maintain an attachment to their mother.

Monkeys can also develop an attachment to an artificial object with certain qualities. This was discovered by the American comparative psychologist Harry Harlow [1905–1981], who developed an extensive and influential research program on the effects of early experience on infant and adult behavior in rhesus monkeys. Harlow (1971; Harlow & Zimmermann 1959) was initially interested in the psychological abilities of infant monkeys, so he developed a procedure for raising them in isolation. It was soon obvious that infants that were separated from their mother 6 to 12 hours after birth exhibited a strong attachment to a blanket used to cover the wire floor of the cage. Infants reacted violently when the piece of cloth was removed from the cage, and their behavior was disturbed for a few days, making them unsuitable subjects for the types of experiments that were being conducted in the laboratory. These observations suggested a procedure for studying the development of affective attachment in monkeys. The feature that seems to have sparked Harlow's attention was the possibility, which his later research confirmed, that attachment to a surrogate mother was a function of tactile stimuli (later known as *contact comfort*). The prevailing idea at the time explained the infant's attachment to its mother as derived, through conditioning, from the satisfaction provided by the mother's milk of the infant's primary motivational states of hunger and thirst. In contrast, Harlow's research suggested that contact comfort itself provided a source of primary reinforcement.

Infants were then exposed to mother surrogates made of either wire or cloth, each with a distinctive face to provide for individuality, as shown in ***Figure 12.7-a.*** These were cylindrical objects, standing at a 45° angle, to which the infants could cling. In one experiment, only one of these surrogates provided milk, and the time spent in contact with each was recorded for a group of infants. The results, shown in ***Figure***

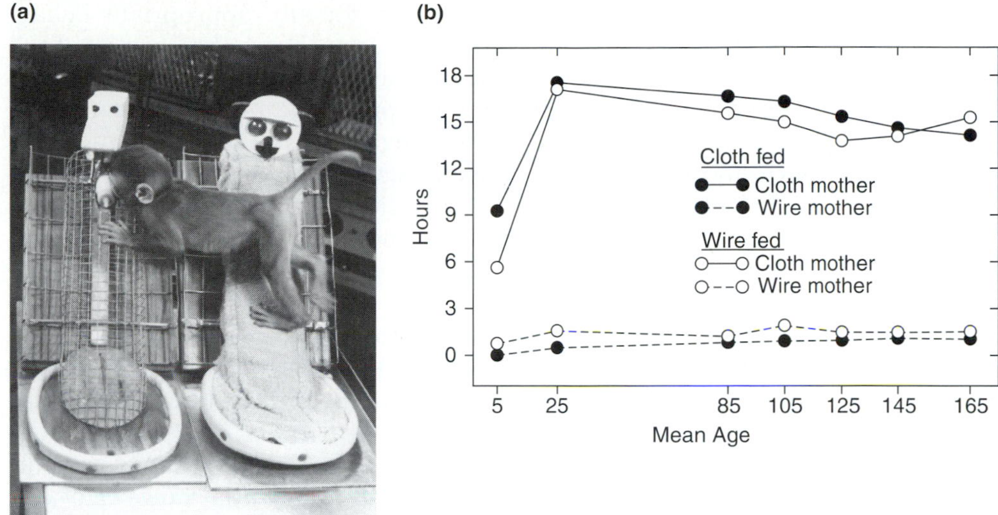

FIGURE 12.7. *(a)* Surrogate mothers used in the classic experiments on attachment in infant rhesus monkeys conducted by Harlow and Zimmerman (1959). The wire mother (left) is a wire cylinder tilted at a 45° angle so that the infant monkey could cling to it. The cloth mother (right) is similar except that it has a different face and the cylinder is covered with cloth. *(b)* Infant monkeys spent most of their time in contact or proximity to the cloth mother, whether milk was provided by the cloth or the wire mother. Experiments like this support the hypothesis that contact comfort is a primary incentive capable of facilitating the development of attachment in infant monkeys.

12.7-b, clearly demonstrated that whether the milk was provided by the wire or cloth surrogate mother, monkeys spent most of their time in contact with the cloth mother. Interestingly, the infants for which the wire mother provided milk did not become attached in time, as would be expected if attachment were acquired through a process of conditioning via milk reinforcement. These infants spent enough time with the wire mothers to obtain nourishment and then shifted to the cloth mother for the remaining time.

Attachment to the cloth mother was further indicated by the infant's behavior in fear-inducing situations. In a typical test situation, infants raised with both surrogates and exposed to a mechanical toy that induced a fear response preferred to seek contact with the cloth mother, independently of whether milk was provided by the cloth mother or the wire mother. Infants exposed to a fear-inducing stimulus with the cloth mother present would usually cling to and rub their bodies against the cloth for a few minutes. Eventually, the fear would decline, and infants would leave the surrogate mother to approach and explore the object. Infants reared exclusively with wire mothers would rapidly develop an attachment to the cloth mother when fear-inducing stimuli were presented in a series of test sessions. Furthermore, given a choice between approaching one of these mothers or avoiding them by hiding in a compartment, infants raised with the cloth mother developed strong approach tendencies. In contrast, infants raised and fed by the wire mother approached her initially, but after 100 days of age begun to show avoidance reactions.

Attachment to the cloth mother was also evident when infants were placed in a novel environment containing several objects known to elicit manipulatory behavior in monkeys (e.g., a roll of paper, wooden blocks, etc.). In this open-field test, monkeys raised with the cloth mother rapidly clutched it as soon as they were placed in the room, yet, again, they soon began to explore the new objects and exhibit manipulative behaviors. Infants would typically return to the cloth mother periodically and before shifting their attention to a new object. These same infants placed in the open-field room without the cloth mother exhibited a totally different set of behaviors, including crouching in a corner, vocalizing, rocking, sucking, and running around the open field on their hind legs while clutching themselves with their arms. Similarly, infants raised with wire mothers showed evidence of distress when placed in the open-field situation, even if their wire mother was present. If the wire mother was present, these infants would typically sit close to her and hold themselves with their arms while rocking their bodies. Infants raised with wire mothers showed very few of the playful and exploratory behaviors that were typical of infants raised by the cloth mother and comforted by her presence.

2.d. Early Experience and Primate Social Behavior. Most primates live in groups. Group living demands from the individual a set of complex social skills and behaviors. Individuals have to be able to adequately interpret signals of dominance and receptivity, and they need to respond to such signals with the socially appropriate behaviors. In return, they share the benefits of the group, including access to resources and protection from predators. As a result, it is not surprising that early social isolation has negative effects upon the ability of the adult primate to adjust to its social environment.

Rhesus monkeys deprived of their mothers during early infancy grow up to exhibit a variety of deficits in their individual and social behavior. A comparison between feral rhesus monkeys and laboratory-reared monkeys (housed in individual cages that prevented physical contact with other monkeys but allowed visual and auditory contact) indicated a substantial number of differences (Mason 1960). For example, feral monkeys displayed longer bouts of grooming, shorter aggressive episodes, and higher frequency of sexual behavior. Sexual behavior of laboratory-reared rhesus monkeys was also qualitatively different from that of feral monkeys, as shown in ***Figure 12.8.*** In this particular study, all males were tested with experienced females. Under these conditions, the deprived monkeys were less efficient in their sexual behavior than the feral ones, usually attempting to mount the female from the side or thrusting against the female's back. Deprived rhesus monkeys also remained fearful of novel situations and interacted little with peers when placed in social situations. Deprived females who became mothers provided deficient maternal care to their own infants and were often aggressive during the initial 2 to 3 months of life of their infants. Sackett (1967) found that 4-year-old rhesus monkeys raised by these motherless mothers displayed significantly higher amounts of aggressive behavior than monkeys raised by normal mothers.

Infants raised with a cloth mother, which, as described previously, provided a source of attachment and encouraged nor-

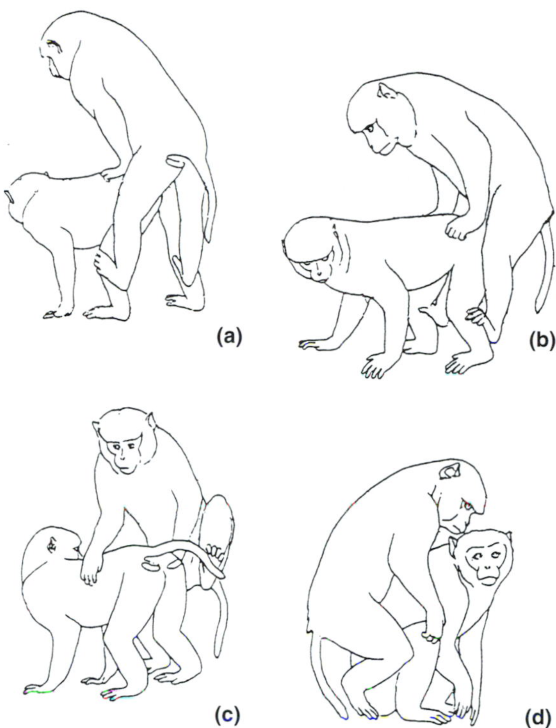

FIGURE 12.8. Sexual behavior of rhesus monkeys (Mason 1960). ***(a, b)*** The normal copulatory responses of feral males. ***(c, d)*** Abnormal and ineffective copulatory responses of males raised under laboratory conditions.

mal exploratory behavior, also displayed deficient social adjustment as adults. Various "therapies" were tried with these infants in an attempt to determine whether the abnormal social behavior of deprived monkeys could be reduced or eliminated. Movement introduced in the surrogate mothers by adding rockers or by moving the model on a track resulted in only modest improvement in social skills. Monkeys raised in the company of dogs developed an attachment to their companions of equal strength to that shown by monkeys raised with moving models (e.g., similar levels of vocalizations emitted upon withdrawal of the object). However, dog-reared monkeys were generally more likely to initiate social interactions, and their social interactions were more complex (Capitanio 1985). ***Figure 12.9*** shows a representation of the social networks developed by dog-reared and hobbyhorse-reared rhesus monkeys. Whereas all dog-reared monkeys exhibited some social preference toward other monkeys in the group, only some of the hobbyhorse-reared monkeys did so. Grooming and its reciprocation were observed in some of the dog-reared monkeys, but not in the monkeys reared with a moving model. Although dogs provided a type of interaction different in many ways to that typically found among rhesus monkeys, these animals engaged in a substantial amount of social interchange, which obviously prepared the monkeys to adjust better to their species-typical social environment.

In the laboratory context, perhaps the most successful treatment of deprived infants was provided by normally reared monkeys; for this reason, they were referred

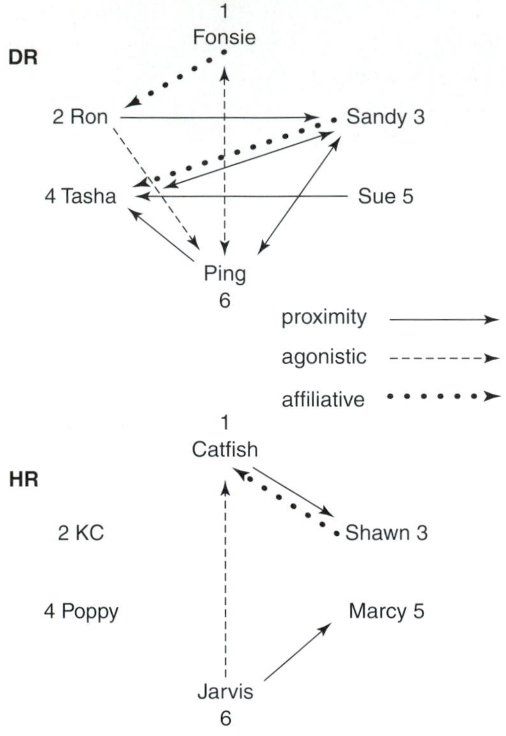

FIGURE 12.9. Networks of social relations in rhesus monkeys exposed during early development to either dogs (***DR***, or dog-reared monkeys) or a wooden hobbyhorse (***HR***, or hobbyhorse-reared monkeys). Although the type of social interaction provided by dogs is very different from that provided by conspecifics, dog-raised monkeys developed a more complex set of relationships among themselves than those observed in hobbyhorse-reared monkeys (Capitanio, 1985).

to as "therapists" (Harlow & Suomi 1971). In one study, 6-month-old, socially isolated monkeys were permitted to join 3-month-old, normally reared monkeys for a period of 2 hours per day. A 3-month-old normal monkey is sufficiently mature to provide clinging contact and yet too young to behave aggressively toward deprived monkeys. Initially, a deprived monkey placed in social contact with a therapist would typically rush to a corner, where it would remain motionless. However, the therapist's reaction would be to follow the deprived monkey and cling to it. In a few weeks, these monkeys were clinging to each other and eventually displaying vigorous, playful interactions. Deprived monkeys gradually stopped displaying maladaptive behaviors, and by the end of their first year of age, their behavior was essentially indistinguishable from that of normally reared monkeys.

3. Development of Vocal Behavior

3.a. Avian Vocalizations. Many different types of animals vocalize by modulating the sounds produced by the release of air from the lungs. This is how human speech, the alarm calls of ground squirrels, and the stereotyped vocalizations of rodents—among other examples covered in previous sections and chapters—are generated. Birds are notable for the evolution of a wide range of developmental programs that produce *vocal behavior* of various levels of complexity. In fact, a group of avian species known as the songbirds (order Passeriformes) has attracted the attention of experts and nonexperts alike because of their refined and melodious singing abilities. Some species, like the canary, have been domesticated solely because of the beauty of their songs, while generations of ornithologists, both amateur and professional, have enjoyed the observation, description, and cataloguing of singing behavior for centuries.

The modern study of bird vocal behavior was perhaps initiated by the English ornithologist William H. Thorpe [1902–1988], who developed a set of procedures to study bird songs in a quantitative manner. Thorpe (1961) recorded the songs of chaffinches (*Fringilla coelebs*) in their natural habitat, using a sound spectrograph to obtain a visual representation of the temporal and spectral properties of each song. The resulting sonogram permits an appreciation of the various components of a song, the range of frequencies modulated during song emission, and the temporal structure of the song (see ***Figure 12.10***).

Thorpe also went beyond mere description. Using a modern version of Spalding's isolation experiment, Thorpe took chaffinch chicks directly from their nests and brought them into the laboratory, where they were hand-raised in acoustic isolation. The scientific controversies of the time centered around the issue summarized by the phrase *nature versus nurture* (see ***Chapter 1, section 5,*** pp. 18–20), so research of this kind aimed to discover which aspects of the song were "innate" and which were "acquired." In reality, and as shown throughout this book, behavior is better understood as resulting from an interaction of information at various levels of organization. Thorpe's research opened the way to an understanding of birdsong development as based upon an interaction of genetic, physiological, and environmental influences more in line with the *epigenetic view* of development that dominates today's scientific thought (see ***Chapter 10, section 1.e.,*** pp. 370–372).

Field observations and experimental research on the vocal behavior of birds has provided a wealth of information since the 1950s. We now know that species differ in developmental profiles, although the extent to which the evolution of different developmental programs relates to ecological factors, phylogenetic constraints, or a complex interplay of both is still unclear. The calls and songs of birds also function in several contexts, including mother-offspring interactions, reproductive activities, and flocking behavior. Vocalizations allow birds to communicate information about aversive internal states (e.g., the distress calls of chicks), food availability, predatory danger (e.g., alarm calls), territorial tendencies, and reproductive readiness, among many others. Depending on the species, the song of a bird may identify it as belonging to a particular species (species-typical song), as inhabiting a particular region within the distribution range of a species (dialect song), or as being a particular individual within a population.

The vocalizations of many nonpasserine species are widely considered to be simple, stereotyped, and largely independent of vocal experience for their development. For example, they tend to be unimpaired by experimental deafening after hatching, which suggests that these vocalizations might be independent even of auditory feedback (Konishi 1963). These vocalizations, usually produced by both males and females, are referred to as *calls* rather than songs. However, research also shows that at least some of these calls are sensitive to various sources of experience, some quite unexpected. In many precocial species, it is possible to distinguish different types of calls for different food items. For example, the

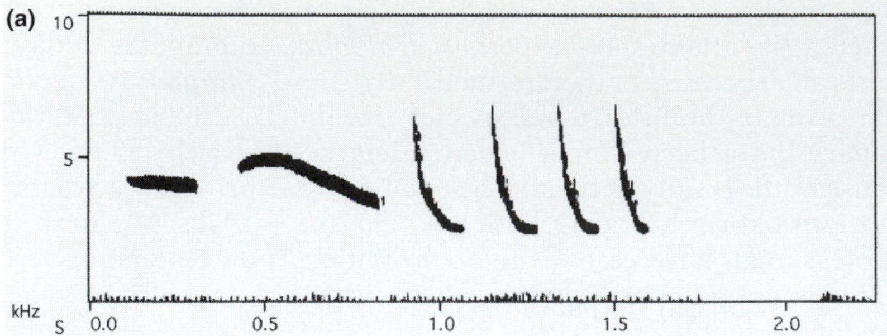

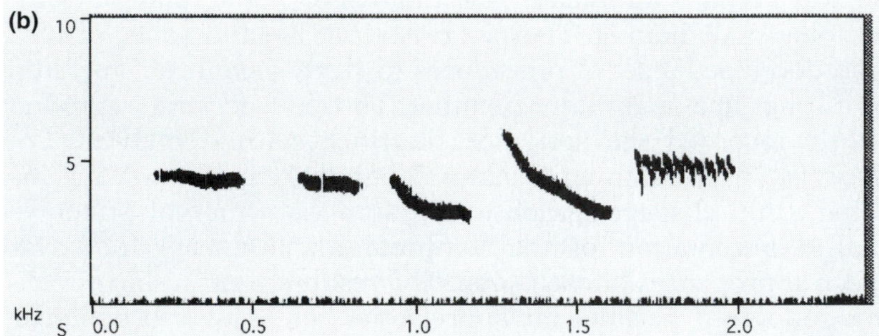

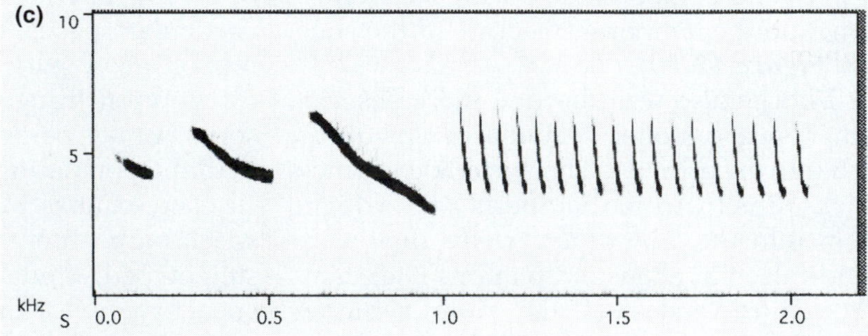

FIGURE 12.10. Sonograms of the song of the rufous-collared sparrow *(Zonotrichia capensis)*. The initial part of the song that included two to four relatively long elements in these samples is called the theme. The ending portion of the song that includes a variable number of fast notes is referred to as the trill. These sonograms were recorded in different regions of Argentina: ***(a)*** and ***(c)*** were recorded in forested habitats, southwest of the Pampas region; whereas ***(b)*** comes from a male living in the highland grasslands of Cordoba, in central Argentina. Differences in trill structure reflect geographic variations in the song, called dialects. (Photograph courtesy of Pablo Tubaro.)

food calls of chickens (*Gallus gallus*) may convey information about the quality of the food (Marler et al. 1986). A hen's food call may attract her chicks to food sources, and a cock's food call may attract hens to his vicinity, increasing courtship opportunities. In the laboratory, high-quality food calls can be released by providing a mealworm, whereas low-quality calls can be induced by providing regular laboratory food. The two calls involve the same note, but the note is repeated at a higher frequency in the high-quality call. It seems that, at least in some species, these food calls can control behavior even before they are associated with high- or low-quality food items. Calls are therefore said to be *prefunctionally organized* (Moffatt & Hogan 1992). In one experiment, chicks of the Burmese red junglefowl (*Gallus gallus spadiceus*) received training in a runway, where they were exposed to two kinds of trials in a random order. In one group, running from the start to the goal box of the runway when the high-quality food call was being played back through a speaker was reinforced with a mealworm, whereas running when the low-quality food call was being presented was nonreinforced. In this condition, therefore, the calls matched the quality of the outcome, and the chicks rapidly learned to run faster in the presence of the high-quality food call. However, in the reverse condition it was the low-quality food call that signaled the mealworm, whereas the high-quality call was paired with nonreinforcement. The speed of running of these animals during the initial trials was higher for the high-quality call than for the low-quality call; but as the chicks experienced the reversed contingencies, their speeds also reversed, eventually running faster in the presence of the low-quality call (which signaled a mealworm). These results suggest that while the chicks have a tendency to respond faster to the high-quality food call, even before ever experiencing a contingency between that type of call and a high-quality food item, the tendency can be reversed by experience. The calls themselves may be simple and stereotyped, but their ability to control behavior by acting as discriminative stimuli is quite malleable.

Maternal calls have also been demonstrated to be highly attractive to chicks of several precocial species soon after hatching. These vocalizations are referred to as *assembly calls* because the chicks or ducklings respond by approaching the source of acoustic stimulation. An extensive series of experiments with Peking ducks (*Anas platyrhynchos*) have uncovered the importance of auditory embryonic experience in the development of such preference (Gottlieb 1981). In order to exhibit preference for the distinctive maternal call, duckling embryos have to be exposed to their own vocalizations and those of their broodmates. This type of stimulation normally occurs in the nesting environment in which embryos develop. The calls emitted by one embryo can be heard both by that embryo inside the egg and by other embryos in adjacent eggs. The importance of these sources of experience has been demonstrated by a combination of experimental manipulations on the embryo, including devocalization, deafening, and individual incubation. When embryonic acoustic experience is prevented, ducklings respond to the maternal calls of a variety of species, exhibiting a loss of specificity in their response to the species-typical assembly call. Interestingly, the embryonic calls that are so important in this process bear little overall resemblance to the assembly call emitted by the hen, containing only isolated features in common (e.g., the range of frequencies, or notes per second, is similar). Moreover, this experience must occur before hatching in order to be effective, suggesting the presence of a sensitive period (Gottlieb 1985). Embryonic learning of the maternal call, similar to the one just described for Peking ducks, has also been observed in several precocial species. Again, this suggests that whereas the calls themselves may be simple and stereotyped, the call's ability to induce behavioral changes in young birds requires prehatching experience.

3.b. Vocal Learning in Birds. *Vocal learning* is demonstrated when the adult vocalization requires some type of auditory experience to develop normally—that is, within the parameters of variability in song production that are typical of the species. As mentioned previously, such demonstrations require convergent evidence from a variety of procedures, including devocalization, deafening, and rearing in isolation, among others. Vocal learning probably occurs in species from many avian orders, but it has so far been clearly observed only in three orders: in parrots and budgerigars (order Psittaciformes), in hummingbirds (order Trochiliformes), and in the songbirds (order Passeriformes). This phylogenetic distribution suggests that the mechanisms subserving vocal learning capacities are likely to have evolved independently in these three orders.

Very little is known about the contribution of learning processes to the development of vocal behavior in budgerigars and hummingbirds. Experiments in which nestling budgerigars (*Melopsittacus undulatus*) are deafened a few days after hatching indicate that auditory feedback is important in the development of complex food-begging calls (Heaton & Brauth 1999) and contact calls (Dooling et al. 1987). For example, deaf budgerigars emit food-begging calls that are significantly longer and less variable than those of control animals. The deleterious effects of post-hatching deafening in budgerigars is analogous to the effects of deafening in songbirds (see below), and it contrasts with the invulnerability of calls that do not depend on vocal learning (see ***section 3.a.*** above) to similar manipulations.

The Passeriformes, or songbirds, produce vocalizations referred to as songs. The difference between a call and a song is to some degree arbitrary. *Songs* are melodious vocalizations, usually (but not always) restricted to the male, and produced in the context of reproductive behavior (e.g., to advertise the occupation of a territory to other males and to attract females). There are two major taxonomic subdivisions of the Passeriformes: suborders Passeri (e.g., mockingbirds, sparrows, finches, etc.; also known as oscines) and Tyranni (e.g., manakins, woodcreepers, ovenbirds, etc.; also known as suboscines). Vocal learning has been extensively studied in oscine species, to which the most familiar songbirds belong. Based on molecular phylogenetic analyses, suboscine species are thought to be relatively more primitive (Sibley & Ahlquist 1990). Their vocalizations are less sensitive to manipulations that restrict experience, a fact suggesting that learning plays a relatively minor role in song production (Kroodsma 1984). Interestingly, these suborders were traditionally established on the basis of anatomical differences in the syrinx (essential for sound modulation) and middle ear oscicles (essential for auditory perception). In both of these sets of traits, the suboscines exhibit a lower degree of complexity than the oscines.

The diversity in profiles for song development among oscine species is astounding, although they tend to share certain properties. For example, oscine song development is greatly impaired by deafening. As mentioned previously, deafening eliminates the ability of a bird to hear its own vocalizations, which is a source of sensorimotor experience vital to the development of singing behavior. However, the effects may vary across species. For example, Konishi (1964, 1965) found that deafening greatly impaired song structure in white-crown sparrows (*Zonotrichia leucophrys*), but had less devastating effects in juncos (*Junco* spp.). A similar conclusion applies to the effects of rearing in acoustic isolation. In most cases, birds that are socially isolated during early development exhibit abnormal vocalizations, but there is a range of effects. ***Figure 12.11*** shows this range in a comparison of song development in swamp sparrows (*Melospiza georgiana*) and song sparrows (*M. melodia*). Whereas acoustic isolation eliminates most features of the song in swamp sparrows, a considerable amount of structure remains in the song of the song sparrow (Marler 1987). Moreover, the songs of song sparrows reared in acoustic isolation elicit some amount of behavior from conspecifics, certainly much more than the songs of deaf animals (although less than the songs of normally-reared animals). Thus, although deafening and acoustic isolation generally impair the structure of the adult song, the effects vary depending on the species; at least in some cases, the song's communicative function is partially spared.

3.c. Age-Dependent Plasticity. Among the species of songbirds that exhibit vocal learning, a major distinction can be established between those exhibiting age-dependent plasticity and those for which plasticity occurs throughout their life (age-independent plasticity is reviewed in ***section 3.e.*** below). *Age-dependent plasticity* occurs in species that acquire the song during early development (Marler 1987). The final product of this learning process is a song that the bird will produce for the rest of its life. The best-studied species in this group is the white-crowned sparrow (*Zonotrichia leucophrys*); however, other species in which the development of the adult song also depends on exposure to a singing adult model (usually the nestling's father) exhibit a similar developmental profile (see ***Figure 12.12***).

Age-dependent song learning passes through two distinct phases. The acquisition of the song occurs during an initial *sensory learning phase,* during which the young

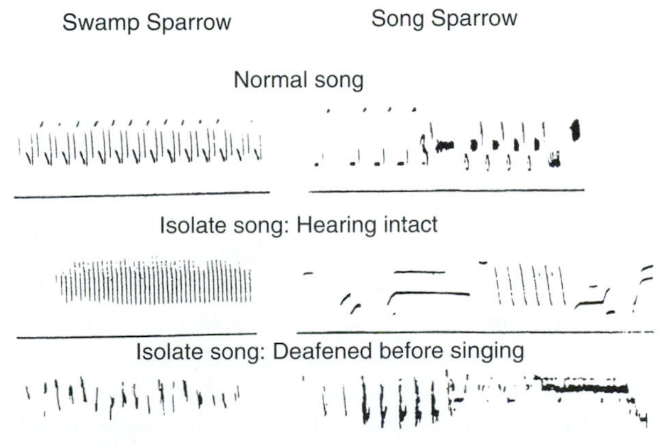

FIGURE 12.11. Effects of deprivation of early experience on song development in sparrows (Marler 1987). Social isolation (lack of an opportunity to hear a model singing) and deafening (lack of an opportunity to hear their own singing) drastically affect the final song of both swamp and song sparrows. However, the song of isolate song sparrows preserves a considerable degree of internal structure and elicits social behavior from conspecifics, suggesting that these two species differ in the processes underlying song development.

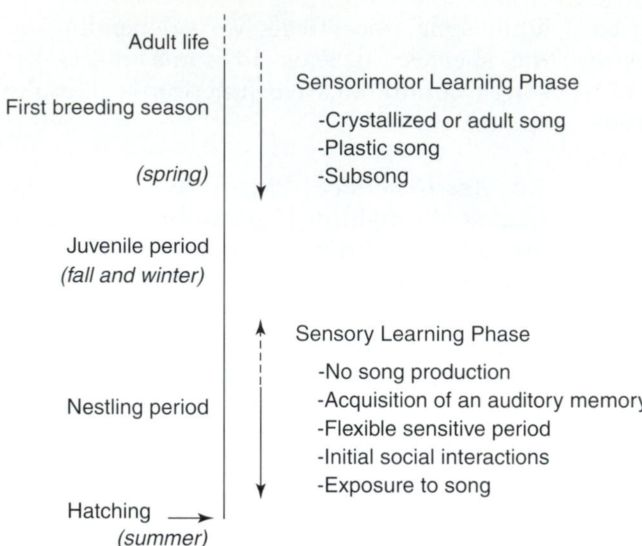

FIGURE 12.12. A schematic representation of the main events in the early development of vocal behavior in species exhibiting age-dependent plasticity. Nestlings learn by mere exposure to the father's song, but they do not themselves produce a song (the sensory learning phase). In the following spring, juveniles start singing and pass through a series of periods known as subsong, plastic song, and crystallized song (the sensorimotor learning phase). Although there is substantial variability across species, many of these features and the order in which these learning phases occur appear to apply to many songbird species.

bird does not itself vocalize. The absence of vocal behavior during this phase indicates a decoupling of learning from performance. As in other cases reviewed in this chapter, acquisition occurs by mere exposure to the model, and it can be accomplished in the laboratory if the real model is replaced by a tape recorder that plays back the song to the nestling (Marler 1970). Such experiments show that adults sing normally if exposed to the songs during a period ranging between 10 and 50 days after hatching but not if exposed to the songs before 10 days of age or after 50 days of age. Obviously, this temporal window suggests the presence of a sensitive period for this form of exposure learning, and, much as in the case of similar learning phenomena (e.g., filial imprinting), the nature of the experience during this sensitive period plays an important role in determining the boundaries of the period. As a result, it cannot be ascertained that the period has rigid limits. For example, white-crowned sparrows exposed to live tutors with which they can interact socially (rather than to songs played back from a tape recorder) are able to acquire the normal song even when exposed beyond the 50 days of age (Baptista & Petrinovich 1984).

The white-crowned sparrow starts emitting vocalizations in its first spring, during the *sensorimotor learning phase.* The song undergoes a series of changes that have been described in terms of three successive transitions in development: subsong, plastic song, and crystallized song (Marler 1991). The *subsong* involves the initial vocal behavior of the songbird. During this period, the song is extremely rudimentary and generally lacks structure. The subsong period probably establishes the basic motor skills involved in song production, as well as the animal's ability to modulate sound production based on auditory feedback. Eventually, the bird starts producing syllables of songs to which it has been previously exposed; this is referred to as the *plastic song.* Plastic songs begin to exhibit some structure, usually a few syllables sung in rapid succession. Some of the syllables acquired during this phase will be eventually discarded, while others will become part of the final repertoire of the adult animal. Finally, a *crystallized song* emerges; this is the song the animal will sing for the rest of its life. Unlike the plastic song, the crystallized song decreases in variability: The number of syllables, range of frequencies, song duration, and rhythm of song production all become highly stereotyped.

A complex set of factors determines the normal transition from subsong to crystallized song in the white-crowned sparrow. Deafening before or during this period leads to an abnormal adult song, which suggests that part of the sensorimotor learning process during this period is related to a matching of the produced song to the song stored in memory and learned by exposure during the initial sensory learning phase. This auditory memory acquired during the nestling period is referred to as the *template*. Final matching of the song to the template may also require hormonal contribution. For example, castrated males exhibit both subsong and plastic song periods, but they do not develop a final song. Administration of the hormone testosterone, which is eliminated by castration, results in the crystallization of a song. This crystallized song remains viable so long as testosterone is kept above a certain level. Therefore, the development of a normal song in species that learn from a model (e.g., the white-crowned sparrow) requires, at least, three things: exposure to the song during a sensitive period early in life, sensorimotor practice and auditory feedback during a subsequent period of vocal production, and a particular internal hormonal milieu that contributes to song crystallization.

Age-dependent plasticity in vocal learning exhibits some peculiar additional properties. For example, white-crowned sparrows can acquire the song from exposure to a tape, but they are selective as to the type of songs they learn (Marler 1970). If exposed to the conspecific song as well as to the song of another species (an allospecific song), white-crowned sparrows acquire only the conspecific song. If exposed only to an allospecific song (e.g., a song sparrow's), the final song resembles that of neither species. Whereas experiential input is required for song development, the process seems to be sensitive to relatively specific properties of the song. Like white-crowned sparrows, zebra finches (*Taeniopygia guttata*) also acquire the song from exposure to a tape, but acquisition is enhanced if the animal is exposed to a live tutor during the sensitive period (35 to 65 days of age). Interestingly, isolating the birds from conspecifics during early development extends the period of plasticity considerably. For example, song learning occurs in isolated birds exposed to a live tutor at 120 days of age (Jones et al. 1996). Social factors are such an important component of the song-learning process that imitation of an allospecific song is possible in some species exposed to a live tutor. For example, a white-crowned sparrow can acquire the song of a song sparrow if exposure is extensive and conditions allow for social interactions (Baptista & Petrinovich 1984).

3.d. Dialects. Vocal learning has resulted in the evolution of song *dialects*—that is, regional differences in a song among populations of the same species. Like the dialects and accents of human populations, those of birds are also the result of social learning and transmission and are, therefore, considered to be cultural traits (Marler & Tamura 1964). Two relatively well-known species that exhibit song dialects are the rufous-collared sparrow (*Zonotrichia capensis*) from Argentina (see **Figure 12.10**, p. 470) and the white-crowned sparrow (*Z. leucophrys*) from western United States (see ***Figure 12.13***). In both species the song can be divided into two basic components: the theme and the trill. The theme is the initial part of the song and is composed of one to a few notes. The trill is the ending part and usually involves a rapid succession of short notes. The sonograms in these figures show greater consistency in trill structure within each area than across areas.

In the rufous-collared sparrow, dialects are defined by such properties as the rate of trill notes. In the Argentinean Pampas, a vast region characterized as a homogeneous herbaceous steppe, trills vary little, with intervals separating successive notes that tend to average about 60 ms (Nottebohm 1969). However, dialect transitions may occur over very short distances when the habitat changes abruptly. For example, rufous-collared sparrows inhabiting a 1-km-wide strip of woodland parallel to the De la Plata River and adjacent to the steppe, in eastern Argentina, display a much slower trill, with intervals reaching an average of 80 ms in some locations (Tubaro et al. 1993). Similar dialectal transitions occur in adjacent habitats that differ in altitude. Since dialects have a communicative function, it seems likely that songs with acoustic properties that tend to maximize signal transmission would be positively selected over less efficient songs. Tubaro et al. point out that slowly modulated sounds tend to be less degraded in a forested environment than rapidly modulated sounds. Dialects may arise because of the differential effectiveness of signals with various acoustic properties as a function of the amount and type of vegetation present in a particular area.

Marler's (1970) isolation and playback experiments demonstrated that white-crowned sparrows learned the dialect of a different area to which they were exposed during the sensitive period. Dialects are thus maintained by imitation of the song heard early in life; there appears to be no selectivity in the learning of dialectal variations in song in this particular species. Because the song is a major component of courtship behavior, it would seem obvious that dialects may encourage mating among individuals born in the same area. A selective mating of this sort also requires that females, which do not sing, would exhibit a preference for males singing the dialect of the female's area of birth. However appealing, this hypothesis does not appear to work for at least some species. For example, pairs of white-crowned sparrows from the San Francisco Bay area that lived in a zone where two different dialects meet were found to be mixed in terms of their origin (Petrinovich & Baptista 1984). Testosterone injections were used to induce singing in the females, in order to determine the dialect to which they were exposed early in their life. Furthermore, mixed pairs had a reproductive success similar to that of pairs in which both birds originated from the same dialect area. Therefore, female white-crowned sparrows do not seem to choose their mate based on the dialect and do not seem to pay a reproductive penalty for choosing males from other areas.

3.e. Social Modulation of Song in Cowbirds. In one group of species the young bird is not exposed to the conspecific song as a nestling: the brood parasites. *Brood parasites* are species in which the female usually lays her eggs in the nest of another species. The nestlings thus produced are exposed to the song of a foster parent rather than to the song of their own father, and so they have no opportunity to acquire the conspecific song in a manner analogous to that of most other songbirds. The development of the song in cowbirds (*Molothrus ater*), one such brood parasite species, is

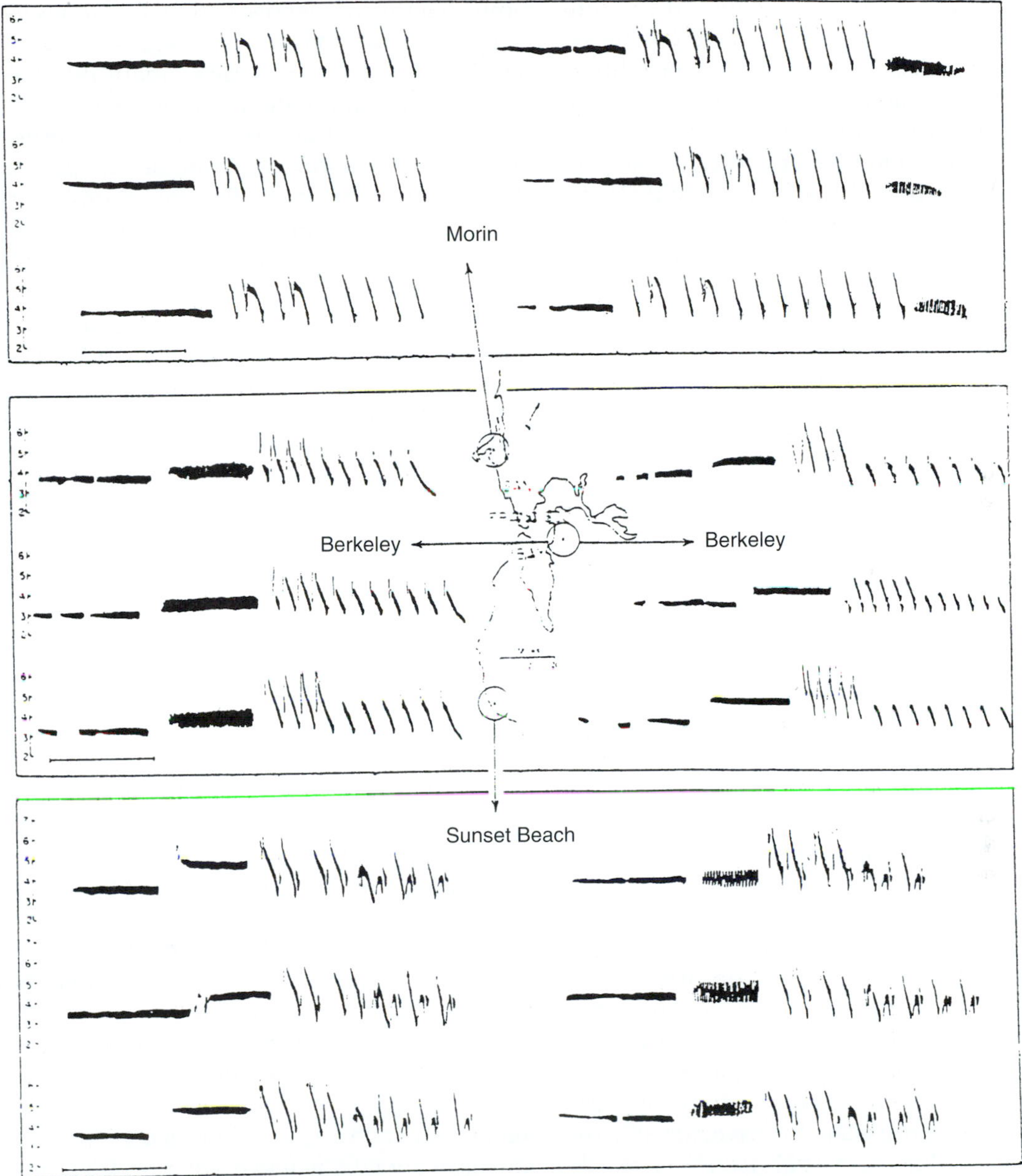

FIGURE 12.13. Dialects of white-crowned sparrows from different areas near San Francisco Bay, California (Marler 1970). Notice that there is more consistency within each area than across different locations.

particularly interesting because these animals are raised by a wide variety of hosts and are, as a result, exposed to very different early experiences. Yet they have to be able to eventually recognize conspecifics to engage in reproductive activities. It has traditionally been assumed that learning plays little or no role in the development of vocal behavior in brood parasites. Isolation experiments with birds taken from their nest at 2 days of age and maintained in social and acoustic isolation until the first breeding season confirm that naive males produce effective songs and naive females respond with the appropriate copulatory posture to a male's song (West et al. 1981).

In the cowbird, however, social isolation induces an unusual effect—it improves the efficiency of the song! Cowbird males reared in isolation are about twice as effective in eliciting the copulatory posture in females as are normally reared males. This is true for both laboratory-reared and wild-caught females. Acoustic analysis shows that the song of males raised in social isolation is more potent and intense than that of males reared in group cages. But the isolation procedure imposes a variety of restrictions upon the developing animal, including limits to its sensory experience and to its social experience; therefore, it is not clear which is the factor responsible for the increased effectiveness of the isolate song. The contribution of various types of experience to this *isolate song effect* was determined by raising males under four different conditions during their first year of life: audiovisual isolation, visual isolation (birds could hear but not see other birds), social isolation (birds could see and hear other birds but not interact with them), and group raising (birds could see, hear, and interact with other birds). The songs produced by these males were recorded and played back to females to ensure similar testing conditions. The results showed that the songs of males that were visually isolated from conspecifics elicited, on average, about twice as many female copulatory responses than the songs of males that could either see other cowbirds interacting in an adjacent cage or that could interact directly with conspecifics. Interestingly, the songs of cowbirds reared in isolation and later transferred into a group lost a significant degree of effectiveness; and, vice versa, the songs of males reared in a group and later placed in isolation cages increased in effectiveness.

The modifiability of the cowbird's song is an example of *age-independent plasticity*. In their natural environment, juvenile cowbirds flock together and learn the song from other males with which they interact intensely. It is this social interaction that shapes the potency of the song. In the laboratory, when isolate males are introduced into an established colony, their singing behavior elicits a substantial amount of aggressive behavior from the resident males. In contrast, socially reared males sing very little and are only occasionally the target of aggressive behavior by the residents. Experiments demonstrate that, within a few days of being introduced into the colony, isolate males significantly decrease the frequency of vocal behavior and, as a result, receive very little or no aggression. These aggressive interactions can result in the isolate male being killed by resident males. In one experiment, 9 of 21 isolate males that sang potent songs were killed by the resident males. An interesting difference in the behavior of socially isolated and normal males is the contextual specificity of singing behavior: Whereas isolate males sing in both the presence or the absence of resident males, socially reared males sing mostly when the resident males are not present in their vicinity. A second difference is that, at least in some cases, isolate males that sing a potent song can lower the potency of the song to a level that elicits few attacks by resident males.

The male cowbird's song is, therefore, subject to subtle social modulation. The song's potency is balanced by opposing factors: Female responsivity raises it, but male aggression lowers it. Males adjust the potency of the song to a level that attracts a number of females for reproductive purposes (by no means the maximum effectiveness possible for the song), balanced by the avoidance of aggressive competition from other males in the group. The cowbird's song appears to be shaped by reinforcement contingencies analogous to those established in typical instrumental conditioning situations. Additional evidence of such sensitivity to instrumental contingencies comes from experiments in which males from one region are housed with females from a different region. Cowbirds also exhibit dialects, although little is known about the mechanisms that give rise to such geographical variation. In one experiment (King & West 1983), male cowbirds trapped in North Carolina were housed individually with female cowbirds from Texas, with females from North Carolina, or with birds from a different species. Female cowbirds raised in Texas and North Carolina had been exposed to very different songs, and the question was which of these songs would be produced by North Carolina males in the following breeding season. The answer was clear: Males tended to produce a song that resembled the dialect of the female's area of origin. This indicates again that adult males are capable of modifying their vocal behavior and, even more interestingly, that such vocal behavior can be shaped by the female. In the natural environment, the juvenile male's song is shaped during the winter months, when they associate closely with females within the flock. Careful observations indicate that females respond to a male singing a particular song by moving her wings. The same songs that elicit such wing movements during the winter also elicit the copulatory response during the breeding season (West & King 1988). The potency and type of male song is thus shaped by a complex combination of appetitive factors (the female's copulatory responses and wing movements) and aversive factors (aggressive behavior from other males).

3.f. Brain Mechanisms. It was noted previously that white-crowned sparrow females, which do not normally sing, can be induced to sing by the administration of testosterone. This effect is achieved by actions of testosterone on membrane receptors located in neurons distributed in several regions of the telencephalon. In fact, oscine species are characterized by the presence of androgen and estrogen receptors in brain nuclei that are known to control vocal behavior, which implies that these hormones exert control over a variety of reproductive functions, including vocal behavior. In species that exhibit age-independent plasticity, such as the canary (*Serinus canaria*), testosterone is also responsible for seasonal changes in the volume of brain nuclei important for vocal behavior (Nottebohm et al. 1987). What are these nuclei?

The neurobiology of vocal behavior in songbirds is the target of intensive research in several species. Numerous brain nuclei participate in the control of vocal behavior in songbirds. A number of components of this neural circuit are shared across species that exhibit either age-dependent plasticity, such as zebra finches, or age-independent plasticity, such as the canaries. A simplified version of the vocal behavior network of songbirds is presented in ***Figure 12.14.*** Afferent information from the inner ear enters into the nucleus ovoidalis of the thalamus (NO) and then into a critical area known as the *higher vocal center* (*HVC*). Axons from HVC neurons generate two parallel circuits. The first circuit involves connections from the HVC to the robust nucleus of the archistriatum (RA) and then to the motor control of syrinx muscles, mediated by the hypoglossus nerve (cranial nerve XII). The second circuit involves connections from the HVC to area X, to the medial part of the dorsolateral nucleus of the thalamus (DLM), to the lateral part of the magnocellular nucleus of the anterior neostriatum (LatMAN), and to RA, from which the motor output is controlled. Both of these circuits participate in vocal behavior in a variety of ways.

The size of some of these nuclei is related to the amount of song production. In species in which the male sings but the females does not sing, such as in zebra finches, the HVC and RA can be five times larger in males than in females (Nottebohm & Arnold 1976). Such sexual dimorphism is not so marked in the canary, a species in which females are known to occasionally sing, and is greatly reduced or even eliminated in songbird species in which both male and female engage in singing behavior (Brenowitz & Arnold 1986). As I pointed out previously, there are also seasonal variations; Nottebohm (1981) discovered that the HVC and RA nuclei of male canaries were significantly larger during the spring, when singing is at its peak, than during the fall, when singing declines. Several features of these brain nuclei are responsible for the enlargement, including the number and size of neurons and the extent of their dendritic arborizations. Most interesting is the fact that the annual cycle—the shrinking and enlargement of the HVC and other areas of the circuit in the canary—involves *neurogenesis*. New neurons produced in the area adjacent to the cerebral ventricles migrate into areas of the vocal circuit, including HVC (Goldman & Nottebohm 1983). Neurogenesis occurs at a high rate in species that acquire new songs throughout their lives (i.e., age-independent plasticity, such as in the canary) and during the time of the year when new songs are being acquired. The discovery of neurogenesis in the adult canary brain was surprising and extremely important since it forced a change in the prevailing view that new neurons are not produced in adult brains. Since then, neurogenesis has been observed in several species and brain areas.

Additional evidence supports the hypothesis that some of the components of the circuit described in ***Figure 12.14*** are critical in the production of vocal behavior. For example, lesions of the HVC cause severe deficits in song production, whereas recording of neuronal activity in HVC and RA demonstrates a degree of synchronicity between that activity and ongoing singing behavior. In zebra finches, lesions of area X and LatMAN disrupt song learning; however, song production is not affected if these areas are lesioned after song crystallization (Bottjer et al. 1984). These results have encouraged the generalization (probably simplistic) that the HVC-RA circuit of the posterior telencephalon is more relevant to song production, whereas the area X-LatMAN circuit of the anterior telencephalon is more important for song acquisition.

Brain areas that become more active when the bird is acquiring a song can also be assessed by measuring the degree of activation of a gene family known as immediate-early genes. One such gene, known as ZENK, produces a regulatory protein that modulates transcription of other genes and is a marker for neuronal activation related to synaptic plasticity. In zebra finches, ZENK induction increases during singing in HVC, RA, and area X; however, when songs are

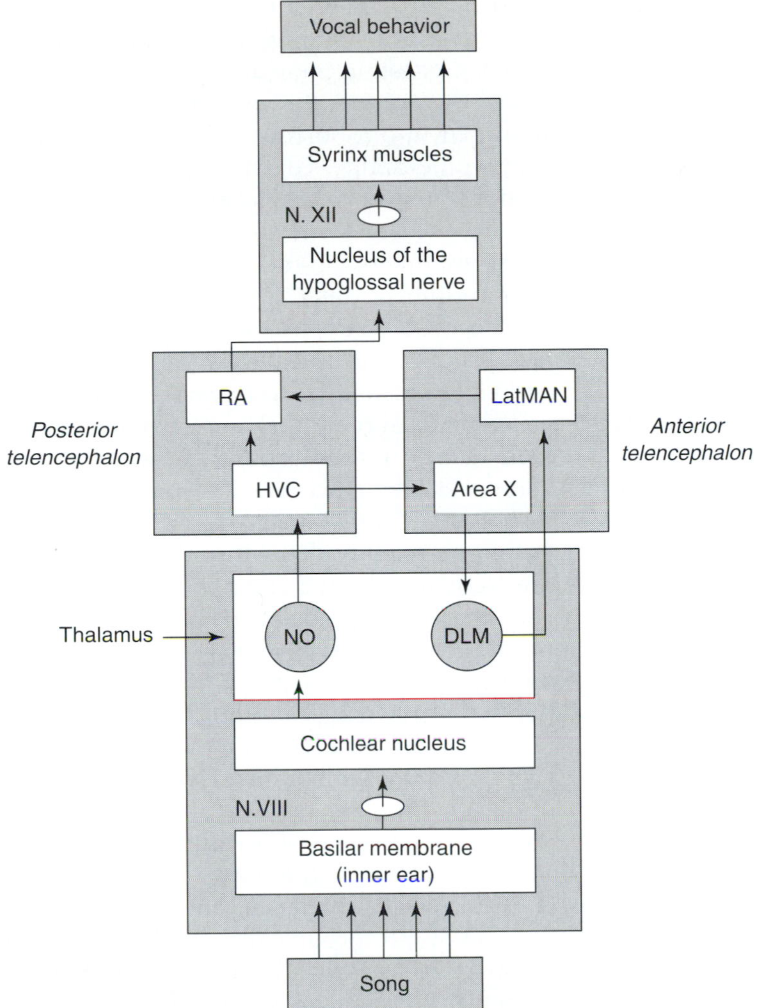

FIGURE 12.14. A schematic representation of the brain circuitry underlying vocal behavior in songbirds. Notice two processing circuits running in parallel. The circuit in the posterior telencephalon is more closely related to song production, whereas that of the anterior telencephalon and thalamus appears to be more involved in the acquisition process. ***DLM:*** medial part of the dorso-lateral nucleus of the thalamus. ***HVC:*** high vocal center. ***LatMAN*** (also known as 1MAN): lateral part of the magnocellular nucleus of the anterior neostriatum. ***NO:*** nucleus ovoidalis of the thalamus. ***N. VIII:*** auditory cranial nerve. ***N. XII:*** hypoglossal cranial nerve. ***RA:*** robust nucleus of the archistriatum.

played back to the animal, ZENK induction is elevated in auditory telencephalic areas such as the caudomedial neostriatum, which projects to both HVC and area X (Jin & Clayton 1997). ZENK induction in the caudomedial neostriatum is high during the sensitive period when the bird is undergoing song acquisition, but levels decay in adult animals after song crystallization. In the canary, ZENK induction is also high in the caudomedial neostriatum when males are hearing a new song (Mello et al. 1992).

3.g. Vocal Learning in Mammals. Several instances of vocal behavior in mammals were discussed in various sections of this book: the alarm calls of ground squirrels and vervet monkeys (***Chapter 4, sections 4.e.*** and ***4.f.,*** pp. 113–117); and speech (***Chapter 9, section 4,*** pp. 349–357, and ***Chapter 14, section 3.d.,*** pp. 572–576). Of course, there are many other examples of vocalizations in mammals, both complex and varied (e.g., the songs of whales) and seemingly stereotyped and simple (e.g., the distress vocalizations of rodents described in ***section 2.b.,*** above). The fact that vocalizations may be described as rigid does not necessarily imply that their development is simple and that no experience is involved in their production. A case in point is provided by the alarm calls of ground squirrels and vervet monkeys.

Ground squirrels (*Spermophilus beldingi*) emit *alarm calls* in the presence of predators. Such calls alert other members of the colony, which would ideally rush into their burrow for protection. But these reactions do not emerge spontaneously during development. Juveniles, for example, are particularly vulnerable to predation, which suggest they are not responding in the appropriate way to the calls. Playback experiments demonstrate that juveniles that are just emerging from the burrow tend to respond to all types of calls, including those made by birds, a fact suggesting poor discrimination of call types. In addition, they tend to freeze, rather than run into a burrow, which may explain their vulnerability. Ground squirrels learn to respond appropriately to alarm calls by observing the reactions elicited by the calls in other members of the colony, particularly their mothers (Mateo 1996).

Vervet monkeys (*Cercopithecus aethiops*) also produce alarm calls that are specific to particular predators. In response to an eagle call (an aerial predator), vervets move down from a tree to the ground, whereas in response to a leopard call (a terrestrial predator), vervets move up a tree. While, for example, the eagle calls of juveniles and adults are acoustically indistinguishable, juvenile vervets do not produce them in the appropriate context and do not respond to them appropriately (Seyfarth & Cheney 1986). Experience may also facilitate the production of calls. Groups of vervet monkeys defend their territory against intrusion by members of other groups. Vervets alert the group about the presence of an intruder by emitting a specific intergroup call. Hauser (1989) reported evidence that both the production of intergroup calls and the juvenile's reaction to these calls improve with age. Moreover, the improvement is faster for animals that have a higher frequency of exposure to intergroup encounters.

Human speech probably represents the best example of vocal learning among the mammals. Some aspects of the development of human language were described previously, so here I would like to emphasize some interesting parallels with song learning in passerine birds. Human speech and oscine singing represent pinnacles of vocal evolution and animal communication. Sound production is achieved in both cases according to the same basic process—that is, by blowing air from the lungs while modulating its passage by subtle muscular coordination. The range of frequencies produced is very similar, as is the auditory sensitivity (roughly ranging between 10 Hz and 20 kHz). Human speech and oscine singing also share various other properties, including their dependence on experience and auditory feedback for normal development; the presence of sensitive periods for learning; the ability to generate new vocalizations through imitation; the large repertoire of words in the case of humans and of songs in the case of some species, notably the mockingbirds; the presence of cerebral lateralization—that is, the predominance of the left hemisphere in the control of both human speech and oscine singing; and the existence of dialects maintained by social learning across generations.

4. KEY TERMS

age-dependent plasticity 473
age-independent plasticity 478
alarm calls 482
assembly calls 471
attachment 462
begging response 456
brood parasitism 476
calls 469
caravaning behavior 458
chemical imprinting 457
contact comfort 464
critical period 446
crystallized song 475
dialect 475
distress calls 448
dithering behavior 459
double sexual imprinting 459
ectothermy 461
embryonic experience 448
endothermy 461
epigenetic view 469
fear reaction 443
filial imprinting 443
following reaction 443
food calls 471
higher vocal center (HVC) 480
hormones 460
hypothalamo-pituitary-adrenal axis 464
individual recognition 463
instrumental conditioning 447
intermediate-medial hyperstriatum ventrale (IMHV) 453
isolate song effect 478
latent learning 458
master-yoked design 448
maternal behavior 460
maternal imprinting 457
mother-infant bond 460
nature *versus* nurture 469
neurogenesis 480
omission training 447
perceptual learning 446
plastic song 474
prefunctional organization 471
scallop 447
secondary imprinting 446
sensitive period 446
sensitized maternal behavior 462
sensorimotor learning phase 474
sensory learning phase 474

5. References

Ainsworth, M. D. S. (1972). Attachment and dependency: A comparison. In J. L. Gewirtz (Ed.), *Attachment and dependency* (pp. 97–137). Washington: Winston & Sons.

Bailey, M. T., & Coe, C. L. (1999). Maternal separation disrupts the integrity of the intestinal microflora in infant rhesus monkeys. *Developmental Psychobiology,* **35,** 146–155.

Baptista, L. F., & Petrinovich, L. (1984). Social interaction, sensitive phases, and the song template hypothesis in the white-crowned sparrow. *Animal Behaviour,* **32,** 172–181.

Bolhuis, J. J., & Honey, R. C. (1994). Within-event learning during filial imprinting. *Journal of Experimental Psychology: Animal Behavior Processes,* **20,** 240–248.

Bolhuis, J. J., Johnson, M., Horn, G., & Bateson, P. P. G. (1989). Long-lasting effects of IMHV lesions on social preferences in domestic fowl. *Behavioral Neuroscience,* **103,** 438–441.

Bottjer, S. W., Miesner, E. A., & Arnold, A. P. (1984). Forebrain lesions disrupt development but not maintenance of song in passerine birds. *Science,* **224,** 901–903.

Brenowitz, E. A., & Arnold, A. P. (1986). Interspecific comparisons of the size of neural song control regions and song complexity in duetting birds: Evolutionary implications. *Journal of Neuroscience,* **6,** 2875–2879.

Brock, J., Wolf, A., & Braun, K. (1996). Influence of the N-methyl-D-aspartate receptor antagonist DL-2-amino-5-phosphonovaleric acid on auditory filial imprinting in the domestic chick. *Neurobiology of Learning & Memory,* **65,** 177–188.

Cairns, R. B., & Johnson, D. L. (1965). The development of interspecies social attachments. *Psychonomic Science,* **2,** 337–338.

Capitanio, J. P. (1985). Early experience and social processes in rhesus macaques (*Macaca mulatta*): II. Complex social interaction. *Journal of Comparative Psychology,* **99,** 133–144.

Cheney, D. L., & Seyfarth, R. M. (1980). Vocal recognition in free-ranging vervet monkeys. *Animal Behavior,* **28,** 362–367.

Coe, C. L., Mendoza, S. P., Smotherman, W. P., & Levine, S. (1978). Mother-infant attachment in the squirrel monkey: Adrenal response to separation. *Behavioral Biology,* **22,** 256–263.

Crews, D., & Moore, M. C. (1986). Evolution of mechanisms controlling mating behavior. *Science,* **231,** 121–125.

DePaulo, P., & Hoffman, H. S. (1981). Reinforcement by an imprinting stimulus versus water on simple schedules in ducklings. *Journal of the Experimental Analysis of Behavior,* **36,** 151–169.

Dooling, R. J., Gephart, B. F., Price, P. H., McHale, C., & Brauth, S. E. (1987). Effects of deafening on the contact call of the budgerigar (*Melopsittacus undulatus*). *Animal Behaviour,* **35,** 1264–1266.

Eiserer, L. A. (1980). Development of filial attachment to static visual features of an imprinting object. *Animal Learning & Behavior,* **8,** 159–166.

Eiserer, L. A. (1980). Long-term potential for imprinting in ducks and chickens. *Journal of the Experimental Analysis of Behavior,* **33,** 383–395.

Eiserer, L. A., & Swope, R. L. (1980). Acquisition of behavioral control by static visual features of an imprinting object: Species generality. *Animal Learning & Behavior,* **8,** 481–484.

Freeberg, T. M., King, A. P., & West, M. J. (1995). Social malleability in cowbirds (*Molothrus ater artemisiae*): Species and mate recognition in the first 2 years of life. *Journal of Comparative Psychology,* **109,** 357–367.

Goldman, S., & Nottebohm, F. (1983). Neuronal production, migration and differentiation in a vocal control nucleus of the adult female canary brain. *Proceedings of the National Academy of Sciences,* (USA), **80,** 2390–2394.

Gottlieb, G. (1978). Development of species identification in ducklings: IV. Change in species-specific perception caused by auditory deprivation. *Journal of Comparative & Physiological Psychology,* **92,** 375–387.

Gottlieb, G. (1981). Roles of early experience in species-specific perceptual development. In R. N. Aslin, J. R. Alberts, & M. R. Petersen (Eds.), *Development of perception* (Vol. 1, pp. 5–44). New York: Academic Press.

Gottlieb, G. (1985). Development of species identification in ducklings: XI. Embryonic critical period for species-typical perception in the hatchling. *Animal Behaviour,* **33,** 225–233.

Grassman, M. (1993). Chemosensory orientation behavior in juvenile sea turtles. *Brain, Behavior, & Evolution,* **41,** 224–228.

Grassman, M., Owens, D. W., McVey, J. P., & Marquez, R. (1984). Olfactory-based orientation in artificially imprinted sea turtles. *Science*, **224**, 83–84.

Gray, P., & Chesley, S. (1984). Development of maternal behavior in nulliparous rats (*Rattus norvegicus*): Effects of sex and early maternal experience. *Journal of Comparative Psychology*, **98**, 91–99.

Gubernick, D. J. (1981). Maternal "imprinting" or maternal "labelling" in goats? *Animal Behavior*, **28**, 124–129.

Gubernick, D. J., Jones, K. C., & Klopfer, P. H. (1979). Maternal "imprinting" in goats? *Animal Behaviour*, **27**, 314–315.

Harlow, H. F. (1971). *Learning to love*. San Francisco: Albion Press.

Harlow, H. F., & Suomi, S. J. (1971). Social recovery by isolation-reared monkeys. *Proceedings of the National Academy of Sciences, USA*, **68**, 1534–1538.

Harlow, H., & Zimmermann, R. R. (1959). Affectional responses in the infant monkey. *Science*, **130**, 421–432.

Hasler, A. D., & Scholz, A. T. (1983). *Olfactory imprinting and homing in salmon*. Berlin, Germany: Springer-Verlag.

Hauser, M. D. (1989). Ontogenetic changes in the comprehension and production of vervet monkey (*Cercopithecus aethiops*) vocalizations. *Journal of Comparative Psychology*, **103**, 149–158.

Heaton, J. T., & Brauth, S. E. (1999). Effects of deafening on the development of nestling and juvenile vocalizations in budgerigars (*Melopsittacus undulatus*). *Journal of Comparative Psychology*, **113**, 314–320.

Hofer, M. E. (1975). Infant separation responses and the maternal role. *Biological Psychiatry*, **10**, 149–153.

Hoffman, H. S. (1987). Imprinting and the critical period for social attachments: Some laboratory investigations. In M. H. Bornstein (Ed.), *Sensitive periods in development* (pp. 99–121). Hillsdale, NJ: Erlbaum.

Hoffman, H. S., Eiserer, L. A., & Singer, D. (1972). Acquisition of behavioral control by a stationary imprinting stimulus. *Psychonomic Science*, **26**, 146–148.

Hoffman, H. S., & Ratner, A. M. (1973). A reinforcement model of imprinting: Implications for socialization in monkeys and men. *Psychological Review*, **80**, 527–544.

Hoffman, H. S., Schiff, D., Adams, J., & Searle, J. (1966). Enhanced distress vocalization through selective reinforcement. *Science*, **151**, 352–354.

Hoffman, H. S., Stratton, J. W., & Newby, V. (1969a). Punishment by response-contingent withdrawal of an imprinting stimulus. *Science*, **163**, 702–704.

Hoffman, H. S., Stratton, J. W., & Newby, V. (1969b). The control of feeding behavior by an imprinted stimulus. *Journal of the Experimental Analysis of Behavior*, **12**, 847–860.

Horn, G. (1985). *Memory, imprinting, and the brain*. Oxford, UK: Clarendon Press.

Horn, G. (1991). Cerebral function and behaviour investigated through a study of filial imprinting. In P. Bateson (Ed.), *The development and integration of behaviour. Essays in honour of Robert Hinde* (pp. 121–148). Cambridge, UK: Cambridge University Press.

Horn, G., Bradley, P., & McCabe, B. J. (1985). Changes in the structure of synapses associated with learning. *Journal of Neuroscience*, **5**, 3161–3168.

Immelmann, K. (1972). Sexual and other long-term aspects of imprinting in birds and other species. *Advances in the Study of Behavior*, **4**, 147–174.

Insel, T. R. (1992). Oxytocin: A neuropeptide for affiliation—evidence from behavioral, autoradiographic, and comparative studies. *Psychoneuroendocrinology*, **17**, 3–35.

Jin, H., & Clayton, D. F. (1997). Localized changes in immediate-early gene regulation during sensory and motor learning in zebra finches. *Neuron*, **19**, 1049-1059.

Johnson, M. H., & Horn, G. (1988). Development of filial preferences in dark-reared chicks. *Animal Behaviour*, **36**, 675–683.

Jones, A. E., ten Cate, C., & Slater, P. J. B. (1996). Early experience and plasticity of song in adult male zebra finches (*Taeniopygia guttata*). *Journal of Comparative Psychology*, **110**, 354–369.

Junco, F. (1993). Acquisition of a filial preference in an altricial bird without food reinforcement. *Animal Behaviour*, **46**, 1237–1239.

Junco, F. (1988). Filial imprinting in an altricial bird: The blackbird (*Turdus merula*). *Behaviour*, **106**, 25–42.

Kaplan, J., & Russell, M. (1974). Olfactory recognition in the infant squirrel monkey. *Developmental Psychobiology*, **7**, 15–19.

Kendrick, K. M., Levy, F., & Keverne, E. G. (1992). Changes in the sensory processing of olfactory signals induced by birth in sheep. *Science*, **256**, 833–836.

King, A. P., & West, M. J. (1983). Epigenesis of cowbird song: A joint endeavor of males and females. *Nature*, **305**, 704–706.

Kling, A., Lloyd, R., Tachiki, K., Prince, H., Klimenko, V., & Korneva, E. (1992). Effects of social separation on immune function and brain neurotransmitters in cebus monkey (*C. apella*). *Annals of the New York Academy of Sciences*, **650**, 257–261.

Konishi, M. (1963). The role of auditory feedback in the vocal behaviour of the domestic fowl. *Zeitschrift für Tierpsychologie*, **20**, 349–367.

Konishi, M. (1964). Effects of deafening on song development in two species of juncos. *Condor*, **66**, 85–102.

Konishi, M. (1965). The role of auditory feedback in the control of vocalization in the white-crowned sparrow. *Zeitschrift für Tierpsychologie*, **22**, 770–783.

Kroodsma, D. E. (1984). Songs of the alder flycatcher (*Empidonax alnorum*) and willow flycatcher (*Empidonax traillii*) are innate. *Auk*, **101**, 13–24.

Leon, M. (1975). Dietary control of maternal pheromone in the lactating rat. *Physiology & Behavior,* **14,** 311–319.

Lorenz, K. Z. (1937). The companion in the bird's world. *Auk,* **54,** 245–273.

Marler, P. (1970). A comparative approach to vocal learning: Song development in white-crowned sparrows. *Journal of Comparative & Physiological Psychology Monograph,* **71**(No. 2, Part 2), 1–25.

Marler, P. (1987). Sensitive periods and the roles of specific and general sensory stimulation in birdsong learning. In J. P. Rauschecker & P. Marler (Eds.), *Imprinting and cortical plasticity* (pp. 99–135). New York: Wiley & Sons.

Marler, P. (1991). Differences in behavioural development in closely related species: birdsong. In P. Bateson (Ed.), *The development and integration of behaviour. Essays in honour of Robert Hinde* (pp. 41–70). Cambridge, U.K.: Cambridge University Press.

Marler, P., Dufty, A., & Pickert, R. (1986). Vocal communication in the domestic chicken: I. Does a sender communicate information about the quality of a food referent to a receiver? *Animal Behaviour,* **34,** 188–193.

Marler, P., & Tamura, M. (1964). Culturally transmitted patterns of vocal behavior in sparrows. *Science,* **146,** 1483–1486.

Mason, W. A. (1960). The effects of social restriction on the behavior of rhesus monkeys: I. Free social behavior. *Journal of Comparative & Physiological Psychology,* **53,** 582–589.

Mateo, J. M. (1996). The development of alarm-call response behaviour in free-living juvenile Belding's ground squirrels. *Animal Behaviour,* **52,** 489–505.

McCabe, B. J., & Horn, G. (1988). Learning and memory: Regional changes in N-methyl-D-aspartate receptors in the chick brain after imprinting. *Proceedings of the National Academy of Sciences, USA,* **85,** 2849–2853.

McCabe, B. J., Horn, G., & Bateson, P. P. G. (1981). Effects of restricted lesions of the chick forebrain on the acquisition of filial preferences during imprinting. *Brain Research,* **205,** 29–37.

McCabe, B. J., Cipolla-Neto, J., Horn, G., & Bateson, P. P. G. (1982). Amnesic effects of bilateral lesions placed in the hyperstriatum ventral of the chick after imprinting. *Experimental Brain Research,* **48,** 13–21.

Mello, C. V., Vicario, D. S., & Clayton, D. F. (1992). Song presentation induces gene expression in the songbird forebrain. *Proceedings of the National Academy of Sciences, U.S.A.,* **89,** 6818–6822.

Moffatt, C. A., & Hogan, J. A. (1992). Ontogeny of chick responses to maternal food calls in the Burmese red junglefowl (*Gallus gallus spadiceus*). *Journal of Comparative Psychology,* **106,** 92–96.

Moltz, H., & Stettner, L. J. (1961). The influence of patterned light deprivation on the critical period for imprinting. *Journal of Comparative & Physiological Psychology,* **54,** 279–283.

Morin, P.-P., Dodson, J. J., & Doré, F. Y. (1989). Cardiac responses to a natural odorant as evidence of a sensitive period for olfactory imprinting in young Atlantic salmon, *Salmo salar. Canadian Journal of Fisheries and Aquatic Sciences,* **46,** 122–130.

Nottebohm, F. (1969). The song of the chingolo, *Zonotrichia capensis,* in Argentina: Description and evaluation of a system of dialects. *Condor,* **71,** 299–315.

Nottebohm, F. (1981). A brain for all seasons: Cyclical anatomical changes in song-control nuclei of the canary brain. *Science,* **214,** 1368–1370.

Nottebohm, F., & Arnold, A. P. (1976). Sexual dimorphism in vocal control areas of the songbird brain. *Science,* **194,** 211–213.

Nottebohm, F., Nottebohm, M. E., Crane, L. A., & Wingfield, J. C. (1987). Seasonal changes in gonadal hormone levels of adult male canaries and their relation to song. *Behavioral & Neural Biology,* **47,** 197–211.

Panksepp, J., Vilberg, T., Bean, N. J., Coh, D. H., & Kastin, A. J. (1978). Reduction of distress vocalizations in chicks by opiate-like peptides. *Brain Research Bulletin,* **3,** 663–667.

Peterson, N. (1960). Control of behavior by presentation of an imprinted stimulus. *Science,* **132,** 1395–1396.

Petrinovich, L. (1974). Individual recognition of pup vocalization by northern elephant seal mothers. *Zeitschrift für Tierpsychologie,* **34,** 308–312.

Petrinovich, L., & Baptista, L. F. (1984). Song dialects, mate selection, and breeding success in white-crowned sparrows. *Animal Behaviour,* **32,** 1078–1088.

Polan, H. J., & Hofer, M. A. (1999). Maternally directed orienting behaviors of newborn rats. *Developmental Psychobiology,* **34,** 269–279.

Ratner, A. M. (1976). Modification of duckling's filial behavior by aversive stimulation. *Journal of Experimental Psychology: Animal Behavior Processes,* **2,** 266–284.

Rosenblatt, J. S., & Siegel, H. I. (1980). Maternal behavior in the laboratory rat. In R. W. Bell & W. P. Smotherman (Eds.), *Maternal influences and early behavior* (pp. 155–199). New York: Spectrum Publications.

Sackett, G. P. (1967). Some persistent effects of different rearing conditions on preadult social behavior of monkeys. *Journal of Comparative & Physiological Psychology,* **64,** 363–365.

Salzen, E. A., & Meyer, C. C. (1968). Reversibility of imprinting. *Journal of Comparative & Physiological Psychology,* **66,** 269–275.

Scott, J. P., & Fuller, J. L. (1965). *Genetics and the social behavior of the dog.* Chicago: University of Chicago Press.

Seyfarth, R. M., & Cheney, D. L. (1986). Vocal development in vervet monkeys. *Animal Behaviour,* **34,** 1640–1658.

Sibley, C. G., & Ahlquist, J. E. (1990). *Phylogeny and classification of birds: A study in molecular evolution*. New Haven: Yale University Press.

Smith, J. C., & Sales, G. D. (1980). Ultrasonic behavior and mother-infant interactions in rodents. In R. W. Bell & W. P. Smotherman (Eds.), *Maternal influences and early behavior* (pp. 105–133). New York: Spectrum Publications.

Smotherman, W. P., Wiener, S. G., Mendoza, S. P., & Levine, S. (1977). Maternal pituitary-adrenal responsiveness as a function of differential treatment of rat pups. *Developmental Psychobiology,* **10,** 113–122.

Spalding, D. A. (1873/1954). Instinct; with original observations on young animals. In J. B. S. Haldane (Ed.), Introducing Douglas Spalding. *British Journal of Animal Behaviour,* **2,** 1–11.

Stern, J. M., & Johnson, S. K. (1989). Perioral somatosensory determinants of nursing behavior in Norway rats (*Rattus norvegicus*). *Journal of Comparative Psychology,* **103,** 269–280.

ten Cate, C. (1986). Sexual preferences in zebra finch (*Taeniopygia guttata*) males raised by two species (*Lonchura striata* and *Taeniopygia guttata*): I. A case of double imprinting. *Journal of Comparative Psychology,* **100,** 3, 248–252.

Tsuji, K., & Ishikawa, T. (1984). Some observations of the caravaning behavior in the musk shrew (*Suncus murinus*). *Behaviour,* **90,** 167–183.

Tsuji, K., Matsuo, T., & Ishikawa, T. (1986). Developmental changes in the caravaning behaviour of the house musk shrew (*Suncus murinus*). *Behaviour,* **99,** 117–138.

Tubaro, P. L., Segura, E. T., & Handford, P. (1993). Geographic variation in the song of the rufous-collared sparrow in eastern Argentina. *Condor,* **95,** 588–595.

Vidal, J.-M. (1980). The relations between filial and sexual imprinting in the domestic fowl: Effects of age and social experience. *Animal Behaviour,* **28,** 880–891.

West, M. J., & King, A. P. (1988). Female visual displays affect the development of male song in the cowbird. *Nature,* **334,** 244–246.

West, M. J., King, A. P., & Eastzer, D. H. (1981). The cowbird: Reflections on development from an unlikely source. *American Scientist,* **69,** 56–66.

Wiesner, B. P., & Sheard, N. M. (1933). *Maternal behavior in the rat*. London: Oliver & Boyd.

PART IV
Comparative Analysis of Learning

The two chapters in ***Part IV*** deal with what is perhaps the most traditional area of research in comparative psychology: the processes and skills that allow animals to acquire information and use it in their attempts to adjust to changing environmental conditions. It was the connection between intelligence and evolution that prompted the birth of this field during the 19th century. Darwin, Romanes, Morgan, and others in their time looked at the abilities of a wide variety of animals to deal with change in their environment as part of a search for evidence of mental continuity. Darwin's notion that all biological traits evolved by the slow accumulation of useful variations suggested that even the "higher mental powers" displayed by our own species ought to be present in "lower" animals, at least in rudimentary form. This idea provided the initial impetus for the research described in the following chapters. ***Chapter 13*** concentrates on general aspects of learning; it introduces a basic vocabulary, a taxonomy of learning phenomena, and a general review of learning processes across situations and species. ***Chapter 14*** deals with species comparisons in learning and cognitive abilities and mechanisms. These chapters provide an overview of the evolution of learning abilities in animals.

CHAPTER 13

General Learning Processes

MAIN GENERALIZATIONS OF CHAPTER 13

- *Associative learning processes are preeminently based on temporal contiguity between events such as stimuli in the environment (classical conditioning) or between the animal's behavior and its consequences (instrumental conditioning).*
- *Many factors modulate the acquisition of associative learning and its expression in terms of behavioral changes, including the salience of the stimuli, the distribution of practice, and the nature of prior experience.*
- *There is an impressive degree of generality in conditioning processes both across situations and across species.*

All environments are characterized by a mixture of stability and change. Learning mechanisms are designed to acquire information about food distribution, predators, shelters, territories, social interactions, and other resources that may ultimately be critical for reproductive success. As was shown in many of the preceding chapters, learning plays a fundamental role in the development and emergence of behavior in many different species and situations. Two broad categories of learning phenomena are generally recognized. One of them involves experience with a single event, and thus it is usually referred to as *nonassociative learning.* Habituation and sensitization (see ***Chapter 7***) are the most common examples, but perceptual or exposure learning, as in the case of imprinting and vocal learning (see ***Chapter 12***), could also be included in this category. The second category, *associative learning,* includes *classical* and *instrumental conditioning* and is the one on which Chapters 13 and 14 concentrate. It should be emphasized that these categories are not mutually exclusive. Scientific analysis of natural phenomena allows a distinction among a variety of factors and mechanisms; however, this should not be taken to imply that these mechanisms act in isolation. Behavioral changes demanded by environmental challenges probably depend on a convergence of actions from several learning mechanisms, as well as from other processes including genetic predisposition, maturation, motivation, changes in stimulus conditions, and so on. Even under the controlled conditions of the laboratory experiment, it may be difficult, for example, to separate the contribution of classical and instrumental conditioning processes in a particular instance of learning. I begin with a description of these two forms of conditioning and of the manner in which their relative contribution to behavior can be determined.

1. Forms of Associative Learning

1.a. Defining Associative Learning. Associative learning is generally defined in terms of the acquisition, storage, and retrieval of information about events that occur in close temporal or spatial *contiguity. Acquisition* refers to the gaining of information through experience. *Storage* refers to the translation of acquired information into a more or less permanent neural record. *Retrieval* refers to the reactivation of information previously stored.

Several assumptions underlie this definition of learning. The first one is that learning is different from behavior. Learned information can potentially affect behavior, but the effect may not be immediate. This was clear in the cases of sexual imprinting and age-dependent vocal learning described in ***Chapter 12.*** A classic demonstration of this *learning-performance dichotomy* is provided by the phenomenon of latent learning illustrated in ***Figure 4.3,*** p. 94 (Tolman & Honzik 1930). Rats exposed to a complex maze without receiving food reinforcement explored the environment without showing any obvious change in behavior. However, when food was introduced in the goal-box of the maze, preexposed animals exhibited faster acquisition of the correct itinerary than nonpreexposed animals. The faster acquisition rate of preexposed rats demonstrates that despite the absence of obvious performance changes, rats were acquiring and storing information during the preexposure trials. That information was later retrieved in order to solve the task when food became available in that environment. The learning-performance dichotomy makes any conclusion regarding the absence of conditioning particularly problematic. Apparent failures of acquisition must be treated with caution because they may represent failures of performance.

The second assumption of the present definition of associative learning is that acquisition, storage, and retrieval refer to processes that occur in the CNS, which implies that learning is an animal phenomenon. Organisms lacking neural tissue (e.g., sponges, plants, unicellular organisms) and machines (e.g., artificial intelligence) may exhibit "behavioral" change, and the processes may present interesting parallels with those observed in animals. But the resemblance is necessarily superficial and will not be discussed further.

The third assumption is that whereas acquisition, storage, and retrieval are general labels for physiological processes occurring within the CNS, the particular way in which these processes are instantiated may depend on the type of neural organization of a particular species. The mechanisms by means of which learning is actually achieved in specific animals depend on the organization of the organism's nervous system and on the functions it is capable of performing. The comparative analysis of learning is concerned primarily with the study of common and unique aspects of learning processes across species.

1.b. Classical and Instrumental Conditioning. Situations vary in the extent to which an animal can alter its immediate surroundings by means of its own behavior. At one extreme lie situations in which the environment changes independently of the animal's actions and control, as in the case of daily cycles. New events may also arise as unexpected consequences of the animal's own behavior. A foraging animal may come across a new source of food or become the target of intense aggressive behavior after stepping into the territory of a conspecific. An animal may be helpless to deal with such situations, but it still has the ability to learn the connection between biologically important events and their preceding cues. Thus, signs of the new type of food may induce salivation and approach responses in later encounters, whereas a hint indicating the presence of a conspecific male may provoke freezing and withdrawal responses. At the other extreme are situations in which the animal's own behavior brings it into contact with resources such as food and water. This behavior is said to be instrumental in the sense that it is influential in producing a change in the conditions of the environment. It is also referred to as operant, a term implying active control over some feature of the environment.

Scientists have modeled a vast array of laboratory procedures after these two basic situations. In a typical experiment in classical conditioning, an animal is repeatedly exposed to a sequence of two events. The first event in the sequence is a stimulus, initially neutral, that may not even support overt responses. This is referred to as the conditioned stimulus (CS). The second element in the sequence is a relatively strong or intense stimulus capable of eliciting one or several responses (e.g., movements or autonomic reactions). This is referred to as the unconditioned stimulus (US). Such CS-US pairings are separated by an intertrial interval, are presented several times within a particular session, and eventually convey to the CS an ability it did not have before: the ability to elicit a conditioned response (CR).

This basic procedure, called *delay* or *forward conditioning,* was developed and studied in great detail by the Russian physiologist Ivan P. Pavlov [1849–1936]. Pavlov (1927) viewed conditioning as a procedure that allowed for a quantitative and reliable way of accessing higher brain functions. What is unique about the procedure used in classical conditioning experiments is that the occurrence of a response during the CS is not required for the delivery of the US.

For this reason, CS-US pairings are said to be response-independent pairings. Obviously, this feature makes the learning-performance dichotomy especially relevant in classical conditioning situations. Suppose you expose an animal to several CS-US pairings, videotape the session so as to have a real-time record of behavior, and find no particular behavioral change during the CS. The conclusion that the animal has not been able to learn that the CS signals the US must be considered with caution. Since no behavior is required during CS, the animal is not forced to perform any type of specific activity. Special efforts may be needed to detect conditioning in this situation, such as, for example, recording physiological reactions that may provide a more sensitive dependent measure (e.g., perhaps the animal's heart rate changes when the CS is presented).

Another way in which conditioning can be detected in the absence of behavioral changes is by using the CS's ability to act as a *secondary reinforcer,* that is, a stimulus that has acquired the ability to sustain behavior. USs can both elicit responses (called unconditioned responses, URs) and reinforce a CS-US association. Likewise, CSs can both elicit CRs and reinforce a CS-CS association, but only after CS-US conditioning has occurred. Failure to provoke a CR does not imply that the CS is unable to act as a secondary reinforcer. The response-eliciting and motivational properties of a CS are independent from each other, although both depend on a successful conditioning history. In one experiment, pigeons (*Columba livia*) received pairings between a tone (the CS) and access to mixed grain (the US) during several sessions (Rescorla 1980). No particular behavior was observed to occur when the tone was presented, even after many tone-grain pairings. Subsequently, pigeons were exposed to two spatially localized lights; one was consistently followed by the tone, while the other was presented by itself. After a few trials, the pigeons started to peck significantly more at the light signaling the tone than at the light presented alone. Unlike diffuse tones, localized lights that signal food can induce pecking responses in pigeons (an animal that feeds on seeds). This phenomenon, called *second-order conditioning,* is based on the reinforcing properties of a CS that, in turn, can be acquired only by prior CS-US training.

The other basic method for studying associative learning is instrumental conditioning. The unique feature of instrumental training is the dependency of reinforcement upon the occurrence of an instrumental response. Thus instrumental conditioning is said to involve response-dependent training. Although the actual events may be the same, the terminology used to refer to such events changes depending on whether the procedure is classical or instrumental. CS, US, CR, and UR are used exclusively to refer to classical conditioning events. Within an instrumental training procedure, a discriminative stimulus (S^D) is said to set the occasion for the response rather than to elicit it; an instrumental response (R) is said to be emitted rather than elicited or provoked; and reinforcement (S^R) is said to strengthen prior responses rather than prior stimuli. The term *reinforcer* refers to the actual object (e.g., food, water, electric shock, etc.), whereas the organism's reception of a reinforcer is termed *reinforcement.*

Instrumental learning was first studied in detail by the American comparative psychologist Edward L. Thorndike [1874–1949], who labeled it *trial-and-error learning* to emphasize the tentative nature of the behavior when an animal is solving a specific problem. In Thorndike's view (1911), instrumental learning was an ideal procedure for studying the acquisition and development of new behavioral skills. Thorndike suggested that new behaviors are acquired via a gradual process involving the strengthening of successful responses and the weakening of unsuccessful ones, where "success" is defined in terms of achieving a goal object such as food or water. Thorndike (1911, p. 244) referred to this principle as the *law of effect:*

> Of several responses made to the same situation, those which are accompanied or closely followed by satisfaction to the animal will, other things being equal, be more firmly connected with the situation, so that when it recurs, they will be more likely to recur; those which are accompanied or closely followed by discomfort to the animal will, other things being equal, have their connections with that situation weakened, so that, when it recurs, they will be less likely to occur. The greater the satisfaction or discomfort, the greater the strengthening or weakening of the bond.

This formulation is usually referred to as the theoretical law of effect because Thorndike suggested an explanation of the behavioral change based on the formation of a hypothetical association between the situation (or stimulus) and the response, or S-R association. A more inductive formulation, dispossessed of the intervening variable and known as the empirical law of effect, simply states that responses followed by appetitive reinforcers tend to increase in strength, whereas responses followed by aversive reinforcers tend to decrease in strength.

1.b. Distinguishing Among Conditioning Processes. The procedural distinction between classical and instrumental conditioning was first clearly noted by the Polish physiologists Miller and Konorski (1928), who also suggested that the underlying processes were different. Whereas there is an obvious distinction of procedures, the more substantial hypothesis that the processes subserving these two types of conditioning are different has been disputed by many. Indeed, every time an animal responds in an instrumental training situation, a reinforcer is delivered in the presence of a discriminative stimulus. As a result, there is a parallel between this S^D-S^R pairing and the CS-US pairing of a Pavlovian situation. As this simple analysis indicates, classical conditioning is embedded into instrumental learning, so disentangling the two and identifying which one is the source of a specific instance of behavioral change is a rather complicated task.

Suppose you are conducting a classical conditioning experiment in which a rat receives pairings between a light (the CS) and a piece of food (the US). Further suppose that every time the light is turned on during a trial, the rat orients toward it, approaches it, and sniffs it. As the rat is sniffing the light, the food is delivered according to a Pavlovian, response-independent rule scheduled by you, the experimenter. Does the rat sniff at the light because the light has become a Pavlovian signal for food? Or does the rat sniff at the light because sniffing is being instrumentally reinforced by contingent food? Although technically speaking this experiment involves a response-independent contingency between light and food (i.e., that is how it was designed by the experimenter), from the rat's perspective there is a consistent number of sniffing-food pairings (i.e., "accidental" response-reinforcer pairings) that may lead to an instrumental effect upon behavior.

The key difference between the Pavlovian and instrumental accounts lies in the extent to which the response, sniffing, is sensitive to the light-food (S-S) contingency versus the sniff-food (R-S) contingency. The best way to decide between these two alternative accounts is by introducing an *omission contingency* on sniffing (Sheffield 1965). According to the logic of the omission experiment, if a response is sensitive to the presentation of the reinforcer, then it should also be sensitive to its contingent omission. That is, if the rat sniffs because of the sniff-food instrumental pairing, then it should stop sniffing when the response produces the elimination of food. However, notice that because the rat may sniff in some trials but not in others, the omission contingency would result in a mixture of light-food trials (when it does not sniff) and light-only trials (when it sniffs). Therefore, the omission condition must be compared with a control condition in which the rat receives exactly the same frequency and distribution of light-food and light-only trials, but independently of sniffing. This is achieved by the now familiar *master-yoked procedure* (see ***Figure 8.6-b,*** p. 277, for another example).

There are two possible outcomes in an omission experiment. If the omission and control groups do not differ from each other, then the implication is that sniffing is entirely under the control of the Pavlovian light-food contingency. Groups are matched in terms of light-food pairings but vary in the degree to which the response affects food delivery. Similar acquisition functions across groups imply that the consequences of the response do not control the occurrence of that response. Pavlovian responses are impervious to their consequences but are sensitive to the S-S contingency.

By contrast, if omission training leads to a relatively low response frequency compared to the control, then the implication is that sniffing is under the control of instrumental contingencies. Since omission does not permit response-reinforcer pairings, the frequency of sniffing tends to remain low. The degree of S-S contingency prevailing in the situation is insufficient to sustain a high level of behavior. This result was obtained in an experiment on filial imprinting described in ***Chapter 12, section 1.c.,*** pp. 446–448: Ducklings rapidly learned to stay away from the imprinting object in order to keep that object moving.

Omission experiments in which several responses are changing simultaneously demonstrate that whereas some are decreased by omission contingencies, other responses do not seem sensitive to their consequences, occurring at high rates even though they prevent appetitive reinforcers from being administered. For example, rats (*Rattus norvegicus*) exposed to delay conditioning with a burst of white noise as the CS and food as the US exhibit an increase in the frequency of at least three different responses during the CS: They tend to startle (i.e., a sudden body movement), they exhibit short and rapid head-jerk movements oriented to the food magazine, and they tend to stand motionless in front of the magazine where food will be delivered shortly (Holland 1979). The three panels in ***Figure 13.1*** show the effects, on each of these three responses, of imposing an omission contingency in one of them at a time. There were four groups in each of these experiments, but only two are relevant in the present discussion: the groups labeled O (omission) and Y (yoked). These groups were matched in terms of their exposure to and temporal distribution of CSs and USs. Omission contingencies have absolutely no effect on the startle response ***(a)***, an intermediate effect on head jerk responses ***(b)***, and a markedly suppressive effect on magazine behavior ***(c)***. Interestingly, then, some responses within the same training situation are instrumental (magazine, head jerks) while others are Pavlovian (startle).

The reason why behaviors differ in the degree to which they are sensitive to their consequences is unclear. However, omission experiments demonstrate that the dis-

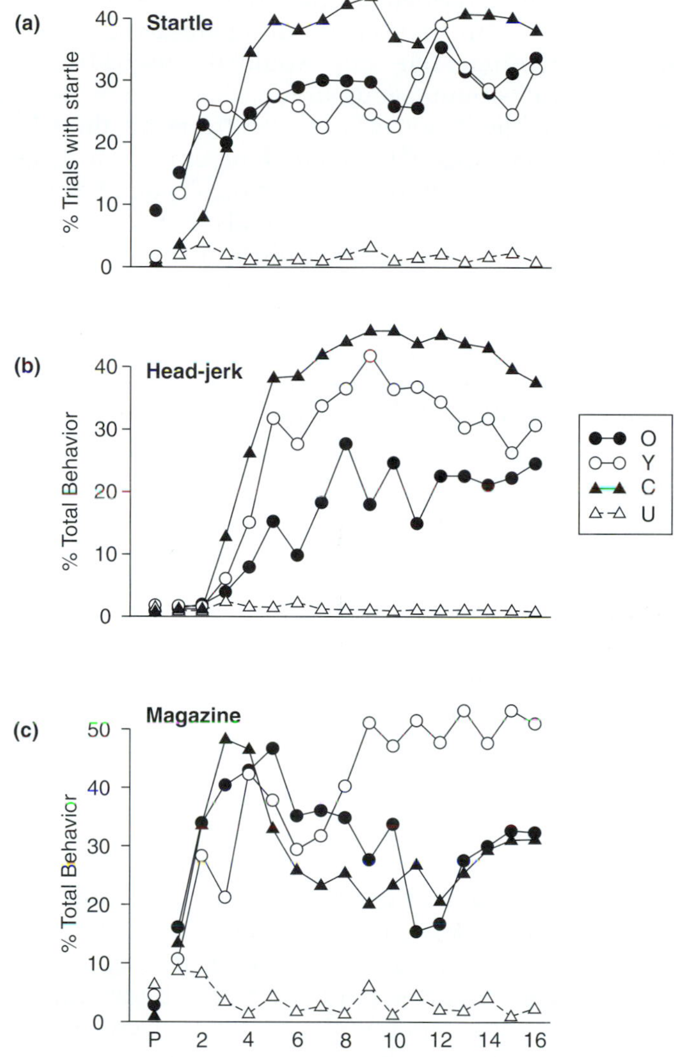

Figure 13.1. Effects of omission training on three different responses in appetitive conditioning with rats (Holland 1979). The same set of responses were scored in these three experiments, but omission contingencies were enforced on startle ***(a)***, head-jerk ***(b)***, or magazine responses ***(c)***. Four groups were included in each of these experiments: a master or omission group (O), a yoked control (Y), a group receiving continuous reinforcement (C), and an unpaired control group (U). The main outcome is that different responses developing in the same conditioning situation may be differentially sensitive to omission contingencies. A comparison of groups O and Y indicates that omission has no effect on startle (a Pavlovian response), but it decreases the frequency of head-jerk and magazine responses (instrumental).

tinction between classical and instrumental conditioning goes beyond simple matters of procedure. This distinction notwithstanding, many of the variables that affect conditioning have similar effects in both types of situations.

2. Classical Conditioning

2.a. Processes Mimicking Conditioning. A proper demonstration of *excitatory conditioning*—that is, of the ability of CS-US pairings to influence behavior—requires a distinction between the effects on behavior of the relationship between CS and US from the effects of the individual events per se. Some CSs elicit responses that may be based on the same effector system as that of the CR and that may increase in frequency during CS-only training. These responses, called *alpha responses,* are an example of a behavioral change not caused by conditioning. For example, in the eyelid-response preparation, a tone or a light (the usual CS) is paired with a puff of air to the eye or a paraorbital shock (the usual US). After some pairings, rabbits or rats (the species usually trained under these conditions) start closing their eyelids in the presence of the CS; however, the CS may itself induce eyelid closure. Such alpha responses usually have a shorter latency of occurrence than true CRs, a property that allows researchers to discriminate between them (Gormezano 1966). The unconditioned response to the CS may also increase as a result of exposure to the US, an effect called *sensitization.* In yet other cases, the repeated elicitation of a response by the US may increase the probability that other stimuli would elicit that same response. This is called *pseudoconditioning.*

Notice that in all of these situations the CS develops the ability to induce the response after some training. In alpha conditioning, the response to the CS increases because of exposure to just the CS. In sensitization, it is the administration of the US that intensifies the original response to the CS. In pseudoconditioning, the response originally elicited by the US transfers to the CS. These behavioral changes occur even in the absence of CS-US pairing experience and simply because of repeated exposure to either the CS or the US.

Several procedures have been suggested to control for nonassociative influences that can mimic the conditioning process. Single-stimulus controls are appropriate to eliminate a particular effect (e.g., a CS-only control can be used to eliminate alpha conditioning), but they would be insensitive to the simultaneous influence of two or more of these nonassociative effects on the CR. The *explicitly unpaired procedure* involves the presentation of both the CS and US, but with interstimulus intervals that do not support conditioning. Unfortunately, this procedure may provide a misleading picture of the size of the conditioning effect in comparison with a group exposed to the CS-US pairing procedure. The reason is related to the possibility that the CS in an explicitly unpaired procedure provides information for the nonoccurrence of the US, at least for some amount of time after the CS. This type of learning is called *inhibitory conditioning* (see ***section 2.d.*** below), and the possibility of its occurrence implies that the control procedure may not be neutral. The same issue arises with another popular control procedure: *differential conditioning.* In an A+/B– situation, and provided the validity of the stimuli are *counterbalanced* (i.e., some animals receiving A+/B– while others B+/A–), discriminative performance provides evidence for specificity, a hallmark of conditioning and a property missing from the nonassociative alternatives discussed above. However, response in B– trials may be exaggeratedly suppressed by inhibitory conditioning, a possibility that may overestimate the true conditioning effect observed in A+ trials. Control procedures supposed to provide a baseline that is equidistant from both excitatory and inhibitory conditioning, such as the so-called *truly random control* procedure (i.e., CS and US are randomly presented throughout the session), have turned out to implicate a variety of effects, leaving the CS far from neutral (Papini & Bitterman 1990).

Unfortunately, the issue of the appropriate control procedure for demonstrating excitatory conditioning cannot be treated in absolute terms. The choice of a control condition depends on theoretical and procedural considerations. Despite their potential problems, the explicitly unpaired and differential procedures are among the most frequently used controls for nonassociative factors.

2.b. Basic Acquisition Phenomena. Although delay conditioning is the most common paradigm for studying conditioning, many different arrangements have been developed to deal with specific problems and to explore the generality of excitatory conditioning. For example, in *trace conditioning* there is a temporal gap between the offset of the CS and the onset of the US. The name given to this procedure by Pavlov (1927) refers to the possibility that excitatory conditioning occurs to the sensory trace left by the CS after its presentation. It is the trace of the CS, rather than the CS itself, that becomes associated with the US. In *simultaneous conditioning* the onset and offset of both CS and US coincide in time, whereas in *backward conditioning* the US occurs before the CS (opposite to delay or forward conditioning). Although these conditioning paradigms are generally considered less powerful than delay conditioning, evidence of excitatory conditioning has been obtained with all of them in a variety of experiments. This, in turn, suggests that the CS need not bear a forward relation with the US, nor even be strictly contiguous with it, for excitatory conditioning to occur.

As noted previously, because of the learning-performance dichotomy one must exercise caution when interpreting evidence of seemingly weak conditioning effects, as in the case of some of these paradigms. The apparent weakness of trace, simultaneous, and backward paradigms may result from a performance deficit rather than a learning deficit. Matzel et al. (1988) argued that acquisition may occur in simultaneous and backward paradigms, but it may not be expressed in terms of the response-evoking properties of the CS. An ingenious design, based on a phenomenon known as *sensory preconditioning,* was used to demonstrate this point with rats as subjects. ***Figure 13.2*** shows some of the essential features of this design (the actual effects were illustrated in two experiments, and several control groups were added that are not shown in this figure). Clicks and tones served as CSs and electric shock as the US. These stimuli were presented in a forward (F), simultaneous (S), backward (B), or unpaired (U) fashion. The effects of these training regimes were assessed in test sessions in which the CSs were presented while the rat was drinking. Since the CS was paired with an electric shock, the greater the suppression of drinking, the greater the conditioning of the CS.

During Phase 1, the three key groups (F-F, F-S, and F-B) received forward pairings of the two CSs, clicks and tones. This was designed to establish an association between the click and tone CSs. In Phase 2, the second CS in the sequence, the tone, was paired with shock according to forward, simultaneous, or backward temporal arrangements. Sensory preconditioning is demonstrated by Group F-F, which shows robust responding to the click, never itself paired with shock but only "paired" indirectly via the mediation of the tone. Interestingly, robust responding was also observed in Groups F-S and F-B, in which the tone had been paired with the shock in simultaneous and backward paradigms, respectively. Control groups, such as Group U-U shown in this figure, determined that paired exposure to these stimuli was necessary for this effect, thus discarding nonassociative factors. Furthermore, a second

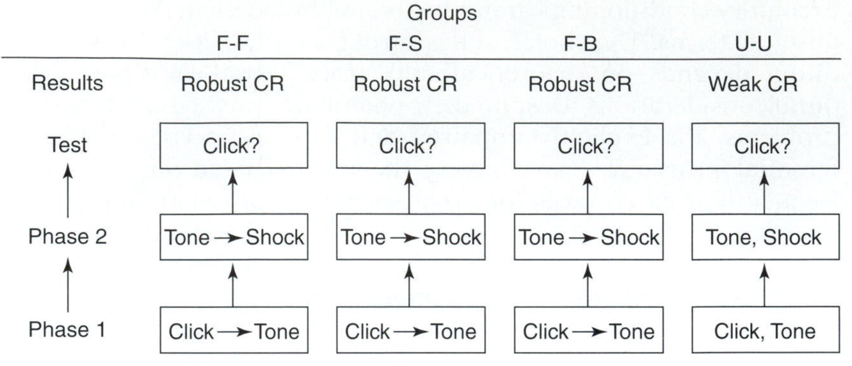

FIGURE 13.2. Does conditioning occur when CS and US are arranged in a simultaneous or backward paradigm? Research with rats (Matzel et al. 1988) suggests that conditioning does occur, but its detection requires special measurement procedures. In this experiment, a sensory preconditioning technique is used for this purpose. Groups are labeled according to whether the treatment received in Phase 1 and 2 involved forward (F), simultaneous (S), backward (B), or unpaired (U) presentations of the CS and US. Notice that Phase 1 involves forward pairings of two relatively neutral stimuli, the click and tone (except for the U-U control group). In Phase 2, the second stimulus, the tone, is given either F, S, or B treatment. In a final test, the first stimulus, the click, is presented. A robust CR indicates both that an association between click and tone developed in Phase 1 and that F, S, and B treatments resulted in equivalent conditioning strength.

test (not shown in ***Figure 13.2***) in which the tone alone was presented demonstrated robust responding in Group F-F, as expected because of its forward training, but not in Groups F-S and F-B. Therefore, a CS that commands weak responding due to its simultaneous or backward conditioning with the US is nonetheless capable of supporting levels of sensory preconditioning analogous to those of a forward CS. At least within certain limits, the temporal relationship between CS and US is not important as long as there is temporal contiguity between the two. However, forward- or delay-conditioning arrangements endow the CS with maximum response-eliciting power.

In addition to temporal contiguity, other factors intrinsic to a CS-US pairing event are important modulators of acquisition. For example, generally speaking, the intensity of both CS and US is positively related to the speed of acquisition. Within limits, the greater the intensity of these stimuli, the faster the emergence of a CR during training. Contiguity also affects conditioning in an interesting manner. As the temporal relationship between the CS and the US is manipulated, the speed of acquisition follows a nonmonotonic function, with CRs peaking at an optimal value and decreasing at values smaller and greater that the optimal. ***Figure 13.3*** illustrates the ef-

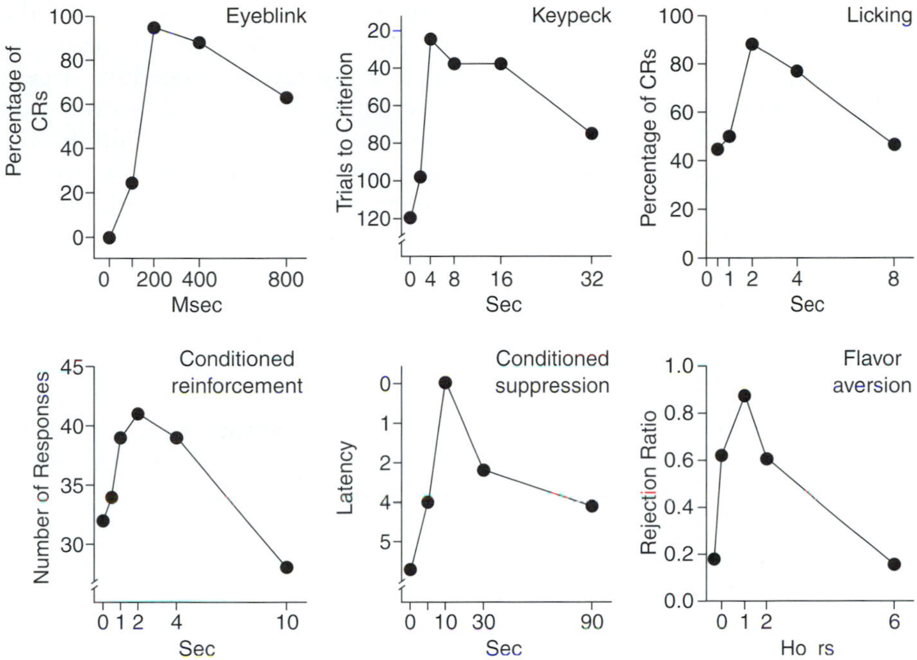

FIGURE 13.3. CS-US interval functions in a variety of Pavlovian conditioning preparations (see Rescorla 1988 for the original sources). An inverted U-shaped function is evident in each case, although the specific values in the abscissa vary from ms to hours.

fect of varying the *CS-US interval* in different conditioning preparations. Notice that the general shape of these functions is similar, but the specific values for the CS-US interval range from milliseconds (as in eyelid conditioning in rabbits), to seconds (as in most conditioning preparations), and to minutes for flavor aversion in rats (a flavor paired with a toxin that leads to suppression of flavor consumption). Whereas there is no unique, absolute value that fits all these conditioning situations, there is an optimal value for which the effectiveness of the CS to evoke a CR is maximum in each case. This effectiveness of the CS decreases as the interval changes in either direction of the optimal value, which implies that the response-eliciting effectiveness of simultaneous conditioning (i.e., with a CS-US interval equal to zero) is lower than that of the optimal value.

The type of conditioning paradigm, the intensity of the stimuli, and the CS-US interval are factors that characterize the conditioning trial. But trials are, in turn, embedded in the context provided by the training session, which usually includes several trials separated by a variable interval. The amount of responding in a given trial depends not only on the conditions of that trial but also on the context in which that trial is embedded. Perfectly effective forward pairings may support a substantial amount of behavior or very little if any behavior, depending, for example, on the length of the intertrial interval. A robust outcome of learning experiments is that, other things equal, the longer the intertrial interval, the faster the acquisition. The importance of this effect, known as the *trial-spacing effect,* lies in that it challenges the sufficiency of temporal contiguity for associative learning. Otherwise effective learning conditions result in greatly impaired acquisition when trials occur in rapid succession. In one experiment (McAllister et al. 1974), rats received 25 trials in each of which a light was paired with an electric shock delivered to the animal's feet, all in a single session and in a white compartment. Trials were separated by 15, 45, 75, 105, 165, 225, and 285 s in independent groups. Fear conditioning was assessed the following day by giving the animals the possibility of escaping from the white compartment into a safe gray box when the light CS was presented. During the test session, escape speeds increased as the intertrial interval enforced in training increased, up to a value of 105 s, and then the speeds became stable and high. Thus, a perfectly viable conditioning procedure leads to weak escape responses when trials are 15 s apart but leads to strong escape responses when trials are 105 s apart.

There are several other situations in which otherwise effective CS-US temporal contiguity fails to support normal levels of responding. In ***Chapter 11*** (see ***Figure 11.6,*** p. 419), I mentioned the phenomenon known as *latent inhibition*: nonreinforced preexposure of a stimulus retards its subsequent acquisition when the stimulus is used as a CS in Pavlovian training. Latent inhibition has been demonstrated in several species of mammals and in a variety of situations. It is generally accepted that retardation of acquisition is related to the innocuous nature of nonreinforced CS presentations. In a typical demonstration, a rat may be exposed to a tone for dozens of trials without anything else occurring in the situation. This procedure is analogous to the familiar habituation procedure except that the effects of repeated stimulation are assessed in a subsequent conditioning phase (in habituation experiments, the effects of repeated stimulation on the occurrence of some response are assessed during stimulation per se). Since tones do not bear any significant motivational value, animals may learn to disregard them; more technically, this treatment may induce a decrement in attention to the CS (Lubow 1989). Later, when the situation changes and the CS precedes the presentation of an important event (such as food or shock), preexposed animals have to overcome an attentional deficit before they can show evidence of CRs.

Just as learning about a CS-US pairing is modulated and affected by other pairings that occur in the situation (as, e.g., in the trial-spacing effect), responding to the CS is also affected by the value of the context in which training takes place. When a US is presented, it always occurs in a particular situation, surrounded by static cues that, unlike the CS, are constantly present. These so-called contextual stimuli include any of a variety of visual, auditory, tactual, and olfactory properties of the environment in which conditioning occurs and to which the animal is sensitive. Thus, in every occasion in which a CS is presented, it occurs in compound with contextual cues. If a CS-US pairing is represented as an A+ episode ("A" stands for the CS and "+" for the US), and the context is represented with an X, then, in fact, a pairing should be represented as AX+. Extending this idea, a nonreinforced presentation of the CS, as in the first phase of a latent inhibition experiment, can be represented as AX– ("–" stands for the absence of the US), and the presentation of an unsignaled US would then be an X+ trial (e.g., a US with no discrete CS preceding it). X+ trials lead to *contextual conditioning.*

This terminology suggests that contextual conditioning can modulate CS conditioning, given its ubiquitous presence. Manipulations of the context can have significant consequences on CS learning, as shown in ***Table 13.1.*** For example, in a latent inhibition experiment, a change in context between phases restores the CS's ability to condition (e.g., AX– followed by AY+ training, where X and Y are different contexts). Moreover, unsignaled USs result in context inflation that, in turn, decreases the rate of subsequent conditioning to the CS. This is known as the *US-preexposure effect.* Finally, unsignaled USs intermixed with CS-US pairings reduce the response-evoking properties of the CS, a phenomenon known as the *contingency-degradation effect.* Notice, again, that in these situations the target CS bears a temporal relationship with respect to the US that is itself appropriate to sustain responding, as demonstrated by control groups. Yet the response of the animal to the CS is significantly modulated by the strength of contextual conditioning.

Pavlovian acquisition processes are complicated by the sensitivity of CS-US pairings to both intrapairing factors (such as CS-US interval and stimulus intensity) and extrapairing factors (such as the spacing of trials and contextual conditioning). However, there is a surprising degree of order in the emergence of responding, as was shown by an extensive reanalysis of published data presented by Gibbon and Balsam (1981). They simply assumed that the strength of the CS could be indexed by its duration (called T, for "trial"), whereas the strength of the context in which the CS-

Table 13.1 Three Examples of Contextual Modulation in Classical Conditioning

(a) Disruption of Latent Inhibition by a Context Shift

Group	***Phase 1***	***Phase 2***	***Result***
1—No Shift	AX–	AX+	Group 1 more retarded in Phase 2 than Group 2
2—Shift	AY–	AX+	

Reference: Lubow et al. (1976)

(b) The US-Preexposure Effect

Group	***Phase 1***	***Phase 2***	***Result***
1—No Shift	X+	AX+	Group 1 more retarded in Phase 2 than Group 2
2—Shift	Y+	AX+	

Reference: Tomie (1976)

(c) The Contingency-Degradation Effect

Group	***Training***	***Result***
1—Unsignaled USs	AX+, X+	Group 1 exhibits less responding to A than Group 2
2—No unsignaled USs	AX+, X–	

Reference: Rescorla (1968)

US pairing occurred could be indexed by the length of the interval between successive reinforcements (called C, for "cycle"). There is independent evidence from appetitive conditioning situations supporting the assumptions that the shorter the value of T, the faster the acquisition of conditioning to the CS (Gibbon et al. 1977), and that the shorter the value of C, the greater the conditioning of the context (Mustaca et al. 1991). What Gibbon and Balsam (1981) found was an orderly negative correlation between the emergence of the CR and what they called the *expectancy ratio,* that is, the ratio of cycle to trial duration, or C/T ratio. ***Figure 13.4*** shows their reanalysis of the results reported in several published experiments plotted in double logarithmic scales so that the function appears as a straight line. As the C/T ratio increases (and quite independently of the absolute values of C and T), the CR emerges earlier and after a progressively smaller number of CS-US pairings.

In conclusion: Acquisition itself appears to depend strongly on temporal contiguity, whereas the expression of learning into performance requires the contribution of several factors intrinsic to the CS-US pairing event, including temporal contiguity and a delay arrangement, and extrinsic to the CS-US pairing event, such as the temporal distribution of pairings within a session and the value of the context in which CS-US pairings occur.

2.c. Compound Conditioning. The previous discussion implies that even the simplest of all conditioning procedures involves a compound presentation of the CS and the contextual cues. However, we have also seen that most naturalistic stimuli are in fact patterns of multisensory stimulation. For example, the critical stimulus in a filial imprinting situation may include auditory, visual, and thermal elements, among others. The study of *compound conditioning*—that is, the way in which animals learn about the elements of a complex cue—suggests that the conditioning of an element may be importantly affected by the strength of accompanying elements in the complex cue.

Suppose a compound CS that includes two elements, say a tone and a light, is reinforced according to a delay-conditioning procedure (TL+) until the animal responds consistently. In a subsequent test, the elements presented in isolation would command some level of responding, but usually the level will be lower than that of a control condition in which only the element has been reinforced during acquisition. For example, after TL+ training, responding to, say, T is generally lower than responding after just T+ training. Pavlov (1927) discovered this effect, called *overshadowing,* which also questions the sufficiency of temporal contiguity to support acquisition. Overshadowing is particularly strong when the accompanying stimulus is of greater intensity than the overshadowed one; a relatively weak stimulus may be left completely incapable of eliciting a CR when conditioned in compound with a strong element.

A similar deficit occurs when one of the elements in a compound stimulus received prior reinforcement individually, or is individually reinforced in separate trials within the same session. Suppose, for example, that animals receive pretraining with the light (L+) during Phase 1, followed by conditioning with the tone-light compound (TL+) in Phase 2. In this case, a subsequent test of the tone's strength (T) may indicate poor responding in comparison with a control condition exposed only to the TL+ trials. Prior L+ training has interfered with the conditioning of T, an effect called *blocking* (Kamin 1969). Similarly, when Phases 1 and 2 of a blocking experiment are inter-

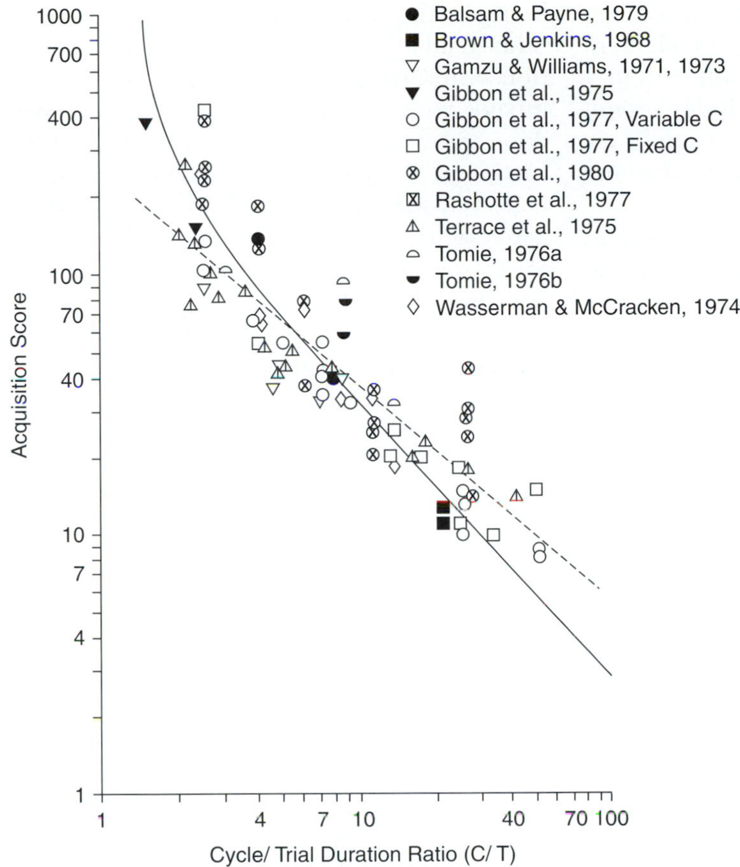

Figure 13.4. Acquisition of Pavlovian responses as a function of the expectancy ratio (see Gibbon & Balsam 1981 for the original sources). In this extensive reanalysis of published data, acquisition was assessed in terms of the number of trials to a criterion (called "acquisition score"). The expectancy ratio results from dividing the duration of the interreinforcement interval (cycle, C) and the duration of the CS (trial, T). The logarithmic axes result in a linear relation. The dashed line is the minimum variance regression line. The solid line is a theoretically derived function. In general, acquisition rate is faster as the expectancy ratio increases, independently of the actual absolute values of C and T.

mixed within the same session, subsequent tests of the strength of the target element generally indicate less conditioning than a group for which there was no independent reinforcement of the light. This special case of blocking is referred to as the *cue-validity effect* (Wagner 1969).

Figure 13.5 illustrates an experiment based on the eyeblink conditioning preparation in rabbits (*Oryctolagus cuniculus*). Rabbits were assigned to four different groups. In Group I, the key condition, a tone-light compound, was paired with paraorbital shock (TL+) in some trials, whereas light-shock pairings (L+) were presented in other trials. There were three control conditions. In Group I/II, TL+ trials were intermixed with unsignaled shocks; this was done to equate the groups in terms of USs. In Group II there were only TL+ trials. Finally, Group III received TL+ trials intermixed with L– trials. The question of interest was how much learning of the tone, T, was there in each of the groups. Notice that T was equally paired with shock in all the groups, so group differences can be attributed only to the conditioning of the light. As the figure shows, T was blocked in Group I,

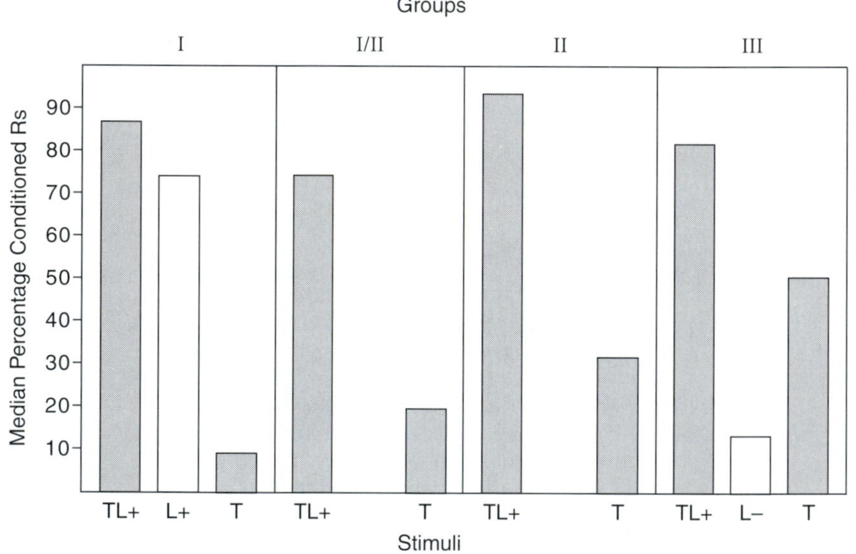

FIGURE 13.5. The cue-validity effect in eyelid conditioning with rabbits (Wagner 1969). During a phase of training not shown in this figure, Group I received TL+ trials intermixed with L+ trials. Groups I/II, II, and III were controls. This figure shows the results of a test session in which rabbits received nonreinforced trials with TL, T, and L. The critical comparison is that involving T, which did not differ in its treatment across groups. In Group I, the separate reinforcement of L leads to relatively less learning about the accompanying T element. This is the cue-validity effect—that is, a CS perfectly paired with the US fails to acquire control of the CR because of the strength of its accompanying element in the compound.

which received additional L+ trials, to a greater extent than in the other groups. Thus, increasing the strength of a cue (either by prior conditioning, as in blocking, or by concurrent reinforcement, as in cue validity), detracts from the ability of accompanying cues in the compound to gain strength from their pairings with the US.

Overshadowing, blocking, cue validity, and their attenuation have played an important role in theoretical developments. Most theories interpret these effects as failures of acquisition. For example, Rescorla and Wagner (1972) suggested that the US supports a fixed amount of conditioning given its intensity. Acquisition by one element of the compound detracts from the ability of other elements to acquire strength. This principle, known as *shared associative strength,* suggests that conditioning of a cue progresses in inverse relation to the strength and salience of concurrently presented cues. In overshadowing, the more salient or intense CS rapidly acquires strength at the expense of the weaker element. In blocking and cue validity, the stronger CS (made stronger by virtue of separate training) interferes with the ability of the less trained element to acquire strength. As with other instances of poor conditioning, the question must be raised as to whether overshadowing and blocking reflect acquisition versus retrieval failure; the evidence at this point is ambiguous (Holland 1999; Kaufman & Bolles 1981).

2.d. Extinction and Inhibitory Conditioning. *Extinction* was among Pavlov's most important discoveries. Just as the pairing of a CS and US results in a progressive increase in some behavior, the subsequent presentation of the CS alone, without the US, results in a progressive decrease in the same behavior. In some sense, extinction is the reversal of acquisition. But, does extinction undo the CS-US association established in acquisition?

Pavlov noticed that a dog that had undergone extinction of the salivary response would exhibit a recovery of the CR after a variety of treatments. Since before the recovery the CR was essentially nil, the recovery meant that the absence of the CR was not necessarily an indication that the effects of acquisition had been completely reversed by the extinction procedure. In several of Pavlov's (1927) experiments, extinction was obtained simply by exposing the dog to powdered meat (the US) that had been previously available (acquisition) and was now presented at a distance and made available only in terms of sight and smell (the CSs). Pavlov (1927) noticed that a period of rest after extinction, during which no events were presented to the animal, could result in the reemergence of the CR when the CS was presented again. This effect is called *spontaneous recovery* and is analogous to a similar finding in habituation experiments (see ***Chapter 7, section 3.a.,*** pp. 244–247). Pavlov (1927) described a second procedure that results in the recovery of the CR. In this case, after extinction of the salivary response to food, the dog was stimulated with a few drops of acid in its mouth, which also elicited salivation. The next presentation of the CS resulted in a substantial recovery of the CR. This was called *disinhibition* by Pavlov and is analogous to the dishabituation of habituated reflexes, also described in ***Chapter 7.*** Other events that by themselves induce no salivation could also result in the disinhibition of an extinguished CR. In one experiment, Pavlov himself entered the room where the dog was being trained, approached and talked to the animal, staying there for about two minutes. A following test revealed a substantial disinhibition of the salivary response. Pavlov (1927) also reported that an extinguished CR recovers its strength if extinction is followed by an unsignaled presentation of the US used during original acquisition training. This effect is called *reinstatement.*

While seemingly simple, these extinction phenomena are not yet fully understood. For example, whereas some experiments indicate that these effects are modulated by contextual cues, other studies demonstrate that this may not be the case. Obviously, it is possible for the nature of the learning process to differ radically depending on the conditions of training. Experiments involving *within-group designs*—that is, designs in which the same set of animals is exposed to the key manipulations in the same context—demonstrate both spontaneous recovery (Rescorla 1997) and reinstatement (Delamater 1997). In these experiments, rats received training in the same context with two CSs, light and tone, each paired with a different US, food pellets and sucrose solution. Then both CSs were extinguished. In the case of spontaneous recovery, one CS was extinguished immediately before the test (the control CS), while the other was extinguished 6 days before the test. The control CS was the light for half the rats, the tone for the other half, and each was paired with the pellets for half the animals and with the sucrose solution for the rest. Stimulus and reinforcer counterbalance ensure that the results of the experiment do not depend on the actual stimuli used but on their conditioning treatment. ***Figure 13.6-a*** shows that the CS for which there was a 6-day rest period (S1) manifested substantial spontaneous recovery relative to the CS extinguished immediately before the test (S2). In the case of reinstatement, the day after extinction rats were exposed to one of the USs (pellets for half the rats, sucrose solution for the rest) and subsequently tested with both CSs. As shown in ***Figure 13.6-b,*** there was selective reinstatement of the response controlled by the CS paired to the exposed US (CSr), whereas the CS that had been paired to the nonreinstated US exhibited a response level similar to that shown at the end of extinction (CSnr).

In the previous experiments, the use of a within-group design ensures that the context in which the animals receive the treatments is the same for both CSs. Still, in the case of reinstatement, the presentation of an unsignaled US may affect the current value of the context. *Between-group designs* in which different sets of animals receive different treatments demonstrate that reinstatement and extinction itself can be both context-specific phenomena. For example, exposure to unsignaled USs in the same context in which the rats had been trained and extinguished resulted in a significantly greater reinstatement of fear than did exposure to the US in a different context (Bouton 1984). Moreover, if rats receive CS-US pairings in one context and CS-only extinction in another context, presentation of the CS in either the original acquisition context or in a third, new context results in the recovery of the response (Bouton & Bolles 1979). This phenomenon, called *renewal,* adds to the other response recovery phenomena in providing support for Pavlov's hypothesis that extinction does not completely eliminate the CS-US association established in acquisition. Furthermore, renewal suggests that extinction is rather specific to the context in which it occurs; the same cannot be said of acquisition, since a well-trained CS would generally transfer well its response-eliciting properties to new contexts.

In Pavlov's (1927) view, extinction results in the development of an opposing process that temporarily blocks the CR. Pavlov called this process inhibition and interpreted spontaneous recovery, disinhibition, and reinstatement as manipulations that would remove the inhibitory influence, permitting the reemergence of the CR.

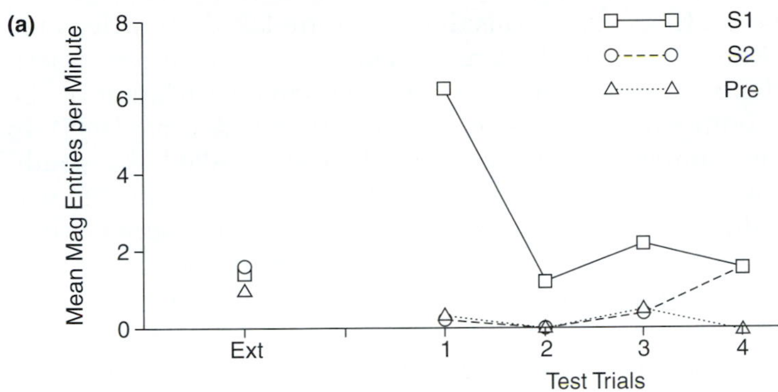

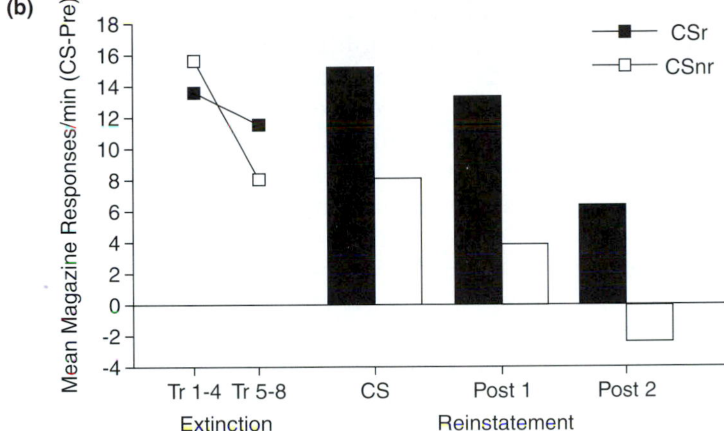

Figure 13.6. Within-group designs demonstrate that extinction phenomena may be relatively independent of the context in which training takes place. ***(a)*** Rats exposed to two CSs, each paired with a different US and both extinguished, exhibit spontaneous recovery in the CS tested after a 6-day interval (S1), but not in the CS tested immediately after extinction (S2) (Rescorla 1997). ***(b)*** Rats exposed to two CSs, each paired with a different US, received extinction of both CSs followed by the unsignaled presentation of one of the USs. Rats exhibited a greater recovery of the CR to the reinstated signal (CSr) than to the nonreinstated signal (CSnr) (Delamater 1997).

Pavlov (1927) also developed training procedures that led to a more permanent type of inhibition. In such inhibitory conditioning procedures, events are arranged such that the US occurs at times other than when the target CS is present. Animals would seem to learn that the CS is followed by a US-free period. Pavlov's main example was a procedure known as conditioned inhibition training, which can be represented as an A+/AB– discrimination. Notice that A becomes excitatory due to its pairing with the

US in A+ trials; in AB– trials, however, B becomes a signal for the absence of an otherwise expected US (expected on the basis of A). Pavlov suggested that in AB– compound trials, the excitation elicited by A is counteracted by the inhibition conditioned to B, thus eliciting a low level of responding.

A major problem with inhibitory conditioning is that of its very detection. In some cases, it may be that a stimulus paired with the omission of a US induces a response opposite to that induced by one paired with the presentation of the US. For example, in an appetitive situation, a CS paired with food would tend to elicit approach to either the CS (*sign tracking*) or to the location where the US will be presented (*goal tracking*). By contrast, a CS paired with food omission would tend to elicit withdrawal responses (Wasserman et al. 1974). However, in other cases, inhibitory CSs may be behaviorally silent—that is, they induce no obvious change in behavior. In these cases, indirect procedures are required to detect the presence of inhibitory conditioning.

Several indirect procedures for detecting inhibitory conditioning have been developed, but two have become particularly popular, the so-called summation and retardation-of-acquisition procedures. Both share the idea that in order to detect inhibitory conditioning there has to be a source of excitation from which the putative inhibitor may detract some strength. In the *summation test,* the stimulus suspected to be inhibitor because of some prior training is compounded with a known excitor. Since excitation and inhibition are opposites, then the summation of these two should result in less responding to the compound than that induced by the excitor alone. In the *retardation test,* the stimulus suspected to be an inhibitor is now paired with the US; inhibition should make it harder for the CS to become excitatory, thus retarding acquisition.

Consider the complex design depicted in ***Figure 13.7-a*** of an appetitive experiment with rats involving a variation of the A+/AB– procedure (Pearce & Kaye 1985). In the experimental group (called the conditioned inhibition group, CI), a tone (T) was made excitatory by virtue of a serial conditioning procedure in which it preceded a reinforced trial with a clicker (C+). A compound of the tone and a light (TL–) was never reinforced. The key question was whether L became inhibitory in this experimental group. The control group (referred to as a latent inhibition group, LI) received the same treatment except that T was unpaired with respect to the C+ trial. Notice that both groups received equal exposure to all the stimuli involved, and the only difference between them lies in the relationship between T and C+ (serial vs. unpaired).

Half the animals were exposed to a summation test, shown in ***Figure 13.7-b,*** and the rest to a retardation test, shown in ***Figure 13.7-c.*** The summation test showed greater disruption of the CR (goal tracking) during the LC trial of the experimental group than during the LC trials of the control group, in both cases relative to the strength of the known excitor (C). The retardation test (L+ trials) indicated a lower (i.e., more retarded) level of goal tracking CRs in the experimental group than in the control group. The implication of these results is that the treatment administered to L in the experimental group led to inhibitory conditioning.

A second major difficulty in the study of inhibitory conditioning is related to the fact that inhibition is only one of a multitude of processes that can lead to response suppression. The solution consists of eliminating alternative explanations by incorporating appropriate control groups, but the task is quite complex (Papini & Bitterman 1993). Consider just a few possibilities. Perhaps

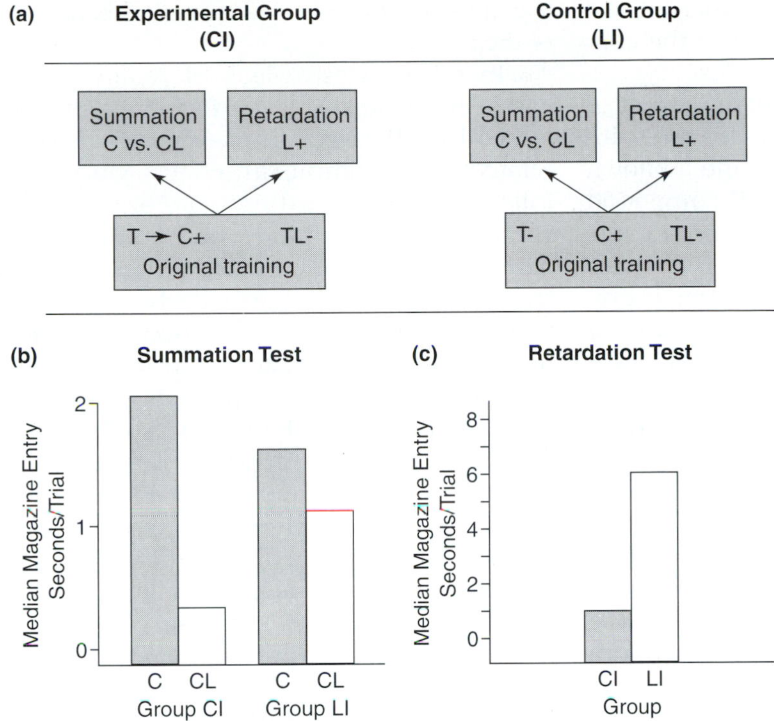

Figure 13.7. Appetitive inhibitory conditioning in rats (Pearce & Kaye 1985). ***(a)*** The design of this experiment involves two groups receiving the same number of CSs and USs. The only difference is whether T preceded a reinforced trial (as in the experimental group, CI) or was presented by itself and nonreinforced (as in the control group, LI). The excitation gained by T in the experimental condition supports inhibitory conditioning to L during TL– trials. ***(b)*** A summation test indicates that L, the putative inhibitor, suppressed responding to a known excitor, C, more in the experimental group than in the control group. ***(c)*** A retardation-of-acquisition test indicates that L+ led to less responding after inhibitory training than after control treatment. Together, these tests suggests that the original training had endowed L with inhibitory properties.

the most traditional concern has been that of distinguishing between inhibitory conditioning and reduced generalized excitation. Because all stimuli can be assumed to share some common elements, the reinforcement of one stimulus would lead to some amount of *generalization* of excitation to other stimuli in proportion to the number of shared elements. Generalized excitation would tend to be extinguished when the CS is nonreinforced, as it generally is in inhibitory training procedures. As a result, it is often difficult to determine if the experimental group shows more inhibition than the control group, or simply less excitation.

Consider a second difficulty inherent to the summation test. In a summation test involving a putative inhibitor, B, and a known excitor, C, responding to the BC compound may be reduced relative to the excitor alone, C, because the addition of B changes C. This is known as generalization decrement, that is, a reduction in the amount of stimulus generalization from C to BC as a result of the presence of B in the compound. Finally, ponder a difficulty of retardation tests. When acquisition of the CR by the putative inhibitor is retarded, it is possible in some cases to attribute such a retardation to an attentional deficit (i.e., latent inhibition effect) induced during training by the nonreinforced presentation of the CS. Convergent evidence from two or more tests may be needed to determine whether a particular treatment endows a CS with inhibitory conditioning.

3. Instrumental Conditioning

3.a. Learning Versus Performance. Many of the factors that affect acquisition in classical conditioning also have an effect on the acquisition of instrumental responses. The learning-performance dichotomy mentioned previously (see ***section 1.a.***) also introduces an element of complexity in the study of instrumental learning. In part, the danger of overlooking this issue lies in the fact that instrumental learning involves by definition the reinforcement of a specific response; thus, it may be tempting to identify learning with performance. One example is, of course, the latent learning experiment considered previously (see ***Figure 4.3,*** p. 94), in which a shift in incentive conditions is required to detect a learning effect on the instrumental behavior of the rat.

In other cases, a lack of group differences in acquisition performance maintained by different parameters may be correlated with significant effects during a following phase of extinction. For example, variations in magnitude of reinforcement many times do not produce differential effects in acquisition, particularly in the asymptotic portion of the function, when behavior is stable. Yet, a transition to extinction may be accompanied by large effects. ***Figure 13.8*** shows one such result from an experiment in which rats received training to run in a runway for a food pellet weighing either 45 mg or 500 mg (McCain et al. 1971). In this figure, the lower the scores, the better the performance. Obviously, the acquisition process of animals trained with different reinforcement magnitudes must be different, despite the absence of any noticeable difference in performance, given the large behavioral differences found in extinction. Since in extinction both groups receive exactly the same treatment (i.e., animals run the same runway and encounter an empty goal box), behavioral differences must be attributable to the different acquisition treatments (e.g., large vs. small rewards). Perhaps the behavioral measure—time to reach the goal box in this case—rapidly reaches its floor (i.e., the lower end of the scale) and can no longer discriminate among conditions. *Floor effects* (and *ceiling effects,* when the behavioral change is incremental) may reflect either a lack of sensitivity of the response measure or the presence of a biological limit for a particular response. For example, rats can run up to some maximum speed.

A third example supporting the dichotomy between learning and performance re-

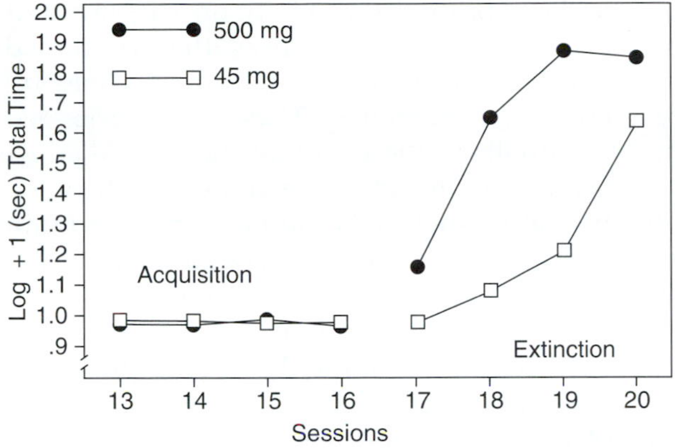

FIGURE 13.8. Floor effect in instrumental learning (McCain et al. 1971). Rats trained in a runway with different reward magnitudes show very similar terminal acquisition performance. However, when shifted to extinction the rats trained with large rewards exhibited faster extinction of the instrumental response than rats trained with small rewards. Behavioral differences were hidden during terminal acquisition by a floor effect. Ceiling effects may be observed when the behavioral changes are incremental.

lates to the notion that the acquisition of new information can influence instrumental performance only when the associative strength surpasses a *response threshold*. Consider a simultaneous visual discrimination problem in a T-shaped maze, in which a rat is reinforced with food for approaching the lighted arm (L+), but nonreinforced for approaching the darkened arm (D–). In such experiments, the right and left position of L and D are varied from trial to trial, more or less randomly, to make it impossible for the rat to rely on spatial cues. Under these conditions, sometimes rats display a consistent choice for, say, the left arm, which translates into a 50% level of correct responses because the left arm is L+ in about half the trials. This is called a *position habit*. Is the rat learning anything about the L+/D– discrimination while exhibiting a position habit?

A simple and ingenious procedure can be implemented to determine whether random-level instrumental performance may involve some amount of measurable acquisition (Spence 1945). The procedure consists of reversing the validity of the cues (from L+/D– to D+/L–, in this example) while the animal is engaged in a position habit. If random choice reflects no learning, then the reversal should pose no additional difficulties. However, rats exposed to such reversals exhibit significant retardation in the development of the visual discrimination. This retardation implies that the animal was indeed learning something about the contingencies of reinforcement, but not enough for performance to be affected (hence the notion that such learning was below a response threshold).

3.b. Instrumental Contingencies. A general definition of instrumental conditioning must refer to the relationship between responses and their consequences. Previous descriptions have emphasized the most typical case in which a response, such as pressing a lever or running in a runway, leads to an outcome, such as a piece of food. Under many conditions, response-reinforcer contingencies lead to an increase in the amplitude, frequency, or probability of the response. But, obviously, this represents only one of several possible instrumental contingencies, all of which have some degree of influence upon the animal's behavior.

A more complete view of the basic contingencies of instrumental learning can be attempted by distinguishing between appetitive and aversive reinforcers and by characterizing the process of reinforcement in terms of either the response-contingent presentation of the reinforcer or its withdrawal. These dimensions yield a 2 × 2 table with four possible combinations, as shown in ***Table 13.2.*** I have used the terms "appetitive" and "aversive" previously without attempting any rigorous definition, but now it is possible to use instrumental principles to characterize the hedonic value of a reinforcer. *Appetitive reinforcers,* such as food and water, can be defined as events that support instrumental behavior when their presentation is made contingent on the occurrence of the response. In contrast, *aversive reinforcers,* such as electric shock, support instrumental behavior when their withdrawal is made contingent on the occurrence of the response. Perhaps such events as food, water, and electric shock can be correctly classified as appetitive or aversive even without much thought. However, these definitions allow for the classification of events that, a priori, could not be clearly placed in one of these categories. For example, Olds and Milner (1954) first reported that rats rapidly acquired a lever-pressing response reinforced by the delivery of a weak electric current through an electrode that had been surgically inserted into a deep brain location. Soon afterward it was found that responses that prevented stimulation of other brain areas could increase in frequency. These discoveries led eventually to the idea that there are distinct brain areas for pleasure and pain. The attribution of such hedonic properties to brain structures was possible because of the instrumental effects of response-contingent intracranial stimulation.

Let's consider the 2 × 2 table in detail. The top left panel corresponds to the case of *positive reinforcement*—that is, the case in which the occurrence of a R is paired with the occurrence of a S^R and the absence of R is paired with the absence of the S^R. As already noted, such a contingency usually, although not always, leads to an increase in some dimension of the response. Skinner (1935) noted that instrumental responses are defined more in terms of the function they achieve than in terms of the specific coordination of muscles involved in the actual production of the movement. Similarly, the stimulus conditions under which instrumental behavior occurs can be quite complex and dynamic. Hence, Skinner suggested that the stimuli and responses relevant in instrumental learning could be better conceptualized as classes of events. For example, lever-pressing responses, a common operant used in learning experi-

TABLE 13.2 Instrumental Contingencies

	Hedonic Value of the Reinforcer	
	Appetitive	***Aversive***
Presentation	Positive reinforcement $R \rightarrow S^R$, $noR \rightarrow noS^R$ Response increases	Punishment $R \rightarrow S^R$, $noR \rightarrow noS^R$ Response decreases
Withdrawal	Omission training $R \rightarrow noS^R$, $noR \rightarrow S^R$ Response decreases	Negative reinforcement $R \rightarrow noS^R$, $noR \rightarrow S^R$ Response increases

ments, is defined as a class of responses that result in the closing of an electronic circuit that activates the feeder; the rat could use a forepaw, its nose, or push the lever accidentally with its tail and still receive the scheduled reinforcement.

In freely-behaving animals, instrumental reinforcement does indeed result in the activation of several responses, at least early in training. As training continues, response variability may be drastically reduced, only to emerge again when the conditions of reinforcement change, such as in extinction (Antonitis 1951). This effect of instrumental reinforcement upon response variability is what permits the development of new skills from behavioral precursors, a process referred to as *shaping*. In the shaping of a target response, such as training a rat to run in circles, the experimenter may define a very remote precursor of the target response, such as turn the head toward one side, and reinforce it consistently until the response increases in frequency. At this point, the experimenter may require a head turn with some forward locomotion and differentially reinforce these new responses while extinguishing the previously reinforced one. The rat's behavior gradually develops into the target response; at each point, however, a family of responses increases in strength and provides precursor responses for the next stage of shaping.

Although extended positive reinforcement may result in a highly stereotyped operant response, it can also be used specifically to generate response variability, as illustrated in the following examples. Pryor et al. (1969) used food reinforcement to generate novel behaviors without shaping in a rough-toothed porpoise (*Steno bredanensis*). Although one new response, as judged by two independent observers, was scheduled to be reinforced per session, there were sessions in which up to four new responses were observed (e.g., aerial spin, beaching, tail walk, tail wave, etc.). In more conventional experiments, pigeons (*Columba livia*) trained to peck eight times on two keys, a right and a left key, in any sequence, rapidly learned to emit novel sequences (e.g., LLRLRRRL). Pigeons can generate new response sequences even when the criterion is set such that reinforcement is administered only when a sequence differs from the previous 50 sequences! Moreover, yoked controls receiving the same frequency of reinforcement independently of the novelty of their sequences exhibit significantly less response variability (Page & Neuringer 1985).

The lower left cell in ***Table 13.2*** describes the case of omission training, also considered in previous chapters and discussed above in ***section 1.c.*** as an important procedure to distinguish between classical and instrumental responses. To the extent that a response is instrumental and, therefore, sensitive to its consequences, the effect of omission training is to suppress behavior. As I mentioned before, Pavlovian responses are less sensitive to omission contingencies, occurring at relatively high levels even though their occurrence eliminates the very appetitive reinforcer that supports them in the first place.

The top right cell in the table corresponds to *punishment*—that is, the presentation of an aversive reinforcer contingent upon the occurrence of the instrumental response. Punishment contingencies result in the suppression of behavior, but they are effective only under very special conditions. Experiments with pigeons (Azrin & Holz 1966) and rats (Church 1969) have contributed to identify some of the factors that facilitate the suppressive effects of punishment on behavior. In a typical experiment, a response is first shaped and maintained with an appetitive reinforcer (e.g., lever pressing reinforced with food) and subsequently subjected to a punishment schedule (e.g., the same lever-pressing response now punished with electric shock). Among the factors affecting the effectiveness of punishment are the intensity of the punisher stimulus, the temporal relationship between the response and the punisher, and the frequency of the response-punisher pairing. For example, very intense shocks introduced with their maximum intensity from the outset of the punishment phase are maximally effective. Similarly, the longer the duration of the punisher, the stronger the suppression of behavior. In contrast, gradually increasing the intensity of the punisher is relatively ineffective in suppressing behavior, even if eventually the punisher reaches a high intensity. Delayed and partial punishment are also particularly ineffective ways of suppressing behavior. Effective punishment then involves the delivery of highly noxious stimuli, consistently for each response, and with a close temporal contiguity with respect to the response. Likely natural counterparts of laboratory experiments on punishment are predator-prey encounters and territorial aggression among conspecifics (Stamps 1998).

The last cell in ***Table 13.2*** corresponds to the case of *negative reinforcement*—that is, the situation in which the response removes an otherwise present or potentially present aversive stimulus. Such a response would tend to increase in frequency, probability, or amplitude. There are two major examples of negative reinforcement: escape conditioning and avoidance conditioning. In *escape conditioning,* the response removes an aversive stimulus already present in the situation or removes the organism from the aversive situation. In *avoidance conditioning,* the response prevents the occurrence of an aversive event or situation that would occur in the absence of the response. These instances of learning are described below in ***section 3.d.***

Notice that these contingencies are defined in terms of the occurrence or omission of events external to the animal. For example, positive reinforcement involves the occurrence of food contingent on some response, and negative reinforcement involves the omission of an electric shock contingent on some response. There are correlated internal states that also vary. For example, food removes an aversive state of hunger, and pain removes an appetitive state of comfort. It is the external events, however, and not their correlated internal states that define these contingencies. For example, addiction to drugs such as nicotine and cocaine results in the development of an aversive internal state when the drug is removed, called drug-withdrawal symptoms. Drug procurement and consumption behaviors may then be instrumentally reinforced because the drug eliminates an aversive internal state. Is this a case of positive or negative reinforcement? According to the criterion used here, it is a case of positive reinforcement because the drug (i.e., the external event) is the reinforcer, not the removal of the withdrawal symptoms (i.e., an internal state).

3.c. Some Basic Procedures and Phenomena. Thorndike's (1911) law of effect opens a wide set of possible circumstances under which behavior is reinforced. These so-called *schedules of reinforcement* have been studied in great detail by B. F. Skinner [1904–1990] and many others (e.g., Ferster & Skinner 1957; Skinner 1938). Essentially, any situation involving the occurrence or omission of reinforcers contingent upon some behavior can be characterized in terms of some schedule. Skinner studied the behavioral properties of many such schedules by introducing the animal (a rat or a pigeon) into a chamber in which the operation of some device (pressing of a lever in the case of rats, pecking at an illuminated disk in the case of pigeons) led to the automatic delivery of a piece of food. Skinner's procedure became known as *free-operant training* because the animal is free to emit the instrumental response at any moment during the session. (This is contrasted with *discrete-trial training* in which the reinforcement of a response can occur only during a trial; most of the experiments reviewed previously involved discrete-trial procedures.)

In free-operant procedures, reinforcement can be delivered according to several criteria. The two most basic rules are *continuous reinforcement* (one reinforcer per response) and extinction (nonreinforcement for every response), but between these two extremes lie a variety of schedules in which not every response results in the delivery of a reinforcement. Accordingly, these are schedules of *partial* or *intermittent reinforcement*. Partial reinforcement can be scheduled in two basic ways: Either as a function of responses emitted or as a function of time. ***Table 13.3*** illustrates some of the most popular schedules.

These schedules of reinforcement may be arranged so that they mimic natural situations. For example, time-based schedules are analogous to food resources that either take time to replenish after being consumed by the animal (such as the nectar of a flower) or appear according to a certain cycle (such as prey that become active at a certain time of day). Response-based schedules resemble a foraging situation in which an animal is collecting food in a particular patch. The higher the rate of responding (or searching in a patch), the higher the rate of reinforcement. Depletion of food by the animal's own foraging behavior can be simulated by progressive ratio schedules in which the number of responses required to obtain a reinforcement increases from one cycle to the following (e.g., usually in steps of fixed magnitude, 2–4–6–8– . . .).

Reinforcement schedules also have definite behavioral properties. I have mentioned the fixed-interval scallop (see ***Chapter 12, section 1.c.,*** pp. 446–448), a patterned distribution of responses that occurs after extensive training on fixed-interval schedules. In this situation, the first response that occurs after a given interval of time receives reinforcement. Immediately after reinforcement, animals typically show response suppression called the postreinforcement pause, which is followed by either a gradual or an abrupt transition to a higher response rate. The length of the postreinforcement pause tends to be directly proportional to the size of the temporal interval. *Timing* processes (i.e., the estimation of the interval's length), play an important role in the adjustment to fixed-interval schedules. In a fixed-interval schedule, the highest degree of temporal control is represented by a subject that waits to respond until the interval is over, whereas the poorest is represented by a subject that responds constantly at the same rate. Lejeune and Wearden (1991) found the highest degree of temporal control in mammals (e.g., rats, woodmice, cats, and monkeys), whereas nonmammalian species exhibited poorer temporal control (e.g., pigeons, doves, turtles, and tilapia fish). However, the fixed-interval scallop pattern was obtained in all the species.

Simple schedules such as those shown in ***Table 13.3*** can also be combined to yield complex schedules of reinforcement. For example, discrimination learning can be studied by arranging two simple schedules, each with its own discriminative stimulus, present either at the same time (called a concurrent schedule) or in succession (called a mul-

Table 13.3 Some Examples of Response-Based and Time-Based Simple Schedules of Reinforcement

Schedule	*Abbreviation*	*Definition*	*Main Behavioral Effects*
Fixed Ratio	FR	S^R for 'x' Rs, with 'x' having always the same value.	Postreinforcement pause, followed by high response rate.
Variable Ratio	VR	S^R for 'x' Rs, with 'x' varying from cycle to cycle.	Steady, high response rate.
Differential Reinforcement of High Rates	DRH	S^R for a R provided it occurs within a certain time since the previous R.	High response rates.
Differential Reinforcement of Low Rates	DRL	S^R for a R provided it occurs after a minimum time since the previous R.	Low response rates.
Differential Reinforcement of Other Responses (Omission Training)	DRO	S^R delivered provided a R does not occur within a certain time.	Response suppression.
Progressive Ratio	PR	S^R for 'x' Rs, with 'x' increasing according to some defined value.	Used to mimic depletion of food resources.
Fixed Interval	FI	S^R for a R occurring after a fixed time elapses.	Postreinforcement pause, followed by gradual increase in response rate (called the *FI scallop*).
Variable Interval	VI	S^R for a R occurring after a variable time elapses.	Steady, intermediate response rate.
Fixed Time and Variable Time	FT, VT	Analogous to FI and VI except there is no response requirement (i.e., Pavlovian).	Used to control for S^R distribution.
Progressive Interval	PI	Analogous to PR except based on a time interval.	Response-independent depletion.

tiple schedule). The development and maintenance of response chains can be studied by implementing a sequence of simple schedules, each with its own discriminative stimulus, that provides food reinforcement only after the last component is satisfied. These are called chain schedules.

The temporal relationship between the occurrence of the response and the delivery of the reinforcer is a powerful determinant of instrumental learning. This *delay of reinforcement gradient* has been studied in a variety of procedures. For example, Grice (1948) trained rats in a simultaneous brightness discrimination in a T-shaped maze. After making a choice, animals were detained for various lengths of time. The results demonstrated a very steep gradient: Delays beyond 0.5 s deteriorated choice performance significantly. Similar effects have been described in many other situations, including the free-operant lever-pressing situation with rats (Dickinson et al. 1992). Although the absolute values vary across training conditions, as they did in the CS-US delay function described previously (see ***Figure 13.3,*** p. 499), increasing the delay of reinforcement tends to retard the acquisition of the instrumental response.

There are, however, many ways of bridging such temporal delays so that reinforcement can still strengthen the instrumental response. One procedure involves limiting the occurrence of competing responses that occur during the delay period. In one experiment, rats detained in a small box learned faster with long delays compared to rats detained in a larger box that allowed for a substantial amount of exploratory activity (Spence 1956). A second procedure involves making the cues present during the delay interval a signal for reinforcement. These cues can then act as secondary reinforcers. For example, the presentation of a tone during the delay and only after the rat has made a correct choice results in better acquisition with delays of 3 and 6 s than either not presenting the tone or presenting it after both correct and incorrect responses (Williams 1991). Presenting the tone after a correct choice and, therefore, before reinforcement endows it with Pavlovian secondary reinforcing properties. A third procedure for bridging the delay of reinforcement consists of introducing a stimulus change (called a *marking stimulus*) both after the choice is made and before the outcome for that trial. In one experiment (Lieberman et al. 1979), an intense light stimulus was presented for a brief period immediately after the rat entered the delay compartment and again immediately before it was released to enter the goal box. This was done for correct as well as incorrect choices, a procedure that reduces the chances that the stimulus acts as a secondary reinforcer. With this marking procedure it is possible to obtain discriminative performance with a level of accuracy bordering on 90% even with temporal delays of 60 s between the response and the reinforcer.

The mere temporal contiguity between the instrumental response and the reinforcer can have a powerful effect upon behavior. In a famous experiment, Skinner (1948) left a few pigeons exposed to a fixed-time 15 s schedule of food delivery—that is, a piece of food was administered every 15 s independently of the pigeon's behavior. After several hours under these conditions, pigeons were exhibiting peculiar responses. One was circling counterclockwise, another was thrusting its head into one of the upper corners of the chamber, and another was moving its head vertically. Skinner suggested that the accidental delivery of food when the animal happened to be performing a particular behavior resulted in the strengthening of that behavior, which made it, in turn, more likely that the response would be occurring at the time of the next reinforcement, thus leading to the spontaneous shaping of relatively complex activities. These responses were referred to as *superstitious behaviors.*

There is little doubt that accidental reinforcement may have measurable effects upon behavior in the manner suggested by Skinner (1948). However, subsequent analogous experiments demonstrated less response idiosyncrasy than expected for superstitious behavior. In one such study with pigeons, Staddon and Simmelhag (1971) carried out detailed observations of several behavioral categories during the interreinforcement interval, also using fixed-time schedules of reinforcement. They found two sets of responses that increased in frequency at different moments during the interval. *Terminal responses* peaked toward the end of the interval, before food delivery, and involved such activities as goal tracking and pecking at the food cup. *Interim responses* occurred early in the interval, after the previous food delivery, and involved such behaviors as turning away from the proximity of the food cup and pecking at the floor. Since the pigeons had learned that food was never delivered early in the interreinforcement interval, interim responses may correspond to responses induced by signals of food omission. I have previously mentioned the withdrawal responses induced by signals of reward omissions (see ***section 2.d.***). One possibility is that interim responses are natural components of the feeding behavior of animals facing food depletion, whereas terminal responses are part of the animal's repertoire for dealing with food (Timberlake & Lucas 1985). The superstitious behavior experiment has contributed to highlight the interrelation between classical and instrumental contingencies in the shaping of behavior. The resulting behavioral changes have such a degree of organization that individual responses may be described as part of a *behavior system* for dealing with the reinforcer (e.g., the feeding behavior system in the examples reviewed here).

3.d. Escape and Avoidance Learning. Escape and avoidance learning were first thoroughly studied by the Russian psychologist Vladimir Bechterev [1857–1927]. In the typical training preparation, a dog was exposed to pairings of a light and an electric shock delivered to its leg, which was resting on the electrodes. Leg flexion was the response to the footshock, and it was also the response to the light once conditioning had occurred. Similarly, human subjects were trained in a situation in which the flexion of a finger was the avoidance response. Although Bechterev thought of his procedure as analogous to Pavlov's classical conditioning of the salivary response, it is obvious that Bechterev's preparation involved a response-dependent component that made it instrumental. The leg or finger flexion responses allowed the subject to either escape from the shock or to avoid it when the response occurred during the presentation of the signal.

Several procedures are used to study escape-avoidance learning. The techniques used by Bechterev are referred to as *active avoidance* procedures because shock avoidance depends on the occurrence of a response. It can also be arranged for the avoidance of the shock to depend on the omission of a particular response, a procedure called *passive avoidance.* For example, an animal exposed to shocks in a black compartment may subsequently be placed in an adjacent white compartment and the time to cross to the black box measured. Shocked animals take longer to cross, or they do not reenter the black compartment at all. The distinction between discrete-trial and free-operant procedures also extends into avoidance training. In discrete-trial procedures, an explicit S^D precedes shock delivery; an avoidance response that occurs during the S^D terminates the S^D and prevents the shock. In free-operant avoidance training, there is no explicit S^D; animals receive electric shocks at a given rate unless they emit a specific response, in which case the shocks are delayed for some period of time (Sidman 1953). When the appropriate parameters are used, this so-called *Sidman avoidance training* leads to a steady response rate that is often used as a baseline to measure the effects of various manipulations on avoidance learning.

The contribution of Pavlovian and instrumental contingencies to avoidance learning can be studied by means of the master-yoked design. Under these conditions, the master animal receives an instrumental treatment while the yoked animal receives a Pavlovian treatment matched in terms of the frequency and distribution of reinforcements. From a purely Pavlovian analysis of the avoidance situation, every trial in which the animal fails to respond there is a CS-US pairing, while trials in which the animal responds represent a CS-only trial. Thus, avoidance training could be thought of as involving partial reinforcement; this is exactly what the yoked group experiences in the absence of the response contingency present in the master group. Many experiments with such a design involving a variety of species (e.g., rats, goldfish) and a variety of responses (e.g., wheel turning, swimming over a barrier) show that while Pavlovian contingencies may support some amount of behavior, the addition of response-dependent, instrumental reinforcement leads to a substantially higher performance level. In one experiment (Overmier & Papini 1986), master-yoked pairs of goldfish (*Carassius auratus*) were placed in tanks with two compartments separated by a barrier located in the middle. Photocells at each side of this barrier detected where the animal was in each trial. Master goldfish rapidly acquired the avoidance response (crossing over a barrier from one side of the tank to the other), preventing about 80% of the shocks from being delivered. In contrast, yoked goldfish responded only in about 15% of the trials.

Notice that avoidance learning ultimately depends on the elimination of the shock from the situation. However, how could the absence of an event, in this case the electric shock, be directly responsible for any kind of learning? One possibility is that the avoidance response is not reinforced by shock omission but by the reduction in an aversive internal state of fear induced by the S^D (Mowrer 1947). Fear conditioning develops because in those trials without avoidance responding the animal experiences Pavlovian pairings that endow the S^D with the ability to act as a signal for shock. Subsequently, as the avoidance response eliminates the S^D, fear is reduced and the response is instrumentally reinforced by such reduction. Mowrer's theory is an example of the *two-process theory* approach: Learned behavior is explained as arising from the joint engagement of Pavlovian and instrumental mechanisms. In this case, the Pavlovian process results in the acquisition of fear to the S^D, while the instrumental process results in the reinforcement of the avoidance response by fear reduction.

Several factors affect the course of acquisition in avoidance conditioning. An experiment described previously shows the reinforcing power of fear reduction (McAllister et al. 1974). In the first phase of that experiment, animals were enclosed in a box where they received tone-shock pairings. In a second phase, the animals were again exposed to the tone, but now there was a second compartment where they could escape (no shocks were administered during this second phase). Escape from the tone is rapidly acquired under certain conditions, suggesting that responses that remove the source of fear are instrumentally reinforced. Avoidance is also drastically impaired if the response does not terminate the S^D immediately, even if the shock is actually prevented (Kamin 1956). In fact, a typical delay of reinforcement gradient is obtained if the interval elapsing between the occurrence of the response and the offset of the S^D is lengthened (Kamin 1957).

Avoidance learning is also harmed by prior experience with inescapable shocks, a phenomenon called *learned helplessness* (Overmier & Seligman 1967). Three groups are included in a typical learned-helplessness experiment, which spans over two successive phases. All groups receive the same treatment in Phase 2: escape-avoidance training. However, the treatments differ during Phase 1. Two of the groups involve a master-yoked comparison, with the yoked group being the target procedure in this case. Master and yoked groups are matched in terms of the number and distribution of shocks, but they differ in terms of response contingencies. The master animals are usually trained in an escape-conditioning situation, whereas the regime for the yoked animals is purely Pavlovian. The response and the apparatus are usually different from those of Phase 2, which is why learned helplessness is characterized as a transituational phenomenon. The third group is exposed to the same situation and treated in the same way as the master and yoked groups, except that no shocks are ever delivered to these animals. Therefore, this no-shock control group provides information on the extent to which the conditions of Phase 2 support avoidance learning in untreated animals.

The typical outcome of this experiment is that the master and no-shock groups acquire the avoidance response at about the same speed, and both are significantly better than the yoked animals. Learned helplessness is therefore not the product of being exposed to painful stimuli per se, because the master animals show little or no deficit in acquisition when compared to the no-shock controls. It is rather the product of being exposed to inescapable painful stimuli. As the master-yoked design shows, what matters is the animal's ability to control the shocks, a feature referred to as *controllability*.

The first phase of a learned-helplessness experiment, also called the induction phase, has provided researchers with a rich spectrum of behavioral and physiological effects. Helplessness itself seems to involve deficits in a variety of functions (Maier & Jackson 1979). For example, experience with inescapable shocks may lead the animal to learn that there is no connection between its own behavior and the aversive stimulation. Such learning may subsequently discourage active coping with situations involving aversive stimuli; hence the label "helplessness" for this phenomenon. The induction phase may also reduce general activity levels, making it difficult for the animal to cope with novel situations. Although such a reduction in activity may contribute significantly in some situations, learned helplessness cannot be explained solely in these terms because it occurs in situations requiring response inhibition (e.g., passive avoidance training in Phase 2) and in situations in which the motor demands of alternative responses are equated (e.g., choice situations). The induction phase also seems to lead to attentional deficits that make it difficult for the animal to discriminate its own responses. Increasing response discriminability by marking the behavior with an exteroceptive stimulus sometimes totally eliminates learned helplessness. Alternatively, exposure to uncontrollable shocks does not necessarily imply that the animal cannot partially attenuate the impact of the shock by means of some postural adjustment. The helplessness deficit may arise as a result of the acquisition of a response during the induction phase that reduces the pain elicited by shock (and is thus instrumentally reinforced). Such a response could actively compete with the response required during the second phase. In one experiment (Balleine & Job 1991), rats that were explicitly shaped to remain inactive in order to escape from shock were more impaired than yoked controls (i.e., the opposite of a helplessness effect), provided they were required to remain inactive for a relatively long time.

As noted in the case of punishment (see ***section 3.b.*** above), such aversive stimuli as electric shocks mimic the experience an animal may face in natural situations involving predators and intraspecific aggressive encounters. In one experiment, yoked rats (Y) given training with inescapable shocks were later placed as intruders into a well-established colony of conspecifics (Williams & Lierle 1986). As shown in ***Figure 13.9,*** Y animals were defeated more frequently by resident males and received a greater number of bites in aggressive encounters than either master animals (M) that had experienced escapable shocks or nonshocked, restrained controls (R). Just as in the case of regular avoidance training, providing escapable-shock training before inescapable training reduced the frequency with which these intruder rats were defeated by the residents. Such a treatment is called immunization because it renders inescapable training less effective in generating helplessness. Moreover, repeated defeat by an aggressive resident male leads to deficits in escape learning. Williams and Lierle (1988) exposed groups of male rats to established colonies with either aggressive or nonaggressive males. In one

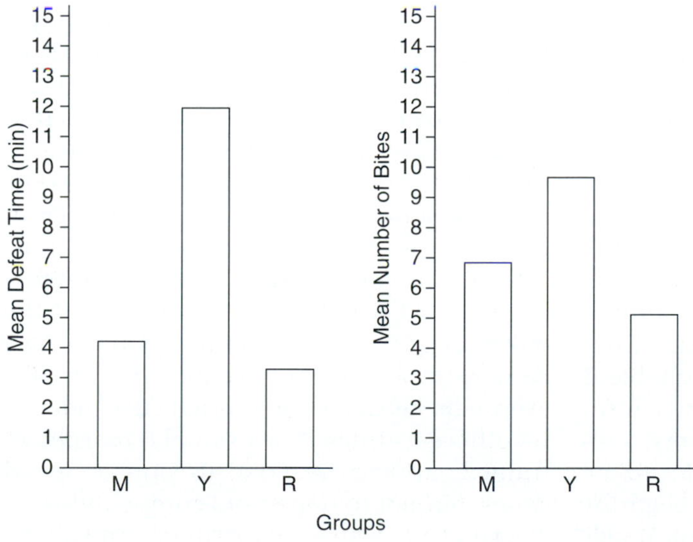

Figure 13.9. Effects of inescapable shocks on agonistic interactions in rats (Williams & Lierle 1986). Rats received preexposure training with either escapable (master rats, M) or inescapable (yoked rats, Y) shock according to a master-yoked design. An additional control group was restrained but not shocked (R). All these males were subsequently exposed to aggressive colonies as intruders. Exposure to inescapable shocks (Group Y) led to a greater level of submissive behaviors than either of the two control conditions.

case, intruders that were repeatedly defeated by aggressive residents (about 25 such encounters were administered) exhibited more defensive behavior and gained less body weight than intruders that did not experience defeat but had equal exposure to established colonies. In subsequent escape training, defeated animals exhibited performance deficits, relative to nondefeated rats, when required to jump twice over a barrier to escape from the footshocks. Defeat in aggressive encounters has, therefore, consequences similar to those of inescapable shock.

4. Generality of Associative Learning

4.a. Situational Generality. What is the usefulness of classifying a particular phenomenon as an instance of conditioning? Among other things, it implies that the phenomenon should have most, or even all, of the known properties of conditioning processes. In turn, this is a source of knowledge that may lead to new discoveries, theoretical integration, and applied interventions. Consider some of the conditioning preparations that have been described in the present and previous chapters (see ***Table 13.4***). These preparations vary in terms of the sensory modality of the stimulus conditions under which training occurs, the type of reinforcer, and the type of response. The question of interest is whether the same types of conditioning phenomena are observed in situations involving stimuli, reinforcers, and responses different from the typical ones, as described in the table. I will concentrate on examples drawn from classical conditioning experiments, although this central argument applies to associative learning in general. Let's begin by considering the stimulus conditions under which conditioning occurs.

The typical conditioning preparations studied under laboratory conditions use a wide variety of visual and auditory stimuli as CSs or S^Ds. These stimuli are easily manipulated and can be defined in precise terms. However, conditioning can be supported by less obvious stimulus conditions. Consider interoceptive stimuli, that is, a type of stimulus which originates internally, unlike exteroceptive visual and auditory cues. For example, rats can be trained to use cues arising from different levels of food deprivation as Pavlovian CSs for shock. In one experiment (Davidson et al. 1992), two groups of rats were placed in a box after either 0 or 24 hr of food deprivation. For one group, the 0-hr deprivation condition was paired with shock, and the 24-hr deprivation condition was paired with no shock (i.e., 0+/24–); for the other group the conditions were reversed (i.e., 24+/0–). After three trials of each type, the rats received a series of extinction sessions, and their freezing behavior was measured (e.g., the rat remains motionless, crouching on the floor). In the 0+/24– group, there was a greater level of freezing during extinction sessions in which the animals were nondeprived; in contrast, the freezing level was higher after one day of food deprivation in the 24+/0– group. Drugs can also be used to induce internal cues that serve as CSs or S^Ds in Pavlovian or instrumental training situations (Riley 1997). For instance, a rat given CS-US pairings after an injection of morphine, but CS-only trials after an injection of saline solution, rapidly develops a CR only when administered the morphine. Drug discrimination studies also demonstrate that rats have the ability to discriminate between the internal cues induced by different drugs. For example, morphine-trained rats may respond to similar opioid drugs, but not to nonopioid compounds.

I have described experiments involving reinforcers other than the more conven-

TABLE 13.4 Main Conditioning Preparations Described in the Present and Previous Chapters

Preparation	*CS*	*US*	*CR*	*Species*
(1) *Classical Conditioning*				
Salivary conditioning	Visual, auditory	Food	Drops of saliva	Dogs
Autoshaping	Visual	Food	Key pecking	Pigeons
Appetitive training	Visual, auditory	Food	Various response categories	Rats
Goal tracking	Visual, auditory	Food	Magazine entry	Rats
Eyelid conditioning	Visual, tactual, auditory	Air puff, shock	Anticipatory eyelid closure	Rabbits
Conditioned suppression	Visual, auditory	Shock	Suppression of lever pressing or drinking	Rats
Fear conditioning	Tone, context	Shock	Freezing, preference test	Rats
Flavor aversion	Flavor	Toxin	Flavor intake	Rats
Preparation	S^D	S^R	***R***	***Species***
(2) *Instrumental Conditioning*				
Runway	Spatial cues	Food	Latency	Rats
T-maze	Spatial, visual	Food	Percentage correct	Rats
Skinner box	Visual, auditory	Food	Lever pressing, key pecking	Rats, pigeons
Shuttlebox training	Visual, auditory	Shock	Latency to escape or avoid shock	Rats, goldfish

tional ones listed in ***Table 13.4***. Among these are various types of social interaction in fish, birds, and primates (see ***Chapter 5, section 1.b.,*** pp. 126–127), sources of heat for chicks (see ***Chapter 11, section 2.g.,*** pp. 430–432), and imprinting stimuli (see ***Chapter 12, section 1.c.,*** pp. 446–448). Of the many studies that have used relatively unusual reinforcer stimuli, perhaps the most detailed series of studies involves *sexual reinforcement* in Japanese quail (*Coturnix japonica*). Quail are polygynous birds that exhibit a high frequency of mating behavior. Pavlovian conditioning of sexual behavior in both male and female quail has been extensively documented (Domjan 1998). In a prototypical experiment, males are exposed to a trial in which a visual stimulus (the CS) is paired with the release of a receptive female followed by copulation (the US). Control groups may receive unpaired presentations of the CS and US. Conditioning is assessed in terms of goal-tracking behavior—that is, approach to the area immediately proximal to the site where the female will be released. Using such a procedure, sexual conditioning has been shown to display some of the properties that were described previously for more conventional preparations, including a CS-US interval gradient, second-order conditioning, and blocking. For example, the goal-tracking response reaches its maximum strength with CS-US intervals of 30 s and becomes progressively weaker with intervals of up to 1200 s (Akins et al. 1994). However, longer CS-US intervals support a more general search response. As in the case of more conventional preparations, it would be wrong to assume that the absence of one response implies the absence of sexual conditioning.

Experiments with taxidermic models suggest that males may be predisposed to develop copulatory responses by simple exposure. Such predisposition indicates that processes other than classical conditioning contribute to the organization of sexual behavior in quail. Particularly effective are models that include the head, neck, and approximate body shape of a female (see ***Figure 13.10 on back inside cover***), compared to similar models lacking the taxidermically prepared head and neck region. If such a model is paired with copulatory experience with a live female (i.e., used as a CS), the strength of copulatory responses directed at the model (i.e., the CR) increases even further. Such predisposition to develop sexual responses toward naturalistic models is also evidenced in the blocking paradigm (Köksal et al. 1994). As mentioned previously, blocking is observed in this sexual conditioning preparation, unless the added cue is the taxidermic model with head and neck. Male quail were given pairings between an audiovisual cue (the CS) and access to a receptive female (the US) during a first phase of training. In a second phase, the audiovisual CS was compounded with the taxidermic model and again paired with the US. Occasional trials with the model alone demonstrated about equal amounts of approach behavior as those observed in control groups given either unpaired CS and US presentations in phase 1 or no training at all during phase 1.

Associative processes are known since the time of Pavlov and Thorndike to affect glandular secretions (e.g., salivation) as well as skeletal responses (e.g., running in a maze). Conditioning procedures in fact affect a variety of responses, not all of them changing simultaneously and none being necessarily a better index of learning than the others. This point was perhaps first clearly demonstrated by Zener (1937), who replicated the procedure used by Pavlov with harnessed dogs, but allowed the dogs to freely move in the laboratory room. A wide set of CRs was apparent under Zener's free-moving conditions, including orienting responses toward the location of the CS (sign tracking) and toward the location where the food was going to be delivered (goal tracking). Experiments in which several responses are simultaneously recorded sometimes demonstrate a set of roughly synchronized behavioral changes, whereas, in other cases, changes in one CR may precede changes in a second CR by a substantial number of pairings. For example, eyelid conditioning in the rabbit may take dozens of trials before anticipatory eyelid responses develop; however, the same animals simultaneously show changes in heart rate after only a few pairings (Schneiderman 1972). Moreover, the effectiveness of conditioning can vary dramatically depending on the response system. Whereas eyelid CRs condition optimally with CS-US intervals ranging between 0.25 and 1 s, depending on the behavioral measure, heart rate CRs condition optimally with CS-US intervals of about 7 s (a similar effect was described above for sexual conditioning; Atkins et al 1994). Simultaneously changing behaviors may also obey different underlying processes, some being sensitive to omission contingencies (i.e., instrumental) and others not (i.e., Pavlovian), as is shown in ***Figure 13.1*** (p. 495).

Classical conditioning also contributes to an understanding of neural-immune interactions—that is, the influence of neural processes on the activity of the immune system. The immune system includes a set of organs and functions that evolved to provide protection against invading microorganisms. In one experiment, mice were administered flavor-aversion training in which access to a saccharine solution (the CS) was followed by an injection of the drug cyclophosphamide (the US). This drug has several effects, including a toxic effect that induces gastrointestinal discomfort, which the experimenters had in mind when they chose it to carry out flavor-aversion experiments. However, mice given the paired treatment died at an unexpectedly high rate. Further research showed that cyclophosphamide also had an unconditioned suppressive influence on immune function that was conditioned to saccharine as a CR (Ader & Cohen 1982). This effect can be observed by challenging a conditioned animal with an antigen and measuring the immune system's ability to generate antibodies. Under some conditions, however, Pavlovian pairings may result in an enhancement of immune function. For example, mice administered cyclophosphamide in the presence of a distinctive set of visual and auditory cues (as different from a taste stimulus) and later challenged with sheep red blood cells exhibited enhanced antibody production in the presence of the conditioned environmental cues, compared to unpaired, saline, and no-CS controls (Krank & MacQueen 1988). Since Pavlovian CSs may suppress or enhance immune function, this phenomenon is known as *conditioned immunomodulation.*

Classical conditioning may also modulate the development of allergies. A role of conditioning in allergy is suggested by a medical report of a patient who was allergic to roses and exhibited symptoms when exposed to an artificial rose. Experiments in both rats (MacQueen et al. 1989) and humans (Gauci et al. 1994) suggest that exteroceptive cues paired with substances that elicit allergic reactions can acquire the ability to induce similar cellular responses. Mast cells located in various regions of the body release specific enzymes (the UR) in response to allergens (the US). A CS paired with such allergens can acquire the ability to induce the release of the same enzymes (the CR), thus suggesting a neural control of mast cell function.

The repeated administration of many drugs of abuse, such as heroin, cocaine, and alcohol, results in the development of withdrawal symptoms after a period of abstinence. Withdrawal symptoms often involve aversive internal feelings that promote relapse. Many experiments with human and nonhuman animals document the presence of withdrawal symptoms and relapse in subjects exposed to cues previously paired with the consumption of such drugs. An additional consequence of periodic drug administration is the development of tolerance for the drug. Tolerance occurs when increasing doses are required to obtain the same result initially produced by a relatively small dose. Stimuli present before and during the administration of a drug can acquire control over many of these responses, causing withdrawal symptoms, cravings for the drug that may lead to relapse, and tolerance.

Figure 13.11 shows a Pavlovian analysis of the development of tolerance for the effects of administration of a drug such as morphine (Siegel 1999). Notice that tolerance is based on the development of a *compensatory response*; for example, the analgesic unconditioned effects of morphine are

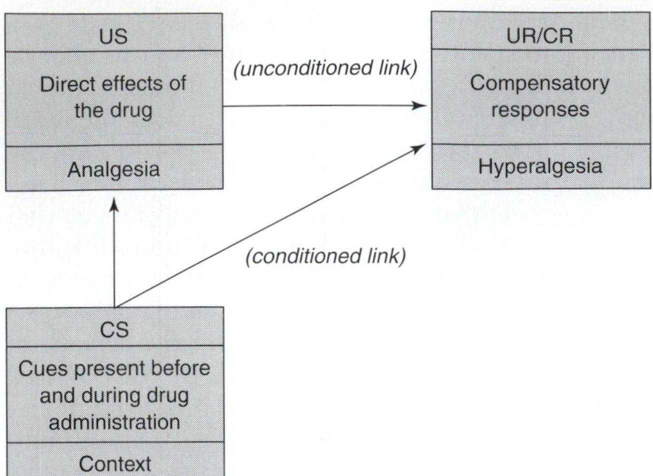

FIGURE 13.11. Pavlovian model of the development of tolerance to the analgesic effects of morphine based on Siegel (1999).

tolerated because of a superimposed hyperalgesic response that cancels out the analgesic US. This compensatory response is both a UR induced directly by the drug and a CR induced by preceding and concurrent signals of the US. Several tests have been devised to measure hyperalgesia. For example, a rat's paw may be placed on top of a heated plate, and the latency to withdraw and lick the paw may be recorded as a measure of pain perception. The shorter this paw-lick latency, the higher the hyperalgesia (i.e., the faster the pain is experienced by the rat). Using such a procedure, Siegel et al. (1978) demonstrated that morphine tolerance results in a conditioned hyperalgesic response. Rats given morphine injections in a novel context and exposed to the context alone during a series of test sessions exhibited shorter paw-lick latencies, and hence greater hyperalgesia, than did rats given unpaired context and morphine experience. In a dramatic demonstration of the role of compensatory responses (Siegel et al. 1982), rats were made tolerant to relatively large doses of heroin by pairing this drug with a conditioning context during many trials. In a subsequent test, animals that received the terminal heroin dose (to which they had become tolerant) in a novel context died in significantly greater numbers than did rats tested in the familiar environment. Lacking the "benefits" of a conditioned compensatory response triggered by the familiar context, the rats tested in the novel situation were susceptible to the lethal effects of heroin.

The examples reviewed in this section demonstrate the generality of classical conditioning across a wide range of stimulus conditions, reinforcers, and response systems. Similar generality has been found in studies of instrumental conditioning. Despite such degree of applicability, associative learning processes are not applicable to all possible situations. Some of the limits of conditioning techniques to modify behavior are reviewed in ***Chapter 14.*** Let's now turn to the issue of the species generality of conditioning processes.

4.b. Species Generality. The original experiments on conditioning involved domesticated species: Pavlov used dogs and Thorndike cats. These animals were rapidly replaced by rats, which together with pigeons, continue to be the most common experimental models. Other species have been used to a lesser degree, including monkeys, rabbits, mice, quail, and goldfish; and many other species have served as models occasionally in learning experiments. Many of the conditioning phenomena described in this chapter have routinely been found in experiments with lower vertebrates, including reptiles, amphibians, and fish (for a review, see Macphail 1982). Indeed, a set of basic Pavlovian and instrumental phenomena have been described in some detail in invertebrate species from several phyla. The emergent view is that the remarkable generality of associative learning processes may be the result of a limited set of cellular and molecular mechanisms that are perhaps common to a wide variety of species and highly conserved in evolutionary terms.

Conditioning has been studied in a variety of invertebrates, although rarely has behavioral analysis of learning capacities progressed beyond basic manipulations. In general, the main attractiveness of invertebrates is their relatively simple nervous systems that allow for the study of the cellular correlates of learning. In this section, however, I concentrate on behavioral evidence. Many modern animal phyla are represented in fossil faunas of the early Cambrian period, about 540 Mya, and some lineages may predate the Cambrian fauna by another hundred million years. Therefore, there has been a considerable amount of time for independent evolution of the animal phyla. Moreover, the common ancestor of living animals must have been a very simple organism indeed.

Sea anemones, coral, and jellyfish (Cnidaria) are generally considered to possess the simplest nervous systems of all animals, a diffuse nerve net without any clear distinction between central and peripheral systems. Nonetheless, cnidarian neurons exhibit many of the physiological properties that are familiar from research with other animals, including mammals, and show evidence of nonassociative learning (see ***Chapter 7, section 1.b.,*** pp. 225–229). However, there is no evidence of classical or instrumental learning in these animals. Much controversy was generated by research on classical conditioning in planaria (Platyhelminthes; Thompson & McConnell 1955), perhaps the simplest extant bilaterals. Although this issue is of considerable evolutionary importance given the taxonomic status of planaria, the question of whether these animals are capable of associative learning remains open. Reasonably good demonstrations of conditioning have been reported for species from a handful of phyla, including nematodes (Nematoda), segmented worms (Annelida), gastropods and cephalopods (Mollusca), and insects and crustaceans (Arthropoda). There is virtually no information from the majority of invertebrate phyla (see ***Table 7.1,*** p. 224, for a review of animal phyla).

The nematode *Caenorhabditis elegans* demonstrates both appetitive and aversive classical conditioning. In the appetitive task, a salt-based solution (the CS) was paired with access to food (a layer of *E. coli* bacteria, the US). In a subsequent test, nematodes showed a preference for a location marked with the CS solution (Wen et al. 1997). In the aversive task, diacetyl odor (the CS) was paired with exposure to an acetic acid solution (the US). While nematodes were initially attracted to the diacetyl odor (e.g., they tracked a small spot of this odor placed in front of them), pairing experience reduced this tracking response significantly below the level of unpaired controls exposed to both CS and US but separated by a 30-s long interval (Morrison et al. 1999). With a CNS containing just 302 neurons, *C. elegans* is a valuable model for cellular and genetic studies of learning, although it will probably offer only limited behavioral plasticity for analysis. In any event, these experiments suggest that classical conditioning can be supported by a relatively simple neural machinery.

Annelid worms have been the subject of some early experiments involving classical conditioning procedures; while the results were suggestive, many of the experiments included only single-stimulus controls (CS-only and US-only) instead of unpaired controls, making it difficult to interpret the behavioral changes as being truly associative. Subsequent research with earthworms (*Lumbricus terrestris*) shows that pseudoconditioning may play a large role in aversive training situations (Abramson & Buckbee 1995). Pseudoconditioning occurs when a neutral stimulus has the ability to induce the UR (thus giving the impression of conditioning) after US-only training. Another annelid species, the leech (*Hirudo medicinalis*), shows evidence of Pavlovian conditioning in a training situation involving tactile stimulation (the CS) paired with electric shock (the US) applied to the posterior end of the animal. After training, the CS potentiates the shortening reflex, a defensive response that can be easily measured (Sahley & Ready 1988).

The bulk of conditioning research with invertebrates involves species of molluscs and arthropods. Two groups of molluscs have been studied in some detail, the cephalopods (e.g., octopuses, cuttlefish) and the gastropods (e.g., snails). Cephalopods have traditionally been considered among the behaviorally and neurologically most complex of all invertebrates. Classical conditioning of approach and attack to a visual stimulus paired with food has been observed in octopuses (*Octopus cyanea*; Papini & Bitterman 1991) and cuttlefish (*Sepia officinalis;* Purdy et al. 1999). Indeed, octopuses are famous for their behavioral flexibility and problem-solving capacities. In one experiment (Fiorito et al. 1990), animals (*Octopus vulgaris*) given access to a closed transparent jar with a crab inside rapidly learned to unscrew the lid and seize the crab (***Figure 13.12***). There is a trade-off between behavioral and neural complexity: Species that show complex behavior also have complex CNSs that are generally hard to approach given current neuroscience techniques. For this reason, the emphasis has been on research based on species that are in the opposite end of this continuum—that is, relatively simple at the behavioral level but with neural properties that make the cellular analysis of learning viable.

Gastropod molluscs such as the sea hare *Aplysia californica,* the nudibranch mollusc *Hermissenda crassicornis,* and the terrestrial snail *Limax maximum* are among the most popular invertebrate species used in learning research. These animals are characterized by the presence of large neurons, some of which are easy to locate and can be individually labeled (see also ***Chapter 7, section 2.a.,*** pp. 231–233). Aversive classical conditioning has been demonstrated in these species in several training situations; a brief description of an experiment with each of them demonstrates the relatively broad spectrum of stimuli and response measures used in these experiments. For example, *Aplysia* exhibits the gill-withdrawal reflex when stimulated in the tail with a strong electric shock (the US). If weak tactile stimuli are applied to different regions, such as the siphon and the mantle, and these CSs are differentially paired with a tail shock in an A+/B– paradigm, animals quickly learn to retract the gill in A trials, but not on B trials (Carew et al. 1983). The identity of A and B is irrelevant (e.g., siphon

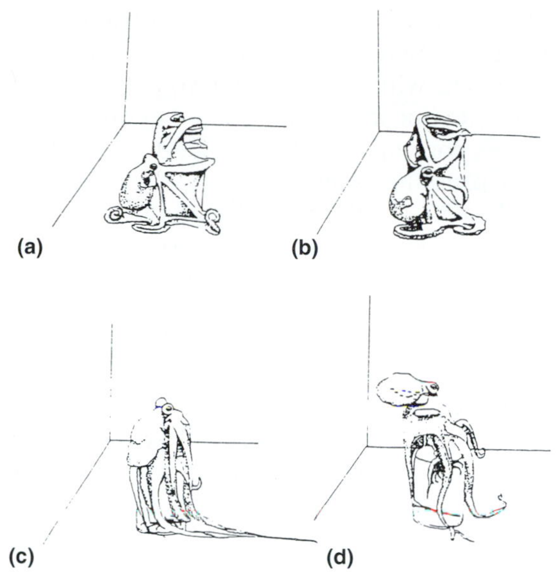

FIGURE 13.12. Problem-solving behavior in *Octopus vulgaris* (Fiorito et al. 1990). The octopus attacks a clear jar, explores it, opens the lid, and seizes the crab.

or mantle), which demonstrates that the behavioral change is specific to the pairing history of the CS.

In a series of experiments with the terrestrial snail *Limax,* Sahley et al. (1981) provided evidence for second-order conditioning, blocking, and the US-preexposure effect, all well-known learning phenomena from experiments with vertebrates. In the first phase of the second-order conditioning study, carrot odor (the first-order CS) was paired with quinidine sulfate (the US), a bitter substance with aversive properties. In the second phase, the carrot odor was paired with potato odor, and in the subsequent test, animals were given a preference test between the potato odor (the second-order CS) and a neutral odor (rat chow). Two standard controls received unpaired training either in phase 1 or in phase 2. Only the experimental animals exhibited an aversion to the second-order CS, the potato odor, during the test session, spending significantly less time in that side of the apparatus.

The nudibranch mollusc *Hermissenda* demonstrates Pavlovian conditioning in a training situation in which high-speed rotation is used as the US. Rotation stimulates the statocysts, the animal's vestibular organ, inhibiting locomotion and inducing a shortening of the foot (the URs). Pairing of a light (the CS) with rotation (the US) reduces the normal positive phototactic response of *Hermissenda* (the CR), whereas pairing of a food substance (the CS) with rotation (the US) inhibits feeding reflexes (the CR) normally elicited by contact of the food with the animal's mouth (Farley et al. 1997). In other instances of classical conditioning in invertebrates described above (e.g., *Hirudo, Aplysia*), the eventual CR is a behavior caused, in a weak form, by the CS before training; the pairing experience seems to merely enhance the CS's ability to elicit the response. This is referred to as alpha conditioning. In these experiments with *Hermissenda,* the effects of training are measured on a CR that is different from the UR elicited by rotation, thus discarding alpha conditioning as the process responsible for these behavioral changes.

Aplysia also demonstrates appetitive differential conditioning (Colwill et al. 1997). Tactile stimuli manually applied to the animal's mouth and differing in texture were used as CSs (i.e., one smooth and the other rough). Food (a small piece of seaweed) served as the US in an A+/B– design (of course, half of the animals received the counterbalanced B+/A– arrangement). Biting responses rapidly increased during A+ trials, whether the stimulus was the smooth or the rough surface, but decreased during B– trials. Interestingly, a reversal of the validity (e.g., A+/B– followed by A–/B+), led to a reversal in differential responding to the CSs. Pavlovian conditioning can also lead to the development of an attraction for an odor after pairings of the odor CS with food US. Experiments with the snail *Helix aspersa* indicate that contact with food elicits a response consisting of lowering the posterior tentacles toward the food source. This response can be conditioned to an initially neutral odor by simple pairing, occurs at a lower frequency in unpaired controls, and decreases during extinction (Ungless 1998). Moreover, the CR is unchanged by omission training, a finding suggesting that these tentacle responses are not influenced by instrumental contingencies.

Among the arthropods, the crustaceans (e.g., crabs) have received some attention as research models. The green crab *Carcinus maenas* shows both Pavlovian and instrumental conditioning (Abramson & Feinman, 1988, 1990). Pairings of a mild tactile stimulus applied to the carapace (the CS) with an air puff to the eye (the US) result in anticipatory eye-withdrawal responses. Such CRs occurred at a higher frequency in crabs exposed to CS-US pairings than in unpaired, backward, US alone, and CS alone controls. Crabs can also be trained to press a lever with a claw by using food reinforcement in a Skinner box situation resembling that used with rats. Master-yoked comparisons demonstrate that the response-reinforcer contingency is critical to maintain lever-pressing behavior.

Insects are the most frequently used invertebrate species in learning research. The use of several species of flies in genetic experiments was described in ***Chapter 3*** (see, for example, ***section 3.b.***, pp. 74–77, on learning mutants). Insects are equipped with relatively sophisticated sensory systems that make them amenable to deal with a wide range of stimuli. This allows for relatively complex demonstrations of learning that rival the designs used with vertebrates, as has been extensively demonstrated in experiments with honeybees (*Apis mellifera*) trained under both Pavlovian and instrumental contingencies (Bitterman 1988, 1996).

Of the several training procedures used with bees, the free-flying training situation has been the most versatile. The procedure was first introduced by the German ethologist Karl von Frisch [1886–1982], who used it to study sensory-perceptual processes in bees. In this situation, free-flying bees drink to repletion from a cup containing a highly concentrated sucrose solution and then depart to the hive. They digest a minimal part of this solution, regurgitate the rest in the colony, and are back at the location usually after about 5 min. One or more trials can be administered in each of these visits; a honeybee can fly many times between the lab and the hive in a single day, so that a substantial amount of practice can be provided. Visual (colors, shapes, spatial cues), olfactory, and magnetic stimuli have been successfully used in a wide variety of compound conditioning experiments to demonstrate such familiar phenomena as overshadowing, blocking, summation of excitation, and within-compound associations.

Consider, for example, the following demonstration of within-compound associations (Couvillon & Bitterman, 1982). The design involves compound stimuli including a color (either orange, O, or yellow, Y) and an odor (either jasmine, J, or lemon, L) administered adjacent to the location where the bee found the drop of sucrose solution. (Although stimulus validity was counterbalanced in this experiment, I will ignore this feature in the following description for simplicity.) In the first phase, bees found either OJ+ or YL+ targets in random sequence across several visits. This training is designed to establish associations between the color-odor elements of the compound (O-J and Y-L), as well as between each CS and the US. During the second phase, the colors were omitted and a discrimination was enforced with the odors: J+/L–. This discrimination was introduced to maintain the strength of one of the elements by pairing it with reinforcement while reducing the strength of the other by means of nonreinforcement. In a final, critical test, bees faced a choice between the two colors, O and Y. Despite the fact that these colors had been equally reinforced during the first phase, bees showed a greater responding to O than to Y. This preference indicates that nonreinforcement of L had reduced the value of its paired Y color via the Y-L within-compound association.

The free-flying technique has been used to study parameters of reward, including amount (the total volume of sucrose solution), magnitude (the concentration), and probability (partial reinforcement), as well as spatial learning involving the use of landmarks. Perhaps the most notable conclusion of this research is the striking similarity in conditioning phenomena between bees and vertebrates. ***Table 13.5*** shows a partial list of learning phenomena that have been demonstrated in bees and that are also familiar from experiments involving mammals and birds as subjects. In addition to the appetitive free-flying technique, this table lists phenomena observed with several other preparations, including appetitive and aversive procedures with harnessed bees, and several response measures, including dipping for food into a hole, shuttling, and proboscis-extension responses. The response measures include choice accuracy, latency, probability of response, and response frequency. Not all the learning phenomena listed in this table have been described in the present or previous chapters, so a brief characterization is provided. The main point of ***Table 13.5*** is that the learning phenomena observed in bees, pigeons, and rats bear a substantial degree of similarity despite the remote phylogenetic relationships between these species.

4.c. Some Implications. What are the main implications of the remarkable generality of conditioning phenomena across situations and species? From a comparative perspective, the situational and species generality of learning phenomena may imply a great deal of evolutionary conservation (i.e., homology) in basic associative processes. But this conclusion is not forced by the data reviewed in this section because, as was repeatedly shown throughout this book, character similarity may result from either *homology* (i.e., common ancestry) or *homoplasy* (i.e., independent evolution). When confronted with such a problem, evolutionary scientists determine how the character in question is organized, how it develops, and how it functions in the species being compared. For example, similarities in the "wings" of birds, bats, and the extinct pterosaurs can be considered homoplastic based on, among other things, the differences in the way in which the soft tissue is supported by the digits. In birds, the first

TABLE 13.5 Partial List of Learning Phenomena Known from Experiments with Honeybees and Vertebrates

Phenomenon	*Brief Characterization*
Blocking	Phase 1: A+ Phase 2: AB+ Test: B
Compound-component discrimination	AB+/A–/B–
Conditional discrimination	X: A+/B–, Y: A–/B+
Context conditioning	X: +, Y: –
Discrete-trial avoidance learning	A: R->no shock, no A
Escape learning	Shock -> R -> no shock
Free-operant avoidance learning	X: R -> shock postponed
Latent inhibition	Phase 1: A– Phase 2: A+
Omission training	X: R-> no reward, no R-> reward
Overlearning extinction effect	Faster extinction after additional acquisition training
Overshadowing	Less response to B after AB+ than B+ training.
Partial delay of reinforcement extinction effect	Random mixture of immediate and delayed reward leads to slower extinction than immediate reward always
Partial reinforcement extinction effect	Slower extinction after acquisition with partial reinforcement, rather than continuous reinforcement.
Potentiation	More response to B after AB+ than B+ training.
Probability matching	Choice of an alternative matches the probability of reinforcement for that alternative.
Progressive improvement in spatial reversals	Faster A+/B– discrimination after repeated validity reversals (e.g., A+/B–, B+/A–, A+/B–, etc.).
Second-order conditioning	Phase 1: A+ Phase 2: B–>A Test: B
Spontaneous recovery in extinction	Recovery of the CR after a period of rest.
Successive negative contrast	Rejection of a small reward after a large reward.
Summation of excitation	Greater response to AB after individual training with A+ and B+.
Transfer along a continuum	An easy discrimination with stimuli from the same sensory modality facilitates a subsequent difficult discrimination with stimuli from the same modality.
US-preexposure effect	Unsignaled USs retard subsequent A+ acquisition.
Within-compound associations	Associations between the elements of a compound stimulus.

Note. The control groups were omitted for brevity. A and B refer to discrete CSs, whereas X and Y refer to static contextual stimuli. Treatments separated by a slash were provided within the same visit. See Bitterman (1988, 1996) for extensive reviews on learning in honeybees.

digit is free, digits two and three are fused to support the wing, while digits four and five are missing; in bats, the first digit is also free, whereas fingers two through five are extended and provide major support for the wing; and in pterosaurs, digits one to three were free and the wing was supported primarily by a highly elongated fourth digit. Likewise, it seems plausible that the behavioral similarities that we call "conditioning" and that arise from a general sensitivity to temporal contiguity among events are only superficial, based on entirely different mechanisms that evolved in response to similar ecological pressures. As pointed out by Dickinson (1980), the generality of conditioning processes may be related to their function of detecting and acquiring information about cause-effect relationships between events. Such relationships are expected to occur under most, if not all, ecological conditions.

This simple analogy highlights the need to differentiate between learning phenomena and learning mechanisms. *Learning phenomena* include such empirical findings as acquisition, extinction, generalization, latent inhibition, second-order conditioning, and the fixed-interval scallop. These are the results of specific types of experience within particular situations. *Learning mechanisms* are processes hypothesized to be responsible for the learning phenomena, and they may be phrased in terms of psychological, neurobiological, neurochemical, or molecular intervening variables (see ***Figure 14.1,*** p. 542). It is these mechanisms that are subject to evolutionary forces. For example, acquisition during CS-US training may be said to occur because of the formation of a stimulus-stimulus association (a psychological mechanism), because of the convergence of sensory input from the CS and US pathways on a particular brain nucleus (a neurobiological mechanism), because of a particular synaptic process (a neurochemical mechanism), or because of the engagement of a cellular process that leads to synaptic plasticity (a molecular mechanism). Depending on the level of analysis, conditioning phenomena may seem similar or dissimilar.

Consider, for example, classical fear and appetitive conditioning in rats in which a light CS is paired, respectively, with electric shock and food. Such pairings are likely to lead to the establishment of stimulus-stimulus associations, which makes these two conditioning phenomena similar to each other. However, from the physiological point of view, brain function tends to be somewhat localized. As a result, the rat brain deals with information concerning shock and food in different areas, perhaps on the basis of different neurochemical systems, and stores the critical information in different sites. These features make the two conditioning phenomena different. Indeed, some species comparisons may even be meaningless given the lack of shared homologies in terms of brain areas. For example, the CNSs of vertebrates and arthropods evolved largely independently, and so they exhibit no homologies in terms of areas. Bees (protostomes) and rats (deuterostomes) share a common ancestor that lived in deep time, more than 540 Mya, and that probably resembled extant planaria in terms of neural organization and behavior. While the neurons may be considered homologous, the networks have certainly been assembled independently, making it likely that at least some of the similarities in learning phenomena arise from the operation of different mechanisms.

What about the molecular level of analysis? Given the strong functional and morphological correspondence between the neurons of cnidarians (the most primitive animals with nervous systems) and those of other animals, it may be argued that some fundamental features of the cellular machinery of neurons were established very early in animal phylogeny. Such molecular processes may thus have a great deal of generality both across situations and across species. One such process involves the role of so-called *second-messenger systems* in long-term behavioral changes of the type observed in conditioning experiments. In chemical synapses, the neurotransmitter molecule acts as a first messenger, inducing electrochemical potentials in the postsynaptic cell. In addition, repeated activation of a synaptic pathway engages second messengers, such as cyclic adenosine-monophosphate (cAMP), which have the ability to induce gene transcription. The products of such transcription are necessary for morphological changes in neurons that support the long-term synaptic plasticity required in conditioning (see ***Figure 3.7,*** p. 77).

cAMP plays a role in the acquisition of classically conditioned responses in species from three widely divergent phyla: the fruit fly *Drosophila* (Arthropoda), the sea hare *Aplysia* (Mollusca), and the rodents (Chordata). Kandel and Abel (1995) pointed out that cAMP is present in bacteria, and it may be among the most ancient second-messenger systems. Its cooption into playing a role in associative learning may have occurred early in animal phylogeny. Such a hypothesis would imply that the generality of learning processes across situations and species may be based, at least in some basic respects, on homologous cell-molecular processes. The acquisition of different tasks (e.g., fear and appetitive conditioning) involving different brain areas, pathways, and neurochemical systems, as well as the acquisition process in species with widely divergent nervous systems, may still be based on homologous molecular processes. Ultimately, research on the role of these molecular modules may provide a biological basis for the notion of general learning processes, derived entirely from the comparative analysis of learning phenomena.

5. Key Terms

acquisition 490
active avoidance 518
alpha responses 496
appetitive reinforcers 512
associative learning 490
aversive reinforcers 512
avoidance conditioning 514
backward conditioning 497
behavior system 518
between-group designs 506
blocking 502
classical (or Pavlovian) conditioning 490
compensatory response 525
compound conditioning 502
conditioned immunomodulation 525
contextual conditioning 501
contiguity 490
contingency-degradation effect 501
continuous reinforcement 515
controllability 520
counterbalance 496
CS-US interval 499
cue-validity effect 504
delay (or forward) conditioning 491
delay of reinforcement gradient 517
differential conditioning 496
discrete-trial training 515
disinhibition 505
escape conditioning 514

6. References

Abramson, C. I., & Buckbee, D. A. (1995). Pseudoconditioning in earthworms (*Lumbricus terrestris*): Support for nonassociative explanations of classical conditioning phenomena through an olfactory paradigm. *Journal of Comparative Psychology,* **109,** 390–397.

Abramson, C. I., & Feinman, R. D. (1988). Classical conditioning of the eye withdrawal reflex in the gree crab. *Journal of Neuroscience,* **8,** 2907–2912.

Abramson, C. I., & Feinman, D. A. (1990). Lever-press conditioning in the crab. *Physiology & Behavior,* **48,** 267–272.

Ader, R., & Cohen, N. (1982). Behaviorally conditioned immunosuppression and murine systemic lupus erythematosus. *Science,* **215,** 1534–1536.

Akins, C. K., Domjan, M., & Gutiérrez, G. (1994). Topography of sexually conditioned behavior in male Japanese quail (*Coturnix japonica*) depends on the CS-US interval. *Journal of Experimental Psychology: Animal Behavior Processes,* **20,** 199–209.

Antonitis, J. J. (1951). Response variability in the white rat during conditioning, extinction, and reconditioning. *Journal of Experimental Psychology,* **42,** 273–281.

Azrin, N. H., & Holz, W. C. (1966). Punishment. In W. K. Honig (Ed.), *Operant behavior: Areas of research and application* (pp. 380–447). New York: Appleton-Century-Crofts.

Balleine, B., & Job, R. F. S. (1991). Reconsideration of the role of competing responses in demonstrations of the interference effect (learned helplessness). *Journal of Experimental Psychology: Animal Behavior Processes,* **17,** 270–280.

Bitterman, M. E. (1988). Vertebrate-invertebrate comparisons. In H. J. Jerison & I. Jerison (Eds.), *Intelligence and evolutionary biology* (pp. 251–275). Berlin: Springer-Verlag.

Bitterman, M. E. (1996). Comparative analysis of learning in honeybees. *Animal Learning & Behavior,* **24,** 123–141.

Bouton, M. E. (1984). Differential control by context in the inflation and reinstatement paradigms. *Journal of Experimental Psychology: Animal Behavior Processes,* **10,** 56–74.

Bouton, M. E., & Bolles, R. C. (1979). Contextual control of the extinction of conditioned fear. *Learning & Motivation,* **10,** 445–466.

Carew, T. J., Hawkins, R. D., & Kandel, E. R. (1983). Differential classical conditioning of a defensive withdrawal reflex in *Aplysia californica. Science,* **219,** 397–400.

Church, R. M. (1969). Response suppression. In B. A. Campbell & R. M. Church (Eds.), *Punishment and aversive behavior* (pp. 111–156). New York: Appleton-Century-Crofts.

Colwill, R. M., Goodrum, K., & Martin, A. (1997). Pavlovian appetitive discriminative conditioning in *Aplysia californica. Animal Learning & Behavior,* **25,** 268–276.

Couvillon, P. A., & Bitterman, M. E. (1982). Compound conditioning in honeybees. *Journal of Comparative & Physiological Psychology,* **96,** 192–199.

Davidson, T. L., Flynn, F. W., & Jarrard, L. E. (1992). Potency of food deprivation intensity cues as discriminative stimuli. *Journal of Experimental Psychology: Animal Behavior Processes,* **18,** 174–181.

Delamater, A. R. (1997). Selective reinstatement of stimulus-outcome associations. *Animal Learning & Behavior,* **25,** 400-412.

Dickinson, A. (1980). *Contemporary animal learning theory.* Cambridge: Cambridge University Press.

Domjan, M. (1998). Going wild in the laboratory. Learning about species typical cues. *Psychology of Learning & Motivation,* **38,** 155–186.

Farley, J., Reasoner, H., & Janssen, M. (1997). Potentiation of phototactic suppression in *Hermissenda* by a chemosensory stimulus during compound conditioning. *Behavioral Neuroscience,* **111,** 320–341.

Ferster, C. B., & Skinner, B. F. (1957). *Schedules of reinforcement.* New York: Appleton-Century-Crofts.

Fiorito, G., von Planta, C., & Scotto, P. (1990). Problem-solving ability of *Octopus vulgaris* Lamarck (Mollusca, Cephalopoda). *Behavioral & Neural Biology,* **53,** 217–230.

Gauci, M., Husband, A. J., Saxarra, H., & King, M. G. (1994). Pavlovian conditioning of nasal tryptase release in human subjects with allergic rhinitis. *Physiology & Behavior,* **55,** 823–825.

Gibbon, J., & Balsam, P. D. (1981). Spreading association in time. In C. M. Locurto, H. S. Terrace, & J. Gibbon (Eds.), *Autoshaping and conditioning theory* (pp. 219–253). New York: Academic Press.

Gibbon, J., Baldock, M. D., Locurto, C. M., Gold, L., & Terrace, H. S. (1977). Trial and intertrial durations in autoshaping. *Journal of Experimental Psychology: Animal Behavior Processes,* **3,** 264–284.

Gormezano, I. (1966). Classical conditioning. In J. B. Sidowski (Ed.), *Experimental methods and instrumentation in psychology* (pp. 385–420). New York: McGraw-Hill.

Grice, G. R. (1948). The relation of secondary reinforcement to delayed reward in visual discrimination learning. *Journal of Experimental Psychology,* **38,** 1–16.

Holland, P. C. (1979). Differential effects of omission contingencies on various components of Pavlovian appetitive conditioned responding in rats. *Journal of Experimental Psychology: Animal Behavior Processes,* **5,** 178–193.

Holland, P. C. (1999). Overshadowing and blocking as acquisition deficits: No recovery after extinction of overshadowing or blocking cues. *Quarterly Journal of Experimental Psychology,* **52B,** 307–333.

Kamin, L. J. (1956). The effects of termination of the CS and avoidance of the US on avoidance learning. *Journal of Comparative & Physiological Psychology,* **49,** 420–424.

Kamin, L. J. (1957). The gradient of delay of sencondary reward in avoidance learning. *Journal of Comparative & Physiological Psychology,* **50,** 445–449.

Kandel, E., & Abel, T. (1995). Neuropeptides, adenylyl cyclase, and memory storage. *Science,* **268,** 825–826.

Kaufman, M. A., & Bolles, R. C. (1981). A nonassociative aspect of overshadowing. *Bulletin of the Psychonomic Society,* **18,** 318–320.

Köksal, F., Domjan, M., & Weisman, G. (1994). Blocking of the sexual conditioning of differentially effective conditioned stimulus objects. *Animal Learning & Behavior,* **22,** 103–111.

Krank, M. D., & MacQueen, G. M. (1988). Conditioned compensatory responses elicited by environmental signals for cyclophosphamide-induced suppression of antibody production in mice. *Psychobiology,* **16,** 229–235.

Lejeune, H., & Wearden, J. H. (1991). The comparative psychology of fixed-interval responding: Some quantitative analyses. *Learning & Motivation,* **22,** 84–111.

Lieberman, D. A., McIntosh, D. C., & Thomas, G. V. (1979). Learning when reward is delayed: A marking hypothesis. *Journal of Experimental Psychology: Animal Behavior Processes,* **5,** 224–242.

Lubow, R. E., Rifkin, B., & Alek, M. (1976). The context effect: The relationship between stimulus preexposure and environmental preexposure determines subsequent learning. *Journal of Experimental Psychology: Animal Behavior Processes,* **2,** 38–47.

MacQueen, G., Marshall, J., Perdue, M., Siegel, S., & Bienenstock, J. (1989). Pavlovian conditioning of rat mucosal mast cells to secrete rat mast cell protease II. *Science,* **243,** 83–85.

Macphail, E. M. (1982). *Brain and intelligence in vertebrates.* Oxford: Oxford University Press.

Maier, S. F., & Jackson, R. L. (1979). Learned helplessness: All of us were right (and wrong): Inescapable shock has multiple effects. *Psychology of Learning & Motivation,* **13,** 155–218.

Matzel, L. D., Held, F. P., & Miller, R. R. (1988). Information and expression of simultaneous and backward associations: Implications for contiguity theory. *Learning & Motivation,* **19,** 317–344.

McAllister, W. R., McAllister, D. E., Weldin, G. H., & Cohen, J. M. (1974). Intertrial interval effects in classically conditioning fear to a discrete conditioned stimulus and to situational cues. *Journal of Comparative & Physiological Psychology,* **87,** 582–590.

McCain, G., Dyleski, K., & McElvain, G. (1971). Reward magnitude and instrumental responses: Consistent reward. *Psychonomic Monograph Supplements,* **3,** No. 16 (Whole No. 48).

Miller, S., & Konorski, J. (1928). Sur une forme particuliere des reflexes conditionnels. *Compte Rendu Hebdomadaire des Seances et Memoires de la Societe de Biologie,* **99,** 1151–1157.

Morrison, G. E., Wen, J. Y. M., Runciman, S., & van der Kooy, D. (1999). Olfactory associative learning in *Caenorhabditis elegans* is impaired in *lrn-1* and *lrn-2* mutants. *Behavioral Neuroscience,* **113,** 358–367.

Mowrer, O. H. (1947). On the dual nature of learning—a reinterpretation of "conditioning" and "problem-solving." *Harvard Educational Review,* **17,** 102–148.

Mustaca, A. E., Gabelli, F., Papini, M. R., & Balsam, P. D. (1991). The effects of varying the interreinforcement interval on appetitive contextual conditioning. *Animal Learning & Behavior,* **19,** 125–138.

Olds, J., & Milner, P. (1954). Positive reinforcement produced by electrical stimulation of septal area and other regions of the rat brain. *Journal of Comparative & Physiological Psychology,* **47,** 419–427.

Overmier, J. B., & Papini, M. R. (1986). Factors modulating the effects of teleost telencephalon ablation on retention, relearning, and extinction of instrumental avoidance behavior. *Behavioral Neuroscience,* **100,** 190–199.

Overmier, J. B., & Seligman, M. E. P. (1967). Effects of inescapable shock upon subsequent escape and avoidance learning. *Journal of Comparative & Physiological Psychology,* **63,** 23–33.

Page, S., & Neuringer, A. (1985). Variability is an operant. *Journal of Experimental Psychology: Animal Behavior Processes,* **11,** 429–452.

Papini, M. R., & Bitterman, M. E. (1990). The role of contingency in classical conditioning. *Psychological Review,* **97,** 396–403.

Papini, M. R., & Bitterman, M. E. (1991). Appetitive conditioning in *Octopus cyanea. Journal of Comparative Psychology,* **105,** 107–114.

Papini, M. R., & Bitterman, M. E. (1993). The two-test strategy in the study of inhibitory conditioning. *Journal of Experimental Psychology: Animal Behavior Processes,* **19,** 342–352.

Pavlov, I. P. (1927). *Conditioned reflexes.* Oxford: Oxford University Press.

Pearce, J. M., & Kaye, H. (1985). Strength of the orienting response during inhibitory conditioning. *Journal of Experimental Psychology: Animal Behavior Processes,* **11,** 405–420.

Pryor, K. W., Haag, R., & O'Reilly, J. (1969). The creative porpoise: Training for novel behavior. *Journal of the Experimental Analysis of Behavior,* **12,** 653–661.

Purdy, J. E., Roberts, A. C., & Garcia, C. A. (1999). Sign tracking in cuttlefish (*Sepia officinalis*). *Journal of Comparative Psychology,* **113,** 443–449.

Rescorla, R. A. (1968). Probability of shock in the presence and absence of the CS in fear conditioning. *Journal of Comparative & Physiological Psychology,* **66,** 1–5.

Rescorla, R. A. (1980). *Pavlovian second-order conditioning: Studies in associative learning.* Hillsdale: Erlbaum.

Rescorla, R. A. (1988). Behavioral studies of Pavlovian conditioning. *Annual Review of Neuroscience,* **11,** 329–352.

Rescorla, R. A. (1997). Spontaneous recovery after Pavlovian conditioning with multiple outcomes. *Animal Learning & Behavior,* **25,** 99–107.

Rescorla, R. A., & Wagner, A. R. (1972). A theory of Pavlovian conditioning: Variations in the effectiveness of reinforcement and nonreinforcement. In A. H. Black & W. F. Prokasy (Eds.), *Classical conditioning II* (pp. 64–99). New York: Appleton-Century-Crofts.

Riley, A. L. (1997). Drug discrimination learning: Assessment of opioid receptor pharmacology. In M. E. Bouton & M. S. Fanselow (Eds.), *Learning, motivation, and cognition. The functional behaviorism of Robert C. Bolles* (pp. 225–254). Washington: American Psychological Association.

Sahley, C. L., & Ready, D. F. (198). Associative learning modifies two behaviors in the leech, *Hirudo medicinalis. Journal of Neuroscience,* **8,** 4612–4620.

Sahley, C. L., Rudy, J. W., & Gelperin, A. (1981). An analysis of associative learning in a terrestrial mollusc. I. Higher-order conditioning, blocking, and a transient US preexposure effect. *Journal of Comparative Physiology-A,* **144,** 1–8.

Schneiderman, N. (1972). Response system divergencies in aversive classical conditioning. In A. H. Black and W. F. Prokasy (Eds.), *Classical conditioning, II: Current research and theory* (pp. 341–376). New York: Appleton-Century-Crofts.

Sheffield, F. D. (1965). Relations between classical conditioning and instrumental learning. In W. F. Prokasy (Ed.), *Classical conditioning: A symposium* (pp. 302–322). New York: Appleton-Century-Crofts.

Sidman, M. (1953). Avoidance conditioning with brief shock and no exteroceptive warning signal. *Science,* **118,** 157–158.

Siegel, S. (1999). Drug anticipation and drug addiction. *Addiction,* **94,** 1113–1124.

Siegel, S., Hinson, R. E., & Krank, M. D. (1978). The role of predrug signals in morphine analgesic tolerance: Support for a Pavlovian conditioning model of tolerance. *Journal of Experimental Psychology: Animal Behavior Processes,* **4,** 188–196.

Siegel, S., Hinson, R. E., Krank, M. D., & McCully, J. (1982). Heroin "overdose" death: The contribution of drug-associated environmental cues. *Science,* **216,** 436–437.

Skinner, B. F. (1935). The generic nature of the concepts of stimulus and response. *Journal of General Psychology,* **12,** 40–65.

Skinner, B. F. (1938). *The behavior of organisms.* New York: Appleton-Century.

Skinner, B. F. (1948). "Superstition" in the pigeon. *Journal of Experimental Psychology,* **38,** 168–172.

Spence, K. W. (1945). An experimental test of continuity and non-continuity theories of discrimination learning. *Journal of Experimental Psychology,* **35,** 253–266.

Spence, K. W. (1956). *Behavior theory and conditioning.* New Haven: Yale University Press.

Staddon, J. E. R., & Simmelhag, V. L. (1971). The "superstition" experiment: A reexamination of its implications for the principles of adaptive behavior. *Psychological Review,* **78,** 3–43.

Stamps, J. (1998). Territoriality. In G. Greenberg & M. Haraway (Eds.), *Comparative psychology: A handbook* (pp. 761–770). New York: Garland.

Thompson, R., & McConnell, J. V. (1955). Classical conditioning in the planarian *Dugesia dorotocephala. Journal of Comparative and Physiological Psychology,* **48,** 65–68.

Thorndike, E. L. (1911). *Animal intelligence.* New York: MacMillan.

Timberlake, W., & Lucas, G. A. (1985). The basis of superstitious behavior: Chance contingency, stimulus substitution, or appetitive behavior? *Journal of the Experimental Analysis of Behavior,* **44,** 279–299.

Tolman, E. C., & Honzik, C. H. (1930). Introduction and removal of reward and maze performance in rats. *University of California Publications in Psychology,* **4,** 257–275.

Tomie, A. (1976). Retardation of autoshaping: Control by contextual stimuli. *Science,* **192,** 1244–1246.

Ungless, M. A. (1998). A Pavlovian analysis of food-attraction conditioning in the snail *Helix aspersa. Animal Learning & Behavior,* **26,** 15–19.

Wagner, A. R. (1969). Stimulus selection and the "modified continuity theory." *Psychology of Learning & Motivation,* **3,** 1–41.

Wasserman, E. A., Franklin, S. R., & Hearst, E. (1974). Pavlovian appetitive contingencies and approach versus withdrawal to conditioned stimuli in pigeons. *Journal of Comparative & Physiological Psychology,* **86,** 616–627.

Wen, J. Y. M., Kumar, N., Morrison, G., Rambaldini, G., Runciman, S., Rousseau, J., van der Kooy, D. (1997). Mutations that prevent learning in *C. elegans. Behavioral Neuroscience,* **111,** 354–368.

Williams, B. A. (1991). Marking and bridging versus conditioned reinforcement. *Animal Learning & Behavior,* **19,** 264–269.

Williams, J. L., & Lierle, D. M. (1986). Effects of stress controllability, immunization, and therapy on the subsequent defeat of colony intruders. *Animal Learning & Behavior,* **14,** 305–314

Williams, J. L., & Lierle, D. M. (1988). Effects of repeated defeat by a dominant conspecific on subsequent pain sensitivity, open-field activity, and escape learning. *Animal Learning & Behavior,* **16,** 477–485.

Zener, K. (1937). The significance of behavior accompanying conditioned salivary secretion for theories of the conditioned response. *American Journal of Psychology,* **50,** 384–403.

CHAPTER 14

Comparative Learning and Cognition

MAIN GENERALIZATIONS OF CHAPTER 14

- *Comparative research on learning and cognition aims at distinguishing the contribution to performance made by learning and cognitive processes from the contribution made by contextual factors (e.g., sensory-perceptual, motivational, and motor processes).*
- *Comparative studies suggest that learning mechanisms may be relatively conserved; ecologically appropriate behavior often seems to arise from the fine-tuning of contextual factors.*
- *Macroevolutionary transitions in learning processes have been suggested in several areas of research, including the attentional and emotional modulation of instrumental behavior in mammals and the evolution of rule learning in apes.*
- *Studies with a handful of animals (apes, marine mammals, and birds) suggest that they are capable of acquiring abstract concepts, some degree of numerical competence, and linguistic skills.*

It has always been obvious to the lay person that animals differ in terms of their behavioral abilities. While many would be willing to attribute humanlike capacities to chimpanzees, dogs, or dolphins, few would see any evidence of such resemblance when the comparison involves frogs, earthworms, or sea anemones. However obvious these differences may appear to the amateur observer, comparative psychologists have found it difficult to conclusively demonstrate the existence of dissimilar processes that generate species differences in learning and cognitive skills. In fact, as previous chapters demonstrate (especially ***Chapters 7*** and ***13***), there is conclusive evidence that at least some basic forms of both associative and nonassociative learning processes are similar across a wide range of species. Such similarity may even be based on homologous cellular mechanisms, a remarkable possibility given the remoteness of the common ancestor.

Chapter 14 further explores these issues—namely, whether there are species differences in learning and cognitive processes that may be attributed to evolutionary divergence in mechanisms and whether, when similarities are found, they are to be understood as evolutionary homologies or homoplasies. These are not easy questions to answer. The difficulties raised by the study of learning and cognitive processes from a comparative perspective have resulted in the development of many ingenious procedures and approaches that provide convergent evidence on specific research phenomena. Complex testing procedures and experimental designs are used to distinguish learning factors from a variety of other processes that can affect performance in any specific situation. Brain-behavior and ecology-behavior correlations have also been used as a source of information in the comparative analysis of learning and cognitive phenomena. I begin with a consideration of methodological problems.

1. Comparative Methodology

Divergence, homology, and homoplasy are the three major evolutionary outcomes. *Divergence* refers to the split of lineages with regard to a particular trait; evolutionary divergence produces phenotypic dissimilarity. One example is the evolution of the bipedal posture in hominids, relative to the ancestral quadrupedal posture. *Homology* refers to phenotypic similarity attributable to common ancestry, as in the pentadactyl hand of primates; whereas *homoplasy* refers to phenotypic similarity attributable to common adaptations, as in the convergent species of marsupials and placentals (see ***Figure 6.14,*** p. 207).

These concepts provide a general framework upon which to conceptualize comparative studies of learning. When different learning phenomena are found in different species, the question of interest is whether the underlying mechanisms of learning have diverged. The principal alternative hypothesis maintains that the behavioral differences are caused by divergence in nonlearning mechanisms that affect behavior, including sensory-perceptual, motivational, motor, and so forth. When similar learning phenomena are found in different species, the main issue is to determine whether the underlying mechanisms are the same (thus suggesting homology) or whether the behavioral changes are achieved via different mechanisms (thus suggesting homoplasy). Let's consider first the case in which different learning phenomena are discovered in different species.

Learning mechanisms must be inferred from behavioral observations, but many processes other than learning can influence behavior. An animal may stop eating a particular type of food because it has learned an aversion, or because it cannot detect the presence of food in the situation, or because it is satiated, or because it cannot perform the actions necessary to obtain the food. Sensory-perceptual, motivational, and motor processes, among other so-called *contextual variables,* can influence the animal's behavior independently of learning. Therefore, any species comparison in terms of learned performance must take into account the possibility that these nonlearning factors are responsible for the observed differences. This is another instance of the *learning-performance dichotomy* emphasized in ***Chapter 13*** and applied here to the case of a comparison across species.

A major obstacle for comparative research on learning originates in the impossibility to equate contextual factors across species—or *control by equation.* For example, if rats and turtles are reinforced with three pellets of food for running down a runway, and rats show better performance, is it because the rats' learning mechanisms are more efficient or because three pellets have a greater motivational impact for the rats than for the turtles? Perhaps turtles reinforced with six pellets would perform at the same level as rats. One corollary of the inviability of control by equation is that it would be virtually impossible to compare different species in absolute terms (i.e., the performance of species A versus that of species B).

An alternative method consists of comparing functional relationships between variables across species (Bitterman 1975). Instead of asking whether the rat learns the runway task faster than the turtle, one may ask whether the runway task depends on the same set of variables in rats and turtles. For example, although rats and turtles may perform at different speeds, acquisition may improve in both species as the size of the reinforcer is increased. This direct relationship between acquisition rate and reinforcer magnitude implies that, depending on the values used, acquisition may proceed faster in the rat or in the turtle. This method is referred to as *control by systematic variation.* Variables suggested by previous research or by theoretical considerations to be important determinants of learned behavior (e.g., reinforcer magnitude) can be systematically manipulated across species to determine whether the behavioral adjustments are similar or dissimilar.

The potential role of contextual variables to explain the presence of different learning phenomena in a comparison of two different species may be difficult to dismiss completely, independently of the number of variables systematically manipulated. Therefore, the conclusions in most of the topics reviewed in this chapter are expressed in tentative terms. A hypothesis of divergence in learning mechanisms may be strengthened by extending the analysis both across species and across related learning situations. If species differences in a particular learning phenomenon fit a meaningful phylogenetic pattern or co-vary with other phenomena thought to depend on the same underlying mechanisms, then it may be difficult to explain the behavioral differences in terms of contextual variables.

Further problems arise when one considers the case of similarity in learning phenomena across species. Similarities can be characterized at various levels of analysis, including psychological, neurobiological, neurochemical, and molecular. Homology requires that the learning phenomena observed in two different species be dependent on the same mechanisms, no matter what the level of analysis may be. Thus, a particular learning phenomenon that occurs under analogous conditions in two different species would be based on homologous mechanisms if it is sensitive to the same independent variables (e.g., manipulations of training parameters, neurobiological structures, neurochemical systems, cell-molecular processes, etc.). As a source of phenotypic similarity, homology would tend to be more likely when the comparison involves closely related species.

A learning phenomenon may be similar across two different species but be caused by the operation of different mechanisms that give rise to similar behavioral outcomes under analogous environmental conditions. Character similarity based on homoplasy would generally be more likely when the species being compared are distantly related. Notice, however, that mechanistic levels are hierarchically nested, as shown in ***Figure 14.1.*** Molecular (e.g., second-messenger systems), neurochemical (e.g., neurotransmitter systems), neurobiological (e.g., CNS sites of plasticity), and psychological (e.g., associative structures) levels of analysis can be distinguished. The implication is that a particular cell-molecular module may be activated by the opera-

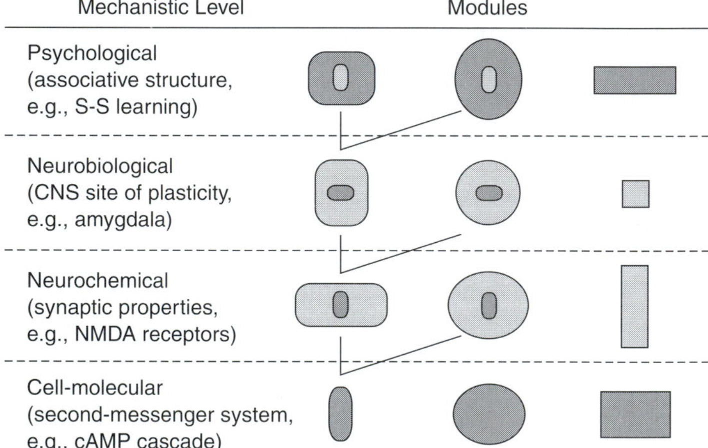

FIGURE 14.1. A representation of several levels of learning mechanisms. Each geometric shape represents a different module. A given module in one level may participate in one or more modules of the next level. For example, a second-messenger cascade system (e.g., cAMP) may be activated in cells that respond to different neurotransmitter systems (e.g., NMDA receptors). In turn, the same neurotransmitter and cell-molecular systems may contribute to learning in different brain sites (e.g., amygdala, hippocampus, cerebellum, etc.), supporting different psychological processes (e.g., S-S associations, attention, etc.). Similarity in learning phenomena across species may be considered homologous when the same modules control behavior, and homoplastic when modules differ at least at one level.

tion of different neurotransmitters in different neurobiological sites. Homoplasy would be implied when there is a difference at some level of the underlying mechanistic machinery that supports a similar phenomenon in different species. However, since brain mechanisms are generally conservative, it is possible for convergent phenomena to share some homologous modules, particularly at the cell-molecular level. So, for example, similar learning phenomena observed in two different species may be based on different neurotransmitter systems and yet share the same cell-molecular processes for synaptic plasticity.

The tools to apply the comparative method to the study of learning are the familiar procedures of systematic variation in training parameters, brain lesions, stimulation, and drug administration. Molecular biological procedures will be increasingly applied to determine the type of cellular processes that accompany conditioning in different species.

2. COMPARATIVE LEARNING

2.a. Food-Aversion Conditioning. Several experimental findings suggest the possibility that learning mechanisms are adaptively specialized for the resolution of species-specific ecological problems. This *ecological view* of learning has traditionally been portrayed as opposite to the *general-process view,* according to which the same learning processes operate throughout the animal kingdom. Key findings for the ecological view relate to interactions between CS and US in Pavlovian conditioning situations (this section) and to the generality of the law of effect (next section). The main alternative possibility is that these findings are explained in terms of species or situational differences in contextual variables (e.g., sensory-perceptual, motivational, or motor differences).

Rats exposed to a taste or an audiovisual CS followed by either a US that induces gastrointestinal distress (e.g., X-ray irradiation or the administration of a toxin such as lithium chloride, LiCl) or one that causes peripheral pain (e.g., electric shock) appear to display selective learning (Garcia & Koelling 1966). Rats reject the taste after taste-LiCl pairings, but show little concern for the audiovisual CS after audiovisual-LiCl pairings. In contrast, they respond to the audiovisual CS after audiovisual-shock pairings, but exhibit little rejection of the taste after taste-shock pairings. Additionally, the results showed that food-aversion learning can occur even after a single trial and with CS-US intervals as long as one hour. Experiments with pigeons demonstrate similar CS-US interactions. Pigeons exposed to pairings of an audiovisual compound CS with either food or shock later show more responding to the auditory element when shock was the US, but more responding to the visual element when food was the US (Shapiro et al. 1980). Results such as these suggest that each of the CSs and USs is capable of supporting conditioning, but some CS-US combinations work better than others. These stimulus-reinforcer interactions, referred to as *selective associations,* contradict the classic notion of *equipotentiality,* according to which any CS can be associated with any US as long as the parameters of training are appropriate. In addition, the acquisition of food-aversions with long temporal delays disagrees with the classic view of the importance of close temporal contiguity between CS and US.

Selective associations and long-delay learning have been interpreted as representing limits of applicability of general principles, reflecting the presence of adaptive specializations in learning. This view finds support in reports that demonstrate a degree of congruence between the natural behavior of a species and the outcome of learning experiments. For example, rats guide their feeding behavior predominantly on the basis of gustatory and olfactory cues and learn food-aversions relatively fast; in contrast, bobwhite quail (*Colinus virginianus*) find food largely on the basis of visual cues and easily learn to associate a visual CS (water made blue by the addition of vegetable food coloring) with drug-induced illness (Wilcoxon et al. 1971). One problem with a comparison involving such distantly related species as rats and bobwhite quail is that they differ not only in terms of their respective ecology, but also in phylogenetic terms. In order to determine whether ecological pressures lead to evolutionary divergence in learning mechanisms, the ideal approach is to compare closely related species that have adapted to radically different environments (Domjan & Galef 1983).

Selective associations and long-delay learning could be considered adaptive mechanisms for animals with a generalized diet that are likely to sample novel food items constantly. Such a generalist tendency would make it likely that an animal may encounter and ingest poisonous foods unless it can develop an aversion rapidly, selectively to the food's taste (thus avoiding the intake of a large amount of poison), and even when there is a considerable temporal delay between initial consumption and sickness. This hypothesis can be tested, for example, in rodent species that differ in their feeding preferences according to a specialist-generalist dimension. Some rodents exhibit generalized preferences, while others restrict their diet to a narrow variety of foods. A case in point is provided by species of kangaroo rats of the genus *Dipodomys* (e.g., *D. merriami*), most of which consume grains, seeds, and a variety of plant materials; in contrast, the diet of *D. microps* is almost exclusively restricted to the leaves of chenopod plants (e.g., shadscale). One study compared the development of food-aversions in these two species of kangaroo rats that differ in diet specialization but belong to the same genus, are sympatric (they are both found in the Owens Valley of California), are similar in body size and shape, and can be maintained in the laboratory under very similar conditions. To the extent that food-aversion conditioning reflects adaptation to a generalist diet, *D. merriami* (a generalist) should learn faster than *D. microps* (a specialist). Indeed, pairings of a novel food, sunflower seeds (the CS), with LiCl injections (the US) generated a stronger aversion in the generalist *D. merriami* than in the specialist *D. microps* (Daly et al. 1982).

As pointed out in the previous section, however, direct comparisons between species may incorrectly assume that contextual factors are equated. For example, in the experiment just described, species differed not only in the strength of their food-aversion learning but also in their initial reaction to the sunflower seeds. *D. microps,* which exhibited a weak aversion, also showed greater consumption of sunflower seeds during the first trial. It is plausible that the more generalist of these two species of kangaroo rats, *D. merriami,* shows better food-aversion because it is reluctant to consume novel food items, a phenomenon called *neophobia.* When *D. merriami* is exposed to a different novel food for which it is less neophobic (wheat grain), then there is no evidence of food-aversion and no difference from the specialist *D. microps.* Rapid food-aversion conditioning could thus result from an unconditioned neophobic reaction rather than from a specialized learning mechanism.

In the original demonstrations of selective associations in food-aversion conditioning, rats given access to a saccharin solution and shocked immediately afterwards exhibited little or no aversion to the solution. The implication that no learning had occurred with this particular combination of CS and US was challenged by a study in which the saccharine-shock delay was either 5, 30, or 210 s (Krane & Wagner 1975). While no aversion was detected at 5 s, a substantial aversion to the saccharin paired with shock developed when the CS-US interval was 30 s or even 210 s long. It appears thus that taste solutions require a considerable CS-US interval in order to be associated with postingestional consequences, independently of whether the US is sickness or peripheral pain. One reason why long delays may be efficient in this situation is that the stimulus trace of a tasty solution decays at a much slower rate than that of audiovisual stimuli. A *stimulus trace* is the internal representation of a stimulus that remains active after the stimulus no longer activates the peripheral receptor. Poor conditioning with short CS-US intervals in the case of a taste stimulus could be explained in terms of the forward association being offset by the development of a backward association between the US and the trace of the CS. This backward association could result in the acquisition of some inhibitory conditioning to the CS. The forward association would prevail when the CS-US interval is relatively long, thus resulting in the development of an aversion to the taste CS.

Similarly, although the initial results demonstrated a difficulty of the audiovisual stimulus to become associated with toxicosis, subsequent studies showed that such associations are indeed established. In one experiment, rats were placed in a novel environment characterized mainly in audiovisual terms and given LiCl injections during a first training phase; in a second phase, they were given saccharin-LiCl pairings in the same environment. These rats later exhibited evidence of blocking of the saccharin-LiCl association by the context-LiCl association established during the initial phase of training (Batson & Best 1979). In addition to this blocking effect, food-aversion conditioning exhibits many of the properties known from other conditioning situations, and it is thus widely considered to be based, at least in part, upon general learning processes (Domjan 1980; Logue 1979). One implication of this research is that natural selection can result in the fine-tuning of a particular behavioral process by adjusting contextual factors (e.g., neophobia, stimulus trace dynamics) without modifying the processes that result in the acquisition of information.

2.b. Misbehavior. Equipotentiality was traditionally assumed to apply also to the response-reinforcer contingency operating in instrumental conditioning situations. Accordingly, any response, no matter how arbitrary, was assumed to be influentiable by contingent instrumental reinforcement. Several sources of data suggest that some responses are more sensitive to instrumental reinforcement than others, some responses appear to actually deteriorate after extended reinforcement, and some responses appear to be just insensitive to reinforcement.

Breland and Breland (1961), who had developed a company that provided trained animals for use in commercial advertising, reported several cases in which positive reinforcement failed to increase the frequency of particular behaviors. In one situation, a pig was trained to take a token in its mouth, walk a short distance, and drop the token into a toy bank; the sequence of behaviors was shaped by means of regular food reinforcement procedures. Initially, the pig performed the behavioral sequence quite normally and gained food reinforcement immediately after releasing the token into the bank. However, as training progressed, the pig increasingly refused to release the token, holding it in its mouth and taking longer and longer to perform the entire sequence. As a consequence, the pig lost a large number of reinforcements for failing to emit the target instrumental response. The word *misbehavior* has been used to label responses that are relatively insensitive to instrumental reinforcement and thus violate Thorndike's law of effect.

Several learning phenomena involve similar apparent violations of the law of effect. For example, rats have difficulty in learning to press a lever to avoid shock, while the same response can be easily conditioned using positive reinforcement (Bolles 1970). Similarly, Shettleworth (1978) showed that punishment suppressed face washing but actually increased the occurrence of open rearing responses in golden hamsters (*Mesocricetus auratus*). Bolles (1970) argued that the presentation of any biologically powerful event, such as electric shocks or food, activates a set of preorganized behaviors that have evolved to deal with that particular event. These responses form what is known as a *behavior system.* A representation of the rat's defensive system is shown in ***Figure 14.2.***

When a rat deals with electric shocks, the fear response conditioned to cues of the environment in which training takes place induces the activation of a defensive behavior system. In this case, it is assumed that the electric shock is a substitute for a predator and the defensive behaviors are part of a *species-specific defense response* (*SSDR*) repertoire. If the instrumental avoidance response coincides with the SSDRs of the rat, then acquisition would proceed fast; however, when the instrumental response and the SSDRs are incompatible, then there would be considerable interference. For example, rats typically freeze in a fear-inducing situation (e.g., they crouch in a corner and remain motionless); freezing is a response that interferes with lever-pressing behavior, thus causing retardation of acquisition. In contrast, avoidance conditioning is very rapid when rats are required to freeze in order to prevent the delivery of shocks. Similarly, in the example of the pig described above, there were accidental pairings between the token (a CS) and food (a US) that may explain the reluctance of the pig to release the token. Animals often treat a CS for food as a surrogate for food.

Interestingly, whereas rats respond with passive freezing to a signal for shock, they typically engage in a variety of defensive and even aggressive responses immediately after receiving shock (e.g., defensive attack). One interpretation of this switch from freezing to defensive attack relies on the idea that the rat's behavior depends on the degree of predatory imminence (Blanchard 1997). Experiments with wild rats exposed to a cat show that freezing is dominant when the predator is more than 1 m away; in learning experiments, this may fit the situation in which the animal is exposed to a signal for shock rather than to the shock itself. Freezing is replaced by defensive attack when the distance between the rat and the predator is 0.5 m or less. The structure of the situation may also determine whether active or passive responses are observed. The presence of a predator in a situation in which there are escape routes almost invariably induces flight responses, whether the predator is close or far away.

Misbehavior then appears to arise as a result of conflicting requirements of the instrumental contingencies scheduled by the experimenter and the activation of a system of behaviors designed to deal with a partic-

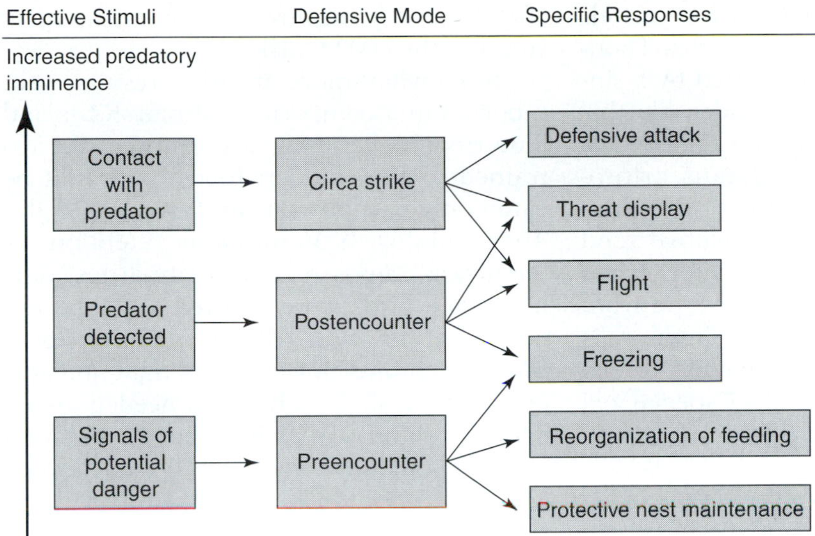

FIGURE 14.2. The rat's defensive behavior system. Three levels are represented in this figure: effective stimuli, defensive modes, and specific responses. (Based on Fanselow 1994.)

ular reinforcer. The components of such a system may fall under the control of Pavlovian signals that, therefore, acquire the ability to induce specific behaviors. Misbehavior arises in situations in which Pavlovian responses compete for expression with target instrumental responses. In contrast, rapid conditioning is obtained when the Pavlovian and instrumental responses are compatible. Therefore, misbehavior appears to depend on the manner in which responses induced by the conditions of training happen to interact (i.e., a contextual factor) rather than on adaptive learning processes.

2.c. Spatial Learning. While studies of food-aversion and misbehavior have been framed in terms of adaptive significance, research has rarely involved explicit species comparisons. As was noted previously, the central idea of the ecological view of learning is that selective pressures cause the divergent evolution of specialized learning mechanisms. In principle, specialized mechanisms are detectable by means of a systematic comparison of learning abilities in closely related species adapted to different ecological conditions. Such a comparative approach is being used to determine whether passerine birds that display food-hoarding behavior have evolved specialized mechanisms of spatial learning (see ***Chapter 4, section 3.g.,*** pp. 100–101, for a description of food-hoarding behavior).

Species within several avian orders, including raptors (hawks and owls), woodpeckers, and passerines have evolved various degrees of food-hoarding behavior. Experiments with passerine species, such as marsh tits (*Parus palustris*) and Clark's nutcrackers (*Nucifraga columbiana*), indicate that food-storing behavior is based on spatial learning abilities. In these food-storing birds, consumption is deferred for periods ranging between hours and months. Thousands of food items may be stored by a single bird, sometimes at a considerable distance from the place in which the food is found. These items (e.g., seeds, nuts, arthropods) are recovered by means of spatial information during periods of relative food scarcity, such as during the winter, when nutcrackers obtain most of their food from food caches. The question of interest is whether the food-storing behavior of tits and nutcrackers is the result of specialized learning mechanisms not present in closely related nonstoring species.

Some experiments comparing storing and nonstoring tit species in spatial learning tasks show similar sensitivity to variables that affect performance in memory situations. In one experiment, marsh tits (storer) and great tits (*P. major,* nonstorer) were trained in a so-called *delayed matching to sample* (*DMTS*) problem with stimuli varying in shape and color (Healy & Krebs 1992a). In this DMTS task, a sample stimulus was presented for a given time and then, after a delay interval, the animal was exposed to two test stimuli. One of these test stimuli matched the sample in location, appearance, or both. Choice of the test stimulus that matched the sample stimulus was reinforced with food. Correct choices reflect memory of the sample stimulus across the delay interval. A set of 100 stimuli was used in this experiment; only 20 of them were used per day, implying that any given stimulus was repeated every fifth session. The variable of interest was the length of the temporal delay between the presentation of the sample and that of the test stimuli: 30 s, 5 min, or 15 min. Accuracy was surprisingly stable and significantly above chance across temporal delays, but storer and nonstorer species were equally effective. Thus, there was no evidence that food-hoarding habits correlate with improved memory, as measured in the DMTS task.

Somewhat more positive results were reported in a comparison of marsh tits and blue tits (*P. caeruleus,* a nonstorer species) trained to find hidden food that could be eaten only partially (Healy & Krebs 1992b). After training, a 30-min-long retention interval was imposed before a final test during which birds were allowed a second opportunity to find the remaining food. Storers exhibited fewer errors than nonstorers in this task, but they still needed an average of about two visits to locate the food versus about three visits by the nonstorers. The difference does not appear very outstanding. Still other experiments point to perceptual differences in the relative salience of spatial cues (Brodbeck 1994). The storer black-capped chickadee (*P. atricapillus*) and nonstorer dark-eyed junco (*Junco hyemalis*) were trained to locate food on the basis of a spatial-color compound stimulus. In subsequent test trials, animals were exposed to stimuli made different either in terms of their spatial location or of their color. This dissociation of the elements of the compound stimulus revealed that storers responded first on the basis of spatial location rather than color, whereas nonstorers exhibited no bias toward spatial or color components.

Nutcrackers have also been tested in a variety of spatial and nonspatial tasks, and their behavior has been compared to that of other corvids, which are reportedly less dependent on cache food to survive during the winter but nonetheless store substantial amounts of food (Olson 1991). In one spatial task, called delayed nonmatching to sample, the correct test stimulus was the one that was different from the sample stimulus presented previously (i.e., the opposite to the DMTS task). In this task, nutcrackers performed more accurately than scrub jays (*Aphelocoma coerulescens*) and pigeons (*Columba livia*) at a range of temporal delays. However, scrub jays, which store substantial amounts of food, performed at about the same level as the nonstorer pigeons. Moreover, comparison of four different storer corvids showed significant differences in accuracy in several spatial tasks (e.g., Kamil et al. 1994). So in some spatial tasks at least, storer and nonstorer species may not differ, while different storer species may exhibit significant differences in performance.

An experiment comparing nutcrackers with pinyon jays (*Gymnorhinus cyanocephalus*), also a food-storing species, provides a clue about one potentially important contextual variable that might explain species differences in spatial tasks. Pinyon jays performed significantly better than nutcrackers in a seed storing and recovering task, and the difference in accuracy could be traced to the jays' tendency (not observed in nutcrackers) to store seeds in close proximity in the test arena (Balda & Kamil 1989). While the evidence in favor of divergent spatial learning mechanisms is intriguing, the possibility remains that at least in part, the evolutionary solution to the problem of food storage may have been achieved by modifications of sensory-perceptual biases or by the use of response strategies coupled with general-purpose learning mechanisms.

Perhaps the best evidence that spatial learning skills in food-storing passerines evolved by divergence is not behavioral but rather neurobiological. The *hippocampal formation* is known to be involved in spatial learning in a variety of vertebrates. For example, males of polygynous species of voles (genus *Microtus*) maintain large breeding territories and exhibit relatively large hippocampal size and greater spatial learning abilities than closely related monogamous species in which the male's territory is significantly smaller (Sherry et al. 1992). In teleost fish, lesions of a homologous region located in the lateral telencephalon selectively impair behavior in spatial learning tasks but not in visual discrimination tasks (Salas et al. 1996). Thus, the hippocampus is a prime candidate to subserve food-storing behavior in passerines, and, as already mentioned (see ***Chapter 4, section 3.g.,*** pp. 100–101), the hippocampal formation of food-storing species is relatively larger than that of nonstoring species. In a study involving species from 13 families of passeriform birds, three storing species (black-capped chickadee, *P. atricapillus*; blue jay, *Cyanocitta cristata*; red-breasted nuthatch, *Sitta canadensis*) exhibited a larger hippocampus relative to both body size and telencephalic size than nonstoring species from 10 different families (Sherry et al. 1989). Among species of the tit family (Paridae), species variation in the degree of food-storing behavior is positively correlated with hippocampal size but not with the size of the body or telencephalon (Healy & Krebs 1996).

2.d. Another Look at Comparative Methodology. Studies of food-aversions, misbehavior, and spatial learning abilities (described in the previous three sections), suggest that behavioral plasticity with obvious adaptive significance may be produced in a variety of ways. Natural selection may affect sensory-perceptual, motivational, and motor processes, in addition to learning mechanisms, to fine-tune behavior to the resolution of specific ecological problems. The fact that adaptive behavior seems to be often achieved by evolutionary changes in contextual (rather than learning) factors suggests that there might be relatively more rigid developmental constraints to modify learning mechanisms. One possible advantage of adjusting contextual factors may be that the needed genetic changes may have relatively restricted phenotypic effects. For example, a perceptual bias toward spatial cues affects only the visual system. In contrast, a genetic change that alters a mechanism of neural plasticity, particularly if it affects a cell-molecular module, can potentially influence several behavior systems and cause maladaptive effects.

The generality of some learning processes may require comparisons between distantly related species in order to discover instances of evolutionary divergence. The further back in time the common ancestor of two species, the more likely learning processes will be based on divergent mechanisms. Such comparisons rely on the hypothesis that the taxonomic status of a particular species determines the learning skills available to the animal. Animals within a particular taxon (e.g., an order, a class, a phylum) would then share a set of common processes (independently of their lifestyle), and they may lack certain other processes present in different taxa. Common learning mechanisms may transcend specific ecological conditions if they are adaptations for aspects of the environment common to many different niches, such as detecting cause-effect relationships (Dickinson 1980). Divergent learning mechanisms do not imply that the learning skills of one species are biologically better adapted than those of the other but simply that adaptive behavior may involve either different forms of plasticity or, in some species, no behavioral plasticity at all.

A biological analogy may be drawn in terms of thermoregulation. All vertebrates share a variety of thermoregulatory mechanisms (e.g., basking behavior—that is, exposure to sunlight in cold environments). In addition to these common processes, birds and mammals have evolved endothermy, a metabolic capacity to generate heat that keeps the internal milieu at a relatively constant temperature despite environmental fluctuations. Endothermy does not vary dramatically with changes in ecological conditions for different species of birds and mammals; instead, it is an adaptation common to all members of these taxa. Furthermore, it would be inaccurate to say that birds and mammals are better adapted than, say, reptiles because of their possession of endothermy; rather, the problem of thermoregulation is resolved in different ways by different species. The next three sections point to possible macroevolutionary transitions in learning processes.

2.e. Attention and Learning. Experience with compound stimuli may lead to changes in the manner in which specific elements of the compound control the animal's behavior. While all the components may be equally effective as signals for a biologically important event, behavior may fall under the exclusive control of a single element of the compound. Such selectivity of stimulus control suggests a process of *attention.* Conditioning treatments can either enhance or disrupt attention to a particular stimulus.

Attentional decrement may be one of the causes of the phenomenon known as *latent inhibition* (see ***Figure 11.6,*** p. 419, for a description of the basic design). Briefly, latent inhibition refers to a retardation of CS-US acquisition (phase 2) after the CS is repeatedly presented by itself (phase 1). Despite the simplicity of this procedure, the species generality of latent inhibition may be restricted. For example, there is evidence suggesting that this effect does not occur in teleost fish. In a series of experiments with goldfish (*Carassius auratus*), Shishimi (1985) found no clear evidence of latent inhibition after systematic variation of the type of stimulus (visual vs.

auditory), reinforcer (electric shock vs. food), number of preexposure trials (from 0 to 160 trials), and contingencies (classical vs. instrumental). In some experiments, preexposure to one stimulus (a flickering red light, R) did retard conditioning relative to a nonpreexposed groups, but not relative to a group preexposed to a different stimulus (a steady white light, W). In experiments with mammals, latent inhibition is notoriously specific, occurring only to the stimulus that has been preexposed during the initial phase of training.

In mammals, preexposure to a CS also retards conditioning when the CS is used as the negative stimulus in a conditioned inhibition paradigm (i.e., A+/AB–, with B representing the preexposed CS). This result is important because it suggests that the effect does not involve inhibitory conditioning (as the name latent "inhibition" would suggest), but rather involves an attentional deficit that affects the processing of the CS independently of its role in a conditioning situation (Rescorla 1971). In goldfish, however, nonreinforced preexposure does not affect the course of conditioned inhibition training. Goldfish acquired a W+/WR– discrimination equally well whether R (the flickering red light acting as the negative stimulus) was preexposed or not, as shown in ***Figure 14.3.*** In this experiment, animals received classical conditioning training in a shuttle-box situation in which visual stimuli (the white and red lights) were used as CSs and swimming over a barrier as the CR. Notice that the performance of preexposed goldfish was generally lower than that of nonpreexposed goldfish, although the discrimination was equally efficient. This group difference suggests that the effect of preexposure is to reduced the animal's general responsiveness to stimuli in the situation, rather than modify attention to a particular stimulus.

In some cases, nonreinforced preexposure to a CS can actually enhance subsequent CS-US conditioning—a sort of reversed latent-inhibition effect. In one experiment (Morin et al. 1990), Atlantic salmon (*Salmo salar*) were preexposed to an olfactory stimulus (L-cysteine diluted in water) during 20 trials, followed the next day by 20 pairings of the same olfactory stimulus (the CS) with electric shock (the US). Changes in heart rate during the CS were measured as the CR. Preexposure actually enhanced acquisition during CS-US pairing training. Such a reversed latent-inhibition effect was also reported in 10-day-old rats after relatively few preexposure trials (see ***Figure 11.6-b,*** p. 419, a result that offers an interesting parallel between comparative and developmental data.

Do teleost fish demonstrate other effects thought to depend on attentional processes? Suppose that a group of animals is trained in a visual discrimination involving compound stimuli. The elements of the compound are colors (red, R, and yellow, Y) and lines (horizontal, H, and vertical, V). The training is such that color is relevant and line irrelevant; there are four types of trials, as follows: RH+/RV+/YH–/YV– (the correct strategy is to respond to R, not to respond to Y, and to ignore H and V). The question of interest is how would these animals learn a subsequent discrimination in which either the previous relevant dimension continues to be relevant (*intradimensional transfer*), or the previously irrelevant dimension now becomes relevant (*extradimensional transfer*). The group is thus divided into two subgroups and given discrimination training involving new colors (green, G, and blue, B) and new lines (slash, S, and backslash, B). For the intradimensional condition, color continues to be relevant: GS+/GB+/BS–/BB– (respond to G). However, for the extradimensional condi-

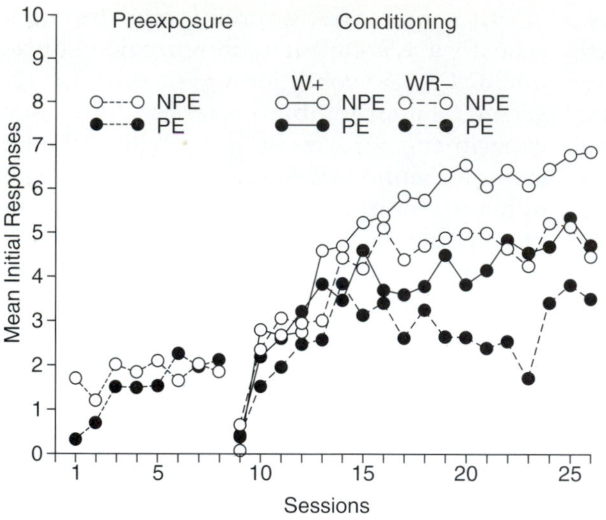

FIGURE 14.3. Discrimination learning after nonreinforced preexposure to the stimuli in goldfish (Shishimi 1985). Filled symbols represent the performance of subjects receiving nonreinforced preexposure (PE) to the stimuli, whereas open symbols represent the performance of nonpreexposed (NPE) controls. While PE goldfish generally responded below the level of NPE controls, discrimination developed at the same rate in both conditions, thus providing no evidence of latent inhibition.

tion, line orientation has now become relevant: GS+/BS+/GB–/BB– (respond to S). Experiments with monkeys and rats suggest that intradimensional transfer is easier than extradimensional transfer because the initial training results in attentional decrement to the irrelevant perceptual dimension of the visual compound (Sutherland & Mackintosh 1971). In the above example, a reduction of attention to line orientation during the initial phase causes a retardation of acquisition when the diagonal line orientations become relevant during the second phase of training. Interestingly, goldfish learn these complex transfer problems, but their performance is equally effective whether the transfer is intradimensional or extradimensional (Couvillon et al. 1976).

These results suggest the possibility that attentional modulation of associative learning involves mechanisms that are not available to teleost fish. It is possible that the behavioral differences observed across species in latent inhibition and dimensional transfer experiments tap into an evolutionary divergence of underlying learning processes. Perhaps these mechanisms evolved in the ancestors of extant mammals and are thus not available to other species. The alternative hypothesis would suggest that the behavioral differences reflect species differences in contextual factors rather than a divergence in learning mechanisms. For example, the absence of latent inhibition in experiments with fish may be attributable to the use of inappropriate conditions of preexposure training.

2.f. Emotion and Learning. Mammals exposed to signals for appetitive events (e.g., food, water) develop expectancies for those events. However, when the signals are present and the rewards fail to occur, or occur in a degraded fashion (degraded either in quality or quantity), mammals exhibit a variety of behavioral and physiological responses that can be collectively characterized as aversive and emotional. Such a shift in reward conditions, referred to as *surprising nonreward* (surprising because the signals predicted a more favorable event), has two basic properties: it elicits a state of *primary frustration,* which induces a variety of immediate consequences; and it supports the acquisition of *anticipatory frustration* (Amsel 1992).

Evidence that primary frustration has aversive properties is found in the fact that rats rapidly learn a new response that removes them from a situation in which they have experienced surprising nonreward. For example, rats trained to approach a goal box where they received a few pellets of food, subsequently learned to jump over one of the walls and into a different compartment when the food was either omitted or reduced in amount (Daly 1974). This type of escape learning indicates that the situation is aversive. The emotional consequences of surprising nonreward are illustrated by an experiment in which pigs first received training to press a panel with their snout to receive food and then were shifted to extinction (i.e., pressing led to nonreward). Extinction sessions were carried out with pairs of pigs that had received the same treatment. These animals exhibited increased plasma levels of corticosteroid hormones (which are good markers of stress) and displayed substantial amounts of aggressive behavior, including pushing, biting, and fighting (Dantzer et al. 1980). Extinction-induced aggression has also been observed in primates and rodents.

In addition, there is good evidence from a variety of training situations that rats and other mammals exposed to a surprising shift from a large (or more preferred) reward to a small (or less preferred) reward reject the downshifted reward significantly more than control animals exposed only to the lesser reward. This phenomenon, called *successive negative contrast* (*SNC*), has been described in human babies, monkeys, rats, mice, and opossums and in situations involving instrumental responses (e.g., running in a maze) and consummatory responses (e.g., consumption of a sweet solution). ***Figure 14.4-a*** shows a deterioration of instrumental performance in an experiment in which rats received training in a complex maze where they experienced a downshift in reward quality from bran mash to sunflower seeds (Elliott 1928). ***Figure 14.4-b*** shows a similar deterioration but in the consummatory behavior of two species of didelphid marsupials exposed to a quantity shift in the concentration of a sucrose solution from a 32% to a 4% solution (Papini et al. 1988). Further experiments with rodents demonstrate that SNC is correlated with high plasma levels of corticosteroid hormones (Flaherty et al. 1986) and can be reduced by treatment with anxiolytic drugs such as diazepam (Mustaca et al. 2000). SNC reflects, at least in part, the suppressive effects of anticipatory frustration on behavior. The conditions of training are exactly the same in both groups after the downward shift in reward (either both groups working for sunflower seeds or for the 4% sucrose solution); however, performance is disrupted when animals have experienced better reward conditions in the same environment.

SNC has failed to appear in experiments with a variety of nonmammalian vertebrates. ***Figure 14.5*** maps the distribution of SNC on a tree depicting the phylogenetic relationship of the species used in these experiments. These experiments involve analogous conditions of training, including the reinforcer (food or water), responses (runway running or swimming, key-pecking in pigeons, consummatory behavior), and the use of widely spaced conditions of training (e.g., one trial per day). Only mammals show the spaced-trial SNC effect, represented in this figure as an undershooting of performance during the postshift phase of training. In other vertebrates, behavior is sensitive to the difference in reward magni-

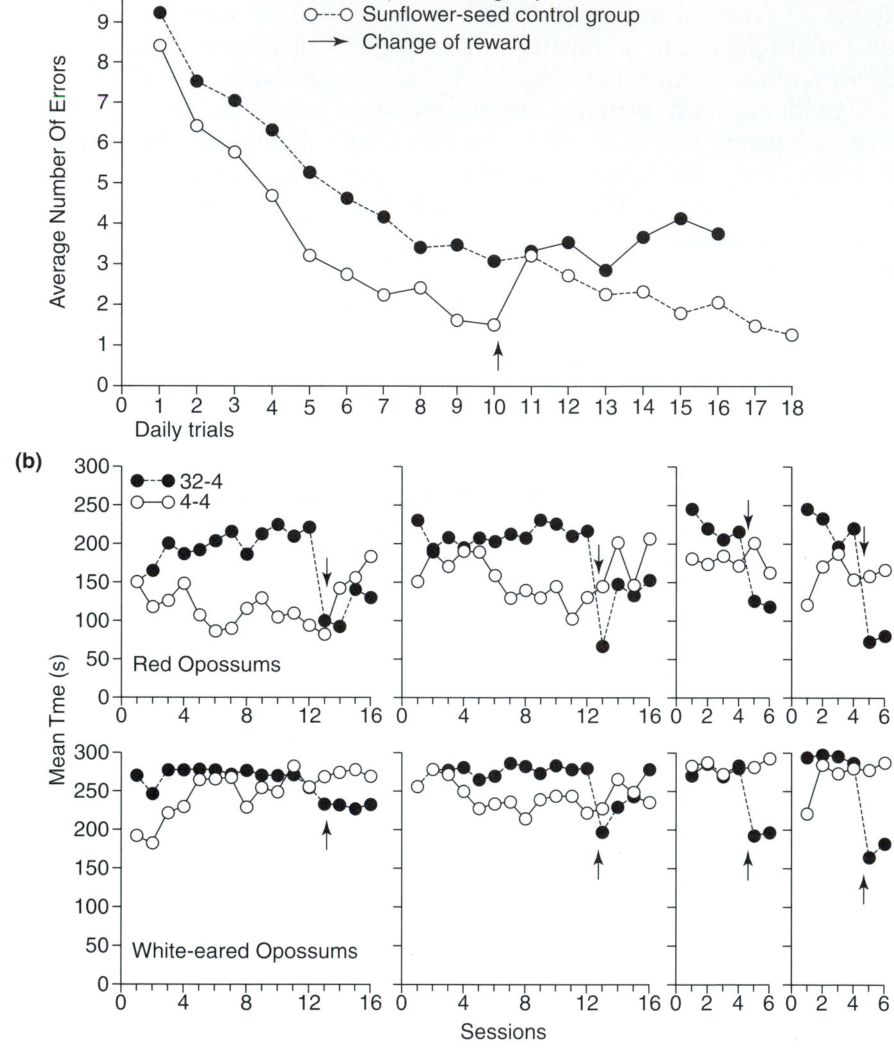

FIGURE 14.4. Successive negative contrast. ***(a)*** The original demonstration of this effect in rats trained in a complex maze for either bran mash (highly preferred) or sunflower seeds (less preferred) at a rate of one trial per day (Elliott 1928). A shift from the more to the less preferred reward (see arrow) results in a deterioration of performance above the number of errors exhibited by unshifted controls. ***(b)*** Repeated contrast in consummatory behavior in two species of marsupial mammals (Papini et al. 1988). Opossums received access to either 32% or 4% sucrose solutions during daily sessions. The arrows mark the sessions in which the 32% solution was shifted to 4%. Consummatory contrast is observed in terms of a reduced amount of time drinking in shifted groups relative to unshifted controls.

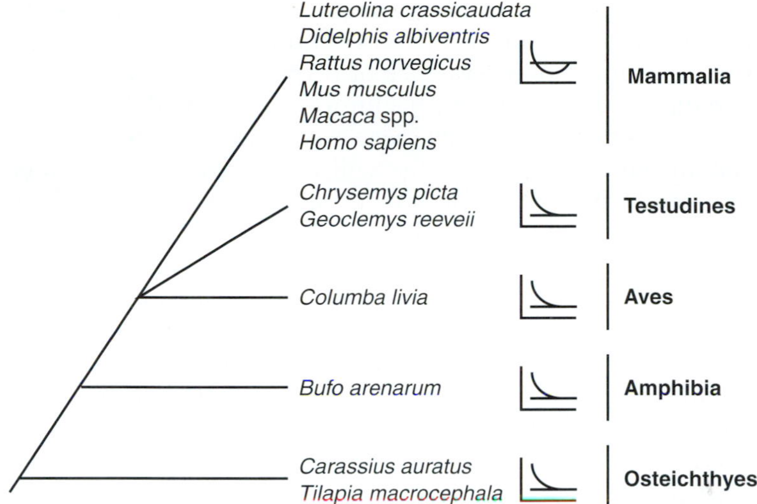

Figure 14.5. Phylogenetic tree showing the taxonomic relationships between species of several vertebrate classes that have been systematically studied in the successive negative contrast paradigm. This phenomenon occurs only in mammals. (See Papini 1997 for references.)

tude, thus discarding the possibility that the absence of SNC is due to the animal's inability to perceive the difference among rewards; however, the shift leads either to a gradual adjustment in the animal's behavior, without the undershooting characteristic of contrast, or to no change in behavior whatsoever.

As an example, consider an experiment involving goldfish (*Carassius auratus*) as subjects (Lowes & Bitterman 1967). Goldfish were trained to swim from a start-box to a goal-box of a straight alley for a food reward consisting of either 4 or 40 worms. Response latencies decreased faster for the group receiving the large reward, suggesting that the magnitude difference had an appreciable impact upon the instrumental behavior of these animals. Subsequently, a shift from 40 to 4 worms per trial resulted in virtually no change in performance. These results are typical of experiments involving lower vertebrates (e.g., turtles, toads, and teleost fish).

Do lower vertebrates also fail to exhibit other effects thought to depend on anticipatory frustration? At least two other learning phenomena have also failed to appear in spaced-trial experiments with lower vertebrates: the *partial reinforcement extinction effect* (*PREE*, greater persistence in extinction after training with partial, rather than continuous, reinforcement) and the *magnitude of reinforcement extinction effect* (*MREE*, greater persistence in extinction after training with small, rather than large, reinforcement). All these effects (i.e., PREE, MREE, and SNC) also fail to appear in infant rats (see ***Table 11.2***, p. 428), again demonstrating an interesting parallel between comparative and developmental studies of learning. In addition, adult rats can be induced to exhibit a performance analogous to that of nonmammalian vertebrates and infant rats by exposure to several treatments. For example, treatment with anxiolytic drugs and lesions of several structures within the limbic system eliminate the SNC and PREE (Feldon & Gray 1981; Franchina & Brown 1971).

These results suggest the possibility that the mechanisms underlying such effects as the SNC and PREE, responsible for the acquisition of information about the emotional reaction to surprising nonreward, have evolved in the mammalian lineage and are thus not present in nonmammalian vertebrates. Again, however, it is also possible that some as yet unidentified contextual factor could be responsible for the absence of these effects in lower vertebrates, infant rats, and adult rats treated with anxiolytic drugs.

2.g. Problem-Solving Behavior. The work of two prominent comparative psychologists, Edward L. Thorndike [1874–1949] and Wolfgang Köhler [1897–1967], gave rise to an influential controversy about the nature of learning. Thorndike's (1911) experiments on the acquisition of new skills by a variety of species led him to suggest that learning progressed gradually as a result of a trial-and-error process now called instrumental conditioning. For example, cats exposed to a puzzle box in which only the operation of a latching device allowed them to open the door and have access to food, showed a gradual decline in the time it took for them to open the door across practice trials. This view, known as the *continuity view* of learning, was contradicted by experiments that showed that animals may acquire a new skill suddenly and abruptly by a process called *insight*. Köhler (1925) reported a wide variety of experiments with chimpanzees in which, as in Thorndike's puzzle box situation, access to a piece of food required a relatively complex sequence of responses. In a famous experiment, a chimpanzee named Koko was shown an inaccessible piece of fruit hanging from the ceiling of his cage, together with a familiar small box. Koko's initial behavior involved all sorts of attempts to reach the fruit, except that he paid no attention to the box. After a few sessions of exposure to this situation, Koko exhibited a variety of behaviors toward the box: he threw it, sat on it, and violently attacked it. In a subsequent session, and after a few unsuccessful attempts at reaching the fruit, Koko turned toward the box, seized it, dragged it beneath the fruit, stepped on it, and took the fruit.

While the problem-solving abilities of Koko were impressive, equally impressive performance can be obtained provided the animal is given extensive training. Of course, Koko and the other chimpanzees used by Köhler in his experiments exhibited insightful behavior only after extensive practice with all the elements involved in the problem-solving situation.

Consider again the insight phenomenon, but this time with a pigeon as the subject. Epstein (1987) separately trained four different responses in a pigeon by reinforcing each with food according to regular procedures of instrumental shaping. First, the pigeon was trained to peck at a small cardboard box so that the box would move toward a green spot placed on the floor. Second, the pigeon learned to open the door of an enclosure. Third, the pigeon was taught to step on the cardboard box, which had been previously fixed in a particular location. Finally, a plastic banana was suspended out of reach, but any movement toward it was reinforced with food. Importantly, only the object appropriate to the performance of whichever response was being shaped was present during shaping session (i.e., movable box, enclosure, fixed box, or banana). In a subsequent test session, the movable box was placed inside the enclosure, and the banana was suspended out of the animal's reach and over the test apparatus. ***Figure 14.6*** describes the pigeon's behavior during the test session.

The pigeon's initial reaction was to stretch toward the banana. This was followed by approaching and pecking at the enclosure's door until it opened. About 100 s into the session, the pigeon started to push the cardboard box that had been placed inside the enclosure in the direction of the banana. When the box was about midway between its original position and the banana, the pigeon stepped on it and stretched toward the banana. Subsequently, the pigeon pushed again at the box, climbed on it, and pecked at the plastic banana. The entire sequence took 237 s to complete. Although the individual components of this response sequence were trained in isolation, the test situation seems to have induced their spontaneous interconnection. The entire process is reminiscent of Koko's insightful problem-solving behavior and suggests that such a behavioral capacity need not be considered restricted to primates.

A number of training paradigms have been developed that exploit the ability of

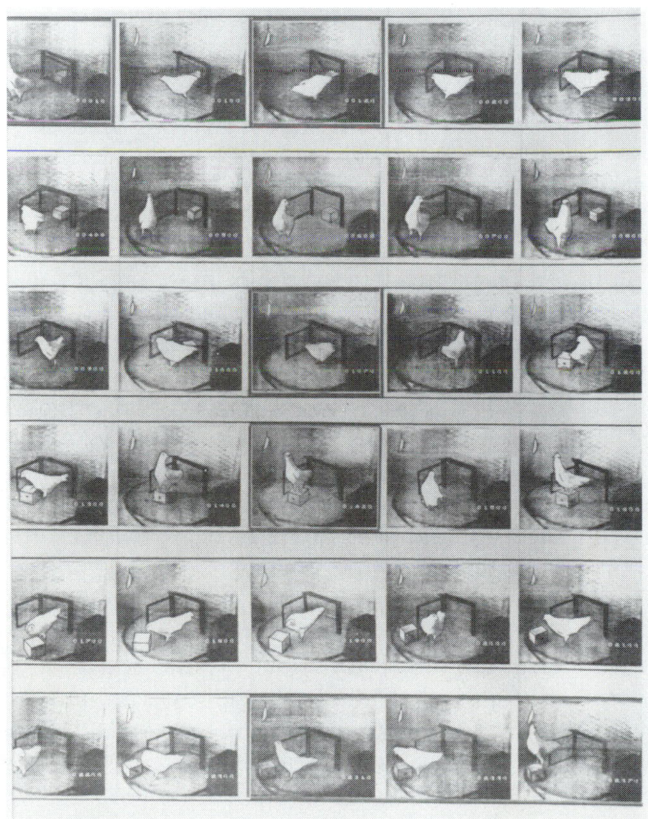

FIGURE 14.6. Spontaneous interconnection of previously trained responses (Epstein 1987). See text for details.

animals to transfer previously acquired information into new situations. These paradigms illustrate the effects of extensive problem-solving training on the adjustment to new situations in a more systematic fashion than that characterizing the experiments reviewed above. In the *learning set* paradigm, animals are trained in a sequence of simple discriminations, each one involving a pair of stimuli. In each case, choice of one of the two stimuli is reinforced with food, whereas choice of the other is not reinforced: A+/B–, followed by C+/D–, E+/F–, etc. While the resolution of the initial discriminations is achieved gradually by a process of trial and error, eventually the animal's behavior appears to be insightful. A sophisticated animal facing an X+/Y– discrimination after having successfully solved many similar problems may behave as if it were following a *win-stay, lose-shift rule:* (1) choose any of the two stimuli randomly in the first trial and verify the corresponding outcome (either food or no food, depending on whether the choice was correct or incorrect), and (2) stay with the stimulus if the choice was correct, but shift to the other stimulus if the choice was incorrect (Harlow 1949).

Comparative learning set studies demonstrate that contextual variables are important determinants of performance in this paradigm. Sensory-perceptual factors are particularly important determinants of the performance level attained by a particular species. For example, rats trained to discriminate between two-dimensional visual stimuli perform rather poorly, even after hundreds of problems. However, the learning set performance of rats exposed to discrimination problems involving tridimensional visual stimuli, spatial locations, or olfactory stimuli is comparable to that obtained in studies involving primates (see ***Chapter 8**, **section 4.e.,*** pp. 309–314). It appears, then, that there is nothing like an absolute performance level for a given species in the learning set paradigm.

Rumbaugh (1997) suggested that the contribution of contextual variables could be minimized by comparing species in terms of their ability to transfer from an original problem to a new problem. *Transfer* occurs in any situation in which the performance in one problem is affected by prior experience. Prior experience can either facilitate subsequent learning (i.e., positive transfer) or interfere with it (i.e., negative transfer). In primates, for example, reversal learning tends to lead to negative transfer in prosimians and New world monkeys, but to positive transfer in Old World monkeys and apes, even when the original discrimination is equally difficult and acquired to what is an operationally identical criterion (see ***Figure 8.19,*** p. 313). Rumbaugh (1997) extended these studies of reversal learning by comparing the strict reversal condition with two additional conditions in which a novel stimulus substitutes one of the two stimuli used in the original discrimination. Each animal, from a variety of primate species, received training in the original A+/B– discrimination, followed by training in three different reversal problems. One set of trials involved the strict reversal of the original problem (i.e., A–/B+); a second set of trials involved a pair in which a new stimulus replaced the previously positive stimulus (i.e., C–/B+); and a third set of trials involved replacement of the previously negative stimulus by a new stimulus (i.e., A–/D+). The key outcome was that the strict reversal of the original discrimination (A–/B+) was more difficult than any of the discriminations involving a new stimulus (C–/B+ or A–/D+) in prosimians (lemur) and monkeys (squirrel monkeys, talapoins, rhesus monkeys), but the discriminations were more similar in difficulty for apes (gorillas and chimpanzees).

One interpretation of these results is that negative transfer reflects the learning of response tendencies developed gradually, strengthened by reinforcement (to the A+ stimulus), and weakened by nonreinforcement (to the B– stimulus). The strict reversal condition requires the gradual reversal of these response tendencies and therefore leads to a relatively greater contribution of negative transfer to reversal performance. According to this interpretation, this would be the manner in which prosimians and monkeys learn discriminations. In contrast, discrimination learning in apes would seem to be based on the acquisition of a rule. Rule learning in a situation like this one would result in equal levels of difficulty for these three reversal discriminations (A–/B+, C–/B+, and A–/D+) because they involve the same win-stay, lose-shift rule acquired in the original problem. Furthermore, the fact that these animals reach the acquisition criterion for the original discrimination (9 correct out of 10 successive trials) at about the same rate suggests that there are probably no major differences in terms of contextual variables.

Whereas these experiments on discrimination learning seem to imply a qualitative difference in learning processes among species (e.g., apes vs. monkeys and prosimians), the assessment is not as simple as it would appear in a first analysis. Acquired associative structures can be quite complex and can give rise to phenomena that would be hard to anticipate, as is shown in the next section.

3. Comparative Cognition

3.a. Associative Versus Cognitive Views. Associative views of learning have their roots in philosophical traditions. During the initial decades of experimental research on learning, associative processes provided a parsimonious view and even suggested plausible neural processes as candidates for physiological mechanisms. Thorndike (1911) suggested that learning involves the establishment of associations between the stimulus (S) conditions and the successful responses (R) that occurred under those conditions. These so-called *S-R associations* were conceived not merely as psychological entities but as based on "connections between neurons and neurons, whereby the disturbance or neural current arising in the former is conducted to the latter across their synapses" (Thorndike 1911, p. 247).

Alternatives to this S-R standpoint were rapidly developed by those who viewed the S-R associative process as too primitive, simple, and mechanical to account for the full repertoire of behaviors that could be observed in animals attempting to solve problems. One such example is Köhler's insight learning discussed in the previous section. Another example is provided by the influential view of learning developed by the American comparative psychologist Edward C. Tolman [1886–1959]. Out of Tolman's laboratory came a variety of experiments cleverly designed to expose the so-called cognitive abilities of rats. Tolman's (1932) central argument replaced the learning of S-R connections by the acquisition of cognitive expectations that came to be framed in terms of associations between stimuli, or *S-S associations.* According to this view, the delivery of a reinforcer in a particular situation results in the establishment of an expectation of that reinforcer. Behavior is then guided by acquired expectations.

A key piece of evidence was provided by the contrast experiment described previously (see ***Figure 14.4-a***) and carried out in Tolman's laboratory by his student Elliott (1928). This experiment demonstrated that reinforcers not only strengthen an instrumental response, as required by a simple S-R account, but that animals also encode the reinforcer as part of the associative structure acquired during training. The disruption of instrumental behavior after a shift in reward parameters (e.g., quality, magnitude) strongly suggests the presence of S-S associations that allow the rat to anticipate the type of reinforcer to be encountered in the goal box. Another of Tolman's students, Tinklepaugh (1928), reported a similar outcome using monkeys and qualitative shifts in reward from a more preferred type—a piece of banana—to a less preferred, but still acceptable, reward—a piece of lettuce. As shown in ***Figure 9.2*** (p. 328), monkeys accepted both bananas and lettuce when they expected to find these rewards. However, if it expected a banana, the monkey found the lettuce unacceptable; it displayed searching behavior and became aggressive toward the experimenter. Interestingly, single-cell recordings from the prefrontal cortex of monkeys that are working on this problem demonstrate the presence of neurons that fire predominantly when the animal is expecting a specific reward (Watanabe 1996). Therefore, there appears to be a cellular correlate of Tolman's concept of expectancy.

During the decades spanning the 1920s and the 1950s, a strong debate between the S-R and S-S proponents led to an impressive series of theoretical and empirical developments. In addition to Tolman, a major figure in this debate was Clark L. Hull [1884–1952], whose theoretical efforts were directed at offering explanations based on S-R principles for many of the new discoveries stimulated by Tolman's cognitive view. Hull (1931) also suggested that expectancies could be thought of as *anticipatory goal responses*—that is, miniature versions of the response directed at the reinforcer (e.g., salivating and swallowing while we go over the items on the menu in a restaurant, in anticipation of the meal). In some cases, these internal responses were defined as pure-stimulus acts—that is, ideas that can guide behavior and provide for what we call "purpose, desire, or wish" (Hull 1931, p. 505).

During the peak of this debate, the S-R and S-S associative structures were conceptualized as mutually exclusive. It was hoped that experiments would provide unambiguous support for one of these views, and it was also hoped that learning would be based on just one type of principle. Subsequent research showed that the manner in which animals represent their experience, even in terms of associative structures, can be far more complex than any of these views anticipated. Three examples will suffice to demonstrate this point. First, consider the possibility that a food-aversion can be established without ever directly pairing the CS and US, as shown in an experiment described in ***Table 14.1*** (Holland 1981). The key group in this experiment, Group TT, received pairings of a tone (the CS) with food (the US) during phase 1 until the tone became a reliable signal of food. In a second phase of training, the tone was now paired with an aversive US, an injection of LiCl. Holland reasoned that since the tone would activate an internal representation of the food by virtue of its prior training, LiCl would in fact be paired with the tone and also with this internal representation of the food. As a result, the food itself should become aversive. To test this hypothesis, rats received access to food after tone-LiCl pairings, and, as expected, they showed a significant aversion relative to three control groups as described in the table. Apparently, then, associations can be established even when one of the components is present during the trial only as an expectancy.

Table 14.1 Representation-Mediated Food Aversions

Group	*Phase 1*	*Phase 2*	*Test Results*
TT	T-food, L-nothing	T-LiCl, L-nothing	71*
TL	T-food, L-nothing	T-nothing, L-LiCl	94
LT	T-nothing, L-food	T-LiCl, L-nothing	91
BT	food-T, L-nothing	T-LiCl, L-nothing	86

Note. T, tone. L, light. LiCl, lithium chloride, a toxin that causes gastrointestinal distress. Notice that all animals received the same exposure to T and L (the CSs), and to food and LiCl (the USs), but they differ in the pairings of these stimuli. The number of food pellets consumed by the rats is shown in the Test Results column. The asterisk denotes that this number was significantly lower than the amount consumed by the rats in the three control groups. (From Holland 1981, Experiment 1.)

A second experiment suggested by the notion that expectancies guide behavior just as much as external stimuli relates to the resolution of conditional discrimination problems. In a *conditional discrimination,* two response alternatives are present in every trial; one of them is correct in the presence of one stimulus, but the other is correct in the presence of a different stimulus. Trapold (1970) asked whether conditional discriminations would be facilitated when each of the correct choices was rewarded by a different outcome. Three groups of rats received training in which two different auditory stimuli (a tone and a click), two different responses (right and left retractable levers), and two different rewards (dry food pellets and sucrose solution) were combined in different ways. In the critical group, described in ***Figure 14.7-a,*** each stimulus was associated to one response and reinforced with a different outcome. It was expected that S-S pairings between each stimulus and its unique outcome (tone-pellet, click-sucrose) would also establish a unique outcome expectancy. These differential expectancies would contribute to make the conditional discrimination easier than that of control groups in which the outcome was always either pellet or sucrose. In these control groups, the common expectancy induced by both the tone and the click would make it more difficult for the animal to retrieve the appropriate information regarding the correct response for each trial. The results, shown in ***Figure 14.7-b,*** confirmed the prediction. This so-called *differential-outcome effect* has been observed in a variety of appetitive and aversive experiments, with rats, pigeons, and children. Like the previous example, this effect illustrates the stimulus properties of expectancies.

A final example demonstrates a similar effect while using a different technique, one based on the ability of stimuli to transfer control over a response with which they have never been paired in the past, by virtue of a common expectancy. ***Table 14.2*** shows the design of a study with rats reported by Kruse et al. (1983). During the first phase of training, rats received training in a conditional discrimination in which a tone (T) signaled that choice of the right lever (R) would be reinforced with pellets, whereas a click (C) signaled that choice of the left lever (L) would be reinforced with a sucrose solution. In each trial, the presentation of a discriminative stimulus (either T or C) was followed a few seconds later by the insertion of both levers (R and L) in the box until the rat chose one of them. These two

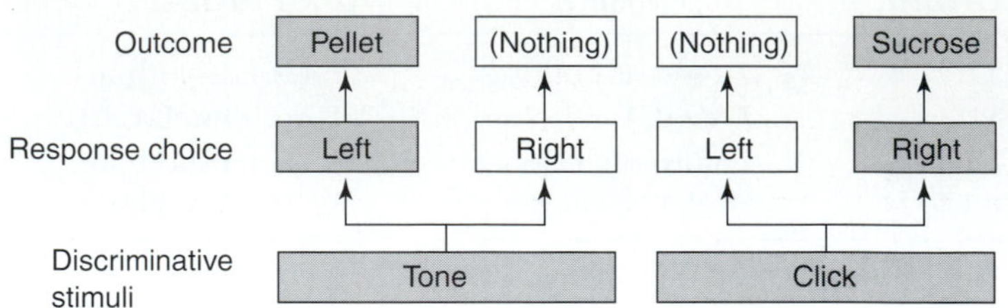

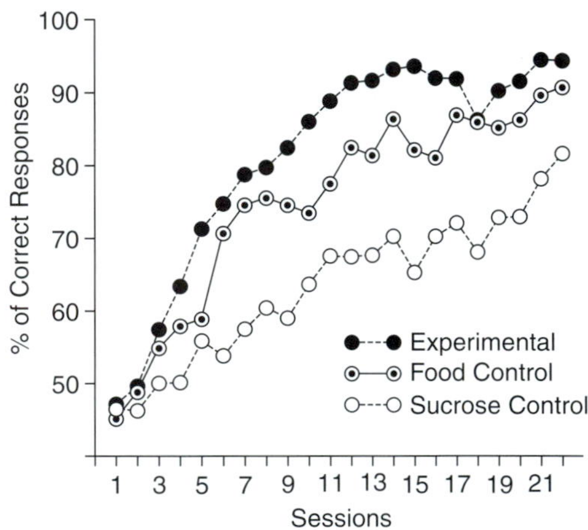

FIGURE 14.7. The differential-outcome effect in rats (Trapold 1970). ***(a)*** The procedure used with the experimental group. It is a conditional discrimination with two conditional stimuli (tone, click), two responses (right lever, left lever), and two reinforcers (dry pellet, sucrose solution). Each correct response leads to a different outcome. ***(b)*** Acquisition rate is facilitated by this differential-outcome procedure. Control groups always receive the same outcome for both correct responses, either the dry pellets or the sucrose solution.

groups differed only in terms of the Pavlovian US with which a white noise (N) was paired during the second phase. The response levers were not available during this second phase and no specific response was required to obtain the reward. In a final transfer-of-control test, the Pavlovian CS was presented while the two levers were available and under extinction to avoid any further conditioning. In 74% of the test trials rats chose the lever that had been paired with the same reinforcer during the first

TABLE 14.2 Transfer-of-Control Experiment

Group	*Phase 1: Instrumental*	*Phase 2: Pavlovian*	*Test (in extinction): Transfer of Control*
Pellet	T-R-pellet / C-L-sucrose	N-pellet	N: R̲ vs. L
Sucrose	T-R-pellet / C-L-sucrose	N-sucrose	N: R vs. L̲

Note. T, tone. C, click. R, right lever. L, left lever. N, absence of white noise. The slash implies that the trials were presented within the same session. During the test phase, several trials were presented while the rats had access to both levers and under extinction conditions to avoid any further learning. The key result is that the Pavlovian CS, N, invigorates the response with which it shares the reinforcer (i.e., R̲ in Group Pellet and L̲ in Group Sucrose). (Kruse et al. 1983.)

phase (i.e., R in Group Pellet, but L in Group Sucrose). Therefore, choice performance is mediated by expectancies, whether these are activated by the discriminative stimuli established during original training or by Pavlovian CSs established independently.

These examples demonstrate the need to incorporate Tolman's notion of expectancy into the associative process. But does this imply that S-R associations are irrelevant to an understanding of learned behavior? Several lines of evidence suggest that S-R associations also contribute to behavioral change. For example, appetitive experiments in which the reinforcer used during an initial phase of training is subsequently devalued (e.g., by pairing it with LiCl until the animal rejects it) assess the extent to which reinforcer-specific expectancies contribute to performance. Typically, such experiments show a significant loss of power by a stimulus previously paired with the (now devalued) reinforcer, either in a Pavlovian or an instrumental task. However, the response level is often well above zero and in some cases totally unaltered, indicating a residual ability of the stimulus to evoke the response even when the appetitive reinforcer associated with a Pavlovian CS or an instrumental response has become aversive (Colwill & Rescorla 1986). A possible interpretation suggests that the underlying associative structure involves S-R associations that are impervious to the reward-devaluation procedure since they do not encode information about the reward itself.

The techniques illustrated by these examples have been extremely useful in detecting a variety of associations that are established during both Pavlovian and instrumental training situations (Colwill & Rescorla 1986; Trapold & Overmier 1972). Other well-established learning phenomena should be added to this list of examples, including latent learning (see ***Figure 4.3,*** p. 94) and sensory preconditioning (see ***Figure 13.2,*** p. 498). The main conclusion to be drawn from these examples is that caution must be exercised to avoid oversimplification of the associative view of learning in any discussion involving higher cognitive processes. *Cognition* means literally "knowing," and it has traditionally embraced such processes as perceiving, learning, memorizing, thinking, and judging. A traditional assumption behind the study of cognitive processes is that they are not reducible to associative processes, even of the type suggested by Tolman. As will become apparent in the following sections, associative processes are treated as contextual factors in experiments designed to demonstrate higher-level cognitive phenomena, including concept formation, numerical competence, and language.

3.b. Concept Learning. In most of the experiments exploring the ability of animals to learn discriminations described so far, the number of stimuli included was relatively small. For example, in a simple A+/B– discrimination, the animal needs to deal with only two stimuli to solve the problem. What would happen if A and B referred to sets of stimuli, rather than individual stimuli? Could animals learn to correctly categorize relatively large sets of stimuli? Obviously, such a categorization underlies the use of concepts in humans. When we correctly label a new stimulus as an instance of some category (i.e., this is a picture of a Greek temple), we are using a concept (i.e., we have the concept of "Greek temple"). A *concept* is a category of related exemplars, such as a set of objects that share some feature, either perceptual (e.g., "flowers" or "songs"), functional (e.g., "vehicles" or "furniture"), or abstract (e.g., "sameness" or "greater-than").

Herrnstein and Loveland (1964) first reported an ingenious attempt at teaching the concept of "human" to pigeons. Since then, most experiments studying the acquisition of visual concepts have been carried out with pigeons, taking advantage of their superb vision. Pigeons were exposed to two large sets of slides, one of them containing persons and the other not. The slides were selected such that the sharing of sensory features would be minimized. For example, in some of the slides, a person was clearly visible, whereas in others people would be in the background or periphery of the picture; some were color pictures, some were black and white; and pictures included children or adults, men or women, fully clothed or naked persons, a single person or a group. As many variations as possible were included in the set of pictures. Pecking at a slide containing a person was reinforced with food, whereas pecking at a slide without a person was nonreinforced. Pigeons rapidly learned to categorize these two sets, pecking at a high rate when the slide being presented included humans. To discard the possibility that pigeons were learning the contingencies of reinforcement for each individual slide, a new set of slides was introduced during a transfer test. Pigeons readily transferred their correct categorization to the new stimuli.

This ability of pigeons to categorize large sets of slides was extended to a variety of objects, some of which could be considered a priori as natural categories for pigeons to learn (e.g., "trees"), while others are clearly arbitrary for a pigeon (e.g., "fish"). Categorization abilities appear to be applicable to a variety of stimulus sets, independently of the extent to which one would expect pigeons to be prepared to process the stimuli based on their natural history. While the ability of pigeons to categorize is not doubted, whether such behavior is based on the development of a concept is a matter of debate. For example, despite the efforts of the experimenter, the pictures within a set could share one or a few perceptual features on the basis of which the pigeons would be able both to discriminate during training and to generalize to new instances during transfer testing. In fact, these two processes (i.e., discrimination across categories and generalization within a given category) are essential components of concepts as they are used in the context of human language. We discriminate between "chairs" and "tables," but would include a wide variety of objects in each of these categories, even if some of them share very few stimulus features with the majority of objects included in the category (e.g., most tables have legs, but a trunk can sometimes be classified as a table).

The concept of generalization is commonly used in reference to the transfer of control from the training stimulus to other stimuli based on the degree of physical similarity. For example, an animal reinforced for responding in the presence of a green light would respond with diminishing strength to wavelengths progressively more dissimilar to green in either direction of the spectrum. This generates a bell-shaped response distribution with a peak at the green wavelength (i.e., a *generalization gradient*). Some experiments involving visual stimuli demonstrate that categorization, and transfer to new stimuli may be based on a generalization process of this type. For example, monkeys (*Cebus apella*) trained with a procedure similar to that used with pigeons by Herrnstein and Loveland learned to discriminate "human" and "nonhuman" slides and transferred successfully to new instances (D'Amato & Van Sant 1988). However, an analysis of the errors demonstrated that the monkeys tended to respond to slides that had a patch of reddish coloration, which turned out to be a common feature of stimuli containing humans. Since the goal of these experiments is to demonstrate the use of abstract concepts in nonhuman animals, then factors such as stimulus control and generalization are considered contextual variables.

Generalization among the components of a particular category may be also mediated by the sharing of a common response, even if the stimuli are visually dissimilar. Hull (1943) referred to this as *secondary generalization*—that is, generalization attributable to common elements among sets of associations. Can animals generalize beyond physical similarity? There is evidence that a common response induces the formation of a single category even when the stimuli involved are very different (Wasserman et al. 1992). This is a complex experiment involving three phases of training. In phase 1, pigeons learned to choose one response, R1, when exposed to slides containing either a "person" or a "car," and to choose the other response, R2, when exposed to slides of "flowers" or a "chair." In phase 2, one component from each category was withheld while the pigeon learned to choose one of two new responses, R3 or R4, when exposed to the other component—for example, people-R3-food (car withheld) and flower-R4-food (chair withheld). In both phases, choosing the incorrect response led to nonreward. In phase 3, the two stimuli withheld during phase 2 (e.g., car and chair) were reintroduced, but this time only R3 and R4 were available for choice; that is, the stimuli (presented in phase 1) and response alternatives (available in phase 2) had not been trained explicitly. The results indicated that pigeons tended to choose R3 during car trials, whereas they tended to choose R4 during chair trials. Since these responses were not available during phase 1, when pigeons first learned about these slides, their choices must reflect the experience acquired during phase 2. One interpretation of these results maintains that the training administered during phase 1 established a single category for [people + car] and another single category for [flower + chair], based on their sharing of the same response, R1 and R2, respectively. Then, during testing, the presentation of a "car" slide was equivalent to presenting a "people" slide; thus, selecting R3 was the appropriate response. Similarly, the presentation of a "chair" slide was equivalent to presenting a "flower" slide, thus evoking R4.

In solving the types of problems described previously, pigeons rely on their ability to generalize across stimuli based either on physical similarity or other common elements. But can animals learn an abstract concept, such as the *same/different concept*? Suppose animals are exposed to a large set of pairs of stimuli that can be either identical or different, and they are reinforced for choosing one alternative when the stimuli are equal, but a different alternative when they are different. In one experiment, two rhesus monkeys (*Macaca mulatta*) were trained to categorize sounds as being the same or different using a relatively simple procedure (Wright et al. 1990). Examples of the sounds included the following: door buzzer, cuckoo clock, siren, car engine, telephone ring, monkey calls, metronome, coyote howls, and rooster crows, among many others. Sounds were presented serially, and monkeys learned to press one key when the sounds were the same and a different key when the sounds were different. A correct response when the sounds were the same resulted in the delivery of a banana pellet, whereas a correct response when the sounds were different caused the presentation of orange drink. Occasional transfer trials with novel stimuli indicated a level of accuracy indistinguishable from that obtained with training stimuli; in both cases, the percentage of correct responses was above 75%.

Demonstrations of abstract concepts have been attempted with a variety of species (e.g., primates, dolphins, pigeons), using procedures similar to the one described above and either visual or auditory stimuli. As pointed out previously in this chapter, the contribution of contextual variables to the phenomenon under analysis can be best assessed by convergent evidence provided by different approaches. In the study of concept learning, one such piece of evidence comes from a long series of studies of a single, very peculiar subject: Alex, an African Grey parrot (*Psittacus erithacus*). Prior to the research reported in an article on the same/different concept (Pepperberg 1987), Alex had received training in the use of English vocalizations to identify, request, refuse, or comment on as many as 80 different objects. For example, Alex would correctly use phrases such as "Come here" or "I want X," where X refers to an appropriate object. Training on the same/different task involved a rather complex procedure, from which I will summarize some of the key features (see Pepperberg 1987 for a full account of the training procedure).

During training trials, Alex was presented with two objects while the trainer asked either "What's same?" or "What's different?" The objects could differ in terms of color (red, green, or blue), shape (triangular or square), or matter (rawhide or wood). The correct response was to name the dimension on which the objects were the same or different, but not the actual stimulus. For example, when confronted with a "red, wooden triangle" and a "blue, wooden triangle," and asked "What's different?", the correct response was "color." The rewards for a correct response were praise from the trainer and an opportunity to interact with the object. Correct responses were recorded by an observer who could hear Alex but could not see the actual stimuli that were being presented. In addition, the trainer presenting the stimuli was not familiar with the same/different task. These precautions were taken to avoid cueing effects of the type that vitiated early attempts to train animals in complex tasks (see the case of Clever Hans in ***Chapter 1, section 3***, p. 13). Tests on the same/different task were interspersed with training trials related to other problems, and they involved both familiar and novel objects. ***Figure 14.8*** shows the results. Correct responses for familiar and novel objects, and in terms of the "same" and "different" problems, are aligned in the diagonal, whereas incorrect responses lie off the diagonal. Alex was correct in 75% or

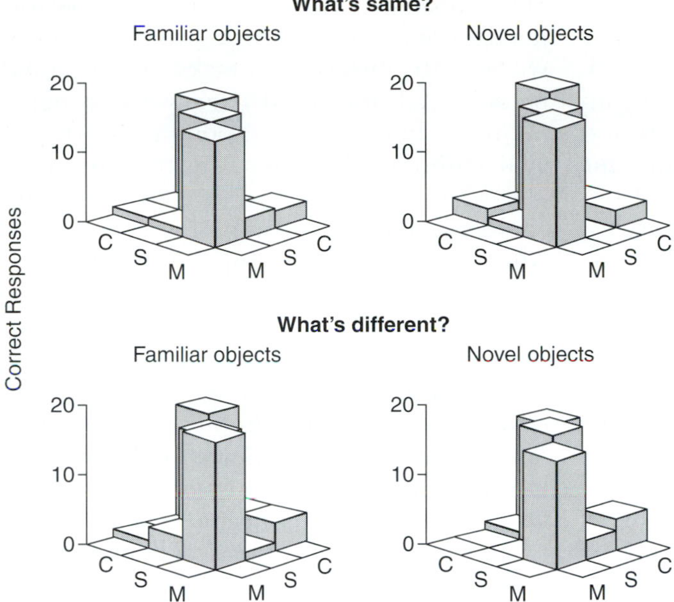

FIGURE 14.8. Same/different concept acquisition by Alex (Pepperberg 1987). Objects could be similar or different in terms of their color (C), shape (S), or material (M). The two test questions were "What's same?" and "What's different?", and they referred to either familiar or novel objects. Correct performance is plotted in the diagonal.

more of the test trials, even when stimuli were novel.

In yet another type of test trial, called probe trials, Alex faced two objects that were equal in two of the three attributes and was asked to judge sameness or difference when two of the three alternatives were correct. For example, Alex faced a "yellow, wooden triangle" and a "blue, wooden triangle," and was asked "What's same?" There are two correct responses to this question: "matter" and "shape." Notice that if Alex had been responding to the physical attributes of the stimuli, rather than the verbal question, his prior training would have prompted the incorrect response "color." This is so because color is the only attribute that differs, and all training trials involved pairs of stimuli differing in only one attribute. But the question made it such that there were two correct answers in probe trials; in this example, giving the question "What's same?" both "matter" and "shape" are correct. In addition, the ambiguity in the correct response for these probe trials tended to further dilute any cueing effects from the trainers. Probe trial performance was impressive: overall, Alex was correct in 90% of the trials. Furthermore, the performance was similarly high for "same" and "different" questions and for color, shape, and matter problems.

Once considered the exclusive domain of primates, abstract concepts now appear to have been demonstrated in birds as well. Given the remote evolutionary relationship of the avian and mammalian lineages and the extensive set of biological traits for which these species show convergence (e.g., relative brain size, sleep-wakefulness cycles, parental care patterns, etc.), it would not be surprising to find evidence of further homoplasy in terms of the mechanisms underlying concept learning.

3.c. Counting and the Concept of Number. *Number* provides another example of an abstract concept. One of the central properties of mathematical operations is their independence from physical objects. The numbers signifying specific quantities, as well as the operations that we can do with those numbers (e.g., addition), are detached from any specific reality, can be applied to almost any aspect of the real world, and can even be acquired in the absence of any specific relationship to physical realities, as students who take a course on calculus know. While it is obvious that people vary in their mathematical skills, most if not all healthy adults can acquire some minimum set of basic quantitative operations. Are similar skills available to other species?

Some quantitative skills that allow for the solution of numerical problems may be available even to organisms lacking the concept of number (Davis & Pérusse 1988). When the goal is to demonstrate that the animal arrives at the solution of the problem by using the number concept, such quantitative skills are treated as contextual factors. Suppose, for example, that an animal is trained to discriminate a specific quantity from other quantities in trials involving different kinds of objects: 2–/4+, 4+/8–, 1–/4+, etc. The objects could be marbles, raisins, pencils, etc. Correct performance (i.e., choosing the alternative that involves four objects) in a task like this could be achieved not only by using the concept of "four" but also by responding to the visual stimulus characterizing the area usually covered by four objects. The second choice would not require the use of any concept but only the simple use of a visual correlate common to most sets of four objects; therefore, the latter would be a more parsimonious process. Similarly, the time it takes to process the stimulus, the temporal rhythm with which stimuli are presented, and a number of other perceptual aspects of the task may be used to solve the problem without involving concepts. As in other types of comparative studies, such contextual factors must be eliminated before it can be safely concluded that nonhuman animals use numerical concepts.

There are at least two levels of operation regarding the use of numerical concepts. The lowest level is one in which an organism can count the number of occurrences of some event or order a set of events according to their numerical properties. *Counting* occurs when an animal (1) assigns a different tag or label to collections of objects differing in the number of elements (e.g., "one," "two," etc.), (2) can use that tag independently of the elements being counted (e.g., four marbles, four books, four cardinal points), and (3) demonstrates ordinal abilities (e.g., "three" is always less than "four" and more than "two"). Tags may be words or numbers within human languages, but it is possible that species that lack a symbolic system of communication use nonlinguistic tags. The highest level of numerical competence is one in which the organism can exploit the operational properties of numbers, such as addition and subtraction. Would animals that are capable of counting, say, 6 responses be able to understand that 3 plus 3 and 8 minus 2 are both equal to 6? Such is the evidence required to argue that any animal possesses the concept of number.

The counting ability of animals has been studied using a variety of procedures. A series of experiments reported by Breukelaar and Dalrymple-Alford (1998) illustrates one approach to evaluating the role of a contextual factor—in this case, timing of signal duration. Rats received training in a conditional discrimination with two available responses and two conditional stimuli in which count and time were confounded. One of the stimuli involved 2 pulses and lasted for 2 s, whereas the other stimulus involved 8 pulses and lasted for 8 s. R1 was correct in the presence of one signal, but R2 was correct in the presence of the other signal. Rats were reinforced with a food pellet for correct responses. Since rats could solve this conditional discrimination either in terms of counting or timing, test trials were administered to determine which dimension had acquired control over discriminative behavior. In one type of test trial, duration was held constant at 4 s (an intermediate value relative to training stimuli), but the number of pulses was varied between 2 and 8. In a second type of test trial, count was held constant at 4 pulses, but the duration of the signal was varied between 2 and 8 s in 1-s intervals. Rats demonstrated clear control by timing, but not by counting. Thus, when number and duration are confounded, rats respond preferentially to the duration of the stimulus.

What if all duration cues were eliminated? This was achieved in a subsequent phase of training in which all stimuli were of the same total duration but contained either 2 or 8 events; in addition, and most importantly, the duration of each pulse event within the trial was varied randomly. This generated unique stimuli for each trial as far as timing parameters were concerned. In a final test phase, a similar procedure was used to generate unique stimuli varying in terms of the number of events, and now also in terms of total duration. The results suggest that both number of events (counting) and duration (timing) acquired control over behavior. Therefore, rats appear to be able to count, but they tend to rely on timing if temporal cues are available. The issue of whether counting is used as a last-resort process (as these results suggest) or is routinely performed by animals, perhaps in the context of foraging, is still not fully resolved.

Rhesus monkeys (*Macaca mulatta*) also exhibit ordinal abilities—that is, they can respond according to the particular numerical order of stimuli encountered during training (either ascending, 1—›2—›3—›4, or descending, 4—›3—›2—›1) and later transfer the appropriate order (ascending or descending) to numbers beyond the original set (e.g., 5-6-7-8-9 or 9-8-7-6-5). In these studies (Brannon & Terrace 2000), the training stimuli varied in terms of the number of elements between 1, 2, 3, or 4. Elements were geometric forms such as circles, squares, ellipses, and rectangles. The stimuli were carefully matched for size, shape, foreground color, and background color; in addition, the position of the four stimuli in the screen and the position of the elements within each stimulus were randomized across trials. These precautions were taken to eliminate the potential use of these nonnumerical contextual factors to solve the problems. In any particular trial, four stimuli were presented on a computer screen; each stimulus included 1, 2, 3, or 4 elements. For two of the animals, reinforcement (a food pellet) was contingent upon touching the stimuli according to the number of elements and in an ascending order (1—›2—›3—›4), whereas the third monkey was reinforced for touching the stimuli in a descending order (4—›3—›2—›1). Monkeys developed the ascending or descending response sequence and transferred this ability to new stimuli readily in occasional nonreinforced test trials. This is not in itself particularly striking since, as the authors noted, these same monkeys had previously learned to respond to a set of pictures in a specific sequence and without any reference to ordinality (e.g., cat—›rose—›apple—› beetle).

In a subsequent phase of training, however, these monkeys were presented with pairs of stimuli and required to respond in an ordinal manner (ascending or descending, depending on their previous training). During this phase, novel stimuli were introduced that involved 5, 6, 7, 8, or 9 elements—that is, numbers above the range to which the monkeys had been trained before. Trials involving two familiar stimuli were reinforced according to the ascending or descending rule, but no reinforcement was provided for responding in trials in which one or both stimuli were novel. Using this procedure, two of the three monkeys (both trained with an ascending series) exhibited positive transfer in trials involving two novel stimuli, responding, for example, 5—›6, 6—›8, 7—›9. The performance of the monkey trained in a descending series was at chance level. Notice that these results are more consistent with the hypothesis of counting as a first-resort strategy—that is, one spontaneously and routinely used by animals. Moreover, in yet a subsequent phase in which reinforcement was provided for correct performance with all the stimuli, choice performance reflected the numerical distance between the stimuli. For example, when the trial involved 6 and 7 elements (i.e., a numerical distance of 1), accuracy was lower and responses slower than in trials involving stimuli with 1 and 9 elements (i.e., a numerical distance of 8). This phenomenon, known from similar experiments with human subjects, provides compelling evidence of control by the numerical properties of the stimuli.

Ordinal capacities have also been demonstrated in chimpanzees (*Pan troglodytes*) using procedures analogous to those described previously for monkeys. But chimpanzees trained to count objects by assigning Arabic numerals can display *addition,* at least in a rudimentary form. In one experiment, a chimpanzee named Sheba was trained to move through three different locations in the lab, as shown in ***Figure 14.9*** (Boysen & Berntson 1989). In a first task, Sheba found oranges hidden in two of the three locations. The task required that Sheba add the total number of oranges (up to a maximum of four, since she had been trained to recognize numerals 0–4) and point to the appropriate Arabic numeral in a test stand. Although the initial intention of the experimenters was to train Sheba in this task, she surprised them by performing significantly above chance from the very first session. In a subsequent phase, the oranges were replaced by plastic cards with an Arabic number between 0 and 4 written on it. As before, two of the three locations had a card, and Sheba's task was to visit the three sites and then choose the Arabic numeral that corresponded to the sum of the two numbers hidden in these sites. In these trials, the experimenter scoring Sheba's performance stayed behind her so as to be unable to intervene in the choice process; in addition, the numbers were placed in each site by a different experimenter. This double-blind procedure considerably reduced opportunities for cueing. Again, Sheba performed above chance from the first session, choosing the number representing the sum of the two numbers she had previously seen hidden in each of two different locations.

FIGURE 14.9. Addition in the chimpanzee Sheba (Boysen & Berntson 1989). The setting included three locations Sheba was trained to search before choosing a card. In the initial tests, two of the three locations have different numbers of oranges, and the correct response was to point to the Arabic number that equaled the sum of oranges. In the situation represented in this figure, plastic cards with Arabic numbers replaced the oranges, and Sheba was asked to add the numbers and point to the appropriate card. Sheba performed above chance in both tasks from the first session.

Performance was also above chance independently of whether the correct sum equaled 1, 2, 3, or 4. Overall, Sheba was correct in 81% of the trials!

The experiments reviewed in this section suggest that the concept of number is within reach of at least some nonhuman primates. The subtlety of contextual factors has forced the development of ingenious procedures of testing that greatly reduce the chances that the problem-solving behavior could be based on nonconceptual sources of information. It is yet unclear whether counting and other aspects of numerical competence are routinely used by animals, perhaps in foraging situations or in social contexts, or whether exposing such skills would demand the design of procedures that preclude the use of nonconceptual strategies. Particularly striking is the "spontaneous" appearance of problem-solving behavior (e.g., ordinal tasks by rhesus monkeys, addition by Sheba). This phenomenon suggests the presence of a *generative process* that allows for the integration of acquired information resulting in behavioral skills beyond those that were specifically trained (Rumbaugh et al. 1996).

3.d. Language Production. Perhaps the most obvious difference between the behavior of human and nonhuman animals is the presence of language in the former and the absence of anything that obviously resembles language in the latter. Not surprisingly, therefore, scholars have entertained the possibility of teaching language to nonhuman animals for centuries. The seminal idea was originally suggested by the French philosopher Julien de La Mettrie [1709–1751], who speculated that properly educated chimpanzees might be able to learn a human language (see ***Chapter 1, section 2,*** p. 8. In modern times, perhaps the first to tackle this possibility empirically was the American comparative psychologist Robert M. Yerkes [1876–1956], who during the 1910s, in collaboration with William Furnes, attempted to teach chimpanzees and orangutans to speak. The attempt met with some success; for example, an orangutan was reported capable of producing a few recognizable words, including "cup" and "papa." Similar spoken words were later produced by Viki, a chimpanzee raised by anthropologists Keith and Cathy Hayes in their home during the 1940s. These and similar efforts suggested that the anatomy of the vocal tract probably makes it difficult for apes to display the rich repertoire of sounds required by spoken language (see ***Figure 9.13,*** p. 355).

While spoken language has since then been ruled out for apes, new generations of comparative psychologists have developed novel approaches to the study of language acquisition in nonhuman animals. One premise of these studies was the hypothesis that linguistic skills could be uncovered by using behaviors that are independent of sound modulation. Impressed by the rich repertoire of gestures exhibited by apes, Yerkes (1916) suggested that perhaps chimpanzees could be taught to use their fingers to communicate, much as hearing-impaired people use theirs. Starting in the 1960s, with Allen and Beatrix Gardner's training of a chimpanzee named Washoe with a simple version of American Sign Language, comparative psychologists developed a wide variety of training procedures in their attempts to teach linguistic skills to such animals as chimpanzees (*Pan troglodytes*), bonobos (*Pan paniscus*), gorillas (*Gorilla gorilla*), orangutans (*Pongo pygmaeus*), dolphins (*Tursiops truncatus*), sea lions (*Zalophus californianus*), and even an African Grey parrot (*Psittacus erithacus*). Human-animal communication is mediated by a variety of means, including English language, gestures, plastic tokens placed on a magnetic board, and computer-controlled symbols manipulated from a specially designed keyboard. In some studies, the emphasis has been on *language production*—that is, the creation of syntactically appropriate strings of symbols (whether word or arbitrary geometric symbols called lexigrams). In other studies, research has been concerned with *language comprehension* (see next section), the extent to which linguistically trained animals are able to correctly follow commands presented to them in a symbolic manner, whether with spoken words, gestures, or lexigrams (Hillix & Rumbaugh 1998).

The original research endeavors emphasized language production. Projects involving some form of sign language with chimpanzees Washoe (Gardner & Gardner 1969) and Nim (Terrace 1979), a gorilla named Koko (Patterson 1990), and an orangutan named Chantek (Miles 1983) demonstrated their ability to acquire a relatively large repertoire of signs that referred to specific objects (e.g., apple, ball) and actions (e.g., tickle, give). Washoe was reported to have acquired approximately 130 such signs, to use them in the appropriate context, and to follow specific sequences in their use. Similar success was obtained with Koko and Chantek. Sequential structure is important because it suggests the presence of *syntax,* a major feature of human language. In English, for example, it is correct for the adjective to precede the noun (e.g., "beautiful day"), while the opposite is meaningless (e.g., "day beautiful"). Sequential rules may vary, but human languages always contain sequential constraints in the ordering of symbols. In addition, the order of the words in a sentence may convey a specific meaning that could be altered if the sequence is reversed. For example, "Romulus killed Remus" conveys the opposite information from "Remus killed Romulus."

Signing apes reportedly exhibited some consistency in their sequential use of signs which led to the suggestion that they had acquired the rudiments of linguistic proficiency. Terrace et al. (1979) ignited a controversy when they suggested that language-trained apes were not using language at all but were simply performing appropriate actions to obtain a variety of rewards, much as animals do in instrumental conditioning situations. Their argument was based on data they collected from their own chimpanzee, Nim, which had received strict instrumental training, as well as on a reanalysis of videotape evidence collected from Washoe's training sessions, which were less structured and often involved no food reinforcement for correct actions. Terrace et al. noted that many signs produced by these chimpanzees matched similar signs produced by their trainers shortly before, which suggested that mimicking played a role in sign production. In addition, these chimpanzees often produced long strings which involved the pointless repetition of signs. For example, an answer to a question such as "do you want to eat an apple?" could take the form: "apple eat eat apple eat apple hurry apple hurry hurry." They also offered alternative interpretations for a number of striking examples of apparent linguistic proficiency. For example, Washoe had been reported to articulate the signs for "water" and "bird" upon seeing a duck swimming in a lake. Since a sign for "duck" was lacking, this was originally interpreted as evidence of creativity, an important property of language that allows us to combine known words to refer to new objects (e.g., "flying saucer"). Terrace et al. suggested that Washoe may have been simply signing two familiar objects, bird and water; no creativity is assumed in this case.

Premack (1976) used an alternative method based on plastic tokens that his chimpanzees could manipulate and place on a magnetic board. Four chimpanzees participated in this project; a female named Sarah was the most intensively studied. The tokens varied widely in shape, color, size, and texture; some were totally arbitrary, while others were letters. Each token correlated with an English word and made reference to an object, an action, or some abstract concept such as "same/different." The tokens were placed in vertically arranged strings according to an explicit set of sequential constraints that simulated a syntax. This procedure had at least two advantages over the sign language method. First, the sentence created by the animal could be recorded and analyzed more objectively and easily than a sequence of hand gestures, an important methodological advantage. Second, since the tokens were under the animal's continuous view, sentence formation placed a light burden on short-term memory. In contrast, meaningful signing requires the animal to remember the early signs of a sentence, thus placing a heavier demand on memory.

Using this token procedure, chimpanzees were trained in progressively more complex tasks. With a repertoire of about

130 tokens, Sarah's vocabulary allowed for the design of a wide variety of problems, including naming, the use of interrogative mode, and the classification of objects. Premack's chimpanzees were trained to comprehend commands involving two-, three-, and four-word sentences. For example, when shown a piece of apple, they were required to place the tokens for "give apple" in the board; subsequently, the chimpanzee had to correctly choose the token corresponding to its name from two different names and place it at the end of the string ("give apple Sarah"); and finally, a token corresponding to a trainer's name was added so as to form a request of the form "Debbie give apple Sarah." Performance was notoriously correct when sentences involved two words, surpassing the 90% effectiveness in test trials. However, correct responses dropped below 75% correct immediately after a shift to strings involving four words. Errors included not only choosing the wrong token but also placing the tokens in an incorrect sequence (e.g., "give Debbie apple Sarah"). With sufficient training, performance in four-word sentences exhibited some improvement, but, curiously, the chimpanzees refused to continue the training.

Sarah was also trained in a series of concept-learning tasks, such as a series of trials aimed at teaching the concept of "causality." ***Figure 14.10*** shows three types of test trials designed to study causality. In each case, the top line represents a sequence (from left to right) of the following type: object—›cause—›effect. There were two types of problems. In one type (***Figure 14.10-a***), the instrument that can cause a certain effect is missing and Sarah was required to choose it from a sample of three objects (a vase, a pencil, and a knife). Sarah was administered 12 problems of this type, involving different objects (e.g., apple, cookie, towel, etc.) and different actions (e.g., cut, wash, draw, etc.), and selected the correct instrument from the sample in 9 of these tests. In a second type (***Figure 14.10-b***), the question mark replaces the effect and Sarah was required to select the appropriate effect, given the object and cause elements. Sarah was correct in 8 out of 12 tests of this modality. Finally (***Figure 14.10-c***), the instrument (e.g., knife) is replaced by the token corresponding to the action performed with that instrument (e.g., cut). Moreover, tokens also replace the instruments in the set from which Sarah had to choose the correct option. Sarah was correct in 10 of 11 tests of this type. Similar results were obtained with a second chimpanzee, Peony, tested under the same conditions, but somewhat lower accuracy was recorded for yet two other chimpanzees, Elizabeth and Walnut, trained in only some of these problems.

These results show two striking features, both suggesting a level of abstraction beyond that implied by direct associations between objects and tokens. One is that the actions themselves (e.g., cutting) were completely absent in these tests and represented only by a static instrument (e.g., knife). Sarah was able to relate the perceived object with a particular way in which this object could be used (though not demonstrated directly), so that the appropriate effect would be produced. Another remarkable feature of these results is the choice of the correct instrument in trials in which the options involved actions that Sarah had never in fact experienced. For example, the sentence "sponge—›?—›halves sponges" was correctly solved by choosing the knife, although Sarah had never actually seen a sponge being cut into two halves with a knife. The action of cutting must have been thus represented independently of the objects with which the action was first

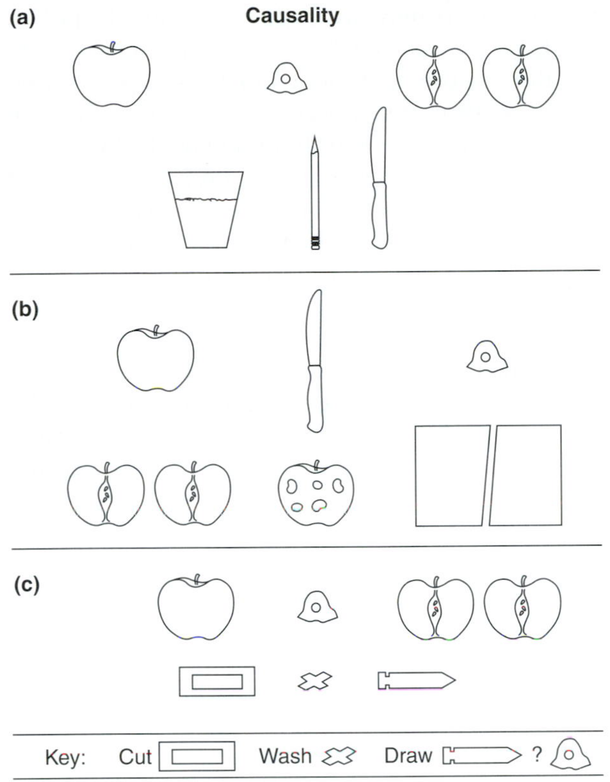

Figure 14.10. Causality concept in the chimpanzee Sarah (Premack 1976). ***(a)*** Some tests presented a whole object on the left and that object split into two halves on the right. Sarah was required to choose one of three instruments that could be used to produce the effect (in this example, the correct answer is the knife). ***(b)*** In other tests, the effect was omitted, and Sarah had to choose the correct one from three different objects (in this case, the two halves of an apple). ***(c)*** Eventually, the instrument (knife) was replaced by the symbol for the appropriate action (symbol for "cut"). Sarah had to choose the correct symbol out of a sample of three action symbols.

learned, so that it could be applied to new problems.

A somewhat more elaborated procedure involved the used of lexigrams (arbitrary geometric patterns symbolizing objects and actions). Lexigrams were presented as keys in a keyboard; chimpanzees were trained to press the keys in order to form strings that could be roughly translated into English phrases such as "please machine give piece of apple." In an interesting study combining language comprehension and production, chimpanzees Sherman and Austin were first trained to share food (e.g., apple) and instruments (e.g., wrench) and subsequently exposed to situations that required their cooperation to obtain a particular reward. In one such situation, one of these chimpanzees learned to request the appropriate tool from the other in order to obtain a specific food, all by using the correct tool and food lexigrams. Once obtained, the food was shared (Savage-Rumbaugh et al. 1978).

Notice that the procedure used by Premack (1976) aimed mainly at the resolution of problems posed to the animal in terms that the experimenter defined as linguistic. But the use of symbols during these training sessions was essentially noncommunicative, thus lacking an important feature of language. So it is not surprising that the performance of these chimpanzees, impressive as it is, can still be understood in terms of more basic processes. Sign-language training procedures had the communicative properties, but the results of such training are difficult to evaluate. In particular, the possibility of experimenter cueing is hard to eliminate. One attempt to bypass this problem involved the introduction of an infant named Loulis into a group of chimpanzees that had previously received sign language training, including Washoe (Fouts & Fouts 1989). Loulis did acquire a repertoire of signs from his interactions with other chimpanzees (human trainers never signed in Loulis's presence), a fact suggesting that these gestures, once established, can spread in a group via social learning. However, the linguistic properties of Loulis's vocabulary have not been fully assessed.

3.e. Language Comprehension. The lexigram procedure used with Sherman and Austin was applied to other apes. In one such project, there was an unexpected consequence that turned out to have remarkable importance for our understanding of linguistic capacities in nonhuman primates. A new feature of this project involved the use of a bonobo in a linguistic study for the first time. Bonobos are closely related to chimpanzees and have only recently been recognized as a distinct species. In their natural environment, bonobos appear to be more social and communicative than common chimpanzees, frequently using vocalizations, sharing food, and exhibiting a high level of tolerance with one another. The first bonobo trained with the lexigram procedure, Matata, was a wild-caught female that showed little progress in learning to use symbols during four years of training. Matata's training took place in the presence of her infant, a male named Kanzi, born in 1980. Whereas Kanzi was not specifically trained to manipulate lexigrams, he soon showed an ability to use symbols in the appropriate manner. Most interestingly, Kanzi demonstrated an understanding of spoken English that parallels that of human infants during the first stages of language acquisition, thus becoming the focus of intensive study (Savage-Rumbaugh et al. 1993).

There were several unique aspects of Kanzi's training. First, and perhaps most obvious, is the fact that Kanzi was a bonobo. Second, Kanzi's training was informal and spontaneous; there was no attempt to teach any lexigram in particular, or any spoken word. Rather, Kanzi acquired these skills by growing up in a rich linguistic environment in which the use of lexigrams and speech was part of the daily routine. Third, unlike his mother Matata and many of the apes that participated in language training projects, Kanzi was exposed to language from a very early age. Kanzi was 6-months-old and still with his mother when first exposed to both lexigrams and spoken English, whereas most of the other chimpanzees were 2½ years old or older when their language training started.

More recently, training designed in the same informal setting as that experienced by Kanzi (also characteristic of human infants) was extended to two other bonobos and a chimpanzee. These animals also started training at a very early age, showed comparable progress in language comprehension, and exhibited a proficiency level that is generally considered higher than that achieved by chimpanzees whose training started at an age of 2½ years or later. These findings suggest that the bonobo-chimpanzee species difference is probably not as important as the age at which exposure to language starts and the type of training environment. It is possible that early exposure is beneficial because of greater neural plasticity in the developing brain or because of the presence of a sensitive period for learning related to communicative functions. Such plasticity may be more restricted in brains that have undergone substantial development (see ***Chapter 10, section 3.d.,*** pp. 393–395).

Kanzi showed the first signs of comprehension of spoken English at about 2 years of age. After Kanzi was separated from his mother (2½ years old), he began to spontaneously use lexigrams for communicative purposes. As is normally the case with human infants, language comprehension was evident before Kanzi became proficient with the use of lexigrams (i.e., comprehension precedes production). Moreover, comprehension of a particular word usually occurred before the acquisition of the lexigram that corresponded to that word. Kanzi's day consisted of a daily walk through a 50-acre area surrounding the laboratory where different types of foods and objects could be found at predictable locations. Caretakers accompanied Kanzi during these trips and provided informal training by talking, pointing to lexigrams when that was possible, and interacting with others as the opportunities arose. Activities were organized around Kanzi's interests to keep him motivated to interact.

At 8 years of age, Kanzi was exposed to a series of systematic tests of language comprehension, and his performance was compared to that of a human female infant, Alia, who was then between 1½ and 2 years old. Care was taken during these tests to avoid Clever Hans effects. For example, the trainer who provided the stimulus (a sentence in spoken English) was located in a room separated from the subject's room by a one-way mirror. This removal of the trainer from the subjects' visual field prevented any kind of visual cueing. When the task involved a third participant (e.g., when the subjects were asked to give a specific object to a specific person), this participant was equipped with headphones through which loud music was presented in order to mask the verbal requests and make the participant unaware of what the subject was required to do. Finally, different trainers tested Kanzi and Alia during a period of months; throughout testing, each trainer was unaware of the results obtained in analogous tests by the other trainer. Approximately 400 blind trials were administered to each subject.

The general procedure consisted of giving the subjects a verbal request and recording whether the subject carried out the requested action correctly or not. Neither Kanzi nor Alia were specifically reinforced for responding correctly, although food, toys, and other objects were continuously available in the room during test sessions. Several types of sentences were administered, as shown in ***Table 14.3,*** and several aspects of the results are interesting. First, the performance of both Kanzi and Alia in these tests was not perfect, but it was generally quite accurate and very similar across subjects. On the basis of the overall similarity in scores, it is tempting to conclude that Kanzi's English comprehension skills are approximately similar to those of a 2-year-old human infant, which is, in fact, remarkable. Third, some of the correct responses by Kanzi indicate a very accurate use of word order within a sentence. For example, Kanzi performed well in contrasting sentences such as "place object X in object Y" versus "place object Y in object X," indicating that he was not responding merely to the actual words used in the sentence, but to their order. Fourth, when the accuracy level differed substantially across subjects (e.g., by a difference of 20% or greater), as it did in four sentence types (2B, 5B, 5C, and 7), Kanzi generally outperformed Alia.

A major difference between the communicative behavior of Kanzi and Alia appears to lie in the extent to which they engaged in a conversation. For example, in the an-

TABLE 14.3 Sentence Types for Testing Language Comprehension in Kanzi and Alia

	Description	*% Correct (blind trials only)*	
Type	*"example"*	*Kanzi*	*Alia*
1A	Put object X in/on transportable object Y "put the ball on the pine needles"	63	73
1B	Put object X in nontransportable object Y "put the ice water in the potty"	77	71
2A	Give (or show) object X to animate A "give the lighter to Rose"	78	84
2B	Give object X and object Y to animate A "give the peas and the sweet potatoes to Kelly"	37	57
2C	Do action A on animate A "give Rose a hug"	91	91
2D	Do action A on animate A with object X "get Rose with the snake"	76	61
3	Do action A on object X with object Y "knife the sweet potato"	82	63
4	Announce information "the surprise is hiding in the dishwasher"	67	83
5A	Take object X to location Y "take the snake outdoors"	78	71
5B	Go to location Y and get object X "go to the refrigerator and get a banana"	82	45
5C	Go get object X that is in location Y "go get the carrot that's in the microwave"	77	52
6	Make pretend animate A do action A on recipient Y "make the doggie bite the snake"	67	56
7	All other sentence types	78	33

Note. Examples and results from Savage-Rumbaugh et al. (1993).

nouncement sentences (type 4), Alia often added some verbal comments during the test. If the sentence was "Alia is going to chase mommy," then Alia responded, "Chase me, chase me," indicating a degree of communicative engagement that was not observed in Kanzi. It seems possible that Kanzi or other apes that have been exposed to linguistic environments may eventually show some level of engagement in a conversation, although this may turn out to be a relatively unique property of human language. Whatever the case, it seems obvious that at least some aspects of language lie well within the capabilities of apes.

A degree of language comprehension has also been observed in a variety of nonprimate species. Using an artificial gestural language with a relatively small set of gestures that allowed the experimenter to produce a large number of sentences, language comprehension has also been demonstrated with dolphins. In a typical test situation with a dolphin named Ake (Herman et al.

1993), a sequence of gestures presented on a television screen required the animal to perform an action in relation to a particular object present in the tank. Understanding of the sequential properties of these sentences was evidenced by correct responding to complementary sentences. For example, Ake performed correctly when asked "take the Frisbee on your left to the hoop on your right," and also when asked the complementary sentence "take the Frisbee on your right to the hoop on your left." Similarly, Ake correctly executed actions that resulted from interchanging "Frisbee" and "hoop" in the sentence. In some trials, dolphins are reported to rearrange their environment in order to be able to execute a specific request. For example, a dolphin asked to swim through a hoop was observed to lift a hoop that was lying on the bottom of the tank and subsequently swim through it as requested. Analogous performance was reported in California sea lions also trained to respond to gestural instructions by performing a variety of actions (Schusterman & Krieger 1984). For example, the sequence "water, white small bottle fetch" requested a female sea lion named Rocky to take the white, small bottle and place it in a stream of water. Like Ake, Rocky received a fish reward for a correct response.

Alex, the African Grey parrot whose ability to acquire abstract concepts was described previously (see ***section 3.b.***), is especially interesting because his behavior provides evidence of both comprehension and production of spoken English. Alex began vocal training when he was approximately 13 months of age, in 1977, and eventually acquired the English words for a wide variety of colors ("green," "rose," "blue," etc.), shapes ("2-cornered" in reference to a football-shaped object, "three-cornered" for triangle, etc.), materials ("cork," "wood," "rock," etc.), a variety of objects ("key," "cup," "truck," etc.), and labels for abstract categories such as "color," "shape," and "material." Alex's vocabulary reached approximately a hundred words. In one experiment, two to seven objects (in different trials) were placed in a tray, and Alex was asked one of four possible questions (Pepperberg 1993). Two of the questions concerned the color attribute of objects: "What color is X?" and "What object is color A?"; the other two questions concerned the shape of objects: "What shape is X?" and "What object is shape B?" As usual, extensive precautions were taken to avoid Clever Hans effects. Alex's overall effectiveness for the color questions was 80%, whereas for the shape questions was 89%.

Is it possible that such a seemingly linguistic performance such as that exhibited by Kanzi, Ake, Rocky, Alex, and other similarly trained animals reflects the operation of complex, yet nonlinguistic, cognitive processes? This is not a question that can be answered unambiguously at this time; in fact, it sparks substantial controversy. Despite the similarity in training procedures, there are important distinctions in the experimental protocols used with these species and also in the role played by linguistic material in the lives of these animals. Savage-Rumbaugh (1993) pointed out a variety of differences, including the relatively rich variety of consequences that linguistic interactions had for Kanzi. In contrast, Ake and Rocky performed all their tasks for the sole consequence of receiving the reward of a fish. Perhaps even greater cognitive capacities could be revealed if these marine mammals could be trained under conditions more analogous to those used with apes. In addition, the performance of Rocky in tests involving sentences with anomalous syntax have led Gisiner and Schusterman (1992) to argue that sentence comprehension can be accounted for in nonlinguistic terms as the acquisition of conditional discriminations (see ***Figure 14.7-a,*** p. 562). In the artificial gestural language used with Rocky, signs referring to objects (O) and those referring to actions (A) are exclusively combined in an O—›A sequence. Rocky was trained to perform different responses when given O and A signs. For example, when the trainer produced the sign for an object (e.g., "bottle"), Rocky turned around and visually scanned the pool while remaining close to the trainer. In contrast, a sign for an action (e.g., "fetch") required Rocky to remain in position, facing the trainer, until the sentence was concluded (this was signaled when the trainer dropped one foot on the water). When given a sentence with the reversed sequence, A—›O, Rocky either showed a scanning response first (appropriate for O, but not for A) or remained close to the trainer without scanning the pool. Despite the fact that some of the anomalous sentences contained enough information to induce responses, Rocky tended to remain close to the trainer in these trials. That is, Rocky showed little evidence of transfer when the stimulus conditions were modified. Whether accounts such as this one can be usefully extended to other linguistically trained animals remains controversial.

Studies of the higher cognitive abilities of nonhuman animals, such as those reviewed in the preceding sections on concept formation, numerical competence, and language, as well as the additional studies on self-awareness, deception, and similar topics, raise the Darwinian issue of *mental continuity* across species (see ***Chapter 1, section 3,*** pp. 11–15). They seem to demonstrate that some of the most characteristic features of human psychology are not unique to our species but, rather, are shared by other species. Mental continuity refers, of course, to the idea that some fundamental mechanisms of higher cognitive processes are shared by humans and at least some nonhuman animals or, in other words, that there is a degree of homology in underlying mechanisms. A reflection on what is required to demonstrate that similar behaviors are indeed based on homologous mechanisms indicates how much still needs to be done (see ***Figure 14.1***). For example, little or nothing is known about how such psychological capacities as the acquisition of concepts (visual, abstract, numerical, or linguistic) are realized in terms of cell-molecular and neurochemical processes. At the neurobiological level, human language is known from studies of patients suffering from brain damage to be lateralized into the left hemisphere for most people, as it was first shown by the neurologists Paul Broca [1824–1880] and Carl Wernicke [1848–1905] in the 19th century. Is there any similar evidence for linguistically trained non–human subjects? Sherman and Austin, two chimpanzees trained with the lexigram procedure, reacted faster to brief presentations of known lexigrams on the right visual field (i.e., left hemisphere) than on the left visual field; such an asymmetry is not observed with unfamiliar lexigrams (Hopkins & Morris 1993). Whether or not this result implies a homologous lateralization process between linguistically trained chimpanzees and humans, it is this type of data that will be relevant for an ultimate testing of mental continuity.

4. COMPLEXITY

Complexity may be hard to measure rigorously, but it has a relatively clear meaning when viewed at the conceptual level. Phenomena in which many distinct parts or processes can be discriminated, and relationships and interconnections established between these parts, are usually referred to as complex. Human societies, behaviors, and brains are almost prototypical examples of complexity, and comparative psychology, as a discipline, is expected to provide a set of theories that account for the evolutionary and developmental origin of such complexity. As a result, comparative psychologists have developed a wide variety of procedures and concepts to study complex forms of behavior, including learning, problem solving, concept formation, language, and others. However, a few caveats are in order when considering the issue of complexity in the natural world.

First, complexity of systems and functions is not an inevitable consequence of evolutionary and developmental processes. For example, trends toward increasing body size (usually taken as a proxy of complexity; Bonner 1988) can be identified in almost every evolutionary lineage; but so can trends toward miniaturization in body size. Quantitative studies of specific traits, such as the vertebral column of mammals (McShea 1993), demonstrate that trends toward complexity and simplicity tend to occur at similar rates. Although complexity is not an inevitable evolutionary outcome, increases in complexity do characterize the evolution of some traits. For example, and according to the same set of measures, the vertebral column of mammals is significantly more complex than that of reptiles and fish (McShea 1996).

Second, complexity (and simplicity) should not be used to characterize an entire species (e.g., humans are more complex than lizards), but only to characterize homologous traits across taxa (e.g., mammalian dentition is more complex than reptilian dentition). Because of the mosaic nature of evolution, any individual organism is a heterogeneous mixture of traits that have evolved at different rates and in different directions of specialization. Some of such traits may have increased in complexity, others may have become simplified or reduced, and still others may exhibit evolutionary stasis. In humans, for example, the neocortex is generally viewed as having increased in complexity to support the evolution of language, whereas the vermiform appendix, the muscles of the ear, and the wisdom teeth are vestigial or simplified traits; and the number of digits in our hands and feet has remained stable since the pentadactyl limb evolved in primitive tetrapods.

Third, complexity in structure and function arises directly from natural selection. Alleles determining different degrees of complexity in a particular structure or function, however indirect this influence may be, contribute differentially to inclusive fitness and thus spread through the population or are eliminated. This process may result in species that differ in complexity. However, the fact that a particular structure is more complex in species A than in species B does not imply that species A is better adapted to its environment than species B. Adaptation is a major driving force of evolution, whereas complexity is better viewed as one of the possible outcomes of adaptive processes.

Fourth, the existence of complex behavior does not necessarily imply that the underlying processes are complex. Indeed, the real scientific challenge is to account for as much complex behavior as possible within the constraints of relatively simple assumptions. Comparative psychologists have kept themselves faithful to Morgan's canon, which demands that our explanations of behavior be based on the simplest process possible. Adherence to parsimony provides a great impetus for creativity and careful experimental research, as scientists struggle to provide strong evidence for complex psychological processes and develop increasingly clear criteria to distinguish among behavioral skills (Thomas 1980).

The foregoing four points about complexity provide a general framework for conceptualizing the examples of trends in behavioral evolution and development described in this book—the central theme of comparative psychology. As discussed in ***Chapter 2,*** the amount of DNA needed to build an eukaryote organism is greater than that needed by prokaryote bacteria. The evolution of the first eukaryotes and, consequently, their descendants (including the animals) involved an increase in phenotypic complexity, paralleled by a larger genome. However, the C-value paradox warns us against any simplistic notion of progressive evolution: There is extensive overlap in the amount of DNA material across animals of vastly different degree of phenotypic complexity. In ***Chapter 5,*** the societies of insects and higher vertebrates were treated as complex, evolving from simpler modes of organization. Kinship and reciprocity, among other factors, are thought to have played a major role in social evolution. In ***Chapter 6,*** the history of the animal kingdom provides a monumental example of a transition in complexity with the relatively sudden emergence of most of the known phyla in Cambrian fossils. Similar adaptive radiations have occurred a multiplicity of times in specific lineages, including the mammalian radiation of the early Tertiary, when most of the modern orders of mammals were established.

Chapter 7 deals with simple nervous systems and behavior by focusing on research involving invertebrates. The fossil trails of bilaterals provide compelling evidence of an increase in behavioral complexity across the Vendian-Cambrian boundary. Still, the simplicity of neural organization in some extant invertebrates has been extremely appealing and useful. Nervous systems with relatively few components (e.g., the 302 neurons of *C. elegans*!) are ideal for the cellular and molecular analysis of simple behavioral outputs, including some forms of plasticity. Knowledge of the manner in which these simple systems operate is also useful in understanding the workings of more complex systems, such as those of higher vertebrates.

As shown in ***Chapter 8,*** vertebrate nervous systems have evolved complex networks that subserve a wide variety of behavioral functions by using the same building blocks, the neurons, that are found in invertebrate nervous systems. Both character stability and novelty are combined in the evolution of the vertebrate nervous system. A transition from simple to relatively more complex nervous systems and sensory systems is documented in the agnathans, or jawless fish. Just as the social insects represent a zenith of behavioral complexity for the invertebrates, the primates constitute one of the vertebrate pinnacles in neural and behavioral complexity, as described in ***Chapter 9.*** Primate history is characterized by several episodes of increase in relative brain size. Primates have larger brains than most mammals, and hominids have, in turn, larger brains than nonhominid species. The evidence for tool making in early *Homo* spp. and the emergence of language, culture, and worldwide migrations provide striking evidence of behavioral complexity. These also stand as major examples of biological complexity.

Many instances of transitions in complexity were described in connection with developmental processes. Among the animals, a major transition involved the emergence of mesoderm in the earliest bilaterals, or triploblastic animals, which allowed for the emergence of a wide variety of body plans. ***Chapter 10*** also reviewed the role of hormones and experience in the development of the vertebrate brain, whereas ***Chapters 11*** and ***12*** discussed the extensive effects of early learning on adult behavior, particularly in birds and mammals, and the emergence of complex behaviors such as tool use in primates. Neural systems and behavior illustrate the intricate set of coactions among levels of organization that characterize epigenetic development.

Finally, evidence presented in ***Chapter 14*** also points to the evolution of complex behaviors in the food-storing behavior of birds and its correlation with an enlarged hippocampal formation (***section 2.c.***); the attentional and emotional modulation of instrumental behavior in mammals (***sections 2.e.*** and ***2.f.***); the greater reliance of apes on rule learning (***section 2.g.***); and the existence of higher cognitive abilities in a handful of animals intensively trained in the acquisition of abstract concepts, numerical competence, and linguistic communication (***section 3***).

Despite enormous progress during the 20th century, any reasonable assessment of the current state of comparative psychology would probably conclude that we have only scratched the surface. Our understanding of the evolution and development of behavior is in its infancy. The advancement of comparative psychology now requires a new generation of researchers who can make contact with the fundamental principles of evolutionary and developmental biology, neuroscience, ecology, paleontology, and many other areas, without losing the perspective provided by psychology.

5. KEY TERMS

addition 570
anticipatory frustration 553
anticipatory goal responses 560
attention 550
behavior system 546
cognition 563
complexity 580
concept 564
conditional discriminations 561
contextual variables 541
continuity view 556
control by equation 541
control by systematic variation 541
counting 568
delayed matching to sample (DMTS) 548
differential-outcome effect 561
divergence 540
ecological view 543
equipotentiality 543
extra-dimensional transfer 551
generalization gradient 565
general-process view 543
generative process 571
hippocampal formation 549
homology 540
homoplasy 540
insight 556
intra-dimensional transfer 551
language comprehension 572
language production 572
latent inhibition 550
learning-performance dichotomy 541
learning set 558

magnitude of reinforcement extinction effect (MREE) 555
mental continuity 580
misbehavior 546
neophobia 544
number 568
partial reinforcement extinction effect (PREE) 555
primary frustration 553
same/different concept 566
secondary generalization 565
selective associations 543
species-specific defense responses (SSDRs) 546
S-R associations 559
S-S associations 559
stimulus trace 545
successive negative contrast (SNC) 553
surprising nonreward 552
syntax 573
transfer 558
win-stay, lose-shift rule 558

6. References

Amsel, A. (1992). *Frustration theory.* Cambridge: Cambridge University Press.

Balda, R. P., & Kamil, A. C. (1989). A comparative study of cache recovery by three corvid species. *Animal Behaviour,* **38,** 486–495.

Batson, J. D., & Best, P. J. (1979). Drug-preexposure effects in flavor-aversion learning: Associative interference by conditioned environmental stimuli. *Journal of Experimental Psychology: Animal Behavior Processes,* **5,** 273–283.

Bitterman, M. E. (1975). The comparative analysis of learning. *Science,* **188,** 699–709.

Blanchard, D. C. (1997). Stimulus, environmental, and pharmacological control of defensive behaviors. In M. E. Bouton & M. S. Fanselow (Eds.), *Learning, motivation, and cognition. The functional behaviorism of Robert C. Bolles* (pp. 283–303). Washington: American Psychological Association.

Bolles, R. C. (1970). Species-specific defense reactions and avoidance learning. *Psychological Review,* **77,** 32–48.

Bonner, J. T. (1988). *The evolution of complexity by means of natural selection.* Princeton: Princeton University Press.

Boysen, S. T., & Berntson, G. G. (1989). Numerical competence in a chimpanzee (*Pan troglodytes*). *Journal of Comparative Psychology,* **103,** 23–31.

Brannon, E. M., & Terrace, H. S. (2000). Representation of the numerosities 1–9 by rhesus macaques (*Macaca mulatta*). *Journal of Experimental Psychology: Animal Behavior Processes,* **26,** 31–49.

Breland, K., & Breland, M. (1961). The misbehavior of organisms. *American Psychologist,* **16,** 681–684.

Breukelaar, J. W. C., & Dalrymple-Alford, J. C. (1998). Timing ability and numerical competence in rats. *Journal of Experimental Psychology: Animal Behavior Processes,* **24,** 84–97.

Brodbeck, D. R. (1994). Memory for spatial and local cues: A comparison of a storing and a nonstoring species. *Animal Learning & Behavior,* **22,** 119–133.

Colwill, R. M., & Rescorla, R. A. (1986). Associative structures in instrumental learning. *Psychology of Learning & Motivation,* **20,** 55–104.

Couvillon, P. A., Tennant, W. A., & Bitterman, M. E. (1976). Intradimensional vs. extradimensional transfer in the discriminative learning of goldfish and pigeons. *Animal Learning & Behavior,* **4,** 197–203.

Daly, H. B. (1974). Reinforcing properties of escape from frustration aroused in various learning situations. *Psychology of Learning & Motivation,* **8,** 187–231.

Daly, M., Rauschenberger, J., & Behrends, P. (1982). Food-aversion learning in kangaroo rats: A specialist-generalist comparison. *Animal Learning & Behavior,* **10,** 314–320.

D'Amato, M. R., & Van Sant, P. (1988). The person concept in monkeys (*Cebus apella*). *Journal of Experimental Psychology: Animal Behavior Processes,* **14,** 43–55.

Dantzer, R., Arnone, M., & Mormade, P. (1980). Effects of frustration on behaviour and plasma corticosteroid levels in pigs. *Physiology & Behavior,* **24,** 1–4.

Davis, H., & Pérusse, R. (1988). Numerical competence in animals: Definitional issues, current evidence, and a new research agenda. *Behavioral & Brain Sciences,* **11,** 561–615.

Dickinson, A. (1980). *Contemporary animal learning theory.* Cambridge: Cambridge University Press.

Domjan, M. (1980). Ingestional aversion learning: Unique and general processes. In J. S. Rosenblatt, R. A. Hinde, C. Beer, & M. C. Busnel (Eds.), *Advances in the study of behavior* (Vol. 11, pp. 276–330). New York: Academic Press.

Domjan, M., & Galef, B. G. Jr. (1983). Biological constraints on instrumental and classical conditioning: Retrospect and prospect. *Animal Learning & Behavior,* **11,** 151–161.

Elliott, M. H. (1928). The effect of change of reward on the maze performance of rats. *University of California Publications in Psychology,* **4,** 19–30.

Epstein, R. (1987). The spontaneous interconnection of four repertoires of behavior in a pigeon (*Columba livia*). *Journal of Comparative Psychology,* **101,** 197–201.

Fanselow, M. S. (1994). Neural organization of the defensive behavior system responsible for fear. *Psychonomic Bulletin & Review,* **1,** 429–438.

Feldon, J., & Gray, J. A. (1981). The partial reinforcement extinction effect after treatment with chlordiazepoxide. *Psychopharmacology,* **73,** 269–275.

Flaherty, C. F., Becker, H. C., & Pohorecky, L. (1985). Correlation of corticosterone elevation and negative contrast varies as a function of postshift day. *Animal Learning & Behavior,* **13,** 309–314.

Fouts, R. S., & Fouts, D. H. (1989). Loulis in conversation with the cross-fostered chimpanzees. In R. A. Gardner, B. T. Gardner, & T. E. Van Cantfort (Eds.), *Teaching Sign Language to Chimpanzees* (pp. 293–307). Albany: State University of New York Press.

Franchina, J. J., & Brown, T. S. (1971). Reward magnitude shift effects in rats with hippocampal lesions. *Journal of Comparative & Physiological Psychology,* **76,** 365–370.

Garcia, J., & Koelling, R. A. (1966). Relation of cue to consequence in avoidance learning. *Psychonomic Science,* **4,** 123–124.

Gardner, R. A., & Gardner, B. T. (1969). Teaching sign language to a chimpanzee. *Science,* **165,** 664–672.

Gisiner, R., & Schusterman, R. J. (1992). Sequence, syntax, and semantics: Responses of a language-trained sea lion (*Zalophus californianus*) to novel sign combinations. *Journal of Comparative Psychology,* **106,** 78–91.

Harlow, H. (1949). The formation of learning sets. *Psychological Review,* **56,** 51–65.

Healy, S. D., & Krebs, J. R. (1992a). Delayed-matching-to-sample by marsh tits and great tits. *Quarterly Journal of Experimental Psychology,* **45B,** 33–47.

Healy, S. D., & Krebs, J. R. (1992b). Comparing spatial memory in two species of tit: Recalling a single positive location. *Animal Learning & Behavior,* **20,** 121–126.

Healy, S. D., & Krebs, J. R. (1996). Food storing and the hippocampus in Paridae. *Brain, Behavior & Evolution,* **47,** 195–199.

Herman, L. M., Pack, A. A., & Morrel-Samuels, P. (1993). Representational and conceptual skills of dolphins. In H. L. Roitblat, L. M. Herman, & P. E. Nachtigall (Eds.), *Language and communication: Comparative perspectives* (pp. 403–442). Hillsdale: Erlbaum.

Herrnstein, R. J., & Loveland, D. H. (1964). Complex visual concept in the pigeon. *Science,* **146,** 549–551.

Hillix, W. A., & Rumbaugh, D. M. (1998). Language in animals. In G. Greenberg & M. Haraway (Eds.), *Comparative psychology. A handbook* (pp. 837–848). New York: Garland.

Holland, P. C. (1981). Acquisition of representation-mediated conditioned food-aversions. *Learning & Motivation,* **12,** 1–18.

Hopkins, W. D., & Morris, R. D. (1993). Hemispheric priming as a technique in the study of lateralized cognitive processes in chimpanzees: Some recent findings. In H. L. Roitblat, L. M. Herman, & P. E. Nachtigall (Eds.), *Language and communication: Comparative perspectives* (pp. 291–309). Hillsdale: Erlbaum.

Hull, C. L. (1931). Goal attraction and directing ideas conceived as habit phenomena. *Psychological Review,* **38,** 487–506.

Hull, C. L. (1943). *Principles of behavior.* New York: Appleton-Century-Crofts.

Kamil, A. C., Balda, R. P., & Olson, D. J. (1994). Performance of four seed-caching corvid species in the radial-arm maze analog. *Journal of Comparative Psychology,* **108,** 385–393.

Köhler, W. (1925). *The mentality of apes.* London: Routledge & Kegan Paul.

Krane, R. V., & Wagner, A. R. (1975). Taste aversion learning with delayed shock US: Implications for the "generality of the laws of learning." *Journal of Comparative & Physiological Psychology,* **88,** 882–889.

Kruse, J. M., Overmier, J. B., Konz, W. A., & Rokke, E. (1983). Pavlovian conditioning stimulus effects upon instrumental choice behavior are reinforcer specific. *Learning & Motivation,* **14,** 165–181.

Logue, A. W. (1979). Taste aversion and the generality of the laws of learning. *Psychological Bulletin,* **86,** 276–296.

Lowes, G., & Bitterman, M. E. (1967). Reward and learning in the goldfish. *Science,* **157,** 455–457.

McShea, D. W. (1993). Evolutionary change in the morphological complexity of the mammalian vertebral column. *Evolution,* **47,** 730–740.

McShea, D. W. (1996). Metazoan complexity and evolution: Is there a trend? *Evolution,* **50,** 477–492.

Miles, H. L. W. (1990). The cognitive foundations for reference in a signing orangutan. In S. T. Parker & K. R. Gibson (Eds.), *Language and intelligence in monkeys and apes: Comparative developmental perspectives* (pp. 511–539). Cambridge: Cambridge University Press.

Morin, P.-P., Dodson, J. J., & Doré, F. Y. (1990). Facilitative effect of preexposure on heart-rate conditioning to an olfactory cue in Atlantic salmon (*Salmo salar*). *Journal of Comparative Psychology,* **104,** 340–344.

Mustaca, A. E., Bentosela, M., & Papini, M. R. (2000). Consummatory successive negative contrast in mice. *Learning & Motivation,* **31.**

Olson, D. J. (1991). Species differences in spatial memory among Clark's nutcrackers, scrub jays, and pigeons. *Journal of Experimental Psychology: Animal Behavior Processes,* **17,** 363–376.

Papini, M. R. (1997). Role of reinforcement in spaced-trial operant learning in pigeons (*Columba livia*). *Journal of Comparative Psychology,* **111,** 275–285.

Papini, M. R., Mustaca, A. E., & Bitterman, M. E. (1988). Successive negative contrast in the consummatory responding of didelphid marsupials. *Animal Learning & Behavior,* **16,** 53–57.

Patterson, F. L. (1990). Language acquisition by a lowland gorilla: Koko's first ten years of vocabulary development. *Word,* **41,** 97–143.

Pepperberg, I. M. (1987). Acquisition of the same/different concept by an African Grey parrot (*Psittacus erithacus*): Learning with respect to categories of color, shape, and material. *Animal Learning & Behavior,* **15,** 423–432.

Pepperberg, I. M. (1993). Cognition and communication in an African Grey parrot (*Psittacus erithacus*): Studies on a nonhuman, nonprimate, nonmammalian subject. In H. L. Roitblat, L. M. Herman, & P. E. Nachtigall (Eds.), *Language and communication: Comparative perspectives* (pp. 221–248). Hillsdale: Erlbaum.

Premack, D. (1976). *Intelligence in ape and man.* Hillsdale: Erlbaum.

Rescorla, R. A. (1971). Summation and retardation tests of latent inhibition. *Journal of Comparative & Physiological Psychology,* **75,** 77–81.

Rumbaugh, D. M., Washburn, D. A., & Hillix, W. A. (1996). Respondents, operants, and emergents: Toward an integrated perspective on behavior. In K. Pribram & J. King (Eds), *Learning as a self-organizing process* (pp. 57–73). Hillsdale: Erlbaum.

Salas, C., Broglio, C., Rodriguez, F., Lopez, J. C., Portavella, M., & Torres, B. (1996). Telencephalic ablation in goldfish impairs performance in a spatial constancy problem but not in a cued one. *Behavioural Brain Research,* **79,** 193–200.

Savage-Rumbaugh, E. S. (1993). Language learnability in man, ape, and dolphin. In H. L. Roitblat, L. M. Herman, & P. E. Nachtigall (Eds.), *Language and communication: Comparative perspectives* (pp. 457–484). Hillsdale: Erlbaum.

Savage-Rumbaugh, E. S., Murphy, J., Sevcik, R. A., Brakke, K. E., Williams, S. L., & Rumbaugh, D. M. (1993). Language comprehension in ape and child. *Monographs of the Society for Research in Child Development,* **58**(3–4), Serial No. 233.

Savage-Rumbaugh, E. S., Rumbaugh, D. M., & Boysen, S. (1978). Symbolic communication between two chimpanzees (*Pan troglodytes*). *Science,* **201,** 641–644.

Schusterman, R. J., & Krieger, K. (1984). California sea lions are capable of semantic comprehension. *Psychological Record,* **34,** 3–23.

Shapiro, K. L., Jacobs, W. J., & LoLordo, V. M. (1980). Stimulus-reinforcer interactions in Pavlovian conditioning of pigeons: Implications for selective associations. *Animal Learning & Behavior,* **8,** 586–594.

Sherry, D. F., Jacobs, L. F., & Gaulin, S. J. C. (1992). Spatial memory and adaptive specialization of the hippocampus. *Trends in Neuroscience,* **15,** 298–303.

Sherry, D. F., Vaccarino, A. L., Buckenham, K., & Herz, R. S. (1989). The hippocampal complex of food-storing birds. *Brain, Behavior & Evolution,* **34,** 308–317.

Shettleworth, S. J. (1978). Reinforcement and the organization of behavior in golden hamsters: Punishment of three action patterns. *Learning & Motivation,* **9,** 99–123.

Shishimi, A. (1985). Latent inhibition experiments with goldfish (*Carassius auratus*). *Journal of Comparative Psychology,* **99,** 316–327.

Sutherland, N. S., & Mackintosh, N. J. (1971). *Mechanisms of animal discrimination learning.* New York: Academic Press.

Terrace, H. S. (1979). *Nim.* New York: Knopf.

Terrace, H. S., Petitto, L. A., Sanders, R. J., & Bever, T. G. (1979). Can an ape create a sentence? *Science,* **206,** 891–902.

Thomas, R. K. (1980). Evolution of intelligence: An approach to its assessments. *Brain, Behavior, & Evolution,* **17,** 454–472.

Thorndike, E. L. (1911). *Animal intelligence.* New York: Macmillan.

Tinklepaugh, O. L. (1928). An experimental study of representative factors in monkeys. *Journal of Comparative Psychology,* **8,** 197–236.

Tolman, E. C. (1932). *Purposive behavior in animals and men.* New York: Irvington.

Trapold, M. A. (1970). Are expectancies based upon different positive reinforcing events discriminably different? *Learning & Motivation,* **1,** 129–140.

Trapold, M. A., & Overmier, J. B. (1972). The second learning process in instrumental learning. In A. H. Black & W. F. Prokasy (Eds.), *Classical conditioning. II. Current research and theory* (pp. 427–452). New York: Appleton-Century-Crofts.

Wasserman, E. A., DeVolder, C. L., & Coppage, D. J. (1992). Non-similarity-based conceptualization in pigeons via secondary or mediated generalization. *Psychological Science,* **3,** 374–379.

Watanabe, M. (1996). Reward expectancy in primate prefrontal neurons. *Nature,* **382,** 629–632.

Wilcoxon, H. C., Dragoin, W. B., & Kral, P. A. (1971). Illness-induced aversions in rat and quail: Relative salience of visual and gustatory cues. *Science,* **171,** 826–828.

Wright, A. A., Shyan, M. R., & Jitsumori, M. (1990). Auditory same/different concept learning by monkeys. *Animal Learning & Behavior,* **18,** 287–294.

Yerkes, R. M. (1916). *The mental life of monkeys and apes.* New York: Holt.

Glossary of Key Concepts

acceleration An example of peramorphosis in which a particular trait develops earlier in the descendant than it did in the ancestor.

Acheulean technology The tool kit characteristic of later hominids (e.g., *Homo ergaster*), consisting of stones modeled on both sides, and including hand axes, picks, and cleavers.

acoelomates Triploblastic animals (e.g., planarians) that lack a coelom—an internal cavity with organs.

acquisition Gaining of information through experience.

action potential (AP) An all-or-none electrochemical potential transmitted through the neuron's axon at constant speed and amplitude.

activating and organizing effects of hormones Hormones can have relatively fast and transient activating effects on cells, or they may affect the organization of tissue, particularly when acting during early developmental stages.

adaptation A trait that evolved by natural selection.

adaptationism A view that maintains that an organism is a collection of traits that evolved by natural selection.

adaptive landscape A metaphor of speciation that includes hills and valleys. Populations are supposed to be pushed up a hill by natural selection into a specialized set of traits. Moving down the hill represents maladaptive change. Such movement may be driven by nonselective factors, such as genetic drift.

adaptive radiation The relatively abrupt emergence of taxonomic diversity over a geologically short period of time.

adaptive significance Contribution of a particular trait to the individual's inclusive fitness. One of the four causal levels in the study of behavior according to Tinbergen's (1963) classification.

addition Ability to summate quantities that follows from the acquisition of the number concept.

age-dependent or age-independent plasticity Vocal learning in different species of birds that occurs either during a sensitive period (i.e., age dependent) or throughout the life of the animal (i.e., age independent).

aggressive behavior Potentially or actually harmful agonistic interactions between conspecifics.

aggressive mimicry Crypticity of a sit-and-wait predator.

agonistic behavior Spectrum of behaviors that may be activated in an aggressive-defensive situation, including aggressive responses, threat displays, and submissive behavior.

alarm calls Vocalizations that induce antipredator defensive behavior in the recipient.

alarm substance Substances (e.g., pheromones) that induce defensive behavior.

alleles Different versions of homologous genes (genes located in the same locus in homologous chromosomes) present in different animals within a population.

allometric growth The positive correlation, computed on a sample of species, that exists between the size of individual organs and the size of the body. The relationship is described by the allometric equation $\mathbf{E = aS^b}$, in which **E** represents the size of an organ (the brain, in this case), **S** is body size, and **a** and **b** are parameters derived from the analysis. When $\mathbf{b = 1}$, the organ is said to exhibit isometric growth—that is, it increases one unit for each unit of increase in body size. Positive allometry occurs when $\mathbf{b > 1}$, whereas negative allometry occurs when $\mathbf{b < 1}$.

alpha responses Responses elicited by the CS and based on the same effector system as that of the CR.

alternative mating strategies The different reproductive behaviors in which males of the same species may engage. In some cases, alternative strategies demand different phenotypes, whereas in other cases males adopt different behaviors depending on what other males are doing.

altricial young Young animals born with eyes closed and minimal locomotor abilities.

altruism A social interaction between an agent and a recipient in which the agent engages in a behavior at a cost, whereas the recipient is the beneficiary of that behavior. Cost and benefit are ultimately measured in terms of inclusive fitness.

amniotic egg The main synapomorphy of the amniotes (i.e., reptiles, birds, and mammals). The amniotic egg provides yolk to the embryo and includes the amnion and allantois, two membranes that reduce dehydration.

anagenesis Speciation within a single lineage, without divergence.

Animalia (or Metazoa) A kingdom that includes multicellular eukaryotes that obtain nutrients by ingestion (e.g., animals).

antennapedia mutant A mutant *Drosophila* for homeotic gene number 6, known as antennapedia because it produces a pair of legs in place of the normal pair of antennae.

anticipatory goal responses Responses similar to those exhibited in the goal area when in contact with the reinforcer, but occurring in advance. Such a response could also be interpreted as an expectancy of the reinforcer if the responses are conceptualized as internal.

apomorphy Derived trait.

apoptosis Selective neuronal death.

aposematic coloration Presence of bright colors and clear patterns of stripes in the body of certain animals.

appetitive stimuli and reinforcers Appetitive stimuli are events that induce approach responses. Appetitive reinforcers are events that support instrumental learning when they are presented immediately after the occurrence of a response.

appetitive-consummatory behavior Components of instinctive behavior. Consummatory responses (e.g., eating, drinking) are relatively fixed and stereotyped, whereas appetitive responses (e.g., searching, orienting) are flexible and complex.

arboreal life A tree-dwelling lifestyle characteristic of many primates.

artificial selection Selective breeding of animals and plants carried out by humans with the purpose of domestication, animal or plant production, or scientific research.

asexual reproduction The production of new individuals without meiosis or fertilization. Two examples of asexual reproduction include budding (reproduction by outgrowth of a part, as in cnidarians) and parthenogenesis (reproduction from unfertilized eggs, as in some lizards).

assembly calls Maternal vocalizations that induce approach behavior in the offspring.

association cortex Areas in the neocortex of mammals that are primarily concerned with neither sensory nor motor functions.

attachment Mother-infant bond involving individual recognition, a preference for the attached organism, and an aversive response to separation.

attention Ability to focus selectively on a subset of all the stimuli present at one time.

autonomic nervous system (ANS) A part of the peripheral nervous system that includes a sympathetic branch, responsible for changes associated with escape behaviors (e.g., increase in heart rate), and the parasympathetic branch, generally having effects that are opposite to those of the sympathetic branch (e.g., decrease in heart rate).

aversive stimuli and reinforcers Aversive stimuli are events that induce withdrawal responses. Aversive reinforcers are events that support instrumental learning when they are withdrawn immediately after the occurrence of a response.

avoidance conditioning, active and passive In an active avoidance task, the animal acquires a response that terminates a signal (e.g., a tone) for an aversive primary reinforcer (e.g., a shock). In a passive avoidance task, the animal learns to avoid a location previously paired with an aversive primary reinforcer. Avoidance responses also prevent the delivery of the primary reinforcer.

backward conditioning A classical conditioning situation in which the US precedes the CS.

basicraneal flexure Orientation of several points at the base of the cranium of hominids that permits an appreciation of the way in which muscles controlling the movements of the vocal apparatus were inserted.

Bateman's principle Inverse relationship between parental investment and variation in reproductive success of males versus females.

Batesian mimicry Convergence in coloration of mimic, edible species with their unpalatable, toxic models.

begging response A response typical of altricial birds. Upon arrival of a parent to the nest, the nestlings vigorously open their mouths and induce their parent to deliver food.

behavior system A view according to which responses designed to deal with a particular resource (e.g., feeding responses to deal with food) are organized into a system.

behavioral neophenotypes The development of new phenotypic traits as a result of a change in behavior (e.g., nutrition preferences) that induces the expression of previously silent genes.

behaviorism An approach to psychology that emphasizes behavior as the object of study and concentrates on observable events (e.g., stimuli and responses) that can be measured and manipulated objectively.

below-zero habituation Habituation involves the complete elimination of a particular response (i.e., zero frequency of occurrence). If the stimulus continues to be presented for an additional number of trials, then, although no further changes occur, the response will exhibit lower levels of recovery (e.g., spontaneous recovery is reduced) as if the response would have fallen below a zero frequency.

between-group and within-group design Designs in which subjects are either assigned to only one of the conditions of the experiment (between group) or tested under all the conditions of the experiment (within group).

bilateral symmetry Organisms that exhibit an anterior-posterior axis and paired bodily parts (e.g., humans).

bimanual dexterity Differential use of the hands during object manipulation.

binaural audition A comparison of auditory information reaching both ears that is used to locate the source of a stimulus.

biological intelligence The capacity of animals to develop internal representations of the environment based on sensory-perceptual information.

bipedality Locomotion on the hind legs. A trait unique to hominids among the primates.

biogenetic law Haeckel's generalization, according to which ontogeny recapitulates phylogeny.

bithorax mutant A mutant fruitfly (*Drosophila*) characterized by the development of two pairs of wings (the wild type exhibits one pair).

blastopore The point at which cells invaginate to form the endoderm during the gastrula stage.

blastula stage A stage of embryonic development arising soon after fertilization and characterized as a hollow ball of cells.

blocking Previous conditioning of one element, A+, impairs (or blocks) later conditioning of an added element, B, to an AB+ compound stimulus.

body plan (or Bauplan) A basic set of homologous structural traits common to all the species in a particular taxon.

brachiation The use of hands and arms to move from one tree branch to another.

brain An anterior enlargement of the CNS. In vertebrates, the size (weight or volume) of the brain can, in some cases, be measured or estimated from fossil crania, an important source of data for an understanding of brain evolution.

brainstem A portion of the rhombencephalon of vertebrates that includes the medulla, pons, and tegmentum.

Broca's aphasia Impairment of speech articulation produced by lesions of the frontal cortex.

brood parasitism In several species of birds, females lay eggs in the nests of other species. These eggs are thus incubated by foster parents that also eventually care for the chicks.

Burgess Shale fauna Fossil fauna from the mid-Cambrian (about 520 Mya) first discovered at Burgess Shale, Canada, and now known to have worldwide distribution. Specimens attributable to several extant phyla have been clearly identified.

calls Relatively simple vocalizations.

cAMP (cyclic adenosine monophosphate) A second-messenger system present in the cytoplasm of a variety of cells, including neurons. When activated, cAMP production can ultimately induce gene transcription in the cell nucleus and thus affect the density of membrane receptors at the synapse. The cAMP pathway has been implicated in a variety of functions, including associative learning.

canalization Extent to which a particular trait develops relatively independently of environmental pressures.

caravaning behavior A physical attachment of mother and offspring observed in insectivore mammals of the family Crocidurinae. During a period after giving birth, the mother stimulates her offspring to grab her fur with their teeth, and to grab each other; this results in a tandem formation.

cellular differentiation Cells diverging in morphology and becoming specialized for a particular function.

central and peripheral nervous system The central nervous system (CNS) includes the neural tissue located in the ganglia (invertebrates) or in the brain and spinal cord (vertebrates). It is distinguished from the peripheral nervous system, a set of nerves that connect the CNS with receptors, organs, and muscles in the periphery of the body.

central pattern generator (CPG) A neural network that controls a sequentially organized series of behaviors without relying on sensory feedback from each individual component.

central place foraging A situation in which a foraging animal carries food items to a location different from that in which the item was found or seized (e.g., burrow, nest).

central sulcus A sulcus that divides the frontal lobe from the parietal lobe.

cerebellum A structure located dorsally with respect to the brainstem and posteriorly with respect to the cerebral hemispheres. The cerebellum has a cortex and subcortical nuclei, and it participates in a wide variety of functions, including sensory processing (e.g., electroreception) and motor control (e.g., fine coordination of movement).

cerebral cortex An external layer of cell bodies in the telencephalon of reptiles, birds, and mammals. Three types are recognized. The archicortex involves the hippocampal formation of amniotes. The paleocortex contains up to three cell layers, and it is present in amniotes. The neocortex contains up to six cell layers, and it is clearly present only in mammals.

character displacement Natural selection favors the evolution of anatomical and physiological specializations that optimize resource exploitation. When animals compete for the same resource, competitive exclusion may lead to the evolution of distinct phenotypes and even speciation by displacing homologous characters away from each other in competing populations.

character similarity Degree of similarity in morphological and functional characters across species within a given taxon—a major source of information in the development of taxonomies and phylogenetic histories.

chemical imprinting The establishment of a preference for the place where an organism spent the early period of its development based on chemical cues present in that location.

chemoaffinity hypothesis The theory that ameboid movements of the growth cones of neurons are guided by molecular gradients of substances released by target neurons.

chimeric animal An animal created with DNA fragments from more than two animals.

circadian and circannual rhythms Behavioral or physiological cycles with periods close to either 24 hr or 1 year.

clade A monophyletic group of lineages.

cladogenesis Speciation by divergence.

cladogram A hypothesis of divergence among the lineages within a clade based on synapomorphies (i.e., shared derived characters).

classical (or Pavlovian) conditioning An instance of associative learning based on exposure to two or more stimuli that occur in close temporal or spatial contiguity.

classical conditioning theory of imprinting The proposal that initially neutral features of an imprinting stimulus acquire significance by virtue of their contiguity with initially salient features (e.g., movement) of the same imprinting stimulus.

claustrum A sheet of neurons located underneath the insular lobe and unique to primates. Its functions are poorly known.

cleavage Initial cell divisions of the zygote.

clonal species Species in which all individuals are genetically identical by virtue of asexual reproduction.

coaction Interactions among existing components of a developing organism that may give rise to new properties. Horizontal coactions occur within a given level (e.g., cell-molecular), whereas vertical coactions occur across levels (e.g., behavioral-morphological).

coadaptation The alleles controlling a particular phenotype may become associated into clusters by the action of natural selection. This coadaptation of gene clusters is disrupted in artificial selection experiments, so that when the selective pressure is relaxed the trait tends to exhibit genetic homeostasis.

coalitions A group of unrelated individuals that provide assistance to one another (i.e., reciprocity).

coefficient of relatedness (r) Proportion of genes shared by two individuals.

coefficient of variation (CV) A measure of variability independent of the mean size (CV = standard deviation / mean).

coelomates A group of phyla characterized by the possession of an internal cavity called a coelom (e.g., arthropods, chordates). The coelom allowed for the evolution of larger internal organs and stronger muscles.

coevolution The evolution of species associations (e.g., flowering plants and their polinators; predators and their prey). Each component of a coevolving system evolves adaptations that either facilitate or interfere with the association.

cognition The ability to know. As an area of psychology, cognition is traditionally involved with the processes of perception, learning, memorizing, thinking, and judging.

cognitive map An internal representation of the spatial features of a particular environment that allows the animal efficient movement across locations.

collothalamus A field of thalamic nuclei (diencephalon) characterized by afferent input from the superior and inferior colliculi.

command neuron A unit, or a small network, responsible for activating a pattern of behavior.

communication The release of a message encoded in a medium that a recipient (usually a conspecific) is able to decode and interpret. Messages may involve scents, vocalizations, visual signals, etc.

comparative psychology The study of the evolutionary and developmental basis of behavior. Almost an interdisciplinary area by definition, it originated during the 19th century from the intersection of experimental psychology and evolutionary biology.

compensatory response A response, conditioned or unconditioned, that opposes a physiological reaction induced by a stimulus.

competitive exclusion Specialization in the exploitation of resources that may lead to divergent evolution.

complexity The quality, or state, of a system having many different components and interrelations among the components.

compound conditioning Conditioning of the individual elements of a complex cue.

concept A category of related exemplars.

conditional discriminations Discriminations in which one stimulus, A, signals that one response, R, is correct and another response, L, is incorrect, whereas another stimulus, B, signals the opposite arrangement. In abbreviated notation: A—›R+/A —›L– and B—›L+/B—›R–.

conditioned analgesia A stimulus (e.g., a tone) that predicts the imminent presentation of a painful event (e.g., electric shock) elicits an analgesic response that raises the animal's threshold for pain.

conditioned immunomodulation Ability of conditioning processes to modulate (i.e., enhance or interfere with) immune responses.

conditioned suppression A complex training situation: Animals receive training in some form of appetitive task (e.g., licking water from a tube). Then, while water is not present, animals receive Pavlovian pairings between a CS and an aversive US (e.g., tone-shock pairings). Finally, animals are reexposed to the appetitive task, and eventually the CS is presented. The degree of suppression in the appetitive response (e.g., suppression of licking) reflects the strength of the CS.

consistency index In cladistic analysis, a measure of the goodness of fit between the minimum tree length possible, given the number of characters analyzed, and the tree length actually obtained (i.e., the number of character changes assumed in a cladogram).

constraints In optimal foraging models, constraints refer to aspects of the situation that limit the animal's decisions about foraging. For example, a foraging animal may need to allocate time and effort to detecting the presence of predators, at the expense of feeding itself.

contact comfort Touch among animals, particularly in primates, that provides an important source of information for the development of attachments.

contextual conditioning Conditioning of the static cues present in the situation where training takes place.

contextual variables In the comparative analysis of learning, contextual variables are nonlearning factors that can affect behavior independently of learning, including sensory-perceptual, motivational, and motor factors. In the analysis of cognitive phenomena, associative learning processes are often treated as contextual factors. Explanations based on contextual factors are considered more parsimonious and must thus be excluded before a difference in behavior across species can be safely attributed to different learning or cognitive processes.

contiguity A fundamental determinant of associative learning that refers to events occurring close together in time or space.

continental drift The movement of continental masses that rest on rigid tectonic plates. The plates float on a layer of melted rock called the mantle, approximately 100 km beneath the earth's surface. They move slowly, changing places, colliding with one another, and modifying the distribution of land masses.

contingency-degradation effect An impairment of response to a CS that results from the presentation of unsignaled USs intermixed with regular CS-US pairings.

continuity view of learning The view according to which associative learning progresses gradually (i.e., trial-and-error learning).

continuous and partial reinforcement Conditioning procedures in which every CS or every response is paired with the presentation of the reinforcer (continuous) or in which only some subset of CSs or responses is paired with the reinforcer (partial).

control by equation The assumption that equal conditions of training applied to different species equate all contextual factors, thus allowing for a direct species comparison in performance. This assumption is generally impossible to substantiate.

control by systematic variation Manipulation of training variables in learning experiments with different species that permits an assessment of the extent to which animals from different species exhibit similar functional regularities between such variables and their behavior.

controllability A psychological dimension that refers to the animal's expectation that events in the environment will be under the control of its own behavior.

convergence Character similarity across species that evolves independently from different primitive characters. An instance of homoplasy.

cooperation The combined efforts of two or more animals to achieve a benefit that is not available to one alone.

Cope's law The hypothesis that lineages tend to the evolution of species of increasing body size.

copulatory behavior Sexual intercourse between male and female.

correlated traits A trait that evolves not because it is directly under positive selective pressure, but because it is genetically associated to other traits that are themselves positively selected.

cortex An external, peripheral laminar sheet, usually including several distinct layers of cell somas.

cost-benefit analysis An approach used by optimal foraging models in particular, and by adaptive-functional approaches to behavior in general, according to which adaptations evolve as a trade-off between reproductive benefits and costs.

counterbalance In learning experiments, a procedure designed to demonstrate that the associations between events, and not the events themselves, are responsible for the observed behavioral changes. For example, in a differential conditioning task of the form A+/B–, counterbalancing stimulus assignments would involve to expose half of the animals to the A+/B– problem and the remaining animals to the B+/A– problem. If the discrimination occurs in both conditions, then it cannot be attributed to the individual stimuli, A and B, having unique behavioral properties. Rather, the discrimination is attributable to the relationship between each stimulus and the reinforcer.

counting Ability to assign a numerical tag to a set of objects, to use the same tags independently of the objects being counted, and to assign ordinal properties to those tags.

creationism The biblical postulate according to which all species were created simultaneously and independently by a superior being.

critical period A concept introduced by the classic ethologists (e.g., Lorenz and Tinbergen) to describe cases in which learning is preprogrammed to occur during a specific period of time. Since the onset and offset of such periods are more malleable than originally thought, the term "sensitive period" has come into common use.

cross-sectional design A type of developmental research in which independent groups of animals differing in age are observed under a certain set of conditions to determine changes in behavior as a function of age.

crypticity Ability to match external appearance with the background.

crystallized song An adult bird song that is the result of a process of vocal learning.

CS-US interval The time between onset of the CS and onset of the US. An important determinant of the strength of the CR in classical conditioning situations.

cue-validity effect Intermixing of AB+ and A+ trials impairs conditioning of B.

culture A set of standardized practices acquired or developed by one or a few individuals that disseminate to other members of the group and are passed across generations via social learning.

C-value paradox The fact that the number of base pairs (or C value) in the genotype of a wide variety of animals appears to bear no correlation to the degree of phenotypic complexity of the animal.

darting behavior In a reproductive context, the behavior of a female rodent. She may run and stop in front of a male, adopting a copulatory posture known as lordosis.

Darwinian (or direct) fitness Traits that contribute to maximize the number of offspring produced by an organism are said to have high Darwinian fitness.

deception Providing incorrect information about the availability of food or other resources to a potential competitor. Deception implies intentionality, a difficult issue to resolve in animal behavior research.

delay (or forward) conditioning A basic procedure in classical conditioning according to which the CS is presented before the US.

delay of reinforcement gradient The longer the temporal gap between the occurrence of the instrumental response and the delivery of the reinforcer, the slower the acquisition of the response.

delayed matching to sample (DMTS) A task designed to measure short-term memory. The presentation of a sample stimulus is followed by a retention interval and by the presentation of two or more choice stimuli. Choice of the stimulus that matches the sample is reinforced.

delayed response task A task in which a temporal interval is interpolated between the presentation of a signal and the opportunity to respond in order to obtain a reward.

depolarization A change in the resting potential of a neuron that makes the interior of the cell electrically less negative or positive, in relation to the extracellular space.

depth perception Visual estimation of the distance between the organism and objects in the environment.

detour task A task in which the animal learns to move temporarily away from a visible but inaccessible reward in order to reach it.

deuterostomes A group of phyla characterized because the anus develops at (or near) the blastopore (i.e., the point in which cells invaginate during the gastrula stage).

development The ontogenetic process of individual animals that spans from egg fertilization to death.

developmental causes Processes along the lifespan of an organism that result in the emergence of a particular behavior. One of the four causal levels in the study of behavior according to Tinbergen's (1963) classification.

developmental constraints Restriction in the development of one trait by other traits that are developing concurrently.

dialect Geographical variations in song (birds) or language (humans), maintained by social learning.

diapause A temporary arrest of embryonic development.

diastema A gap in the lower jaw interpolated between the incisors and the canines. The absence of diastema is typical in hominids.

diencephalon A segment in the organization of the CNS of vertebrates located between the telencephalon (more anterior) and the mesencephalon (more posterior).

diet selection An animal's ability to decide which food items to consume and which to leave.

differential conditioning A classical conditioning situation of the form A+/B–.

differential-outcome effect In conditional discriminations of the form A—›R+/A—›L– and B—›L+/B—›R–, where A and B are different stimuli and R and L are different responses, acquisition is facilitated when each stimulus-response sequence is paired with a different reinforcer or outcome (e.g., when "+" represents food pellets after A—›R+, but sucrose solution after B—›L+).

diploblastic animals Animals having a body organization involving two cell layers called ectoderm and endoderm. Cnidarians and ctenophorans are diploblastic phyla.

diploid, haploid, diplodiploidy, haplodiploidy In sexually reproducing animals, germ cells contain a single set of chromosomes and are referred to as haploid. By contrast, somatic cells contain pairs of homologous chromosomes and are called diploid. During fertilization, haploid sperm and egg cells join and the diploid number is reinstated. This duplication of chromosomes in somatic cells is referred to as diplodiploidy (i.e., offspring are produced by diploid parents, as in human reproduction). In some species of insects (e.g., ants), males are produced directly from unfertilized eggs laid by the queen, whereas females are produced by fertilized eggs. Thus, whereas males are haploid (all cells in their body contain a single set of chromosomes), females are diploid. This system is referred to as haplodiploid.

directional dominance A better response in one direction (e.g., high line) than in the other (e.g., low line) in artificial selection studies. Directional dominance may reflect the absence of variability in a trait that prevents its change in a given direction.

directional selection Selection that increases (or decreases) the population mean for a particular trait across generations.

discrete-trial and free-operant procedures Conditioning training procedures in which the opportunity for responding may be limited to a particular period (discrete trial) or continuously available (free operant).

dishabituation A resurgence of a habituated response after the presentation of a novel, relatively intense stimulus.

disinhibition After extinction of a conditioned response, the administration of a novel and relatively intense stimulus often causes the resurgence of the response the next time the CS is presented.

discrimination reversal A task involving the acquisition of a discrimination of the type A+/B– followed by training with the opposite discrimination, B+/A–.

displacement Responses observed in one context (e.g., courtship) may resemble behaviors performed under a different context (e.g., feeding). A displacement of a behavior from one context to another may be involved in the evolution of some displays.

disruptive selection Selection against the average version of a particular trait. Extreme phenotypes have greater fitness than intermediate ones. Disruptive selection results in the evolution and maintenance of polymorphisms.

distress vocalizations Vocalizations induced by aversive stimuli, particularly in young animals.

dithering behavior Directing courtship and social behaviors to members of more than one species.

divergence An evolutionary outcome representing the split of taxa from a common ancestor. Divergent evolution results in the dissimilarity of homologous traits.

DNA (deoxyribonucleic acid) A sequence of nucleotides (adenine, thymine, guanine, and cytosine) that encodes information necessary to build proteins. In animals, the DNA molecule is enclosed in the chromosomes, and these in a membrane-bound nucleus.

DNA fingerprinting A technique used to determine genetic relatedness among individuals of the same population.

DNA-DNA hybridization A technique used to develop phylogenies at the taxonomic level of order or family.

dodging behavior Behavior aiming at defending a captured prey from a conspecific competitor.

domestication The reproduction of animals (dogs, cats, cattle) and plants (wheat, corn, rice) in order to improve some character in their descendants.

dominance In a social group, access to resources may depend on a relatively strict order (sometimes called a pecking order).

dopamine A neurotransmitter implicated (in mammals) in a variety of behavioral processes, including reinforcement and drug addiction.

double sexual imprinting Sexual imprinting to more than one species.

dwarfism An example of heterochrony in which the morphology of the descendant species is similar to that of the ancestor species but smaller in body size.

echolocation The tracking of objects in the environment by generating a sound and processing its echo.

ecological niche The group of factors necessary to sustain the life of a particular population of animals, including physical factors (e.g., temperature), biological factors (e.g., food sources), and behavioral factors (e.g., patterns of daily activity).

ecological view of learning A view according to which learning processes are adaptations at the species level.

ectoderm An external layer of cells present in all animals.

ectothermy The fluctuation of an animal's internal temperature with that of the environment. Ectothermy is characteristic of lower vertebrates.

Ediacaran fauna A fossil assemblage first discovered in the Ediacara Hills of southern Australia and now known to have worldwide distribution. The oldest Ediacaran fossils are estimated to be 555 Mya. Whereas the animal status of some fossils is disputed, others appear to correspond to cnidarian animals similar to extant jellyfish and sea anemones.

electrical synapse A synapse in which the electrochemical potential crosses directly from the presynaptic to the postsynaptic neuron, without neurotransmitter release.

embryo A developing organism in which the structures characteristic of the adult are being formed.

embryonic experience Events that affect the animal and that occur during embryonic development.

embryonic stem cells Nondifferentiated cells from an embryo in the morula stage.

emotionality A tendency of animals to exhibit affective reactions under testing conditions. In artificial selection experiments based on learned performance, researchers often find that animals change in their tendency to be disturbed by the conditions of training rather than in some general learning ability.

encephalization Evolutionary trend toward an increase in the relative size of the brain not attributable entirely to allometric growth.

encephalization quotient (EQ) A measure of relative brain size. The brain size of a particular species is divided by the expected brain size for the class to which that species is assigned. The expected brain size is derived from the equation of allometric growth.

endoderm An internal layer of cells present in all animals.

endothermy Ability to maintain a constant internal temperature. Endothermy is characteristic of higher vertebrates.

environmental enrichment Exposure to an early environment with a variety of objects including, in some cases, conspecifics.

epigenesis A view of development according to which structures and functions in an organism arise as a result of complex interactions between genetic and nongenetic factors.

episodic culture The ability to share the contents of episodic memories among members of a group and the means developed for that purpose.

episodic memory Memory for specific episodes or events.

equipotentiality The assumption made by the general-process view of learning, according to which any stimulus or response is equally associable with any reinforcer.

escape conditioning The acquisition of a response that allows an animal to terminate an aversive primary reinforcer (e.g., electric shock).

ethology A branch of biology dedicated to the study of behavior.

eukaryotes In the five-kingdom classification, eukaryotes include the unicellular protists (e.g., amoeba) and the multicellular plants, fungi, and animals. They are distinguished from the prokaryotes by their larger size, by the presence of a membrane-bound nucleus that encloses the chromosomes containing the DNA molecule, and by cytoplasmatic organelles.

eusociality A pattern in animal societies that exhibit parental care, overlapping generations, and sterile castes.

evagination and eversion Divergent patterns of telencephalic development. In evagination, the telencephalon closes toward the middle line, leading to the formation of the lateral ventricles. This is typical of sharks and tetrapods. In eversion, the telencephalon folds externally. This is typical of bony fish. The topographical distribution of telencephalic areas vary depending on whether the telencephalon develops by evagination or eversion.

evolution Many definitions of this central concept are available. In a succinct way, it could be defined as descent with modification. More technically, it is defined as an outcome of evolutionary processes that generate change (e.g., natural selection, genetic drift, etc.) and evolutionary patterns that constrain that change (e.g., phylogenetic history).

evolutionarily stable strategy Alternative strategies with equal fitness displayed by animals within a population.

evolutionary inertia The persistence of a trait in a descendant species that was adaptive in the ancestors.

evolutionary patterns The phylogenetic history of specific lineages of ancestors and descendants. Phylogenetic patterns may be viewed as conservative forces that determine which traits are open to change given the prior history of the population.

evolutionary processes The rules that determine evolutionary change in a population, including natural selection, genetic drift, and allometry. Processes may be viewed as the innovative forces of evolution that produce novelty and change.

evolutionary rate A measure (in units called darwins) of the speed of phenotypic change in a lineage. Evolutionary rates can be assessed in fossil lineages as well as in living lineages both in the natural environment and in artificial selection experiments.

excitatory and inhibitory conditioning CSs may acquire the ability to predict the presentation (excitatory) or the omission (inhibitory) of a US.

excitatory and inhibitory postsynaptic potential (EPSP and IPSP) A depolarizing (EPSP) or hyperpolarizing (IPSP) gradual potential induced in the postsynaptic neuron by the release of neurotransmitter by the presynaptic neuron.

exons and introns The DNA molecule is organized in coding segments called exons and noncoding segments called introns. Although the entire sequence is transcribed from DNA into RNA, introns are subsequently excised to give rise to messenger RNA in a process called splicing.

exon shuffling Crossing-over of introns that leads to exon duplication and exchange between genes.

expectancy ratio (C/T) A ratio of the cycle (i.e., interreinforcement interval) divided by the trial (i.e., duration of the CS). Acquisition rate is an inverse function of the size of this ratio.

expectancy-specific neurons Frontal cortex neurons that become activated when the animal expects the impending occurrence of a specific event.

explicitly unpaired procedure A frequently used nonassociative control condition consisting of presenting the CS and US such that they are never close in time.

exploratory behavior Behavior that results in the acquisition of information about an environment. The information may be used immediately, or it may become relevant later when the situation changes. The latter effect is known as latent learning.

extinction A procedure (continuous nonreinforcement after acquisition training) and a learning phenomenon (decrease in response strength after a shift from reinforcement to continuous nonreinforcement).

eye-hand coordination Skillful reaching for and manipulation of objects.

fear conditioning A classical conditioning situation in which organisms receive pairings of a signal (e.g., a tone) and a painful event (e.g., electric shock). Fear conditioning is usually measured in terms of freezing responses.

fear An intervening variable postulated to account for behavioral changes in conditioning situations involving aversive primary reinforcers (e.g., electric shock).

fear reaction In the imprinting situation, the tendency of young chicks deprived of social experience to withdraw from moving objects.

fearfulness A tendency to exhibit a variety of fear-induced behaviors (e.g., tonic immobility).

female choice Active selection of sexual partners by females in polygynous species. Male choice may be observed in polyandrous species.

fertilization, external and internal The joining of a sperm and egg cell into a zygote. In some aquatic species, male and female eject their germ cells in the water, where fertilization occurs. In others, specialized organs and copulatory behavior have evolved to allow fertilization to occur inside of the female's body.

fetus An unborn mammal that is growing in size and in which the internal systems become functional.

figure-background discrimination The ability to detect a stimulus, which increases as the stimulus differs in some perceptual dimension (e.g., color, pattern) from its background.

filial imprinting A learning process wherein a young bird learns to recognize its mother.

final common path A term for the spinal cord motoneurons, the ones ultimately responsible for stimulating peripheral muscles to generate behavior.

fixed action pattern (FAP) A concept postulated by classic ethologists (e.g., Lorenz and Tinbergen) to refer to innate responses that, once initiated, would continue to completion without interference from external stimuli. These patterns were considered to be fixed both across individuals in any given species and across instances in a single individual. Because these patterns are in fact more variable than originally postulated, they are now referred to as modal action patterns.

flavor- or food-aversion learning A training situation in which a flavor (e.g., saccharin solution) or some type of food is paired in a Pavlovian fashion with the administration of an event that intoxicates the animal, inducing nausea and gastric discomfort (e.g., X-irradiation, lithium chloride). Animals reject the flavor or food previously paired with a state of toxicosis.

flight-fight reaction An active antipredator behavior. The switch from flight to fight response depends on the proximity of the predator. Animals tend to escape from a situation in which the predator is relatively far away, but they may turn to aggressive defense when the predator is within reach.

floor and ceiling effects Loss of measurement sensitivity when scales with fixed floor and/or ceiling limits (e.g., probability of response, varying from zero to one) fail to detect behavioral changes as scores approach these limits.

following reaction In the imprinting situation, the tendency of young chicks to follow their mother (or the imprinting object).

food calls Vocalizations that convey information about the quality of a food source.

food-hoarding behavior Storage of food items in locations different from those in which the food was found and for some period of time before consumption.

food recognition Ability to identify appropriate food items.

foramen magnum The opening through which the spinal cord enters into the cranial cavity. In hominids, the relative position of the foramen magnum provides a clue as to the degree of bipedality.

forgetting Inability to remember previously acquired information.

fossil traces The fossilized remains of animal tracks. Fossil traces allow for inferences regarding morphological and behavioral features of the animals that made them.

founder effect Substantial genetic change due to genetic drift in a small portion of a population that becomes isolated from the rest. This effect could be a relatively common scenario preceding the evolution of new species.

fovea A region in the retina with a high concentration of cone receptors allowing for the formation of sharp visual images. The presence of a fovea is a marker for a diurnal lifestyle, whereas its absence suggests a nocturnal lifestyle.

freezing response A motionless state induced in an animal exposed to a stimulus that disrupts its ongoing behavior. Freezing is usually elicited by fear-inducing stimuli.

frequency-dependent selection The fitness of a particular phenotype may depend on the frequency with which that phenotype is present in a population.

frontal cortex Neocortex of the frontal lobe, involved in motor coordination, planning, and expectancy formation.

frustration, primary and anticipatory An intervening variable postulated to account for behavior in situations involving surprising nonreward. Primary frustration refers to the reaction that follows surprising nonreward, whereas anticipatory frustration is a conditioned form of that reaction.

functional disconnection A reduction in the efficacy of a synapse as a result of habituation training.

functional localization Allocation of a brain area to a relatively specific function.

Fungi A kingdom that includes multicellular eukaryotes that obtain nutrients by absorption (e.g., mushrooms).

ganglion A cluster of neurons in the CNS of invertebrates.

gastrula stage A stage of embryonic development following the blastula stage and characterized by an invagination of cells that forms an internal cavity. This cavity eventually becomes the gut.

gene A section of DNA coding for a particular protein.

gene knockout A technique that allows for the blocking of a particular gene. The animal carrying that "silent" gene does not express a specific phenotypic product (e.g., a specific neurotransmitter receptor).

general-process view of learning A view according to which the same learning processes operate throughout the animal kingdom.

generalization A tendency to respond in like manner to similar stimuli. Response strength tends to decrease as the test stimuli differ from the training stimulus, giving rise to a generalization gradient.

generalization of habituation Habituation to a stimulus that transfers to other stimuli in direct proportion to their degree of similarity.

generative process The integration of previously acquired information that results in the emergence of a behavioral skill that has not been specifically trained.

genetic assimilation Selection for the ability to produce a particular phenotype in response to an environmental pressure, resulting in the eventual development of the phenotype independently of the environment.

genetic code A sequence of three bases in the DNA molecule that results in the transcription of a specific amino acid. The triplet of bases is called a codon. Amino acids, in turn, are the building blocks of proteins. As far as it is known, all animals use the same genetic code (see ***Table 2.1***).

genetic drift Random (i.e., nonselective) change in allele frequency in a population. Genetic drift is particularly important in relatively small populations of sexually reproducing animals.

genetic homeostasis High and low strains for a specific trait can usually be developed by artificial selection relatively rapidly. When the selection criterion is relaxed and animals are allowed free interbreeding, the trait distribution tends to regress to values that were typical of the parental population. Such regression is said to reflect genetic homeostasis.

genotype The genetic information contained in the DNA of an organism.

geotaxis A tendency to orient in reference to gravity either toward the ground (positive geotaxis) or away from the ground (negative geotaxis).

giant neurons Neurons of large size that have served as models to understand the neuron's electrochemical properties (e.g., the squid's giant axon).

giantism An example of heterochrony in which the morphology of the descendant species is similar to that of the ancestor species but larger in body size.

gill slits Part of the breathing system of chordates. One of the four traits defining the chordate body plan.

goal- and sign-tracking responses CRs directed either at the site where the US was presented previously (goal tracking), or at the CS (sign tracking).

grade A certain degree of resemblance exhibited by taxa sharing derived characters that have evolved independently. Mammals and birds are usually placed in a same grade, referred to as higher vertebrates, because of the sharing of several characters independently evolved (e.g., endothermy).

graded potential A change in the electrochemical potential of a neuron proportional to the stimulus that provoked it.

grasping An adaptation for prehension (e.g., brachiation) involving the hand or foot with opposable thumb or big toe.

grooming Care of the body. The term "allogrooming" is used when the caring is of one animal by another. In primates grooming behavior may also serve to establish and strengthen social bonds.

group care In some species, the caring of the young that is undertaken by several individuals within a group.

group selection A view that suggests that in most animal social behavior is directed at avoiding the overexploitation of resources that are important for the survival of the species.

growth cones The tips of the axons of vertebrate neurons. Growth cones display an ameboid movement toward a target area during the development of the nervous system.

gyrencephalic Mammalian neocortex characterized by the presence of convolutions.

habituation A decrease in the response to a stimulus that results from its repetitive presentation. The short-term version of this effect is considered to be an example of nonassociative learning. Long-term habituation may involve associative learning between the habituating stimulus and the contextual cues present at the time of training.

habituation of dishabituation The degree of response recovery that will tend to diminish when a response is repeatedly dishabituated.

habituation of habituation A period of rest after habituation of a response that results in the spontaneous recovery of that response. If, however, several such resting periods are introduced, response recovery decreases.

hammer-anvil tool A combination of two relatively hard objects, one to hit and the other as a base, used to break apart food-bearing items (e.g., nuts, bones).

handedness Preferential use of one hand during object manipulation.

handicap principle The idea that costly ornaments and behaviors convey information about the bearer's fitness.

Hardy-Weinberg equilibrium In a population in which there are no mutations, no gene migration, a large number of animals, random mating, and equally viable alleles, the frequency of alternative alleles does not change across generations.

heat-seeking behavior The main mechanism for temperature regulation in young birds and mammals—to approach a source of heat (usually the mother).

helpers Sexually mature individuals that postpone their own reproduction and allocate their time to provide care for the chicks of other animals. Helpers usually contribute to the raising of genetically related animals.

heritability (h^2) A measure of the effectiveness of artificial selection. Heritability is directly related to the difference in a trait expressed in the filial generation relative to the parental generation (called gain, G), and inversely related to the difference between the trait distribution in the parental population relative to that of the subpopulation selected for inbreeding (called selection differential, S). Thus, $h^2 = G/S$. When heritability is estimated after several generations of selective breeding, it is referred to as realized heritability.

heterochrony Evolutionary changes in the rate of development and in the relative time of appearance of traits in descendant species compared to their ancestors.

heterosis (or hybrid vigor) A condition in which heterozygous individuals exhibit a higher fitness than homozygous counterparts.

heterosynaptic facilitation The facilitation of transmission through a synapse as a result of a third neuron modifying the excitability of the presynaptic neuron via an axo-axonic synapse. Heterosynaptic facilitation has been proposed as the mechanism underlying some instances of dishabituation.

heterozygous In a diploid organism, heterozygosity occurs when dominant and recessive alleles combine for a particular gene.

higher vertebrates A taxonomic term that refers to birds and mammals.

higher vocal center (HVC) An area of the avian telencephalon involved in vocal learning.

hippocampal formation A structure located in the telencephalon of vertebrates that has been implicated in a variety of functions (e.g., spatial learning).

home range A nondefended area where an animal may look for resources.

homeotic (or Hox) genes Regulatory genes that control the identity of the various segments of the animal body.

homing behavior The ability of some breeds of animals (e.g., homing pigeon) to return to their home when released at distant places.

homology Similarity in genotype (DNA sequence) or phenotype (morphology or function) based on shared ancestry.

homoplasy Character similarity across species that evolved independently. Parallelism, convergence, and reversal are the three instances of homoplasy.

homosynaptic depression A decrease in the excitability of a synapse. Homosynaptic depression has been proposed as a mechanism underlying some instances of short-term habituation.

homozygous In a diploid organism, having two dominant or two recessive alleles for a particular gene.

hormones Proteins synthesized by glands, secreted into the blood stream, and widely distributed in the body. Hormones can influence cells, including neurons, in a variety of ways.

hyoid bone A bone that supports muscles in the larynx that are important for speech.

hypermorphosis An example of peramorphosis in which the onset of sexual maturity occurs later in the descendant than it was in the ancestor.

hyperpolarization Action potentials that cause the interior of the postsynaptic neuron to become more negative than it is during a resting potential.

hypersexuality A tendency to engage in copulatory behavior with a variety of sexual partners, including animals of different species.

hypothalamic-pituitary-adrenal axis Structures linked through the action of hormones that participate in the organism's response to emotionally arousing situations.

inbreeding depression The deleterious effect of inbreeding on the expression of a particular trait across generations.

inclusive fitness The sum of direct (or Darwinian) and indirect fitness.

increased excitability An ability exhibited by some neurons to increase the amount of neurotransmitter released in the synapse by lengthening the time during which calcium channels remain open. Increased excitability has been proposed as a mechanism underlying some instances of dishabituation.

independent assortment During meiosis (cellular division leading to a haploid germ cell), pairs of alleles located in different chromosomes are segregated without regard to other alleles located in different chromosomes. As a result, the chromosomes in germ cells are a mosaic of intermixed alleles from both parents.

index of extracortical neurons (Nc) An estimation of the number of cortical neurons available for processing information other than that concerned with the body (i.e., sensory and motor information).

indirect fitness Traits that contribute to the fitness of genetically related organisms, at the expense of direct (or Darwinian) fitness, are said to confer high indirect fitness.

individual recognition The ability to distinguish a particular animal from other conspecifics.

infantile amnesia Failure to remember events that occurred early in one's life.

information center The sharing of information among a group of animals about prey availability.

ingroup In cladistic analysis, the set of lineages within the clade under study.

inheritance of acquired traits A theory advanced by Lamarck in the early 19th century according to which the use and disuse of parts determined the degree to which they were passed across generations. The Lamarckian view of evolution survived until the early 20th century, when it was displaced by the so-called modern synthesis view. In this view, information circulates in a one-way manner from the genotype to the phenotype; thus, phenotypic changes cannot affect genetic information such that the modified trait is passed to the offspring.

insight The sudden resolution of a problem.

instincts Traditionally, a concept used to refer to behaviors that develop independently of experience, that are common to a particular species, and that serve a specific function. Contemporary views of instinctive behavior stress the fact that these are species-typical responses that develop as a result of complex interactions between genetic and nongenetic factors.

instrumental (or operant) conditioning An instance of associative learning based on exposure to a contingency between a response and a reinforcer that occur in close temporal contiguity.

intervening variable A variable postulated to explain functional relationships between independent variables (e.g., stimulus conditions) and dependent variables (e.g., behavior).

intradimensional and extradimensional transfer A discrimination between compound stimuli with elements from two different dimensions (e.g., line orientation and color) can be arranged so that one dimension is relevant while the other is irrelevant (e.g., respond to orientation, ignore color). Once this discrimination is acquired, a new discrimination is presented with the same dimensions but different elements (i.e., different orientations and colors from those used originally). In this new discrimination, the relevant dimension may be the same that was relevant before (intra dimensional), or the dimension that was previously irrelevant (extra dimensional).

intrauterine position In mammals in which several embryos develop simultaneously in uterus, the location of the embryo and the gender of adjacent developing embryos may affect various developmental processes.

intermediate-medial hyperstriatum ventrale (IMHV) An area of the avian telencephalon involved in learning.

invertebrates All the animals except the vertebrates.

irritability A basic property of living organisms that allows for reactions to stimulus conditions. According to Lamarck, organisms without nervous systems exhibit irritability, but are incapable of initiating movement from within.

ISI effect The shorter the interstimulus interval (ISI), the faster the habituation.

isolate song effect A greater-than-normal efficacy of the song of male cowbirds reared in social isolation.

kin recognition Ability to discriminate relative from nonrelative conspecifics.

kinship theory The proposal that the probability for altruistic behavior to evolve is directly related to the number of genes shared by the agent and recipient in the altruistic interaction.

labyrinthine tooth A tooth structure characterized by the folding of the enamel, typical of lobe-fin fish and early tetrapods.

language comprehension and production Language comprehension refers to the ability to correctly follow commands presented in a symbolic format, whereas language production involves the creation of syntactically appropriate strings of symbols.

latent inhibition A learning phenomenon in which nonreinforced preexposure to a stimulus subsequently retards conditioning when that stimulus is paired with a reinforcer.

latent learning Exploratory behavior that results in the acquisition of knowledge about the spatial features of the environment that is not immediately used, but becomes relevant after a change in the environment (e.g., when food becomes available).

lateral inhibition A neuron with axon collaterals that inhibit neighboring neurons.

lateralization Equivalent areas of the neocortex may subserve different functions depending on the hemisphere.

law of effect The assertion that successful responses are strengthened, whereas unsuccessful responses are weakened.

law of segregation Mendel's statement that alleles controlling a particular trait segregate from each other during the production of germ cells (sperm and eggs) and are restored after fertilization without losing their identity. Mendel postulated this law in opposition to the then-current view that inheritance involved a sort of blending. The law of segregation allowed Mendel to account for the apparent loss of a recessive character in the F_1 that reappears in the F_2.

leadership In social species, the tendency to occupy specific positions in relation to other members of the group. Leadership may determine the priority of access to resources.

learned helplessness Experience with inescapable aversive reinforcers impairs later acquisition in other situations, including situations in which the reinforcer is escapable or avoidable.

learning (associative and nonassociative) Acquiring, storing, and retrieving information that results from experience. These processes occur in the CNS. Associative learning results from repeated experience with two or more events that occur in temporal or spatial contiguity. Nonassociative learning occurs when organisms modify their response to a single event after repeated presentations.

learning mutants Animals carrying mutations that affect learning processes.

learning-performance dichotomy Learning must not be equated with performance or behavior. This is particularly important when dealing with putative instances of learning failure. The absence of a behavior does not imply the absence of learning.

learning phenomena and mechanisms Empirical findings (phenomena) are explained in terms of underlying processes (mechanisms).

learning sets The successive acquisition of discriminations (e.g., A+/B- followed by C+/D-, E+/F-, etc., where letters represent stimuli).

leg-flexion reflex Stimuli applied to the skin or tendons of a leg that produce the flexion of the limb.

lek polygyny A form of polygyny in which males defend a specific piece of courtship ground or area, called the lek, itself having no resources.

lemnothalamus A field of thalamic nuclei (diencephalon) characterized by the reception of afferent fibers from the lemniscal system.

life-dinner principle The inequality of motivation in the predator-prey relationship: Whereas the predator runs for its dinner, the prey runs for its life. This asymmetry highlights the differential strength of the selective pressures operating on predators and preys.

life-history strategy Evolutionary changes in sets of traits. For example, selection for increased body size may also result in a variety of changes in reproductive biology and behavior, longevity, and social behavior.

lifetime reproductive success (LRS) Direct (or Darwinian) fitness measured across the organism's entire lifespan.

limbic system A set of nuclei and areas located in the core of the telencephalon known to be involved in many functions relevant for an understanding of behavior (e.g., learning, memory, emotion, motivation, etc.).

lissencephalic Pertaining to a mammalian neocortex characterized by the absence of convolutions.

locomotion Movement based on use of legs.

longitudinal design A type of developmental research in which a single group of animals is repeatedly observed at various periods during development.

lordosis In rodents, a female copulatory posture consisting of curving of the back to expose the genital area.

lower vertebrates A taxonomic label that refers to the various classes of fishes, amphibians, and reptiles.

macroevolution Pattern of evolution above the species or genus taxonomic level.

magnitude of reinforcement extinction effect (MREE) Greater persistence of behavior during extinction after training with small, rather than large, reinforcement.

male-male competition An aspect of sexual selection. Competitive behavior among males in a polygynous species. Female-female competition may occur in polyandrous species.

marginal value theorem An adaptive-functional model of foraging behavior that makes predictions regarding the factors that affect certain types of foraging decisions. The model assumes the animal has knowledge of the distribution of a food resource in a patchy environment, and predicts that the decision to leave a particular patch is influenced by the rate of prey capture in the patch relative to the environment as a whole and by the cost of traveling between patches.

marking stimulus In a delay-of-reinforcement situation, a stimulus that occurs after the response and again before the delivery of the reinforcer.

mass action The extent to which brain damage affects a specific function depends on the size of the damage, rather than on its location.

mass extinction The disappearance of lineages in the fossil record during a relatively brief geological period.

master-yoked procedure A control procedure used to match a pair of animals in terms of environmental events, while allowing one of them (the master animal), but not the other (the yoked), to experience control of these events by its own behavior.

mate-defense polygyny A form of polygyny in which males actively defend females from other males.

maternal behavior Caring behavior of a mother directed at her offspring.

maternal factors Substances from the mother's body that contribute to the formation of the egg and to which the embryo is exposed during development. Maternal factors may support some types of exposure learning.

maternal imprinting The formation of an attachment of the mother toward her offspring soon after birth.

meaning Semantic content of human language.

mechanicism A biological view according to which the functional properties of living organisms, including behavior, arise from actions and processes of the bodily components. Mechanicism opposed Vitalism, eventually becoming the dominant view in the biological and psychological sciences.

mechanism Processes that account for the occurrence of particular behaviors (e.g., neural mechanisms). One of the four causal levels in the study of behavior according to Tinbergen's (1963) classification.

Mendelian genetics Traits that depend on one or a few genes can be studied in terms of the same procedures used by Mendel with garden peas, including hybridization, backcross, and quantitative analysis of the distribution of phenotypes.

mental continuity Darwin's view, according to which seemingly unique human attributes (e.g., imagination, language, moral judgment, etc.) should be found in nonhuman species, although perhaps in rudimentary form. Mental continuity follows from Darwin's emphasis on gradual evolutionary change.

mesencephalon A segment of the CNS of vertebrates located between the diencephalon (more anterior) and the rhombencephalon (more posterior).

mesoderm Intermediate layer of cells present in all the animals that exhibit bilateral symmetry.

metamorphosis Morphological and functional reorganization of the developing animal that eliminates adaptations appropriate for a previous ontogenetic niche, while inducing traits that are needed in the new environment.

microevolution Pattern of evolution at the species or genus level.

migratory orientation The initial direction taken by migratory animals.

mimesis Ability to reenact an event as the actor viewed it.

mimetic culture The ability to communicate events to the members of a group via mimesis.

mind-body dualism Descartes' view that the subjective, mental experience induced by sensory stimuli (e.g., the hot feeling aroused when we touch a flame) cannot be explained in terms of brain processes. These bodily mechanisms account only for behavior and reflexes.

misbehavior Responses that are relatively resistant to positive reinforcement.

mitochondrial DNA DNA present in the mitochondria (i.e., cytoplasmatic organelles). Sequential analysis of mitochondrial DNA can be used to develop phylogenies at the taxonomic level of subspecies.

mobbing Antipredator grouping behavior induced by the presence of a predator. During mobbing, the potential prey may act aggressively toward the predator.

modal-action pattern (MAP) Sequentially organized behaviors that, once activated, develop in a more or less ballistic manner. MAPs are said to be species-typical behaviors.

molecular clock The accumulation of changes (e.g., mutations) in the DNA molecule that may be used as a time scale to assess the age of a particular evolutionary event. The key assumption is that DNA changes occur at a constant rate in time.

Monera A kingdom that includes all the bacteria.

monogamy An exclusive reproductive bond maintained by a male and female for a relatively long period (e.g., an entire breeding season or longer).

monogyny A term applied to monogamous and polyandrous mating systems.

monophyletic group A group of lineages stemming from a common ancestor.

monosynaptic reflex A reflex arc based on two neurons and a single synapse (a sensory-motor synapse).

Morgan's canon Also known as parsimony, the canon emphasizes that explanations of behavioral capacities should be based on the simplest possible mechanisms.

morphogenesis The development of the general shape of the organism.

morphotype A set of traits hypothesized to typify the common ancestor of a clade.

morula stage A stage of development following cleavage that is characterized by the formation of a blastula.

mosaic evolution Different traits may evolve at different rates, demonstrating a certain degree of independence.

mother-infant bond The affective association between mother and infant, particularly important in mammals.

motor primacy theory The proposal that movement occurs first in the developing animal, even in the absence of sensory feedback.

mounting A rear approach by males with elevation of forepaws and grasping of the female by the flanks, accompanied by intromission of the penis into the female's vagina and ejaculation of sperm.

mouthing Exploration of an object with the mouth.

Mousterian technology The tool kit characteristic of Neanderthals and modern humans; it includes a wide variety of tools.

Müllerian mimicry Convergence in coloration across unpalatable, toxic species.

multicausality The idea that many factors, and their interactions, determine most instances of behavior. Environmental stimuli, hormones, gene products, neural activity, etc., can affect behavior in complex ways. Thus behavior is said to be caused by a multiplicity of factors.

multicellular organisms Organisms that include cell types that differ in morphology and function. Only eukaryotes have evolved multicellularity (i.e., animals, plants, and fungi).

multiregional evolution hypothesis The proposition that populations of archaic humans evolved locally into *Homo sapiens* in several regions of the world.

muscular fatigue Exhaustion of the muscles after repeated stimulation, resulting in the inability to perform a response.

mutation Random alterations in the sequence of bases in the DNA molecule produced by copying errors, radiation, chemical substances, etc.

mutualism A symbiotic relationship between animals from different species that benefits both partners.

myelinization Developmental process that results in the partial occlusion of the axon by myelin cells. Myelinization is a major determinant of the speed of action potentials.

natural selection Natural selection occurs when individuals within a population exhibit phenotypic variation in some trait, when alternative traits possess differential reproductive success, and when the traits under selection have a genetic basis.

nature-nurture dichotomy Conflicting opinion regarding the origins of behavior. Originally intended as distinct categories of behavior, nature referred to instinctive responses that are presumably fixed and genetically determined, whereas nurture referred to acquired behaviors that originate in individual experience. Currently these are viewed as extremes of a continuum and as developing from complex interactions of both genetic and nongenetic factors. This interactionist view is known as epigenesis.

negative reinforcement A contingency between an instrumental response and the withdrawal of an aversive reinforcement (escape conditioning), or a signal of an aversive reinforcer (avoidance conditioning).

nematocyst A coiled structure present in cnidarians (e.g., jellyfish) that can be released to seize a prey.

neocortex ratio Volume of the neocortex divided by the volume of the rest of the brain.

neophobia An unconditioned reluctance to deal with novel stimuli or situations.

neoteny An example of paedomorphosis in which descendant and ancestor exhibit similar onset in development, but the descendant shows a slower rate of development and delayed emergence of sexual maturity.

nerve cord The CNS of a developing chordate, located dorsally with respect to the digestive apparatus. One of the four traits defining the chordate body plan.

neurochemical systems Pathways in the CNS of vertebrates that use a specific neurotransmitter.

neurogenesis Production of new neurons.

neuromeres Subdivisions of the CNS that are evident during development of the vertebrate embryo.

neurotransmitter A chemical substance released at the axon's terminals by an incoming action potential. Neurotransmitters diffuse in the synapse and reach the membrane of the postsynaptic neuron, where they activate specific receptors. Such activation may induce gradual potentials in the postsynaptic neuron.

neuron doctrine The theory according to which neural networks are formed by discrete cells, called neurons, that communicate with each other through tiny gaps called synapses.

neurula stage A stage of vertebrate development in which the mesoderm is differentiated and the embryo develops a dorsoventral axis.

neutral theory The view suggesting that most of the molecular variation in DNA sequence is basically neutral—that is, unrelated to natural selection.

nictitating membrane response Many species of tetrapods possess a second eyelid, called the nictitating membrane, that closes passively when the eye retracts. This response can also be conditioned using Pavlovian procedures.

NMDA (N-methyl-D-aspartate) A neurotransmitter involved in learning.

nocturnal niche An ecological niche presumably exploited by the ancestor of extant mammals.

norm of reaction The expression of genotypic information is modulated by nongenetic factors.

notochord A stiff rod located dorsally that provides support. One of the four traits defining the chordate body plan.

nucleus A cell cluster in the CNS with relatively clear anatomical boundaries.

number concept An abstract concept allowing an organism to qualify a particular set of objects in terms of its quantitative properties. Acquisition of the number concept should also give rise to the ability to perform mathematical operations based on those numbers (e.g., addition).

object investigation Active approach and exploration of an object by an animal.

object-object combination Using one object to modify another object.

object permanence The ability to remain focused on an object even when it disappears temporarily from the visual field.

observer In a social learning situation, the animal that acquires information from viewing a conspecific engaged in a particular situation.

occipital condyle The portion of the skull that articulates with the first vertebra. In hominids, the relative position of the occipital condyle reveals the degree of bipedality.

occipital cortex Neocortex of the occipital lobe, critically involved in visual perception.

Oldowan technology The tool kit characteristic of early *Homo* spp., including hammer stones, choppers, and scrapers.

omission contingency A contingency between an instrumental response and the withdrawal of an appetitive reinforcer. The reinforcer is presented when the target response does not occur.

one-zero sampling An observational procedure that consists of determining the presence (one) versus the absence (zero) of a particular behavior during a specific time interval.

ontogenetic adaptations Traits present in developing animals that allow them to survive and develop until sexual maturity.

ontogenetic niche Environment in which a developing animal must survive (e.g., egg, uterus).

ontogeny The origin of individuals through development.

optic tectum A dorsal structure of the mesencephalon that plays a key role in vision.

optimal foraging models A family of models based on the assumption that the foraging behavior of animals is based on decisions that optimize some currency (e.g., maximize energy intake, minimize time delays, etc.) that ultimately correlates positively with inclusive fitness.

organogenesis The formation of functionally specialized structures called organs.

orienting response Ability to adjust body posture so as to maximize contact with a source of stimulation.

out-of-Africa hypothesis The hypothesis that *Homo sapiens* originated in a single population in southern Africa and their descendants spread to northern Africa, Europe, the Middle East, and the rest of the world.

outgroup In cladistic analysis, an outgroup is the most closely related lineage outside of the clade under study.

overshadowing The more intense of the elements of a compound CS impairs conditioning of other elements in the compound.

paedomorphosis An example of heterochrony in which development in the descendant species stops at a stage that corresponds to an early phase in its ancestor.

pallium Structures located in the medial, dorsal, and lateral portions of the telencephalon of vertebrates.

parallelism Character similarity across species that evolves independently from similar primitive characters. An instance of homoplasy.

paralogous genes A set of genes that has been duplicated. For example, the homeotic genes of vertebrates have been duplicated twice to yield four sets of paralogous genes.

paraphyletic group A taxonomic group that does not include all of its descendants (e.g., Reptilia does not include birds and mammals).

parasitism A symbiotic relationship between animals from different species that benefits one partner and causes a detriment for the other.

parent-offspring conflict An evolutionary conflict induced by divergent interests. Whereas parents need to invest just enough time and effort to generate independent offspring and then reproduce again, offspring seek as much care as possible.

parental (paternal, maternal, or biparental) care In some species, parental investment in the offspring is carried out exclusively by the father (paternal) or mother (maternal). In other species, both parents contribute to the caring of the young.

parental investment Any contribution of a parent to the fitness of some offspring at the expense of the parent's ability to invest in other offspring.

parietal cortex Neocortex of the parietal lobe, involved in somatosensory perception and spatial learning and memory.

partial reinforcement extinction effect (PREE) Greater persistence of behavior during extinction after training with partial, rather than continuous, reinforcement.

paternal uncertainty The degree to which a father can be certain that the female carries his offspring rather than the offspring of another male.

peramorphosis An example of heterochrony in which development in the descendant species exhibits the addition of features not present in the ancestor.

pentadactyle hand A hand with five digits. A primitive trait of tetrapods.

perceptual learning Acquisition of information by mere exposure.

peripheral reflex arc A reflex arc completely organized at the periphery, capable of functioning even when separated from the CNS.

pharyngula stage The phylotypic stage of chordates during which the four basic traits of the chordate body plan are first observed (gill slits, notochord, tail, and a dorsal nerve cord).

phenogram A representation of a phylogenetic history based on the overall degree of character similarity among taxa.

phenotype Collection of traits characterizing a particular organism. The phenotype develops as a result of a complex set of interactions between genetic and nongenetic factors.

phenotypic plasticity Exhibition of different phenotypes by animals of the same species that have been exposed to different environments during development.

phylogeny The origin of taxa.

phylogenetic history The evolutionary history of a particular lineage or of a particular trait (e.g., a behavior). One of the four causal levels in the study of behavior according to Tinbergen's (1963) classification.

phylogenetic tree A phylogenetic pattern of ancestor and descendant taxa that is captured by the tree analogy. Common ancestors are represented by the trunk of the tree, whereas divergent lineages are represented by the branches. Information from a variety of sources (e.g., DNA sequence, protein structure, morphological similarity, etc.) can be used to build phylogenetic trees. A phylogenetic tree may be viewed as a hypothesis of genealogical relationships between the lineages of a particular taxon.

phylotypic stage The stage at which characters unique to a particular phylum first appear during development.

phylum A monophyletic group of animals that exhibit a unique body plan.

Plantae A kingdom including multicellular eukaryotes that obtain nutrients by photosynthesis (e.g., algae, plants).

planum temporale A region of the temporal cortex located inside the Sylvian sulcus that exhibits hemispheric asymmetry, being larger in the left hemisphere of humans and chimpanzees. It is involved in auditory perception.

plastic song The initial production of syllables of the song to which the bird was exposed during the early sensory learning phase, as a nestling.

plasticity Malleability of certain synapses based on their degree of activation.

play behavior Social interactions that are energetically costly but serve no immediate apparent function.

pleiotropy The effect of a single gene on the development of several traits.

plesiomorphy Primitive traits.

polarity In cladistic analysis, the directionality of character change across taxa.

polyandry A mating system in which females compete for reproductive access to males.

polygeny Many genes contribute to the development of a trait.

polygynandry A mating system in which several males and females share their reproductive potential.

polygyny A mating system in which males compete for reproductive access to females.

polygyny threshold Properties of the habitat that determine the propensity of a female to engage in a polygynic system.

polymorphism The stable coexistence of alternative phenotypes in a population.

polyphyletic group A group of taxa derived from different ancestors.

polysynaptic reflex A reflex arc that includes sensory neurons, motor neurons, and interneurons.

population bottleneck A drastic reduction in population size that may cause the loss of alleles due to genetic drift.

position habit A tendency to respond on the basis of position (right or left) in a visual discrimination task in which the stimuli (e.g., red light vs. blue light) vary randomly in position from trial to trial. Position habits typically precede the solution of the problem (i.e., respond to the positive alternative).

positive reinforcement A contingency between an instrumental response and the presentation of an appetitive reinforcer that increases the strength of the response.

postdisplacement An example of paedomorphosis in which the rate of development of a trait and the onset of sexual maturity are similar in descendant and ancestor, but the trait's onset of development is delayed in the descendant species.

preadaptation Traits that evolve for one function may eventually be coopted into acquiring new functions. For example, the feathers of birds may have evolved as temperature-regulating structures and later become important in courtship displays.

precocial young Young animals born in a relatively mature state of development.

predator-prey system A major example of coevolution. Natural selection favors the evolution of more efficient means of detecting, capturing, and consuming prey, but this creates a pressure for the evolution of countertraits in prey species.

predisplacement An example of peramorphosis in which development of a particular trait starts earlier in the descendant than it did in the ancestor.

prefunctional organization Behavioral patterns that appear in the appropriate context (e.g., feeding) even in the absence of specific experience.

prehension A reaching movement of the arm toward an object and a grasping movement of the hand to grab the object.

principle of terminal addition Haeckel's notion that descendants evolve by the addition of further developmental stages not present in the ancestors.

profitability In optimal foraging models, profitability is defined as the ratio between the amount of energy, nutrients, or other currency that is being maximized and the time and energy invested in handling the prey.

progenesis An example of paedomorphosis in which the onset and rate of development are similar in descendant and ancestor, but sexual maturity is precocious in the descendant species.

prognathism Forward projection of the jaws typical of many mammals, including the apes and australopithecines.

prokaryote In the five-kingdom classification, prokaryotes are referred to as Monera. They include all the bacteria, distinguished from the eukaryotes by their smaller size and by the absence of a membrane-bound nucleus. Prokaryotes have not evolved multicellular forms.

proper mass The amount of neural tissue allocated to a particular function is correlated with the importance of that function in the animal's life.

Protista (or Protozoa) A kingdom that includes all the unicellular eukaryotes.

protostomes A group of phyla in which the mouth of the animal develops at (or near) the blastopore (i.e., the point in which cells invaginate during the gastrula stage).

proximate causes In Tinbergen's (1963) classification of causal levels, proximate causes refer to mechanisms and developmental causes. These are proximate in the sense that they refer to processes operating in the organism under observation.

pseudocoelomates A heterogeneous group of phyla possessing an internal cavity similar to a coelom but lacking a mesoderm lining (e.g., nematodes).

pseudoconditioning A response originally elicited by the US that transfers to the CS nonassociatively.

psychology A discipline concerned with the study of behavior in a broad sense, from social behavior and the properties of social groups to the physiological basis of simple motor movements.

punctuated equilibria A pattern of evolution characterized by geologically short periods of phenotypic change intermixed with geologically long periods of phenotypic stasis.

punishment A contingency between an instrumental response and the presentation of an aversive reinforcer.

quantum evolution The hypothesis that macroevolution occurs rapidly and in relatively small populations.

radial symmetry A body organized around one (or more) central axis (e.g., jellyfish).

reactivation treatment Exposure to a part of a situation previously experienced by an animal that alleviates otherwise detectable forgetting.

reciprocity (or reciprocal altruism) Tit-for-tat strategy. Reciprocity occurs when an animal (the agent) procures some benefit to another animal (the recipient) at one time, while the agent-recipient roles reverse at a later time. An important feature of reciprocity is that the animals are not closely genetically related.

recombinant inbred strains A line of animals produced by brother-sister pairings of descendants from separately inbred lines.

reflex arc A unit of behavior that includes a sensory component that provides afferent information from some specific stimulus and a motor component that activates a specific organ or muscle in the periphery. Monosynaptic (sensory-motor direct connection) and polysynaptic reflexes (sensory, motor, and interneurons) can be distinguished.

reflex chain A neural network that controls a sequence of responses based on the sensory feedback provided by each element in the sequence.

regression Display of a behavior typical of a younger stage in a situation involving conflict.

reinforcers, primary and secondary Motivationally significant events that display this property either with little or no prior training (primary) or by virtue of a conditioning history (secondary).

reinstatement After extinction of a conditioned response, the unsignaled presentation of the US often causes a resurgence of the response the next time the CS is presented.

releasing factors Hypothalamic hormones that stimulate the release of other hormones from the pituitary gland.

renewal A resurgence of a CR after a shift to a context other than that present during extinction.

repetitive DNA Sections of DNA with the same coding sequence.

reproductive isolation Absence of gene flow between populations; reproductive isolation is a fundamental component of speciation.

resource-defense polygyny A form of polygyny in which males actively compete for some resource and defend it from other males.

response threshold An intervening variable postulated to explain abrupt changes in behavior that correlate with gradual changes in the conditions of training.

resting potential The electrochemical potential of a nonstimulated neuron.

restless response A behavior exhibited by some caged migratory birds that reflects their migratory orientation.

retardation test A test of inhibitory conditioning. The putative inhibitory CS is paired with the US. Inhibition is suggested by a relatively slow rate of acquisition.

retention interval An interval of time between original acquisition training or exposure to a stimulus and testing for the retention (or forgetting) of the task or stimulus.

reticular formation An area of the brainstem of vertebrates involved in the regulation of activity cycles. Neurons located in various nuclei of the reticular formation give rise to some of the most important neurochemical systems.

retrieval and retrieval failure Retrieval is a memory process that allows for the reactivation of previously acquired information. A failure of retrieval, rather than a failure of acquisition, has been shown to underlie many instances of forgetting.

reversal Evolution in a descendant species of a character that was present in a remote ancestor. An instance of homoplasy.

rhombencephalon A segment of the CNS of vertebrates located between the mesencephalon (more anterior) and the spinal cord (more posterior). It includes the cerebellum and the brainstem.

ribosomal RNA (rRNA) Sequential analysis of rRNA demonstrates a very low rate of change that has been used to develop phylogenies of distantly related taxa (e.g., phyla).

ritualizations Displays that are salient, stereotyped, and unambiguous.

RNA (ribonucleic acid) DNA information is transcribed into RNA in the cell nucleus. The RNA molecule, called messenger RNA, leaves the nucleus and enters the cell cytoplasm where it is used as a template to produce a protein. The RNA molecule is a sequence of the bases adenine, thymine, guanine, and uracil.

rules of thumb Whereas natural selection favors the evolution of mechanisms that result in optimal behaviors, the currency that is being optimized need not be measured directly. Some variables can be assessed indirectly. For example, the caloric content of a particular solution may be assessed indirectly by its sweetness.

same/different concept Training to discriminate pairs of perceptually identical stimuli from pairs of perceptually dissimilar stimuli may endow the animal with the conceptual ability to extrapolate this notion to novel exemplars.

sampling In foraging situations, the allocation of time to gather information about the distribution of resources.

satellite male An inconspicuous male that sneaks in a sexual interaction involving another male.

scala naturae The Aristotelian view according to which living organisms can be ordered along a single dimension from the simplest to the most complex. Humans occupy the pinnacle of this ladder.

scallop A pattern of response distribution observed in fixed-interval schedules of reinforcement. Responses stop after reinforcement and resume either gradually or abruptly until the end of the interval.

scent marking Deposition of scent in different locations of a territory.

schedules of reinforcement The various forms that the contingency between an instrumental response and a reinforcer may adopt.

search image An interval representation that allows predators to concentrate on prey they have captured recently.

second-messenger system A cell-molecular process activated, in neurons, by specific patterns of stimulation that may result in DNA transcription.

second-order conditioning Pairing of two relatively neutral stimuli (e.g., light —› tone) that may support conditioning to the initial stimulus (e.g., the light) if the second stimulus was previously paired with a reinforcer (e.g., tone —› food).

secondary generalization Generalization among sets of associations based on common responses.

secondary imprinting Development of a second attachment.

secondary sexual characters Traits involved in reproductive behavior (e.g., body size, feather ornamentation, fur coloration, etc.). These are to be distinguished from primary sexual characters such as the genital organs.

segmentation A pattern of body organization characterized by the repetition of a particular unit in the anterior-posterior axis.

segmented germ band stage The phylotypic stage of arthropods, during which the distinct traits of the arthropod body plan are first observed (head, thorax, and abdominal segments).

selective associations Functional preorganization of certain combinations of stimuli that makes their association easily established.

self-recognition The ability to identify self from others.

selfish gene view The view according to which natural selection acts at the level of individual genes.

sensitive period A period in early development during which the animal is particularly susceptible to a source of experience.

sensitization An increase in the strength of a response as a result of the repeated presentation of a relatively intense stimulus. Whereas the short-term sensitization effect is generally thought to be an instance of nonassociative learning, the nature of the long-term sensitization effect is not yet well understood.

sensitized maternal behavior Maternal behavior induced by sensory stimulation from infants in an animal other than the mother.

sensorimotor intelligence A series of four stages of intellectual development, according to Piaget's theory, involving the emergence of reflexes, object exploration, reaching responses, and object permanence.

sensorimotor learning phase A phase in the vocal learning process of birds during which the animal starts emitting vocalizations. The song develops through a series of phases known as subsong, plastic song, and crystallized song.

sensory adaptation As a result of repeated stimulation, a sensory receptor may decrease or even stop firing in response to a stimulus.

sensory learning phase A phase in the vocal learning process of birds during which the chick acquires the species-typical song. No singing occurs in this phase.

sensory preconditioning The pairing of two neutral stimuli (e.g., light —› tone), followed by classical conditioning of the second stimulus (e.g., tone —› food), endows the first stimulus with the ability to evoke a CR.

sentinel behavior Patrolling a territory and emitting alarm calls when predators are detected.

sequential hermaphroditism The capacity of females in some fish species to turn into males under certain environmental conditions.

serotonin A neurotransmitter implicated (in mammals) in a variety of behaviors, including circadian rhythms, aggressive behavior, impulsivity, etc.

sexual dimorphism Morphological (e.g., body size) or functional (e.g., behavior) differences across genders within a given species.

sexual imprinting In some species, early social experience that affects species recognition in the adult.

sexual maturity A stage in development during which the animal becomes capable to reproduce.

sexual reinforcement Access to a sexually receptive conspecific (or to a model of a conspecific) acts as a reinforcer analogous to food or water in that it supports conditioning.

sexual reproduction The production of new individuals by the joint contribution of germ cells from a male and a female.

sexual selection A special case of natural selection related to the evolution of sexual characters.

sham-operated control A control group in experiments involving lesions of the brain. Sham animals receive exactly the same treatment as animals prepared for brain lesion (e.g., anesthesia, skull opening, etc.), but brain tissue is spared.

shaping Development of a target response with a particular form by the instrumental reinforcement of successive approximations of that target response.

shared associative strength A learning principle according to which the elements of a compound stimulus compete for a fixed amount of associative strength such that the more strength is gained by one of the elements, the less strength remains to be acquired by the others.

Sidman avoidance training Training in which shocks occur at a constant rate unless the animal performs an avoidance response, in which case the shocks are postponed for a fixed period of time. All the shocks can be avoided by performing the response at an appropriate given rate.

sign stimulus A concept suggested by classic ethologists (e.g., Lorenz and Tinbergen) that refers to a sensory influence that releases a particular behavioral pattern. For example, a specific movement during courtship may induce the partner to respond in a specific manner. Sign stimuli are often components of the complete configuration (e.g., female European robins react to any patch of red feathers).

simple parsimony A rule applied to the selection of alternative cladograms based on the assumption that the best cladogram is the one requiring the lowest number of hypotheses of character change.

simple systems approach A research strategy based on the selection of a relatively simple instance of behavior and a simple neural circuit to understand the cellular basis of behavior.

simultaneous conditioning A classical conditioning situation in which there is temporal overlap in the presentation of the CS and US.

singing behavior Vocal behavior of songbirds.

sister groups Taxa with an immediate common ancestor.

sit-and-wait predators Predators that use passive behavior to capture prey. Many sit-and-wait predators have evolved striking specializations for crypticity and for luring their prey into their proximity.

social enhancement The feeding behavior of an animal may induce another animal to search for food in the same location.

social learning The acquisition of information by interacting with conspecifics.

social reinforcement Ability to learn about situations in which the motivationally important event (i.e., the reinforcer) is the presence of a conspecific or the opportunity to interact with it.

somatotopic organization The orderly mapping of a sensory organ (e.g., the retina) to the structure in the CNS that receives the projection (e.g., lateral geniculate nucleus of the thalamus).

songs Vocal output produced by songbirds.

spatial learning Acquisition of information about the features (e.g., landmarks) that characterize a particular environment.

speciation, allopatric and sympatric Evolution of a new species. There are two major speciation scenarios. Allopatric speciation involves the geographic isolation of previously interbreeding populations for a number of generations sufficient to result in reproductive isolation. Islands, lakes, a mountain range, and changes in continental land masses are some of the possible geographical barriers that may lead to allopatric speciation. Sympatric speciation involves the emergence of reproductive isolation within subpopulations of animals occupying the same habitat. Mutations affecting species recognition, changes in resource exploitation, and similar factors may induce sympatric speciation.

species recognition Ability to recognize conspecifics.

species-specific defense responses (SSDRs) Functionally preorganized behaviors aroused by the presentation of aversive reinforcers.

species-typical patterns Behavioral patterns that are observed in most members of a particular species.

sperm competition When females copulate with more than one male, sperm may compete for fertilization.

spike broadening The slowing down of potassium outflow by some neurons that lengthens the time during which a neurotransmitter is released after an action potential. Spike broadening has been proposed as a mechanism underlying some instances of sensitization.

spinal cord A cylinder of neural tissue enclosed in the vertebral column of vertebrates. A part of the CNS concerned with the processing of afferent sensory and efferent motor impulses, as well as with the organization of reflexes.

spinal preparation A surgical preparation in which the spinal cord is severed at an anterior level in order to isolate it from the rest of the CNS.

spontaneous generation A belief held by some ancient philosophers (e.g., Lucretius) that living organisms could originate directly out of the moist soil or in decaying bodies.

spontaneous recovery In habituation or extinction experiments, a resurgence of the response following a period of rest introduced after the response being measured has decreased in strength.

S-R and S-S associations Intervening variables postulated to account for a variety of associative learning phenomena. S-R associations involve connections between internal representations of a stimulus and a response. Their main property is that the stimulus selects a response, whereas their main problem is that they leave out knowledge about the reinforcer—the event that sets them up in the first place. S-S associations involve connections between internal representations of stimuli. Their main property is that they provide an associative account of expectancy formation, whereas their main problem is that they do not account for response selection.

stabilizing selection Selection against extreme versions of a particular trait.

sterile castes Nonreproductive individuals that provide care for the eggs or young, forage for food, and defend the nest.

stimulus intensity Habituation is an inverse function of the intensity of the habituating stimulus. However, in other forms of learning, acquisition is usually a direct function of the intensity or magnitude of the stimuli involved.

stimulus-response habits An acquired tendency to respond in a certain way when confronted with a particular stimulus or situation.

stimulus trace A representation of an external stimulus that remains active for some time after the stimulus has been turned off. Traces are generally assumed to decay spontaneously in time.

storage Translation of acquired information into a more or less permanent neural record.

stotting display A behavior observed in African gazelles threatened by a predator, consisting in jumping with all four legs extended and detached from the ground.

stretching response A response exhibited by rat fetuses involving the dorsal flexion of the body accompanied by the extension of the rear limbs.

structural and regulatory genes Structural genes involve a DNA sequence that encodes the information necessary to build proteins that participate in cell differentiation, tissue development, and the organization of the phenotype. Regulatory genes give rise to proteins that regulate other genes in terms of their timing of transcription.

subpallium Structures located in the ventral portions of the telencephalon of vertebrates.

subsocial A category of insect species that exhibit parental care and overlapping generations.

subsong Vocalization displayed by a bird during the early stages of the sensorimotor learning phase.

successive negative contrast (SNC) Behavioral disruption that follows a downward shift in the magnitude or quality of an appetitive reinforcer. The performance measure can be either instrumental (e.g., speed of running in a runway) or consummatory (e.g., amount of a solution drunk during a session).

successive reversal learning After acquiring an A+/B– discrimination, animals are trained in its reversal, B+/A–, to a criterion, and then the discrimination is reversed again, and so on. The main interest is to determine whether there is progressive improvement in the acquisition of these discriminations after many reversals.

summation test A test of inhibitory conditioning. The putative inhibitor CS is compounded with a known, separately trained excitor. Inhibitory conditioning is suggested by a lower response strength to the compound than to the excitor alone.

supernormal stimulus A concept introduced by classic ethologists (e.g., Lorenz and Tinbergen) to describe cases in which animals exhibit a preference for a stimulus that is larger or more conspicuous than the species-typical stimulus. For example, some birds prefer abnormally large eggs to their own.

superstitious behavior A behavior strengthened by accidental pairing with a reinforcer.

surprising nonreward The total or partial omission of an appetitive reinforcer in a situation previously paired with that reinforcer.

Sylvian sulcus A sulcus that separates the temporal lobe from the frontal and parietal lobes.

symbiosis Associations between animals of different species that may benefit both parts (mutualism) or may benefit one to the detriment of the other (parasitism).

sympatric distribution Populations of different species that coexist in the same habitat and exhibit overlapping distributions.

synapomorphy Derived traits shared exclusively by two or more lineages.

synapse (chemical or electrical) A synapse is the point at which neurons communicate. Neurons are not in physical contact at the synapse; rather, the synapse can be viewed as a gap between neurons. Communication is typically (but not always) unidirectional, from the presynaptic to postsynaptic neuron. In chemical synapses, communication is mediated by the release of neurotransmitters by the presynaptic neuron and activation of neurotransmitter receptors in the postsynaptic neuron. In electrical synapses, action potentials travel with minimal or no delay through the synapse.

synaptogenesis Establishment of synaptic connections between neurons during development.

syntax or grammar Rules for the sequential organization of human language.

tabula rasa Literally, "erased tablet." British and French philosophers of the 18th and 19th centuries proposed that the human mind at birth is like a blank slate on which sensory events write the content of experience by means of associative processes.

tail A post-anal structure used in swimming. One of the four traits defining the chordate body plan.

taxes A concept postulated by classic ethologists (e.g., Lorenz and Tinbergen) to refer to movements that depend on continuous sensory feedback. For example, the approach of flies to sources of light is referred to as positive phototaxis.

taxon A unit of taxonomic analysis.

telencephalon The most anterior portion of the CNS of vertebrates.

template Auditory memory of the adult song acquired by the bird during the sensory learning phase, early in its life.

temporal cortex The neocortex of the temporal lobe that plays a key role in auditory perception, including language comprehension in humans.

temporal fenestrae Openings in the skull of amniotes (reptiles, birds, and mammals).

terminal and interim responses Responses that tend to peak during the later (terminal) or earlier (interim) portions of the interreinforcement interval.

territory A portion of the environment actively defended by the resident. Defense may involve direct or ritualized aggression.

timing Ability to estimate the duration of an event.

tonic immobility A passive antipredator behavior induced in a potential prey by contact with a predator and consisting on a total absence of movement (e.g., the opossum's feigned death).

tool kit A set of tools characteristic of a particular species.

tool use and manufacturing Many animals use a variety of objects as mediators to achieve a particular goal (e.g., reach a food item, protection from conspecifics, etc.). In some cases, the object is selected and modified in a specific manner to achieve the goal. These objects are called tools.

tooth replacement pattern In reptiles, tooth replacement is a continuous process. In contrast, mammals' teeth are replaced only once (milk teeth to adult teeth). These differences provide clues as to the identity of fossils in the therapsid-mammal lineage.

trace conditioning A classical conditioning situation in which there is a temporal gap between the presentation of the CS and US.

trait Morphological (e.g., length of the giraffe's neck) or functional characters (e.g., capacity of pandas to process sugar cane leaves) that constitute the phenotype of an organism.

transfer (positive and negative) The learning of one task may facilitate (positive) or interfere (negative) with the acquisition of a subsequent task.

transfer index (TI) An index used in discrimination reversal tasks to assess the extent to which overtraining in the original discrimination, A+/B–, facilitates (positive transfer) or interferes (negative transfer) with the acquisition of the reversed discrimination, B+/A–.

trial-and-error learning Another term for instrumental conditioning.

trial spacing effect Faster acquisition of conditioning when trials are separated by relatively long intertrial intervals.

tribosphenic molar A molar characterized by the presence of three main cusps, a variable number of accessory cusps, and crests with sharp edges. It first appears in therian mammals (the ancestors of extant marsupials and placentals).

triploblastic animals All the bilaterally symmetrical animals that possess three layers of cells: ectoderm, endoderm, and mesoderm.

trophallaxis In mammals, the interchange of stimulation between mother and offspring. In insects, the interchange of food among individuals.

truly random control A classical conditioning training situation in which the CS and US are presented independently from each other; occasional pairings may occur in this situation.

two-process theory Any theory that explains behavior as arising from a combination of classical and instrumental conditioning processes.

ultimate causes In Tinbergen's (1963) classification of causal levels, ultimate causes include adaptive significance and phylogenetic history. These are ultimate causes in the sense that they operated in the ancestors of the animal currently under observation.

ultrasonic vocalizations Acoustic signals emitted by some animals (e.g., rodents) characterized by a frequency that is above the upper auditory threshold of humans.

unicellular organisms Single-cell organisms, including the bacteria (prokaryotes) and the protists (eukaryotes).

US-preexposure effect Unsignaled preexposure to the US retards subsequent delay conditioning.

ventricular system A series of cavities in the CNS of vertebrates, filled with cerebrospinal fluid, that provides support, buffers neural tissue against potentially damaging movements of the head, and mobilizes a variety of chemical substances.

vertebrates A phylum or subphylum (depending on the taxonomist) of animals characterized, among other things, by a cranium in the anterior end that encloses the brain.

vitalism A biological view according to which a force, called the élan vital, permeates living organisms and is responsible for variation, adaptation, and reproduction. These functions were considered essential features of life by 18th- and 19th-century biologists. Vitalism was held in opposition to Mechanicism.

vocal behavior Communication based on the emission of vocalizations.

vocal learning Vocal behavior dependent on specific acoustic learning.

von Baer's theorem The idea that traits that develop relatively early in ontogeny tend to be generalized and primitive, whereas those developing relatively late tend to be derived.

waist-to-hip ratio (WHR) The length of the hip divided by the length of the waist. The WHR has been suggested to be a proxy used by men to assess a woman's fitness.

weaning In mammals, the period in which the young animal becomes independent of the mother for feeding.

Wernicke's aphasia An impairment of language comprehension caused by lesions of the temporal cortex in humans.

win-stay/lose-shift strategy A response strategy useful to resolve A+/B– discriminations, as observed in some experiments on learning sets.

wiping response A response exhibited by rat fetuses involving the sliding of one or both arms toward the snout, generally induced by solutions with a strong olfactory component.

within-compound associations Associations established among the elements of a compound stimulus.

words Symbolic units of communication in human language.

zootype A set of highly conserved regulatory genes that determine the identity of the bodily parts during the development of all animals.

zygote A fertilized egg.

PHOTO CREDITS

Chapter 4 **Front inside cover:** T. Matsuzawa/Primate Research Institute.

Chapter 5 **Front inside cover:** J.A.L. Cooke, Oxford Scientific Films/Animals Animals/Earth Scenes.

Chapter 6 **Page 185:** Harvard University OEB; **front inside cover:** J. Schauer/Aquatic Life Sculptures.

Chapter 8 **Page 291:** Ruben Muzio; **p. 291:** Rubin Muzio.

Chapter 11 **Back inside cover:** I. Gazit and J. Terkel; **back inside cover:** W. Ferguson; **back inside cover:** N. Inoue-Nakamura/T. Matsuzawa/Primate Research Institute; **back inside cover:** N. Inoue-Nakamura/T. Matsuzawa/Primate Research Institute.

Chapter 12 **back inside cover:** Keiichiro Tsuji; **p. 465:** Harlow Primate Laboratory; **p. 470:** Pablo Luis Tubaro.

Chapter 13 **Back inside cover:** Michael Domjan.

Chapter 14 **Page 557:** Robert Epstein.

TEXT CREDITS

Page 32, *Figure 2.1:* Reprinted with permission from Fitch, W.M. & Margoliash, E., Construction of Phylogenetic Trees, SCIENCE. Copyright (c) 1967, American Association for the Advancement of Science. **p. 35, *Figure 2.3:*** Adapted from BIOLOGY by H. Curtis and N.S. Barnes (c) 1989, by Worth Publishers. Used with the permission of W.H. Freeman and Company. **p. 46, *Figure 2.6:*** Raff, R.A. and Kaufman, T.C., EMBRYOS, GENES AND EVOLUTION. Copyright (c) 1983 by Indiana University Press. Reprinted with permission. **p. 51, *Figure 2.8:*** T.H. Clutton-Brock, ed. REPRODUCTIVE SUCCESS. Copyright (c) 1988 by the University of Chicago Press. Reprinted with permission.

Page 67, *Figure 3.3:* Copyright (c) 1983 by the American Psychological Association. Reprinted with permission. **p. 70, *Figure 3.4:*** Copyright (c) 1988 by the American Psychological Association. Reprinted with permission.

Page 94, *Figure 4.3:* Tolman, E.C. and Honzik, C.H., (1930), "Introduction and Removal of Reward and Maze Performance in Rats," UNIVERSITY OF CALIFORNIA PUBLICATIONS IN PSYCHOLOGY, 4, p. 257-275. **p. 97, *Figure 4.5:*** Reprinted with permission from Pietriewicz, A.T., and Kamil A.C. (1979), Search Image Formation in the Blue Jay (Cyanocitta Cristata), SCIENCE. Copyright (c) 1979 American Association for the Advancement of Science.

Page 129, *Figure 5.1a:* From Gutierrez, G. and Domjan, M. (1996), "Learning and Male-Male Sexual Competition in Japanese Quail (coturnix japonica)," JOURNAL OF COMPARATIVE PSYCHOLOGY, 97, p. 56, fig. 3. **p. 129, *Figure 5.1b:*** Hollis, Dumas, Singh, and Fackelman (1995), "Pavlovian Conditioning of Aggressive Behavior in Blue Gourami Fish (Trichogaster trichopterus): Winners become Winners and Loosers stay Loosers," JOURNAL OF COMPARATIVE PSYCHOLOGY, 109, p. 223, fig. 3 (*bottom*). **p. 133, *Figures 5.2:*** Andromeda Oxford Limited. Reprinted with permission. **p. 135, *Figure 5.3:*** T.H. Clutton-Brock (ed.), Reproductive success. Copyright (c) 1988 by the University of Chicago Press. Reprinted with permission. **p. 145, *Figure 5.6:*** BEHAVIOUR by D. MORRIS. Copyright 1956 by BRILL ACAD PUBS. Reproduced with permission of BRILL ACAD PUBS in the format Textbook via Copyright Clearance Center. **p. 147, *Figure 5.7:*** Copyright (c) 1993 by the American Psychological Association. Reprinted with permission. **p. 151, *Figure 5.8:*** Copyright (c) 1993 by the American Psychological Association. Reprinted with permission.

Page 177, *Figure 6.2:* Reprinted with permission from A. Knoll and S. Carroll, 1999, Science, 284: 2129–2137. Copyright (c) 1999, American Association for the Advancement of Science. **p. 182, *Figure 6.3:*** Smith, A.G., Smith, D.G., & Funnell, Brian M., ATLAS OF MESOZOIS AND CENOZOIC COASTLINES. Copyright (c) 1994 Cambridge University Press. Reprinted with the permission of Cambridge University Press. **p. 186, *Figure 6.5:*** Briggs, Erwin, & Collier, THE FOSSILS OF THE BURGESS SHALE, Smithsonian Institution Press, 1994. Reprinted with permission. **p. 205, *Figure 6.13:*** Modified from Gingerich, 1984. Gingerich, P.D. (1984) Primate Evolution, in Mammals. Notes for a Short Course (eds P.D. Gingerich and C.E. Badgeley), University of Tennessee Studies in Geology, vol. 8, University of Tennessee, Knoxville, pp. 167-81. **p. 207, *Figure 6.14:*** Young, J.Z. (1981), THE LIFE OF VERTEBRATES, 3/e, Oxford University Press, by permission of Oxford University Press. **p. 208, *Figures 6.15:*** Based on various sources, including Marshall et al., 1982 and Marshall, 1988 and others. Marshall L.G., Webb, S.D., Sepkoski, J.J., and Raup, D.M. (1982), Mammalian evolution and the Great American Interchange. Science, 215, 1351–7. Marshall, L.G. (1988), Land mammals and the Great American Interchange, American Scientist, 76, 380–8. **p. 216, *Figure 6.17a:*** Reprinted from ANIMAL BEHAVIOUR, Vol. 51, Appendix 2, "Hop, Step, and Gape: Do the Social Displays of the Pelecaniformes Reflect Phylogeny?" pp. 273–291, 1996, by permission of the publisher Academic Press London. **p. 216, *Figure 6.17b:*** Reprinted from ANIMAL BEHAVIOUR, Vol. 51, Appendix 2, "Hop, Step, and Gape: Do the Social Displays of the Pelecaniformes Reflect Phylogeny?" pp. 273–291, 1996, by permission of the publisher Academic Press London.

Page 227, *Figure 7.1:* JOURNAL OF NEUROPHYSIOLOGY Volume/Edition 53 by Anderson, P.A.V. Copyright 1985 by AM PHYSIOLOGICAL SOC. Reproduced with permission of AM PHYSIOLOGICAL SOC. in the format Textbook via Copyright Clearance Center. **p. 230, *Figure 7.2:*** J.H. Lipps & P.W. Signor, eds., ORIGIN AND EARLY EVOLUTION OF THE METAZOA. Copyright (c) 1992 by Kluwer Academic/Plenum Publishers. Reprinted with permission. **p. 234, *Figure 7.3:*** Reprinted with permission from Kupferman, I., Pinsker, H., Castellucci, V., & Kandel, E. R., "Central and peripheral control of gill movements in Aplysia," SCIENCE. Copyright (c) 1971 American Association for the Advancement of Science. **p. 235, *Figure 7.4:*** JOURNAL OF NEUROPHYSIOLOGY by Byrne, J., Castelucci, V., & Kandel, E. Copyright 1974 by AM PHYSIOLOGICAL SOC. Reproduced with permission of AM PHYSIOLOGICAL SOC. in the format Textbook via Copyright Clearance Center. **p. 237, *Figure 7.5:*** Copyright (c) 1986 by the American Psychological Association. Reprinted with permission. **p. 248, *Figure 7.10:*** JOURNAL OF COMPARATIVE PHYSIOLOGY A, "Habituation in the crab Chasmagnathus granulatus: effect of morphine and naloxone," by Brunner, D., & Maldonado, H., Vol. 162, fig. 7, p. 691, copyright 1988 by Springer-Verlag. Reprinted with permission. **p. 250, *Figure 7.11:*** Original figures drawn by K.W. Mah and S.R. Wicks. Reprinted with permission. **p. 256, *Figure 7.14:*** Reprinted with permission from Pinsker, H.M., et al, "Long-term sensitization of a defensive withdrawal reflex in Aplysia," SCIENCE. Copyright (c) 1973 American Association for the Advancement of Science. **p. 258, *Figure 7.15:*** W.G. Wright, "Phylogenetic analysis of learning-related neuromodulation in molluscan mechanosensory neurons," EVOLUTION, Dec. 1996, vol. 50, pp. 2248–2263. Reprinted with permission. **p. 260, *Figure 7.16:*** Adapted from BEHAVIORAL BIOLOGY OF APLYSIA by Eric R. Kandel (c) 1979 by W.H. Freeman and Company. Used with permission.

Page 282, *Figure 8.7:* Copyright 1984 by the Society for Neuroscience. **p. 286, *Figure 8.9:*** BRAIN, BEHAVIOR & EVOLUTION, "The Dorsal Thalamus of Jawed Vertebrates: A Comparative Viewpoint," by Butler, A.B., vol. 46, fig. 4, p. 220, copyright 1995 by S. Karger AG. Reprinted with permission. **p. 292, *Figure 8.12:*** BRAIN, BEHAVIOR & EVOLUTION, "THE FOREBRAIN OF GNATHOSTOMES: IN SEARCH OF A MORPHOTYPE," by Northcutt, R.G., vol. 46, fig. 11, p. 306, copyright 1995 by S. Karger AG. Reprinted with permission. **p. 293, *Figure 8.13:*** BRAIN, BEHAVIOR & EVOLUTION, "The Telencephalon of Tetrapods in Evolution," by Striedter, G.F., vol. 49, fig. 15, p. 205, copyright 1997 by S. Karger AG. Reprinted with permission. **p. 296, *Figure 8.14:*** From Comparative Vertebrate Neuroanatomy: Evolution and Adaptation, by Butler/Hodos, Copyright (c) 1996 by John Wiley & Sons. Reprinted by permission of John Wiley & Sons. **p. 296, *Figure 8.14:*** Figure from "Central Nervous System of Marsupials" by J.I. Johnson, Jr. in THE BIOLOGY OF MARSUPIALS, edited by D. Hunsaker II, copyright (c) 1977 by Academic Press, reproduced by permission of the publisher. **p. 306, *Figure 8.18:*** From JOURNAL FUR HIRNFORSCHUNG, 30, p. 662. Copyright (c) 1989. Reprinted with permission. **p. 313, *Figure 8.19:*** Roitblat, et. al., eds., ANIMAL COGNITION. Copyright (c) 1984 by Lawrence Erlbaum Associates, Inc. Reprinted with permission.

Page 325, *Figure 9.1:* BRAIN, BEHAVIOR & EVOLUTION, "Correlations of Cerebral Indices for 'Extra' Cortical Parts and Ecological Variables in Primates," by Sawaguchi, T., vol. 32, fig. 1, p. 132, copyright 1988 by S. Karger AG. Reprinted with permission. **p. 328, *Figure 9.2:*** Courtesy Katsuo and Chiharu Tomita. **p. 330, *Figure 9.3:*** Figure from "Fossile Prosimians" in PRIMATE ADAPTATION AND EVOLUTION by J.G. Fleagle, copyright (c) 1988 by Academic Press, reproduced by permission of the publisher. **p. 332, *Figure 9.4:*** Simons, E. (1992), "The fossil history of primates" in S. Jones, R. Martin & D. Pilbeam, eds., CAMBRIDGE ENCYCLOPEDIA OF HUMAN EVOLUTION, p. 206. Reprinted with the permission of Cambridge University Press. **p. 343** ***Figure 9.10:*** Fran-Cois Bordes, THE OLD STONE AGE, copyright (c) 1977, reproduced with permission of The McGraw-Hill Companies, Inc. **p. 343,** ***Figure 9.10:*** D.A.E. Garrod and D.M.A. Bate THE STONE AGE OF MOUNT CARMEL, Oxford University Press, 1937, by permission of Oxford University Press. **p. 352,** ***Figure 9.12a & b:*** Dumbar, R.I.M. (1993), Coevolution of neocortical size, group size, and language in humans, BEHAVIORAL AND BRAIN SCIENCES, 16, fig. 1, p. 683, & fig. 3, p. 688. Reprinted with the permission of Cambridge University Press. **p. 355,** ***Figure 9.13:*** Lieberman, P. (1992), "Human Speech and Language," in S. Jones, R. Martin & D. Pilbeam, eds., CAMBRIDGE ENCYCLOPEDIA OF HUMAN EVOLUTION, p. 135. Reprinted with the permission of Cambridge University Press.

Page 363, ***Figure 10.1:*** From Garstand, W. (1928), "The morphology of the tunicata, and its bearing on the phylogency of the chordata," QUARTERLY JOURNAL OF MICROSCOPICAL SCIENCE, 75, pp. 51–187. Reprinted with permission from the Company of Biologists, Ltd. **p. 366,** ***Figure 10.3:*** Conklin, E.G., 1932. The embryology of Amphioxus , J. Morph. 54: 69–151. Hein, W. 1900. Untersuchungen uber die Entwicklung von Aurelia aurita , Z. wiss. Zool. 67: 401–438, pls. 24–25. Shearer, C. 1911. On the development and structure of the trochophore of Hydroides uncinatus (Eupomatus). , W. Jl microsc. Sci., N.S. 56: 543–590, pls. 21–23. **p. 371,** ***Figure 10.5:*** From NATURE, 361, copyright 1993 by Nature Publishing Group. Reprinted with permission. **p. 374,** ***Figure 10.6:*** From NATURE, 183, copyright 1959 by Nature Publishing Group. Reprinted with permission. **p. 379,** ***Figure 10.9:*** Adapted from BIOLOGY by H. Curtis and N.S. Barnes (c) 1989 by Worth Publishers. Used with the permission of W.H. Freeman and Company. **p. 382,** ***Figure 10.11:*** McKinney, M.L. and Schoch, R.M., "Titanothere Allometry, Heterochrony, and Biomechanics: Revising an Evolutionary Classic," EVOLUTION, 39. Copyright (c) 1985. Reprinted with permission. **p. 386,** ***Figure 10.13:*** Saunders, M. W. Jr., Animal morphogenesis. Copyright (c) 1968. Reprinted with permission of the author. **p. 392,** ***Figure 10.15:*** Reprinted with permission from Finlay, B.L. and Darlington, R.B., "Lined Regularities in the Development and Evolution of Mammalian Brains," SCIENCE. Copyright (c) 1955 American Association for the Advancement of Science.

Page 404, ***Figure 11.1:*** Tyndale-Biscoe, H. (1973) LIFE OF MARSUPIALS, Elsevier, p. 81, fig. 2.13 as it originally appeared in A.G. Lyne, Marsupials and Monotremes of Australia, 1967. Reprinted with permission. **p. 407,** ***Figure 11.2:*** Figure from "Association Between Chemosensory Stimuli and Cesarean Delivery in Rat Fetuses: Neonatal Presentation of Similar Stimuli Increases Motor Activity," by Molina, J.C. and Chotro, M.G., in BEHAVIORAL AND NEURAL BIOLOGY, vol. 55, p. 54, copyright (c) 1991 by Academic Press, reproduced by permission of the publisher. **p. 417,** ***Figure 11.5:*** Copyright (c) 1978 by the American Psychological Association. Reprinted with permission. **p. 419,** ***Figure 11.6b:*** ANIMAL LEARNING AND BEHAVIOR, 17, p. 68, reprinted by permission of Psychonomic Society, Inc. **p. 423,** ***Figure 11.8b:*** Copyright (c) 1979 by the American Psychological Association. Reprinted with permission. **p. 425,** ***Figure 11.9b:*** Copyright (c) 1976 by the American Psychological Association. Reprinted with permission. **p. 404,** ***Figure 11.10b:*** Copyright (c) 1981 by the American Psychological Association. Reprinted with permission. **p. 429,** ***Figure 11.11:*** Campbell, B.A., and Campbell, E.H. (1962), "Retention and Extinction of Learned Fear in Infant and Adult Rats," JOURNAL OF COMPARATIVE AND PHYSIOLOGICAL PSYCHOLOGY, vol. 55, fig. 1, p. 3. **p. 431,** ***Figure 11.12:*** Copyright (c) 1974 by the American Psychological Association. Reprinted with permission. **p. 437,** ***Figure 11.14:*** Copyright (c) 1997 by the American Psychological Association. Reprinted with permission.

Page 444, ***Figure 12.1:*** From ANIMAL LEARNING AND BEHAVIOR, 8, p. 483, reprinted by permission of Psychonomic Society, Inc. **p. 444,** ***Figure 12.1:*** Copyright (c) 1985 by the American Psychological Association. Reprinted with permission. **p. 445,** ***Figure 12.2:*** tables from Johnson, M.H., and Horn. G. (1988), "Development of Filial Preferences in Dark-Reared Chicks," ANIMAL BEHAVIOR, vol. 36, p. 676, fig. 1A, p. 678, figs. 2A,C,E,G. Reprinted with permission. **p. 454,** ***Figure 12.5a:*** Reprinted from BRAIN RESEARCH, 205, McCabe, Horn, and Bateson, p. 34, Copyright 1981, with permission from Elsevier Science. **p. 454,** ***Figure 12.5b:*** EXPERIMENTAL BRAIN RESEARCH, "Amnesic Effects of Bilateral Lesions Placed in the Hyperstriatum Ventral of the Chick After Imprinting," by McCabe, Cipolla-Heto, Horn and Bateson, 48, 2, p. 16, 1982, copyright Springer-Verlag. Reprinted with permission. **p. 465,** ***Figures 12.7:*** Reprinted with permission from Harlow H., and Simmerman, R.R., "Affectional Responses in the Infant Monkey," SCIENCE. Copyright (c) 1959 American Association for the Advancement of Science. **p. 467,** ***Figure 12.8:*** Mason, W.A. (1960), "The Effects of Social Restriction on the Behavior of Rhesus Monkeys: I. Free Social Behavior," Journal of Comparative & Physiological Psychology, Fig. 2, p. 587. **p. 473,** ***Figure 12.11:*** From IMPRINTING AND CORTICAL PLASTICITY by J.P. Rauschecker & P. Marler, eds., Copyright (c) 1987 by John Wiley & Sons. Reprinted by permission of John Wiley & Sons. **p. 477,** ***Figure 12.13:*** Copyright (c) 1970 by the American Psychological Association. Reprinted with permission.

Page 495, ***Figure 13.1:*** Copyright (c) 1979 by the American Psychological Association. Reprinted with permission. **p. 499,** ***Figure 13.3:*** With permission, from the Annual Review of Neuroscience, Volume 11 (c) 1988 by Annual Reviews www.AnnualReviews.org. **p. 503,** ***Figure 13.4:*** figure from "Spreading Association in Time" by Gibbon, J. and Balsam, P.D. in AUTOSHAPING AND CONDITIONING THEORY, edited by C.M. Locurto, H. S. Terrace and J. Gibbon, copyright (c) 1981 by Academic Press, reproduced by permission of the publisher. **p. 504,** ***Figure 13.5:*** Figure from "Stimulus Selection and the 'Modified Continuity Theory'," by Wagner, A.R. in THE PSYCHOLOGY OF LEARNING AND MOTIVATION: ADVANCES IN RESEARCH AND THEORY, vol. 3, copyright (c) 1969 by Academic Press, reproduced by permission of the publisher. **p. 507,** ***Figure 13.6a:*** From ANIMAL LEARNING AND BEHAVIOR, 25, p. 101, reprinted by permisison of Psychonomic Society, Inc. **p. 507,** ***Figure 13.6b:*** From ANIMAL LEARNING AND BEHAVIOR, 25, p. 404, reprinted by permisison of Psychonomic Society, Inc. **p. 509,** ***Figure 13.7b:*** Copyright (c) 1985 by the American Psychological Association. Reprinted with permission. **p. 511,** ***Figure 13.8:*** From PSYCHONOMIC MONOGRAPH SUPPLEMENTS, 3, no. 16 (Whole No. 48), p. 252, reprinted by permission of Psychonomic Society, Inc. **p. 521,** ***Figure 13.9:*** From ANIMAL LEARNING AND BEHAVIOR, 16, p. 309, reprinted by permisison of Psychonomic Society, Inc. **p. 529,** ***Figure 13.12:*** Figure from "Problem-solving ability of Octopus Vulgaris Lamarck (Mollusca, Cephalopoda)" by Fiorito, von Planta, and Scotto in Behavioral and Neural Biology, Volume 53, p. 223, copyright (c) 1990 by Academic Press, reproduced by permission of the publisher.

Page 561, ***Figure 14.1:*** table from "Acquisition of Representation-Mediated Conditioned Food Aversions," by P.C. Holland in LEARNING & MOTIVATION, vol. 12, 1–18, copyright (c) 1981 by Academic Press, reproduced by permission of the publisher. **p. 563,** ***Figure 14.2:*** table from "Pavlovian conditioning Stimulus Effects Upon Instrumental Choice Behavior are Reinforcer Specific," by Kruse, Overmier, Konz, and Rokke in LEARNING & MOTIVATION, vol. 14, 165–181, copyright (c) 1983 by Academic Press, reproduced by permission of the publisher. **p. 552,** ***Figure 14.3:*** Copyright (c) 1985 by the American Psychological Association. Reprinted with permission. **p. 554,** ***Figure 14.4a:*** Elliott, M.H. (1928) "The Effect of Change of Reward on the Maze Performance of Rats" UNIVERSITY PUBLICATIONS IN PSYCHOLOGY, 4, p. 26, fig. 4. **p. 554,** ***Figure 14.4b:*** From ANIMAL LEARNING AND BEHAVIOR, 16, p. 56, reprinted by permisison of Psychonomic Society, Inc. **p. 562,** ***Figure 14.7b:*** table from "Are Expectancies Based Upon Different Positive Reinforcing Events Discriminably Different?" by Trapold, M.A. in LEARNING & MOTIVATION, Volume 1, 134, copyright (c) 1970 by Academic Press, reproduced by permission of the publisher. **p. 567,** ***Figure 14.8:*** From ANIMAL LEARNING AND BEHAVIOR, 15, p. 28, reprinted by permission of Psychonomic Society, Inc. **p. 571,** ***Figure 14.9:*** Copyright (c) 1989 by the American Psychological Association. Reprinted with permission. **p. 575,** ***Figure 14.10:*** From Premack, D. (1976), INTELLIGENCE IN APE AND MAN. Reprinted by permission of Lawrence Erlbaum Publishers.

Name Index

Subject Index

Species Index

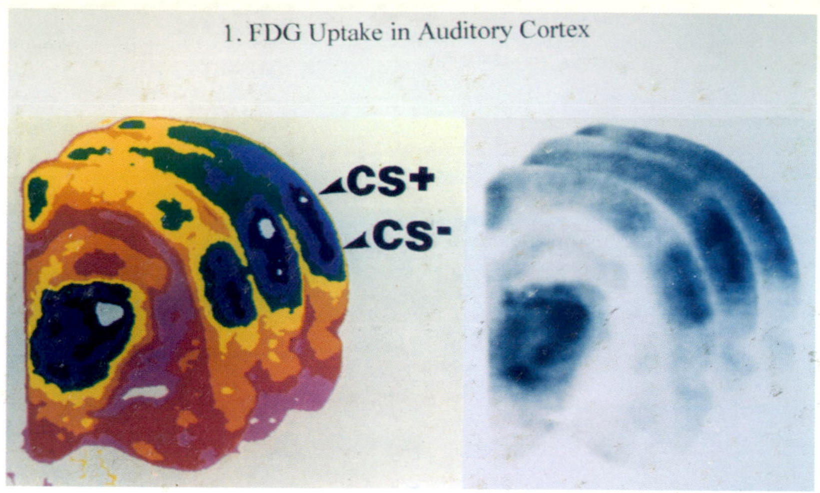

Figure 8.17. An example of cortical plasticity detected by a non-invasive technique known as autoradiography. Animals exposed to classical conditioning are given an injection of a radioactively labeled glucose analog followed by a test trial with the conditioned stimulus. Immediately after the test, the animals are sacrificed, the brain is prepared in slices, and the slices are mounted on top of special film. Regions of the brain that have taken up more of the glucose analog appear as dark regions. This technique permits the identification of brain regions that are active at the time the animal was processing the conditioned stimulus. Thus, these regions are assumed to be sites of plasticity. (Photograph courtesy of Francisco González-Lima.)

Figure 11.13. A young chimpanzee cracking an oil palm nut at Bossou, Guinea, by using the hammer-anvil stone tool. (Photograph courtesy of Tetsuro Matsuzawa.)